THE ECONOMICS OF ACCOUNTING POLICY CHOICE

EDITED BY

Ray Ball
Clifford W. Smith, Jr.

*William E. Simon Graduate School
of Business Administration
University of Rochester*

McGRAW-HILL, INC.

New York   St. Louis   San Francisco   Auckland
Bogotá   Caracas   Lisbon   London   Madrid   Mexico
Milan   Montreal   New Delhi   Paris   San Juan
Singapore   Sydney   Tokyo   Toronto

McGraw-Hill Series in Advanced Topics in Finance and Accounting

CONSULTING EDITORS
Ray Ball
Clifford W. Smith, Jr.

THE ECONOMICS OF ACCOUNTING POLICY CHOICE

1 2 3 4 5 6 7 8 9 0 DOH   DOH 9 0 9 8 7 6 5 4 3 2

ISBN 0-07-003586-5

The editor was Kenneth A. MacLeod;
the production supervisor was Al Rihner.
The cover was designed by Karen K. Quigley.
Project supervision was done by Caliber/Phoenix Color Corp.
R. R. Donnelley & Sons Company was printer and binder.

Library of Congress Cataloging-in-Publication Data

The Economics of accounting policy choice / edited by Ray Ball,
   Clifford W. Smith, Jr.
      p.   cm.—(McGraw-Hill series in advanced topics in finance
   and accounting)
      Includes bibliographical references.
      ISBN 0-07-003586-5
      1. Accounting.   2. Accounting—Standards.   3. Disclosure in
   accounting.   I. Ball, Ray, (date).   II. Smith, Clifford W.
   III. Series.
   HF5629.E26   1992
   658.15'11—dc20
                                                92-4237

CONTENTS

IV APPLICATION TO SPECIFIC ACCOUNTING CHOICES

INTRODUCTION

This collection brings together thirty-four previously-published articles on the economics of accounting policy choice. These articles adopt a *costly-contracting* perspective. The collection is designed for use in Intermediate Accounting courses (in conjunction with texts that explain the mechanics but not the economics of accounting policies) and in Accounting Theory or other research-level courses.

As the mechanics of Generally Accepted Accounting Principles (GAAP) become increasingly complicated, it becomes increasingly difficult to obtain a comprehensive knowledge of accounting by learning its mechanics. It becomes natural to turn to more systematic ways of acquiring accounting knowledge. The contracting-cost literature provides a systematic attempt to understand accounting, as it is practiced. It studies the economics of accounting policy choice. While the literature is still at a formative stage, it already has achieved important results and offers promise of much more.

To be selected for the core collection, an article has to meet three criteria:

1. *Topic is accounting policy choice*: the article seeks to explain how GAAP are determined, why different corporations choose different accounting techniques from among GAAP, or why they change their choices over time;

2. *Approach is empirical*: the article either utilizes data on accounting policy choices, their determinants or their effects, or it develops empirically testable propositions; and

3. *Underlying theory assumes costly contracting*: the tested or testable propositions arise from the economic theory of costly contracting.

In addition, we have included several survey articles. These surveys deal with a literature that is wider than can be contained in this collection and they add a perspective to the articles included.

The articles are organized into four sections. The first section introduces the costly-contracting literature in accounting. It contains pioneering contributions and two literature survey articles. The second and third sections cover the influence of debt and compensation contracts on accounting, respectively. The fourth section focusses on particular accounting technique choices. Because the section themes are not mutually-exclusive, the organization we have chosen is unlikely to be optimal for all courses of study. We therefore recommend that instructors experiment with the order in which the articles are prescribed. Each section begins with an introduction that places the section in perspective and briefly describes the articles contained in it. In each section's introduction, references to articles reproduced in this collection are set in bold. Other references are to sources that are listed at the end of the collection.

The articles originally were published in *The Accounting Review, Australian Journal of Management, Journal of Accounting and Economics, Journal of Accounting Research* and *Journal of Financial Economics*. We acknowledge the cooperation of all of the authors and publishers represented in the collection. We also acknowledge the encouragement and support of Ken MacLeod at McGraw-Hill and the secretarial assistance of Jane Muellner.

McGraw-Hill and the authors would like to thank Jang Y. Cho, University of Nebraska, Lincoln, for his many valuable comments and suggestions in reviewing this manuscript.

Ray Ball
Clifford W. Smith, Jr.

ACKNOWLEDGMENTS

The editors wish to thank the following authors for permission to reprint their articles:

Professor Sanjai Bhagat, College of Business Administration, University of Colorado.
Professor James A. Brickley, William E. Simon Graduate School of Business Administration, University of Rochester.
Professor Chee W. Chow, School of Accountancy, San Diego State University.
Professor Andrew A. Christie, William Simon Graduate School of Business Association, University of Rochester.
Professor Lane A. Daley, Carlson School of Management, University of Minnesota.
Professor Linda Elizabeth DeAngelo, Department of Accounting, University of Southern California.
Professor Victor J. Defeo, Wharton School, University of Pennsylvania.
Professor Dan S. Dhaliwal, College of Business and Public Administration, Department of Accounting, University of Arizona.
Professor Joanne C. Duke, Graduate School of Business, San Francisco State University.
Professor Robert L. Hagerman, Department of Accounting, School of Management, SUNY Buffalo.
Professor Paul M. Healey, Sloan School of Management, Massachusetts Institute of Technology.
Professor David A. Hsieh, Fuqua School of Business, Duke University.
Professor Herbert G. Hunt III, School of Business Administration, University of Vermont.
Professor Eugene A. Imhoff, Jr., School of Business Administration, University of Michigan.
Professor Michael C. Jensen, Graduate School of Business Administration, Harvard University.
Professor Avner Kalay, Graduate School of Business, The University of Utah.
Professor Sok-Hyon Kang, Graduate School of Industrial Management, Carnegie-Mellon University.
Professor Richard A. Lambert, Graduate School of Business, Stanford University.
Professor David F. Larcker, Wharton School, University of Pennsylvania.
Professor Ronald C. Lease, Graduate School of Business, University of Utah.
Professor Chi-Wen Jevons Lee, A. B. Freeman School of Business, Tulane University.
Professor Richard Leftwich, Graduate School of Business, University of Chicago.
Professor Thomas Lys, Kellogg Graduate School of Management, Northwestern University.
Professor Shehzad L. Mian, School of Business Administration, Emory University.
Professor Susan E. Moyer, School of Business, University of Washington.
Professor Gerald L. Salamon, School of Business, Indiana University.

The editors wish to acknowledge the sources of the articles reprinted in this volume:

American Accounting Association:
Ross L. Watts and Jerold L. Zimmerman, "Towards a Positive Theory of the Determination of Accounting Standards," *The Accounting Review*, 53 (1978), pp. 112-134.
Jerold L. Zimmerman, "The Cost and Benefits of Cost Allocations," *The Accounting Review*, 54 (1979), pp. 504-521.
Richard Leftwich, "Accounting Information in Private Markets: Evidence from Private Lending Agreements," *The Accounting Review*, 58 (1981), pp. 23-42.
Michael C. Jensen, "Organization Theory and Methodology," *The Accounting Review*, 58 (1983), pp. 319-339.
Chee W. Chow, "The Impacts of Accounting Regulation on Bondholder and Shareholder Wealth: The Case of the Securities Acts," *The Accounting Review*, 58 (1983), pp. 485-520.
Susan E. Moyer (Liberty) and Jerold L. Zimmerman, "Labor Union Contract Negotiations and Accounting Choices," *The Accounting Review*, 61 (1986) pp. 692-712.
Victor J. Defeo, Richard A. Lambert and David F. Larcker, "The Executive Compensation Effects of Equity-for-Debt Swaps," *The Accounting Review*, 64 (1989), pp. 201-227.
Elizabeth Linda DeAngelo, "Equity Valuation and Corporate Control," *The Accounting Review*, 65 (1990), pp. 93-112.
Ross L. Watts and Jerold L. Zimmerman, "Positive Accounting Theory: A Ten Year Perspective," *The Accounting Review*, 65 (1990), pp. 131-156.

Australian Graduate School of Management:
Ross L. Watts, "Corporate Financial Statements, A Product of the Market and Political Processes," *Australian Journal of Management*, 2 (1977), pp. 53-75
Clifford W. Smith, Jr. and Ross L. Watts, "Incentives and Tax Effects of Executive Compensation Plans," *Australian Journal of Management*, 7 (1982), pp. 139-157.

Institute of Professional Accounting:
Richard W. Leftwich, Ross L. Watts and Jerold L. Zimmerman, "Voluntary Corporate Disclosure: The Case of Interim Reporting," *Journal of Accounting Research*, 19 (1981), Supplement), pp. 50-77.
Chi-Wen Jovons Lee and David A. Hsieh, "Choice of Inventory Accounting Methods: Comparative Analyses of Alternative Hypotheses," *Journal of Accounting Research*, 23 (1985), pp. 468-485.
Richard A. Lambert and David F. Larcker, "An Analysis of the Use of Accounting and Market Measures of Peformance in Executive Compensation Contracts," *Journal of Accounting Research*, 25 (1987, Supplement), pp. 85-125.

North Holland Publishing Co.:
Clifford W. Smith, Jr. and Jerold B. Warner, "On Financial Contracting: An Analysis of Bond Covenants," *Journal of Financial Economics*, 7 (1979), pp. 117-161.

Richard Leftwich, "Evidence of the Impact of Mandatory Changes in Accounting Principles on Corporate Loan Agreements," *Journal of Accounting and Economics*, 7 (1981), pp. 3-36.

Mark E. Zmijewski and Robert L. Hagerman, "An Income Strategy Approach to the Positive Theory of Accounting Standard Setting/Choice," *Journal of Accounting and Economics*, 3 (1981), pp. 129-149.

Dan S. Dhaliwal, Gerald S. Salamon and E. Dan Smith, "The Effect of Owner Versus Management Control on the Choice of Accounting Methods," *Journal of Accounting and Economics*, 4, (1982), pp. 41-53.

Avner Kalay, "Stockholder-Bondholder Conflict and Dividend Constraints," *Journal of Financial Economics*, 10, (1982), pp. 211-233.

David F. Larcker, "The Association Between Performance Plan Adoption and Corporate Capital Investment," *Journal of Accounting and Economics*, 5 (1983), pp. 3-30.

Lane A. Daley, and Robert L. Vigeland, "The Effects of Debt Convenants and Political Costs on the Choice of Accounting Methods: The Case of Accounting for R&D Costs," *Journal of Accounting and Economics*, 5 (1983), pp. 195-211

Thomas, Lys, "Mandated Accounting Changes and Debt Covenants: The Case of Oil and Gas Accounting," *Journal of Accounting and Economics*, 6 (1984), pp. 39-65.

Paul M. Healy, "The Effect of Bonus Schemes on Accounting Decisions," *Journal of Accounting and Economics*, 7 (1985), pp. 85-107.

James A. Brickley, Sanjai Bhagat and Ronald C. Lease, "The Impact of Long-Range Managerial Compensation Plans on Shareholder Wealth," *Journal of Accounting and Economics*, 7 (1985), pp. 115-129.

Sanjai Bhagat, James A. Brickley and Ronald C. Lease, "Incentive Effects of Stock Purchase Plans," *Journal of Financial Economics*, 14 (1985), pp. 195-215.

Ian Zimmer, "Accounting for Interest by Real Estate Developers," *Journal of Accounting and Economics*, 8 (1986), pp. 37-51.

Paul M. Healy, Sok-Hyon Kang and Krishna G. Palepu, "The Effect of Accounting Procedure Changes on CEOs' Cash Salary and Bonus Compensation," *Journal of Accounting and Economics*, 9 (1987), pp. 7-34.

Jilnaught Wong, "Economic Incentives for the Voluntary Disclosure of Current Cost Financial Statements," *Journal of Accounting and Economics*, 10 (1988), pp. 151-167.

Eugene A. Imhoff, Jr. and Jacob K. Thomas, "Economic Consequences of Accounting Standards: The Lease Disclosure Rule Change," *Journal of Accounting and Economics*, 10 (1988), pp. 277-310.

Jacob K. Thomas, "Why do Firms Terminate Their Overfunded Pension Plans?" *Journal of Accounting and Economics*, 11 (1989), pp. 361-398.

Andrew A. Christie, "Aggregation of Test Statistics: An Evaluation of the Evidence on Contracting and Size Hypotheses," *Journal of Accounting and Economics*, 12 (1990), pp. 15-36.

Joanne C. Duke and Herbert G. Hunt III, "An Empirical Examination of Debt Covenant Restrictions and Accounting-Related Debt Proxies," *Journal of Accounting and Economics*, 12 (1990), pp. 45-63.

Shehzad L. Mian and Clifford W. Smith, Jr., "Incentives for Unconsolidated Financial Reporting," *Journal of Accounting and Economics*, 12, (1990a), pp. 141-171.

Shehzad L. Mian and Clifford W. Smith, Jr., "Incentives Associated with Changes in Consolidated Reporting Requirements," *Journal of Accounting and Economics*, 13 (1990b), pp. 249-266.

I

CONTRACTING–COST THEORIES OF ACCOUNTING POLICY CHOICE

1 Watts, Ross L., "Corporate Financial Statements, A Product of the Market and Political Processes," *Australian Journal of Management*, 2 (1977), pp. 53–75.

2 Watts, Ross L. and Jerold L. Zimmerman, "Towards a Positive Theory of the Determination of Accounting Standards," *The Accounting Review*, 53 (1978), pp. 112–134.

3 Watts, Ross L. and Jerold L. Zimmerman, "Positive Accounting Theory: A Ten Year Perspective," *The Accounting Review*, 65 (1990), pp. 131–156.

4 Christie, Andrew A., "Aggregation of Test Statistics: An Evaluation of the Evidence on Contracting and Size Hypotheses," *Journal of Accounting and Economics,* 12 (1990), pp. 15–36.

5 Jensen, Michael C., "Organization Theory and Methodology," *The Accounting Review*, 58 (1983), pp. 319–339.

6 Zimmerman, Jerold L., "The Costs and Benefits of Cost Allocations," *The Accounting Review*, 54 (1979), pp. 504–521.

7 DeAngelo, Linda Elizabeth, "Equity Valuation and Corporate Control," *The Accounting Review*, 65 (1990), pp. 93–112.

The seminal work of Coase (1937) established the fundamental proposition that all economic institutions (Coase called them "firms," following general usage in economics) owe their existence to costs of contracting. The impact of Coase's paper, entitled "The Nature of the Firm," has been enduring. It was instrumental in earning its author the 1991 Nobel Prize in Economics, some 54 years after its publication. Like all important propositions, Coase's is deceptively simple. He observes that, in the absence of contracting costs, firms would be irrelevant: consumers could contract directly with the owners of factors of production; there would be no demand for firms to intermediate between them; and all decisions would be based on a complete set of costlessly observable market prices. This proposition is no less than a *general institutional irrelevance theorem*, in a hypothetical world without costs of contracting.

The theorem is so fundamental that it appears, under various guises, in several literatures. In corporate finance, for example, it appears as the Fisher Separation Theorem, that (given the value of the firm) the timing of its cash distributions to shareholders is irrelevant to them, provided it is costless for them to transact (that is, to contract in the capital market). Miller and Modigliani (1961) proved the related theorem, that corporate dividend policy is irrelevant when transactions costs are assumed away. Modigliani and Miller (1958) had earlier proven the irrelevance of corporate capital structure under the same assumption. These are examples of *specific institutional irrelevance theorems*, addressing specific institutional details in a hypothetical world without costs of contracting.

Institutional irrelevance theorems provide important insights. To the researcher who is interested in explaining why the economy is structured in a particular fashion, the Coasian analysis suggests that contracting costs be studied. Economic theories that assume an absence of contracting costs cannot explain even the existence of firms, let alone whether they are diversified or divisionalized or incorporated or pay dividends or calculate their income in a particular fashion. An implication of the general institutional irrelevance theorem is that no "institutional fact," such as the existence of a corporation or a corporate policy on debt, can be explained by an economic theory that assumes away contracting costs.

The converse of the irrelevance proposition is that, in an unregulated economy, the institutional structure that we observe is contracting-cost-efficient. Contracting costs *do* exist and institutional form is economically relevant. Decades, centuries, and even millennia of competitive innovation in institutional forms leads to the more efficient contracting technology tending to replace the less efficient.[1] At the most general level, Coase (1937, p. 390) reasoned that firms exist because "there is a cost of using the price mechanism." More specifically, individual institutional details are explained, under this theory, in terms of their contracting-cost efficiency.

Researchers seeking to explain the existence of an enormous range of institutional facts, ranging from the existence of firms in general through the existence of particular detailed practices, therefore have turned their attention toward *efficiency in contracting* as an hypothesis. For example, Fama and Jensen (1983) seek contracting-cost explanations for the dominance of non-profit corporations in areas that attract donations of time and money (charities, hospitals, universities), of professional partnerships in "ethical" areas (law, public accounting, medicine) and of other basic institutional forms. Brickley and Dark (1987) study the decision to franchise versus own the operating units of a chain (restaurants, travel agencies, etc). In the absence of regulation, such choices are dictated by contracting costs alone. The literature started by Coase (1937) now is substantial.

One branch of the contracting-cost literature focuses on the *economics of agency relationships*. Within this there are two distinct sub-branches, commonly labelled the "modelling" and the "empirical" agency literatures. The research reproduced in this volume focuses on the latter branch, which builds on important work by Alchian and Demsetz (1972) and Jensen and Meckling (1976). While these branches share a common objective (scientific investigation of economic institutions) and increasingly utilize each other's results, the empirical branch is more likely to emphasize the consistency of theory with a rich range of institutional "facts" and less likely to emphasize the formal completeness and internal consistency of the theory. An analysis of this literature, with particular reference to accounting research, is provided by **Jensen (1983).**

No theory completely explains or is approximately consistent with all the "facts" with which it is confronted. A normal response is to modify the theory for important omitted vari-

---

[1]See Alchian (1950) for an analysis of innovation in economics and Rosenberg and Birdzell (1986) for an account of institutional innovation since the Middle Ages.

ables. In seeking to explain the existence and form of economic institutions, researchers have found it necessary to modify their analysis of voluntary contracting among economic agents, to allow for the *regulation of economic activity* by the political process. Coase (1937, p. 393) himself observed that "transactions on a market and the same transactions organized within a firm are often treated differently by Governments or other bodies with regulatory powers." While regulation in principle can create both costs and benefits, the literature has focused on the latter, using the term *political costs*. Hence, contracting costs arise from two sources in this literature: private and political.

Coase's general theorem applies equally to accounting. Whether expressed in its irrelevance form ("nothing matters without contracting costs") or its preference form ("the observed institutional structure can be explained in terms of contracting-cost efficiency"), the theorem applies to all areas of institutional form, including the existence and detailed shape of accounting. In principle, the economics of costly contracting, modified to allow for economic regulation, can be used to explain the existence of accounting, the form taken by the profession, the existence of GAAP, the process that determines GAAP, the content of GAAP, the selection from GAAP by corporations, and the most detailed institutional facts in accounting. In practice, the theory and the data never appear perfectly consistent, no matter how successful the literature is, thus presenting the research challenges for further literature development.[2]

In a world without contracting costs, accounting would be irrelevant: all prices relevant to all decisions would be costlessly observable; prices would be sufficient for all decisions; and thus no resources would be devoted to producing accounting numbers for use in decision-making. In a world with contracting costs, to explain the general existence and the specific forms of accounting rules and accounting numbers, one must investigate the contracting contexts in which accounting numbers are used. These determine the demand for the accounting product. Supply considerations (that is, the nature of accounting as a specialist producer of information) must be considered also.[3]

These ideas were introduced to the accounting literature by **Watts and Zimmerman (1978)** and **Watts (1977)**. Their work builds upon the principal/agent analysis of Jensen and Meckling (1976) and examines both contracting in an agency setting and political costs. Surveys of this literature are presented by **Watts and Zimmerman (1990)** and **Christie (1990)**. Christie's survey utilizes formal statistical techniques for aggregating results across empirical studies, whereas Watts and Zimmerman provide a more typical overview. In spite of their differences in approach, the surveys reach a similar conclusion. They conclude that there are reliable statistical relations between a firm's preferred accounting policies and properties of its debt contracts, properties of its management compensation contracts, and its size (the latter is offered as a proxy for political costs). The directions of the relations are as predicted by the theory. The contracting-cost and the political-cost explanations of accounting "institutional facts" thus have much to offer.

Compared to the accounting literature that preceded it, the contracting-cost literature

---

[2]For an analysis of the interaction between theory and data in this literature, see Ball and Foster (1982).

[3]The role of contracting costs in a theory of accounting is strengthened by Hayek's (1945) observation that information costs are significant determinants of the way the economy is organized. The accounting system is a specialist supplier of information.

offers many new insights, including:

1. Broadening the previously nearly-exclusive focus on reporting to shareholders, to encompass a range of users of accounting information;
2. Demonstrating the existence of a *market* for accounting information, albeit a regulated market;
3. Demonstrating that corporations and parties that contract with them act in their own interest in making accounting policy choices;
4. Demonstrating that regulation of accounting is not necessarily motivated by altruism; and
5. Demonstrating a demand for diversity in accounting policies.

By adapting economic theories of contracting and regulation to accounting, this literature continued the process of successfully merging accounting and economics, a process that essentially commenced with the "capital markets" research on accounting and stock prices. As in the capital markets area, this accounting research relied upon and contributed to underlying breakthroughs in economic thought.

A major problem confronting researchers in this literature is the unobservability of both contracting costs and political costs. Researchers tend to rely upon *proxies* for these costs. For example, a corporation's observed debt/equity ratio is taken as a proxy for the closeness of the observed ratio to the maximum ratio prescribed in a contract to raise long-term debt. The latter in turn is a proxy for the expected value of the costs arising from any restrictions imposed upon the corporation under its debt contracts, should it breach the agreement to maintain a maximum debt level. These costs include the costs of renegotiating the debt agreement and the costs of opportunities foregone as a result of the agreed restrictions upon new investment, new financing, etc.[4] A second example is size, which frequently is used as a proxy for the political costs arising from accounting policy choice. Potential research design problems arise from two sources: (1) the likelihood that the proxy measures the construct (contracting costs or political costs) with error; and (2) the possibility that the error is correlated with omitted variables. Random measurement error frequently causes true relations to be underestimated, perhaps to the point of not being observed. Correlated measurement error can cause the researcher to falsely attribute an observed relation to the theory under investigation. These problems are described in the **Watts and Zimmerman (1990)** survey article.

A related problem in this literature lies in distinguishing between *opportunism* and *contracting efficiency* as determinants of accounting policy choice. In theory, they are not clearly distinguishable, because in the presence of positive contracting costs there will be a positive optimal (efficient) amount of opportunism. In empirical work. the two explanations can be difficult to distinguish as well. For example, consider the relation between accounting policy choice and a dummy variable that indicates whether or not a corporation has a formal plan that ties executive compensation to reported earnings. (A selection of studies on compensation is contained in the third section of this collection). A statistically significant relation could indicate that managers whose compensation is formally tied to reported earnings act opportunistically in selecting accounting policies that influence reported earnings. Alternatively, it could indicate that corporations for which a particular accounting technique set is efficient also tend to be those for which it is efficient to utilize a formal compensation plan that uses reported income as a performance measure.

---

[4]This issue is studied in Duke and Hunt (1990).

One area that has resisted detailed empirical research from a contracting-cost perspective is "managerial" accounting. **Zimmerman (1979)** asks the question: "Why do corporations allocate overheads?" His answer is based on the principal/agent model. In a sense, the "institutional fact" that corporations do allocate overhead is evidence in favor of the model he proposes. Zimmerman's work stands almost alone in a potentially important area of research. Empirical research in "management" accounting from a contracting-cost perspective seems likely to be limited, until richer data sets become available.

DeAngelo (1990) investigates the role of accounting in corporate control transactions. She reports evidence that accounting numbers are used in valuing equities in this context. DeAngelo views the demand for accounting numbers in this context as distinct from the demand modelled in the costly-contracting and capital markets literatures. This distinction is not clear, in that corporate control changes can be viewed as shareholders recontracting for the management of the corporation, which is a right attaching to their equity contract with the corporation.[5]

The articles reproduced in this section provide an introduction to the empirical literature applying contracting-cost economics to accounting. This literature addresses an increasingly rich set of institutional facts over time, as researchers learn how to adapt the theory to a wider and deeper set of issues. It offers much insight and further promise.

---

[5]A related issue is the relation between the demands for accounting information studied in the costly-contracting and capital markets literatures. Watts and Zimmerman (1986) point out that, in the absence of regulation, the supply of information to equity investors by corporations would be a matter of private contracting between them. This does not preclude negotiation by institutions acting on behalf of individual investors, such as security analysts' associations, trustees or stock exchanges (which establish disclosure requirements), or by holders of large blocks of shares. In this sense, the issues studied in the two literatures are equivalent. **Watts and Zimmerman (1978)** and **Watts (1977)** point to pre-regulatory economies, in which corporations voluntarily contracted to supply audited reports.

CORPORATE FINANCIAL STATEMENTS, A PRODUCT OF THE MARKET AND POLITICAL PROCESSES

by
Ross L. Watts*

Abstract:

An outline for a theory of financial statements is presented. Financial statements are viewed as products of both markets and political processes and the interactions among individuals and groups in these processes. Individuals are assumed to maximize their self-interests. Various hypotheses and data are provided to illustrate the theory. It relies heavily on theories of agency, economic regulation and public choice. At this stage, the theory has great promise in explaining the form and contents of financial statements. The theory contrasts with earlier "normative" theories of financial statements and offers an explanation for the forms they take.

Keywords:

ACCOUNTING PROCEDURES; ACCOUNTING THEORY; AGENCY; ECONOMIC REGULATION; FINANCIAL STATEMENTS; PUBLIC CHOICE

*Graduate School of Management, University of Rochester. An early version of this paper was presented at the Annual Congress of the New South Wales Branch of the Institute of Chartered Accountants in Australia in June, 1974. Many of the ideas in that early paper evolved from discussions I had with M. Jensen while we were trying to write a paper on accounting theory. The concepts in this paper are substantially more developed than in the original paper. Some of those developments were conceived during attempts by J. Zimmerman and myself to test hypotheses generated by the 1974 paper. A major development, the structure of the Agency Problem, was provided by Jensen and Meckling (1976). Thus, I owe a great deal to Jensen, Meckling and Zimmerman. However, they are not responsible for any errors in the paper. I am also indebted to G. Benston, R. Holthausen, M. Krasney, R. Leftwich and C. Smith for their helpful comments and suggestions.

1. INTRODUCTION

The financial accounting literature concentrates on prescriptions: on what "should" be the content of financial statements.[1] Very little attention is given to developing a theory to explain many interesting observed phenomena; in particular to explain why financial statements take their current form. In other words, the literature is unscientific.[2] We have no theory of corporate financial statements, in the form of a group of internally consistent, interrelated hypotheses which have been subjected to formal tests and "confirmed".

Prescriptions in the accounting literature are based on hypotheses about observed phenomena in capital markets, political process, and other areas. Rarely do any of the prescribers suggest that the hypotheses be tested formally, let alone perform such tests. Moreover, the hypotheses are often inconsistent with currently accepted theories in finance and economics.[3]

Even that part of the accounting literature which relies on the empirically-based efficient market hypothesis and the capital-asset-pricing models of finance does not include any tests of hypotheses which directly explain why financial statements take their current form. Instead, the emphasis in that finance-based literature is on stock market reaction to the content of financial statements.[4]

The development of prescriptions and the development of theory are not incompatible. The development of prescriptions which are likely to achieve their objectives requires an underlying theory which explains observed phenomena: which predicts the effects of particular prescriptions. Thus, given the concentration on prescriptions, the lack of development of theory in financial accounting is an enigma.

The purpose of this paper is to provide an outline for a theory of financial statements and to provide examples of some of its constituent hypotheses. The approach is based upon price theory. It assumes that individuals maximize their own expected utilities and that they are innovative and creative in doing so.[5] Financial statements are viewed as resulting from interaction among these maximizing individuals in both markets and the political process. No one individual or group of individuals is viewed as determining the form of financial statements. The outline relies heavily on theories of agency, public choice and economic regulation.[6] A justification for these assumptions and for the reliance

---

[1]For example see Sanders, Hatfield and Moore (1938), Paton and Littleton (1940), Edwards and Bell (1961), Sprouse and Moonitz (1962), Gordon (1964), American Accounting Association (1966), Chambers (1966), and Ijiri (1967).

[2]This observation is also made by Jensen (1976, p.11). Jensen also argues for a positive theory of accounting.

[3]For example, Chambers (1966, p.293) asserts: "Statutes and regulations secure the rights of investors, potential investors, their advisers, their agents, and the public generally, to authenticated financial information, with the object of creating a fair and informed market in securities." This implies that the object of securities statutes and regulations is what is called in economics "the public interest". Convincing evidence that this is not the objective of statutes and regulations is supplied by Posner (1974) among others. Chambers does not present any evidence to support his assertion.

[4]See Gonedes and Dopuch (1974) for a review of this literature.

[5]For a discussion of the importance of this assumption, see Meckling (1976b).

[6]See Jensen and Meckling (1976b) for a theory of the firm based upon the agency relationship, Mueller (1976) for a summary of the theory of public choice and

on these other theories is the rich set of testable hypotheses generated about corporate financial statements and the extent to which those hypotheses are consistent with observed phenomena. Casual empiricism confirms some of these hypotheses. The few that have been formally tested have been confirmed.[7]

Another purpose is to propose an hypothesis which explains the enigma of the accounting literature: the emphasis on prescriptions and the simultaneous lack of emphasis on accounting theory (i.e. explanation of observed phenomena) which is necessary for successful prescription. This hypothesis is explored in greater depth in Watts and Zimmerman (1977).

The next section of this paper discusses the market interaction of individuals associated with the corporation. Hypotheses about the content of financial statements are drawn from that discussion. In section 3, the political interaction of expected-utility maximizing individuals is examined and additional hypotheses about the content of financial statements are provided. Examples of observed phenomena which these hypotheses can explain are also contained in sections 2 and 3. Section 3 also provides an hypothesis to explain the abundance of prescriptions without theory in the accounting literature. The conclusions are set out in section 4.

The reader should bear in mind that I am only proposing hypotheses. These proposals are based on theories drawn from finance and economics and apparently are consistent with a range of observed phenomena. Thus I believe there is a high likelihood that a theory can be developed from the approach adopted in the paper. Whether that belief is justified or not will be determined by the ability of my hypotheses to withstand formal empirical testing.

2.   CORPORATE FINANCIAL STATEMENTS AND THE MARKET PROCESS

2.1 The Agency Relationship and Financial Statements

Corporations listed on stock exchanges are owned by shareholders, but they typically are managed by individuals who own only a small fraction of the outstanding shares. Because I assume that all individuals, including shareholders and managers, maximize their own expected utilities, this situation implies a conflict: actions that maximize managers' expected utilities do not necessarily maximize shareholders' expected utilities.

The relationship between shareholders and managers is an agency relationship. Jensen and Meckling (1976b, p.308) define an agency relationship as "a contract under which one or more persons (principal(s)) engage another person (the agent) to perform some service on their behalf which involves delegating some decision making authority to the agent". Shareholders are principals in the relationship and managers are agents.

There is a growing literature in economics on the agency relationship.[8] Most of it addresses the reconciliation of conflict: construction of incentives for the agents to act in the principal's interest. In other words, most of the literature is normative. In contrast, Jensen and Meckling (1976b) have investigated the positive aspects of the agency relationship as it applies to corporations. They define the concept of agency costs, analyze the incentives of principals and agents and derive formal hypotheses about the contractual arrangements one would expect to observe in equilibrium. Further, they suggest

---

[6](cont'd.) Posner (1974) for a summary of alternative theories of economic regulations.

[7]See Watts and Zimmerman (1977b).

[8]See Berhold (1971), Ross (1973, 1974), Wilson (1968, 1969) and Heckerman (1975).

that audited corporate financial statements are part of an equilibrium result.

I believe that an analysis of the role of corporate financial statements in the agency relationship can contribute much to our understanding of the development of accounting (i.e. to a theory of accounting). In this section of the paper I provide the grounds for that belief. I investigate the implications of Jensen and Meckling's analysis for the content of financial statements and provide examples of hypotheses which can be derived from their analysis. These hypotheses appear to be consistent with observed phenomena. Finally, I examine the relationship between the function of corporate financial statements in the agency relationship and the information function of financial statements which has been proposed frequently in the accounting literature.

2.1.a The costs of the agency relationship and who bears them

Jensen and Meckling (1976b, p.308) define the costs of the agency relationship (agency costs) as the sum of three components:

1.   monitoring expenditures by the principal

2.   bonding expenditures by the agent

3.   the residual loss.

Monitoring expenditures are expenditures by the principal to "control" the agent's behaviour (e.g. costs of measuring and observing the agent's behaviour, costs of establishing compensation policies, etc.). The agent has incentives to make expenditures to guarantee that he will not take certain actions to harm the principal's interest or that he will compensate the principal if he does. These are bonding costs. Finally, even with monitoring and bonding expenditures, the actions taken by the agent will differ from the actions the principal would take himself. Jensen and Meckling define the wealth effect of this divergence in actions as the "residual loss".

Jensen and Meckling analyze the effect of both outside equity and debt on agency costs. They compare the behaviour of a manager when he owns 100 per cent of the equity in a firm (owner-manager) with his behaviour after he sells off some of that equity. They show that if the equity market is competitive and makes unbiased estimates of the effects of monitoring and bonding expenditures, then the owner-manager bears the total wealth effect of the expected agency costs of creating outside equity. Thus, the manager has an incentive to reduce expected agency costs. He writes contracts for monitoring and bonding as long as the marginal benefits of those contracts (in terms of reduction of residual loss) are greater than the marginal costs (direct costs of the covenants and the utility of the perquisites foregone).

There are agency costs involved in debt financing also. Jensen and Meckling show (p.335) how, in the absence of monitoring or bonding contracts, an owner-manager can increase his wealth at the expense of bondholders by first selling bonds with the loose promise to invest in a project with a low variance of return and by then investing in a project with the same systematic risk but a higher variance of return.[9] However, Jensen and Meckling argue, the bondholders realize that he will do so, as a wealth-maximizer, and they will price the bond accordingly. In addition, if the high variance project has a lower expected return than the low variance project then the total value of the firm is reduced by the manager investing in the high variance project. This wealth loss is the "residual loss" portion of the agency costs of debt. This "residual loss" is borne by the owner-manager, so he has an incentive to reduce the total agency costs of debt by

---

[9]The term "systematic risk" is used as in the Sharpe (1964)-Lintner (1965) capital asset pricing model.

offering monitoring and bonding contracts.[10]

There are abundant examples of monitoring and bonding arrangements which are consistent with the hypothesis that managers seek to reduce the agency costs of both debt and equity. One of the most common examples is the covenant that restricts the payment of dividends. Without this restriction we would expect managers and shareholders to "steal" the assets of the corporation and leave the debt-holders with the "shell" of the corporation.[11] This covenant is not only common; it is also old. As early as 1620, a corporate charter included a limitation that dividends only be paid from profits.[12] Since we observe some company charters after that date and not including the dividend covenant, it appears that this company's covenant was voluntarily included by its promoters.[13]

An example of monitoring and bonding activities to reduce the agency costs of equity, is a management compensation plan which ties management wealth to shareholder wealth, directly via stock options or indirectly by bonus plans in which the bonus depends on net income.[14] Management compensation plans of this kind have existed for many years. For example, in 1887 the Leeds Estate Building and Investment Company's articles included a provision whereby the manager and the directors were entitled to a bonus based on the amount of profits available for dividends.[15] Another example is provided in the Spanish Prospecting Company case of 1911. An officer of the Spanish Prospecting Company was entitled to salary "only in the case of there being sufficient profits arising from the business to provide for its payment" [Hatfield (1927, p.281)]. I suspect that these are not isolated examples; in fact, I hypothesize that the management compensation of U.K. companies in the nineteenth century usually was tied to the "profits" of the company.[16]

2.1.b The role of audited financial statements in reducing agency costs

Jensen and Meckling (1976b, p.338) provide an example of the way in which audited financial statements can reduce agency costs:

> Suppose, for example, that the bondholders (or outside equity holders) would find it worthwhile to produce detailed financial statements such as those contained in the usual published accounting reports as a means of monitoring the manager. If the manager himself can produce such information at lower costs than they (perhaps because he is already collecting much of the data for his own internal decision making purposes), it would pay him to agree in advance to incur the cost of

---

[10]The agency costs of debt and the manager's incentives to reduce them are also analyzed by Black, Miller and Posner (1974) and Myers (1976).

[11]For a statement of the purpose of dividend covenants see "Excerpts from Manual on Framing Loan Covenants" in Black, Miller and Posner (1974). Black and Scholes (1973), Black, Miller and Posner (1974) and Myers (1976) investigate the implications of dividend restrictions for the valuation of debt.

[12]The company was the New River Company. See Kehl (1941, p.4).

[13]Kehl (1941, p.4) states that the inclusion of such dividend covenants in corporate charters began in the 1600's and that they became "increasingly more common" during the eighteenth century. This suggests that not all corporate charters included them in the 1600's.

[14]Conference Board (1974).

[15]See Edwards (1968, p.148).

[16]I discuss the definition of "profits" and its relationship to shareholder wealth later in this section of the paper.

providing such reports and to have their accuracy testified to by an
independent outside auditor.

In an unregulated economy, without legally-required corporate financial
statements, we could observe corporate financial statements fulfilling the
function of reducing agency costs. An opportunity to test this hypothesis is
provided by the nineteenth century, in which corporations in both the U.S. and
the U.K. were not generally required to present financial statements.[17] Were
corporate financial statements used in that period to reduce agency costs? Did
promoters/managers voluntarily contract at the time of selling debt or equity to
supply outside equity and debt-holders with information useable for monitoring
their own actions? Whether or not the types of informatiion observed in
financial statements in the nineteenth century could serve to reduce agency costs
is relevant to these questions. Since this depends on the form on the monitoring
and bonding contracts, we first note some of the contracts existing in the
nineteenth century.

One such contract is the compensation scheme. Jensen and Meckling (1976b, p.323)
hypothesize that monitoring and bonding contracts which tie the incentives of the
manager more closely to the outside equity holders' interests (such as
compensation schemes dependent on shareholder wealth) can reduce agency costs. I
have noted the existence of such contracts in the U.K. in the late nineteenth and
early twentieth centuries.

I have indicated that covenants restricting the payment of dividends to the
amount of profits reduce the agency costs of debt. They also reduce the agency
costs of preferred equity capital. Such covenants were common in the articles of
corporations in the nineteenth century.[18] Indeed the famous nineteenth century
cases on the definition of profits arose because of such covenants.[19]

A third covenant which also reduced the agency costs of debt and preferred equity
existed in the articles of some U.K. corporations in the nineteenth century.
That covenant restricted the payment of dividends to the amount of profits
remaining after deducting a reserve fund for maintenance, repairs, depreciation
and renewals. An example of the covenant is the 104th article of London Tramways
Company as reported in the action Davison vs. Gillies (1879).[20] The articles of
some other corporations did not require a deduction for depreciation (e.g. the
Neuchatel Asphalt Company).[21] The courts took the presence or absence of this
covenant on depreciation seriously. They did or did not require depreciation to
be deducted before determining profits available for dividend depending on
whether the articles did or did not include the covenant.[22] I predict that in the
nineteenth century the articles of U.K. corporations included many other types of
covenants which reduced agency costs of outside equity and debt. Detailing all
those covenants is beyond the scope of this paper. The important point is that
in order to monitor the three forms of covenant mentioned above, the outside

---

[17]See Benston (1976, chapter 2, pp.14-22).

[18]The U.K. Companies Act of 1862 did not require dividends to be paid only out of
profits [Brief (1976, p.17)].

[19]See Brief (1976) and Hatfield (1927) for descriptions of these cases.

[20]See Dent vs. The London Tramways Company (Limited) in Brief (1976, p.193).

[21]See Lee vs. Neuchatel Asphalt Company in Brief (1976, p.19).

[22]Ibid. Also see Litherland (1968). Litherland is quite explicit (p.171): "the
question of depreciation was a matter of internal management with which the law
had nothing to do. The Articles of the given company were to govern".

equity holders and debt holders need an observable estimate of what they understand to be profits. Moreover, that estimate can not be under the sole control of management. Thus, if managers offered those covenants on bonding contracts in the nineteenth century, I expect that they also bonded themselves to provide audited financial statements.

During the period 1856 to 1900, U.K. corporations were not required by law to provide financial statements to shareholders or to bondholders. If supplied, they were not required by law to be audited.[23] However, the Joint Stock Companies Act of 1856 did include a model set of articles. Those articles were also included in the 1862 Companies Act as Table A. The articles required directors to present to the annual general meeting of a company a Statement of Income and Expenditure including, among other things, a balance of profit or loss and a Balance Sheet.[24] The articles also required the appointment of auditors and required those auditors to report upon the Balance Sheet and accounts. The court decided in 1887 that the articles made the auditor responsible for the soundness of the "profit available for dividend" number reported in the financial statements.[25]

During the 44-year period 1856 to 1900 many promoters of managers or corporations voluntarily bonded themselves by accepting the model articles or at least articles including the requirement to present audited financial statements. It was "not unusual" for the accounts of well-known corporations to be audited in that period and by the end of the period the professional auditor was "an accepted part of the scene".[26]

2.1.c Implications for financial statements in an unregulated economy

The argument, that a function of audited financial statements in an unregulated economy is to reduce agency costs, could explain which corporations present financial statements and how the contents of those statements vary across corporations. Thus, Jensen and Meckling's analysis has the potential to produce a theory of corporate financial statements. Whether or not it does so depends upon the ability of derived hypotheses to withstand empirical testing. In this section I provide examples of derived hypotheses which can be tested.

If the function of financial statements is to present numbers for monitoring covenants, then I expect to observe nineteenth century corporations voluntarily presenting financial statements when such covenants exist.

> Hypothesis 1: The greater the number of bonding covenants dependent on financial numbers entered into by the corporation, the greater the likelihood that the corporation presented financial statements.

The above test of the proposed theory is not very strong. Covenants could exist for reasons other than to reduce agency costs and the financial statements could exist purely because of the covenants. A stronger test would be to predict which corporations in an unregulated economy are likely to have bonding covenants and hence are likely to present financial statements. The analysis of Jensen and Meckling (1976b) enables such a prediction. They predict (pp.346-7) that the

---

[23]See Edey (1968, p.137) and Edey and Panitpakdi (1956). However, note that auditing was required for banks by the Companies Act of 1879 and life insurance companies were required by the Life Assurance Companies Act of 1870 to provide financial statements upon request to shareholders and policyholders.

[24]See Edey and Panitpakdi (1956, pp.362-364).

[25]See the Leeds Estate Building Company case in Edwards (1956, p.148).

[26]Edey (1968, p.137).

optimum level of monitoring increases as the ratio of the managers' share of equity to outside equity falls. Further, they also predict (p.347) that (holding the managers' share of equity constant) the larger the corporations' outside debt the larger the optimum level of monitoring. Both of these predictions provide hypotheses which could be tested using nineteenth century data on corporations which were not required by statute to present financial statements.

> Hypothesis 2: The smaller the managers' total relative share of the corporation's equity the greater the likelihood that the corporation presented financial statements.[27]

> Hypothesis 3: The larger the absolute amount of the corporation's outside risky debt, the greater the likelihood that the corporation presented financial statements.

The analysis of agency costs can provide predictions on the contents as well as the existence of financial statements in the absence of statutory requirements. The contents will vary across corporations as bonding covenants vary.

Consider management compensation schemes as illustrating how a particular type of covenant can vary across corporations and as illustrating the effect of that variation on financial statements. The ability of a particular compensation scheme to reduce agency costs depends upon the extent to which the index used for compensation correlates with the interest of the outside shareholders and upon the cost of calculating and applying that index. The degree of correlation and the costs of calculation and application of a particular index will vary across corporations and industries. Hence I expect to observe compensation indexes varying across corporations.

One index used for management compensation in the nineteenth century was "profits". Examples are found in the articles of the Leeds Estate Building Company and the Spanish Prospecting Company reported earlier. According to Litherland (1968, p.171) "profit was calculated in the trading section of the balance sheet as the excess of revenue receipts over properly chargeable expenditures". The accrual concept was not recognized.[28] Further, as I have indicated depreciation was a matter for management and generally was treated as an allocation of profit.[29] Hence "profits" generally were calculated to approximate operating cash flows.

Changes in a corporation's earnings and operating cash flows are highly associated with changes in the market value of the corporations' shares.[30] Thus

---

[27]Jensen and Meckling analyze the agency costs involved in a single manager situation. In practice corporations usually have many managers. This undoubtedly makes the analysis more complex. I consider the Jensen and Meckling analysis as a simplification which is justified if it produces implications which are consistent with observed phenomena. If a corporation has more than one manager we could sum all the equity shares of the managers for the purpose of testing this hypothesis.

[28]Litherland (1968, pp.171-172).

[29]This statement is based on the writings of accounting historians. To check whether it is correct I examined the annual reports of the U.S. non-railroad corporations in the Commercial Chronicle in the last decade of the nineteenth century and the first decade of this century. Since there was a close relationship between U.K. and U.S. accounting practices at that time, the practices of those U.S. corporations should provide evidence on U.K. practices. I found that the majority of those U.S. corporations which did take depreciation charged it to Retained Earnings.

the "profits" index would correlate with the interests of outside shareholders. However, it also provides an important incentive for the manager to act against the shareholders' interests. For example, the manager can increase current operating cash flows (and hence his income) at the expense of future cash flows (and the market value of shares) by reducing maintenance expenditures and allowing fixed assets to deteriorate.

One way to reduce this imperfection of the "profits" index is to adjust the index: i.e., to re-define the index as "profits" less an allowance for repairs and maintenance and depreciation of fixed assets. Since articles did include covenants requiring the deduction of such allowances in order to determine profits available for dividend (e.g. the London Tramways Company referred to earlier), I would predict that some management compensation schemes also used "profits" after depreciation as their index. In fact, since the agency cost of calculating cash flow "profits" would increase as the amount of the corporations' fixed assets increased, I would predict that the greater the value of the corporation's fixed assets the more likely it is that the corporation's management compensation scheme used profits after depreciation as its index of shareholder interest. This prediction in turn provides an hypothesis about the variation of the content of financial statements across corporations in the nineteenth century.

> Hypothesis 4: The greater the value of a corporations' fixed assets, the greater the likelihood that its financial statements included an allocation of profits for renewals, repairs, maintenance or depreciation.

It is interesting to note that a covenant requiring a manager to allocate profits for renewal, repairs, maintenance or depreciation could also reduce the agency costs of debt. Myers (1976) analyzes the effects of agency costs on corporate borrowing. He concludes (p.30) that relatively more debt will be used to finance "assets-in-place" (assets already owned) than will be used to finance growth opportunities (future investments). This conclusion comes from an assumption that greater restrictions can be placed on management's discretion in the case of existing assets and hence agency costs of debt used to finance existing assets will be lower. The requirement to set aside profits for renewal, repairs, maintenance or depreciation of existing assets is one such restriction.

2.1.d The effect of regulation of financial statements on agency costs

The above hypotheses illustrate the way in which accounting practices can be explained by a theory of agency costs. Many more hypotheses can be generated from that theory, about current practice as well as practice in the nineteenth century. The nineteenth century is chosen because the influence of the market on accounting practice in that time period is more readily apparent. There were fewer legal requirements and fewer effects of the political process.

In a regulated economy, the manager of a corporation still has the incentive to reduce agency costs. We observe him engaging in bonding activities. Also, we can observe the corporation's published audited financial statements being used to monitor bonding covenants.[31] However, regulations and statutes now have an impact on the contents of those statements. The agency cost theory of accounting

---

[30]See Ball and Brown (1968).

[31]For example, Brunswick Corporations' Note Agreement with the Prudential Insurance Company of America (dated May 11, 1976) includes (page 5) an affimative covenant requiring the corporations' management to deliver quarterly and annual financial statements to Prudential. The annual financial statements must be certified by the auditors who must also certify that they have no knowledge of any defaults on the covenants in the note agreement.

is rich enough to predict effects of changes in financial statements, due to the political process, on actions of managers and investors.

An examination of U.S. lending agreement covenants indicates that the impact of regulation on the contents of financial statements has not always been to the advantage of investors.   For example in Brunswick Corporation's May 11, 1976 Note Agreement with Prudential Insurance Company of America, the definition of earnings available for dividends excludes certain gains (non-cash items) which have been required to be included in reported net income by various U.S. accounting standard setting bodies.[32]

I hypothesize that had reported profits consisted of operating cash flows as in the nineteenth century, the extra bonding costs of devising these exclusions would not have been incurred.   These extra bonding costs were borne by the residual-claim holders (shareholders and management) at the time the accounting standards were announced.

The proposition that accounting standards have increased legal costs can be tested.   An examination of U.S. accounting standards since the standard setting process began with the Committee on Accounting Procedure (C.A.P.) in 1939 should identify standards which could cause reported profits to increase by the inclusion of non-cash accruals (income-increasing standards).   By comparing a sample of loan agreements before and after the announcement of income-increasing standards I can test the following hypothesis.

> Hypothesis 5: Loan agreements made after the requirements of an income increasing standard are more likely to incorporate covenants eliminating the particular accrual from the profits available for dividend.

I hope that the above examples have made it clear that an agency cost theory of corporate financial statements is potentially a rich source of hypotheses about accounting practice.   However, it does not explain the form and nature of the regulations and statutes that affect financial statements.   A theory with the potential to explain regulations and statutes is outlined in section 3.

2.1.e The agency relationship in the accounting literature

Accountants have long been aware of the importance of the agency relationship in explaining observed accounting practice.   Yamey (1962, p.15) suggests that accounting began because of the agency relationship: "The origins of accounting and indeed of written records are probably to be found in the need of an 'accounting' officer to render a statement of money and other assets received in his charge on behalf of his employer or disbursed on his behalf.   There was a need for a check on the honesty and reliability of subordinates."   De Ste Croix (1956, p.38) states that the purpose of Greek and Roman accounting was to disclose any "loss due to dishonesty or negligence" of subordinates (i.e., agents).

The idea that the purpose of accounting is to check the honesty and reliability

---

[32]Examples of those gains which are excluded in the agreement include: (1) gains from "the sale, conversion or other disposition of capital assets" which could have been credited to Retained Earnings instead of Income if the U.S. Securities and Exchange Commission (S.E.C.) had not adopted a "clean-surplus" policy; and (2) income arising from accounting for investment by the equity method required by the Accounting Principles Board (A.P.B.): i.e., the corporation's share of the profits retained by a subsidiary.

Note that while accounting standard setting-bodies like the A.P.B. did not have legal power to enforce their standards, they did have the backing of the S.E.C. which did have the power [see Horngren (1976)].

of agents is called the "stewardship" concept in the accounting literature. It
has been used to explain, among other things, feudal accounting in England
[Littleton and Zimmerman (1962, p.23) and Yamey (1962, p.15)] and the financial
reporting provisions of the British Companies Act of 1847 [Littleton and
Zimmerman (1962, p.84)]. Thus the idea that the agency relationship can explain
accounting practice is not new. What is new in this paper is recognition of the
relationship between agency costs and financial statements: the recognition that
promoters and managers of corporations offering new issues of shares or debt have
incentives to reduce agency costs, to contract (e.g. in corporate articles) to
reduce those costs and to contract to supply monitoring information in financial
statements. This formal structuring of the role of financial statements in the
agency relationship makes it possible to formulate consistent, interrelated
hypotheses about accounting practice and to test them. It provides a means of
carrying out the suggestions of Edey and Panitpakdi (1956, n.14) that accountants
study "the extent to which the pressure of the market brought about voluntary
improvements in the presentation of corporate accounting information in the late
nineteenth century."

2.2 The Information Hypothesis as an Explanation of Financial Statements

Many papers in the accounting literature argue that the function of corporate
financial statements is and should be to provide information useful to investors
in their investment decisions (the information function).[33] Information for
monitoring bonding covenants is useful information to investors, so the functions
overlap. However, the emphasis is different. Information for monitoring bonding
covenants is contracted for in advance as part of a mechanism by which the
manager restricts the extent to which his actions deviate from the interests of
shareholders or bondholders. The emphasis is on information as part of a
management control mechanism. In the alternative information function the
emphasis is on the provision of information to investors to enable them to value
securities and make "rational" investment decisions.[34] The emphasis is on
information for market valuation.

I argue in section 3 that the emphasis in the accounting literature on the
information function of financial statements is the result of actions of
individuals in the political process: that it is the result of the Congress (or
Parliament) and regulatory agencies such as the S.E.C. stating that corporate
financial statements should provide information useful to investors in valuing
securities in the capital markets. I doubt that the information hypothesis has
as much potential as the agency cost hypothesis for explaining corporate
financial statements in an economy without such government intervention. I have
this doubt for several reasons.

> 1. The evidence suggests that corporate financial statements convey
> relatively little information which causes the capital markets to change
> the values of corporations' securities.[35]
>
> 2. Managers are likely to have little incentive to supply information in
> corporate financial statements. Individuals who are the first to discover
> information relevant to the valuation of a corporation's securities (e.g.,
> that oil has been discovered) can trade on that information and increase

---

[33]For example, see the American Accounting Association, Committee on External
Reporting (1969) and the American Institute of Certified Public Accountants Study
Group on the Objectives of financial Statements (1973, p.13).

[34]For examples of the emphasis see Staubus (1969, p.651) and Chambers (1968).

[35]For U.S. evidence see Ball and Brown (1968) and Foster (1977). For Australian
evidence see Brown (1970).

their wealths. I expect them to trade until the prices of corporations'
securities are equal to their estimates of the equilibrium prices of the
securities, given the information. People will invest in the production
of such information until they earn a "normal" return on the marginal
dollar invested. Thus, corporate managers can only supply information in
corporate financial statements if two conditions are met. The first
condition is that they have access to information about corporations'
values (e.g., their future cash flows) before outsiders gathering such
information discover it or surrogate information (a plausible assumption).
The second condition is that they be able to maintain exclusive access to
that information until the financial statements are published (an
implausible assumption). If managers cannot supply information relevant to
the valuation of the corporations' securities to the capital markets in
financial statements, they will not be rewarded for such information
production.[36] Note that they are rewarded for contracting to supply
information for monitoring bonding covenants at the times of entering into
the covenants. They are rewarded by being able to sell the shares or
bonds at higher prices with the covenants than without them.

3.   CORPORATE FINANCIAL STATEMENTS AND THE POLITICAL PROCESS

3.1   The Political Process and Financial Statements

In the previous section I examined the determination of corporate. financial
statements in an unregulated economy. Modern economies are regulated. There are
Companies Acts in the U.K. and Australia which require disclosure of particular
items in financial statements and there are government agencies such as the
Securities and Exchange Commission (S.E.C.) which regulate the contents of
financial statements. A theory of corporate financial statements should explain
the extent to which such government requirements and regulations affect financial
statements. Ideally it should predict the government requirements and
regulations themselves.

There has been substantial interest in the theory of government in recent years.
Much of this interest was stimulated by Downs (1975a and 1957b) and Buchanan and
Tullock (1962). The prime contribution of economists to this literature has been
to introduce the assumption that individuals in the political process (e.g.,
voters, elected and appointed officials) maximize their own self-interests (i.e.
expected utilities).[37] The literature on the application of economics to the
political process has been classified into two non-mutually exclusive sets:
Mueller (1976) describes one set as the literature on "public choice"; and Posner
(1974) describes another set as "theories of economic regulation."

The theory of government is not yet developed to the stage that we can predict
when and how corporate financial statements will be regulated. However, we can
identify some variables involved in that process and hence can formulate some
hypotheses about disclosure regulations and managers' reactions to them. In this
section I demonstrate how one can generate such hypotheses on the basis of the
assumption that individuals maximizing their expected utilities.

3.1.a   Information in the political process

One important variable in the theory of government is identified by Downs (1957a
and 1957b). That is that the probability of one individual's vote affecting an

---

[36]This result does not require the assumption that has been popularized by
Gonedes and Dopuch (1974), that information in financial statements is a public
good.

[37]See Buchanan and Tullock (1962, pp.17-39) and Meckling (1976a).

election outcome usually is very small. Hence, the expected value of the voter's own vote is trivial. As a result, he has little incentive to incur costs to gather information relevant to his vote. Further, the number of bills proposed by a legislative body during a legislative term is large. The costs to the individual of keeping track of his representative's vote on each bill and of determining the effect of that bill on his own expected utility are likely to be large. Thus, I expect that the information an individual uses in making voting decisions is acquired as a by-product of other activities. Examples of these other activities would be trade-union membership, watching television news reports for entertainment, etc.

Jensen (1976b) and Meckling (1976a) argue that if individual voters have little incentive to demand information on the effects of their representative's actions and related political phenomena, then the media have little incentive to supply such information. As a consequence, Jensen (1976b) predicts that news programs on television, newspapers, etc. would tend to provide simple explanations of the political process: explanations which entertain rather than inform. For example, he suggests that such entertainment would lead to some groups in any political conflict being cast as "good" and other groups as "evil".

Jensen (1976b, pp.20-22) argues that crises (impressions of impending disaster caused by natural phenomena or by individuals) are entertainment and thus the news media has incentives to create them. Jensen and Meckling (1976a, pp.21-22) argue that politicians also have incentives to create crises. Politicians create crises and then come to the rescue with simple legislative "solutions". For example, the crisis that unions and monopolies are creating inflation requires price controls [see Meckling (1976a, p.21)]. These "solutions" almost invariably increase the resources controlled by government and hence the resources controlled by elected representatives.

It is instructive to contrast information production in the political sector with information production in the capital market. It is often argued that small investors have little incentive to acquire information relevant to the valuation of securities.[38] Nevertheless, security prices reflect such information. Since entrepreneurs can capture the benefits of the information by trading on it, they bear the costs of production . Hence security prices can reflect information and serve as efficient signals for resource allocation. However, it is costly for political entrepreneurs to capture the benefits of information relevant to the political process. They can not directly buy votes, or claims to the effects of votes like the entrepreneur in the capital market who can buy securities. Hence information produced for political decisions is not likely to be of the same calibre as information on which security prices are based. Crises and simple "solutions" will abound.

3.1.b Crises and the regulation of corporate financial statements

Crises have a long history in justifying legislative actions which affect corporations. For example: the South Sea Bubble, which was blamed on speculators, led to an Act of the U.K. Parliament in 1720 which prohibited the formation of joint-stock companies;[39] the failure of the City of Glasgow Bank "under conditions of fraud," led to the U.K. Companies Act of 1879;[40] the U.S. stock market crash, combined with the published attacks on corporate disclosure by Ripley and others, led to the Securities Act of 1933 and the Securities

---

[38]For example, see Lorie and Hamilton (1973, chapter 5).

[39]Littleton and Zimmerman (1962, p.80). Also see Alchian (1976), who reports that the law did not effectively prevent the formation of joint-stock companies.

[40]Edey (1968, p.138).

Exchange Act of 1934;[41] the recent mining boom and bust in Australia led to the Rae Committee Report and to the recent proposals for federal regulation of securities markets. There is no doubt that significant economic events did occur at these times. What is doubtful is the validity of the simplistic explanations used by legislators to justify legislative actions to remedy the crisis.[42]

Many crises which led to corporate regulation and, in particular, to regulation of corporate financial statements were blamed by political entrepreneurs on the lack of adequate corporate disclosure or misleading corporate disclosure. For example, U.S. politicians claimed that inadequate corporate disclosure was partially to blame for the stock market "crash" of 1929. Benston (1969, p.23) reports that the idea "that investors had been defrauded or, at least seriously misled by inadequate disclosure of the financial affairs of corporations" was an important rationale for the U.S. Securities Exchange Act of 1934 which established the S.E.C. Mundheim (1964, p.648) puts the idea succinctly: "The theory of the Securities Act is that if investors are provided with sufficient information to permit them to make a reasoned decision concerning the investment merits of securities offered to them, investor interests can be adequately protected without unduly restricting the ability of business ventures to raise capital."

Empirical evidence suggests that the stock market uses information from sources

---

[41]Benston (1969, pp.52-53) reports that despite Ripley's attacks on corporations for releasing confusing financial reports, a careful examination of the Senate hearings that preceded the Securities Act of 1933 [U.S. Congress, Senate (1933)] turned up only one citation of fraudulently prepared financial statements.

[42]Neither the U.S. Senate Hearings [U.S. Congress, Senate (1933)] prior to the Securities Act of 1933 nor the Rae Report [Australia, Senate (1974)] provides systematic evidence to support their conclusions. Benston (1969) deals with the U.S. Senate Hearings. In Australia, the Rae Report [Australia, Senate (1974, p.1.1)] states that:

> The main finding of this Committee is that the regulation of the securities markets, of the intermediaries which operate in these markets, and of some of the activities of public companies and investment funds, is in need of fundamental reform. Our essential recommendation is that an Australian Securities Commission be established forthwith by the Federal Government to carry out this reform.

The objectives of such legislation and thus presumably the criteria for the establishment of the commission are listed on page 16.15:

> (i) The first is to maintain, facilitate and improve the performance of the capital market in the interests of economic development, efficiency and stability.

> (ii) The second is to ensure adequate protection of those who invest in the securities of public companies and in the securities markets.

At least one of the objectives appears to be economic efficiency. Yet nowhere in the Rae Report is there any attempt to systematically estimate the resource cost of such legislation or to assess the benefits. All that is provided is a series of case studies of a few frauds (the same cases appear in several chapters). The mere existence of fraud is not sufficient to show a "need" for legislation since we would not expect it to be optimal to eliminate all fraud (because of costs). Moreover, in a period of uncertainty about future cash flows following apparent new mineral discoveries, the optimal rate of fraud is likely to be higher than normal.

other than the financial statements in valuing securities. Numbers in financial statements (e.g., sales and net income) are reflected in stock prices before the numbers are announced.[43] While some of the price adjustment is caused by "leaking" of the numbers in the financial statements, some of the adjustment occurs because the information is available from alternative sources (e.g., trade information such as that included in the Commercial Chronicle in the U.S. in the nineteenth century).

It is highly unlikely that the 1929 "crash" (or any other widespread drop in security prices) was due to inadequate disclosure by corporations. Further, the U.S. Senate Hearings preceding the U.S. Securities Acts do not provide any systematic evidence to support the conclusion that inadequate disclosure led to the 1929 crash.[44] It appears that blaming the crash on the lack of disclosure and then regulating disclosure was a convenient "solution" for political entrepreneurs.

3.1.c The effect of crisis regulation on bureaucratic behaviour

I assume bureaucrats appointed to administer corporate disclosure laws maximize their own expected utilities. The bureaucrats' careers and hence their expected utilities are affected by the likelihood of being blamed for future "crises". Thus, I expect bureaucrats to consider the effects of alternative regulations on the likelihood of blame when they draft and interpret regulations on corporate financial statements. Consequently, in order to predict the regulations of agencies such as the S.E.C. I must predict the effects of different regulations on the likelihood of blame for crises.

Losses due to actions are more apparent than losses due to inactions. Hence it is easier for politicians to attach blame for the former type of losses (i.e., the story is easier to sell). For example, when a drug is issued, the losses it causes (e.g. loss of life or deformed babies) become apparent. If a drug is not issued, the lives lost due to the unavailability of the drug are not apparent. Consequently, we would expect the bureaucrats in charge of allowing new drugs to be issued (e.g. the U.S. Federal Drug Administration) to weigh potential losses due to issuance heavier than potential losses due to withholding. Hence they would make the tests of drugs more stringent than might otherwise be optimal.

I expect a similar bias in the regulation of disclosure of corporate financial statements. Failures of large corporations are potential political crises. The losses to shareholders are apparent. Ex post it is easy to claim that assets were overvalued. On the other hand, undervaluing assets is unlikely to lead to any political crises if the corporation is successful. It is much more difficult for the shareholders and voters to observe any losses due to the undervaluation. As a consequence, I would expect bureaucrats to specify rules which encourage management to undervalue assets in corporate financial statements.

A bias towards undervaluation of assets in corporate financial statements would also be expected in an unregulated economy in inflation. Market values of assets for use in monitoring covenants are costly to obtain. There might not be a readily-observable market price for fixed assets and an independent assessment can be costly. Hence, in an unregulated economy I would not expect to observe continuous revaluation of assets. Revaluations would occur when the effect on agency costs of the disparity between market value and book value exceeded the cost of revaluation.

---

[43]See Fama (1976) for a summary of evidence on the efficient markets hypothesis and Gonedes and Dopuch (1974) for a summary of the evidence on the relationship between numbers in financial statements and stock prices.

[44]See n. 42.

When the bureaucratic bias towards undervaluation in the regulated economy is added to the bias caused by the costs of revaluation, I would expect the extent of undervaluation to increase. This provides a testable hypothesis about the effect of the political process on corporate financial statements.

> Hypothesis 6: The assets in corporate financial statements are more undervalued in an economy in which disclosure regulations are set by bureaucrats than in an unregulated economy.

The hypothesis is consistent with observed phenomena in the U.S. Soon after the S.E.C. came into existence it effectively outlawed upward revaluations of assets.[45] Recently, that restriction appears to have been eased. In 1976 the S.E.C. issued Accounting Series Release No. 190 which required large listed corporations to disclose the replacement cost of inventories and gross property, plant and equipment.[46] However, the required disclosure is not in the financial statements themselves. It is by note or in a separate section of the report. The basis for asset valuation in the financial statements is still historical cost.

Hypothesis 6 could be tested in economies other than the U.S. where the content of corporate financial statements is subject to regulation by bureaucrats. However, in performing such tests one would have to be careful to select economies where the basis of valuation is set by bureaucrats and is not specified by statute. In the latter case the bureaucrat can blame the statute for crises "caused" by accounting procedures.

3.1.d The effect of crisis regulation on managers' behaviour

Watts and Zimmerman (1978) investigate the reaction of corporate managers to regulation of the contents of financial statements when information for voting decisions is costly. They argue that the corporate manager has an incentive to select accounting procedures and to lobby with politicians and bureaucrats for accounting procedures which reduce the net income reported in financial statements. Political entrepreneurs use "high" profits to create "crises". For example, the profits of U.S. oil corporations during the recent Arab oil embargo were used to justify bills to "break-up" large oil corporations.[47] Watts and Zimmerman (1978, p.8) also argue that the likelihood that reported net income will be used to justify political action increases with the size of the corporation.[48] Thus the manager of a large corporation is more likely to favour an accounting standard which decreases the net income reported in the corporation's financial statements than is the manager of a small corporation. This argument provides Watts and Zimmerman with a testable hypothesis.

> Hypothesis 7: The larger the size of a corporation whose net income is increased (decreased) by a proposed accounting standard, the greater the likelihood that its managers will lobby against (for) the standard.

---

[45]See Zeff (1972, pp.156-160) for an account of the circumstances leading to this action.

[46]Ernst and Ernst (1976). The requirement applies to listed corporations whose total iventories and gross property, plant and equipment are more than $100 million and more than 10% of total assets.

[47]For example see a bill introduced into the Senate by Senator Bayh [U.S. Congress, Senate, Subcommittee on Anti-trust and Monopoly (1975, pp.5-13) and (1976, p.1,893)]. Note that it is absolute size and profits which are used as justification. On this point also see the "Curse of Bigness", Barrons, June 30, 1969, pp.1 and 8. Also see Alchian and Kessel (1962, p.162).

[48]Watts and Zimmerman (1978). See also n. 47.

Watts and Zimmerman observe the submissions to the U.S. Financial Accounting Standard Board concerning its discussion memorandum on general price level adjustments (issued February 15, 1974). They identify 26 non-utility corporations whose net incomes would be decreased by those adjustments. They are able to reject the null hypothesis that the attitude of the management of those firms towards the standard is independent of the firm's asset size at the .001 level. The management of the larger corporations tended to favor the proposed standard.

I am confident that the political process affects the choice of accounting procedures in Australia as well as in the U.S. For example, the use of replacement cost depreciation by Australia's largest corporation (The Broken Hill Proprietary Company Limited) is most likely due to that corporation's size and sensitivity to the political process. By reducing its reported profit, the corporation's managers are able to reduce the costs imposed by political entrepreneurs.

3.1.e Other effects

There are other effects of the political process on financial statements, in addition to those caused by "crisis" regulation. For example, corporate income taxes apparently had an important impact on the treatment of depreciation in corporate financial statements in the U.S. I noted earlier that at the beginning of the nineteenth century depreciation was regarded as an allocation of profits instead of an expense.[49] When depreciation was taken, usually it was charged to Retained Earnings and not to Income.[50]

Depreciation came to be generally regarded as an expense in the U.S. and hence it came to be charged to Income during the early part of the twentieth century. It is highly likely that this change in attitude was due to the U.S. Revenue Act of 1913 which allowed depreciation as a deduction for the purpose of determining taxable income. Hatfield (1927, p.140) ascribes the change to that Act.

The Corporation Excise Tax Law of 1909 was passed in an effort to avoid a U.S. Supreme Court decision holding that an income tax law enacted in 1894 was unconstitutional. This law was itself declared unconstitutional, but it had a significant impact on the 1913 tax law passed after the Sixteenth Amendment to the Constitution. The Treasury (which administered the 1909 Act) ruled that "depreciation to be admitted as a deduction in calculating income must be recorded unequivocally on the books as such".[51] A March, 1912 editorial in the Journal of Accountancy reports that, after the ruling, many corporate officials began charging depreciation as an expense in the corporate financial statements.[52]

It is difficult to hypothesize why the Treasury required that depreciation be recorded as an expense. A potential hypothesis is that accountants lobbied for such a ruling because it reduced their costs of convincing corporate management to charge depreciation.[53]

3.2   The Function of the Accounting Literature in the Political Process

If individuals involved in the political process maximize their own expected

---

[49]Litherland (1968, p.171).

[50]See n.29.

[51]Carey (1969, p.64).

[52]Carey (1969, p.68).

[53]Note that auditors were legally liable for breach of covenants, some of which involved depreciation.

utilities, why does the accounting literature tend to assume otherwise?[54] The reason is that the function of the contemporary accounting literature is something other than to explain observed accounting practices. I will use the U.S. experience in the regulation of corporate financial statements to explain the real function of the accounting literature.

The S.E.C. was established as a "solution" to the crisis "caused" by inadequate corporate disclosure. One of the "inadequacies" of that disclosure was the diversity of accounting procedures used by corporate management.[55] The bureaucrats at the S.E.C. were motivated to reduce the diversity to avoid the blame for future crises.

The diversity of accounting procedures does not occur by chance. For example, in section 2 I predicted that accounting procedures would vary across corporations because of differences in agency problems (see Hypothesis 4). Accounting procedures can also vary across firms because of income tax rules.[56] Hence, changes in accounting procedures in order to reduce their diversity will impose costs on individuals. Those changes might increase agency costs or they might increase corporate taxes.[57] Consequently corporate managers will be motivated to lobby against attempts to reduce the diversity of accounting procedures.

The bureaucrats involved in reducing the diversity of accounting procedures have conflicting incentives. They have an incentive to appear to reduce diversity in order to avoid blame. They also have an incentive to avoid imposing costs on corporate managers and other individuals. Those managers could lobby with members of Congress to offset the bureaucrats' decisions, to reduce the S.E.C.'s budget, etc. The bureaucrats will choose the course which maximizes their own expected utilities.

The S.E.C. temporarily avoided the problem by delegating the responsibility for setting accounting standards to a committee of the American Institute of Certified Public Accountants, known as the Committee on Accounting Procedure (C.A.P.), soon after the S.E.C.'s formation.[58] But the C.A.P. failed to significantly reduce the diversity of accounting procedures.[59] The Institute then replaced the C.A.P. by the Accounting Principles Board (A.P.B.) which also failed in its task of reduction of the diversity of procedures. The Institute then replaced the A.P.B. by the semi-autonomous Financial Accounting Standards Board (F.A.S.B.) which currently sets standards in the U.S. However, Arthur Andersen and Co. recently has instituted a law suit which could force the S.E.C. to set accounting standards.[60]

The C.A.P., the A.P.B. and the F.A.S.B. all tried to formulate a set of consistent principles to justify their selection of accounting standards. That is, they tried to formulate a story which could be used to forestall political

---

[54]See n. 1.

[55]Ripley (1927, pp.208-228) criticizes the lack of comparability of corporate financial statements in the 1920's.

[56]For example in the U.S. corporations which use the last-in-first-out method of inventory valuation for tax purposes are also required to use that method in corporate financial statements.

[57]See Watts and Zimmerman (1978) for a discussion of the types of costs which can be imposed on corporate management as a result of an accounting standard.

[58]Zeff (1972, p.133).

[59]Moonitz (1974, p.15).

[60]See The C.P.A. Letter September 13, 1976, p.2.

action by individuals affected by the standards. The C.A.P. and the A.P.B. failed.[61] The F.A.S.B. has not used an underlying set of principles to justify the standards it has issued to date. The reason the C.A.P. and the A.P.B. were unable to find such a set of principles is that the only consistent explanation of the standards of the C.A.P., the A.P.B. and the F.A.S.B. would be based on the individuals involved in the process (managers, bureaucrats, accountants etc.) maximizing their own self-interests. However, it is not in the self-interest of the individuals on the C.A.P., the A.P.B. or the F.A.S.B. to justify the selection of accounting standards on that basis. I argued previously that voters would only tend to acquire their information on political choices as a by-product of some other activity. As a result, news media have incentives to entertain rather than inform; news stories are portrayed as a conflict between "good" and "bad" parties. Individuals motivated by self-interest are portrayed as "bad".[62] Consequently, explaining the choice of an accounting standard on the basis of self-interest of accountants and corporate managers would not be an effective defense against the political actions of individuals harmed by the standard.

Because the only possible consistent explanation of a standard-setting group's selection of accounting procedures is politically costly, the group demands other explanations. These explanations must of necessity be inconsistent and must vary from circumstance to circumstance because they are not the underlying reasons. There is a demand for diverse prescriptions for accounting standards. I hypothesize that one of the major functions of academic accounting research since 1939 has been to supply those diverse prescriptions.[63] Because it is the "story" per se which is important and not the explanation of observed phenomena, there has been little incentive to confirm the hypotheses upon which any particular set of prescriptions is based.

Thus, the major function of the academic accounting literature is not the typical function of theory for an applied area. For example, the literature does not function to provide practitioners with a structure for choice among alternative practices and recommendations to clients. Instead, it functions to provide excuses. As a consequence, the academic literature does not lead practice except by chance, and it is little wonder that, after studying the history of the determination of accounting standards, Zeff comes to the same conclusion:

> A study of the U.S. experience clearly shows that the academic literature has had remarkably little impact on the writings of practitioners and upon the accounting policies of the American Institute and the SEC. I seriously doubt that practitioners in this country, including especially the members of the American Institute's accounting principles committees, look to academics or to the American Accounting Association for inspiration, insight, or counsel. The evidence suggests that accounting theory is invoked more as a tactic to buttress one's preconceived notions, rather than as a genuine arbiter of contending views.[64]

---

[61]See Moonitz (1974) and Zeff (1972) for accounts of these attempts.

[62]See Jensen (1976, p.11).

[63]Watts and Zimmerman (1977) trace the major developments in accounting theory this century and link them to the demand for "stories" (i.e., to the demand for excuses).

[64]Zeff (1973). Zeff's investigation of the determination of accounting principles is given in Zeff (1972).

4. CONCLUSION

I have endeavoured to outline the basic structure of a theory of financial statements and to provide examples of its constituent hypotheses. The apparent consistency of the hypotheses derived in this paper with observed phenomena confirms that the theory has great promise as an explanation of observed phenomena in accounting.

Watts and Zimmerman (1978) have tested one of the hypotheses provided in this paper. I hope that the Watts and Zimmerman paper proves to be the beginning of a literature in accounting whose aim is to explain accounting practice.

I cannot see the accounting professional bodies ever publicly accepting the theory outlined here. It assumes that accountants act in their own self-interests. Hence any endorsement is likely to impose substantial political costs on practicing accountants. Despite this, I have found that individual practitioners in both the U.S. and Australia agree privately with the idea that the contents of financial statements are the equilibrium outcome of individuals maximizing their own self-interests. Further, students who understand the elements of this theory have found the selection of alternate accounting procedures less confusing and have gone into practice with an analytical base which proves useful. This suggests that there might be a demand for this theory in professional education.

REFERENCES

Alchian, A., 1976, "On Corporations: A Visit With Smith," paper presented at the Mont Pelerin Meeting in St. Andrews, Scotland, August.

Alchian A. and R. Kessel, 1962, "Competition, Monopoly and the Pursuit of Money," in: Aspects of Labor Economics (N.B.E.R., Princeton University Press, Princeton).

American Accounting Association, Committee on External Reporting, 1969, "An Evaluation of External Accounting Practices," Accounting Review, 44 (supplement), 79-123.

American Institute of Certified Public Accountants, Study Group on the Objectives of Financial Statements, 1973, (A.I.C.P.A., New York).

Australia, Senate, Select Committee on Securities and Exchange, 1974, Australian Securities Markets and their Regulation (Australian Government Publishing Service, Canberra).

Ball, R. and P. Brown, 1968, "An Empirical Evaluation of Accounting Income Numbers," Journal of Accounting Research, 6, 159-77.

Benston, G.J., 1969, "The Effectiveness and Effects of the S.E.C.'s Accounting Disclosure Requirements," in: Henry G. Manne, ed., Economic Policy and the Regulation of Corporate Securities (American Enterprise Institute, Washington, D.C.)

Benston, G.J., 1976, Corporate Financial Disclosure in the U.K. and the U.S.A. (Saxon House, Westmead, U.K.).

Berhold, M., 1971, "A Theory of Linear Profit Sharing Incentives," Quarterly Journal of Economics, 84, 460-82.

Black, F. and M. Scholes, 1973, "The Pricing of Options and Corporate Liabilities," Journal of Political Economy, 81, 637-54.

Black, F., M.H. Miller and R.A. Posner, 1974, "An Approach to the Regulation of

Bank Holding Companies", unpublished paper, University of Chicago.

Brief, R.P., ed., 1976, The Late Nineteenth Century Debate Over Depreciation, Capital and Income (Arno Press, New York).

Brown, P., 1970, "The Impact of the Annual Net Profit Report on the Stock Market," The Australian Accountant, 6, 277-83.

Buchanan, J.M. and G. Tullock, 1962, The Calculus of Consent (University of Michigan Press Ann Arbor).

Carey, J.L., 1969, The Rise of the Accounting Profession, Vol. 1 (American Institute of Certified Public Accountants, New York).

Chambers, R.J., 1966, Accounting, Evaluation and Economic Behavior (Prentice-Hall Inc., Englewood Cliffs, New Jersey).

Chambers, R. J., 1968, "Measures and Values - A Reply to Professor Staubus," Accounting Review, 42, 239-47.

de Ste Croix, 1956, "Greek and Roman Accounting," in: Littleton, A.C. and B.S. Yamey, eds., Studies in the History of Accounting (Richard D. Irwin Inc., Homewood, Illinois).

Downs, A., 1957a, "An Economic Theory of Political Action in a Democracy," Journal of Political Economy, 65, 135-50.

Downs, A., 1957b, An Economic Theory of Democracy (Harper and Row, New York).

Edey, H.C., 1968, "Company Accounting in the Nineteenth and Twentieth Centuries," in: M. Chatfield, ed., Contemporary Studies in the Evolution of Accounting Thought (Dickenson Publishing Company Inc., Belmont, California).

Edey, H.C. and P. Panitpakdi, 1956, "British Company Accounting and the Law 1844-1900," in: A.C. Littleton and B.S. Yamey, eds., Studies in the History of Accounting (Sweet and Maxwell, London).

Edwards, E.O. and P. W. Bell, 1961, The Theory and Measurement of Business Income (University of California Press, Berkeley and Los Angeles).

Edwards, J.D., 1968, "The Antecedents of American Public Accounting," in: M. Chatfield, ed., Contemporary Studies in the Evolution of Accounting Thought (Dickenson Publishing Company, Belmont, California).

Ernst and Ernst, 1976, Financial Reporting Developments (Ernst and Ernst, New York), April.

Fama, E. F., 1976, Foundations of Finance (Basic Books Inc., New York).

Foster, G., 1977, "Quarterly Accounting Data: Time Series Properties and Predictive Ability Results," Accounting Review, 52, forthcoming.

Gonedes, N. and N. Dopuch, 1974, "Capital Market Equilibrium, Information Production, and Selecting Accounting Techniques: Theoretical Framework and Review of Empirical Work," Studies on Financial Objectives: 1974, Journal of Accounting Research, 12 (supplement), 48-129.

Gordon, M.J., 1964, "Postulates, Principles and Research in Accounting," Accounting Review, 39, 251-63.

Hatfield, H.R., 1927, Accounting (D. Appleton-Century Company, New York).

Heckerman, D.G., 1975, "Motivating Managers to Make Investment Decisions," Journal of Financial Economics, 2, 273-92.

Horngren, C. T., 1976, "Setting Accounting Standards in 1980," unpublished speech before the Arthur Young Professors Roundtable, March 30-31.

Ijiri, Y., 1967, The Foundations of Accounting Measurement (Prentice-Hall Inc., Englewood Cliffs, New Jersey).

Jensen, M., 1976a, "Reflections on the State of Accounting Research and the Regulation of Accounting," paper presented at the Stanford Lectures in Accounting, May 21, 1976.

Jensen, M. 1976b, "Towards a Theory of Press," unpublished paper, Graduate School of Management, University of Rochester.

Jensen, M. and W. H. Meckling, 1976a, "Can the Corporation Survive?" Public Policy Working Paper Series, Center for Research in Government Policy and Business, Graduate School of Management, University of Rochester.

Jensen, M. and W. H. Meckling, 1976b, "Theory of the Firm: Managerial Behavior, Agency Costs and Ownership Structure," Journal of Financial Economics, 3, 305-60.

Kehl, D., 1941, Corporate Dividends (The Ronald Press Company, New York).

Lintner, J., 1975, "Security Prices, Risk, and Maximal Gains from Diversification," Journal of Finance, 20, 587-616.

Litherland, D.A., 1968, "Fixed Asset Replacement a Half Century Ago," reprinted in: M. Chatfield, ed., Contemporary Studies in the Evolution of Accounting Thought (Dickenson Publishing Company Inc., Belmont, California).

Littleton, A.C. and V.K. Zimmerman, 1962, Accounting Theory: Continuity and Change (Prentice-Hall Inc., Englewood Cliffs, New Jersey).

Lorie, J. H. and M. T. Hamilton, 1973, The Stock Market: Theories and Evidence (Richard D. Irwin Inc., Homewood, Illinois).

Meckling, W.H., 1976a, "Towards a Theory of Representative Government," paper presented at the Third Annual Conference on Analysis and Ideology, Interlaken, Switzerland, June 4.

Meckling, W.H., 1976b, "Values and the Choice of the Model of the Individual in the Social Sciences," Revue Swisse d´Economic, Politique et de Statistique, December.

Moonitz, M. 1974, Obtaining Agreement on Standards, Studies in Accounting Research No. 8 (American Accounting Association, Sarasota, Florida).

Mueller, D. C., 1976, "Public Choice: A Survey." Journal of Economic Literature, 14, 395-433.

Mundheim, R.H., 1964, "Foreword, Symposium on Securities Regulation," Law and Contemporary Problems, 29, 647-52.

Myers, S. C., 1976, "Determinants of Corporate Borrowing," unpublished paper, Massachusetts Institute of Technology.

Paton, W.A. and A.C. Littleton, 1940, An Introduction to Corporate Accounting Standards (American Accounting Association, Sarasota, Florida).

Posner, R.A., 1974, "Theories of Economic Regulation," The Bell Journal of Economics and Management Science, 5, 335-58.

Ripley, W.Z., 1927, Main Street and Wall Street (Little, Brown and Company, Boston).

Ross, S.A., 1973, "The Economic Theory of Agency: The Principals Problems," American Economic Review, 62, 134-9.

Ross, S.A., 1974, "The Economic Theory of Agency and the Principle of Similarity," in: Balch et.al., eds., Essays on Economic Behavior Under

Uncertainty (North Holland Publishing, Amsterdam).

Sanders, T. H., H.R. Hatfield and Underhill Moore, 1938, Statement of Accounting Principles (American Institute of Certified Public Accountants, New York).

Sharpe, W.F., 1964, "Capital Asset Prices: A Theory of Market Equilibrium Under Conditions of Risk", Journal of Finance, 19, 425-42.

Smith, C., 1976, "On the Theory of Lending," unpublished paper, Graduate School of Management, University of Rochester.

Sprouse, R.T. and M. Moonitz, 1962, A Tentative Set of Broad Accounting Principles for Business Enterprises, Accounting Research Study No. 3 (American Institute of Certified Public Accountants, New York).

Staubus, G., 1967, "Current Cash Equivalent For Assets: A Dissent," Accounting Review, 42, 650-61.

United States--Conference Board, 1974, Top Executive Compensation (Conference Board, New York).

U.S. Congress, Senate, Committee on Banking and Currency, 1933, Hearings on 5.875, 73rd Congress, 1st Session (U.S. Congress, Washington).

U.S. Congress, Senate, Subcommittee on Anti-trust and Monopoly of the Committee of the Judiciary, 1975, Hearings, the Petroleum Industry, Part I, 94th Congress, 1st Session (U.S. Congress, Washington).

U.S. Congress, Senate, Subcommittee on Anti-trust and Monopoly of the Committee on the Judiciary, 1976, Hearings, the Petroleum Industry, Part III, 94th Congress, 1st Session (U.S. Congress, Washington).

Watts, R. and J. Zimmerman, 1977, "The Demand for and Supply of Accounting Theories: The Market for Excuses," unpublished paper, Graduate School of Management, University of Rochester.

Watts, R. and J. Zimmerman, 1978, "Towards a Positive Theory of the Determination of Accounting Standards," Accounting Review, 53, forthcoming.

Wilson, R., 1968, "On the Theory of Syndicates," Econometrica, 36, 119-32.

Wilson, R., 1969, "La Decision: Aggregation et Dynamique des Orders de Preference, Extrat (Editions du Centre National de la Recherche Scientifique, Paris).

Yamey, B.S., 1962, "Some Topics in the History of Financial Accounting in England 1500-1900," in: W.T. Baxter and S. Davidson, eds., Studies in Accounting Theory (Sweet and Maxwell, London).

Zeff, S., 1972, Forging Accounting Principles in Five Countries: A History and Analysis of Trends 1971, Arthur Andersen Lecture Series (Stipes Publishing Company, Champaign, Illinois).

Zeff, S., 1973, "Comments on Accounting Principles - How They are Developed," in: Robert Sterling, ed., Institutional Issues in Public Accounting (Scholars Book Company, Lawrence, Kentucky).

Towards a Positive Theory of the Determination of Accounting Standards

Ross L. Watts and Jerold L. Zimmerman

ABSTRACT: This article provides the beginnings of a positive theory of accounting by exploring those factors influencing management's attitudes on accounting standards which are likely to affect corporate lobbying on accounting standards. Certain factors are expected to affect a firm's cashflows and in turn are affected by accounting standards. These factors are taxes, regulation, management compensation plans, bookkeeping costs, and political costs, and they are combined into a model which predicts that large firms which experience reduced earnings due to changed accounting standards favor the change. All other firms oppose the change if the additional bookkeeping costs justify the cost of lobbying. This prediction was tested using the corporate submissions to the FASB's Discussion Memorandum on General Price Level Adjustments. The empirical results are consistent with the theory.

ACCOUNTING standards in the United States have resulted from a complex interaction among numerous parties including agencies of the Federal government (notably the Securities and Exchange Commission and Treasury Department), state regulatory commissions, public accountants, quasi-public accounting standard-setting boards (the Committee on Accounting Procedures (CAP), the Accounting Principles Board (APB), and the Financial Accounting Standards Board (FASB)), and corporate managements. These parties have, in the past, and continue to expend resources to influence the setting of accounting standards. Moonitz [1974], Horngren [1973] and [1976], Armstrong [1976] and Zeff [1972] document the sometimes intense pressure exerted on the "private" accounting standard-setting bodies (i.e., CAP, APB, FASB). These pressures have led to several reorganizations of the standard-setting boards.

Ultimately, we seek to develop a positive theory of the determination of accounting standards.[1] Such a theory will help us to understand better the source of the pressures driving the accounting standard-setting process, the effects of various accounting standards on different groups of individuals and the allocation of resources, and why various groups are willing to expend resources trying to affect the standard-setting process. This understanding is necessary to determine if prescriptions from normative theories

We wish to thank members of the Finance Workshop at the University of Rochester, members of the Accounting Seminar at the University of Michigan and, in particular, George Benston, Ken Gaver, Nicholas Gonedes, Michael Jensen, Keith Leffler, Martin Geisel, Cliff Smith and an anonymous referee for their helpful suggestions.

[1] See Jensen [1976] and Horngren [1976].

Ross L. Watts and Jerold L. Zimmerman are Assistant Professors of Accounting at the University of Rochester.

(e.g., current cash equivalents) are feasible.

Watts [1974] and [1977] has started to develop such a theory. This paper expands on this initial work by focusing on the costs and benefits generated by accounting standards which accrue to managements, thereby contributing to our understanding of the incentives of management to oppose or support various standards. Management, we believe, plays a central role in the determination of standards. Moonitz supports this view:

> Management is central to any discussion of financial reporting, whether at the statutory or regulatory level, or at the level of official pronouncements of accounting bodies. [Moonitz, 1974, p. 64]

Hence, it seems appropriate that a precondition of a positive theory of standard-setting is understanding management's incentives.

The next section introduces those factors (e.g., tax, regulatory, political considerations) which economic theory leads us to believe are the underlying determinants affecting managements' welfare and, thereby, their decision to consume resources trying to affect the standard-setting process. Next, a model is presented incorporating these factors. The predictions of this model are then tested using the positions taken by corporations regarding the FASB's Discussion Memorandum on General Price Level Adjustments (GPLA). The last section contains the conclusions of the study.

FACTORS INFLUENCING MANAGEMENT ATTITUDES TOWARDS FINANCIAL ACCOUNTING STANDARDS

In this paper, we assume that individuals act to maximize their own utility. In doing so, they are resourceful and innovative.[2] The obvious implication of this assumption is that management

lobbies on accounting standards based on its own self-interest. For simplicity, (since this is an early attempt to provide a positive theory) it could be argued that we should assume that management's self-interest on accounting standards is congruent with that of the shareholders. After all, that assumption has provided hypotheses consistent with the evidence in finance (e.g., the risk/return relationship of the various capital asset pricing models). However, one function of financial reporting is to constrain management to act in the shareholders' interest. (For example, see Benston [1975], Watts [1974], and Jensen and Meckling [1976a].) Consequently, assuming congruence of management and shareholder interests without further investigation may cause us to omit from our lobbying model important predictive variables. To reduce this possibility, we will examine next the effects of accounting standards on management's self-interest without the congruence assumption. The purpose of the examination is to identify factors which are likely to be important predictors of lobbying behavior so that we can include them in our formal model.

The assumption that management selects accounting procedures to maximize its own utility is used by Gordon [1964, p. 261] in an early attempt to derive a positive theory of accounting. There have been several attempts to test empirically Gordon's model, or variants of it, which we call the "smoothing" literature.[3] Problems in the specification of the em-

---

[2] Many economic models assume a rather limited version of economic man. In particular, they assume that man maximizes his own welfare when he is constrained to play by certain rules and in certain institutional settings, ignoring his incentives to avoid or change the rules, setting, etc. Meckling [1976] analyzes this issue.

[3] Ball and Watts [1972]; Barefield and Comiskey [1972]; Barnea, Ronen and Sadan [1975]; Beidleman [1973]; Copeland [1968]; Cushing [1969]; Dasher and Malcom [1970]; Gordon [1964]; Gordon, Horwitz and Meyers [1966].

pirical tests in the smoothing literature leave the Gordon model essentially unconfirmed.[4] Also, certain aspects of the Gordon model contribute to the model's lack of confirmation. Essentially, Gordon [1964] assumed that shareholder satisfaction (and, presumably, wealth) is solely a positive function of accounting income. This assumption avoids the conflict between shareholders and management by implying that increases in stock prices always accompany increases in accounting income. However, recent research casts serious doubt on the ability of management to manipulate directly share prices via changes in accounting procedures.[5]

We assume that management's utility is a positive function of the expected compensation in future periods (or wealth) and a negative function of the dispersion of future compensation (or wealth). The question is how do accounting standards affect management's wealth?[6] Management's total compensation from the firm consists of wages, incentive compensation (cash bonuses and stock or stock options), and nonpecuniary income, including perquisites (discussed in Jensen-Meckling, 1976a). Since it is unclear what role accounting standards play in the level of nonpecuniary income, we exclude it and focus on the first two forms of compensation. To the extent that management can increase either the level of incentive compensation or the firm's share price via its choice of accounting standards, they are made better off.

This analysis distinguishes between mechanisms which increase management's wealth: 1) via increases in share price (i.e., stock and stock options are more valuable) and 2) via increases in incentive cash bonuses. The choice of accounting standards can affect both of these forms of compensation indirectly

through i) taxes, ii) regulatory procedures if the firm is regulated, iii) political costs, iv) information production costs, and directly via v) management compensation plans. The first four factors increase managerial wealth by increasing the cashflows and, hence, share price. The last factor can increase managerial wealth by altering the terms of the incentive compensation. Each of these five factors are discussed in turn.

Factors Affecting Management Wealth[7]

Taxes. Tax laws are not directly tied to financial accounting standards except in a few cases (e.g., the last-in-first-out inventory valuation method). However, the indirect relationship is well documented Zeff [1972] and Moonitz [1974]. The adoption of a given procedure for financial accounting does not decrease the likelihood of that procedure's being

---

[4] For these defects see Ball and Watts [1972], Gonedes [1972] and Gonedes and Dopuch [1974].

[5] Fama [1970] and Goedes and Dopuch [1974]. Further, the results of studies by Kaplan and Roll [1972], Ball [1972] and Sunder [1975] which address the specific issue support the hypothesis that the stock market can discriminate between real events and changes in accounting procedures. Given that the market can on average discriminate, then it must be concluded that managers (on average) expect the market to discriminate. Obviously, managers do and will attempt to influence their share price by direct accounting manipulation, but if these attempts consume resources, then incentives exist to eliminate these inefficient allocations.

[6] For earlier discussions of this question see Watts [1974] and Gonedes [1976].

[7] We have purposefully excluded from the set of factors being examined the information content effect of an accounting standard on stock prices. We have done this because at present the economic theories of information and capital market equilibrium are not sufficiently developed to allow predictions to be made regarding the influence an accounting standard on the capital market's assessment of the distributions of returns (see Gonedes and Dopuch, 1974). We believe that a theory of the determination of account ng standards can be developed and tested ignoring the information content factor. If at some future date, the information content factor can be specified and included in the theory, then the predictions and our understanding of the process will be improved. But we see no reason to delay the development of a theory until information content is specified.

adopted in future Internal Revenue codes, and more likely, will increase the chance of adoption. To the extent that management expects a proposed financial accounting procedure to influence future tax laws, their lobbying behavior is affected by the future tax law effects.

Regulation.[8] Most public utility commissions base their rate-setting formulas on accounting determined costs. A new accounting standard which reduces a utility's reported income may provide its management with an "excuse" to argue for increased rates. Whether the utility commission grants the increase depends on whether groups opposed to the rate increase (e.g., consumer groups) are able to exert political pressure on the commission.[9] This depends on such factors as information costs (to be discussed later). However, to the extent that there is some probability of a rate (and hence cashflow) increase (either temporary or permanent) as the result of an accounting standards change, utilities have an incentive to favor that change. Similarly, they have an incentive to oppose changes in accounting standards which might lead to a rate decrease.

Political Costs. The political sector has the power to effect wealth transfers between various groups. The corporate sector is especially vulnerable to these wealth redistributions. Certain groups of voters have an incentive to lobby for the nationalization, expropriation, break-up or regulation of an industry or corporation.[10] This in turn provides an incentive for elected officials to propose such actions. To counter these potential government intrusions, corporations employ a number of devices, such as social responsibility campaigns in the media, government lobbying and selection of accounting procedures to minimize reported earnings.[11] By avoiding the attention that "high" profits draw because of

the public's association of high reported profits and monopoly rents, management can reduce the likelihood of adverse political actions and, thereby, reduce its expected costs (including the legal costs the firm would incur opposing the political actions). Included in political costs are the costs labor unions impose through increased demands generated by large reported profits.

The magnitude of the political costs is highly dependent on firm size.[12] Even as a percentage of total assets or sales, we would not expect a firm with sales of $100 million to generate the same political costs (as a percentage of sales) as a firm with $10 billion of sales. Casual empiri-

---

[8] We deal in this paper with public utility regulation and the forms of rate regulation employed. Other industries (e.g., banking and insurance) are regulated differently and these industries are ignored in this paper to simplify the analysis.

[9] For the economic theory of regulation upon which this discussion is based see Stigler [1971], Posner [1974] and Peltzman [1975]. Also, Horngren [1976].

[10] Stigler [1971], Peltzman [1975], and Jensen and Meckling [1976b]. An example of an industry facing such action is the oil industry.

[11] For an alleged example of this, see Jack Anderson, Syndicated Column, United Features (New York, April 10, 1976).

[12] Several studies document the association between size and anti-trust [Siegfried 1975]. In proposed anti-trust legislation, size *per se* has been mentioned specifically as a criterion for action against corporations. See the "Curse of Bigness," *Barron's*, June 30, 1969, pp. 1 and 8. Also see a bill introduced into the Senate by Senator Bayh (U.S. Congress, Senate, Subcommittee on Anti-trust and Monopoly (1975), pp. 5–13) would require divesture for oil firms with annual production and/or sales above certain absolute numbers. In the hearings on that bill, Professor Mencke of Tufts University argued that absolute and not relative accounting profits are the relevant variable for explaining political action against corporations.

Menke said, "Nevertheless, precisely because the actions of large firms are so visible, the American public has always equated absolute size with monopoly power. The major oil companies are among the very largest and most visible companies doing business in the United States.

Huge accounting profits, but not high profit rates, are an inevitable corollary of large absolute firm size. This makes these companies obvious targets for public criticism." (U.S. Congress, Senate, Subcommittee on Anti-trust and Monopoly (1976), p. 1893).

cism suggests that Superior Oil Company (1974 sales of $333 million) incurs considerably less costs from anti-trust, "corporate responsibility," affirmative action, etc., than Exxon with sales of $42 billion.

Information Production (i.e., bookkeeping) Costs. Changes in accounting procedures are not costless to firms. Accounting standard changes which either increase disclosure or require corporations to change accounting methods increase the firms' bookkeeping costs (including any necessary increases in accountants' salaries to compensate for additional training).[13]

Management Compensation Plans. A major component of management compensation is incentive (bonus) plan income (Conference Board [1974]), and these plans are based on accounting income. Our survey of 52 firms in our sample indicates that the majority of the companies formally incorporate accounting income into the compensation plan.[14] Hence, a change in accounting standards which increase the firm's reported earnings would, *ceteris paribus*, lead to greater incentive income. But this would reduce the firm's cashflows and share prices would fall. As long as the per manager present value of the after tax incentive income is greater than the decline in each manager's portfolio, we would expect management to favor such an accounting change.[15] But this assumes that the shareholders and nonmanager directors do not oppose such an accounting change or do not adjust the compensation plans for the change in earnings.[16] In fact, the increased cashflows resulting from the political costs, regulatory process and tax effects of an accounting change assumes that various politicians/bureaucrats (i.e., the electorate) do not fully adjust for the change. A crucial assumption of our analysis is that the shareholders and nonmanaging directors have more incentive to adjust for and control increases in reported earnings due to changes in accounting standards than do politicians and bureaucrats.

Incentives for Various Groups to Adjust for a Change in Accounting Standards

An individual (whether a shareholder, nonmanaging director, or politician) will adjust a firm's accounting numbers for a change in accounting standards up to the point that the marginal cost of making the adjustment equals the marginal benefits. Consider the incentives of the outside directors to adjust bonus compensation plans due to a change in accounting standards. If these directors do not adjust the plans, management compensation rises and share price falls by the full discounted present value of the additional compensation.[17] Each outside director's wealth declines to the extent of his ownership in the firm and there is a greater chance of his removal from the board.[18]

[13] We are assuming that any change in accounting standards does not reduce the firm's information production costs. Although there may be cases where a firm is using a costly procedure which is eliminated by a simpler, cheaper procedure, information production costs in this case may decline, but we expect these situations to be rare.

[14] The frequency is 69 percent.

[15] At this early stage in the development of the theory, we assume that management of the firm is composed of homogeneous (i.e., identical) individuals to simplify the problem.

[16] Our examination of the description of 16 management compensation plans indicated that all the plans were administered by the nonmanaging directors.

[17] Likewise, we would expect the outside directors to adjust the incentive compensation targets in those circumstances when it is in the shareholders' interest to report lower earnings (e.g., LIFO), thereby not reducing the managers' incentive via bonus earnings to adopt LIFO.

[18] Our analysis indicates that outside (nonmanaging) directors are "efficient" monitors of management, Watts [1977]. If this were not the case, the capital market would quickly discount the presence of outside directors. As far as we can determine, firms are not required by the New York Stock Exchange listing requirements or Federal regulations to have outside directors. Paragraph 2495G

If nonmanaging directors did not control management (including adjusting the compensation plans for changes in accounting standards), the decline in firm value offers incentives for an outsider or group to tender for control of the firm and install outside directors who will eliminate those managerial activities which are not in the best interest of the shareholders.[19] This group would then gain a proportionate share of the full capitalized value of the eliminated abuses (e.g., the present value of the incremental compensation resulting from the change in accounting standards). Therefore, the benefits for shareholders and nonmanaging directors to adjust compensation plans for changes in accounting standards are immediate and direct, if there is an efficient capital market for equity claims.

However, for the politicians and bureaucrats, our analysis suggests that the lack of a capital market which capitalizes the effects on the voters' future cashflows reduces the benefits accruing to the politicians of monitoring accounting standards, and the result is that they will perform less adjustments for changes in accounting standards.[20] For example, what are the benefits accruing to a utility regulator for adjusting a utility's accounting numbers for a change in standards? In the previous case of an outside director, the share price will fall by the discounted presented value of the increased compensation resulting for an incomplete (or inaccurate) adjustment of the compensation plan. But if the regulator does not completely adjust for a change in accounting standards and allows the utility's rates to increase (resulting in a wealth transfer from consumers to the utility's owners), then the only cost the regulator is likely to incur is removal from office due to his incomplete adjustment. He incurs no direct wealth change.

For small rate increases, the *per capita* coalition costs each consumer (or some group of consumers) would bear lobbying for the regulator's removal would vastly outweigh the small *per capita* benefits they would receive via lower regulated rates. Hence, rational consumers would not incur large monitoring costs of their regulators and other politicians (Downs [1957]; Alchian [1969]; and Alchian and Demsetz [1972]). Knowing this, it is not in the regulators' and politicians' interests to adjust changes in accounting standards as fully as if they were confronted with the same change in accounting standards in the role of outside directors or shareholders in the firm. The benefits of adjusting for changes in accounting standards are lower in the political sector than in the private sector.[21] Hence, there is a greater likelihood that a given accounting standard change will result in increased tax, regulatory, and political benefits than will the same change result in increased management compensation. For a given accounting standard change, managers should expect their own shareholders and outside di-

---

of Commerce Clearing House, Volume 2, New York Stock Exchange encourages listed firms to appoint outside directors. "Full disclosure of corporate affairs for the information of the investing public is, of course, normal and usual procedure for listed companies. Many companies have found this procedure has been greatly aided by having at least two outside directors whose functions on the board would include particular attention to such matters." This listing statement is consistent with our observation that outside directors provide monitoring benefits.

[19] This assumes, of course, that such takeovers earn a fair rate of return net of transactions costs.

[20] See Zimmerman [1977] and Watts [1977] for further discussion of this issue.

[21] It could also be argued that politicians and regulators have a higher marginal cost of adjusting than do shareholders, nonmanaging directors, and other capital market participants since the former group does not necessarily have a comparative advantage of adjusting financial statements, whereas, existing capital market participants probably have a comparative advantage at such activities.

rectors to make a more complete adjustment than politicians.

Given this analysis, we predict that managers have greater incentives to choose accounting standards which report lower earnings (thereby increasing cashflows, firm value, and their welfare) due to tax, political, and regulatory considerations than to choose accounting standards which report higher earnings and, thereby, increase their incentive compensation. However, this prediction is conditional upon the firm being regulated or subject to political pressure. In small, (i.e., low political costs) unregulated firms, we would expect that managers do have incentives to select accounting standards which report higher earnings, if the expected gain in incentive compensation is greater than the foregone expected tax consequences. Finally, we expect management also to consider the accounting standard's impact on the firm's bookkeeping costs (and hence their own welfare).

The next section combines these five factors into a model of corporate lobbying standards.

A POSITIVE THEORY OF MANAGEMENT LOBBYING ON ACCOUNTING STANDARDS

Given a proposed accounting standard, management's position depends on the size of the firm (which affects the magnitude of the political costs) and whether the proposed standard increases or decreases the firm's reported earnings.[22] Figure 1 separates the standard's impact on earnings into decreases (1A) and increases (1B). The curve GB in Figure 1A (earnings decrease) denotes the proposed accounting standard's present value to management including the tax, regulatory, political, and compensation effects as a function of firm size. For small firms (below size E), not subject to much political pressure, these managers

have an incentive to oppose the standard since their bonus compensation plans will have to be adjusted (a costly process), if their incomes are to remain unchanged by the new standard. Above size E, the political, regulatory, and tax benefits of reporting lower earnings due to the new standard are assumed to dominate the incentive compensation factor.

The benefits (costs) of a proposed accounting standard are expected to vary with the firm's size. This relationship can exist for two reasons: (1) the magnitude of the reported income change may be larger for larger firms and (2) for an income change of a given magnitude, the benefits (costs) vary with firm size.[23] Hence, the present value of the stream of benefits (or costs) to the firm, GB, are an increasing function of firm size.[24]

Information production costs, curve IC, are also expected to vary to some extent with firm size due to the increased complexity and volume of the larger

[22] The expected effect of an accounting standard could vary over time (i.e., it could increase current reported income and decrease some future reported income). In that case, the analysis is slightly more complex, but the criterion is still the same (i.e., the effect on the manager's wealth). However, for simplicity, the remainder of the paper refers to standards increasing or decreasing reported income as though the whole time series of future income shifts up or down.

[23] Whether the magnitude of the income change does vary with firm size depends on the particular accounting standard in question. For certain accounting standards (e.g., requiring all firms to report depreciation based on current replacement costs) it is apparent *a priori* that there will be a correlation between the income change and firm size. For other standards (e.g., general price level accounting) *a priori*, it is not obvious that a relationship will exist (e.g., net monetary gains may offset depreciation in larger firms). However, since political costs depend on firm size then we expect the benefits (costs) of standard changes to vary with firm size. For example, if all firms earnings decline by $1 million (due to a standards change) then we would expect larger firms to incur larger benefits since the likelihood of anti-trust actions are expected to be associated with firm size.

[24] We would expect firms in different industries to be subject to different political pressures, tax structures, and regulation. Hence, Figure 1 is developed for firms in the same industry that only differ by size.

FIGURE 1

A MODEL OF FIRMS' SUBMISSIONS TO THE FASB

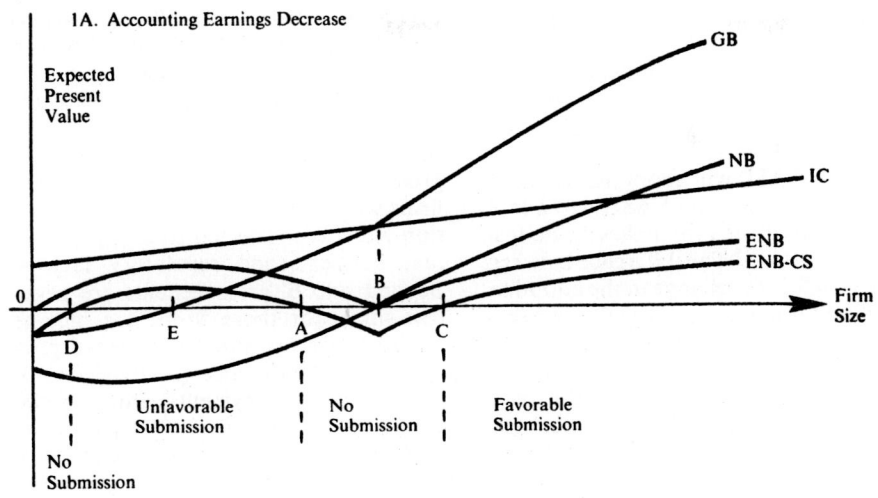

1A. Accounting Earnings Decrease

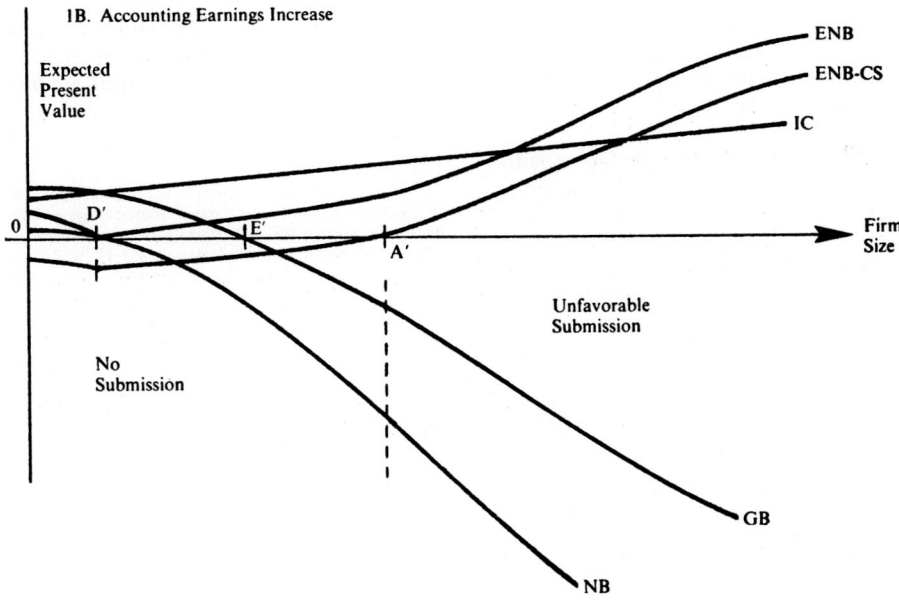

1B. Accounting Earnings Increase

firm's accounting system. The difference between the gross benefits, GB, and the additional information costs, IC, yields the net benefits curve, NB.

If the firm size is in the region OB, the net benefits curve, NB, is negative, and the firm will consider making an unfavorable submission to the FASB. Before the firm makes a submission, management holds beliefs regarding the likelihood the FASB will adopt the standard and the likelihood the FASB will adopt the standard if the firm makes an opposing submission.[25] The difference between these beliefs is the change in the adoption likelihood if management makes a negative submission. The product of this difference and the negative net benefits, NB, (i.e., the present value[26] of the cashflows arising from the five factors) is the expected present value of the net benefits curve, ENB. For example, a firm will incur negative net present value benefits of $100,000 if the standard is adopted. They believe the likelihood of adoption is .60. By making a negative submission to the FASB the likelihood falls to .59. The expected net present value of the benefits of the submission is then +$1000.

Firms larger than size B face positive net benefits if the standard is adopted. They will consider supporting the standard to the FASB, thereby increasing the standard's likelihood of adoption.[27] Hence, the expected net benefits curve is also positive beyond point B since it is the product of a positive net benefit and a positive change in the FASB's likelihood of adoption given a favorable submission.

If the cost of the submission is $CS, consisting primarily of the opportunity cost of the manager's time, then the total expected net benefits of a submission given the submission cost is a vertical downward shift in the ENB curve by the amount CS, ENB—CS. A firm will make a submission if ENB − CS is positive. This occurs in the regions DA, where opposing submissions occur, and beyond C, where favorable submissions are made. Between O and D and between A and C no submissions are made.

In Figure 1B, the proposed standard increases reported income. This case is similar to the previous one except the gross benefits are only positive for small firms where the management compensation plans are expected to dominate the tax, political, and regulatory factors. Beyond size E' gross benefits are negative since, for those firms, the income increases are expected to increase governmental interference (political costs), raise future tax payments, and lead the public utility commission to reduce the firm's revenues (if the firm is regulated). The net benefits curve is again the algebraic sum of GB (gross benefits) and IC (information costs) and the submission's expected net benefits less submission costs, ENB − CS, cuts the axis at A'. Accordingly, firms with asset sizes in the interval OA' make no submissions and firms of sizes beyond A' make unfavorable submissions.

---

[25] In this situation, it is possible that management will lobby on an accounting standard because of secondary (or gaming) effects (i.e., vote trading thereby influencing subsequent FASB pronouncements). We chose not to introduce gaming because it complicates the model and such complication is only justified if it improves or is likely to improve the empirical results. We are able to predict corporate behavior without considering gaming, and we do not consider it likely to improve these results.

[26] The firm is discounting the future cashflows with the appropriate, risk-adjusted discount rate. Furthermore, we are assuming that this discount rate is not increasing in firm size which is consistent with the available evidence.

[27] We are assuming that the likelihood of the FASB adopting the standard, if the firm makes a submission, is independent of firm size. This is unrealistic since large firms, we expect, would have more influence with the Board. However, inclusion of this additional dependency does not change the results; in fact, it strengthens the predictions.

When we consider the implications of both figures, we see that larger firms (firms larger than size C in Figure 1) will make favorable submissions if their incomes are decreased by the accounting standard, and unfavorable submissions if their incomes are increased. Smaller firms (firms smaller than size C in Figure 1) will either not submit or make unfavorable submissions.

While Figures 1A and 1B reflect the general tendency of costs and benefits of an accounting standard to vary with firm size, there will be exceptions to this relationship. We have omitted variables, some of which we recognize. In particular, regulation costs borne by utilities depend not only on net income but also on operating earnings.[28] The effect of an accounting standard on operating earnings may vary with firm size.

The increment to a regulated firm's value of an accounting change which reduces operating earnings is increasing in firm size. Most public utility commissions set revenues according to the following type of equation:

Revenues = Operating Expenses
+ Depreciation + Taxes + $r \cdot$ Base   (1)

where r is the accepted rate of return allowance on the investment base (usually the historic cost of net plant and working capital) [Haskins and Sells 1974.] Interest is not directly included in the rate-setting formula. The approach is to work on a return to total assets. Since all the terms on the right-hand side of equation (1) are highly correlated with firm size, any accounting standard that increases reported operating expenses, depreciation, or the recorded value of the asset base proportionally will, in general, result in an increase in the utility's revenues. And these increments to the utility's cashflows will, in general, be increasing in firm size.

When an accounting standard increases net income and decreases operating earnings of utilities, as does price-level adjustments [See Davidson and Weil, 1975b], we would not necessarily expect the relationship between management's attitude to the standard and firm size to be as we specified above (i.e., larger firms favoring or opposing the standard depending upon the effect on net income and smaller firms opposing the standard). As a consequence, we concentrate on testing that relationship for unregulated firms.

Another omitted variable is the political sensitivity of the firm's industry which clearly affects the political cost of an accounting standard change. We do not have a political theory which predicts which industries Congress singles out for wealth transfers (For example, why was the oil industry subject to intensive Congressional pressure in early 1974 and not the steel industry?[29] Consequently, we do not consider it formally in our model. As we shall see, political sensitivity has an impact on our results (only one steel company submitted on price-level accounting compared to seven oil companies submitting), but it does not eliminate the general relationship between firm size and management's accounting lobbying behavior.

EMPIRICAL TESTS

Data

On February 15, 1974, the FASB issued the discussion memorandum "Re-

---

[28] Operating earnings, although explicitly defined by each public utility commission, are generally, utility revenues less operating expenses, including depreciation but excluding interest and taxes. We assume that the adoption of GPLA would mean that price-adjusted depreciation would affect operating earnings while the gain or loss on monetary assets would be treated like interest and would only affect net income.

[29] This does not mean we do not have any ideas as to which variables are important. For example, in the case of consumer goods industries, we suspect that the relative price change of the product is important.

porting the Effects of General Price-Level Changes in Financial Statements" and scheduled a public hearing on the topic for April 25, 1974. Public comments and position papers were solicited. One hundred thirty-three accounting firms, public corporations, industry organizations, and government agencies filed written comments.

We assume the submission indicates the position of corporate management. Clearly, this assumption could introduce some error into our tests. For example, some controllers of corporations may submit not because of corporate effects, but because they receive nonpecuniary income from the submission (e.g., if they are officers in their local chapter of the National Association of Accountants). However, we expect the error to be random. Ignoring this error biases our tests of management's attitudes on accounting standards towards rejecting the theory.

Almost all the corporations making submissions (49 out of 53) were New York Stock Exchange firms. Of the remaining four firms, one was listed on the American Stock Exchange, one was traded over the counter, and the other two were not traded. Of the 53 firms, 18 submitted opinions expressing favorable views on general price level adjustments whereas 34 expressed opinions ranging from strong objection to discussions of the merits of current costing to skepticism and feelings that GPLA was premature. These 34 were classified as opposing GPLA. For one firm, Transunion, an opinion could not be ascertained, and this firm was subsequently dropped from the sample. The firms making submissions and their position on the issue are listed in Table 1.

Once the sample of firms was identified from their submissions to the FASB, 1972 and 1973 financial data was obtained from the COMPUSTAT tape and the 1974 Moody Manuals. In addition, data on the existence of management incentive compensation plans was obtained by a questionnaire mailed to the chief

TABLE 1

FIRMS MAKING SUBMISSIONS TO THE FASB ON GENERAL PRICE LEVEL ADJUSTMENTS*

Firms Advocating GPLA	Firms Opposing GPLA
Regulated Firms	
AT&T	Aetna Life & Casualty (M)
Commonwealth Edison	Commerce Bank of Kansas City
Consumer Power (M)	Liberty Corporation (M)
Detroit Edison	Northeast Utilities
Duke Power	Peoples Gas
Indiana Telephone	Southern Natural Resources (M)
Iowa Illinois Gas & Electric	
Northwestern Telephone	Pennzoil
Southern Company	Texas Eastern Transmission (M)
	Texas Gas Transmission
Unregulated Firms	
Exxon (M)	Continental Oil (M)
Gulf Oil (M)	Standard Oil of Indiana (M)
Shell Oil (M)	Texaco (M)
Standard Oil of California (M)	Rockwell International (M)
Caterpillar Tractor	United Aircraft (M)
Dupont E. I. DeNemours (M)	Automated Building Components
General Motors (M)	Copeland Corporation (M)
Ford Motor Company (M)	General Electric (M)
Marcor (M)	General Mills (M)
	Gillette
	W. R. Grace (M)
	Harsco (M)
	Inland Steel (M)
	International Harvester (M)
	American Cyanamid (M)
	IT&T (M)
	Eli Lilly & Co. (M)
	Masonite (M)
	Merck (M)
	Owens-Illinois, Inc. (M)
	Reliance Electric (M)
	Seagrams Sons, Inc. (M)
	Sears Roebuck (M)
	Texas Instruments (M)
	Union Carbide (M)

* Transunion Corporation made a submission, but they did not state a position on GPLA. It made two technical comments.

M denotes the firm has a management compensation plan.

financial officer of each firm. Missing data on the nonresponses (30 percent of the firms) was obtained from the firms' proxy statements and annual reports. If no mention of an incentive plan was found, we assumed the firm did not have one. Firms classified as having management incentive compensation plans based on accounting earnings[30] are denoted by an (M) in Table 1.

The precise impact of reported earnings on executive incentive compensation is difficult to estimate simply because the firm has such a plan. The most common procedure companies use is to take some fraction of reported earnings after deducting a return on invested capital as a pool out of which incentive compensation is paid. However, most companies do not pay out all of this pool each year. The important point, though, is that managers in firms with management compensation plans which report higher adjusted earnings will not suffer a decline in their incentive compensation and it may actually increase their compensation (depending on the monitoring by the outside directors).

Methodology

The FASB's General Price Level Adjustment (GPLA) standard would require supplementary price adjusted statements. Even though the supplementary statements will not replace conventional reports, users of the information will obviously make comparisons [See Ijiri, 1976] and if adjusted income is above (below) unadjusted income, we expect our previous reasoning to hold, and we assume the effect is the same as an increase (decrease) in reported income.

A price-level adjusted income figure does not exist for all firms in our sample. Since only a few firms voluntarily published GPLA statements, income proxies must be constructed. Fortunately, a

previous series of studies by Davidson and Weil (1975a and 1975b) and Davidson, Stickney, and Weil (1976) developed an adjusting procedure which relies solely on published financial statements and GNP deflators. Using either their published figures for 1973 financial statements or using their procedures, we were able to obtain estimates of the direction of change in reported price-level income.[31]

In addition to using the Davidson and Weil results or procedures, we constructed proxy variables based on unadjusted depreciation and net monetary assets. Both of these variables have a direct negative impact on GPLA earnings (i.e., the larger depreciation or net monetary assets, the lower the adjusted income and the smaller or more negative the difference between GPLA adjusted income and unadjusted income). If we assume that our sample of firms has the same age distribution of depreciable property, then (cross-sectionally) depreciation and net monetary assets can serve as a surrogate for the effect of GPLA earnings.[32] Those numbers are readily

---

[30] If the firm had an incentive plan, but it was not tied to reported earnings then this firm was coded as not having an incentive plan (Gillette).

[31] 1973 was a period of high inflation. If firms based their FASB lobbying position on the price adjustments produced by high unexpected inflation without considering more "typical" years, then this would introduce errors into the data and finding a statistically significant result becomes more difficult. If these errors are systematic with respect to firm size, then our results could be biased. We do not expect this to be the case. To control partially for this, statistical tests are performed which are independent of the magnitude of the price change. Net monetary assets in 1973 may still be abnormally small (large) due to the high rate of inflation, but these preliminary tests suggest that our results are not dependent upon 1973 being atypical.

[32] The assumption that the age distribution of depreciable property is the same across our firms is reasonable. The firms who submitted to the FASB on the GPLA issue, generally, were large, capital-intensive and long-established firms. Moreover, the results using these surrogates are consistent with the results using Davidson and Weil's estimates.

available for our sample.

Davidson and Weil [1975c] also estimate the effect of GPLA on income for 1974 (which was in the future at the time of the submissions). Even though the adjustment procedure was slightly different, only two of our 19 firms in the combined samples reverse the direction of the income effect between 1973 and 1974. Similarly, all of the utilities, (24), and 35 of the 50 other companies in their sample have income effects of the same sign in both years. Since the effects of income changes in the immediate future are less heavily discounted, these results suggest that the error introduced by our assumption of stationary income changes is not likely to be severe.

Tests of the Theory

In the reported tests, we use asset size as the surrogate for firm size.[33] Based on our model, we can make predictions about the relationship between asset size and firm submissions. We predict that firms whose earnings are increased by GPLA will oppose GPLA regardless of their size (i.e., there will be no association between size and submission). However, for firms whose earnings are decreased by GPLA, we predict that they will either support GPLA or will not make a submission depending on where asset size C (Figure 1) occurs in their industry. Since we cannot determine the asset size corresponding to point C, we are in a position analogous to being able to predict the sign of a regression coefficient but not its magnitude. Consequently, our test of the model does not include asset size C (analogous to the magnitude of the coefficient). The test is only of the prediction that there is a positive relationship between asset size and submission for firms with income decreases.

Firms making submissions were classified according to the direction of change

in their net income and ranked by their asset size (Table 2). Of the 26 firms with income decreases, eight voted yes and 18 no.[34] The eight yes votes came from the larger firms, thus supporting our prediction. To test the null hypothesis that the eight firms which voted yes are drawn from the same population of firms (with respect to size) as the 18 that voted no, we performed a Mann-Whitney U test. Our tables indicate that we can reject the null hypothesis at the .001 level.[35]

Of the eight firms with income increases or no changes in net income, seven voted no. Thus, the general ten-

[33] In this case, firm size is measured by the firm's *Fortune* 500 rank in assets. The results are identical when rank in sales is used. Furthermore, the intent of government intervention depends on the metric used by the courts, legislators, and regulators. Market share, concentration and size are among the commonly used indicators. Absolute size is important in explaining government regulation for both theoretical and empirical reasons. An implication of Peltzman's (1975, p. 30) theory of regulation is that the amount of wealth redistributed from firms by government intervention is a positive function of economies of scale. Since we expect large firm size to indicate the presence of economies of scale, implication of Peltzman's theory is that government intervention will be greater for larger firms. Empirically, we observe numerous cases of politicians and regulators echoing the conventional wisdom of certain segments in society, that big business is inherently bad. (See, "Curse of Big Business," *Barron's* June 16, 1969 and footnote 12).

[34] We use the term "vote" to mean responding to a discussion memorandum by issuing a corporate opinion.

[35] Siegel [1956], p. 274. Even after any reasonable adjustment for the degrees of freedom lost due to previous statistical analysis, this result is still significant.

An intuitive idea of the strength of the relationship between management's attitude and firm size can be obtained by considering an analogy. Suppose we put 26 balls in an urn representing the firms with earnings decreases; eight red balls representing the firms that voted yes; and 18 black balls, representing the firms that voted no. Now, we randomly draw 13 balls out of the urn without replacement representing the largest 13 firms (out of the 26). The probability that we draw eight red balls (analogous to the probability of the eight firms voting yes being the "large" firms if the null hypothesis of no association between votes and size is correct) is .001. If the votes of firms are not independent, as in the case of gaming, this analogy is inappropriate. But we do not have any evidence of vote dependence (via gaming or otherwise).

TABLE 2

ASSET SIZE, DIRECTION OF EARNINGS EFFECT AND CORPORATE POSITION ON GPLA

Rank on Asset Size	Firm	Rank in Fortune 500 (1973)	Corporate Position, Classified by Earnings Change†	
			Increase or no change	Decrease
1	Exxon	1		Yes
2	General Motors	2		Yes
3	Texaco	3	No	
4	Ford	4		Yes
5	Sears Roebuck (Rank 1 in retail sales)	7		No
6	IT&T	8	No	
7	Gulf Oil	9		Yes
8	Standard Oil of California	10		Yes
9	General Electric	11	No	
10	Standard Oil of Indiana	12		No
11	Shell Oil	16		Yes
12	Dupont E.I. Nemours	18		Yes
Point C*				
13	Union Carbide	22		No
14	Continental Oil	26		No
15	Marcor (Rank 2 in retail firms)	33	Yes	
16	International Harvester	34		No
17	Caterpillar Tractor	47		Yes
18	Rockwell International	54	No	
19	W. R. Grace	55	No	
20	Owens-Illinois	80	No	
21	Inland Steel	85		No
22	American Cyanamid	92		No
23	United Aircraft	107		No
24	Seagrams Sons Inc.	108		No
25	Eli Lilly & Co.	135		No
26	Merck	143		No
27	General Mills	156	No	
28	Texas Instruments	164		No
29	Gillette	167		No
30	Reliance Electric	332		No
31	Harsco	368		No
32	Masonite	386		No
33	Automated Building Components	Not Ranked		No
34	Copeland Corporation	Not Ranked		No

* Point C in Figure 1 is determined by minimizing the number of misclassifications.

† Yes = Favored GPLA

No = Opposed GPLA

dency of these firms is to vote no as predicted by our model.

The results in Table 2 are consistent with the implications of our model including our assumption that the management compensation factor is dominated by political and tax considerations. Of the 31 unregulated firms with management compensation plans, eight had increases or no change in income and 23

had decreases in income as a result of price-level adjustments. If management compensation dominates tax and political factors, then firms with increases in income would be more likely to support price-level adjustments than firms with decreases. In fact, the reverse is true. The frequency of firms with income decreases which support price-level adjustment is seven out of 23 (30 percent) while the frequency of firms with income increases that support price-level adjustments is one out of eight (12.5 percent).

The above results support the relationship between management's attitudes on GPLA and firm size for the 23 unregulated firms. However, if we assume that firm size and the direction of the income change are independent (Table 2 supports this assumption), then (if there is no size effect) the average size of firms supporting GPLA should be the same as the average size of firms opposing. Thus we can use the voting behavior of all 52 firms in our sample to test the size relationship.

Table 3 presents the median rank on asset size for both regulated and unregulated firms favoring and opposing GPLA. The median rank in the *Fortune* 500 of the nine unregulated firms supporting GPLA is 10. The median rank of the 25 unregulated firms opposing GPLA is 92.

TABLE 3

MEDIAN RANKS OF FIRM SIZE BY REGULATION AND POSITION ON GPLA*

	Regulated (N = 18)		Unregulated (N = 34)	
	In Favor (9)	Against (9)	In Favor (9)	Against (25)
Median Rank	13	38	10	92

* *Fortune* [May and July, 1974].

For regulated firms, there also appears to be a relationship between size and management attitudes. The net incomes for all the utilities investigated by Davidson and Weil [1975b] are increased by GPLA suggesting none of the utilities should favor GPLA. However, as noted in the preceding section, operating earnings are relevant to rate determination. Those earnings fall for all the utilities investigated by Davidson and Weil [1975b] and this could explain why rela-

tively larger regulated firms favor GPLA.

If we assume our model is correct and that asset size C is the same for all industries, we can estimate C by minimizing the number of prediction errors (analogous to estimating a regression coefficient by minimizing the sum of squared errors). This estimate provides information on the relative importance of political and/or tax costs for different size firms. Given the data, C is between the 18th and 22nd largest firms in the *Fortune* 500 in 1973 (see Table 2). This suggests that reduced political and/or tax costs outweigh information production and/or management compensation factors in determining management's position on GPLA only for very large firms. For most other firms, information production costs dominate.

Are the major benefits of reporting lower adjusted incomes derived from tax or political considerations? It is very difficult to differentiate between these two factors, but one possible way is the following. Is the change in adjusted income proportional to firm size? If it is, then both the tax and political factors may be operating. But if there is no association between firm size and the magnitude of the income change, then the tax effect cannot explain why larger firms favor GPLA. Therefore, this result could only be due to political costs. We can obtain estimates of the income effect of GPLA for 11 of the firms whose incomes would be reduced by GPLA (six supporting, five opposing).[36] The average reduction in income for the six firms which supported GPLA is $177.7 million, while the average reduction for the five which opposed GPLA is $38.5 million. Thus, it appears that the income change does vary with size and the pre-

[36] This test was performed on 11 firms with income decreases which Davidson and Weil reported 1973 adjusted earnings. Firms which were manually adjusted by us for Table 2 were excluded from this test since only the sign of the earnings change was calculated.

ceding results are consistent with both the tax and political costs affecting management's attitudes.

The preceding results test only whether the size effect exists for firms which did submit to the FASB. It is interesting to examine the effect of GPLA on firms which did not submit. In particular, the firms of asset size above our estimated C which did not submit are of interest since our model predicts they would submit on the basis of the income effect. Dupont is the last firm above asset size C in Table 2 to vote. It is ranked 18th in the *Fortune* 500 in 1973. There are seven firms ranked higher than 18th which did not make a submission to the FASB. They are IBM (ranked 5th), General Telephone (6th), Mobil Oil (7th), U.S. Steel (13th), Chrysler (14th), Tenneco (15th), and Atlantic Richfield (17th).

The size of the income change is crucial to determining why these seven firms did not submit. If changes are not associated with firm size, the expected benefits of a submission could be very small and may not exceed the submission costs. Unfortunately, Davidson and Weil only estimated the change in earnings in 1973 for three of these seven firms: IBM, U. S. Steel, and Chrysler. All three have income reductions with GPLA and their average reduction is $88 million. This is less than the average reduction for the six firms with income reductions which did submit ($177 million), but it is not trivial. Further, the reductions for two of the three nonsubmissions (IBM and General Telephone) exceed the reductions for four of the six submissions. Consequently, it is difficult to attribute the fact that the three firms did not submit to the lack of an income effect.[37]

In summary, these tests confirm the relationship between size and management attitudes on GPLA. Political costs and, perhaps, tax effects influence management's attitudes on accounting standards. Although we are not able to explain some of the notable nonsubmitting firms' decisions, we would point out that most of the firms submitting are large, and the likelihood of submission increases with asset size (12 of the 18 firms ranked 1–18 in the *Fortune* 500 submitted, four of the 18 firms ranked 19–36 submitted, two of the 18 firms ranked 37–54 submitted, one of the 18 firms ranked 55–72 submitted, etc.).

Discriminant Analysis

The preceding tests were based on the direction of the earnings change, not the magnitude of the change. A discriminant analysis is conducted including management compensation, depreciation, and net monetary assets as independent variables, and using data on 49 of the 53 firms making submissions to ensure consistency of the Davidson and Weil procedures.

The change in price-adjusted income is correlated with the magnitudes of depreciation and net monetary assets. The larger both of these variables in unadjusted terms, the larger will be the decline (in absolute dollars) in adjusted net income. We do not perform an actual price-level adjustment, but rely on the unadjusted magnitudes of depreciation and net monetary assets.

[37] A more likely explanation of U.S. Steel's failure to submit is the fact that the steel industry was not as politically sensitive as the oil industry (for example) at the time. In other words, a given earnings effect has less political cost or benefit. This possibility is not included in our model. This could also explain Chrysler's failure to submit. As number three after General Motors and Ford they may be subject to less political pressure (and hence cost). In addition, the "free rider" effect may explain some of these nonsubmissions.

While we can only expect a positive theory to hold on average, the failure of IBM to submit is puzzling. That firm has anti-trust suits outstanding and some economists allege that it earns monopoly profits. For a discussion of one of these suits and statements by economists that IBM earns monopoly profits, see "The Breakup of IBM" *Datamation*, October 1975, pp. 95-99.

The general form of the discriminant function we estimate is[38]

$$p_i = \alpha_1 + \alpha_2 \frac{DEP_i}{MKTVL_i} + \alpha_2 \frac{NMA_i}{MKTVL_i} + \alpha_3 (SALES_i) CHG_i$$

$$+ \alpha_4 \left(\frac{SALES_i}{TSALES_i} \right) CHG_i + \alpha_5 MCOMP_i + \alpha_6 REG_i \qquad (2)$$

where

$$p_i = \begin{cases} \dfrac{\text{Number of opposing firms}}{\text{Total firms in sample}} & \text{if the } i^{\text{th}} \text{ firm favored GPLA} \\[2ex] \dfrac{\text{Number of supporting firms}}{\text{Total firms in sample}} & \text{if the } i^{\text{th}} \text{ firm opposed GPLA} \end{cases}$$

$MKTVL_i =$ the market value of the firm's equity (number of common shares outstanding × average share price)

$$REG_i = \begin{cases} 1 & \text{if the } i^{\text{th}} \text{ firm was regulated} \\ 0 & \text{otherwise} \end{cases}$$

$$MCOMP_i = \begin{cases} 1 & \text{if the } i^{\text{th}} \text{ firm had a management incentive scheme} \\ 0 & \text{otherwise} \end{cases}$$

$DEP_i =$ unadjusted depreciation expense in 1973 for the ith firm

$NMA_i =$ net monetary asset position in 1973 for the ith firm

$$CHG_i = \begin{cases} +1 & \text{if price-level adjusted income is below unadjusted income or if the firm is regulated} \\ -1 & \text{if price-level adjusted income is above unadjusted income} \\ 0 & \text{otherwise} \end{cases}$$

$SALES_i =$ Sales of the ith firm

$TSALES_i =$ Total sales of the Compustat firms with the same SIC code as firm i.

$\dfrac{SALES_i}{TSALES_i} =$ a proxy variable for market share

Table 4 presents the results of various functional forms of equation (2) fitted over various subsets of the data.[39] The first two terms,

$$\frac{NMA}{MKTVL} \quad \text{and} \quad \frac{DEP}{MKTVL},$$

normalize the unadjusted figures by the market value of the equity[40] and the estimated coefficients measure the extent to which an increase in relative depreciation or net monetary assets affect voting behavior. These coefficients, which should

[38] Northwestern Telephone, Commerce Bank of Kansas City, and Indiana Telephone were dropped from the sample due to a lack of data.

[39] The discriminant function is estimated using ordinary least squares. t-statistics on the coefficients are reported. The usual t-tests cannot be performed since the dependent variable is not normally distributed nor can asymptotic properties of large samples be used. However, the t-statistic is still useful as an index of the relative importance of the independent variable.

[40] Normalizing by the market value of the common stock introduces some error since we are not including the market value of the debt or preferred stock. However, since the market value of the common is highly correlated with total market value of the firm, we do not expect serious problems except that there may be some systematic, negative understatement of normalized net monetary assets.

TABLE 4

DISCRIMINANT ANALYSIS

Coefficients (*t*-statistics)

Model Number	N	Sample	Constant	DEP/ MKTVL	NMA/ MKTVL	SALES × CHG	$\frac{SALES}{TSALES} \times$ CHG	MCOMP	REG	R^2	Yates Adjusted Chi Square*
1	49	total sample	−.0241 (−.12)	122.6 (.60)	−38.9 (−1.62)	.000044 (3.67)	−.4131 (−1.11)	−.2355 (−1.42)	−.3443 (−1.29)	.358	9.25
2	49	total sample	−.0855 (−.44)	160.4 (.79)	−14.2 (−.98)	.000043 (3.53)	−.4381 (−1.17)	−.1619 (−1.03)		.332	9.25
3	49	total sample	−.0973 (−.50)	143.0 (.70)	−15.6 (−1.07)	.000034 (3.58)		−.1601 (−1.02)		.311	9.25
4	34	unregulated firms	.0431 (.19)	74.0 (.27)	−36.5 (−1.06)	.000044 (3.58)	−.3271 ′−.89)	−.2186 (−.89)		.366	19.96
5	34	unregulated firms	.0412 (.18)	86.2 (.32)	−35.3 (−1.03)	.000038 (3.73)		−.2335 (−.96)		.347	13.16
6	49	total sample	−.0079 (−.04)	215.3 (1.09)		.000033 (3.44)		−.2365 (−1.39)	.0077 (.05)	.293	11.74
7	49	total sample	−.0662 (−1.03)			.000033 (3.44)				.201	5.98

* The Yates correction for continuity is useful in establishing a lower bound on the χ^2 statistic.

capture the tax effects, are predicted to be positive under that hypothesis (the larger the depreciation and net monetary assets the greater the decline in adjusted income and the greater the tax benefits).

The sign on normalized depreciation is as predicted, but normalized net monetary assets is of the wrong sign. One of the following three hypotheses explain this result: the tax effect is only operating via depreciation;[41] depreciation and net monetary assets, being inversely related (correlation coefficient ranging from −.41 to −.55), are entering the regression with opposite signs; or the tax effect is not an explanatory factor. Since our sample is very small, it is not possible to use a holdout subset to distinguish between these hypotheses.

The next two variables,

$$(SALES) \, CHG \text{ and } \left(\frac{SALES}{TSALES}\right) CHG,$$

are proxies for political costs. These two variables, assume that political costs are symmetric for both earnings increases and decreases. The multiplicative dummy, CHG, is positive if earnings decline (based on the Davidson-Weil [1975a] results) or if the firm is regulated.[42]

The sign on SALES × CHG is as predicted, positive, and in addition has the highest *t*-statistic of all the independent variables. In addition, the coefficient on SALES × CHG is the most stable coefficient across various realizations and subsamples which leads us to conclude that firm size is the most important variable. The sign of

[41] That is, this sample of firms does not expect the tax laws to be changed to include in taxable income gains/losses on net monetary assets.

[42] Since the regulatory commission bases rates on depreciation, net monetary assets are not expected to be an important consideration, hence operating earnings decline for regulated firms.

$$\frac{SALES}{TSALES} \times CHG$$

is of the wrong sign. But this is probably due to the crude metric of market share,

$$\frac{SALES}{TSALES},$$

this variable is attempting to measure.[43] When the market share proxy is eliminated, the model's predictive ability is not impaired.

MCOMP, a dummy variable for management compensation schemes is expected to have a negative sign regardless of the change in earnings. Prior research indicates that executive compensation is more highly associated with operating income (which includes depreciation) than net income (which includes gains/losses on monetary assets).[44] Therefore, MCOMP is not multiplied by CHG. The sign of MCOMP being negative is consistent with our predictions.

If the firm is regulated, the dummy variable, REG, is one. Regulated firms' price-level adjusted operating incomes decline, unambiguously, and therefore these firms should tend to favor GPLA if the regulatory factor is operating. Yet, the sign of the coefficient of REG is negative in Model 1. This sign is negative because REG is inversely related to

$$MCOMP \quad and \quad \frac{NMA}{MKTVL}$$

(correlation coefficients of $-.60$ and $-.86$ respectively). When

$$\frac{NMA}{MKTVL}$$

is deleted from the model (Model 6), the sign of REG reverses, the importance of

$$\frac{DEP}{MKTVL}$$

increases, and the discriminatory power of the model improves from a Chi-Square of 9.25 to 11.74. However, the multicolinearity between

$$REG, MCOMP, and \frac{NMA}{MKTVL}$$

precludes our drawing any conclusions regarding the impact of management compensation or regulation on lobbying behavior.

Models 4 and 5 are fitted using only the unregulated firms ($N = 34$). REG and then

$$\frac{SALES}{TSALES} \times CHG$$

have been deleted. The R^2 statistic still remains high and the Yates adjusted Chi Square is significant at the 1 percent level. In fact, Model 4 correctly classifies the voting behavior for 32 out of the 34 firms.

The constant should be capturing the partial effect of information production costs after controlling for the other factors. When the total sample is used in the estimation, the constant is negative as expected. When the regulated firms are excluded, the constant is positive. But in

---

[43] Our measure of industry sales does not include firms in the industry not on the COMPUSTAT tape and furthermore all the firm's sales are assumed to be in the firm's dominant SIC category.

[44] Our examination of management compensation plans indicates that although the minimum and maximum amounts transferred to the bonus pool depend on the final net income number, we find that the actual bonus paid is most highly associated with operating or current income (depreciation is included, but extraordinary gains and losses are excluded). We correlated the change in management incentive compensation expense for 271 COMPUSTAT firms with changes in operating income and changes in net income after extraordinary items. The correlation coefficient for changes in operating income exceeded that for changes in net income after extraordinary items for over two-thirds of the firms. Gains or losses on monetary assets are not included in operating income. Consequently, only adjusted depreciation (ignoring inventory adjustments) are expected to affect management compensation and the effect is to reduce management pay.

all models the constant is close to zero.

The estimated discriminant functions are consistent with the tests of the theory. All of the discriminant functions are statistically significant and the intervening variable driving these findings is firm size. In fact, firm size explains over half the explained variance in voting behavior (Model 7).

These results are consistent with those using the Davidson and Weil findings. The discriminant functions indicate that the political cost factor is more important than the tax factor in affecting management's attitudes.

The major empirical problem in the discriminant analysis is the rather small sample size which precludes using a hold-out sample and, furthermore, does not allow more sophisticated econometric techniques to control for the multicolinearity. Hence, it is difficult to control for the interaction between the underlying factors. However, these preliminary results are encouraging and suggest that additional research in this area is warranted.

SUMMARY AND CONCLUSIONS

We have focused in this paper on the question of why firms would expend resources trying to influence the determination of accounting standards. The histories of the Committee on Accounting Procedures, the Accounting Principles Board, and FASB are replete with examples of managements and industries exerting political pressure on the standard-setting bodies.

A possible answer to this question is provided by the government intervention argument, namely, that firms having contact (actual or potential) with governments, directly through regulation (public utility commissions, Interstate Commerce Commission, Civil Aeronautics Board, etc.) or procurement, or indirectly through possible governmental intervention (antitrust, price controls, etc.), can affect their future cashflows by discouraging government action through the reporting of lower net incomes. The empirical evidence with respect to the position 52 firms took before the FASB on price level restatements is consistent with respect to this hypothesis.

The single most important factor explaining managerial voting behavior on General Price Level Accounting is firm size (after controlling for the direction of change in earnings). The larger firms, *ceteris paribus*, are more likely to favor GPLA (if earnings decline). This finding is consistent with our government intervention argument since the larger firms are more likely to be subjected to governmental interference and, hence, have more to lose than smaller corporations.

The existence of costs generated by government intervention may have more fundamental and important effects on the firm's decisions than just its lobbying behavior on financial accounting standards. Not only would we expect the firm to manage its reported earnings, but also to alter its investment-production decisions if the potential costs of government interference become large. For example, government intervention costs may lead the firm to select less risky investments in order to eliminate the chance of high returns which then increase the likelihood of government intervention. If the total risk of these less risky investments tends to be positively correlated with the systematic risk of the firm, then we would expect the beta (the estimate of the covariance between the return on the stock and the market return normalized by the variance of the market) on the common stock to be significantly below one (average risk) for those firms facing large government intervention costs. The evidence from the sample of firms making submissions to the FASB on GPLA is consistent with this hypothesis. The average β is .67. Furthermore, firms favoring GPLA tend to have lower betas than the firms in opposition.[45]

Our findings, in a preliminary extension of these results, tend to confirm the decline in systematic risk as firm size increases and as government intervention costs rise. These tentative findings are suggestive of fertile research possibilities of examining the effects of politically motivated factors on the maximizing behavior of firms' managements and shareholders.

We believe that the general findings in this paper, if confirmed by other studies, have important implications for the setting of financial accounting standards in a mixed economy. As long as financial accounting standards have potential effects on the firm's future cashflows, standard setting by bodies such as the Accounting Principles Board, the Financial Accounting Standards Board, or the Securities and Exchange Commission

will be met by corporate lobbying. The Committee on Accounting Procedures and the Accounting Principles Board could not withstand the pressure. The former Chairman of the FASB also has complained of the political lobbying, and the FASB has been forced to defer the controversial GPLA topic. The SEC has, until recently, avoided direct involvement in the setting of accounting standards. One could hypothesize that this was in their own interest. By letting the American Institute of Certified Public Accountants be the scapegoat, the Securities and Exchange Commission could maintain their "credibility" with Capitol Hill and the public.

[45] The average betas of various subclasses are:

	Regulated	Un-regulated	Combined
Firms opposing GPLA	.67	.72	.71
Firms favoring GPLA	.50	.65	.59
Combined	.59	.70	.67

Note that as a firm grows via diversification its beta should tend to one.

REFERENCES

Alchian, A. A., "Corporate Management and Property Rights," in *Economic Policy and the Regulation of Corporate Securities* (H. Manne, ed.), (American Enterprise Institute, 1969).

———— and H. Demsetz, "Production, Information Costs and Economic Organization," *American Economic Review* (December 1972), pp. 777–795.

Armstrong, Marshall S., "The Politics of Establishing Accounting Standards," A speech before the Third Annual Securities Regulation Institute in San Diego, California, January 16, 1976, as reported in Arthur Andersen & Co., *Executive News Briefs*, (February 1976), p. 1.

Ball, R., "Changes in Accounting Techniques and Stock Prices," *Empirical Research in Accounting: Selected Studies, 1972.* Supplement to *Journal of Accounting Research* (1972), pp. 1–38.

———— and Ross Watts, "Some Time Series Properties of Accounting Income," *Journal of Finance* (June 1972), pp. 663–82.

Barefield, R. M., and E. E. Comiskey, "The Smoothing Hypothesis: An Alternative Test," THE ACCOUNTING REVIEW (April 1972), pp. 291–298.

Barnea, A., J. Ronen, and S. Sadan, "The Implementation of Accounting Objectives—An Application to Extraordinary Itens," THE ACCOUNTING REVIEW (January 1975), pp. 58–68.

Beidleman, C. R., "Income Smoothing: The Role of Management," THE ACCOUNTING REVIEW (October 1973), pp. 653–667.

Benston, George J., "Accountants Integrity and Financial Reporting," *Financial Executive* (August 1975), pp. 10–14.

The Conference Board, *Top Executive Compensation* (Conference Board, 1974).

Copeland, Ronald M., "Income Smoothing," *Empirical Research in Accounting: Selected Studies.* Supplement to *Journal of Accounting Research* 1968, pp. 101–116.

Cushing, B. E., "An Empirical Study of Changes in Accounting Policy," *Journal of Accounting Research* (Autumn 1969), pp. 196–203.

Dasher, B. E. and R. E. Malcom, "A Note on Income Smoothing in the Chemical Industry," *Journal of Accounting Research* (Autumn 1970), pp. 253–259.

Davidson, Sidney, Clyde P. Stickney and Roman L. Weil, *Inflation Accounting* (McGraw-Hill, 1976).

——— and Roman L. Weil, "Inflation Accounting: What Will General Price Level Adjusted Income Statements Show?" *Financial Analysts Journal*, (January–February 1975a) pp. 27–31; 70–81.

——— and Roman L. Weil, "Inflation Accounting: Public Utilities," *Financial Analysts Journal*, (May–June 1975b), pp. 30–34; 62.

——— and Roman L. Weil, "Inflation Accounting: Some 1974 Income Measures," *Financial Analysts Journal*, (September–October 1975c), pp. 42–54.

Downs, A., *An Economic Theory of Democracy*," (Harper and Row, 1957).

Fama, Eugene F., "Efficient Capital Markets: A Review of Theory and Empirical Work," *Journal of Finance*, (May 1970), pp. 383–417.

Gonedes, N., "Income-smoothing Behavior Under Selected Stochastic Processes," *Journal of Business* (October 1972), pp. 570–584.

———, "Class Discussion Notes: Section 8," unpublished manuscript, University of Chicago (January 1976).

——— and N. Dopuch, "Capital Market Equilibrium, Information Production, and Selecting Accounting Techniques: Theoretical Framework and Review of Empirical Work," *Studies on Financial Accounting Objectives: 1974*. Supplement to *Journal of Accounting Research* (1974).

Gordon, M. J., "Postulates, Principles and Research in Accounting," THE ACCOUNTING REVIEW (April 1964), pp. 251–263.

———, B. N. Horwitz, and P. T. Meyers, "Accounting Measurements and Normal Growth of the Firm," *Research in Accounting Measurement*, eds. Jaedicke, Ijiri and Nielsen (American Accounting Association, 1966), pp. 221–231.

Haskins and Sells. *Public Utilities Manual* (New York, 1974).

Horngren, Charles T., "The Marketing of Accounting Standards," *Journal of Accountancy* (October 1973), pp. 61–66.

———, "Setting Accounting Standards in 1980," unpublished speech before the Arthur Young Professors Roundtable (March 30–31, 1976).

Ijiri, Yuji, "The Price-Level Restatement and its Dual Interpretation," THE ACCOUNTING REVIEW, (April 1976), pp. 227–243.

Jensen, Michael C., "Reflections on the State of Accounting Research and the Regulation of Accounting," Presented at the Stanford Lectures in Accounting, May 21, 1976.

———, and William H. Meckling, "Theory of the Firm: Managerial Behavior, Agency Costs and Ownership Structure," *Journal of Financial Economics* (October 1976a), pp. 305–360.

———, and William H. Meckling, "Can the Corporation Survive?" Public Policy Working Paper Series, PPS76-4, Graduate School of Management, University of Rochester, (April, 1976b).

Kaplan, R. S., and R. Roll, "Investor Evaluation of Accounting Information: Some Empirical Evidence," *Journal of Business* (April 1972), pp. 225–57.

Meckling, William H., "Values and the Choice of the Model of the Individual in Social Sciences," *Revue Suisse d' Economic Politique et de Statistique* (December 1976).

Moonitz, Maurice, *Obtaining Agreement on Standards*. Studies in Accounting Research No. 8 (Sarasota, Florida: American Accounting Association, 1974).

Peltzman, S., "Toward a More General Theory of Regulation," *Journal of Law and Economics*, (August 1976), pp. 221–240.

Posner, Richard A., "Theories of Economic Regulation," *The Bell Journal of Economics and Management Science*, (Autumn 1974), pp. 335–358.

Siegel, Sidney, *Nonparametric Statistics* (McGraw-Hill, 1956).

Siegfried, John, "Determinants of Antitrust Activity," *Journal of Law and Economics* (October 1975), pp. 559–581.

Stigler, G. J., "The Theory of Economic Regulation," *The Bell Journal of Economics and Management Science*, (Spring 1971), 3–21.

Sunder, S., "Empirical Analysis of Stock Price and Risk as They Relate to Accounting Changes in Inventory Valuation," THE ACCOUNTING REVIEW (April 1975), pp.305–315.

U.S. Congress, Senate, Subcommittee on Antitrust and Monopoly of the Committee on the Judiciary, *Hearings, The Petroleum Industry*, Part I, 9th Congress, 1st Session, 1975.

U.S. Congress, Senate, Subcommittee on Antitrust and Monopoly of the Committee on the Judiciary, *Hearings, The Petroleum Industry*, Part III, 9th Congress, 1st Session, 1976.

Watts, Ross, "Accounting Objectives," Working Paper Series No. 7408, Graduate School of Management, University of Rochester, (April 1974).

Watts, Ross, "Corporate Financial Statements: Product of the Market and Political Processes," *Australian Journal of Management* (April 1977), pp. 53–75.

Zeff- Stephen, *Forging Accounting Principles in Five Countries: A History and an Analysis of Trends*, Arthur Andersen Lecture Series (Stipes Publishing Company, 1972), pp. 110–268.

Zimmerman, Jerold, "The Municipal Accounting Maze: An Analysis of Political Incentives," Supplement to the *Journal of Accounting Research* (1977).

Positive Accounting Theory: A Ten Year Perspective

Ross L. Watts and Jerold L. Zimmerman
University of Rochester

ABSTRACT: This paper reviews and critiques the positive accounting literature following publication of Watts and Zimmerman (1978, 1979). The 1978 paper helped generate the positive accounting literature which offers an explanation of accounting practice, suggests the importance of contracting costs, and has led to the discovery of some previously unknown empirical regularities. The 1979 paper produced a methodological debate that has not been very productive. This paper attempts to remove some common misconceptions about methodology that surfaced in the debate. It also suggests ways to improve positive research in accounting choice. The most important of these improvements is tighter links between the theory and the empirical tests. A second suggested improvement is the development of models that recognize the endogeneity among the variables in the regressions. A third improvement is reduction in measurement errors in both the dependent and independent variables in the regressions.

I T is more than a decade since our two papers, "Towards a Positive Theory of the Determination of Accounting Standards" and "The Demand for and Supply of Accounting Theories: The Market for Excuses" were published in *The Accounting Review*. The intervening time allows us to look back on these papers and the ensuing literature with some perspective.

The two papers were controversial ten years ago and remain so today. The papers (primarily Watts and Zimmerman 1978) contributed to a literature that has uncovered empirical regularities in accounting practice (Christie forthcoming; Holthausen and Leftwich 1983; Leftwich forthcoming; Watts and Zimmerman 1986). The empirical regularities have been replicated in different settings

Financial support was provided by the John M. Olin Foundation and the Bradley Policy Research Center at the University of Rochester. The comments of Ray Ball, James Brickley, Andrew Christie, Linda DeAngelo, Robert Hagerman, S. P. Kothari, Richard Leftwich, Tom Lys, Clifford Smith, Jerold Warner, and Greg Whittred are gratefully acknowledged. We thank William Kinney for encouraging us to pursue this project. An earlier version of this paper was presented at the Accounting Association of Australia and New Zealand, July 4, 1989, Melbourne, Australia.

Manuscript received May 1989.
Revision received September 1989.
Accepted September 1989.

(Christie forthcoming) and it is clear there is a relation between firms' accounting choice and other firm variables, such as leverage and size and the signs of the relations are mostly consistent across studies. Positive accounting research guided the search for the empirical regularities and provided explanations for them. To date, there are no *systematic* alternative sets of *explanations* for those regularities articulated and tested in the literature. Further, the literature has moved beyond the first simple exposition of the theory in the 1978 paper. The explanation for accounting choice is now richer and more sophisticated.

Our first objective in this paper is to convey our perspective on the evolution and current state of positive accounting theory and to summarize the evidence on systematic empirical regularities in accounting (Section I). The second objective is to evaluate the research methods and the methodology used to document the empirical regularities. We discuss criticisms of the original papers and of the subsequent positive accounting literature in Section II. While the positive accounting literature has explained some accounting practice, much remains unexplained. Our third objective is to provide our views about future directions for positive accounting literature (Section III).

I. Evolution and State of Positive Accounting Theory

Evolution

Modern positive accounting research began flourishing in the 1960s when Ball and Brown (1968), Beaver (1968), and others introduced empirical finance methods to financial accounting. The subsequent literature adopted the assumption that accounting numbers supply information for security market investment decisions and used this "information perspective" to investigate the relation between accounting numbers and stock prices.[1] The "information perspective" has taught us much about the market's use of accounting numbers. But, except for the choice of inventory methods, the "information perspective" has not provided hypotheses to predict and explain accounting choices. The "information perspective" has not provided hypotheses to explain why entire industries switch from accelerated to straight-line depreciation without changing their tax depreciation methods.

An important reason that the information perspective failed to generate hypotheses explaining and predicting accounting choice is that in the finance theory underlying the empirical studies, accounting choice *per se* could not affect firm value. Information is costless and there are no transaction costs in the Modigliani and Miller (1958) and capital asset pricing model frameworks. Hence,

---

[1] The "information perspective" views accounting data (usually earnings, dividends, and cash flows) as providing information on inputs to valuation models (e.g., discounted cash flows) and tests for associations between accounting disclosures and stock prices or returns. In the contracting approach adopted in the literature and discussed in this paper, accounting methods are primarily determined by the use of accounting numbers in contracts between parties to the firm. Under this approach accounting disclosures directly affect parties' (including stockholders') contractual claims and, hence, the values of those claims (including stock prices). To the extent accounting disclosures are correlated with attributes investors use in valuing securities, these disclosures contain information and affect stock prices. Thus, under both an "information perspective" and a "contracting perspective," accounting disclosures have the potential to alter securities prices (Holthausen forthcoming).

if accounting methods do not affect taxes they do not affect firm value. In that situation there is no basis for predicting and explaining accounting choice. Accounting is irrelevant.

To predict and explain accounting choice accounting researchers had to introduce information and/or transactions costs. The initial empirical studies in accounting choice used positive agency costs of debt and compensation contracts and positive information and lobbying costs in the political process to generate value effects for and, hence, hypotheses about accounting choice. Finance researchers had introduced costs of debt that increase with the debt/equity ratio (Jensen and Meckling 1976) to explain (in combination with differential taxes) how optimal capital structures could vary across industries. The debt costs first introduced were bankruptcy and agency costs. The agency costs were of particular interest to accountants because accounting appeared to play a role in minimizing them. Debt contracts apparently aimed at reducing dysfunctional behavior use accounting numbers (Smith and Warner 1979; Leftwich 1983). Accounting researchers recognized the implications for accounting choice and began using the accounting numbers in debt contracts to generate hypotheses about accounting choice (Watts 1977).[2]

Accounting numbers also are used in manager's compensation contracts and it is hypothesized that such use again minimizes agency costs (Smith and Watts 1982). This use of accounting numbers in bonus plans suggested the possibility that accounting choice could affect wealth and so accounting researchers began employing that use to explain accounting choice. Watts and Zimmerman (1978) is an early example of this approach.

Borrowing from the industrial organization literature in economics (Stigler 1971; Peltzman 1976) which assumes positive information costs and lobbying costs, accounting researchers postulated that the political process generated costs for firms. These political costs are a function of reported profits. Thus, incentives are created to manage reported accounting numbers. Information and lobbying costs are part of the costs of "contracting" in the political process. The extent and form of the wealth transfers created by the political process (such as the tax code) are affected by these contracting costs.

While the early literature concentrated on using debt and compensation contracts and the political process to explain and predict accounting choice, the theory underlying the empirical work was more general and had its foundation in an economic literature on the theory of the firm. Since the 1970s, economists have strived to develop a theory of the firm by attempting to explain the organizational structure of the firm (e.g., choice of corporate form, structure of contracts, management compensation, centralization-decentralization). The underlying notion (Alchian 1950) is that competition among different forms of institutions leads to the survival of those forms most cost-effective in supplying goods and services. Productive activity can occur via the marketplace or by the inclusion of several activities within a firm (Coase 1937; Alchian and Demsetz 1972). In the marketplace, direction of productive activity and cooperation is by

---

[2] Prior to that time other studies investigate accounting choice without explicit recognition of contracting effects (e.g., Gordon 1964; Gordon et al. 1966; Sorter et al. 1966; Gagnon 1967).

market prices; within the firm alternative mechanisms such as standard costs are used (Ball 1989). Which productive activities are carried out by markets and which by firms depends on which arrangement is cost effective.[3] In competition among firms, those that organize themselves to minimize contracting costs are more likely to survive (Fama and Jensen 1983a, 1983b). It was a short step to suggest that accounting methods affect the firm's organizational costs and so the accounting methods that survive are the result of a similar economic equilibrium (Watts 1974, 1977).[4] Accounting researchers have recently returned to using that notion of an efficient set of accounting methods to explain accounting choice (Zimmer 1986).

As noted above, the agency costs associated with debt and management compensation contracts and the agency, information, and other contracting costs associated with the political process provided the hypotheses tested in the early empirical accounting choice studies (bonus plan, debt/equity, and political cost hypotheses). However, the more general approach suggested agency and other costs associated with other contracts (e.g., sales contracts) could also affect accounting choice.[5] This potential for many contracts to play a role in explaining organizational choice (including accounting choice) and the fact that agency costs used to explain the contracts often arise in contractual scenarios that differ from those of the standard agency problem led researchers to start to use the term "contracting costs" instead of agency costs (Klein 1983; Smith 1980). The concept of contracting costs and the notion of accounting methods as part of efficient organizational technology play key roles in contemporaneous positive accounting theory.

Contemporaneous Positive Accounting Theory

Contracting costs arise in (1) market transactions (e.g., selling new debt or equity requires legal fees and underwriting costs), (2) transactions internal to the firm (e.g., a cost-based transfer price scheme is costly to maintain and can produce dysfunctional decisions), and (3) transactions in the political process (e.g., securing government contracts or avoiding government regulation requires lobbying costs). Contracting costs consist of transaction costs (e.g., brokerage

---

[3] Coase (1937) suggests that economies of scale in long-term contracting are what cause activity to be organized in firms. Alchian and Demsetz (1972) point out that those economies are not sufficient since market arrangements could achieve the same economies (e.g., contracting consultants). What is necessary is some unique advantage of firm organization over market arrangements. Alchian and Demsetz suggest it is the advantage firms have in metering inputs to team production that generates firms. Monitors meter individual inputs and the monitors' incentive problem is solved by giving them the residual claim to the firm (hence, the firm structure). Klein et al. (1978) suggest firms emerge to solve post contractual opportunism associated with specialized assets. Meckling and Jensen (1986) suggest that firms have an advantage in generating information by aggregating data and using that information. Difficulties in capturing the information's benefits in the market result in the firm being the optimal form of organization.

[4] Watts adopted such a view in "Accounting Objectives" which he presented to the Annual Congress of the N.S.W. branch of the Institute of Chartered Accountants in Australia in 1974. The paper was later substantially revised given Jensen and Meckling (1976) and joint work with Zimmerman and published in Watts (1977).

[5] The influence of sales contracts on accounting choice is considered by Watts and Zimmerman (1986, 207) and by Zimmer (1986) and joint venture contracts by Zimmer (1986). Further, Ball (1989) suggests intrafirm transactions affect internal accounting choice (e.g., the basis for transfer prices).

fees), agency costs (e.g., monitoring costs, bonding costs, and the residual loss from dysfunctional decisions), information costs (e.g., the costs of becoming informed), renegotiation costs (e.g., the costs of rewriting existing contracts because the extant contract is made obsolete by some unforeseen event), and bankruptcy costs (e.g., the legal costs of bankruptcy and the costs of dysfunctional decisions). Throughout this paper, we use the term "contracting costs" to incorporate this wide variety of costs. The term "contracting parties" is meant to include all parties to the firm including "internal" employees and managers and "external" parties, such as suppliers, claim holders, and customers.[6]

The existence of contracting costs is crucial to models of both the organization of the firm and accounting choice. Meckling and Jensen (1986) suggest that within the firm the lack of a market price is replaced by systems for allocating decisions among managers, and measuring, rewarding, and punishing managerial performance. Accounting plays a role in these systems and so appears to be part of the firm's efficient contracting technology. Trying to predict and explain the organization of the firm with zero contracting costs is pointless (Coase 1937; Ball 1989). How the firm is organized, its financial policy, and its accounting methods, are as much a part of the technology used to produce the firm's product as are its production methods. Hence, modelling accounting choice while assuming zero contracting costs is not productive.

The extent to which accounting choice affects the contracting parties' wealth depends on the relative magnitudes of the contracting costs. For example, *assume* accounting-based debt agreements have higher renegotiation costs than accounting-based bonus plans. Then, mandatory changes in accounting procedures by the FASB impose greater relative costs on firms with debt agreements than on firms with bonus plans, *ceteris paribus*. And, firms with debt agreements will conduct more lobbying and undertake more (costly) accounting, financing, and production changes to undo the effects of the mandatory change than firms with only bonus plans. Thus, developing a positive theory of accounting choice requires an understanding of the relative magnitudes of the various types of contracting costs.

Contracts that use accounting numbers are not effective in aligning managers' and contracting parties' interests if managers have complete discretion over the reported accounting numbers. If managers know (or can determine) which accounting methods best motivate subordinates, then the contracting parties want managers to have some discretion over the accounting numbers. Hence, we expect some restrictions on managers' discretion over accounting numbers, but some discretion will remain. When managers exercise this discretion it can be because (1) the exercised discretion increases the wealth of all contracting parties, or (2) the exercised discretion makes the manager better off at the expense of some other contracting party or parties. If managers elect to exercise discretion to their advantage *ex post*, *and* the discretion has wealth redistributive effects among the contracting parties, then we say the managers acted "opportunistically."

---

[6] See Watts (1974) for an earlier and Ball (1989) for a later discussion of contracting parties other than capital suppliers and managers.

Ex ante, the set of accounting choices restricted by the contracting parties is determined by "efficiency" reasons (to maximize firm value). One cost of allowing managers more rather than less discretion is the increased likelihood of some *ex post* managerial "opportunism" (i.e., wealth transfers to managers) via accounting procedures. However, *ex ante* the contracting parties expect some redistributive effects and reduce the price they pay for their claims. *Ex post*, wealth is redistributed by managerial opportunism, but *ex ante* some redistribution was expected and the parties price protected themselves. Price protection does not eliminate the incentive to act opportunistically nor does price protection eliminate the dead weight costs of managers taking opportunistic actions. The extent to which contracts can be written *ex ante* to preclude such *ex post* behavior that causes dead weight costs increases the chance the firm will survive in a competitive environment (Klein 1983, fn. 2).

The set of accounting procedures within which managers have discretion is called the "accepted set." It is voluntarily determined by the contracting parties. Managerial discretion over accounting method choice (i.e., the "accepted set") is predicted to vary across firms with the variation in the costs and benefits of restrictions. These restrictions produce the "best" or "accepted" accounting principles even without mandated accounting standards by government. The restrictions are enforced by external auditors. Reacting to the incentive of managers to exercise accounting discretion opportunistically, the accepted set includes "conservative" (e.g., lower of cost or market) and "objective" (e.g., verifiable) accounting procedures (Watts and Zimmerman 1986, 205–206).

Figure 1 represents the concept of the "accepted set" of accounting methods as a Venn diagram. $A1$ denotes the accepted set of methods for firm 1. *Ex ante*, the accepted set is determined jointly by the contracting parties to maximize the value of the firm (e.g., set $A1$ vs. $A2$ in Fig. 1). Managers have discretion to choose any method within the accepted set (e.g., $X1$). Also, managers in firm 2 are constrained *ex ante* to the set $A2$ and choose $X2$ *ex post*. For example, within the accepted set of procedures used for bonus plans managers might select the method that maximizes their utility, even if it comes at another contracting party's expense. Managers' *ex post* choice can either increase the wealth of all contracting parties or redistribute wealth among the parties. Empirically, it is difficult to separate *ex ante* from *ex post*. Contracts are continually being written, rewritten, and revised.

Variations across sets of accepted accounting procedures (e.g., $A1$ and $A2$ in Fig. 1) explain some cross-sectional variation in accounting choice (e.g., managers in firm 2 cannot choose method $X1$). For example, Zimmer (1986) argues Australian real estate development firms are restricted by accepted practice from capitalizing interest except for cost plus contracts that allow interest as a cost. His evidence is consistent with that hypothesis.

Most accounting choice studies assume managers choose accounting methods to transfer wealth to themselves at the expense of another party to the firm because they can take the firm's observed contracts as given and then determine managers' incentives for accounting choice. Some research studies assume accounting methods are chosen for efficiency reasons (i.e., they increase the pie available being shared among all parties to the firm (Watts 1974, 1977; Leftwich

Figure 1
Relation Between the Accepted Set of Accounting Methods
and the Choice of Method from within the Accepted Set

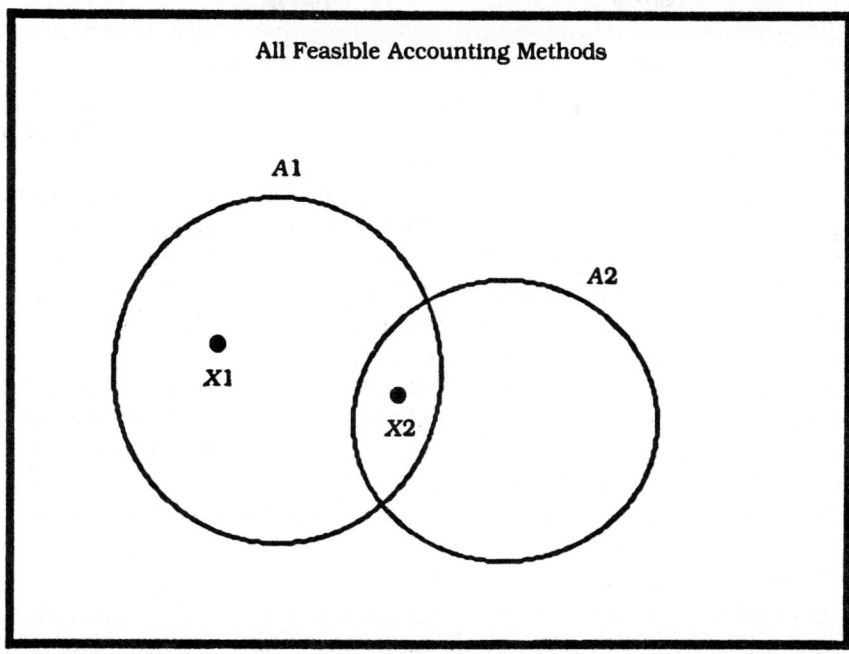

*A*1 denotes the set of accepted methods for firm 1
*A*2 denotes the set of accepted methods for firm 2
*X*1 denotes the choice of method from within the accepted set by firm 1
*X*2 denotes the choice of method from within the accepted set by firm 2

et al. 1981; Zimmer 1986; Whittred 1987; Ball 1989; Malmquist forthcoming; Mian and Smith forthcoming). However, no study to date has explained both the *ex ante* choice of the accepted set and the *ex post* choice of accounting method from within the accepted set. Most studies that assume opportunistic choice of accounting methods do not control for the fact that managers in different firms likely are choosing accounting methods from different constrained accepted sets.

The accepted set of accounting methods is one part of the firm's implicit and explicit contracts including the firm's capital structure, compensation plans, and ownership structure. All the contracting provisions (including the accounting policies) are endogenous. Capital structure choice is related to compensation policy and to accounting policy. But, the relation is not necessarily causal. Capital structure changes do not *cause* changes in the accepted set of accounting methods. Rather, some exogenous event, such as a new invention or government deregulation occurs and this causes changes in the contracting variables including accounting methods (Ball 1972; Smith and Watts 1986).

Evidence on the Theory

Two types of tests of the theory have been conducted: stock price tests and accounting choice tests. The stock price tests have been reviewed extensively elsewhere (Foster 1980; Ricks 1982; Holthausen and Leftwich 1983; Lev and Ohlson 1982; Watts and Zimmerman 1986; Bernard 1989). Stock price tests of the theory reveal some price reactions to mandatory accounting changes, especially involving oil and gas accounting (Lys 1984).[7] Stock price studies are probably relatively weak tests of the theory (Watts and Zimmerman 1986). The more promising ones are accounting choice studies.

Most accounting choice studies attempt to explain the choice of a single accounting method (e.g., the choice of depreciation) instead of the choice of combinations of accounting methods. Focusing on a single accounting method reduces the power of the tests since managers are concerned with how the combination of methods affects earnings instead of the effect on just one particular accounting method (Zmijewski and Hagerman 1981). Some studies seek to explain accounting accruals (the difference between operating cash flows and earnings). Accounting accruals aggregate into a single measure the net effect of all accounting choices (Healy 1985; DeAngelo 1986, 1988a; Liberty and Zimmerman 1986). But use of accruals as a summary measure of accounting choice suffers from a lack of control of what accruals would be without managerial accounting discretion.

Most accounting choice studies use combinations of three sets of variables: variables representing the manager's incentives to choose accounting methods under bonus plans, debt contracts, and the political process. Bonus plan and debt contract variables are used because they're observable. The three particular hypotheses most frequently tested are the bonus plan hypothesis, the debt/equity hypothesis, and the political cost hypothesis. The literature has tended to state each of these hypotheses as managers behaving opportunistically. The bonus plan hypothesis is that managers of firms with bonus plans are more likely to use accounting methods that increase current period reported income. Such selection will presumably increase the present value of bonuses if the compensation committee of the board of directors does not adjust for the method chosen.

The choice studies to date find results generally consistent with the bonus plan hypothesis (Watts and Zimmerman 1986, chap. 11; Christie forthcoming).

---

[7] Using Lys' own calculations, Frost and Bernard (1989, 20) and Bernard (1989, 14) conclude Lys' evidence is inconsistent with a link between stock price reactions to mandated oil and gas accounting and the violation of debt covenants. However, that conclusion is unwarranted. Lys estimates the average cost of violations as 2.5 percent of the stock value, the same order of magnitude as the stock price reactions observed. Frost and Bernard argue that given an average cost of violation of 2.5 percent, the average stock price reaction should be much less since according to Foster (1980) very few firms have a debt covenant violation as a result of the mandated accounting change. There are at least three problems with the Frost and Bernard argument. First, the Lys point estimates are likely to have large standard errors. Second, to obtain an estimate of the stock price reaction, the estimated cost of a violation has to be weighted not by the relative frequency of violation but by the change in the likelihood of violation. While few firms violated covenants, many firms' probability of violation likely increased substantially. Third, Malmquist (forthcoming) suggests Foster's description of oil and gas firms' covenants is incorrect. Frost and Bernard (1989) also use their own empirical study's results to argue that there is no link between the stock price reaction and debt covenants. Because of selection biases, however, their study provides little evidence on the issue (Begley forthcoming).

The early tests of the bonus hypothesis are not very powerful tests of the theory because they rely on simplifications of the theory that are not appropriate in many cases. For example, a bonus plan does not always give managers incentives to increase earnings. If, in the absence of accounting changes, earnings are below the minimum level required for payment of a bonus, managers have incentive to reduce earnings this year because no bonuses are likely paid. Taking such an "earnings bath" increases expected profits and bonuses in future years. By using bonus plan details to identify situations where managers are expected to reduce earnings, Healy's (1985) tests encompass more kinds of manipulation. His results are consistent with managers manipulating net accruals to affect their bonuses.

The debt/equity hypothesis predicts the higher the firm's debt/equity ratio, the more likely managers use accounting methods that increase income. The higher the debt/equity ratio, the closer (i.e., "tighter") the firm is to the constraints in the debt covenants (Kalay 1982). The tighter the covenant constraint, the greater the probability of a covenant violation and of incurring costs from technical default. Managers exercising discretion by choosing income increasing accounting methods relax debt constraints and reduce the costs of technical default.

The evidence is generally consistent with the debt/equity hypothesis.[8] The higher firms' debt/equity ratios, the more likely managers choose income increasing methods. Press and Weintrop (forthcoming) and Duke and Hunt (forthcoming) find that debt/equity ratios are correlated with closeness to bond covenants as assumed in the debt/equity hypothesis.[9] Some studies, however, have avoided using the debt/equity ratio as a proxy variable for closeness to the covenant constraint by using more direct tests. For example, Bowen et al. (1981) examine whether accounting choice varies with tightness of the dividend constraint as specified in the debt covenant and measured by "unrestricted retained earnings." The association between leverage and accounting method choice is an empirical regularity unknown prior to the positive accounting studies.

The political cost hypothesis predicts that large firms rather than small firms are more likely to use accounting choices that reduce reported profits. Size is a proxy variable for political attention. Underlying this hypothesis is the assumption that it is costly for individuals to become informed about whether accounting profits really represent monopoly profits and to "contract" with others in the political process to enact laws and regulations that enhance their welfare. Thus, rational individuals are less than fully informed. The political process is no different from the market process in that respect. Given the cost of information and monitoring, managers have incentive to exercise discretion over accounting profits and the parties in the political process settle for a rational amount of *ex post* opportunism.

[8] Holthausen (1981) and Healy (1985) fail to reject the null hypothesis of no association between leverage and accounting method choice (see Christie forthcoming, table 1).

[9] Researchers are beginning to distinguish between how close the firm is to a given covenant constraint versus the existence of the covenant. For example, Press and Weintrop (forthcoming) find the existence of a covenant has additional explanatory power in a model predicting accounting choice after including a leverage variable.

The evidence is consistent with the political cost hypothesis. However, the result only appears to hold for the largest firms (Zmijewski and Hagerman 1981) and is driven by the oil and gas industry (Zimmerman 1983). Difficulties with using firm size to proxy for political costs, including the likelihood that it can proxy for many other effects, such as industry membership, are discussed in Ball and Foster (1982). The interesting finding is the consistency of the sign of the relation between size and accounting choice across a variety of studies. The largest firms tend to use income decreasing accounting methods. Presently, there is no alternative theory for the empirical regularity between firm size and accounting choice other than the political cost hypothesis.

Bonus plan, debt contract, and political process variables other than bonus plan existence, leverage, and size have also been found to be associated with accounting choice. Christie (forthcoming) aggregates test statistics across the various studies and concludes ". . . six variables common to more than one study have explanatory power. These variables are managerial compensation, leverage, size, risk, and interest coverage and dividend constraints. Another conclusion is that the posterior probability that the theory taken as a whole has explanatory power is close to one."

While bonus, debt, and political process variables tend to be statistically significant (p-values smaller than .10), in many studies the explanatory power (R^2) of the models is low. In Zmijewski and Hagerman (1981), the model of cross-sectional choice of accounting methods is not significantly better than picking the most common combination, although Press and Weintrop (forthcoming) achieve slightly improved explanatory power. The alternative predictive model is that each firm uses the most common combination of accounting methods, a model with little explanatory appeal. The alternative model begs the question of what determines the majority accounting choice. Many accounting teachers would be uncomfortable with the explanation that managers choose their accounting procedures based on what most other firms are doing. The real issue is the lack of an alternative model with greater explanatory power, not the low explanatory power of the extant theory. Several problems with the existing research methods contribute to the low explanatory power. These are discussed next.

II. Criticisms of Positive Accounting Research

Table 1 lists most of the published papers with critical comments on our 1978 and 1979 papers. The second and third columns list the number of explicit references made by the authors to our 1978 and 1979 papers. These columns indicate which of the two papers is the primary focus of the article. The fourth column lists the general topic of the paper and the fifth column lists the major criticisms raised in the paper.

The criticisms in Table 1 can be dichotomized into two mutually exclusive sets: those concerning research methods (including the inferences drawn) and those concerning methodology (including the philosophy of science). For example, Ball and Foster (1982), Holthausen and Leftwich (1983), and McKee et

Table 1

Summary of Papers Reviewing Watts and Zimmerman (1978 and 1979)

Authors	Number of References		Topic	Major Criticisms
	WZ (1978)	WZ (1979)		
Ball and Foster (1982)	13	1	Review of Empirical Accounting Research	• Firm size and bonus plans can proxy for omitted variables • Weak theoretical underpinning for size-political cost construct • Holdout sample not used
Tinker et al. (1982)	1	4	Positive versus normative theories	• Positive theories are value-laden and mask a conservative bias • Ignores underlying class struggles
Christenson (1983)	6	9	Methodology of Positive Accounting	• Logical Positivism is an obsolete methodological approach • Approach is a "sociology of accounting" instead of accounting theory • Tests introduce *ad hoc* arguments to excuse the exceptions to the theory • Inappropriate methods are used for constructing explanatory theories
Holthausen and Leftwich (1983)	7	0	Review of "Economic Consequences Literature"	Interpretation of results limited because: • Incomplete political and contracting theories • Specification problems in left-hand-side and right-hand-side variables
Lowe et al. (1983)	0	12	WZ (1979)	• Economic framework is unjustified • Positive approach open to dispute • Nature of proof is unscientific • Contrary evidence presented

TABLE 1—*Continued*

| Authors | Number of References | | Topic | Major Criticisms |
	WZ (1978)	WZ (1979)		
McKee et al. (1984)	4	0	Replication of WZ (1978)	• Results do not hold in a new sample • Holdout sample not used • Foreknowledge of sample proportions biases parameter estimates
Whittington (1987)	0	7	Review of WZ (1986)	• Presentation of arguments and evidence is unbalanced • Extreme methodological stance • Positive theories are value-laden • Approach is a "sociology of accounting" instead of accounting theory
Hines (1988)	4	0	Christenson (1983) and Methodology	• Popper is not a practical evaluative guideline for empirical accounting research

al. (1984)[10] discuss research methods problems and not philosophy of science issues. The remaining authors concentrate on philosophy of science issues to the near exclusion of problems with research methods. Except for Holthausen and Leftwich (1983), all the reviews of positive accounting ignore the accumulating body of evidence consistent with the theory. For example, Hines (1988) cites McKee et al. (1984) as contradictory evidence to Watts and Zimmerman (1978). Yet, she ignores 21 studies reviewed in Watts and Zimmerman (1986, chaps. 11, 12) and Christie (forthcoming) that present evidence generally consistent with the theory.

The research method issues are important and future research must attempt to address them. However, it is unlikely that the positive accounting literature or any other empirical literature will ever totally eliminate such issues. We do not agree with many of the philosophy of science issues raised and seek to eliminate the common misconceptions they reflect. Research method issues, some raised by others and some by us, are discussed first in this section and philosophy of science issues are discussed second.

Research Method Issues

The first research method issue involves the tests' lack of power. The second issue involves the possibility that the results obtained in the positive accounting literature are due to unrecognized alternative hypotheses, not the stated hypotheses.

Reductions in the tests' power. Tests of the theory lack power for several reasons: problems with model specification, problems specifying the left-hand-side and right-hand-side variables, and omitted variables. Each of these are discussed next.

Model specification. All the studies to date have assumed accounting choice results either from efficiency reasons or managerial opportunism. This produces two model specification errors. First, in probit type regressions where the choice of accounting method depends on the effect of the choice on the manager's wealth, the right-hand-side or explanatory variables reflect the wealth effects of the choice via compensation plans, debt agreements, and the political process. Implicitly researchers are holding constant the firm's investment opportunity set and contracts and interpret the compensation plan variable as managerial opportunism. But, the debt and political variables can represent both efficiency and opportunism. Thus, the model is misspecified. The second specification error results from ignoring the interaction effects among the right-hand-side variables. Higher earnings impose political costs and so reduce the size of the pie for the contracting parties and at the same time increase the manager's bonus compensation. The manager's increased share of the smaller pie might be larger than a smaller share of the larger pie. The bonus plan and political process effects inter-

---

[10] McKee et al. (1984) discuss problems of the tests in Watts and Zimmerman (1978), extend the tests to another sample of firms, and offer some statistical refinements. The only satistically significant explanatory variable in our 1978 paper was firm size. McKee et al. find that their refined measure of firm size, (SALES/MAXSALES)DTREND, is statistically significant in both our sample and their sample and remains statistically significant after various refinements are made. They do not discuss the importance of this finding.

act. However, in the empirical models the right-hand-side variables are treated as additive and interaction effects are ignored. Solving these two specification problems requires researchers to specify the intertemporal interaction between opportunism (including managerial reputation incentives) and efficiency effects (see Christie 1987).

Left-hand-side variable. Problems specifying the accounting choice variable reduce the power of the tests. One such problem mentioned earlier is the use of single method choices as the left-hand-side variable. Zmijewski and Hagerman (1981) and Press and Weintrop (forthcoming) use sets of accounting methods and still achieve relatively low explanatory power. However, ranking the effects of various portfolios of accounting methods on earnings requires assumptions about the relative effects on earnings of the various accounting choices (e.g., the effect of depreciation choice vs. inventory choice). These assumptions induce error in the left-hand-side variable. Healy (1985) tries to overcome this problem by using net accruals as his left-hand-side variable. But, the variable "net accruals" is a noisy measure of the net accruals manipulated by managers. Some accounting decisions that affect accruals have been made earlier and are probably beyond the manager's discretion at the time of the measurement. Ideally, net accruals should be measured relative to what they would be without manipulation, so these variations are excluded from the left-hand-side variable. This requires a model of accruals that currently does not exist (Moyer 1988; McNichols and Wilson 1988; DeAngelo 1988b).

Right-hand-side variables. Some variables in accounting choice studies are mismeasured. For example, both the closeness to the covenant (i.e., the difference between the number specified in the covenant and the actual number) and the existence of the covenant are likely important determinants of accounting choice. But the debt/equity ratio by itself is an imprecise measure of both closeness to the constraint and the existence of a constraint. Also, the use of a zero-one variable to measure a bonus plan effect is simplistic. Ball and Foster (1982, 184) point out that other components of pay, such as salary, can depend on accounting earnings without a formal compensation plan and that even with a formal accounting-based plan the outside directors can adjust the incentive pay for accounting changes. However, finding an association between an indicator variable representing a bonus plan and choice of accounting methods is informative and suggests that further research with more refined measures based on the bonus plans' details will yield stronger results than the zero-one variable. Also, more direct measures of political sensitivity than firm size (Wong 1988; Jones 1988; Sutton 1988) provide more powerful tests of the political cost hypothesis.

Omitted variables. There are three different omitted variable problems in the current literature: omitting standard accounting-based contracts, omitting less standard contracts, and omitting variables representing the accepted set. First, contracting cost variables for standard contracts, such as bonus plans occasionally are omitted because such variables are costly to collect. For example, Daley and Vigeland (1983) omit a variable representing accounting-based management compensation plans from their regression. Because leverage, compensation contracts, and accounting policy are part of the firm's efficient contracting technology, these variables covary and also vary with firm size. Omitting a right-hand-side variable correlated with included variables causes the existing right-hand-side variables to become surrogates for the omitted variables. This produces biased coefficients of the estimated right-hand-side variables and hampers their interpretation.

A second omitted variables problem is that to a large degree, the literature to date focuses only on debt and compensation contracts. Other contracts influence management's choice of accounting methods, but these are omitted in most tests. For example, the existence of a bonus plan is likely correlated with other organizational devices such as stock option plans. These other organizational structures might be driving the accounting choice rather than bonus plans (Ball and Foster 1982, 185). And, it is incorrect to ascribe all the explanatory effect of the bonus plan indicator variable results to the bonus plan. Corporate control issues also are often omitted as explanatory variables in seeking to explain accounting choices. DeAngelo (1988a) finds that net accruals are more positive (i.e., higher reported earnings) during proxy fights. Zimmerman (1979) and Ball (1989) argue that accounting numbers are part of the internal control process and, thus, affect manager's choice of accounting methods (e.g., cost allocations). Ignoring these, other less frequently researched informal contracts can produce biased coefficients.

Third, as discussed under specification problems above, the left-hand-side variable in most studies is the manager's choice of accounting methods. Even without a government regulatory defined set of accounting methods, this choice is made from within the "accepted set of methods" (see Fig. 1).[11] Yet, most studies do not control for differences across firms' accepted sets. Such control requires a theory of how the sets of accepted accounting methods vary and such a theory does not exist. Failure to control for differences in accepted sets induces another correlated omitted variables problem in the tests. The severity of this correlated omitted variables (and model specification) problem is likely to be larger in studies in which the sampled firms are drawn from several industries than in studies where the sampled firms are drawn from the same industry.

Alternative hypotheses. Alternative hypotheses can explain the bonus, debt/equity, and size results found in the positive accounting literature. Several scenarios illustrate how this problem might arise:

1. If the accounting system is part of the firm's efficient set of implicit and explicit contracts, accounting choice is endogenous. Contracting, investment, and production decisions are determined jointly. The type of contracts used (including the accounting methods) depends on the firm's investment opportunity set. Hence, the firm's investment opportunity set (e.g., whether it includes growth options or not) is correlated with the firm's financial, dividend, compensation, and accounting policies. Smith and Watts (1986) find significant cross-sectional correlations among

---

[11] Mian and Smith (forthcoming) find that accounting policy decisions regarding consolidations vary by type of organization structure. Consumer finance subsidiaries are more prevalent where the parent is in the financial services industry and choice of consolidation is more homogeneous within like organization structures than in dissimilar structures. Also, operating interdependencies between the parent and subsidiary drive some accounting choices.

firms' investment opportunity sets, financial policies, dividend policies, and compensation policies. The documented correlations between debt/equity and accounting choice and between bonus plans and accounting choice could be due to the correlation between financial and compensation policies and the optimal set of accounting procedures for contracting. Most researchers, however, interpret these associations as resulting from opportunistic actions by managers and have not considered efficiency-based hypotheses.

2. Accounting choice also is endogenous in the political process. The potential costs of a proposed accounting standard affect the standard before it is released. The correlation between financial and compensation policies and accounting policy is likely affected by the firm's tax accounting policies. While some financial accounting method choices do not affect taxes, reducing bookkeeping costs by keeping one set of books and the possibility that tax audits or future taxes might be levied using reported income induce a relation between financial accounting and tax accounting methods.[12]

One cannot test claims that variables like debt/equity and size are surrogates for alternative explanations until those alternatives are identified and the relation specified. Given the investment opportunity set and taxes are identified as possible explanatory variables, future research can investigate their implications as alternative hypotheses to those currently advanced. For example, changing accounting methods can result from a change in the firm's investment opportunity set causing the efficient contracts and accounting methods to change. Or, some exogenous event occurs (such as reduced demand for the firm's products) and managers take opportunistic actions to undo the adverse compensation and debt contract effects of the exogenous event. Accounting changes likely are due to both efficiency reasons and managerial opportunism. Probing the relative importance of efficiency and opportunism for accounting method changes requires more refined theories and more linkage between the theory and the tests.

Philosophy of Science Issues

Positive theories are value-laden. Tinker et al. (1982, 167) argue that all research is value-laden and not socially neutral. Specifically, "Realism, operating in the clothes of positive theory, claims theoretical supremacy because it is born of fact, not values" (p. 172). We concede the importance of values in determining research; both the researcher's and user's preferences affect the process.

Competition among theories to meet users' demands constrains the extent to which researcher values influence research design. Positive theories are "If . . . , then . . ." propositions that are both predictive and explanatory. Researchers choose the topics to investigate, the methods to use, and the assumptions to make. Researchers' preferences and expected payoffs (publications and citations) affect their choice of topics, methods, and assumptions. In this sense, all re-

---

[12] The Corporate Alternative Minimum Tax under the Tax Reform Act of 1986 requires a portion of reported income be in the tax base. This act increases the tax incentives on financial reporting. Research to date has not documented the effect of 1986 tax reform on financial reporting incentives.

search, including positive research is "value-laden." The usefulness of positive theories depends on their predictive and explanatory power and on the user's preferences or objective function. To the extent that the researcher's values interfere with the theory's ability to predict and explain, the theory's usefulness is reduced.

Approach is a "sociology of accounting" instead of accounting theory. Christenson (1983, 5) writes, "The program of the Rochester School is concerned with describing, predicting, and explaining the behavior of accountants and managers, not that of accounting entities." His definition of an "accounting entity" is "A business enterprise or other economic unit, or any subdivision thereof for which a system of accounts is maintained" (Kohler 1975, 14). Christenson (1983, 6) supports his criticism with an analogy from the physical sciences, "Chemical theory consists of propositions about the behavior of chemical entities (molecules and atoms) not about the behavior of chemists." In chemistry, chemical reactions exist without chemists and one can study reactions without studying chemists. But, there would be no accounting without accountants, managers, or preparers of the numbers; there would be no numbers or systems to investigate because people "*maintain*" the system (Lavoie 1989). Analogously, there would be no study of political science if politicians and voters were ignored.

The study of accounting (or political science) is a social science (Christenson 1983, fn. 5). An accounting theory that seeks to explain and predict accounting cannot divorce accounting research from the study of people. The contracting approach to studying accounting requires researchers to understand the incentives of the contracting parties.

Inappropriate methods are used for constructing explanatory theories. We apply traditional, generally accepted research methods and methodology from accounting, finance, and economics. Christenson (1983, 6) states, "The Rochester School has drawn its concept of 'positive theory' from that guru of the Chicago School of Economics, Milton Friedman."[13] Whittington (1987, 331) states, ". . . Watts and Zimmerman are not unique in owing intellectual allegiance to the Chicago view. . . . The majority of North American empirical accounting researchers would fall into this category, and their collective achievements are formidable."

The economic approach we and many others use applies a simple proposition: To predict and explain individual behavior, people (including accountants, regulators, and researchers) consider the private costs and benefits (broadly defined) of an action and choose the action if the benefits exceed the costs. This economics-based research methodology may be fundamentally flawed in ways we do not now understand. But, accounting research using this methodology has produced useful predictions of how the world works (e.g., association between earnings and stock prices, random walk model of earnings, contracting and size variables associated with accounting choice). A methodology that yields useful results should not be abandoned purely because it *may* not predict *all* human

---

[13] Christenson is referring to Milton Friedman's views on scientific methodology as expounded in Friedman (1953). In our opinion, Friedman places too much emphasis on prediction vis-á-vis explanation.

behavior. Do we discard something that works in some situations because it *may* not work in every circumstance? Despite what the critics think methodology *should be*, the methodologies that survive are the ones that produce useful theories. Competition in the marketplace of ideas will produce future research that uncover the errors of our present ways. Time will tell whether our approach is inappropriate.

Choice of the term "Positive Accounting Theory." Positive accounting research existed long before the publication of our 1978 and 1979 papers. Early examples include Gordon (1964), Gordon et al. (1966), and Gagnon (1967). We applied the label "positive" to a set of existing research studies. The prime reason we attached this adjective in "Towards a Positive Theory of the Determination of Accounting Standards" was to emphasize that accounting theory's role is to provide explanations and predictions for accounting practice.

In Watts and Zimmerman (1986, 2) we state the objective of an accounting theory is to explain and predict accounting practice. Neither prediction nor explanation is preeminent. We adopted the label "positive" from economics where it was used to distinguish research aimed at explanation and prediction from research whose objective was prescription. Given the connotation already attached to the term in economics we thought it would be useful in distinguishing accounting research aimed at understanding accounting from research directed at generating prescriptions. In the 1960s researchers were still debating various normative theories of accounting (Chambers 1966; Sprouse and Moonitz 1962).

Our use of the term "positive" differentiated our and other people's (positive) research from traditional normative theories by emphasizing the importance of prediction and explanation. It helped place normative theories and their role in a clearer perspective. Our work was not directly related to the debate over alternative normative theories and we wanted to differentiate our work from that debate. The phrase "positive" created a trademark and like all trademarks it conveys information. "Coke," "Kodak," "Levis" convey information. A positive theory differs from a normative theory, though a positive theory can have normative implications once an objective function is specified (Jensen 1983).

In retrospect, the term "positive" generated more confusion than we anticipated. For example, some thought we meant logical positivism (Christenson 1983). We merely intended to distinguish positive propositions from the extant normative propositions in the literature. While the term "positive" avoided debates over normative uses of the work, the term "positive" generated considerable debate over philosophical issues.

Despite its problems, we prefer "positive accounting literature" to alternative terms that have arisen, particularly the term "economic consequences literature." This latter term suggests accounting standards are decided on some higher basis and that economic consequences are a secondary factor only considered after the initial decision is made on the higher basis.[14]

---

[14] Some have suggested the term "contracting theory." While descriptive of most of the elements in the existing theory, it seems to preclude noncontractual variables that might be discovered later (e.g., taxes or information for the capital markets, Holthausen forthcoming).

Debate over methodology. Several papers listed in Table 1 involve a debate over what constitutes "proper" methodology (Tinker et al. 1982; Christenson 1983; Lowe et al. 1983; Whittington 1987; Hines 1988). For example, Christenson (1983, 1) concludes, ". . . [T]he standards advocated by the Rochester School for appraisal of their own theories are so weak that those theories fail to satisfy Popper's (1959) proposal for demarking science from metaphysics." Hines (1988) then criticizes Christenson for relying on Popper (1959) which later philosophers of science have questioned. Hines (1988, 658) argues these methodology issues are important and if ignored will "harmfully limit the nature and domain of accounting research."

The methodology criticisms have failed the market test because they have had little influence on accounting research. Researchers have not changed their approach. Referees and editors of journals have not asked researchers to alter their methodology based on these published critiques. There are at least three reasons these criticisms have had little effect on published research. First, the criticisms are written in an abstract fashion. Instead of just criticizing extant papers, if the critics would repeat studies without making the alleged errors, then users of the corrected research would demand such procedures be followed in the future. If the alleged errors are important to users, then other researchers, editors, and referees would adopt the suggestions. Second, critics who place unreasonable demands on studies cause other researchers to disregard their complaints. For example, Hines (1988, 661) argues that Watts and Zimmerman (1978) should have: (1) avoided crude proxies, (2) avoided unrealistic assumptions, (3) investigated the anomalies, (4) clarified their theories, and (5) rigorously tested their theories against competing hypotheses. All these standards are relevant, but if all were applied rigorously to individual papers (especially early papers in an area of thought), no research would be published. Third, to most researchers, debating methodology is a "no win" situation because each side argues from a different paradigm with different rules and no common ground. Our reason for replying here is that some have mistaken our lack of response as tacit acceptance of the criticisms.

III. Summary and Conclusions

Our prime objective in this paper is to provide a perspective on our 1978 and 1979 *Accounting Review* papers. The 1978 paper has proven more important than the "Excuses" paper. Based on citations, the 1978 paper has received over three times as many citations as the 1979 paper (Brown and Gardner 1985, 97). The 1978 paper was a catalyst for research into the choice of accounting methods. Except for generating debates over methodology, the 1979 "Excuses" paper has remained outside the mainstream of accounting research probably because of the more subjective type of evidence necessary to test theories of the effect of accounting research on policy.

The debate over methodology has been less useful than the discovery and explanation of empirical regularities. The positive accounting literature has discovered several empirical regularities in accounting choice and provided an explanation for them. Critics of the 1978 and 1979 papers raise issues involving research methods and philosophy of science. The methodology we and the subsequent literature use is the methodology of economics, finance, and science generally. This methodology has been successful in accounting and we feel no necessity to apologize for it. Under this methodology, a theory is not discarded merely because of some inconsistent observations. The best theory is determined in a competition to meet the demand from students and practitioners for theories that explain and predict accounting choice. It is unlikely an accounting or a social science theory with perfect predictions will ever exist. Researchers are influenced by their values. But, to the extent those researchers are competing to meet student and practitioners' demand for theories, they have incentives to reduce that influence. Further, the careful dichotomy between theory and prescription helps reduce that influence. Lastly, accounting is an activity carried out by people and one cannot generate a theory that predicts and explains accounting phenomena by ignoring the incentives of the individuals who account. In this final section we summarize the contributions made by this literature, our views on promising research directions, and some conclusions.

Positive Accounting Literature Contributions

Discovering systematic patterns in accounting choice outlined in the preceding sections and providing specific explanations for the patterns are the literature's major contributions. However, we believe the literature has made other contributions: it provides an intuitively plausible framework for understanding accounting. A plausible framework is a useful pedagogy for teaching accounting. The literature also encourages researchers to address accounting issues and emphasizes the central role of contracting costs in accounting theory.

The literature explains why accounting is used and provides a framework for predicting accounting choices. Choices are not made in terms of "better measurement" of some accounting construct, such as earnings. Choices are made in terms of individual objectives and the effects of accounting methods on the achievement of those objectives. For example, some accounting instructors teach that certain accounting methods (e.g., current cost) are better than others (e.g., historical cost). But, no explanation is offered why these "better" measures are not adopted. The positive accounting literature takes as given the proposition that the accepted set maximizes the wealth of the contracting parties and then seeks to understand how wealth is affected by specific accounting methods.

The literature's emphasis on predicting and explaining accounting phenomena encourages research that is relevant to accounting. One of the first questions one pursuing this approach asks of a new model is whether it has any relevance to predicting and explaining accounting practice.

Another contribution of the literature is to highlight the importance of contracting costs (including information, agency, bankruptcy, and lobbying costs). Contracting costs have long been important in economics and date to Coase (1937). Positive accounting research has more recently recognized the importance of contracting costs to explain accounting. In the late 1960s and 1970s, financial economists derived pricing models (capital asset pricing models, option pricing models, arbitrage pricing models). These models were developed under assumptions of costless information and such models explain why different securities sell for different relative prices. Such models do not explain institutional differences, such as open- and closed-end mutual funds. To explain such institutional differences requires assumptions of costly information and contracting. Likewise, accounting would not exist without contracting costs and so it is difficult to produce a theory that predicts and explains accounting without making assumptions about the relative magnitudes of these costs. The central role of contracting costs highlighted by positive accounting research makes it difficult to ignore these costs in accounting theories. It directs researchers' attention to the appropriate issues.

Future Research Directions

Section II discussed two major research methods issues: the lack of power of the tests and alternative economic explanations for the empirical regularities. The following research suggestions focus on these two issues. We believe these suggestions will be more fruitful in advancing the understanding of accounting choice than "merely conducting more studies using existing formulations of the theory and existing ways of measuring variables" (Christie forthcoming) (also see Holthausen and Leftwich 1983, 109–114).

First, the single most important task facing positive accounting researchers is improving the linkage between the theory and empirical tests. The theory predicts that the magnitude of debt renegotiation costs will affect managers' choice of accounting methods and will set an upper bound on the magnitude of the default costs. To date, researchers have been unable to document the magnitude of the costs imposed by a technical violation of a debt covenant or the magnitude of renegotiation costs (Holthausen 1981; Leftwich 1981; Lys 1984; Leftwich forthcoming). Greater attention has to be placed on developing a unified theory that incorporates both the *ex ante* efficient restrictions on the managers' accepted set of accounting methods and the *ex post* exercise by managers of their discretion to choose accounting methods from within the accepted set. The empirical tests can no longer assume accounting choice is made for either efficiency or opportunistic reasons. Both must be incorporated into the tests. Also, estimates of the relative magnitudes of the various components of contracting costs can help to further refine the linkage between the theory and tests by identifying those costs most influential in driving accounting choice.

Developing and testing alternative hypotheses for the existing empirical regularities also will enhance the linkage between the theory and the tests. Hypotheses can be developed to predict new empirical regularities. Under the contracting approach, debt and compensation contracts are only some of the contracts that affect firms' cash flows. Other (explicit and implicit) contracts can be used to develop new predictions (DeAngelo 1988a). Particularly promising is the effect of accounting procedures for internal control on external reporting (Ball 1989). For example, Mian and Smith (forthcoming) find that the prevalence of consolidated reporting of financing subsidiaries depends on the extent to which the subsidiary is interdependent with the parent's main business. How the firm is organized internally (e.g., functionally or by product line), the type of internal compensation systems, and the investment opportunity set are likely associated with the type of internal accounting performance measurement systems. Internal contracting parties may well turn out to be as important a determinant of external financial reporting as the external contracting parties.

Finally, the political process can affect firms' cash flows other than via the simple political cost hypotheses. More detailed specification of government regulatory processes that rely on accounting numbers can be used to develop new hypotheses and a tighter linkage between the theory and tests by suggesting more precise proxy variables other than firm size (Sutton 1988; Wong 1988; Jones 1988).

Second, when accounting choice is cast as part of the efficient contracting technology, variables often used to explain and predict accounting choice are endogenous. For example, changes in accounting procedures occur simultaneously with changes in the firm's investment opportunity set, its financial and compensation contracts, its organizational structure, and even in its political environment. Managers choose packages of accounting policy, financial policy, and organizational structure (including performance evaluation and reward systems). Theoretical and empirical models have to be developed to sort out the endogeneity problems among the variables and, thereby, increase the power of the tests. While this is no easy task, it seems essential to significant advances in both the theories of the firm and of accounting.

Accounting numbers are used in different ways across industries. Besides the obvious regulatory uses of accounting numbers in financial institutions and public utilities, differences in industries' opportunity sets are likely to affect the accepted set of accounting methods. Two types of studies are likely to prove useful and again increase the tests' power. First, studies investigating differences in investment opportunity sets (e.g., the relative amount growth opportunities to assets in place, Myers 1977), accounting policies, organizational structures, and financial policies across industries are likely to produce information useful for the modelling suggested in the preceding paragraph. Second, intra-industry studies of accounting choice while requiring significant amounts of industry-specific knowledge by the researcher, have the potential of generating useful insights about the magnitude of contracting costs.

Third, measurement errors in net accruals can be reduced to increase the tests' power. This requires a model of net accruals not subject to managerial accounting discretion (Kaplan 1985; McNichols and Wilson 1988; DeAngelo 1988b; Moyer 1988). Also, replacing the simple indicator variables used to represent a bonus plan or an accounting-based debt covenant with continuous variables that better measure the relative magnitudes of various contracting costs will probably increase the theory's predictive power.

Conclusions

While the positive accounting literature has yielded empirical regularities and explanations for these regularities, it is clear there are many research opportunities available beyond those currently exploited. The tests of the debt, bonus, and political cost hypotheses represent very limited exploration. Incorporating both *ex ante* contracting efficiency incentives with *ex post* redistributive effects is likely to prove useful. Likewise, investigating the implications of internal contracts and external contracts other than debt and bonus contracts is likely to be productive. The major breakthroughs are likely to come from viewing accounting as a choice that is endogenous with the choice of organization, contracting, and financial structures. Such a breakthrough will be difficult to achieve, but important foundations can be laid by stressing the linkage between the theory and the empirical tests and by investigating inter- and intra-industry variations in accounting methods and other organizational choices.

References

Alchian, A. A. 1950. Uncertainty, evolution and economic theory. *Journal of Political Economy.* (June): 211–221.

———, and H. Demsetz. 1972. Production, information costs and economic organization. *American Economic Review.* (December): 777–795.

Ball, R. 1972. Changes in accounting techniques and stock prices. *Journal of Accounting Research.* (Supplement): 1–38.

———. 1980. Discussion of accounting for research and development costs: The impact of research and development expenditures. *Journal of Accounting Research.* (Supplement): 27–37.

———. 1989. Accounting, auditing and the nature of the firm. Working paper, William E. Simon Graduate School of Business Administration, University of Rochester.

———, and P. Brown. 1968. An empirical evaluation of accounting income numbers. *Journal of Accounting Research.* (Autumn): 159–178.

———, and G. Foster. 1982. Corporate financial reporting: A methodological review of empirical research. *Journal of Accounting Research.* (Supplement): 161–234.

Beaver, W. 1968. The information content of annual earnings announcements. *Journal of Accounting Research.* (Supplement): 67–92.

Begley, J. 1990. Debt covenants and accounting choice. *Journal of Accounting & Economics.* (Forthcoming).

Bernard, V. 1989. Capital markets research in accounting during the 1980s: A critical review. Manuscript, University of Michigan.

Bowen, R. M., E. W. Noreen, and J. M. Lacey. 1981. Determinants of the corporate decision to capitalize interest. *Journal of Accounting & Economics.* (August): 151–179.

Brown, L. D., and J. C. Gardner. 1985. Using citation analysis to assess the impact of journals and articles on contemporary accounting research (CAR). *Journal of Accounting Research.* (Spring): 84–109.

Chambers, R. J. 1966. *Accounting, evaluation, and economic behavior.* Prentice-Hall.

Christie, A. A. 1987. On cross-sectional analysis in accounting research. *Journal of Accounting & Economics.* (December): 231–258.

———. 1990. Aggregation of test statistics: An evaluation of the evidence on contracting and size hypotheses. *Journal of Accounting & Economics.* (Forthcoming).

Christenson, C. 1983. The methodology of positive accounting. *The Accounting Review.* (January): 1–22.

Coase, R. H. 1937. The nature of the firm. *Economica.* (November): 386–405.

Daley, L. A., and R. L. Vigeland. 1983. The effects of debt covenants and political costs on the choice of accounting methods: The case of accounting for R&D costs. *Journal of Accounting & Economics.* (December): 195–211.

DeAngelo, L. E. 1986. Accounting numbers as market valuation substitutes: A study of management buyouts of public stockholders. *The Accounting Review.* (July): 400–420.

———. 1988a. Managerial competition, information costs, and corporate governance: The use of accounting performance measures in proxy contests. *Journal of Accounting & Economics.* (January): 3–36.

———. 1988b. Discussion of evidence of earnings management from the provision for bad debts. *Journal of Accounting Research.* (Supplement): 32–40.

Duke, J., and H. Hunt. 1990. An empirical examination of debt covenant restrictions and accounting-related debt proxies. *Journal of Accounting & Economics.* (Forthcoming).

Fama, E. F., and M. C. Jensen. 1983a. Separation of ownership and control. *Journal of Law and Economics.* (June): 301–325.

——, and ——. 1983b. Agency problems and residual claims. *Journal of Law and Economics.* (June): 327–349.

Foster, G. 1980. Accounting policy decisions and capital market research. *Journal of Accounting & Economics.* (March): 29–62.

Friedman, M. [1953] 1966. *The methodology of positive economics, essays in positive economics.* Reprint, Phoenix Books.

Frost, C. and V. Bernard. 1989. The role of debt covenants in assessing economic consequences of limiting capitalization of exploration costs. *The Accounting Review.* (October): 788–808.

Gagnon, J. M. 1967. Purchase versus pooling of interest: The search for a predictor. *Journal of Accounting Research.* (Supplement): 187–204.

Gordon, M. J. 1964. Postulates, principles and research in accounting. *The Accounting Review.* (April): 251–263.

——, B. N. Horwitz, and P. T. Meyers. 1966. Accounting measurements and normal growth of the firm. *Research in accounting measurement.* Eds. R. K. Jaedicke, Y. Ijiri, and O. Nielsen, 221–231. American Accounting Association.

Healy, P. M. 1985. The effect of bonus schemes on accounting decisions. *Journal of Accounting & Economics.* (April): 85–107.

Hines, R. D. 1988. Popper's methodology of falsificationism and accounting research. *The Accounting Review.* (October): 657–662.

Holthausen, R. W. 1981. Evidence on the effect of bond covenants and management compensation contracts on the choice of accounting techniques: The case of the depreciation switch-back. *Journal of Accounting & Economics.* (March): 73–109.

——. 1990. Accounting method choice: Opportunistic behavior, efficient contracting and information perspectives. *Journal of Accounting & Economics.* (Forthcoming).

——, and R. W. Leftwich. 1983. The economic consequences of accounting choice: Implications of costly contracting and monitoring. *Journal of Accounting & Economics.* (August): 77–117.

Jensen, M. C. 1983. Organization theory and methodology. *The Accounting Review.* (April): 319–339.

——, and W. H. Meckling. 1976. Theory of the firm: Managerial behavior, agency costs and ownership structure. *Journal of Financial Economics.* (October): 305–360.

Jones, J. 1988. The effect of foreign trade regulation on accounting choices, and production and investment decisions. Working paper, University of Michigan.

Kalay, A. 1982. Stockholder-bondholder conflict and dividend constraints. *Journal of Financial Economics.* (July): 211–233.

Kaplan, R. S. 1985. Comments on Paul Healy: Evidence on the effect of bonus schemes on accounting procedure and accrual decisions. *Journal of Accounting & Economics.* (April): 109–113.

Klein, B. 1983. Contracting costs and residual claims: The separation of ownership and control. *Journal of Law & Economics.* (June): 367–374.

——, R. Crawford, and A. Alchian. 1978. Vertical integration, appropriable rents, and the competitive contracting process. *Journal of Law & Economics.* (October): 297–326.

Kohler, E. L. 1975. *A dictionary for accountants.* 5th ed. Prentice-Hall.

Lavoie, D. 1989. The accounting of interpretations and the interpretation of accounts: The communicative function of "the language of business." *Methodology and accounting research: Does the past have a future.* Ed. O. Johnson, 107–149. Orace Johnson.

Leftwich, R. 1981. Evidence of the impact of mandatory changes in accounting principles on corporate loan agreements. *Journal of Accounting & Economics.* (March): 3–36.

——. 1983. Accounting information in private markets: Evidence from private lending agreements. *The Accounting Review.* (January): 23–42.

——. 1990. Aggregation of test statistics: Statistics vs economics. *Journal of Accounting & Economics.* (Forthcoming).

——, R. L. Watts, and J. L. Zimmerman. 1981. Voluntary corporate disclosure: The case of interim reporting. *Journal of Accounting Research.* (Supplement): 50–77.

Lev, B., and J. A. Ohlson. 1982. Market-based empirical research in accounting: A review, interpretation, and extension. *Journal of Accounting Research.* (Supplement): 249–322.

Liberty, S. E., and J. L. Zimmerman. 1986. Labor union contract negotiations and accounting choices. *The Accounting Review.* (October): 692–712.

Lowe, E. A., A. G. Puxty, and R. C. Laughlin. 1983. Simple theories for complex processes: Accounting policy and the market for myopia. *Journal of Accounting and Public Policy.* (Spring): 19–42.

Lys, T. 1984. Mandated accounting changes and debt covenants: The case of oil and gas accounting. *Journal of Accounting & Economics.* (April): 39–65.

Malmquist, D. 1990. Efficient contracting and the choice of accounting method in the oil and gas industry. *Journal of Accounting & Economics.* (Forthcoming).

McKee, A. J., Jr., T. B. Bell, and J. R. Boatsman. 1984. Management preferences over accounting standards: A replication and additional tests. *The Accounting Review.* (October): 647–659.

McNichols, M., and G. Wilson. 1988. Evidence of earnings management from the provision for bad debts. *Journal of Accounting Research.* (Supplement): 1–31.

Meckling, W., and M. Jensen. 1986. Knowledge, control and organizational structure. Working paper, University of Rochester.

Mian, S., and C. Smith. 1990. Incentives for unconsolidated financial reporting. *Journal of Accounting & Economics.* (Forthcoming).

Modigliani, F., and M. H. Miller. 1958. The cost of capital, corporation finance and the theory of investment. *American Economic Review.* (June): 261–297.

Moyer, S. 1988. Accounting choices in commercial banks. Dissertation, University of Rochester.

Myers, S. 1977. Determinants of corporate borrowing. *Journal of Financial Economics.* (November): 147–175.

Peltzman, S. 1976. Toward a more general theory of regulation. *Journal of Law and Economics.* (August): 211–240.

Popper, K. R. [1959] 1965. *The logic of scientific discovery.* Reprint, Harper & Row.

Press, E., and J. Weintrop. 1990. Accounting-based constraints in public and private debt agreements: Their association with leverage and impact on accounting choice. *Journal of Accounting & Economics.* (Forthcoming).

Ricks, W. 1982. Market assessment of alternative accounting methods: A review of the empirical evidence. *Journal of Accounting Literature.* (59–102).

Smith, C. W. 1980. On the theory of financial contracting: The personal loan market. *Journal of Monetary Economics.* (July): 333–357.

——, and J. B. Warner. 1979. On financial contracting: An analysis of bond covenants. *Journal of Financial Economics.* (June): 117–161.

——, and R. Watts. 1982. Incentive and tax effects of U.S. executive compensation plans. *Australian Journal of Management.* (December): 139–157.

——, and ——. 1986. Investment opportunity set and corporate policy choices. Working paper, University of Rochester.

Sorter, G. H., S. W. Becker, T. R. Archibald, and W. H. Beaver. 1966. Accounting and financial measures as indicators of corporate personality—some empirical findings. *Research in accounting measurement.* Eds. R. K. Jaedicke, Y. Ijiri, and O. Nielsen, 200–210. American Accounting Association.

Sprouse, R., and M. Moonitz. 1962. A tentative set of broad accounting principles for business enterprises. *Accounting Research Study No. 3.* American Institute of Certified Public Accountants.

Stigler, G. J. 1971. The theory of economic regulation. *Bell Journal of Economics and Management Science.* (Spring): 3–21.

Sutton, T. G. 1988. The proposed introduction of current cost accounting in the U.K.: Determinants of corporate preference. *Journal of Accounting & Economics.* (April): 127–149.

Tinker, T. A. M., B. D. Merino, and M. D. Neimark. 1982. The normative origins of positive theories: Ideology and accounting thought. *Accounting, Organizations and Society* 2: 167–200.

Watts, R. L. 1974. Accounting objectives. Working paper, University of Rochester.

———. 1977. Corporate financial statements, a product of the market and political processes. *Australian Journal of Management.* (April): 53–75.

———, and J. L. Zimmerman. 1978. Towards a positive theory of the determination of accounting standards. *The Accounting Review.* (January): 112–134.

———, and ———. 1979. The demand for and supply of accounting theories: The market for excuses. *The Accounting Review.* (April): 273–305.

———, and ———. 1986. *Positive accounting theory.* Prentice-Hall.

Whittington, G. 1987. Positive accounting: A review article. *Accounting and Business Research.* (Autumn): 327–336.

Whittred, G. 1987. The derived demand for consolidated financial reporting. *Journal of Accounting & Economics.* (December): 259–285.

Wong, J. 1988. Economic incentives for the voluntary disclosure of current cost financial statements. *Journal of Accounting & Economics.* (April): 151–167.

Zimmer, I. 1986. Accounting for interest by real estate developers. *Journal of Accounting & Economics.* (March): 37–51.

Zimmerman, J. L. 1979. The costs and benefits of cost allocations. *The Accounting Review.* (July): 504–521.

———. 1983. Taxes and firm size. *Journal of Accounting & Economics.* (August): 119–149.

Zmijewski, M., and R. Hagerman. 1981. An income strategy approach to the positive theory of accounting standard setting/choice. *Journal of Accounting & Economics.* (August): 129–149.

AGGREGATION OF TEST STATISTICS
An Evaluation of the Evidence on Contracting and Size Hypotheses

Andrew A. CHRISTIE*

University of Rochester, Rochester, NY 14627, USA

Received January 1986, final version received January 1989

More powerful tests of a theory of choice of accounting methods and the effect of changes in these choices on equity values are provided. The power increase comes from efficiently aggregating results across studies. One conclusion is that at least six variables common to more than one study have explanatory power. These variables are managerial compensation, leverage, size, risk, and constraints on interest coverage and dividends. Another conclusion is that the posterior probability that the theory taken as a whole has explanatory power is close to one. This conclusion includes the effect of variables that only appear in one study.

1. Introduction

Holthausen and Leftwich (1983) and Watts and Zimmerman (1986) conduct recent evaluations of the aggregate knowledge gained from empirical studies of the so-called positive (or economic consequences) theories of accounting.[1] Both reviews conclude there are empirical regularities consistent with the theory. In particular, they conclude financial leverage (a contracting variable) and size (often hypothesized to be a proxy for political exposure) have explanatory power. This paper extends the review process by providing formal tests of the hypothesis that the theory can explain choice of accounting procedures and/or valuation effects of changes in accounting procedures.[2]

*I am indebted to Ray Ball, Bill Beaver, Steve Brown, Delores Conway, Steve Crow, Eric Noreen, Adrian Pagan, Bill Schwert (referee), Bert Steece, Greg Waymire, Ross Watts (the editor), Mark Weinstein, Arnold Zellner, Jerry Zimmerman, and especially Jay Shanken (referee) for their comments and suggestions.

[1] While the theory is 'positive' and has economic consequences, these are not its salient features. The distinguishing feature of the theory is that it relies on use of accounting numbers in contracts and in the political arena. Although size has been used as a proxy for political exposure, a size variable can arise for reasons other than political costs. Therefore, the terms contracting and size are used to describe the theory in this paper.

[2] In the process of discussing the reported effects of a given variable across studies, both reviews provide extensive methodological analyses. Methodological evaluations of this literature are also conducted by Ball and Foster (1982) and Christie (1987). The purpose of the Ball and Foster (1982) study is to review methodology rather than content, and hence they do not purport to judge the aggregate knowledge obtained from these studies.

This paper shows that six variables have explanatory power across studies, a much stronger conclusion than that of Holthausen and Leftwich and Watts and Zimmerman. Further, the evidence supporting the contracting and size hypotheses is overwhelming when the theory is defined more broadly than just variables that are common to two or more studies.

The previous reviews are extended in two ways. First, the paper provides formal tests of the proposition that specific contracting and size variables have an effect on firm value or affect choice of accounting procedure. These tests are more powerful than the tests emanating from any one study and more powerful than the informal approach of prior reviewers. Second, the study examines both the proposition tested in the earlier reviews of whether specific variables have explanatory power, and the broader proposition of whether the contracting and size theory taken as a whole contributes to our understanding of the role of accounting numbers in economics.

The paper provides three different methods of aggregating across studies. These three methods have different statistical properties that, in part, reflect different ways of viewing the evidence from the contracting and size literature. Ensuing sections discuss the connections between the theory and the tests in more detail.

The first of the three tests is an exact chi-square test that assumes independence of the test statistics being aggregated. It is based on aggregation of a transform of significance (probability) levels.

The second procedure is an asymptotic test that aggregates test (say Student t) statistics directly using a central limit theorem. This test has the advantage that, unlike the chi-square test, it readily adapts to situations where the test statistics being aggregated are dependent. For reasons discussed later, the paper uses this extension. Although this is nominally an asymptotic test, in this study it is, for all practical purposes, exact. Also, the null and alternative in the asymptotic test differ from those in the chi-square test.[3]

The third procedure is Bayesian and differs in important ways from the other two, both of which emanate from classical statistics. One difference stems from the different ways in which a classicist and a Bayesian treat the tradeoff between type I and type II errors. A classicist holds the probability of a type I error constant and reduces the probability of a type II error as degrees of freedom increase. In the limit the probability of a type II error goes to zero and the power of the test goes to unity. In contrast, a Bayesian reduces the probability of both type I and type II errors as degrees of freedom increase in a manner consistent with the assessed costs of the two types of error. This difference can lead to the classicist and Bayesian forming different conclusions when faced with the same data and is known as the Jeffreys–Lindley paradox.

---

[3] The form of analysis used in this paper is termed meta analysis in some disciplines. Wolf (1986) provides an extensive discussion of methodological problems inherent in meta analysis and examples of its application in other social sciences.

The second important difference between the Bayesian and classical approaches is that the Bayesian assigns posterior probabilities to the null and alternative. This procedure, which has no analogy in classical statistics, permits an overall evaluation of the theory. That is, the two classical tests ignore information contained in specialized hypotheses that are peculiar to one study, since they focus on variables that are common to two or more studies. Most studies contain such specialized hypotheses and these are encompassed by the Bayesian test.

Sections 2, 3, and 4 discuss the finite-sample, asymptotic, and Bayesian tests, respectively. The fifth section discusses potential selection biases and the effect of commonalities in research design. Discussion of other methodological issues, particularly dependence, is scattered throughout the paper at points where it arises naturally.

The final section contains some concluding comments. The broad conclusions are, first, that six contracting and size variables have explanatory power across studies. Second, the posterior probability in favor of the contracting and size theories is close to one. Evidence is presented that these conclusions are robust to potential violations of independence assumptions and to potential selection biases in published works.

2. Exact test

This section evaluates the explanatory power of contracting and size variables that are common to two or more studies using an exact chi-square test.

The chi-square test stems from the fact that the integral of any continuous density function is uniform on $[0, 1]$ and from the fact that minus twice the natural log of a uniform random variable is distributed as chi-square with two degrees of freedom [Johnson and Kotz (1970, ch. 25)]. The sum of K independent chi-square variables with two degrees of freedom is distributed as chi-square with $2K$ degrees of freedom. Therefore, one can aggregate significance levels across any number of *independent* tests. The required chi-square statistic is minus twice the sum of the natural logarithms of the significance levels.[4]

The above test is originally due, independently, to K. Pearson and R.A. Fisher, and is discussed at length by E.S. Pearson (1938) and Wallis (1942). In particular, Wallis (1942, sects. 1, 2) shows that, in combining independent tests of significance, it is not sufficient to multiply together the probabilities emanating from the individual tests. Since smaller products are more likely than larger ones, the probability for judging significance is not the product of the individual probabilities but a function thereof. This chi-square statistic is

---

[4] It is important to emphasize that these results hold only for *continuous* density functions. The chi-square test must be modified to aggregate statistics that have discrete probability functions; see Wallis (1942).

the requisite function. The probability associated with the above chi-square statistic is the probability of observing a product of probabilities as small as the product of the individual probabilities (significance levels) to be aggregated.[5]

Since probabilities are being aggregated, and each probability depends on the underlying hypothesis, the null hypothesis is that each of the probabilities is drawn from a uniform distribution. One can also think of the null as being the joint hypothesis that the t-statistic on a given variable in each study is less than or equal to zero. Rejection of the null implies that at least one of the t-statistics is strictly greater than zero. In other words, rejection of the null implies that the theory works in at least one situation.

Economic aspects of the null and alternative are also important. A review of any literature that purports to test a theory requires that the theory be the same across studies, independent of the statistical methods used in the review. This paper, in common with prior reviews, therefore treats the contracting and size model as a unified theory. The terms of contracts can change through time and differ across industries, and different accounting changes can affect contracts in different ways. However, the underlying notion that contracts generate a demand for accounting numbers and that changes in accounting numbers can, through contracts, affect firm value is common to all the studies. The chi-square test is now applied to variables that are common to two or more studies.

Table 1 summarizes significance levels and associated chi-square statistics for six variables taken from studies that investigate contracting and/or size hypotheses.[6] The table includes only studies where, in the judgement of this author, there is a close relation between the theory and the tests. Clearly there is some unavoidable subjectivity involved in this judgement. On the other

---

[5] There are many aggregation methods one can derive. For a given size of rejection region, these tests will have different power. However, under conditions discussed by Pearson (1938), this chi-square procedure is the uniformly most powerful (UMP) test. Loosely, the chi-square is UMP if the null and alternative differ by location but not scale. Shanken (1985) uses an alternative aggregation method. He converts probabilities to unit normal variables using the inverse normal transformation and then sums the normal variables. Gibbons and Shanken (1987) investigate the relative power of the chi-square and inverse normal tests. While they find a slight power advantage for the inverse normal test, their data do not meet the condition necessary for the chi-square test to be UMP. One interpretation of their results is that the power of the chi-square test is robust to departures from the condition required for it to be UMP. Note that, among all possible aggregation methods, only the chi-square test has the interpretation discussed by Wallis (1942). The probability of observing the chi-square statistic is the probability of obtaining, under the null, a product of the individual probabilities as small as that observed.

[6] The significance levels in table 1 are not always those reported in the original studies. First, authors sometimes report significance levels based on two-tailed tests where directional hypotheses are involved, for which one-tailed tests are appropriate. Second, authors often report significance levels as 'at least 0.01' rather than the actual level of say 0.0014. Such a policy may reflect either convention or an author's lack of faith in the specification of a test. All such cases are, within the limits of numerical accuracy and existing tabulations, restated to the actual levels.

Table 1

Exact test of explanatory power of contracting and size variables across studies: Aggregation of independent probability levels. [a]

Study	Accounting topic	Significance levels for variables common to two or more studies						Source
		Managerial compensation	Interest coverage	Leverage	Size	Dividend constraint	Risk	
Watts & Zimmerman (1978)	Price levels	0.20	—	—	0.015	—	—	Table 4, Model 1
Zmijewski & Hagerman (1981)	Depn, Inventory, ITC, Pensions	0.02	—	0.023	0.003	—	0.30	Table 2, 7 Strategy
Bowen, Noreen & Lacey (1981)	Interest capitalization	0.89	0.09	0.09	0.94	0.02	—	Table 6, Model 1
Holthausen (1981)	Depreciation	0.66	—	0.80	0.29	0.29	—	Table 4, Model 1 (& footnotes)
Leftwich (1981)	Purchase/Pooling	—	—	0.00001	0.00001[b]	—	—	Table 5, Average regression
Dhaliwal, Salamon & Smith (1982)	Depreciation	—	—	0.002	0.15	—	—	Table 5
Lilien & Pastena (1982)	Oil & Gas	—	—	0.04	0.02	—	0.02	Table 6
Daley & Vigeland (1983)	R&D	—	0.33	0.02	0.015	0.034	—	Table 4
Healy (1983)	Accruals	0.00001	—	0.98	0.000001	—	—	Table 6.5, (1956—1980)
Hughes & Ricks (1984)	Installment sales	—	—	0.43	—	—	0.15	Table 5, Model 4
		—	—	0.33	—	—	0.09	Event 6
		—	—	0.002	—	—	0.87	Event 7
		—	—	0.006	—	—	0.001	Event 8
Lys (1984)	Oil & Gas	—	—	—	—	0.27	—	Table 5, Model 1
Ayres (1986)	Foreign currency translation	—	0.052	—	0.0007	0.0054	—	Table 5
El-Gazaar, Lilien & Pastena (1986)	Leasing	0.00013	—	0.000012	—	—	—	Table 5, Model 3
Zimmer (1986)	Interest capitalization	—	—	0.174	0.007	—	—	Table 5
Francis & Reiter (1987)	Pension funding	—	—	0.031	0.255	—	—	Table 5, Panel A 1980
		—	—	0.92	0.132	—	—	1981
Whittred (1987)	Consolidations	—	—	0.091	—	—	—	Table 11, OLS
Wong (1988)	Export tax credits	—	0.204	—	0.004	—	—	Table 5, Model 1
Chi-square[c]		53.03	16.13	131.80	135.57	30.12	32.94	
Degrees of freedom		12	8	34	28	10	12	
Probability		<0.00001	0.04	<0.00001	<0.00001	0.0008	<0.001	

[a] The probabilities in the main body of the table are the significance levels associated with the t-statistics reported in each study. Probability levels are not necessarily those reported by the authors, as some authors report two-tailed significance levels when one-tailed tests are appropriate. This is of particular importance when coefficients have the 'wrong' sign as in Holthausen (1981). The probability associated with the chi-square statistic is the probability of observing a probability at least as small as the product of the probabilities in each column.

[b] Two-tailed test; all other tests are one-tailed.

[c] The chi-square statistic is minus twice the sum of the logs of the probabilities in each column. The probability of observing the chi-square is the probability of obtaining, under the null, a product of the probabilities in each column as small as that observed.

hand, since a unified theory is being tested, one does not want to include results that are not tests of the theory being examined. Similar statements apply to selection of a regression from each study to include in table 1.

In cases such as the 'oil and gas accounting' studies, where several papers use an essentially common set of data, table 1 includes only the most recent study to be published in a major journal. This policy is partly motivated by the need to avoid dependence among the studies included in the review. Another motivation is the premise that, for a study on the same subject as previous papers to be published in a major journal, it must be an improvement in some dimension. Therefore, table 1 includes Lys (1984) and excludes the earlier oil and gas studies by Collins and Dent (1979), Dyckman and Smith (1979), and Collins, Rozeff, and Dhaliwal (1981).

Only those variables common to two or more studies are included in table 1. Variables are treated generically, since specific definitions of variables like 'leverage', 'size', and 'risk' vary across papers. Variation in definitions of dependent or independent variables across studies means that the interpretation of coefficients differs across studies. However, such variation does not present any problems for this review, since all variables are standardized (converted to t-statistics) prior to aggregation. Standardized variables are scale-free and summing them does not create an 'apples and oranges' problem.

Assume that the twenty sets of results included in table 1 are mutually independent and that each set is well specified. Well specified implies absence of measurement error, correlated omitted variables, random coefficients, and simultaneous equation relations. Jointly, the independence and specification assumptions imply that reported test statistics can be taken literally.

Five of the variables included in table 1 – managerial compensation, leverage, size, dividend constraint, and risk – are significant at least at the 0.001 level. The probability of observing the chi-square statistic on the remaining variable, interest coverage constraint, is 0.04.

Observe that the chi-square test implicitly weights each study differently, since the test's inputs are probability levels that depend on degrees of freedom. The larger the degrees of freedom in a given study, the greater the weight ascribed to that study. This partly makes operative the Holthausen and Leftwich (1983) statement that more powerful studies should be given greater weight.

There are two basic difficulties with this analysis. The first is specification error in the studies and the second is dependence among some or all of the studies.

Ball and Foster (1982), Holthausen and Leftwich (1983), Watts and Zimmerman (1986), Bernard (1987), and Christie (1987) discuss specification in the contracting and size studies at length. Noreen (1988) shows that tests of individual coefficients using both probit and ordinary least squares are well specified under the null in a contracting setting. Collectively, there is no evidence in these papers that the studies in table 1 are seriously misspecified. In any case, a reviewer is forced to accept the procedures adopted by individual authors and hence can do nothing about potential specification error.

Theil (1971, ch. 7) demonstrates that, in a system of regression equations, independence of residuals across equations is a sufficient condition for independence of coefficient estimators and t-statistics across equations. This result does not depend on the properties of the data matrix. In this context, 'across equations' means across studies, so independence of residuals across studies is a sufficient condition for independence of coefficient estimators and t-statistics across studies.[7]

The methods of selecting studies in table 1 discussed earlier in this section eliminate (or at least substantially mitigate) dependence from this analysis. Three of the seventeen studies – Zmijewski and Hagerman (1981), Holthausen (1981), and Dhaliwal, Salamon, and Smith (1982) – examine choice of depreciation method. However, dependence among these three studies is more ostensible than real. Zmijewski and Hagerman examine choice of accounting method for a random sample of 300 listed firms in 1975. Their dependent variable reflects the joint effect of choice of accounting methods for pensions, the investment tax credit, inventories, and depreciation. Dhaliwal, Salamon, and Smith use 1962 data for a random sample of 83 firms that were listed on the NYSE in 1954. Their dependent variable reflects choice of depreciation method for reporting purposes, given that accelerated depreciation is used for tax purposes. Not only is the probability of substantial overlap between the Zmijewski and Hagerman sample and the Dhaliwal, Salamon, and Smith sample small, but the difference in construction of the dependent variable also reduces the likelihood of residual dependence between the two studies. Holthausen examines the effect on equity values of changes in depreciation method that occur between 1962 and 1978. Out of 125 data points, Holthausen's sample only includes one observation from 1962 and one from the 1975 through 1978 period.

Twelve of the other fourteen studies examine diverse topics in diverse time periods and countries: interest capitalization, research and development, installment sales, inflation accounting, purchase/pooling, leasing, foreign currency translation, pension funding, export tax credits (New Zealand), elections to consolidate (Australia), and total accruals. The remaining two studies are of oil and gas accounting. The Lys (1984, table 5, model 1) analysis is of the stock price reactions of oil and gas firms to the exposure draft of Financial Accounting Statement 19 on 7/19/77. Lilien and Pastena (1982) examine

---

[7]Although independence of residuals across equations is a sufficient condition for independence of the coefficients across equations, it is not a necessary condition. Even with cross-equation residual dependence, the coefficients and t-statistics can be independent if the data matrix has the 'right' properties. Christie (1982) provides an example of this phenomena.

choice of accounting method in the oil and gas industry in 1978 pursuant to Accounting Series Releases 253 and 258.

Even if these latter two studies suffer from residual dependence, excluding one or the other of them is not of great consequence. For example, excluding the Lilien and Pastena study from the analysis, the risk variable is significant at the 0.005 level rather than 0.001. Excluding the Lys study drops the risk variable from 0.001 to about the 0.03 level and slightly increases the significance of the dividend constraint variable. Whichever of the two studies one excludes, the leverage and size variables are still significant at least at the 0.00001 level. Thus, dependence does not materially affect an inference that at least the managerial compensation, leverage, size, dividend constraint, and risk variables have some explanatory power.[8] Alternative ways of handling dependence are possible and are discussed in section 3.

It is important to note the partial nature of the theory. The debt contracting and size theory is a theory of extremes (e.g., 'closeness' to covenants), which therefore cannot explain the choices of the mass of firms not near the extremes. Further, many other contracts of the firm are not included in the empirical studies because their terms are not observable. Therefore, not only is there reason to expect low R-squares, but the theory predicts only that certain variables matter. Low R-square does not, per se, negate the explanatory power of the theory. It simply reflects the tautology that the theory is incomplete. In other words, statistical significance of a variable or variables is the relevant consideration in evaluating the explanatory power of the theory, not R-square.

3. Asymptotic tests

The chi-square test in the previous section that each probability comes from a uniform distribution cannot be extended to aggregation of dependent tests. Another way to examine the explanatory power of the contracting and size hypotheses is to base the aggregation directly on the test statistics rather than on probability levels. Sums of independent test statistics with finite variances converge to normality under standard limiting arguments. For example, with appropriate adjustments for degrees of freedom, $N^{1/2}$ times the sample mean t-statistic can be compared with the unit normal distribution. Patell (1976) and Christie (1982) use variations of this approach.

Such asymptotic tests have the advantage that they extend readily to situations where the statistics to be aggregated are dependent. White (1984) provides an extensive discussion of central limit theorems with dependent and/or nonidentically distributed variables.

---

[8] Riffe (1988) conducts a more extensive sensitivity analysis of the results of table 1, to the extent of including different results from the individual papers. In all cases, the chi-square tests are trivially different from those reported here.

Another difference between the chi-square and asymptotic tests stems from the nature of the null and alternative in the two tests. In the chi-square test the null is that the test statistic from *each* study is less than or equal to zero. In the asymptotic test the null is that the *mean* value of the test (t) statistics from the individual studies is less than or equal to zero. The alternative is that the mean value of the t-statistics is strictly positive. This null and alternative are consistent with the view expressed in section 2 that the theory is the same across studies. Under the null, each t-statistic (appropriately adjusted for degrees of freedom) is a drawing from a population with a zero mean and unit variance. These drawings need not be independently distributed and they need not be identically distributed under the alternative. The chi-square and asymptotic tests therefore differ in two respects: the nature of the null and alternative and their ability to cope with dependence among observations.

Central limit theorems for dependent random variables are valid with the kinds of correlation one typically finds in economic data.[9] Consider aggregation of dependent test statistics where each statistic is drawn from Student's t distribution with v_i degrees of freedom. Then, asymptotically,

$$Z_D = Z\{1 + (N-1)\bar{p}\}^{-1/2} \tag{3.1}$$

is distributed $N(0, 1)$, where

$$Z = \bar{t} N^{1/2}, \tag{3.2}$$

$$\bar{t} = \sum t_i w_i / N \tag{3.3}$$

is the mean t-statistic adjusted for degrees of freedom,

$$w_i = \{(v_i - 2)/v_i\}^{1/2} \tag{3.4}$$

is the inverse of the standard deviation of t_i, and

$$\bar{p} = \sum_{i \neq j}\sum p_{ij}/\{N(N-1)\} \tag{3.5}$$

---

[9]Loosely, limit theorems for dependent random variables require correlation that does not 'persist' indefinitely. In a time-series context, first-order autocorrelation satisfies this condition. In a cross-section, a block-diagonal correlation matrix, say where each block constitutes an industry, will support the limiting arguments. White (1984) provides an extensive discussion of limit theorems for dependent and nonidentically distributed random variables.

is the grand mean of the off diagonal elements of the correlation matrix among the t-statistics.[10]

Using (3.1) there are three approaches one can take. The first is to assume independence and use (3.2) rather than (3.1). The second is to find some way of estimating the p_{ij}. The third is to ask the question: given Z, how large would $\bar{p}$ have to be for Z_D to be insignificant? One can impute the required number, p^*, from eq. (3.1).[11] However, the small number of time-series observations typical in this literature precludes use of the second approach, since it requires there be more time-series observations than cross-sections. Further, the second approach is not feasible in a review, since, even with enough time-series observations, one would need all the original data to estimate the necessary correlations. In a review, therefore, only the first and third approaches are feasible.

Table 2 reports the asymptotic parallel to table 1 under the assumption of independence.[12] From table 2 the significance levels associated with the compensation, leverage, size, risk, and dividend constraint variables range from < 0.000001 to 0.002. The probability level associated with the interest coverage variable is 0.0174. Given independence, it is concluded that the mean values of the test statistics associated with these six variables are significantly different from zero.

Now consider the third of the three possible approaches to coping with potential dependence. One asks how large $\bar{p}$ would have to be for the statistics that appear significant under independence to be insignificant at conventional levels. For this purpose, an insignificant Z-statistic is deemed to be one that is no greater than 1.5. Table 2 also includes the mean correlations (p^*) necessary to lower the Z's from their reported levels to 1.5. The p^*'s needed to make the Z's insignificant are greater than 1.0 for four of the six variables. For the remaining variables, the p^* associated with the interest coverage is equal to 0.33, while that associated with the risk variable is 0.56. That is, in four of the six cases, even perfectly positively correlated t-statistics across studies would not invalidate the conclusion that these variables have explanatory power. All of the p^*'s seem to be much greater than the degree of correlation one would expect to find in these data. Therefore, potential violation of the independence

---

[10] Note that $\bar{p}$ is a sufficient statistic for the full correlation matrix in this test. Observe that these limiting results do not require that the t-statistics have a common mean under the alternative, but assuming they do simplifies interpretation.

[11] Christie (1982) uses all three of these approaches and uses a seemingly unrelated regression on two random subsets of his data to estimate the mean correlation among his test statistics.

[12] Different studies do not always hypothesize the same sign on a given variable, yet aggregation of test statistics across studies requires that hypothesized signs be the same across studies. Therefore, the signs of all estimators and test statistics are transformed so that they are positive if in agreement with the directional hypothesis and negative if there is disagreement. Then, when say Student t-statistics are aggregated, 'correct' signs are rewarded and 'incorrect' signs are penalized.

Table 2

Asymptotic tests of explanatory power of contracting and size variables across studies: Aggregation of t-statistics.[a]

Variables common to two or more studies	Z under independence	Prob(Z)	Number of studies	Number of studies with insignificant results needed to make Z insignificant[b]	Mean correlation among t-statistics needed to to make Z insignificant[c]
Managerial compensation	4.41	0.000005	6	46	1.53
Interest coverage	2.11	0.0174	4	4	0.33
Leverage ratio	6.69	< 0.000001	17	321	1.18
Size	10.01	< 0.000001	14	609	3.35
Dividend constraint	3.65	0.0001	5	25	1.23
Risk	2.93	0.002	6	17	0.56

[a] This table is an alternative test of the explanatory power of the contracting/size theory to that of table 1, and uses the same data. The null hypothesis is that the mean t-statistic is less than or equal to zero, while the alternative is that the mean t-statistic is greater than zero. This hypothesis is tested by comparing the reported Z-statistic with a unit normal distribution, where $Z = \bar{t}N^{1/2}$, $\bar{t} = \sum_i t_i w_i / N$ is the mean t-statistic adjusted for degrees of freedom and $w_i = \{(v_i - 2)/v_i\}^{1/2}$ is the inverse of the standard deviation of t_i. $\bar{p}$ is the average (off-diagonal) element of the correlation matrix among the t-statistics. The mean correlation ($\bar{p}$) that would be necessary to reduce each Z to 1.5, that is to insignificance by usual standards, is inferred from $Z_D = Z\{1 + (N - 1)\bar{p}\}^{-1/2}$. Z_D is the statistic that arises when the t-statistics to be aggregated are dependent.

[b] This column reports the number of independent studies having a mean t-statistic of zero that would be needed to reduce the Z-statistic to 1.5.

[c] Note that a mean correlation greater than unity implies that even perfect positive correlation does not invalidate the conclusions, that is does not make Z insignificant.

assumptions underlying the chi-square and asymptotic tests is unlikely to affect the inferences in this review.[13]

Given the results so far, it is useful to compare the procedures used here with those of Holthausen and Leftwich (1983) and Watts and Zimmerman (1986). Neither study discusses what null or alternative is being tested when it compares results across studies. Holthausen and Leftwich (1983, sect. 4) are somewhat more specific when they talk about the 'consistency' of results across studies. They also consider weighting studies and seem to have some notion of 'counting' the number of 'significant' and 'insignificant' coefficient

[13] The tests used in sections 2 and 3 can also be used within a study to aggregate test results from independent time periods or independent firms. These tests have the advantage that they do not constrain coefficients to be equal across time or firms as 'pooled' or 'average' tests often do. If the coefficients are not equal across tests, then the chi-square and asymptotic tests will be more efficient than a corresponding pooled or average regression. Loosely, the average test is akin to using ordinary least squares (OLS), whereas the aggregated test amounts to weighted least squares (WLS). Often, such intra-study tests permit evaluation of a finer set of hypotheses than inter-study tests. Earlier versions of this paper applied both tests to the nine cross-sectional regressions in Leftwich (1981). The results are available from the author.

estimates. Such an approach could be formalized by doing some variant of a sign test on the coefficient estimates (or t-statistics) of a given explanatory variable, say leverage. However, the null and alternative in a sign test are the same as those in the above asymptotic test. Therefore, the sign test is just an inefficient version of the asymptotic test [see Hollander and Wolfe (1973, ch. 3)]. Intuitively, the inefficiency arises because the sign test ignores information about magnitudes of effects contained in individual estimators. The sign test also fails to adjust for differing degrees of freedom (and hence power) across studies. Another way to view the efficiency issue is that an efficient aggregate test will use all the information available. Available information includes the power of the individual tests to be aggregated and the magnitude of the coefficients and/or t-statistics.[14]

As discussed earlier, Holthausen and Leftwich (1983) also advocate giving more weight to more powerful tests. The chi-square and asymptotic tests both have this property, since both tests adjust for differing degrees of freedom across studies. Of course, within the context of classical statistics, there is no mechanism to weight studies to reflect power differences that stem from differences in research design rather than degrees of freedom. Both forms of weighting are implicit in Bayesian analysis, which is discussed in the next section.

4. Bayesian tests of overall explanatory power

The tests of the previous two sections provide important insights into explanatory power of the contracting and size hypotheses as reflected in estimated t-statistics on specific variables. However, these tests fail to address two potentially important issues.

First, the preceding tests do not address the tradeoff between type I and type II errors in a systematic manner. Second, they ignore information in coefficient estimates of variables that are peculiar to only one study and consequently do not provide an overall assessment of the contracting and size model. Even if a few variables have explanatory power, systematic failure of study specific subsidiary hypotheses leads to reservations about the overall usefulness of the theory. One might conclude that the significant coefficients are attributable to misspecification or chance. On the other hand, systematic support for the subsidiary hypotheses reinforces the conclusions from the preceeding tests. Bayesian tests provide an opportunity to address the tradeoff between type I and type II errors and to provide an overall assessment of the contracting and size model.

---

[14]Holthausen and Leftwich and Watts and Zimmerman discuss why some of the tests on compensation variables are of low power. Healy's (1983) tests were explicitly designed to increase power with respect to the compensation variable.

The use of Bayesian tests raises questions about how one should go about specifying priors on the models and on the distributions of the parameters of the models. The view that priors are subjective and hence the conclusions are subjective is often expressed. This may seem to be of particular concern in a review.

Fortunately, reservations about subjectivity of priors are more apparent than real, since one can always incorporate diffuse priors on both the models and the parameter distributions. Loosely, diffuse priors allow the data to dominate the priors.

Two recent papers, Klein and Brown (1984) and Brown and Klein (1985), enhance incorporation of diffuse priors. These two papers consider the form of the posterior odds ratios of models when measures of prior information are minimized. They obtain an expression for the posterior odds ratio that is invariant to the parameterization of the models. This expression is valid for comparison of nested and nonnested models and can account for directional hypotheses on coefficients. That is, it rewards consistency of the sign of coefficient estimates with the alternative hypothesis and penalizes inconsistency with the alternative. The Klein and Brown expression also reflects a tradeoff between parsimony and data fit. Further, under conditions met by some of the studies in this review, the criterion can be interpreted as a likelihood ratio test in which the size of the test is a declining function of sample size. The criterion reduces both type I and type II errors as sample size increases. The classical tests of the earlier sections hold the size of the test constant as degrees of freedom change.

Klein and Brown (1984, theorems 1, 2) show that when one minimizes a measure of prior information on the models and parameters, the posterior odds ratio in favor of model 1 (the null hypothesis, H1) with respect to the alternative model (H2) is

$$O_{12} = T^{d/2} \cdot L_1^* / L_2^*, \tag{4.1}$$

where T is the sample size, $d = (K_2 - K_1)$ is the difference between the number of parameters in models 1 and 2, and L_1^*/L_2^* is the ratio of maximized likelihoods. The term $T^{d/2}$ reflects a tradeoff between parsimony and data fit.[15]

---

[15]The information measure minimized by Klein and Brown is not derived from axioms of individual behavior in the same way that, for example, utility theory is. Hence, it may be better to view eq. (4.1) as a useful heuristic. However, by letting the sample size go to infinity, Schwarz (1978) derives the same odds ratio in (4.1) that Klein and Brown obtain by letting the information in the priors become small. This suggests that the criterion (4.1) may be robust to both the priors and to departures from normality. Essentially, Klein and Brown and Schwarz pick different ways of letting the data dominate the priors.

With a symmetric loss function, one would choose model 1, the null in this case, if the posterior odds ratio is greater than 1 and model 2 (the alternate) if the posterior odds ratio is less than 1 [Zellner (1971, s.10.1)].[16] Alternatively, one can restate the odds ratio as a posterior probability of the alternative hypothesis H2. The odds ratio and the associated posterior probabilities on the two models have no analogy in classical hypothesis testing.

Brown and Klein (1985) extend (4.1) to account for the situation where there is a directional hypothesis on one of the parameters. They show that one should divide the odds ratio in (4.1) by $2 \cdot Q(-\hat{t})$, where $Q(\cdot)$ is the distribution function of univariate Student's t and the hypothesized sign on the parameter is negative. This adjustment varies between 0 and 2; it is > 1 when $\hat{t}$ has the right sign and < 1 when $\hat{t}$ has the wrong sign. Therefore the test rewards correct signs and penalizes incorrect signs in evaluating the competing hypotheses.

One can extend these results to the case of interest here where multiple parameters are subject to one tail tests and where hypothesized signs can be positive or negative. Using results in Klein and Brown (1984) about nested hypotheses, the odds ratio becomes

$$O_{12} = T^{d/2} \cdot \left[1 + d \cdot F / (T - K_2)\right]^{-T/2} / \left\{2 \cdot G_H(s_h \cdot \hat{t}_h)\right\}, \qquad (4.2)$$

where s_h is the hypothesized sign on parameter h, H is the number of parameters subject to directional hypotheses, F is the F-statistic on the hypothesis that the H contracting and size variables are zero, and $G_H(\cdot)$ is the joint distribution of the H test statistics subject to directional hypotheses. That is, under the above conditions, the odds ratio with minimal prior information in (4.2) reduces to a transformation of an F test. When the H explanatory variables are independent,

$$G_H(\cdot) = \prod_h Q(s_h \cdot \hat{t}_h). \qquad (4.3)$$

From the discussion in sections 2 and section 3, independence across studies seems to be a reasonable assumption. The tests of the overall theory discussed in this section require consideration of another potential source of dependence, the joint distribution of the t-statistics of the explanatory variables in a given study. The 'one-tail' results in this section assume independence of regressors, since a reviewer can observe only the product of the marginal distributions and not the joint distribution of the explanatory variables within a study. This assumption is reflected in eq. (4.3).

---

[16]A symmetric loss function is one in which the losses associated with type I and type II errors are equal.

Armed with (4.2) and (4.3) one can test whether the contracting and size theory in its entirety has explanatory power. The odds ratio in (4.2) can be cumulated over all the studies available. Provided the studies are independent, the posterior odds ratio for the first study becomes the prior odds ratio for the second study etc. One ends up with a posterior odds ratio over the whole set of studies that translates to a posterior probability on the model of primary interest. This procedure has the advantage that it accounts for variables that appear in only one study. It is a test of the overall explanatory power of the theory rather than a test of whether variables common to more than one study have explanatory power.

Implicit in the cumulation approach above is an assumption that, at each step, prior studies provide no information about distributions on parameters. That is, each step assumes that diffuse priors on the parameters are appropriate. Given the substantial variations in research design and variable definitions that exist across studies this seems a reasonable way to proceed.[17]

Not all the studies evaluated in the earlier parts of the paper satisfy the conditions necessary for the application of (4.2), which is an extension of Klein and Brown's theorem 2. Theorem 2 assumes application of least squares so it cannot be applied to studies that use logit, probit, or jackknife methods.[18] Also, one must exclude studies, such as Holthausen (1981), that report an *F*-statistic that includes noncontracting and size variables such as unexpected earnings. The Bayesian results for the studies that use least squares and that report the requisite *F*-statistics are in table 3.

The first thing to observe from table 3 is that the cumulative posterior probability that the contracting and size model has explanatory power, calculated over the fifteen regressions in the table, is 0.99 for both the one- and two-tail versions of the test. Overall the data strongly support the contracting and size model. Note that these (very strong) results exclude most of the 'choice' studies, since these studies do not use least squares. Choice studies are, on a study-by-study basis, generally viewed as providing stronger support for the theory than 'returns' studies.

The one-tail test is not a test of the incremental explanatory power of the study-specific variables. However, one can obtain some feel for this incremental explanatory power by comparing the one- and two-tail results. Recall the one-tail results reflect consistency of actual with predicted signs of coefficient

---

[17]This cumulation, which lets there be nondiffuse priors on the theory and diffuse priors on the parameters, does not meet the letter of the Klein and Brown procedure. Adapting it in this way is similar in spirit to using a consistent estimator in a finite sample. One case where one might reasonably have nondiffuse priors on the parameters is the oil and gas studies, since there is a sequence of relatively similar research designs.

[18]This constraint can possibly be relaxed by exploiting the fact that the chi-square statistic reported in the logit etc. studies is minus twice the log of the likelihood ratio. Doing this produces results that are not qualitatively different from those reported in the paper.

Table 3

Bayesian tests: Posterior probabilities that the contracting and size theory has explanatory power.[a]

Source	One-tail[b]	Two-tail	Prob(F)	Sample size (T)
Leftwich (1981) – event #1	0.00005	0.00001	0.37	338
Leftwich (1981) – event #4	0.26	0.17	0.001	338
Leftwich (1981) – event #9	0.00001	0.00003	0.15	338
Leftwich (1981) – event #13	0.99	0.93	0.0001	338
Leftwich (1981) – event #15	0.005	0.004	0.002	338
Leftwich (1981) – event #16	0.0	0.0	0.55	338
Leftwich (1981) – event #18	0.15	0.03	0.001	338
Leftwich (1981) – event #19	0.0004	0.0002	0.03	338
Leftwich (1981) – event #21	0.04	0.14	0.001	338
Healy (1983)	0.99	0.99	0.00001	1725
Hughes and Ricks (1984) – event #6	0.99	0.91	0.004	30
Hughes and Ricks (1984) – event #7	0.99	0.99	0.001	30
Hughes and Ricks (1984) – event #8	0.99	0.99	0.0005	30
Lys (1984)	0.56	0.17	0.009	34
Whittred (1987)	0.99	0.99	0.00001	70
Cumulative posterior probability	0.99	0.99		

[a] This table differs from the previous two in that it tests the overall explanatory power of the theory rather than the explanatory power of specific variables.

[b] The one-tail posterior probabilities account for consistency (or lack thereof) of actual with predicted signs of coefficients. The posterior probability in favor of the alternative hypothesis is $1/(1 + O_{12})$ where O_{12}, the odds ratio in favor of the null, is $O_{12} = T^{d/2}[1 + dF/(T - K_2)]^{-T/2}/\{2G_{II}(s_h \hat{t}_h)\}$, where F is the F-statistic on the hypothesis that the H contracting and size variables are zero, T is the sample size, $d = (K_2 - K_1)$ is the difference between the number of parameters under the alternative and null, s_h is the predicted sign of a given coefficient, and $G_{II}(\cdot)$ is the product of H univariate Student t-distribution functions on those coefficients subject to one-tail tests.

estimators under an assumption that regressors are independent. Observe the posterior probabilities that the alternative hypothesis is true are greater for the one-tail test in thirteen of the fifteen cases. Therefore, in all except two cases, accounting for study-specific hypotheses leads a Bayesian to revise his posterior probability in the direction of the contracting and size theory.

For seven of the fifteen regressions the one-tail posterior probability on the contracting and size model is > 0.5. It is interesting to compare these results with the number of observations and probabilities of the F-statistics, which are also in table 3. Twelve of the fifteen F-statistics are significant at the 5% level and eleven are significant at better than the 1% level. Casual scanning of table 3 then reveals that the regressions that have highly significant F-statistics and posterior probabilities on the model of less than 0.5 tend to be those where the number of observations is large. Leftwich's events 4, 15, 18, 19, and 21 are examples. This difference between the Bayesian and classical results is just the Jeffreys–Lindley paradox at work. The Bayesian and classicist make different tradeoffs between type I and type II errors as sample size increases. In sum, however, the two approaches basically convey the same message; overall the data are consistent with the contracting and size theory.

5. Methodological issues

This section discusses methodological issues other than independence of data sets that are germane to the issues at hand.

5.1. Selection bias

A general difficulty with aggregation across studies is that it can be subject to a form of selection bias. It is often claimed that editors tend to publish, and authors tend to submit, papers with 'positive' findings [see Wolf (1986)].

Part of the concern is that authors keep varying data selection, research design, and variable definitions until they 'find' something. One's perception of the seriousness of this problem depends on one's view of the competence of specific editorial boards, but other factors are relevant as well. Claims of selection bias should be evaluated within the context of (i) the natural progression of the scientific process and (ii) the nature of the theory.

5.1.1. The scientific process

A literature's life cycle affects selection biases. When a theory is in the early stages of its development, marginally significant or difficult to interpret results are not surprising. As the theory and methodological tools develop, significance levels initially increase. However, as finer (more detailed) implications are tested, often on smaller and smaller data sets, significance levels tend to decline.

In the early stages of a literature, one is typically more interested in regularities than anomalies. Eventually, however, this interest reverses. Once researchers accept the central core of a theory, development can only proceed by exploring the anomalies. Studying anomalies leads to enhancement of the theory and/or the empirical methods. A useful example is provided by the asset pricing/market efficiency literature, which is well into its anomalies stage. At one point, it was 'fashionable' to publish evidence in support of the efficient markets hypothesis. Now the situation is reversed and there are numerous published studies of asset pricing/market efficiency anomalies.

Given the reviews and methodological analyses by Ball and Foster (1982), Holthausen and Leftwich (1983), Watts and Zimmerman (1986), and Christie (1987) and the results in this paper, it seems reasonable to characterize the contracting and size literature as being in the 'finding regularities' phase.

Regularities are currently more valuable than anomalies, but this does not, per se, imply a selection bias exists. In fact, the oral tradition surrounding this literature is that the results in many of the published studies are *not* statistically significant. The consensus seems to be that editors are not reluctant to publish insignificant results.

To put any potential selection bias in perspective, one can use the data in table 2 to determine whether unpublished studies with insignificant results could affect the conclusions in this study. For each of the six variables common to two or more studies, table 2 reports the number of additional studies with a mean t-statistic of zero that would be needed to reduce each Z-statistic to 1.5. The number of insignificant studies needed ranges from 4 for the interest coverage variable to 609 for the size variable. Another way to view this is to calculate the ratio of the number of unpublished insignificant studies needed to reduce Z to insignificance by conventional standards to the sample size of published studies. These ratios range from $1:1$ to $44:1$ across the six variables. The number of active researchers in this area and the number of potential data sets is relatively small. Even if one were to believe that all potential unsubmitted studies were powerful and well specified, it seems inconceivable that there are enough unsubmitted insignificant studies to affect the conclusions.

5.1.2. The nature of the theory

Selection biases are more prone to exist where there is either no theory, or where the theory does not predict signs of coefficient estimators. Selection bias is harder for editors to control when hypotheses require two-tail tests. Two-tail tests make it harder to detect 'data mining'. The tests aggregated here are buttressed by a theory that is essentially the same in all studies, and almost exclusively makes directional predictions. Further, a wide variety of data sets have been used to test the theory.

Given the results of this paper, at the very least there is an interesting set of empirical regularities to explain. Further, only a theory with greater explanatory power can displace the current theory. In light of these characteristics and the results of this study, it is incumbent on any advocate of the selection bias hypothesis to provide a dominant competing theory and to explain how so many directional hypotheses could be satisfied by chance.

5.2. Commonalities in research design

Commonalities in research design across studies are closely related to the above discussion of potential selection biases. The topic that any researcher chooses to investigate, his/her research design, and sample selection procedures are influenced by the designs and outcomes of prior studies and by the comments of authors of related studies. Such commonality is not an accident, but rather is a consequence of research studies not being costless to conduct. In the face of such costs, random sampling from the population of possible studies is unlikely to be optimal. One chooses the research design and data set that will ex ante maximize the power of the tests, given what has been learned from previous studies.

Such research design choices do not, per se, generate either dependencies across studies or selection biases. The only relevant source of dependence across studies is dependence among the residuals of different studies. In other words, it is properties of the data that are crucial, not properties of research designs.

Many sciences, such as physics, astrophysics, and chemistry conduct replications on different data sets using identical research designs, and some statisticians advocate similar replications for the social sciences. The fact that replications are not conducted as a matter of course in the social sciences is probably an implicit statement about the net benefit of the replications. See Freedman (1979), Leamer (1983), and Burgstahler (1987) for related discussions.

6. Concluding remarks

This paper uses an exact chi-square test, an asymptotic normal test, and a Bayesian procedure to evaluate the ability of contracting and size theories to explain the data. One conclusion is that six variables, managerial compensation, leverage, size, risk, and interest coverage and dividend constraints have significant explanatory power.[19] While the size variable is often included as a proxy for political exposure, this is not exclusively the case [Holthausen (1981), Leftwich, (1981)], and it may be proxying for other unspecified factors.

The tests used here are more powerful than the tests emanating from any one study, since they aggregate results across studies. This is of particular importance in evaluating the evidence of concern in this review as many of the studies are of low power, mainly because of difficulties specifying and measuring explanatory variables. Since both classical and Bayesian tests require examination of a joint distribution, only studies whose data appear to be independent are included.

A Bayesian evaluation of the contracting and size theory taken as a whole is also conducted. In contrast to the evaluation of the six variables common to two or more studies, this overall evaluation takes account of finer hypotheses

---

[19]One can also conduct Bayesian versions of the tests in section 3 using special cases of (4.1). These tests account for the increase in degrees of freedom as one aggregates across studies in trading off the probabilities of type I and type II errors. The posterior probabilities that the mean *t*-statistics on the six variables in table 2 are strictly positive range from 0.90 to 0.99 and hence support the classical results.

that are peculiar to specific contexts. The posterior probability that the contracting and size theory has explanatory power, calculated over the regressions that satisfy the conditions of the theorem used, is 0.99.

Evidence is presented that the conclusions of this study are robust. It is shown that neither dependence across studies nor selection bias in the types of results authors submit for publication is likely to invalidate the results.

Since the tests used in this study are general, one can also use them to aggregate tests within a study, either across firms or through time. Also, note that the tests are not limited to studies that use regression procedures, they can be applied any time significance levels are obtained.

It is important to note that the difference between the conclusions in this paper and those in earlier reviews stems solely from the use of more powerful tests. The difference does not come from incorporating more (or more recent) studies in the review. The results here are qualitatively unchanged from (though somewhat stronger than) earlier versions of the paper, which incorporated only studies that were in Holthausen and Leftwich (1983) and Watts and Zimmerman (1986).

The conclusions of this review that the contracting and size theory provides a partial explanation of the demand/supply/use of accounting numbers have implications for the directions of future work in this area. There is little to be gained by merely conducting more studies using existing formulations of the theory and existing ways of measuring variables.[20] Instead, effort should be devoted to developing the theory and finding better ways to measure independent variables. For example, the early studies, such as Leftwich (1981) and Holthausen (1981), view the leverage ratio as a proxy for the magnitude of contracting costs, while many consumers of the literature appear to regard leverage as a proxy for 'closeness to covenants'. Determining what leverage is measuring and determining what are appropriate measures of 'closeness to covenants' would be useful steps forward. El-Gazzar, Lilien, and Pastena (1985) is in this vein, as is Whittred (1987).

There are also a number of anomalous results in the literature. One example is the failure of Leftwich's hypothesis that the coefficient on his public debt variable should be larger in absolute value than that on the private debt variable. Exploring this and other anomalies is a useful way to develop the literature.

As with any theory, there are omitted variables with probability one. In particular, it is possible that at least leverage and size are proxying for characteristics of the production/investment opportunity set that influence accounting choices other than through the debt and compensation contracts.

---

[20] This paper is a casual application of the methods of sequential analysis, which, loosely, provides a stopping rule for sampling. That is, when have we sampled enough either to accept or reject the null?

However, as discussed in section 5.1, only an enhanced theory can displace the current theory. Similar statements about profitable directions for future research can be found in Holthausen and Leftwich (1983) and Watts and Zimmerman (1986). The findings of this study reinforce their appeals.

References

Ayres, F.L., 1986, Characteristics of firms electing early adoption of SFAS 52, Journal of Accounting and Economics 8, 143–158.

Ball, R. and G. Foster, 1982, Corporate financial reporting: A methodological review of empirical research, Supplement to Journal of Accounting Research, 161–234.

Bernard, V., 1987, Cross-sectional dependence and biased inference in market based accounting research, Journal of Accounting Research 25, 1–48.

Bowen, R., E. Noreen, and J. Lacey, 1981, Determinants of the corporate decision to capitalize interest, Journal of Accounting and Economics 3, 151–179.

Brown, S.J. and R.W. Klein, 1985, Model selection in the federal courts: An application of the posterior odds ratio criterion, Working paper.

Burgstahler, D., 1987, Inference from empirical research, The Accounting Review 62, 203–214.

Christie, A.A., 1982, The stochastic behavior of common stock variances: Value, leverage and interest rate effects, Journal of Financial Economics 10, 407–432.

Christie, A.A., 1987, On cross-sectional analysis in accounting research, Journal of Accounting and Economics 9, 231–258.

Collins, D.W. and W.T. Dent, 1979, The proposed elimination of full cost accounting in the extractive petroleum industry, Journal of Accounting and Economics 1, 3–44.

Collins, D.W., M.S. Rozeff, and D.S. Dhaliwal, 1981, The economic determinants of the market reaction to proposed mandatory accounting changes in the oil and gas industry: A cross-sectional analysis, Journal of Accounting and Economics 3, 37–71.

Daley, L.A. and R.L. Vigeland, 1983, The effect of debt covenants and political costs on the choice of accounting methods: The case of accounting for R&D costs, Journal of Accounting and Economics 5, 195–211.

Dhaliwal, D., G. Salamon, and E. Smith, 1982, The effect of owner versus management control on the choice of accounting methods, Journal of Accounting and Economics 4, 41–53.

Dyckman, T.R. and A.J. Smith, 1979, Financial accounting and reporting by oil and gas producing companies: A study of information effects, Journal of Accounting and Economics 1, 45–75.

El-Gazzar, S.M., S.B. Lilien, and V.S. Pastena, 1985, The influence of external reporting choices on private debt agreements, Working paper (Baruch College of CUNY, New York, NY).

El-Gazzar, S.M., S.B. Lilien, and V.S. Pastena, 1986, Accounting for leases by leasees, Journal of Accounting and Economics 8, 217–237.

Francis, J.R. and S.A. Reiter, 1987, Determinants of corporate pension funding strategy, Journal of Accounting and Economics 9, 35–59.

Freedman, D., 1979, Statistics and scientific method, Working paper (University of California, Berkeley, CA).

Gibbons, M.R. and J. Shanken, 1987, Subperiod aggregation and the power of multivariate tests of portfolio efficiency, Journal of Financial Economics 19, 389–394.

Healy, P., 1983, The impact of bonus schemes on accounting choices, Unpublished doctoral dissertation (University of Rochester, Rochester, NY).

Hollander, M. and D.A. Wolfe, 1973, Nonparametric statistical methods (Wiley, New York, NY).

Holthausen, R.W., 1981, Evidence on the effect of bond covenants and management compensation contracts on the choice of accounting techniques: The case of the depreciation switch-back, Journal of Accounting and Economics 3, 73–109.

Holthausen, R.W. and R. Leftwich, 1983, The economic consequences of accounting choice: Implications of costly contracting and monitoring, Journal of Accounting and Economics 5, 77–117.

Hughes, J.S. and W.E. Ricks, 1984, Accounting for retail land sales: Analysis of a mandated change, Journal of Accounting and Economics 6, 101–132.

Johnson, N.L. and S. Kotz, 1970, Distributions in statistics: Continuous univariate distributions – 2 (Wiley, New York, NY).

Klein, R.W. and S.J. Brown, 1984, Model selection when there is 'minimal' prior information, Econometrica 52, 1291–1312.

Leamer, E.E., 1983, Let's take the con out of econometrics, American Economic Review 73, 31–43.

Leftwich, R., 1981, Evidence of the impact of mandatory changes in accounting principles on corporate loan agreements, Journal of Accounting and Economics 3, 3–36.

Lilien, S. and V. Pastena, 1982, Determinants of intramethod choice in the oil and gas industry, Journal of Accounting and Economics 4, 145–170.

Lys, T., 1984, Mandated accounting changes and debt covenants: The case of oil and gas accounting, Journal of Accounting and Economics 6, 39–66.

Noreen, E., 1988, An empirical comparison of probit and OLS regression hypothesis tests, Journal of Accounting Research 26, 119–133.

Patell, J.M., 1976, Corporate forecasts of earnings per share and stock price behavior: Empirical tests, Journal of Accounting Research 14, 246–276.

Pearson, E.S., 1938, Tests based on the probability integral transform, Biometrika 30, 134–148.

Plosser, C.I., 1981, Serial correlation corrections and distributed lag models in the presence of measurement error, Working paper no. 7830 (Graduate School of Management, University of Rochester, Rochester, NY).

Riffe, S., 1988, An analysis of: 'Aggregation of test statistics: An evaluation of the evidence on contracting and size hypotheses', Working paper (University of Southern California, Los Angeles, CA).

Schwarz, G., 1978, Estimating the dimension of a model, Annals of Statistics 6, 461–464.

Shanken, J., 1985, Multivariate tests of the zero-beta CAPM, Journal of Financial Economics 14, 327–348.

Theil, H., 1971, Principles of econometrics (Wiley, New York, NY).

Wallis, W.A., 1942, Compounding probabilities from independent significance tests, Econometrica 10, 229–248.

Watts, R. and J. Zimmerman, 1978, Towards a positive theory of the determination of accounting standards, The Accounting Review 53, 112–134.

Watts, R. and J. Zimmerman, 1986, Positive accounting theory (Prentice-Hall, Englewood Cliffs, NJ).

Wetherill, G.B., 1975, Sequential methods in statistics, 2nd ed. (Wiley, New York, NY).

White, H., 1984, Asymptotic theory for econometricians (Academic Press, New York, NY).

Whittred, G., 1987, The derived demand for consolidated financial reporting, Journal of Accounting and Economics 9, 259–285.

Wolf, F.M., 1986, Meta analysis: Quantitative methods for research synthesis (Sage Publications, Beverly Hills, CA).

Wong, J., 1988, Political costs and an intraperiod accounting choice for export tax credits, Journal of Accounting and Economics 10, 37–51.

Zellner, A., 1971, An introduction to Bayesian inference in econometrics (Wiley, New York, NY).

Zimmer, I., 1986, Accounting for interest by real estate developers, Journal of Accounting and Economics 8, 37–51.

Zmijewski, M. and R. Hagerman, 1981, An income strategy approach to the positive theory of accounting standard setting/choice, Journal of Accounting and Economics 3, 129–149.

Organization Theory and Methodology

Michael C. Jensen

ABSTRACT: The foundations are being put in place for a revolution in the science of organizations. Some major analytical building blocks for the development of a theory of organizations are outlined and discussed in this paper. This development of organization theory will be hastened by increased understanding of the importance of the choice of definitions, tautologies, analytical techniques, and types of evidence. The two literatures of agency theory are briefly discussed in light of these issues. Because accounting is an integral part of the structure of every organization, the development of a theory of organizations will be closely associated with the development of a theory of accounting. This theory will explain why organizations take the form they do, why they behave as they do, and why accounting practices take the form they do. Because such positive theories as these are required for purposeful decision making, their development will provide a better scientific basis for the decisions of managers, standard-setting boards, and government regulatory bodies.

I. INTRODUCTION

A major challenge facing social scientists is the development of a body of theory to explain why organizations take the form they do and why they behave as they do. My objective is to outline some aspects of this emerging line of research on organizations and to call attention to a number of related methodological issues that play an important role in this research: the relation between positive and normative theories, the importance to the research effort of the choice of tautologies and definitions, the nature of evidence, and the role of mathematics. I conclude with a brief discussion of the two literatures of agency theory.

I have two basic propositions that directly bear on accounting:

(1) Accounting is an integral part of the structure of every organization, and

(2) a fundamental understanding of why accounting practices evolve as they do and how to improve them requires a deeper understanding about organizations than now exists in the social sciences.

By way of background, I shall digress briefly to discuss the relation between positive and normative research.

II. POSITIVE AND NORMATIVE THEORY AND DECISION MAKING

In the period prior to the mid-1970's accounting theory was predominantly normative. It focused on policy prescrip-

I am indebted to Charles Christenson, Robert Kaplan, and to my colleagues, George Benston, Andrew Christie, Ann Coughlan, Martin Geisel, Clifford Holderness, John Long, William Schwert, Clifford Smith, René Stulz, Jerold Warner, and especially Ross Watts, William Meckling and Jerold Zimmerman for their comments and suggestions.

Michael C. Jensen is Professor and Director, Managerial Economics Research Center, University of Rochester.

tions for management or public policy—questions involving the appropriate treatment of inflation, exchange rates, inventories, leases, and so on. These policy questions are, of course, both interesting and important, and they are best answered with knowledge of a wide range of positive theory—that is, knowledge about how the world behaves. For example, accountants have been justifiably concerned with the effects of General Price Level Adjusted accounting (GPLA) on accounting numbers. But a manager interested in maximizing the value of his firm also must estimate either explicitly or implicitly how such accounting procedures will affect firm value. And how GPLA affects firm value is a purely positive issue in the sense that the term is used in the social sciences.[1] Normative questions take the form: "How should price level changes be reflected in the accounting statements?" Positive questions take the form: "How does GPLA affect the value of the firm?" Answers to normative questions always depend on the choice of the criterion or objective function which is a matter of values. Therefore, normative propositions are never refutable by evidence. Answers to positive questions, on the other hand, involve discovery of some aspect of how the world behaves and are always potentially refutable by contradictory evidence.

Considerable discussion and disagreement have occurred over methodological issues associated with the emerging literature on positive accounting theory, and my purpose here is to try to clarify some of these issues. In the end, of course, we are all interested in normative questions; a desire to understand how to accomplish goals motivates our interest in these methodological topics and in positive theories.

An interesting relationship between normative and positive issues often goes unrecognized. Consider the general structure of a decision problem:

$$\max_{\{X_i\}} V = V(Y_1, Y_2, \ldots, Y_N;\ Z_1, Z_2, \ldots, Z_L)\ \{X_1, X_2, \ldots, X_K\}$$

Subject to the following constraints:

$$\begin{bmatrix} \text{Accounting and other} \\ \text{identities (such as budget} \\ \text{constraints, time constraints, etc.)} \end{bmatrix}$$

Positive theories

$$\begin{bmatrix} Y_1 = f_1(X_1, X_2, \ldots, X_K; \\ \qquad Y_2, Y_3, \ldots, Y_N; \\ \qquad Z_1, Z_2, \ldots, Z_L) \\ Y = f_2(X_1, X_2, \ldots, X_K; \\ \qquad Y_1, Y_3, \ldots, Y_N; \\ \qquad Z_1, Z_2, \ldots, Z_L) \\ \vdots \\ Y_N = f_N(X_1, X_2, \ldots, X_K; \\ \qquad Y_1, Y_2, \ldots, Y_{N-1}; \\ \qquad Z_1, Z_2, \ldots, Z_L) \end{bmatrix}$$

where V is the objective function to be maximized, the X's are the decision variables, the Y's are the arguments of the objective function that are determined within the system (the "endogenous" variables), and the Z's are the variables determined outside the system (the "exogenous" variables).

The constraints of the problem are of great interest here, and we can break them into two general categories. The first category contains all accounting and other identities (such as budget constraints, time constraints [24 hours in a day] and so on). The second category of

[1] The use of the term "positive" in this context has had the unfortunate effect of linking accounting researchers who have been engaged in the effort to develop "positive" theories with "logical positivism," a school of thought in philosophy which has been controversial. The proposal to focus on positive theories of accounting does not commit those who propose it to logical positivism.

constraints given by the functions, f_i, determine how the decision variables, X, and the exogenous variables, Z, affect the values of the endogenous variables, Y, in the objective function.

The second set of constraints is made up of positive theories about the way the world works:[2] for example, how decisions on accounting practices, organizational structure, advertising, pricing, and production policies combine with physical laws affecting production and the exogenous variables such as weather, interest rates, governmental regulatory policies, and human behavior to determine the endogenous variables, Y, that affect the value of the firm. Suppose the value of the firm is a function of expected net cash flows, their riskiness and the interest rate. To choose among alternative accounting policies, a manager desiring to maximize the value of the firm wants to know how those alternative choices affect the expected net cash flows and their riskiness. Answers to such questions require positive theories.

Positive theory enters the decision process in one more way. While the choice of the objective or maximand (firm value in our example) is a value judgment and therefore a normative issue, knowledge of the valuation function itself (that is, the function that relates the value of the maximand to the values of the endogenous and exogenous variables) is a positive issue and requires a theory.

It is obvious from the logical structure of decision making that purposeful decisions cannot be made without the implicit or explicit use of positive theories. You cannot decide what action to take and expect to meet your objective if you have no idea about how alternative actions affect the desired outcome—and that requires positive theory. Furthermore, using incorrect positive theories or ignoring important constraints leads to decisions that have unexpected and undesirable outcomes. This is equally true for the manager, the auditor, the FASB or the governmental regulatory body.

The history of operations research provides an interesting example of the importance of positive theories. I believe a major reason for the early successes of operations research and its later failure to live up to the promise offered by those successes can be traced to the nature of the theories given emphasis in those efforts. The operations research literature seems to evidence careful attention to the constraints that positive physical or engineering theories impose on decision making. When such physical phenomena are the dominant constraining force, ignoring other constraints given by market forces, information costs, and the peculiarities of human behavior can still lead to highly successful results. Witness the successes in using linear programming to help run oil refineries or to solve feed-mixture problems. In these problems prices could reasonably be taken as fixed because of the competitive nature of the markets involved. Furthermore, the fact that human beings do not always do what they are told or even do what they agree to do is less important in a highly mechanized process. In this sense refining and diet problems, where most of the important constraints involve chemical or other physical phenomena, are very special. The application of operations research to marketing and finance and to the management of people has been less successful. The paucity of successful applications in these areas stems not from deficiencies in the techniques or lack of technical expertise, but from the fact that researchers generally

---

[2] And often involve the result of other individuals' maximization process.

ignored the task of developing and incorporating as constraints in their problems robust positive theories of the market, organizational and human behavioral phenomena that were important to the problems.[3] This is also the reason why as scientists we cannot successfully use a straightforward operations research approach to choose accounting procedures or accounting standards; we do not know the necessary positive theories well enough to predict the effects of alternative choices.

All purposeful actions must (at least implicitly) involve positive theory, that is, a presumption that the chosen action will bring about the desired results. However, it is not necessary to presume that these positive theories are explicitly contemplated by the agents we study. In fact, as Alchian [1950] long ago pointed out, we need not even assume that agents are engaged in purposeful activity for our models to work. As an extreme case, suppose agents do not learn from observation and randomly choose strategies and actions. Suppose also that the environment rewards with survival those who happen to select strategies that are closer to optimal and grants extinction to those who are unlucky enough to choose dominated strategies or actions. In such an environment, observed behavior and institutions will tend toward the optimal because those far from it will continually tend towards extinction. In the less extreme and more realistic case where agents learn from empirical observation and engage in purposeful action, we can expect surviving institutions and practices to be an even better source of information to the scientist seeking to discover the relevant positive theories. Finally, science itself can affect the world. As our scientific understanding of the world is improved, our ability to relate actions to

desired outcomes is improved. Pareto [1935, §1785] summarizes the point quite succinctly:

> In the Middle Ages master-masons built marvelous edifices by rules of thumb, by empiricism, without the remotest knowledge of any theory as to the resistance capacities of building materials—merely by trying and trying again, rectifying mistakes as they went along. Now thanks to such theories, modern engineers not only eliminate the losses incident to the old mistakes, but erect buildings that the master-masons and other artisans of past centuries could not possibly have built. Practice had taught physicians certain remedies that were oftentimes better than those recommended by quacks or alchemists. Sometimes again they were altogether worthless. Nowadays chemical theories have eradicated not all, but a very large number, of those mistakes, and biology has made it possible to make better use of many substances that chemistry places at the disposal of medicine. Only a few years back, in making cast iron in a blast-furnace it was wiser to follow the directions of an empiricist than the prescriptions of theory. Today the iron industry is no longer carried on without consultant chemists and other theorists. The same may be said of the dyeing industry and of many others.

As a result of the subtle interactions of the continual striving by purposeful individuals and the natural selection properties of the environment, extremely complicated and sophisticated institutions and practices can arise. And, as Hayek [1979, pp. 153ff] emphasizes, most of the complex and sophisticated phenomena that make up human culture (markets and mores are examples) were never consciously invented by any indi-

---

[3] This conjecture, of course, is a positive theory and capable of being tested.

vidual. Indeed, much of human culture is still not well understood.

The general decision structure delineated above also clarifies the criteria for accepting or rejecting theories. Theories are not rejected in a vacuum. If a theory predicts poorly but still better than the best available alternative, it will not be abandoned by the decision maker because doing so will reduce his welfare. As the old saying goes, "you can only beat a theory with another theory." The choice among competing theories will be based on which is expected to yield the highest value of the objective function when used for decision making. Single observations inconsistent with a theory will not necessarily bring rejection, nor is there a "natural" significance level such as 5% that brings rejection. Thus, care must be taken in interpreting the significance tests often used by scientists who are not in a decision making capacity and therefore do not have a well-defined objective function to use for deciding among contending theories.

How does one go about developing a positive theory of accounting, one that will ultimately aid in normative choices? I start by focusing on the relationship between organizational form and accounting practice—to recognize formally that accounting is a basic part of the structure of every organization. I then discuss the emerging research on an economic theory of organization.

III. ACCOUNTING AND ORGANIZATIONAL FORM

Accountants have long recognized the importance accounting has played in the stewardship or control of organizations, and this is consistent with the notion that accounting is a basic part of organizational structure and that accounting practice and organizational form are related. Accounting practices clearly differ across organizations—profit vs. nonprofit, for example. Frequently nonprofits do not record capital assets on their balance sheets and do not calculate depreciation. Fund accounting, of course, is very different from the usual for-profit system. Satisfactory explanations of these differences do not exist.[4] But this is not surprising, considering that social scientists have not generated satisfactory explanations for why nonprofit organizations exist and why they seem to dominate some activities like education and religion and not others like manufacturing.[5] Taxes are not sufficient to explain their existence, because nonprofits existed long before income taxes became important. Moreover, many other types of organizational forms exist and tend to be related to the type of production activities the organization undertakes. Publicly held or open corporations are dominant in large, complex, capital-intensive activities like manufacturing. Partnerships are dominant in sensitive service activities like law and public accounting, and nonprofits in religion, education, and classical music.

Moreover, within broad organizational categories, specific organizations differ along many dimensions such as performance evaluation, compensation, budgeting, costing, pricing, capital structure, distribution, and sales practices. There is little scientific understanding about why organizations of a given general type differ along these dimensions. And if accounting practices are significantly affected by an organization's structure, then without a fundamental understanding of why organizations dif-

---

[4] See Zimmerman [1977].

[5] See Hansmann [1980, 1981] and Fama and Jensen [1982, 1983a, 1983b] for several recent attempts to understand where nonprofit organizations survive and why.

fer we have no fundamental understanding about why accounting policies differ across organizations.[6]

Consider, for example, the use of profit centers vs. cost centers as the basis for defining divisions of an organization. Although economists and accountants have analyzed both of these organizational devices, no satisfactory theory exists that will predict when an activity within an organization will be organized as a cost center and when as a profit center.[7] Though the accounting procedures employed for each type of organization are well known, the relation of the accounting procedures to the development of the firm's organization is worthy of research. In addition, there is evidence in Chandler's [1962, pp. 61, 145 ff] work that the organizational innovations that led to the large, integrated, multi-divisional American firms in the early 1900's were accompanied by substantial innovations in accounting practices.

We are almost as ignorant regarding why financial reporting practices differ among organizations. Again, to the extent that little theory exists to explain why organizations differ in their financial reporting practices and what the effects of those different practices are, little scientific basis exists to advise management, the FASB, or the SEC on how to improve such practices through changes in accounting standards or regulation.[8] This brings me back to my main topic, the emerging research in economics that is related to organizations.

IV. THE IMPENDING REVOLUTION IN ORGANIZATION THEORY

I believe a revolution will take place over the next decade or two in our knowledge about organizations. This process will involve accounting researchers as well as economists and other social scientists. Accounting theory has bene-

fited greatly from advances in our knowledge of finance and financial markets over the last two decades—advances in which accounting researchers have played an important role. I foresee advances in organization theory which will have an even larger impact on accounting research, and the effects will extend beyond accounting to finance, economics, and management education and practice.

The last decade has been marked by a growing interest in organizations within the economics profession. The work of several dozen scholars comes to mind, and I am sure[9] there is much work unknown to me.[9] The science of organizations is still in its infancy, but the foundation for a powerful theory of organizations is being put into place. In a parallel development there is a growing body of accounting literature addressing related problems that generally goes under the label of positive research in accounting.[10] The existence of empirical

[6] For a number of studies that address these issues see Watts [1977], Watts and Zimmerman [1978, 1979], Leftwich [1983], and Holthausen [1981].

[7] This means, incidentally, that as scientists we have little advice to offer management regarding whether cost or profit centers would be best to use in any given activity.

[8] Understanding why the FASB and the SEC behave as they do and their effects on accounting requires a positive theory of the political process—another difficult area which is experiencing great scientific progress. The research on financial reporting evidences an understanding of this and I shall ignore these political/regulatory issues here.

[9] See, for example, Williamson [1964, 1975, 1979, 1981], Arrow [1963, 1974], Alchian [1950, 1969, 1981], Alchian and Demsetz [1972], Pejovich [1969], Furubotn and Pejovich [1973], Jensen and Meckling [1976, 1979], Lazear [1979], Lazear and Rosen [1981], Klein, Crawford and Alchian [1978], Harris and Raviv [1978], Harris, Kriebel and Raviv [1981], Fama and Jensen [1982a, 1982b, 1983], Fama [1980], Smith and Warner [1979], Chandler [1962, 1977], Chandler and Daems [1980], Daems [1978], Hansmann [1980, 1981], Demsetz [1982], Reagan and Stulz [1982], Marvel [1982], Meckling [1976], and Mayers and Smith [1981, 1982a, 1982b].

[10] See, for example, Benston [1963, 1975a, 1975b, 1979–80], Watts [1977, 1981], Watts and Zimmerman [1978, 1979, 1982a], Hagerman and Zmijewski [1979],

regularities between the choice of accounting procedures and organizational characteristics such as size and capital structure is beginning to be documented in that literature. A healthy and prospering journal, the *Journal of Accounting and Economics*, has been founded by my colleagues Ross Watts and Jerold Zimmerman to further encourage the development of a positive accounting literature.

A. The Dimensions of Organizations

Bill Meckling, my colleague and Dean, and I have spent a half dozen years investigating the application of the principles of economics to the analysis of organizations and in the process have developed a new course entitled Coordination and Control in Organizations. One of the frustrating aspects of that effort has been the difficulty associated with developing an understanding and definition of the relevant dimensions to use in characterizing the structure of an organization. Organizations are complex systems. If we are to make progress in understanding them we must order that complexity. We must find and articulate a set of organizational characteristics which can explain why various organizations function as they do.

In developing our coordination and control course, we have arrived at a three-part taxonomy to characterize organizations:

1. the performance measurement and evaluation system,
2. the reward and punishment system,
3. the system for partitioning and assigning decision rights among participants in the organization.

I do not have space here to discuss the importance of this classification scheme, but notice that the accounting and control system plays a major role in all three

dimensions. Viewing the organization from this perspective helps provide structure to the notion of the stewardship role of accounting in the organization. Furthermore, differences in these three dimensions across organizations are highly likely to result in differences in accounting systems. This also indicates that accounting is an integral part of the structure of every organization and that a thorough understanding of organizational forces is important to a theory of accounting.

In addition to the requirement for a better understanding of the relevant dimensions of organizations, progress in the development of a theory of organizations will also be aided by understanding why economics has not already yielded such a theory.

B. Limitations of the Economic Theory of the Firm

Unfortunately, the vast literature of economics that falls under the label of "Theory of the Firm" is not a positive theory of the firm, but rather a theory of markets. The organization or firm in that theory is little more than a black box that behaves in a value- or profit-maximizing way. In most economic analyses, the firm is modeled as an entrepreneur who maximizes profits in an environment in which all contracts are perfectly and costlessly enforced. In this firm there are no "people" problems or information problems, and as a result the research based on this model has no implications

Leftwich, Watts and Zimmerman [1981], DeAngelo [1981a, 1981b], Collins, Rozeff and Dhaliwal [1981], Holthausen [1981], Zmijewski and Hagerman [1981], Dhaliwal [1980], Lilien and Pastena [1982], Bowen, Noreen and Lacey [1981], Healy [1982], Dhaliwal, Salamon and Smith [1982], Jarrell [1979], and Lys [1982]. Useful reviews of this literature are provided by Holthausen and Leftwich [1982], Zimmerman [1980], and Watts and Zimmerman [1982b].

for how organizations are structured or how they function internally. The firm is, in effect, assumed to be an elementary component of the analysis even though in fact it is an exceedingly complex subsystem. This is not necessarily wrong. When it is appropriate for a scientist to treat a complex subsystem as an elementary component is a subtle and difficult issue. Herb Simon's article on "The Architecture of Complexity" contains an excellent analysis of the issue. As Simon [1962, p. 469] poses the problem:

> ... In most systems in nature, it is somewhat arbitrary as to where we leave off the partitioning, and what subsystems we take as elementary. Physics makes much use of the concept of "elementary particle" although particles have a disconcerting tendency not to remain elementary very long. Only a couple of generations ago, the atoms themselves were elementary particles; today, to the nuclear physicist they are complex systems. For certain purposes of astronomy, whole stars, or even galaxies, can be regarded as elementary subsystems. In one kind of biological research, a cell may be treated as an elementary subsystem; in another, a protein molecule; in still another, an amino acid residue.

Just as astronomers can usefully abstract from the complexities inside a star or a galaxy for certain purposes, the classical economic notion of the firm has usefully abstracted from the internal complexities of organizations. It has yielded a robust theory of markets that is of great value. However, precisely because the definition of the firm abstracts from most of the real problems and complexities of organizations, it provides no insights to the construction of a theory of organizations. The concepts of marginal analysis, competition, opportunity cost, and equilibrium that have been useful in the development of a theory of markets will also be valuable in the development of a theory of organizations. They are not, however, enough to accomplish the job. This raises the question of what we use to replace the black box view of the firm.

V. THE NEXUS OF CONTRACTS VIEW OF ORGANIZATIONS

I believe it is productive to define an organization as a legal entity that serves as a nexus[11] for a complex set of contracts (written and unwritten) among disparate individuals (see Jensen and Meckling [1976, pp. 310ff]). The multilateral contracts between agents that characterize market relations are supplanted within an organization by a system in which the relationships among the cooperating agents are largely effected through unilateral contracts with the legal entity that serves as the contracting nexus. These contracts specify the rules of the game within the organization, including the three critical dimensions outlined above: the performance evaluation system, the reward system, and the assignment of decision rights. This view of organizations focuses attention on the nature of the contractual relations among the agents who come together in an organization—including suppliers of labor, capital, raw materials, riskbearing services, and customers.

The nexus of contracts view helps us to see organizations in a way that can provide useful insights. It leads to inquiry about why certain contractual relations arise and how those relations respond to changes in the environment. For example, it leads us to see the shopping center as an organizational form that is an interesting alternative to a collection of indepen-

[11] "A connection, tie or link between individuals of a group, members of a series, etc." Webster's [1978].

dently owned stores grouped together in a shopping district or as an alternative to a large department store where there is no independent ownership of individual departments. The department store is an organizational device that internalizes the externalities generated by locating certain types and qualities of stores together and providing certain services centrally—so too is a supermarket. On the other hand, as such organizations grow in size, shirking problems grow larger and so do other problems associated with providing department managers, buyers, etc. with the correct incentives. The shopping center with common ownership of buildings and parking facilities coupled with contractual procedures that control the types of stores in the center, their quality, and so on, can also internalize many of the externalities of pure independent ownership. Some of the incentive problems are solved in the shopping center structure by maintaining independent ownership of the individual stores and charging for participation in the organization through a fixed fee rental plus a percentage of revenues or profits.

Although this is not the place to pursue it, it is easy to see how comparisons of such organizational forms lead to questions regarding the factors that give competitive advantages to each of these three organizational types (shopping centers, department stores, and independently owned specialty stores) at various times and at various locations. Such questions are relevant because we know all three types of organizations continue to compete and survive. Close examination should also reveal differences in accounting systems in these organizations (differences that arise from the problems and opportunities peculiar to each of them) and the role accounting plays in permitting these organizations to survive. Understanding such differences and why they arise will add another set of elements to the theory of accounting.

The nexus of contracts view of organizations also helps to dispel the tendency to treat organizations as if they were persons. Organizations do not have preferences, and they do not choose in the conscious and rational sense that we attribute to people. Anyone who has served on committees understands this fact. Usually no single person on a committee has the power to choose the outcome, and the choices that result from committee processes seldom resemble anything like the reasoned choice of a single individual. The voting paradox examined at length in the political science literature is an example of this point. The old description of the camel as a "horse designed by a committee" also captures the point.

The behavior of the organization is the equilibrium behavior of a complex contractual system made up of maximizing agents with diverse and conflicting objectives. In this sense, the behavior of the organization is like the equilibrium behavior of a market. We do not often characterize the steel market or the wheat market as having preferences and motives or making choices like an individual, but this mistake is commonly made about General Motors, Peat, Marwick, Mitchell & Co., and so on. Construction of a theory of organizations involves creating a theory that describes the equilibrium behavior of these complex contractual systems where the individual agent is the elementary unit of analysis.[12]

[12] See Meckling [1976] for a discussion of alternative models of man as the elementary unit of analysis. Sociobiologists, however, find it useful for analysis of some questions to view the gene as the elementary maximizing entity. See Hirshleifer [1978] and Dawkins [1976] and the references therein for discussions of this alternative model.

As Simon emphasizes, the definition of the elementary unit of analysis in science is not a matter of "right" or "wrong" but rather one of usefulness. Whether one chooses the "black box" or "nexus of contracts" definition of an organization depends on the question at hand. Some questions, like how outputs of a firm or industry respond to price changes, are more productively addressed with the former. Other questions, such as those involving organizational problems like the choice of accounting practices, are more productively addressed in the nexus of contracts perspective. However, when using the black box approach it is important to remember that it is a convenient abstraction that is appropriate only for analysis of some questions. The danger in its use arises because it further encourages the tendency to personalize organizations by attributing motives and preferences to what is in fact a complex equilibrium system. Such personalization of organizations easily leads to uncritical application of the black box approach to questions it cannot handle.

VI. SOME RECENT RESULTS ON CONTROL

Eugene Fama and I have been working for several years to understand the characteristics that give survival value to different organizational forms. One of our concerns has been to understand the factors that give survival value to organizations like large public corporations characterized by separation of "ownership and control," or, more precisely, separation of the decision management and residual riskbearing functions. Scholars from Adam Smith [1776] to Berle and Means [1932] have pointed out the inconsistency of interests between managers and outside stockholders and have emphasized the costs these conflicts generate. Yet, even though other organizational forms such as proprietorships,

small partnerships, and closed corporations compete with corporations and do so without the handicap of the costs of separation of ownership and control, the evidence is clear: in the production of a wide range of activities, the corporation continues to win the competition for survival.

In fact, the large, publicly-held corporation is not unique in its separation of "ownership and control." Separation of decision management and residual riskbearing characterizes many organizational forms, for example, financial mutuals and large professional partnerships. Nonprofit organizations which have no alienable residual claims constitute the extreme form of separation of ownership from control.

Fama and I conclude that separation of decision management (the initiation and implementation of decisions) from decision control (the ratification and monitoring of decisions) in the organization is the major device that limits the costs due to separation of "ownership and control." The evidence indicates that open corporations, financial mutuals, large partnerships, and nonprofit organizations are all characterized by separation of decision management and decision control functions. Moreover, all these organizations use a common device—boards of directors, trustees, or managing partners—to accomplish such separation at the top level of the organization. These boards have the rights to ratify and monitor the decisions that are initiated and implemented by top-level managers. In addition, they always have the power to hire, fire, and set the compensation of the top-level managers. This top-level separation of decision management from decision control and the separation and diffusion of decision management and decision control rights among agents throughout lower levels of the organization are the contractual responses that limit the costs of the separation of "ownership and control" and therefore foster survival of these organizations (Fama and Jensen [1983b]).

Watts and Zimmerman have pointed out that our separation proposition mirrors the standards recommended in the auditing and control literature. Stettler's [1977] auditing text, for example, urges that operations responsibility be separated from accounting responsibility by vesting the two functions in different people.[13] In handling cash, the recommendation is to separate the responsibility for the record-keeping function from the person who receives the cash, and similarly for authorizing and drawing checks in the payout process. These widely practiced principles have evolved from long experience with conflicts of interest and evidently have survival value. Since Fama and I derived our propositions about control in a quite different context, these common practices for handling cash, accounts payable, and so on, are encouraging evidence consistent with our thesis. It is exciting that, appropriately generalized, some of the same principles that apply to the conflict of interest problem in the handling of cash also apply to the conflict of interests between managers and stockholders and boards of directors of corporations, financial mutuals, large partnerships, and even nonprofit organizations. It gives hope that the next decade will witness success in the construction of a rich and general theory of control.

VII. Methodological Issues

Whether the potential to develop a science of organizations will be exploited depends, of course, on many factors. I would like to discuss some important methodological issues: (1) the importance of tautologies and definitions, (2) the difficulty but desirability of dealing with qualitative institutional evidence, and (3) the role of mathematics.

A. The Importance of Tautologies

In the language of science, a tautology is a statement that is true by definition and can never be refuted by evidence.[14] Therefore, it is not an hypothesis or a theory. A definition declares that a newly-introduced symbol means the same as another combination of symbols whose meaning is already known; it, therefore, also cannot be refuted by evidence.

The choice of tautologies or definitions has a large impact on the success or failure of research efforts—a fact that often goes unrecognized. Discussion of new research efforts often meets with resistance on the grounds that the effort is purely definitional, or the propositions are tautological and devoid of empirical content. Yet thorough and careful attention to definitions and tautologies is often extremely productive in the early stages of research, especially if the research is a radical departure from the past. On the other hand, it is also common to observe talented manpower devoted to sterile research on toy problems or characterizations of problems that bear little relation to the world and the rich variety of options that people face. The sterility of this research can often be traced to the choice of definitions and tautologies that focus the effort. Unfortunately, there is no obvious criterion we can apply to help us select more productive rather than less productive tautologies or definitions.

[13] "In general, no one department should be responsible for handling all phases of a transaction, and if possible, the division of responsibility should keep operations and custodianship separate from accounting." Stettler [1977, p. 56].

[14] Philosophers have a precise definition of tautology. I use the term here more loosely and more in accord with its use in the social sciences.

Perhaps such choices will remain one of the "artistic" or creative parts of science.

Alfred Whitehead and Bertrand Russell [1910, pp. 11 ff] emphasize the importance of the choice of definitions:

> In spite of the fact that definitions are theoretically superfluous, it is nevertheless true that they often convey more important information than is contained in the propositions in which they are used. This arises from two causes. First, a definition usually implies that the *definiens* [the meaning in terms of the combination of already known symbols] is worthy of careful consideration. Hence the collection of definitions embodies our choice of subjects and our judgment as to what is most important. Secondly, when what is defined is (as often occurs) something already familiar, such as cardinal or ordinal numbers, the definition contains an analysis of a common idea, and may therefore express a notable advance. Cantor's definition of the continuum illustrates this: his definition amounts to the statement that what he is defining is the object which has the properties commonly associated with the word "continuum," though what precisely constitutes these properties had not before been known. In such cases, a definition is a "making definite"; it gives definiteness to an idea which had previously been more or less vague.
>
> For these reasons, it will be found, in what follows, that the definitions are what is most important, and what most deserves the reader's prolonged attention.

The mathematical biologist, A. J. Lotka [1956, pp. 3f], provides another example when he characterizes the enunciation of the survival of the fittest as one of the fundamental advances of science. It is a tautology because the fit is defined to be that which survives. The Coase Theorem [1960] is another important tautology that has helped us to see the importance

of transactions costs in a fundamentally different fashion. (See Demsetz [1982, ch. 2]). The proposition that consumers make choices so as to maximize their utility is also a tautology that has proved useful in understanding human behavior and markets. Another tautology that accountants will agree is important is the proposition that assets equal liabilities plus equity—at least as long as I'm not doing the arithmetic. The usefulness and power of double-entry bookkeeping is testified to by its survival since at least the 15th century and its continuing widespread use. Viewing double-entry bookkeeping this way leaves me believing that we still do not thoroughly understand why it is a powerful organizing device. I am so used to thinking of assets and the claims on them, equities and liabilities, as a way of organizing thoughts about companies that it is hard to conceive of alternatives.[15]

The word tautology has strong pejorative overtones in our profession—to be accused of stating a tautology is practically the highest of professional insults. Therefore, I hasten to add that while a tautology of one form or another lies at the heart of all useful theory, this does not mean that such theory has no refutable, i.e., positive, implications. Darwin and the biologists who followed him as well as economists using the Coase Theorem and utility maximization have thoroughly demonstrated the empirical content of their theories.

The manner in which we use tautologies to develop positive theories is closely related to the nature of the scientific process itself. The process involves the use of the definitions and the underlying tautology (such as the survival of the

---

[15] I am left with questions; for example why don't we organize our thoughts about the family through the double-entry tautology? Perhaps someday these issues will be better understood.

fittest) and a subset of the available data on surviving and extinct species to develop propositions about the important aspects of the environment and their relation to traits contributing to survival. When successful, the result is a theory that is consistent with the utilized data. This theory can then be tested with as yet unused data. In addition, the theoretical structure can be manipulated to derive additional nonobvious propositions which can also be confronted with new or previously unused data to provide tests. When the data is substantially inconsistent with the predictions, the theory is revised or replaced and the process continues. This is a continuing process, of course, and takes place over a series of studies and papers.

Finally, note how Whitehead and Russell's emphasis on the importance of definitions applies to the economic notion of the firm. Defining the firm as a black box diverts attention away from what is going on within the firm. The nexus of contracts definition of organizations, on the other hand, focuses attention on the problems that the contracts are intended to solve, i.e., on how things get done within the organization. Whether the nexus of contracts view will be as productive as I think it will be is itself an empirical question. However, the relatively recent development of the positive theory of agency lends encouragement to the view that the nexus of contracts approach will be productive.

B. Two Useful Tautologies—Agency Costs are Minimized and Survival of the Fittest

The positive theory of agency also derives from several definitions and a simple tautology. Cooperative behavior between human beings is viewed as a contracting problem among self-interested individuals with divergent interests.

Agency costs are defined as the sum of the costs of structuring, bonding, and monitoring contracts between agents. Agency costs also include the costs stemming from the fact that it doesn't pay to enforce all contracts perfectly. Recognizing that one or more of the contracting parties can capture the benefits from reducing the agency costs in any relationship provides the analytical device, the tautology, that yields implications for the forms of the contracts that evolve[16]—maximizing agents minimize the agency costs in any contracting relationship (Jensen and Meckling [1976]). Notice how conveniently this dovetails with the notion of organizations as a nexus of contracts; its application there implies that the organizational form, its contracts, will be those that minimize the agency costs.

Adding two more elements, (1) the notion that competition is a general phenomenon that takes place over many dimensions, including organizational form, and (2) the survival of the fittest tautology,[17] completes most of the major building blocks of the analytical framework for creating a theory of organizations. The view is one of organizations competing with each other to deliver the activities demanded by customers. Those organizations survive that are able to deliver the activities or products at the lowest price while covering costs. Understanding the survival process involves understanding how the contracts of par-

[16] For some interesting applications of this approach see Smith and Warner [1979] who use it to explain covenants in bond indentures, Mayers and Smith [1981, 1982a, 1982b], who examine contracting and organizational practices in the insurance industry, and Leftwich [1983], who examines the private contractual specification of accounting procedures. Holthausen [1981] uses the approach to derive hypotheses about management decisions to change depreciation methods. His tests indicate the data are not consistent with the hypotheses.

[17] Alchian [1950] long ago argued for the use of the natural-selection principle in economic analysis.

ticular organizations achieve low cost control of agency problems and how they combine with the production technology of an activity to enable the organization to survive (Fama and Jensen [1982a, 1983a, 1983b]).

C. The Nature of Evidence

Since a theory of organizations is in essence a special case of a general theory of contracting, it is likely that some confusion and disagreement will arise in the profession over the nature of evidence bearing on the theory. Indeed, this disagreement is already becoming evident in the research on organizations and in positive research in accounting.

Economists, financial economists, accounting researchers and behavioral scientists are well indoctrinated in the methodology associated with the use of quantitative evidence in the testing of theories. We have been fortunate, for example, that the theory of efficient markets yields direct predictions about the characteristics of the probability distributions of asset price changes and returns—predictions for which a rich variety of data and statistical theory are conveniently available for testing purposes. However, many important predictions of the research on positive organization theory and positive accounting theory will be characterizations of the contracting relations, and much of the best evidence on these propositions will be qualitative and institutional evidence. that is, evidence on the forms of the contracts, their provisions, and on other organizational and accounting practices. By its nature, much of this institutional evidence cannot be summarized by measures using real numbers. We simply do not know how to aggregate such evidence, nor can we calculate formal measures of central tendency and standard errors of estimate. This means, of

course, that regression equations cannot be estimated, and this will not bring comfort to those empiricists who clutch regression equations to their breasts like security blankets. Statisticians and econometricians are likely to react because it violates a long and venerable tradition of formal testing.

Whenever feasible, of course, it is desirable to obtain quantitative predictions of a form amenable to the usual testing procedures. However, since the theory is aimed at explaining the contract structures and practices of organizations, it seems unwise to ignore evidence on such structures in testing the theory. It seems especially unwise in the early stages of development because any theory that is likely to be useful and worthy of detailed consideration should not be vastly inconsistent with the readily available institutional evidence. Not all such theories will, however, be acceptable and herein lies a serious inference problem. The fact is that a well developed theory of inference for dealing with quantitative data exists and it is of great value. Such a theory is not nearly as well developed for dealing with the qualitative institutional data that characterize the organizational field, and therefore the likelihood of misuse of data and incorrect inferences is higher.

Nonparametric statistics provide only limited help in dealing with institutional evidence because these procedures generally presume independence in sample observations—a condition seldom satisfied. In addition, it is often difficult to know what procedures were followed in selecting a sample of institutional evidence, and this raises serious questions about the existence of selection bias and therefore about the inferences to be made from the evidence. Finally, because institutional evidence consists of non-commensurable items we do not know how to formally weight the individual pieces of evidence; they cannot be simply counted or added up. Yet this does not mean the observations are not evidence, and most people intuitively understand this when it comes to the issues considered in a criminal trial. With the help of statisticians and philosophers, perhaps some progress will be made in resolving these inference problems.

Meanwhile, it is unwise to ignore important institutional evidence while paying great attention to unimportant quantitative evidence simply because its dimensions are more familiar. The practice of using pejorative labels such as "casual," "anecdotal," or "ad hoc" to describe such institutional or qualitative evidence is counterproductive to the research process. Such labels suggest uncaring or sloppy methods or unimportant evidence. "Readily available" or "institutional" evidence are reasonable substitutes for these emotion-laden terms. "Incomplete," or "inappropriate" evidence are reasonable descriptive labels to use when the researcher's methods are in fact uncaring or sloppy. Not all institutional evidence is readily available; much of it requires a great deal of effort to gather. On the other hand, stock price data, accounting data and national income data are readily available to the scientist but they are not given pejorative labels such as "casual." For several carefully executed and useful studies using institutional evidence, I recommend the study of the covenants in bond indentures by Smith and Warner [1979], the Mayers and Smith [1981, 1982a, 1982b] work on organizations and contractual practices in the insurance industry, the study of the market for accounting theories by Watts and Zimmerman [1979], and the study of private specification of accounting procedures by Leftwich [1983].

D. The Role of Mathematics

Mathematics is a very useful language, but not universally so. It is often useful in the derivation of non-obvious implications that are difficult to develop by other techniques. The propositions of portfolio theory and asset pricing are examples. The unaided human mind and the English language are not well suited to handling the complexities of the notion of a covariance matrix and solutions to sets of simultaneous equations. Without the help of the language of mathematics, the insights of portfolio theory and asset pricing along with many others would likely remain unknown.

Sometimes, however, the use of mathematics is counterproductive in the research process. This is especially true in dealing with new and uncharted areas such as organization theory and accounting theory. As implied by the previous discussion of definitions and tautologies, a great deal of work has to be done in a new area of analysis that represents a radical departure from current knowledge before the dimensionality of the problem and the major variables can be defined. Mathematics seems to be useless for solving these problems. My impression is that attempts to use it at such an early stage in the development of an area are often counterproductive because authors are led to assume the problem away or to define sterile "toy" problems that are mathematically tractable.

Unfortunately, there exists in the profession an unwarranted bias towards the use of mathematics even in situations where it is unproductive or useless. One manifestation of this is the common use of the terms "rigorous" or "analytical" or even "theoretical" as identical with "mathematical." None of these links is, of course, correct. Mathematical is not the same as rigorous, nor is it the same as analytical or theoretical. Propositions can be logically rigorous without being mathematical, and analysis does not have to take the form of symbols and equations. The English sentence and paragraph will do quite well for many analytical purposes. In addition, the use of mathematics does not prevent the commission of errors—even egregious ones.

There will always be some people who think and produce better in one language than another. And there will be problems and problem areas where one language or analytical approach is more productive than another. Nevertheless, some researchers take the attitude that analysis is worthwhile and important only if accomplished through the language of mathematics. Others are antagonistic toward analysis that uses mathematics. Hopefully, as the profession matures, more tolerance, understanding, and consideration of these issues will prevail. As our knowledge of organizations and accounting theory grows I expect to see increased productive use of mathematics.

VIII. THE TWO AGENCY LITERATURES

Since the original papers by Spence and Zeckhauser [1971] and Ross [1973], substantial attention has been given to the development of the theory of agency. Interestingly, that development has resulted in two almost entirely separate and valuable literatures that nominally address the same problem. However, the two literatures differ in many respects, and they reference each other less than one might expect given the closeness of their topics. Being actively involved in one of these efforts and a neophyte in the other, I am not the best person to provide an unbiased comparison of them, but some discussion seems appropriate at this point.

Earlier, I briefly discussed one of the agency literatures—what I have labeled the "positive theory of agency." The other literature has acquired the label "principal-agent."[18] Both literatures address the contracting problem between self-interested maximizing parties and both use the same agency cost minimizing tautology (although not necessarily stated in that form). They differ, however, in many respects. The principal-agent literature is generally mathematical and non-empirically oriented, while the positive agency literature is generally non-mathematical and empirically oriented (although neither literature is entirely so).

The principal-agent literature has generally concentrated on modeling the effects of three factors on contracts between parties interacting in the hierarchical fashion suggested by the term principal-agent: (1) the structure of the preferences of the parties to the contracts, (2) the nature of uncertainty, and (3) the informational structure in the environment. Attention is generally focused on risk sharing and the form of the optimal contract between principal and agent, and on welfare comparisons of the equilibrium contracting solutions in the presence of information costs vis-à-vis the solutions in the absence of such costs.

The positive agency literature has generally concentrated on modeling the effects of additional aspects of the contracting environment and the technology of monitoring and bonding on the form of the contracts and organizations that survive. Capital intensity, degree of spe-

[18] Some representative but far from exhaustive references are Spence and Zeckhauser [1971], Ross [1973, 1974], Raviv [1979], Harris and Raviv [1978], Mirrlees [1976], Harris and Townsend [1981], Townsend [1979], Holmstrom [1979], and Shavell [1979]. Demski and Kreps [forthcoming] review the accounting-related literature in this area.

cialization of assets, information costs, capital markets, and internal and external labor markets are examples of factors in the contracting environment that interact with the costs of various monitoring and bonding practices to determine the contractual forms.[19]

Each of the agency literatures has its strong and weak points, and on occasion tension has surfaced between them. In some sense the reasons are understandable. Part is due to the "tyranny of formalism" that develops when mathematically inclined scholars take the attitude that if the analytical language is not mathematics, it isn't rigorous, and if a problem cannot be solved with the use of mathematics, the effort should be abandoned. Part is due to the belief that the lack of the use of mathematics in the positive agency literature results in ex post facto theorizing that assures the hypotheses will not be rejected. Part is also due to the problems associated with the use of qualitative and institutional evidence, discussed earlier.

Though much of the principal-agent literature seems to be produced in the normative mode, most of it can be interpreted in a positive fashion. However, some believe that so little is put into the current principal-agent models that there is little hope of producing results that will explain much of the rich variety of observed contracting practices. Tractability problems seem to limit the richness of the input to the principal-agent models, especially when it comes to analyzing the effects of markets on the contracting process—for example, capital and labor markets and the market for control. It also seems difficult to analyze within the principal-agent models the effects of complex equilibrium systems in the contracting milieu, for example, mutual monitoring systems like the collegial system so familiar to academics.

The issue boils down to an empirical question regarding how useful the preference, stochastic structure, and information structure variables are in explaining observed contracting practices. The positive agency literature proceeds on the implicit assumption that the variables emphasized in the principal-agent literature are relatively unimportant in understanding the observed phenomenon when compared with richer specifications of information costs, other aspects of the environment, and the monitoring and bonding technology.

On the other hand, the methods of the positive agency literature justifiably seem unconstrained and often perilously close to tautological to some. In part this arises from a misunderstanding by some of the nature of the scientific process—the manner in which we use tautologies to develop positive theories. At the risk of oversimplifying, the ideal process proceeds by using the agency definitions and the cost-minimizing tautology described earlier and a subset of the observed contract structures to develop propositions about the important aspects of the environment and the monitoring and bonding technology—that is, to derive a theory that is consistent with those contracts. If successful, that effort provides a structure that can be manipulated to derive additional non-obvious positive propositions, i.e., hypotheses. Confronting these propositions with previously unknown or unused data provides a test of the theory. If the data are substantially inconsistent with the predictions, the theory is then revised or replaced with a new alternative and the

---

[19] See, for example, Jensen and Meckling [1976], Myers [1977], Smith and Warner [1979], Fama [1980], Holthausen [1981], Mikkelson [1981], Leftwich [1981, 1983], Mayers and Smith [1981, 1982], Watts and Zimmerman [1982a, 1982b], and Fama and Jensen [1982a, 1983a, 1983b].

process continues. This is the scientific process. In the initial stages we should take care to avoid requiring researchers to accomplish all this in a single study or paper—an undesirable requirement from the standpoint of the progress of science. It is important as colleagues, referees, and editors to avoid applying standards to individual papers that are appropriately applied only to the scientific process as a whole.

On the other hand, it is appropriate to be suspicious of results obtained from "too much" fishing in the data—including the institutional data—although it is often difficult to tell how much of that has taken place. The appropriate response is to treat the results of early studies as more like a set of relatively untested hypotheses than a well-tested and surviving theory.

As a result of the continued gradual development of our empirical and conceptual knowledge, I expect to see the two agency literatures become closer, partly because the intellectual efforts devoted by both groups will result in a clearer understanding of the definitions of the important concepts and the relevant dimensions upon which to order the complexity of the world. Mathematics will then be of great help in the generation of non-obvious testable propositions and as a language for use in communicating the important aspects of the theoretical structure.

In the end, competition in research is as important to innovation and progress as competition in the product markets. Scholars will make their own judgments of what are currently useful results and where the productive and exciting research approaches and opportunities are. I have little doubt that with the passage of time, the "fit" (that is, the productive and useful results and approaches) will "survive."

REFERENCES

Alchian, Armen A., "Uncertainty, Evolution and Economic Theory," *Journal of Political Economy*, Vol. 58, No. 3 (June 1950), pp. 211–221.

———, "Corporate Management and Property Rights," *Economic Policy and the Regulation of Corporate Securities*, Henry Manne, Editor (American Enterprise Institute, 1969), pp. 337–360.

———, "Property Rights, Specialization and the Firm," unpublished mimeo (November 1981).

——— and Harold Demsetz, "Production, Information Costs, and Economic Organization," *The American Economic Review*, Vol. LXII, No. 5 (December 1972), pp. 777–795.

Arrow, K. J., "Control in Large Organizations," *Management Science*, Vol. 10 (April 1964), pp. 397–408.

———, *The Limits of Organization* (Norton and Company, Inc., 1974).

Benston, George J., "The Role of the Firm's Accounting System for Motivation," THE ACCOUNTING REVIEW, (April 1963), pp. 347–354.

———, "Accountants' Integrity and Financial Reporting," *Financial Executive*, Vol. XLIII (August 1975a), pp. 10–14.

———, "Accounting Standards in the U.S. and U.K.: Their Nature, Causes and Consequencies." *Vanderbilt Law Review*, Vol. 28 (January 1975b), pp. 235–268.

———, "The Market for Public Accounting Services: Demand, Supply and Regulation," *The Accounting Journal*, Vol. II, No. 1 (Winter 1979–80), pp. 1–46.

Berle, A. A., and G. C. Means, *The Modern Corporation and Private Property* (Macmillan, 1932).

Bowen, R. E., Noreen, and J. Lacey, "Determinants of the Corporate Decision to Capitalize Interest," *Journal of Accounting and Economics*, Vol. 3 (August 1981), pp. 151–179.

Chandler, Alfred D., Jr., *Strategy and Structure* (MIT Press, 1962; Doubleday and Co., 1966).

———, *The Visible Hand: The Managerial Revolution* (Belknapp Press, 1977).

———, and Herman Daems, *Managerial Hierarchies: Comparative Perspectives on the Rise of the Modern Industrial Enterprise* (Harvard University Press, 1980).

Coase, Ronald, "The Problem of Social Cost," *Journal of Law and Economics* (October 1960), pp. 1–44.

Collins, Daniel W. Michael S. Rozeff, and Dan S. Dhaliwal, "The Economic Determinants of the Market Reaction to Proposed Mandatory Accounting Changes in the Oil and Gas Industry: A Cross Section Analysis," *Journal of Accounting and Economics*, Vol. 3, No. 1 (March 1981), pp. 37–71.

Daems, Herman, *The Holding Company and Corporate Control* (Martinus Nijhoff, 1978).

Dawkins, Richard, *The Selfish Gene* (Oxford University Press, 1976).

DeAngelo, Linda E., "Auditor Independence, 'Low Balling,' and Disclosure Regulation," *Journal of Accounting and Economics*, Vol. 3, No. 2 (August 1981a), pp. 113–127.

―――, "Auditor Size and Audit Quality," *Journal of Accounting and Economics*, Vol. 3, No. 3 (December 1981b), pp. 183–200.

Demsetz, Harold, *Economic, Legal, and Political Dimensions of Competition* (North-Holland Publishing Company, 1982).

Demski, Joel S., and David M. Kreps, "Models in Managerial Accounting," Supplement to *Journal of Accounting Research* [forthcoming, 1982].

Dhaliwal, D., "The Effect of the Firm's Capital Structure on the Choice of Accounting Methods," THE ACCOUNTING REVIEW, Vol. 55 (January 1980), pp. 78–84.

―――, G. Salamon, and E. D. Smith, "The Effect of Owner Versus Management Control on the Choice of Accounting Methods," *Journal of Accounting and Economics*, Vol. 4 (July 1982), pp. 41–53.

Fama, Eugene F., "Agency Problems and the Theory of the Firm," *Journal of Political Economy*, Vol. 88, No. 2 (April 1980), pp. 288–307.

―――, and Michael C. Jensen, "Residual Claims and Investment Decisions in Organizations," unpublished manuscript (July 1982a).

―――, and ―――, "Agency Problems and Residual Claims," Graduate School of Management, University of Rochester, Managerial Economics Research Center Working Paper No. MERC 82-16, and University of Chicago, Graduate School of Business, Center for Research in Security Prices Working Paper No. 88 (forthcoming in the *Journal of Law and Economics*, June 1983a).

―――, and ―――, "Separation of Ownership and Control," Graduate School of Management, University of Rochester, Managerial Economics Research Center Working Paper No. MERC 82-14 and University of Chicago, Graduate School of Business, Center for Research in Security Prices Working Paper No. 89 (Forthcoming in the *Journal of Law and Economics*, June 1983b).

Furubotn, E. G., and S. Pejovich, "Property Rights, Economic Decentralization and the Evolution of the Yugoslav Firm, 1965–1972," *Journal of Law and Economics*, Vol. 16 (October 1973), pp. 275–302.

Hagerman, R., and M. Zmijewski, "Some Economic Determinants of Accounting Policy Choice," *Journal of Accounting and Economics* (August 1979). pp. 141 161.

Hansmann, Henry B., "The Role of Nonprofit Enterprise," *The Yale Law Journal*, Vol. 89, No. 5 (April 1980), pp. 835–901.

―――, "Nonprofit Enterprise in the Performing Arts," *The Bell Journal of Economics*, Vol. 12, No. 2 (Autumn 1981), pp. 341–361.

Harris, M., C. H. Kriebel, and A. Raviv, "Asymmetric Information, Incentives and Intrafirm Recource Allocation," unpublished manuscript (July 1981).

―――, and A. Raviv, "Some Results in Incentive Contracts with Applications to Education and Employment, Health Insurance, and Law Enforcement," *American Economic Review*, Vol. 68 (March 1978), pp. 20–30.

―――, and R. Townsend, "Resource Allocation Under Asymmetric Information," *Econometrica*, Vol. 49, No. (January 1981), pp. 33–64.

Hayek, F. A., *The Political Order of a Free People*, Volume 3 of a series *Law, Legislation and Liberty* (The University of Chicago Press, 1979).

Healy, Paul, "The Impact of Bonus Schemes on the Selection of Accounting Principles," unpublished dissertation proposal, Graduate School of Management, University of Rochester (1982).

Hirshleifer, J., "Competition, Cooperation, and Conflict in Economics and Biology," *The American Economic Review*, Vol. 68, No. 2 (May 1978), pp. 238–243.

Holmstrom, B., "Moral Hazard and Observability," *The Bell Journal of Economics*, Vol. 10 (Spring, 1979), pp. 74–91.

Holthausen, Robert W., "Evidence on the Effect of Bond Covenants and Management Compensation Contracts on the Choice of Accounting Techniques: The Case of the Depreciation Switch-Back," *Journal of Accounting and Economics*, Vol. 3 (March 1981), pp. 73–109.

————, and Richard W. Leftwich, "The Economic Consequences of Accounting Choice: Implications of Costly Contracting and Monitoring," University of Chicago Graduate School of Business, Center for Research in Security Prices Working Paper No. 87 (October 1982).

Jarrell, G. A., "Pro-Producer Regulation and Accounting for Assets: The Case of Electric Utilities," *Journal of Accounting and Economics* (August 1979), pp. 93–116.

Jensen, Michael C., and William H. Meckling, "Theory of the Firm: Managerial Behavior, Agency Costs and Ownership Structure," *Journal of Financial Economics*, Vol. 3 (October 1976), pp. 305–360.

————, and ————, "Rights and Production Functions: An Application to Labor-Managed Firms and Codetermination." *Journal of Business*, Vol. 52, No. 4 (October, 1979), pp. 469–506.

Klein, Benjamin, Robert Crawford, and Armen A. Alchian, "Vertical Integration, Appropriable Rents, and the Competitive Contracting Process," *Journal of Law and Economics*, Vol. XXI, No. 2 (October 1978), pp. 297–326.

Lazear, Edward P., "Why is There Mandatory Retirement?," *Journal of Political Economy*, Vol. 87, No. 6 (December 1979), pp. 1261–1284.

————, and Sherwin Rosen, "Rank-Order Tournaments as Optimum Labor Contracts," *Journal of Political Economy*, Vol. 89, No. 5 (October 1981), pp. 841–864.

Leftwich, Richard, "Evidence of the Impact of Mandatory Changes in Accounting Principles on Corporate Loan Agreements," *Journal of Accounting and Economics*, Vol. 3, No. 1 (March 1981), pp. 3–36.

————, "Accounting Information in Private Markets: Evidence from Private Lending Agreements," THE ACCOUNTING REVIEW (January 1983).

————, Ross L. Watts, and Jerold L. Zimmerman, "Voluntary Corporate Disclosure: The Case of Interim Reporting," *Journal of Accounting Research*, Supplement to Volume 19 (1981), pp. 50–77.

Lilien, S., and V. Pastena, "Determinants of Intramethod Choices in the Oil and Gas Industry," *Journal of Accounting and Economics* (December 1982).

Lotka, Alfred J., *Elements of Mathematical Biology* (Dover Publications, 1956).

Lys, Thomas, "Selection of Accounting Procedures and Implications of Changes in Generally Accepted Accounting Principles: A Case Study Using Oil and Gas Accounting," unpublished Ph.D. dissertation, University of Rochester (1982).

Marvel, Howard P., "Exclusive Dealing," *Journal of Law and Economics*, Vol. XXV, No. 1 (April 1982), pp. 1–25.

Mayers, David, and Clifford W. Smith, Jr., "Contractual Provisions, Organizational Structure, and Conflict Control in Insurance Markets," *Journal of Business*, Vol. 54, No. 3 (July 1981), pp. 407–434.

————, and ————, "On the Corporate Demand for Insurance," *Journal of Business*, Vol. 55, No. 2 (April 1982a), pp. 281–296.

————, and ————, "Toward a Positive Theory of Insurance," Monograph Series in Finance and Economics, Salomon Brothers Center for the Study of Financial Institutions, New York University, Graduate School of Business Administration, Monograph 1982–1, Ernest Bloch and Paul Wachtel, Editors (1982b).

Meckling, William H., "Values and the Choice of the Model of the Individual in the Social Sciences (REMM)," *Schweizerische Zeitschrift fur Volkswirtschaft und Statistik*, Vol. 4 (December 1976), pp. 545–560.

Mikkelson, Wayne H., "Convertible Calls and Security Return,s," *Journal of Financial Economics*, Vol. 9, No. 3 (September 1981), pp. 237–264.

Mirrlees, J., "The Optimal Structure of Incentives and Authority Within an Organization," *The Bell Journal of Economics*, Vol. 7, 1 (Spring 1976), pp. 105–131.

Myers, Stewart C., "Determinants of Corporate Borrowing," *Journal of Financial Economics*, Vol. 5, No. 2 (November 1977).

Pareto, Vilfredo, *The Mind and Society*, Arthur Livingston, Editor (Harcourt, Brace and Company, 1935).

Pejovich, S., "The Firm, Monetary Policy and Property Rights in a Planned Economy," *Western Economics Journal*, Vol. 7, No. 3 (September 1969), pp. 193–200.

Raviv, A., "The Design of an Optimal Insurance Policy," *American Economic Review*, Vol. 69 (March 1979), pp. 84–96.

Reagan, Patricia B., and René M. Stulz, "Rish Sharing, Labor Contracts, and Capital Markets," Graduate School of Management, University of Rochester, Center for Research in Government Policy and Business Working Paper No. GPR 82-1 (January 1982).

Ross, Stephen A., "The Economic Theory of Agency: The Principals Problem," *American Economic Review*, Vol. LXII (May 1973), pp. 134–139.

————, "The Economic Theory of Agency and the Principle of Similarity," in *Essays on Economic Behavior Under Uncertainty*, M. D. Balch, et al., Editors (North-Holland Publishing Company, 1974).

Shavell, S., "Risk Sharing and Incentives in the Principal and Agent Relationship," *The Bell Journal of Economics*, Vol. 10 (Spring 1979), pp. 55–73.

Simon, Herbert A., "The Architecture of Complexity," *Proceedings of the American Philosophical Society* (December 1962), pp. 467–482.

Smith, Adam, *The Wealth of Nations*, 1776. Canaan ed. (New York: Modern Library, 1937).

Smith, Clifford, W., Jr., and Jerold B. Warner, "On Financial Contracting: An Analysis of Bond Covenants," *Journal of Financial Economics*, Vol. 7 (July 1979), pp. 117–161.

Spence, Michael, and R. Zeckhauser, "Insurance, Information and Individual Action," *American Economic Review*, Vol. LXI, No. 2 (May 1971), pp. 380–387.

Stettler, Howard P., *Auditing Principles* (Prentice-Hall, 1977).

Townsend, R. M., "Optimal Contracts and Competitive Markets with Costly State Verification," *Journal of Economic Theory*, Vol. 21 (October 1979), pp. 265–293.

Watts, Ross L., "Corporate Financial Statements, A Product of the Market and Political Processes," *Australian Journal of Management*, Vol. 2 (April 1977), pp. 53–75.

————, "The Political Economics of the Determination of Accounting Standards," in R. Hoyt (ed.) *The Relationship of Accounting Theory to the Standard Setting Process* (Faculte des Sciences de l'Administration, Universite Labal, 1981).

————, and Jerold L. Zimmerman, "Towards a Positive Theory of the Determination of Accounting Standards," THE ACCOUNTING REVIEW, Vol. 53 (January 1978), pp. 112–134.

————, and ————, "The Demand for and Supply of Accounting Theories: The Market for Excuses," THE ACCOUNTING REVIEW (April 1979), pp. 273–305.

————, and ————, "Agency Problems, Auditing and the Theory of the Firm: Some Evidence," University of Rochester, Graduate School of Management, unpublished manuscript (July 1982a).

————, and ————, "Positive Theories of the Determination of Accounting Procedures," unpublished manuscript, Graduate School of Management, University of Rochester (1982b).

Webster's New World Dictionary, Second College Edition (William Collins and World Publishing Co., Inc., 1978).

Whitehead, Alfred N., and Bertrand Russell, *Principia Mathematica* (Cambridge University Press, original ed. 1910; paperback ed. 1973).

Williamson, Oliver E., *The Economics of Discretionary Behavior: Managerial Objectives in a Theorf of the Firm* (Prentice-Hall, 1964).

————, *Markets and Hierarchies: Analysis and Antitrust Implications* (Free Press, 1975).

————, "Transaction-Cost Economics: The Governance of Contractual Relations," *Journal of Law and Economics*, Vol. 22, No. 2 (October 1979), pp. 233–261.

————, "The Modern Corporation: Origins, Evolution, Attributes," *Journal of Economic Literature* (December 1981), pp. 1537–1568.

Zimmerman, Jerold L., "The Municipal Accounting Maze: An Analysis of Political Incentives," in "Studies in Measurement and Evaluation of the Economic Efficiency of Public and Private Nonprofit Institutions," Supplement to *The Journal of Accounting Research*, Vol. 15 (1977), pp. 107–144.

————, "The Costs and Benefits of Cost Allocations," THE ACCOUNTING REVIEW (July 1979), pp. 504–521.

————, "Positive Research in Accounting," in R. D. Nair and T. H. Williams (eds.), *Perspectives on Research* (Graduate School of Business, University of Wisconsin, 1980).

Zmijewski, M., and R. Hagerman, "An Income Strategy Approach to the Positive Theory of Accounting Standard Setting/Choice," *Journal of Accounting and Economics*, Vol. 3 (August 1981), pp. 129–149.

The Costs and Benefits
of Cost Allocations

Jerold L. Zimmerman

ABSTRACT: This paper raises the often-ignored, positive question of why firms continue to allocate costs for internal reporting purposes in spite of educators' continual admonitions to the contrary. Two examples are constructed. These cases illustrate that cost allocations can act as a lump-sum tax which reduce the manager's consumption of perquisites and that cost allocations can serve as useful proxy variables for certain difficult-to-observe costs. These examples suggest that cost allocations might be useful devices for controlling and motivating managers.

COST allocations has been a pervasive topic in the accounting literature for over 75 years.[1] Usually, cost allocations are discussed within the context of inventory costing and pricing decisions. However, the allocation problem also arises under the guise of transfer pricing, divisional performance evaluation, and line of business reporting. The issue of cost allocations is a principal concern of the Cost Accounting Standards Board (CASB).[2]

The prevailing views of most accounting researchers vary from the position that the determination of how to allocate costs is essentially an arbitrary decision to the view that cost allocations are so highly firm-specific that no general rule can be determined.[3] For example, Dopuch [1977, p. 81] claims that "practically every cost accounting text stresses the arbitrary nature of many cost allocations...." Kaplan [1977, p. 52] goes further and asserts that "[m]any accountants and almost all economists argue that any allocation of joint costs

(including overhead and depreciation over time) is arbitrary and serves no use-

---

[1] Solomons [1968] describes the early development of cost allocations. In addition the following references are illustrative of the later literature: Clark [1923], Vatter [1945], Brummet [1957], Thomas [1969], Fekrat [1972], Hart [1973], Moriarity [1975], Hamlen, *et al.* [1977].

[2] Of the first six standards promulgated by the CASB since its inception in 1970, three dealt directly with cost allocations and the other three were indirectly related. See Joint Financial Management Improvement Program [1974].

[3] See Thomas [1971], Dopuch, Birnberg, Demski [1974, p. 32], and Horngren [1977, p. 508].

This research was supported by the Managerial Economics Research Center, Graduate School of Management, University of Rochester. The author gratefully acknowledges the suggestions of George Benston, Chandra Kanodia, Nicholas Dopuch, Robert Holthausen, Michael Jensen, Melvin Krasney, Richard Leftwich, William Meckling, Robert McCormick, Clifford Smith, Shyam Sunder, Thomas Russell, Ross Watts, Prem Prakash, and William R. Scott.

Jerold L. Zimmerman is Assistant Professor of Accounting and Information Systems, University of Rochester.

Manuscript received June, 1978.
Revision received September, 1978.
Accepted November, 1978.

ful purpose." Some researchers even take the rather novel position of not advocating cost allocations while they simultaneously introduce a new technique by which costs can be allocated.[4] Except for inventory valuation for financial and tax reporting, government contracting, rate-setting, cost documentation for possible antitrust suits (*e.g.*, the Robinson-Patman Act), or cost-plus pricing, the accounting literature generally recommends avoiding cost allocations.

The general thrust of the vast majority of the literature generically labeled "cost allocation" is predominantly normative. The literature is aimed at prescribing how firms should or should not allocate costs. Accounting researchers typically ignore the positive question[5] of why firms persist in allocating costs in spite of the continual admonitions by educators against doing so.

This paper addresses this positive question. It identifies some plausible reasons why rational, maximizing individuals would want to allocate costs. Other authors have noted possible benefits from the allocation of costs. Horngren [1977, p. 508], for example, concludes:

Whether to include uncontrollable or indirect costs is a difficult question, which must ultimately be resolved in terms of how the given alternatives *influence management behavior* in a particular organization. In one organization, allocation may be desirable because it induces the desired behavior. In another organization, the same allocation procedure may cause an opposite behavioral effect (emphasis in original text).

Kaplan [1977, pp. 52–53] also recognizes the schism between practice and theory:

A desire for cost allocations . . . must arise because of decentralization. . . . One approach that might prove interesting is to assume that central management has a simple, but not complete, representation of the pro-

duction and sales opportunities available for each of its divisions or product lines. . . . One would hope to be able to show that the solution arrived at by the local managers incorporating the allocated costs is superior to the solution which they would have obtained in the absence of any cost allocations.

Notice that both Horngren and Kaplan believe that cost allocations are linked to managerial behavior. That is, managers will behave differently if costs are allocated. This paper provides some concrete examples and sufficient conditions which support Horngren's and Kaplan's conjectures. Two cost-allocation situations and the associated costs and benefits are described: controlling a manager's discretionary spending on perquisites and rationing an internal service (*e.g.*, a payroll department). An analysis of these situations shows that cost allocations, managerial behavior, and the structure of the organization, including the incentives facing the managers, are inextricably linked. This suggests that in practice cost allocations are used, at least in part, to solve certain organizational control problems.

Furthermore, this paper demonstrates that situations exist in which cost allocations yield positive net benefits to the firm. Clearly, in such cases, cost allocations are not arbitrary decisions, and the myth should be dispelled that a firm's allocating costs for internal purposes is *prima facie* evidence of irrational behavior.

The paper consists of three sections.

---

[4] For example, Kaplan and Welam [1974, p. 478] state: "[T]his paper should not be construed as a defense for allocating traditional overhead costs to goods. Rather, it provides methods so that, if management *wants* to allocate traditional overhead costs to goods, the relative profitability of the goods is not distorted" (emphasis in original text).

[5] See Jensen [1976]. Such a positive approach has been applied to several financial accounting topics, see Benston [1975], Watts [1977], and Watts and Zimmerman [1978].

Section I is mainly pedagogic, showing how a firm's organization can be conceptualized as a complex of interacting, self-interested agents, and how Williamson's ideas [1964] of using a tax scheme to drive an agent to reduce discretionary spending carries over to cost allocations achieving similar ends in the firm. Section II analyzes cost allocations in a product costing situation, thereby illustrating the rationality of such practices. Section III concludes the study with a brief summary of the main arguments of the paper, and indicates directions for further research.

I. Cost Allocations and the Agency Problem

Whenever one person (the principal) engages another person (the agent) to perform some tasks on his behalf, an agency problem exists.[6] If all individuals are assumed to be resourceful, evaluative, maximizing men (or REMMs),[7] we would expect (as should the principal) that the agent will try to improve his welfare by engaging in activities which are not necessarily in the principal's best interest (e.g., shirking, on-the-job leisure, consumption of perquisites, theft).[8] The principal can install monitoring devices (e.g., security guards, auditors, time clocks, supervisory personnel) and incentive schemes (e.g., piece rates, bonuses, promotions) to discourage the agent from selecting actions which increase the agent's welfare at the principal's expense. Likewise, the agent can enter into contracts (bonding arrangements) which reduce the likelihood of his choosing actions which harm the principal, or which compensate the principal if those actions are selected. However, since bonding and monitoring are costly, we expect the agent, even given optimum levels of bonding and monitoring, to select some actions which reduce the principal's welfare. The dollar-value

equivalent of the reduction in the principal's welfare is defined as the "residual loss" by Jensen and Meckling [1976, p. 308] and comprises the third component of agency costs (the other two are monitoring and bonding costs).

The firm can be conceptualized as a series of agent-principal relationships. Jensen and Meckling [1976] analyze the agency problems which exist among the various classes of capital holders and management, where management is assumed for purposes of their analysis to be either a single individual or a homogeneous group. However, their theory applies as well to subordinate-superior managerial relationships within the firm. The divisional vice president, for example, is faced with an agency problem since the subordinate manager can divert resources by shirking and by expending firm resources to improve his working conditions (e.g., thick carpets, air conditioning, congenial employees) beyond the level that maximizes the superior's welfare. The principal (or superior) attempts to structure a system of incentives to induce the agent to choose actions which maximize the principal's welfare. Given the incentive and monitoring structure faced by the superior (i.e., each superior is also an agent) the superior's welfare usually depends in part on the agent's productivity, the agent's compensation, and the agency costs associated with the superior-subordinate relationship. The internal accounting system in general and cost allocations in particular affect these agency costs in the following manner.

Consider a firm using responsibility centers where superiors use the formal reporting system to assess their subordinates' performance, and this assessment

---

[6] Jensen and Meckling [1976].
[7] Meckling [1976].
[8] Alchian and Demsetz [1972] and Williamson [1964].

affects the subordinate's compensation.[9] Managers of these centers are given budgets and objectives. Their welfare depends on their ability to manage the resources at their discretion to achieve these objectives. The manager of the responsibility center derives utility not only from pecuniary compensation but also from non-pecuniary factors. The size and decor of the manager's office, the number of subordinates reporting to the manager, the number of hours he works, *etc.*, are typical non-pecuniary items which enter into the manager's utility function. The manager is usually given the discretion to decide how much to spend on these and the other input factors of production within his responsibility center. If the manager's utility function depends only on pecuniary compensation, which is a function of his performance to achieve the stated objectives, then the manager will select the level of each factor of production which maximizes his center's and hence the firm's (and his principal's) objective function. But if the manager's (the agent's) utility function also depends on non-pecuniary items, and if the manager cannot replicate these outside the firm, then he will substitute some of his center's output (or profits) for additional perquisites (*i.e.*, the agent will "overconsume" certain inputs).[10]

For example, suppose a one-period world and let the curve denoted ABCD in Figure 1 be the production possibility frontier between the reported responsibility center's profits and dollars of a given factor of production that the manager also values as a perquisite (*e.g.*, computer utilization). Holding all other factor inputs constant, firm profits rise as the first dollars are spent on this input (*i.e.*, marginal cost is less than the marginal value of the product), but subsequently total profits fall since the marginal cost exceeds the marginal value of the product. The center's profits are maximized by spending E^* on the perquisite. Since the manager is assumed to receive non-pecuniary income from this factor input (*i.e.*, his utility function has two arguments, center profits and this factor input), his indifference curves are represented by I, I', and I''. If there are perfect substitutes for perquisites outside the firm which the manager could purchase dollar for dollar, then the indifference curves would be straight lines (ignoring taxes). But as long as the manager cannot spend corporate resources on anything he wants or cannot "steal" resources, the indifference curves are convex towards the origin.[11] Such a manager will not select the center's profit maximizing level of perquisites (*e.g.*, E^*), but rather will trade off some profits for additional perquisites by selecting point C where $E > E^*$.

The exact shape of the indifference curves in Figure 1 depends on the trade-offs perceived by the individual manager. Impounded into the indifference curves is the incentive compensation plan (*i.e.*, the formula defining the manager's share of the division's profits). Furthermore, the analysis assumes there are no trading opportunities arising from the differential tax treatment of the corporation and manager. Mathematically, the utility function, U, has two arguments, division profits, π, and dollars of perquisites, E, and $U(\pi, E)$ displays a diminishing marginal rate of substitution between E and π as E increases.[12]

The principal has at his disposal numerous monitoring and incentive de-

[9] See Benston [1963] pertaining to this assumption.

[10] Williamson [1964].

[11] Jensen and Meckling [1976, p. 316].

[12] For the indifference curves in Figure 1 to be convex a sufficient condition in the two-good case (E and π) is that the marginal utility of each is positive but decreasing, as E increases and the cross-partial, $U'_{E\pi}$, is zero.

FIGURE 1
OVERHEAD AS A LUMP-SUM TAX TO REDUCE
DISCRETIONARY SPENDING

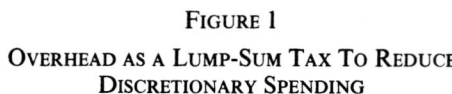

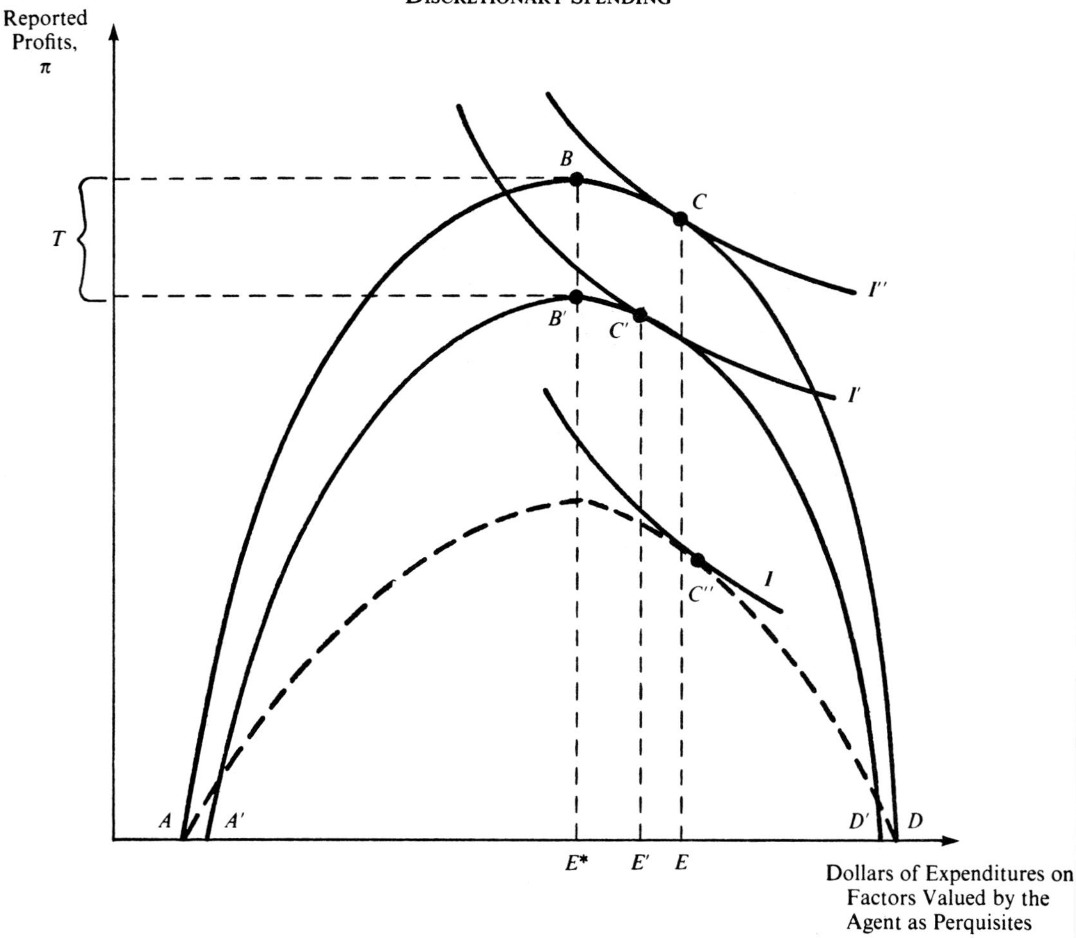

vices to control the agent's overconsumption of perquisites including direct observation, formal reporting schemes, competition among subordinates, *etc*. However, since all these monitoring devices are costly, they will only be used up to the point that marginal costs and benefits are equated. Although the principal can reduce the agent's overconsumption from what it would be in the absence of any monitoring, it is unlikely that all of the overconsumption will be eliminated.[13] Since the firm is already

calculating cost allocations for tax and external reporting purposes, the additional bookkeeping costs of reporting these allocations internally are minimal. The question is, can cost allocations further reduce the overconsumption of perquisites?

Williamson [1964, Ch. 4] established

[13] In particular, unless the monitoring cost functions are such that a corner solution results (*i.e.*, all perquisite overconsumption is eliminated), monitoring will proceed to where marginal costs and benefits are equated, which need not be where overconsumption is eliminated.

that under certain assumptions, an agent's discretionary spending on perquisites can be reduced by a lump-sum tax. Cost allocations can act as a lump-sum tax. Refer again to Figure 1. Assume that home office expenses are allocated to responsibility centers. In effect, the principal is "taxing" the responsibility center by allocating T of the principal's overhead to the responsibility center. The responsibility center manager faces a new opportunity set, $A'B'C'D'$. ($A'B'C'D'$ is a vertical downward shift in $ABCD$ by T.) The new optimum level of perquisites (from the agent's perspective) after the allocation of T is C', and the level of perquisites is reduced from E to E'.[14]

If the tax (or allocation scheme) is tied to profits, the analysis becomes more complex. Williamson [1964] demonstrates that a tax tied to profits leads to an indeterminate effect on the manager's discretionary behavior (*i.e.*, the direction of the effect depends on the substitution and income effects) and hence, additional assumptions must be made if cost allocations are to reduce perquisite consumption. The dashed curve $AC''D$ is generated if overhead is allocated based on profitability (*i.e.*, $AC''D$ is $(1-t)$ times $ABCD$ where $0 < t < 1$ is the overhead rate on center profits). In this example, the quantity of perquisites chosen actually increases.

Williamson's analysis provides a plausible reason as to why, in practice, noncontrollable costs are allocated to managers (*i.e.*, to reduce their consumption of perquisites). However, using Williamson's model in the cost-allocation context has some shortcomings. If the principal is using overhead as a tax to reduce perquisites, why not set the tax equal to total expected profits, thereby driving the agent to E^*? This is not done because, unless the agent is receiving wages and perquisites at least equal to his next best

employment alternative, he will leave the firm. Williamson's analysis ignores equilibrium in the labor markets (*i.e.*, $U = U^0$, where U^0 is the agent's opportunity utility). Also, it does not include alternative (costly) monitoring schemes and the tradeoff among the alternatives. Although Williamson's model has faults, it does raise an interesting, possible beneficial role of cost allocations.

Several testable implications are suggested by this agency cost model. First, cost allocations are more likely in situations when other monitoring costs are high, for example, where the agent and principal are geographically dispersed. Since the costs of direct observation by the principal are higher when the agent and principal are geographically separated, there is greater expected overconsumption of perquisites. Accordingly, cost allocations, to the extent that they reduce the overconsumption problem, are more likely to be used. Second, since a proportional tax (*e.g.*, an overhead scheme tied to profits) can cause the agent actually to increase his overconsumption of perquisites, we should observe fewer such schemes than of the lump-sum overhead allocation variety.

Cost allocations also can reduce the agency costs associated with perquisite consumption by inducing the subordinate to act as a monitor of his superior. By allocating the superior's expenditures to the subordinate, incentives are created for the subordinate to monitor these expenditures, since his welfare is now affected by his superior's overconsumption of perquisites. The subordinate is indirectly the agent of his superior's principal, and, through the allocation

---

[14] This result depends on the sign of the rate of change of the marginal rate of substitution between perquisites and profits. If perquisites are normal goods, then a lump-sum tax on profits results in a new tangency moving in the southwest direction.

process, bears some of the cost (in terms of his welfare) of the superior's expenditures. Since the subordinate is evaluated against other department managers on the basis of, in part, internal accounting statements employing allocated costs, the subordinate's future promotions are negatively affected by his superior's excessive consumption of perquisites.[15] As the superior's decisions start to impinge on the subordinates' welfare, the subordinates either try to convince their superior to eliminate the wealth-reducing expenditures or they go directly to their superior's principal.

The subordinate will by-pass his superior only if the expected benefits (*i.e.*, the increased chances of promotions by either disclosing his superior's indulgences or having larger discretionary profits) outweigh the costs which the subordinate will incur from such monitoring activities. Overhead allocations create incentives for the subordinate to monitor his superior's expenditures since his own welfare is affected. In addition, if the subordinate has access to local information and can specialize regarding his department's production process, then he may be the minimum-cost monitor of his superior.

The purpose of the preceding discussion is *not* to derive optimum allocation schemes or to present a complete formal model of the problem, but rather to suggest a possible benefit of allocating costs and to stimulate further work in the area. The Williamson model should be expanded to include income tax effects, incentive compensation plans, competition in the market for managers, *etc.*[16]

II. MANUFACTURING OVERHEAD COSTS

This section analyzes cost allocations in the typical product costing situation. But before discussing manufacturing overhead costs, some prefatory comments are in order.

A. Cost Allocations as Proxies for Externalities Arising from Decentralization

First, in this section, the overconsumption-of-perquisites problem (previously discussed) is ignored.

Second, to illustrate the central theme of this section, consider the following simplified example. The firm leases from the telephone company a WATS (Wide Area Telephone Service) line for $3800 per month, expecting to use the line 100 hours per month. This service allows the firm unlimited toll-free long distance calls within the United States. Although each individual long distance call is not billed by the phone company, only one call at a time can be placed. The $3800 is a "fixed" cost; the "variable" cost of a call is zero. Should the firm allocate this $3800 internally among the users?

One argument goes that the cost should not be allocated, for any charge will discourage use and since the marginal cost is zero, the value of the resource is not being maximized. However, the "correct" marginal cost (*i.e.*, the opportunity cost) of using the resource is not zero. It equals the cost imposed by forcing others who want to use the WATS line to either wait or place a regular toll call. Hence, the correct price to charge is the cost which the user imposes on others by tying up the scarce resource. But this cost varies between zero (if no one is delayed) to, at most, the cost of a regular toll call if a user cannot use the WATS line. This cost changes from instant to instant throughout the day. To measure it exactly is not easy,[17] requiring either a

---

[15] Even if his future promotion is not affected by the superior's excessive spending, he still has incentive to monitor his superior if the subordinate is forced to reduce his consumption of perquisites because his department is charged for his superior's consumption of perquisites via cost allocations.

[16] Here, the papers by Berhold [1971], Ross [1973, 1974], Jensen and Meckling [1976], Demski and Feltham [1978], and Kanodia [1978] should prove useful.

[17] See Dolan [1977].

real-time information system or a sophisticated statistical analysis of hourly arrival rates, distribution of calls, *etc.* Both of these solutions are costly. An alternative to either charging a zero price or charging a price based on an elaborate (costly) system is to charge $38 per hour (*i.e.*, a constant price based on the full allocated cost of the $3800 divided by the expected utilization of 100 hours). A side benefit of such a full-cost allocation is that information is generated regarding the value of the service. If more than $3800 in overhead is absorbed, the purchase of an additional WATS line should be investigated. If less than $3800 is absorbed, then discontinuance of the service might be warranted.

The major points of this example are:

1. there are costly-to-observe non-zero opportunity costs (or externalities) associated with resource utilization within the firm;
3. cost allocations can proxy these opportunity costs; and
3. cost allocations can be the optimum pricing scheme for internal resource utilization, given the costs of implementing and operating alternative systems.

These opportunity costs can take one of at least three forms:

1. One user's use of a resource causes other users to wait, thereby forcing them to incur delay costs. The sum of these delay costs is a measure of the opportunity cost of utilizing the resource. Batch-operated computer systems, maintenance shops, and typing pools are all examples where delay costs are generated.

2. Degradation of service (*i.e.*, turnaround time or quality) to other users can often result when a "fixed" resource is shared. Supervision is an example. As the number of workers being supervised rises, holding the number of supervisors fixed, each worker's average (and marginal) productivity is likely to fall. Hence, there is a degradation of service. A new supervisor is hired when the cost of the new supervisor is less than the value of the degradaion. This suggests that certain step-costs do not really follow steps. Although the *reported* cost of the resource follows a step function, as in Figure 2, the *total* cost, including the degradation in in service (the dashed line, ABC), which need not be linear, is not a step function. The dotted portions represent degradation costs in excess of the costs of an added supervisor. Degradation costs are often found in time-share computer systems.

3. As service is degraded, queues develop, users seek alternative solutions, often purchasing additional resources external to the firm. If the backlog at the central computer facility forces a user to incur delay costs, as soon as these delay costs exceed the user's cost of the next best alternative (*e.g.*, install a minicomputer or purchase time external to the firm), the rational user will make these substitutions. If economies of scale exist, the central computer facility will be expanded.

Thus, a given user, permanently expanding his utilization of a shared resource, is likely to impose costs on all other users which probably will result in a future scale expansion of the resource. Overhead allocations can act as proxies for these future expansions, delay costs, *etc.* This problem is similar to the common resource or fishing example in economics—where the individual users have incentives to overconsume the common resource.[18] Perhaps additional insights to cost allocations can be gleaned by applying these economic analyses

[18] See Gordon [1954] for the classic analysis of the common resource problem and Cheung [1970] for a more recent discussion of these externalities.

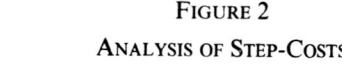

FIGURE 2

ANALYSIS OF STEP-COSTS

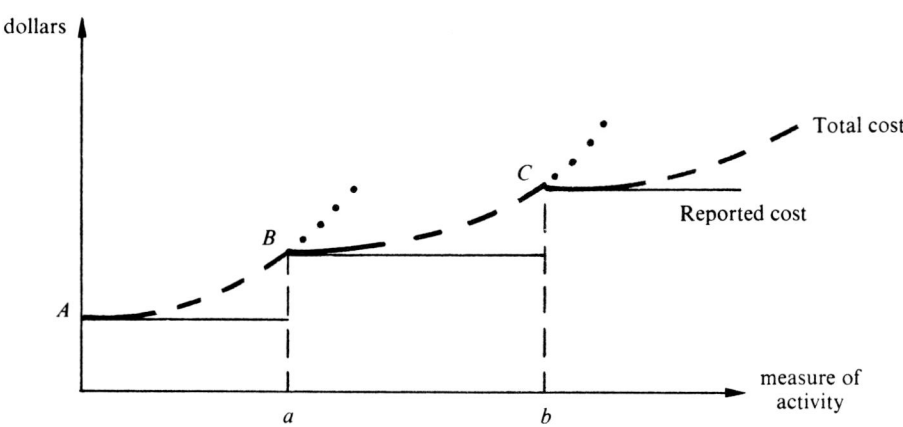

within the firm. We now turn to the manufacturing overhead example.

B. A Product Costing Situation

The typical textbook portrayal[19] presents a multi-department manufacturing concern with several service departments and production departments. Within each production department a job order (or process) costing system accumulates the prime costs—labor and materials— used in manufacturing the job (or product).[20] Each department's overhead costs as well as the department's share of the service departments' costs are allocated to each job by using direct labor hours as the allocation base. The department managers are evaluated as cost centers. This section explores how such an allocation scheme can increase the value of the firm.

Overhead application problems usually assume that the ith decentralized production manager chooses factor inputs, x_1^i (labor) and x_2^i (materials), to produce a single output $\bar{q}^i$ at minimum cost. If the two inputs cost P_1 and P_2 respectively, then the standard microeconomics solution is to equate the ratio of the factor prices to the rate of technical substitution

(i.e., the ratio of the marginal productivities of the inputs). In Figure 3, S is the point of tangency between the isocost line (having a slope $-P_1/P_2$) and the isoquant; denote the corresponding mix of inputs, $(\hat{x}_1^i, \hat{x}_2^i)$. If overhead is allocated based on x_1^i (e.g., direct labor hours) and since, by assumption, the manager minimizes total reported cost,[21] then the isocost curve facing the manager has slope $-P_1-R/P_2$ where R is the overhead rate per unit of x_1^i. The new point of tangency occurs at T, $(\hat{x}_1^i, \hat{x}_2^i)$, with the manager substituting materials for labor. By allocating overhead to the manager, the cost of x_1^i is raised, thus causing a different mix of inputs to be selected. The question becomes one of determining whether the correct marginal cost of x_1^i to manager i is P_1 or P_1+R; i.e., under what conditions does R serve as a useful

[19] For examples, see Chapters 4, 15 and 16 in Horngren [1977] or Chapter 13 in Dopuch, Birnberg, and Demski [1974].

[20] For purposes of this analysis, we will assume that standard costs are not used. The introduction of standard costs does not basically alter the results, but does substantially add to the complexity.

[21] A fundamental assumption in this section, which appears consistent with casual observation, is that managers attempt to minimize reported costs.

FIGURE 3

THE *i*th PRODUCTION MANAGER'S FACTOR
MIX DECISION

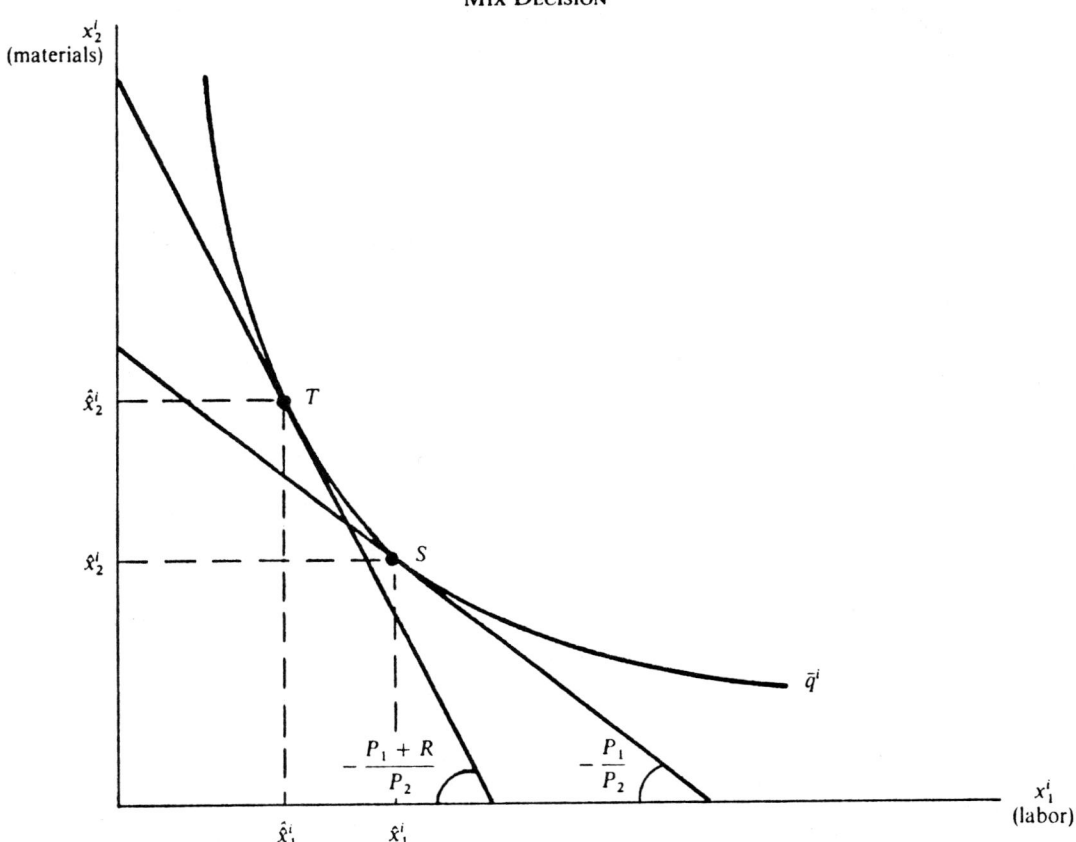

proxy for some of the previously discussed externalities?

To address this question, additional structure must be imposed on the problem in order to explore what conditions could lead to point T being preferred to point S (*i.e.*, which point produces larger firm-wide cashflows?).

C. Organizational Structure and Decentralization

The first question to be addressed is: Why does the *i*th production manager exist; that is, why is a decentralized organizational structure employed? The literature on decentralization[22] suggests that, in general, limited cognitive capacity

of the principal and the existence of investment alternatives with positive net present values leads the principal to delegate (or assign) decision-making responsibility to an agent: hence, decentralization. As outlined above, overhead allocations can serve a useful role, even in the situation where the agent's preferences are congruent with the principal's (*i.e.*, the maximization of shareholder wealth). The role of overhead allocations in this situation is to increase the reported factor cost (*e.g.*, direct labor) by an amount which approxi-

---

[22] Some representative papers include Alchian and Demsetz [1972], Benston [1963], and Hirshleifer [1964].

mates certain difficult-to-observe costs that arise from decentralization.

Assume a multi-product manufacturing firm, where each of the m products requires two inputs, say labor and materials, and a commonly shared input such as a personnel department, corporate treasurer, accounting department, maintenance department, purchasing, *etc.*[23] To simplify the analysis without loss of generality, assume the firm is a price taker in all markets.

The firm must select the input and output quantities. The decision regarding who actually makes the decisions (*i.e.,* the delegation of decision-making authority) is the organization design problem. Numerous alternatives exist, including: one individual makes all decisions; each of m individuals select the output quantity, q^i, and the mix of inputs to produce q^i; or one individual or department (*e.g.,* marketing) could select the output quantities while each of m manufacturing managers selects the mix of the two factor inputs to achieve the desired output for each of the m products. The choice of organization structure involves trading off the gains of specialization, communication costs, alternative uses of the peak coordinator's time, *etc.,* against the additional costs of having m agents (*e.g.,* the additional coordination costs, salaries, agency costs, *etc.*).

This is obviously a complicated decision problem, one that has not been solved analytically. But firms have developed organization structures: decisions do get made. For purposes of this paper, assume that the "optimum" organization structure (*i.e.,* that structure which maximizes firm value) has evolved over time and involves a vice president of manufacturing who oversees m production managers, each of whom is responsible for meeting the production quota for one of the m products set by marketing. Furthermore, the manufacturing vice president selects the scale of the common factor of production.[24]

Notice that the production quotas selected by marketing may not and probably do not maximize firm profits at each point in time since in the decentralized organization being assumed, marketing does not have complete (or up-to-date) information on all factor costs and production technologies. The foregone profits from marketing not setting quantities which maximize profits is just one component of the costs of decentralization. In this example, it is assumed that alternative organizational structures result in even larger costs.

The decision to organize the firm with a centralized service department which provides S units of service per unit of time, controlled by the manufacturing vice president, is also an organizational design problem. Each manufacturing manager could conceivably perform all service-related functions (*e.g.,* payroll, purchasing, hiring, security) at some cost. However, the existence of significant economies of scale can justify the centrali-

---

[23] Mathematically, the quantities of the m products are denoted by the vector $Q = (q^1, q^2, \cdots, q^m)$. The vector function, $Q = F(x_1^1, x_2^1, x_1^2, x_2^2, \cdots, x_1^m, x_2^m, S)$ describes the production function. Each output, q^i, requires two inputs, x_1^i and x_2^i as well as a commonly shared input S. x_1^i and x_2^i are purchased at constant prices, P_1 and P_2.

[24] The ith production manager specializes in selecting the optimum mix of factors for the ith product. That is, each production manager faces his own production function, $q^i = f^i(x_1^i, x_2^i, S)$, where S is determined by the vice president. Notice that such a decentralization of the manufacturing decision assumes that the firm's m-vector production function, $F(\cdot)$, is mathematically separable into m-scalar functions. It is unlikely that $F(\cdot)$ is mathematically separable in this fashion. Positive and negative externalities in $F(\cdot)$ are not captured by the m-scalar functions. For example, idle laborers in the ith product line who can be shifted to the jth line or crowding effects are formally captured in $F(\cdot)$ but are excluded in $f^i(\cdot)$, $i = 1, \cdots, m$. These externalities impose costs on the manufacturing vice president which presumably were considered in his decision to decentralize.

zation of certain service activities.[25] It is assumed that providing the service from a centralized pool is the least-cost alternative.

The size of the service department is determined in this example by the vice president of manufacturing. In the "short-run," the scale of the service department is fixed. But in the "long-run" the vice president can vary the scale to minimize total manufacturing costs (which is assumed equivalent to maximizing his utility).[26] For any given "fixed" scale of the service department, a given production manager who expands his utilization of the service department imposes costs on his peers by reducing the amount of the "fixed" service available for the other departments, thereby generating delay costs and costs of degraded service. This crowding effect is an externality created by the manufacturing vice president when he delegated the factor mix decisions to the m agents. Assuming that the size of the labor force affects the utilization of the shared resource, if a production manager expands his labor force, and the scale of the common resource is not instantly adjusted, the other $m-1$ managers are affected. Over time the vice president will adjust the scale of the service department by equating at the margin the costs of changing the scale to the costs of delay and degraded performance of the service department. Each of the m managers does not directly consume the common resource but rather indirectly affects it by his utilization of the prime inputs, (x_1^i, x_2^i). For example, the ith production manager does not consume payroll services directly, but rather indirectly by expanding his labor force which then places more demands on the payroll department.

Given the organization structure as described, the value of the firm is larger (as is the manufacturing vice president's utility) if each production manager takes account of the costs which he imposes on the other managers by consuming more of the fixed resource when choosing his mix of inputs. That is, instead of just looking at the reported costs of the factors, each manager should also consider all the costs he generates via delays, degradation and eventual expansion costs in the service departments.

For each manager to choose the principal's (vice president's) cost minimizing mix of inputs requires either a centralized solution or an iterative solution to the problem unless the "total" marginal cost of the service department (*i.e.*, the marginal cost, including all externalities) is constant. That is, if the "total" marginal cost of the common resource varies as managers change the level of their production (thereby varying the utilization of the common resource), then each manager cannot select the "total" cost minimizing input mix until all the other managers have selected their input mixes, because the "total" marginal cost of the common resource is not known.

As in the WATS telephone example, several estimates of the "total" marginal cost of the shared resource exist. At one extreme, the marginal cost can be assumed to be zero. At the other extreme is a periodic and expensive cost analysis of all the externalities. Between these two extremes is an allocated cost. The problem which the vice president faces is to choose the optimum estimator of "total" marginal cost. As in selecting among statistical estimators, the cost of one estimator over another must be traded

[25] See Hirshleifer [1964].

[26] In this example, the overconsumption of perquisites problem discussed in the preceding section is ignored. Specifically, each individual's utility function is assumed to depend only on pecuniary income, which in turn is a function of reported costs.

off against the cost of the difference in decisions that result from using one estimator or another. In particular, we are interested in determining a set of conditions under which point T (full-cost allocations) in Figure 3 strictly dominates point S (direct costing).

D. Full Costing versus Direct Costing

Under an overhead recharge scheme, the manufacturing vice president structures an incentive system whereby the production manager is compensated for minimizing *reported* costs, including overhead. When the reported cost of the shared resource is allocated to the production managers on the basis of their utilization of one of their factors of production, each manager will reduce his use of that factor as depicted in Figure 3. This system estimates the "total" marginal cost of the shared resource, using the average cost of the shared resource and produces a minimum "total" cost (as opposed to minimum *reported* cost) only if the allocated cost happens to equal the "total" marginal cost of the shared resource.

The crucial question is: under what conditions does applying an overhead charge to the production manager maximize the value of the firm? If overhead is not allocated, then each manager presumably will consider only the factor prices (and the isoquant) in his production decisions. The vice president's decision to allocate overhead affects the reported costs facing the managers. Do conditions exist such that cost allocations strictly dominate no allocations? The graphical analysis in Figure 4 is used to examine these conditions.

The step function in Figure 4 represents the reported cost of the service department and in reality can take any shape—step-fixed (as drawn), step-variable (see Horngren [1977, p. 783]), *etc.* The curve, $K(X_1)$, denoted *dabc* represents the "total" cost of the service departments (*i.e.*, the sum of the reported costs and any incremental crowding externalities). The total cost of the service department, $K(X_1)$, is a function of all the managers' utilization of the shared resource, which in this example depends on their total direct labor,

$$X_1 = \sum_{i=1}^{m} x_1^i.$$

The step size (which is controlled by the vice president and need not be constant) is determined when the "total" costs just equal the reported costs. That is, if collectively all the managers are incurring opportunity costs slightly greater than the cost of expanding the service department, then it is in everyone's best interest to expand the service department. Hence, *dabc* is an upper bound to the reported costs.

As alternative way of viewing the relationship between the reported cost and "total" cost curves is as follows. The long-run reported cost of the service department is the step function. Over time, the scale of the service is adjusted whenever the cost of changing the scale is less than the cost of degraded service. If the scale can be varied instantly and in sufficiently small increments, then the reported costs and "total" cost curves in Figure 4 would be identical. But if these conditions do not hold, then the two curves are different.

At the beginning of each accounting period, the vice president estimates the overhead rate R by estimating the expected quantity of direct labor, X_1, and the expected reported cost of S.[27,28]

[27] Normal (expected) volume is the total expected demand for the first factor (*e.g.*, direct labor hours). In this example, the estimated quantity of X_1 and expected reported service costs are assumed to be unbiased forecasts of the actual usage of X_1 and actual reported costs. That is, all overhead variances are expected to be zero.

[28] At the preliminary stage of this analysis, the important question of the choice of allocation basis is

FIGURE 4

THE LONG-RUN RELATIONSHIP BETWEEN THE OVERHEAD ALLOCATION FUNCTION,
OC, AND THE "TOTAL" COSTS OF A SERVICE DEPARTMENT, $K(X_1)$

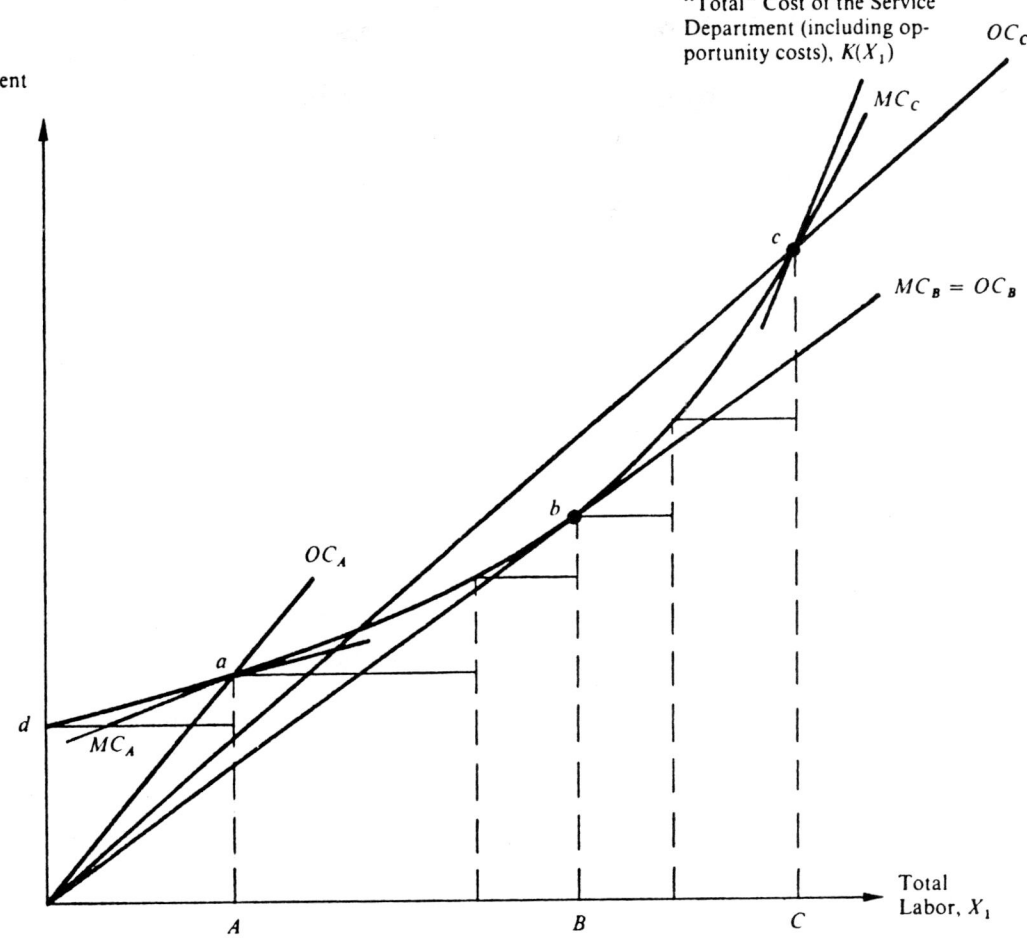

Slope of MC_{X_1} = "Total marginal cost of the service department when total labor input is X_1
Slope of OC_{X_1} = Reported overhead cost per unit of labor when normal volume is X_1
                  = Reported cost at X_1 divided by X_1
                  = R

The ratio of these estimates yields the overhead rate, R. Graphically, if the expected quantity of X_1 (normal volume) by chance happens to be estimated at $X_1 = B$ and the estimated cost is $K(B)$ (reported and total costs coincide), then the overhead rate R is $K(B)/B$. Point B, given the shape of K as drawn, is the only point where marginal cost (the slope at

ignored. To keep this analysis simple, degradation of service is asserted to depend only on the amount of direct labor, X_1. Whether to use direct labor or materials or some other basis to allocate the cost of the shared resource, depends on the sensitivity of the externality to the basis of allocation. We observe allocation bases being selected because of their causality with respect to the costs being allocated. [Solomons, 1968, p. 29]. The additional complexity that arises when a shared factor varies with two or more inputs must await future analysis.

B) and the average reported cost (the slope of the overhead cost function which equals R) coincide. If X_1 is expected to be at any other point, then the overhead allocation scheme does *not* coincide with "total" marginal costs and the agent's (reported) cost-minimizing mix of inputs does not minimize the principal's costs. If the expected quantity of X_1 does not equal B, then we are faced with a theory of second best: does an internal reporting system which employs an overhead recharge outperform one without recharges (*i.e.*, direct costing) in terms of maximizing the value of the firm?[29] There are two cases to consider:

Case 1. The expected quantity of direct labor, X_1, is greater than B (Figure 4) for example, point C. Since the "total" marginal cost, in this case MC_c, is greater than the average reported cost, OC_c, direct labor is over-utilized by each manager. The total price ($P_1 + R$) being charged for labor by the accounting system is too low. But, since R is greater than zero, the over-utilization of x_1^i is still not as great as it would be if overhead is not allocated (*i.e.*, $R=0$). Under direct costing, the reported incremental cost of the service generated by an increment to x_1^i is zero ($R=0$), but the manager is aware of the benefits, and overconsumes direct labor. Under case 1, the overhead scheme unambiguously dominates the no-overhead (*e.g.*, direct costing) scheme. That is, point T in Figure 3 strictly dominates point S.[30]

Case 2. Expected volume is below point B, for example, $X_1 = A$. Direct labor will be under-utilized by all departments if overhead is allocated. The price which each manager is being charged by the accounting system for the service per unit of x_1^i is greater than its "total" marginal cost. In this case the overhead recharge does not unambiguously dominate direct costing. In certain situations,

it may be better not to charge the production manager for his incremental cost of the service, if by charging him, direct labor is reduced so drastically that the value of the firm falls from his slight over-utilization to a large under-utilization of x_1^i.

Even though an overhead allocation system does not strictly dominate no allocations, it can do so under certain situations (*e.g.*, $X_1 \geq B$ in Figure 4). Furthermore, firms can devise alternative allocation techniques to the average cost procedure implicit in full-absorption costing. For example, instead of basing the overhead rate on the total reported costs of the service department, if only some portion of the resource's cost (*e.g.*, variable costs) is used, then, under-utilization of direct labor is reduced. These alternative schemes result in lower overhead rates than the one computed by using full-absorption costing, thereby reducing the over-utilization of x_1^i (which occurs if overhead is not allocated). Yet, direct labor is not so under-utilized as to reduce the value of the firm below what it would have been if allocations were not performed. Besides devising hybrid overhead formulas, the vice president can place constraints on the minimum amount of direct labor which the manager must hire to prevent under-utilization or can place a limit on the amount of x_2^i (*e.g.*, materials or capital) which each manager can substitute for labor.

---

[29] Since the firm is already calculating the cost allocations for external reporting and taxes, this analysis assumes that the incremental costs of reporting these allocations internally are minimal.

[30] Under direct costing, the variable overhead component of the service department is charged to the users. But in this example with step-fixed reported costs, variable overhead is zero.. Furthermore, even if a step-variable reported cost curve was assumed, the variable overhead component, by definition, is always less than or equal to "total" marginal costs since, by assumption, the variable overhead component does not measure all the opportunity costs or crowding externalities.

This example demonstrates that manufacturing overhead allocations can increase the value of the decentralized firm. This situation arises when the firm has incomplete or imperfect information regarding the "true" shadow prices of all factors of production; in this case the true shadow price of direct labor includes the externality created by managers sharing a common resource. If top management has complete and perfect knowledge of all the cost functions, exact shadow prices could be calculated, overhead approximations become unnecessary, but then all decisions could be made centrally. Complete information is usually not the case and is an important reason for decentralization.[31]

In addition, this model suggests the following testable implications: we expect to find overhead allocations more prevalent in situations where average service costs (including all externalties) are increasing with increases in direct labor than in situations where average costs are decreasing. In these latter situations, we expect to find fewer full-cost systems, more hybrid overhead systems (*i.e.*, less than full cost overhead rates) and a greater frequency of centrally administered constraints imposed on the operating managers.

III. SUMMARY AND CONCLUSIONS

This paper examines the reasons why firms allocate costs. Much of the past literature dwells on the erroneous decisions resulting from managers basing their decisions on data containing cost allocations. Yet, few researchers have sought to explain why cost allocations are so prevalent in practice. Horngren [1977, p. 508] and Kaplan [1977, pp. 52–53] are two notable exceptions. They suggest that cost allocations are desirable mechanisms for motivating and controlling managers. Their suppositions are

extended and amplified by this paper.

The important point emerging from this analysis is that cost allocations appear to proxy for certain hard-to-observe costs that arise when decision-making responsibilities are assigned to and vested in various individuals (*i.e.*, decentralized) within the firm. That is, when the rights to make certain decisions are assigned among the firm's managers, control and coordination problems arise. Cost allocations, when coupled with incentive schemes that induce the managers to pay attention to reported costs, help mitigate some of these control and coordination problems.

Two specific situations are discussed: (1) controlling the agent's overconsumption of perquisites and (2) proxying the costs of degraded service, delay, and future expansion that arise when a common resource is shared by several decision makers.

It is unlikely that cost allocations are "perfect" in the sense that they eliminate all the agent's overconsumption of perquisites or that allocated costs measure "exactly" all the costs arising from decentralization. However, as long as the benefits from cost allocations (*e.g.*, reduced perquisite consumption or less delay costs) exceed the costs of cost allocations (*e.g.*, the additional book-keeping costs and the costs of erroneous decisions), then we expect rational individuals to employ allocation techniques. Likewise, if we observe voluntary, widespread, and persistent use of an accounting technique, it is likely that the technique is yielding benefits that exceed its costs.

Ultimately, this positive research will produce new normative allocation procedures—techniques that either increase

---

[31] All cost functions could be known, but still a decentralized structure chosen if the costs of communication were sufficiently high.

the benefits or decrease the costs, or both. However, before new normative procedures can be devised, much more positive analysis, only begun in this paper, is required.

The major obstacle to developing this positive analysis is in gaining access to data in order to test theories, which will generate new insights and produce richer theories, thereby better assessing the empirical magnitudes of the various costs and benefits. Even though the empirical tests will likely be based on a single firm or an industry, the results will still be generalizable. If the links between organizational structure, incentive schemes, agency costs, and cost allocations are correctly modeled, the empirical tests will control for these other variables and, the theory can be generalized to other organizational structures and incentive schemes.

Out of such a positive analysis, a better understanding of the role of cost allocations in solving various organizational problems, such as the agency and decentralization problems discussed in this paper, is likely to emerge. Then, more realistic normative procedures which descriptively better model the underlying phenomena can be constructed, thereby leading to improved allocation schemes.

REFERENCES

Alchian, A. A. and H. Demsetz, "Production, Information Costs, and Economic Organization," *American Economic Review* (December 1972), pp. 777–795.

Benston, G. J., "The Role of the Firm's Accounting System for Motivation," THE ACCOUNTING REVIEW (April 1963), pp. 347–354.

Benston, G. J., "Accountants' Integrity and Financial Reporting," *Financial Executive* (August 1975), pp. 10–14.

Berhold, M., "A Theory of Linear Profit Sharing Incentives," *Quarterly Journal of Economics* (August 1971), pp. 460–482.

Brummet, R. L., *Overhead Costing* (Ann Arbor: University of Michigan Press, 1957).

Cheung, S. N. S., "The Structure of a Contract and the Theory of a Non-Exclusive Resource," *Journal of Law and Economics* (April 1970), pp. 49–70.

Clark, J. M., *Studies in the Economics of Overhead Costs* (University of Chicago Press, 1923).

Demski, J. and G. Feltham, "Economic Incentives in Budgetary Control Systems," THE ACCOUNTING REVIEW (April 1978), pp. 336–359.

Dolan, R. J., "Incentive Mechanisms for Priority Queuing Problems," unpublished manuscript, University of Chicago (September 1977).

Dopuch, N., "Discussion of 'Application of Quantitative Models in Managerial Accounting,'" in *Management Accounting—State of the Art* (University of Wisconsin Press, January 25, 1977), pp. 74–83.

Dopuch N., J. Birnberg, and J. Demski, *Cost Accounting* (Harcourt Brace Jovanovich, Inc., 1974).

Fekrat, M. A., "The Conceptual Foundations of Absorption Costing," THE ACCOUNTING REVIEW (April 1972), pp. 351–355.

Gordon, H. S., "The Economic Theory of a Common Property Resource: The Fishery," *Journal of Political Economy* (April 1954), pp. 124–142.

Hamlen, S. S., W. A. Hamlen, and J. T. Tschirhart, "The Use of Core Theory in Evaluating Joint Cost Allocation Schemes," THE ACCOUNTING REVIEW (July 1977), pp. 616–627.

Hart, H., *Overhead Costs: Analysis and Control* (Heinemann, Ltd., 1973).

Hirshleiter, J., "Internal Pricing and Decentralized Decisions," in Bonini, Jaedicke, and Wagner (Eds.) *Management Controls: New Directions in Basic Research* (McGraw-Hill, Inc., 1964), pp. 27–37.

Horngren, C., *Cost Accounting: A Managerial Emphasis*, Fourth Edition (Prentice-Hall, Inc., 1977).

Jensen, M. C., "Reflections on the State of Accounting Research and the Regulation of Accounting," presented at the Price Waterhouse Lectures in Accounting, Stanford University, May 21, 1976.

Jensen, M. C. and W. H. Meckling, "Theory of the Firm: Managerial Behavior, Agency Costs and Owner-ship Structure," *Journal of Financial Economics* (October 1976), pp. 305–360.

Joint Financial Management Improvement Program, *Financial Management Functions in the Federal Government*, U.S. General Accounting Office, (September 1974).

Kanodia, C., "Effects of Shareholder Information on Corporate Decisions and Capital Market Equi-librium," unpublished manuscript, University of Chicago (April 1978).

Kaplan, R., "Application of Quantitative Models in Managerial Accounting: A State of the Art Survey," in *Management Accounting—State of the Art* (University of Wisconsin Press, January 25, 1977), pp. 30–71.

Kaplan, R. and U. P. Welam, "Overhead Allocation with Imperfect Markets and Non-Linear Tech-nology," THE ACCOUNTING REVIEW (July 1974), pp. 477–484.

Mautz, R., *Financial Reporting by Diversified Companies* (Financial Executives Research Foundation, 1968).

Meckling, W. H., "Values and the Choice of the Model of the Individual in Social Sciences," *Revue Suisse d'Economie Politique et de Statisque*, (December 1976).

Moriarity, S., "Another Approach to Allocating Joint Costs," THE ACCOUNTING REVIEW (October 1975), pp. 791–795.

Ross, S. A., "The Economic Theory of Agency: The Principal's Problem," *American Economic Review* (May 1973), pp. 134–139.

Ross, S. A., "The Economic Theory of Agency and the Principle of Similarity," in M. D. Balch, et al. (Eds.) *Essays on Economic Behavior Under Uncertainty* (North-Holland, 1974).

Solomons, D., "The Historical Development of Costing," in David Solomons (Ed.) *Studies in Cost Analysis*, Second Edition (Sweet & Maxwell, 1968), pp. 3–49.

Thomas, A., "The Allocation Problem in Financial Accounting Theory," *Studies in Accounting Research, Number 3* (American Accounting Association, 1969).

Thomas, A., "Useful Arbitrary Allocations," THE ACCOUNTING REVIEW (July 1971), pp. 472–479.

Vatter, W. J., "Limitations of Overhead Allocation," THE ACCOUNTING REVIEW (April 1945) in W. E. Thomas (Ed.) *Readings in Cost Accounting, Budgeting and Control* Second Edition (South-Western, 1960), pp. 239–258.

Watts, R. L., "Corporate Financial Statements, A Product of the Market and Political Processes," *Australian Journal of Management* (April 1977), pp. 53–75.

Watts, R. L. and J. L. Zimmerman, "Towards a Positive Theory of the Determination of Accounting Standards," THE ACCOUNTING REVIEW (January 1978), pp. 112–134.

Williamson, O., *The Economics of Discretionary Behavior: Managerial Objectives in a Theory of the Firm* (Prentice-Hall, Inc., 1964).

Equity Valuation and Corporate Control

Linda Elizabeth DeAngelo
University of Michigan

ABSTRACT: The proliferation of control contests for large public corporations at 50% + premiums above market illustrates the wide divergence between open-market stock prices and equity exchange values. This paper considers equity valuation in corporate control transactions—e.g., management buyouts and hostile takeovers—that engender potentially severe manager-stockholder conflicts. These conflicts generate a demand for independent assessments of equity values by investment bankers who specialize in these appraisals. The paper provides evidence from (1) a large sample of fairness opinions on management buyouts, and (2) a small sample of investment bankers' working papers which indicates that investment bankers' valuation techniques make extensive use of accounting data. This demand for accounting information in equity valuation is distinct from that previously recognized in the capital markets or contracting literatures.

EQUITY exchange values in corporate control transactions—e.g., mergers, tender offers, management buyouts, leveraged recapitalizations—routinely deviate substantially from open-market stock prices. For example, management buyouts of exchange-listed corporations typically occur at a 50% + premium above the pre-offer stock price (DeAngelo et al. 1984), as do interfirm tender offers (Comment and Jarrell 1987). Moreover, multiple bids for the same firm often differ substantially from each other, and open-market stock prices do not at each moment equal the highest current (or eventual winning) bid (Bradley 1980).

Helpful comments were received from Vic Bernard, Fischer Black, Jim Brickley, Paul Danos, Harry DeAngelo, Cliff Holderness, Gene Imhoff, Bill Kinney, Bob Lipe, Susan Moyer, Eric Noreen, Pat O'Brien, Gita Rao, Ed Rice, Jay Ritter, Jim Sington, René Stulz, Jake Thomas, Ross Watts, Eric Wruck, Karen Wruck, Jerry Zimmerman, two anonymous referees, and workshop participants at Harvard, Iowa, Michigan, Minnesota, Ohio State, and Wisconsin. Financial support for this project was provided by the Michigan Business School, the Arthur Young Foundation, the Managerial Economics Research Center at the University of Rochester, and the John M. Olin Foundation.

Manuscript received September 1987.
Revisions received May 1988, November 1988, and July 1989.
Accepted September 1989.

THE ACCOUNTING REVIEW
Vol. 65, No. 1
January 1990
pp. 93–112

How are equity exchange values determined? The answer is important because these values divide the gains from a change in corporate ownership between stockholders and other corporate claimants, hence they affect the feasibility of control transactions. The answer is empirically important, given the proliferation of takeovers of large public corporations at 50% + premiums above market. Obviously, a target corporation's pre-offer stock price is an inadequate measure of its acquisition value. Perhaps less obviously, its post-offer stock price is also inadequate, given uncertainty about the outcome of the current bid, the price the current bidder is ultimately willing to pay, and the existence of other bidders and their possible offer terms. In short, capital market efficiency does not ensure that market prices perfectly reveal equity values in *each* feasible alternative use, and to each feasible alternative user.

The inability to rely on anonymous capital markets to value a given control transaction generates disagreement among stockholders over the exchange values of their claims. Since stockholders' cooperation is required to effect these transactions, such disagreement can potentially cause the failure of transactions that are overall value-increasing. This difficulty is exacerbated because equity exchange values can be negatively affected by the actions of managers who have (1) inside information about the value of target shares in alternative uses, and (2) interests that conflict with those of their stockholder constituents. Manager-stockholder conflicts are especially severe in management buyouts and in hostile takeover attempts that offer target stockholders a substantial premium, while potentially costing managers their jobs.

In this paper it is argued that managerial conflicts of interest in corporate control transactions generate a demand for an independent valuation of shares. The evidence presented indicates that the terms of management buyouts are evaluated by investment bankers whose valuation techniques predominantly rely on accounting information. For example, discounted cash flow techniques employed in practice use historical accounting relations to estimate future cash flows. By imposing impartial, external constraints on equity exchange values, an independent valuation helps ensure these values are perceived as "fair" by the outside stockholders whose cooperation is required to effect a control transaction.[1] This process facilitates transactions that increase overall firm value, yet that also generate manager-stockholder conflicts of interest.

Section I develops the demand for an independent valuation of shares. Section II describes the valuation process and generally accepted valuation techniques. Section III reports evidence from a large sample of management buyouts that investment bankers unanimously cite accounting information as influencing their evaluations of the terms of these transactions. Section IV reports evidence from detailed case studies of a small sample of investment bankers' working papers, recently required to be filed with the SEC for management buyouts, that virtually all valuation techniques used by investment bankers rely on accounting information. Section V provides a brief summary.

---

[1] It is impossible to ascertain whether the primary motivation of participants in this valuation process is to estimate equity values, or simply to justify selected values to outside stockholders and the courts. In either case, accounting information affects equity values to the extent that it defines the feasible range of "fair" values. These issues are discussed in Section II.

I. The Demand for an Independent Valuation of Shares

Insider-managers of corporations with equity claims in place have some ability to take actions that reduce the value of outsiders' claims (Jensen and Meckling 1976). One such action is to issue or redeem equity at other than "intrinsic" value, given managers' superior information. Competitive capital markets imperfectly protect outside stockholders from these welfare-reducing transactions when information is costly (Myers and Majluf 1984). Stock prices reflect the *expected* value of managers' inside information, conditional on the proposed transaction. While expectations should be realized on average, the shares of a *given* firm will trade at other than intrinsic value. Thus, issuing and redeeming shares at market prices does not ensure "fair" treatment of all stockholders or resolve all intra-stockholder conflicts over share values.[2]

When a corporation originally sells shares to outsiders, the offer price will reflect investors' perceptions of managers' ability to effect welfare-reducing equity transactions. Hence, managers have incentives to contractually pre-commit to limit their discretion over the terms of these transactions. Such responses include corporate charter provisions that pre-specify permissible transactions, e.g., anti-greenmail provisions and preemptive rights that provide proportionate access to future equity issuances.[3] They also include valuation formulas for equity exchange terms, e.g., common stock redemption rights (so-called "poison pill" securities), conversion features for convertible preferred stock and debt, and fair price provisions that stipulate a minimum offer price in mergers with a substantial stockholder (Smith 1978).

Not all future circumstances are foreseeable, however, nor are all potential manager-stockholder conflicts amenable to resolution via simple *ex ante* numerical sharing rules. Moreover, the technology for resolving intra-claimant conflicts can change over time, such as via changes in the legal system. Unforeseen financial innovations—including a wide variety of corporate control transactions—can expand the set of feasible equity transactions. For example, hostile cash tender offers were first attempted in the 1960s. Management buyouts were a rare occurrence until the late 1970s, and only recently have financing innovations such as "junk" bonds made these buyouts feasible for the largest corporations. The first leveraged recapitalization was proposed in the 1980s.

Table 1 describes the major corporate control transactions and the managerial conflicts they generate. These conflicts are likely to be relatively mild in friendly acquisitions, especially those that involve multiple bidders with equal access to information about the target firm.[4] At the other end of the spectrum are management buyouts and hostile takeovers, in which managerial conflicts are

---

[2] For open-market trades among anonymous individuals, a well-functioning capital market harmonizes the interests of all stockholders (H. DeAngelo 1981). Stockholder unanimity fails in the current case because managers with monopolistic access to firm-specific information can influence the terms of subsequent equity issuances and redemptions.

[3] Proportionate stock issuances and redemptions mitigate intra-stockholder conflicts by providing all stockholders with equal or "fair" access to the offer.

[4] A competitive auction is *not* sufficient to guarantee that target stockholders receive "fair" value for shares, however, except in the unlikely case that managers can (and do) costlessly reveal and credibly verify all relevant inside information to all potentially relevant bidders.

Table 1
Corporate Control Transactions and
Managerial Conflicts of Interest

Arm's Length Acquisitions:

1. *Friendly merger or tender offer* in which target management negotiates the offer terms with one or more bidders. Managers have incentives to favor bidders that promise them the most lucrative future employment opportunities. Mergers require voting approval of target stockholders, convey judicial appraisal rights, and target managers virtually always provide an investment banker's fairness opinion. Tender offers are ratified by target stockholders' tendering decisions.

2. *Hostile tender offer* in which target management opposes the takeover attempt. Managers have incentives to resist external bids that they believe will cost them their jobs, at the loss of a premium payment to their stockholders. Managerial takeover resistance is virtually always justified by an investment banker's opinion that the offer price is inadequate.

Non-Arm's Length Acquisitions and Partial Acquisitions:

1. *Parent-subsidiary acquisition* in which parent management purchases the public (often, the minority) shares of a partially-owned subsidiary. Parent managers have incentives to propose offer terms that favor parent over subsidiary stockholders. These acquisitions generally require subsidiary stockholder approval, convey judicial appraisal rights, and parent managers virtually always provide an investment banker's opinion that the terms are fair to subsidiary stockholders. These acquisitions require extensive disclosure under SEC Rule 13e-3.

2. *Management or leveraged buyout* in which managers (perhaps with the help of third party equity investors) purchase all shares held by outsiders. As purchasers, managers have incentives to minimize the price paid, and these incentives conflict with their fiduciary duty to obtain the best terms for outside stockholders. The disclosure and procedural requirements are the same as for parent-subsidiary acquisitions.

3. *Leveraged recapitalization* in which managers cause the corporation to pay out substantial cash to stockholders that is financed with new borrowing. Managers have incentives to "front-end" load the cash portion of these offers to compete with a hostile bid. In general, recapitalizations require stockholder approval and are accompanied by an investment banker's fairness opinion.

potentially severe. In management buyouts, managers have a fiduciary duty to negotiate the best possible terms for stockholders, offset by incentives as purchasers to pay the lowest possible price. Moreover, managers have some ability to suppress favorable inside information in order to purchase shares at less than "fair" value.[5] Similar conflicts of interest characterize acquisitions of a subsidiary's publicly-traded stock by a parent corporation.

In non-arm's length acquisitions, the target's post-offer stock price reflects market expectations about insiders' valuations, but it does not fully *reveal* those valuations to outside stockholders. Critically, stock prices understate "fair" value because they reflect *all* publicly-available information, *including* managers' perceived ability to buy shares at "unfair" terms and to otherwise

---

[5] As a theoretical matter, there is no unique "fair" value for shares when a control transaction generates gains whose realization requires the cooperation of more than one claimant group—in this case, managers and outside stockholders. Rather, the manager-stockholder relation is a bilateral monopoly, for which no unique sharing rule for joint gains exists.

reduce outside stockholder welfare.[6] Similar difficulties plague a target's stock price during a hostile takeover attempt. Outside stockholders cannot rely on stock prices to indicate definitively whether they should tender because market prices will not fully reveal managers' inside valuation of shares, either as an independent entity or if auctioned to the highest bidder.

Even absent these information problems, the target's post-offer stock price will not fully reveal the market's evaluation of its acquisition value, given uncertainty about the success of the current bid, the price the current bidder is ultimately willing to pay, and the existence of other bidders and their offer terms. To see this latter difficulty, consider the post-offer market price as a probability-weighted average of the values expected to accrue to target stockholders under different outcomes:

$$P_M = \pi_A P_A + (1 - \pi_A) P_S \qquad (1)$$

where:

$P_M =$ the open-market stock price after an offer is announced, but before it expires,

$\pi_A =$ the market-assessed probability the target will ultimately be acquired (by the current or another bidder),

$P_A =$ the market's expectation of the ultimate acquisition price conditional on the current bid,[7] and

$P_S =$ the post-offer expiration market price expected to obtain if the target remains independent, which capitalizes target stockholders' expected values under all other perceived outcomes.

Equation (1) reveals that, while the target's post-offer stock price *incorporates* the market's assessment of its ultimate acquisition value, P_A, it does not perfectly *reveal* that value to outsiders, who observe only P_M. Individuals cannot costlessly invert market prices, which are weighted averages of conditional expected values, to obtain *one* of the priced components. Such inversion requires knowledge of the market-assessed probabilities and stockholder values under *all* other priced outcomes. The very characteristic that makes open-market stock prices good trading prices (they incorporate all publicly-available information) makes them inadequate measures of acquisition values, i.e., makes them insufficient to themselves *determine* the terms at which corporate control will (or should) be exchanged.

The failure of market prices to perfectly reveal acquisition values implies that potential bidders must themselves formulate an offer price for shares—they cannot rely on the capital market to costlessly provide it. Similarly, outside

---

[6] Lev (1988) discusses how investors' perceptions of the fairness of open-market trading prices determine their willingness to trade shares. The current paper argues that their perceptions of the fairness of future equity issuance and redemption terms determine their willingness to invest equity capital in public corporations. Both effects are likely to be important determinants of economically relevant variables, such as open-market stock prices, equity exchange values, and bid-ask spreads.

[7] Equation (1) is a simplification, since P_A is itself a weighted average of the target's acquisition value to various bidders, each of which may put target assets to different uses or effect different synergistic combinations of target and bidder assets.

stockholders and the board of directors must incur resource costs to evaluate that price—a service the market does not costlessly provide.[8] In other words, the parties to a control transaction cannot infer the relevant P_A (which can differ according to attributes of the bidder, as well as the target firm) from the target's open-market stock price. The function of the equity valuation process is to generate an independent estimate of the relevant value.

This paper emphasizes the demand for accounting information in the process through which acquisition values are determined. It is not directly concerned with the effect of accounting information on open-market stock prices as in capital markets research (e.g., Beaver 1973, 1981; Lev 1988). Because stock prices aggregate *all* public information, accounting data can have a relatively small marginal impact on open-market prices. In contrast, acquisition values are neither directly observable nor invertible from open-market stock prices, so that accounting data can be relatively important in determining acquisition values. The role for accounting information discussed here is conceptually distinct from its role in determining open-market stock prices.[9]

II. The Equity Valuation Process

Managers of firms engaged in a wide variety of control transactions hire an independent investment banker to evaluate the fairness of the transaction to the firm's outside stockholders. An investment banker's fairness opinion is virtually always provided to target stockholders in arm's length and non-arm's length mergers, and in leveraged recapitalizations. Managers who resist a hostile bid typically rely on an investment banker's opinion that the offer terms are inadequate. In short, corporate control transactions motivate a target firm's internal governance system to provide an independent valuation of shares. The extent to which this valuation process (1) is itself fair, and (2) generates fair equity values, is subject to review by the judicial system and the SEC.[10]

Evaluating the fairness of a corporate control transaction is complex, since the gains from these transactions require the cooperation of multiple groups of corporate claimants. Akin to the usual analysis of bilateral monopoly, there is *no* one theoretically correct way to divide joint gains in these cases, hence no one "fair" price for shares. Moreover, while managers and investment bankers may claim that a given offer price represents fair value, their actual beliefs are not observable. One possibility is that these parties believe what they claim. Another

---

[8] The shares originally sold to outsiders should be priced to reflect the expected resource costs of evaluating future control transactions. Because such price protection is *sunk* in future periods, it does not alter managers' *future* incentives to engage in welfare-reducing transactions. Hence, outsiders face ongoing evaluation costs, which managers have incentives to reduce by providing a governance process that helps ensure that outsiders receive fair value in corporate control transactions.

[9] Of course, these two perspectives are not mutually exclusive, but rather they are related via the specification in equation (1). In particular, to the extent that accounting information affects P_A, it has a feedback effect on P_M.

[10] The landmark *Smith v. Van Gorkom* (1985) case highlights the importance of an internal governance process that appears capable of generating fair value for stockholders. The Delaware court found the directors of Trans Union Corp. had breached their fiduciary duty by approving an arm's length merger, even though the offer price was at a 48 percent premium to market, without "formal analysis" of the offer price or an investment banker's fairness opinion (Fischel 1985).

is that investment bankers simply "rubber stamp" whatever equity values managers select. In this latter view, investment bankers judiciously manipulate elaborate financial models to generate numbers that rationalize managements' chosen equity values to public stockholders and the courts.

Absent an ability to infer individuals' actual beliefs, this "excuse" motivation is not refutable. Hence, one cannot rule out the possibility that the primary function of the valuation process is to justify managerially-dictated terms to outsiders. It is, however, worth noting that this view is analogous to the assertion one sometimes hears that certified public accountants routinely "rubber stamp" whatever income figure management selects. In fact, the parallels between the investment banking and auditing professions are striking. Each certifies the fairness of managements' financial representations, each relies to some extent on data compiled by managers, and each has economic incentives to maintain a reputation for independence and quality work (L. DeAngelo 1981).[11] The economic benefits from that reputation give investment bankers and auditors incentives to avoid "rubber stamp" approvals of managerial representations.[12]

It is important to note that *whichever* motivation for an independent appraisal is the dominant one—whether the process generates a good faith estimate of fair value or simply justifies managerially-dictated terms—the valuation techniques used in this process affect real resource allocation, hence stockholder wealth. To see this point, consider the extreme case in which the *sole* motivation for an independent valuation is to justify equity values that are *entirely* chosen by other means. Even in this extreme scenario, the valuation information that justifies the selected exchange values to outside stockholders and the courts helps *determine* those values because it sets bounds on the feasible range of equity exchange values. Hence, the investment banker's valuation techniques affect stockholder wealth even if the valuation process simply serves as an elaborate "excuse" to justify managerially-imposed decisions.

Finally, the information used to determine equity exchange values need not be the same as that used to justify those values to outsiders who possess neither (1) managers' inside information about the firm's future prospects, nor (2) investment bankers' valuation expertise. Outsiders who lack these advantages rationally demand (and insiders will therefore supply) valuation data that incorporate well-understood, external constraints on managers' ability to disadvantage outside stockholders via the exchange values set on corporate equity.

Table 2 summarizes the major equity valuation techniques for corporate control transactions. A common element of the comparable firms (row 1) and comparable acquisitions (row 2) approaches is that both use historical pricing relations from a trading market in shares (companies). For example, comparable firms analysis mimics the capital market's pricing function for earnings or book value, while comparable acquisitions analysis mimics the control market's pric-

---

[11] The differences are also striking. Investment bankers have no codified rules for gathering and evaluating the evidence that underlies their opinion. Nor do they prohibit contingent fees, which are both routine and substantial.

[12] Investment bankers do sometimes refuse to issue a fairness opinion. In the Fort Howard management buyout analyzed in Section IV, management's initial $50 offer was judged unfair by the banker representing the outside directors, and management subsequently raised the offer to $53.

Table 2
Alternative (Nonmarket) Valuation Approaches
Used to Value Publicly-Traded Equity
in Corporate Control Transactions

1. *Comparable firms approaches* that develop an average relation between open-market prices and accounting variables. The primary method is to capitalize the current firm's per-share earnings at an average price/earnings ratio for comparable publicly-traded firms. Market-to-book and market-to-sales ratios are also sometimes employed.

2. *Comparable acquisitions approaches* that develop an average relation between prior acquisition prices and open-market prices or accounting variables. The primary method is to multiply an acquisition target's pre-offer stock price by an average premium paid in comparable acquisitions of publicly-traded corporations.

3. *Discounted cash flow* (*DCF*) *analysis*, sometimes operationalized as the capitalization of forecasted earnings or dividends (these approaches are detailed in Brealey and Myers (1988) and Weston and Copeland (1986)).

4. *Asset-based approaches* that develop an estimate of company value based on the appraised value of its assets, e.g., liquidation value. Liquidation values are not used to value going concerns, although asset appraisals are sometimes used to value companies with material real estate and/or natural resource holdings.

Sources: Banks (1972, 1974), Brudney and Chirelstein (1974), Chazen (1981), Fischel (1983, 1985), Giuffra (1986), Greenhill (1977), Harris (1981), Herzel and Colling (1984), Lipton (1979), Rosenbloom (1981), and Saffer (1984).

ing function for entire companies. Courts in the important state of Delaware have typically relied on the former approach, and have only recently begun to accept the latter. Discounted cash flow (DCF) techniques (row 3) are commonly used by investment bankers, but have only recently become acceptable in court.[13] Asset valuations (row 4) are rarely used, primarily to value real estate or natural resource holdings.

On the surface, it is puzzling that DCF analysis is not the *sole* equity valuation technique, given its prominence in finance textbooks (e.g., Brealey and Myers 1988; Weston and Copeland 1986). One plausible explanation is that DCF-generated equity values are sensitive to the cash flow and discount rate assumptions of insider-managers. Thus, while DCF analysis may be useful in assessing equity values in a given use or to a given bidder, it is not a very credible means of convincing outside stockholders that those values are fair.

In practice, DCF techniques are largely *accounting*-based valuation approaches. First, DCF valuations use historical accounting relations to forecast future earnings, from which future cash flows are estimated. Second, the terminal values that typically constitute the majority of DCF-generated values are commonly estimated from projections of future earnings. Finally, investment bankers rely on historical accounting relations to evaluate the reasonableness of managerial earnings forecasts, a practice that appears designed to reduce the

[13] In the landmark *Weinberger v. UOP* (1983) case, the Delaware court initially "rejected the plaintiff's discounted cash flow method of valuing UOP's stock as not corresponding with 'either logic or the existing law.'" The Delaware Supreme Court reversed upon appeal, paving the way for future acceptance of the DCF and comparable acquisitions approaches.

credibility problems with DCF analysis. These facts suggest that it is inappropriate to view DCF analysis as a *substitute* for accounting-based valuation methods, since it is itself largely an accounting method in practice.

Several other aspects of the valuation process seem designed to protect outside stockholders from managerial opportunism. First, investment bankers' valuations rely to a large extent on publicly-available, objective and verifiable data, such as market prices, acquisition values, and accounting data. Managers would seem to have little discretion over market prices, while their discretion over accounting data is limited by impartial institutional and regulatory constraints, including GAAP. When investment bankers use managerial forecasts, they attempt to evaluate their reasonableness. Thus, much of the evidence underlying a fairness opinion is either outside managers' control or incorporates well-understood, external constraints on managers' ability to affect that evidence.

Second, while there may be debate about cash flow and discount rate assumptions, investment bankers use explicit valuation models that generate arguably objective, mechanical share values. Third, they use a number of such models. The use of multiple, semi-independent valuation techniques avoids reliance on any one imperfect (potentially biased) approach. It thereby reduces the likelihood that a given control transaction is welfare-reducing for outside stockholders. The output of this process is a set of valuation working papers that typically runs 100–300 pages, and that generates a range of values that underlies the investment banker's opinion. This opinion serves as one basis upon which the board of directors evaluates a proposed control transaction.

If outside stockholders are not satisfied that their firm's internal governance process and/or the equity values it generates are fair, they can seek redress in court. Because the courts are a costly means of resolving conflicts, all parties have incentives to settle their disputes privately. Whether or not the parties to a given transaction actually go to court, court-sanctioned valuation methods set bounds on the feasible exchange values. In other words, managers can reduce the resource costs of litigation by structuring the transaction and its terms to satisfy the relevant court's fairness tests.

Legally, managers have the right (in fact, the obligation) to resist external offers they evaluate as inadequate (Easterbrook and Fischel 1981). Directors can be held liable for breach of fiduciary duty if they fail to consider explicit valuation evidence before acting on a bid. This standard of care is usually satisfied by an investment banker's opinion that the offer is inadequate (Giuffra 1986, 124–125; Lipton 1979; McAtee 1977).

Stockholders who dissent to a management buyout can demand the court-appraised value of their shares. Before *Weinberger v. UOP* (1983), Delaware courts assessed fair value via a weighted average of pre-offer stock prices, net asset value, and the capitalized value of historical earnings (Fischel 1983; Banks 1972, 1974). Since *Weinberger*, Delaware courts can accept other valuation approaches, e.g., comparable acquisitions and DCF techniques.[14]

---

[14] Delaware courts have recently held that, once a decision is made to sell the firm, the board has a duty to facilitate an auction (*MacAndrews & Forbes Holdings, Inc. v. Revlon, Inc.* 1986). An auction does not eliminate the demand for an independent equity valuation since outside stockholders cannot be sure that the information managers provide external bidders ensures the auction is "fair."

III. Equity Valuation in Management Buyouts: Some Preliminary Evidence

This section provides evidence on the valuation information cited as influencing investment bankers' fairness evaluations of management buyouts. The source documents are 60 fairness opinions from the DeAngelo (1986) sample of 64 buyout proposals for New York and American Stock Exchange firms. As detailed in DeAngelo (1986), the initial sample was obtained by direct inspection of *The Wall Street Journal* over the ten-year period 1973–1982. While proxy materials for 61 (95 percent) of the 64 buyout proposals reference a fairness opinion, one firm did not supply its text and, therefore, was dropped for this analysis.

Thirty-one of the 64 buyout proposals do not include third party equity investors. These non-leveraged buyouts tend to involve firms that are majority controlled by management—in the 31 non-leveraged buyouts, management owned a mean 50.1% (median, 51.7%) of the common stock. The potential for a majority owner to coerce the minority to accept an "unfair" acquisition proposal has led to the popular term "minority freezeout" for these buyouts.[15] Proxy materials for 28 proposals (90.3%) contain the text of a fairness opinion. Pre-offer managerial ownership averages 24.5% (median, 15.4%) for the 33 leveraged buyouts, and proxy materials for 32 (97.0%) contain the text of a fairness opinion.

Table 3 reports the information cited in the investment banker's fairness opinion and/or management's proxy discussion as influencing the buyout terms. Column (1) reports data for the 28 non-leveraged buyouts, and column (2) reports data for the 32 leveraged buyouts. For both subsamples, 100 percent of the proxy materials cite accounting information as influencing the banker's evaluation of the offer terms. The same percent cites open-market prices as influential. Prices paid in other acquisitions are also widely cited (64.3% of the non-leveraged, and 81.3% of the leveraged buyouts), as are managerial forecasts (67.9% and 62.5%, respectively). The latter are probably used in DCF analysis, which will also include some portion of the 17.9% (and 9.4%) incidence reported for cash flow analysis (the two categories most likely overlap).

Dividend capacity and asset appraisals are less frequently cited. For example, the firm's dividend capacity or past dividend record is referenced in 39.3% of the non-leveraged and 25.0% of the leveraged buyouts. Other influences on fairness opinions in leveraged buyouts are the buyout specialist's memo to investors, exchange values for other negotiated transactions in the firm's equity, and the results of the investment banker's attempt to "shop" the company. The latter is not cited in any of the non-leveraged buyouts, perhaps because of the high degree of managerial stock ownership in these firms.

The Table 3 evidence indicates that investment bankers unanimously cite accounting information as influencing their fairness evaluations of management buyouts. Unfortunately, the data do not indicate exactly *how* accounting information is used in equity valuation. However, the SEC has recently strongly encouraged firms contemplating a management buyout to file the valuation infor-

---

[15] There is a very limited role for a competitive auction in these cases, since the majority owner often does not want to, and cannot be forced to sell its interest to another party.

Table 3

**Valuation Evidence Cited as Influencing the Terms of a Management
Buyout: 60 Management Buyouts (1973–1982) with Text of
Investment Bankers' Fairness Opinions Published
in Proxy Materials**

	28 Non-Leveraged Buyouts with No Outside Equity Participants		32 Leveraged Buyouts with Outside Equity Participants	
	n	Percent	n	Percent
Accounting information	28	100.0	32	100.0
Open-market stock price	28	100.0	32	100.0
Prices paid in other acquisitions	18	64.3	26	81.3
Management forecasts	19	67.9	20	62.5
Cash flow analysis	5	17.9	3	9.4
Dividend history or capacity to pay	11	39.3	8	25.0
Asset appraisal	8	28.6	6	18.8
Buyout specialist's memo to investors	n/a	n/a	10	31.3
Actual or contemplated price of prior equity transaction	6	21.4	5	15.6
Banker's attempt to shop the company	0	0.0	8	25.0

mation presented to the board of directors by their financial advisers in their
Schedule 13e-3 filings.[16] These documents, the investment banker's equivalent
to the auditor's working papers, can be analyzed via a case study approach to
shed light on the manner in which valuation methods incorporate accounting
data.[17]

IV. Equity Valuation in Management Buyouts: A Closer Look

I obtained a list of 1988 Schedule 13e-3 filings from Disclosure and requested
valuation information for six firms that are reasonably representative of recent
buyouts, according to consultations with investment bankers. Disclosure was
able to supply the relevant filings for three of these firms—Bell & Howell Com-

[16] According to the SEC Office of Tender Offers, this valuation information has been included in
firms' Schedule 13e-3 filings since 1987. According to Disclosure, firms sometimes receive confidentiality from the SEC so that this information is only available (at considerable delay and expense) under
the Freedom of Information Act.

[17] The approach here is similar to the one used by Leftwich (1983) to analyze the role of accounting
information in private debt agreements. Leftwich studies *Commentaries on Indentures*, which provides a menu of potential debt covenants, combined with detailed inspection of actual lending documents from five private lenders. I study a large sample of fairness opinions, combined with detailed
inspection of four sets of investment bankers' working papers. The ability to generalize from such
studies is, of course, limited (Leftwich 1983, 30–31).

Table 4

**Valuation Techniques Used by Four Investment Bankers
to Evaluate the Fairness of a Management Buyout
According to Details of Rule 13e-3 Filings[a]**

Valuation Approach	Morgan Stanley	Salomon Bros.	Dillon Read	First Boston
Comparable firms analysis	yes	yes	yes	yes
Comparable acquisitions analysis	yes	yes	yes	yes
Discounted cash flow analysis	yes	yes	yes[d]	yes
Asset appraisal	no	no	no	no
Investment banker's attempt to shop the company	yes[b]	yes	no	no
Dividend history or capacity to pay	no	no	no	yes
Leveraged buyout model	no	yes	yes	yes
Leveraged recapitalization model	no	yes[c]	no	yes

[a] These filings are for the proposed 1988 management buyouts of Bell & Howell Company (investment bankers, Morgan Stanley and Salomon Bros.), Foodmaker, Inc. (Dillon Read), and Fort Howard Corporation (First Boston).

[b] Morgan Stanley did not itself shop the company, but its opinion refers to the Salomon Bros. attempt to solicit other offers.

[c] Salomon Bros. had performed this analysis for management before any external bidder made its intentions public.

[d] Dillon Read cautions that DCF analysis is of limited usefulness in leveraged acquisitions because of the sensitivity of its results to changes in its assumptions.

pany, Foodmaker, Inc., and Fort Howard Corporation.[18] Managers of all three companies proposed a buyout in 1988 and all have since gone private. Their filings contain fairness opinions with valuation documentation from four different "blue chip" investment bankers. Foodmaker and Fort Howard each provide one fairness opinion, and Bell & Howell provides two opinions.[19]

This section's case study analysis is, therefore, based on four sets of valuation documents—Morgan Stanley's and Salomon Brothers' reports on the Bell & Howell management buyout, Dillon Read's report on the Foodmaker buyout, and First Boston's on the Fort Howard Corp. buyout. These documents range from 92 to 309 pages in length, and detailed tables of numbers and sensitivity analyses comprise most of that length. I also rely on the investment banker's discussion of the factors that influenced the fairness evaluation, contained in the proxy statement or offering document, and on the fairness opinion itself. The Appendix reproduces Morgan Stanley's fairness opinion on the Bell & Howell management buyout.

Table 4 categorizes the valuation approaches used by each investment

[18] The three firms for which I was unable to obtain valuation data are Jewelcor Inc., Plantronics Inc., and Trans World Airlines Inc.

[19] The first opinion is from management's investment banker, while the second is from the financial adviser to the special committee of outside directors that evaluated management's proposal. Such committees are typically formed to negotiate with management on behalf of outside stockholders. See DeAngelo and DeAngelo (1987) for a comprehensive discussion of the extensive checks on the manager-outside stockholder bargaining process in management buyouts.

banker, according to my reading of these source documents. These materials exhibit the wide range of valuation techniques and sensitivity analyses that underlie a fairness opinion. The table cannot convey the large volume of financial data that support these opinions. It does, however, report the major approaches taken by the four investment bankers to highlight their differences and similarities.

With respect to the latter, all four investment bankers provide analyses of comparable firms, comparable acquisitions, and DCF analyses. As detailed below for the Fort Howard management buyout, all these valuation approaches (*including* DCF techniques) rely heavily on published accounting information. None of the investment bankers performs or relies upon direct asset appraisals.

Both investment bankers that evaluated the Bell & Howell management buyout acknowledge the Salomon Bros. attempt to solicit competing acquisition proposals in their fairness opinions (see Morgan Stanley's opinion, reproduced in the Appendix). The directors of the other two firms had not actively solicited competing bids at the time the fairness opinion was issued, and both investment bankers cite that fact in their opinions.[20] The observation that all four bankers' opinions discuss the solicitation of competing bids highlights the importance placed by courts in recent years on whether the directors held an open auction for the company. To some degree, a competitive auction substitutes for the valuation process discussed here, but not completely (see fns. 4 and 14).

Table 4 indicates that First Boston is the only banker to use a dividends capitalization approach. They use it to estimate stock prices if the company were to remain publicly-traded. Three bankers perform a leveraged buyout analysis and two also estimate equity values under a leveraged recapitalization. Leveraged buyout models assess financial feasibility under various assumptions about the offer price, proceeds from asset dispositions, and financing terms. The general approach is to project net income under various scenarios. Interest coverage ratios are then calculated, based on both earnings and cash flows, to assess financial risk. Returns to equity investors are also computed, and their sensitivity assessed to changes in underlying assumptions.

Table 5 reports the summary valuation of one investment banker to give readers a better feel for (1) the range of equity values generated by the valuation process, and (2) specific valuation techniques. First Boston's summary valuation of Fort Howard Corp. reports a preliminary price range of $35–62 per share, obtained from nine different valuation approaches (management's offer was $53 per share). They provide two DCF analyses of the entire firm. The first relies on management's long-run projections, while the second incorporates First Boston's adjustments to those projections (the "upside case"). The upside scenario assumes higher product prices, sales growth, and operating profit margins than do management's long-run projections.

Terminal values typically constitute a large portion of DCF-generated values. Consequently, investment bankers typically use several approaches to estimate

---

[20] Dillon Read's opinion on the Foodmaker management buyout states that "the Agreement and Plan of Merger does not prohibit the Special Committee from soliciting competing proposals, and the Special Committee has advised us that it intends to request us to do so." First Boston's opinion on the Fort Howard management buyout states that "We were not requested to, and did not, solicit third party indications of interest in acquiring all or any part of the Company."

Table 5
Summary Valuation for the 1988 Management Buyout of
Fort Howard Corporation: Prepared by
The First Boston Corporation

Valuation Approach	Preliminary Range Per Share[1]
1. Consolidated DCF analysis[2]— Base case (management's long-range plan)	$49–$54
2. Consolidated DCF analysis[2]— Upside case (First Boston adjustments to managerial projections)	57– 62
3. Break-up value[3]	46– 57
4. Comparable company analysis	45– 53
5. Comparable acquisition analysis	38– 46
6. Dividend discount model	50– 60
7. Historical multiples	35– 50
8. LBO analysis	50– 54
9. Recapitalization analysis	49– 54

Sources: Exhibits (b)(4) and (d)(1) to the Schedule 13e-3 filing of Fort Howard Corporation dated July 1, 1988.

[1] The price at which the company went private in 1988 was $53 per share.

[2] Derived by estimating terminal values as multiples of 14–16 times 1998 projected unlevered net income and using a 12.0% discount rate.

[3] Derived using DCF and comparable publicly-traded company analyses for each of the four business segments, and comparable acquisition analysis for the two segments for which acquisition data were available.

these values. For the Fort Howard buyout, First Boston used three methods to estimate terminal values—a multiple of 1998 unlevered income, a multiple of 1998 book value, and a perpetual growth model applied to 1998 cash flows. As an example of the impact of terminal value assumptions on DCF equity values, First Boston's terminal value estimates constitute (1) 53–71 percent of equity values when estimated as a multiple of earnings, (2) 56–73 percent of equity values when estimated as a multiple of book value, and (3) 53–80 percent of equity values using a perpetual growth model.

Table 5 reports equity values of $49–62 from First Boston's DCF analysis, assuming terminal values of 14–16 times 1998 projected unlevered net income and a 12 percent discount rate. This range widens to $39–133 under the full set of assumptions considered by First Boston. First Boston points out in the offer materials that this wide range of values "demonstrates the sensitivity of discounted cash flow analysis" to terminal value assumptions and expresses a preference for the earnings multiple approach.[21]

[21] First Boston is not the only investment banker to cite the limitations of DCF analysis. The offer materials for the Foodmaker buyout report that "Dillon Read indicated that it regarded the discounted cash flow analysis as less useful in this instance, because the company is highly leveraged and small changes in certain assumptions can produce large changes in per share values."

First Boston's $46–57 estimate of Fort Howard's break-up value is derived from DCF and comparable company analyses of each of the company's four major segments, and from comparable acquisition analysis of the two segments for which acquisition data were available. As noted in Table 5, First Boston also uses comparable company and comparable acquisition techniques on the entire firm. Company-wide comparable firm analysis generates equity values of $45–53, while First Boston's analysis of historical multiples generates values of $35–50. Their valuation working papers use data on the price/sales, price/cash flow, price/operating income, price/earnings, and price/book value multiples of Fort Howard compared to those of Scott Paper Company, James River Corp., and Kimberly-Clark Corp. These are clearly accounting-based valuation approaches.

First Boston also performs extensive additional analyses on the P/E ratios of Fort Howard compared to those of Scott Paper, James River, and Kimberly-Clark, and to the P/E ratios of 11 other paper companies that they deem less comparable. These analyses consider market prices and P/E ratios both before and after the October 1987 market crash. They use both historical EPS figures (as of June 30 and December 31, 1987) and the average Institutional Brokers' Estimate System (I/B/E/S) earnings forecast. First Boston also compares Fort Howard's monthly and quarterly P/E multiples since 1983 to averages for the Standard & Poor 400, using both actual earnings and I/B/E/S forecasts. These analyses generate a range of P/E (and price-to-book) multiples that First Boston applies to Fort Howard's projected EPS and book values to estimate equity values.

First Boston's comparable acquisition analysis describes the attributes of nine acquisitions of (and by) companies in the paper industry. These attributes are not acquisition premiums—rather they all relate acquisition values to various accounting variables. Specifically, First Boston reports acquisition values as a multiple of the latest 12-month net income, book value, sales, operating income, and operating cash flow. They also summarize attributes of completed tender offers in 1988 (as of May 1988), partitioned into hostile and friendly offers. These attributes include acquisition premiums—measured relative to market prices one day, one week, and four weeks prior to announcement. They also include acquisition values as a multiple of accounting variables—the latest 12-month sales, net income, and book value.

First Boston uses a "dividend discount" model to estimate the trading value of the company, should it remain public in substantially unchanged form. Despite the "dividend discount" label, this approach in essence capitalizes future *earnings*. Future dividends are assumed to be 40 percent of earnings projections for five years, and terminal value is a multiple of 1992 earnings.[22] Earnings projections are based on (1) management's long-run plan, and (2) First Boston's upside case. First Boston estimates trading values as the present value of expected dividends and terminal values under various discount rates. They also estimate trading values should the firm engage in a leveraged recapitalization.

---

[22] Dillon Read takes a similar approach to estimate the trading value of Foodmaker equity in substantially unchanged form. (Foodmaker paid no dividends as a public company.) Dillon Read estimates equity value in 1993 as a multiple of terminal earnings, assuming managers' earnings projections are realized, and discounts that value using various required rates of return on equity.

Finally, First Boston performs a leveraged buyout analysis of the company (under various assumptions about offer prices, proceeds from future asset sales, and financial terms) to assess the financial feasibility of the proposed transaction. Their general approach is to project future earnings based on (1) management's long-range plan, (2) management's projections, assuming divestiture of certain assets, and (3) First Boston's upside scenario. Table 5 reports a range of $50–54 which is based on *assumed*, not derived equity values under this approach. First Boston's leveraged buyout analysis leads them to conclude that $54 is at the upper range of financial feasibility, and the offer materials report their opinion that "in light of the corresponding financial projections, it would be difficult to finance a leveraged buyout at higher prices."

The available evidence does not allow determination of the precise effect of a given valuation method on the final transaction price of $53 per share paid for Fort Howard equity. However, it does appear that $53 falls in the approximate mid-range of equity values generated by First Boston. Specifically, $53 lies within the range of values generated by six (two-thirds) of the nine valuation methods summarized in Table 5. Importantly, it lies below the range only for DCF-generated values in the upside case (and above the range implied by comparable acquisitions and historical multiples). In short, it appears that the ultimate transaction price is constrained to fall within the approximate range of values implied by a broad variety of valuation techniques.

Overall, accounting information and accounting statement formats—balance sheets, income statements, analysis of funds flows—permeate investment bankers' valuation techniques. Importantly, their use of accounting data is not confined to analysis of historical P/E or market-to-book multiples. Rather, accounting variables and relations are used in *every* valuation technique documented here. They are used in DCF analysis to evaluate managers' earnings projections and to estimate the terminal values that commonly drive DCF values. They are used to evaluate cash flow forecasts for leveraged buyout and leveraged recapitalization analyses, and in dividend and equity valuation models. They are used in comparable acquisition analysis to link acquisition values to firm-specific attributes. In fact, the equity valuation process can be reasonably characterized as one that predominantly employs accounting information to estimate fair compensation to outside stockholders.

V. Summary

The proliferation of control contests for large public corporations at 50% + premiums above market illustrates the wide divergence between open-market stock prices and equity exchange values. This paper considers equity valuation in corporate control transactions—e.g., management buyouts and hostile takeovers—that engender potentially severe managerial conflicts of interest. These conflicts generate a demand for independent assessments of equity values by investment bankers who specialize in these appraisals. The paper provides evidence on the valuation information used by investment bankers to evaluate the fairness of a large sample of management buyouts. It also provides a closer look at their valuation techniques via a detailed case study of investment bankers' valuation working papers.

This evidence indicates that accounting information permeates the valuation process for management buyouts. It is, therefore, consistent with the hypothesis that accounting information affects real resource allocation, hence stockholder wealth, via the terms of corporate control transactions. Importantly, this inference holds whether the valuation process documented here is actually used to estimate equity exchange values, or whether it serves primarily to justify values selected via other means to public stockholders and the courts. The evidence also suggests that accounting information may affect equity valuation in other control transactions—e.g., hostile tender offers and leveraged recapitalizations—that represent promising areas for future research.

Finally, the analysis suggests that accounting information plays a more extensive role in the governance of manager-stockholder relations than previously recognized in the contracting or capital markets literatures. Specifically, it isolates a potentially important demand for accounting information beyond that associated with managerial wage agreements, debt contracts, and the political process (Watts and Zimmerman 1986). Moreover, the demand for accounting data in equity valuation is conceptually distinct from that posited in the capital markets literature, which restricts attention to open-market stock prices. In short, the role of accounting information in equity valuation (and corporate governance) is broader than previously thought.

Appendix

Morgan Stanley & Co. Incorporated
1251 Avenue of the Americas
New York, New York 10020

December 14, 1987

Special Committee of the
    Board of Directors
Bell & Howell Company
5215 Old Orchard Road
Skokie, Illinois 60077-1076

Dear Sirs and Madam:

We understand that Bell & Howell Company ("Bell & Howell" or the "Company") is entering into a Merger Agreement, dated December 14, 1987 (the "Merger Agreement"), with BHW Acquisition Corp. ("Parent"), a Delaware corporation formed and controlled by a group of investors led by Robert M. Bass Group, Inc. and including certain members of the Company's management (the "Bass Group"), and BHW Merger Corp. ("Merger Sub"), a Delaware corporation and a directly or indirectly wholly-owned subsidiary of Parent. Pursuant to the Merger Agreement, on the terms and subject to the conditions thereof, Merger Sub will be merged with and into the Company (the "Merger"), and each then outstanding share of the Company's Common Stock, without par value (the "Common Shares") and each then outstanding share of the Company's Cumulative Convertible Preferred Stock, Series A, without par value (the "Preferred Shares" and collectively with the Common Shares, the "Shares"), other than Shares owned by Parent, Merger Sub, any other direct or indirect subsidiary of Parent and Shares held by stockholders of the Company who properly exercise any appraisal rights available under applicable law, will be converted in the Merger into the right to receive $64 in cash (the "Merger Consideration").

You have asked for our opinion as to whether the Merger Consideration to be received by the holders of Shares is fair to such holders (other than Parent and its affiliates) from a financial point of view.

For the purposes of this opinion we have, among other things,

(i) reviewed the audited and unaudited financial statements for the three most recent fiscal years and interim periods to date and certain other financial and operating data relating to Bell & Howell made available to us by Bell & Howell;

(ii) analyzed certain internal financial and operating data of Bell & Howell, including financial projections for the period 1987–1997 prepared by Bell & Howell management relating to the earnings, cash flow, assets, and prospects of the Company's business;

(iii) conducted discussions with members of senior management of Bell & Howell and its subsidiaries with respect to the Company's business, operating performance, and prospects;

(iv) reviewed the financial terms, to the extent publicly available, of certain recent acquisition transactions deemed relevant;

(v) compared the financial information relating to certain of the Company's businesses with published financial information concerning certain companies whose businesses we deemed to be comparable, in whole or in part, to those of the Company;

(vi) analyzed the market price and trading characteristics of Bell & Howell common stock for recent periods to date;

(vii) reviewed the Certificate of Designation relating to the Preferred Stock;

(viii) reviewed the Merger Agreement; and

(ix) performed such other analyses and examinations and conducted such other discussions as we have deemed appropriate.

In preparing our opinion, we have relied upon the accuracy and completeness of all information supplied or otherwise made available to us by Bell & Howell, and we have not independently verified such information or made or obtained an independent evaluation or appraisal of the Company's business. We have also assumed that the Company's projections have been reasonably prepared, and have been generated on bases reflecting the best currently available estimates and judgments of the future financial performance of the Company's business segments. We have relied on your counsel with respect to legal matters relating to the Merger Agreement and the transactions contemplated thereby. It should be noted that our opinion is necessarily based upon market conditions prevailing, and other circumstances and conditions existing at the present time.

As you know, we have been retained, and have received a fee therefor, solely for the purpose of rendering to you our opinion as to the fairness, from a financial viewpoint, of the consideration to be received by the Company's stockholders (other than Parent and its affiliates) pursuant to the Merger Agreement. Accordingly, we were not requested to solicit, and did not solicit, other potential purchasers for the Company or any of its business segments. Nor have we participated in any of the discussions or negotiations with the Bass Group or any other potential purchasers of the Company or any of its business segments with respect to the Merger Agreement or other possible alternative transactions. We understand that Salomon Brothers Inc. conducted a solicitation of acquisition proposals for the Company during November-December 1987, and we have discussed the results of such solicitation with Salomon Brothers Inc.

As we have advised you, in the past we have rendered financial advisory and investment banking services to Robert M. Bass Group, Inc. and certain affiliated entities (in matters not relating to the Company) for which we have received customary compensation.

Based upon the foregoing, and such other factors as we deem relevant, including our assessment of general economic, market, and monetary conditions, we are of the opinion that the Merger Consideration to be received by the holders of Shares is fair to such holders (other than Parent and its affiliates) from a financial point of view.

Very truly yours,

MORGAN STANLEY & CO. INCORPORATED

By: _____

Steven Rattner
Managing Director

(Source: proxy statement dated April 16, 1988 for Bell & Howell Company)

References

Banks, W. E. 1972. A selective inquiry into judicial stock valuation. *Indiana Law Review.* (No. 1): 19–44.

——. 1974. Measuring the value of corporate stock. *California Western Law Review.* (Fall): 1–59.

Beaver, W. H. 1973. What should be the FASB's objectives? *Journal of Accountancy* (August): 49–56.

——. 1981. *Financial reporting: An accounting revolution.* Prentice-Hall.

Bradley, M. 1980. Interfirm tender offers and the market for corporate control. *Journal of Business* (October): 345–376.

Brealey, R. A., and S. C. Myers. 1988. *Principles of corporate finance.* 3d ed. McGraw-Hill.

Brudney, V., and M. A. Chirelstein. 1974. Fair shares in corporate mergers and takeovers. *Harvard Law Review.* (December): 297–346.

Chazen, L. 1981. Fairness from a financial point of view in acquisitions of public companies: Is "third-party sale value" the appropriate standard? *The Business Lawyer.* (July): 1439–1481.

Comment, R., and G. A. Jarrell. 1987. Two-tier and negotiated tender offers: The imprisonment of the free-riding shareholder. *Journal of Financial Economics.* (December): 283–310.

DeAngelo, H. 1981. Competition and unanimity. *American Economic Review.* (March): 18–27.

——, and L. DeAngelo. 1987. Management buyouts of publicly-traded corporations. *Financial Analysts' Journal.* (May/June): 38–49.

——, ——, and E. M. Rice. 1984. Going private: Minority freezeouts and stockholder wealth. *Journal of Law and Economics.* (October): 367–401.

DeAngelo, L. 1981. Auditor size and audit quality. *Journal of Accounting and Economics.* (December): 183–199.

——. 1986. Accounting numbers as market valuation substitutes: A study of management buyouts of public stockholders. *The Accounting Review.* (July): 400–420.

Easterbrook, F. H., and D. R. Fischel. 1981. The proper role of a target's management in responding to a tender offer. *Harvard Law Review.* (April): 1161–1204.

Fischel, D. R. 1983. The appraisal remedy in corporate law. *American Bar Foundation Research Journal.* (Fall): 875–902.

——. 1985. The business judgment rule and the Trans Union case. *The Business Lawyer.* (August): 1437–1455.

Giuffra, R. J., Jr. 1986. Investment bankers' fairness opinions in corporate control transactions. *Yale Law Journal.* (November): 119–141.

Greenhill, R. F. 1977. Structuring an offer. *The Business Lawyer.* (May): 1305–1309.

Harris, R. A. 1981. Determining the right price to pay. *Handbook of mergers, acquisitions and buyouts.* Eds. S. J. Lee and R. D. Colman, 149–169. Prentice-Hall.

Herzel, L., and D. E. Colling. 1984. Establishing procedural fairness in squeeze-out mergers after *Weinberger v. UOP. The Business Lawyer.* (August): 1525–1539.

Jensen, M. C., and W. H. Meckling. 1976. Theory of the firm: Managerial behavior, agency costs, and ownership structure. *Journal of Financial Economics.* (October): 305–360.

Leftwich, R. 1983. Accounting information in private markets: Evidence from private lending agreements. *The Accounting Review.* (January): 23–42.

Lev, B. 1988. Toward a theory of equitable and efficient accounting policy. *The Accounting Review.* (January): 1–22.

Lipton, M. 1979. Takeover bids in the target's boardroom. *The Business Lawyer.* (November): 101–134.

McAtee, J. J., Jr. 1977. The role of the dealer manager in the disclosure process. *The Business Lawyer.* (May): 1331–1335.

MacAndrews & Forbes Holdings, Inc. v. Revlon, Inc., 501 A.2d 1239 (Del. Ch. 1985), affirmed, 506 A.2d 173 (Del. 1986).

Myers, S. C., and N. S. Majluf. 1984. Corporate financing and investment decisions when firms have information that investors do not have. *Journal of Financial Economics.* (June): 187–221.

Rosenbloom, A. H. 1981. A hypothetical going private transaction. *The Journal of Corporate Law.* (April/May): 601–637.

Saffer, B. H. 1984. Touching all bases in setting merger prices. *Mergers and Acquisitions.* (Fall): 42–48.

Smith, C. B. 1978. Fair price and redemption rights: New dimensions in defensive charter provisions. *Delaware Journal of Corporate Law.* (No. 1): 1–38.

Smith v. Van Gorkum, 488 A.2d 858 (Del. 1985).

Watts, R. L., and J. L. Zimmerman. 1986. *Positive accounting theory.* Prentice-Hall.

Weinberger v. UOP, Inc., 457 A.2d 701 (Del. Supr. 1983).

Weston, J. F., and T. E. Copeland. 1986. *Managerial finance.* 8th ed. The Dryden Press.

II

DEBT CONTRACTS AND
ACCOUNTING POLICY CHOICE

1 Smith, Clifford W., Jr., and Jerold B. Warner, "On Financial Contracting: An Analysis of Bond Covenants," *Journal of Financial Economics*, 7 (1979), pp. 117–161.

2 Kalay, Avner, "Stockholder-Bondholder Conflict and Dividend Constraints," *Journal of Financial Economics*, 10 (1982), pp. 211–233.

3 Chow, Chee W., "The Impacts of Accounting Regulation on Bondholder and Shareholder Wealth: The Case of the Securities Acts," *The Accounting Review*, 58 (1983), pp. 485–520.

4 Leftwich, Richard, "Evidence of the Impact of Mandatory Changes in Accounting Principles on Corporate Loan Agreements," *Journal of Accounting and Economics*, 3 (1981), pp. 3–36.

5 Leftwich, Richard, "Accounting Information in Private Markets: Evidence from Private Lending Agreements," *The Accounting Review*, 58 (1981), pp. 23–42.

6 Duke, Joanne C. and Herbert G. Hunt III, "An Empirical Examination of Debt Covenant Restrictions and Accounting-Related Debt Proxies," *Journal of Accounting and Economics*, 12 (1990), pp. 45–63.

A firm's accounting reports are of potential use to all parties who contract with it, or who potentially could contract with it. Contracting parties include suppliers of factors of production (debt and equity capital, labor, management, goods and services, etc.) as well as customers. For large, publicly-listed corporations, the range of actual and potential contracting parties can be wide enough to justify supplying accounting reports to any party—that is, to imply full public disclosure. While in most countries the supply of accounting reports to the public is regulated, it nevertheless is an economic activity which arises because there is a demand for it.

One source of demand for accounting information arises from contracts between corporations and suppliers of debt capital. If suppliers of debt had no interest in controlling the actions taken by managers or in the outcomes from their actions, then debt contracts would be different than those we observe. **Smith and Warner (1979)** show that suppliers of risky debt do have an interest in manager's actions and their outcomes. They argue that suppliers of risky debt therefore contract to receive some rights to monitor and control manager's actions. The interest of suppliers of debt arises from the possibility that managers, acting on behalf of the stockholders who appoint them, can increase the wealths of stockholders at the expense of decreasing the wealths of debtholders. That is, there are potential conflicts of interest between stockholders and bondholders. For example, unless they are constrained, managers might distribute the corporation's assets to shareholders and leave suppliers of debt capital holding claims on a "shell." There will be a contracting-cost-efficient amount (and form) of contractual provisions to limit the risk of wealth transfers of this type. Debt with longer maturities is more exposed to the risk of wealth transfer, so longer-term corporate bonds typically give bondholders the right to receive information that is used to monitor managers, as well as various rights to control managers' actions under certain circumstances. These rights are defined in the covenants to debt agreements. **Smith and Warner** developed several testable propositions about the form such convenants take.

If contracting was costless, then contracts with all parties (managers, shareholders, and bondholders included) could simply prescribe a set of optimal managerial actions in all feasible future states, as well as a costless mechanism for monitoring managers' actions and enforcing the contracted-for optimal actions. The conflicts of interest described by **Smith and Warner** would be costlessly controlled. In reality, there are positive contracting costs, so potential conflicts are costly and debt contracts incorporate a contracting-cost-efficient set of monitoring and controlling rights. Short-term debt contracts (e.g., callable bank overdrafts) tend to have fewer rights for monitoring and restricting managers, but longer-term debt contracts (e.g., public bond issues) tend to have more. Some of the contractual provisions are expressed in terms of numbers contained in independently-certified (audited) accounting reports, such as reported debt/total assets ratios, retained earnings and earnings/interest coverage ratios. The underlying hypothesis in the costly-contracting literature is that the firm uses accounting information in debt contracts because it is contracting-cost efficient to do so.

Kalay (1982) studies restrictions on dividends and other distributions to stockholders that are contained in corporate bond indentures. These include distributions via stock repurchases. Kalay argues that a testable implication of the theory that dividend restrictions in debt contracts arise from latent conflicts of interest between stockholders and bondholders is that such restrictions are not observed when potential stockholder/bondholder conflict does not arise. He presents evidence consistent with this hypothesis. Specifically, bond covenants generally differentiate between dividends financed by equity (in which case there is no conflict) and those financed by issuing debt or by depleting the firm's investment base (in which case there is). This suggests that conflicts of interest, which only occur in the presence of contracting costs, are the source of dividend restrictions. The demand for accounting reports in this context arises from the need to monitor the amount and source of financing via stockholders' equity versus debt. This requires an accounting not only for equity issues and repurchases, but also for profits and losses as well as dividend distributions.

Leftwich (1981) investigates the effect on equity prices, for firms with risky debt, around the time of a change in GAAP for business combinations. The hypothesized effect occurs because debt covenants frequently restrict the proportion of debt financing of the firm's assets and because in public debt contracts the relevant amounts for assets and debt typically are those reported in the firm's public accounts (i.e., they are determined by GAAP). An accounting change that reduces reported assets therefore has the effect of increasing reported leverage and thus of making existing debt covenants more restrictive, other things remaining equal. This makes existing debt more valuable and equity less valuable. Assuming the change to be exogenously imposed, **Leftwich (1981)** hypothesizes that APB 16 and 17 were associated with decreases in firm's equity prices, with the decrease being a function of the firm's proportion of debt finance. (The effect on bond prices is not observed, because bonds are not traded sufficiently frequently.) The evidence partially supports the hypothesis. **Leftwich (1981)** recognizes several research design problems in this type of study, including the difficulty of identifying the dates at which the sharemarket substantially revised its estimates of the likelihood of the accounting change. Other problems include the endogeneity of the accounting change, the adequacy of the debt-asset ratio as a proxy for the cost imposed on shareholders, and the possibility that the hypothesized effects are very small relative to exogenous variance in share prices (and thus difficult to detect).

Leftwich (1983) provides evidence that private debt contracts frequently deviate from GAAP in determining relevant numbers, such as the amounts of debt and assets for the purpose of leverage restrictions. The data in this study are the actual negotiated terms of private loan agreements. They are not proxy variables. Observed deviations from GAAP in private debt contracts appear to be consistent with the incentives of the contracting parties (borrowers and lenders). Note that the corporation here is contracting to provide accounting information in addition to, and calculated on, a different accounting basis than that reported to the public at large in its published financial statements.[1]

Following **Leftwich (1981, 1983)** and Benston (1973), **Chow (1983)** investigates the effects of the Securities Acts of 1933 and 1934 on the wealths of stockholders and bondholders. Assuming the Acts to be exogenously imposed on investors, he argues that the legislation increased the amount of information to investors, by requiring additional disclosure, increasing the cost of fraudulent disclosure, and increasing the cost to managers of manipulating accounting methods to escape bond indenture restrictions. Other things remaining equal, this should transfer wealth from equity to debtholders. The evidence is partly consistent with this hypothesis.

An issue that frequently arises in this literature is whether the debt-asset ratio is a valid proxy for the costs associated with accounting policy choice. **Duke and Hunt (1990)** in part address this issue by collecting data on how close a company is to the actual restrictions in its debt convenants and by observing the relation of this variable with the company's leverage ratio. While they find a significant relation between the leverage ratio proxy and the tightness of the actual covenant, this does not imply that:

1. The relation is perfect and the proxy is without error; or
2. The tightness of the covenant is a perfect proxy, in turn, for the expected cost of moving closer to violating it.

The six papers in this section demonstrate the existence of a demand for accounting numbers in debt contracts. They provide some initial insight into the form of that demand. They also highlight many of the research design issues that await future research.

[1]Leftwich equates GAAP with *regulation* of accounting methods. The correspondence is not obvious. Professional and trade associations, franchise chains and organizations in general promulgate rules to which voluntarily-contracting parties agree, in the absence of political effects. Leftwich's results show that one does not have to buy hamburgers cooked under the rules of a hamburger franchise.

ON FINANCIAL CONTRACTING

An Analysis of Bond Covenants*

Clifford W. SMITH, Jr. and Jerold B. WARNER

University of Rochester, Rochester, NY 14627, USA

Received September 1978, revised version received May 1979

With risky debt outstanding, stockholder actions aimed at maximizing the value of their equity claim can result in a reduction in the value of both the firm and its outstanding bonds. We examine ways in which debt contracts are written to control the conflict between bondholders and stockholders. We find that extensive direct restrictions on production/investment policy would be expensive to employ and are not observed. However, dividend and financing policy restrictions are written to give stockholders incentives to follow a firm-value-maximizing production/investment policy. Taking into account how contracts control the bondholder stockholder conflict leads to a number of testable propositions about the specific form of the debt contract that a firm will choose.

1. Introduction and summàry

The conflict of interest between the firm's bondholders and its stockholders has been discussed by a number of authors. For example, Fama/Miller (1972, p. 179) indicate that under certain circumstances 'it is easy to construct examples in which a production plan that maximizes shareholder wealth does not maximize bondholder wealth, or vice versa'.[1] Citing an extreme case of the bondholder–stockholder conflict, Black (1976) points out that 'there is no easier way for a company to escape the burden of a debt than to pay out all of its assets in the form of a dividend, and leave the creditors holding an empty shell'.

In this paper, we examine how debt contracts are written to control the bondholder–stockholder conflict. We investigate the various kinds of bond covenants which are included in actual debt contracts. A bond covenant is a provision, such as a limitation on the payment of dividends, which restricts the firm from engaging in specified actions after the bonds are sold.

*This research is supported by the Managerial Economics Research Center, Graduate School of Management, University of Rochester. We are indebted to numerous colleagues, both those at the University of Rochester and elsewhere, for their help on this paper. We are especially grateful to Michael C. Jensen for his assistance.

[1]See also, Modigliani/Miller (1958, p. 293), Black/Cox (1976), Jensen/Meckling (1976), Miller (1977a), and Black/Miller/Posner (1978).

Our description of the specific provisions in debt contracts is based primarily on an American Bar Foundation compendium entitled *Commentaries on Indentures*. This volume contains both the standardized provisions which are included in the debt contract (the 'boilerplates') and a practitioner-oriented discussion of their use.

1.1. Sources of the bondholder–stockholder conflict

Corporations are 'legal fictions which serve as a nexus for a set of contracting relationships among individuals'.[2] To focus on the contract between the bondholders and the corporation, we assume that costs of enforcing other contracts are zero. For example, we assume that contracts between stockholders and managers costlessly induce managers to act as if they own all the firm's equity.

The corporation has an indefinite life and the set of contracts which comprise the corporation evolves over time: as the firm's investment opportunity set changes decisions are made about the real activities in which the firm engages and the financial contracts the firm sells. With risky bonds outstanding, management, acting in the stockholders' interest, has incentives to design the firm's operating characteristics and financial structure in ways which benefit stockholders to the detriment of bondholders. Because investment, financing, and dividend policies are endogenous, there are four major sources of conflict which arise between bondholders and stockholders:

Dividend payment. If a firm issues bonds and the bonds are priced assuming the firm will maintain its dividend policy, the value of the bonds is reduced by raising the dividend rate and financing the increase by reducing investment. At the limit, if the firm sells all its assets and pays a liquidating dividend to the stockholders, the bondholders are left with worthless claims.

Claim dilution. If the firm sells bonds, and the bonds are priced assuming that no additional debt will be issued, the value of the bondholders' claims is reduced by issuing additional debt of the same or higher priority.

Asset substitution. If a firm sells bonds for the stated purpose of engaging in low variance projects[3] and the bonds are valued at prices commensurate

---

[2]Jensen/Meckling (1976, p. 310).

[3]The importance of the variance rate is derived from the option pricing analysis of Black/Scholes (1973). In section A.1 of the appendix we discuss the determinants of the value of a bond issue where the bonds are single-payment contracts, and the market is efficient and competitive, without transactions costs, information costs, other agency costs, or taxes. The option pricing analysis assumes that the value of the firm will be independent of its financial structure. Our concern in this paper is with a world in which covenants can change the value of the firm. Hence a critical assumption of the option pricing analysis is violated; the value of the firm will, in general, be a function of the covenants which are offered. The option pricing

with that low risk, the value of the stockholders' equity rises and the value of the bondholders' claim is reduced by substituting projects which increase the firm's variance rate.[4]

Underinvestment. Myers (1977) suggests that a substantial portion of the value of the firm is composed of intangible assets in the form of future investment opportunities. A firm with outstanding bonds can have incentives to reject projects which have a positive net present value if the benefit from accepting the project accrues to the bondholders.

The bondholder–stockholder conflict is of course recognized by capital market participants. Rational bondholders recognize the incentives faced by the stockholders. They understand that after the bonds are issued, any action which increases the wealth of the stockholders will be taken. In ricing the bond issue, bondholders make estimates of the behavior of the stockholders, given the investment, financing, and dividend policies available to the stockholders. The price which bondholders pay for the issue will be lower to reflect the possibility of subsequent wealth transfers to stockholders.[5] The pricing of the bond issue is discussed in more detail in the appendix.

1.2. Control of the bondholder–stockholder conflict: The competing hypotheses

There seems to be general agreement within the finance profession that the bondholder–stockholder relationship entails conflict and that the prices in security markets behave as if all security-holders form rational expectations about the stockholders' behavior after the bonds are issued. However, there is disagreement about whether the total value of the firm is influenced by the way in which the bondholder–stockholder conflict is controlled. There are

---

analysis does not address the issue of the endogeneity of the stockholders' behavior because variables such as the value of the firm's assets or the variance rate are treated as fixed rather than as decision variables. Therefore, the implications drawn from the option pricing model are only suggestive. In section A.2 of the appendix, we suggest how the endogeneity of investment policy affects the optimal choice of financial structure and the value of the firm's financial claims.

[4]The mere exchange of low-risk assets for high-risk assets does not alter the value of the firm if both assets have the same net present values. However, stockholders will have incentives to purchase projects with negative net present values if the increase in the firm's variance rate from accepting those projects is sufficiently large. Even though such projects reduce the total value of the firm, the value of the equity rises.

[5]Similarly, the value of the common stock at the time the bonds are issued will be higher to reflect possible transfers which shareholders will be able to effect. However, this is not to suggest that there is always a positive price at which the bonds can be sold. If the probability of a complete wealth transfer to stockholders prior to required payments to bondholders is 1, then the bonds will sell for a zero price.

two competing hypotheses. We call them the Irrelevance Hypothesis and the Costly Contracting Hypothesis.

1.2.1. The Irrelevance Hypothesis

The Irrelevance Hypothesis is that the manner of controlling the bondholder–stockholder conflict does not change the value of the firm.

Irrelevance under a fixed investment policy. In the Modigliani/Miller (1958) or Fama/Miller (1972) models the firm's investment policy is assumed fixed.[6] As long as the firm's total net cash flows are fixed, the value of the firm will not be changed by the existence or non-existence of protective covenants; with fixed cash flows, any gain which covenants give bondholders is a loss to stockholders, and vice versa. Covenants merely alter the distribution of a set of payoffs which is fixed to the firm's claimholders as a whole, and the choice of specific financial contracts is irrelevant to the value of the firm.

Irrelevance when investment policy is not fixed. Dividend payout, asset substitution, and underinvestment all represent potential opportunities for wealth transfer to stockholders. When these opportunities are available, the firm's investment policy cannot be regarded as fixed because it is likely to be altered by the presence of risky debt. The total value of the firm could be reduced if stockholders engage in actions which maximize the value of their own claims, but not the total value of the firm. However, even if investment policy cannot be regarded as fixed, mechanisms other than covenants exist which could be sufficient to induce the firm's stockholders to choose a firm-value-maximizing production/investment policy.

The forces exerted by external markets could induce the stockholders to maximize the value of the firm. Long (1973) suggests that the firm will accept all projects with a positive net present value if recapitalization is costless. Fama (1978a) argues that if takeovers are costless, the firm's owners always have an incentive to maximize the value of the firm. Additionally, ongoing firms have other incentives to follow a value-maximizing policy. Cases can be constructed in which a firm with a long history of deviating from such a policy in order to maximize only shareholder wealth will be worth less than it would have, had a value-maximizing policy been followed and expected to continue.

Ownership of the firm's claims could be structured in a way which controls the stockholders' incentive to follow a strategy which does not maximize the total value of the firm. Galai/Masulis (1976) suggest that if all investors hold equal proportions of both the firm's debt and the firm's equity

---

[6]The mechanism by which this fixity occurs is not well specified. However, the assumption of zero transactions costs in these models suggests that contractual provisions which fix investment policy and control the bondholder–stockholder conflict can be costlessly written and enforced.

issues, wealth redistributions among claimholders leave all investors indifferent. In such a case, bondholder–stockholder conflict arising over investment policy is costlessly controlled, and, even with risky debt, the stockholders will still follow a firm-value-maximizing strategy.

Thus, even when the firm's investment policy is not fixed, under the Irrelevance Hypothesis the stockholders' behavior is not altered by the presence of the bondholder–stockholder conflict. The influence of external markets or the possibility of restructuring the firm's claims implies that the choice of financial contracts is irrelevant to the value of the firm.

1.2.2. The Costly Contracting Hypothesis

The Costly Contracting Hypothesis is that control of the bondholder–stockholder conflict through financial contracts can increase the value of the firm. Like the Irrelevance Hypothesis, the Costly Contracting Hypothesis recognizes the influence which external markets and the possibility of recapitalization exert on the firm's choice of investment policy. However, this hypothesis presupposes that those factors, while controlling to some extent the bondholder–stockholder conflict, are insufficient to induce the stockholders to maximize the value of the firm rather than maximizing the value of the equity. The Costly Contracting Hypothesis underlies the work of Jensen/Meckling (1976), Myers (1977), and Miller (1977a).

Financial contracting is assumed to be costly. However, bond covenants, even if they involve costs, can increase the value of the firm at the time bonds are issued by reducing the opportunity loss which results when stockholders of a levered firm follow a policy which does not maximize the value of the firm. Furthermore, in the case of the claim dilution problem (which involves only a wealth transfer), if covenants lower the costs which bondholders incur in monitoring stockholders, the cost-reducing benefits of the covenants accrue to the firm's owners. With such covenants, the firm is worth more at the time the bonds are issued.

Under the Costly Contracting Hypothesis, there is a unique optimal set of financial contracts which maximizes the value of the firm. Note, however, that the bondholder–stockholder conflict would be resolved and its associated costs driven to zero without bond covenants if the firm never issued any risky debt. But for the firm to follow such a policy is costly if it is optimal to have risky debt in the firm's capital structure. Thus, the Costly Contracting Hypothesis presupposes that there are benefits associated with the inclusion of risky debt. Others have suggested benefits associated with issuance of risky debt which relate to, for example, (1) information asymmetries and signalling [Stiglitz (1972) and Ross (1977)], (2) taxes [Modigliani/Miller (1958, 1966)], (3) agency costs of equity financing [Jensen/Meckling (1976)], (4) differential transactions and flotation costs, and (5) unbundling of riskbearing and capital ownership [Fama (1978b)]. We do not address the issue of the exact nature of the benefit from the issuance of risky debt.

1.3. Evidence provided by an examination of bond covenants

In this paper, we use the data base provided by the *Commentaries* to distinguish between the Irrelevance and the Costly Contracting Hypotheses. Much of our evidence is qualitative rather than quantitative. Many social scientists are reluctant to consider such observations as evidence. However, qualitative evidence such as that provided by the *Commentaries* is frequently employed in the social sciences and in particular the property rights/economic analysis of law literature [see Alchian/Demsetz (1972), Cheung (1973), Coase (1960), Demsetz (1967), Manne (1967), and Posner (1972)]. Furthermore, qualitative evidence appears to have been instrumental in the development of the natural sciences [e.g., Darwin (1859)].[7]

Observation of persisting institutions represents important empirical evidence. However, we must specify precisely the nature of the evidence afforded by the observations under a particular hypothesis. After all, evidence (whether qualitative or quantitative) is useful only if it distinguishes among competing hypotheses;[8] what separates good empirical evidence from bad is not whether it can be reduced to numbers, but whether it increases our knowledge of how the world functions.

Debt covenants are a persistent phenomenon. They have been included in debt contracts for hundreds of years,[9] and over time the corporate debt contract which contains them has evolved into 'undoubtedly the most involved financial document that has been devised'.[10] The covenants discussed in *Commentaries* are representative of the covenants found in actual practice. As discussed by Rodgers (1965) and in the preface to the *Commentaries*, specific sections of the *Commentaries* were written by those considered to be the leading practitioners in their field. To check the correspondence between *Commentaries* and observed contractual provisions, we selected a random sample of 87 public issues of debt which were

---

[7]Darwin is perhaps the most familiar example; however, it is not the best. Although Darwin presents no quantitative evidence to support his hypotheses, his discussions are typically phrased in quantitative terms, referring to testable propositions about population sizes, etc. However, other areas of biology were developed totally without quantitative evidence. For example, see von Baer's work on embryology, Barnard's work in physiology, and Cuvier's work on taxonomy. For a general description of the development of the science of biology, see Coleman (1971).

[8]This proposition is well established in the philosophy literature. See Kuhn (1970), Nagel (1961), and Popper (1959).

[9]Rodgers (1965) discusses the evolution of debt contracts; he also discusses the history of the American Bar Foundation's Corporate Trust Indenture Project, under which the *Commentaries* were written.

[10]Kennedy (1961, p. 1).

registered with the Securities and Exchange Commission between January, 1974 and December, 1975. The standardized provisions of the type discussed in *Commentaries* are used frequently: 90.8 percent of the bonds contain restrictions on the issuance of additional debt, 23.0 percent have restrictions on dividend payments, 39.1 percent restrict merger activities, and 35.6 percent constrain the firm's disposition of assets. Furthermore, we found that when a particular provision is included, a boilerplate from *Commentaries* is used almost exclusively.

It seems reasonable that the covenants discussed in *Commentaries* have not arisen merely by chance; rather, they take their current form and have survived because they represent a contractual solution which is efficient from the standpoint of the firm.[11] As Alchian (1950) indicates, 'success (survival) accompanies relative superiority';[12] and 'whenever successful enterprises are observed, the elements common to those observed successes will be associated with success and copied by others in their pursuit of profits or success'.[13] Hence the *Commentaries* represents a powerful piece of evidence on efficient forms of the financial contract.

However, Miller (1977b, p. 273) indicates an important constraint on the use of this evidence: 'The most that we can safely assert about the evolutionary process underlying market equilibrium is that harmful heuristics, like harmful mutations in nature, will die out. Neutral mutations that serve no function, but do no harm, can persist indefinitely.' In addition to observing the persistence of covenants, we must demonstrate that the covenants involve out-of-pocket or opportunity costs for the firm, since the mere existence of covenants is consistent with both the Irrelevance and the Costly Contracting Hypotheses. But if covenants are costly, as we find in this paper, we must reject the Irrelevance Hypothesis. Similarly, the existence of the costly incentive-related covenants we discuss is inconsistent with the argument that external market forces and the possibility of restructuring the firm's claims provide a sufficient incentive for stockholders to follow a firm-value-maximizing policy. On the other hand, costly incentive-related covenants are exactly what would be expected under the Costly Contracting Hypothesis.

Given that the costs of restrictive covenants are positive, an important question is whether those costs are economically significant. The costs of particular covenants cannot easily be measured, and we present no direct evidence on the dollar magnitude of the costs. In a number of instances we use the assumption that such costs are important to generate testable propositions about the firm's capital structure. Although the evidence on the

---

[11]See Alchian (1950) and Stigler (1958) for a discussion of the survivorship principle.

[12]Alchian (1950, p. 213).

[13]Alchian (1950, p. 218).

importance of the bondholder–stockholder conflict is by no means conclusive, in several cases where the predictions of the analysis have been tested, the evidence is consistent with the theory. It appears that the Costly Contracting Hypothesis, which explains how firms reduce the costs of the bondholder–stockholder conflict, helps to account for the variation in debt contracts across firms. In contrast, the Irrelevance Hypothesis, while consistent with any observed set of contracts, yields no predictions about the form of the debt contract.

1.4. Overview of the paper

Observed debt covenants are discussed in section 2. To facilitate the discussion, observed covenants are grouped into four categories: production/investment covenants, dividend covenants, financing covenants, and bonding covenants. We use a common format for the discussion of each covenant; a particular type of covenant is first described, and its impact then analyzed.

Covenants which directly restrict the shareholders' choice of production/investment policy, are discussed in section 2.1. These covenants impose restrictions on the firm's holdings of financial investments, on the disposition of assets, and on the firm's merger activity. The observed constraints place few specific limitations on the firm's choice of investment policy. However, it is important to realize that, because of the cash flow identity, investment, dividend, and financing policy are not independent; they must be determined simultaneously. Thus, covenants which restrict dividend and financing policy also restrict investment policy.

Bond covenants which directly restrict the payment of dividends are considered in section 2.2. The dividend restriction does not take the form of a constant dollar limitation. Instead, the maximum allowable dividend payment is a function of both accounting earnings and the proceeds from the sale of new equity. The analysis suggests that the dividend covenant places an implicit constraint on the investment policy of the firm and provides the stockholders with incentives to follow a firm-value-maximizing production/investment policy.

Financing policy covenants are discussed in section 2.3. These covenants restrict not only the issuance of senior debt, but the issuance of debt of any priority. In addition, the firm's right to incur other fixed obligations such as leases is restricted. These restrictions appear to reduce the underinvestment incentives discussed by Myers (1977). In section 2.4, convertibility, callability, and sinking fund provisions are also examined. These provisions appear to specify payoffs to bondholders in a way which also controls bondholder–stockholder conflict.

In section 2.5, we analyze covenants which specify bonding activities –

expenditures made by the firm which control the bondholder–stockholder conflict. These bonding activities include the provision of audited financial statements, the specification of accounting techniques, the required purchase of insurance, and the periodic provision of a statement, signed by the firm's officers, indicating compliance with the covenants.

Just as the covenants described in section 2 are persistent phenomena, so are the institutions for enforcing these contractual restrictions. The enforcement of bond covenants within the existing institutional arrangements is the subject of section 3. The Trust Indenture Act of 1939 restricts the provisions of the debt contract for public issues in a way which makes the enforcement of tightly restrictive covenants very expensive. Another enforcement cost emanates from the legal liability which bondholders incur when they exercise control over the firm. Default remedies which are available to the firm, and their associated costs, are also discussed.

Our conclusions are presented in section 4.

2. A description and analysis of bond covenants

We group observed covenants into four categories: production/investment covenants, dividend covenants, financing covenants, and bonding covenants. Our discussion of the covenants covers all the restrictions reported in *Commentaries*; we have not singled out only particular types of covenants for discussion.[14]

2.1. Restrictions on the firm's production/investment policy

The stockholders' production/investment decisions could be directly constrained by explicitly specifying the projects which the firm is allowed to undertake. Alternatively, if it were costless to enforce, the debt contract could simply require the shareholders to accept all projects (and engage in only those actions) with positive net present values. Although certain covenants directly restrict the firm's investment policy, debt contracts discussed in *Commentaries* do not generally contain extensive restrictions of either form.

2.1.1. Restrictions on investments

Description. Bond covenants frequently restrict the extent to which the firm can become a claimholder in another business enterprise. That restriction, known as the 'investment' restriction, applies to common stock investments, loans, extensions of credit, and advances.[15] Alternative forms of this cov-

---

[14]However, note that we do not discuss the standard contractual provisions governing procedural matters (e.g., face amount, redemption procedure) which are necessary to define the firm's obligations as debt.

[15]Investments in direct obligations of the United States of America, prime commercial paper, and certificates of deposit are frequently excepted. *Commentaries* (p. 461, sample covenant 1A).

enant suggested in *Commentaries* either (1) flatly prohibit financial investments of this kind, (2) permit these financial investments only if net tangible
assets meet a certain minimum, or (3) permit such investments subject to
either an aggregate dollar limitation or a limitation representing a prespecified percentage of the firm's capitalization (owners' equity plus long-
term debt).

Analysis.   We suggest that stockholders contractually restrict their ability to
acquire financial assets in order to limit their ability to engage in asset
substitution after the bonds are issued.[16,17] However, the inclusion of the
investment covenant imposes opportunity costs. First, if there are economies
of scale in raising additional capital, or costs associated with changing
dividends, then allowing the purchase of financial assets can reduce these
costs.[18] Second, if a firm is involved in merger activities, the purchase of
equity claims of the target firm prior to the merger can also provide benefits.
Thus, the Costly Contracting Hypothesis predicts that bond contracts of
firms involved in merger activities, for which the opportunity cost of
restricting 'investments' is therefore high, will contain less restrictive investment covenants. However, our analysis does not predict which of the above
forms the investment restriction will take.

2.1.2. Restrictions on the disposition of assets

Description.   'The transfer of the assets of the obligor substantially as an
entirety' can be restricted by a standard boilerplate.[19] The contract can also
require that the firm not 'otherwise than in the ordinary course of business,
sell, lease, transfer, or otherwise dispose of any substantial part of its
properties and assets, including...any manufacturing plant or substantially
all properties and assets constituting the business of a division, branch, or
other unit operation'.[20] Another restriction is to permit asset disposition only

---

[16]Given that stockholders of most corporations are subject to double taxation of their returns,
financial assets are negative net present value projects whose acquisition reduces the value of the
firm. However, shareholders will have an incentive to purchase such assets if acquiring them
increases the variability of the firm's cash flows by enough to offset the reduction in the value of
the firm. Thus, the investments covenant raises the price to the stockholders of increasing the
variability of the firm's cash flows.

[17]An alternative explanation for the investment restriction is that it reduces the conflict
between managers and stockholders. The investment restriction typically applies to 'any person'.
Hence managers are restricted from making loans to themselves, as well as from investing the
firm's resources in firms which the managers own. We cannot reject this explanation for the
investment restriction. However, it is not clear why bondholders have a comparative advantage
(over stockholders) in policing managerial behavior of this form.

[18]That the purchase of short-term riskless assets is often allowed under the investments
restriction is consistent with this explanation. Stockholders cannot increase the variability of
cash flows with riskless assets. Furthermore, Treasury Bills dominate cash, which has a zero
pecuniary return.

[19]*Commentaries* (p. 423).

[20]*Commentaries* (p. 427, sample covenant 2).

up to a fixed dollar amount, or only so long as (1) the proceeds from the sale are applied to the purchase of new fixed assets, or (2) some fraction of the proceeds is used to retire the firm's debt.[21]

Analysis. The Costly Contracting Hypothesis suggests that restrictions on the sale of substantial units of the firm's assets are observed because, in general, the proceeds if assets are sold piecemeal will be less than if sold as a going concern.[22] By imposing the higher cost of piecemeal sale, this covenant also raises the cost to stockholders of substituting variance increasing assets for those currently owned by the firm.

One cost associated with flat prohibitions on the sale of particular assets rises from the fact that the firm is not permitted to divest itself of those assets whose value to others is greater than the value to itself. Thus the restriction which permits asset sale if the proceeds are applied to the purchase of new fixed assets lowers this opportunity cost. However, a provision which permits such asset exchange is costly because it allows for the possibility of obtaining variance increasing negative net present value assets in the exchange. The stipulation that a fraction of the proceeds from the sale of assets be used for the retirement of the firm's debt makes asset substitution more expensive for stockholders by requiring a concurrent increase in the coverage on, and thus the value of, the outstanding debt.

2.1.3. Secured debt

Description. Securing debt gives the bondholders title to pledged assets until the bonds are paid in full. Thus, when secured debt is issued the firm cannot dispose of the pledged assets without first obtaining permission of the bondholders.

Analysis. We suggest that the issuance of secured debt lowers the total costs of borrowing by controlling the incentives for stockholders to take projects which reduce the value of the firm; since bondholders hold title to the assets, secured debt limits asset substitution. Secured debt also lowers administrative costs and enforcement costs by ensuring that the lender has clear title to the assets and by preventing the lender's claim from being jeopardized if the borrower subsequently issues additional debt. In addition, collateralization

---

[21]Such provisions typically apply to the retirement of the firm's funded (i.e., long-term) debt. The covenant in a particular bond issue requires that *all* the firm's debt be retired on a prorated basis. To require that only the particular bond issue containing the covenant be retired might well violate the firm's other debt agreements.

[22]Given that selling substantial portions of the firm's assets can be illegal under, for example, the Uniform Fraudulent Conveyance Act, the standard boilerplate would seem redundant. Our theory does not explain the redundancy of the terms of the bond contract and the constraints implied by the legal system. But in the case of this boilerplate, we suggest that, should the assets of the firm be sold, subjecting the firm's managers to civil and criminal liability alone is a more costly remedy than allowing the bondholders to put the firm in default.

reduces expected foreclosure expenses because it is less expensive to tsae possession of property to which the lender already has established title.

However, secured debt involves out of pocket costs (e.g., required reports to the debt-holders, filing fees, and other administrative expenses). Securing debt also involves opportunity costs by restricting the firm from potentially profitable dispositions of collateral.

The Costly Contracting Hypothesis leads to two predictions about the use of secured debt. First, if the firm goes into bankruptcy proceedings and the collateral is judged necessary for the continued operation of the firm, the bankruptcy judge can prohibit the bondholders from taking possession of the property. Thus for firms where liquidation is more likely than re-organization (e.g., for smaller firms), the issuance of secured debt will be greater. Second, we would expect more frequent use of secured debt the less specialized the firm's resources. To the extent that assets (such as a patent right) are highly specialized and firm-specific, their value is greater to the firm than in the market place. Consequently, it will be costly to the stockholders if they dispose of such assets in order to engage in asset substitution. The more specialized the assets, the more costly is asset substitution to stockholders, the tighter the implicit constraint on asset sale, and thus the less likely is the use of secured debt.[23]

2.1.4. Restrictions on mergers

Description. Some indenture agreements contain a flat prohibition on mergers. Others permit the acquisition of other firms provided that certain conditions are met. For example, *Commentaries* suggests restrictions in which the merger is permitted only if the net tangible assets of the firm, calculated on a post-merger basis, meet a certain dollar minimum, or are at least a certain fraction of long-term debt. The merger can also be made contingent on there being no default on any indenture provision after the transaction is completed.

The acquisition and consolidation of the firm into another can be permitted subject to certain requirements. For example, the corporation into which the company is merged must assume all of the obligations in the initial indenture. Article 800 of the American Bar Foundation *Model Debenture Indenture Provisions* also requires that there be no act of default after completion of the consolidation, and that the company certify that fact through the delivery to the trustee of an officer's certificate and an opinion of counsel.

Analysis. Since the stockholders of the two firms must approve a merger, the market value of the equity claims of both the acquired and acquiring firm must be expected to rise or the merger will not be approved by

---

[23]For a further discussion of secured debt, see Scott (1977) and Smith/Warner (1979).

stockholders of the respective firms.[24] A merger between two firms usually results in changes in the value of particular classes of outstanding claims because both the asset and liability structure of the resulting firm differ from that of the predecessor firms. The effects of a merger on the value of particular claims depend upon: (1) the degree of synergy brought about by the merger, (2) the resources consumed in accomplishing the merger, (3) the variance rates of the pre-merger firms' cash flows, (4) the correlation coefficient between the merged firms' cash flows, and (5) the capital structure (i.e., ratio of face value of debt to market value of all claims) of the respective firms. A merger leaves the value of outstanding debt claims unaffected if (1) the merger involves no synergy, (2) there are no transactions costs, (3) the pre-merger firm's cash flows have equal variance rates, (4) the correlation coefficient between the merged firms' cash flows is $+1$, and (5) the pre-merger firms have the same capital structure.

With no contractual constraints against mergers, the value of the bondholders' claims can be reduced due to the effect of a difference in variance rates or a difference in capital structures. Our analysis implies, then, that merger restrictions limit the stockholders' ability to use mergers to increase either the firm's variance rate or the debt to asset ratio to the detriment of the bondholders. Note that to the extent that synergistic mergers are prevented by this covenant, the firm suffers an opportunity loss.[25]

2.1.5. Covenants requiring the maintenance of assets

Description. The covenants we have discussed constrain production/investment policy by prohibiting certain actions. However, the firm's operating decisions can also be limited by *requiring* that it take certain actions, that it invest in certain projects, or hold particular assets. Examples of such covenants are those requiring the maintenance of the firm's properties and maintenance of the firm's working capital (i.e., current assets less current liabilities).[26] *Commentaries* offers covenants which require the firm to maintain working capital above a certain minimum level. Frequently, activities

---

[24]This is consistent with the evidence of Dodd/Ruback (1977) and Bradley (1978). They find that, on average, there is positive abnormal performance for common stocks of both acquiring and acquired firms.

[25]As we discuss in section 2.3, the indenture agreements typically require that the firm comply with one or more tests (such as minimum ratios of net tangible assets to funded debt) in order to issue additional debt. According to *Commentaries*, when additional debt obligations are incurred through a merger, for purposes of the tests, the debt incurred can be treated as having been issued as of the merger. Thus, financing policy covenants can be employed to control mergers.

[26]Another restriction on increases in the risk of the firm's activities is a covenant requiring that the firm stay in the same line of business. For example, the Associated Dry Goods Credit Corporation Notes of 1983 require that the firm 'not engage in any business other than dealing in Deferred Payment Accounts'. This covenant thus makes it more costly to engage in asset substitution.

such as mergers are made contingent upon the maintenance of working capital

Analysis. While a covenant can require that the firm maintain its properties, such a covenant will not have much impact if it is expensive to enforce. However, if the maintenance is performed by an independent agent, enforcement costs are expected to be lower and such a restriction will be effective. For example, in the shipping industry, where maintenance services are typically provided through third parties, bond covenants frequently explicitly include service and dry-docking schedules in the indenture.

We suggest that the working capital requirement is included because any violation of the covenant provides a signal to the lender. This signal can result in renegotiation of the debt contract, an alternative preferable to default when bankruptcy is more costly than renegotiation. This hypothesis is consistent with the interpretation of the working capital covenant in *Commentaries* (p. 453): 'If a breach of the covenant occurs, the lender is in a position to use this early warning to take whatever remedial action is necessary.'

2.1.6. Covenants which indirectly restrict production/investment policy

Stockholder use (or misuse) of production/investment policy frequently involves not some action, but the failure to take a certain action (e.g., failure to accept a positive net present value project). Because of this, investment policy can be very expensive to monitor, since ascertaining that the firm's production/investment policy does not maximize the firm's market value depends on magnitudes which are costly to observe. Solutions to this problem are not obvious. For example, if the indenture were to require the bondholders (rather than the stockholders) to establish the firm's investment policy, the problem would not be solved; the bondholders, acting in their self interest, would choose an investment policy which maximized the value of the bonds, not the value of the firm.[27] In addition, there are other costs associated with giving bondholders a role in establishing the firm's investment policy. For instance, as we discuss in section 3, legal costs can be imposed on bondholders if they are deemed to have assumed control of the corporation.

However, direct restrictions on the stockholder's choice of production/investment policy are only one way to limit the projects in which the firm can engage. Covenants constraining the firm's dividend and financing policies can also be written in a way which serves a similar function, since the firm's production/investment, dividend, and financing policies are linked through the cash flow identity. If direct restrictions on production/investment policy

---

[27]Jensen/Meckling refer to this as the symmetry property.

were sufficiently expensive to enforce, dividend and financing policy covenants would be the only efficient way of constraining the firm's actions.

2.2. Bond covenants restricting the payment of dividends

Description. Cash dividend payments to stockholders, if financed by a reduction in investment, reduce the value of the firm's bonds by decreasing the expected value of the firm's assets at the maturity date of the bonds, making default more likely. Thus, it is not surprising that bond covenants frequently[28] restrict the payment of cash dividends to shareholders.[29] Since the payment of dividends *in cash* is just one form which distributions to stockholders can take, actual dividend covenants reflect alternative possibilities. For example, if the firm enters the market and repurchases its own stock the coverage on the debt decreases in exactly the same way as it would if a cash dividend were paid. The constraints discussed in *Commentaries* relate not only to cash dividends, but to 'all distributions on account of or in respect of capital stock...whether they be dividends, redemptions, purchases, retirements, partial liquidations or capital reductions and whether in cash, in kind, or in the form of debt obligations of the company'.[30]

The dividend covenant usually establishes a limit on distributions to stockholders by defining an inventory of funds available for dividend payments over the life of the bonds.[31] The inventory is not constant; rather, it is allowed to change as a function of certain variables whose values can be influenced by the stockholders. Typically, the inventory of funds available for the payment of dividends in quarter τ, D_τ^*, can be expressed as

$$D_\tau^* = k\left(\sum_{t=0}^{\tau} E_t\right) + \left(\sum_{t=0}^{\tau} S_t\right) + F - \left(\sum_{t=0}^{\tau-1} D_t\right), \tag{1}$$

[28]Kalay (1979) reports that in a sample of 150 randomly selected industrial firms, every firm had a dividend restriction in at least one of its debt instruments.

[29]According to Henn (1970, pp. 648–656) most states have also limited the source of dividends to legally prescribed funds. Various laws define the funds legally available for dividends in terms of (1) earned surplus, (2) net profits or net earnings, (3) non-impairment of capital, (4) insolvency, or some combination. Directors are often made liable by statute (and possibly subject to criminal penalties) for dividends paid out of funds not legally available. Even apart from statutes expressing such limitation, distribution of dividends which would render the corporation insolvent is probably wrongful in most jurisdictions on principles of the law of creditors' rights.

[30]*Commentaries* (p. 405). It should be noted that the problem of constraining the firm's investment in financial assets, which we discussed in section 2.1, is sometimes handled within the dividend covenant. Distributions restricted under the dividend covenant can be defined to include purchases of securities by the firm. Under this definition, the stockholders of the firm can choose to hold any amount of financial investments so long as they give up an equal amount of dividends.

[31]Kennedy (1961, p. 137). In his study of dividend covenants, Kalay (1978) finds that most of them take the form discussed here.

where, for quarter t,

E_t is net earnings,
S_t is the proceeds from the sale of common stock net of transactions costs,
F is a number which is fixed over the life of the bonds, known as the 'dip',
k is a constant, $0 \leq k \leq 1$.

Hence the inventory of funds is a positive function of the earnings which the firm has accumulated, a positive function of the extent to which the firm has sold new equity claims, and a negative function of the dividends paid since the bonds were issued at $t = 0$.

The payment of a dividend is not permitted if its payment would cause the inventory to be drawn below zero. The inventory can become negative if the firm's earnings are negative. In that case, no dividend is permitted. However, stockholders are not required to make up the deficiency.[32] Thus the dividend payment in quarter τ, D_τ, must satisfy the constraint

$$D_\tau \leq \max[0, D_\tau^*]. \tag{2}$$

Analysis. This form of dividend covenant has several interesting features. The dividend restriction is not an outright prohibition on the payment of dividends. In fact, the stockholders are permitted to have any level of dividends they choose, so long as the payment of those dividends is financed out of new earnings or through the sale of new equity claims. The dividend covenant acts as a restriction not on dividends *per se*, but on the payment of dividends financed by issuing debt or by the sale of the firm's existing assets, either of which would reduce the coverage on, and thus the value of, the debt.

The dividend covenant described in eqs. (1) and (2) coupled with the cash-flow identity that inflows equal outflows constrain investment policy.[33] The cash-flow identity for the firm can be expressed as

$$D_t + R_t + P_t + I_t \equiv \phi_t + S_t + B_t, \tag{3}$$

where, for quarter t,

D_t is the dividend paid,
R_t is interest paid,
P_t is debt principal paid,
I_t is new investment,
ϕ_t is the firm's cash flow.

---

[32]Given limited liability, a covenant requiring that a positive balance be maintained in the inventory and that individual shareholders be assessed for deficiencies is probably not enforceable without considerable cost.

[33]We would like to thank John Long for suggesting this expositional model and for helpful discussions on this point.

S_t is the proceeds from the sale of equity net of transactions cost,
B_t is the proceeds from the sale of bonds net of transactions cost.

The firm's cash flow, ϕ_t, can be expressed as[34]

$$\phi_t \equiv E_t + d_t + R_t + L_t, \tag{4}$$

where, for quarter t,

E_t is the firm's net earnings,
d_t is depreciation,
L_t is the book value of any assets liquidated.[35]

Substituting (3) into (4) and solving for D_t yields

$$D_t \equiv E_t + d_t + R_t + L_t - I_t + S_t + B_t - R_t - P_t. \tag{5}$$

To see how the dividend covenant constrains investment policy, consider the simplest case. Assume that an all equity firm sells bonds at par with a covenant that it will issue no additional debt over the life of the bonds (i.e., $B_t = 0$ for $t \neq 0$, and $P_t = 0$ for $t \neq T$). If we also assume that $F \equiv 0$, and $k \equiv 1$, then substituting (5) and (1) into (2) yields the condition for dividends in quarter τ to be positive,

$$B_0 \leq \sum_{t=0}^{\tau} (I_t - L_t - d_t). \tag{6}$$

The right-hand side of (6) is simply the cumulative change in the book value of the firm's assets since the bonds were sold. Thus in this simple case, the dividend covenant requires that for dividends to be paid in the quarter the bonds are issued, investment must be large enough that the net change in the book value of the firm's assets be no less than the net proceeds from the sale of the debt – the firm cannot borrow to pay dividends. The constraint also requires that in subsequent quarters investment be large enough for the book value of the firm's assets to be maintained at that level.

If the assumptions that $k = 1$ and $F = 0$ are now relaxed, then eq. (6) becomes

$$B_0 + (1-k)\left(\sum_{t=0}^{\tau} E_t\right) - F \leq \sum_{t=0}^{\tau} (I_t - L_t - d_t). \tag{7}$$

---

[34]For purposes of illustration we assume that the accrual is depreciation and that all items other than depreciation, interest payments, and liquidations affect cash flows and earnings in the same way.

[35]L_t is defined as the book value of assets liquidated when earnings includes gains or losses on the sale of assets. If such gains or losses are not included in earnings, then L_t is the proceeds from the liquidation.

Setting k between zero and one requires that if the firm has positive earnings, the book value of the assets of the firm must actually increase in order for dividends to be paid.[36]

By placing a maximum on distributions, the dividend covenant effectively places a minimum on investment expenditures by the owners of the firm, as Myers and Kalay (1979) argue. This reduces the underinvestment problem discussed by Myers, since so long as the firm *has* to invest, profitable projects are less likely to be turned down.

While having a tight dividend constraint controls the stockholders incentives associated with the dividend payout problem, there are several associated costs. An outright prohibition on dividends or allowing dividends but setting k less than one increases the probability that the firm will be forced to invest when it has no available profitable projects. Investment in securities of other firms is not always possible, since purchases of capital market instruments (which in the absence of corporate taxes have zero net present value) are frequently prohibited by the investments covenant we discussed in section 2.1. Even if financial investments are not restricted, Kalay argues that if the firm pays income taxes on its earnings, the taxation of the returns from the financial assets makes them negative net present value projects.[37]

The tighter restriction on dividends implied by a lower k also increases the stockholders' incentives to engage in asset substitution, and increases the gain to the firm's shareholders from choosing high variance, negative net present value projects. Assume that negative net present value projects generate negative accounting earnings. Then from the first term of eq. (1), the inventory available for dividends will be reduced by taking such a project. The lower the value of k, the smaller the reduction in the inventory. To the extent that dividends transfer wealth to stockholders, the marginal impact of lowering k is thus to increase the gain (or decrease the loss) to shareholders from accepting such projects. However, as we discuss below, a lower k also confers benefits, since it reduces the stockholders' incentive to engage in 'creative accounting' to increase reported earnings.

If it is costly to restrict dividends, not all debt agreements will include a dividend restriction. Dividend covenants would be expected only if there are offsetting benefits. One prediction of our analysis is that the presence of a dividend covenant should be related to the maturity of the debt. Thus, short-

---

[36]The value of k is less than 1 in about 20 percent of the dividend covenants which Kalay (1979) examines. According to *Commentaries* (p. 414), the 'dip', F, is equal to about a year's earnings. Kalay finds that the mean value of the dip, as a fraction of earnings, is indeed approximately 1.

[37]We conjecture that the specification of a positive F in the debt contract is directed at reducing the costs of temporarily having no profitable investment projects and being unable to pay dividends. In spite of the increased payouts it allows, the dip permits a dividend to be paid to shareholders even when earnings are negative and the firm has not sold new equity.

term debt instruments (such as commercial paper) are less likely to contain dividend restrictions than long-term debt; if liquidation of the firm's assets within a short period of time is sufficiently costly to the shareholders, they are better off not selling the firm's assets for cash in order to pay themselves a dividend. This implicit constraint on dividend payout becomes less restrictive the longer the time to maturity of the debt, and the cost-offsetting benefits of an explicit dividend constraint thus become greater as a function of maturity.

Evidence. Kalay develops and tests a number of propositions about how the dividend constraint will be set. He argues that the shareholders' incentive to sell assets for cash is greater the higher the fraction of the firm consisting of debt: the higher that fraction, the greater the potential wealth transfer to stockholders. Consistent with the argument that the dividend constraint involves costs, he finds a significant negative cross-sectional relationship between the dividends which can be paid out under the constraint and the firm's debt/equity ratio.[38]

Kalay also reports that firms do not always pay out all of the dividends to which they are entitled under the indenture agreement. He argues that firms maintain such an 'inventory of payable funds' because having an inventory reduces the probability that the firm will be unable to pay dividends and thus be forced to invest when there are temporarily no profitable investment projects. However, if stockholders maintain an inventory and fail to pay out all funds available for dividends, wealth transfers from bondholders are foregone. On this basis, Kalay posits that the shareholders' incentive to maintain an inventory is lower the higher the firm's leverage. That proposition is consistent with his finding that there is a significant negative relationship between the firm's debt/equity ratio and the (size adjusted) 'inventory of payable funds'.

2.2.1. Control of investment incentives when the inventory is negative

Throughout the above analysis we have assumed that the inventory of funds available for the payment of dividends, D_{τ}^{*}, is positive. If the firm has been experiencing negative earnings, the inventory can become negative; with a negative inventory, no dividends can be paid. The negative earnings which lead to a dividend prohibition are likely to be associated with a fall in the value of the firm, and an increase in both its debt/equity ratio and the probability of default on its debt. Hence at the times when a dividend

---

[38]The effective constraint on dividends cannot be determined without considering dividend covenants across all the firm's bond issues. Kalay treats the tightness of the dividend constraint with this in mind; the negative relationship he postulates is between the amount which can be paid out (adjusted for firm size) under the firm's *most* restrictive dividend constraint and its leverage.

prohibition comes into play, the firm is also likely to be faced with greater incentives to engage in asset substitution and claim dilution.

When the firm is doing poorly, the dividend constraint is not capable of controlling the investment and financing policy problem induced by the presence of risky debt. But the direct limitations on production/investment policy we discussed in section 2.1 can limit the stockholders' actions when the inventory for payment of dividends is negative. In addition, financing policy covenants not only address the claim dilution problem, but independently reinforce the effect of the dividend covenant in restricting production/investment policy.

2.3. Bond covenants restricting subsequent financing policy

2.3.1. Limitations on debt and priority

Description. In section 1 we discussed the stockholders' incentives to reduce the value of the outstanding bonds by subsequently issuing additional debt of higher priority, thereby diluting the bondholders' claim on the assets of the firm. Covenants suggested in *Commentaries* limit stockholders actions in this area in one of two ways: either through a simple prohibition against issuing claims with a higher priority, or through a restriction on the creation of a claim with higher priority unless the existing bonds are upgraded to have equal priority. The latter restriction requires, for example, that if secured debt is sold after the issuance of the bonds, the existing bondholders must have their priority upgraded and be given an equal claim on the collateral with the secured debtholders.

In addition to restricting the issuance of debt of higher priority, there are sample covenants in *Commentaries* restricting the stockholders' right to issue *any* additional debt. Issuance of new debt can be subject to aggregate dollar limitations. Alternatively, issuing debt can be prohibited unless the firm maintains minimum prescribed ratios between (1) net tangible assets and funded (i.e., long-term) debt, (2) capitalization and funded debt, (3) tangible net worth[39] and funded debt, (4) income and interest charges (referred to as earnings tests), or (5) current assets and current debt (referred to as working capital tests). There are also provisions requiring the company to be free from debt for limited periods (referred to as 'clean-up' provisions). Combinations of two or more of these limitations are sometimes included in the indenture agreement.

It is important to note the scope of the restrictions imposed through the

---

[39]Some definitions of net worth include subordinated debt and thus treat it as equity. Thus the issuance of debt of equal priority is limited, and the constraint on the issuance of junior debt is relaxed. Our theory does not explain which alternative definition of net worth will be appropriate for a given firm.

covenants limiting the issuance of additional debt. In addition to money borrowed, the covenants also apply to other liabilities incurred by the firm. Other debt-like obligations which can be limited by the covenants are: (1) assumptions or guarantees of indebtedness of other parties,[40] (2) other contingent obligations which are analogous to, but may not technically constitute, guarantees; (3) amounts payable in installments on account of the purchase of property under purchase money mortgages, conditional sales agreements or other long-term contracts; (4) obligations secured by mortgage on property acquired by the company subject to the mortgage but without assumption of the obligations.

Since the claims of the firm in subsidiary corporations are like that of a stockholder, if a subsidiary issues debt or preferred stock the coverage afforded the bondholders of the parent firm is reduced. Thus the limitations on debt usually apply to the debt of the consolidated firm.[41]

Analysis. Our analysis suggests that it is generally not optimal to prevent all future debt issues. If, as the firm's opportunity set evolves over time, new investments must be financed by new equity issues or by reduced dividends, then with risky debt outstanding part of the gains from the investment goes to bondholders, rather than stockholders. Those investments increase the coverage on the debt, and reduce the default risk borne by the bondholders. To the extent such reductions are unanticipated, they result in an increase in the value of outstanding bonds at the expense of the stockholders. So a prohibition of all debt issues would reduce the value of the firm because wealth maximizing stockholders would not take all positive net present value projects. The possibility of asset substitution increases the costs of outright prohibition on debt issues and makes variance reducing positive net present value projects less attractive. However, our analysis suggests that contractually agreeing to have *some* degree of restriction on future debt issues is in the interests of the firm's owners. By merely restricting the total amount of *all* debt which can be issued, the perverse investment incentives associated with debt discussed by Myers (1977) are limited.

---

[40]The third edition of Dewing (1934, p. 105) discusses the Denver Rio Grande Railroad, which is the 'classic case' of a guaranteed bond which brought a severe test of the strength of the guarantor:

> 'The old Western Pacific Railway was built for strategic reasons in order to complete a Pacific coast extension for the Denver and Rio Grande Railroad – all a part of Gould's contemplated transcontinental railway system. The bonds of the Western Pacific were guaranteed, principal and interest, by the Denver and Rio Grande. When it developed that the Western Pacific failed to earn the interest charges, default occurred, and the Western Pacific passed into the hands of receivers.
>
> The Denver and Rio Grande Railroad, having failed to meet the guarantees, was ordered to pay over to the trustees of the Western Pacific bonds the sum of $38,000,000. Thereupon the Denver and Rio Grande itself failed.'

[41]Borrowing by a subsidiary from the company or another subsidiary is excluded.

Financing-policy covenants also impact on investment incentives in other ways. In section 2.1, we discussed the direct limitations on financial investments included in bond covenants. Financial investments can also be restricted through the debt covenant. For example, when debt is limited to a specific percentage of net tangible assets, financial investments are sometimes excluded from the definition of net tangible assets for purposes of the covenant. This definition allows the firm to hold a portion of its assets as financial investments, but requires the firm to reduce the debt and its capital structure to do so, thus controlling the asset substitution problem associated with financial investments.

Financing policy impacts on production/investment policy through the dividend covenant. If the level of outstanding debt changes over the life of the bonds, eq. (6) (which presumes that no additional debt is either issued or repaid) must be modified,

$$\sum_{t=0}^{\tau} (B_t - P_t) \leqq \sum_{t=0}^{\tau} (I_t - L_t - d_t), \qquad (8)$$

where

B_t is the proceeds from the sale of bonds net of transactions costs,
P_t is debt principal paid,
I_t is new investment,
L_t is the book value of any assets liquidated,
d_t is depreciation.

The left-hand side of eq. (8) is simply the cumulative change in the book value of the firm's debt since the sale of this bond issue at $t = 0$. For dividends to be paid the cumulative change in the book value of the assets must be no less than the cumulative change in the book value of the debt. Thus the stockholders cannot borrow to finance dividend payments.

2.3.2. Limitations on rentals, lease, and sale-leasebacks

Description. Commentaries offers alternative restrictions on the stockholders' use of lease or rental contracts. The covenant typically restricts the firm from the sale-leaseback of property owned prior to the date of the indenture.[42] Some covenants also exclude individual leases or sale-leasebacks below a specified dollar total. Lease payments can also be limited to a fraction of net income. Finally, leasing and renting can be controlled through the debt covenant by capitalizing the lease liability and including it in both

---

[42]This restriction sometimes applies only to specific property (e.g., manufacturing property or heavy equipment) or applies except for items specifically exempted (e.g., office space, warehouses, or automobiles). Alternatively, only long-term leases are covered, with a condition that for short-term leases the company discontinue the use of the property after the term of the lease.

the long-term debt definition and asset definitions. In this case, the covenant specifies the procedure for computing the capitalized value of the asset and liability.[43]

Analysis. Continued use of leased or rented assets by the firm is contingent on making the lease or rental payments. These payments represent liabilities to the firm, and are a claim senior to that of the debtholders: such obligations reduce the value of the outstanding bondholders' claim. For this reason, the Costly Contracting Hypothesis predicts restrictions on the stockholders' subsequent use of leases in the indenture agreement. However, we are unable to explain the specific form which the restriction will take for a particular set of firm characteristics.

2.4. Bond covenants modifying the pattern of payoffs to bondholders

There are several provisions which specify a particular pattern of payoffs to bondholders in a way which controls various sources of stockholder–bondholder conflict of interest.

2.4.1. Sinking funds

Description. A sinking fund is simply a means of amortizing part or all of an indebtedness prior to its maturity. A sinking fund bond is like an installment loan.[44] In the case of a public bond issue, the periodic payments can be invested either in the bonds which are to be retired by the fund or in some other securities. The sinking fund payments can be fixed, variable or contingent. For the years 1963–1965, 82 percent of all publicly-offered issues included sinking fund provisions.[45]

Analysis. A sinking fund affects the firm's production/investment policy through the dividend constraint. From eq. (8) we see that if a sinking fund is included in the indenture, principal repayment, P_t, will be positive prior to the maturity date of the bond; the book value of the assets of the firm can decline over the life of the bond issue without violating the dividend constraint. A sinking fund reduces the possibility that the dividend constraint will require investment when no profitable projects are available. One potential cost associated with the dividend constraint is thus reduced.

Myers (1977) has suggested that sinking funds are a device to reduce

---

[43]See *Commentaries* (p. 440).

[44]In a private placement, the amortization may simply require periodic partial payments to the holder. An alternative to a sinking fund it to provide for serial maturities with part of the issue maturing at fixed dates. This practice is rarely used in the corporate bond market presumably because with fewer identical contracts, maintenance of a secondary market in the bond contracts is more expensive.

[45]See Norgaard/Thompson (1967, p. 31). Note also that in enforcing the Public Utilities Holding Company Act, the SEC requires a sinking fund to be included.

creditors' exposure in parallel with the expected decline in the value of the assets supporting the debt. Myers' analysis implies that sinking funds would be more likely to be included in debt issues (1) the higher the fraction of debt in the capital structure, (2) the greater the anticipated future discretionary investment by the firm and (3) the higher the probability that the project will have a limited lifetime. One industry which illustrates an extreme of the last of these characteristics is the gas pipeline industry. The sinking fund payments required in some gas pipeline debentures are related to the remaining available gas in the field.[46]

Not all debt issues have sinking funds; their exclusion from some contracts can be explained by anticipated costs which sinking funds can impose on the trustee if there is a default. Although the application of sinking fund monies is set forth in the covenant, should default occur the applicable law is not clear.[47] Even where only one series of bonds is involved, application of funds to the retirement of specific bonds with knowledge of a default might involve participation by the trustee in an unlawful preference for which the trustee might be held liable.

2.4.2. Convertibility provisions

Description. A convertible debenture is one which gives the holder the right to exchange the debentures for other securities of the company, usually shares of common stock and usually without payment of further compensation. The convertible must contain provisions specifying:

[46]The model indenture provision on this point from the American Bar Foundation (1971) states:

> 'The Company will file with the Trustee on or before..., and on or before each [insert month and day] thereafter so long as the Debentures shall remain Outstanding, a Certificate of Available Gas Supply. In the event that any such Certificate shall show that the date of exhaustion of available gas supply of the Company is a date earlier than..., the aggregate of the Sinking Fund installments due on the next succeeding Sinking Fund Date and each Sinking Fund Date thereafter up to and including the Sinking Fund Date immediately preceding a date (herein called the Margin Date) two years prior to said date of exhaustion of available gas supply shall be increased by an amount equal to the aggregate of the Sinking Fund instalments due on and after the Margin Date, each such Sinking Fund Instalment coming due between the date of such Certificate and the Margin Date being increased proportionately, as nearly as may be, so that each increased installment shall be multiple of $1,000 and the Sinking Fund installments due on and after the Margin Date shall be eliminated and the schedule of Sinking Fund installments thus revised shall constitute the schedule of Sinking Fund installments under this Indenture until further revised as hereinafter provided.'

[47]If specific bonds have been selected for purchase or redemption by the sinking fund, and all necessary steps have been taken except the actual surrender of the bonds, the funds in the hands of the trustee become specifically allocated to the selected bonds. In the event of subsequent default the holder is entitled to payment upon surrender of the bonds, regardless of the payoff to the other bondholders. If default occurs before all steps necessary for retirement of a specific bond have been concluded, all further action is typically suspended. Any preliminary steps taken are revoked, and the funds are retained by the trustee until the default is cured or the trustee receives judicial direction as to the disposition of the funds.

(1) The type of security issuable upon conversion. This is usually common stock of the company, but occasionally it has been stock of a parent or affiliated corporation.

(2) The duration of the conversion period. This may start at the time of issuance or after a specified date, and run until maturity, redemption, or some specified earlier date. The New York Bond Exchange will not permit the designation 'convertible' on the issue unless the privilege extends for the life of the debenture. The exchange will permit the formal designation to be followed by '(convertible prior to...)'.

(3) The conversion price at which the stock can be acquired. The conversion price may be the same for the entire period or increase at stated intervals. The conversion price is normally payable only by surrender of a like principal amount of the debentures but occasionally the payment of cash in a fixed ratio to debentures is also required.

(4) Additional Procedural Points. E.g., where must the issue be surrendered for conversion? Does the debenture holder receive accrued interest upon conversion? Will the firm issue fractional shares?

(5) Antidilution Provisions. Provisions which protect the conversion privilege against certain actions by the stockholders such as stock splits, stock dividends, rights offerings, issuance of other convertible securities, mergers, and the distribution of assets.

Analysis. Jensen/Meckling (1976) and Mikkelson (1978) discuss the use of convertible debt as a way to control aspects of the bondholder–stockholder conflict of interest. With non-convertible debt outstanding, the stockholders have the incentive to take projects which raise the variability of the firm's cash flows. The stockholders can increase the value of the equity by adding a new project· with a negative net present value if the firm's cash flow variability rises sufficiently. The inclusion of a convertibility provision in the debt reduces this incentive. The conversion privilege is like a call option written by the stockholders and attached to the debt contract. It reduces the stockholders' incentive to increase the variability of the firm's cash flows, because with a higher variance rate, the attached call option becomes more valuable. Therefore the stockholders' gain from increasing the variance rate is smaller with the convertible debt outstanding than with non-convertible debt.

However, not all debt contracts include a convertibility provision since it is costly to do so.[48] For example, the underinvestment problem is exacerbated with convertible debt outstanding.

---

[48]If part of the incentive for issuing debt comes from the tax deductibility of interest payments, then the tax treatment of interest payments by the Internal Revenue Service can be important and is affected by whether the debt is convertible. Where the capitalization of a corporation is largely debt, the IRS under Section 385 of the Tax Code can contend that some of the 'loans' are in fact capital contributions, and will deny the deduction of 'interest' on the loans. While debt-equity ratios of as much as 700 to 1 have been allowed for tax purposes, the

Evidence. Mikkelson (1978) presents cross-sectional evidence that the probability of the inclusion of the conversion privilege is positively related to (1) the firm's debt/equity ratio, (2) the firm's level of discretionary investment expenditure, and (3) the time to maturity of the debt. Each of these relationships is consistent with the Costly Contracting Hypothesis, and the hypothesis that the benefits of convertible debt are related to a reduction in the bondholder–stockholder conflict.

2.4.3. Callability provisions

Description. The firm's right to redeem the debentures before maturity at a stated price is typically included in the indenture agreement. Without the inclusion of the callability provision in the indenture agreement, a debenture holder cannot be compelled to accept payment of his debenture prior to its stated maturity date. In the usual case, the call price is not constant over the life of the bonds. The redemption price in a callable bond normally is initially set equal to the public offering price plus one year's interest on the bond. The schedule of call prices then typically scales the call premium to zero by a date one year prior to the maturity of the bonds, although it is sometimes as early as two to five years prior to maturity.

Analysis. We have suggested that if agency costs of equity are zero and recapitalization of the firm is costless, the firm will accept all projects with positive net present values and thus the stockholder–bondholder conflict of interest will be solved. One cost of buying out bondholders in a recapitalization results from the additional premium the bondholders demand for the firm to repurchase the bonds. Since the firm cannot vote bonds which it repurchases, a bilateral monopoly results from the attempt to repurchase

---

Treasury is inclined to look askance at 'loans' by stockholders in proportion to their stockholdings to a corporation with a high debt-equity ratio.

Whether stockholder advances to a corporation are loans or equity is a question of fact under the Tax Code. The taxpayer has the burden of proof as to this fact. The Treasury has issued guidelines for determining whether a corporate obligation is equity or debt. The major factors are: (1) the ratio of debt to equity of the corporation; (2) the relationship between holdings of stock and holdings of debt; (3) whether the debt is convertible into the stock of the corporation; (4) whether there is a subordination or preference over any indebtedness of the corporation; and (5) whether there is a written, unconditional promise to pay on demand, or on a specified date a sum of money in return for adequate compensation, and to pay a fixed rate of interest.

If the IRS determines that the 'debt' is really equity there are a number of tax consequences. (1) The 'interest' deduction to the corporation is disallowed. (2) All payments of 'interest' and 'principal' are treated as dividend income to the shareholder/lender. (3) The shareholder/lender is denied a bad debt deduction if the corporation is unable to pay the principal.

The guidelines point out a potential cost in making all debt convertible. Even if the agency costs of debt are reduced to zero when stockholders and bondholders are the same, there can be an associated increase in taxes paid by the firm and its claimholders. It should be kept in mind, however, that factors other than taxes are necessary to explain why, prior to the corporate income tax, firms typically did not issue proportional claims, and not all debt was convertible.

the outstanding bonds. With a bilateral monopoly it is indeterminate how the gains will be divided between stockholders and bondholders. As Bodie/Taggart (1978) and Wier (1978) argue, a call provision places an upper limit on the gains which the bondholders can obtain. Wier notes further that if side payments can be negotiated costlessly, then the bondholder monopoly is unimportant from the standpoint of the value of the firm; the callability provision merely redistributes the property rights to the monopoly from bondholders to stockholders. Implicit in the argument that the call provision affects the total value of the firm is the notion that the bilateral monopoly implies real resource expenditures on negotiation.

It should also be noted that our argument cannot represent the only reason for callable bonds: after all, government bonds are often callable but there is no obvious investment incentive problem which such a provision addresses.[49]

2.5. Covenants specifying bonding activities by the firm

Potential bondholders estimate the costs associated with monitoring the firm to assure that the bond covenants have not been violated, and the estimate is reflected in the price when the bonds are sold. Since the value of the firm at the time the bonds are issued is influenced by anticipated monitoring costs, it is in the interests of the firm's owners to include contractual provisions which lower the costs of monitoring. For example, observed provisions often include the requirement that the firm supply audited annual financial statements to the bondholders. Jensen/Meckling call these expenditures by the firm bonding costs.

2.5.1. Required reports

Description. Indenture agreements discussed in *Commentaries* normally commit the company to supply financial and other information for as long as the debt is outstanding. Typically, the firm agrees to supply the following types of information: (1) all financial statements, reports, and proxy statements which the firm already sends to its shareholders; (2) reports and statements filed with government agencies such as the SEC or Public Utility Commissions; (3) quarterly financial statements certified by a financial officer of the firm and (4) financial statements for the fiscal year audited by an independent public accountant.

Analysis. Our analysis suggests that bondholders find financial statements to be useful in ascertaining whether the provisions of the contract have been (or are about to be) violated. If the firm can produce this information at a

---

[49]In addition, since virtually all debt is callable, there is little cross-sectional variation in its use. For a discussion of the empirical testability of arguments for callable debt, see Wier (1978).

lower cost than the bondholders (perhaps because much of the information is already being collected for internal decision making purposes), it pays the firm's stockholders to contract to provide this information to the bondholders. The market value of the firm increases by the reduction in agency costs.[50]

Jensen/Meckling (1976) and Watts (1977) point out that firms have the incentive to provide financial statements which have been audited by an external accounting firm if the increase in the market value of the bonds is greater than the present value of the auditing fees, net of any nominal benefits which accrue in internal monitoring. If bonding activities which are related to the bondholder–stockholder conflict involve incremental costs, then since the conflict increases with the debt in the firm's capital structure, the use of externally audited financial statements should be positively related to the firm's debt/equity ratio. Auditing expenditures should be associated with the extent to which covenants are specified in terms of accounting numbers from financial statements.[51,52]

2.5.2. Specification of accounting techniques

Description. As indicated, covenants restricting dividend, financing, and production/investment policy are frequently specified in terms of income or balance sheet numbers.[53] For public debt issues, other than stating that they should be consistent with generally accepted accounting principles (GAAP), covenants frequently do not specify how the accounting numbers will be computed.

Analysis. Restrictions on the shareholders' behavior can be relaxed by manipulating the accounting numbers which define the constraints.[54] For example, the impact of a change in accounting techniques on dividend and investment policy can be seen by referring to eq. (1) defining the inventory of funds for payment of dividends. The change in allowed dividend payments in quarter τ resulting from a change in earnings in quarter τ is proportional to k (i.e., $\partial D_\tau^* / \partial E_\tau = k$). If accounting earnings are overstated, then required current investment is increased by $(1-k)$ times the change in reported earnings. After the bonds have been sold, shareholders have an incentive to use whichever method of calculation inflates stated earnings. However, this

---

[50]See Jensen/Meckling (1976, p. 338) and Watts (1977).

[51]For a further discussion of the incentives to employ external auditors, see Watts (1977).

[52]Furthermore, this analysis leads Leftwich/Watts/Zimmerman (1979) to predict that voluntary public disclosure of financial statements prior to required provision by the exchanges or regulation should be associated with the level of debt in the firm's capital structure.

[53]See Holthausen (1979) and Leftwich (1979) for more comprehensive analyses of the use of accounting definitions in bond covenants.

[54]One case where accounting manipulations may have been made to prevent the firm from violating its debt covenants is that of Pan American World Airways. See Foster (1978, p. 354).

argument overstates the incentive to manipulate accounting earnings if current earnings can only be increased by reducing future earnings. To illustrate, since the total amount of depreciation on a machine is fixed, taking less depreciation now implies that future accounting earnings will be reduced. In this case the shareholders can only lower required current investment by increasing required future investment. The magnitude of the gain to the shareholders from manipulation of accounting numbers is on the order of the discount rate multiplied by k times the change in reported earnings and this is likely to be relatively small.

It is expensive to specify the accounting procedure by contract and, if the specified procedure differs from GAAP, it is expensive to prepare an additional set of accounting statements for the bondholders. Such detailed procedures can be a more costly mechanism for the bondholders to protect themselves against 'creative accounting' than by requiring external auditing and reflecting any risk of accounting manipulations in the price paid for the bonds.

Holthausen (1979) argues that the firm's decision to change depreciation methods could result in a change in reported earnings which relaxes contractual constraints and results in a transfer of wealth to stockholders. Furthermore, Leftwich (1979) argues that restricting stockholders to GAAP involves costs since over time, accounting principles change. Mandated changes in GAAP can cause the constraints on the stockholders' behavior to change and in some cases to be violated.[55] Leftwich's analysis predicts that certain changes in GAAP should be associated with wealth losses to the firm's claimholders. Moreover, the extent of the loss should be related to the extent to which the contracts are specified in terms of GAAP.

2.5.3. Officers' certificate of compliance

Description. Commentaries suggests that in addition to submitting the reports indicated above, the firm usually promises to provide an annual certificate as to whether there has been any default under the indenture. The Certificate of Compliance must be signed both by the president or vice-president, and by either the treasurer, assistant treasurer, controller or assistant controller of the company. The statement indicates that the signing officer has reviewed the activities of the company for the year, and that to the best of his knowledge the firm has fulfilled all of its obligations under the indenture. If there has been a default, the nature and status of the default must be specified. Some indentures also call for certificates or opinions as to compliance to be supplied by independent accountants. Normally it is provided that the accountants' statement certify that during the examination the accountants 'obtained no knowledge' of any default. The accountants are

---

[55]Fogelson (1978) discusses several cases where this has occurred.

often expressly relieved of all liability for failure to obtain knowledge of a default.

Analysis. The Costly Contracting Hypothesis suggests that the certificate of compliance is a way of reducing the monitoring costs of the bondholders. It is less expensive to have officers of the firm or the firm's accountants, who already will be knowledgeable of any defaults, contract to call such defaults to the attention of the bondholders than to let bondholders themselves ascertain if a default has occurred.

2.5.4. The required purchase of insurance

Description. Indenture agreements frequently include provisions requiring the firm to purchase insurance. The sample covenants in *Commentaries* specify that the firm will purchase insurance 'to substantially the same extent as its competitors'. The stockholders sometimes retain the right to self-insure if the plan is certified by an actuary. Typically, the indenture requires the firm to maintain liability insurance.

Analysis. In a world with perfect markets, there is no corporate demand for insurance; the corporate form effectively hedges insurable risk.[56] Our analysis suggests that the corporate purchase of insurance is a bonding activity engaged in by firms to reduce agency costs between bondholders and stockholders (as well as between the managers and the owners of a corporation). If insurance firms have a comparative advantage in monitoring aspects of the firm's activities, then a firm which purchases insurance will engage in a different set of activities from a firm which does not.

For example, a frequently purchased line of corporate insurance is boiler insurance. Insurance companies hire and train specialized inspectors to monitor the operation and maintenance of boilers, and the loss control program which is provided by the insurance company constrains the actions of the stockholders and managers of the firm. A covenant requiring the purchase of insurance gives stockholders the incentive to engage in the optimal amount of loss control projects. If the purchase of a sprinkler system were a positive net present value project it could still be rejected by stockholders of a levered firm because it reduces the variance rate of the firm's cash flows and thereby increases the value of the debt. But if the firm is contractually required to purchase insurance and if the insurance industry is competitive, the firm has the incentive to take any loss control project where the present value of the premium reductions is greater than the cost of the project. With the purchase of insurance the corporation's cash flow variability is unaffected by the purchase of loss control projects.

---

[56]See Mayers/Smith (1978).

3. The enforcement of bond covenants

The covenants we have discussed do not completely control the conflict between bondholders and stockholders; they do not go nearly so far as they could in restricting the firm's actions. The covenants could require that the firm secure permission of the bondholders for each action it takes, or that the firm 'accept all profitable projects, and only those projects'. However, as Jensen/Meckling (1976, p. 338) and Myers (1977, p. 158) argue, if such covenants are sufficiently expensive to enforce, it will not be in the interests of the firm's owners to offer them.

To specify types of enforcement costs, we must examine the institutional framework within which covenant enforcement takes place for further insight into why certain kinds of covenants are observed – and others not. Our analysis takes the institutional arragements as given. A deeper issue relates to the endogeneity of the institutions themselves. To the extent that the existing legal institutions represent an efficient solution to the problem of financial contracting, enforcement costs are lowered. But regardless of whether or not existing institutions imply 'minimum' costs, the types of contracts we observe depend on the level of these institutionally-related costs.

3.1. The legal liability of bondholders

Description. When bondholders exercise a significant degree of 'control' over the firm, they become legally liable to both the firm (i.e., the shareholders) and to third parties for losses incurred as a result of certain of their actions.[57] Although acts such as the seizure of collateral do not, in general, subject the creditor to liability,[58] creditor liability still occurs under a variety of conditions. For example, it can arise when a creditor who controls the firm is responsible for mismanagement. One of the leading cases is *Taylor versus Standard Gas Company*,[59] in which the court held the firm's creditor responsible for abuses which resulted from the exercise of control.

Creditors whose debt contracts contain restrictions which cause the firm to breach its contract with third parties, such as suppliers, employees, and other creditors, can also be held liable. One notable case in which a covenant

---

[57]Much of the discussion of the liability issue is based on the survey article of Douglas-Hamilton (1975). The liability of bondholders depends critically on the definition of 'control'. In the case of liability for securities law violations, 'a creditor would be considered in control of a corporate debtor even it if only indirectly possessed the power to direct the management or the policies of the debtor'. See Douglas-Hamilton (pp. 346–347).

That the courts frown upon bondholder control is not a new notion. Dewing (1953, pp. 188–189) indicates that the 'exclusion of bondholders from all voice in the management of the corporation...has been sanctioned by centuries of legal authority' and is a 'time honored legal theory'.

[58]Douglas-Hamilton (p. 364).

[59]306 U.S. 307 (1939). See Douglas-Hamilton (p. 348).

B

violated the rights of third parties is that of *Kelly versus Central Hanover Bank and Trust Company.*[60] There, the bondholders of the debtor corporation brought suit against another class of claimants, namely the creditor banks of the debtor. The bondholders charged that the banks, in obtaining a covenant pledging stock as security for their loans, violated the terms of the indenture agreement between the bondholders and the debtor. According to Douglas-Hamilton (1975, p. 364):

> 'It appears that the case against the banks was later settled on terms which included a payment of $3,435,008 by the banks to the bondholders and the withdrawal by the banks of claims aggregating $42,887,500 in the debtor corporation's bankruptcy proceedings.'

Creditors can also incur liability for Federal Securities Law violations. For example, under Rule 10b–5 of Section 10 of the Securities Act of 1934, which deals with fraud, a creditor incurs liability for failing to disclose material information about the firm. Creditor liability even arises in cases where there has been inadequate 'policing by a creditor of press releases of its troubled debtor to insure that they do not depict an inaccurate optimistic picture to the public'.[61]

Analysis. Covenants which have the effect of assigning legal liability to the bondholders represent a real cost to the firm's owners if bondholders, or their agent, are more likely than the firm's management to be held responsible for actions which result in losses and if the legal process which establishes liability is costly. In that case, giving bondholders control is a more costly way to run the firm simply because of the legal costs involved in the determination of bondholder liability. The firm's owners are better off simply not issuing those types of debt which are likely to result in such costs being incurred. While we have no direct evidence on the costs of creditor liability, one comment from the legal literature which suggests that those costs are not trivial is the warning that 'whenever a creditor contemplates taking a hand in the management of a financially troubled debtor, it should think of its deeper pockets and keep its hands there'.[62]

3.2. The role of the trust indenture and the trustee

Description. Debt contracts discussed in *Commentaries* typically appoint an independent 'trustee' to represent the bondholders and act as their agent in covenant enforcement. This is done under a device known as a corporate trust indenture, which specifies the respective rights and obligations of the

---

[60]85 F 2d 61 (2d Cir. 1936).
[61]Douglas-Hamilton (p. 354).
[62]Douglas-Hamilton (p. 364).

firm, the individual bondholders, and the trustee. Although the trustee is an agent of the bondholders, in practice he is actually compensated by the firm.[63]

Analysis.   If the firm's debt is not held by a single borrower, then a number of problems related to enforcement of the debt contract arise. For example, any individual's holdings of the firm's debt may be so small that no single bondholder has much incentive to expend resources in covenant enforcement. But it is not the case that individual bondholders necessarily expend 'too few' resources in covenant enforcement. If the number of bondholders is small, then there can actually be overinvestment in enforcement in the sense that there is either a duplication of effort, or that creditors expend resources which simply result in change in the distribution of the proceeds. Our analysis implies that the firm's owners offer a contract which appoints a trustee to help assure that the optimal amount of covenant enforcement will take place.

Having the firm pay the trustees directly solves the 'free-rider' problem which would be inherent in making individual bondholders pay the trustee for enforcing the covenants. However after the bonds have been sold, the stockholders have an incentive to bribe the trustee so that they can violate the debt covenants. There are several factors which prevent such bribery from taking place.

Bribing the trustee is expensive if the trustee's reputation has significant value in the marketplace. *Ex ante*, it is in the interests of the firm's owners to choose an 'honest' trustee – that is, one who is expensive to bribe. This is because the value of the firm at the time it issues the debt contract reflects the probability of covenant enforcement. To the extent that enforcement by an 'honest' trustee reduces the problems of adverse borrower behavior induced by risky debt, the value of the firm is higher. Our analysis therefore implies that those chosen as trustees stand to lose much if they are caught accepting bribes. In fact, the indenture trustee is 'generally a large banking institution',[64] which has significant revenues from activities unrelated to being a trustee and which also depend on the market's perception of its trustworthiness. Furthermore, the behavior of the trustee is restricted by both trust and contract law.[65]

3.2.1. The Trust Indenture Act of 1939

Description.   Publicly issued debt obligations must comply with the requirements of the Trust Indenture Act of 1939 (TIA).[66] Although the TIA does

---

[63]For a further discussion of the trustee's compensation, see Kennedy (1961, p. 49).

[64]Obrzut (1976, p. 131).

[65]For a further discussion, see Kennedy, especially chapter 2.

[66]There are minor exceptions. For example, issues of less than $1 million are exempted. The TIA is enforced by the Securities and Exchange Commission. For the bonds to be sold, the terms of the indenture must be 'qualified' by the SEC.

not explicitly regulate the restrictive covenants which the bond contract can include, the TIA does impose certain standards of conduct on the trustee. The trustee must meet certain minimum capital requirements. The trustee is not permitted to have a serious conflict of interest; with some minor exceptions, he may not act as the agent for two different classes of bondholders of the same firm, and he may not himself be a creditor in the firm for whose debt contract he acts as trustee.[67]

Analysis. In spite of these restrictions on the behavior of the trustee, it can still be very costly to write a contract where the bondholders are represented by such an agent. The trustee will still not act entirely in the bondholders' interest. This is particularly true because the extent to which the trustee can be held negligent is limited: while the trustee must act in good faith, his responsibilities often go no further unless there is a default. Under the TIA, when a default has occurred the trustee is only required to 'use the same degree of care and skill...as a prudent man would exercise' in enforcing the covenants. Furthermore it is not clear whether, prior to the TIA, the legal standards for either pre- or post-default conduct of trustees were significantly different.[68]

3.2.2. Public versus private placements

Description. Section 4(2) of the Securities Act of 1933 provides that a sale of securities not involving any public offering is exempt from registration. Such exempt issues are referred to as private placements or direct placements. Private placements are not typically subject to the TIA. They represent an alternative to publicly placed debt.

Analysis. Since the enforcement of tightly restrictive covenants through a trustee is difficult, the benefit from private (rather than public) placement of the firm's debt issues can be substantial. Our analysis suggests that private placements will contain more detailed restrictions on the firm's behavior than do public issues.[69] In addition, we would expect that the riskier the debt, the more likely that it will be privately placed. Because of the costs associated with the enforcement of trust indentures, the covenants in debt issues are not likely to eliminate the problems induced by the presence of risky debt.

---

[67]Kennedy (p. 35) claims that the standards of conduct contained in the TIA 'had been accepted and followed by the more responsible trust companies for a long time prior to the enactment of the legislation, so that no abrupt or sudden change was effected'. A major proponent of the legislation which resulted in the TIA was the Securities and Exchange Commission [Obrzut (1976, p. 133)].

[68]For a further discussion, see Johnson (1970).

[69]That private issues contain more restrictive covenants than public issues is consistent with the observations of the authors of *Commentaries* (p. 11 and p. 14). Note that private issues may also have trustees, even though the number of claimholders is typically small.

Evidence. Consistent with the hypothesis that privately placed debt contracts contain more extensive provisions than public, Leftwich (1979) presents evidence that variations from generally accepted accounting procedures occur more frequently in private than public debt issues. The adjustments to GAAP are systematic; they generally eliminate non-cash gains. However they do not restrict non-cash losses. For example, restatement of asset values which result in gains are typically eliminated from computed earnings while those resulting in losses are not.

Cohan (1967, p. 1) finds evidence of a shift to private placements during the 1930s: 'In the thirty-four years from 1900 to 1934, about 3 percent of all corporate debt cash offerings, or approximately $1 billion were directly (privately) placed. However, in the ensuing thirty-one years, from 1935 to 1965, 46 percent, or $85 billion, were directly placed.' While our analysis does predict such a shift to private placements after the TIA, this shift is also consistent with Benston's (1969) suggestion that the inception of the SEC in 1934 increased the cost of public versus private issues.

3.3. Default remedies

The debt contract typically gives the firm a strong incentive to live up to the restrictive covenants: any breach of the covenants is considered an act of default. Not only is the firm normally required to report any such breach, but the lender is given the right to engage in certain actions (e.g., seizure of collateral, acceleration of the maturity of the debt) to protect his interest.

3.3.1. Renegotiation

Description. Since actions such as the seizure of collateral consume real resources, the debt contract is often renegotiated in order to eliminate the default. In public debt issues the contract can be changed by the use of a 'supplemental indenture'. The supplement must be approved by the bondholders, and must meet the requirements of the TIA.

Changes in the specific covenants cannot usually be made without the consent of the holders of two-thirds in principal amount of the outstanding debt[70] (the firm itself is not allowed to vote any debt it holds). Moreover, the consent of 100 percent of the debtholders is required in order to change the maturity date or principal amount of the bonds. In private placements involving few lenders, renegotiation is typically easier.[71]

---

[70]See *Commentaries* (p. 307) and Section 902, American Bar Foundation Model Debenture Indenture Provisions – All Registered Issues.

[71]According to Zinbarg (1975): 'My own institution's experience [Prudential Insurance Co. of Am] may serve as an illustration. In any given year, we will, on average, receive one modification request per loan on the books. In no more than five per cent of these cases will we refuse the request or even require any quid pro quo, because the vast majority of corporate requests are perfectly reasonable and do not increase our risk materially.'

Analysis. The seemingly lower renegotiating costs of privately placed debt issues further re-inforce our earlier prediction that such private placements will contain tighter restrictions on the firm's behavior than will public issues.

3.3.2. Bankruptcy

Description. Should renegotiation fail, a default also gives the lender the right to put the firm into legal bankruptcy proceedings. Several features of the bankruptcy process bear on the enforcement of debt contracts. For example, since the bankruptcy process gives the firm temporary protection from acts of foreclosure and lien enforcement, some enforcement mechanisms are no longer available to the lender.

Analysis. Our theory suggests that it is more efficient to have some ambiguities in the initial debt contract, and to let them be resolved in bankruptcy should default ever occur. Since it is the firm's owners who bear the total costs associated with enforcing the debt contract, it is in their interests to find the most efficient balance between expenditures on drafting the debt contract and expected legal expenditures in bankruptcy. In a world where contracting is costly, that balance will imply less than complete specification of the payoff to be received by claimholders in every possible future state of the world.

As Warner (1977) discusses, bankruptcy courts recognize the priorities specified in the firm's debt agreements in only a limited sense. There are many cases where 'junior' claimants are compensated before claimants 'senior' to them are paid in full. Since 'priorities' are not always enforced, it will not always pay the firm to indicate the priority of a given debt issue with much specificity (e.g., creditor A is forty-seventh in line).

4. Conclusions

4.1. The role of bond covenants

We have examined the specific provisions which are included in corporate debt contracts. Since covenants are a persistent phenomena, we can therefore assume that these provisions are efficient from the standpoint of the firm's owners, and thus we can draw inferences about the role of these contractual forms in the firm's capital structure.

Observed debt covenants reduce the costs associated with the conflict of interest between bondholders and stockholders; the ingenuity with which debt contracts are written indicates the strong economic incentives for the firm's owners to lower the agency costs which can result from having risky debt in the firm's capital structure.

The existence of standardized debt contracts such as those found in

Commentaries suggests that the out-of-pocket costs of drafting observed bond contracts are small indeed. However, the direct and opportunity costs of complying with the contractual restrictions appear to be substantial. We have presented no evidence on the precise dollar magnitudes, and we emphasize that a particular covenant included in a given debt contract will not impose opportunity costs with probability one. But our analysis indicates that observed bond covenants involve expected costs which are large enough to help account for the variation in debt contracts across firms. This is consistent with the Costly Contracting Hypothesis. On the other hand, it is inconsistent with the Irrelevance Hypothesis, which predicts that total resource expenditures on control of the bondholder–stockholder conflict will be negligible.

Our analysis also sheds some light on the relative costs of the alternative types of restrictions which can be written into the debt contract. We conclude that production/investment policy is very expensive to monitor. Stockholder use (or misuse) of production/investment policy frequently involves not some explicit act, but the failure to take a certain action (e.g., failure to accept a positive net present value project). It is expensive even to ascertain when the firm's production/investment policy is not optimal, since such a determination depends on magnitudes which are difficult to observe. The high monitoring costs which would be associated with restrictive production/investment covenants, including the potential legal costs associated with bondholder control, dictate that few production/investment decisions will be contractually proscribed. For the firm's owners to go very far in directly restricting the firm's production/investment policy would be inefficient.

On the other hand, we conclude that dividend policy and financing policy involve lower monitoring costs. Stockholder use of these policies to 'hurt' bondholders involves acts (e.g., the sale of a large bond issue) which are readily observable. Because they are cheaper to monitor, it is efficient to restrict production/investment policy by writing dividend and financing policy covenants in a way which helps assure that stockholders will act to maximize the value of the firm.

4.2. Implications for capital structure

With more fixed claims in the capital structure, the benefits to the stockholders from asset substitution, claim dilution, underinvestment, and dividend payout increase; with higher benefits, the stockholders will expend more real resources 'getting around' any particular set of contractual constraints. This, in turn, will increase the benefits of increased tightness of the covenants. Accordingly, the costs associated with the bondholder–stockholder conflict rise with the firm's debt/equity ratio. Simply limiting the debt in the capital structure is an efficient mechanism for controlling this conflict. Because of this, the costs associated with writing and enforcing covenants influence the level of debt the firm chooses.

Since observed debt covenants involve real costs, there must be some benefit in having debt in the firm's capital structure; otherwise, the bondholder–stockholder conflict can be costlessly eliminated by not issuing debt. Hence our evidence indicates not only that there is an optimal form of the debt contract, but an optimal *amount* of debt as well. The benefits from issuing risky debt are not well understood, and even though the costs we have discussed in this paper provide a lower bound on their magnitude, our analysis has not permitted us to distinguish between alternative explanations of the benefits: (1) information asymmetries and signalling, (2) taxes, (3) agency costs of equity financing, (4) differential transactions and flotation costs, and (5) unbundling of riskbearing and capital ownership.

4.3. Some possible extensions

While our analysis of debt covenants is a useful start at explaining certain aspects of the firm's capital structure, there are a number of issues which have not been explored here which, we believe, merit further attention. We have attempted to indicate the interrelationship between covenants restricting dividend, financing, and production/investment policy. However, we have not developed a theory which is capable of explaining how, for a given debt issue, the total 'package' of covenants is determined. Further work on the substitutability or complementarity of the specific contractual provisions is necessary before it is possible to predict, for any set of firm-specific characteristics, the form which the debt contract will take.

Second, we emphasize that bond covenants are but one way in which the behavior of the stockholders is constrained. For example, both the legal system and the possibility of takeovers are factors which make it more expensive for stockholders to engage in actions aimed at maximizing the value of their own claim but not the total value of the firm. The relative importance of these factors, and how they affect the firm's choice of debt covenants, is not yet well understood.

Finally, it is important to remember that in focusing on the bondholder–stockholder conflict, we have ignored other conflicts, such as that between managers and stockholders, which also exist. To the extent that the contracts comprising the firm are interdependent and simultaneously determined, the bondholder–stockholder conflict should not be viewed in isolation. The impact of the bondholder–stockholder conflict on the firm's total contracting costs cannot be fully understood until the nature of these contractual interdependencies is explored.

Appendix

In this appendix, we consider in more detail the results presented in section 1. First, we discuss the valuation of the debt of a levered firm when the relevant variables in the valuation equations can be specified parametrically over the life of the bonds. We then expand the analysis to the case where stockholders can change these variables after they obtain the proceeds from the sale of the debt, and where both the stockholders and bondholders are aware of this possibility when the bonds are originally issued.

A.1. Option pricing valuation of the firm's financial claims

The valuation of the equity and debt of a levered firm is examined by Black/Scholes (1973) and Merton (1974). Where the bonds are single-payment contracts and the market is efficient and competitive, without transactions costs, information costs, other agency costs, or taxes, the analysis is straightforward. Consider a bond contract which promises to repay a lump sum, X, covering both principal and interest at a specified date in the future, t^*. When the bond issue is sold, the proceeds from the sale equal the current value of the bondholders' claim, B, on the firm's assets. Assume that the firm's financial claims consist of this bond issue and common stock. Thus, the current value of the stock, S, is the difference between the current value of the firm's assets, V, and the value of the bonds, B,

$$S \equiv V - B. \tag{A.1}$$

Given this contract, the optimal strategy for the firm's shareholders at the maturity date of the bonds can be specified: if the value of the firm's assets at the maturity date, V^*, is greater than the face value of the bonds, X, then repay the bonds; the stockholders equity at that date, S^* will be the difference between the value of the firm's assets and the face value of the bonds, $V^* - X$. On the other hand, if at the maturity date of the bonds the value of the firm's assets is less than the face value of the bonds, then default on the bonds; the bondholders do not receive the face value of the bonds, they receive only the firm's assets, V^*. Given limited liability, the shareholders' equity is zero. Thus, at t^* the value of the stock, S^*, is

$$S^* = \max[0, V^* - X], \tag{A.2}$$

and the value of the bonds is

$$B^* = \min[V^*, X]. \tag{A.3}$$

This bond issue is equivalent to the sale of the firm's assets to the bondholders for a package containing: (1) the proceeds from the sale of the bonds, B, (2) a claim which allows the stockholders to receive the dividends paid by the firm over the life of the bonds, and (3) a European call option[72] to repurchase the assets at the maturity date of the loan T time periods later ($T = t^* - t$), with an exercise price equal to the face value of the bonds, X. Those variables which affect the value of call options are also important in valuing the financial claims of firms.

To derive an explicit solution for the market value of the bonds given the other variables, make the following assumptions:

(1) There are homogeneous expectations about the dynamic behavior of the value of the firm's assets. The distribution at the end of any finite time interval is lognormal. The variance rate, σ^2, is constant.

(2) The dynamic behavior of the value of the assets is independent of the face value of the bonds, X.

(3) There are no transactions costs associated with default.

(4) The firm pays a continuous flow of dividend payments to the shareholders. The dividend payment, per unit time D, is a constant fraction, δ, of the market value of the assets: $\delta = D/V$.

(5) Capital markets are perfect. There are no transactions costs or taxes. All participants have free access to all available information. Participants are price takers.

(6) There is a known constant riskless rate of interest, r.[73]

Under these assumptions, Merton (1974) has shown that the value of the bonds, B, can be written as

$$B = Ve^{-\delta T}N\left\{\frac{-\ln(V/X) - (r - \delta + \sigma^2/2)T}{\sigma\sqrt{T}}\right\}$$

$$+ Xe^{-rT}N\left\{\frac{\ln(V/X) + (r - \delta - \sigma^2/2)T}{\sigma\sqrt{T}}\right\} \qquad (A.4)$$

[72]A European call option is a contract which gives the owner the right to purchase a specified asset at a specified price, called the exercise price, on a specified date, called the maturity date. Since the option is only exercised if it is in the best interest of the owner, it will be exercised only if the value of the asset is above the exercise price at the maturity date; otherwise it will expire worthless.

[73]Merton (1973) has modified the Black/Scholes contingent claims analysis to account for time series variability in interest rates. His solution retains the basic form of this analysis. Since the effects of the variability of the riskless rate and term structure are not of primary concern here, this simpler assumption will be maintained.

where $N\{\ \}$ is the cumulative standard normal distribution function. In general form,

$$B = B(V, X, T, \delta, \sigma^2, r), \tag{A.5}$$

where

$$\frac{\partial B}{\partial V}, \frac{\partial B}{\partial X} > 0 \quad \text{and} \quad \frac{\partial B}{\partial T}, \frac{\partial B}{\partial \delta}, \frac{\partial B}{\partial \sigma^2}, \frac{\partial B}{\partial r} < 0.$$

A.2. The nature of the covenants to be included in the debt contract

As we discussed in section 1, in pricing the bonds the bondholders must ascertain the values of the variables in eq. (A.5). These variables can be changed after the bonds are issued; the bondholders make assessments of likely stockholder actions, given whatever restrictions the debt contract places on the stockholders. The particular covenants written are those which maximize the wealth of the firm's current owners. This is the set of covenants which maximizes the with-dividend value of the firm when the bonds are issued.

For explicit analysis of the incentives faced by the shareholders and bondholders in drafting the debt contract, the analysis of the valuation of claims must be expanded.[74] The firm's objective is assumed to be the maximization of current equity, S, and the current dividend, D,

$$W \equiv S + D. \tag{A.6}$$

For an all equity firm which has decided to sell bonds, the value of the stock, S, can be expressed as the total ex-dividend value of the firm, V, minus the value of the claim sold to the new bondholders, B,

$$S \equiv V - B. \tag{A.7}$$

The value of the claim sold to the new bondholders is a function of the projects chosen, and the terms of the contract. More specifically, let the firm choose a vector of activities, α, and a vector of provisions in its financial contracts, f (e.g., f includes the face value of the debt, X, and the time to maturity of the bonds, T, as well as covenants such as restrictions on dividend payments). In general, the value of the firm's assets, the variance rate, and the dividend payments area function of the activities and contractual provisions chosen. Thus the value to the stockholders of the claim sold to the bondholders can be expressed as

$$B = B(\alpha, f). \tag{A.8}$$

---

[74]The following analysis was suggested by John Long.

The cash flow identity that inflows equal outflows can be used to re-express the dividend payment, D, as the sum of the internally generated cash flow before interest expense, ϕ, plus the net proceeds from the sale of the new bonds, B, minus the new investment expenditures, I,

$$D \equiv \phi + B - I. \tag{A.9}$$

The proceeds from the sale of the new bonds will depend on the financial covenants, f, chosen. Let $\alpha(f)$ represent the activity that, given the choice of financial contract, f, maximizes the with-dividend value of the shareholder's equity. The bondholders will assume that if the contractual provisions are f, then the stockholders will act in their own self-interest and choose the vector of activities, $\alpha(f)$. Thus, the proceeds from the sale of the new bonds will be

$$B = B(\alpha(f), f). \tag{A.10}$$

Substituting (A.7), (A.8), (A.9) and (A.10) into (A.6) allows us to re-express shareholder wealth as

$$W = V(\alpha, f) - B(\alpha, f) + B(\alpha(f), f) + \phi(\alpha, f) - I(\alpha, f). \tag{A.11}$$

Thus, for a given financial structure, f, the optimal activity choice, α, to maximize shareholder wealth is

$$W(\alpha(f), f) = V(\alpha(f), f) + \phi(\alpha(f), f) - I(\alpha(f), f). \tag{A.12}$$

From (A.12) it is clear that the optimal financial structure, f^*, will be that structure for which the with-dividend value of the firm is maximized subject to the available set of financial structures; i.e.,

$$V[\alpha(f^*), f^*] + \phi[\alpha(f^*), f^*] - I[\alpha(f^*), f^*]$$
$$\geqq V[\alpha(f), f] + \phi[\alpha(f), f] - I[\alpha(f), f],$$

for all feasible f.

This can be illustrated graphically. Let (α^{**}, f^{**}) be the point where the with-dividend value of the firm is maximized; i.e., where

$$V(\alpha^{**}, f^{**}) + \phi(\alpha^{**}, f^{**}) - I(\alpha^{**}, f^{**})$$
$$\geqq V(\alpha, f) + \phi(\alpha, f) - I(\alpha, f),$$

for all choices of financial structure and activities, assuming that the magnitudes could be independently set. We call this point the 'idealized' capital structure/activity choice for the firm. In fig. 1 the with-dividend value of the firm is represented in (α, f) space as level sets. The set of optimal activity choices as a function of financial structure, $\alpha(f)$, is also represented. The agency costs described by Jensen/Meckling (1976) are $[V(\alpha^{**}, f^{**}) + \phi(\alpha^{**}, f^{**}) - I(\alpha^{**}, f^{**})] - [V(\alpha(f^*), f^*) + \phi(\alpha(f^*), f^*) - I(\alpha(f^*)f^*)]$, i.e., the difference between the with-dividend value of the firm given the idealized capital structure and the idealized activity choice minus the value of the firm given the optimum (feasible) choice of activities and capital structure.

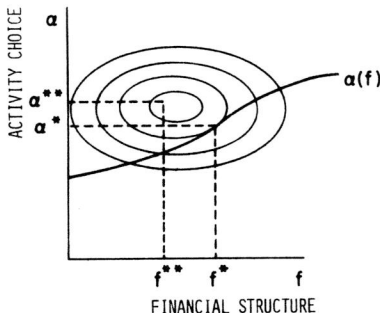

Fig. 1. Determination of the optimal financial structure, f^*, and activity choice, α^*. The collection of level sets represent different with-dividend market values of the firm, assuming the activity choice, α, and financial structure, f, can be set independently. The point (α^{**}, f^{**}) is the maximum with-dividend firm market value. The function $\alpha(f)$ represents the choice of activity which maximizes shareholder wealth for a given financial structure. Agency costs are $\{[V(\alpha^{**}, f^{**}) + \phi(\alpha^{**}, f^{**}) - I(\alpha^{**})] - [V(\alpha(f^*), f^*) + \phi(\alpha(f^*), f^*) - I(\alpha(f^*), f^*)]\}$.

References

Alchian, Armen, 1950, Uncertainty, evolution, and economic theory, Journal of Political Economy 58, 211–221.

Alchian, Armen and Harold Demsetz, 1972, Production, information costs, and economic organization, American Economic Review 62, 777–795.

American Bar Foundation, 1971, Commentaries on model debenture indenture provisions 1965, Model debenture indenture provisions all registered issues 1967, and Certain negotiable provisions which may be included in a particular incorporating indenture (Chicago, IL).

Benston, George J., 1969, The effectiveness and effects of the SEC's accounting disclosure requirements, in: Henry G. Manne, ed., Economic policy and the regulation of corporate securities (American Enterprise Institute, Washington, DC), 23–79.

Black, Fischer, 1976, The dividend puzzle, Journal of Portfolio Management 2, 5–8.

Black, Fischer and John C. Cox, 1976, Valuing corporate securities: Some effects of bond indenture provisions, Journal of Finance 31, 351–367.

Black, Fischer, Merton H. Miller and Richard A. Posner, 1978, An approach to the regulation of bank holding companies, Journal of Business 51, 379–412.

Black, Fischer and Myron Scholes, 1973, The pricing of options and corporate liabilities, Journal of Political Economy 81, 637–659.

Bodie, Zvi and Robert Taggart, 1978, Future investment opportunities and the value of the call provision on a bond, Journal of Finance 23, 1187–1200.

Bradley, Michael, 1978, An analysis of interfirm cash tender offers, Unpublished manuscript (University of Chicago, Chicago, IL).

Cheung, Steven, 1973, The fable of the bees: An economic investigation, Journal of Law and Economics 16, 11–33.

Coase, Ronald, 1960, The problem of social cost, Journal of Law and Economics 3, 1–44.

Cohan, Avery G., 1967, Yields on corporate debt directly placed (National Bureau of Economic Research, New York).

Coleman, William, 1971, Biology in the nineteenth century: Problems of form, function, and transformation (Wiley, New York).

Darwin, Charles, 1859, The origin of species by means of natural selection or the preservation of favoured races in the struggle for life. Reprinted in 1962 (Collier Books, New York).

Demsetz, Harold, 1967, Toward a theory of property rights, American Economic Review 57, 347–359.

Dewing, Arthur, 1934, 1953, The financial policy of corporations (Ronald Press, New York).

Dodd, Peter and Richard Ruback, 1977, Tender offers and stockholder returns: An empirical analysis, Journal of Financial Economics 5, 351–373.

Douglas-Hamilton, Margaret H., 1975, Creditor liabilities resulting from improper interference with the management of a financially troubled debtor, Business Lawyer 31, 343–365.

Fama, Eugene F., 1978a, The effect of a firm's investment and financing decisions on the welfare of its security holders, American Economic Review 68, 272–284.

Fama, Eugene F., 1978b, Agency problems and the theory of the firm, Unpublished manuscript (University of Chicago, Chicago, IL).

Fama, Eugene F. and Merton Miller, 1972, The theory of finance (Holt, Rinehart and Winston, New York).

Fogelson, James H., 1978, The impact of changes in accounting principles on restrictive covenants in credit agreements and indentures, Business Lawyer 73, 769–787.

Foster, George, 1978, Financial statement analysis (Prentice-Hall, Englewood Cliffs, NJ).

Galai, Dan and Ronald W. Masulis, 1976, The option pricing model and the risk factor of stock, Journal of Financial Economics 3, 53–81.

Henn, Harry H., 1970, Handbook of the law of corporations and other business enterprises (West Publishing Company, St. Paul, MN).

Holthausen, Robert, 1979, Toward a positive theory of choice of accounting techniques: The case of alternative depreciation methods, Unpublished manuscript (University of Rochester, Rochester, NY).

Jensen, Michael C. and William H. Meckling, 1976, Theory of the firm: Managerial behavior, agency costs, and capital structure, Journal of Financial Economics 3, 305–360.

Johnson, William A., 1970, Default administration of corporate trust indentures: The general nature of the trustee's responsibility and events of default, St. Louis University Law Journal 15, 203–236.

Kalay, Avner, 1979, Toward a theory of corporate dividend policy, Unpublished Ph.D. thesis (University of Rochester, Rochester, NY).

Kennedy, Joseph C., 1961, Corporate trust administration (New York University Press, New York).

Kuhn, Thomas S., 1970, The structure of scientific revolutions (University of Chicago Press, Chicago, IL).

Leftwich, Richard, 1979, Accounting principles and bond indentures: The role of private contracts, Unpublished manuscript (University of Rochester, Rochester, NY).

Leftwich, Richard, Ross Watts and Jerold L. Zimmerman, 1979, A theory of voluntary corporate disclosure, Unpublished manuscript (University of Rochester, Rochester, NY).

Long, John B., 1973, Book review of the theory of finance by Eugene Fama and Merton Miller, Journal of Money, Credit and Banking 5, 229–235.

Manne, Henry, 1967, Our two corporation systems: Law and economics, Virginia Law Review 53, 259–284.

Mayers, David and Clifford W. Smith, 1978, Towards a positive theory of insurance, Unpublished manuscript (University of Rochester, Rochester, NY).

Merton, Robert C., 1973, Theory of rational option pricing, Bell Journal of Economics and Management Science 4, 141–183.

Merton, Robert C., 1974, On the pricing of corporate debt: The risk structure of interest rates, Journal of Finance 29, 449–470.

Mikkelson, Wayne, 1978, An examination of the agency cost rationale for convertible bonds, Unpublished manuscript (University of Rochester, Rochester, NY).

Miller, Merton, 1977a, The wealth transfers of bankruptcy: Some illustrative examples, Special issue on the economics of bankruptcy reform, Law and Contemporary Problems 41, Autumn, 39–46.

Miller, Merton, 1977b, Debt and taxes, Journal of Finance 22, 261–275.

Miller, Merton and Franco Modigliani, 1966, Some estimates of the cost of capital to the electric utility industry, American Economic Review 56, 334–391.

Modigliani, Franco and Merton Miller, 1958, The cost of capital, corporation finance, and the theory of investment, American Economic Review 48, 261–297.

Myers, Stewart C., 1977, Determinants of corporate borrowing, Journal of Financial Economics 5, 147–175.

Nagel, Ernest, 1961, The structure of science: Problems in the logic of scientific explanation (Harcourt, Brace & World, New York).

Norgaard, Richard L. and F. Corine Thompson, 1967, Sinking funds: Their use and value (Financial Executives Research Foundation, New York).

Obrzut, Frederica R., 1976, The trust indenture act of 1939: The corporate trustee as creditor, UCLA Law Review 24, 131–159.

Popper, Karl, 1959, The logic of scientific discovery (Hutchinson, London).

Posner, Richard A., A theory of negligence, Journal of Legal Studies 1, 29–96.

Rodgers, Churchill, 1965, The corporate trust indenture project, Business Lawyer 20, 551–571.

Ross, Stephen A., 1977, The determination of financial structure: The incentive signalling approach, Bell Journal of Economics 8, 23–40.

Scott, James H., Jr., 1977, Bankruptcy, secured debt, and optimal capital structure, Journal of Finance 32, 1–19.

Smith, Clifford W., 1976, Option pricing: A review, Journal of Financial Economics 3, 3–51.

Smith, Clifford W. and Jerold B. Warner, 1979, Bankruptcy, secured debt, and optimal capital structure: Comment, Journal of Finance 34, 247–251.

Stigler, George J., 1958, The economies of scale, Journal of Law and Economics 1, 54–71.

Stiglitz, Joseph E., 1972, Some aspects of the pure theory of corporate finance: Bankruptcies and takeovers, Bell Journal of Economics 3, 458–482.

Warner, Jerold B., 1977, Bankruptcy, absolute priority, and the pricing of risky debt claims, Journal of Financial Economics 4, 239–276.

Watts, Ross, 1977, Corporate financial statements, a product of the market and political processes, Australian Journal of Management 2, 53–75.

Wier, Peggy, 1978, Callable debt, Unpublished manuscript (University of Rochester, Rochester, NY).

Zinbarg, Edward, 1975, The private placement loan agreement, Financial Analysts Journal 31, July/Aug., 33–52.

STOCKHOLDER–BONDHOLDER CONFLICT
AND DIVIDEND CONSTRAINTS

Avner KALAY*

New York University, New York, NY 10003, USA

Received July 1981, final version received February 1982

This paper examines a large, randomly chosen, sample of bond indentures focusing on the constraints they set on dividend payments that have the potential to transfer wealth from the bondholders (i.e., payments which are financed by a new debt issue or reduced investment). The nature of these restrictions support the hypothesis that bond convenants are structured to control the conflict of interest between stockholders and bondholders. Further, the empirical evidence suggests that these constraints are not binding — i.e., stockholders do not pay themselves as much dividends as they are allowed to. Explanations of this puzzling empirical regularity are suggested.

1. Introduction and summary

Corporate dividend policy has long been an issue of interest in the financial literature. Thus far, this issue has been examined under the assumption that the firm is one homogeneous unit whose clear objective is to maximize its market value [Brennan (1970), Miller–Modigliani (1961), Miller–Scholes (1978)]. However, in a growing body of recent literature [Black (1976), Fama (1978), Fama–Miller (1972), Galai–Masulis (1976), Jensen–Meckling (1976), Kalay (1979a, b), Myers (1977), Smith–Warner (1979)] researchers have recognized that the firm is a collection of groups whose interest can, and do, conflict. Thus, the renewed interest in corporate dividend policy expressed in this paper stems from their important role in this conflict.

Of the groups comprising the firm, the largest and perhaps the most important two are the bondholders and the stockholders. The stockholders, who control the firm, are expected to choose investment and financial decisions that maximize their own wealth. In particular, they could, if permitted, attempt to transfer wealth from bondholders by choosing policies which increase the risk of the outstanding bonds. The stockholders can effect

*I would like to thank Ernest Bloch, Kenneth Garbade, Kose John, Richard Leftwich, William Schwert, Ronald Singer, Marti Subrhamanyam, Jerold Warner, Ross Watts, the referee, Clifford Smith, and especially John Long and Michael Jensen for their helpful comments.

such a transfer by utilizing two dividend related mechanisms.[1] First, stockholders can reduce planned investment or deplete existing assets and pay the 'saved' outlays as dividends (hereafter pay 'investment financed dividends'). Secondly, stockholders can pay out the proceeds of a new issue of senior debt as dividends (hereafter pay 'debt financed dividends'); thereby, increasing the risk of the outstanding bonds. If these payments were not anticipated by the bondholders, wealth would be transferred from them to the stockholders. Clearly, these two wealth transfer mechanisms depend on stockholders' ability to pay out funds.[2] Moreover, as Jensen and Meckling (1976) and Myers (1977) demonstrate, stockholders can choose to finance dividend payments by rejecting investment projects with positive net present value (NPV). These potential costs associated with the conflict can be reduced (or avoided) by stockholders' precommitment to limit the level of future dividend[3] payments.

The above rationale for the existence of dividend constraints is suggested in the financial literature [see Jensen–Meckling (1976), Myers (1977), Smith–Warner (1979), Kalay (1979a, b)], although the exact form of the constraint, the details of its properties, its variations across firms and the extent to which it is likely to be binding, are yet to be documented. This paper addresses these issues by examining limitations on dividend payments in a large, randomly chosen, sample of bond indentures.

Overview of the paper

Examination of the bond indentures reveals that the dividend decisions of levered firms are constrained. Section 2 contains a documentation and analysis of the typical direct dividend constraint. Most of the firms in the sample choose a constraint of the same form in which the limitations apply to all forms of payout — i.e., share repurchases and other distributions to the stockholders are treated as cash dividends. Most importantly, the typical direct dividend constraint limits only dividend payments that have the potential to cause a wealth transfer, i.e., it limits debt and investment financed dividends while allowing for unlimited amounts of dividend

---

[1]As Black and Scholes (1973) suggest, stockholders of a levered firm can be viewed as holders of an European call option on their firm whose exercise price is equal (in the case of a pure discount bond) to the face value of the debt. Thus, by increasing the investment's risk (other things constant) the value of this call option — i.e., the value of the equity — increases. The availability of this wealth transfer mechanism, however, is not related to the dividends and therefore is not investigated here.

[2]If dividend payments are constrained, the proceeds of any new debt issue must be invested. In this case the market value of the old bonds is affected favorably by the increment in the investment and negatively by the increment in the leverage ratio. The net effect is unclear.

[3]Since we expect the payout constraints to apply to all forms of cash distributions to the stockholders, we use the words 'payout' and 'dividends' interchangeably. In other words, 'dividends' are defined to be the sum of all cash distributions to the stockholders.

payments which are financed by new issues of equity (hereafter 'equity financed dividends'). Finally, the constraint is cumulative; namely, stockholders' legal ability to pay dividends can be postponed into the future.

The sample of bond indentures studied in this paper reveals that dividend payments are constrained indirectly as well — for example, through stockholders' precommitment to maintain a minimum level of working capital or a minimum ratio of assets to liabilitites. Similar to the direct dividend constraint, the indirect constraints are cumulative and place additional restrictions *only* on the payment of debt and investment financed dividends. Usually, firms are subject to several direct and indirect constraints. This makes the estimation of the effective dividend constraint — i.e., the amount of debt or investment financed dividends that can be paid under the most restrictive constraint — difficult. Fortunately, *Moody's Industrial Manual* contains corporate reports as to what we shall call their 'reservoir of payable funds'. This reservoir is defined to be the maximum amount of debt or investment financed dividends that stockholders can pay under the most restrictive direct or indirect dividend constraint at a given point in time. Hence, at a given point in time the reservoir measures a deviation from a preimposed constraint. When the reservoir becomes zero the effective constraint can be said to be binding.

As reported in section 3, all the firms in the sample maintain positive reservoirs continuously for periods of ten to twenty years. These reservoirs are of non-trivial magnitude. They can, therefore, be used to increase the risk of the outstanding bonds by increasing the existing leverage ratio substantially. If the bonds are priced expecting no reservoirs to be maintained, any positive level of reservoir would transfer wealth from the stockholders *to* the bondholders. It is, therefore, surprising to find that the stockholders do not pay themselves the maximum allowed debt or investment financed dividends. Moreover, a precommitment by stockholders to pay no dividends would ensure that no reservoirs would be maintained and eliminate any possible tax related costs of paying dividends. The question which naturally arises is why would stockholders choose a constraint which allows for future dividend payments and, given that they do, why would they maintain reservoirs?

Section 4 contains an examination of possible explanations for these puzzling empirical regularities. It is suggested that if the corporation has a limited supply of non-negative net present value projects, a precommitment to pay no dividends in the future and therefore to maintain no reservoirs can result in *overinvestment* (i.e., forced acceptance of projects with negative net present value). The choice of a constraint that allows for investment financed dividends, and, consequently, for the existence of reservoirs reduces the likelihood of overinvestment. In periods in which the dividend constraint implies a minimum investment that would cause overinvestment, stockholders can use the reservoir to pay investment financed dividends, thereby avoiding the losses associated with overinvestment.

2. The typical direct dividend constraint

To investigate the form and potential uniformity of the dividend constraints, the debt indentures of 150 corporations as reported in *Moody's Industrial Manual* were randomly selected. All of them include restrictions on stockholders' future ability to pay dividends. The direct dividend constraint is reported for 135 firms of which 128 have the following form:

$$D_t \leqq \max \left\{ 0, \sum_{j=0}^{t} S_j + \sum_{j=0}^{t} \alpha NE_j + F - \sum_{j=0}^{t-1} D_j \right\}, \tag{1}$$

where

$j \quad = 0, 1, \ldots, T$ ($j = 0$ is the bond's issue date, $j = T$ is the debt maturity),

$D_j \quad =$ dividends (defined to be the sum of cash dividends, share repurchase and all other distribution to the stockholders) at j,

$S_j \quad =$ proceeds from sales of stock at j,

$NE_j =$ net earnings at j,

α and F are constant over the life of the bond.

2.1. Analysis

The direct dividend constraint has several interesting features. First, it constrains all forms of payments and does not distinguish between cash dividends and share repurchase. Second, as the formulation of the direct dividend constraint into eq. (1) indicates, corporations are not forced to pay negative dividends (i.e., issue new equity) in periods of successive negative earnings. In such periods the dividends would be zero. However, dividends cannot be paid unless the right-hand side of eq. (1) is positive. It is interesting to note that the constraint is cumulative; namely, the legal ability to pay dividends can be postponed into the future. In other words, under this constraint stockholders can maintain a reservoir of funds which are legally available for dividend payments. The direct dividend constraint not only enables the maintenance of a reservoir but also defines the initial reservoir which is the dip [F in eq. (1)].

The direct dividend constraint limits only investment and debt financed dividends while allowing unlimited amounts of equity financed dividends. This can be shown by an examination of the firm's cash flow identity.[4] The firm's cash inflows at time t are

$$NE_t + \Delta_t + L_t + S_t + B_t, \tag{2}$$

[4] I am indebted to John Long for suggesting this expositional model to me.

where NE_t is net earnings, Δ_t is depreciation, L_t is proceeds from sale of assets, S_t is proceeds from sale of new equity, and B_t is proceeds from sale of new debt. The firm's outflows at time t are

$$D_t + I_t + P_t, \tag{3}$$

where I_t is new investment, P_t is repayment of debt principal, and D_t is the dividend (defined to include all payments to the stockholders). At time t the firm's inflows must equal its outflows. Hence, the cash flow identity can be rewritten as

$$D_t = NE_t + \Delta_t + L_t + S_t + B_t - I_t - P_t. \tag{4}$$

Alternatively,

$$D_t = \sum_{j=0}^{t} (NE_j + \Delta_j + L_j + S_j + B_j - P_j - I_j) - \sum_{j=0}^{t-1} D_j. \tag{5}$$

Substituting the right-hand side of eq. (1) for D_t yields

$$\sum_{j=0}^{t} (NE_j + \Delta_j + L_j + S_j + B_j - P_j - I_j) - \sum_{j=0}^{t-1} D_j$$

$$\leq \max\left\{0, \sum_{j=0}^{t} (S_j + \alpha NE_j) + F - \sum_{j=0}^{t-1} D_j\right\}. \tag{6}$$

If the right-hand side of (6) is positive,[5] the inequality simplifies to

$$\sum_{j=0}^{t} (I_j + \Delta_j - L_j) \geq \sum_{j=0}^{t} [(1-\alpha)NE_j + B_j - P_j] - F. \tag{7}$$

The left-hand side of (7) is the firms' cumulative net investment; namely, the cumulative amount by which new investments exceeds the sum of depreciation and proceeds from sale of assets. Hence, the direct dividend constraint can be viewed as a minimum investment constraint. To illustrate this point, assume the firm issues a pure discount bond (i.e., $P_t = 0$ for any t which is less than the maturity date T, and $B_t = 0$ for any positive t) which includes a direct dividend constraint with $\alpha = 1$. In this case eq. (7) simplifies to

$$\sum_{j=0}^{t} (I_j - \Delta_j - L_j) \geq B_0 - F, \tag{8}$$

[5]If the right-hand side of eq. (6) is zero, the proceeds of new equity or debt issued as well as net earnings must be invested. Clearly, in this case the firm cannot pay any debt or investment financed dividends.

where B_0 is the market value of the debt on the contracting date. Thus, the firm can pay dividends if and only if the net cumulative investment, during the life of the bond, exceeds the proceeds from the sale of the debt minus the initial reservoir, F. The implications of eqs. (7) or (8) are obvious. On the contracting date, debt financed dividends are constrained[6] to F and the minimum investment to be maintained is restricted to $B_0 - F$.

Finally, note that if the right-hand side of eq. (1) is positive, the firm can pay out its proceeds from sale of new equity. Hence, anticipating non-negative cumulative earnings, the direct dividend constraint limits only dividend payments that have the potential to cause a wealth transfer — debt and investment financed dividends.

2.2. Empirical characteristics of the direct dividend constraints

A sample of 150 firms, all of which are included in *Moody's Industrial Manual*, were chosen randomly. For each firm, the details of the direct dividend constraint, as reported in *Moody's Industrial Manual* for the period 1956–1975, were collected. Of these firms the direct dividend constraint of 128 is of the form quantified by eq. (1).[7] This section contains the cross-sectional description of the two parameters α and F. Table 1 depicts the cross-sectional distribution of the unconstrained portion of net earnings, α, reported by the firms. I found 106 firms to have α equal to 1, and the lowest α is 0.5. The sample mean is 0.95 and its standard deviation is 0.1. This evidence indicates that in most cases stockholders maintain the ability to pay a large fraction of future net earnings.

To estimate the magnitude of F, the initial reservoir, the 80 firms in the sample for which net annual earnings (at the year the debt was issued) are available in the *Compustat Industrial File*, were examined. For each firm, the ratio $F/$(net annual earning at the year the debt was issued) was calculated, thereby obtaining a size adjusted measure of F. The histogram of the resulting 90 observations[8] is given in fig. 1. The sample mean is 1.235 and the ratio ranges in value from 0 to 8.7. The evidence suggests that firms choose F to be, on average, slightly greater than net annual earnings.[9]

---

[6]Since the new debt issued can include other and more restrictive constraints, the amount of funds available for debt or investment financed dividends on the contracting day can be smaller than F.

[7]The debt indentures of the other 22 firms contain dividend constraints as well. However, of them 15 firms do not report the form of the direct constraints and 7 report a form similar to eq. (1) — i.e., a cumulative constraint which restricts only debt and investment financed dividends and all methods of distribution.

[8]Some firms have more than one F in the period covered.

[9]It is interesting to note that the American Bar Foundation's *Commentaries on Indentures* (1971) contains a description of suggested restrictive covenants to be included in the debt indentures. It contains a suggestion for a dividend constraint identical to eq. (1). In it the suggested F is annual net earnings. For an analysis of these covenants, see Smith and Warner (1979).

Table 1

The distribution of α, the coefficient of net earnings in the direct dividend constraint, as reported in *Moody's Industrial Manual* for 128 corporations, in the period 1956 to 1975.

Number of firms	Value of α
106	1.00
1	0.85
4	0.80
8	0.75
7	0.7
1	0.6
1	0.5

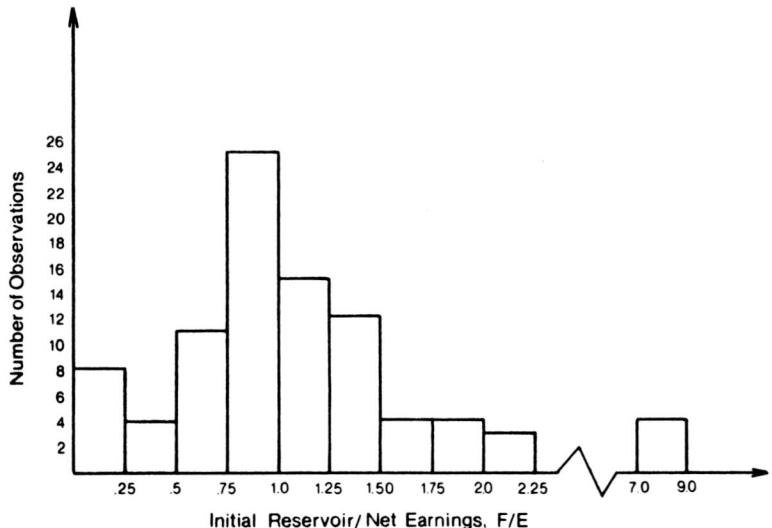

Fig. 1. Histogram of the initial reservoir of payable funds, F, to net annual earnings for 90 debt indentures issued in the period 1951 to 1976. F is the constant in the direct dividend constraint, and net annual earnings used are from the *Compustat Industrial File* tape for the year the debt was issued.

Since F is the initial reservoir of payable funds, F/B_0 is the fraction of the market value of the debt outstanding on the contracting date which can be paid out as investment or debt financed dividends. It is interesting to examine the magnitude of this ratio; however, this estimation involves several problems. First, almost all the firms in our sample have several issues of debt outstanding on the contracting date, and data on the market value of these issues of debt is unavailable. I therefore estimate B_0 as the sum of the book values of all outstanding debt issues on the contracting day as reported in the *Compustat Industrial File*. The resulting histogram of F/B_0 for the 128 firms in the sample is reported in fig. 2. The sample mean is 0.318 and the estimates range from 0 to 3.402. Hence, on average, the direct dividend constraint implies that roughly 68% of the book value of the debt could not have been paid out.

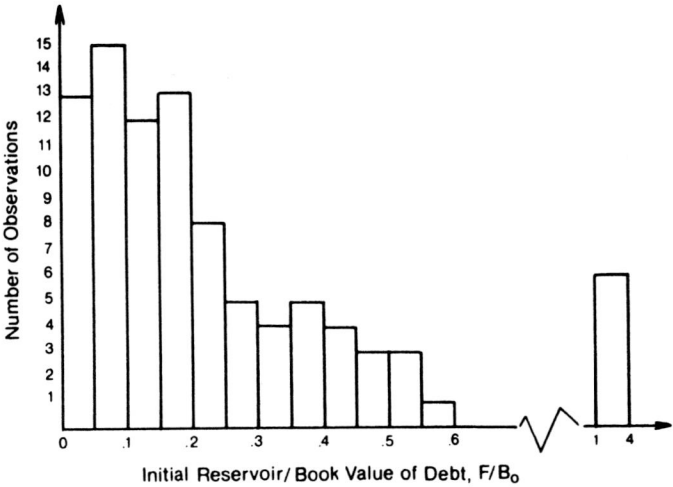

Fig. 2. Histogram of the initial reservoir of payable funds, *F*, to the book value of debt for 92 debt indentures issued in the period 1951 to 1976. *F* is the constant in the direct dividend constraint, and the book values of debt used are from the *Compustat Industrial File* tape for the year in which the debt which includes this constraint is issued.

3. The indirect dividend constraints and the reservoir of payable funds

3.1. The indirect dividend constraints

The sample of bond indentures reveals that dividend payments are constrained indirectly as well as directly. Indirect dividend constraints are restrictions generated by items such as the contractual obligations of stockholders to maintain a minimum level of working capital or net worth and a minimum ratio of assets to liabilities. The indirect dividend constraints place additional restrictions only on the payment of debt and investment financed dividends. For example, the obligation to maintain minimum net worth limits the allowed amount of debt and investment financed dividends, while a commitment to maintain a minimum ratio of current assets to current liabilities restricts only the allowed amount of investment financed dividends. Hence, depending on which of its indirect dividend constraints are binding, the maximum amount of debt financed dividends the firm is allowed to pay can differ from the allowed amount of investment financed dividends, even if the new debt issued to finance the dividends contains no new restrictions.

A complete documentation, quantification and analysis of the major forms the indirect dividend constraint takes is contained in the appendix where it is shown that the indirect dividend constraints differ from the direct dividend constraint in one important aspect — they can force the firm to pay *negative dividends* (i.e., to issue new equity).

3.2. The reservoir of payable funds

Moody's Industrial Manual contains corporate reports specifying their legal ability to pay dividends at a given point in time under the most restrictive dividend constraint. For example, the report of Kelsey–Hayes Company [*Moody's Industrial Manual* (1967, page 443)] is:

> 'Company may not pay cash dividends in excess of consolidated net income after September 1, 1963, plus $6,000,000; also agrees to maintain consolidated current assets of at least twice consolidated current liabilities and consolidated working capital of at least the greater of $17,000,000 or 140% of long term debt. On August 31, 1966, $16,400,000 of retained earnings were not so restricted.'

Note that Kelsey–Hayes Company can pay out unlimited amounts of equity financed dividends. However, as of August 31, 1966, this company can pay out $16,400,000 worth of debt *or* investment financed dividends, which is its reservoir of payable funds.

3.3. The sample

To document the magnitude of the reservoir, a subset of 100 firms, which are included in the sample and report their reservoirs in *Moody's Industrial Manual*, is selected. The reservoir is reported once a year. Thus, a time series of annual reservoirs was collected for each firm in this sample. Fig. 3 describes the sample. The number of reservoirs reported for the company is plotted on the horizontal axis and the number of firms is plotted on the vertical axis. For example, 34 firms in our sample had 10 years of reservoirs reported. As can be seen in fig. 3 the number of observations (i.e., reservoirs) varies from 5 to 20. Six firms have as little as 5 observations, while 20 firms report 20 reservoirs.

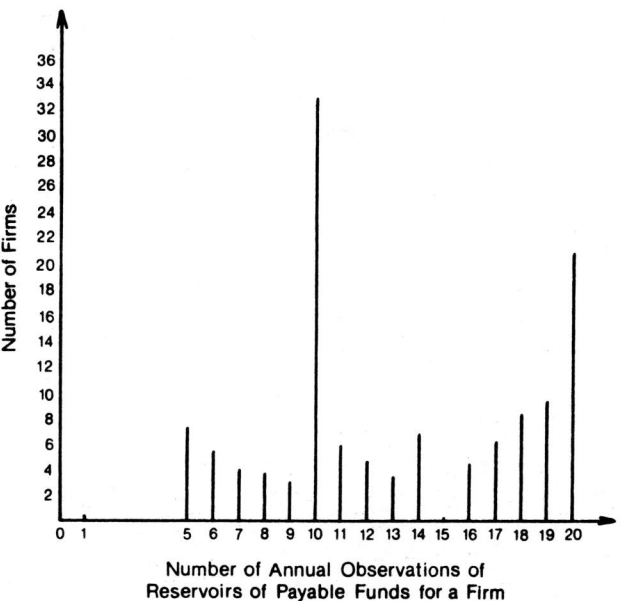

Fig. 3. Frequency distribution of the number of annual observations on reservoirs of payable funds maintained by 100 firms and reported in *Moody's Industrial Manual* for the period 1955 to 1976.

3.4. The cross-sectional description

The magnitude of the reservoir is estimated by standardizing it by an estimate of the market value of the firm. This size adjusted reservoir is estimated for each firm in the sample in the following way:

$$R_j = (1/T_j) \sum_{t=1}^{T_j} (RPF_{j,t}/PMV_{j,t}), \qquad j = 1, 2, \ldots, 100,$$

where

$RPF_{j,t}$ = reservoir of payable funds for firm j at time t,

$PMV_{j,t}$ = market value of the equity plus book value of debt for firm j at time t,

T_j = number of observations available for firm j,

and the data on the standardizing variables is from the *Compustat Industrial File*.

These ratios were sorted from low to high and divided into deciles. Decile 1 contains the lowest ratios and decile 10 contains the highest. An equally weighted average of the corporate ratios was calculated in each decile. Table 2 depicts the results. The average ratio in the ith decile, $\bar{R}_i$, is as low as 0.031 for decile 1 and as high as 0.273 for decile 10. These ratios vary from about 0.02 (see column 4) to about 0.44 (see column 5). Thus, the size adjusted reservoir exhibits large cross-sectional variability.[10] The overall mean of these ratios is 0.117, i.e., firms hold, on average, a reservoir equal to 11.7% of their market value (as estimated by the proxy employed). Hence, the magnitude of the reservoir is a non-trivial fraction of total firm value.

Table 2

Distribution of the average ratios of reservoir of payable funds to market value of the firm for 100 corporations.

Decile	Average size adjusted reservoir[a]	Standard deviation	Minimum size adjusted reservoir	Maximum size adjusted reservoir
1	0.031	0.008	0.017	0.041
2	0.050	0.003	0.043	0.057
3	0.066	0.005	0.059	0.075
4	0.081	0.004	0.076	0.087
5	0.099	0.003	0.091	0.102
6	0.112	0.005	0.103	0.120
7	0.130	0.006	0.121	0.137
8	0.148	0.007	0.138	0.159
9	0.176	0.012	0.161	0.190
10	0.273	0.076	0.198	0.437
Total sample	0.117	0.071	0.107	0.437

[a]The average size adjusted reservoir in the ith decile, $\bar{R}_i$, is an equally weighted average of the individual size adjusted reservoirs, R_j, in that decile. R_j is estimated as follows:

$$R_j = (1/T_j) \sum_{t=1}^{T_j} (RPF_{j,t}/MVF_{j,t}),$$

where $RPF_{j,t}$ is the reservoir of payable funds of firm j at time t, $MVF_{j,t}$ is the market value of equity plus the book value of debt of firm j at time t, and T_j is the number of reservoirs available for firm j.

3.5. Time series description

To describe the time series profile of the RPF's the sample was limited to firms having at least 16 observations. This requirement reduces the sample of 100 firms, described in fig. 3, to 40 firms, and the period covered to 1956–

[10]An alternative measure of size adjusted reservoir — a ratio of the average RPF divided by the average of the standardizing variable — resulted in similar cross-sectional variability. Furthermore, the adjustments of the reservoir for size with net earnings and cash dividends resulted in a similar large cross-sectional variability.

1975. For any given year the average RPF, I_t, is calculated as follows:

$$I_t = (1/N_t) \sum_{j=1}^{N_t} RPF_{j,t},$$

where N_t is the number of firms reporting their reservoirs for year t.

Fig. 4 describes the time series profile of I_t. The evidence suggests that the average RPF increases with time. The average size adjusted RPF at year t, IM_t, is estimated by

$$IM_t = (1/N_t) \sum_{j=1}^{N_t} (RPF_{j,t}/PMV_{j,t}).$$

Fig. 5 describes its time series profile which suggests that the average size adjusted RPF is around 12% per year. Additionally, the size adjusted RPF does not exhibit an upward trend.

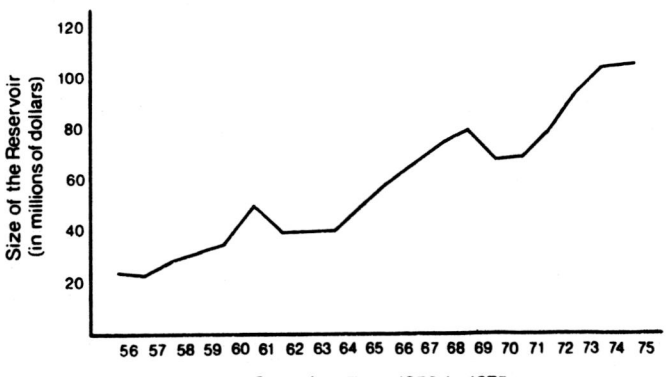

Fig. 4. Time series behavior of the average reservoir of payable funds (in millions) for 40 firms over the period 1956 to 1975.

3.6. The behavior of the reservoir around new debt issues

Frequently firms issue new debt while the old debt is still outstanding. The new issue can contain a different set of constraints thereby changing the magnitude of the reservoir maintained. To address this issue a subset of 61 firms, each having a new debt issue and at least 8 annual reservoirs reported for the period 1957–1975, was selected. Since the reservoirs are reported once a year, the date of the new issue is rounded to the nearest calendar year. For

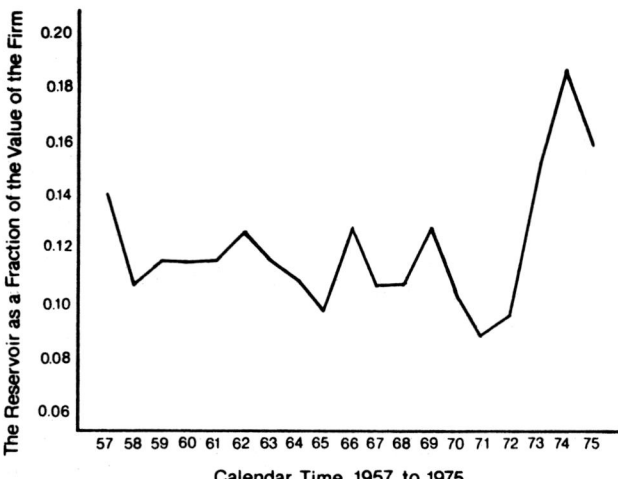

Fig. 5. The time series behavior of the average reservoir of payable funds as a fraction of the market value of the firm for 40 firms over the period 1957 to 1975.

example, July 1975 is changed to 1976 while May 1975 is changed to 1975. Defining the issue date as time 0, I calculate

$$I_t = (1/N_t) \sum_{j=1}^{N_t} RPF_{j,t},$$

where

t = number of years before and after the new issue (t ranges in value from -9 to 10),

N_t = number of firms reporting their reservoirs for year t.

Table 3 depicts the results. The average reservoir around the new debt issue seems to be similar to that usually maintained.

3.7. Potential increments in the risk of the outstanding bond

The reservoir of payable funds could be utilized to pay debt or investment financed dividends. These payments would, in turn, increase the leverage ratio and therefore the risk of the outstanding bonds. To estimate these potential increments of the leverage ratio it is assumed that the stockholders can eliminate the *RPF* by paying debt financed dividends.[11] The potential

---

[11]Assuming that the reservoir can be eliminated only by the payment of investment financed dividends would result in a similar potential change in the leverage ratio. This method will be used if the existing debt is protected by a 'me first' rule.

Table 3

The average reservoir of payable funds for 61 firms for the period 1957 to 1975 during which each had issed new debt. The date of the new issue is denoted as zero. The average reservoir is the cross-sectional average of the reservoirs available at time t for the relevant firms.

Number of years relative to the date of the new debt issue, t	Average reservoir (in millions)	Number of firms
−9	$29.25	13
−8	51.18	19
−7	33.58	22
−6	34.42	22
−5	24.29	26
−4	34.15	36
−3	33.17	44
−2	35.98	45
−1	46.75	44
0	45.76	61
1	42.36	55
2	53.66	53
3	57.81	56
4	64.04	55
5	71.33	51
6	71.82	44
7	91.98	43
8	80.05	30
9	82.88	26
10	95.13	23

change in the leverage ratio is therefore estimated by

$$PL_j - L_j = \left((1/T_j) \sum_{t=1}^{T_j} RPF_{j,t} \right) \Big/ \left((1/20) \sum_{t=1}^{20} PMV_{j,t} \right)$$

and

$$L_j = \sum_{t=1}^{20} (\text{Book value of debt})_{j,t}/PMV_{j,t},$$

where

L_j = estimated leverage ratio of the jth firm $(j = 1, 2, \ldots, 100)$,
PL_j = estimated leverage ratio the firm can achieve by eliminating the RPF.

T_j and $PMV_{j,t}$ are the number of observations for firm j and the sum of the market value of equity and the book value of debt as defined above. The period covered is from 1956 (i.e., $t = 1$) to 1975 (i.e., $t = 20$). Both PL_j and L_j were estimated for each firm in the sample. The results are reported in table 4.

A. Kalay, Dividend constraints in bond covenants

Table 4

The estimated average leverage ratio of 100 corporations and the average of their potential leverage ratios.

Variable[a]	Average	Standard deviation	Lowest	Highest
(1) Leverage ratio	0.299	0.142	0.051	0.852
(2) Potential leverage	0.425	0.144	0.115	0.859
(3) Difference [(2)−(1)]	0.126	0.081	0.006	0.547

[a]The Spearman rank correlation between (1) and (3) is −0.213 whose z value is −2.128, i.e., significant at the 5% level.

The estimated leverage ratios of the 100 firms examined ranged from 0.051 to 0.852 with a mean of 0.299. The high ratio indicates that the sample of firms investigated contains firms which have risky bonds outstanding. These ratios can be increased on the average by 12.6 percentage points to 0.425 by the elimination of the reservoirs. These potential increments range from 0.006 to 0.547, and are larger for firms with low leverage ratios. The histogram of the potential increments in the leverage ratios is depicted in fig. 6. Clearly, the levels of the reservoirs maintained imply that the leverage ratios, and therefore the risk of the outstanding bonds, can be increased substantially.

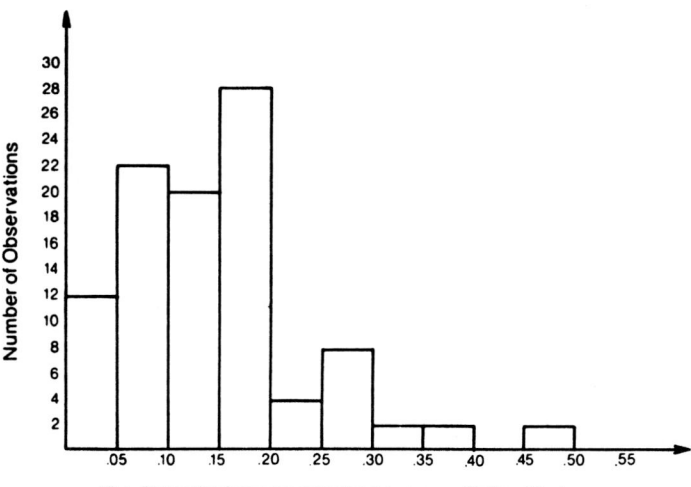

Fig. 6. Histogram of the potential increments in the leverage ratio, $PL_j − L_j$, for 100 firms. PL_j is the potential leverage ratio, i.e., the leverage ratio firm j can achieve if it eliminates its reservoir by paying debt financed dividends. L_j is the current leverage ratio of firm j.

4. The *RPF*'s, wealth transfers and potential explanations

As the sample of bond indentures reveals, stockholders impose restrictions on themselves by constraining their future ability to pay debt and investment financed dividends. At the time of issuance of the bonds, the potential bondholders would expect a certain level of future dividend payments. Obviously, bondholders' wealth is unaffected if actual dividend payments coincide with their expectations. However, if stockholders pay themselves less than the expected dividends, wealth is transferred from them to the bondholders. It is, therefore, surprising to find that stockholders do not pay themselves as much debt or investment financed dividends as they are allowed to. If the bonds are priced at issue under the expectation that no reservoir will be maintained, any positive level of reservoir maintained through the life of the bond transfers wealth *to* the bondholders. The obvious question is: Why do stockholders maintain these reservoirs?

Moreover, the existence of these reservoirs stems from stockholder's choice of dividend constraints which allow for positive payment of future dividends. In other words, stockholders can ensure that no reservoir would be maintained by precommitting themselves to pay no dividends. By doing that they would also avoid any possible tax related costs of paying dividends. In this case bonds are priced expecting no reservoir to be maintained and no dividends to be paid. The question which therefore arises is: Why do stockholders choose a constraint which allows for some dividend payments?[12]

If the typical corporation faces an unlimited supply of investment projects with non-negative net present value, stockholders can resolve these issues costlessly by precommitting themselves to pay no dividends. Indeed, investment in financial instruments trading in a perfect capital market provides the firm with unlimited supply of projects with zero net present value. However, when taxes are introduced, investment in the financial market by the corporations for the stockholders is subject to double taxation.[13] This investment, therefore, can impose negative net present value

---

[12]Notice that the reservoir is the maximum amount of debt *or* investment financed dividends that can be paid under the most restrictive dividend constraint. Thus, one cannot rule out the possibility that the reservoirs documented here are of funds available only for the payment of investment financed dividends. These payments, in turn, could require the rejection of projects with positive net present value. In this case the costs of eliminating the reservoir can exceed the benefits from increasing the risk of the outstanding bonds. Furthermore, in pricing the bonds the potential bondholders would rationally anticipate that such a reservoir would be maintained and price the debt accordingly. Therefore, the ex-post maintenance of such a reservoir would not involve any wealth transfer.

Unfortunately, due to data limitations, we are unable to determine what kinds of dividends can be paid under the maintained reservoir. However, all the firms in our sample have maintained reservoirs continuously over periods of ten to twenty years. Is it possible that *all* of them have found it *always* too costly to pay investment financed dividends?

on the stockholders. In this case the corporation has a limited supply of non-negative NPV projects and its precommitment to pay no dividends and therefore to maintain no reservoirs can result in *overinvestment* (i.e., forced acceptance of projects with negative NPV) in the future. To avoid such costs, stockholders would choose a constraint which allows for dividend payments and consequently they would maintain reservoirs. For in periods in which the minimum investment implied by the dividend constraint would have caused overinvestment, stockholders would avoid it by using the reservoirs.[14]

5. Conclusions and implications

This paper investigates a large sample of bond indentures focusing on the effects of the conflict of interests between the bondholders and the stockholders on the dividend decision of levered firms. The traditional examination of corporate dividend policy assumes that the firm is one homogeneous unit. The examination of dividend policy has therefore centered around stockholders' choice of the level of payout and the method of payout (i.e., cash dividends versus share repurchase). However, when dividends are examined in the context of their role in the bondholders-stockholders conflict, they are distinguished by their method of financing (i.e., debt, investment or equity). Indeed, the evidence presented here indicates that the stockholders of levered firms choose to limit the ability to pay *only* dividends which are financed in a way that has the potential to generate a wealth transfer from the bondholders — i.e., debt and investment financed dividends. Furthermore, these restrictions of future payouts do not distinguish between dividends and share repurchases.

My evidence indicates that the stockholders do not pay out all the allowed amount of debt and investment financed dividends. All the firms in my

---

[13]In addition to the issue of double taxation the tax on 'improper profit accumulation' [see Bittker and Eustice (1971, pp. 8-3, 8-18)] can affect the supply of zero net present value projects. By retaining earnings beyond the 'reasonable needs of the business' the corporation is providing evidence of its intent to avoid income tax paid by its stockholders. Among the major elements determining whether the tax avoidance purpose is present, are the corporation's dividend history and investment of undistributed earnings in assets unrelated to the corporation's business. Investment in the financial market is viewed as investment not related to the purpose of the business. Hence, including the expected costs due to the accumulated earnings' tax, those projects can have negative net present value. Admittedly, very few publicly held corporations have been prosecuted under this law. However, this can be an equilibrium result; firms can avoid this cost by paying dividends. Moreover, investing in assets having no reasonable connection with the purpose of the business can bring on a searching inquiry. Thus, costs can be imposed even if investigation is not followed by an actual prosecution.

[14]This potential explanation for the choices of the level of the dividend constraint and the magnitude of the reservoir maintained is developed in Kalay (1979a, b). In it the analysis is extended, a model is developed, and its empirical implications are found to be consistent with the empirical evidence.

sample maintain reservoirs of substantial magnitude. The existence of these reservoirs stems from a choice of a dividend constraint which allows for future dividend payouts. If the corporation faces a limited supply of non-negative NPV projects a precommitment to pay no dividends would result in overinvestment. In this case the choice of a constraint which allows for future payouts and the maintenance of the reservoirs reduces this cost. Hence firms can find it optimal to pay out funds, even if these payments involve tax and transaction related costs.

The analysis does not provide an answer to the 'dividend puzzle' — i.e., an explanation for the payment of cash dividends which are taxed more heavily than realized capital gains. The argument is that some form of payment should be used to avoid taking negative net present value projects. Since the dividend constraint allows for both share repurchase and cash dividends, corporations should only use share repurchase as a method of distribution if the effective tax on cash dividends is always higher than that on realized capital gains.

The effective tax on cash dividends, however, is not always higher than that on *realized* capital gains. Miller and Scholes (1978) point out a way in which investors can avoid the tax payments on dividends by converting them to tax deferred capital gains. In this case the effective tax on dividends would be *lower* than that on realized capital gains. Furthermore, the use of share repurchases as a method of distribution is subject to limiting regulation (SEC rule 13 e-2) and can lead to charges of violations of the insider trading rules. Hence, it is not necessarily a less costly method of distribution than cash dividends. It can, therefore, be optimal for the corporation to use both. Extending this argument, it can be optimal for the corporation to pay cash dividends even if these payments involve tax related costs as long as the alternative method of distribution is not less costly.

Finally, the empirical evidence presented in this paper is encouraging in several respects. It is consistent with rational maximizing behavior and constitutes powerful evidence in support of the importance of the control of the conflict of interest between the bondholders and the stockholders to corporate financial policies. But perhaps more importantly, it details sophisticated solutions discovered long ago by the financial community to problems that have attracted attention in the academic literature only recently.

Appendix: The indirect dividend constraints

This appendix details and quantifies the various forms the indirect dividend constraints take. For ease of exposition I will focus my analysis on a firm with a simplified balance sheet as shown in table 5.

Table 5[a]

Assets	Liabilities
$CA_t =$ 740	$CL_t = 300$
	$LD_t = 700$
$FA_t = 1,300$	
	$TL_t = 1,000$
$TA_t = 2,000$	$NW_t = 1,000$
	$TCF_t = 2,000$

[a]CA_t = current assets at time t,
FA_t = fixed assets at time t,
TA_t = $CA_t + FA_t$ = total assets at time t,
CL_t = current liabilities at time t,
LD_t = long-term debt at time t,
TL_t = $CL_t + LD_t$ = total liabilities at time t,
NW_t = net worth at time t,
TCF_t = $TL_t + NW_t$ = total claims on the firms' assets at time t.

Furthermore, throughout this appendix I assume (without loss of generality):

Assumption 1. The book values of this firm's assets and liabilities are equal to their respective market values.

Assumption 2. In paying investment financed dividends, stockholders forego projects with zero net present value (or deplete assets and pay out their proceeds without any liquidation costs).

Assumption 3. When new debt is issued to finance dividend payments it is issued at par and the coupon payments are equal to the required rate of return on that debt.

Assumption 4. The firm will not buy back all or parts of its outstanding debt.

As revealed by the examination of our sample, the indirect dividend constraints place additional restrictions only on the payment of debt and investment financed dividends. These constraints, in turn, can be grouped into five categories.

First, stockholders often precommit themselves to maintain a minimum level of net worth during the life of the outstanding debt. This restriction can be quantified as

$$NW_t > a, \qquad \forall t < T, \qquad\qquad (A.1)$$

where T is the debt maturity and a is the minimum net worth.

This constraint specifies the maximum allowed amount of investment financed dividend, D_t^I, to be

$$D_t^I \leq NW_t - a = TA_t - TL_t - a. \qquad\qquad (A.2)$$

If, for example, (A.2) is the most binding dividend constraint and $a = 400$, the stockholders of our firm can pay 600 dollars worth of investment financed dividends. Similarly, under Assumptions 1–4 they can pay 600 dollars worth of debt financed dividends. Note that this constraints and, as will be shown shortly, each of the other indirect dividend constraints can force the firm to issue new equity. If the net worth falls below the promised minimum, stockholders must issue new equity to meet their obligation. Hence, the indirect dividend constraints differ from the direct dividend constraint in that they can imply negative dividends.

The second type of indirect dividend constraint found is stockholder's obligation to maintain a minimum level of working capital throughout the life of the bonds. Formally,

$$WC_t = CA_t + CL_t \geq b, \qquad \forall t < T, \qquad\qquad (A.3)$$

where WC_t is the working capital at time t.

Hence,

$$D_t^I \leq TA_t - (b + CL_t). \qquad\qquad (A.4)$$

If (A.4) is the most binding investment financed dividend constraint and $b = 400$, our stockholders can pay 1300 dollars worth of investment financed dividends, D_t^I. This constraint, however, allows for unlimited payments of debt financed dividends, D_t^D, as long as these payments are financed by the issue of long-term debt.

The third form the indirect dividend constraint takes is similar to the second. In it stockholders precommit to maintain a minimum level of working capital which is no less than the greater of a given constant or some fraction of long-term debt. Formally,

$$WC_t = CA_t - CL_t \geq \max[c, \gamma LD_t], \qquad\qquad (A.5)$$

where γ and c are constants. We can rewrite (A.5) as

$$CA_t \geq \max[c + CL_t, \gamma LD_t + CL_t].\tag{A.6}$$

Thus the allowed amount of investment financed dividends is

$$D_t^I \leq TA_t - \max[c + CL_t, \gamma LD_t + CL_t].\tag{A.7}$$

If (A.7) is the most binding investment financed dividend constraint and $\gamma = 2$, $D_t^I \leq 300$. Moreover, an identical amount of debt financed dividends can be paid if it is financed by an increase in current liabilities. However, only 150 dollars of dividends financed by the issue of long-term debt can be paid.

The fourth indirect dividend constraint is stockholders' precommitment to maintain the ratio of total liabilities to total assets below an agreed upon maximum. Formally,

$$TL_t/TA_t \leq L^*.\tag{A.8}$$

Thus, for a given level of TL_t, the investment financed dividends the stockholder can pay are restricted by

$$D_t^I \leq TA_t - TL_t/L^*.\tag{A.9}$$

Hence, if (A.9) is the most restrictive dividend constraint, the stockholders of our firm can pay $2000 - 1000/0.7 = 571$ dollars of investment financed dividends, D_t^I. On the other hand, for a given level of total assets, TA_t, debt financed dividends, D_t^D, are restricted by

$$D_t^D \leq TA_t(L^* - TL_t/TA_t).\tag{A.10}$$

The stockholders of our firm can therefore pay themselves 400 dollars worth of D_t^D.

Finally, the fifth indirect dividend constraint is similar to the fourth. It contains the stockholders' obligation to maintain a ratio of current liabilities to current assets that will not exceed an agreed upon maximum during the life of the bond. This restriction can be quantified as follows:

$$CL_t/CA_t \leq e^*.\tag{A.11}$$

Thus, for a given level of CL_t, stockholders can pay

$$D_t^I \leq TA_t - CL_t/e^*.\tag{A.12}$$

Hence, if (A.12) is the most binding dividend constraint and $e^* = 0.5$, our firm can pay $2000 - 300/0.5 = 1,400$ dollars worth of D_t^l. This constraint, however, allows for unlimited payment of debt financed dividends as long as these payments are financed by the issue of a new long-term debt.

In summary, like the direct dividend constraint, the documented indirect dividend constraint places restrictions only on the payment of investment and debt financed dividends. Moreover, under these constraints, stockholders can postpone the payment of dividends into the future without 'losing' their right to pay them — i.e., these indirect dividend constraints (like the direct) are cumulative. Hence, they enable the creation and the maintenance of a reservoir of payable funds. Unlike the direct dividend constraint, the indirect constraint can force the stockholders to pay negative dividends. Finally, under the same indirect dividend constraint the maximum allowed amount of debt financed dividends can differ from the allowed amount of investment financed dividends.

References

American Bar Foundation, 1971, Commentaries on indentures, (American Bar Foundation, Chicago, IL).

Black, F. and M. Scholes, 1973, The pricing of options and corporate liabilities, Journal of Political Economy 81, 637–659.

Black, F., 1976, The dividend puzzle, Journal of Portfolio Management 2, 5–8.

Brennan, M.J., 1970, Taxes, market valuation and corporate financial policy, National Tax Journal 23, 417–427.

Bittker, B.I. and J.S. Eustice, 1971, Federal income taxation of corporations and shareholders (Warren, Gorham and Lamont, Boston, MA).

Fama, E.F. and M.H. Miller, 1972, The theory of finance (Holt, Rinehart and Winston, New York).

Fama, E.F., 1978, The effects of a firm's investment and financing decisions on the welfare of its security holders, American Economic Review 68, 272–284.

Galai, D. and R.W. Masulis, 1976, The option pricing model and the risk factor of stocks, Journal of Financial Economics 3, 53–81.

Jensen, M.C. and W.H. Meckling, 1976, Theory of the firm: Managerial behavior, agency costs, and capital structure, Journal of Financial Economics 3, 305–360.

Kalay, A., 1979a, Corporate dividend policy: A collection of related essays, Ph.D. dissertation (University of Rochester, Rochester, NY).

Kalay, A., 1979b, Towards a theory of corporate dividend policy, Unpublished paper (New York University, New York).

Long, J.B., Jr., 1973, Book review of the theory of finance by Eugene Fama and Merton Miller, Journal of Money, Credit and Banking 5, 229–235.

Long, J.B., Jr., 1978, The market valuation of cash dividends: A case to consider, Journal of Financial Economics 6, 235–264.

Mikkelson, W., 1981, Convertible calls and security returns, Journal of Financial Economics 9, 237–264.

Miller, M.H. and F. Modigliani, 1961, Dividend policy, growth and the valuation of shares, Journal of Business 34, 411–433.

Miller, M.H. and M. Scholes, 1978, Dividends and taxes, Journal of Financial Economics 6, 333–364.

Miller, M.H., 1977, Debt and taxes, Journal of Finance 32, 261–275.

Modigliani, F. and M.H. Miller, 1958, The cost of capital, corporation finance and the theory of investment, American Economic Review 48, 261–297.

Myers, S.C., 1977, Determinants of corporate borrowing, Journal of Financial Economics 4, 147–175.

Ross, S., 1977, The determination of financial structures: The incentive-signalling approach, The Bell Journal of Economics 8, 23–40.

Smith, C.W. and J.B. Warner, 1979, On financial contracting: An analysis of bond convenants, Journal of Financial Economics 7, 117–161.

The Impacts of Accounting Regulation on Bondholder and Shareholder Wealth: The Case of the Securities Acts

Chee W. Chow

ABSTRACT: This study shows that the 1933 and 1934 Securities Acts significantly, and unexpectedly, increased firms' required financial disclosure while curtailing their accounting alternatives. These constraints are postulated to have affected the nature of outstanding bondholder-shareholder contracts and the future costs of entering into such contracts. These changes are hypothesized to have affected bondholder and shareholder wealth through shareholder-to-bondholder wealth transfers, modifying firms' investment, financing, and production opportunity sets, reducing shareholder-bondholder contracting costs, and through wealth transfers across firms. Empirical tests were performed on daily stock and bond returns during the deliberation period of each Act. The sample consisted of New York Stock Exchange stocks and bonds, and over-the-counter stocks. The evidence is consistent with the '33 Act having reduced shareholder wealth through interfirm wealth transfers, out-of-pocket compliance costs, and reduced opportunity sets. The evidence weakly suggests that the '33 Act enhanced bondholder wealth. However, this effect does not appear to have been due to a wealth transfer from shareholders. There is no evidence of a significant effect due to the '34 Act.

I. INTRODUCTION

THIS study investigates how the accounting provisions of the 1933 and 1934 Securities Acts affected investor wealth around the time of their enactment. While numerous authors have analyzed how the Acts changed underwriting practices,[1] little attention has been paid to how the Acts' accounting provisions affected investor wealth.[2] The few studies that exist in this area all have serious methodological limitations.[3] Further, they focus only on shareholder wealth; the Acts' impacts on other investors, such as bondholders, remain unexplored.

This study improves upon past related research in several ways. First, it extends

[1] A sampling of this literature can be obtained by referring to Carosso [1970], Gourrich [1937], and Halleran and Calderwood [1959].

This paper is based on my Ph.D. dissertation at the University of Oregon. I am indebted to the members of my committee for their advice and encouragement: Robert G. Bowman, Helen Morsicato Gernon, Robert E. Smith, and especially my chairman, Barry H. Spicer. I have also benefited enormously from the many suggestions of Garth Blanchard, Robert Bowen, Helen Kong, Richard Leftwich, Eric Noreen, Glenn Pfeiffer, Gary Sundem, and the members of the Manuscript Award Committee, especially James Patell and Mark Wolfson. Any remaining shortcomings of this paper are my responsibility.

Chee W. Chow is Associate Professor of Accounting, The University of North Carolina at Chapel Hill.

Manuscript received June 1982.
Revision received February 1983.
Manuscript accepted February 1983.

the coverage to bondholder wealth. Second, it incorporates recent methodological refinements in accounting-event studies. Finally, its hypotheses are based on an agency framework;[4] thus, the empirical results not only address whether investor wealth was affected by the Acts' accounting provisions, but also shed some light on how these changes (if they existed) could have come about.

Section II of this study shows that the Securities Acts brought significant accounting requirements which were generally unanticipated. Using an agency framework, Section III develops hypotheses about bondholder and shareholder wealth changes due to these requirements. Section IV describes the data-collection procedures. Section V delineates the empirical results. Conclusions and recommendations for future research are set forth in Section VI.

II. THE PROBABLE IMPACTS OF THE SECURITIES ACTS ON EXISTING FINANCIAL DISCLOSURE PRACTICE

The 1933 Securities Act was introduced into Congress on March 29 and signed into law on May 27. It required exchange-listed firms to register new security issues with the Federal Trade Commission (FTC). Firms were required to include the following financial information in their registration statements:

A balance sheet . . . showing all of the assets of the issuer, the nature and cost thereof, whenever determinable, *in such detail and in such form as the Commission shall prescribe* (with intangible items segregated), . . . [a]ll the liabilities of the issuer in such detail and such form as the Commission shall prescribe, including surplus of the issuer showing how and from what sources such surplus was created, . . . *certified by an independent public or certified accountant*, . . . [a] profit-and-loss statement . . . showing

earnings and income, the nature and source thereof, and the expenses and fixed charges in such detail and such form as the Commission shall prescribe for the latest fiscal year for which such statement is available and for the two preceding years, . . . *such statement shall show what the practice of the issuer has been during the three years* . . . as to depreciation, depletion, and maintenance charges. . . . Such statement shall also differentiate between any recurring and non-recurring income and between any investment and operating income. [Schedule A, para. 25, 26. Emphasis added.]

Carey [1969, p. 183] reports that the '33 Act caught the accounting profession by surprise.[5] An examination of the financial press (the *Wall Street Journal* (WSJ) and the *Commercial and Financial Chronicle*) from July 1932 to March 1933 found no mention of impending federal securities legislation.[6] Thus, it seems reasonable to assume that the '33 Act was generally unanticipated.

[2] Stigler [1964] concluded that public regulation of the securities markets did not benefit investors in new issues. Benston [1969a, 1973] concluded that the Securities Acts did not significantly affect security prices or firms' use of the securities markets. Deakin [1976] noted a shift in stock price relatives around the effective date of the 1934 Act's disclosure requirements, but cautions against attributing this to the Act.

[3] Evaluations of Stigler's [1964] study are provided by Friend and Herman [1964, 1965] and Schwert [1981]. Gonedes and Dopuch [1974] and Friend and Westerfield [1975] discuss the methodological limitations of Benston's [1973] study. Deakin [1976] lists some major limitations of his own investigation.

[4] Agency theory analyzes the conflicts of interests that can arise when resource owners ('principals') delegate resource allocation decisions to other individuals ('agents'). Recent examples of this literature include Jensen and Meckling [1976], Myers [1977], Demski and Feltham [1978], and Fama [1980].

[5] McCormick [1948] notes that the Securities Acts were not the first attempts at federal regulation of the securities markets. Several bills with this objective had been presented to Congress in the preceding two decades. None of these had passed or received much support.

[6] On March 24, 1933, a *WSJ* report discussed President Roosevelt's plans to regulate the securities market and firms' financial disclosure practices. Five days later, the 1933 Act was introduced into Congress.

Descriptions of common accounting practices preceding the '33 Act indicate that the Act's accounting provisions were a significant departure from the status quo. Even though many states had previously enacted corporation laws which required financial disclosure,[7] these seldom contained content or accounting procedure specifications [Hawkins, 1968, p. 254]. Stock exchanges similarly had few accounting requirements.[8] This lack of restrictions was reflected in firms' financial disclosure practices in the period just prior to the '33 Act. Hoxsey [1930, pp. 259–261] notes that firms often made no distinction between operating income and other income. Littleton and Zimmerman [1962, p. 101] report that firm managements frequently created secret reserves and made questionable adjustments to surplus and profits without revealing these to the public. Summarizing this state of affairs, Chatfield [1977, p. 279] observes:

> . . . throughout this period managements had almost complete control over the selection of financial information distributed in published reports.

In addition to controlling the extent of financial disclosure, managements also seemed to dominate accounting technique choices. Ripley's [1927] survey of annual reports led him to conclude that companies could manipulate their reported results almost at will. Carey [1969, p. 182] makes a similar observation, as does Hawkins [1968], who states (p. 273):

> . . . accounting practice placed few restrictions on industrial management. There was an inviting variety of alternatives approved by accountants and employed by businessmen. For example, there still were many different theories of depreciation. No consensus of opinion yet existed as to the degree of ownership which warranted consolidation. Frequently, no distinction was made between operating income and other income. And a variety of methods pertaining to the recording of asset values persisted.

In view of this historical background, it seems that the '33 Act both increased the general extent of financial disclosure and reduced the available accounting alternatives.[9] Incentives for compliance were probably considerable, as external auditing was mandated, and both the issuers of securities and external auditors were held potentially liable for investor damages arising out of fraudulently or negligently prepared registration statements [Benston, 1969a].

The accounting provisions of the '33 Act applied only to issuers of new, publicly traded securities. The 1934 Securities and Exchange Act extended these requirements to all exchange-listed firms. This Act was probably less of a surprise than the '33 Act because President Franklin Roosevelt had revealed his plans for such a law in early 1933 (see Section IV). The '34 Act did add a major new accounting requirement—sales disclosure [Benston, 1973; Carey, 1969]. In addition, it reduced somewhat the legal liability of external auditors, imposed regulations on margin trading and the activities of securities traders, and created a Securities and Exchange Commission

---

[7] See Wise [1934], Smith [1937], and Carosso [1970] for detailed descriptions of these laws.

[8] Edwards [1960, p. 150] notes that the New York Stock Exchange did not require listed firms to file audited financial statements until January 1933. Zeff [1972, p. 125] reports that listed firms did not have to reveal their accounting methods.

[9] The '33 Act gave the Federal Trade Commission authority over financial disclosure practices. Whether the public expected the Commission to use this power is uncertain, though McCormick [1948] and Zeff [1972] note that the Commission had engaged in standardizing accounting practices in the past. Given the *laissez faire* environment preceding the '33 Act, any movement towards standardization was likely to reduce management's accounting discretion.

(SEC) to administer both Securities Acts.[10]

III. Impacts of the Securities Acts' Accounting Requirements on Bondholder and Shareholder Wealth

This section uses the agency framework to analyze how the Acts' accounting provisions may have affected bondholder and shareholder wealth. Nine hypotheses are generated for empirical testing.

Numerous authors have shown that within business firms, a conflict of interests exists between shareholders and bondholders; shareholders have incentives to make resource allocations which benefit themselves at the expense of bondholders [Fama and Miller, 1972; Galai and Masulis, 1976; Jensen and Meckling, 1976; Myers, 1977].[11] This conflict is a negative-sum game because some resource allocations which benefit the shareholders reduce not only the value of the debt, but also the value of the firm [Jensen and Meckling, 1976; Myers, 1977; Smith and Warner, 1979]. Thus, incentives exist for voluntary contracting among shareholders and bondholders to control their interest conflict. Smith and Warner [1979] and Leftwich [1980] show that many accounting-based debt covenants can be interpreted as serving this function. These authors further note that such covenants (especially those for public debt) usually rely on prevailing generally accepted accounting principles (GAAP) at the time of financial statement preparation, and not at the issue date of the debt. Since GAAP typically allows several alternative treatments of the same transaction, this arrangement does not totally eliminate shareholders' flexibility to circumvent debt covenants through "creative accounting." Smith and Warner [1979] and Leftwich [1980] suggest that more rigid accounting specifications are not used because of costs.[12]

In an informationally efficient securities market, the expected resource allocation implications of such accounting discretion will tend to be incorporated in share and bond prices. If the available accounting alternatives are unexpectedly reduced, the costs and nature of existing debt covenants may be affected; the expected impacts of these changes will also tend to be reflected in share and bond prices.

Benston [1969a, p. 527] reports that almost all corporate debt was publicly placed before 1934—only about three percent was privately placed between 1900 and 1934. Even though many of the debt covenants in this period were based on accounting numbers,[13] the previously reviewed historical accounts suggest that few restrictions were placed on how the accounting numbers were to be computed. The restrictions placed on accounting alternatives by the Securities Acts may have changed the nature of these outstanding covenants, and through this, the wealth of shareholders and bondholders.

The Acts probably reduced share-

---

[10] The non-accounting requirements of the Securities Acts will not be studied in this paper. These requirements applied to the securities markets as a whole, and are unlikely to affect the security portfolio comparisons in this study. Also, there is no strong reason to suspect a systematic relation between their effect and that of the accounting-related firm characteristics examined here

[11] A conflict of interests also exists between the firm manager and shareholders. This will not be addressed in this paper. Relative to the value of the firm, the manager's wealth is probably immaterial, and leaving it out of the analysis is not likely to significantly change the results. Also, the manager-shareholder interest conflict probably can be controlled relatively cheaply by the manager dealing with the board of directors.

[12] These costs include impairment to the firm's flexibility in pursuing profitable projects, and accounting costs in keeping track of a long time-series of GAAP for firms with multiple debt issues.

[13] Dewing [1926], Kehl [1941], Rodgers [1965], and Chow [1982] provide numerous examples of popular debt covenants from the 1800s and early 1900s which were based on accounting numbers such as current assets and liabilities, quick assets, and accounting earnings.

holders' flexibility in satisfying debt covenants through accounting means. This could have unexpectedly curtailed their ability to benefit at the expense of bondholders. Shareholder wealth could also have decreased if accounting reports conforming to the new requirements were costly to prepare (e.g., necessitated new accounting procedures and external auditing), or if they abridged the firm's permissible financing, investment, and production alternatives.[14] While all of these adverse effects appear likely, the net result of the new accounting requirements may not have been reduced shareholder wealth. Shareholders could have benefited from the Acts through a reduction in shareholder-bondholder contracting costs. Before the Securities Acts, shareholders and bondholders may have been deterred from using more accounting-based debt covenants due to competitive disadvantage considerations; information provided to a firm's investors can be used by competitors to its disadvantage.[15] Conceivably, some degree of uniformity in financial disclosure practices could have substantially neutralized this concern, thus reducing shareholder-bondholder contracting costs in general.[16] Since the Securities Acts not only prescribed some standardization of financial disclosure practices, but also provided an enforcement mechanism, they could have brought about just such a benchmark, to the benefit of both shareholders and bondholders. Given that the Acts could have both benefited and imposed costs on shareholders, their net impact on shareholder wealth is, on average, indeterminate. Thus, the following hypothesis is specified:

Hypothesis 1:

Ceteris paribus, firms covered by the Securities Acts experienced a change in shareholder wealth.[17]

The Acts' compliance costs and restric-

tive effects on firm resource allocations could have reduced bondholder wealth by affecting the mean and variance of firm cash flows. However, if these costs were substantial, bondholders could agree to modify the existing debt covenants. Thus, the Acts probably affected bondholders more directly through an unexpected wealth transfer to them from the shareholders and through reducing contracting costs.

Hypothesis 2:

Ceteris paribus, firms covered by the Securities Acts experienced an increase in bondholder wealth.

In addition to the average effects postulated in Hypotheses 1 and 2, the Acts' wealth impacts are also expected to differ cross-sectionally. Leftwich [1981] notes that the costs to renegotiate debt

---

[14] Leftwich [1981, p. 7] observes that shareholders have incentives to minimize the impact of an unexpected tightening of restrictive covenants. They can try to renegotiate the existing covenants, redeem the debt, or change the firm's resource allocation activities to avoid violating the covenants. All of these alternatives are potentially costly, and Leftwich postulates that shareholders will not be able to avoid some reduction in wealth. Dhaliwal [1980] provides evidence that accounting and investment, financing, and production decisions are interdependent.

[15] Mautz and May [1978] report that concern over competitive disadvantage motivated many multi-segment firms to oppose mandatory segmented financial disclosure. Foster [1980] and Beaver [1981] also discuss the effects of financial disclosure on competitive disadvantage.

[16] Leftwich [1983] also observes that having a benchmark set of accounting standards can facilitate shareholder-bondholder contracting. Beaver [1981] suggests that accounting regulation can be beneficial in establishing such a benchmark.

[17] For this and the remaining hypotheses, the alternate hypothesis is that no impact or relationship existed. Note that failure to support Hypothesis 1 does not necessarily imply that the Securities Acts did not affect shareholder wealth, since the opposing effects could have been about equal in absolute value. Finding that shareholder wealth was decreased would be consistent with the Acts having imposed significant compliance and/or wealth transfer costs on shareholders. A significant increase in shareholder wealth would support the hypothesis that the Acts reduced shareholder-bondholder contracting costs.

covenants, redeem outstanding debt, and default on debt agreements all increase with the amount of debt outstanding. This implies that, other things being equal, more highly levered firms face higher costs in adapting to new accounting requirements. Consequently, such firms are also more likely to have been affected by the Acts' accounting requirements.

Hypothesis 3:

Ceteris paribus, bondholders' increase in wealth due to the Securities Acts varied directly with their firms' leverage.

The directional link between leverage and shareholder wealth changes is less certain. The previous discussion suggests that the new accounting requirements induced greater shareholder-to-bondholder wealth transfers in firms with higher leverage. However, shareholders in such firms could also have benefited proportionally more from the new accounting requirements. Fama and Miller [1972] and Jensen and Meckling [1976] show that the severity of the shareholder-bondholder interest conflict increases with leverage. To the extent that the Acts' accounting requirements reduced shareholder-bondholder contracting costs, more-highly levered firms probably were more likely to take advantage of this by initiating or expanding their use of accounting-based debt covenants. Considering both the Acts' costs and benefits, the following hypothesis results:

Hypothesis 4:

Ceteris paribus, shareholders' wealth changes due to the Securities Acts were proportional to their firms' leverage.

It also appears likely that debt covenants which used many different accounting indices (e.g., earnings, current

assets) were more likely to have been affected by the new accounting constraints.[18] Thus,

Hypothesis 5:

Ceteris paribus, bondholders' wealth gains due to the Securities Acts increased with the number of different accounting indices in their firms' debt covenants.

In the case of shareholder wealth, offsetting influences appear likely. Unexpected shareholder-to-bondholder wealth transfers were probably larger, and/or more likely, for firms with more accounting-based debt covenants. At the same time, the Acts' accounting requirements could have unexpectedly reduced their competitive disadvantage versus firms with more sketchy previous disclosure. As a result, shareholders of the former type of firms could have reaped a wealth transfer from the shareholders of the latter type. In addition, it is likely that firms with scanty previous disclosure faced higher costs to comply with the new accounting requirements (e.g., additional bookkeeping, external auditing). Given these other possible effects, shareholders whose firms had more accounting-based debt covenants may not have been affected more adversely than shareholders whose firms had less reliance on such covenants. Thus:

Hypothesis 6:

Ceteris paribus, firms covered by the Securities Acts experienced a change in shareholder wealth which was proportional to the number of different accounting indices in their debt covenants.

Even firms with exactly the same accounting-based debt covenants may not

[18] The study by Collins, Rozeff and Dhaliwal [1981] of oil and gas accounting regulation provides support for this hypothesis.

have been affected by the new accounting requirements to the same degree. In the case of dividend constraints, Kalay [1978] reports that firms typically maintain an inventory of payable funds rather than pay out all dividends permitted by the debt covenants. He suggests that such an inventory helps firms to avoid being forced by the covenants to undertake suboptimal investments. Using similar reasoning, Leftwich [1981] and Collins, Rozeff and Dhaliwal [1981] postulate that firms which are farther from the constraints in lending agreements are less likely to be affected by a given accounting requirement—the distance reduces the probability of debt covenants becoming binding or violated under the new accounting rules. In the case of the Securities Acts, this implies that firms which were more distant from their debt covenant constraints are less likely to have experienced a shareholder-to-bondholder wealth transfer or a drastic reduction in permissible financing, investment, and production alternatives. Thus:

Hypothesis 7:

Ceteris paribus, firms covered by the Securities Acts experienced an increase in bondholder wealth which was inversely related to their distance from debt covenant provisions.

Hypothesis 8:

Ceteris paribus, firms covered by the Securities Acts experienced a reduction in shareholder wealth which was inversely related to their distance from debt covenant provisions.

All of the firm characteristics discussed thus far have been suggested by agency contracting considerations. Though firm size plays no explicit role in this framework, it may still account for some cross-sectional variation in the Acts' wealth impacts. If the new accounting require-

ments had significant fixed start-up costs or decreasing marginal compliance costs, shareholders of larger firms would have experienced a proportionally smaller wealth decrease relative to smaller-firm shareholders.[19] Bondholders, on the other hand, should not have been affected significantly since they are not the residual claimants. Thus:

Hypothesis 9:

Ceteris paribus, firms covered by the Securities Acts experienced a decrease in shareholder wealth which was proportionally smaller for larger firms.

The following section will describe how data were collected to test the nine stated hypotheses.

IV. Sample Selection and Data Collection

This section describes the sample, the time-period selected for study, and variable definition and measurement.

A. Sample Selection

1. *Stocks*. The "treatment" sample of common stocks came from industrial New York Stock Exchange (NYSE) firms listed in the December 28, 1935 *Wall Street Journal* (*WSJ*). To ensure a sufficient time-series of financial data, continuous NYSE listing and inclusion in *Poor's Industrial Volume* from 1926 to 1935 were required.[20] Out of 371 firms considered, 259 satisfied these criteria. This number was further reduced to 196 for the following reasons:

[19] Benston [1969b, p. 62] summarizes SEC statistics from 1951, 1953, and 1955 which show that accounting fees as a percentage of proceeds from publicly offered debt issues decrease with size of issue. Benston suggests this is consistent with there being significant fixed compliance costs to the Securities Acts' accounting requirements. Some recent evidence in Banz [1981] also suggests that information costs are proportionally higher for smaller firms.

[20] These two criteria could have introduced a selection bias which works against the stated hypotheses. *Poor's* may have included only firms which exceed certain

1) Two firms were excluded because, unlike the rest, they were not externally audited as of 1933 fiscal year end, yet constituted too small a sample for statistical analysis.

2) Forty-seven firms were dropped because, unlike the other firms, their fiscal years did not end on December 31. Only firms with a common fiscal year end date were retained because this helped to control for confounding effects, such as those associated with year-end announcements.[21]

3) Fourteen firms were excluded because they had made new public securities offerings at various times during the interim between the Securities Acts. The security returns to these firms would have included significant confounding effects in this period.[22]

A control sample of stocks was selected from the 66 industrial over-the-counter (OTC) firms listed in the December 28, 1935 *WSJ*. The inclusion criteria listed above were used, with two exceptions:

1) Both audited and non-audited OTC firms were retained.
2) The firm had to have remained unlisted until at least 1940.

Twenty-six firms satisfied all the inclusion criteria. If non-audited firms had been excluded, the OTC sample would have dropped to 16. The requirement for remaining unlisted was designed to limit potential impacts on the control firms due to their impending plans to list with an exchange (thus coming under the coverage of the Securities Acts).

Selected characteristics of the treatment and control samples are summarized in Table 1, Panels A and B, respectively. The data source was the 1933 *Poor's Industrial Volume*. From this table, it appears that the OTC sample had lower financial disclosure standards, on

average, than the NYSE sample—sales disclosure, external auditing, and accounting-based debt covenants were all less prevalent for this group. For hypothesis testing in this study, such differences between the two samples should not pose a major problem. Because security portfolio returns are compared between a control and an event period (see Section V), systematic return differences due to different disclosure characteristics should occur in both periods. If the OTC firms turn out to be an inappropriate control group (i.e., they were also affected by the new accounting requirements), comparing the treatment and control portfolio returns will bias the results against, rather than in favor of, the hypotheses.

---

minimum standards in financial disclosure. If this is the case, the accounting requirements of the Securities Acts could have had a below-average impact on these firms. Further, some firms may have anticipated such high costs under the Securities Acts, so that it was less costly for them to delist from the NYSE. The firms that remained on the Exchange would then be those less drastically affected by the Acts. Benston [1973, p. 150] reports that of the 484 corporations listed on the NYSE in 1929, ten went over-the-counter in 1933 and four did so in 1934. The small number of delistings suggests that this potential selection bias is unlikely to be large.

[21] This was motivated by Rozeff and Kinney's [1976] finding of seasonal patterns in monthly returns to NYSE firms. These authors postulate that this phenomenon may be due to firms' accounting announcements related to their fiscal year-ends. In the present study, security return comparisons use the same calendar time across firms. Having only December 31 year-end firms can help equalize the effects of year-end announcements, thus improving the power of empirical tests.

[22] Data on new securities offerings were collected from *Poor's, The Commercial and Financial Chronicle, National Stock Summary, National Bond Summary*, and *Capital Change Reporter*. It may appear that since these 14 firms came under the 1933 Act's requirements with their new securities offerings, they could be used directly to assess wealth changes due to the Act's requirements. However, the potential for confounding is great. If a firm realized that a new securities offering would require compliance with the '33 Act, but still decided to proceed, it probably expected the benefits from the new offering to exceed its costs. Thus, the effects of new financing could mask those of the '33 Act.

TABLE 1

SELECTED CHARACTERISTICS OF THE TREATMENT
AND CONTROL SAMPLES AT 1932
FISCAL YEAR-END

Panel A
NYSE Firms

		Disclosed Sales		
		Yes	No	Total
Had Public Debt Outstanding and Accounting-based Debt Covenants	Yes	38	28	66
	No	62	68	130
		100	96	196

Panel B
OTC Firms
Externally Audited

		Disclosed Sales		
		Yes	No	Total
Had Public Debt Outstanding and Accounting-based Debt Covenants	Yes	3	4	7
	No	3	6	9
		6	10	16

Not Externally Audited

		Disclosed Sales		
		Yes	No	Total
Had Public Debt Outstanding and Accounting-based Debt Covenants	Yes	1	1	2
	No	2	6	8
		3	7	10

2. *Bonds.* Only bonds listed in the *WSJ* from January 1933 to July 1935 were included. The following additional criteria were imposed to limit the influence of omitted variables:[23]

1) The bond was not convertible into equity shares.
2) The bond had no warrants attached.
3) The bond interest was not in arrears at 1932 fiscal year-end.
4) The bond was not serial.

In order to keep the observations as cross-sectionally independent as possible, only one bond per firm was included. Out of 82 NYSE bonds examined, 46 satisfied the price data availability requirement. Of these, four were deleted due to criteria one and two, three were excluded due to default of interest, and one was eliminated because it was serial. The 38 remaining bonds constituted the treatment sample. Major characteristics of these bonds are reported in Table 2.

TABLE 2

SELECTED CHARACTERISTICS OF THE BOND
TREATMENT SAMPLE

	Bonds With Accounting-based Covenants (N = 23)	Bonds With No Accounting-based Covenants (N = 15)
Average coupon rate	5.4%	5.25%
Average years to maturity	13.6	10.0
Proportion with sinking fund provisions	.82	.73
Proportion with trustees	.95	.93
Proportion with call provisions	.87	.93

Table 2 suggests that the bonds with and without accounting-based debt covenants were quite similar on the selected characteristics. The average coupon rate and maturity for the accounting-based bonds were 5.4 percent and 13.6 years, respectively, while for the non-accounting-based bonds these were 5.25 percent and 10 years, respectively. The other provisions were also rather evenly distributed between the two groups.

[23] Van Horne [1978] summarizes an extensive theoretical and empirical literature on the factors affecting bond returns. Mikkelson [1978] shows that convertible bonds reduce the shareholder-bondholder interest conflict.

A control portfolio of bonds was not available because only three of the OTC sample firms had bond-price data in the *WSJ*. As the following discussion will show, a control period-event period comparison is used to overcome this handicap.

B. Time-Period of Study

Much evidence exists that security prices anticipate the effects of new regulation [Rice, 1978; Collins and Dent, 1979; Noreen and Sepe, 1981]. This prompted selection of the deliberation period for analysis.[24]

Congressional deliberations on the Securities Acts occurred during the Great Depression; they also coincided with numerous other executive and legislative activities.[25] Stock market returns were particularly volatile around this time [Officer, 1973; Deakin, 1976]. Given this background, daily events were selected for study so as to minimize confounding by other factors.

1. Selecting the Critical Dates. Following the approach of Noreen and Sepe [1981] and Leftwich [1981], the *WSJ* from July 1, 1932 to May 30, 1933 was examined for reports of federal activities to regulate the securities markets and financial disclosure. Out of these, 11 were subjectively selected as having been "critical" to the '33 Act (i.e., they significantly affected market assessment of its probability of enactment and/or the stringency of its accounting requirements). These critical events were further classified into favorable (i.e., they increased the Act's assessed probability of enactment and/or accounting stringency) and unfavorable (i.e., they decreased the Act's assessed probability of enactment and/or accounting stringency) categories, consisting of eight and three events, respectively. The reason for this favorable/unfavorable partitioning was to per-

mit two independent tests—the Act's effects should reverse directions between the two categories of events.[26]

Critical events relating to the '34 Act were similarly selected from *WSJ* reports between January 1 and June 30, 1934. The 23 selected events were split into 14 favorable and nine unfavorable.

Appendices A and B summarize the *WSJ* reports relating to the selected 1933 and 1934 critical events.

2. Defining the Event Periods. A five-day event period was defined around each critical event date, consisting of the two

---

[24] Contrary to modern times, the securities markets in the 1930s may have been less efficient with respect to public information, and price reaction to the Securities Acts may not have occurred until compliance, or even later. This would cause the impact period of this study to be mis-specified and bias the results towards insignificance. However, recent evidence in Jarrell [1981] suggests that securities markets were at least semi-strongly efficient prior to the Securities Acts.

[25] Congressional consideration of the 1933 Securities Act occurred around the time when President Roosevelt declared a bank holiday and signed an Emergency Banking Act. Significant pieces of legislation which were either enacted or under consideration in the March–June 1933 period included the Economy Bill, the Farm Relief Bill, the Home Mortgage Bill, the Reforestation Relief Bill, the Rail Coordination Bill, and abandonment of the gold standard. Consideration of the 1934 Securities and Exchange Act coincided with the Gold Reserve Act, the Commodity Exchange Bill, amendments to the Agricultural Act, the Bankhead Cotton Control Bill, the Wagner Bill which made the National Labor Board a permanent agency, the Administration Tariff Bill, a sugar bill, a bill to create credit banks for industry, and a bill to guarantee the Home Owners' Loan Corporation's bonds and interest.

[26] Subjective selection of critical events is not without drawbacks. It necessitates subjective judgment as to which events were critical and, given that an event was critical, whether it was favorable or unfavorable. Erroneous inclusion of non-critical events and exclusion of critical ones would bias the results towards insignificance. Also, some events which appear to be favorable (unfavorable) may have been less favorable (unfavorable) than the market had expected at the time. This would cause these events to be misclassified and bias the results against the hypotheses. Neither of these effects is desirable. However, in view of the potential problems with using an extended study period, it was decided that subjective classification of events represented the preferred alternative.

days before, the day of, and the two days following the event.[27] These event periods were judged to be long enough to capture anticipatory and subsequent market reactions to each event, and yet specific enough to attribute security price changes to the event.[28] For each Securities Act, the overall favorable (unfavorable) event period was defined as the union of all the five-day periods surrounding each favorable (unfavorable) critical event. These overall event periods are the focal points of the empirical tests.

In addition, a 40-day control period was established for each Act. These 40 days were selected from the same calendar time as the event periods without overlapping the latter. The selection criterion was that no *WSJ* report concerning the Securities Acts appeared on these dates. Thus, security returns on both event and control days should include the influence of other economic circumstances, while their differences should reflect the Securities Acts' impacts.

Exhibits 1 and 2 display the calendar dates of the favorable, unfavorable, and control periods for the '33 and '34 Acts, respectively. (See pages 515 and 516.)

C. Variable Definition and Measurement

1. Dependent Variables. Changes in daily stock and bond returns were used as proxies for changes in shareholder and bondholder wealth. Gross returns were used because the Acts were hypothesized to have affected all listed securities. Since available "market" indices are based on such securities, regressing out "market"-wide effects would net out many of the return changes being analyzed here. Daily returns were calculated as follows:

$$S_{i,t} = \frac{SP_{i,t+1} - SP_{i,t} + D_{i,t}}{SP_{i,t}},$$

$$B_{i,t} = \frac{BP_{i,t+1} - BP_{i,t}}{BP_{i,t}} + CR_i.$$

where

$S_{i,t}$ = return to stock i on day t,

$SP_{i,t+1}$ = opening price per share of stock i on day $t+1$,

$SP_{i,t}$ = opening price per share of stock i on day t,

$D_{i,t}$ = dividend per share payable to stock i owners of record on day t,

$B_{i,t}$ = return to bond i on day t,

$BP_{i,t+1}$ = opening price for bond i on day $t+1$,

$BP_{i,t}$ = opening price for bond i on day t, and

CR_i = average daily coupon rate for bond i.

All returns were adjusted for capital changes. For NYSE stocks and bonds, the average of bid and asked prices substituted for the opening price when the latter was not available. Only bid and asked prices were reported for OTC stocks, so the average of these prices was used for the OTC stocks throughout. In all cases, returns to days with missing data were estimated through apportionment.[29]

---

[27] If two event dates were within four calendar days of each other, the event period was from two days before the earlier event to two days after the later event.

[28] Dann, Mayers and Raab [1977] and Foster [1978, Ch. 11] present evidence that security prices adjust to new public information very rapidly. These studies are based on recent events. If the securities markets were less efficient in the 1930s, the five-day event period may not fully capture the effects of a particular event. This would bias the results toward insignificance.

[29] Missing data was not a serious problem. Typically, only several days of missing data occurred within each type of event period (i.e., favorable, unfavorable, control). Since the apportionment usually takes place among days within the same event period, it does not affect the comparison across types of periods. Apportionments which involved splitting a multi-day return among different types of event periods were rare.

2. *Independent Variables* (*Firm Characteristics*). For each sample firm, data were gathered for four characteristics: leverage (LEVG), firm size (SIZE), number of different accounting indices included in debt covenants (NUMCOV), and distance from existing accounting-based debt constraints (LOOSNS). The data sources were the *Poor's Industrial Manuals* from 1926 to 1935 and, in the case of market values, the *WSJ* and the *Commercial and Financial Chronicle*.

Leverage and firm size were measured as follows:[30]

$$LEVG_{i,T} = \frac{DEBT_{i,T} + PFDSTK_{i,T}}{EQUITY_{i,T}},$$
$$SIZE_{i,T} = DEBT_{i,T} + PFDSTK_{i,T} + EQUITY_{i,T}$$

where

$LEVG_{i,T}$ = leverage of firm i at the end of year T,
$DEBT_{i,T}$ = book value of debt of firm i at the end of year T,
$PFDSTK_{i,T}$ = book value of outstanding preferred stock of firm i at the end of year T,
$EQUITY_{i,T}$ = market value of outstanding equity stock of firm i at the end of year T, and
$SIZE_{iT}$ = size of firm i at the end of year T.

T was set at the 1932 and 1933 fiscal year ends for the '33 and '34 Acts, respectively.

NUMCOV was obtained by counting the number of different accounting indices (e.g., current assets, earned surplus, net worth) across all of a firm's outstanding debt covenants, as summarized in the 1933 *Poor's Industrial Volume*. The permissible cash dividends under each of these constraints was also calculated for each firm. (Some dividend constraints are explicit, such as permit-

ting cash dividends only out of earned surplus; others are implicit, such as requiring current assets to equal at least twice current liabilities—a firm cannot pay a cash dividend which reduces current assets below this minimum. See Smith and Warner [1979] and Kalay [1982] for more detailed discussions of dividend constraints.) The smallest permissible dividend across all of a firm's debt covenants was divided by SIZE to yield its LOOSNS measure. For analyzing the '33 ('34) Act, financial data from *Poor's* up to the 1932 (1933) fiscal year end were used in these calculations. Out of the 66 treatment firms with accounting-based debt covenants, 44 were bound by explicit dividend constraints; for the remaining 22, implicit dividend constraints were the tightest accounting-based restrictions.

It should be noted that both NUMCOV and LOOSNS have potential limitations as proxies for their conceptual counterparts. In the former case, simply adding up the number of different accounting indices probably does not fully reflect how different accounting-based constraints work as a package. The LOOSNS measure has a similar shortcoming because it considers each constraint in isolation. Also, LOOSNS only focuses on dividend restrictions (though these are the most prevalent; see Kalay [1978] and Chow [1982]) to the exclusion of other types of restrictions (e.g., mer-

---

[30] Both LEVG and SIZE are partially based on the book value of debt, and are therefore likely to have measurement errors. However, these errors are probably not very severe. Malkiel [1966, p. 8] reports that around 1932–1933, the average yield on long-term corporate bonds was about 4.5 percent. Since the sample bonds had coupon rates which averaged only slightly above five percent and their average maturity was around ten years, the difference between book and market values probably was not enormous. Also, Bowman [1980] suggests that leverage measures based on book value of debt can be very satisfactory surrogates for measures based on market values.

gers, disposing of the firm's assets, issuing new debt or equity shares). Because of these limitations, test results based on NUMCOV and LOOSNS are suggestive rather than conclusive. These proxies are used only because no theoretical guidance exists for developing better aggregate measures.

Table 3 presents the mean, median, and standard deviation of each independent variable for the control and treatment samples, and selected subsets of the latter.

Table 3 reveals some rather large differences in firm characteristics across subsamples. For 1933, median firm size for the OTC sample was $3.31 million; the NYSE sample had a median firm size of $14.27 million, or about four times as much. Within the NYSE sample, median LEVG for 1933 was .093 for the 130 firms without accounting-based debt covenants, and .817 for the 66 firms with such covenants. These apparent differences motivated statistical tests for cross-sectional differences in firm characteristics. Some of the hypothesis tests are based on cross-sectional return comparisons; in order for these tests to yield meaningful results regarding the Securities Acts, potential confounding due to differences in sample characteristics needs to be assessed.

Kolmogorov-Smirnov goodness-of-fit tests indicated that many of the firm characteristics were non-normally distributed (indicated by asterisks in Table 3). As a result, the cross-sectional comparisons were done with the nonparametric Wilcoxon rank sum test.[31] The results indicated that the treatment firms were significantly larger than the control firms in both 1933 and 1934. The dividend constraint was also significantly tighter (i.e., LOOSNS was smaller) for the treatment firms in 1934. Within the treatment sample, the 66 firms with accounting-

based debt covenants were significantly more highly levered than the remaining 130 firms in both years. Focusing on the 38 treatment firms in the bond sample, the 23 firms with accounting-based debt covenants had significantly higher leverage than the 15 remaining firms in both 1933 and 1934. None of the other pairwise comparisons approached statistical significance at conventional levels.

A formal test for multicollinearity among firm characteristics was not performed. However, within each subsample, simple pairwise correlations among firm characteristics were generally low in absolute value.[32] This suggests that multicollinearity may not be a major problem in this study.

V. EMPIRICAL METHODS AND RESULTS

The empirical results are presented in three sections. Stock returns are analyzed first with portfolio-pair comparisons and cross-sectional regressions. The same tests are then applied to bond returns. Finally, correlational tests are performed on the stock and bond returns.

A. Stock Return Tests

The portfolio return comparisons focus on the returns to the control firms, which should not have been affected by the Acts, and the treatment portfolio of listed stocks, which is hypothesized to have been affected. These comparisons shed light on the average impact of each

---

[31] Hollander and Wolfe [1973] provide a detailed discussion of the Kolmogorov-Smirnov and Wilcoxon rank-sum tests. Lehmann [1975] observes that even if the normality assumption is correct, use of an appropriate nonparametric test would result in only a five percent loss of efficiency.

[32] For both the accounting- and non-accounting-based treatment subsamples, all pairwise correlations were below .2 in absolute value. For the 23 accounting-based firms in the bond sample, the exceptions were correlations of $-.355$ between LEVG and SIZE in 1933, and $-.416$ between these two variables in 1934. The corresponding figures for the 15 non-accounting-based firms in the bond sample were $-.484$ and $-.438$, respectively.

TABLE 3

MEANS, MEDIANS, AND STANDARD DEVIATIONS OF THE INDEPENDENT VARIABLES FOR THE CONTROL AND TREATMENT SAMPLES AND SUBSETS OF THE TREATMENT SAMPLE

		OTC Control Sample (N=26)		Total NYSE Treatment Sample (N=196)		NYSE Treatment Firms without Debt or Accounting-based Debt Covenants (N=130)		NYSE Treatment Firms with Accounting-based Debt Covenants (N=66)		NYSE Treatment Firms in the Bond Sample (N=38)		NYSE Treatment Firms in the Bond Sample with Accounting-based Debt Covenants (N=23)		NYSE Treatment Firms in the Bond Sample without Accounting-based Debt Covenants (N=15)	
		1933	1934	1933	1934	1933	1934	1933	1934	1933	1934	1933	1934	1933	1934
LEVG	Mean	.442	.406	.436*	.354*	.284*	.224*	.734*	.610	.703*	.608	.784*	.698	.578*	.471
	Median	.465	.340	.402	.251	.093	.057	.817	.639	.852	.667	.893	.782	.328	.375
	(Standard Deviation)	(.406)	(.399)	(.383)	(.346)	(.350)	(.305)	(.244)	(.272)	(.283)	(.298)	(.214)	(.224)	(.332)	(.344)
NUMCOV	Mean	.692*	.692*	.612*	.612*	0	0	1.818*	1.818*	1.368*	1.368*	2.261	2.261	0	0
	Median	.222	.222	.254	.254	0	0	1.471	1.471	1.063	1.063	2.375	2.375	(0)	(0)
	(Standard Deviation)	(1.192)	(1.192)	(1.034)	(1.034)	(0)	(0)	(.991)	(.991)	(1.404)	(1.404)	(1.096)	(1.090)	(0)	(0)
LOOSNS	Mean	.695*	.438*	.148*	.061*	NA	NA	.440*	.180*	.207*	.087*	.265*	.102*	NA	NA
	Median	.007	.006	.000	.000	NA	NA	.000	.001	.002	.003	.003	.005	NA	NA
	(Standard Deviation)	(2.069)	(1.466)	(.501)	(.222)	NA	NA	(.788)	(.355)	(.519)	(.256)	(.573)	(.272)	NA	NA
SIZE (Millions)	Mean	3.99	5.42*	50.53*	74.34*	53.89*	83.06*	43.91*	57.18*	98.59*	124.21*	61.58*	70.50*	152.02*	203.99*
	Median	3.31	3.53	14.27	21.82	11.80	21.33	14.53	21.83	35.09	37.15	30.01	30.43	39.26	42.57
	(Standard Deviation)	(3.72)	(5.69)	(118.49)	(184.92)	(129.17)	(209.53)	(94.56)	(122.50)	(179.40)	(239.70)	(62.91)	(75.95)	(266.60)	(356.85)

NOTE: NA = Not applicable.
* = Significant departure from normality at the 10% (2-tailed) level based on the Kolmogorov-Smirnov goodness-of-fit test.

Act. The cross-sectional regressions then explore the moderating effect of each firm characteristic.

The major findings are as follows:

a) The '33 Act significantly reduced listed stock returns; no effect due to the '34 Act was detected.

b) The '33 Act's impact on stock returns was negatively related to firm size and number of accounting indices in debt covenants, and positively related to leverage. Distance from accounting-based debt constraints, as measured, did not have a significant moderating effect.

1. Portfolio Return Comparisons. These tests involved three steps for each Act:

a) In each study period (i.e., favorable, unfavorable, and control), arithmetically weighted daily returns were calculated for the control portfolio (denoted portfolio C), the treatment portfolio (denoted portfolio T), and two mutually exclusive and collectively exhaustive subsets of the treatment portfolio: portfolio TND, consisting of the 130 treatment firms with no

debt or accounting-based debt covenants, and portfolio TD, made up of the 66 treatment firms with such covenants. These daily portfolio returns are denoted $S_{C,t}$, $S_{T,t}$, $S_{TND,t}$, and $S_{TD,t}$, respectively, where t stands for day t. Table 4 reports the means and standard deviations of these distributions for each study period. Kolmogorov-Smirnov goodness-of-fit tests indicated that nine of the 24 distributions (four portfolios × two Securities Acts × three study periods per Act) departed significantly from normality. These distributions are identified with asterisks in Table 4.

b) Daily return differences were calculated between selected portfolio pairs as follows:

$S_{T,t} - S_{C,t} =$ Excess return (either positive or negative) on day t to the treatment portfolio over the control portfolio.

$S_{TD,t} - S_{C,t} =$ Excess return on day t to the accounting-based treatment subsample

TABLE 4

AVERAGE DAILY STOCK RETURNS TO THE CONTROL AND TREATMENT SAMPLES AND SELECTED
SUBSETS OF THE TREATMENT SAMPLE
(Standard Deviations in Parentheses)

	OTC Control Sample (N=26)		Entire NYSE Treatment Sample (N=196)		NYSE Firms with Accounting-based Debt Covenants (N=66)		NYSE Firms without Accounting-based Debt Covenants (N=130)	
	1933	1934	1933	1934	1933	1934	1933	1934
Control period	.0124* (.020)	.0039* (.0044)	.0147 (.0170)	.0028* (.0094)	.0174 (.0188)	.0022* (.0127)	.0133 (.0159)	.0031* (.0073)
Favorable event period	.0151 (.0166)	−.0009 (.0030)	.0126 (.0111)	−.0017 (.0036)	.0126 (.0112)	−.0014 (.0042)	.0126* (.0110)	−.0019 (.0032)
Unfavorable event period	−.0010 (.0256)	.0016* (.0052)	.0168 (.0211)	.0012* (.0037)	.0152 (.0147)	.0012 (.0035)	.0177 (.0238)	.0011* (.0038)

NOTE: * Significant departure from normality at the 10% (2-tailed) level based on the Kolmogorov-Smirnov goodness-of-fit test.

TABLE 5

WILCOXON RANK—SUM COMPARISONS OF DAILY STOCK PORTFOLIO
RETURN DISTRIBUTIONS ACROSS STUDY PERIODS

1. The 1933 Securities Act

Panel A

Inter-Period Comparisons of Portfolio-pair Return Differences

Comparison Set Number	Return Series	Average Rank, Control Period	Average Rank, Favorable Period	Average Rank, Unfavorable Period	Z-Score	2-tailed Probability
A1	$S_T - S_C$	39.5	30.17		1.899	.058
		23.88		33.73	−1.947	.052
A2	$S_{TD} - S_C$	39.24	30.52		1.774	.076
		24.27		32.27	−1.581	.113
A3	$S_{TND} - S_C$	38.80	31.10		1.566	.117
		23.25		36.00	−2.520	.011

Panel B

Inter-period Comparisons of Average Daily Portfolio Returns

Comparison Set Number	Return Series	Average Rank, Control Period	Average Rank, Favorable Period	Average Rank, Unfavorable Period	Z-Score	2-tailed Probability
B1	S_C	32.30	39.77		−1.519	.128
		27.87		19.18	1.718	.085
B2	S_T	37.04	33.45		.730	.465
		24.45		28.00	− .504	.614
B3	S_{TD}	37.77	32.47		1.080	.280
		26.20		25.27	.183	.854
B4	S_{TND}	36.70	33.90		.569	.568
		24.92		29.91	− .985	.324

over the control portfolio.

$S_{TND,t} - S_{C,t} =$ Excess return on day t to the non-accounting-based treatment subsample over the control portfolio.

$S_{TD,t} - S_{TND,t} =$ Excess return on day t to the accounting-based over the non-accounting-based treatment subsample.

The means of these return differences can be calculated from Table 4, hence they are not reported separately.

TABLE 5—(*Continued*)

II. The 1934 Securities and Exchange Act

Panel C

Inter- Period Comparisons of Portfolio-pair Return Differences

Comparison Set Number	Return Series	Average Rank, Control Period	Average Rank, Favorable Period	Average Rank, Unfavorable Period	Z-Score	2-tailed Probability
C1	$S_T - S_C$	48.75	46.57		.382	.701
		41.76		37.13	.902	.367
C2	$S_{TD} - S_C$	47.37	47.59		− .038	.969
		40.97		37.95	.591	.554
C3	$S_{TND} - S_C$	48.52	46.74		.313	.753
		41.88		37.00	.952	.341
C4	$S_{TD} - S_{TND}$	43.20	50.69		− 1.317	.187
		38.32			− .471	.637

Panel D

Inter-period Comparisons of Average Daily Portfolio Returns

Comparison Set Number	Return Series	Average Rank, Control Period	Average Rank, Favorable Period	Average Rank, Unfavorable Period	Z-Score	2-tailed Probability
D1	S_C	67.67	32.56		6.184	.000
		46.95		31.66	2.990	.003
D2	S_T	53.50	43.06		1.837	.066
		44.52		34.21	2.014	.044
D3	S_{TD}	51.70	44.39		1.286	.198
		43.60		35.18	1.643	.100
D4	S_{TND}	53.10	43.35		1.715	.086
		44.40		34.34	1.964	.050

Kolmogorov-Smirnov tests indicated that $S_T - S_C$, $S_{TND} - S_C$, and $S_{TD} - S_{TND}$ all deviated significantly from normality in the 1933 and 1934 control periods. $S_{TND} - S_C$ also departed significantly from normality in the 1934 control period. In further tests, first-order time series regressions detected no significant serial correlation in any of the return or return difference series.[33]

c) If an Act affected stock returns significantly, the return differences between the control and treatment firms should have either increased or decreased in each event period relative to the control period (when events were presumably neutral with respect to the Act). Accordingly, the return difference distributions were compared between the control period and the favorable and unfavorable event periods, respectively. Similar inter-period comparisons were performed on each portfoilo return (as distinguished from return difference) distribution; since gross returns were used as the dependent variable, these additional comparisons can illuminate whether inter-period changes in portfolio-pair return differences were due to the Securities Acts or to factors such as market-wide conditions and different sample-firm characteristics.

The inter-period comparisons used the Wilcoxon rank-sum test to accommodate the numerous non-normal distributions. Panels A and B of Table 5 present the results for the '33 Act. Panels C and D of this table apply to the '34 Act.

The 1933 Securities Act. In Panel A of Table 5, comparison set A1 indicates that the daily return differences between the treatment and control portfolios (i.e., $S_T - S_C$, which could have been either positive or negative) had a smaller median value in the favorable event period than in the control period. This difference is significant at the .058 (two-tailed) level. It indicates that when events were favorable to the '33 Act, returns to the treatment firms declined relative to the control firms. This finding is corroborated by the control period-unfavorable period comparison. When events were unfavorable to the '33 Act, returns to the treatment portfolio increased relative to the control portfolio (i.e., $S_T - S_C$ was higher in the unfavorable

event period relative to the control period). This inter-period difference is significant at the .052 (two-tailed) level. Thus, both comparisons are consistent with Hypothesis 1, and indicate that the '33 Act had an adverse effect on the returns to listed stocks. Similar results are obtained when the control portfolio is compared to each subset of treatment firms: those with accounting-based debt covenants (i.e., portfolio TD) and those without such covenants (i.e., portfolio TND). Comparison sets A2 and A3 have a pattern similar to A1, though three of the four comparisons have somewhat reduced levels of significance.[34]

The results in Panel A are based on gross returns and could have been due to market-wide events rather than the '33 Act. Suppose other economic events (aside from the '33 Act) had increased market-wide returns in the favorable event period and reduced them in the unfavorable event period. Since the OTC firms were significantly smaller than the NYSE sample firms, they probably had a higher systematic risk, on average, than the latter.[35] Accordingly, returns to the control portfolio would have mirrored these market changes more substantially

[33] These first-order time-series regressions were based on all the usable days in each study period. For example, a five-day segment of an event period would yield four daily returns and four lagged daily returns. The number of days used in the regressions for 1933 were 31 for the control period, 26 for the favorable event period, and 10 for the unfavorable event period. The corresponding numbers for 1934 were 13, 44, and 33, respectively.

[34] $S_{TD} - S_{TND}$ was also compared across periods. Relative to the control period, this distribution was lower in the favorable and unfavorable periods at the .021 and .136 (two-tailed) significance levels, respectively. The 66-firm TD portfolio was also compared to a 66-firm TND portfolio matched to it on leverage. Again, returns were lower in both event periods, at the .161 and .177 levels, respectively. Since the differences do not reverse directions between the favorable and unfavorable periods, this evidence casts some doubt on the role of accounting-based debt covenants in this analysis.

[35] For example, Beaver, Kettler and Scholes [1970] found that firms with smaller asset sizes had higher systematic risk.

than returns to the treatment portfolio. This could have produced the results in Panel A.

The return comparisons in Panel B explore whether market-wide events were the likely cause of the Panel A results. First, comparison set B1 indicates that, relative to the control period, daily returns to the control portfolio were higher in the favorable event period and lower in the unfavorable event period. These inter-period differences are significant at the .128 and .085 (two-tailed) levels, respectively. This evidence moderately suggests that market returns increased in the favorable period and decreased in the unfavorable period. Comparison set B2 shows an opposite pattern to B1. Returns to the treatment portfolio were lower in the favorable event period and higher in the unfavorable event period. Taken by itself, the B2 pattern of inter-period differences is consistent with the '33 Act having adversely affected listed stock returns. However, since neither difference is statistically significant, comparisons B1 and B2 together do not rule out the possibility that market-wide factors caused the Panel A results.

If market-wide factors were the main cause of the observed stock return fluctuations, returns to the treatment stocks should at least have mirrored the pattern of market movements. More specifically, returns to NYSE firms of higher systematic risk should have followed the pattern in B1 more closely. As established in earlier discussion, portfolio TD had significantly higher leverage than portfolio TND. Given previous research into the relationship between leverage and systematic risk [Hamada, 1969; Bowman, 1980], TD firms should have had higher systematic risk than TND firms. Yet comparison B3, which uses only TD firms, still has a pattern opposite to that in B1, as does comparison B4 which uses

only the TND portfolio. Considering also that it was highly unlikely for market return increases and decreases to have coincided with the favorable and unfavorable periods (since the calendar dates for the control and event periods were intermingled), it was concluded that the Panel A results were due to the '33 Act rather than to other economy-wide factors.[36]

The 1934 Securities and Exchange Act. Panel C of Table 5 contains the interperiod comparisons of portfolio-pair return differences; Panel D provides these comparisons for portfolio returns. All of the comparisons in Panel C are far from statistically significant. Panel D shows that for every portfolio, returns were lower in both event periods than in the control period. All but one of these inter-period comparisons is statistically significant. Given the insignificant results in Panel C, the failure of the inter-period differences to reverse directions between the favorable and unfavorable periods is more indicative of market-wide changes than the influence of the '34 Act. Thus, it is concluded that *within the time-span selected for study*, the '34 Act did not significantly affect listed stock returns. This result is not surprising, since President Roosevelt had discussed his plans for such legislation the year before. Even if the '34 Act's accounting requirements

---

[36] The directional changes in OTC stock returns in the favorable and unfavorable periods may have reflected more than just market-wide events. The Acts could have benefited the OTC firms with a shift in competitive advantage to them, given that listed firms would have to disclose more financial data. The OTC firms could also have gained from a reduction in future bondholder-shareholder contracting costs due to the benchmark accounting practices set up by the Acts. These effects are incorporated into the control portfolio-treatment portfolio comparison. Another reason for portfolio returns to diverge is industry factors. Though a formal classification of firms by industry was not conducted, *Poor's* description of the sample firms' businesses suggests that each portfolio contains numerous industries. Thus, it is unlikely that the portfolio return differences were due to industry-specific factors.

did affect stock returns, these anticipated effects were likely to have been incorporated into stock returns the previous year and added to the observed effects of the '33 Act.[37]

2. Cross-sectional Regressions. Two cross-section regressions (one for each event period) were used to test whether changes in listed stock returns were proportional to leverage (Hypothesis 4) and number of different accounting indices in debt covenants (Hypothesis 6), and negatively related to distance from accounting-based debt constraints (Hypothesis 8) and firm size (Hypothesis 9):

$$\bar{S}_{i,F-C}=a_0+a_1 LEVG_i+a_2 NUMCOV_i +a_3 LOOSNS_i+a_4 SIZE_i, \quad (1)$$
$$\bar{S}_{i,UF-C}=b_0+b_1 LEVG_i+b_2 NUMCOV_i +b_3 LOOSNS_i+b_4 SIZE_i, \quad (2)$$

where

$\bar{S}_{i,F-C}=$ the average daily return to stock i in the 1933 favorable event period minus its average daily return in the 1933 control period,

$\bar{S}_{i,UF-C}=$ the average daily return to stock i in the 1933 unfavorable event period minus its average daily return in the 1933 control period, and

$LEVG_i$, $NUMCOV_i$, $LOOSNS_i$ and $SIZE_i$ are as previously defined.

Regressions (1) and (2) focused on the 66 treatment firms with accounting-based debt covenants because only these firms had data on all four independent variables. Supplementary analyses were performed by including both the control sample and the treatment firms with no accounting-based constraints, and the results were consistent with the ones reported here.[38] Only the 1933 results will be presented; as may be expected, none of the 1934 regressions was statistically significant.

The dependent variable in Equation (1) reflects the change in firm-specific stock returns due to the '33 Act.[39] The dependent variable in Equation (2) is the opposite of this measure; it is the change in firm-specific stock returns when events were unfavorable to the '33 Act's passage and/or accounting stringency. Thus, the two regressions provide independent tests of the cross-sectional hypotheses. Table 6 displays the results in four panels. Panels A and B are for Equation (1). The former is based on all 66 accounting-based treatment firms; the latter uses only the 44 treatment firms bound by explicit accounting-based dividend constraints. Panels C and D apply to Equation (2). They are also based on the 66-firm and 44-firm samples, respectively.

Each panel in Table 6 contains two regressions. The second regression of each pair omits the size variable. This is done to assess the reliability of the coefficients for the three agency-theory-based variables. In no case does the inclusion or exclusion of SIZE significantly affect the conclusions regarding these variables.

[37] In a separate set of tests (not reported here), the '34 Act's sales disclosure requirement was found to have affected previously non-sales-disclosing firms adversely, relative to sales-disclosing firms.

[38] These tests involved estimating versions of Equations (1) and (2), using the control stocks and the non-accounting-based treatment stocks separately, and a dummy-variable regression using all 196 treatment stocks. Details of these tests are available from the author on request.

[39] It may appear that, rather than deducting each treatment firm's average return in the control period from its average return in the critical event period, the average return to the control portfolio in the critical event period should be deducted. However, this results in subtracting the same constant from every treatment firm's average return in the critical event period. Consequently, it will not fulfill the objective of isolating the Securities Acts' differential impacts on each treatment firm for use in a cross-sectional regression. A viable alternative is to match the control and treatment firms, and deduct the return to the matched control firm from the treatment firm's return in the same period. The problem with this approach is that it will reduce the sample size by more than half.

TABLE 6

PARAMETER ESTIMATES FROM CROSS-SECTIONAL STOCK RETURN REGRESSIONS BASED ON THE TREATMENT
FIRMS WITH ACCOUNTING-BASED DEBT COVENANTS

Dependent Variable: Event period average daily return −
Conttol period average daily return

(T-statistics in parentheses)

I. 1933 Favorable Event Period

Panel A
All 66 Firms with Accounting-based Debt Covenants

	INTERCEPT	LEVG	NUMCOV	LOOSNS	SIZE ($\times 10^{10}$)	R^2	F (Significance)	Kolmogorov-Smirnov Z for the residuals (Significance)
Predicted Sign	?	?	?	+	+			
	−.0018	−.0211	.0064	−.0022	.4266	.101	2.838	.747
	(−.191)	(−1.904)*	(2.365)***	(−.663)	(1.491)#		(.032)	(.632)
	.0016	−.0229	.0062	−.0020		.084	2.984	.790
	(.167)	(−2.062)**	(2.273(**	(−.589)			(.038)	(.560)

Panel B
44 Firms with Dividend Constraints Being the Tightest Accounting-based Constraints

	INTERCEPT	LEVG	NUMCOV	LOOSNS	SIZE ($\times 10^{10}$)	R^2	F (Significance)	Kolmogorov-Smirnov Z for the residuals (Significance)
Predicted Sign	?	?	?	+	+			
	−.0022	−.0246	.0079	−.0013	.4118	.136	2.694	.531
	(−.217)	(−2.015)**	(2.398)**	(−.379)	(1.529)#		(.045)	(.940)
	.0012	−.0259	.0077	−.0012		.107	2.721	.700
	(.124)	(−2.093)**	(2.279)**	(−.332)			(.057)	(.710)

II. 1933 Unfavorable Event Period

Panel C
All 66 Firms with Accounting-based Debt Covenants

	INTERCEPT	LEVG	NUMCOV	LOOSNS	SIZE ($\times 10^{10}$)	R^2	F (Significance)	Kolmogorov-Smirnov Z for the residuals (Significance)
Predicted Sign	?	?	?	−	−			
	−.0167	.0320	−.0039	.0016	−.5958	.084	2.504	.363
	(−1.003)	(2.323)**	(−1.171)	(.388)	(−1.679)#		(.051)	(.999)
	−.0215	.0345	−.0036	.0013		.057	2.330	.481
	(−1.425)	(2.488)**	(−1.075)	(.306)			(.083)	(.975)

TABLE 6—(Continued)

Panel D
44 Firms with Dividend Constraints Being the Tightest Accounting-based Constraints

	INTERCEPT	LEVG	NUMCOV	LOOSNS	SIZE ($\times 10^{10}$)	R^2	F (Significance)	Kolmogorov-Smirnov Z for the residuals (Significance)
Predicted Sign	?	?	?	-	-			
	−.0199	.0376	−.0063	.0015	−.5508	.120	2.476	.447
	(−.886)	(2.395)**	(−1.488)	(.326)	(−1.591)#		(.060)	(.988)
	−.0189	.0394	−.0059	.0013		.087	2.367	.656
	(−1.248)	(2.466)**	(−1.377)	(.277)			(.085)	(.782)

** Significant at .05, two-tail test.
* Significant at .10, two-tail test.
# Significant at .10, one-tail test.

Hence, only the result of the first (full) regression in each pair will be discussed. Table 6 also shows that all the regression equations are statistically significant at (at least) the .10 level. In addition, Z statistics from Kolmogorov-Smirnov goodness-of-fit tests are reported. These do not indicate significant departures from normality in the residuals. Hence, the F and t tests should be reasonably reliable.

In Panel A of Table 6, the predicted signs of a_1 (for LEVG) and a_2 (for NUMCOV) are indeterminate because Hypotheses 4 and 6 are non-directional. Coefficients a_3 (for LOOSNS) and a_4 (for SIZE), on the other hand, are predicted to be positive: the Acts' impacts were hypothesized to vary inversely with LOOSNS and SIZE. Since the '33 Act reduced returns to listed stocks, firms with higher values for LOOSNS and SIZE should have experienced smaller declines in, and hence higher levels of, return.

LEVG has a statistically significant coefficient; hence, Hypothesis 4 is supported. The negative sign of this coefficient indicates that more highly levered firms experienced greater stock return decreases due to the '33 Act.[40] Consistent with Hypothesis 6, NUMCOV has a sta-

tistically significant coefficient. The positive sign of this coefficient implies that firms with more accounting indices in their debt covenants underwent smaller reductions in shareholder wealth.[41] SIZE has a positive and significant coefficient as implied by Hypothesis 9. This means that larger firms experienced smaller proportional declines in shareholder wealth.[42]

[40] Leftwich's [1981] study of mandatory changes in accounting for business combinations obtained a similar result. He found that the costs of the new requirements were higher for firms with larger amounts of debt outstanding. Apparently, the importance of leverage depends on the accounting regulation being studied. Collins, Rozeff and Dhaliwal [1981] found this variable to have little explanatory power for changes in share returns related to oil and gas accounting regulation.

[41] Collins, Rozeff and Dhaliwal [1981] included a dummy variable for the existence of debt covenants or a management compensation plan defined in terms of reported accounting numbers. They found this variable to be significantly and negatively related to stock returns associated with a proposed change in oil and gas accounting regulation. One reason for their result being opposite to that of the present study is that in their case, both accounting alternatives being considered by the policymakers were widely used, and the accounting numbers could be easily translated between the two. In the present study, both the extent of disclosure and the available accounting alternatives were affected, so that the compliance costs and competitive advantage considerations take on special significance.

[42] Leftwich [1981] obtained a similar result. Collins, Rozeff and Dhaliwal [1981] report that firm size has a marginally significant negative impact in their study.

Contrary to Hypothesis 8, the LOOSNS coefficient is neither positive nor statistically significant. This result is not due to multicollinearity among the independent variables. Equation (1) was re-estimated using each independent variable separately as well as all possible combinations of them; the sign and statistical significance of each coefficient remained substantially unchanged. The effect of measurement errors was probed by estimating Equation (1) with subsets of treatment firms being bound by relatively homogeneous dividend constraints. Panel B shows that for the 44 firms bound by explicit accounting-based dividend constraints, the conclusions are unchanged from the 66-firm regression. Regressions using the 22 firms bound by implicit dividend constraints are statistically insignificant. Thus, distance from accounting-based debt constraints, *as measured in this study*, did not significantly affect changes in stock returns. However, only dividend constraints were used in calculating LOOSNS. More comprehensive definitions of this variable may yield different results, and should be incorporated into future research.

Since the dependent variable in Panels C and D is the opposite of that in Panels A and B, the signs of the coefficients should be reversed between these panel-pairs. This is observed in every case. LEVG and SIZE have statistically significant coefficients, but the coefficient for NUMCOV is only significant at about the .30 (two-tailed) level in the 66-firm regression, and at about the .15 (two-tailed) level in the 44-firm regression. LOOSNS again fails to have a significant coefficient.

Overall, the results in Table 6 strongly support the importance of firm size and leverage, moderately support the hypothesized role of number of accounting indices in debt covenants, and fail to uphold the role of distance from ac-

counting-based dividend constraints. The relatively weak results for accounting-based debt covenants may have been due, at least in part, to the measurement problems discussed earlier. Conversely, the significant effects of firm size and leverage may have been induced by market-wide events (through the links among these firm characteristics and systematic risk). This possibility was investigated with additional regressions which included all the control- and treatment-sample stocks (see footnote 38). The results indicate that the leverage and firm size effects are probably due to the '33 Act rather than to other economy-wide phenomena.

As a whole, the stock return evidence has the following interpretations:

a) At least part of the '33 Act's effects was transmitted through accounting-based debt covenants.

b) Even if the '33 Act reduced shareholder-bondholder contracting costs, this benefit was small relative to the costs of the new accounting provisions.

c) The significant coefficient for NUMCOV could have come about due to the compliance costs of the new accounting requirements: firms with extensive previous disclosure could have complied with these more cheaply than firms with sketchy previous disclosure. The former could also have reaped an unexpected gain in competitive advantage over the latter.

d) The moderating effect of leverage could have resulted from the new accounting requirements restricting investment, financing, and production alternatives permissible under outstanding debt covenants (thus reducing firm value), or from a wealth transfer from shareholders to bondholders. Both of these interpretations assume that more highly levered firms have higher debt covenant renegotiation costs which make them less able to cushion the impacts of new accounting requirements.

e) The size effect suggests that the costs of the new accounting requirements had a substantial fixed component, and/ or a decreasing marginal relationship to size.

Note that it is possible to ascribe all of the cross-sectional stock return findings to the '33 Act's compliance costs and/or curtailment of firms' opportunity sets. The following two subsections focus more specifically on whether a shareholder-to-bondholder wealth transfer was likely to have occurred.

B. Bond Return Tests

As in the case of stock returns, portfolio returns were first compared across study periods. Regressions then probed the effect of each firm characteristic. The sample was the 38 firms whose bonds satisfied the various inclusion criteria.

The major findings are as follows:

a) The evidence weakly suggests that the '33 Act increased bondholder wealth; the '34 Act had no significant bond return impact.

b) The '33 Act's effect was probably

due to a change in compliance costs or other causes, but not to a shareholder-to-bondholder wealth transfer.

1. *Portfolio Return Comparisons.* These tests involved three steps for each Act:

a) In each study period (favorable, unfavorable, control), the following arithmetically weighted portfolio daily returns were calculated:

$B_{TD,t}$ = Average return on day t to the 23 bonds with accounting-based debt covenants.

$B_{TND,t}$ = Average return on day t to the 15 bonds with no accounting-based debt covenants.

Table 7 reports the means and standard deviations of these 12 distributions (two portfolios × two Securities Acts × three study periods per Act). Kolmogorov-Smirnov goodness-of-fit tests indicated that B_{TD} and B_{TND} departed significantly from normality in both the 1933 and 1934 control periods. Neither B_{TD} nor B_{TND} was significantly autocorrelated in 1933, but both were significantly autocorrelated in all three 1934 study periods.

TABLE 7

AVERAGE DAILY RETURNS TO THE ACCOUNTING-BASED AND
NON-ACCOUNTING-BASED BOND TREATMENT SUBSAMPLES
(Standard Deviations in Parentheses)

	Accounting-based Treatment Subsample (N=23)		Non-accounting-based Treatment Subsample (N=15)	
	1933	1934	1933	1934
Control period	.0064* (.0047)	.0010* (.0029)	.0041* (.0039)	−.0001* (.0029)
Favorable event period	.0042 (.0058)	.0002 (.0015)	.0031 (.0043)	−.0004 (.0019)
Unfavorable event period	.0014 (.0060)	.0012 (.0017)	−.0003 (.0047)	.0014 (.0017)

* Significant departure from normality at the 10-percent level indicated by the Kolmogorov-Smirnov goodness-of-fit test.

b) Daily return differences were computed between the 23-firm accounting-based portfolio and the 15-firm non-accounting-based portfolio.

$$B_{TD,t} - B_{TND,t} = \text{Excess return on day } t \text{ to the accounting-based over the non-accounting-based bond portfolio.}$$

Kolmogorov-Smirnov tests indicated that this return difference distribution departed significantly from normality in the 1933 and 1934 control periods. Its autocorrelation was significant at the .15 level in the 1934 control period.

c) The portfolio return and return difference distributions were compared across periods with the Wilcoxon rank-sum test. Table 8 reports the 1933 and 1934 results in Panels A and B, respectively.

TABLE 8

WILCOXON RANK—SUM COMPARISONS OF DAILY BOND PORTFOLIO
RETURNS AND RETURN DIFFERENCES ACROSS EVENT PERIODS

Panel A
1933 Securities Act

Return Series	Control Period Average Rank	Favorable Event Period Average Rank	Unfavorable Event Period Average Rank	Z-Score	2-Tailed Probability	1-Tailed Probability
B_{TD}	36.47	34.20		.4639	.643	##
	27.60		20.18	1.466	.142	.071
B_{TND}	36.85	33.70		.641	.522	##
	27.69		19.86	1.547	.122	.061
$B_{TD} - B_{TND}$	35.10	36.03		−.189	.849	.425
	25.91		26.32	−.0802	.936	##

Panel B
1934 Securities and Exchange Act

Return Series	Control Period Average Rank	Favorable Event Period Average Rank	Unfavorable Event Period Average Rank	Z-Score	2-Tailed Probability	1-Tailed Probability
B_{TD}	51.72	44.37		1.294	.196	##
	40.44		38.51	.375	.707	.354
B_{TND}	52.72	43.63		1.599	.109	##
	39.86		39.12	.145	.885	.443
$B_{TD} - B_{TND}$	48.40	46.83		.276	.783	##
	43.81		34.96	1.728	.084	.042

Not significant for a one-tailed test. The direction of this difference is contrary to prediction.

In Panel A, comparison set A1 shows that B_{TD} did not differ significantly between the 1933 control and favorable periods. However, there was a significant decrease from the control period when events were unfavorable to the '33 Act's enactment and/or accounting stringency. Since the favorable and unfavorable period comparisons are substantially independent, the latter result may be taken to imply that the '33 Act was beneficial to bondholders. However, any such interpretation has to be tempered by the results of comparisons A2 and A3. The former indicates that B_{TND} had the same pattern of inter-period differences as B_{TD}. Comparison set A3 shows that the return difference distributions were not significantly different across the three study periods. Thus, assuming that the return reduction in the unfavorable period was not due to market-wide phenomena,[43] the '33 Act appears to have affected listed bonds the same way regardless of whether they had accounting-based debt covenants. A possible reason for this finding is differences in firm characteristics between the accounting-based and non-accounting-based firms in the bond sample. This is explored in the cross-sectional tests.

The comparisons in 1934 (Panel B) show that neither B_{TD} nor B_{TND} differed significantly across the three study periods. This evidence is inconsistent with Hypothesis 2, and is not unexpected given the stock return results for 1934. The portfolio return difference did register a significant decline between the control and unfavorable periods. However, the significance level of this difference is probably inflated due to the significant autocorrelations in the portfolio return and return difference series. A manifestation of this problem is that all of the 1934 cross-sectional regressions were statistically insignificant.

2. Cross-sectional Regressions. Following the analysis of stock returns, two cross-sectional regressions (one for each event period) were used to test whether changes in bond returns were positively related to leverage (Hypothesis 3) and number of different accounting indices in debt covenants (Hypothesis 5), and negatively related to distance from accounting-based debt constraints (Hypothesis 7). Even though firm size was not hypothesized to have a significant effect, it was included in some of the regressions for exploratory purposes.

$$\bar{B}_{i,F-C} = e_0 + e_1 LEVG_i + e_2 NUMCOV_i + e_3 LOOSNS_i + e_4 SIZE_i, \quad (3)$$

$$\bar{B}_{i,UF-C} = f_0 + f_1 LEVG_i + f_2 NUMCOV_i + f_3 LOOSNS_i + f_4 SIZE_i, \quad (4)$$

where

$\bar{B}_{i,F-C}$ = the average daily return to bond i in the 1933 favorable event period minus its average daily return in the 1933 control period,

$\bar{B}_{i,UF-C}$ = the average daily return to bond i in the 1933 unfavorable event period minus its average daily return in the 1933 control period, and

$LEVG_i$, $NUMCOV_i$, $LOOSNS_i$, and $SIZE_i$ are as defined previously.

Both Regressions (3) and (4) focused on the 23 firms with accounting-based debt covenants because only they have data on all four independent variables. Supplementary analysis which included the 15 non-accounting-based bond sam-

---

[43] The evidence from the previous subsection suggests that this is a reasonable assumption. To shed more light on this issue, daily returns to long-term government bonds were collected for ten randomly-selected days in each study period. No significant difference was found across the three periods. This suggests that market factors did not cause the observed differences.

TABLE 9

PARAMETER ESTIMATES FROM CROSS-SECTIONAL BOND RETURN REGRESSIONS BASED ON THE
23 BONDS WITH ACCOUNTING-BASED DEBT COVENANTS FOR 1933 EVENT PERIODS

Dependent Variable = Event period average daily return –
Control period average daily return

(T-statistics in Parentheses)

Panel A
1933 Favorable Event Period

	INTERCEPT	LEVG	NUMCOV	LOOSNS	SIZE ($\times 10^{10}$)	R^2	F (Significance)	Kolmogorov-Smirnov Z for the residuals (Significance)
Predicted Sign	?	+	+	−	?			
	.0027	−.0019	−.0013	−.0015	.0140	0	.355 (.837)	.454
	(.388)	(−.266)	(−1.022)	(−.611)	(.057)			(.805)
	.0029	−.0020	−.0013	−.0015		.073	.499	.726
	(.489)	(−.314)	(−1.049)	(−.630)			(.687)	(.547)

Panel B
1933 Unfavorable Event Period

	INTERCEPT	LEVG	NUMCOV	LOOSNS	SIZE ($\times 10^{10}$)	R^2	F (Significance)	Kolmogorov-Smirnov Z for the residuals (Significance)
Predicted Sign	?	−	−	+	?			
	−.0045	−.0054	−.0003	.0041	.5644	.212	2.485	.716
	(−.629)	(−.748)	(−.254)	(1.604)#	(2.300)**		(.080)	(.685)
	.0035	−.0112	−.0003	.0039		.034	1.263	.623
	(.508)	(−1.494)	(−.209)	(1.375)			(.315)	(.832)
	−.0052	−.0054		.0042	.5638	.251	3.462	.765
	(−.831)	(−.771)		(1.698)#	(2.357)**		(.037)	(.601)
	−.0037	−.0041	−.0006		.5502	.147	2.267	.808
	(−.498)	(−.546)	(−.464)		(2.156)**		(.110)	(.532)
	−.0051	−.0041			.5485	.180	3.427	.723
	(−.774)	(−.556)			(2.193)**		(.052)	(.692)
	−.0091		−.0003	.0039	.6285	.230	3.201	.807
	(−2.444)		(−.267)	(1.547)#	(2.765)**		(.047)	(.533)
	−.0099			.0039	.6282	.266	4.998	.820
	(−4.786)			(1.638)#	(2.831)**		(.017)	(.512)
	−.0072		−.0006		.5998	.177	3.370	.756
	(−1.988)		(−.471)		(2.560)**		(.055)	(.617)
	−.0086				.5979	.207	6.769	.726
	(−4.328)				(2.601)**		(.017)	(.701)

** Significant at .05, two-tail test.
# Significant at .10, one-tail test.

ple firms did not significantly change the conclusions of these regressions.[44] Only the 1933 results will be discussed; the 1934 regressions were all statistically insignificant.

Similar to Regressions (1) and (2), Regressions (3) and (4) provide substantially independent tests of the hypotheses. The results of these regressions are presented in Table 9 as Panels A and B, respectively.

In Panel A, both regressions (with and without SIZE) are statistically insignificant, as are all the individual regression coefficients. Thus, Hypotheses 3, 5, and 7 are not supported. Together with the insignificant inter-period comparisons for the 1933 favorable event period, this evidence casts doubt on the notion that the '33 Act affected bond returns through accounting-based debt covenants.

Panel B contains nine regressions. Seven of these are statistically significant at at least the .10 level, and none has residuals that deviate significantly from normality. The first regression is based on the full model. It shows that the coefficients for LEVG, NUMCOV and LOOSNS all have the predicted signs. Among these, however, only the LOOSNS coefficient is statistically significant. On the other hand, SIZE, which was not predicted to have a significant effect, has a positive and statistically significant coefficient. In fact, SIZE is the most important independent variable; when it is excluded from the second regression, the entire regression becomes statistically insignificant.

The effects of multicollinearity were explored by using all possible subsets of the independent variables in separate regressions. Only the statistically significant ones are included in Panel B. SIZE appears in every regression, the coefficients for LEVG and NUMCOV remain insignificant, and LOOSNS has a margi-

nally significant positive coefficient in each case. The LOOSNS coefficient is unlikely to be affected by the pairwise correlation ($-.083$) between LOOSNS and SIZE in 1933. However, given that the regressions are statistically significant only when SIZE is included, the impact of LOOSNS is, at best, a minor one. In view of the insignificant results in Panel A and the insignificant LOOSNS coefficients in the stock return regressions, the '33 Act probably did not affect bondholder wealth significantly through affecting accounting-based debt covenants (i.e., a shareholder-to-bondholder wealth transfer).

The significant and positive coefficient for SIZE in the unfavorable period (when returns to the sample bonds decreased) indicates that the '33 Act affected larger firms proportionally less. This finding is consistent with the stock return regressions, and may be a reflection of the Act's compliance costs independent of bondholder-shareholder contracting issues. These costs could have reduced firm value (both shareholder and bondholder wealth) by reducing firms' expected cash flows. The size effect could have arisen if these compliance costs had a large fixed component, and/or increments which decreased with firm size.

C. Correlational Tests

The correlational tests seek to shed additional light on whether the '33 Act's accounting requirements caused a shareholder-to-bondholder wealth transfer. If such a transfer took place, changes in stock and bond returns would have been negatively correlated in each event period.

[44] These tests were similar to the supplementary regressions on stock returns. Versions of Equations (3) and (4) were estimated using the 15 non-accounting-based bonds, and a dummy-variable regression using all 38 bonds in the treatment sample. The results are available on request.

The 38 firms in the bond sample were used in these tests. For each firm, changes in average daily returns for stocks and bonds were calculated between the control and favorable, and control and unfavorable periods. For each event period, Pearson and Spearman correlations were computed between the stock and bond return changes. The results were not substantially different between the two correlations. The nonparametric Spearman correlations are presented in Table 10, since these are more appropriate for non-normal distributions.

TABLE 10

SPEARMAN RANK CORRELATIONS BETWEEN CHANGES IN
AVERAGE DAILY STOCK AND BOND RETURNS WITHIN
EACH CRITICAL EVENT PERIOD IN 1933
(Two-tailed Significance Levels in Parentheses)

Panel A All 38 Firms in the Bond Sample		
	Favorable Event Period	Unfavorable Event Period
Favorable Event Period	.058 (.364)	
Unfavorable Event Period		.182 (.138)

Panel B 23 Firms in the Bond Sample with Accounting-based Debt Covenants		
	Favorable Event Period	Unfavorable Event Period
Favorable Event Period	.143 (.258)	
Unfavorable Event Period		.299 (.083)

Panel C 15 Firms in the Bond Sample Without Accounting-based Debt Covenants		
	Favorable Event Period	Unfavorable Event Period
Favorable Event Period	.064 (.410)	
Unfavorable Event Period		−.064 (.410)

Panel A of Table 10 shows the results based on all 38 treatment firms. In the favorable event period, the changes in average daily stock and bond returns (from the control period) have a positive correlation of .058, which is significant at the .364 level. The correlation in the unfavorable event period is likewise positive, with a value of .182 which is significant at the .138 level. Thus, neither correlation is indicative of a shareholder-to-bondholder wealth transfer. If anything, they suggest that shareholder and bondholder wealth were affected in the same direction. However, note that the impacts of other factors (e.g., compliance costs and reductions in opportunity sets) have not been eliminated from the changes in stock and bond returns; consequently, correlations between these changes afford only a crude assessment of the hypothesized shareholder-to-bondholder wealth transfer.

Panels B and C provide some additional insights into the wealth transfer issue. Since bondholders' gains were hypothesized to be due to accounting-based debt covenants, the correlations should be more negative for firms with such covenants than for those without them. This is not observed. Panel B shows that the accounting-based firms not only have positive correlations in both event periods, but the coefficient in the unfavorable period is statistically significant. The non-accounting-based firms have statistically insignificant correlations in both periods, and the coefficient in the unfavorable period is negative. This evidence is inconsistent with the '33 Act having caused a shareholder-to-bondholder wealth transfer through affecting accounting-based debt covenants.

A major limitation of the above tests is that they have not controlled for market-wide influences. Since both stock and bond returns respond to changes in market returns, this co-movement can swamp effects due to wealth transfers. Refinements to control for such market-induced co-movements were not introduced in view of the previous subsections' strong implication that either a shareholder-to-bondholder wealth transfer did not occur, or its magnitude was too small to be statistically detectable.

VI. SUMMARY AND IMPLICATIONS

The findings of this study are consistent with the 1933 Securities Act's accounting provisions having reduced returns to exchange-listed stocks. There is very limited evidence that returns to listed bonds were increased due to this Act. Within the time-span selected for study, the 1934 Securities and Exchange Act was not associated with a significant change in average returns to listed stocks and bonds.

Results from multiple regressions suggest that at least part of the '33 Act's impact on stock returns arose through affecting accounting-based debt covenants. This evidence is consistent with the '33 Act having significant out-of-pocket compliance costs, having affected the competitive relationships across firms, or having reduced firms' available investment. financing, and production opportunities by tightening existing accounting-based debt covenants. The findings on bonds, in conjunction with correlational tests based on changes in stock and bond returns, suggest that a shareholder-to-bondholder wealth transfer did not result from the Act. This implies that the changes in bond returns were due to factors outside of this study.

In addition to examining the Securities Acts, this study provides an assessment of agency contracting explanations for the security price effects of accounting

regulation. As such, it complements the work of Leftwich [1981] and Collins, Rozeff and Dhaliwal [1981], both because it tests the agency theory variables in a different setting and because it extends the empirical investigation to bond returns.

Even though this study has incorporated numerous methodological improvements over previous related work, much room remains for additional refinements. These apply to future studies of the Securities Acts as well as other accounting regulations. One area for improvement is variable measurement. Some of the variables in this study are measured rather crudely (e.g., distance from debt constraints, and number of accounting indices in debt covenants). Reducing the measurement errors in these variables can significantly enhance the power of empirical tests. Another desirable betterment is more extensive controls for omitted variables, such as market-wide events and systematic risk. Controlling for such factors had to be done indirectly in this study due to the extensive coverage of the Securities Acts, but should be easier when the regulation being studied only applies to a small subset of firms. Finally, the relatively modest adjusted R^2 statistics found in studies by Leftwich [1981], Collins, Rozeff and Dhaliwal [1981], and in this study, suggest that alternate explanations for the effects of accounting regulations should be explored. Collins, Rozeff and Dhaliwal [1981] suggest estimation risk theory as an alternative to agency contracting theory. The present study also introduces the informational role of accounting regulation through its impact on the competitive relationships across firms. Neither study, however, develops tests that differentiate between the contracting and informational roles of required accounting disclosure. Efforts to test these and other competing theories can do much to advance this line of research.

EXHIBIT 1

CALENDAR DATES OF THE FAVORABLE, UNFAVORABLE, AND CONTROL EVENT PERIODS FOR THE 1933 SECURITIES ACT

March		April		May		June	
17	C	1	• F	1		1	C
18	C	2	F	2		2	C
19	C	3	+ F	3	+	3	C
20	C	4	UF	4	F	4	C
21	C	5	UF	5	+ F	5	C
22	F	6	• UF	6	• F	6	C
23	F	7	+ UF	7	F	7	C
24	• F	8	+ UF	8	F	8	C
25	• F	9	UF	9	C	9	C
26	F	10	• UF	10	C	10	C
27	F	11	UF	11	C	11	C
28	F	12	• UF	12	C	12	C
29	F	13	UF	13	C	13	C
30	• F	14	UF	14	C	14	C
31	+ F	15		15	C	15	C
		16	F	16	C		
		17	F	17	C		
		18	• F	18	C		
		19	+ F	19	C		
		20	F	20	C		
		21	C	21	F		
		22	C	22	F		
		23	C	23	• F		
		24	C	24	F		
		25	C	25	• F		
		26	C	26	F		
		27		27	F		
		28	+	28			
		29		29	+		
		30		30	C		
				31	C		

Note: • = A selected critical event date.
C = Belongs to 40-day control period.
F = Belongs to favorable event period (N = 30 days).
UF = Belongs to unfavorable event period (N = 11 days).
+ = A *WSJ* report relating to the Act appeared on this date.

EXHIBIT 2

CALENDAR DATES OF THE FAVORABLE, UNFAVORABLE, AND CONTROL EVENT PERIODS FOR THE 1934 SECURITIES AND EXCHANGE ACT

January					February					March				
1					1	+		F		1	+			UF
2					2		C			2	•			UF
3					3		C			3	+			UF
4					4		C			4				UF
5					5		C			5				UF
6					6		C			6	+			UF
7					7	+				7	•			UF
8					8	+		F		8	+			UF
9					9			F		9	•			UF
10		C			10	•		F		10	+			UF
11		C			11			F		11				UF
12		C			12	+		F		12	+			
13		C			13				UF	13	+		F	
14		C			14	+			UF	14			F	
15		C			15	•			UF	15	•		F	
16		C			16	+			UF	16	•		F	
17		C			17	+			UF	17			F	
18		C			18					18			F	
19		C			19	+				19			F	
20		C			20	+				20	+		F	
21		C			21	+				21	•		F	
22		C			22	+				22	+		F	
23		C			23					23	+		F	
24		C			24	+				24	+			
25		C			25					25			F	
26		C			26	+				26	+		F	
27			F		27	+				27	•		F	
28			F		28	+			UF	28	+		F	
29	•		F							29			F	
30	•		F							30	+			
31	+		F							31				

April					May					June				
1					1	•			UF	1	+		F	
2	+				2				UF	2	•		F	
3	+			UF	3	+		F		3			F	
4	+			UF	4	•		F		4			F	
5	•			UF	5	•		F		5		C		
6	+			UF	6			F		6		C		
7	+			UF	7	+		F		7	+			
8					8	+				8		C		
9				UF	9	+				9		C		
10	+			UF	10	+		F		10		C		
11	•			UF	11	+		F		11		C		
12	+			UF	12	•		F		12		C		
13	•			UF	13			F		13		C		
14	+			UF	14	•		F		14		C		
15				UF	15	+		F		15		C		
16	+				16	+		F		16		C		
17	+				17	+				17		C		
18	+				18	+				18		C		
19	+				19	+				19		C		
20	+				20					20		C		
21	+				21	+		F		21		C		
22					22			F		22		C		
23	+				23	•		F		23		C		
24	+			UF	24	+		F						
25	+			UF	25	+		F						
26	•			UF	26	+		F						
27	+			UF	27			F						
28	+			UF	28	•		F						
29				UF	29			F						
30	+			UF	30			F						
					31			F						

Note: • = A selected critical event date.
C = Belongs to 40-day control period.
F = Belongs to favorable event period (N = 54 days).
UF = Belongs to unfavorable event period (N = 38 days).
+ = A *WSJ* report relating to the Act appeared on this date.

APPENDIX A

SUBJECTIVELY SELECTED CRITICAL EVENTS RELATING TO THE 1933 SECURITIES ACT

Panel A

FAVORABLE EVENTS

Event Number	Event Date	Headline or Summary of Wall Street Journal *Report*
1	March 24	President Roosevelt is considering a program of regulations which include requiring fullest disclosure of facts in the prospectus for any security and independently audited statements for securities already issued.
2	March 25	"Provisions for full publicity touching upon transactions of officers and directors in the stocks of their own company is . . . likely to be covered in the legislation . . . in addition to requirements for uniform, complete and frequent statements of the affairs of the company itself."
3	March 30	"Both Houses Get Securities Bill." The President indicated that this was but the first step of a legislative program. The proposed legislation provided for the registration of new securities with the Federal Trade Commission and extensive financial disclosure in the registration statements.
4	April 1	Leading senators interpret the securities bill to apply to old as well as new security issues.
5	April 18	The senate version of the bill requires registrants to provide more financial data than the original version demanded.
6	May 6	The House had passed the bill without dissent on May 5. The bill now goes to the Senate, which has its own version of the bill.
7	May 23	The House has repassed a compromise bill with the Senate.
8	May 25	The final draft of the bill has passed the Senate.

Panel B

UNFAVORABLE EVENTS

Event Number	Event Date	Headline or Summary of Wall Street Journal *Report*
1	April 6	Original framers of the bill limited the role of the Federal Trade Commission. The administration sought revocation of the retroactive clause. The liability of registration statement signers was reduced.
2	April 10	The Senate Banking and Currency Committee's new print of the bill exempts old securities and limits the liability of registration statement signers to the price paid for securities.
3	April 12	Senate committee curbs the Federal Trade Commissioner's power to revoke securities.

APPENDIX B

SUBJECTIVELY SELECTED CRITICAL EVENTS RELATING TO THE 1934 SECURITIES AND EXCHANGE ACT

Panel A

FAVORABLE EVENTS

Event Number	Event Date	Headline or Summary of Wall Street Journal *Report*
1	January 29	A report was submitted to President Roosevelt by the Committee on Stock Exchange Regulations. Legislation to regulate stock exchanges is expected in the Senate soon.
2	January 30	The report of the Committee on Stock Exchange Regulations recommends licensing stock exchanges, regulating the activities of securities traders, and extensive financial disclosure by listed securities on a regular basis.
3	February 10	A bill to regulate stock exchanges was introduced in the Senate the day before. An identical bill will be introduced in the House today. The bill provided for stock exchange licensing, restrictions on trading activities, extensive and frequent financial disclosure by listed firms, and potential liability of firm officers, directors, and accountants for investor losses due to misleading or false information.

APPENDIX B—(*Continued*)

4	March 15	Sponsors of the bill will yield on some points, but frequent company reports will remain.
5	March 16	President Roosevelt desires passage of the bill. Changes will be made to ensure the bill's passage.
6	March 21	The revised bill includes extensive financial disclosure by listed firms, certified by independent public accountants or as the Federal Trade Commission may prescribe.
7	March 27	President Roosevelt has endorsed the revised bill.
8	May 4	"Moves to Alter Stock Bill Lose. Passage Today Likely."
9	May 5	"House Passes Exchange Bill. Compromise with Senate Likely."
10	May 12	"Senate Debates Exchange Bill. Many Liberalizing Measures Shouted Down as Chamber Speeds Measure."
11	May 14	The Senate passed the bill on May 12. The bill now enters the conference stage with the House.
12	May 23	The conferees have settled their differences regarding reporting and registration requirements. "Any further financial statements which the commission may deem necessary" must also be filed.
13	May 28	The conferees have reached full agreement on May 26. A new, five-member Federal Securities Commission was provided for.
14	June 2	Both Houses passed the bill the previous day.

Panel B

UNFAVORABLE EVENTS

Event Number	Event Date	Headline or Summary of Wall Street Journal Report
1	February 15	The bill will be substantially modified before it can be passed. Chairman Rayburn of the House Interstate Commerce Committee emphasized the tentative nature of the bill.
2	March 2	The Senate Banking and Currency Committee counsel indicated the required financial reports may be made less frequent.
3	March 7	Opposition within the Administration to the bill was revealed. Doubt is expressed in the Senate about enactment of the bill at the current session of Congress.
4	March 9	Sharp revisions of the whole bill before it can pass either house of Congress are regarded as a certainty.
5	April 5	"Protests on Corporation Report Requirements Get Support in the House."
6	April 11	Revisions are expected to require only annual audited reports.
7	April 13	The House version removed the Federal Trade Commission's authority to dictate accounting standards. The Senate version is expected to approach the House version.
8	April 26	"House Battle on Stock Bill Sure."
9	May 1	House opponents of the bill will seek to liberalize the measure and to curb the Federal Trade Commission's power over corporations.

REFERENCES

Banz, R. W. (1981), "The Relationship Between Return and Market Value of Common Stocks," *Journal of Financial Economics* (March 1981), pp. 3–18.

Beaver, W. H. (1981), *Financial Reporting: An Accounting Revolution* (Prentice-Hall, 1981).

———, P. Kettler and M. Scholes (1970), "The Association Between Market Determined and Accounting Determined Risk Measures," THE ACCOUNTING REVIEW (October 1970), pp. 654–682.

Benston, G. J. (1969a), "The Value of the SEC's Accounting Disclosure Requirements." THE ACCOUNTING REVIEW (July 1969), pp. 515–532.

——— (1969b), "The Effectiveness and Effects of the SEC's Accounting Disclosure Requirements," in Henry G. Manne (Ed.), *Economic Policy and the Regulation of Corporate Securities* (Washington:

American Enterprise Institute for Public Policy Research, 1969), pp. 23–79.

—— (1973), "Required Financial Disclosure and the Stock Market: An Evaluation of the Securities and Exchange Act of 1934," *The American Economic Review* (March 1973), pp. 132–155.

Bowman, R. G. (1980), "The Importance of a Market-Value Measurement of Debt in Assessing Leverage," *Journal of Accounting Research* (Spring 1980), pp. 242–254.

Carey, J. (1969), *The Rise of the Accounting Profession 1896–1936* (AICPA, New York, 1969).

Carosso, V. (1970), *Investment Banking in America—A History* (Cambridge, MA., 1970).

Chatfield, M. (1977), *A History of Accounting Thought* (Robert E. Krieger Publishing Co., 1977).

Chow, C. W. (1982), "The Demand for External Auditing—Size, Debt and Ownership Influences," THE ACCOUNTING REVIEW (April 1982), pp. 272–291.

Collins, D. W. and W. T. Dent (1979), "The Proposed Elimination of Full Cost Accounting in the Extractive Petroleum Industry," *Journal of Accounting and Economics* (March 1979), pp. 3–44.

——, M. Rozeff and D. Dhaliwal (1981), "The Economic Determinants of the Market Reaction to Proposed Mandatory Accounting Changes in the Oil and Gas Industry," *Journal of Financial Economics* (January 1981), pp. 3–22.

Dann, L. Y., D. Mayers and R. J. Raab, Jr. (1977), "Trading Rules, Large Blocks and the Speed of Price Adjustment," *Journal of Financial Economics* (January 1977), pp. 3–22.

Deakin, E. B. (1976), "Accounting Reports, Policy Interventions and the Behavior of Security Returns," THE ACCOUNTING REVIEW (July 1976), pp. 590–603.

Demski, J., and G. Feltham (1978), "Economic Incentives in Budgetary Control Systems," THE ACCOUNTING REVIEW (April 1978), pp. 336–359.

Dewing, A. (1926) *The Financial Policy of Corporations*, Revised Edition (The Ronald Press Co., 1926).

Dhaliwal, D. (1980), "The Effect of the Firm's Capital Structure on the Choice of Accounting Methods," THE ACCOUNTING REVIEW (January 1980), pp. 78–84.

Edwards, J. (1960), *History of Public Accounting in the United States* (Michigan State University Press, 1960).

Fama, E. F. (1980), "Agency Problems and the Theory of the Firm," *Journal of Political Economy* (April 1980), pp. 288–307.

——, and M. H. Miller (1972), *The Theory of Finance* (Holt Rinehart and Winston, 1972).

Foster, G. (1978), *Financial Statement Analysis* (Prentice-Hall, 1978).

—— (1980), "Externalities and Financial Reporting," *Journal of Finance* (May 1980), pp. 521–533.

Friend, Irwin and E. S. Herman (1964), "The SEC Through a Glass Darkly," *Journal of Business* (October 1964), pp. 382–405.

——, and —— (1965), "Professor Stigler on Securities Regulation: A Further Comment," *The Journal of Business* (January 1965), pp. 106–110.

——, and R. Westerfield (1975), "Required Disclosure and the Stock Market: Comment," *The American Economic Review* (June 1975), pp. 467–472.

Galai, D. and R. Masulis (1976), "The Option Pricing Model and the Risk Factor of Stock," *Journal of Financial Economics* (March 1976), pp. 53–81.

Gonedes, N. and N. Dopuch (1974), "Capital Market Equilibrium, Information Production, and Selecting Accounting Techniques: Theoretical Framework and Review of Empirical Work," *Studies on Financial Accounting Objectives: 1974*, Supplement to the *Journal of Accounting Research* (1974), pp. 48–129.

Gourrich, P. (1937), "Investment Banking Methods Prior to and Since the Securities Act of 1933," *Law and Contemporary Problems*, Volume 4 (1937), pp. 51–71.

Halleran, T. and J. Calderwood (1959), "Effect of Federal Regulation on Distribution of and Trading in Securities," *George Washington Law Review* (October 1959), pp. 97–99.

Hamada, R. S. (1969), "Portfolio Analysis, Market Equilibrium and Corporation Finance," *Journal of Finance* (March 1969), pp. 13–31.

Hawkins, D. (1968), "The Development of Modern Financial Reporting Practices Among American Manufacturing Corporations," in M. Chatfield (Ed.), *Contemporary Studies in the Evolution of Accounting Thought* (Dickenson Publishing Co., 1968), pp. 247–279.

Hollander, M. and D. Wolfe (1973), *Nonparametric Statistical Methods* (John Wiley and Sons, 1973).

Hoxsey, J. M. B. (1930), "Accounting for Investors," *Journal of Accountancy* (October 1930), pp. 251–284.

Jarrell, G. A. (1981), "The Economic Effects of Federal Regulation of the Market For New Security Issues," *Journal of Law and Economics* (December 1981), pp. 613–675.

Jensen, M. and W. Meckling (1976), "Theory of the Firm: Managerial Behavior, Agency Costs and Ownership Structure," *Journal of Financial Economics* (October 1976), pp. 305–360.

Kalay, A. (1978), "Towards a Theory of Corporate Dividend Policy," Unpublished manuscript, New York University (December 1978).

——— (1982), "Stockholder-Bondholder Conflict and Dividend Constraints," *Journal of Financial Economics* (July 1982), pp. 211-233.

Kehl, D. (1941), *Corporate Dividends* (The Ronald Press, 1941).

Leftwich, R. (1980), "Accounting Regulation, Market Failures and Market Solutions: Some Evidence," Working Paper No. MER C 80-09, University of Rochester (1980).

——— (1981), "Evidence of the Impact of Mandatory Changes in Accounting Principles on Corporate Loan Agreements," *Journal of Accounting and Economics* (March 1981), pp. 3-36.

—— (1983), "Accounting Information in Private Markets: Evidence from Private Lending Agreements," THE ACCOUNTING REVIEW (January 1983), pp. 23-42.

Lehmann, E. L. (1975), *Nonparametrics: Statistical Methods Based on Ranks* (Holden-Day, 1975).

Littleton, A. C. and V. K. Zimmerman (1962), *Accounting Theory: Continuity and Change* (Prentice-Hall, 1962).

Malkiel, B. (1966), *The Term Structure of Interest Rates: Expectations and Behavior Patterns* (Princeton University Press, 1966).

Mautz, R. and W. G. May (1978), *Financial Disclosure in a Competitive Economy* (Financial Executives Research Foundation, 1978).

McCormick, E. (1948), *Understanding the Securities Act and the S.E.C.* (American Book Company, 1948).

Mikkelson, W. (1978), "An Examination of the Agency Cost Rationale for Convertible Bonds," Unpublished manuscript, University of Rochester (1978).

Myers, S. C. (1977), "Determinants of Corporate Borrowing," *Journal of Financial Economics* (November 1977), pp. 147-175.

Noreen, E. and J. Sepe (1981), "Market Reactions to Accounting Policy Deliberations: The Inflation Accounting Case," THE ACCOUNTING REVIEW (April 1981), pp. 253-269.

Officer, R. R. (1973), "The Variability of the Market Factor of the New York Stock Exchange," *Journal of Business* (July 1973), pp. 434-453.

Rice, S. J. (1978), "The Information Content of Fully Diluted Earnings Per Share," THE ACCOUNTING REVIEW (April 1978), pp. 429-438.

Ripley, W. Z. (1927), *Main Street and Wall Street* (Little Brown, 1927).

Rodgers, C. (1965), "The Corporate Trust Indenture Project," *Business Lawyer* (April 1965), pp. 551-571.

Rozeff, M. and W. Kinney (1976), "Capital Market Seasonality: The Case of Stock Returns," *Journal of Financial Economics* (October 1976), pp. 379-402.

Schwert, G. W. (1981), "Using Financial Data to Measure Effects of Regulation," *The Journal of Law and Economics* (April 1981), pp. 121-158.

Smith, C. W., Jr. and J. B. Warner (1979), "On Financial Contracting: An Analysis of Bond Covenants," *Journal of Financial Economics* (June 1979), pp. 117-161.

Smith, R. (1937), "The Relation of Federal and State Securities Laws," *Law and Contemporary Problems*, Volume 4 (1937), pp. 241-255.

Stigler, G. J. (1964), "Public Regulation of the Securities Market," *Journal of Business* (April 1964), pp. 117-142.

Van Horne, J. C. (1978), *Financial Market Rates and Flows* (Prentice-Hall, 1978).

Wise, R. (1934), *Blue Sky Legislation* (Commerce Clearing House, Inc., 1934).

Zeff, S. A. (1972), *Forging Accounting Principles in Five Countries: A History and an Analysis of Trends* (Stipes Publishing Co., 1972).

EVIDENCE OF THE IMPACT OF MANDATORY CHANGES IN ACCOUNTING PRINCIPLES ON CORPORATE LOAN AGREEMENTS

Richard LEFTWICH*

The University of Chicago, Chicago, IL 60637, USA

Received August 1980, final version received December 1980

The theory in this paper predicts that mandatory changes in accounting principles can affect the measurement rules defined in restrictive covenants in firms' lending agreements. Consequently, those mandatory changes can have an impact on the value of a firm's equity, even if the changes appear to be merely 'cosmetic'. This contracting cost theory is tested by examining both event-related and cross-sectional abnormal performance of the equity of a sample of firms when the Accounting Principles Board changed accounting principles for business combinations. The theory provides, at best, an incomplete explanation of the observed abnormal performance.

1. Introduction

The purpose of this paper is to present a theory to explain why some apparently 'cosmetic' mandatory changes in accepted accounting principles have an impact on firms' cash flows and on the value of debt and equity. The theory focuses on the use of accounting numbers in lending contracts which reduce the potential conflict of interest between stockholders and bondholders.[1] Empirical tests of the theory are conducted. The tests are based on the mandatory changes in accounting for business combinations brought about by Accounting Principles Board *Opinion no. 16* and *Opinion no. 17*.

*This paper is part of my Ph.D. dissertation at the University of Rochester. I would like to thank the members of my committee for their advice and encouragement: Michael Jensen (Chairman), William Schwert, Ross Watts and Jerry Zimmerman. Robert Holthausen provided valuable comments on several earlier drafts, and I have benefited from the comments of Gary Biddle, William Beaver, Daniel Collins, Nicholas Gonedes, Myron Scholes, and participants of the accounting workshops at the University of Arizona and Cornell University. Financial support for the dissertation was provided by the Ernst and Whinney Foundation and the Managerial Economics Research Center of the Graduate School of Management at the University of Rochester. I am grateful for that financial support.

[1]Holthausen (1981) presents a similar theory to predict the impact of *voluntary* changes in accounting principles. He tests the theory using firms which changed depreciation methods. After I completed the empirical analysis in this paper, I was made aware of a study by Collins, Rozeff and Dhaliwal which relies on agency theory to predict the cross-sectional effects obtained in Collins and Dent (1979).

A number of recent studies attempt to measure the effect of mandatory changes in generally accepted accounting principles on the equity values of firms.[2] However, many of these mandatory changes are apparently cosmetic or neutral. They have no obvious impact on firms' cash flows, and they provide little, if any, new information to investors; i.e., the information provided by applying the new principles was available prior to the mandatory change, either in footnotes to annual accounts or in other published sources. If equity markets are efficient, available information is incorporated in stock prices and the mandatory changes in accounting principles should not result in abnormal price movements unless the change induces unanticipated effects on cash flows to or from the firm and its equityholders.[3]

Until recently, little attention has been devoted to explaining why equity values would be affected by apparently neutral mandatory changes in generally accepted accounting principles and to predicting whether the impact of a particular change differs across firms systematically.[4] Accounting for business combinations is a contentious issue that aroused considerable opposition and the existence of that opposition suggests that the rule change was associated with real costs for firms affected by it.[5] Langer (1976) and Zeff (1972) provide a detailed history of the business combination deliberations from the time of an initial Accounting Research Study (June 1963) to the announcement of the final ruling in July 1970. I review the history of the deliberations and select 21 'events' during the deliberation period. The selected events involve press releases about the proposed accounting rules, testimony at congressional hearings, APB meetings and publication of exposure drafts. I then examine abnormal performance of a sample of firms for several days before and after each of the 21 events to determine which events resulted in a revision of expectations concerning the form of the final rule. By examining abnormal performance for only several days before and after each of the events, the entire deliberation period can be studied and the risk of including other news items in the investigation period is reduced. I identify statistically significant abnormal performance around 9

---

[2]See, for example, Collins and Dent (1979), Dyckman and Smith (1979), and Lev (1979).

[3]Fama (1976) discusses the efficient market hypothesis and reviews empirical tests of market efficiency.

[4]Watts and Zimmerman (1978) present a theory to explain management's choice of accounting principles and their response to mandatory changes in those principles. They test their predictions by examining corporate submissions on the General Price Level Accounting Discussion Memorandum of the Financial Accounting Standards Board. Collins and Dent (1979) and Lev (1979) offer some concluding remarks to explain why some firms are affected by apparently cosmetic mandatory changes. They present no formal tests of their explanations.

[5]Some argue that the dispute over business combinations led to the demise of the APB; see Langer (1976). Although accounting for business combinations is not topical, it remains on the FASB agenda. A discussion memorandum was issued in 1976 and public hearings were held in 1977.

of the 21 events, and I examine the performance of the sample firms around those 9 events to determine whether the cross-sectional variation in the impact of the mandatory change is consistent with the contracting theory outlined in this paper. Some confirmation of the contracting theory is obtained, but it is concluded that contracting theory provides, at best, an incomplete explanation of the observed abnormal performance for firms during the APB deliberation period.

Outline of the paper

In section 2, predictions are made concerning the impact of a mandated accounting rule change on firms. Those predictions are based on the effect of the rule change on accounting numbers in lending contracts. In section 3, a simple expectations model is developed to explain the effect of unexpected changes in accounting rules on measures of both event-related and cross-sectional abnormal performance. The data used to test the contracting theory predictions are described in section 4, and the results of the empirical tests are presented in section 5. In section 6, the results are interpreted and brief conclusions are presented. The appendix contains a detailed explanation of the calculation of the abnormal performance measures used in the study.

2. Contracting theory predictions

Corporate lending agreements restrict the financing and investment decisions of borrowing firms. Measurement rules used in those restrictions rely in whole or in part on generally accepted accounting principles. Thus, mandatory changes in accepted principles can change the restrictions in lending agreements and affect the value of the equity of firms with debt outstanding. Section 2.1 explains the purpose of restrictions in lending agreements and the consequences of changing those restrictions. Section 2.2 contains a set of hypotheses concerning the effect of a change in negotiated restrictions brought about by a change in generally accepted accounting principles.

2.1. Lending agreements and accounting numbers

There is a conflict of interest between bondholders and stockholders of firms with debt outstanding — decisions which are in the best interest of stockholders are not necessarily in the best interests of bondholders.[6] Lending agreements impose restrictions on borrowing firms' financing and

[6]See Fama and Miller (1972, pp. 150–188). Further discussion of the consequences of the conflict of interest between bondholders and stockholders is contained in Black and Scholes (1973), Galai and Masulis (1976), Jensen and Meckling (1976), and Myers (1977).

investment decisions, and control activities which favor stockholders at the expense of bondholders. Activities subject to restrictive covenants include:[7]

(i)   payment of dividends,
(ii) incurrence of additional debt,
(iii) maintenance of working capital,
(iv) merger activity,
(v)   disposition of all or part of the assets of the firm, and
(vi) the purchase of certain securities.

The constraints imposed by restrictive covenants, particularly restrictions on paying dividends and issuing additional debt, depend on the firm's performance and financial position as reflected by accounting numbers such as: net income, net tangible assets, tangible net worth, current assets, and current liabilities. Accounting principles concerning asset valuation and income determination; i.e., accounting measurement rules used to calculate the accounting numbers, partially determine the level of the constraints.

Lending agreements define the measurement rules used to calculate accounting numbers for the purposes of restrictive covenants. Leftwich (1980b) presents evidence of the types of measurement rules contained in lending agreements. A summary of that evidence follows:

(i)   Definitions of accounting numbers in lending agreements consistently refer to generally accepted accounting principles (GAAP). GAAP is used as a benchmark and any modifications to those principles consist of specific inclusions and exclusions.
(ii) The definitions of accounting numbers require that contractual accounting numbers be determined by generally accepted accounting principles in force at the date of calculation, not at the date of issue of the debt;[8] i.e., the definitions rely on 'rolling' GAAP, not 'frozen' GAAP.
(iii) Variations from generally accepted accounting principles are more frequent (and more elaborate) in private debt agreements than in public debt indentures.

---

[7]Smith and Warner (1979) analyze common forms of restrictions contained in loan agreements, and offer explanations of how particular covenants reduce the conflict of interest between bondholders and stockholders. A discussion of typical bond covenants is contained in American Bar Foundation (1971), Maycock and Jenkins (1958), Fryling (1964), and Simmons (1972).

[8]Fogelson (1978, pp. 780–781) discusses some contrary examples of recent indentures which do rely on generally accepted principles at the time of issue of the debt. He suggests that the increased 'activism' of the FASB and the SEC induced the firms to tie the definitions to existing accounting rules. It is difficult to assess whether the instances he reports are isolated, or part of a general response by firms.

(iv) If modifications to generally accepted accounting principles are made in lending agreements, those modifications state that certain *increases* in income and asset values are *not* allowed, and ensure that other *decreases* in income and asset values *are* recorded.

When an accounting rule change is mandated for particular transactions (e.g., accounting for leases), lending agreements are affected if they rely on generally accepted accounting principles to record those transactions. Thus, even apparently cosmetic changes in generally accepted accounting principles can alter the terms of the contract between borrowers and lenders; i.e., even if the new accounting rule has no direct impact on a firm's cash flows.[9]

2.2. Hypotheses

It is hypothesized that alterations to a lending agreement caused by a mandatory change in accounting principles can affect the value of a firm's debt and equity. If the new rule results in lower reported income and asset numbers (or higher liability numbers), restrictive covenants are tightened and the probability of violating the terms of the lending agreement is increased.[10] Managers can modify production, investment or financing activities to avoid contract violations, or renegotiate the lending agreement. Such responses impose costs on the firm and it is predicted that the value of the firm falls if restrictions are tightened by a mandatory change in generally accepted accounting principles. The maximum reduction in the value of the firm is the lowest of the cost of renegotiating the agreement, redeeming the debt, defaulting on the loan agreement, or changing the firm's operations to avoid violating the covenants.

The value of the equity can fall by more than the decline in the value of the firm if the tighter restrictions transfer wealth from stockholders to bondholders. Tighter restrictions can favor bondholders (and harm stockholders) because the new restrictions prevent assets from being transferred out of the firm to the stockholders (by way of increased dividends, for example).

Hypothesis 1. An unanticipated mandated income-reducing change in generally accepted accounting principles reduces the value of the equity of a

---

[9]The *magnitude* of the changes in cash flows caused by restrictions in lending agreements is an empirical issue. Tests of the theory in this paper presume that the costs are sufficiently large to be detected by the methodology employed. If, however, the changes are small (because, for example, contract renegotiation is virtually costless), the theory adds little to our understanding of why firms are affected by apparently cosmetic accounting changes.

[10]Many mandated accounting rule changes alter the timing of charges to income; e.g., *Financial Accounting Standard*, No. 2, required that all research and development costs be expensed when incurred, rather than capitalized and amortized. Those rule changes result in tighter restrictive covenants in some periods, and looser restrictive covenants in others.

firm with debt outstanding, even if the accounting change has no direct effect on a firm's cash flows.

Some predictions can be made concerning the cross-sectional effects of income-reducing mandated changes. If the cost of default, redemption and renegotiation[11] is an increasing function of the amount of debt that is outstanding, the decline in the value of the equity of firms is an increasing function of the amount of debt outstanding. Furthermore, it is predicted that the costs of renegotiation and default are lower for private issues than for public issues.[12] The *Trust Indenture Act* of 1939 requires that, whenever a corporation issues debt to the public, a trustee for the debtholders must be appointed and an indenture agreement entered into by the firm and the trustee. Trustees cannot approve subsequent modifications to an indenture unless they submit the proposed modifications to a vote of debtholders and obtain favorable votes from holders of a substantial majority (usually two-thirds) of the debt outstanding — a costly procedure when debt is widely held. By contrast, private debt agreements can be modified by mutual consent between the issuer and the small number of purchasers.

Hypothesis 2. The decline in value of the equity is an increasing function of the amount of the firm's outstanding debt.

Hypothesis 3. The decline in value of the equity is larger if the outstanding debt is publicly held than if it is privately held.

If the firm's debt is callable, the firm can avoid costly renegotiation or default by calling the debt. Thus, the mandated rule change cannot impose costs that are in excess of the redemption costs (the excess of the call price over the market value of the debt).[13] Loan contracts for callable debt are no more costly to renegotiate than contracts for non-callable debt, and the call provision can provide a lower cost alternative to renegotiation.

Hypothesis 4. The decline in value of the equity is smaller if the outstanding debt is callable.

If the firm's debt is convertible, any decline in the value of the firm caused by the mandatory accounting change reduces the value of the conversion

---

[11]Renegotiation costs include more than the out-of-pocket costs associated with drawing up a revised loan agreement. Renegotiation costs are defined to include any extra protection or interest payments the lender demands as a price for renegotiation. If interest rates have increased since the debt was issued, the lender may be able to set a high price on renegotiation.

[12]Zinbarg (1975) argues that lower negotiation costs are one of the major advantages of private issues.

[13]A firm can repurchase its public debt in the market, but that does not avoid the renegotiation costs. Public debt indentures can be modified only if approval is obtained from holders of two-thirds of the *outstanding* debt. Repurchase of some of the debt increases the bargaining power of the remaining holders.

privilege and lowers the probability that the debt will be converted. Thus, part of the reduction in the value of the firm is absorbed by the debtholders if the debt is convertible.

Hypothesis 5. The decline in value of the equity is smaller if the debt is convertible.

Firms can avoid costly recontracting by changing production, financing, or investment decisions to avoid violating restrictive covenants while the debt is outstanding. Changing the firm's activities itself involves costs, but, once the debt matures, the original set of activities can be resumed.[14] Thus, the shorter the term to maturity of the debt, the lower are the costs of changing the firm's activities.

Hypothesis 6. The decline in value of the equity is greater for firms which have outstanding debt with longer time to maturity.

In the next section of the paper, some of the problems associated with testing the impact of mandatory accounting changes are discussed. A simple expectations model is then developed to allow tests of Hypotheses 1–6 to be conducted.

3. Expectations of mandatory accounting changes

There are three fundamental limitations associated with empirical tests of the impact of mandatory accounting changes on the equity value of firms.[15]

(i) Studies of abnormal performance around the time of a mandated change in accounting methods rely on some variation of the cumulative average residual technique developed by Fama, Fisher, Jensen and Roll (1969). That technique captures not only the impact of the mandated change, but also the effect of any other information released at the same calendar time. Consequently, the measured abnormal performance is not necessarily attributable to the mandated change. In addition, test statistics may be overstated because of cross-sectional dependence in

---

[14]Resuming the original set of activities is not costless either. However, the option to resume them sooner cannot make firms worse off.

[15]Foster (1980) independently discusses the limitation of empirical tests of the impact of mandatory changes, particularly in studies related to oil and gas accounting. Foster examines the problems caused by 'confounding' events, sample selection, and the absence of any theory about why firms are affected by the accounting changes.

measured abnormal returns.[16] Lev (1979) and Foster (1980) discuss these problems. They reveal that, during the period surrounding the release of the Financial Accounting Standards Board (FASB) exposure draft on oil and gas accounting, there were many 'news' items concerning oil and gas firms which could produce the results obtained by Collins and Dent (1979) and Dyckman and Smith (1979).

(ii) The choice of a set of mandatory accounting rules is endogenous to a particular economic environment. Changes in those rules are not imposed exogenously, but result from economic forces.[17] Firms affected by the accounting rule changes are likely to be affected by the same economic forces that bring about the new accounting rules. It is thus difficult to identify the cause of measured abnormal performance of affected firms — some (or none) of the abnormal performance may be attributable to the accounting rule change per se, some (or none) of it may be attributable to the economic forces that motivated the rule change.

(iii) If the equity market is efficient, the market response to any piece of news reflects only the unexpected component of that news, i.e., the deviation of the actual outcome from the expected outcome. If market participants form expectations of a mandatory accounting change prior to the actual announcement of the change, the abnormal performance observed when the change is announced reflects only the extent to which the final ruling departs from the expected ruling. In the perverse extreme, if the final ruling imposes lower costs on firms than were expected, positive abnormal performance can be observed when the ruling is announced, even though the mandatory change adversely affects all firms. Most accounting rule changes do not come as a complete surprise to market participants. Typically, the rule changes are preceded by a long period of deliberations during which discussion memoranda are issued, public hearings are held and exposure drafts are circulated. Market participants have several months' warning of a likely change and, based on various releases of information, they revise their

---

[16]The problem is, of course, less severe when the cumulative average residual technique is applied to study the performance of firms which experience an 'event' (such as a tender offer) at different points in calendar time. In general, the net effect of any other information should be zero when the residuals are averaged across many firms in event time and the measured abnormal performance can be attributed to the event being studied with more confidence. See Brown and Warner (1980) for a discussion of the effect of the distribution of event dates on the power of the cumulative average residual technique.

[17]Watts and Zimmerman (1978) develop a model of how accounting rule changes are mandated. In their model, a particular accounting rule is endorsed by members of a standard-setting body acting in their own self-interest. Changes in economic variables, such as the inflation rate, alter the tradeoffs associated with particular accounting rules. As a result, users and producers of accounting numbers lobby for particular rule changes and members of the standard-setting body respond to that lobbying activity.

expectations concerning the form of the final rule and its effect on firms. To cope with this problem of revised expectations, abnormal performance can be calculated over a period long enough to capture the initial major revision of expectations concerning the rule change. However, selecting the length of the period poses a dilemma. The problem discussed in (i) is accentuated when the period is lengthened, because other news items affecting firms are likely to be encountered and abnormal performance associated with these pieces of information can mask or reinforce any abnormal performance associated with the accounting rule change.[18]

A simple expectations model provides some insight into the effect of changes in expectations on abnormal performance measures. An expectations model is developed for event-related abnormal performance in section 3.1, and cross-sectional abnormal performance in section 3.2.

3.1. Event-related abnormal performance

Consider a world where the entire feasible set of accounting rules for a particular transaction (such as a business combination) has been discovered and is known to investors. In this world, the accounting standard-setting body does not invent or create 'new' rules. Instead, the rule-making body decides which rules it will endorse as acceptable, and rule changes occur when that body deems a currently-endorsed rule no longer acceptable. Investors estimate the expected cost or benefit associated with changes in accounting rules and investors revise their expectations as they receive new information about criticisms of the currently-endorsed rule and the response of accounting regulators to those criticisms.

The cost (or benefit) of a rule change for a particular firm includes all of the effects that the rule change has on the firm's cash flows.[19] The cost (or benefit) is measured by the difference between the market value of the firm if investors are certain that the currently-endorsed rule will remain in effect and the market value of the firm if investors are certain that the rule change will be endorsed. Assume investors have homogeneous expectations and let MV_i^*

---

[18]Schwert (1980) discusses this dilemma and other problems associated with drawing inferences from market-based studies of the effect of regulation.

[19]For example, the contracting cost theory in section 2 predicts that accounting rule changes impose costs or benefits on firms depending on whether restrictive covenants are tightened or relaxed. Moreover, the cost (or benefit) of an accounting rule change for a particular firm depends on some characteristics of the firm, and this is developed further when cross-sectional abnormal performance is discussed in section 3.2. Throughout the discussion, it is assumed that those characteristics of the firm do not change for the time period under consideration.

be the market value of firm i if investors are certain that there will be no rule changes. Thus, at time t,

$$MV_{it} = MV_i^* - \sum_{j=1}^{J} p_{jt} C_{ij},$$

where

MV_{it} = market value of firm i at time t,
p_{jt} = investors' estimate of the probability of state j,
C_{ij} = cost of the change in accounting rules in state j to firm i, and
J = number of states.[20]

Suppose we consider a time period during which investors receive information causing them to revise their expectation of the cost of a forthcoming rule change. Then, assuming MV_i^* remains unchanged,[21]

$$\Delta MV_i = \sum_{j=1}^{J} C_{ij}(p_{jt} - p_{jt+1}),$$

where

$$\Delta MV_i = MV_{it+1} - MV_{it}.$$

Note that, if $\Delta MV_i \neq 0$, we can conclude that investors have revised their expectations about the cost of a rule change. However, if $\Delta MV_i = 0$, we cannot determine whether expectations are unchanged (i.e. $p_{jt} = p_{jt+1}$ for all j), or have changed without affecting the market value of the firm [i.e., $p_{jt} \neq p_{jt+1}$ for some j but $\sum_{j=1}^{J} C_{ij}(p_{jt} - p_{jt+1}) = 0$]. Thus, if we use cumulative average residual techniques and discover that firms experience abnormal performance when news of a forthcoming rule change is released, we can conclude that the proposed rule change is 'costly' or 'beneficial', i.e., $C_{ij} \neq 0$ for at least some j. However, such methodology does not shed any light on the source of the costs (or benefits) associated with the proposed rule change.

[20]For simplicity, the model is expressed in discrete terms, but a continuous model can be developed without changing the inferences drawn from the results. An equivalent interpretation of the expectations model is given in Leftwich (1980a). In that model, there are R rules each imposing costs of C_{ij} on firm i. Investors do not revise their estimates of the cost of the rules during the deliberation period. Instead, they revise their estimates of the probabilities that various rules will be endorsed. That model leads to the same inferences that are drawn from the model in this paper.

[21]This is a very strong assumption. If accounting rule changes are endogenous, as is discussed above, the value of the firm, MV_i^* may be affected by the same economic forces that induce the rule change.

A theory must be developed to identify the effect of the rule change on the firm's cash flows. To test that theory, we must consider the cross-sectional effect of a change in expectations about a forthcoming accounting rule change.

3.2. Cross-sectional abnormal performance

Suppose we develop a theory (similar to the one developed in section 2) that predicts that the cost of a particular accounting rule change for firm i is a linear function of N characteristics of the firm, i.e., we hypothesize that the value function is

$$C_{ij} = \sum_{k=1}^{N} b_{jk} D_{ik},$$

where

D_{ik} = the kth characteristic of firm i (such as its debt–equity ratio), and
b_{jk} = the coefficient of the kth characteristic in the value function for C_{ij}.

Thus, the change in market value of firm i, ΔMV_i, when there is a change in expectations, is

$$\Delta MV_i = \sum_{j=1}^{J} \sum_{k=1}^{N} b_{jk} D_{ik} (p_{jt} - p_{jt+1})$$

$$= \sum_{k=1}^{N} D_{ik} \sum_{j=1}^{J} b_{jk} (p_{jt} - p_{jt+1}).$$

Our theory makes predictions about the sign or magnitude of the coefficients, b_{jk}, of some observable characteristics of the value function. The change in market value of the firm is observable, so we could estimate (using, say, OLS regression for a sample of F firms)

$$\Delta MV_i = \sum_{k=1}^{N} \beta_k D_{ik}, \qquad i = 1, \ldots, F.$$

Notice that the estimated coefficients are estimates of $\sum_{j=1}^{J} b_{jk}(p_{jt} - p_{jt+1})$; i.e., the estimated coefficients are an average of the coefficients of all value functions weighted by the change in expectations. However, our theory makes predictions about the sign and magnitude of the coefficients of particular states.

To yield more precise results, we can simplify the model further. Suppose that investors are perfectly certain at time t that a forthcoming rule change will cost firm i, C_{i1} (i.e., $p_{1t}=1$). At time $t+1$, investors completely revise their expectations and are perfectly certain that there will be *no* rule changes (i.e., the probability of the state with no costly rule changes is 1 and the probability of all other states is zero). Thus,

$$\Delta MV_i = C_{i1} \quad \text{and} \quad \hat{\beta}_k = b_{1k}.$$

However, if we assume that investors initially expect no costly rule changes (i.e., the status quo will be preserved) and then, at $t+1$, are perfectly certain that a rule change will cost C_{i1},

$$\Delta MV_i = -C_{i1} \quad \text{and} \quad \hat{\beta}_k = -b_{1k}.$$

Thus, the sign of the estimated coefficient depends on the direction of the change in expectations. Even with the restrictive assumptions in this model, drawing inferences from the cross-sectional tests is difficult.

The highly-simplified expectations model we have developed here provides some warnings about empirical tests of the effect of mandated rule changes on firms. The following precautionary steps are warranted:[22]

(1) If $(p_{jt} \approx p_{jt+1})$ for all j, $E(\hat{\beta}_k)=0$, even if $b_{jk} \neq 0$. Thus, a two-stage procedure is appropriate. First, investigate the abnormal performance of firms' securities to determine whether particular events caused investors to revise their expectations. Second, estimate cross-sectional regressions around those events where expectations have been substantially revised.

(2) The sign of $\hat{\beta}_k$ depends on the direction of the change in expectations. For example, the theory in section 2 predicts that the sign of the coefficient depends on whether the rule change tightens or relaxes restrictions in bond covenants. Consequently, the sign of the estimated coefficient must be considered in conjunction with whether expectations shifted towards, or away from, a more restrictive accounting rule.

(3) Several changes in expectations can be identified for particular accounting rule changes, e.g., expectations can change when an exposure draft is issued and can change again, for example, when the Securities and Exchange Commission (SEC) announces that it does not support the exposure draft. Separate cross-sectional regressions can be estimated for each of the events associated with a change in expectations. However, unless the change in expectations is approximately equal for each event,

---

[22]Estimating ΔMV_i presents further difficulties. The cumulative average residual technique provides a proxy, but the cross-sectional dependence in the values of the proxy hampers significance testing. These problems are addressed subsequently.

we should not expect the estimated coefficients to be equal across events because those estimated coefficients depend on the change in expectations.

The next section of the paper discusses the data used for the two-stage empirical tests of the impact of a mandatory accounting change on the equity value of firms.

4. Data

4.1. Timetable of the APB decision process

In August 1970, the Accounting Principles Board (APB) issued *Opinion no. 16*: 'Accounting for Business Combinations', and a related pronouncement, *Opinion no. 17*: 'Accounting for Intangible Assets'. These opinions restrict the circumstances under which the pooling method can be used, and require that, if the purchase method is used, any difference between the purchase price and the net book value of the acquired assets must be allocated to specific assets if identifiable. Any residual ('goodwill on consolidation') must be amortized in the income statement over a period not exceeding 40 years. Furthermore, firms can no longer inflate their annual earnings number by merging with a profitable company late in the fiscal year — the merged firm's earnings are pooled only for that part of the year that the companies are combined. *Opinion no. 16* and *Opinion no. 17* are designed to reduce management's ability to use purchase and pooling of interests accounting to boost reported income numbers.[23]

The APB found the purchase-pooling issue difficult to resolve. Langer (1976) and Zeff (1972) discuss the controversy associated with APB proposals on accounting for business combinations. Leftwich (1980a, app. A) contains a brief summary of events related to the APB rulings. The APB deliberations commenced in June 1969 and a final ruling was not issued until August 1970. Prior to the APB deliberations, two Accounting Research Studies were released — *Accounting Research Study no. 5*: 'A Critical Study of Accounting for Business Combinations' [Wyatt (1963)], and *Accounting Research Study no. 10*: 'Accounting for Goodwill' [Catlett and Olson (1968)]. Those studies called for drastic changes in the accounting rules for business combinations and the studies were severely criticized, especially by the research directors for the studies. The APB rejected the recommendations of those studies, but the Board was under pressure to make substantive changes in business combination accounting rules. For example, a vocal

---

[23]There is some dispute as to whether the strict requirements of *Opinion no. 16* and *Opinion no. 17* are enforced and whether those opinions deter the use of pooling. For example, see Libby (1972) and Rayburn (1975).

critic of accounting principles, Briloff, published articles in *Barron's* on July 15, 1968 and April 28, 1969 detailing alleged abuses associated with pooling. The Chairman of the SEC testified before a congressional committee on February 25, 1969 and claimed that the SEC would establish accounting rules for business combinations unless the APB acted promptly. Initially, the APB tried to impose strict conditions on the use of pooling, and then moved to eliminate pooling entirely. After intensive lobbying from corporations and informal pressure from the SEC, the APB abandoned its attempt to eliminate pooling, and reverted to imposing stringent conditions on pooling. One of those restrictions, the size test, encountered strong opposition.[24] The 3:1 test proposed by the APB in December 1969 was relaxed to 9:1 in June 1970 and was dropped entirely in the final opinion in August 1970.

The history of the APB rulings on business combinations illustrates several of the difficulties encountered when researchers attempt to measure the effect of a mandated change in accounting rules. First, the time period is long, extending from July 1968 to August 1970. Second, an event subsequent to the final APB ruling could also have an impact on firms. In October 1970, both the NYSE and ASE announced that they intended to monitor firms' compliance with the APB opinion. Both exchanges required that listing applications for shares used in pooling transactions must be accompanied by an opinion from the firms' independent accountants detailing the compliance of the transaction with the criteria in the APB ruling. Third, although the final APB ruling restricted the use of pooling, the restrictions were less severe than those proposed earlier in the deliberations. Thus, expectations of any adverse effect of the ruling may have been incorporated in equity values months prior to August 1970. If a stock price study were restricted to the date of the final ruling, little effect may be observed. The detected effect could even be in the opposite direction to that predicted if the final ruling contained good news relative to expectations already incorporated in prices.[25] Fourth, it is difficult to determine when news of the various proposals was released because APB deliberations were supposed to be confidential.

I selected 21 events from the deliberation history summarized in Leftwich (1980a). Those events are listed in table 1. The events were not selected randomly, but they were selected before any abnormal performance tests were performed. I endeavored to select events which could have induced market participants to revise their expectations concerning the form of the

---

[24]Under the proposed size tests, pooling could be used only if the two firms in the business combination were 'approximately' the same size. As a compromise, a ceiling of 3:1 was proposed for the ratio of sizes, and eventually a 9:1 maximum ratio was suggested.

[25]*Wall Street Journal* reports can be similarly misleading. For example, reports published on October 31, 1969 and August 3, 1970 suggested that the new proposals were restrictive. Those proposals were restrictive in comparison with the existing accepted accounting methods, but were lenient in comparison with previous proposals.

final APB ruling. The selected events consist of the initial public announcement dates of proposals by the SEC, the APB and the Federal Trade Commission (FTC).[26] In addition, I included the publication dates of two antipooling articles by Briloff in *Barron's* to determine whether those articles had an impact on investors' expectations.[27]

4.2. Sample of NYSE firms

Rayburn (1975) describes a sample of 423 NYSE firms that engaged in a total of 1,790 mergers from November 1968 through December 1972. Pooling was used to account for 82% of the mergers, and virtually all of the firms used pooling at least once. Corporations in the sample were the ones most likely to be affected by the mandatory change in accounting for business combinations, and they were included in this study provided that they were listed on the NYSE on August 31, 1970, had at least the previous 36 months of data available on the CRSP file, and were unregulated. There were 338 such firms and they engaged in 1,139 mergers from November 1968 through December 1972. Approximately 90% of the mergers were accounted for as poolings, and virtually all of the firms used pooling at least once.

Details of the sample firms' debt issues and book values of debt and equity were collected from the 1970 edition of *Moody's Industrial Manual*. Three-hundred and twenty-five of the firms had some long-term debt. There were 1,684 issues of debt outstanding and 338 of those issues were publicly held. The book value of the public debt comprised 34% of the total book value of long-term debt for the sample.[28]

5. Methodology and results

A two-stage procedure is employed to control for the problems discussed in section 3 above. First, abnormal performance measures are calculated for the sample of firms around each of the 21 events listed in table 1 to classify the events into 'revision in expectations', or 'non-revision in expectations' categories. Second, for those events in the revision category, cross-sectional regressions are estimated to test whether the effects of the rule changes vary across firms as predicted by Hypotheses 2–6 above.

---

[26]Discussion at APB meetings was supposed to be confidential. Accordingly, when the meeting dates and public announcement dates are available (and not contiguous), they are included in table 1 as separate events.

[27]Evidence in Foster (1979) suggests that Briloff's criticisms of firms' accounting methods caused the market to revalue the equity of those firms.

[28]Further details of types of debt issues and book values of debt and equity are contained in Leftwich (1980a, tables 2 and 3).

Table 1

Selected events associated with APB ruling on accounting for business combinations (July 1968–October 1970).[a]

Event no.	No. of trading days	Dates and description
1	1	*July 15, 1968.* Briloff article ('Dirty Pooling') appeared in *Barron's*.
2	1	*February 25, 1969.* SEC Chairman Budge testified before the House Interstate and Foreign Commerce Committee and threatened that the SEC would establish accounting rules for business combinations unless the APB acted promptly.
3	1	*April 28, 1969.* Briloff article ('Much Abused Goodwill') appeared in *Barron's*.
4	3	*June 25–27, 1969.* APB meeting proposed stringent conditions for the use of pooling (e.g., only common stock for the transaction, at least 95% of the voting stock acquired, and a 60:40 size test). Amortization of goodwill was to be compulsory if purchase accounting was used.
5	1	*July 11, 1969.* Draft of June 25–27 proposals was circulated to APB members.
6	2	*August 6–7, 1969.* APB meeting abandoned June 25–27 draft. Instead pooling was to be prohibited, 'fair value' pooling substituted and the maximum period for goodwill amortization in purchase accounting set at 40 years.
7	1	*August 27, 1969.* Draft of August 6–7 proposals was released publicly.
8	3	*September 10–13, 1969.* APB meeting discussed SEC's informal response to August 6–7 proposals. APB decided to drop 'fair value' pooling and require purchase accounting for all combinations.
9	1	*September 24, 1969.* WSJ report of APB September 10–13 meeting: 'End to "Pooling of Interests" in Takeovers Favored by Accountants' Rule-Making Unit'.
10	1	*October 8, 1969.* APB released draft opinion of September 10–13 proposals.
11	2	*October 23–25, 1969.* APB meeting decided to drop previous proposals. Instead combinations would be recorded at 'fair value' only if 90% of the acquired's common were obtained solely for the acquirer's common. All other combinations would be treated as purchases with compulsory amortization of goodwill.
12	2	(a) *October 31, 1969.* WSJ report: '"Pooling of Interests" in Merger Accounting is Likely to be Ended'. (b) *November 3, 1969.* Federal Trade Commission Staff Report recommended that pooling be eliminated.
13	4	(a) *December 3, 1969.* WSJ report: 'Battling Bookkeepers: CPA Institute Team is Split As It Begins to Rewrite Rules for Merger Accounting'. According to the report, there wasn't a 2/3 majority in favor of the proposed ruling and the SEC was no longer insisting on a decision by January 1, 1970. (b) *December 3–6, 1969.* APB discussed the SEC's response to the October 23–25 proposals and dropped its attempt to eliminate pooling. Instead, strict conditions were proposed for pooling (e.g., 90% of the

Table 1 (continued)

Event no.	No. of trading days	Dates and description
		acquired's common must be obtained for the acquirer's common only, no treasury stock or contingent consideration could be used, and the acquired company must satisfy a 3:1 size test).
		(c) *December 8, 1969. WSJ* report of December 3–6 APB meeting: 'Accounting Board Approves Keeping Interest Pooling'.
14	3	*January 21–24, 1970.* APB meeting agreed to issue a formal exposure draft based on the December 3–6 proposal.
15	3	(a) *February 18, 1970.* SEC Chairman Budge testified before the Senate Judiciary Committee and endorsed the forthcoming exposure draft. Budge said the restrictions on pooling would be severe and the SEC encouraged those restrictions.
		(b) *February 23, 1970.* APB released the exposure draft incorporating the December 3–6 proposals.
16	1	*May 14, 1970.* (a) SEC Chairman Budge testified before a congressional subcommittee and said that the exposure draft involved severe restrictions, 'some' of which the SEC encouraged.
		(b) *WSJ* report summarizing Arthur Andersen's opposition to exposure draft: 'Arthur Andersen & Co. Raps Planned Changes in Merger Accounting'.
17	1	*June 1, 1970.* Two congressmen read anti-exposure draft journal articles into the *Congressional Record.*
18	4	(a) *June 24, 1970. WSJ* report that there was no clear majority among the APB members to support the proposed opinion: 'Mergers Accounting Fight at a Stalemate; Principles Board is Likely to Compromise'.
		(b) *June 24–27, 1970.* APB meeting substituted 9:1 size test for 3:1 when informed of SEC opposition.
		(c) *June 29, 1970. WSJ* report of June 24–27 APB meeting: 'Accounting Group Moves to Tighten Rules on Mergers'.
19	1	*July 10, 1970.* SEC Chairman Budge testified before the Joint Economic Committee that the SEC was indifferent between a 9:1 size test and no size test.
20	4	(a) *July 29, 1970. WSJ* report of prediction by a member of the APB that the size test would not survive a formal vote: 'Merger Accounting Shifts Aren't Set Yet, In Disputed View of One of Rule Makers'.
		(b) *July 29–31, 1970.* APB meeting dropped size test completely. APB *Opinion no. 16* and *Opinion no. 17* narrowly approved.
		(c) *August 3, 1970. WSJ* report of the APB compromise: 'Accountants' Top Rule-Making Body Drops Plan to Limit Pooling-of-Interest Mergers'.
21	1	*October 23, 1970. WSJ* report: 'Two Major Exchanges Demand Assurances Firms Use New Merger-Accounting Rules'. NYSE and ASE required that listing applications for shares used in pooling transactions must be accompanied by an opinion from the firm's independent accountants detailing the compliance of the transaction with the APB criteria.

[a]*Source:* Leftwich (1980a, app. A).

5.1. Event-related abnormal performance

The impact of the mandated accounting change on the rate of return of the sample firms is investigated using the market model,[29]

$$\tilde{R}_{it} = \alpha_i + \beta_i \tilde{R}_{Mt} + \tilde{\varepsilon}_{it}, \tag{1}$$

where $\tilde{R}_{it}$ is the rate of return on security i over period t (in this paper, t is one day), $\tilde{R}_{Mt}$ is the rate of return on a value-weighted market portfolio over period t, and $\tilde{\varepsilon}_{it}$ is the disturbance term with a zero mean and constant variance. For each firm i, prediction errors, PE_{it}, are calculated for the 5 trading days before and after each of the 21 events in table 1 and for each trading day during the event. Thus,

$$PE_{it}^m = R_{it} - (\hat{\alpha}_i + \hat{\beta}_i R_{Mt}),$$

for

$$m = 1, 2, \ldots, 21 \quad \text{and} \quad t = -5, -4, \ldots, -1, EP, +1, \ldots, +5,$$

where EP is the event period itself. The number of trading days during each event period ranges from 1 to 4. (See table 1.)

The prediction errors, PE_{it}^m are estimates of the abnormal returns to the stockholders of the sample of firms for the days surrounding the 21 stages in the evolution of the final APB ruling. The estimates of α_i and β_i from eq. (1) are calculated for the period starting at least 500 days before and ending 5 days prior to event 1. Data for the entire APB deliberation period (i.e., from 5 days prior to event 1 to 5 days after event 21) are not used in the estimation because the expected value of the disturbance term, $E(\tilde{\varepsilon}_{it})$, is not equal to zero during this period if the rule change has an impact on stockholders' returns.[30]

An average prediction error for the sample of 338 firms is calculated for each of the 5 days *before* each event, for trading days during each event, and for each of the 5 days *after* each event. The procedure results in 11 averages for each of the 21 events: 5 for the days prior to the event, 1 for the event

---

[29]The market model is widely used in empirical studies of abnormal performance in accounting and finance. Fama, Fisher, Jensen and Roll (1969) introduced the methodology of abnormal performance studies to the finance literature. Fama (1976, pp. 151–168) reviews some subsequent applications of the methodology.

[30]Scholes and Williams (1977) show that OLS estimates of α_i and β_i in eq. (1) are biased and inconsistent if true returns follow the market model but the securities do not trade continuously. Consequently, in this study, estimates of α_i and β_i are obtained using *weekly* data which should be less affected by the non-synchronous trading problem. For all firms, α_i and β_i are estimated using a minimum of 100 and a maximum of 200 weeks of data. All estimates of α_i are converted from a weekly rate of return to a daily rate of return by adjusting for the number of trading days per week during the estimation period.

period, and the remaining 5 for the days subsequent to the event. These averages are then cumulated to provide a series of cumulative average prediction errors for each event.[31]

To provide a test of the statistical significance of the cumulative prediction errors, the daily standard deviation of the prediction errors for the portfolio of 338 firms (σ_p) is calculated over a 100 day period prior to the first event. Under the assumption that the daily prediction errors are serially independent, the standard error of the cumulative prediction errors of the portfolio for N days is $\sigma_p\sqrt{N}$.[32] The null hypothesis to be tested is that the cumulative prediction error for the event period is significantly different from zero. The test statistic used is

$$t^m = CPE^m_{+5}/(\sigma_p \cdot \sqrt{N_m + 10}), \qquad m = 1, 2, \ldots, 21,$$

where CPE^m_{+5} is the cumulative average prediction error calculated from 5 trading days before to 5 trading days after the event period for event m, and N_m is the number of trading days in event m.

Under the null hypothesis that the average predictions errors are serially independent and normally distributed, the test statistic t^m has a student's t-distribution with 99 degrees of freedom.

Table 2 contains the cumulative average prediction errors calculated for each of the 21 events during the APB deliberations.

Hypothesis 1 predicts that the value of the equity of the sample of firms will fall if the unanticipated mandatory accounting change tightens restrictions in lending agreements. The results in table 2 support this hypothesis. The 21 events in table 1 occupy 41 trading days. When prediction errors for the 5 trading days before and after each of these events are considered also, a deliberation period of 261 days is obtained. The sample of 338 firms experienced a below normal rate of return of -6.84% for those 261 days, an average of -0.55% for the average event period of 12.43 days.[33] The abnormal performance is significantly less than zero at the 1% level for a one-tail test.[34]

When abnormal performance around each of the 21 events is investigated, it appears that events 1, 4, 13, 15, 16, 18, 19 and 21 contained unanticipated

---

[31] See the appendix for details of the calculation of the average and cumulative average prediction errors.

[32] This assumption is violated if the daily value-weighted index is serially dependent because of non-synchronous trading. Violation of the assumption results in t-statistics which are overstated.

[33] As is discussed below, 16 of the 261 days during the deliberation period are counted twice; e.g., days -5 and -4 for event 5 are the same calendar days as days $+4$ and $+5$ for event 4. The average daily abnormal performance for those 16 days is 0.03% and double counting those days does not influence the results in table 2.

[34] The daily standard error of the average prediction error for the 338 firms (σ_p) is 0.177%. Hence the standard error of the sum of the average prediction errors for the portfolio of 338 firms for a period of 261 days is 2.86%, assuming the prediction errors are serially independent.

Table 2

Cumulative prediction errors (CPE^m) for sample of 338 firms for 5 trading days before and after 21 events during APB deliberations on accounting for business combinations (%).

Event no.	Time [trading days relative to event period (EP)]											t-statistic	No. of trading days
	−5	−4	−3	−2	−1	EP	+1	+2	+3	+4	+5		
1	−0.10	−0.43	−0.78	−0.90	−0.82	−0.91	−0.96	−1.22	−1.25	−1.52	−1.65	−2.81[a]	11
2	0.07	0.04	0.32	0.17	−0.04	−0.16	−0.32	−0.35	−0.43	−0.56	−0.66	−1.16	11
3	−0.24	−0.50	−0.51	−0.39	−0.56	−0.71	−0.78	−0.45	−0.25	−0.41	−0.53	−0.92	11
4	−0.02	−0.12	−0.32	−0.88	−1.11	−1.55	−1.58	−1.61	−1.86	−1.99	−1.85	−2.92[a]	13
5	−0.13	0.01	0.48	0.36	0.45	0.06	0.14	−0.17	−0.46	−0.46	−0.31	−0.51	11
6	0.03	−0.07	0.15	0.40	−0.01	0.14	−0.01	0.27	0.30	−0.18	−0.21	−0.35	12
7	−0.05	−0.08	−0.38	−0.00	−0.09	−0.09	−0.36	−0.32	−0.35	−0.38	−0.23	−0.37	11
8	−0.03	0.12	0.30	0.41	−0.08	−0.33	−0.37	−0.20	0.22	0.09	0.04	0.06	13
9	0.42	0.29	0.24	0.09	0.40	0.30	0.74	0.91	0.99	1.04	1.12	1.91[b]	13
10	0.08	−0.10	−0.28	−0.32	−0.28	−0.49	−0.79	−0.77	−0.34	−0.29	−0.07	−0.14	11
11	0.23	0.38	0.28	0.41	0.27	0.41	0.54	0.63	0.72	0.50	0.48	0.81	12
12	−0.07	0.06	0.15	0.24	0.02	−0.07	0.05	−0.07	−0.14	−0.58	−0.55	−0.89	12
13	0.26	0.14	0.01	0.05	0.05	−0.44	−0.61	−0.99	−1.07	−1.30	−1.12	−1.70[b]	14
14	−0.30	−0.53	−0.30	0.31	0.44	0.57	0.37	0.41	0.72	0.80	0.90	1.39	13
15	−0.42	−0.18	−0.19	−0.10	0.10	−1.01	−0.99	−1.25	−1.19	−1.16	−1.07	−1.68[b]	13
16	−0.04	−0.10	−0.37	−0.18	−0.23	−0.59	−1.15	−1.31	−1.00	−1.02	−1.05	−1.77[b]	11
17	−0.32	−0.58	0.00	0.18	−0.03	−0.37	−0.25	0.54	0.47	0.42	0.36	0.63	11
18	0.00	−0.64	−0.59	−0.62	−0.31	−1.19	−1.66	−2.18	−2.47	−2.31	−2.15	−3.26[a]	14
19	−0.29	−0.13	0.03	−0.98	−0.87	−0.99	−0.69	−0.90	−1.07	−1.12	−1.40	−2.41[a]	11
20	0.24	−0.15	0.39	0.64	0.62	1.09	0.70	0.61	0.44	0.16	0.57	0.85	14
21	−0.23	−0.20	−0.69	−0.68	−0.95	−1.33	−1.17	−1.43	−1.67	−1.79	−2.21	−3.78[a]	11
Avg.	−0.04	−0.13	−0.10	−0.09	−0.15	−0.37	−0.44	−0.47	−0.46	−0.57	−0.55	−2.39[a]	12.43

[a]Significant at 2% level, two-tail test.
[b]Significant at 10% level, two-tail test.

bad news — the cumulative prediction errors for those events are -1.65%, -1.85%, -1.12%, -1.07%, -1.05%, -2.15%, -1.40% and -2.21%, all of which are significantly different from zero at the 10% level for a two-tail test. Event 9 contained unanticipated good news — the cumulative prediction error is 1.12%, which is significantly different from zero at the 10% level for a two-tail test.[35]

Cross-sectional dependence in security returns can produce 'too many' statistically significant *t*-values in calendar time event studies. In addition, serial dependence in the prediction errors can result in overstated *t*-statistics. To determine whether the results in table 2 are evidence of more than cross-sectional dependence or even serial dependence, the tests are repeated for the same sample of 338 firms over an equivalent length period prior to the APB deliberations. In that prior period, only 4 of the 21 *t*-statistics are significant at the 10% level for a two-tail test. Only 1 of those 4 *t*-statistics is negative. Consequently, I conclude that the 9 significant *t*-statistics in table 2 are evidence of abnormal performance associated with the APB deliberations.

The simple expectations model developed above in section 3 allows us to interpret the statistically significant performance around 9 events (1, 4, 9, 13, 15, 16, 18, 19 and 21) as evidence that those events induced investors to revise their expectations about APB rule endorsements. The other 12 events could have induced changes in expectations, but the absence of abnormal performance is also consistent with expectations remaining unchanged, unless we impose additional restrictions on the expectations model.

Care must be exercised in providing explanations for the results in table 2 because those explanations could degenerate into a series of ex post rationalizations for every level of observed abnormal performance. Interestingly enough, there is no evidence of any significant change in expectations around the time of the APB meeting when the final form of the rules was determined (event 20). If the study had considered only that meeting, the conclusion would be that the new merger accounting rules had no effect on the value of the equity of the sample firms. The evidence suggests that all of the impact of the rules determined at that meeting had been anticipated.[36]

[35]The abnormal performance measures calculated in table 2 are not independent across events because there is some overlap between the trading days following some events and the trading days preceding the next event. Events 4 and 5 have 2 days in common, events 7 and 8 have 2 days in common, events 8 and 9 have 3 days in common, events 9 and 10 have 1 day in common, events 11 and 12 have 5 days in common and events 18 and 19 have 3 days in common. However, double-counting those days does not affect the results. If the 'overlap' days are assigned prediction errors of zero, the same 9 events display significant abnormal performance.

[36]This evidence is surprising in view of the apparent uncertainty associated with the final APB meeting. Reports of that meeting suggest that the members were sharply divided and the final decision was reached only after prolonged debate and compromise [see Langer (1976)].

5.2. Cross-sectional abnormal performance

The second stage of the procedure suggested by the expectations model in section 3 requires cross-sectional tests to be performed on the sample of firms for those events in the 'revision in expectations' category.

An average prediction error, $\overline{PE}_i^m$, is calculated for each firm i for the period from 5 days before each event to 5 days after the event. Thus,

$$\overline{PE}_i^m = \sum_{t=-5}^{5} (PE_{it}^m/(N_m+10)),$$

where

$t \quad = -5, -4, \ldots, -1, EP, +1, \ldots, +5,$
$EP \quad =$ the event period for event m,
$PE_{it}^m =$ the prediction error for firm i for day t as defined above,
$m \quad = 1, \ldots, 21,$ and
$N_m \quad =$ the number of trading days in the event period EP.

Table 3 contains summary statistics of the cross-sectional distribution of the average prediction errors. It can be seen from table 3 that the event-related abnormal performance (reported in table 2) pervades the sample of 338 firms, i.e., the measured abnormal performance of the sample is not 'driven' by a small subset of firms. For 8 of the 9 revision in expectations events, the sign of the average prediction error, $\overline{PE}_i^m$, agrees with the sign of the sample t-statistics for a statistically significant number of firms, i.e., for more than the expected number plus 2 standard deviations (188).[37] The studentized range statistics in table 3 indicate some departures from normality, but those departures are present for both revision and non-revision events.[38]

The contracting cost theory developed above yields testable hypotheses about the cross-sectional impact of the mandated accounting rule change for business combinations. To test whether that theory explains the event-related abnormal performance reported in table 2, cross-sectional regressions are estimated. Recall that, in the expectations model, the sign of the estimated coefficient, $\hat{\beta}_k$, depends on the sign of the actual coefficient and the direction of the revision in expectations. Hypotheses 2–6 predict the signs of coefficients for unanticipated income-decreasing rule changes. The abnormal performance results in table 2 suggest that event 9 caused investors to lower

[37]The number of positive or negative averages is statistically significant for only 2 of the 12 non-revision events.
[38]Moreover, the distributions of daily stock returns are fatter-tailed than normal distributions; see Fama (1976, ch. 1).

Table 3

Summary statistics — cross-sectional distribution of average prediction errors for sample of 338 firms for 5 trading days before and after 21 events during APB deliberations on accounting for business combinations.

| Event no. | Portfolio results (from table 2) | | Cross-sectional statistics (average daily prediction errors of 338 firms) | | | | |
	t-statistic	Average daily prediction error (%)	Minimum (%)	Maximum (%)	Studentized range	Number <0	Number >0
Revision							
1	−2.81[b]	−0.15	−1.64	2.15	6.3	208[e]	130
4	−2.92[b]	−0.14	−1.53	2.58	5.7	207[e]	131
9	1.91[a]	0.10	−1.42	3.28	8.0[d]	139	199[f]
13	−1.70[a]	−0.08	−1.97	0.99	6.3	190[e]	148
15	−1.68[a]	−0.08	−2.50	4.27	7.1[c]	193[e]	145
16	−1.77[a]	−0.10	−3.26	2.65	7.5[d]	174	164
18	−3.26[b]	−0.15	−2.14	1.93	6.4	192[e]	146
19	−2.41[b]	−0.13	−3.17	1.91	7.0[c]	193[e]	145
21	−3.78[b]	−0.20	−2.57	4.45	10.5[d]	204[e]	134
Non-revision							
2	−1.16	−0.06	−1.41	1.61	6.9	187	151
3	−0.92	−0.05	−1.76	1.63	6.9	185	153
5	−0.51	−0.03	−2.67	1.61	8.1[d]	167	171
6	−0.35	−0.02	−2.03	2.41	7.8[d]	169	169
7	−0.37	−0.02	−1.70	1.65	7.4[c]	176	162
8	0.06	0.00	−2.09	2.38	8.1[d]	175	163
10	−0.14	−0.01	−1.84	1.51	6.1	173	165
11	0.81	0.04	−2.66	1.77	7.5[d]	157	181
12	−0.89	−0.05	−1.98	1.44	6.5	179	159
14	1.39	0.07	−2.11	2.03	6.7	145	193[f]
17	0.63	0.03	−2.27	3.01	6.9	164	174
20	0.85	0.04	−1.91	1.93	6.7	147	191[f]

[a]Significant at 10% level, two-tail test.

[b]Significant at 2% level, two-tail test.

[c]Greater than 0.95 fractile of Studentized Range in samples of 500 from a Normal distribution.

[d]Greater than 0.99 fractile of Studentized Range in samples of 500 from a Normal distribution.

[e]Number of negative observations is greater than 2 standard deviations from the expected value of 169.

[f]Number of positive observations is greater than 2 standard deviations from the expected value of 169.

their estimate of the probability of an income-decreasing change. Thus, in estimating the cross-sectional regressions, the signs of the abnormal performance measures for event 9 are reversed, and the estimated coefficients should have the signs predicted by Hypotheses 2–6.

The average prediction errors, $\overline{PE_i^m}$, are used as dependent variables in separate regressions for each of the 9 significant events.[39] In addition, the average prediction error for the 9 significant events for each firm $\overline{\overline{PE}}_i$, is used as an independent variable where

$$\overline{\overline{PE}}_i = \left(\sum_{m=1}^{9} PE_i^{m*}(N_m+10)^*S \right) \Big/ \left(\sum_{m=1}^{9} (N_m+10) \right),$$

where

$m = 1, \ldots, 9$ for the 9 significant events in table 2,
$S = -1$ for event 9, the 3rd significant event, and $+1$ otherwise.

Thus, 10 separate regressions are estimated — 1 using the average prediction error, $\overline{\overline{PE}}_i$, as the dependent variable, and 9 using the average prediction errors for each significant event, $\overline{PE_i^m}$.[40]

For the 338 firms in the sample, the following 10 cross-sectional regressions are estimated:

$$\overline{\overline{PE}}_i = \beta_0 + \beta_1 \frac{PUB_i}{MV_i} + \beta_2 \frac{PVT_i}{MV_i} + \beta_3 \frac{CALL_i}{MV_i} + \beta_4 \frac{CONV_i}{MV_i}$$
$$+ \beta_5 LSIZE_i + \varepsilon_i, \tag{2}$$

$$\overline{PE_i^m} = \beta_0^m + \beta_1^m \frac{PUB_i}{MV_i} + \beta_2^m \frac{PVT_i}{MV_i} + \beta_3^m \frac{CALL_i}{MV_i} + \beta_4^m \frac{CONV_i}{MV_i}$$
$$+ \beta_5^m LSIZE_i + \varepsilon_i^m, \qquad\qquad m = 1, \ldots, 9. \tag{3}$$

---

[39] Strictly, the dependent variable is $PE_i^{m*}S$, where $S = -1$ for event 9, and $+1$ for the other 8 significant events.

[40] In Leftwich (1980a) an additional regression is obtained by pooling the observations used in the 9 separate regressions for the significant events. The pooled equation has an intercept and a dummy variable for each of the events, but the coefficients of the independent variables are constrained to be identical across the 9 events. By comparing the sum of squares from the unconstrained regressions (the 9 separate regressions) with the sum of squares from the constrained regression (the pooled regression), an F-statistic is obtained to test whether the vector of coefficients is identical across events. Since the estimated coefficients are a function of the coefficients of the value function and the change in expectations, this is actually a test of whether $\sum_{j=1}^{J} b_{jk}(p_{jt} - p_{jt} - p_{jt+1})$ is the same for different events. For all of the F tests reported in Leftwich (1980a), the F-value exceeds the critical value of the 99th percentile of the F-distribution, so it must be concluded that the estimated coefficients are not equal across events. Thus, either the change in expectations is not equal for each event, or the coefficients of the value function differ across events (or both expectations and coefficients differ across events).

The independent variables are defined in table 4. Estimates of the parameters and their standard errors obtained from the 10 regressions are presented in table 5, together with the adjusted R^2 of the regressions and the studentized ranges of the residuals from the regressions.

Table 4

Definitions of independent variables for each firm in cross-sectional tests.

Independent variable	Definition
PUB	Book value of public debt
PVT	Book value of private debt
CALL	Book value of callable debt
CONV	Book value of convertible debt
MV	Market value of the equity
LSIZE	Natural log of *SIZE* where *SIZE* = market value of equity plus book value of long-term liabilities

Hypothesis 2 predicts that the decline in value of the equity is an increasing function of the amount of the firm's outstanding debt. Thus, the sign of the coefficients of PUB_i/MV_i and PVT_i/MV_i should be negative. Hypothesis 3 predicts that the decline is greater for public debt than for private debt; i.e., the coefficient of PUB_i/MV_i should be greater (in absolute magnitude) than the coefficient of PVT_i/MV_i. Hypotheses 4 and 5 predict that the decline in equity value is lower if the debt is callable or convertible; i.e., the coefficients of $CALL_i/MV_i$ and $CONV_i/MV_i$ should be positive.

Contracting theory does not yield any predictions about size per se. A size variable is included in the regression for two reasons. First, there is some recent evidence that smaller firms earn positive abnormal returns,[41] suggesting a negative coefficient on the $LSIZE_i$ variable in regressions (2) and (3). Second, some studies which examine management's choices of accounting techniques find that the size of the firm has some explanatory power. These studies argue that managers of larger firms prefer techniques which reduce reported income. Larger firms, it is argued, are subject to closer scrutiny by politicians and regulators and increased reported earnings can be used as justification for increased government control of the firm.[42] According to this line of reasoning, the sign of the $LSIZE_i$ coefficient should be positive because the new merger accounting rules reduced reported

[41] For example, Banz (1979) concludes that his results are consistent with the hypothesis that information is more costly for small firms.

[42] See Watts and Zimmerman (1978) and Hagerman and Zmijewski (1979). The explanation of managers' incentives to choose such methods is set out in Watts (1977).

Table 5

Estimates of parameters from cross-sectional regression test on abnormal returns to sample of 338 firms for period of APB deliberation on accounting for business combinations (t-values in parentheses).

$$\overline{\overline{PE}} = \beta_0 + \beta_1 \frac{PUB_i}{MV_i} + \beta_2 \frac{PVT_i}{MV_i} + \beta_3 \frac{CALL_i}{MV_i} + \beta_4 \frac{CONV_i}{MV_i} + \beta_5 LSIZE_i + \varepsilon_i,$$

$$\overline{PE}^m = \beta_0^m + \beta_1^m \frac{PUB_i}{MV_i} + \beta_2^m \frac{PVT_i}{MV_i} + \beta_3^m \frac{CALL_i}{MV_i} + \beta_4^m \frac{CONV_i}{MV_i} + \beta_5^m LSIZE_i + \varepsilon_i^m,$$

$$m = 1, 2, \ldots, 9.$$

Coefficient (Predicted sign)								
β_0 $(-)$	β_1 $(-)$	β_2 $(-)$	β_3 $(+)$	β_4 $(+)$	β_5 $(?)$	$\bar{R}^2$ (%)	F	SR
Average (PE_i)								
0.005 (0.3)	−0.075 (−1.2)	−0.101 (−4.5)[b]	0.103 (1.7)[a]	−0.005 (−0.1)	0.063 (6.6)[b]	18.3	16.1[b]	6.9

Event no.								
1	−0.093 (−1.7)[a]	−0.289 (−1.7)[a]	−0.045 (−0.7)	0.261 (1.5)	0.138 (1.0)	0.035 (1.3)	0.0	1.0	6.3
4	0.000 (0.0)	0.033 (0.3)	−0.140 (−3.1)[b]	0.040 (0.3)	−0.014 (−0.1)	0.065 (3.3)[b]	6.0	5.3[b]	5.7
9	−0.089 (−1.7)[a]	0.204 (1.2)	−0.026 (−0.4)	−0.037 (−0.2)	0.029 (0.2)	0.022 (0.8)	0.9	1.6	7.9[++]
13	0.097 (2.4)[b]	−0.320 (−2.4)[b]	−0.127 (−2.7)[b]	0.279 (2.2)[a]	0.126 (1.2)	0.091 (4.5)[b]	8.3	7.1[b]	5.9
15	0.046 (0.9)	−0.281 (−1.7)[a]	−0.113 (−1.8)[a]	0.381 (2.3)[a]	−0.203 (−1.4)	0.059 (2.2)[a]	3.8	3.7[b]	7.2[+]
16	−0.021 (−0.3)	0.206 (0.9)	0.045 (0.6)	−0.309 (−1.4)	0.047 (0.3)	0.048 (1.4)	0.0	0.8	7.8[++]
18	0.037 (0.7)	−0.234 (−1.3)	−0.169 (−2.6)[b]	0.255 (1.5)	−0.029 (−0.2)	0.085 (3.0)[b]	4.9	4.5[b]	6.3
19	−0.011 (−0.2)	0.059 (0.3)	−0.215 (−2.9)[b]	0.023 (0.1)	0.011 (0.1)	0.029 (0.9)	2.2	2.5[a]	7.1[+]
21	0.034 (0.6)	0.078 (0.4)	−0.081 (−1.2)	−0.093 (−0.5)	−0.143 (−0.9)	0.123 (4.2)[b]	5.8	5.2[b]	11.0[++]

[a]Significant at 10% level, two-tail test for t-statistics, or exceeds 0.95 fractile of F-distribution.
[b]Significant at 2% level, two-tail test or exceeds the 0.99 fractile of F-distribution.
[+(−)]Greater than (less than) 0.95 fractile (0.05 fractile) of Studentized Range (SR) in samples of size 500 from a Normal Distribution.
[++(−−)]Greater than (less than) 0.99 fractile (0.01 fractile) of Studentized Range (SR) in samples of size 500 from a Normal Distribution.

income. The two effects of size operate in different directions and there is no clear prediction for the sign of the $LSIZE_i$ coefficient.

The results in table 5 support some of the hypotheses. For the average regression, the coefficients on PVT_i/MV_i and $CALL_i/MV_i$ have the predicted sign and are significantly different from zero at the 10% level for a two-tail test. The coefficient on PUB_i/MV_i has the correct sign and the coefficient on $CONV_i/MV_i$ has the wrong sign, but none of these coefficients is significant at usual levels of significance. The coefficient of PUB_i/MV_i is numerically smaller than the coefficient of PVT_i/MV_i contrary to Hypothesis 3 but the difference is not statistically significant. The $LSIZE_i$ coefficient is significantly greater than zero at the 2% level for a two-tail test. The adjusted R^2 for the average regression is 18.3% and the F-statistic (to test the hypothesis that the vector of regression coefficients differs from the null vector) is significant at the 1% level.

The explanatory power of the regression is reduced when it is estimated for each separate event date. The highest adjusted R^2 for the separate regressions is 8.3% for event 13. However, 6 of the 9 F-statistics are significant at the 5% level, and 5 of those are significant at the 1% level. There are some sign reversals in the coefficients when estimated for different events, but none of the reversals is significant at usual levels of significance. The PUB_i/MV_i, PVT_i/MV_i and $CALL_i/MV_i$ coefficients are significantly different from zero (in the predicted direction) for several of the separate regressions. Hypothesis 3 predicts that the coefficient of PUB_i/MV_i is negative and numerically greater than the coefficient of PVT_i/MV_i. In only 1 of the 9 separate regressions (event 13), is the difference between the coefficients significantly different from zero — the t-statistic is 1.66. In none of the separate regressions is the coefficient of $CONV_i/MV_i$ different from zero at usual significance levels.

The studentized range (SR) statistics for the separate regressions indicate that the residuals from some of the regressions (events 9, 15, 16, 19 and 21) are not normally distributed. These are the same events for which extreme SR-statistics are obtained in distributions of the dependent variable (reported in table 3 above). The studentized range statistic for the average regression is consistent with the normality assumption.

Regression eqs. (2) and (3) do not control for all of the variables hypothesized to affect the equity value of the firm when there is an accounting rule change. Hypothesis 6 predicts that the decline in equity value is greater for firms which have outstanding debt with longer term to maturity. In addition, Leftwich (1980a) predicts that the decline in equity value is greater for firms which are closer to the constraints in the lending agreements. The cross-sectional regressions in table 5 are re-estimated to test the effect of the additional variables (maturity and distance from the constraints).[43] Leftwich (1980a) concludes that neither of those variables has any explanatory power.

An alternative methodology provides additional insights into the cross-sectional performance of the sample of firms for the 9 significant events. Noreen and Sepe (1981) develop a 'price reversal' methodology to investigate whether individual firm's abnormal returns are correlated when market expectations about rule changes are reversed. That is, they test to see whether firms that experience negative abnormal performance when a rule change is proposed earn, on average, positive abnormal returns when the proposal is abandoned. In the business combinations deliberation sequence, we can identify 9 separate revisions in expectations — 8 inducing negative abnormal performance and 1 inducing positive abnormal performance. These 9 events yield 36 pairwise correlations. The correlation is predicted to be negative for 8 of the pairwise comparisons (i.e., for all comparisons with event 9) and positive for the remaining 28 pairwise comparisons. Of the 36 correlation coefficients[44] for the sample of 338 firms, 11 are greater than 2 standard deviations from zero and 9 of those 11 (25% of the total) are in the predicted direction — 7 of those 9 are positive and the remaining 2 are negative. To provide an interpretation of this result, the correlation matrix is estimated for all 210 of the separate pairwise comparisons for the 21 events. Of the 174 comparisons not involving significant events, 29 (17%) yield correlation coefficients which are more than two standard deviations from zero.[45] Thus, it appears that the 9 significant events have the predicted systematic effect across firms, i.e., on average, the same firms 'lose' for 8 of the events, and the losers from those events 'gain' for event 9.

6. Interpretation and summary of the results

6.1. Interpretation of the results

The final 1970 APB ruling on merger accounting had no direct effects on firms' cash flows, nor did it provide securityholders with additional information; i.e., the ruling appeared to make only cosmetic changes. However, the event-related abnormal performance tests in the previous section indicate that stockholders of a sample of firms experienced negative

---

[43]Two alternative proxies for the distance from the constraints are tested — the rating of a firm's debt and the inventory of payable funds. Kalay (1979) discusses the inventory of payable funds and its role in lending agreements. The inventory number represents the maximum amount of retained earnings that the firm can pay out without violating its lending agreements. The results are insensitive to the proxy that is used.

[44]The tests are performed using both Pearson product-moment and Spearman rank correlation coefficients. The results are insensitive to the definition of the correlation coefficient.

[45]When this test is repeated for the same sample of firms for a period outside the APB deliberation period, 15% of the correlation coefficients are more than 2 standard deviations from zero.

abnormal returns during the APB deliberation process. Those tests support the hypothesis that the APB ruling was not perfectly anticipated and the ruling had a real impact on the equity value of firms, despite its cosmetic appearance.

The results in the previous section provide some insights into the more general problems associated with measuring the impact of mandated accounting changes. Twenty-one events during the APB deliberations on purchase-pooling are identified and abnormal performance is measured around each of those events. Although the abnormal performance is significantly negative when averaged across all events, the evidence suggests that only 9 of the events caused market participants to significantly revise their expectations concerning the final merger accounting rule. The abnormal performance is significantly negative for only 8 events, significantly positive for 1 event and insignificantly different from zero for 12 other events. If a researcher investigated abnormal performance around only 1 of the 21 events, the negative abnormal performance may not be detected — no abnormal performance would be detected if 1 of 12 events were selected, positive abnormal performance would be measured if the one event were chosen, and negative abnormal performance would be detected only if 1 of 8 events were selected.

The cross-sectional tests partially support the argument that there were real effects associated with the APB ruling because the mandated accounting change affected restrictive covenants in firms' lending agreements. However, some caveats are in order. The following types of econometric problems are associated with the cross-sectional regressions:

(i) cross-sectional dependence of dependent variables,
(ii) heteroscedasticity, and
(iii) multicollinearity.

(i) The dependent variables are likely to be cross-sectionally correlated due to the presence of industry effects. Consequently, the disturbance terms are likely to be positively correlated and the reported R^2 and t-statistics are biased upwards. To gauge the severity of the cross-sectional dependence problem, the cross-sectional regressions are estimated for the 12 non-significant events. Of the 60 t-statistics for the independent variables (excluding the constant) from those 12 separate regressions, only 5 are significant at the 10% level for a two-tail test. Only 1 of the adjusted R^2-values exceeds 3%. By contrast, 15 of the 45 t-statistics for the independent variables in table 5 are significant at the 10% level for a two-tail test. Moreover, 5 of the 9 adjusted R^2-values exceed 3%.

Recall that the event-related tests in table 2 are replicated for a prior period and only 4 significant 'events' are discovered. When the cross-sectional tests in table 5 are replicated on those 4 significant events, only

Table 6

Matrix of correlation coefficients between independent variables for sample of 338 firms.

	PUB/MV	PVT/MV	CALL/MV	CONV/MV	LSIZE
PUB/MV	1.000				
PVT/MV	0.466[a]	1.000			
CALL/MV	0.926[a]	0.567[a]	1.000		
CONV/MV	0.456[a]	0.438[a]	0.420[a]	1.000	
LSIZE	0.046	−0.097	0.058	−0.054	1.000

[a]Greater than 2 standard errors from zero.

4 of the 20 t-statistics for the independent variables (excluding the constant) are significant at the 10% level for a two-tail test, and 1 of those has the opposite sign to that revealed in table 5. Only 1 of the adjusted R^2-values exceeds 3% — it is 4.5%.[46] Consequently, I conclude that the results in table 5 can be interpreted as more than an artifact of the cross-sectional dependence.[47]

(ii) The variance of the dependent variables in the cross-sectional regressions is not constant across firms because the residual variance from the market model is not constant. Thus, heteroscedasticity can be induced in the residuals from the cross-sectional regressions. To control for this problem, the cross-sectional regressions are re-estimated by standardizing the individual observations by the square root of the residual variance from the market model. The heteroscedasticity correction does not alter the results.

(iii) The independent variables are correlated. For example, table 6 contains the matrix of the correlation coefficients of the independent variables from the regressions reported in table 5. Six of the 10 correlation coefficients are more than 2 standard deviations from zero — the critical value for a correlation coefficient based on 338 observations is 0.108. If any multicollinearity is induced in the independent variables, the estimated regression coefficients are sensitive to adding or dropping observations and it is difficult to isolate the effects of particular independent variables. To investigate the sensitivity of the results, each of the 10 regressions in table 5 is replicated 10 times and 10% of the observations are deleted for each of the 10 replications. The results are insensitive to deleting those observations. For example, the signs of the

[46]When the cross-sectional tests are replicated on the 17 non-significant 'events' for the prior period, only 11 of the 85 t-statistics for the independent variables (excluding the constant) are significant at the 10% level. Only 5 of the 17 adjusted R^2-values exceed 3%.

[47]Generalized least squares (GLS) estimation could provide a more powerful test. However, estimation of the covariance matrix presents further problems, and it is not clear what assumptions should be made to simplify the structure of the matrix to be estimated.

t-statistics are unchanged across all 10 replications for 35 of the 60 (6 coefficients for 10 separate regressions) sequences, and there is only 1 sign reversal in a further 10 of those sequences.[48] Moreover, not one sign reversal in the entire set of replications is of sufficient magnitude to change the direction of statistical significance. The adjusted R^2 from the regressions is also insensitive to deleting 10% of the observations. In short, dropping 10% of the observations yields 10 sets of results that differ little from those presented in table 5.

6.2. Summary of the results

The contracting cost theory presented in this paper suggests that some mandated changes in accounting principles impose costs on equityholders by altering the accounting numbers defined in the restrictive covenants in the firms' lending agreements. The evidence in this paper only partially supports the contracting cost theory predictions. For example, as predicted, it appears that the costs imposed on a firm by the mandatory change in merger accounting rules were an increasing function of the amount of debt outstanding and were lower if the debt was callable. However, there is little evidence that the costs were higher if the debt was publicly held, and there is no support for the argument that those costs were lower if the debt was convertible or closer to maturity. The evidence suggests that the costs were lower other things equal, for larger firms. The size relationship is disturbingly large and it is difficult to interpret that relationship because size is probably a proxy for some omitted variable(s).

Contracting cost theory provides, at best, an incomplete explanation of the observed abnormal performance of firms during the APB deliberations on business combinations. At present we have few competing theories to explain why apparently cosmetic accounting changes affect the equity value of firms. Some of the ambiguities associated with the results of this study may be resolved by applying similar methodology to examine the impact of other mandated changes in accounting principles on different samples of firms.

Appendix

Calculation of average and cumulative average prediction errors for event-related abnormal performance tests

An average prediction error for the sample of firms is calculated for each of the 5 days *before* each event (BPE_t^m), for the N_m days during each event (DPE^m), and for each of the 5 days *after* each event (APE_t^m). The average

---

[48]This result is even stronger when the magnitude of the *t*-statistics is considered — many of the sign reversal occur for *t*-statistics which are less than $|0.5|$ in table 5.

prediction errors are calculated as[49]

$$BPE_t^m = \sum_{i=1}^{338} PE_{it}^m/338, \qquad m=1,2,\ldots,21, \quad t=-5,-4,\ldots,-1,$$

where PE_{it}^m is the prediction error for firm i at time t relative to meeting m,

$$DPE^m = \sum_{t=0}^{N_m} \sum_{i=1}^{338} PE_{it}^m/338, \qquad m=1,2,\ldots,21,$$

where N_m is the number of trading days in event m,

$$APE_t^m = \sum_{i=1}^{338} PE_{it}^m/338, \qquad m=1,2,\ldots,21, \quad t=+1,+2,\ldots,+5.$$

The averaging procedure results in 11 averages for each of the 21 events, 5 for the days prior to the event (BPE), 1 for the event period (DPE), and the remaining 5 for the days subsequent to the event (APE). To summarize the abnormal performance for each event, an average prediction error is calculated, PE^m, as

$$PE^m = \frac{1}{(N_m+10)}\left\{\sum_{t=-5}^{-1} BPE_t^m + DPE^m + \sum_{t=+1}^{+5} APE_t^m\right\}.$$

Conventionally, studies of abnormal performances report both average and cumulative prediction errors. Calculation and interpretation of cumulative prediction errors are somewhat more complicated in this study because the number of trading days in the event period is not identical across events. The cumulative prediction error for each event is defined as

$$CPE_\tau^m = \sum_{t=-5}^{\tau} BPE_t^m, \qquad\qquad -5 \leqq \tau \leqq -1,$$

$$= \sum_{t=-5}^{-1} BPE_t^m + DPE^m, \qquad\qquad \tau = 0,$$

$$= \sum_{t=-5}^{-1} BPE_t^m + DPE^m + \sum_{t=+1}^{\tau} APE_\tau^m, \qquad +1 \leqq \tau \leqq +5.$$

---

[49]Strictly, the averages are not *always* calculated across all 338 firms. Occasionally, the firm's returns are missing on the file for a particular day. For those days (and the subsequent day), the average prediction error is calculated over the number of firms with data available. The notation is simplified by setting the divisor at 338 in the exposition.

The cumulative prediction error averaged across events, $\overline{CPE_\tau}$, is defined as

$$\overline{CPE_\tau} = \sum_{m=1}^{21} CPE_\tau^m / 21 , \qquad \tau = -5, -4, \ldots, +5.$$

References

Accounting Principles Board, 1970, Opinion no. 16, Accounting for business combinations (American Institute of Certified Public Accountants, New York).

Accounting Principles Board, 1970, Opinion no. 17, Accounting for intangible assets (American Institute of Certified Public Accountants, New York).

American Bar Foundation, 1971, Commentaries on indentures (American Bar Foundation, Chicago, IL).

Banz, Rolf W., 1979, The relationship between market value and return of common stocks, Working paper no. 29 (Center for Research in Security Prices, Graduate School of Business, University of Chicago, Chicago, IL).

Black, Fischer and Myron Scholes, 1973, The pricing of options and corporate liabilities, Journal of Political Economy 81, 637–654.

Briloff, A.J., 1968, Dirty pooling, Barron's (July 15, 1968), 3, 14, 16, 18, 20 and 24.

Briloff, A.J., 1969, Much-abused goodwill, Barron's (April 28, 1969), 1, 9, 10, 12, 14, 16 and 18.

Brown, Stephen J. and Jerold B. Warner, 1980, Measuring security price performance, Journal of Financial Economics 8, 205–258.

Catlett, George R. and Norman O. Olson, 1968, Accounting for goodwill, Accounting research study no. 10 (American Institute of Certified Public Accountants, New York).

Collins, Daniel W. and Warren T. Dent, 1979, The proposed elimination of full cost accounting in the extractive petroleum industry, Journal of Accounting and Economics 1, 3–44.

Collins, Daniel W., Michael S. Rozeff and Dan S. Dhaliwal, 1981, A cross-sectional analysis of the economic determinants of market reaction to proposed mandatory accounting changes in the oil and gas industry, Journal of Accounting and Economics, this issue.

Dyckman, Thomas R. and Abbie J. Smith, 1979, Financial accounting and reporting by oil and gas producing companies: A study of information effects, Journal of Accounting and Economics 1, 45–75.

Fama, Eugene F., 1976, Foundations of finance (Basic Books, New York).

Fama, Eugene F. and Merton M. Miller, 1972, The theory of finance (Holt, Rinehart and Winston, New York).

Fama, Eugene F., Lawrence Fisher, Michael C. Jensen and Richard Roll, 1969, The adjustment of stock prices to new information, International Economic Review 10, 1–21.

Fogelson, James H., 1978, The impact of changes in accounting principles on restrictive covenants in credit agreements and indentures, Business Lawyer 33, 769–787.

Foster, George, 1979, Briloff and the capital market, Journal of Accounting Research 17, 262–274.

Foster, George, 1980, Accounting policy decisions and capital market research, Journal of Accounting and Economics 2, 29–62.

Fryling, Henry H., 1964, Private placement financing — Lenders' procedural guide, Proceedings of Association of Life Insurance Counsel, 797–838.

Galai, Dan and Ronald W. Masulis, 1976, The option pricing model and the risk factor of stock, Journal of Financial Economics 3, 53–81.

Hagerman, Robert L. and Mark E. Zmijewski, 1979, Some economic determinants of accounting policy choice, Journal of Accounting and Economics 1, 141–162.

Holthausen, Robert W., 1981, Theory and evidence on the effect of bond covenants and management compensation contracts on the choice of accounting techniques; The case of the depreciation switch-back, Journal of Accounting and Economics, this issue.

Jensen, Michael C. and William H. Meckling, 1976, Theory of the firm: Managerial behavior, agency costs and ownership structure, Journal of Financial Economics 3, 305–360.

Kalay, Avner, 1979, Toward a theory of corporate dividend policy, Unpublished Ph.D. thesis (University of Rochester, Rochester, NY).

Langer, Russell Davis, 1976, Accounting as a variable in mergers, Unpublished Ph.D. dissertation (University of California, Berkeley, CA).

Leftwich, Richard W., 1980a, Evidence of the impact of mandatory changes in accounting principles on corporate loan agreements, Working paper no. MERC 80-10 (Managerial Economics Research Center, University of Rochester, Rochester, NY).

Leftwich, Richard W., 1980b, Accounting regulation, market failures and market solutions: Some evidence, Working paper no. MERC 80-09 (Managerial Economics Research Center, University of Rochester, Rochester, NY).

Lev, Baruch, 1979, The impact of accounting regulation on the stock market: The case of oil and gas companies, Accounting Review LIV, 485–503.

Libby, Robert, 1972, The early impact of APB Opinions no. 16 and 17 — An empirical study, CPA Journal XLII, 837–842.

Maddala, G.S., 1977, Econometrics (McGraw-Hill, New York).

Maycock, Roland and George P. Jenkins, 1958, Direct loans by life insurance companies to industrial corporations, Proceedings of Association of Life Insurance Counsel (New York) 201–242.

Mikkelson, Wayne, 1981, An examination of the agency cost rationale for convertible bonds, Journal of Financial Economics, forthcoming.

Myers, Stewart C., 1977, Determinants of corporate borrowing, Journal of Financial Economics 5, 147–175.

Noreen, Eric and James Sepe, 1981, Market reactions to accounting policy deliberations: The inflation accounting case, Accounting Review, forthcoming.

Rayburn, Frank R., 1975, Another look at the impact of Accounting Principles Board Opinion no. 16 — An empirical study, Mergers and Acquisitions 10, 7–9.

Scholes, Myron and Joseph Williams, 1977, Estimating betas from nonsynchronous data, Journal of Financial Economics 5, 309–327.

Schwert, G. William, 1980, Using financial data to measure effects of regulation, Journal of Law and Economics, forthcoming.

Simmons, Richard S., 1972, Drafting of commercial bank loan agreements, Business Lawyer 28, 179–208.

Smith, Clifford W. and Jerold B. Warner, 1979, On financial contracting: An analysis of bond covenants, Journal of Financial Economics 7, 117–161.

Watts, Ross L., 1977, Corporate financial statements: A product of the market and political processes, Australian Journal of Management 2, 53–75.

Watts, Ross and Jerold Zimmerman, 1978, Towards a positive theory of the determination of accounting standards, Accounting Review LIII, 112–134.

Wyatt, Arthur R., 1963, A critical study of accounting for business combinations, Accounting research study no. 5 (American Institute of Certified Public Accountants, New York).

Zeff, Stephen A., 1972, Forging accounting principles in five countries: A history and an analysis of trends (Stipes Publishing Company, Champaign, IL).

Zinbarg, Edward D., 1975, The private placement loan agreement, Financial Analysts Journal 31, 33–52.

Accounting Information in Private Markets: Evidence from Private Lending Agreements

Richard Leftwich

ABSTRACT: This paper contains evidence of accounting measurement rules that are negotiated in private corporate lending agreements. The negotiated sets of rules differ from the regulated set of accounting rules (generally accepted accounting principles). Moreover, the differences between regulated and negotiated rules are systematic and consistent with the economic incentives of borrowers and lenders. Private parties in the market for accounting information are able to produce for themselves at least some of the information required for monitoring lending agreements. The evidence and analysis have implications for:

1. The voluntary choice of accounting rules,
2. The superiority of alternative accounting rules, and
3. The demand for a diverse set of accounting rules.

I. INTRODUCTION

THIS paper presents evidence of accounting measurement rules that are negotiated in a private market—the market for information used in restrictive covenants in lending agreements. The evidence indicates that parties to lending agreements select accounting measurement rules that differ from generally accepted accounting principles (GAAP), which can be viewed as the regulated set of accounting measurement rules. For some transactions, the observed, privately negotiated measurement rules differ markedly from the regulated set of measurement rules. For other transactions, the privately negotiated rules prohibit use of some of the generally accepted measurement rules. For transactions not specifically mentioned in the privately negotiated rules, the regulated method is accepted *in toto*. The observed differences between the negotiated set and the regulated set are systematic—the negotiated set of measurement rules restricts management's ability to choose accounting rules that

This paper is part of my Ph.D. dissertation, completed at the University of Rochester. I would like to thank the members of my committee for their advice and encouragement: Michael Jensen (Chairman), William Schwert, Ross Watts, and Jerold Zimmerman. Robert Holthausen provided valuable comments on earlier drafts, and I have benefited from the comments of Bill Baber, Linda DeAngelo, Nicholas Dopuch, George Foster, Lauren Kelly, and Abbie Smith. Two anonymous reviewers of this journal provided constructive criticisms that improved the analysis and exposition in the paper.

Financial support for the dissertation was provided by the Ernst & Whinney Foundation and the Managerial Economics Research Center of the Graduate School of Management at the University of Rochester. I am grateful for that support.

Richard Leftwich is Associate Professor of Accounting and Finance, University of Chicago.

Manuscript received October 1981.
Revision received February 1982.
Accepted March 1982.

favor stockholders at the expense of bondholders.

The evidence and analysis in this paper support two fundamental propositions. First, the choice of accounting rules in private lending agreements is not a matter of indifference to borrowers and lenders when that choice involves economic tradeoffs between the costs and benefits of alternative rules. Second, borrowers and lenders exercise their choice by selecting a set of measurement rules that reduces the potential conflict of interests between stockholders and bondholders.

The results of the analysis have implications for:

1. The voluntary choice of accounting rules,
2. The superiority of alternative accounting rules, and
3. The demand for a diverse set of accounting rules.

1. The voluntary choice of accounting rules.

Criticisms of accounting measurement rules are common in the academic literature and in the financial press.[1] Typically, critics allege that reported accounting numbers are misleading, subject to manipulation, and/or irrelevant. Increased regulation of accounting standards is often proposed as a remedy for some of these alleged defects. However, little attention has been devoted to studying whether, or how, the alleged defects are circumvented in private contracts that rely on accounting numbers. The evidence in this paper suggests that, without regulatory intervention, one group of users of accounting numbers (borrowers and lenders in the private debt market) identifies and remedies many of the perceived defects of accounting numbers.

Those users devise entirely new accounting rules for some transactions and discriminate among existing accounting rules for other transactions. It is incumbent upon critics of accounting measurement rules to explain why users in other markets voluntarily rely on accounting numbers that are misleading, subject to manipulation, or irrelevant.

2. The superiority of alternative accounting rules.

Some researchers devise accounting measurement rules which they claim are superior to existing rules on *a priori* grounds.[2] However, there is a paucity of evidence of the costs and benefits of alternative accounting rules. The sources of some of those costs and benefits can be inferred by examining measurement rules that are endorsed, modified, or rejected in private contracts. As Benston and Krasney [1978, pp. 5–6] observe, if users systematically reject or modify rules with particular properties (e.g., rules allowing upward revaluation of assets), we can infer that those rules are not cost-justified for that group of users:

> Potential lenders in the direct placement market can request any type of financial information from prospective borrowers, regardless of whether it is publicly available.
>
> Prospective borrowers may comply with the modified information requests or terms, or may search for alternative sources of funds instead. . . . One may view the amount and type of information provided as the outcome of a market process in which the supply and demand functions are relatively unconstrained, unlike the public market for financial accounting information.

---

[1] See, for example, Chambers [1965], Sterling [1970], and Briloff [1970 and 1976].

[2] See, for example, Chambers [1966].

3. The demand for a diverse set of accounting rules.

The evidence in this paper suggests that there is a demand for a diverse set of accounting measurement rules. Although borrowers and lenders in the private lending market use GAAP as a "benchmark," or starting point, for negotiated accounting measurement rules, they "undo" some measurement rules, such as equity accounting, endorsed by GAAP. To that extent, the contract-negotiation and record-keeping costs of using GAAP as a benchmark would be lower for those users if GAAP were to exclude the rules. However, it is unlikely that there would be unanimous agreement among users concerning which rules to exclude from GAAP. Accounting measurement rules in the private lending market are tailored for a specific purpose (monitoring compliance with debt agreements). Users in other markets probably choose rules designed for their own particular purposes.[3] Thus, regulators impose costs on some users when they reduce the diversity of GAAP, even if users in other markets prefer the less diverse rules.

In this paper, evidence of the accounting measurement rules negotiated in private lending agreements is obtained from a sample of private lending agreements and from *Commentaries on Indentures* [American Bar Foundation, 1971] (hereafter called *Commentaries*). *Commentaries* contains examples of covenants and definitions of accounting numbers considered to be representative of best practice by lawyers actively engaged in representing issuers and purchasers of corporate bonds. To contrast negotiated measurement rules with GAAP (the regulated set of measurement rules), I first develop a taxonomy of the pro-

nouncements of accounting regulatory bodies during the period 1937 to 1978. Then, for each category, I compare the regulated accounting method with the privately negotiated method to determine whether the negotiated method involves a measurement rule that is (i) entirely outside GAAP, (ii) consistent with GAAP, but excludes one or more of the generally accepted alternatives, or (iii) entirely consistent with GAAP.

I analyze the differences between the regulated and negotiated sets of measurement rules and argue that there is a systematic explanation for the differences. The observed differences between negotiated and regulated measurement rules are consistent with the hypothesis that borrowers and lenders act to restrict management's ability to transfer wealth from stockholders to bondholders. Negotiated measurement rules reduce management's ability to use accounting methods to relax the restrictions imposed in lending agreements—negotiated rules ensure that certain book charges *are* made to *reduce* reported income and asset numbers and that other book charges are *not* made to *increase* reported income and asset numbers. Not only do participants in this market adopt a set of measurement rules that is at variance with GAAP, they adopt a set of rules that appears well-suited to their hypothesized purpose.

Outline of the Paper

Section II, "Contracting in the Lending Market," explains the potential conflict of interest between borrowers and lenders and reviews the costly contracting arrangements that evolve to reduce the potential conflict. The origins of the

---

[3] There is a dearth of empirical evidence concerning the choice of accounting measurement rules in other contracts, such as profit-sharing contracts in the movie industry.

evidence used in this paper are discussed in Section III, "Source and Nature of the Evidence." Section IV, "Data and Analysis," contains summaries of the evidence and the analysis of the evidence: the accounting measurement rules that are negotiated in lending agreements are compared with generally accepted accounting principles, and differences between the negotiated rules and accepted principles are analyzed to provide systematic explanations for the differences. Brief conclusions are contained in Section V, "Conclusions."

II. Contracting in the Lending Market

Corporate loan agreements restrict the borrowing firm's investment and financing decisions. Some of the activities of the borrowing firm which are commonly subject to restrictions are:[4]

a) payment of dividends,
b) incurrence of additional debt,
c) maintenance of working capital,
d) participation in mergers,
e) disposition of all or part of the assets of the firm, and
f) the purchase of certain securities.

The constraints imposed by restrictive covenants, especially those on dividends, debt, and working capital, depend on the corporation's performance and financial position, measured by such accounting numbers as: net income, net tangible assets, tangible net worth, current assets, and current liabilities. Accounting principles of asset valuation and income determination (accounting measurement rules) used in calculating those accounting numbers partially determine the level of the constraints specified in the agreements. Virtually all lending agreements contain specific references to measurement rules that are to be used in calcu-

lating the accounting numbers for the purposes of the agreement.

I argue that the particular forms of accounting measurement rules in lending agreements result from the incentives of both borrowers and lenders. Restrictions on a borrowing firm's activities are included in lending agreements because financing and investment decisions that maximize the market value of a firm's equity do not necessarily maximize the market value of the firm's risky debt, or even the combined market value of the debt and equity when contracting is costly.[5] As a result, there is a conflict of interest between bondholders and stockholders of firms with risky debt outstanding; some decisions that are in the interest of stockholders are not in the interest of bondholders. Subscribers to a new debt issue can protect themselves from anticipated wealth transfers by taking the level of protection offered by the loan contract into account when they forecast the expected payoffs over the life of the loan. If subscribers establish a price for the debt which offers them a normal return, the price approaches zero as the degree of protection (and thus the expected payoffs to debtholders) ap-

---

[4] Smith and Warner [1979] analyze common forms of restrictions found in loan agreements, and offer explanations of how particular covenants reduce the conflict of interest between bondholders and stockholders. A discussion of typical bond covenants is contained in *Commentaries*, Maycock and Jenkins [1958]. Fryling [1964], and Simmons [1972].

[5] Smith and Warner [1979] develop this "costly contracting hypothesis." External markets, such as the market for corporate control, provide incentives for stockholders to maximize the value of the firm rather than the value of the equity, even if costly contracts are not written. (See Fama [1978].) Smith and Warner [1979] argue that those incentives do not *eliminate* the stockholder-bondholder conflict, because restrictions on firms' financing and investment decisions are included in loan agreements, despite the fact that these restrictions are costly to negotiate and enforce. If external markets eliminated the potential conflict of interest, there would be no demand for costly bond covenants.

proaches zero. In this sense, debtholders can rely on "price protection," and thus they are indifferent to the particular level of protection offered by the terms of the debt issue.

Stockholders, however, are not indifferent to the degree of protection offered to debtholders. If the potential wealth transfers were a zero-sum game (i.e., if any decline in the value of the debt were exactly offset by an increase in the value of the equity), stockholders would prefer not to devote any resources to protect debtholders against wealth transfers. Resources devoted to that protection reduce the value of the firm, and this reduction is borne by the residual claimants, the stockholders. However, the conflict of interest constitutes a negative-sum game to the extent that the bondholder-stockholder conflict affects the firm's production, financing, and investment policies. Some wealth transfers can be achieved only through actions that reduce the value of the firm, and the residual claimants (the stockholders) bear the costs of the foregone profit opportunities or the unprofitable projects undertaken.[6] It is in the interest of stockholders to assure bondholders that wealth will not be transferred from the bondholders if such transfers would reduce the value of the firm. Resources devoted to protecting the debtholders from those wealth transfers can increase the value of the firm, and the stockholders capture this increase when the bonds are sold. Restrictions on the firm's investment and financing decisions are then in the interest of stockholders, even though those restrictions are costly.[7]

Just as it is in the interest of stockholders to negotiate restrictions on a firm's financing and investment decisions, it is also in their interest to negotiate accounting measurement rules that reduce management's ability to circumvent the restrictions by a judicious choice of accounting methods.[8] Berle and Means [1932, p. 203] argue that, even in the 1930s, income-participating securities offered holders protection from management's opportunistic choice of accounting methods:

> Securities like, say, participating preferred stock, or income bonds, whose yield is payable only if it is earned, year by year, are substantially meaningless unless they set up provisions definitely regulating the corporation's accounting. *In fact, the more carefully drawn of such securities, where the design is really to protect the holders, include a definition of accounting methods.*[9] [Emphasis added]

Accounting measurement rules in lending agreements affect the value of the borrowing firm, because restricting management's choice of accounting methods

[6] For example, wealth is transferred from bondholders to stockholders when there is an unanticipated increase in cash dividends or an unanticipated increase in the variance of the returns to the firm's investments. However, the value of the firm falls if the increased dividend is financed by a reduction in planned investments which have positive net present values, or if the higher variance projects have negative net present values. See Smith and Warner [1979] for an explanation of how the value of the equity can be increased in such circumstances despite the reduction in the value of the firm.

[7] Strictly speaking, the conflict of interests in a firm's production, investment, and financing decisions is more complicated than the simple bondholder-stockholder conflict. For example, managers' incentives affect the conflict. Moreover, there can be *intra*-bondholder conflicts when there are different classes of debt outstanding. To focus the analysis in this paper on the stockholder-bondholder conflict, I assume that there is only one class of bondholders and that managers act in the stockholders' interests. For ease of exposition, I discuss managers "making decisions" or "being constrained," but it should be kept in mind that I am assuming that managers act as if they are the stockholders.

[8] The extent of managerial opportunism is, of course, governed by managers' concern for the value of their reputations. (See Fama [1980].)

[9] Note that holders of participating securities suffer if management chooses accounting methods that *reduce* reported income below the participation level. In contrast, holders of *fixed* interest securities suffer if management uses accounting methods to report *higher* income and pays higher dividends. This paper examines accounting rules for fixed interest loans.

involves a cost/benefit tradeoff. Precisely defined rules are more costly to negotiate and monitor. In addition, inflexible rules increase the probability of inadvertent contract breaches. However, loosely defined rules introduce ambiguity to the terms of the contract and can result in costly litigation between borrowers and lenders.

It would be very costly to negotiate an entire set of accounting procedures for a debt contract without a benchmark or "starting point." The set of generally accepted accounting principles provides such a benchmark, but GAAP does not define measurement rules rigidly since GAAP usually endorses several alternative procedures to account for a particular transaction. Moreover, the choice among the alternatives is a matter of management discretion (given the costs incurred if an auditor does not issue a "clean" opinion). Managers can exercise that discretion to circumvent some restrictions in lending agreements by their choice of accounting methods.

Restricting managers' choice under GAAP can be costly to enforce, because, if a lending agreement employs accounting rules that differ from those used for external reporting, either duplicate records must be maintained on the firm must change its external reporting practices.[10] Moreover, additional record-keeping and verification costs would be incurred if the negotiated measurement rule requires information outside the scope of the accounting records.[11] Also, rigid rules based on a subset of GAAP can be costly, because covenants in lending agreements may be breached when GAAP is changed unexpectedly.[12] Alternatively, rigid accounting rules can provide incentives for mangers to change previously optimal production-investment decisions to avoid costly covenant breaches. For example, if a firm were in danger of violating cove-

nants due to foreign currency translation losses reported in accordance with Statement of Financial Accounting Standards No. 8 [FASB, 1975], its managers could purchase a currency-hedging contract solely to avoid the covenant violation. The cost of purchasing that hedge would be attributable to the rigid reliance on GAAP in the firm's lending agreements.

Accounting numbers in lending agreements can be insulated from unanticipated mandatory changes in GAAP by defining contractual numbers in accordance with GAAP at the date of issue of the debt. However, such a contract would be costly to monitor, even ignoring the cost of duplicate record-keeping. Debt is often outstanding for 20 years or more, firms often have more than one issue outstanding, and accountants and auditors would require knowledge of an

---

[10] If the choice of accounting principles for external reports affects the firm's cash flows, it is costly for the firm to adopt the lending agreement rules for its external reports. Watts [1977] and Watts and Zimmerman [1978] suggest that, apart from possible tax effects, a firm's cash flows depend on its externally reported accounting numbers because those numbers have an impact on management compensation contracts, legal costs, and political costs.

[11] Not all differences between externally reported numbers and loan agreement numbers are expensive to accommodate, however. For example, if the accounting records already contain details of some revenues and expenses, those revenue items can be excluded from contractual income, and the expenses can be deducted even when they are not normally charged against income. In contrast to such "bottom-line" adjustments to income, other modifications require at least a partial duplication of sets of accounts, even though they use information available within the accounting system.

[12] For example, Accounting Series Release No. 225 [SEC, 1977] requires firms filing financial statements with the Securities and Exchange Commission (SEC) to adhere to Statement of Financial Accounting Standards No. 13 [FASB, 1976] (Accounting for Leases) for fiscal years ending after December 24, 1978. Firms can apply for an exemption if lease capitalization in accordance with that accounting standard would result in default on their loan covenants. A cursory search of approximately 1,200 firms included in the National Automated Accounting Research System reveals that 12 firms acknowledged that they were requesting such an exemption.

extensive time series of accounting principles.[13]

On the other hand, a rigid set of accounting measurement rules benefits the borrowing firm to the extent that it defines the property rights of bondholders and stockholders to a well-specified share of the firm's cash flows. If the definitions of measurement rules in debt agreements are ambiguous, there are incentives for borrowers to bring lawsuits to resolve that ambiguity (in their favor). For example, McConnell and Schlarbaum [1981] discuss two court cases (successfully) brought by income bondholders disputing the accounting methods used to determine income. The legal costs of bringing and defending those suits provide incentives for stockholders to negotiate a well-defined set of measurement rules "up front."

If contracting is costly, I expect that negotiated accounting rules would restrict management's ability to circumvent contractual restrictions by changing accounting methods. Consequently, I predict that accounting measurement rules in lending agreements will contain systematic modifications to GAAP. Negotiated measurement rules reduce management's ability to circumvent restrictions in lending agreements when the rules ensure that (i) reported income and asset values are not increased unless the firm's cash flows increase, and (ii) reported income and asset values are decreased when the firm's cash flows decrease. Thus, observed measurement rules should restrict the use of book entries to "pad" profits. However, when accounting rules are costly to negotiate and monitor, I do not expect to see management's discretion to choose accounting methods *eliminated*. Rather, I expect to observe negotiated restrictions on management's discretion that implicitly recognize the cost-benefit trade-

offs associated with imposing further restrictions. We can test these predictions by analyzing measurement rules negotiated in actual lending agreements.

III. Source and Nature of the Evidence

A. *Source of the Evidence*

Evidence of the accounting methods negotiated in bond indentures for private placements is obtained from *Commentaries*.[14] *Commentaries* is a reference manual designed to provide advice for lawyers who negotiate restrictive covenants in lending agreements.[15] One section of *Commentaries* includes examples of alternative definitions of accounting concepts (such as net income, net tangible assets, and net worth), together with a brief discussion of which circumstances dictate reliance on a particular version of the definition.

To ensure that the measurement rules cited in *Commentaries* are representative of practice and not merely theoretical ideals, I obtained several private loan agreements from five major private lend-

[13] Fogelson [1978, pp. 780–781] discusses some examples of recent indentures that do rely on GAAP at the time of issuance of the debt. He suggests that the increased "activism" of the FASB and the SEC induced the firms to tie the definitions to existing accounting rules. It is difficult to assess whether the instances which he reports are isolated, or part of a general response by firms.

[14] This paper examines almost exclusively the accounting measurement rules that are incorporated in contracts for *private* debt issues. Of course, participants in the market for *public* debt must also contend with the conflict of interests between bondholders and stockholders. However, their choice of a solution to that conflict is constrained by regulatory intervention, primarily SEC regulations and the Trust Indenture Act of 1939 (TIA). The responses of participants in the public debt market to the costs imposed by SEC regulations and the TIA provide additional evidence of how borrowers and lenders select accounting measurement rules that maximize the value of the firm. For a more detailed discussion, see Leftwich [1980a, pp. 13–15].

[15] Rodgers [1965] describes the research project of the American Bar Foundation that culminated in the publication of *Commentaries*.

ers, and compared the accounting defini-tions in the agreements with the examples given in *Commentaries*. A review of the sample indicates that versions of all of the definitions found in *Commentaries* are contained in one or more of the sample loan agreements.[16]

I obtained evidence of what constitutes GAAP (the set of regulated accounting methods) for firms in unregulated industries[17] from the official pronouncements of the Securities and Exchange Commission (SEC), the Committee on Accounting Procedure (CAP), the Accounting Principles Board (APB), and the Financial Accounting Standards Board (FASB), issued during the period 1937 to 1978. In all, these regulatory bodies issued 348 pronouncements dealing with 212 topics during the years 1937–1978.[18]

Most of the topics considered by regulators were the subject of more than one pronouncement, and many of the topics are similar. I classify the topics into 29 distinct categories which I describe later in the paper.[19] The set of 29 categories represents the universe of accounting problems for unregulated firms for which accounting regulatory bodies have proposed formal solutions. That set does not represent the universe of all accounting problems for unregulated firms, because it excludes those disputes that accounting regulators were unable to solve or that were solved informally.[20]

B. *Nature of the Evidence*

The evidence in *Commentaries* is valuable for this paper because it represents what is considered to be best practice in the private lending market. The examples in *Commentaries* have evolved and survived in situations where borrowers and lenders have incentives to discover, and use, those accounting definitions and covenants best suited to particular circumstances.[21] As Maycock and Jenkins [1958, p. 242] observe, the incentives

ensure that, once particular versions of measurement rules are negotiated, those versions are used in subsequent contracts only if the costs of changing them to overcome previously unforeseen deficien-

[16] Sample agreements and covenants were obtained from: Equitable Life, New York Life, John Hancock Mutual Life, Aetna Life, and Prudential. The sample agreements pertain to debt that was issued prior to 1977. In all, ten sample agreements were reviewed. Smith and Warner [1979] examine a sample of over 80 debt agreements and find that the general restrictions on debt, dividends, and working capital as discussed in *Commentaries* are used frequently. Moreover, "when a particular provision is included, a boilerplate from *Commentaries* is used almost exclusively" [Smith and Warner, 1979, p. 123].

[17] Regulated firms such as banks, airlines, and utilities were excluded from consideration because their accounting methods are often prescribed by regulatory bodies such as the Comptroller of the Currency, the Civil Aeronautics Board, and the Federal Power Commission.

[18] From April 1937 to March 1978, the SEC issued 245 Accounting Series Releases (ASRs) which dealt with 67 topics. The remainder of the ASRs dealt with cases brought against accountants practicing before the Commission (81), the content and format of various reports to the SEC (46), rulings regarding auditing practices (18), and various administrative rulings (6). The CAP produced 51 Accounting Research Bulletins (ARBs) covering 73 topics during the period September 1939 to August 1959. The APB issued 31 Opinions relating to 51 topics from June 1962 to June 1973. The first Statement of Financial Accounting Standards (SFAS) was released by the FASB in December 1973 and the latest, SFAS No. 21, in April 1978. The 21 SFASs relate to 18 separate topics.

[19] The set of categories is, of course, not unique, and other observers might classify the pronouncements differently. A classification scheme is adopted in this paper primarily for expositional purposes, and the analysis of the evidence is essentially independent of the particular classification scheme adopted.

[20] Rappaport [1972, pp. 2.14–2.16] argues that the SEC relies on informal rulings on accounting practices. Those rulings are relevant to this study, but they are unobservable or, at least, costly to determine.

[21] Note that, in Section II of the paper, it is argued that lenders can rely on price protection, and, in that sense, are indifferent to the level of protection afforded them in the loan contract. However, if a set of covenants is written to maximize the value of the firm, it is likely that lenders have a comparative advantage in devising those covenants. Presumably, lenders who regularly devise such covenants have more expertise than firms which borrow infrequently. Furthermore, lenders have economic incentives to discover accounting definitions that will maximize the value of the firm. Lenders "sell" advice about structuring loan contracts, in addition to providing credit.

cies are greater than the benefits of revision:

> In a continuous succession of transactions, the applicable terms and conditions are subjected to the keen scrutiny of a variety of borrowers and their able representatives and we are often called upon to justify and defend even those provisions which we have come to regard as more or less standard boiler-plate material.

Mere survival of a set of measurement rules through time would not establish the superiority of that set if all sets of rules were perfect substitutes. If users were indifferent to the choice of measurement rules in loan contracts, some rules would remain in vogue simply because they were copied from one boilerplate to another. Miller [1977, p. 273] warns that Economic Darwinism cannot eliminate "neutral mutations":

> The most, however, that we can safely assert about the evolutionary process underlying market equilibrium is that harmful heuristics, like harmful mutations in nature, will die out. Neutral mutations that serve no function, but do no harm, can persist indefinitely. Neither in nature or in the economy can the enormous variation in forms we observe be convincingly explained in simple Darwinian terms.

The "neutral mutations" argument itself has no refutable implications. However, when alternative measurement rules impose different costs and benefits on contracting parties, some mutations are not "neutral" because those that have the lowest net benefits are "harmful." It is rational to copy rules from one boilerplate to another only if the costs of changing the rules are greater than the expected benefits of revision. If alternative accounting rules offer equal benefits, only the versions that have the lowest record-keeping costs will survive.[22] Thus, if measurement rules used in lending agreements are a matter of indifference to borrowers and lenders, surviving contracts will contain only measurement rules that rely on the least costly information. However, the evidence in the next section reveals that the surviving rules are not always those with the lowest record-keeping costs.[23]

In the next section of the paper, the privately negotiated rules for the measurement of assets, liabilities, and income are discussed, and the differences between the regulated and privately negotiated accounting methods are analyzed. The analysis evaluates whether negotiated measurement rules implicitly recognize the tradeoffs associated with alternative rules. That evaluation can be made only in general terms without a detailed knowledge of the costs and benefits of negotiating special measurement rules for lending agreements. Currently, we do not have a precise specification of the cost function associated with negotiating, recording, and auditing various accounting rules. In addition, the theory of monitoring and contracting (agency theory) is not sufficiently developed to provide us with complete specification of the benefits of various contractual stipulations. Thus, we can develop and test only qualitative predictions about the types of accounting rules that are negotiated and the differences between negotiated and regulated rules.

IV. Data and Analysis

A. *Measurement Rules—Assets, Liabilities, and Income*[24]

I obtained examples of accounting measurement rules from the sample of

---

[22] Some critics allege that inferior accounting measurement rules survive because of "market failures." See Dahlman [1979] and Leftwich [1980b] for discussions of the logical fallacy involved in market failure arguments.

[23] Similarly, Smith and Warner [1979] argue that, consistent with their costly contracting hypothesis, restrictive clauses in loan agreements survive even though they impose costs on borrowers.

[24] Due to space constraints, the discussion of the regulated and negotiated accounting methods is brief.

private loan agreements mentioned above and from the examples cited in *Commentaries*.[25] The examples reveal that, on the one hand, private borrowers and lenders negotiate measurement rules that circumvent accounting problems that are unresolved in the literature (e.g., lease capitalization). On the other hand, the negotiated rules specifically endorse some rules which are often criticized in the accounting literature (e.g., the historical cost rule for valuing fixed assets).

1) Asset Valuation. Loan agreements almost universally rely on depreciated historical cost to value fixed assets. Furthermore, lenders are aware that those values "do not necessarily reflect the realizable or liquidation value of those assets" [*Commentaries*, p. 374]. Typically, any upward revaluation of fixed assets is nullified by excluding from asset value "any write-up of the value of any assets after [date of financial statements prior to the debt issue]" [Sample 2 (c)]. As I discuss below, negotiated measurement rules contain some sophisticated departures from GAAP, so there is every reason to believe that current-cost data would be supplied if its benefits were to exceed its costs. Thus, the evidence suggests that the benefits of current cost-data for fixed assets do not exceed its costs for this group of users of accounting numbers. Benston and Krasney [1978, p. 2] report similar results from their survey of life insurance company investment officers:

> We surveyed a sample of "sophisticated" investors who comprise a large portion of the supply-side of United States capital markets.
>
> We find that these parties generally do not believe that the benefits of current value or price-level-adjusted financial information outweigh the costs of providing, obtaining, and using it.

On the other hand, negotiated measurement rules usually depart from the historical cost rule for inventories and marketable securities in favor of the lower of cost or market rule. For example, the value of current assets includes "inventories of raw materials and supplies, of work, or materials in process and of finished products, all taken at not in excess of costs, or current market value, whichever is less" [Sample 1 (b)]. Private lenders endorse the use of the lower of cost or market rule, despite claims in the accounting literature that, "from the standpoint of accounting theory there is little to justify the lower of cost or market rule" [Kieso and Weygandt, 1977, p. 356].

Asset valuation rules in lending agreements typically provide for the capitalization of leases, and the measurement rules frequently contain elaborate specification of the leases that are to be capitalized, the cash flows to be discounted, and the discount rate to be employed. For example, some definitions of net tangible assets include "the present value of all net rental payments, discounted, at the Company's option, at either (x) $10\frac{1}{8}\%$ per annum or (y) the actual interest rate factor ascribed to the lease ... under agreements to lease ... real or personal property (other than leases of warehouses, offices, ... and data processing, transportation, and office equipment) having an initial term of more than 3 years" [Sample 3]. In addition, it is common to link measurement of the

---

For details of GAAP for particular transactions, see any standard intermediate accounting text. For details of negotiated methods, see the various definitions in *Commentaries*, and in actual debt agreements.

[25] Private lenders who supplied some of the sample agreements requested confidentiality. In order to preserve the anonymity of the source of the examples cited in this section, the quotations are identified only as samples 1 through 4, with the designation (a) or (b) used for different examples provided by the same lender. *Some* private loan agreements are public information. If the private loan is a "material event," the borrower files an 8-K statement with the SEC and the loan agreement is frequently filed with that statement.

asset value of the lease to measurement of the liability for future lease payments. For example: "For purposes of this definition [of asset values], any leasehold interest of the Company shall be deemed to be a tangible asset if the rental obligations of the Company under the lease are included as Funded Debt in the definition of such term" [*Commentaries*, p. 89].

2) *Liability Measurement.* Lending agreements contain definitions of liabilities that are more encompassing than GAAP, especially with respect to contingencies arising from guarantees and "off-balance sheet financing." *Commentaries* [p. 380] warns lenders to consider definitions of debt that are sufficiently wide to capture "creative financing" arrangements:

> Modern financing has produced a number of arrangements under which, for example, a loan to a new corporation is supported by a contract made by a sponsor corporation under which the sponsor corporation agrees to purchase and pay for goods or services furnished by the new corporation.
>
> Such arrangements are sometimes colloquially called "off-balance sheet financing." If there is any likelihood of the Company becoming a sponsoring company in a similar or analogous situation, it is advisable to consider the extent to which the debenture indenture should treat liabilities under such contracts as "Debt."

Definitions of contingencies in at least some lending agreements heed the advice in *Commentaries*. For example, contingencies are defined to include, first, "obligations under any contract for the purchase of materials, supplies, other property or services . . . if such contract . . . requires that payment . . . be made regardless of whether or not delivery . . . is ever made or tendered," and, second, "obligations under any other contract which, in economic effect, is substantially equivalent to a guarantee"[26] [Sample 2 (c)].

Most debt agreements ensure that lease liabilities are counted as debt, not "buried in footnotes." Thus, a firm cannot expand its borrowing capacity merely by leasing an asset instead of borrowing funds to purchase the asset. For example, the liability for lease payments is defined as "the present value of all payments due under any lease or under any other arrangement for retention of title (discounted at the implicit rate if known or 8% per annum otherwise) if such lease or other arrangement is in substance (a) a financing lease . . . (b) an arrangement for the retention of title for security purposes, or (c) an installment purchase"[27] [Sample 1 (b)].

Although observed contracts usually define liabilities more broadly than GAAP, two notable exceptions to this policy occur for pension fund liabilities and the liability for deferred taxes. Definitions of liabilities in lending agreements seldom include pension fund liabilities. Instead, covenants are written to require the borrower to limit unfunded pension liabilities. For example: "The Company will not permit the present value of all employee benefits vested under all Pension Plans maintained by the Company and its Subsidiaries to exceed the present value of the assets allocable to such vested benefits by an amount greater than . . ."[28] [Sample 1 (b)]. It is not clear why lenders do not design an accounting measurement rule to include the pension fund liability. *Commentaries* [p. 72, fn. 25] advises

---

[26] If these off-balance sheet financial arrangements are recent innovations, we could obtain evidence of the adaptive response of lending agreements by examining how quickly new lending agreements expanded the scope of "debt" definitions.

[27] *Commentaries* predates SFAS No. 13 [FASB, 1976]. Some definitions of lease liabilities in *Commentaries* require capitalization of obligations that need not be capitalized under SFAS No. 13.

[28] Sample 3 contains a similar covenant.

that the so-called liability for future tax does not necessarily represent any claim on the firm:

> Deferred tax credits are classified in the balance sheet along with indebtedness and other liabilities under generally accepted accounting principles. Because these deferred credits do not represent current claims to assets by the government nor is their eventual payment determinable, the definition of debt included in the indenture could profitably state whether such deferred credits are included in or excluded from liabilities.

Some definitions of liabilities include deferred taxes. Almost as frequently, others exclude "reserves for deferred income taxes and other reserves to the extent that such reserves do not constitute an obligation" [Sample 4].

Negotiated measurement rules pay attention to the *classification* of liabilities as well as to their scope. The distinction between long-term and current debt is important for restrictive covenants applying to working capital and debt-equity ratios. Under GAAP, there are rules for classifying debt as either long-term or current, with particular emphasis on whether any part of a long-term debt issue about to be repaid should be classified as a current liability. Prior to 1975, various solutions were acceptable, including, for example, classifying a debt issue as long-term if it was to be refinanced or rolled-over, even if the debt fell due in a matter of months. SFAS No. 6 [FASB, 1975] now imposes stringent tests that must be satisfied if debt due to be repaid is to be classed as long-term. *Commentaries* [p. 78] advises that the classification of liabilities as either current or long-term deserves attention because of the "possibility of an unintended result [violation of a covenant even though the firm is financially healthy] if funded debt whose final

maturity is less than one year after the date of determination is treated as a current liability, particularly for the purpose of the working capital covenant." Consequently, liabilities are usually classed as current in covenants if they are due "within a period of one year *from the date of creation thereof"* [Sample 4, emphasis added]. Under such a definition, once debt is classed as long-term, it remains a long-term liability while it is outstanding. Furthermore, typical negotiated definitions of liabilities classify revolving credit arrangements and debt about to be refinanced as *long-term* debt. This is achieved by excluding (from current liabilities) obligations that are "renewable pursuant to the terms . . . of a revolving credit or similar agreement" or "may be payable out of the proceeds of a similar obligation" [Sample 4].

3) Income Measurement. An all-inclusive income statement is required by GAAP; i.e., all charges (except certain prior-period adjustments) must be made against income directly, and thus transfers to and from reserves and retained earnings cannot be made without affecting the income number.

Negotiated definitions of net income (contractual income) almost always restrict management's ability to *increase* contractual income by transfers from reserves. For example, net income "excludes any restoration of any contingency reserve to net income" [Samples 1 (b) and 2 (a)]. Management's ability to *reduce* contractual income is unaffected by the negotiated definitions. Therefore, those negotiated definitions introduce an asymmetry to the measurement process. This asymmetry is consistent with the incentives of stockholders to negotiate only those restrictions that protect bondholders. Reducing contractual income solely by book entries lowers the pool of funds available for dividends. Bondholders are made better off by keeping funds within the firm, and thus stockholders do not offer them "protection" against accounting techniques that arbitrarily reduce contractual income. In the spirit of restricting management's ability to use book entries to report increased net income numbers, negotiated definitions of net income usually exclude "any gains arising from any write-up of assets"[29] [Samples 3 and 4].

Commentaries [p. 85, fn. 36] advises lenders to ensure that *all* contingencies are deducted from net income, even if not required by GAAP:

> Contingency reserves are deducted from gross revenues in determining net income under generally accepted accounting principles only where the outcome of the matter is reasonably foreseeable and the amount can be reasonably measured. Specific provision should be made in the indenture for the deduction of additional general contingencies whose occurrence is not predictable and would not normally be charged against income under generally accepted accounting principles.

Reported net income for merged firms receives special attention in *Commentaries.* Under GAAP, there are two methods of accounting for a business combination—the purchase method and the pooling method. These methods produce different reported income numbers, especially if "instant earnings" can be recognized by using pooling. Negotiated measurement rules seldom restrict management's choice of purchase or pooling for external reporting. Instead, definitions are written to mitigate the impact of the choice on restrictive covenants. For example, consolidated income defined in indentures typically excludes any earnings of an acquired company accruing "prior to the date of such transaction" [Sample 2 (b)]. Thus, "instant earnings" from pooling are seldom included in

contractual income. Moreover, amortization of *negative* goodwill is usually excluded from contractual income, since many negotiated definitions of income exclude "any deferred credit representing the excess of equity in any Subsidiary at the date of acquisition over the cost of the investment in such Subsidiary"[30] [Samples 3 and 4].

Negotiated income measurement rules frequently nullify management's choice of the equity method of accounting for long-term investments that do not represent controlling interests. For example, one definition of contractual income excludes the net earnings of any unconsolidated firm "in which the Company or any Restricted Subsidiary has an ownership interest unless such net earnings shall have actually been received by the Company or such Subsidiary in the form of cash distributions" [Sample 2 (b)].

B. *Overview of the Evidence*

A comparison of even the general form of negotiated measurement rules for assets, liabilities, and income with GAAP provides evidence that rules in lending agreements reflect economic tradeoffs. The results of this comparison are summarized in (i)–(v) below, together with a brief explanation of how the general characteristics of the tradeoffs are reflected in the rules.

> (i) Definitions of accounting numbers in lending agreements consistently refer to GAAP. Any negotiated modifications to those principles consist of specific inclusions and exclusions.

[29] *Commentaries* [p. 85, fn. 32] advises that, "as a matter of convenience, the parties may want to treat occasional minor capital gains or capital losses as ordinary income or losses." Sample 1 (b) includes the gain or loss on fixed assets in income to the extent that the net gain or loss is $75,000 in any one year.

[30] Note that amortization of *positive* goodwill is not mentioned. Thus, the amortization reduces contractual income.

Incorporating GAAP as a benchmark in negotiated measurement rules is apparently less costly than negotiating an entire set of accounting rules for lending agreements.

> (ii) Definitions in lending agreements require that contractual accounting numbers be determined by GAAP in force at the date of the calculation ("rolling" GAAP), not at the date of issuance of the debt ("frozen" GAAP).

The contracting parties' choice of rolling GAAP instead of frozen GAAP suggests that the expected costs of an inadvertent contract breach when GAAP is changed are lower than the monitoring and record-keeping costs associated with frozen GAAP.

> (iii) The modifications to GAAP in lending agreements state that certain increases in income and asset values permitted under GAAP are *not* allowed, and mandate other decreases in income and asset values not necessary under GAAP.

The modifications that are observed reduce management's ability to choose accounting techniques to relax restrictive covenants. This evidence is consistent with the predictions made earlier in the paper that observed negotiated measurement rules should restrict management's ability to circumvent contractual restrictions.[31]

> (iv) When variations to GAAP occur, they usually take the form of bottom-line adjustments rather than complete re-calculation of accounting numbers. Few of the variations require information from outside the accounting system.

Emphasis in bottom-line adjustments is consistent with the prediction that parties to lending agreements trade off the costs and benefits of alternative measurement rules. Significant costs of collection and verification are incurred if the calculations for contractual num-

bers use information from outside the accounting system (e.g., current-cost information). Those costs are even higher if the information cannot be obtained by reference to quoted prices (e.g., it is more expensive to determine the market value of a factory than that of listed securities). Negotiated measurement rules seldom rely on information from outside the accounting system, and, when they do, they rely almost exclusively on information obtained from quoted prices.[32]

> (v) Variations from GAAP are more frequent (and more elaborate) in private debt agreements than in public debt indentures.

As is discussed in *Commentaries* [pp. 11 and 40], higher re-negotiation costs associated with public debt issues provide incentives for firms making such issues to set looser constraints.[33] Allowing management the freedom to choose from among all accepted accounting principles is one way of setting looser constraints.

C. *Classification of the Evidence*

This section contains a detailed classification of the measurement rules contained in *Commentaries* and the sample of private loan agreements. The negotiated rules are compared with the regulated rules for each of 29 categories of the 212 topics of pronouncements by accounting regulatory bodies during the

---

[31] Watts [1977, p. 62] predicts that income-decreasing modifications to GAAP occur in lending agreements more frequently than income-increasing modifications.

[32] Some oil and gas lending agreements provide a notable exception by defining restrictive covenants in terms of proven reserves. Those covenants predate the SEC's ruling requiring reserve valuation.

[33] It is more costly to renegotiate public debt agreements because approval must be obtained from a majority (usually two-thirds) of the holders of *outstanding* debt. As Smith and Warner [1979] observe, this could explain why riskier firms rely on private debt issues and why most public debt issues contain call provisions. There is, of course, a potential bilateral monopoly problem when private debt agreements are re-negotiated. However, lenders who exercise this monopoly power risk the value of their reputation.

period 1937 to 1978.[34] The negotiated accounting methods for each category are classified into one of the following groups:

Group 1: The negotiated method is entirely outside GAAP.

Group 2: The negotiated method is consistent with GAAP, but excludes one or more of the generally accepted alternatives.

Group 3: The negotiated method is entirely consistent with GAAP.

Results of the classification are contained in Table 1. Of the 29 categories, the negotiated method is entirely outside the set of generally accepted accounting principles for seven categories (Group 1). For another eight of the categories, the negotiated method is consistent with GAAP but excludes one or more of the alternatives available under GAAP (Group 2). There are 14 categories which escape mention entirely (Group 3). For that group, the negotiated method is entirely consistent with GAAP. However, as is discussed below, eight of the 14 categories in Group 3 relate to accounting issues either not relevant to the indentures or specific to particular types of firms or events.

(a) Group 1—Entirely Outside GAAP.

Table 2 contains a summary of the negotiated measurement rules that are entirely outside GAAP for:[35]

  (i) business combinations,
  (ii) contingencies,
 (iii) equity investments,
 (iv) foreign currency,
  (v) goodwill and intangibles,
 (vi) income tax, and
 (vii) stock dividends and stock splits.

The negotiated measurement rules that are entirely outside GAAP (i.e., those in

Group 1) provide further evidence consistent with the argument that parties to lending agreements devise accounting measurement rules in a variety of ways to reduce the conflict of interests between borrowers and lenders. Some rules, such as those negotiated for business combinations and contingencies, reduce management's ability to choose accounting methods to circumvent restrictive covenants. Other rules, such as those negotiated for stock dividends and stock splits, ignore distinctions that are made by GAAP but have no significance for lending agreements. Rules used for goodwill and intangibles and equity investments do not impose costly outright restrictions on investment activity but, at the same time, ensure that certain types of investments do not support additional debt. Still other rules exhibit flexibility: for firms in some circumstances, GAAP is discarded; for other firms, GAAP is followed (e.g., deferred income taxes). The variety of these negotiated solutions suggests that the participants in this market have a sophisticated appreciation of alternative accounting measurement rules.

(b) Group 2—Modified GAAP

Table 3 contains a summary of the negotiated measurement rules that are consistent with GAAP but exclude one or more of the generally accepted alternatives for:[36]

---

[34] Note that *Commentaries* was published in 1971 and the sample agreements pertain to debt issued prior to 1977. However, the timing issue is not critical. The negotiated rules which are entirely outside GAAP (i.e., group 1 in Table 3) would remain outside GAAP even if GAAP had not been changed since 1971. Similarly, the rules that exclude some GAAP alternatives(i.e., group 2 in Table 3) exclude some 1971 GAAP alternatives.

[35] For a detailed explanation of each of the negotiated measurement rules in Group 1, see Leftwich [1980a, pp. 31–41].

[36] For a detailed explanation of each of the negotiated measurement rules in Group 2, see Leftwich [1980a, pp. 42–50].

TABLE 1

GROUPING OF 29 CATEGORIES OF ISSUES CONTAINED IN PRONOUNCEMENTS OF ACCOUNTING REGULATORY BODIES
FROM 1937 to 1978 ACCORDING TO TREATMENT IN INDENTURES

CATEGORY #	CATEGORY	Treatment in Indentures		
		Group 1 Entirely Outside GAAP	Group 2 Modified GAAP	Group 3 Entirely Consistent with GAAP
	Accounting Standards:			
1	All-inclusive income statements		X	
2	Business combinations	X		
3	Capital reorganizations			X
4	Contingencies	X		
5	Convertible bonds		X	
6	Depreciation methods			X
7	Earnings per share			X
8	Employee compensation and stock options			X
9	Equity investments	X		
10	Foreign currency	X		
11	Gain or loss on debt redemption		X	
12	Goodwill and intangibles	X		
13	Income tax	X		
14	Inventory valuation			X
15	Leases		X	
16	Pension plans			X
17	Ratio of earnings to fixed charges		X	
18	Stock dividends and stock splits	X		
19	Treasury stock		X	
20	Valuation of fixed assets		X	
21	Working capital		X	
	Reporting Standards:			
22	Cash-flow reporting			X
23	Disclosure and statement presentation			X
24	Funds statements			X
25	Interim reporting			X
26	Segment reporting			X
	Other Standards:			
27	Special industries and firms			X
28	Terminology			X
29	War and special events			X
	Totals	7	8	14

Group 1: The negotiated method is entirely outside the set of generally accepted accounting principles.
Group 2: The negotiated method is consistent with generally accepted accounting principles, but excludes one or more of the generally accepted alternatives.
Group 3: The negotiated method is entirely consistent with generally accepted accounting principles.

(i) all-inclusive income statements, (v) ratio of earnings to fixed charges,
(ii) convertible bonds, (vi) treasury stock,
(iii) gain or loss on debt redemption, (vii) valuation of fixed assets, and
(iv) leases, (viii) working capital.

TABLE 2

SUMMARY OF NEGOTIATED ACCOUNTING RULES THAT ARE ENTIRELY OUTSIDE GAAP (GROUP I)

Category	Negotiated Accounting Rule
(i) Business combinations	Retained earnings of an acquired firm do not relax the negotiated restrictions on funds available for dividends even if pooling is used. Some upward revaluation of the acquired assets is allowed but only if the assets are independently appraised. If upward asset revaluation is allowed, the amount of any revaluation, even if classed as goodwill, can be included in tangible assets.
(ii) Contingencies	All charges for contingencies must be made against income, not against reserve accounts. Specific contingent liabilities, particularly guarantees of third-party indebtedness, are included in balance sheet liabilities.
(iii) Equity investments	Investments, especially short-term investments, are valued primarily at the lower of cost or market. Investments are frequently excluded from the asset base against which firms may borrow. Income from unconsolidated investments is not recognized until it is received; i.e., the equity method is not used.
(iv) Foreign currency	Foreign subsidiaries are seldom consolidated. Income from foreign investments is recognized only when it is actually received.
(v) Goodwill and intangibles	Goodwill and intangibles are frequently excluded from the asset base against which firms may borrow. The accounting double entry is not preserved—goodwill is eliminated from balance sheet numbers but amortization is required in the income statement.
(vi) Income tax	Deferred tax credits are not always classified as a liability. Deferred tax debits are excluded from the firm's asset base.
(vii) Stock dividends and stock splits	No distinction is made between stock dividends and stock splits.

TABLE 3

SUMMARY OF NEGOTIATED ACCOUNTING RULES THAT ARE CONSISTENT WITH GAAP BUT EXCLUDE ONE OR MORE OF THE GENERALLY ACCEPTED ALTERNATIVES (GROUP 2)

Category	Negotiated Accounting Rule
(i) All-inclusive income statements	Specific income-increasing items (e.g., transfers to income from contingency reserves) are excluded from income, and specific income-decreasing items (e.g., depreciation of leasehold improvements) are charged against income.
(ii) Convertible bonds	An issue of stock for debt conversion is valued at the face value of the converted debt.
(iii) Gain or loss on debt redemption	There is no attempt to classify the gain or loss as an ordinary or extraordinary item.
(iv) Leases	Capitalization of most leases is required.
(v) Ratio of earnings to fixed charges	All fixed charges (e.g., sinking fund and lease payments) are included, not just the imputed interest component.
(vi) Treasury stock	Stock repurchases are treated as cash dividends and treasury stock sales are treated as new issues of common.
(vii) Valuation of fixed assets	Fixed assets are valued at depreciated historical cost. Upward revaluations are prohibited, except in some business combinations. Current-cost data are ignored.
(viii) Working capital	Debt is classified as current or long-term by reference to its time to maturity at the date of issue.

The negotiated measurement rules that modify GAAP (i.e., those in Group 2) provide evidence that corroborates the findings discussed above for Group 1. Some rules, such as those negotiated for leases, reduce the incentives of managers to choose particular financing methods merely to avoid contractual restrictions. Moreover, those incentives are reduced without imposing more costly outright prohibition on the financing methods. Other negotiated rules, such as those used to measure working capital, avoid costly contract breaches that can result from a mechanical reliance on GAAP to classify debt as either current or long-term. Some negotiated rules record the economic consequences of transactions by ignoring their form; e.g., treasury stock purchases and sales are treated as dividends and new issues of common stock. Other rules, such as those negotiated for the all-inclusive income statement, reduce management's ability to choose accounting methods to circumvent restrictive covenants.

(c) Group 3—Entirely Consistent with GAAP.

Some of the categories in Table 1 are seldom mentioned in lending agreements. For those categories, management can choose from any of the accepted accounting alternatives. Typically, there are no restrictions on:[37]

    (i) capital reorganizations,
    (ii) depreciation methods,
    (iii) earnings per share,
    (iv) employee compensation and stock options,
    (v) inventory valuation,
    (vi) pension plans,
    (vii) reporting standards, and
    (viii) other standards.

Some of the measurement rules that rely entirely on GAAP support the find-ings discussed above for Groups 1 and 2. Some categories, such as report presentation and earnings-per-share calculations, have no impact on restrictive covenants, and there are no benefits associated with special rules for those categories. Negotiated rules for other categories, such as employee compensation and stock options, implicitly recognize that the costs imposed on lenders by these transactions are low. GAAP allows these transactions to be virtually ignored in the accounts, so lenders do not restrict management's choice of GAAP for the transactions. Pension fund liabilities are subject to separate restrictive covenants, so the negotiated accounting measurement rules allow those liabilities to remain "off balance sheet," consistent with GAAP. Other categories, such as capital reorganizations and wars, affect lenders' claims, but with such a low probability that it may not be in the lenders' interests to negotiate special measurement rules for them.

On the other hand, there are some apparent anomalies. It is not obvious why several negotiated measurement rules (such as those for depreciation and inventories) are consistent with GAAP.[38] It *may* be rational for lenders to rely on GAAP for depreciation and inventory measurement rules. However, such reliance could be anomalous. Existing theories of contracting and monitoring are not developed sufficiently to resolve the ambiguity.

V. CONCLUSIONS

The analysis and evidence in this paper reveal that accounting measurement rules

---

[37] For a more detailed explanation of why management's choice is not restricted for each of these rules, see Leftwich [1980a, pp. 51–57].

[38] However, Maycock and Jenkins [1958, p. 226] report an example of a definition of net income constraining the amount charged for depreciation to be no less than the amount claimed for income tax purposes.

in lending agreements differ systematically from GAAP, the regulated set of accounting rules. Those who participate in this market for accounting information accept some of the regulated measurement rules, modify others, and design some rules of their own. The observed negotiated rules are generally consistent with the hypothesis that the rules reduce the conflict of interest between stockholders and bondholders. Furthermore, the contracting parties implicitly recognize at least some of the costs and benefits of alternative means of reducing the conflict when designing the contract.

The evidence in this paper has evolved from situations where there are economic incentives to discriminate between efficient and inefficient contracts. Individuals with superior skills in selecting appropriate accounting methods can capture the gains associated with those methods by selling advice to borrowers and lenders. Moreover, the evidence reveals that the surviving rules are not always those with the lowest negotiation and record-keeping costs; e.g., rules used for business combinations restructure some of the book entries required by GAAP. Thus, we can reject the argument that the accounting methods incorporated in lending agreements are irrelevant or "neutral," i.e., that some rules are in vogue simply because they are copied from one boilerplate to another. Such an argument is inconsistent with survival arguments if different rules impose different costs on firms.

There are three general implications of the analysis and evidence in this paper. First, those who advocate increased regulation to remedy alleged defects in accounting measurement rules should consider how at least one group of sophisticated users (borrowers and lenders in the private debt market) tailors a set of accounting rules without regulatory intervention. Second, if sophisticated users systematically reject or modify accounting rules with particular properties (such as measurement rules allowing upward revaluation of assets), there is a presumption that any advantages of those rules are not cost-justified for that group of users. Third, if users design sets of accounting rules specifically for their own purposes, it suggests that there is a demand for a diverse set of regulated rules. Consequently, it is unlikely that a unique set of rules can be mandated without imposing costs on at least some users of accounting numbers.

At least two directions for future research are apparent. First, since *Commentaries* provides evidence of only "typical" measurement rules with little indication of the extent to which those rules vary across firms or industries, one could collect a sample of, say, 100 lending agreements and investigate the cross-sectional variability of measurement rules and the "portfolio" of rules for particular firms and industries. Second, one could collect a time series of lending agreements for a particular lender and investigate how accounting measurement rules in the agreements change through time in response to changes in GAAP. This research would provide more powerful tests of the propositions developed in this paper, and would contribute further insights into the tradeoffs among alternative accounting measurement rules. In particular, the research would allow further investigation of the apparent anomalies concerning negotiated accounting measurement rules for pension liabilities, depreciation expense, and inventory valuation.

REFERENCES

American Bar Foundation, *Commentaries on Indentures* (American Bar Foundation, 1971).

Benston, George J., and Melvin A. Krasney, "DAAM: The Demand for Alternative Accounting Measurements," *Journal of Accounting Research* (Studies on Accounting for Changes in General and Specific Prices: Empirical Research and Public Policy Issues, 1978), pp. 1–30.

Berle, Adolph A., Jr., and Gardiner C. Means, *The Modern Corporation and Private Property* (Macmillan Company, 1932).

Briloff, Abraham J., "Castles of Sand," *Barron's* (February 2, 1970), p. 3.

———, *More Debits Than Credits: The Burnt Investor's Guide to Financial Statements* (Harper & Row, 1976).

Chambers, Raymond J., "Financial Information and the Securities Market," *Abacus* (September 1965), pp. 3–30.

———, *Accounting, Evaluation and Economic Behavior* (Prentice-Hall 1966).

Dahlman, Carl J., "The Problem of Externality," *Journal of Law and Economics* (April 1979), pp. 141–162.

Fama, Eugene F., "The Effects of a Firm's Investment and Financing Decisions on the Welfare of its Security Holders," *American Economic Review* (June 1978), pp. 272–284.

———, "Agency Problems and the Theory of the Firm," *Journal of Political Economy* (April 1980), pp. 288–307.

Financial Accounting Standards Board, "Classification of Short-Term Obligations Expected to be Refinanced," *Statement of Financial Accounting Standards No. 6* (FASB, May 1975).

———, "Accounting for the Translation of Foreign Currency Transactions and Foreign Currency Financial Statements," *Statement of Financial Accounting Standards No. 8* (FASB, October 1975).

———, "Accounting for Leases," *Statement of Financial Accounting Standards No. 13* (FASB, November 1976).

Fogelson, James H., "The Impact of Changes in Accounting Principles on Restrictive Covenants in Credit Agreements and Indentures," *The Business Lawyer* (January 1978), pp. 769–787.

Fryling, Henry H., "Private Placement Financing—Lender's Procedural Guide," *Proceedings of Association of Life Insurance Counsel* (December 1964), pp. 797–846.

Kieso, Donald E., and Jerry J. Weygandt, *Intermediate Accounting* (John Wiley & Sons, Inc., 1977).

Leftwich, Richard W., "Accounting Regulation, Market Failures and Market Solutions: Some Evidence," Unpublished working paper No. MERC 80-09, Managerial Economics Research Center, University of Rochester (1980a).

———, "Market Failure Fallacies and Accounting Information," *Journal of Accounting and Economics* (December 1980b), pp. 193–211.

Maycock, Roland, and George P. Jenkins. "Direct Loans by Life Insurance Companies to Industrial Corporations," *Proceedings of the Association of Life Insurance Counsel* (December 1958), pp. 201–242.

McConnell, John J., and Gary G. Schlarbaum, "Returns, Risks, and Pricing of Income Bonds, 1956–76 (Does Money Have an Odor?)," *Journal of Business* (January 1981), pp. 33–63.

Miller, Merton, H., "Debt and Taxes," *Journal of Finance* (May 1977), pp. 261–275.

Rappaport, Louis H., *SEC Accounting Practice and Procedure* (Ronald Press Company, 1972).

Rodgers, Churchill, "The Corporate Trust Indenture Project," *The Business Lawyer* (April 1965), pp. 551–571.

Securities and Exchange Commission, "Lease Accounting and Disclosure Rules," *Accounting Series Release No. 225* (SEC, August 31, 1977).

Simmons, Richard S., "Drafting of Commercial Bank Loan Agreements," *The Business Lawyer* (November 1972), pp. 179–201.

Smith, Clifford W., Jr., and Jerold B. Warner, "On Financial Contracting: An Analysis of Bond Covenants," *Journal of Financial Economics* (June 1979), pp. 117–161.

Sterling, Robert R., "On Theory Construction and Verification, THE ACCOUNTING REVIEW (July 1970), pp. 444–457.

Watts, Ross L., "Corporate Financial Statements, A Product of the Market and Political Processes," *Australian Journal of Management* (April 1977), pp. 53–75.

Watts, Ross L., and Jerold L. Zimmerman, "Towards a Positive Theory of the Determination of Accounting Standards," THE ACCOUNTING REVIEW (January 1978), pp. 112–134.

AN EMPIRICAL EXAMINATION OF DEBT COVENANT RESTRICTIONS AND ACCOUNTING-RELATED DEBT PROXIES*

Joanne C. DUKE

San Francisco State University, San Francisco, CA 94132, USA

Herbert G. HUNT III

University of Vermont, Burlington, VT 05405, USA

Received May 1988, final version received April 1989

Prior studies of discretionary accounting choices have generally relied on one or more proxy variables to measure closeness to debt covenant restrictions without actually examining the existence or extent of restrictive covenants. This study tests the validity of the most commonly used proxy, the debt–equity ratio, by examining its relation to actual debt covenant restrictions for a random sample of U.S. firms. The results indicate that several versions of the debt–equity ratio capture the existence and tightness of retained earnings restrictions and the existence of net tangible asset and working capital restrictions, but are unrelated to four other covenant restrictions.

1. Introduction

Based on the work of Jensen and Meckling (1976), Fogelson (1978), Smith and Warner (1979), and others, a substantial body of accounting literature has emerged in recent years which examines the implications of accounting-based debt covenant restrictions. Included in this literature are attempts to explain, among other things, accounting method choices, management lobbying positions before accounting standard-setting bodies, stock price reactions to mandated accounting changes, and changes in investment, financing, and operating

*The authors gratefully acknowledge the helpful comments of Joy Begley (discussant and Conference referee), Gene Laber, Ross Watts (the editor), Ian Zimmer (the referee), and the participants of the Olin/JAE Conference, especially George Foster, Robert Hagerman, Eric Press, and Joseph Weintrop. Professor Duke also thanks the other members of her dissertation committee at Penn State University, James Thies (Chairman), Richard Bord, and Richard Twark.

decisions resulting from proposed or enacted accounting standards. While these studies attempt to explain observed phenomena based on the existence and tightness of restrictive debt covenants, rarely have the actual existence and provisions of debt covenants been determined. Instead, researchers have typically relied on one or more proxy measures (e.g., debt–equity ratio) as independent variables under the assumption that the proxy adequately reflects the existence and/or tightness of the covenant restrictions.[1]

Watts and Zimmerman (1986) suggest that the testing of a simple hypothesis (e.g., the debt–equity hypothesis) rather than the more theoretically correct hypothesis (e.g., the covenant-based hypothesis) is justified in the early stages of theory development because '... debt covenant details are costly to gather, and simple hypotheses ... are one way to see whether incurring that cost is likely to pay off. (Subsequently) ... as the literature develops, we expect more researchers to concentrate on testing hypotheses that use the details of covenants rather than the debt–equity hypothesis' (p. 216). Holthausen and Leftwich (1983) point out the need to more closely examine specific features of debt contracts that depend on accounting numbers in order to provide evidence that debt covenant negotiation and renegotiation costs are, as hypothesized, related to the leverage proxy. Indeed, as Johnson and Ramanan (1988) point out in a recent study:

> (L)acking detailed information about the contractual provisions of firms' public and private debt agreements ... we can only speculate about the appropriateness of the debt covenant proximity ... Absent precise measures of technical default probability, our empirical procedures must be interpreted as providing an indirect test of the debt covenant explanation for FC adoption.   (p. 108)

The purpose of this paper is to extend the accounting-based debt contracting research by empirically examining the relation between actual debt covenant restrictions and various leverage proxies that have been used by previous researchers. Thus, the study provides a step forward in the development of a positive theory of accounting and sheds additional light on previous studies that have assumed a relation between debt proxies and actual debt covenant restrictions.

The paper is organized as follows. The next section provides a brief background discussion of accounting-based debt contracts. It examines the accounting choice literature that has tested the debt–equity hypothesis, and it

---

[1]However, see Kelly (1985) in which she found higher debt–equity ratios for firms with debt covenants than for firms without covenants, and Press and Weintrop (1988) in which positive correlations were obtained between measures of nearness to actual debt covenant constraints and debt–equity ratios.

discusses issues involved in validating the debt–equity proxy. The third section explains the research methodology, and this is followed by a discussion of the results. A summary and conclusions section is presented last.

2. Background and hypotheses development

The debt contracting literature is based largely on the testable implications arising from the agency theory literature as exemplified by Jensen and Meckling (1976).[2] This literature suggests that contracts between debtholders and owner-managers contain covenants that restrict management behavior because owner-managers have incentives to take actions that may negatively affect the debtholders' wealth position. Based on the American Bar Foundation's (1971) *Commentaries on Indentures* (*Commentaries* hereinafter), Smith and Warner (1979) and Leftwich (1983) provide a detailed description of the more common restrictions contained in debt covenants. These include, for example, dividend and share purchase restrictions, minimum working capital requirements, restrictions on merger activity, restrictions on investments in other firms, restrictions on the disposition of assets, and restrictions on the issuance of additional debt.

Of interest to accounting researchers is the fact that many debt agreements, especially public debt agreements, rely heavily on the accounting numbers reported in audited financial statements in measuring compliance with the covenants. Since generally accepted accounting principles (GAAP) must be used to prepare financial statements, accounting methods that comply with GAAP will generally be allowable under restrictive debt covenants.[3] Thus, to the extent that GAAP rules allow flexibility in the choice of accounting procedures, managers have an opportunity to choose accounting methods so as to avoid violating restrictive debt covenants. Since it is generally assumed that a default on a debt contract is costly, managers are assumed to choose accounting procedures that increase assets and revenues and decrease liabilities and expenses. In the following paragraphs, we briefly discuss previous studies that used a debt contracting argument to hypothesize a positive relation between a firm's debt–equity ratio and the likelihood that the firm's managers would choose (or support) income-enhancing (or other nonconservative) accounting methods. We focus on the accounting choice research here

---

[2] For an overview of the agency theory literature, see Watts and Zimmerman (1986).

[3] However, see Leftwich (1983) for evidence that private lending agreements often require modified generally accepted accounting principles that differ from those used to prepare the financial statements. Although such modifications are sometimes made in public lending agreements, deviations from GAAP are less common and less elaborate than those in private agreements due to the higher renegotiation costs of public debt agreements [*Commentaries* (1971), Smith and Warner (1979), Leftwich (1983)].

simply to illustrate the use of proxy variables in the debt contracting literature. The use of debt proxies is evident in other types of studies as well, and we could just as well have focused on them.[4]

2.1. Previous research of discretionary accounting choices

We restrict our attention here to the role that proxies for debt covenant restrictions have played in the discretionary accounting choice literature. Thus, our objective is not to provide a complete review of this research, but to simply point out the extent to which the results obtained and the conclusions reached in prior studies depend importantly on the assumed proxy relations.

The most frequently used proxy in previous studies of discretionary accounting choices is the debt–equity ratio, and we therefore focus on several variations of this ratio in the current study.[5] As mentioned above, Watts and Zimmerman (1986, p. 216) suggest that researchers using the debt–equity ratio in investigations of discretionary accounting choices are actually testing the debt–equity hypothesis, which they state as follows:

> Ceteris paribus, the larger a firm's debt–equity ratio the more likely the firm's manager is to select accounting procedures that shift reported earnings from future periods to the current period.   (p. 216)

This hypothesis is derived from the more theoretically correct covenant-based hypothesis which suggests that the closer a firm is to a particular accounting-based covenant restriction, the more likely the manager is to choose accounting methods that increase current earnings.

Dhaliwal (1980) was one of the first to suggest using the debt–equity ratio as a proxy for the effects of restrictive debt covenants.[6] In an effort to extend the work of Watts and Zimmerman (1978), he examined the effect of capital structure on a firm's attitudes towards the FASB's proposed elimination of the

---

[4]For example, debt proxies have been extensively used in lobbying studies, stock price studies, and studies of changes in investment, financing and operating decisions. Reviews of these can be found in Holthausen and Leftwich (1983), Kelly (1983), and Watts and Zimmerman (1986). Also see the recent study by Francis and Reiter (1987) in which an inverse relationship was reported between pension-funding level and the debt–equity ratio.

[5]Several other proxies have also been used, but on a limited basis. These include, among others, the ratio of private debt to public debt, the ratio of preferred stock to total equity, a convertible debt ratio, and a dummy variable for the existence of convertible debt.

[6]Deakin (1979) used the debt–equity ratio as an independent variable in a study designed to distinguish between firms using the full cost method and firms using the successful efforts method of accounting for oil and gas exploration costs. However, the ratio was not intended as a proxy for debt covenants and the author did not provide an explanation for his finding that full cost firms were more leveraged than successful efforts firms.

full cost accounting method for oil and gas companies. He suggested:

> (A)n accounting standard which would cause a reduction in reported earnings or net worth may put highly leveraged firms into the position of having to obtain costly amendments to their credit agreements. Thus, firms with high debt-to-equity ratios are hypothesized to oppose such an accounting standard. (p. 60)

Dhaliwal's results supported his hypothesis by showing that more highly leveraged firms used the income-enhancing full cost method and lobbied against its elimination.

Subsequent to the Dhaliwal (1980) study, several accounting choice studies have used arguments similar to those used by Dhaliwal, and have consistently found that firms with higher debt–equity ratios are more likely to use income-enhancing accounting methods. Many of these studies have been reviewed elsewhere [e.g., Holthausen and Leftwich (1983), Kelly (1983), and Watts and Zimmerman (1986)] and are not summarized here. These include examinations of interest capitalization–expense [Bowen, Noreen, and Lacey (1981)], income strategies involving four discretionary accounting methods [Zmijewski and Hagerman (1981)], the full cost–successful efforts methods of accounting by oil and gas companies [Lilien and Pastena (1982)], depreciation methods [Dhaliwal, Salamon, and Smith (1982)] and the method of accounting for research and development expenditures [Daley and Vigeland (1983)].

The trend towards using the debt–equity ratio as a proxy for the probability of violating accounting-based debt covenants has continued in several more recent studies. Hunt (1985) included the debt–equity ratio in an investigation of firms' reluctance to adopt the LIFO inventory method. Not only did Hunt include the debt–equity ratio as an independent variable, he also used it as a basis for eliminating firms from the analysis that had 'insignificant' levels of long-term debt.[7]. The results showed that nonadopters of LIFO were more levered than adopters, thus suggesting that 'nonadopters had financial ratios closer to violating restrictions in debt covenants than firms adopting or extending the use of LIFO' (p. 464).

El Gazzar, Lilien, and Pastena (1986) examined the effect of debt covenant restrictions on the method used for accounting for leases prior to FASB Statement No. 13. Similar to the previous studies, the researchers did not test actual financial constraints within covenants but instead assumed that the debt–equity ratio served as an adequate proxy. As expected, the authors found that high debt–equity ratios were positively associated with the operating lease method.

---

[7]Ayres (1986) used a similar procedure to control for the level of long-term debt in a study of the adoption date of Statement of Financial Accounting Standard No. 52 (foreign currency translation). However, she did not actually test the debt–equity hypothesis.

Johnson and Ramanan (1988) examined voluntary changes from successful efforts (SE) to full cost (FC) accounting by oil and gas firms during the 1970–1976 period. They included the ratio of long-term debt and preferred stock to tangible assets as one of three proxies for closeness to restrictive covenants.[8] The results showed that firms switching from SE to FC had higher leverage and capital expenditures in the two years leading up to, and in the year of, the accounting change. The authors conclude that their results are consistent with the debt covenant hypothesis.

Based on previous studies and recent work by El Gazzar, Lilien, and Pastena (1988) and Press and Weintrop (1988), Rusbarsky (1988) used the debt–equity ratio as a proxy for closeness to restrictive debt covenant restrictions in an examination of changes in depreciation method. As hypothesized, the results show that firms that switched from accelerated to straight-line depreciation in 1968 and 1969 had significantly higher debt–equity ratios than firms that continued using the accelerated method.

2.2. Legitimizing the debt–equity proxy

The results of the studies cited above provide consistent and convincing evidence of a positive relation between the debt–equity ratio and income-enhancing accounting methods. The conclusions reached in these studies, and other studies not discussed here, are based on the ability of the debt–equity ratio to proxy for the probability that a firm will violate an accounting-based debt covenant constraint. However, the validity of the debt–equity proxy as it has been used in previous studies has not been established. The importance of doing this is underscored by a recent study by Zimmer (1986) in which he investigated methods of accounting for interest by Australian real estate developers. Zimmer found that the debt–equity ratio was positively correlated with interest capitalization, but that the relation becomes insignificant when he controls for project-specific financing. This illustrates the point made by Watts and Zimmerman (1986, pp. 359–361) that the leverage ratio may be associated with accounting choice because both are being driven by some other variable (e.g., the investment opportunity set in this case). In other words, if the nature of the firm's production–investment decisions implies both a particular financing structure and a particular set of accounting methods, the accounting methods and the debt–equity ratio will be positively correlated, but both will be proxying for the nature of the firm's assets.

At this point in the development of a positive theory of the firm, especially in light of Zimmer's (1986) findings, the association between the debt–equity

---

[8]The other two proxies used by Johnson and Ramanan (1988) were earnings before interest divided by interest expense and cash dividends to common divided by available unrestricted retained earnings. Neither emerged as a statistically significant explanatory variable.

ratio and closeness to debt covenant constraints must be established to help validate previous studies. A positive relation between the debt–equity ratio and closeness to debt covenant constraints is a necessary, but not sufficient, condition to legitimize the debt–equity proxy as it has been used in previous research. Indeed, the proxy could be correlated with closeness to covenant constraints and not be a good proxy in some studies of accounting choice. For example, in the Daley and Vigeland (1983) paper, the debt–equity ratio was found to be positively correlated with capitalization of research and development costs. However, since many debt covenants require the effective write-off of intangible assets (including research and development costs), the reported leverage ratio used by Daley and Vigeland cannot be expected to proxy for closeness to default, nor provide an incentive to capitalize research and development expenditures (or any other intangible). Thus, even if the debt–equity ratio is found to be an adequate proxy for the probability of violating accounting-based debt covenants, researchers must be selective in its use. The ultimate test of the debt–equity proxy is its performance in empirical studies of accounting choice.

In order to help establish the validity of using the debt–equity proxy in examinations of accounting choice (and other accounting research), this study examines debt covenant restrictions for a sample of firms and tests the correspondence between both the existence and level of covenant restrictions and several variations of the debt–equity ratio. Based on the common assumption in prior research of a positive relation between the debt–equity ratio and the restrictiveness of accounting-based debt covenant provisions, we test two simple hypotheses in this study. First, we test the hypothesis that the debt–equity ratio is positively linked to the existence of restrictive debt covenants. Second, we test the hypothesis that there is a positive correlation between the debt–equity ratio and the restrictiveness of several common accounting-based debt covenant provisions.[9] The next section describes the methodology that we use to test these hypotheses.

3. Research methodology

3.1. Debt covenant restrictions

In order to determine the types of debt covenant restrictions that depend on accounting measurements, and are therefore influenced by accounting tech-

---

[9] We should note that Kalay (1982) presents evidence of a negative relation between the debt–equity ratio and the 'reservoir of payable funds' for a sample of 150 firms. The reservoir of payable funds represents retained earnings unrestricted by debt covenants. Thus, Kalay's findings support our second hypothesis, at least with respect to dividend constraints.

Table 1

Common accounting-based debt covenant restrictions.[a]

Restricted attribute	Covenant restrictions
Retained earnings[b]	Restricted retained earnings (RE)
Net assets[c]	Net tangible assets (NTA) Net assets (NA)
Working capital[d]	Minimum working capital (WC) Current assets divided by current liabilities (CA/CL)
Debt-to-equity[e]	Debt divided by net tangible assets (D/NTA) Debt divided by net assets (D/NA)

[a] Based on a review of the American Bar Foundation's *Commentaries on Indentures* (1971) and the debt covenant restrictions of a random sample of 20 firms chosen from *Moody's* (1985).

[b] The retained earnings restriction generally limits the payments of dividends and other distributions including redemptions and retirements of stock. The restriction is operationalized by requiring the firm to maintain a minimum (restricted) level of retained earnings.

[c] Net asset restrictions generally prohibit specific actions (e.g., investments, dividend payments, additional debt issues, etc.) unless minimum levels of net assets or net tangible assets are maintained.

[d] Working capital restrictions prohibit certain activities when a minimum level of working capital or a minimum ratio of current assets to current liabilities (current ratio) is not maintained. Prohibited activities include incurring additional debt, dividend payments or other distributions with respect to stock, and mergers and acquisitions.

[e] Debt-to-equity restrictions generally prohibit the issuance of additional debt if the action would increase the debt-to-equity ratio above a specified level. For purposes of the prescribed ratio, a restriction specifies debt as one of the following: (1) funded (long-term), (2) secured, (3) senior funded (nonsubordinated long-term), or (4) total. Equity is generally defined as either net assets or net tangible assets.

nique choice, the debt covenant provisions described in *Commentaries* and those included in a pilot sample of 20 firms randomly selected from *Moody's Industrial Manual* (1985) were examined. This examination revealed that four financial statement attributes (retained earnings, net assets, working capital, and the debt–equity ratio) are commonly restricted by debt covenant provisions.[10] These restrictions are operationalized by either a minimum level of the attribute (e.g., retained earnings) or by the use of a minimum-required or maximum-allowed ratio (e.g., a minimum current ratio or a maximum debt–equity ratio). Table 1 lists the four attributes and their related covenant

[10] Several other restrictions not directly affected by accounting numbers were also found. These include restrictions on the creation of liens on special assets, restrictions on the sale or other disposition of assets, restrictions on leasing activities, restrictions on the level of stock investments, extensions of credit, or advances, and limitations on additional debt.

restrictions. The seven covenant restrictions contained in table 1 are examined in this study.

3.2. Sample selection

To generalize this study's results, a random sample of firms was selected from *Moody's Industrial Manual* (1985) (*Moody's* hereinafter). *Moody's* was used because it includes a relatively diverse and representative population of firms. For example, *Moody's* reports information for all publicly traded corporations with the exception of those included in one of the specialized *Moody's* manuals, such as those for banks and finance institutions, utilities, and transportation firms.

While *Moody's* contains information on both public and private debt agreements, detailed descriptions of covenant restrictions are much more extensive and complete for public debt agreements than for private debt agreements [Begley (1989) and Press and Weintrop (1988)]. For example, Begley (1989) found that *Moody's* specifies accounting-based covenant restrictions in detail for public debt issues that have such restrictions, but often does not do so for private debt agreements. Similarly, Press and Weintrop (1988) report that, on average, *Moody's* contains only 50 percent of the accounting-based restrictions contained in a sample of private debt agreements. Consequently, the current study focuses mainly on the restrictions contained in public debt agreements and the results should not be generalized to private agreements. We should point out that it is not obvious whether public or private debt issues have a greater effect on management actions. One argument is that because private debt agreements can be renegotiated more easily and with less cost (in some cases, with a single phone call) than can public debt agreements (which typically require the trustee to obtain agreement by 2/3 of the debtholders before waiving covenant violations or agreeing to changes in restrictions), the restrictions imposed by public debt issues influence management actions more than private debt restrictions. An alternative argument suggests that because the cost of default is higher for public debt issues, they contain fewer and less restrictive covenants than private debt issues, and therefore have significantly less influence on management actions than private agreements.

An initial sample of 232 firms was selected for inclusion in this study. To ensure a random selection process, each firm listed in the index of *Moody's* was assigned a number from one to 1830 (i.e., the population size was 1830 firms). A four-digit random number table [Snedecor and Cochran (1980)] was then searched until 232 matches were obtained between the random numbers and the numbers assigned to the *Moody's* firms. When repeat random numbers were encountered, they were ignored since the firm with that number was already in the sample.

Prior to data collection, 32 sample firms were eliminated for one of three reasons. Nine firms were eliminated because their financial statements were stated in foreign currencies, and they were listed only on foreign stock exchanges.[11] Ten firms were eliminated because they were wholly-owned subsidiaries, and analyzing their financial statements or financial condition in isolation of the parent corporation could be misleading. The remaining 13 firms were eliminated due to their absence from the 1985 Compustat files (which were used as a data source). An investigation of these 13 firms revealed no systematic reasons for their absence from Compustat.

The 200 sample firms remaining after the above eliminations were then screened based on the most recent fiscal year-end disclosed in *Moody's*. Thirteen additional firms were deleted from the sample at this point because their most recent fiscal year-end was 1983.[12] Of the remaining 187 firms, 179 had a year-end during 1984 and eight had a year-end in early 1985.[13] These 187 firms constituted the final sample.

3.3. Data collection

Three sources of data were utilized in this study. *Moody's* served as the principal source of information related to the existence and types of debt covenant restrictions, and the required level or ratio that needed to be maintained to avoid technical default on the debt agreements. *Standard & Poor's Standard Corporate Descriptions* (1985) (*Standard & Poor's* hereinafter) was used to confirm the debt covenant details gathered from *Moody's*. For 51 percent of the sample, the information contained in the two sources was identical, and for 39 percent, *Standard & Poor's* contained consistent information, but less than that contained in *Moody's*. For the remaining 10 percent of the sample, *Standard & Poor's* contained more information than *Moody's*, and this additional information was included in the data set.

The financial data pertaining to the actual levels of restricted items and the data for the calculation of the debt proxies were obtained from the Compustat files. Since previous research has used different variations of the debt–equity ratio as a debt proxy, we examined several versions in this study. For example, debt has been variously defined as total debt, long-term debt, and nonconvertible debt. Equity has been defined to be stockholders' equity and net tangible

---

[11] See Collins and Dent (1979) for a discussion of the exclusion of foreign firms.

[12] The decision was made to eliminate the firms whose most recent year-end in the 1985 *Moody's* was prior to 1984 in order to minimize the problems created by nonsynchronous reporting periods in a cross-sectional analysis [Foster (1986)].

[13] 1984 fiscal-year data were used for the eight firms that had a 1985 fiscal year-end in the 1985 *Moody's* manual.

assets. Several studies have also used the ratio of total debt to total assets as a more general measure of firm leverage. Based on these observations, seven debt–equity ratios were calculated for each sample firm as follows:

1. Long-term debt/stockholders' equity (LTD/SE),
2. Total debt/stockholders' equity (TD/SE),
3. Nonconvertible debt/stockholders' equity (NCD/SE),
4. Long-term debt/net tangible assets (LTD/NTA),[14]
5. Total debt/net tangible assets (TD/NTA),
6. Nonconvertible debt/net tangible assets (NCD/NTA),
7. Total debt/total assets (TD/TA).

The next section discusses the analyses and results.

4. Analyses and results

4.1. Descriptive statistics

Examination of the data sources indicates that 29 (15.5 percent) of the 187 sample firms had no restrictive debt covenants. Another 23 firms (12.3 percent) had nonaccounting economic restrictions only.[15] Thus, for these 52 firms, restrictive debt covenants should be of little consequence to managers' choices of accounting techniques.

For the remaining 135 firms, the debt covenants contained one or more accounting-based restrictions.[16] One hundred three firms (55.1 percent of the sample) had retained earnings restrictions (RE), 65 firms (34.8 percent) had working capital restrictions (WC or CA/CL), 34 firms (18.2 percent) had net asset restrictions (NTA or NA), and 52 firms (27.8 percent) had debt–equity restrictions (D/NTA or D/NA). The breakdown of the specific types of restrictions is summarized in table 2.

---

[14] In calculating the proxy variables, net tangible assets (NTA) was defined as total assets minus intangibles.

[15] These nonaccounting restrictions are designed to preserve the firm's existence by protecting specific assets or by limiting (or requiring the payment of) certain of its obligations. For example, a mortgage agreement might require the maintenance, improvement, or rehabilitation of specific assets of the firm in order to protect debtholders from impairment of asset value. Other types of covenant provisions include prohibitions of liens or encumbrances on assets, prohibition of outright sale of assets, and prohibitions or limitations on sale–leaseback transactions and other rental arrangements. A more detailed description of these, and other, covenant restrictions can be found in Duke (1987).

[16] In all but one case of accounting-based restrictions, economic restrictions were also included in the debt agreements.

Table 2

Frequency of debt covenant restrictions.[a]

Restriction type	Specific restriction[b]	Frequency	Total firms[c]
None	—	29	29
Economic only	—	23	23
Retained earnings	*RE*	103	103
Working capital	*WC*	54	
	CA/CL	19	65
Net assets	*NTA*	18	
	NA	18	34
Debt-to-equity	*D/NTA*	29	
	D/NA	29	52[d]

[a] Based on a random sample of 187 firms taken from *Moody's* (1985).

[b] See table 1 for definitions of specific restrictions.

[c] Total firms sum to more than 187 due to multiple restrictions for some firms.

[d] Of these 52 firms, 22 had covenant restrictions on the ratio of *secured debt* to equity. For 20 of these 22 firms, the covenant required any new issues of secured debt plus current (as of the date of the covenant) secured debt to be less than some percentage (e.g., 5%) of net assets or net tangible assets. Of the remaining two firms, one had debt-to-equity restrictions defined in terms of new secured debt only and the other in terms of current secured debt only. For purposes of this study, our measurements always included *all* secured debt outstanding as of the balance sheet date, regardless of whether the secured debt was issued before or after the covenant date.

4.2. Statistical tests

Tables 3 and 4 summarize the results of tests of the relation between each of the seven proxy variables described earlier and the existence of and closeness to the specific covenant restrictions. Observation of table 3 indicates that all seven proxies capture the existence of restrictions on retained earnings, working capital, and net assets.[17] The debt–equity restrictions are not systematically related to the proxies, at least as measured by the Wilcoxon test.[18] As table 2 shows, the *RE* and *WC* restrictions are the most common types of

---

[17] As pointed out by the referee, one potential explanation for the relatively consistent results of the seven proxy variables is that they may be highly correlated. A correlation analysis indicates Pearson correlation coefficients in the range from 0.669 to 0.999 for proxies with identical denominators and in the range from -0.030 to 0.283 for proxies with dissimilar denominators. Thus, this prediction is at least partly borne out.

[18] Table 3 reports results of the Wilcoxon two-sample test which tests whether the independent groups were drawn from the same population while taking into account the rank value of each observation [Siegel (1956)]. Similar results (not reported here) were obtained using the less powerful Median test which takes into account only the location of each observation with respect to the combined median [Siegel (1956)].

Table 3

Tests of the relation between debt proxies and the existence of accounting-based debt covenant restrictions.[a]

Proxy[c]	Restricted attribute[b]			
	Retained earnings	Working capital	Net assets	Debt/ equity
LTD/SE	2.871 (0.002)	3.062 (0.001)	3.931 (0.001)	0.278 (0.391)
TD/SE	2.715 (0.003)	2.408 (0.008)	3.772 (0.001)	0.596 (0.276)
NCD/SE	2.762 (0.003)	3.305 (0.001)	4.044 (0.001)	0.645 (0.260)
LTD/NTA	2.745 (0.003)	2.651 (0.004)	3.326 (0.001)	0.077 (0.469)
TD/NTA	2.639 (0.004)	1.951 (0.025)	3.284 (0.001)	0.571 (0.284)
NCD/NTA	2.451 (0.007)	2.702 (0.004)	3.207 (0.001)	0.668 (0.252)
TD/TA	2.870 (0.002)	2.365 (0.009)	3.375 (0.001)	0.776 (0.219)

[a] These tests are based on a random sample of 187 firms taken from *Moody's* (1985). The table reports the Z-statistic and the associated probability values (in parentheses) of a one-tailed test (Wilcoxon two-sample test) of the null hypothesis of no difference in population means of the debt proxy groups classified by existence or nonexistence of a restriction on the listed attribute.
[b] Each attribute was assigned a one if restricted by one of the specific covenant restrictions listed in table 1 and a zero otherwise. For example, if *either* a minimum working capital restriction (WC) or a current ratio restriction (CA/CL) existed for a particular sample firm, the working capital attribute was assigned a one, and if neither restriction existed, the attribute was assigned a zero.
[c] The proxies employed are defined as follows: LTD/SE = long-term debt divided by stockholders' equity; TD/SE = total debt divided by stockholders' equity; NCD/SE = nonconvertible debt divided by stockholders' equity; LTD/NTA = long-term debt divided by net tangible assets (in calculating proxy variables, net tangible assets is defined as total assets minus intangibles); TD/NTA = total debt divided by net tangible assets; NCD/NTA = nonconvertible debt divided by net tangible assets; TD/TA = total debt divided by total assets.

restrictions present in our sample of firms. We examined the pattern of covenant restrictions for the 187 sample firms and found that only eight firms had accounting-based restrictions that did not restrict at least one of the three attributes captured by the debt proxies.

In order to examine the relation between the debt proxies and closeness to covenant restrictions, a 'closeness' ratio was calculated for each constraint which included the total (restricted plus unrestricted) and the restricted amounts of each item. These ratios were constructed so that as the ratio approached a value of 1.0, the firm would be moving closer to technical default (i.e., a value of 1.0 indicates technical default), and the ratio was set

Table 4

Correlations between debt proxies and closeness to debt covenant restrictions.[a]

Proxy[d]	n[c]	Closeness to specific covenant restrictions[b,c]						
		RE	WC	CA/CL	NTA	NA	D/NTA	D/NA
		172	152	181	178	178	187	187
LTD/SE		0.270	0.159	0.050	0.203	0.088	0.016	0.040
		(0.001)	(0.051)	(0.506)	(0.007)	(0.241)	(0.825)	(0.591)
TD/SE		0.249	0.119	−0.001	0.177	0.072	0.019	0.075
		(0.001)	(0.147)	(0.991)	(0.018)	(0.342)	(0.795)	(0.309)
NCD/SE		0.275	0.158	0.068	0.209	0.081	0.033	0.057
		(0.001)	(0.052)	(0.366)	(0.005)	(0.285)	(0.654)	(0.443)
LTD/NTA		0.279	0.139	0.056	0.204	0.055	0.025	−0.001
		(0.001)	(0.087)	(0.457)	(0.006)	(0.464)	(0.737)	(0.995)
TD/NTA		0.269	0.122	−0.039	0.151	0.060	0.024	0.053
		(0.001)	(0.134)	(0.604)	(0.045)	(0.426)	(0.749)	(0.469)
NCD/NTA		0.260	0.094	0.079	0.221	−0.002	0.057	0.025
		(0.001)	(0.249)	(0.292)	(0.003)	(0.976)	(0.438)	(0.738)
TD/TA		0.276	0.128	−0.019	0.158	0.055	0.047	0.058
		(0.001)	(0.116)	(0.802)	(0.035)	(0.468)	(0.524)	(0.434)

[a] This table reports Spearman correlation coefficients and the associated probability values (in parentheses) of the correlations between the debt proxies and measures of closeness to covenant restrictions for a random sample of 187 firms taken from *Moody's* (1985).

[b] Measures of closeness to covenant restrictions were calculated as follows: RE = restricted retained earnings divided by total retained earnings for firms with this restriction, = 0 otherwise; WC = restricted working capital divided by total working capital for firms with this restriction, = 0 otherwise; CA/CL = restricted ratio of current assets to current liabilities divided by the total ratio of current assets to current liabilities for firms with this restriction, = 0 otherwise; NTA = restricted net tangible assets divided by total net tangible assets for firms with this restriction, = 0 otherwise; NA = restricted net assets divided by total net assets for firms with this restriction, = 0 otherwise; D/NTA = ratio of total debt to net tangible assets divided by the restricted ratio of debt to net tangible assets for firms with this restriction, = 0 otherwise; D/NA = ratio of total debt to net assets divided by the restricted ratio of debt to net assets for firms with this restriction, = 0 otherwise.

[c] Following general definitions contained in *Commentaries*, in calculating the closeness measures, net tangible assets was defined as total assets (net of reserves for depreciation, depletion, etc.) less the sum of intangible assets and current liabilities (pp. 87–89), and net assets (net worth) was defined as total assets less the sum of current liabilities and long-term liabilities (pp. 89–91).

Also, as pointed out in footnote e to table 1, debt can be specified in one of four ways (funded, secured, senior funded, or total). In calculating the closeness measures, the definition of debt used in the covenant restriction was used, and when more than one debt–equity restriction existed, the *most restrictive* one was used in the analysis.

[d] The proxies employed are defined as follows: LTD/SE = long-term debt divided by stockholders' equity; TD/SE = total debt divided by stockholders' equity; NCD/SE = nonconvertible debt divided by stockholders' equity; LTD/NTA = long-term debt divided by net tangible assets (total assets minus intangibles); TD/NTA = total debt divided by net tangible assets; NCD/NTA = nonconvertible debt divided by net tangible assets; TD/TA = total debt divided by total assets.

[e] n = number of sample firms included in correlation analysis for the last four proxy variables. For the first three proxies, the number of sample firms was one less than the number listed because one firm had no stockholder equity and this resulted in a zero in the denominator of these proxies. For some sample firms, a specific restriction existed, but insufficient data was disclosed in *Moody's* to calculate the closeness measure. These firms were eliminated from the analysis and resulted in an *n* lower than 187 for some restrictions.

equal to zero if the firm had no restrictions. For example, the ratio for the *RE* restriction was calculated by dividing restricted retained earnings by total retained earnings, and so on. Table 4 contains definitions of the closeness measures and shows the correlation coefficients between each of them and the debt–equity proxy variables. The correlation coefficients shown in table 4 generally support the results reported in table 3. All the debt proxies are positively correlated with the *RE* and *NTA* restrictions, and three of the proxies are positively correlated with the *WC* restriction (at the 0.10 level of significance). The proxies do not appear to be related to the closeness measures for the other four restrictions (*CA/CL*, *NA*, *D/NTA*, and *D/NA*).

Although table 4 reports positive correlations between the proxies and closeness measures for three covenant restrictions, because the sample included firms without regard to whether or not they were subject to the particular covenant restrictions, the results are open to two alternative interpretations. Specifically, leverage could be proxying for the incentive to operate closer to covenants as leverage increases, or it could be proxying because as leverage increases, a firm is more likely to include restrictive covenants in debt agreements. In order to provide additional insight into the relation between the closeness measures and the leverage proxies, a correlation analysis was performed on the subsamples of firms subject to each of the seven covenant restrictions. The results are presented in table 5.

The correlations reported in table 5 provide more definitive results than those reported in table 4. With respect to the *RE* restriction, the correlations increased significantly, indicating that as leverage increases, firms operate closer to retained earnings covenant restrictions. Alternatively, the correlations between the *NTA* restriction and the leverage proxies are negative and insignificantly different from zero in table 5, indicating that the positive correlations reported in table 4 are due to the positive relation between leverage and the existence of the covenant. The results for the other five covenant restrictions are generally mixed. Although many of the correlations are higher in table 5 than in table 4, they are insignificantly different from zero. This suggests that the significant correlations reported in table 4 for *WC* were driven by the existence of restrictive covenants rather than a positive relation between leverage and the covenant closeness measure.

The results reported in tables 3, 4, and 5 generally support both hypotheses examined in this paper. Specifically, they indicate a positive relation between the seven debt proxies examined and the existence of several common accounting-based debt covenant restrictions. Furthermore, the results indicate significant correlations between the debt proxies and the restrictiveness of the most prevalent type of accounting-based covenant restriction, the one related to retained earnings. Thus, to the extent researchers are interested in capturing the retained earnings restriction, a debt–equity ratio appears to be a good

Table 5

Correlations between debt proxies and closeness to actual debt covenant restrictions.[a]

Proxy[d]	n^e	Closeness to specific covenant restrictions[b,c]						
		RE	WC	CA/CL	NTA	NA	D/NTA	D/NA
		88	19	13	9	9	31	28
TD/SE		0.401	0.210	0.231	−0.250	0.267	−0.010	0.019
		(0.001)	(0.389)	(0.448)	(0.517)	(0.488)	(0.955)	(0.924)
TD/SE		0.341	0.293	0.253	−0.400	0.250	0.002	0.019
		(0.001)	(0.223)	(0.405)	(0.286)	(0.517)	(0.991)	(0.925)
NCD/SE		0.408	0.220	0.231	−0.133	0.250	−0.056	0.007
		(0.001)	(0.365)	(0.448)	(0.732)	(0.517)	(0.765)	(0.972)
LTD/NTA		0.449	0.019	0.363	−0.117	0.400	0.059	−0.006
		(0.001)	(0.937)	(0.223)	(0.765)	(0.286)	(0.752)	(0.975)
TD/NTA		0.390	0.346	0.170	−0.367	0.133	0.133	0.014
		(0.001)	(0.146)	(0.578)	(0.332)	(0.732)	(0.476)	(0.945)
NCD/NTA		0.412	−0.162	0.363	−0.117	0.050	0.014	−0.030
		(0.001)	(0.507)	(0.223)	(0.765)	(0.898)	(0.942)	(0.879)
TD/TA		0.382	0.322	0.176	−0.250	0.333	0.123	−0.002
		(0.001)	(0.178)	(0.566)	(0.517)	(0.381)	(0.509)	(0.992)

[a] This table reports Spearman correlation coefficients and the associated probability values (in parentheses) of the correlations between the debt proxies and measures of closeness to covenant restrictions for a subsample of firms (drawn from the sample described in table 4) subject to the particular covenant restriction and for which the level (or amount) of the restriction could be determined from *Moody's*.

[b] Measures of closeness to covenant restrictions were calculated as follows: RE = restricted retained earnings divided by total retained earnings; WC = restricted working capital divided by total working capital; CA/CL = restricted ratio of current assets to current liabilities divided by the total ratio of current assets to current liabilities; NTA = restricted net tangible assets divided by total net tangible assets; NA = restricted net assets divided by total net assets; D/NTA = ratio of total debt to net tangible assets divided by the restricted ratio of debt to net tangible assets; D/NA = ratio of total debt to net assets divided by the restricted ratio of debt to net assets.

[c] See footnote c, table 4.

[d] See footnote d, table 4.

[e] n = number of firms included in correlation analysis. For some firms, a specific restriction existed, but insufficient data was disclosed in *Moody's* to calculate the closeness measure. These firms were eliminated from the analysis.

proxy. The same can be said for the WC and NTA restrictions as well, although the proxies appear to be related only to the existence of these restrictions, and not to their restrictiveness.

Two other observations deserve comment. First, the highest correlation reported in tables 4 and 5 is 0.449. This translates to an R^2 of 20.16 percent, indicating that even for the strongest relation reported in this study, there is considerable variation in closeness to covenants unexplained by leverage, and vice versa. Second, it's interesting to note that the results are relatively consistent across all seven proxy variables examined. Thus, the definition of debt–equity does not appear to be a critical research design issue.

5. Summary and conclusion

A substantial body of accounting literature has emerged in recent years which examines the economic implications of accounting-based debt covenant restrictions. Many of the empirical studies have attempted to explain observed phenomena based on the existence and tightness of restrictive debt covenants, but have relied on one or more proxy variables to measure the restrictiveness of the covenants, rather than examining actual covenant restrictions. A necessary, although not sufficient, condition for legitimizing the use of proxy variables rather than the details of actual debt covenants is an association between the proxies and restrictive covenants. This study investigates the relation between seven variations of the most commonly-used debt proxy, the debt–equity ratio, and seven common debt covenant restrictions. The results indicate that all seven versions of the debt–equity proxy are positively related to the existence and tightness of retained earnings restrictions. All seven proxies are also related to the existence of working capital and net tangible asset restrictions. The three restrictions captured by the proxy variables include the two most prevalent types of accounting-based restrictions (retained earnings and working capital) present in the 187-firm sample used in this study.

The evidence presented here provides one of the necessary conditions for using the debt–equity ratio as a proxy for the existence and tightness of debt covenant restrictions. However, the ultimate test of the ability of the debt–equity ratio to proxy for the probability that a firm will violate an accounting-based covenant is its performance in empirical studies of accounting choice. Future research should go one step further to see if the same results are obtained using the debt–equity ratio as with actual covenant restrictions. Nonetheless, the results reported here help validate the conclusions reached in the prior research that assumed a positive relation between the debt–equity ratio and restrictive debt covenants. Furthermore, the fact that our results are generally not sensitive to the definition of the debt–equity ratio suggests that researchers are safe in using any of the versions tested here, and that the comparability of previous studies that used different definitions does not appear to have been compromised.

It should be noted that four of the seven specific restrictions examined in this study are not captured by the debt–equity ratio. Thus, to the extent researchers are interested in investigating the effects of these particular types of restrictions, either a better proxy must be used or the actual covenant restrictions must be examined. Furthermore, it should be noted that this study examines only the validity of using the debt–equity ratio as a proxy for restrictive debt covenants. Still unresolved are the important issues of the costs of violating restrictive covenants and how these costs are related to the tightness of the restrictions. It is hoped that this paper provides a step toward the resolution of these issues.

References

American Bar Foundation, 1971, Commentaries on indentures (American Bar Foundation, Chicago, IL).

Ayres, F.L., 1986, Characteristics of firms electing early adoption of SFAS 52, Journal of Accounting and Economics 8, 143–158.

Begley, J., 1989, The use of accounting and non-accounting based covenants in public debenture agreements: An empirical investigation, Working paper (University of Rochester, Rochester, NY).

Bowen, R.M., E.W. Noreen, and J.M. Lacey, 1981, Determinants of the corporate decision to capitalize interest, Journal of Accounting and Economics 3, 151–179.

Collins, D.W. and W.T. Dent, 1979, The proposed elimination of full cost accounting in the extractive petroleum industry, Journal of Accounting and Economics 1, 3–44.

Daley, L.S. and R.L. Vigeland, 1983, The effects of debt covenants and political costs on the choice of accounting methods: The case of accounting for R&D costs, Journal of Accounting and Economics 5, 195–211.

Deakin, E.B., III, 1979, An analysis of differences between non-major oil firms using successful efforts and full cost methods, The Accounting Review, Oct., 722–734.

Dhaliwal, D.S., 1980, The effect of the firm's capital structure on the choice of accounting methods, The Accounting Review, Jan., 78–84.

Dhaliwal, D.S., G.L. Salamon, and E.D. Smith, 1982, The effect of owner versus management control on the choice of accounting methods, Journal of Accounting and Economics 4, 41–53.

Duke, J.C., 1987, Debt covenant restrictions and accounting technique choice: An empirical study, Unpublished dissertation (Pennsylvania State University, Philadelphia, PA).

El Gazzar, S., S. Lilien, and V. Pastena, 1986, Accounting for leases by lessees, Journal of Accounting and Economics 8, 217–237.

El Gazzar, S., S. Lilien, and V. Pastena, 1988, Does off-balance sheet financing allow firms to circumvent financial covenant restrictions?, Working paper (Baruch College of CUNY, New York, NY).

Fogelson, J.H., 1978, The impact of changes in accounting principles on restrictive covenants in credit agreements and indentures, The Business Lawyer, Jan., 769–787.

Foster, G., 1986, Financial statement analysis (Prentice-Hall, Englewood Cliffs, NJ).

Francis, J.R. and S.A. Reiter, 1987, Determinants of corporate pension funding strategy, Journal of Accounting and Economics 9, 35–59.

Holthausen, R.W. and R.W. Leftwich, 1983, The economic consequences of accounting choice: Implications of costly contracting and monitoring, Journal of Accounting and Economics 5, 77–117.

Hunt, H.G., III, 1985, Potential determinants of corporate inventory accounting decisions, Journal of Accounting Research, Autumn, 448–467.

Jensen, M.C. and W.H. Meckling, 1976, Theory of the firm: Managerial behavior, agency costs and ownership structure, Journal of Financial Economics 4, 305–360.

Johnson, W.B. and R. Ramanan, 1988, Discretionary accounting changes from 'successful efforts' to 'full cost' methods: 1970–1976, The Accounting Review, Jan., 96–110.

Kalay, A., 1982, Stockholder–bondholder conflict and dividend constraints, Journal of Financial Economics 10, 211–233.

Kelly, L., 1983, The development of a positive theory of corporate management's role in external financial reporting, Journal of Accounting Literature, Spring, 111–150.

Kelly, L., 1985, Corporate management lobbying on FAS No. 8: Some further evidence, Journal of Accounting Research, Autumn, 619–632.

Leftwich, R., 1983, Accounting information in private markets: Evidence from private lending agreements, The Accounting Review, Jan., 23–42.

Lilien, S. and V. Pastena, 1982, Determinants of intramethod choice in the oil and gas industry, Journal of Accounting and Economics 4, 145–170.

Moody's Investors Service, 1985, Moody's industrial manual (Moody's Investors Service, Inc., New York, NY).

Press, E.G. and J. Weintrop, 1988, Accounting-based debt constraints and their association with leverage, Presented at the Olin/JAE Conference at the University of Rochester, Nov.; 1990, Accounting-based constraints in public and private debt agreements, Journal of Accounting and Economics, this issue.

Rusbarsky, M., 1988, Motivations for discretionary accounting changes: The case of the switch from accelerated to straight-line depreciation, Working paper (Graduate School of Management, University of California, Riverside, CA).

Siegel, S., 1956, Nonparametric statistics for the behavioral sciences (McGraw-Hill, New York, NY).

Smith, C.W. and J.B. Warner, 1979, On financial contracting: An analysis of bond covenants, Journal of Financial Economics 7, 117–161.

Snedecor, G.W. and W.C. Cochran, 1980, Statistical methods (Iowa State University Press, Ames, IA).

Standard & Poor's Corporation, 1985, Standard corporate descriptions (Standard & Poor's Corporation, New York, NY).

Watts, R.L. and J.L. Zimmerman, 1978, Towards a positive theory of the determination of accounting standards, The Accounting Review, Jan., 112–134.

Watts, R.L. and J.L. Zimmerman, 1986, Positive accounting theory (Prentice-Hall, Englewood Cliffs, NJ).

Zimmer, I., 1986, Accounting for interest by real estate developers, Journal of Accounting and Economics 8, 37–51.

Zmijewski, M.E. and R.L. Hagerman, 1981, An income strategy approach to the positive theory of accounting standard setting/choice, Journal of Accounting and Economics 3, 129–149.

III

COMPENSATION CONTRACTS AND ACCOUNTING POLICY CHOICE

1 Smith, Clifford W., Jr. and Ross L. Watts, "Incentive and Tax Effects of Executive Compensation Plans," *Australian Journal of Management*, 7 (1982), pp. 139–157.

2 Healy, Paul M., " The Effect of Bonus Schemes on Accounting Decisions," *Journal of Accounting and Economics*, 7 (1985), pp. 85–107.

3 Healy, Paul M., Sok-Hyon Kang and Krishna G. Palepu, "The Effect of Accounting Procedure Changes on CEOs' Cash Salary and Bonus Compensation," *Journal of Accounting and Economics*, 9 (1987), pp. 7–34.

4 Larcker, David F., "The Association Between Performance Plan Adoption and Corporate Capital Investment," *Journal of Accounting and Economics*, 5 (1983), pp. 3–30.

5 Bhagat, Sanjai, James A. Brickley and Ronald C. Lease, "Incentive Effects of Stock Purchase Plans," *Journal of Financial Economics*, 14 (1985), pp. 195–215.

6 Brickley, James A., Sanjai Bhagat and Ronald C. Lease (1985), "The Impact of Long-Range Managerial Compensation Plans on Shareholder Wealth," *Journal of Accounting and Economics*, 7 (1985), pp. 115–129.

7 Lambert, Richard A. and David F. Larcker, "An Analysis of the Use of Accounting and Market Measures of Performance in Executive Compensation Contracts," *Journal of Accounting Research*, 25 (1987, Supplement), pp. 85–125.

8 Defeo, Victor J., Richard A. Lambert and David F. Larcker, "The Executive Compensation Effects of Equity-for-Debt Swaps," *The Accounting Review*, 64 (1989), pp. 201–227.

9 Dhaliwal, Dan S., Gerald L. Salamon and E. Dan Smith, "The Effect of Owner Versus Management Control on the Choice of Accounting Methods," *Journal of Accounting and Economics*, 4 (1982), pp. 41–53.

10 Thomas, Jacob K., "Why Do Firms Terminate Their Overfunded Pension Plans?" *Journal of Accounting and Economics*, 11 (1989), pp. 361–398.

11 Moyer (Liberty), Susan E. and Jerold L. Zimmerman, "Labor Union Contract Negotiations and Accounting Choices," *The Accounting Review*, 61 (1986), pp. 692–712.

A second set of contracts that give rise to a demand for accounting information is the corporation's employment contracts with its managers. Management compensation has become an important topic of research, for at least three reasons. First, it has widespread interest: there is an extensive debate in the popular press on the level of management compensation in the U.S. and its sensitivity to corporate performance.[1] For accountants, the topic is interesting because of the role that accounting performance measures play in management compensation and also because of the role managers play in the production of accounting information. Second, large U.S. corporations typically compensate managers under the terms of formal, legally-executed plans that are placed in the public domain, so in consequence the data is abundant, accessible and of high quality. Third, the topic lends itself readily to principal/agent theory, with stockholders modelled as principals and managers as their agents. Given this unusual conjunction of external interest in the topic, available data and available theory, it is not surprising that management compensation is extensively researched in the accounting literature, as well as in the wider financial economics and economics literatures.

In the accounting literature, the research focus has been on the use of accounting information in management compensation plans and on its interaction with competing information (principally, stock price performance). A related issue has been the extent and form of management manipulation of reported accounting performance measures, motivated by compensation effects. There is clear evidence of the use of accounting information in this context and an emerging literature on the form this usage takes.

Smith and Watts (1982) describe the properties of various types of formal compensation plans and the frequencies with which they are observed. Compensation can include salary, bonuses based in part on accounting performance measures, and payoffs based on stock price performance (stock appreciation rights, options, etc.). They develop and test several hypotheses based on the theory that compensation plans are designed to reduce conflicts of interest between managers and shareholders (that is, to align the incentives of managers and shareholders). While there also is evidence that compensation plan design is motivated by tax considerations, the principal/agent hypotheses perform well. **Smith and Watts** observe that one of the advantages of accounting earnings, relative to stock price, is that it can be decomposed into segments (for example, into divisional profits) and thus used in compensating segment managers.

Larcker (1983) distinguishes bonus elements of compensation schemes (using current earnings performance) and long-term elements (using earnings performance over a longer period). For example, long-term plans might make payoffs that are a function of earnings growth, relative to an agreed target or to the performance of competitors, over an extended period. **Larcker** shows that corporations adopting such plans subsequently experience

[1]See Crystal (1991) and Jensen and Murphy (1990).

increases in capital expenditures, relative to a control sample. At the time the plans are announced, the announcing corporations' stock prices on average increase. The implication is that the incentives of managers and stockholders are being aligned more closely by the adoption of the new, more forward-looking plan.[2] Incidentally, this evidence also suggests that these corporations deliberately are not myopically focused on short-term performance, and design their compensation schemes accordingly. The evidence of **Brickley, Bhagat and Lease (1985)** and **Bhagat, Brickley and Lease (1985)** confirms these results with larger and more diverse samples of corporations and compensation plans.

Because management compensation is based in part on reported earnings, and because managers have some discretion over what earnings are reported, it is natural to ask whether (and to what extent) managers exercise their discretion in their self interest. This is the *opportunistic behavior* hypothesis. **Dhaliwal, Salamon and Smith (1982)** assume that straight-line depreciation invariably leads to higher reported earnings, total assets and retained earnings, relative to accelerated depreciation. They report that manager-controlled firms are more likely to choose straight-line depreciation, versus accelerated depreciation, than owner-controlled firms. They interpret the result as evidence of managers acting in their self interest to increase compensation, in conflict with the interests of stockholders. Note that they control, for the depreciation method used for tax purposes, size and leverage, in an attempt to deal with correlated omitted variables.

Healy (1985) and **Healy, Kang and Palepu (1987)** report a range of evidence consistent with the opportunistic behavior hypothesis. The evidence includes:

1. The sign of the effect of accounting accruals on reported income tends to be consistent with the bonus-induced incentives of managers;
2. Changes in accounting policies are correlated with the adoption of bonus plans; and
3. After accounting policy changes in firms with ongoing bonus plans, compensation tends to be based on reported earnings (without adjustment for the effect of the accounting change).

Some of these results do not clearly distinguish the predictions of the opportunistic behavior and efficiency hypotheses. Consider results (2) and (3) above. It is feasible that change in an omitted variable causes both the efficient accounting method and the efficient method of determining management compensation to change. For example, a reduction in the rate of growth of the corporation, as its business matures, could be associated both with a change in optimal depreciation or inventory method and in the desirability of a more-formal compensation plan. Mature businesses tend to have fewer accounting accrual problems, so they seem more likely to base compensation on accounting performance measures. On the other hand, result (1) above, in **Healy (1985)**, appears robust, particularly because **Healy** shows that ceilings on compensation have a predictable effect on accounting accruals. The contribution of correlated omitted variables to the results in this literature remains unclear.

Defeo, Lambert and Larcker (1989) offer some promise of controlling for omitted vari-

---

[2]It does not follow that the previous plan was sub-optimal. The new plan could be a response to an exogenous change in the investment opportunity set of the corporation. Nor does it follow that companies without long-term plans are behaving sub-optimally: they might have other ways of incenting managers to consider the long term; or they might rationally have shorter horizons.

ables. They study compensation as a function of reported earnings, for corporations whose earnings include gains from debt/equity swaps. They find evidence that managers' wealths increase due to the swap gain and interpret this as evidence of successful earnings manipulation. However, even this research design is not "clean," because it is not clear that it would be optimal, in the absence of costs of monitoring managers' opportunism, to ignore swap gains in management compensation. Swap gains typically occur when firms have borrowed at an *ex post* low interest rate. It is not clear that optimal compensation plans fail to reward this.

Lambert and Larcker (1987) adopt a cross-sectional research design that treats the form of the compensation contract as endogenous. They thus shed light on the literature described above that treats plan adoption as exogenous. They build on Holmstrom's (1979) result that, given two imperfect signals for determining compensation, the relative weights used depend on the signals' respective signal-to-noise ratios. **Lambert and Larcker** study accounting earnings (specifically, rate of return on equity) and stock price performance as signals. Their principal conclusion is that the relative weight for earnings is a decreasing function of: (1) the variance of the accounting performance variable, relative to the variance of stock price performance; and (2) growth. The relative accounting variance is a proxy for relative noise. Since accounting accrual problems are a function of growth, it is a similar proxy. Both results therefore suggest that when accounting measures are less noisy they are more used. This result can be presumed to apply in contexts other than management compensation: in debt contracts, by customers, in the stock market, etc.

Lambert and Larcker (1987) also report that more relative weight is attached to accounting performance in compensation, and correspondingly less on stock price performance, as the value of managers' personal stock holdings increase. They interpret this result as indicating that the weight given to stock performance outside of the compensation plan (due to personal stock ownership) is a substitute for weight given inside the plan.

While the evidence used in this literature primarily relates to formal management compensation schemes, for which the data are readily available, it seems likely that corporations' payoffs to (and the wealths of) other employees are a function of accounting performance reports as well. **Moyer (Liberty) and Zimmerman (1986)** study the role of reported earnings in contract negotiations with labor unions. They confine their attention to the hypothesis that managers select accounting methods that reduce reported earnings in order to favorably influence the outcome of the negotiations. They find no reliable evidence to support this hypothesis. **Thomas (1989)** studies the termination of overfunded corporate employee pension plans. He concludes that terminations are motivated by a demand for cash by underperforming corporations. The implication is that overfunding of pension plans allows corporations to build funded but unrecorded ("off balance sheet") reserves during "good" times, to be drawn down in "bad" times. These two studies aside, little knowledge is available concerning the use of accounting numbers in determining bonuses, salaries, promotions, reemployment and other payoffs for employees other than senior managers.

INCENTIVE AND TAX EFFECTS OF
EXECUTIVE COMPENSATION PLANS

by
Clifford W. Smith, Jr.
Ross L. Watts*

Abstract:

The ability of two (non-mutually exclusive) potential explanations for executive compensation plans is examined. One is that the plans reduce the combined tax liability of the corporation and its managers. The other is that the plans encourage the managers to maximize the value of the firm. It is found that the tax effect can explain some of the popularity of compensation plans, some of the variation in their use across firms, and the timing of changes in the provisions of the plans. However, there are variations in the cross-sectional use of the plans which cannot be explained by taxes, which can be explained by incentive effects.

Keywords:

EXECUTIVE COMPENSATION; INCENTIVES; TAXES

*The University of Rochester. We wish to acknowledge the financial support of the Center for Research in Government Policy and Business and the Managerial Economic Research Center, Graduate School of Management, University of Rochester, Rochester, New York, USA.

1. *INTRODUCTION*

Executive compensation plans often include provisions whose stated objective is to encourage the executive to maximize the value of the firm. These plans formally tie the executive's compensation to some measure of firm performance (e.g., earnings, stock price, etc.). In the U.S. these plans are wide-spread and becoming more popular. In 1970, 65 percent of medium-size and larger U.S. manufacturing companies had annual bonus plans, while in 1980, 90 percent of those firms has such plans.[1] Moreover, Larcker (1981) reports that in 1978 and 1979 over 85 percent of the largest 1000 firms had at least one type of incentive plan other than a bonus. In Australia bonus plans are less common, particularly among Australian owned companies, nevertheless they are employed by a significant number of companies. Chandler and Macleod Consultants Pty. Ltd. (1981, p.27) report that 35 percent of their sample of Australian companies had bonus plans.

There are at least two (non-mutually exclusive) potential explanations of the popularity of these compensation plans. One is that the plans reduce the combined tax liability of the corporation and its managers. The other is that the plans do indeed encourage the managers to maximize the value of the firm. The tax effect can explain the popularity of the plans, some of the variation in their use across firms, and the timing of switches in the use of particular provisions. However, there are variations in the cross-sectional use of plans which cannot be explained by taxes; these can be explained by incentive effects as the analysis in this paper demonstrates. Because of the greater availability of data, U.S. incentive plans are used in the analysis.

The paper briefly summarizes the types of compensation plans and their relative frequency in Section 2. Section 3 analyzes the incentive effects of the different types of compensation plans. In Section 4 the tax effects and extent to which taxes and incentives can explain systematic variations in the use of incentive plans across firms and across time is discussed. Finally, Section 5 contains some concluding comments.

2. *COMPONENTS OF COMPENSATION PLANS*

A. *Salary*

The most common component of executive compensation plans is a pre-specified salary. All firms use salary as a means of executive compensation. It typically accounts for more dollars of compensation than any other form. While salary is typically the greatest proportion of compensation it is usually not the only form of compensation. In 1979 each one of the largest 100 firms in the U.S. had at least one type of incentive provision. Salaries vary by firm size both for firms which have bonus plans and those which do not [see Conference Board (1979, p.17)].

It has been suggested that over time salaries vary with the previous year's reported profits and rates of return on shares, because salaries are negotiated prior to the year for which they are paid. However, there is little evidence to confirm this hypothesis; previous empirical studies have lumped salary and bonus together when examining the time series relationship between executive compensation and profits.

There are components of executive compensation other than salary which do not tie the manager's compensation to performance measures ex ante, for example, pension plans and life and medical insurance. However, these are usually either fixed or tied to salary, so for purposes of analyzing the differential effects of incentive plans we consider these other methods as part of the salary method of

---

[1]These numbers are taken from Conference Board (1980, p.4).

compensation.

B. Bonus Plans

While the managerial salaries vary with past performance, they are not formally tied at the beginning of a compensation period to the firm's performance in that period. But incentive plans do formally tie compensation ex ante (before the fact) to performance. The most common type of incentive plan is the bonus plan. Over 75 percent of medium and larger size manufacturing firms have bonus plans. Typically under a bonus plan the executive is rewarded at year-end on the basis of that year's performance, measured as a function of accounting earnings.

Typically the bonus plan specifies a schedule of allowable contributions to the bonus pool. The schedule normally specifies a minimum level of accounting profits which must be reached before anyone in the corporation can receive a bonus award. The plan also specifies the allowable fraction of the excess of earnings over the minimum which can be transferred to the bonus pool. Finally some plans specify a cap on bonus contributions as a function of dividend payments. For example, the General Motors bonus plan (1972) states:

> ... The Corporation shall maintain a reserve for the purposes of this plan and the General Motors Stock Option Plan, to which shall be credited for each year, with a corresponding charge to income for such year, an amount which the independent public accountants of the Corporation determine and report to be 8% of the net earnings which exceed 7% but not 15% of net capital, plus 5% of the net earnings which exceed 15% of net capital, provided that the amount credited to the reserve may not be in excess of the amount paid out as dividends on the common stock of the Corporation during that year ... .

Within this broad outline, specific provisions of the bonus plans vary. The minimum (or bogey) can be set either as a percentage of stockholders' equity or total capital (stockholders' equity plus long-term debt). If the bonus formula is based on pre-tax profits the minimum profit level is approximately 10 percent of stockholders' equity or total capital. If the bonus formula is based on after tax profits, the equivalent number is 8 percent.[2]

The bonus plan is administered by the compensation committee (a committee of the board of directors composed of non-management directors). They determine the contribution to the pool, subject to the constraints of the plan. From the bonus pool, the compensation committee makes awards to individual managers. There are often maximums for the award to any individual. The most common such maximum across all salary levels is 50 percent of base salary [Conference Board (1979, p.11)]. However Towers, Perrin, Forster and Crosby (1980, p.9) separate the bonus and salary of the Chief Executive Officer for 1979 for 36 of the largest 100 U.S. firms. They find the median ratio of bonus to salary is 70 percent. The proportion of bonus to salary increases both with the size of the firm and the manager's rank within the firm.

Generally, the entire bonus is paid out in cash soon after it is awarded, but some plans allow executives to choose to defer the payment until they retire. A few plans require the award to be paid out in installments over several years. As of 1978 only 10 percent of bonus plans required deferred payments [Conference Board (1979, p.25)].

The bonus plan is administered so that top executives typically receive an award. Even in 1975 when the after tax profits of the Fortune 500 firms fell 13 percent,

---

[2]These numbers are the means of percentages given in Conference Board (1979) Tables 9 and 10, pp.19-20.

only 16 percent of those firms with bonus plans did not pay a bonus [Conference
Board (1979, p.18)].

C. Stock Options

Many companies compensate their top executives by providing them with options to
purchase a given number of the firm's shares at anytime within a given period
(exercise period) at a precribed price (the exercise price). (Technically, these
options are warrants since they are issued by the firm itself.) In 1980, 83
percent of the 100 largest companies in the U.S. had option plans. The
popularity of the plans declines with the size of the company. For example, 68
percent of the Conference Board's sample of 478 manufacturing companies had an
option plan in 1980.

The award of options is made by the compensation committee. Option plans
restrict both the total number of options which can be granted in aggregate to
executives and the total number that can be granted to any one individual over
the life of the plan. The exercise price is typically equal to the stock price
at the date the option is granted. Options have a legal time limit of 10 years
for their exercise; however many companies specify a shorter time limit. Some
plans postpone the exercise period to begin after the date of the option grant.
For example, Shell Oil (U.S.) Company's 1971 Plan requires the executive to
remain with the company for 18 months after the grant and the option is not
exercisable until the end of those 18 months. The option typically terminates if
the executive leaves the company. In the case of death, termination of the
option will usually occur some time (e.g., 12 months) after death.

D. Stock Appreciation Rights

Stock appreciation rights are offered by companies along with options. In 1980,
68 of the largest 100 U.S. corporations had stock appreciation rights. Under a
stock appreciation right executives may choose to give up their option and
receive the difference between the stock price and the exercise price (the
appreciation). Providing managers alternatives of options and rights enables
them to reduce transactions costs associated with exercising options and selling
shares should they want cash. If they want shares, options will minimize
transactions costs.

E. Restricted Stock Plans

Under a restricted stock plan the company awards shares to executives subject to
restrictions on sale. These restrictions are removed when the shares are "earned
out" (e.g., when the executive has worked for a specified period following the
grant of the snares). Until the snares are earned out they are usually subject
to forfeiture if the executive leaves the corporation. Restricted stock plans
are sometimes used as part of the bonus plan (e.g., see Gulf Oil Corporation
Incentive Compensation Plan, May 1, 1973, and Texaco, Inc., 1976 Proxy Statement,
p.16). The bonus instead of being paid in cash is converted into restricted
shares at the share price at the time of award.

As of 1980, only 14 of the largest 100 corporations had a restricted stock plan.
However, they are somewhat more common in smaller corporations. In 1980, 19
percent of the 560 firms in the Conference Board sample of manufacturing and
retail firms had restricted stock plans.

F. Phantom Stock Plans

These plans are to restricted stock plans as stock appreciation rights are to
stock options. Instead of being awarded shares, received when they are earned
out as in the restricted stock plan, the executive is merely credited with the
shares and at the end of the restricted period is actually paid the cash value of
the shares. Dividend equivalents on the phantom shares are often converted into

additional phantom shares.

The Conference Board (1980, p.6) finds that 100 corporations in its sample (1153 corporations) use phantom stock plans; 45 of the 100 corporations use the phantom stock plan as part of a bonus plan. If an executive decides voluntarily to defer all or part of the annual bonus, that deferred bonus is converted into phantom shares at the current market value. The phantom shares then accumulate dividend equivalents and at retirement the executive receives the market value of the accumulated phantom stock at that time.

In the case of the other 55 corporations, the phantom stock plan is an incentive plan separate from the bonus plan. Usually in these cases only the appreciation in value of the phantom shares is paid.

G. Dividend Units

Dividend units which are separate from bonus plans are similar to phantom stock plans. The executive is awarded a number of dividend units instead of a number of phantom stock shares. Instead of being compensated in terms of the appreciation of the stock price at the end of the award period, the executive is compensated on the basis of dividends paid. The number of dividend units serves as the basis for the payment of dividend equivalents. In 1980, Towers, Perrin, Forster and Crosby (1980, p.18-19) reported that only 3 of the largest 100 U.S. industrial firms had dividend unit plans.

H. Performance Units

Under these plans performance goals are established in terms of accounting numbers (earnings per share, growth in earnings per share, accounting rate of return on assets, etc.) at the beginning of the award period which usually ranges from four to five years [Conference Board (1980, p.5)]. Each executive in the plan is allocated a given number of units of fixed dollar value at the start of the award period. At the end of the period the executive's compensation is the number of units earned out times the fixed value per unit. The proportion of the number of allocated units which are earned out depends on the extent to which the performance goal is achieved over the award period. Unlike stock options, stock appreciation rights, phantom stock or restricted stock, performance units do not use stock prices to determine compensation. To that extent they are like bonus plans particularly those few bonus plans which defer payment and tie such payment to variables such as growth in earnings per share.

The use of performance units has grown rapidly over the last 10 years. In 1972 none of the largest 100 firms used these plans; by 1980, 29 out of the 100 used them.

I. Performance Shares

Performance shares are similar to performance units in that performance goals are established in terms of accounting numbers over award periods of four to five years. However, instead of being allocated units of fixed value at the beginning of the award period the executive is allocated a number of shares. The proportion of the allocated shares earned out over the period depends on the extent to which the goals are met. The executive's compensation is the number of shares earned out times the market value of the shares at the end of the award period. Compensation under performance share plans as under performance unit plans depends on the extent to which the goals are met. The executive's compensation is the number of shares earned out times the market value of the shares at the end of the award period. Compensation under performance share plans as under performance unit plans depends on performance measured in terms of accounting numbers. However, unlike performance units, performance shares cause compensation to be affected by the change in the stock price over the award period.

Like performance units, performance shares have become much more popular in
recent years. However, performance shares are not as popular as performance
units (29 of the top 100 firms in 1980 had units, 11 had shares). The Conference
Board (1980, p.5) reports that together performance shares and units are less
popular with smaller firms. While 25 percent of the Conference Board´s
manufacturer sample report performance plans, less than 10 percent are reported
by other classifications.

3. INCENTIVES AND COMPENSATION PLANS

The incentive problems of the corporation have long been recognized. Adam Smith
described them two hundred years ago:

> The directors of such [joint-stock] companies, however, being the
> managers rather of other people´s money than of their own, it cannot
> well be expected that they should watch over it with the same anxious
> vigilance with which the partners in a private copartnery frequently
> watch over their own. Like the stewards of a rich man, they are apt
> to consider attention to small matters as not for their master´s
> honour, and very easily give themselves a dispensation from having it.
> Negligence and profusion, therefore, must always prevail, more or
> less, in the management of the affairs of such a company.

> Adam Smith, The Wealth of Nations, 1776, Cannan Edition (Modern
> Library, New York, 1937), p.700.

More recently Berle/Means (1932) revived interest in the problems of the
separation of ownership and control. They claim corporate executives have
incentives to act in their own interests and not those of the shareholders. Yet
the modern theory of corporate finance assumes that corporate managers make
investment and financing decisions with the objective of maximizing the market
value of the firm, and the theory based on that assumption has been successful in
explaining observable behavior.

The seeming contradiction between this successful theory of finance based on the
assumption that corporate managers maximize firm value and the apparent
incentives of managers to act in their own interest suggests that in some manner
this incentive conflict is controlled, at least sufficiently to make maximization
of firm value a reasonable approximation for many purposes. Finance theory
treats the solution of the incentive problems as a black box; it does not explain
what the solution is, or how it is achieved. This has led finance researchers to
investigate incentive problems and control mechanisms more closely.

A. Incentive Control Mechanisms

Market control mechanisms. Researchers have recognized that the extent of top
management divergence from maximizing the market value of the firm is limited by
managerial labor and capital markets. If managers do not own controlling
interests in their corporations and the sum of the effects of their divergent
actions on the market value of the firm plus their compensation is greater than
that of competing potential managers, the only factor preventing their removal is
the cost of that removal. Those costs are not infinite and as a result we see
managers being removed from office by existing shareholders or via mergers.

While the labor and capital markets do place limits on divergent actions, they
cannot drive those actions to zero because of the costs of removing managers.
However, in markets characterized by rational expectations the cost of the
divergent actions will be borne by those taking those actions [i.e., the
manager]. The firm´s claimholders will expect managers to take the divergent
actions and price their claims appropriately. Further, competition in the labor
market will tend to ensure that on average the manager only receives competitive

compensation. The manager who values the decrease in pecuniary compensation more highly than the divergent actions will want to convince shareholders that those actions will not be taken. In addition, the firm's other claimholders want to find means of reducing those divergent actions by the managers because the result would be an increase in the value of their claims. Thus, private incentives exist within the contracting process to reduce the costs of the divergent action.

Contractual Control Mechanisms. One means of controlling managers so that they do not take divergent actions is to establish a compensation scheme for managers which rewards them for taking actions which maximize the value of the firm. Hence, one would expect to observe contracts between managers and the firm (executive compensation plans) which reward value-maximizing behavior and penalize divergent actions.

Salary renegotiation. The most obvious type of compensation plan which provides incentives to the manager to maximize the market value of the firm is one under which the manager's compensation varies with changes in the value of the firm. Compensation by salary can have this characteristic if salaries are renegotiated based on the changes in the value of the firm in prior periods.

There are several problems in relying on salary renegotiation to control managers. One is that the incentive effects of future salaries decrease as the manager is closer to retirement (the horizon problem). In the extreme, the sixty-four year old chief executive with one year's service left will not be motivated by future salary adjustments. A second problem is that the longer the period between renegotiations of salary, the higher the uncertainty for the manager. Renegotiation of salary will inevitably involve errors in the assessment of the manager's productivity. The longer the renegotiation period, the fewer the number of renegotiations over the manager's working life, the larger the sum of the errors and the greater the uncertainty about the manager's total compensation. Given the manager's risk aversion, the less frequent the renegotiation, the higher compensation the firm will have to pay. But the renegotiation process is costly, so the more frequent the renegotiation the higher these costs.

The above two problems with the renegotiated salary solution are controlled by the incentive provisions of compensation plans. Moreover, incentive provisions address explicitly two other incentive problems: the manager's risk aversion and his tendency to underpay dividends. We now turn to the ways in which incentive plans address those four problems.

B. Control of the Horizon Problem

Conditional payments. Incentive plans explicitly tie the manager's compensation to a measure of the firm's value or change in value. The manager's compensation is conditional on the measure. Compensation under bonus plans and some performance plans depends on reported profits; compensation arising from stock options, stock appreciation rights and restricted and phantom stock depends on the market value of the firm's shares; compensation under a dividend units plan depends on dividends paid, etc.

Instead of compensation depending on performance after the fact, (ex post), under an incentive plan it is tied before the fact (ex ante) to some measure of performance. This formal tie to performance reduces the horizon problem for the sixty-four year old manager; the final year's compensation depends on that year's performance (e.g., the bonus depends on that year's reported profits).

The horizon problem is also reduced in incentive plans by deferring compensation to the retirement period. Ninety-eight of the 100 largest industrial firms in the U.S. have bonus plans with 63 of those 98 containing provisions which allow the compensation committee to defer payment of the bonus (either cash or stock) paying it in future installments [Towers, Perrin, Forster and Crosby (1980, pp.12-13)]. Those plans make provisions for forfeiture of any installments not yet paid if and when the compensation committee finds that the manager committed "any act of omission or commission prejudicial or detrimental to the interests"[3] of the firm. Such a provision will affect the incentives of a manager facing retirement.

Managers whose horizons are short because they are considering leaving the firm for other employment will also be influenced by the deferment provisions included in compensation plans. Deferred payments under bonus plans as well as performance unit and share plans are forfeited if the manager leaves the firm or is fired. Similarly, option plans, stock appreciation right plans, restricted stock plans and phantom stock plans carry the threat of forfeiture if the executive leaves the firm before the date of the exercise of the option or right, or the date of removal of the restrictions on the stock. Deferral of compensation with the threat of forfeiture reduces the probability that the manager will cheat or steal from the firm and increases the incentive to be efficient [see Lazear (1979)].

On the other hand, it might be thought that the forfeiture provision would enable the firm to cheat its managers out of their deferred compensation. However, such a policy would impose substantial costs on the firm. Capricious use of the forfeiture provision would cause current and future managers to discount the value of the deferred compensation for potential expropriation. This discounting would force the firm to increase its current and future managerial compensation to retain a management team of a given quality. In addition, discounting of the deferred compensation would reduce the incentive benefits of the plan. The incentive loss alone should be sufficient to ensure that the firm will not use the forfeiture provision to renege on its contracts.[4]

Bonus plans can affect the real investment and financing decisions of the firm. For example, because they are typically tied to annual profits, bonus plans give managers incentives to turn down positive NPV projects with long pay back and to take negative value projects which impose expenses only after the manager retires (such as restoration expenditures after strip mining). If equity and long-term debt is used as the basis for the minimum, managers have incentives to raise short-term debt (e.g., issue commercial paper). Unless lease payments are capitalized, there is an incentive to lease assets. Also, if the minimum earnings for a bonus is based on equity, managers can have incentives to increase the firm's debt/equity ratio.[5]

The deferred compensation provided for in performance units and shares or in deferral of bonus payments, and the use of market value based incentive plans such as stock option plans and stock appreciation rights, control these incentives with respect to investment policy. Provisions which allow a retiring manager to qualify for bonuses for some time after retirement also control these

---

[3]This wording is taken from Gulf Oil Corporation's Incentive Compensation Plan, May 1, 1973, p.12.

[4]See Telser (1980) for a discussion of such self-enforcing agreements.

[5]This statement is based on the effect of the debt/equity ratio on the expected compensation under the bonus plan. Of course, the dispersion of compensation under the plan would also increase. To the extent the bonus plan is analogous to an option on earnings this would increase the expected value of the compensation. On the other hand, because the manager's human capital depends on the success or failure of the firm the manager's risk exposure is increased, offsetting the manager's incentive to increase the debt/equity ratio.

incentives.

Deferred compensation via incentive plans has other effects in addition to the provision of incentives to be efficient and not to cheat. For example, a manager accumulates a lot of knowledge specific to the firm´s industry. Part of that industry-specific human capital is provided (at some cost) by the firm. However, the manager who leaves the firm to work for another firm in the industry will be rewarded for that industry-specific capital in the form of higher compensation. In effect the firm bears the cost and the manager receives the benefit. Without some mechanism to capture the return on that investment the firm would invest less in providing its managers with industry specific capital (e.g., via training programs). The problem can be controlled by deferred compensation subject to forfeiture if the manager leaves the firm. The deferred compensation means the manager is less likely to leave the firm and the firm is therefore more likely to provide the training. Both the firm and the manager benefit.

C. Renegotiation Costs Problem

In addition to controlling the horizon problem present with salary compensation, incentive plans can reduce the renegotiation cost problem. The manager would like more frequent renegotiation, but the higher the frequency of renegotiation the higher the renegotiation costs. Bonus plans, by tying compensation to a measure of performance (i.e., profits), in effect establish an automatic renegotiation procedure, one without the costs of head-to-head renegotiation. Compensation is adjusted periodically, based on the bonus formula.

D. Control of Manager's Risk Aversion

Incentive plans (and to a lesser extent renegotiated salaries) control an incentive problem which is endemic to compensation via a fixed salary, invariant to the value of the firm.[6] If the top executive of a corporation were paid a fixed claim on the firm, the manager would have incentives to take some investment projects which actually reduced the value of the firm. If an investment project reduces the volatility of the firm´s cash flows, it can increase the value of the manager´s fixed claim (and other fixed claims, e.g., debt) while reducing the firm´s value. The reason the value of the fixed claim increases is that the probability of the firm´s cash flows covering the fixed claim increases. However, the expected cash flows to the firm decrease, so the value of the firm falls.

Not only are there incentives for the manager to take negative net present value (NPV) projects which reduce variance when paid a fixed salary, there are also incentives to forego positive NPV projects which increase the volatility of the firm´s cash flows. The increase in the volatility increases the probability that the manager´s fixed claim will not be paid. That effect reduces the value of the fixed claim even though the investment project increases the value of the firm. In essence, the preceding examples suggest the manager who is compensated by a fixed salary will be more risk averse than is optimal in making investment decisions.

To control the manager´s risk aversion, the compensation plan must include provisions with positive incentives to increase volatility. The expected payoff to a stock option increases with the volatility of the stock price. Thus, options or stock appreciation rights provide the manager with incentives to invest in projects which increase the volatility of the firm´s cash flows. As a result, it is possible by augmenting a manager´s fixed salary with the right amount and type of stock options or stock appreciation rights to offset the

---

[6]The salary structure for government bureaucrats might be considered a real life example of such a compensation scheme.

manager's incentives to take volatility reducing negative value projects or turn down volatility increasing positive value projects (i.e., to be too risk averse).

Bonus plans are similar to stock options except (ignoring accounting accrual) they are like options on operating cash flows rather than the stock. The feature that a bonus is not paid unless the earnings reach a specified level (percentage of equity or total capital) is analogous to the exercise price of the stock -- the option is not worth anything at termination if the stock price does not exceed the exercise price. Performance shares and units also have characteristics of an option plan; the achievement of an award under either plan depends on accounting numbers reaching a specified level. Because they have option characteristics, bonus and performance share and unit plans also provide managers with incentives to increase the volatility of the cash flows; these incentives can offset the manager's natural risk aversion.

However, these provisions are blunt tools. The incentive to increase volatility under the option is a function of the market value of the firm and of the time to maturity of the option. Hence, in order to produce the precisely correct incentives the mix of salary and options would have to be adjusted continually as the firm's market value varies and time elapses (i.e., the time to maturity of the options changes). Such continuous adjustment of the package would be very costly. Given the adjustment costs, non-continuously adjusted options offset some of the manager's risk aversion. And, as we shall see below, there is some evidence that is consistent with options and stock appreciation rights fulfilling that function.

Note also that restricted stock or phantom stock plans will not effectively control the manager's risk aversion. For example, if managers were compensated only with restricted stock, as long as their claims were a large fraction of their wealth, their risk aversion would still provide incentives to take volatility-reducing projects. However, the incentive would be weaker than with compensation through fixed salary claims.

Because a given percentage change in share price causes a larger percentage change in the value of an option, the effect of dysfunctional investments on the value of a share converts into a larger relative effect on the value of the option. Further, a reduction in volatility, per se, reduces the value of an option. Thus, options or stock appreciation rights are powerful provisions in controlling the incentives for managers allowing risk effects to interfere with optimal investment decisions.

Costs of controlling risk aversion. While some provisions in compensation plans control the manager's tendency to be too risk averse in investing, they create a problem by increasing the manager's exposure to risk. Here the legal restriction against selling equity claims on human capital becomes important. Managers who hold non-negotiable stock options, stock appreciation rights, restricted stock, phantom stock, performance units and shares, and bonus claims on their firm also have much of their human capital committed to that firm. There is a strong tendency for the value of the manager's human capital to vary with the market value of the firm (i.e., a high positive covariance between the values). There is also a high positive covariance between the firm's value and the value of options and other claims. As a consequence, the value of the manager's portfolio of assets is risky. If these assets were negotiable, much of the risk could be diversified away (e.g., by selling claims on those assets and using the proceeds to invest in other assets whose values do not vary together as highly). However, the manager cannot diversify this risk away because the human capital and the claims under incentive plans are non-marketable. Thus, incentive provisions increase the manager's (often already high) exposure to risk.[7]

Given that managers are risk-averse, they will require additional compensation of the additional risk. We observe that the base salaries for executives of companies paying bonuses tend to be less than for executives of companies not paying bonuses [see Conference Board (1979, p.17)]. However, the <u>total</u> compensation of executives of bonus paying companies tends to be higher than that of executives of non-bonus paying companies. In addition to a compensating differential for the risk, this probably also reflects the fact that managers who exercise greater discretion earn higher levels of compensation and the more discretion employed, the higher the likelihood of the use of incentive provisions in compensation contracts.

E. Controlling the Over-Retention Problem

A fixed salary can lead the manager to be more conservative than optimal on financing decisions. Suppose the firm only has negative NPV investment opportunities if it reinvests the cash flows it earns. In such a case it makes sense for the manager to pay dividends. However, dividends reduce the extent to which cash flows cover the manager's salary. Hence, the manager has incentives not to pay the optimal amount of dividends.

The manager's incentive to be too conservative in paying dividends is controlled by some provisions of compensation plans. As noted earlier, some bonus plans tie the maximum bonus to dividends paid. Hence, reductions in dividends reduce the maximum bonus and eventually reduce the manager's bonus compensation. In addition, a few firms have dividend unit plans which compensate managers directly on the basis of dividends paid.

Compensation plans are also typically written so that they do not reinforce the manager's incentives to be conservative in paying dividends. If they were not adjusted for dividends paid, stock options, stock appreciation rights, restricted stock and phantom stock would provide managers with incentives to withhold dividends. The manager's compensation under those plans depends on the stock price at exercise or at the time of lapse of restrictions. Without adjustments for dividends, the manager, by reducing dividends and increasing the capital gain on the stock, could increase the stock price and his compensation. However, most of these plans provide for an adjustment for dividends paid (e.g., by dividend equivalents being reinvested in phantom stock).

F. Incentive Provisions and Accounting Techniques

Accounting earnings or profits, the measure of performance used by bonus plans, measure the firm value maximization objective with error. Further, the earnings can be affected by the choice of accounting techniques (e.g., accelerated or straight-line depreciation). This provides managers with incentives to lobby for and use accounting techniques which tend to produce higher reported earnings. Hagerman and Zmijewski (1979) provide evidence that U.S. firms with bonus plans are more likely to use earnings increasing techniques than U.S. firms which do not have bonus plans.

Healy (1982) presents evidence that the sign of a firm's accounting accruals for a given year are related to the position of the firm's earnings vis-a-vis the upper and lower bounds in the bonus plan. If earnings are above the upper bound or below the lower bound, net accruals are more likely to be negative. If earnings are between the upper and lower bound net accruals are more likely to be positive. This relationship is consistent with managers using accruals to

---

[7]Note that insider trading rules make illegal any attempt to hedge the risk by selling short the firm's shares.

increase the present value of bonuses.

Occasionaly the incentives to manipulate accounting techniques are controlled by requiring compensation committees to adjust earnings for items which would include changes in accounting techniques.[8] Deferral of compensation and the existence of incentive plans such as performance unit and share plans which measure performance in terms of accounting numbers over periods of four to five years also tend to control the manager's incentives to use accounting techniques to inflate compensation via bonus plans. Different accounting techniques merely affect the timing of accounting profit on any given investment; the sum of the profits over the investment's life is fixed. Hence, extending the number of years over which profits are measured controls the manager's incentive to manipulate profits.

The preceding analysis of compensation plans suggests that the design of incentive plans is consistent with the notion that those plans induce the manager to maximize the value of the firm. This necessarily involves contracting costs and trade-offs. For example, incentive plans trade the manager's risk aversion off against the effect of that risk aversion on investment policy. Another example is the trade-off between the effect of bonus plans on renegotiation costs and the dysfunctional consequences of bonus plans (e.g., potential effects on debt/equity ratios). Because they involve these costs, optimal compensation packages do not control managers perfectly, and will not result in zero divergent actions.

4. TAXES AND COMPENSATION PLANS

A. Tax Effects of Compensation Plans

The Miller/Scholes (1980) analysis finds that the tax effects of plans are often equivalent to the tax effects of two simple types of transactions: (a) the firm or the individual making tax-deductible contributions to a pension plan; and (b) deferred salary payments. Hence, knowledge of the effect of those transactions on an individual's taxes helps understand the tax effect of compensation plans.

Compensation plans affect the taxes of both the corporation and the executive, so both tax effects must be considered when assessing the tax advantages of any type of plan. For example, a particular provision which provides a given compensation could increase the corporate taxes vis-a-vis the same compensation paid in salary, but decrease the executive's personal taxes. One way to study this problem is to assess the effects of the plan on the total of corporate and executive taxes. That approach is used by Hite/Long (1982) to explain the shift in the early 1970's from qualified to non-qualified options.

---

[8]Gulf Oil Corporation's Incentive Compensation Plan (amended May 1, 1973) states:

> ... For the purpose of determining for any year the credit to the Incentive Compensation Account under this Plan, the Net Income of the Corporation and its Subsidiaries Consolidated as shown in the Annual Report for the year made to the Stockholders, shall be adjusted as follows:
>
> Any unusual or non-recurring items of income or loss not arising in the ordinary course of the business of the Corporation or its Subsidiaries Consolidated shall, if the Committee so decides, be eliminated in whole or in part or shall be allocated to such year or years (including the current year) as the Committee in its discretion directs, and the adjustments necessary to carry out such directions of the Committee applicable to any year shall be made. ...

An alternative approach to assess a plan for tax advantages is to set the plan up in such a way that the plan does not affect corporate taxes vis-a-vis an equivalent salary payment and then investigate the implications of the plan for the individual executive's taxes. To achieve tax neutrality in the plan, the firm typically must purchase a security as well as establishing the plan. This approach is used by Miller/Scholes (1980) and is also used below to assess the tax effects of the different types of plans.

Pension plan contributions. The tax effects of a pension plan are best seen by comparing two alternatives. In the first, the firm makes an annual contribution on behalf of an executive to a tax-exempt pension plan. In the second, the firm increases the executive's annual compensation by the amount of the contribution and the executive saves on his own account. If the executive's tax rate is constant over time, the amount the executive has available at retirement in the first plan will be greater than the amount in the second by the tax the executive pays on the interest from saving on his own account.

Consider the contribution (C) one year before the executive's retirement. In the first case this contribution accumulates to $C(1 + r)$ (where r is the interest rate) at retirement. When it is paid out the executive receives after tax $C(1 + r)(1 - \tau)$ where τ is the executive's tax rate. In the second, the executive receives (after tax) $C(1 - \tau)$ one year before retirement. This is invested and after tax is paid on the interest, $C(1 - \tau)(1 + r(1 - \tau))$ remains at retirement. This sum is $\tau r C(1 - \tau)$ less than in the first case. And of course $\tau r C(1 - \tau)$ is the tax on the interest on the executive's savings.

In essence the pension provisions in the tax code are equivalent to making the interest on the executive's savings tax exempt. This result only holds if the individual's tax rate is the same in all periods. If the tax rate is higher during working years than retirement years, the pension plan yields greater consumption in retirement than does tax exemption on the interest. If the tax rate during retirement exceeds the tax rate during the working life, interest exemption provides the greater consumption in retirement.

Deferred salary payments. Under the U.S. tax code, a promise by a firm to pay an employee additional salary payments at specified dates in the future is not taxable income for the employee if the promise is not funded. Nor is it taxable if the promise is funded but subject to "substantial" risk of forfeiture. Further, the promise is not a tax deduction for the firm under those circumstances. Despite this last provision it is likely salary could be deferred and invested in securities without being taxable at the time of deferral.

The deferral case is analogous to the pension contribution discussed above. However, the interest on the securities would be taxed at the corporation's tax rate. If the corporation's and the executive's tax rates are the same there would be no advantage to deferring the income. But if the corporation's tax rate is less than the executive's there would be an advantage. In the extreme, if the corporation's tax rate were zero deferral would be as good as contributing to an exempt pension fund.

Stock options, stock appreciation rights, and stock. Options have been used for many years, but they became popular in the 1950's when changes in tax laws made them attractive [see Lewellen (1968, p.47)]. In the 1960's the qualified stock option became a common element of the executive compensation packages. By 1968 the qualified option was the sole long-term performance plan for 86 of the 100 largest companies in the U.S. Qualified option plans are plans which met certain requirements laid down by the tax code. Changes in the tax code in the years 1969-1976 led to the replacement of qualified options by non-qualified options and other long-term plans, for example stock appreciation rights. The tax effect of the stock appreciation right is the same as that of a non-qualified option (i.e., the appreciation is taxable income to the executive and is a tax deduction for the corporation).

To assess the tax effect of non-qualified stock options[9] and stock appreciation rights, Miller/Scholes (1980, pp.21-26) compare the effect on manager wealth of a straight salary with the manager investing savings in traded or home-made options to a combination of salary and non-negotiable stock options or stock appreciation rights. The comparison yields a tax effect similar to the pension plan example given above. If the manager is paid a straight salary and invests in options, capital gains must be paid on the appreciation of the options over their whole life. However, if the manager's salary is reduced and options awarded, capital gains are avoided on any price appreciation over the exercise period (i.e., prior to exercise). In essence, that appreciation becomes exempt from capital gains tax just as the interest in the pension plan example was exempt from income tax.[10]

The tax advantage of restricted stock or phantom stock over straight salary is the same as the option's tax advantage. The executive avoids the capital gains on the stock over the period from their award to the lapse of the restrictions (or payment in the case of phantom stock).[11]

While bonus plans are in effect options, they are short-term options and hence their tax advantages are not as large as stock options, particularly if payment is made each year. Unless the payment is deferred, income is delayed at most one year, so at best the capital gains tax on one year's appreciation is avoided.

Many bonus plans, while not requiring deferment, give the compensation committee power to defer payment. Presumably, the compensation committee would do this on the executive's (unwritten) request. The tax effect of this deferral depends on the form of the deferral. If, as is common, the deferral involves provision of options, stock appreciation rights, restricted stock or phantom stock, the tax effect is as indicated above for those incentive plans (i.e., equivalent to an exemption from capital gains tax). Then deferral is advantageous for executives in all relevant tax brackets. However, if deferral is straight deferral of cash and involves investment of the funds in securities yielding taxable income, the deferral is only advantageous if the manager's tax rate is greater than the corporation's.

As indicated previously, performance shares and units are analogous to options so their tax effects are the same as options. By reducing the manager's current salary and effectively awarding options, the firm enables the manager to avoid capital gains tax on the de facto option over the period in which the performance plan is earned out.

It should not be assumed that the decreases in the manager's taxes which emerge from the comparison of payments under the incentive plans and salary accrue to the manager. As noted above, the manager's expected compensation will be determined by the market for managerial labor. If most managers' taxes are reduced by a particular incentive plan, competitive forces would lead to a

---

[9]By 1980 all options were non-qualified options.

[10]Note that this is the differential effect of the options on taxes. With options the manager does pay income tax on the difference between stock price and exercise price, but income tax would also have been paid under the alternative (i.e., straight salary).

[11]Because gains on assets held until death may be exempt from capital gains tax there are some extreme circumstances in which the dominance of restricted or phantom stocks may not hold [see Miller/Scholes (1980, p.19)].

reduction in the value of the manager's compensation equal to the value of the tax savings.

B.   Attributes Which Can Be Explained by Taxes

Tax effects can explain a change in the attributes of incentive plans that occurred in the early 1970's.   That change is the switch from qualified to non-qualified options and stock appreciation rights.   This replacement of qualified options occurred before the Tax Reform Act of 1976 outlawed them; it can be explained by a shift in the relative tax effects of qualified and non-qualified options (see Hite/Long, 1982).

As noted, tax effects can also explain why incentive plans have deferral provisions.   If the deferral is in the form of options, stock appreciation rights, etc., capital gains taxes are reduced and if the deferral involves investment by the firm to provide for the deferred compensation, taxes are reduced to the extent the corporate tax rate is less than the manager's tax rate. Further, since managers of larger firms tend to have higher compensation (and have higher tax rates), the deferral provisions and effects of incentive plans could explain why larger firms are more likely to have incentive plans than smaller firms.

Many aspects of the design of compensation plans are consistent with providing managers with incentives to maximize the value of the firm; some design aspects are also consistent with the objective of tax reduction.   For example, deferral of compensation can be explained as a means of inducing greater efficiency, or as a means of reducing taxes if the corporation's tax rate is lower than the manager's tax rate.   The two explanations are not mutually exclusive; both are likely important.   But to establish a convincing case for the existence of the incentive function, it is necessary to present observed attributes of incentive plans which can be explained only by the incentive function, and by the tax reduction function.

There are serious questions about the explanatory power of the tax reduction hypothesis.   First, the very examples used to demonstrate the advantages of incentive provisions show that the same advantages can be obtained without establishing a formal plan tying compensation to performance (i.e., an incentive plan).   Salary compensation plus a pension plan achieves the same tax effects as options, etc.   Salary compensation with some of the salary deferred achieves the tax advantages of deferral with investment.   Hence, why should firms bother with incentive plans?   A tax explanation is that the tax code restrictions on pension contributions are binding.   However, if tax reduction is the sole motivation for incentive plans one would expect, given the manager's risk aversion, for the payments to be conditional on the variable with low dispersion.   For example, bonus plans would use earnings rather than what is actually used, the excess of earnings over a return on equity or assets.

Second, as Miller/Scholes (1980, p.13) point out, most executives to whom deferral provisions apply probably have marginal tax rates below the corporate tax rate, so that deferral with investment would be disadvantageous in tax terms.

The conclusion is that tax effects are at best a partial explanation for the nature, existence and growing popularity of incentive plans and are not likely to be the primary explanation.   Incentive effects would appear to be more important given their ability to explain the nature of, and cross-sectional variations in, the plans.

C.   *Empirical Regularities Which Can Be Explained by*
Incentive Effects But Not by Tax Effects

Disaggregation of performance.   If incentive plans are designed to provide
individual managers with incentives to make decisions in the shareholders´
interests one would expect the manager´s performance and rewards under the plan
to be sensitive to the decisions made.   Measurements of overall firm performance
such as share values, total profits, etc., are appropriate for the President or
Chairman of the Board who is virtually responsible for all the firm´s cash flows.
But, such measurements and compensation based on them may not be well suited for
a divisional manager.   The divisional manager may do an excellent job, but be
responsible for only five percent of the firm´s cash flows.   When an accounting
is made for the impact of the managers of the other 95 percent, rewards based
solely on overall firm performance may provide the manager with little incentive
to maximize the value of the firm.   The effect of personal decisions and efforts
on compensation is swamped by the decisions and efforts of others.   With an
incentive plan based on such measures the manager has incentives to "free ride"
on the efforts of other managers.

Thus, it would be expected that incentive plans which measure performance on a
company-wide basis would be less likely to apply to managers other than top
management than incentive plans in which performance is measured on a divisional
or more disaggregated level.   This expectation is generally consistent with the
evidence.   Performance units and share plans use overall corporate performance
and are usually restricted to top management.   On the other hand, bonus plans do
measure the performance of individual managers and they typically include
divisional and lower level managers.   For example, the Conference Board (1979,
p.6) reports that only 5 percent of bonus plans were restricted to top
management, 38 percent included divisional managers, 43 percent included lower
management and 12 percent of the plans reached first-line supervisors.   It would
appear contrary to the reasoning presented here that options are awarded to lower
levels of management.   However, while the compensation given by options is
dependent on stock price and hence overall performance, the number of options is
frequently used as a way of deferring payment under bonus plans and bonuses also
depend on individual performance.

Taxes cannot explain the differences in the nature of performance measures across
bonus plans.   Indeed, the tax motivation would not even lead to the prediction
that incentive plans isolate individual performance.   But some of those plans do
isolate individual performance, particularly the most popular bonus plans.   In
their 1979 study of 211 manufacturing firms´ bonus plans the Conference Board
(p.15) reported that "only 23 percent (49) of the 211 manufacturers indicated
that the annual bonus award for executives would not be affected by the financial
performance of the organizational unit in which they work rather than purely
corporate results as a whole".

The Conference Board (1979, p.14) reports the factors used to determine the bonus
(personal, division and corporate) and the percentage attributable to the
division factor for the 140 Conference Board firms which consider divisional
performance.   Thirty-one of those firms consider only divisional performance so
that the bonus is determined 100 percent by the divisional performance.   Twenty-
two firms use personal and divisional performance and the median weight on
divisional performance is 50 percent.   Thirty-five firms use both divisional and
corporate performance and the median weight given to the divisional performance
is 75 percent.   Finally, 52 firms use all three factors and the median weight
given by those firms to divisional performance is 35 percent.

Rewarding a manager on the basis of the division´s performance where performance
is measured by accounting profits can create dysfunctional incentives, as well as
providing incentives to maximize the value of the firm.   A manager may be able to

increase the division's profits at the expense of total corporate profits by
various means (e.g., by charging a monopolistic price for goods transferred
between divisions). That effect is perhaps the reason that, while the 162 firms
examined by the Conference Board consider divisional performance, none of them
pays a bonus, even to the head of a successful division, if corporate performance
does not reach the minimum standard [Conference Board (1979, p.3)].

Comparison of performance across the industry.   Given   the   manager's   risk
aversion, it would be beneficial if the performance measure used in a
compensation plan varied only with factors subject to the manager's control.
Variability in the performance measure due to factors beyond the manager's
control would increase the manager's exposure to risk without providing
incentives to maximize the value of the firm.   Thus, performance plans explicitly
try to remove variability beyond the manager's control, often attempting to
remove   uncontrollable   market   and   industry   fluctuations   in   performance   by
comparing the firm's performance to that of other firms in the same industry.
For example, Toro Co.'s plan compares its growth in returns on assets to that of
its competitors, while Champion International Corp.'s plan compares its growth in
earnings per share to that of its competitors.

If tax reduction were the primary motivation for incentive plans one would expect
the plans to try to reduce the manager's exposure to risk.   In fact, it is
apparent that from this dimension, salary plus a pension plan (which did not
invest in the firm) would be superior to incentive plans which tie compensation
to the firm's performance.   By diversifying the pension plan could eliminate risk
specific to the firm and thereby substantially reduce the manager's risk
exposure.   The performance plans which measure performance relative to other
firms in the industry do not do this.   They remove sources of market and industry
volatility, but leave the volatility specific to the firm which, while
diversifiable, is more controllable by the manager.   This suggests that the
incentive advantage of making the manager responsible for the firm specific
variability exceeds the cost of the increased compensation for the increased
exposure to risk.

The cross-sectional distribution of incentive plans.   In Section 3 it was noted
that incentive plans can offset manager's tendencies to select risk-reducing
investments.   If that is the case, one would expect incentive plans to be more
prevalent in unregulated industries (i.e., industries where it is easier to alter
the risk of investment).   In 1980, 68 percent of manufacturing firms, 43 percent
of retail firms, and 55 percent of construction firms in the Conference Board
(1980, p.6) sample had stock options in their compensation packages.   On the
other hand, in the regulated industries stock options were less popular.   In
1980, 23 percent of commercial banking firms, 18 percent of stock insurance
companies, and 8 percent of utilities had stock option plans.

Bonus plans are also less common in regulated industries.   In 1980, 90 percent of
manufacturing firms, 89 percent of construction firms, and 81 percent of retail
firms had bonus plans.   In commercial banking, 55 percent of firms had bonus
plans.   The percentages for insurance companies and gas and electric utilities
were 52 percent and 13 percent respectively [Conference Board (1980, p.4)].   The
relatively greater popularity of bonus plans in banking and insurance than in
utilities can be explained by the fact that investments are more tightly
regulated in the utility industry.   It might be argued that incentive plans are
more prevalent in unregulated than regulated industries because managerial
compensation in those industries is larger, so the tax benefits are likely to be
larger.   However, this doesn't appear likely since even the incomes of top
executives of utilities are large enough to generate tax advantages.   Salaries of
the chief executive officer of the utilities covered in Business Week's Annual
Summary of Executive Compensation (May 11, 1981) all exceed $200,000.

5. CONCLUSION

It is apparent that tax motivations cannot explain the existence of, and variations in, U.S. firms' compensation plans. A combination of salary and pension plan is as efficient as the incentive plans in reducing taxes and does not increase the manager's exposure to risk as much as incentive plans. Further, taxes cannot explain the extent to which bonus plans go to isolate individual performance or why incentive plans are less frequent in regulated industries. On the other hand, the incentive effects of compensation plans can explain these phenomena. This suggests that the stated objective of incentive plans (i.e., to align the manager's incentives with firm value maximization) is principally responsible for the popularity of incentive plans in the U.S.

(Date of receipt of final typescript: June 1982)

REFERENCES

Berle, A. and G. Means, 1932, The Modern Corporation and Private Property (Macmillan, New York).

Brown, P. and R. Ball, 1967, "Some Preliminary Findings on the Association Between the Earnings of a Firm, Its Industry and the Economy," in Empirical Research in Accounting: Selected Studies, 1967, supplement to Volume 5, Journal of Accounting Research, 55-57.

Chandler and Macleod Consultants Pty. Ltd., 1981, Report on Salaries and Executive Remuneration - Chief Executive and General Management, April 1981 (Chandler and Macleod Consultants Pty. Ltd., Melbourne).

Conference Board, 1979, Top Executive Bonus Plans (Conference Board, New York).

Conference Board, 1980, Top Executive Compensation, 1980 Edition (Conference Board, New York).

Hagerman, R. and M. Zmijewski, 1979, "Some Economic Determinants of Accounting Policy Choice," Journal of Accounting and Economics, 1, 141-166.

Healy, P., 1982, "The Impact of Bonus Schemes on the Selection of Accounting Principles," unpublished dissertation proposal, Graduate School of Management, University of Rochester.

Hite, G. and M. Long, 1982, "Taxes and Executive Stock Options," forthcoming in Journal of Accounting and Economics, 4.

Larcker, D., 1981, "The Association Between Performance Plan Adoption and Corporate Capital Investment," unpublished paper, J.L. Kellogg Graduate School of Management, Northwestern University.

Lazear, E., 1979, "Why Is There Mandatory Retirement?," Journal of Political Economy, 87, 1261-1284.

Lewellen, W., 1968, Executive Compensation in Large Industrial Corporations (National Bureau of Economic Research, New York).

Miller, M. and M. Scholes, 1980, "Executive Compensation, Taxes and Incentives," working paper No. 42, Graduate School of Business, University of Chicago.

Telser, L., 1980, "A Theory of Self-enforcing Agreements," Journal of Business, 53, 27-44.

Towers, Perrin, Forster and Crosby, 1980, Executive Compensation Study, 1980 (Towers, Perrin, Forster and Crosby, Chicago).

THE EFFECT OF BONUS SCHEMES ON ACCOUNTING DECISIONS*

Paul M. HEALY

Massachusetts Institute of Technology, Cambridge, MA 02139, USA

Received October 1983, final version received September 1984

Studies examining managerial accounting decisions postulate that executives rewarded by earnings-based bonuses select accounting procedures that increase their compensation. The empirical results of these studies are conflicting. This paper analyzes the format of typical bonus contracts, providing a more complete characterization of their accounting incentive effects than earlier studies. The test results suggest that (1) accrual policies of managers are related to income-reporting incentives of their bonus contracts, and (2) changes in accounting procedures by managers are associated with adoption or modification of their bonus plan.

1. Introduction

Earnings-based bonus schemes are a popular means of rewarding corporate executives. Fox (1980) reports that in 1980 ninety percent of the one thousand largest U.S. manufacturing corporations used a bonus plan based on accounting earnings to remunerate managers. This paper tests the association between managers' accrual and accounting procedure decisions and their income-reporting incentives under these plans. Earlier studies testing this relation postulate that executives rewarded by bonus schemes select income-increasing accounting procedures to maximize their bonus compensation.[1] Their empirical results are conflicting. These tests, however, have several problems. First, they ignore the earnings' definitions of the plans; earnings are often defined so that certain accounting decisions do not affect bonuses. For exam-

---

*I am indebted to Ross Watts for many valuable discussions and for his insightful remarks on this paper. I also wish to thank the remaining members of my Ph.D. committee, Andrew Christie, Cliff Smith and Jerry Zimmerman, for their helpful comments. The paper has benefited from the comments of Bob Kaplan, Rick Antle, George Benston, Tom Dyckman, Bob Holthausen, Michael Jensen, Rick Lambert, David Larcker, Richard Leftwich, Tom Lys, Terry Marsh, Ram Ramakrishnan, and Rick Ruback. I am grateful to George Goddu and Peat Marwick for allowing me to use their library and financing my preliminary data collection, and to Bob Holthausen and Richard Rikert for letting me use their data bases of changes in accounting procedures. Financial support for this paper was provided by the Ernst and Whinney Foundation and the American Accounting Association.

[1] These studies include Watts and Zimmerman (1978), Hagerman and Zmijewski (1979), Holthausen (1981), Zmijewski and Hagerman (1981), Collins, Rozeff and Dhaliwal (1981), and Bowen, Noreen and Lacey (1981).

Journal of Accounting and Economics 7 (1985) 85–107. North-Holland

ple, more than half of the sample plans collected for my study define bonus awards as a function of income before taxes. It is not surprising, therefore, that Hagerman and Zmijewski (1979) find no significant association between the existence of accounting-based compensation schemes and companies' methods of recording the investment tax credit.

Second, previous tests assume compensation schemes always induce managers to select income increasing accounting procedures. The schemes examined in my study also give managers an incentive to select income-decreasing procedures. For example, they typically permit funds to be set aside for compensation awards when earnings exceed a specified target. If earnings are so low that no matter which accounting procedures are selected target earnings will not be met, managers have incentives to further reduce current earnings by deferring revenues or accelerating write-offs, a strategy known as 'taking a bath'. This strategy does not affect current bonus awards and increases the probability of meeting future earnings' targets.[2] Past studies do not control for such situations and, therefore, understate the association between compensation incentives and accounting procedure decisions.

This study examines typical bonus contracts, providing a more complete analysis of their accounting incentive effects than earlier studies. The theory is tested using actual parameters and definitions of bonus contracts for a sample of 94 companies. Two classes of tests are presented: accrual tests and tests of changes in accounting procedures. I define accruals as the difference between reported earnings and cash flows from operations. The accrual tests compare the actual sign of accruals for a particular company and year with the predicted sign given the managers' bonus incentives. The results are consistent with the theory. I also test whether accruals differ for companies with different bonus plan formats. The accrual differences provide further evidence of a relation between managers' accrual decisions and their income-reporting incentives under the bonus plan. Tests using changes in accounting procedures suggest that managers' decisions to change procedures are not associated with bonus plan incentives. However, additional tests find that changes in accounting procedures are related to the adoption or modification of a bonus plan.

Section 2 outlines the provisions of bonus agreements. The accounting incentive effects generated by bonus plans are discussed in section 3. Section 4 describes the sample design and data collection, and section 5 reports the results of accrual tests. Tests of changes in accounting procedures are described in section 6. The conclusions are presented in section 7.

2. Description of accounting bonus schemes

Deferred salary payment, insurance plans, non-qualified stock options, restricted stock, stock appreciation rights, performance plans and bonus plans

---

[2] See Holthausen (1981) and Watts and Zimmerman (1983).

are popular forms of compensation.[3] Two of these explicitly depend on accounting earnings: bonus schemes and performance plans. Performance plans award managers the value of performance units or shares in cash or stock if certain long-term (three or five years) earnings' targets are attained. The earnings' targets are typically written in terms of earnings per share, return on total assets, or return on equity. Bonus contracts have a similar format to performance contracts except that they specify annual rather than long-term earnings goals.

A number of companies operate bonus and performance plans simultaneously. Differences in earnings definitions and target horizons of these two plans make it difficult to identify their combined effect on managers' accounting decisions. I therefore limit the study to firms whose only remuneration explicitly related to earnings is bonuses. Fox (1980) finds that in 1980 ninety percent of the one thousand largest U.S. manufacturing corporations used a bonus plan to remunerate managers, whereas only twenty-five percent used a performance plan. Bonus awards also tend to constitute a higher proportion of top executives' compensation than performance payments. In 1978, for example, Fox reports that for his sample the median ratio of accounting bonus to base salary was fifty-two percent. The median ratio for performance awards was thirty-four percent.

The formulae and variable definitions used in bonus schemes vary considerably between firms, and even within a single firm across time. Nonetheless, there are common features of these contracts. They typically define a variant of reported earnings (E_t) and an earnings target or lower bound (L_t) for use in bonus computations. If reported earnings exceed their target, the contract defines the maximum percentage (p_t) of the difference that can be allocated to a bonus pool. If earnings are less than their target, no funds are allocated to the pool. The formula for the maximum transfer to the bonus pool (B_t) is

$$B_t = p_t \max\{(E_t - L_t), 0\}.$$

Standard Oil Company of California, for example, defines its 1980 bonus formula as follows:

> ... the annual fund from which awards may be made is two percent of the amount by which the company's annual income for the award year exceeds six percent of its annual capital investment for such year.

Standard Oil defines 'annual income' as audited net income before the bonus expense and interest, and 'capital investment' as the average of opening and closing book values of long-term liabilities plus equity. Variations on these definitions are found in other companies' plans. Earnings are defined before or after a number of factors including interest, the bonus expense, taxes, extraor-

---

[3] For a discussion of these types of compensation, see Smith and Watts (1982).

dinary and non-recurring items, and/or preferred dividends. Capital is a function of the book value of equity when incentive income is earnings after interest and a function of the sum of long-term debt and equity when incentive income is earnings before interest. Bonus plans for ninety-four companies are examined in this study and only seven do not use these definitions of earnings and capital.

Some schemes specify an upper limit (U_t') on the excess of earnings over target earnings. When the difference between actual and target earnings is greater than the upper limit, the transfer to the bonus pool is limited, implying the formula for allocation to the bonus pool (B_t') is

$$B_t' = p_t \left\{ \min \left\{ U_t', \max \left\{ (E_t - L_t), 0 \right\} \right\} \right\}.$$

The upper limit is commonly related to cash dividend payments on common stock.[4] The 1980 bonus contract for Gulf Oil Corporation, for example, limits the transfer to the bonus reserve to six percent of the excess of earnings over six percent of capital 'provided that the amount credited to the Incentive Compensation Account shall not exceed ten percent of the total amount of the dividends paid on the corporation's stock'.

Administration of the bonus pool and awards to executives are made by a committee of directors who are ineligible to participate in the scheme. Awards are made in cash, stock, stock options or dividend equivalents.[5] The bonus contract usually permits unallocated funds to be available for future bonus awards. Plans also provide for award deferrals over as many as five years, either at the discretion of the compensation committee or the manager.

3. Bonus plans and accounting choice decisions

Watts (1977) and Watts and Zimmerman (1978) postulate that bonus schemes create an incentive for managers to select accounting procedures and accruals to increase the present value of their awards. This paper proposes a more complete theory of the accounting incentive effects of bonus schemes.[6] The firm is assumed to comprise a single risk-averse manager and one or more

---

[4] Contracts taking this form create an incentive for the manager to increase dividend payments when the upper limit is binding, thereby counteracting the over-retention problem noted in Smith and Watts (1983).

[5] Dividend equivalents are claims which vary with the dividend payments on common stock.

[6] The theory does not explain the form of bonus contracts or why executives are awarded earnings-based bonuses. For a discussion of these issues, see Jensen and Meckling (1976), Holmstrom (1979), Miller and Scholes (1980), Fama (1980), Hite and Long (1980), Holmstrom (1982), Smith and Watts (1983), Larcker (1983), and Demski, Patell and Wolfson (1984).

owners. The manager is rewarded by the following bonus formula:

$$B'_t = p\left\{\min\left\{U', \max\left\{(E_t - L), 0\right\}\right\}\right\},$$

where L is the lower bound on earnings (E_t), U' is the limit on the excess of earnings over the lower bound $(E_t - L)$, and p is the payout percentage defined in the bonus contract. The manager receives $p(E_t - L)$ in bonus if earnings exceed the lower bound and are less than the bonus plan limit (the upper bound) on earnings, U, given by the sum $(U' + L)$. The bonus is fixed at pU' when earnings exceed this upper bound.

Accounting earnings are decomposed into cash flows from operations (C_t), non-discretionary accruals (NA_t) and discretionary accruals (DA_t). Non-discretionary accruals are accounting adjustments to the firm's cash flows mandated by accounting standard-setting bodies (e.g., the Securities Exchange Commission and the Financial Accounting Standards Board). These bodies require, for example, that companies depreciate long-lived assets in some systematic manner, value inventories using the lower of cost or market rule, and value obligations on financing leases at the present value of the lease payments. Discretionary accruals are adjustments to cash flows selected by the manager. The manager chooses discretionary accruals from an opportunity set of generally accepted procedures defined by accounting standard-setting bodies. For example, the manager can choose the method of depreciating long-lived assets; he can accelerate or delay delivery of inventory at the end of the fiscal year; and he can allocate fixed factory overheads between cost of goods sold and inventories.

Accruals modify the timing of reported earnings. Discretionary accruals therefore enable the manager to transfer earnings between periods. I assume that discretionary accruals sum to zero over the manager's employment horizon with the firm. The magnitude of discretionary accruals each year is limited by the available accounting technology to a maximum of K and a minimum of $-K$.

The manager observes cash flows from operations and non-discretionary accruals at the end of each year and selects discretionary accounting procedures and accruals to maximize his expected utility from bonus awards.[7] The choice of discretionary accruals affects his bonus award and the cash flows of the firm. I assume that these cash effects are financed by stock issues or repurchases and, therefore, do not affect the firm's production/investment decisions.

Healy (1983) derives the manager's decision rule for choosing discretionary accruals when his employment horizon is two periods. The choice of discretion-

---

[7] The manager's accrual decision is motivated by factors other than compensation. Watts and Zimmerman (1978) suggest that the manager also considers the effect of accounting choices on taxes, political costs, and the probability and associated costs of violating lending agreements.

ary accruals in period one fixes his decision in the second period because discretionary accruals are constrained to sum to zero over these two periods. Fig. 1 depicts discretionary accruals in the first period as a function of earnings before discretionary accruals. These results are discussed in three cases.

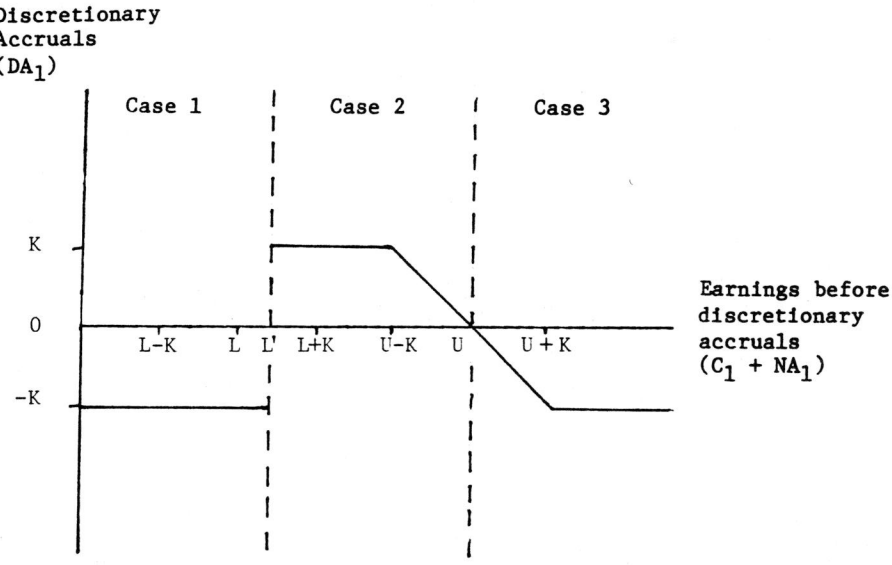

Fig. 1. Managerial discretionary accrual decisions as a function of earnings before discretionary accruals and bonus plan parameters in the first period of a two-period model. L = the lower bound defined in the bonus plan, U = the upper bound on earnings, L' = a cutoff point which is a function of the lower bound, the manager's risk preference, expected earnings in period 2 and the discount rate, K = the limit on discretionary accruals, C = cash flows from operations, and NA = non-discretionary accruals.

Case 1

In Case 1, the manager has an incentive to choose income-decreasing discretionary accruals, that is to take a bath. This case has two regions. In the first, earnings before discretionary accruals are more than K below the lower bound (i.e., $C_1 + NA_1 < L - K$). The manager selects the minimum discretionary accrual ($DA_1 = -K$) because even if he chooses the maximum, reported income will not exceed the lower bound and no bonus will be awarded. By deferring earnings to period two, he maximizes his expected future award.

In the second region of Case 1, earnings before discretionary accruals in period 1 ($C_1 + NA_1$) are within $\pm K$ of the lower bound (L). The manager either selects the minimum ($DA_1 = -K$) or maximum ($DA_1 = K$) discretionary accrual. If he chooses the maximum accrual, he receives a bonus in period 1 but foregoes some expected bonus in period 2 because he is now constrained to report the minimum accrual in that period ($DA_2 = -K$). If he selects the minimum discretionary accrual in period 1 the manager maximizes his expected bonus in period 2, but receives no bonus in the first period. He trades off present value and certainty advantages of receiving a bonus in period 1 against the foregone expected bonus in period 2. Conditional on the bonus plan parameters, expected earnings before discretionary accruals in period 2, the discount rate, and his risk aversion, the manager estimates a threshold (denoted by L' in fig. 1) where he is indifferent between reporting the minimum and maximum accrual in period 1. In fig. 1, the threshold (L') exceeds the lower bound in the bonus plan (L). However, the threshold can also be less than the lower bound, depending on expected earnings in period 2. The manager selects the minimum discretionary accrual ($DA_1 = -K$) when earnings before discretionary accruals are less than the threshold, i.e., $C_1 + NA_1 < L'$.

Case 2

In Case 2, the manager has an incentive to choose income-increasing discretionary accruals. If first-period earnings before discretionary accruals exceed the threshold L', the present value and certainty advantages of accelerating income and receiving a bonus in period 1 outweigh foregone expected awards in period 2. The manager, therefore, selects positive discretionary accruals. When earnings before accounting choices are less than ($U - K$), he chooses the maximum accrual ($DA_1 = K$). When earnings before accounting choices are within K of the upper bound, the manager selects less than the maximum discretionary accrual because income beyond the upper bound is lost for bonus calculations. He chooses $DA_1 = (U - C_1 - NA_1)$, thereby reporting earnings equal to the upper bound. If the bonus plan does not specify an upper bound, the manager selects the maximum discretionary accrual ($DA_1 = K$) when earnings before accounting choices exceed the threshold L'.

Case 3

In Case 3, the manager has an incentive to select income-decreasing discretionary accruals. When the bonus plan upper bound is binding, earnings before discretionary accruals exceeding that bound are lost for bonus purposes. By deferring income that exceeds the upper bound, the manager does not reduce his current bonus and increases his expected future award. When earnings before discretionary accruals are less than $U + K$, he selects $DA_1 = (C_1 + NA_1 - U)$, reporting earnings equal to the upper bound. When earnings before discretionary accruals exceed ($U + K$), he chooses the minimum accrual ($DA_1 = -K$).

In summary, the sign and magnitude of discretionary accruals are a function of expected earnings before discretionary accruals, the parameters of the bonus plan, the limit on discretionary accruals, the manager's risk preferences and the discount rate. Three implications of this theory are tested:

(1) If earnings before discretionary accruals are less than the threshold represented by L', the manager has an incentive to select income-decreasing discretionary accruals.

(2) If earnings before discretionary accruals exceed the lower threshold, denoted by L' in fig. 1, but not the upper limit, the manager has an incentive to select discretionary accruals to increase income.

(3) If the bonus plan specifies an upper bound and earnings before discretionary accruals exceed that limit, the manager has an incentive to select discretionary accruals to decrease income.

Earlier studies on the smoothing hypothesis postulate that discretionary accruals are a function of earnings before accruals.[8] However, the predictions of the compensation theory outlined here differ from those of the smoothing hypothesis: when earnings before accrual decisions are less than the threshold L', the compensation theory predicts that the manager selects income-decreasing discretionary accruals; the smoothing hypothesis implies that he chooses income-increasing accruals.

4. Sample design and collection of financial data

4.1. Sample design

The population selected for this study is companies listed on the 1980 Fortune Directory of the 250 largest U.S. industrial corporations.[9] It is common for stockholders of these companies to endorse the implementation of a bonus plan at the annual meeting. Subsequent plan renewals are ratified, usually every three, five or ten years and a summary of the plan is included in the proxy statement on each of these occasions. The first available copy of the bonus plan is collected for each company from proxy statements at one of three sources: Peat Marwick, the Citicorp Library and the Baker Library at Harvard Business School. Plan information is updated whenever changes in the plan are ratified.

---

[8] See Ronen and Sadan (1981) for an extensive review of the smoothing literature.

[9] Fox (1980) provides evidence that the probability of a corporation employing a bonus plan is not independent of size or industry. The inferences drawn from this study are, therefore, strictly limited to the sample population. Nonetheless, that population is a non-trivial one – the largest 250 industrials account for more than 40 percent of sales of all U.S. industrial corporations.

One hundred and fifty-six companies are excluded from the final sample. The managers of 123 of these firms receive bonus awards but the details of the bonus contracts are not publicly available. Six companies do not appear to reward top management by bonus during any of the years proxy statements are available. A further twenty-seven companies have contracts which limit the transfer to the bonus pool to a percentage of the participating employees' salaries. Since this information is not publicly disclosed, no upper limit can be estimated for these companies.

Some of the sample companies operate earnings-based bonus and performance plans simultaneously. To control for the effect of performance plans on managers' accounting decisions, companies are deleted from the sample in years when both plans are used. This restriction reduces the number of company years by 239.

The useable sample comprises ninety-four companies. Thirty of these have bonus plans which specify both upper and lower bounds on earnings. The contract definitions of earnings, the net upper bound and the lower bound for the sample are summarized in table 1. Earnings are defined as earnings before

Table 1

Summary of useable bonus plan definitions for a sample from the Fortune 250 over the period 1930–1980.

Total number of sample companies	94
Total number of company-years	1527
Number of company-years subject to an upper bound constraint	447
Adjustments to earnings specified in the bonus contract	*Percentage of company-year observations*
Additions to net income	
Income Tax	52.7%
Extraordinary items	27.5
Interest	33.5
Deductions from net income	
Preferred dividends	12.1
Variables used to define lower bounds in the bonus contract	
Net worth	42.0
Net worth plus long-term liabilities	37.2
Earnings per share	8.3
Other	17.8
Variables used to define upper bounds in the bonus contract	
Cash dividends	22.4
Net worth or net worth plus long-term liabilities	2.5
Other	4.5

taxes for 52.7 percent of the company-years and earnings before interest for 33.5 percent of the observations. Bonus contracts typically define the lower bound as a function of net worth (42.0 percent of the observations) or as a function of net worth plus long-term liabilities (37.2 percent). Some contracts define the lower bound as a function of more than one variable. For example, the 1975 bonus contract of American Home Products Corporation defines the lower bound as 'the greater of (a) an amount equal to 12 percent of Average Net Capital or (b) an amount equal to $1.00 multiplied by the average number of shares of the Corporation's common stock outstanding at the close of business on each day of the year'. The upper bound is commonly written as a function of cash dividends.

4.2. Collection of financial data

Earnings and upper and lower bounds for each company-year are estimated using actual bonus plan definitions. The definitions are updated whenever the plan is amended. The data to compute these variables is collected from COMPUSTAT for the years 1964–80 and from Moody's Industrial Manual for earlier years.

Two proxies for discretionary accruals and accounting procedures are used: total accruals and the effect of voluntary changes in accounting procedures on earnings. Total accruals (ACC_t) include both discretionary and non-discretionary components ($ACC_t = NA_t + DA_t$), and are estimated by the difference between reported accounting earnings and cash flows from operations. Cash flows are working capital from operations (reported in the funds statement) less changes in inventory and receivables, plus changes in payables and income taxes payable:

$$ACC_t = -DEP_t - XI_t \cdot D_1 + \Delta AR_t + \Delta INV_t$$

$$- \Delta AP_t - \{\Delta TP_t + D_t\} \cdot D_2,$$

where

DEP_t = depreciation in year t;
XI_t = extraordinary items in year t;
ΔAR_t = accounts receivable in year t less accounts receivable in year $t - 1$;
ΔINV_t = inventory in year t less inventory in year $t - 1$;
ΔAP_t = accounts payable in year t less accounts payable in year $t - 1$;
ΔTP_t = income taxes payable in year t less income taxes payable in year $t - 1$;
DEF_t = deferred income tax expense (credit) for year t;
D_1 = 1 if bonus plan earnings are defined after extraordinary items,
= 0 if bonus plan earnings are defined before extraordinary items;
D_2 = 1 if bonus plan earnings are defined after income taxes,
= 0 if bonus plan earnings are defined before income taxes.

The only accrual omitted is the earnings effect of the equity method of accounting for investments in associated companies.

The second proxy for discretionary accruals and accounting procedures is the effect of voluntary changes in accounting procedures on reported earnings. Accounting changes are collected for sample companies from 1968 to 1980 using two sources: the sample of depreciation changes used by Holthausen (1981) and changes documented by Accounting Trends and Techniques. The effect of each change on current and retained earnings is collected from the companies' annual reports. This data is further described in section 6.

5. Accrual tests and results

5.1. Contingency tests and results

Contingency tables are constructed to test the implications of the theory. Managers have an incentive to select income-decreasing discretionary accruals when their bonus plan's upper and lower bounds are binding. When these bounds are not binding the manager has an incentive to choose income-increasing discretionary accruals. Total accruals proxy for discretionary accruals.

Each company-year is assigned to one of three portfolios: (1) Portfolio UPP, (2) Portfolio LOW, or (3) Portfolio MID. Portfolio UPP comprises observations for which the bonus contract upper limit is binding. Company-years are assigned to this portfolio when cash flows from operations exceed the upper bound defined in the bonus plan. The theory implies that observations should be assigned to portfolio UPP when cash flows from operations plus nondiscretionary accruals exceed the upper bound. Cash flows are a proxy for the sum of cash flows and non-discretionary accruals because nondiscretionary accruals are unobservable. This method of identifying company-years when the upper bound is binding leads to misclassifications which increase the probability of incorrectly rejecting the null hypothesis. Discussion of this problem and tests to control for the bias are presented later in this section.

Portfolio LOW comprises observations for which the bonus plan lower bound is binding. Company-years are assigned to this portfolio if earnings are less than the lower bound specified in the bonus plan. The theory implies that observations should be assigned to portfolio LOW when cash flows from operations plus non-discretionary accruals are less than the lower threshold L'. This threshold is a function of the bonus plan lower bound, the managers' risk preferences and their expectations of future earnings. Since the threshold is unobservable, the method of assigning company-years to portfolio UPP, using cash flows as a proxy for cash flows plus non-discretionary accruals, cannot be used for portfolio LOW. Instead, company-years are assigned to portfolio LOW when earnings are less than the lower bound since no bonus is awarded

Table 2

Summary of the association between accruals and bonus plan parameters.

Portfolio[a]	Proportion of accruals with given sign		Number of company-years	Mean accruals[b]	t-test for difference in means
	Positive	Negative			
Sample A: Plans with a lower bound but no upper bound					
Portfolio LOW	0.38	0.62	74	− 0.0367	2.5652[d]
Portfolio MID	0.36	0.64	1006	− 0.0155	
χ^2 (d.f. = 1)	0.1618				
Sample B: Plans with both a lower bound and upper bound					
Portfolio LOW	0.09	0.91	22	− 0.0671	4.2926[c]
Portfolio MID	0.46	0.54	281	0.0021	8.3434[c]
Portfolio UPP	0.10	0.90	144	− 0.0536	
χ^2 (d.f. = 2)	61.3930[c]				
Sample C: Aggregate of samples A and B					
Portfolio LOW	0.31	0.69	96	− 0.0437	4.3247[c]
Portfolio MID	0.38	0.62	1287	− 0.0117	7.4593[c]
Portfolio UPP	0.10	0.90	144	− 0.0536	
χ^2 (d.f. = 2)	43.7818[c]				

[a] Portfolio LOW comprises company-years when the bonus plan lower bound is binding. Portfolio MID contains observations for which the lower and upper bounds are not binding. Portfolio UPP contains company years when the upper bound is binding.
[b] Accruals are deflated by the book value of total assets.
[c] Significant at the 0.005 level.
[d] Significant at the 0.010 level.

in these years, and managers have an incentive to select income-decreasing discretionary accruals. This assignment method induces a selection bias which increases the probability of incorrectly rejecting the null hypothesis. Discussion of this problem is deferred to later in the section.

Portfolio MID contains observations where neither the upper nor lower bounds are binding. Company-years that are not assigned to portfolios UPP or LOW are included in portfolio MID, and are expected to have a higher proportion of positive accruals than the other two portfolios.

The incidence of positive and negative accruals for portfolios LOW, MID and UPP is presented in the form of a contingency table in table 2. The row denotes the portfolio to which each company-year is assigned. The column denotes the sign of the accrual and each cell contains the proportion of observations fulfilling each condition. Mean accruals, deflated by the book value of total assets at the end of each company-year[10] are also displayed for

[10] Accruals are also deflated by sales and the book value of assets at the beginning of the year. The test results are insensitive to alternative size deflators.

each portfolio. If managers select accruals to increase the value of their bonus compensation, there will be a higher incidence of negative accruals and lower mean accruals for portfolios LOW and UPP than for portfolio MID. Chi-square and t-statistics, testing these hypotheses, are reported in table 2. The chi-square test is a two-tailed test which compares the number of observations in each contingency table cell with the number expected by chance.[11] The t-tests are one-tailed tests of differences in mean deflated accruals for the three portfolios.[12]

Sample A reports results for plans with a lower bound, but no upper bound. There is a lower proportion of negative accruals for portfolio LOW than for portfolio MID, inconsistent with the theory. However, the chi-square statistic is not statistically significant. The mean standardized accruals support the theory: the mean for portfolio LOW is less than the mean for portfolio MID and the t-statistic, comparing the difference in means, is statistically significant at the 0.010 level. This result suggests that managers are more likely to take a bath, that is, select income-decreasing accruals, when the lower bound of their bonus plan is binding than when it is not.

Sample B comprises plans which specify both an upper and lower bound. The chi-square statistic is significant at the 0.005 level, indicating that there is a greater incidence of negative accruals when the bonus plan lower and upper limits are binding than otherwise. Tests of mean standardized accruals reinforce the chi-square results: the means for portfolios LOW and UPP are less than the mean for the MID portfolio. The t-tests, evaluating differences in means, are statistically significant at the 0.005 level. These results are consistent with the hypothesis that managers are more likely to select income-decreasing accruals when the lower and upper bounds of their bonus plans are binding. Sample C aggregates samples A and B and confirms the results.

There are several differences in the results for samples A and B. First, the results for the MID portfolio are stronger for the sample of plans with upper bounds. One explanation is that bonus plan administrators enforce an informal upper bound when one is not specified in the contract. If this informal bound is binding, some of the companies included in the MID portfolio for sample A are misclassified; they should be included in sample B and assigned to

---

[11] The chi-square test assumes that the sample is a random one from the population, and the sample size is large. The statistic is drawn from a chi-square distribution with $(R-1)(C-1)$ degrees of freedom, where R is the number of rows and C the number of columns in the contingency table.

[12] This statistical test assumes that the populations are normal with equal variances. Each t-value is then drawn from a t-distribution with $(N+M-2)$ degrees of freedom, where N is the number of observations in one sample and M the number in the other. Both the t and chi-square tests assume that accruals are independent. This assumption is violated if accruals are autocorrelated or sensitive to market-wide and industry factors. Accruals exhibit significant positive first-order autocorrelation. The test statistics reported in table 2 are therefore overstated.

Table 3

Summary of the association between accrual subcomponents and bonus plan parameters.

Portfolio[a]	Proportion of accrual subcomponents with given sign		Mean accruals[b]	t-test for difference in means
	Positive	Negative		
Change in inventory				
Portfolio LOW	0.59	0.41	0.0096	
Portfolio MID	0.80	0.20	0.0246	2.6880[c]
Portfolio UPP	0.69	0.31	0.0078	4.0515[c]
χ^2 (d.f. = 2)	26.3171[c]			
Change in accounts receivable				
Portfolio LOW	0.59	0.41	0.0092	
Portfolio MID	0.83	0.17	0.0218	3.1152[c]
Portfolio UPP	0.84	0.16	0.0135	2.8119[c]
χ^2 (d.f. = 2)	35.4581[c]			

[a] Portfolio LOW comprises company years when the bonus plan lower bound is binding. Portfolio MID contains observations for which the lower and upper bounds are not binding. Portfolio UPP contains company years when the upper bound is binding.

[b] Accruals are deflated by the book value of total assets.

[c] Significant at the 0.005 level.

portfolio UPP. A second difference between the samples is the stronger result for portfolio LOW for sample B than sample A. I have no explanation for this result.

Contingency tables are constructed for the following subcomponents of accruals: changes in inventory, changes in receivables, depreciation, changes in payables and, where relevant to the bonus award, changes in income taxes payable. The changes in inventory and receivable accrual subcomponents are most strongly associated with management compensation incentives. Contingency table results for the aggregate sample are presented for these two subcomponents in table 3.[13] There are more negative inventory accruals when the upper and lower constraints are binding than for the MID portfolio. The results for receivable accruals confirm the theory for portfolios LOW and MID. However, there is no difference in the proportion of negative accruals for portfolios MID and UPP. The chi-square statistics for both inventory and receivable accruals are significant at the 0.005 level. Differences in mean inventory and receivable accruals for portfolios LOW, MID and UPP are consistent with the theory: the means for portfolios UPP and LOW are significantly lower than the mean for portfolio MID at the 0.005 level.

[13] Results for other subcomponents, and for different plan forms – those with and without an upper bound – are reported in Healy (1983). The upper bound results for depreciation, changes in accounts payable and changes in taxes payable are consistent with the theory, but the lower bound results are inconsistent.

In summary, the evidence in tables 2 and 3 is generally inconsistent with the null hypothesis that there is no association between discretionary accruals and managers' income-reporting incentives under the bonus plan. There is a greater incidence of negative accruals when the upper and lower bounds in the bonus contracts are binding. The contingency tables for decomposed accruals identify changes in inventory and accounts receivables as the accrual subcomponents most highly related to managers' bonus plan incentives.

There are several limitations of the contingency test. First, the method of assigning observations to portfolio LOW induces a selection bias. Company-years are assigned to Portfolio LOW when reported earnings are less than the lower bound. A high incidence of negative accruals are observed for this portfolio, consistent with the theory. However, both reported earnings and total accruals include non-discretionary accruals. Company-years with negative non-discretionary accruals are therefore likely to be assigned to portfolio LOW and they will also tend to have negative total accruals. This selection bias increases the probability of incorrectly rejecting the null hypothesis.

A second limitation of the contingency tests arises from errors in measuring discretionary accruals. Total accruals are used as a proxy for discretionary accruals. Measurement errors for this proxy are correlated with the firm's cash flows from operations and earnings, the variables used to assign company-years to portfolio UPP, MID and LOW. This relation could explain the contingency results. For example, inventory accruals reflect physical inventory levels.[14] If there is an unexpected increase in demand, physical inventory levels and non-discretionary accruals will fall and cash flows from operations increase, consistent with the results reported for portfolio UPP in table 3. However, an unexpected decrease in demand will increase physical inventory levels and nondiscretionary accruals and decrease cash flows from operations, opposite to the theory's predictions for portfolio LOW.

A third limitation of the contingency tests arises from errors in measuring earnings before discretionary accruals. Cash flows are a proxy for this variable and are used to assign company-years to portfolios MID and UPP. Errors in measuring earnings before discretionary accruals are perfectly negatively correlated with measurement errors in discretionary accruals since the sum of the actual variables (earnings before discretionary accruals and discretionary accruals) are constrained to equal the sum of the measured variables (cash flows and total accruals) by the accounting earnings identity. This implies that a disproportionate number of company-years with positive measurement error in earnings before discretionary accruals will be assigned to portfolio UPP. These observations have negative measurement errors in discretionary accruals, increasing the probability of incorrectly rejecting the null hypothesis.

---

[14] Managers therefore have an incentive to manage inventory levels, as well as to select accounting procedures, to maximize the value of their bonus compensation [see Biddle (1980)].

The tests presented in sections 5.2 and 6 are designed to control for the effects on the contingency results of measurement errors in discretionary accruals and in earnings before discretionary accruals.

5.2. Additional tests and results

Additional tests compare accruals for firms whose bonus plans include an upper bound with accruals for firms whose plans contain no upper limit. The theory predicts that managers whose bonus plans include an upper bound have an incentive to select income-decreasing discretionary accruals when that limit is triggered. Ceteris paribus, managers compensated by schemes with no ceilings on earnings are expected to select income-increasing discretionary accruals. This implies that, holding earnings before discretionary accruals constant, discretionary accruals are lower for company plans with a binding upper bound than for firms whose bonus plans exclude an upper bound. This relation reverses when the upper bound is not binding since I assume that discretionary accruals affect only the timing of reported earnings. Discretionary accruals are therefore higher for company plans with a non-binding upper bound than for firms whose plans do not include an upper bound.

Tests of these implications of the theory control for measurement errors in discretionary accruals. They compare measured discretionary accruals (total accruals) for company-years with equivalent cash flows but different bonus plans – plans with and without an upper bound. If the measurement errors are independent of the existence of an upper bound in the bonus plan,[15] the tests isolate discretionary accrual differences between companies with these different types of bonus plans.

The tests also control for errors in measuring earnings before discretionary accruals by comparing accruals for company-years with equivalent measured earnings before discretionary accruals (cash flows) but with bonus plans that include and exclude an upper bound. If measurement errors are independent of the existence of an upper bound in the bonus plan, the estimates of discretionary accrual differences between companies with these two types of bonus plans are unbiased.

The additional predictions of the theory are tested using all company-years for which earnings exceed the lower bound (i.e., portfolios MID and UPP). The observations are divided into two samples: company-years when the bonus plan specifies an upper bound, and company-years when no such limit is defined. The tests are constructed to compare accruals for these two samples holding cash flows constant. The following test design is implemented:

[15] Weak evidence to support this assumption is presented in Healy (1983). He finds that companies whose bonus plans include and exclude an upper limit do not have different means and variances of leverage, firm value, the ratio of gross fixed assets to firm value, and systematic risk. Leverage is defined as the ratio of long-term debt to firm value, and firm value is the sum of the book values of debt and preferred stock and the market value of common stock.

(1) Company-years with a bonus plan upper bound are assigned to one of two portfolios. The first comprises observations whose cash flows exceed the upper bound. The second contains company-years when the upper bound is not binding.

(2) Company-years with a binding upper bound are arrayed on the basis of cash flows (deflated by the book value of total assets) and deciles are constructed. Mean accruals and cash flows (both deflated by total assets) are estimated by decile.

(3) Company-years with no bonus plan upper bound are assigned to one of ten groups. The groups are constructed to have mean deflated cash flows approximately equal to the means of the deciles formed in Step 2. The high and low deflated cash flows for each decile are used as cutoffs to form the ten groups; a company-year with no upper bound is assigned to a group if deflated cash flows are within its cutoffs. Mean deflated accruals and cash flows are estimated for each group.

The mean deflated accruals and cash flows are reported in table 4 by decile for company-years with a binding upper bound and by a group for company-years with no upper bound. The theory predicts that, holding cash flows constant, accruals are lower for companies with a binding bonus plan upper bound, than for companies with no upper bound. The results support the theory: mean accruals are less for company-years with a binding upper bound in nine of the ten pairwise comparisons reported in table 4, panel A. The Sign and Wilcoxon Signed-Ranks tests are used to evaluate whether this result is statistically significant.[16] The Sign test is significant at the 0.0107 level and the Wilcoxon Signed-Ranks test at the 0.0020 level.

The test design is replicated to compare company-years whose upper bound is not binding with company-years whose bonus plan contains no upper bound. The theory predicts that, holding cash flows constant, accruals are higher for companies with a non-binding bonus plan upper bound, than for companies whose plan contains no upper bound. Company-years for which the upper bound is not binding are arrayed on the basis of cash flows and deciles are formed. The high and low cash flows for these deciles are used to form ten groups for company-years with no plan upper bound. Mean deflated accruals and cash flows are reported in table 4, panel B by decile for company-years with a non-binding upper bound, and by group for company-years with no upper bound. The results are consistent with the theory: mean accruals for company-years when the bonus plan upper bound is not binding are greater than mean accruals for company-years with no upper bound in nine of the ten pairwise comparisons. The Sign test is significant at the 0.0107 level and the Wilcoxon Signed-Ranks test at the 0.0068 level.

---

[16] The Sign test and Wilcoxon Signed-Ranks test assume that assignments to test and control groups are random. For a detailed description of the tests see Siegel (1956, pp. 67–83).

Table 4

Results of tests comparing accruals for companies whose bonus plans include and exclude an upper bound holding cash flows constant.

Decile[a]	Average cash flows[b] by decile for company-years whose bonus plan		Average accruals[b] by decile for company-years whose bonus plan		
	Includes an upper bound	Excludes an upper bound	Includes an upper bound	Excludes an upper bound	Difference in average accruals[c]

Panel A: Accruals for company-years when the bonus plan's upper bound is binding compared with accruals for company-years with no upper limit defined in their bonus plan

1	0.0681	0.0658	−0.0044	0.0099	−0.0143
2	0.0912	0.0927	−0.0048	−0.0091	0.0043
3	0.1066	0.1066	−0.0341	−0.0191	−0.0150
4	0.1158	0.1163	−0.0585	−0.0280	−0.0305
5	0.1271	0.1277	−0.0611	−0.0320	−0.0291
6	0.1368	0.1382	−0.0611	−0.0349	−0.0262
7	0.1481	0.1485	−0.0660	−0.0399	−0.0330
8	0.1580	0.1574	−0.0729	−0.0399	−0.0330
9	0.1784	0.1775	−0.0908	−0.0456	−0.0452
10	0.2445	0.2183	−0.0870	−0.0694	−0.0176

	Sign test	0.0107
	Wilcoxon Signed-Rank test	0.0020

Panel B: Accruals for company-years when the bonus plan's upper bound in not binding compared with accruals for company-years with no upper limit defined in their bonus plan

1	−0.0754	−0.0444	0.1235	0.1011	0.0224
2	0.0355	0.0342	0.0277	0.0348	−0.0121
3	0.0612	0.0628	0.0150	0.0099	0.0051
4	0.0857	0.0840	−0.0040	−0.0042	0.0002
5	0.1039	0.1045	0.0055	−0.0161	0.0216
6	0.1257	0.1263	−0.0174	−0.0323	0.0321
7	0.1482	0.1465	−0.0261	−0.0354	0.0093
8	0.1687	0.1675	−0.0314	−0.0449	0.0135
9	0.1953	0.1962	−0.0430	−0.0587	0.0157
10	0.2547	0.2499	−0.0474	−0.0836	0.0362

	Sign test	0.0107
	Wilcoxon Signed-Rank test	0.0068

[a] Company-years for which the bonus plan upper limit is binding (panel A) or not binding (panel B) are arrayed on the basis of cash flows (deflated by total assets) and deciles are formed. The high and low cash flow values for these deciles are used to form ten groups for company-years with no upper bound. Mean cash flows and accruals (both deflated by total assets) are estimated for each group/decile.

[b] Cash flows and accruals are deflated by the book value of total assets.

[c] The compensation theory predicts that the difference is negative (panel A) or positive (panel B).

7. Changes in accounting procedure tests and results

The effect of voluntary changes in accounting procedures on earnings is also used to test the implications of the theory. The proxy used in section 6, accruals, reflects both discretionary and non-discretionary accruals and accounting procedures. Voluntary changes in accounting procedures reflect purely discretionary accounting procedure decisions.

Reported changes in accounting procedures are available from two sources: the sample of depreciation switches used by Holthausen (1981) and changes reported by Accounting Trends and Techniques. Accounting changes are collected from these sources for the sample companies from 1968 to 1980. Procedure changes are decomposed according to the type of change and a summary is presented in table 5 for the full sample (342 changes) and for the changes whose effect on earnings is disclosed in the footnotes (242).

The effect of each accounting procedure change on earnings and equity is collected from the financial statement footnotes. In 100 cases the effect of the change is described as immaterial or not disclosed. A further 49 changes report only the sign of the effect on earnings. These are coded to indicate whether the effect is positive or negative.

7.1. Contingency tests

The contingency tests are replicated using the effect of changes in accounting procedures on earnings available for bonuses as a proxy for discretionary accounting decisions. Earnings available for bonuses are reported earnings, defined in the bonus plan, less the lower bound. If the effect of the accounting change on this variable is positive (negative), the change is classified as income-increasing (income-decreasing). Company-years are assigned to portfolios LOW, MID and UPP using the method adopted in section 6, and contingency tables are constructed to compare the incidence of income-increasing and income-decreasing accounting procedure changes for each portfolio. The results do not support the theory. However, there are several potential explanations of this finding:

(1) Casual evidence suggests that it is more costly for managers to transfer earnings between periods by changing accounting procedures than by changing accruals. Companies rarely change accounting procedures annually – for example, changes to straight line depreciation in one year are typically not followed by a change to other depreciation methods in succeeding years. Managers appear to have greater flexibility to change accruals. For example, they can accelerate or defer recognition of sales, and capitalize or expense repair expenditures.

(2) Changes in accounting procedures affect earnings and the bonus plan lower bound in the current and future years. Managers consider the effect of

alternative accounting methods on the present value of their bonus awards. However, the effect of a procedure change on the accounting numbers is only publicly disclosed for the year of the change. This proxy therefore fails to control for the effect of accounting procedures on bonus awards in future years.

The tests presented in section 7.2 control for these problems.

Table 5

Summary and decomposition of changes in accounting procedures for a sample from the Fortune 250 over the period 1968–1980.

Type of change	Full sample (342 changes)	Subsample with earnings effect disclosed (242 changes)
Miscellaneous	19	12
Inventory		
Miscellaneous	16	9
To LIFO	64	63
To FIFO	3	3
Depreciation		
Miscellaneous	11	6
To accelerated	3	1
To straight-line	27	25
To replacement cost	2	1
Other expenses		
Miscellaneous	20	12
To accrual	12	8
To cash	5	4
Actuarial assumptions for pensions	68	54
Revenue recognition	3	1
Entity accounting		
Miscellaneous	21	8
To inclusion in consolidation	21	1
To equity from unconsolidated	47	34
	$\overline{342}$	$\overline{242}$

Disclosure of effect on net income

Effect on earnings disclosed		242
Estimate given in dollars	193	
Directional effect reported	49	
Effect undisclosed or described as immaterial		100
		$\overline{342}$

Table 6

Association between voluntary changes in accounting procedures and the adoption or modification of a bonus plan.

| Year[a] | Mean number of voluntary accounting changes per firm | | Difference in means |
	Sample changing bonus plan	Sample not changing bonus plan	
1968	0.6364	0.1161	0.5203
1969	1.0000	0.0932	0.9068
1970	1.3333	0.2250	1.1080
1971	0.2000	0.1780	0.0220
1972	0.2000	0.1102	0.0898
1973	0.2500	0.1739	0.0761
1974	0.5000	0.4132	0.0868
1975	0.4000	0.2458	0.1542
1976	0.5000	0.1818	0.3182
1977	0.0000	0.0250	−0.0250
1978	0.0000	0.0417	−0.0417
1980	0.0000	0.1983	−0.1983
	Sign test		0.0730
	Wilcoxon Signed-Rank test		0.0212

[a] No results are reported for 1979 since none of the sample companies adopted or modified their bonus plan in that year.

7.2. Tests of the association between bonus plan changes and changes in accounting procedures

Watts and Zimmerman (1983) postulate that changes in the contracting or political processes are associated with changes in accounting methods. For example, companies are more likely to voluntarily change accounting procedures during years following the adoption or modification of a bonus plan, than when there is no such contracting change. To test this hypothesis, useable sample companies[17] are partitioned into two portfolios for each of the years 1968 to 1980. One portfolio comprises companies that adopt or modify their bonus plan; the other contains companies that have no such contracting change.

Bonus plans are adopted or modified at the annual meeting, which typically occurs three or four months after the fiscal year end. The mean number of voluntary accounting changes per firm reported at the end of the following fiscal year is estimated for companies that modify and adopt bonus plans and for companies with no bonus plan change for each of the years 1968 to 1980. A greater number of voluntary changes are expected for the sample of firms

[17] The sample includes the 94 companies used in earlier tests and the 27 companies formerly excluded because their bonus plan upper limit was a function of participating employees' salaries.

adopting or modifying bonus plans, than for firms with no such change. The Sign and Wilcoxon Ranked-Sign tests are used to evaluate whether the mean number of changes per firm differ for firms with and without a bonus plan change.

The test mitigates one of the limitations of the contingency tests. The proxy for the managers' accounting decisions in those tests, the effect of an accounting procedure change on bonus earnings in the year of the change, ignores the effect on future years' bonus earnings. Tests of the association between bonus plan modifications/adoptions and the incidence of changes in accounting procedures avoid estimating this effect.

Test results are reported in table 6. The mean number of voluntary changes in accounting procedures is greater for firms with bonus plan changes than for firms with no such change in nine of the twelve years. No means are reported for 1979 because no sample companies introduced or modified bonus plans in that year. The Sign and Wilcoxon Signed-Rank tests are statistically significant at the 0.0730 and 0.0212 levels respectively, consistent with the hypothesis that changes in bonus schemes are associated with changes in accounting procedures.

8. Conclusions

Bonus schemes create incentives for managers to select accounting procedures and accruals to maximize the value of their bonus awards. These schemes appear to be an effective means of influencing managerial accrual and accounting procedure decisions. There is a strong association between accruals and managers' income-reporting incentives under their bonus contracts. Managers are more likely to choose income-decreasing accruals when their bonus plan upper or lower bounds are binding, and income-increasing accruals when these bounds are not binding. Results of tests comparing accruals for firms whose bonus plans include and exclude an upper bound further support the theory: holding cash flows constant, accruals are lower for company-years with binding bonus plan upper bounds than for company-years with no upper bound. This difference in the timing or reported earnings is offset when bonus plan upper limits are not binding.

Tests of the theory also use voluntary changes in accounting procedures as a proxy for discretionary accounting decisions. The results suggest that there is a high incidence of voluntary changes in accounting procedures during years following the adoption or modification of a bonus plan. However, managers do not change accounting procedures to decrease earnings when the bonus plan upper or lower bounds are binding.

The paper raises several questions for future investigation. First, why do bonus contracts reward managers on the basis of earnings, rather than stock price? Second, what are the other incentive effects of bonus contracts? Finally, what are the joint incentive effects of bonus schemes and other forms of compensation, such as performance plans?

References

Biddle, Gary C., 1980, Accounting methods and management decisions: The case of inventory costing and inventory policy, Supplement to the Journal of Accounting Research 18, 235–280.

Bowen, Robert M., Eric W. Noreen and John M. Lacy, 1981, Determinants of the corporate decision to capitalize interest, Journal of Accounting and Economics 3, 151–179.

Collins, Daniel W., Michael S. Rozeff and Dan S. Dhaliwal, 1981, The economic determinants of the market reaction to proposed mandatory accounting changes in the oil and gas industry: A cross-sectional analysis, Journal of Accounting and Economics 3, 37–72.

Demski, Joel, James Patell and Mark Wolfson, 1984, Decentralized choice of monitoring systems, Accounting Review, Jan., 16–34.

Fama, Eugene F., 1980, Agency problems and the theory of the firm, Journal of Political Economy 88, 288–307.

Fox, Harland, 1980, Top executive bonus plans (The Conference Board, New York).

Hagerman, Robert L. and Mark E. Zmijewski, 1979, Some economic determinants of accounting policy choice, Journal of Accounting and Economics 1, 141–162.

Healy, Paul M., 1983. The impact of bonus schemes on accounting choices, Dissertation (University of Rochester, Rochester, NY).

Hite, Gailen L. and Michael S. Long, 1980, Taxes and executive stock options, Journal of Accounting and Economics 4, 3–14.

Holmstrom, Bengt, 1979, Moral hazard and observability, Bell Journal of Economics 10, 74–91.

Holmstrom, Bengt, 1982, Managerial incentive problems, in: Essays in economics and management in honor of Lars Wahlbeck (Swedish School of Economics, Helsinki) 209–230.

Holthausen, Robert W., 1981, Evidence on the effect of bond covenants and management compensation contracts on the choice of accounting techniques: The case of the depreciation switch-back, Journal of Accounting and Economics 3, 73–109.

Jensen, Michael C. and William H. Meckling, 1976, Theory of the firm: Managerial behavior, agency costs, and capital structure, Journal of Financial Economics 3, 305–360.

Larcker, David, 1983, The association between performance plan adoption and corporate capital investment, Journal of Accounting and Economics 5, 3–30.

Miller, Merton H. and Myron S. Scholes, 1980, Executive compensation, taxes and incentives, in: W.F. Sharpe and C.M. Cootner, eds., Financial economics: Essays in honor of Paul Cootner (Prentice-Hall, Englewood Cliffs, NJ) 170–201.

Ronen, Joshua and Simcha Sadan, 1981, Smoothing income numbers: Objectives, means, and implications (Addison-Wesley, Reading, MA).

Siegel, Sidney, 1956, Nonparametric statistics for the behavioral sciences (McGraw-Hill, New York).

Smith, Clifford and Ross Watts, 1982, Incentive and tax effects of executive compensation plans, Australian Journal of Management, Dec., 139–157.

Smith, Clifford and Ross Watts, 1983, The structure of executive compensation contracts and the control of management, Unpublished paper (University of Rochester, Rochester, NY).

Watts, Ross, 1977, Corporate financial statements, a product of the market and political processes, Australian Journal of Management, April, 53–75.

Watts, Ross and Jerold Zimmerman, 1978, Towards a positive theory of the determination of accounting standards, Accounting Review, Jan., 112–134.

Watts, Ross and Jerold Zimmerman, 1983, Positive theories of the determination of accounting theories, Unpublished paper (University of Rochester, Rochester, NY).

Zmijewski, Mark E. and Robert Hagerman, 1981, An income strategy approach to the positive theory of accounting standard setting/choice, Journal of Accounting and Economics 3, 129–149.

THE EFFECT OF ACCOUNTING PROCEDURE CHANGES ON CEOs' CASH SALARY AND BONUS COMPENSATION*

Paul M. HEALY and Sok-Hyon KANG

Sloan School of Management, MIT, Cambridge, MA 02139, USA

Krishna G. PALEPU

Harvard Business School, Boston, MA 02163, USA

Received November 1985, final version received October 1986

This paper examines the effect of accounting procedure changes on cash salary and bonus compensation to CEOs. We estimate whether there is an adjustment to the statistical relation between compensation and corporate earnings following changes that lower earnings (FIFO to LIFO inventory valuation) and that raise earnings (accelerated to straight-line depreciation). The results indicate that (1) subsequent to these changes salary and bonus payments are based on reported earnings, rather than earnings under the original accounting method, and (2) the potential compensation effect of the changes is small compared to the effect of economy- or industry-wide changes in compensation.

1. Introduction

In many large U.S. corporations, executives' remuneration is explicitly linked to reported earnings. For example, in 1980 more than 90 percent of the 1000 largest U.S. manufacturing companies used some form of earnings-based compensation plan [see Fox (1980)].[1] Recent studies in accounting hypothesize that these earnings-based plans induce managers to select income-increasing accounting procedures, or impede their selecting income-decreasing procedures, since compensation is imperfectly adjusted for the effect of alternative

*We wish to thank Andrew Christie, Dan Collins (the referee), Linda DeAngelo, Michael Jensen, Bob Kaplan, Rashad Abdel-khalik, Pat O'Brien, Rick Ruback, Ross Watts, Jerry Zimmerman, and the participants at the Stanford Summer Workshop and the MIT Accounting Workshop for their helpful comments on earlier drafts of this paper. We are also grateful to Bob Holthausen and Richard Rikert for letting us use their data bases of changes in accounting procedures.

[1] The most popular schemes included bonus and performance plans. Bonus plans typically award managers cash payments if certain annual earnings targets are attained; performance plans award managers the value of performance units or shares in cash or stock if certain long-term (three- to five-year) earnings targets are achieved. For a more detailed description of bonus plans, see Healy (1985). For a description of performance plans, see Smith and Watts (1982) and Larcker (1983).

0165-4101/87/$3.50 © 1987, Elsevier Science Publishers B.V. (North-Holland)

Journal of Accounting and Economics 9 (1987) 7–34. North-Holland

accounting methods. [See Holthausen and Leftwich (1983) and Watts and Zimmerman (1986) for a summary of these studies.]

This paper examines the statistical relation between cash salary and bonus remuneration to chief executive officers (CEOs), and corporate earnings. We test whether there is an adjustment to this statistical relation subsequent to an accounting procedure change. Two forms of adjustment are considered: (1) those that transform reported earnings under the new accounting method to earnings under the original method, and (2) adjustments to the parameters of the relation that offset the effect of the accounting change. We also examine the effect of an accounting change on CEOs' salary and bonus awards if no adjustment is made to either reported earnings or parameters of the compensation–earnings relation.

We investigate two accounting method changes: from the FIFO to LIFO inventory method, and from accelerated to straight-line depreciation.[2] These are selected for the following reasons. First, they have a large effect on reported earnings. Second, FIFO to LIFO switches typically decrease reported earnings, whereas changes from accelerated to straight-line depreciation usually increase reported earnings.[3] By investigating both income-increasing and income-decreasing changes we are able to increase the power of our tests. Our inventory sample comprises 52 test firms that changed from the FIFO to LIFO inventory method and 50 control firms with no inventory or depreciation method changes. The depreciation sample contains 38 test firms that changed from accelerated to straight-line depreciation and 37 control firms.

We conclude that (1) subsequent to the accounting changes, cash salary and bonus awards are based on reported earnings rather than 'as-if' earnings; (2) the parameters of the compensation–earnings relation change for both the test and control firms subsequent to the accounting changes; and (3) the potential impact of the method changes on salary and bonus payments is small relative to economy-wide changes in compensation.

A number of earlier studies have examined the relation between inventory and depreciation accounting method changes and executive compensation. Their results are mixed. For example, Holthausen (1981) investigates whether the cross-sectional variation in firms' abnormal stock price performance at the date of a change from accelerated to straight-line depreciation is related to the existence of an earnings-based compensation plan. No relation is found.

---

[2] A number of earlier studies that investigate the stock price reaction to accounting changes also focus on these two changes. They include Kaplan and Roll (1972) and Holthausen (1981) in the case of depreciation changes, and Sunder (1973, 1975), Biddle and Lindahl (1982) and Ricks (1982) in the case of inventory changes.

[3] Changes from FIFO to LIFO decrease reported earnings if input prices are rising and physical inventory levels are not depleted. Changes from accelerated to straight-line depreciation increase reported earnings if nominal investments in new depreciable assets are increasing.

However, as Holthausen and Leftwich (1983) point out, this test lacks power because the compensation effects of accounting changes are likely to be small relative to the variability in stock prices and, it is difficult to identify the event dates and specify investors' expectations. Hagerman and Zmijewski (1979) investigate whether companies that have earnings-based compensation plans are more likely to use the FIFO inventory method and straight-line depreciation than companies with no earnings-based plans. They find no relation between the cross-sectional variation in inventory methods and the existence of a compensation plan. However, there is a weak positive relation between the probability that a company uses straight-line depreciation and the probability that it has an earnings-based compensation plan.

Abdel-khalik (1985) estimates a cross-sectional regression of salary and bonus compensation on earnings for a treatment sample of 88 companies that changed to LIFO in 1974, and a control sample of 88 companies that remained on FIFO in that year. He estimates differences in the fixed component of compensation and the elasticity of compensation to reported earnings between these two samples in the two years prior to, the year of, and the year following the accounting change. In the two years prior to the inventory change the compensation parameters do not differ between the treatment and control groups. In the year of the change, the fixed component of compensation is higher for the control group and the elasticity of compensation to reported earnings is higher for the treatment group. These differences persist when reported earnings are replaced by as-if FIFO earnings for the treatment group. Abdel-khalik's findings are therefore mixed.

Our test design differs from that of Abdel-khalik in three ways. First, we examine two accounting changes, one that typically increases earnings (a change to straight-line depreciation) and another that decreases earnings (a change to LIFO). Second, our tests examine earnings and compensation data for as many as ten years following an accounting change. Third, we use a time-series rather than a cross-sectional approach to estimate the relation between compensation and earnings. Murphy (1985) points out that studies that regress compensation on some index of performance across executives at a particular point in time are likely to be misspecified. For these regressions, 'the exclusion of individual-specific factors, such as education and training, perceived ability, performance in previous jobs, firm size, etc., will lead to an omitted variables problem, reflecting factors that are fixed for an executive over time but vary across executives at a point in time' (p. 22). Correlations between the independent variables in a cross-sectional regression and these omitted variables will bias the estimated coefficients. There is some evidence that Abdel-khalik's findings suffer from this form of misspecification because when firm size is included in his cross-sectional regressions, the fixed component of bonus and salary awards and the elasticity of compensation to earnings no longer differ between the treatment and control groups.

The remainder of the paper is organized as follows. Section 2 describes the sample selection and data collection. The statistical tests and results are presented in section 3, and our conclusions are discussed in section 4.

2. Sample selection and data collection

The sample of inventory changes is selected from *Accounting Trends and Techniques* (1970 to 1976). We identify 161 companies that changed from FIFO to LIFO during this period. Our sample of depreciation changes is selected from Holthausen's database [see Holthausen (1981)]. We exclude companies that changed to straight-line depreciation prior to 1967 since compensation data for these companies are incomplete. This restriction limits our sample to 80 of Holthausen's 139 companies.

Bonus and salary data and management changes are collected for the CEOs of our sample companies for the year of the accounting change and the ten years before and after that event from two sources: corporate proxy statements and the annual compensation survey published by *Business Week*. We require that (i) at least five years of consecutive compensation data are available before and after the year of the accounting change, and (ii) a minimum of 14 consecutive years of data are available for each company. These data constraints reduce the test samples to 52 companies that changed inventory policies and 38 companies that changed depreciation methods. The distribution of the changes over the sample period is reported in table 1. The depreciation changes are clustered in 1968 and 1969, and the inventory changes in 1974 and 1975.

Table 2 presents the 2-digit industry breakdown for the test firms. There is some evidence of industry clustering: 23 percent of the firms changing inventory method are in the chemicals industry (SIC 28), and 47 percent of the firms changing depreciation method are in the primary metal industries (SIC 33) and the machinery industry (SIC 35). To control for this industry clustering we collect a matched sample of control firms. The control firms are required to have the same 2-digit industry code as their test firm matches, to have had no inventory or depreciation method changes ten years before and after the years of their test firms' method changes, and to satisfy the compensation data constraints imposed on the test sample. Fifty control firms are found for the inventory sample, and 37 firms for the depreciation sample. The two inventory test firms with no matched control firms available are in the stone, clay, glass and concrete products industry (SIC 32). The one depreciation test firm with no matched control firm available is in the machinery industry (SIC 35). The inventory and depreciation control samples are not independent – 20 of the companies used in the inventory control sample are also included in the depreciation control sample.

Earnings before extraordinary items are collected from COMPUSTAT for the test and control samples for each year that compensation data are

Table 1

Number of test firms changing to LIFO or straight-line depreciation by year in the period 1967–1976.

Year of accounting change	Number of firms changing to LIFO	Number of firms changing to straight-line depreciation
1967	—	2
1968	—	17
1969	—	12
1970	1	1
1971	1	3
1972	0	2
1973	0	0
1974	36	1
1975	10	—
1976	4	—
Total	52	38

Table 2

Number of test firms changing to LIFO or straight-line depreciation in the period 1967–1976 by 2-digit industry.

2-digit SIC code	Industry	Number of firms changing to LIFO	Number of firms changing to straight-line depreciation
20	Food products	3	2
21	Tobacco manufacturers	1	—
22	Textile mill products	—	1
23	Apparels and fabric products	1	—
26	Paper and paper products	2	—
28	Chemicals	12	4
29	Petroleum refining	3	—
30	Rubber and misc. plastic products	1	1
31	Leather and leather products	1	—
32	Stone, clay, glass and concrete products	4	2
33	Primary metal industries	1	9
34	Fabricated metal products, except machinery and transportation equipment	1	—
35	Machinery, except electrical	4	9
36	Electrical and electronic machinery, equipment and supplies	2	4
37	Transportation equipment	7	5
38	Measuring, analyzing, and controlling instruments, photographic, medical and optical goods, watches and clocks	1	—
39	Miscellaneous manufacturing industries	1	—
51	Wholesale trade-nondurable goods	1	—
53	General merchandise stores	3	1
54	Food stores	2	1
59	Miscellaneous retail stores	1	—
	Total	52	38

Table 3

Summary statistics for average annual executive cash salary and bonus, and corporate earnings for sample firms.[a]

	Mean	Mean standard deviation	First quartile	Median	Third quartile
Average executive salary + bonus[b]					
Inventory:					
Test sample[c]	200	49	160	194	234
Control sample[c]	169	40	127	168	206
Depreciation:					
Test sample	176	44	134	178	209
Control sample	165	41	130	165	185
Average corporate earnings[b]					
Inventory:					
Test sample	116,216	47,786	26,312	52,233	89,694
Control sample	73,078	30,495	5,747	36,067	76,179
Depreciation:					
Test sample	52,308	21,293	15,032	31,247	67,877
Control sample	57,736	29,881	14,007	34,395	49,920

[a] These results are for the cross-sectional distribution of time-series averages of annual executive cash salary and bonus, and corporate earnings for each firm in the inventory and depreciation samples. Each time-series contains between 14 and 21 observations.

[b] Both executive salary and bonus, and corporate earnings are in thousands of CPI-deflated (1967 = 100) constant dollars.

[c] The test sample comprises 52 firms that change to LIFO in the period 1970–1976 and 38 firms that change to straight-line depreciation in the period 1967–1974. Each test firm has a matched control firm with the same 2-digit SIC code and with no inventory or depreciation method changes ten years before and after the year of the test firm's method change. Control firms are found for 50 of 52 inventory test firms and 37 of 38 depreciation test firms.

available. Compensation and corporate earnings data are deflated by the CPI to 1967 dollars and time-series averages of these variables estimated for each company. A summary of the cross-sectional distribution of these time-series averages is presented in table 3. The median average salary and bonus in 1967 constant dollars is $194,000 for the inventory test sample and $168,000 for the inventory control sample. The median values for the depreciation test and control samples are $178,000 and $165,000, respectively. The median average corporate earnings in 1967 dollars is $52,233,000 for the inventory test sample and $36,067,000 for the inventory control companies. The median values for the depreciation test and control firms are $31,247,000 and $34,395,000.

The earnings effects of the inventory and depreciation changes are collected for the test firms from the financial statement footnotes for years following the change. Companies that use the LIFO inventory method report the current replacement value of inventory. This value approximates the FIFO inventory value and is used to calculate the difference between reported LIFO income and income that would have been reported had the company continued to use FIFO.

Table 4

Summary statistics for earnings effects of inventory and depreciation method changes as a percentage of 'as-if' earnings for the year of the accounting method changes and the subsequent ten years.[a]

	Year relative to accounting change[b]		
	0	1 to 5	6 to 10
Inventory test sample			
First quartile	− 32.3%	− 10.7%	− 6.4%
Median	− 19.3	− 8.3	− 1.1
Median standard deviation[c]	—	5.3	15.7
Third quartile	− 11.0	− 4.9	5.8
Percent positive	0.0	3.8	48.9
Depreciation test sample			
First quartile	3.6%	5.9%	4.4%
Median	9.6	10.9	7.7
Median standard deviation[c]	—	6.7	4.5
Third quartile	25.7	22.1	23.0
Percent positive	100.0	90.5	100.0

[a] 'As-if' earnings are FIFO earnings following a change to the LIFO inventory valuation method, and earnings computed using accelerated depreciation following a change to straight-line depreciation.

[b] The results in years 1 to 5 and 6 to 10 are for the cross-sectional distribution of time-series averages of the earnings effect of the accounting changes as a percentage of as-if earnings for 52 firms that change to LIFO in the period 1970–1976 and 38 firms that change to straight-line depreciation in the period 1967–1974.

[c] No median standard deviation is reported for year 0 since no time-series standard deviations can be calculated for a single year.

The effect of the depreciation switch from the accelerated to straight-line method is calculated from the deferred tax footnote. All the companies in our depreciation sample continue using the accelerated method for taxes following the reporting change to the straight-line method. The resulting timing difference between book and tax incomes gives rise to an adjustment to deferred taxes which is reported in the tax footnote. We use this value to calculate the difference between reported income and income that would have been reported had the company continued using the accelerated depreciation method.[4,5]

[4] Our depreciation sample includes six companies that changed to straight-line depreciation after 1970. For these companies the deferred tax items after 1981 reflect Accelerated Cost Recovery System (ACRS) rates. ACRS decreased the depreciable lives of fixed assets relative to previous accelerated methods, implying that subsequent to 1981 our adjustments for these companies are not strictly comparable to accelerated depreciation used for reporting purposes. However, this change affects at most three years of data, and is unlikely to alter our conclusions.

[5] None of the companies in our sample reports the deferred tax effect for depreciation prior to 1971. Our as-if earnings series is therefore incomplete for companies that change to the straight-line method prior to this date. These years are treated as missing observations in the empirical tests.

Table 4 reports statistics on the earnings effect of the change to LIFO as a percentage of earnings under FIFO. During the year of change, the median earnings reduction from the inventory policy change is 19.3 percent. Time-series averages of the earnings effect of the inventory change are estimated for each firm for the first five years (years 1 to 5) and the second five years (years 6 to 10) following the LIFO change. The cross-sectional median of these averages is -8.3 percent for the first five years and -1.1 percent for the second five years. The percentage effect of the depreciation change on earnings calculated using accelerated depreciation is also reported in table 4. The median increase in earnings from the depreciation change is 9.6 percent in the year of the change. The cross-sectional median of the average earnings effect for the first five years subsequent to the depreciation change is 10.9 percent, and for the second five years is 7.7 percent.

3. Statistical tests and results

3.1. The compensation model

The statistical tests described below examine whether, subsequent to an accounting change, the relation between CEOs' salary and bonus awards and reported earnings adjusts to fully offset the earnings effect of the accounting change. The tests are based on the following firm-specific compensation model:[6]

$$\ln(COMP_t) = \sum_{i=1}^{n} \alpha_i D_{it} + \beta \ln(EARN_t) + \varepsilon_t, \tag{1}$$

where

$COMP_t$ = salary and cash bonus paid to chief executive officer (CEO) during year t in 1967 constant dollars,

$EARN_t$ = accounting earnings before extraordinary items for the firm during year t in 1967 constant dollars,

D_{it} = 1 if individual i was CEO of the firm during year t, 0 otherwise,

n = number of individuals who held the position of CEO of the firm during the sample period,

β, α_i = firm-specific parameters, to be estimated using time-series data on compensation and earnings ($i = 1, \ldots, n$).

The above compensation model is estimated separately for each firm in the

---

[6] This model is similar to a model presented in Murphy (1985). However, Murphy uses abnormal stock performance as a proxy for management's performance, and constrains the slope coefficient (β) to be constant across firms. For our sample, we reject the hypothesis that the slope coefficient is equal across firms.

sample. There are three features of the model that are worth noting. First, the model is estimated in a logarithmic form since there is some evidence that power transformations perform better than linear regressions in estimating relations between compensation and measures of performance [see Boyes and Schlagenhauf (1979)]. In addition, prior studies have typically used log transformations [e.g., Murphy (1985) and Abdel-khalik (1985)]. The use of a logarithmic form, therefore, makes our results comparable with the findings of these studies.[7]

A second feature of the compensation model is that the intercept term (or the fixed component of compensation), α, is allowed to vary across executives. This enables us to account for differences in manager-specific factors such as age, ability and education. The elasticity of compensation to earnings, β, is assumed to be firm-specific.

The third feature of the model is that the compensation variable is represented by the salary and bonus payments to the chief executive officer. This variable excludes several components of compensation, such as performance awards that are contingent on earnings, and stock option compensation, because disclosures of these awards are frequently incomplete. Their omission limits the conclusions of the study since compensation committees could conceivably adjust these awards, rather than short-term earnings-based awards, to offset the effect of an accounting method change. However, it is worth noting that bonus and salary comprise a non-trivial proportion of executives' total remuneration. For example, in Murphy's study of 461 executives from 1964 to 1981, salary and bonus account for an average 80 percent of total remuneration.

The compensation model in eq. (1) posits that management compensation is in part determined by contemporaneous accounting earnings.[8] A change in the rules used to compute accounting earnings will therefore affect executives' earnings-based compensation unless the compensation committee adjusts for the effect of the accounting change. The committee can insulate salary and bonus compensation from the effects of an accounting rule change in three ways. First, it can continue to use earnings computed under the pre-change accounting rules. In other words, reported earnings under the new accounting rules are adjusted for the effect of the change and the compensation–earnings

---

[7]If earnings are negative, we assume their log value is zero. Twenty of the 90 companies in our sample (29 company-years) are adjusted in this way. The effect of this assumption is to limit managers to receive earnings-dependent compensation only when their company earns profits, consistent with the option characteristics of most bonus contracts [see Healy (1985)]. We also estimate model (1) in linear form, allowing earnings to be negative, and constraining negative earnings to zero. Our conclusions are not sensitive to this adjustment to earnings, or to the logarithmic transformation.

[8]We also test whether lagged earnings are related to salary and bonus awards since salary adjustments could be based on prior years' earnings. We find no evidence that lagged earnings are related to bonus and salary awards.

relation in eq. (1) is applied to the adjusted earnings numbers. Second, the committee can use reported earnings without any adjustment for the accounting change but can modify the parameters α and β in eq. (1) such that, on average, the compensation awarded is unaffected by the accounting change. The tests described below examine whether compensation is insulated from the effects of accounting changes in either of these two ways. The third way for the compensation committee to offset the effect of an accounting change on CEOs' remuneration is through adjustments to stock-based compensation. As noted above, we do not collect data on stock-based awards to CEOs for our sample and therefore do not test this hypothesis.

3.2. Tests of earnings adjustment

To examine whether reported earnings are adjusted for the effect of an accounting change in determining management compensation, we define two earnings variables: reported earnings and 'adjusted' earnings. Reported earnings ($REARN_t$) are based on one set of accounting rules before the accounting policy change, and another set after the change. Adjusted earnings ($AEARN_t$) are computed using the same set of rules both before and after the change. In other words, $AEARN_t$ equal $REARN_t$ for periods prior to the accounting change; $REARN_t$ are adjusted for the effect of the accounting change to generate $AEARN_t$ for periods after the change.

To test whether $AEARN_t$ or $REARN_t$ are used to determine top management compensation subsequent to an accounting change, we estimate the following modified version of eq. (1):

$$\ln(COMP_t) = \sum_{i=1}^{n} \alpha_i D_{it} + \beta \ln(AEARN_t) + \lambda \ln\left(\frac{REARN_t}{AEARN_t}\right) + \varepsilon_t. \quad (2)$$

Eq. (2) modifies (1) by including an additional variable $\ln(REARN_t/ AEARN_t)$. Since $REARN_t$ and $AEARN_t$ are equal before the accounting change, this variable has a value of zero during the pre-change period. In the post-change period, the variable represents the percentage earnings effect of the accounting change on original earnings. If management compensation after the accounting change is computed using earnings under the original rules, and not reported earnings, we expect β to be positive and λ to be zero. If compensation is computed using reported earnings after the accounting change, both β and λ are expected to be positive.

To test the significance of the coefficients for β and λ, eq. (2) is estimated separately for each firm in the sample. The sample distribution of the estimated t-statistics for β and λ are used to test the significance of these parameters. For each parameter, the following sample Z-statistic is computed:

$$Z = \frac{1}{\sqrt{N}} \sum_{j=1}^{N} \frac{t_j}{\sqrt{k_j/(k_j - 2)}},$$

where

t_j = t-statistic for firm j associated with the estimate of the parameter (β or λ),

k_j = degrees of freedom in regression for firm j,

N = number of firms in the sample.

The t-statistic for firm j is distributed Student-t with a variance of $k_j/(k_j - 2)$. Under the Central Limit Theorem, the sum of the standardized t-statistics is normally distributed with a variance of N. The Z-statistic for each of the parameters is therefore a standard normal variate under the null hypothesis that the parameter (β or λ) is not significantly different from zero.

A second and equivalent test compares the explanatory power of eq. (2) with the following restricted form of that equation:

$$\ln(COMP_t) = \sum_{i=1}^{n} \alpha_i D_{it} + \beta \ln(AEARN_t) + \varepsilon_t. \tag{3}$$

Eq. (3) restricts λ in eq. (2) to be equal to zero. An F-statistic is used to test whether this restriction results in a significant reduction in the explanatory power of eq. (2):

$$F_j = \frac{SSR_3 - SSR_2}{SSR_2/k_j},$$

where SSR_3 and SSR_2 are the sums of squares of residuals of eqs. (3) and (2), respectively, and k_j is the degrees of freedom in regression eq. (2) for firm j.

An F-statistic is computed for each firm in the sample. The significance of the sample distribution of F-statistics is tested by the following statistic:

$$\chi^2 = \sum_{j=1}^{N} -2\ln p_j,$$

where p_j is the probability associated with the F-statistic of firm j and N is the number of firms in the sample. Under the null hypothesis that the sample distribution of the F-statistics is no different from that expected by chance, the above statistic is chi-squared distributed with $2N$ degrees of freedom.[9]

---

[9] For a detailed discussion of both these tests, see Christie (1986). Both the tests discussed here are based on the sample distribution of the parameter estimates. In using these tests, it is assumed that the parameters are independent across the firms in the sample. Further discussion of this assumption is deferred to later in the paper.

Table 5

Summary of estimated coefficients for regression tests of the hypothesis that reported earnings are adjusted to FIFO earnings for compensation purposes following a change to the LIFO inventory method.[a]

$$\ln(COMP_{it}) = \sum_{i=1}^{n} \alpha_i D_{it} + \beta \ln(AEARN_t) + \lambda \ln\left(\frac{REARN_t}{AEARN_t}\right) + \varepsilon_t.^b$$

	$\hat{\beta}$	$\hat{\lambda}$
Mean	0.3170	0.3613
Z-statistic[c]	18.12[d]	5.83[d]
First quartile	0.0664	−0.0443
Median	0.2397	0.2701
Third quartile	0.5290	0.8111
Percent positive	92.31%[d]	71.15%[d]
χ^2-statistic (df = 106)	184.54[e]	

[a] These results are for the cross-sectional distribution of time-series regressions for 52 firms that changed to LIFO in the period 1970–1976. Each time-series contains between 14 and 21 observations.

[b] $COMP_t$ = salary + bonus for CEO in year t; $AEARN_t$ = as-if earnings in year t computed using the FIFO inventory method; $REARN_t$ = reported earnings in year t, computed using FIFO before and LIFO after the accounting change; D_{it} = 1 if individual i is CEO of the firm in year t and 0 otherwise; and n = number of individuals who held the CEO position in the sample period.

[c] Under the null hypothesis each Z-statistic is distributed unit normal.

[d] Significant at the one percent level using a two-tailed test.

[e] Significant at the one percent level using a one-tailed test.

3.3. Earnings adjustment test results

3.3.1. Inventory sample

Table 5 presents regression results for the test sample of 52 firms that changed from FIFO to LIFO.[10,11] The estimated coefficient β on the adjusted earnings variable ($AEARN$) is positive for 92 percent (48 of 52) of the sample firms. A binomial test indicates that there is a higher proportion of positive coefficients than expected by chance at the one percent significance level.[12]

[10] The control sample firms are not analyzed in this section because we do not have information on adjusted earnings for these firms.

[11] Twenty-three of the 52 company regression residuals exhibit serial correlation. We use a Cochran–Orcutt transformation for these companies [see Theil (1971) for a description of this technique]. The results do not change significantly. The results reported in table 5 are therefore for the unadjusted estimates.

[12] See Siegel (1956) for a description of the binomial test. The test assumes that the coefficients are cross-sectionally independent. As noted above, further discussion of this assumption is deferred until later in the paper.

The Z-statistic, which tests the joint significance of the *AEARN* coefficients for the 52 sample companies, is significant at the one percent level, enabling us to reject the hypothesis that there is no significant relation between accounting earnings and top management bonus and salary compensation.

The estimated coefficient λ for the variable representing the effect of the change to LIFO (*REARN/AEARN*) on executives' compensation, is positive for 71 percent (37 of 52 firms) of the sample. A binomial test rejects the hypothesis that the proportion of positive coefficients is equal to that expected by chance at the one percent level. The sample Z-statistic, testing the collective significance of the λ coefficients for the 52 firms in the sample, is significant at the one percent level.[13] This evidence is inconsistent with the hypothesis that CEOs' salary and bonus compensation is based on earnings adjusted for the effect of the inventory method change (FIFO earnings).

Finally, the χ^2-statistic shown in table 5 aggregates the probabilities associated with the F-statistics for all firms in the sample. The F-statistic compares the explanatory power of a regression in which λ is restricted to be zero with one in which it is not. The χ^2-statistic for the 52 firms in the sample is 184.5 and is significant at the one percent level. This evidence, consistent with that indicated by the Z-statistic discussed above, suggests that salary and bonus compensation is related to reported earnings, unadjusted for the effect of the change to LIFO. There is no evidence that, for compensation purposes, reported earnings are adjusted to offset the effect of the change in accounting policy for valuing inventory.

3.3.2. Depreciation sample

The results for the 38 test firms that changed from accelerated to straight-line depreciation are similar to the results for the inventory sample. Table 6 reports a summary of the ordinary least squares estimates of model (2). The estimates of the earnings coefficient β are positive for 84.2 percent (32 of 38) of the sample firms. A binomial test indicates that this number of positive estimates is significantly greater than that expected by chance at the one percent level using a two-tailed test. The Z-statistic, which tests the sample significance of the estimates of β, is also significant at the one percent level.

The estimates of λ, the coefficient on the earnings variable that captures the effect of the accounting change, are positive for 60.5 percent (23 of 38) of the companies. The Z-statistic, which tests the significance of the sample estimates of λ, is significant at the one percent level.[14] Consistent with this, the

---

[13] Seventy-seven percent of the estimates of β and 37 percent of the estimates of λ are individually significant at the ten percent level. However, assuming independence across firms in the sample, a more powerful test is to examine the collective significance of the estimated coefficients using the Z-statistic discussed above.

[14] Fifty percent of the estimates of β and 37 percent of the estimates of λ are individually significant at the ten percent level.

Table 6

Summary of estimated coefficients for regression tests of the hypothesis that reported earnings are adjusted to accelerated depreciation earnings for compensation purposes following a change to the straight-line depreciation method.[a]

$$\ln(COMP_t) = \sum_{i=1}^{n} \alpha_i D_{it} + \beta \ln(AEARN_t) + \lambda \ln\left(\frac{REARN_t}{AEARN_t}\right) + \varepsilon_t.[b]$$

	$\hat{\beta}$	$\hat{\lambda}$
Mean	0.1745	0.2752
Z-statistic[c]	15.78[d]	2.16[d]
First quartile	0.0154	−0.6645
Median	0.1642	0.3234
Third quartile	0.2640	0.7393
Percent positive	84.21%[d]	60.53%
χ^2-statistic (df = 76)	164.77[e]	

[a] These results are for the cross-sectional distribution of time-series regressions for 38 firms that changed to straight-line depreciation in the period 1970–1976. Each time-series contains between 14 and 21 observations.

[b] $COMP_t$ = salary + bonus for CEO in year t; $AEARN_t$ = as-if earnings in year t, computed using the accelerated depreciation method; $REARN_t$ = reported earnings in year t, computed using accelerated depreciation before and straight-line depreciation after the accounting change; $D_{it} = 1$ if individual i is CEO of the firm in year t and 0 otherwise; and n = number of individuals who held the CEO position in the sample period.

[c] Under the null hypothesis each Z-statistic is distributed unit normal.

[d] Significant at the one percent level using a two-tailed test.

[e] Significant at the one percent level using a one-tailed test.

χ^2-statistic, which tests whether the accounting change effect variable provides an increase in explanatory power of the sample regressions, is significant at the one percent level. This evidence is inconsistent with the hypothesis that compensation committees continue to use earnings based on accelerated depreciation in determining top management compensation after a change to straight-line depreciation for reporting purposes.

In summary, our results for both inventory and depreciation samples indicate that there is a significant relation between top executive salary and bonus compensation and *reported* accounting earnings. The results indicate that when the two accounting policies are changed, compensation committees do *not* adjust reported earnings for the effects of the accounting changes.

One potential limitation to our findings is that the statistical tests used to aggregate regression results across companies assume the sample observations to be independent. Since the inventory and depreciation changes are clustered in time and concentrated in several industries, this assumption may be violated. To investigate cross-sectional dependence, we estimate the cross-sectional correlations of the residuals from model (2) for 42 companies in the inventory sample with complete data available from 1966 to 1980, and 24 companies in the depreciation sample with data available from 1962 to 1976. There are 861 pairwise residual correlation coefficients for the 42 inventory companies and 276 coefficients for the 24 depreciation companies. The mean correlation coefficient is only 0.0102 for the inventory sample and 0.0193 for the depreciation sample, neither significantly different from zero. We thus find no strong evidence of cross-sectional dependence.

3.4. Tests of compensation model adjustment

The above tests examine whether compensation committees adjust reported earnings for the effects of accounting changes in determining bonus and salary compensation. Committees also have the option of adjusting the fixed component of compensation or the elasticity of compensation to earnings to offset the effect of an accounting change. For example, committees can increase executives' fixed compensation [represented by α in model (1)] or increase the elasticity of compensation to earnings (represented by β) following a change from FIFO to LIFO inventory policy. Executives' remuneration would then be a function of reported earnings, but the compensation effect of using lower LIFO earnings would be approximately offset by higher fixed rewards, or a higher bonus payment for a given percentage increase in earnings.

We test whether there is a change in the parameters of the compensation–earnings relation subsequent to an accounting method change and whether changes on average offset the effect of accounting changes on earnings-based remuneration. Finally, we estimate the potential effect of the accounting changes on bonus and salary awards if no adjustment is made to either reported earnings or parameters of the compensation–earnings relation.

3.4.1. Tests of parameter changes

To test whether the parameters of the compensation models change after an accounting change, we estimate the following regression model for the test samples:

$$\ln(COMP_t) = \sum_{i=1}^{n} \alpha_i D_{it} + \beta_1 \ln(REARN_t) + \beta_2 DUM_t$$

$$+ \beta_3 DUM_t \ln(REARN_t) + u_t, \qquad (4)$$

where DUM_t is 0 in years prior to the accounting method change and 1 after the change, β_2 and β_3 are the adjustments to the intercept and slope parameters of the compensation model following the accounting change, and D_{it}, $REARN_t$, α_i and β_1 are as defined in eq. (2).

Under the null hypothesis that the fixed component of compensation and the elasticity of compensation to earnings are unaltered following an accounting change, both β_2 and β_3 are expected to be zero. We also estimate eq. (4) for control firms using the same dummy variables (DUM_t) as were used for the matched test firms. If there are no economy- or industry-specific changes in the parameters of the compensation model, β_2 and β_3 for the control firms are expected to be zero.

We use a chi-square test to examine the hypothesis that β_2 and β_3 are jointly zero. To compute the chi-square statistic, we estimate the following restricted form of eq. (4) for each firm in the sample:

$$\ln(COMP_t) = \sum_{i=1}^{n} \alpha_i D_{it} + \beta_1 \ln(REARN_t) + w_t. \tag{5}$$

Using the residuals of eqs. (4) and (5) the following statistic is computed for each firm:

$$F_j = \frac{(SSR_5 - SSR_4)/2}{SSR_4/k_j},$$

where SSR_5 and SSR_4 are the sums of squares of residuals for firm j from eqs. (5) and (4), respectively, and k_j is the number of degrees of freedom in regression (4) for firm j. The sample distribution of the above F-statistics is used to test their significance by computing the chi-square statistic discussed in section 3.2.

3.4.2. Tests of relation between parameter changes and accounting changes

We evaluate whether structural changes in the test firms' compensation— earnings relation on average offset the effect of the accounting change on earnings-based remuneration. If compensation committees modify the relation in this way, salary and bonus awards subsequent to the accounting change will approximate awards that would have been paid if there had been no accounting change and no model change.

The log of expected compensation in the absence of accounting and model changes is

$$\ln\{E(COMP_t)\} = \sum_{i=1}^{n} \hat{\alpha}_i D_{it} + \hat{\beta}_1 \ln(AEARN_t), \tag{6}$$

where $\hat{\alpha}_i$ and $\hat{\beta}_1$ are estimates from eq. (4) for the log of fixed compensation and the elasticity of compensation to earnings prior to the accounting change, and $COMP_t$, D_{it} and $AEARN_t$ are defined in eq. (1). Expected compensation is therefore the antilog of the right-hand side of eq. (6). Expected compensation under eq. (6) is estimated for each test firm for years subsequent to the accounting change and percentage prediction errors are computed as follows:

$$PE_t = \frac{COMP_t - \mathrm{E}(COMP_t)}{COMP_t} \times 100. \tag{7}$$

Each prediction error is an estimate of the percentage difference between actual compensation, awarded on the basis of reported earnings and the revised compensation model, and the forecast of compensation in the absence of the accounting change and the model change. Average percentage prediction errors are estimated for each firm as follows:

$$\frac{1}{\tau_2 - \tau_1} \sum_{t=\tau_1}^{\tau_2} PE_t,$$

where τ_1 is the first year following the accounting method change and τ_2 is at least $\tau_1 + 5$, and at most $\tau_1 + 10$, depending upon data availability.

Under the null hypothesis that the compensation committee adjusts the compensation–earnings relation to offset on average the salary and bonus effect of the accounting change, the time-series average percentage prediction error for each firm is zero. If the compensation committee uses reported earnings to award earnings-based compensation and does not adjust the model to offset the effect of the accounting change, the average percentage prediction error is expected to be negative for inventory test firms and positive for depreciation test firms. A Student-t test is used to evaluate the significance of the cross-sectional mean of the average percentage prediction errors.

We also calculate prediction errors for the inventory and depreciation control firms to examine changes in salary and bonus awards induced by industry- and economy-wide factors. The control firms do not make changes in inventory and depreciation methods and therefore do not have adjusted earnings series. We substitute reported earnings for adjusted earnings in eq. (6) and estimate predicted compensation and percentage prediction errors for each control firm during the same calendar years used to predict compensation for its matched test firm. If there are economy- or industry-specific changes in compensation that coincide with but are unrelated to the accounting changes, the time-series average prediction error for the control firms is non-zero.

We compare the average percentage prediction error for each matched pair of test and control firms and use a Student-t test to evaluate the significance of differences between the samples. If the compensation committee adjusts the model parameters to offset the effect of an accounting change on earnings-based compensation, we expect no difference in average prediction errors between these pairs of firms. Alternatively, if there is no adjustment for the accounting change, we expect the average percentage prediction errors for inventory (depreciation) test firms to be lower (higher) than errors for the control firms.

3.4.3. Potential effect of accounting changes on compensation

Finally, we examine the effect of accounting changes on salary and bonus awards if compensation committees do not adjust reported earnings or the parameters of the compensation–earnings relation. CEOs then receive lower earnings-related compensation subsequent to a change to the LIFO inventory method, and higher compensation following a change to straight-line depreciation.

We estimate the percentage effect of the accounting changes on earnings-related compensation (EFF_t), assuming no adjustment to the earnings definition or the compensation–earnings relation, as follows:

$$EFF_t = \frac{\mathrm{E}(COMP_{1t}) - \mathrm{E}(COMP_{2t})}{COMP_t} \times 100, \tag{8}$$

where $COMP_t$ is the actual salary and bonus awarded in year t, and $\mathrm{E}(COMP_{1t})$ and $\mathrm{E}(COMP_{2t})$ are expected compensation in year t based on reported earnings and adjusted earnings, respectively. $\mathrm{E}(COMP_{1t})$ and $\mathrm{E}(COMP_{2t})$ are computed as the antilogs of the right-hand side of the following two equations:

$$\ln(COMP_{1t}) = \sum_{i=1}^{n} \hat{\alpha}_i D_{it} + \hat{\beta}_1 \ln(REARN_t), \tag{9}$$

$$\ln(COMP_{2t}) = \sum_{i=1}^{n} \hat{\alpha}_i D_{it} + \hat{\beta}_1 \ln(AEARN_t), \tag{10}$$

where $REARN_t$ is reported earnings, $AEARN_t$ is adjusted earnings, $\hat{\alpha}_i$ and $\hat{\beta}_1$ are estimates from eq. (4), and D_{it} is a dummy defined in eq. (4). The percentage effects of the inventory and depreciation accounting changes on salary and bonus awards are estimated for each test firm for years subsequent to the method changes.

3.5. Compensation model adjustment results

3.5.1. Inventory sample

Table 7 presents a summary of the estimates of eq. (4) coefficients for the 50 matched pairs of firms in the inventory test and control samples. Parameters

Table 7

Summary of estimated coefficients for regression tests of the hypothesis that the parameters of the compensation–earnings relation change following a change to the LIFO inventory method.[a]

$$\ln(COMP_t) = \sum_{i=1}^{n} \alpha_i D_{it} + \beta_1 \ln(REARN_t) + \beta_2 DUM_t + \beta_3 DUM_t \ln(REARN_t) + u_t.^{[b]}$$

	$\hat{\beta}_1$	$\hat{\beta}_2$	$\hat{\beta}_3$
Test sample[c]			
Mean	0.3937	1.2497	−0.0944
First quartile	0.1238	−2.1906	−0.5467
Median	0.2966	0.9304	−0.0625
Third quartile	0.6465	6.1561	0.2046
Percent positive	92.00%[e]	58.00%	46.00%
χ^2-statistic (df = 100)	193.67[f]		
Control sample[c]			
Mean	0.2282	−0.2296	0.0317
First quartile	0.0048	−2.8636	−0.1963
Median	0.1204	0.0594	0.0425
Third quartile	0.3815	1.9932	0.2317
Percent positive	77.00%[e]	50.00%	56.00%
χ^2-statistic (df = 100)	208.64[f]		
Difference between test and control samples[d]			
Mean	0.1655	1.4793	−0.1261
Z-statistic	3.35[e]	1.84	−1.69
First quartile	−0.0940	−2.5559	−0.6514
Median	0.1326	1.5751	−0.1759
Third quartile	0.5661	7.5306	0.2967
Percent positive	60.00%	60.00%	52.00%

[a] These results are for the cross-sectional distribution of time-series regressions for 50 test firms and 50 control firms. Each time-series contains betwen 14 and 21 observations.

[b] $COMP_t$ = salary + bonus for CEO in year t; $REARN_t$ = reported earnings in year t; $D_{it} = 1$ if individual i is CEO of the firm in year t and 0 otherwise; n = number of individuals who held the CEO position in the sample period; and $DUM_t = 0$ prior to the year of the inventory change and 1 thereafter.

[c] The test sample comprises 50 firms that change to LIFO in the period 1970–1976. Each test firm has a matched control firm with the same 2-digit SIC code and with no inventory or depreciation method changes ten years before and after the year of the test firm's method change. Control firms are found for 50 of 52 inventory test firms.

[d] These distributional statistics are for the differences in coefficients between matched pairs of test and control firms. The Z-statistic tests the significance of the sample mean difference for each coefficient.

[e] Significant at the one percent level using a two-tailed test.

[f] Significant at the one percent level using a one-tailed test.

β_2 and β_3 in the regression are used to examine whether the fixed component of compensation and the elasticity of compensation to earnings change subsequent to a change from FIFO to LIFO. The estimated values of β_2 are positive for 58 percent of the test firms and the mean value is 1.2497. The percent of positive coefficients for the control firms is 50 percent and the mean of the coefficients is -0.2296. Forty-six percent of the estimated values of β_3 are positive for the test firms and the mean estimate is -0.0944. The corresponding values for the control sample are 56 percent and 0.0317. The χ^2-statistics, which test the hypothesis that β_2 and β_3 are jointly zero, are significant at the one percent level for both the test and control firms. Thus, there is some evidence of a structural change in the compensation–earnings relation for the inventory sample.

An examination of the coefficient estimates in table 7 indicates that there are systematic differences in the values for test and control samples. We estimate the differences in coefficients for matched pairs of test and control firms. The sample distributions of these differences are reported in table 7. A Z-test, described earlier in section 3.2, is used to test the significance of the mean coefficient differences. The test firms have a significantly higher compensation–earnings elasticity than the control firms. Subsequent to the accounting change, the test firms experience an increase in fixed compensation and a decrease in their compensation–earnings elasticity relative to the control firms. However, these differences are statistically insignificant. These findings indicate that (1) firms that change to LIFO have higher compensation–earnings elasticities than firms that do not change their inventory method, and (2) the changes in model parameters are not systematically related to the accounting method change.

Results of tests of whether the structural change in the compensation model offsets the effect of the accounting change on earnings-related remuneration are reported in table 8. The cross-sectional mean (median) of the average percent prediction error for compensation is 9.5 (10.5) percent for the test sample. The t-statistic, that evaluates the significance of the mean, is significantly different from zero at the five percent level. The mean (median) for the control sample is 8.3 (11) percent. The t-statistic on the mean is also significantly different from zero. These results indicate that on average there is an economy- or industry-related increase in compensation of eight to eleven percent that coincides with the period following the LIFO changes, the late 1970s and early 1980s. The test firm CEOs have marginally larger average percentage increases in salary and bonus compensation during these same years. However, the t-statistic evaluating the difference in these means is not significant. The results therefore support the null hypothesis that the compensation committee adjusts the model parameters to offset the effect of the accounting change.

Table 8

Summary of average percentage prediction errors for compensation in years subsequent to a change to the LIFO inventory method.[a]

	Test sample[b]	Control sample[b]	Difference between test and control samples
Mean	9.46%	8.31%	1.15%
t-statistic	3.17[c]	2.05[c]	0.49
Mean standard deviation	14.91%	14.07%	0.84%
First quartile	−6.95%	−3.55%	−20.00%
Median	10.48%	11.15%	−0.24%
Third quartile	20.91%	24.70%	16.29%
Median standard deviation	10.11%	8.23%	−1.01%
Percent positive	68.00%	68.00%	48.00%

[a] Percentage prediction errors are the percentage difference between actual compensation and compensation that would have been paid in the absence of a LIFO change and a model change [see eq. (7)]. The results are for the cross-sectional distribution of time-series estimates of mean percentage prediction errors for 50 test firms and 50 control firms. Each time-series contains between six and eleven observations.

[b] The test sample comprises 50 firms that changed to LIFO in the period 1970–1976. Each test firm has a matched control firm with the same 2-digit SIC code and with no inventory or depreciation method changes ten years before and after the year of the test firm's method change. Control firms are found for 50 of 52 inventory test firms.

[c] Significant at the five percent level using a two-tailed test.

An alternative, and we believe equally plausible, explanation for the above finding is that the effect of the accounting change on compensation is not large enough, relative to the effect of the time-dependent change in compensation, to enable us to discriminate between the null and alternative hypotheses. This explanation is consistent with the data. Table 9 reports the distribution of the percentage effect of the LIFO change on salary and bonus awards assuming the compensation committee does not adjust the earnings definition or the parameters of the compensation–earnings relation. The mean and median percent decreases in salary and bonus awards in the year of the LIFO change are 13.9 and 6.7 percent, respectively.[15] A time-series average of the compensation effect of the change is estimated for each firm for an eleven-year period (years 0 to 10) and for the ten years subsequent to the change (years 1 to 10). The cross-sectional mean (median) of these averages is −3.9 (−2.3) percent for the full eleven years, and −2.7 (−1.5) percent for years 1 to 10.

---

[15] This is a sizeable decrease in salary and bonus that far exceeds the effect of the inventory change in subsequent years' compensation. We therefore test whether the compensation committee adjusts reported earnings for the effect of the accounting change in only the year of the change rather than in all following years. We estimate eq. (2) with the explanatory variable $\ln[REARN_t/AEARN_t]$ being set to zero in all years other than the year of the change to LIFO. The coefficient is positive and significant, implying that the compensation committee does not adjust compensation for the effect of the inventory method change even in the year of the change.

Table 9

Summary statistics for compensation effects of inventory method change as a percentage of actual compensation for the year of the inventory change and the subsequent ten years.[a]

	Year relative to accounting change[b]		
	0	1 to 10	0 to 10
Mean	−13.87%	−2.67%	−3.93%
Mean standard deviation[c]	—	5.34	7.32
First quartile	−17.54	−4.52	−6.19
Median	−6.72	−1.48	−2.34
Median standard deviation[c]	—	2.79	3.68
Third quartile	−2.5	−0.02	−0.55

[a] The compensation effect of an inventory method change as a percentage of actual compensation in year t is $[E(COMP_{1t}) - E(COMP_{2t})/COMP_t] \times 100$. $E(COMP_{1t})$ and $E(COMP_{2t})$ are expected compensation using reported and adjusted earnings respectively and are computed from eqs. (9) and (10). $COMP_t$ is the actual compensation paid in year t.

[b] The results in years 1 to 10 and 0 to 10 are for the cross-sectional distribution of time-series averages of the compensation effect of the inventory change as a percentage of actual compensation for 52 firms that change to LIFO in the period 1970–1976.

[c] No mean or median standard deviations are reported for year 0 since no time-series standard deviations can be calculated for a single year.

3.5.2. Depreciation sample

A summary of the estimates of eq. (4) coefficients for the 37 pairs of matched firms in the depreciation test and control samples are reported in table 10. The estimated values of β_2 are positive for 66.7 percent of the test sample and 38.9 percent of the control sample. The mean estimates of β_2 for these samples are 1.8454 and −3.1238, respectively. The percent of positive estimates for β_3 is 36.1 for the test sample and 63.9 for the control sample. The mean estimate of β_3 is −0.1564 for the test firms and 0.3088 for the control firms. The χ^2-statistics that test the joint significance of β_2 and β_3 are significant at the one percent level for both samples, suggesting that there has been a structural change in the relation between compensation and earnings for both the test and control firms.

We also examine whether the coefficient estimates for the test and control samples are significantly different. Table 10 reports the sample distributions of differences in coefficients for matched pairs of test and control firms. On average the depreciation test firms have higher compensation–earnings elasticities than the control firms. The Z-statistic, testing the significance of the mean difference, is significant at the one percent level using a two-tailed test. In addition, relative to the control firms, the test firms experience significant increases in fixed compensation and decreases in their compensation–earnings elasticities subsequent to the accounting change. This indicates that (1) firms

Table 10

Summary of estimated coefficients for regression tests of the hypothesis that the parameters of the compensation–earnings relation change following a change to the straight-line depreciation method.[a]

$$\ln(COMP_t) = \sum_{i=1}^{n} \alpha_i D_{it} + \beta_1 \ln(REARN_t) + \beta_2 DUM_t + \beta_3 DUM_t \ln(REARN_t) + u_t.^{b}$$

	$\hat{\beta}_1$	$\hat{\beta}_2$	$\hat{\beta}_3$
Test sample[c]			
Mean	0.2650	1.8454	−0.1564
First quartile	−0.0008	−2.1288	−0.2866
Median	0.1877	0.5655	−0.0490
Third quartile	0.4658	3.1121	0.2181
Percent positive	75.00%[e]	66.67%	36.11%
χ^2-statistic (df = 74)	166.75[g]		
Control sample[c]			
Mean	0.1612	−3.1238	0.3088
First quartile	0.0031	−4.2258	−0.1335
Median	0.1331	−1.1977	0.1399
Third quartile	0.2813	1.2169	0.4863
Percent positive	77.78%[e]	38.89%	63.89%
χ^2-statistic (df = 74)	161.58[g]		
Difference between test and control samples[d]			
Mean	0.1038	4.9692	−0.4652
Z-statistic	3.55[e]	5.20[e]	−4.88[e]
First quartile	−0.1360	−3.0872	−0.8080
Median	0.0994	2.6294	−0.2809
Third quartile	0.2901	9.3007	0.2827
Percent positive	61.11%	61.11%	38.89%

[a] These results are for the cross-sectional distribution of time-series regressions for 37 test firms and 37 control firms. Each time series contains between 14 and 21 observations.

[b] $COMP_t$ = salary + bonus for CEO in year t; $REARN_t$ = reported earnings in year t; $D_{it} = 1$ if individual i is CEO of the firm in year t and 0 otherwise; n = number of individuals who hold the CEO position in the sample period; and $DUM_t = 0$ prior to the year of the depreciation change and 1 thereafter.

[c] The test sample comprises 37 firms that changed to straight-line depreciation in the period 1967–1974. Each test firm has a matched control firm with the same 2-digit SIC code and with no inventory or depreciation method changes ten years before and after the year of the firm's method change. Control firms are found for 37 of 38 depreciation test firms.

[d] These distributional statistics are for the differences in coefficients between matched pairs of test and control firms. The Z-statistic tests the significance of the sample mean difference for each cofficient.

[e] Significant at the five percent level using a two-tailed test.

[f] Significant at the one percent level using a two-tailed test.

[g] Significant at the one percent level using a one-tailed test.

Table 11

Summary of average percentage prediction errors for compensation in years subsequent to a change to the straight-line depreciation method.[a]

	Test sample[b]	Control sample[b]	Difference between test and control samples
Mean	6.94%	7.93%	−0.99%
t-statistic	2.78[c]	2.40[c]	−0.17
Mean standard deviation	13.41%	15.04%	1.63%
First quartile	−9.49%	−1.19%	−23.43%
Median	4.77%	9.51%	−4.31%
Third quartile	22.75%	15.78%	18.17%
Median standard deviation	9.35%	10.80%	3.11%
Percent positive	56.76%	75.67%	45.94%

[a] Percentage prediction errors are the percentage difference between actual compensation and compensation that would have been paid in the absence of a straight-line depreciation change and a model change [see eq. (7)]. The results are for the cross-sectional distribution of time-series estimates of mean percentage prediction errors for 37 test firms and 37 control firms. Each time-series contains between six and eleven observations.

[b] The test sample comprises 37 firms that changed to straight-line depreciation in the period 1967–1974. Each test firm has a matched control firm with the same 2-digit SIC code and with no inventory or depreciation method changes ten years before and after the year of the test firm's method change. Control firms are found for 37 of 38 depreciation test firms.

[c] Significant at the five percent level using a two-tailed test.

that change depreciation accounting policies have higher compensation–earnings elasticities than firms that do not change their depreciation method, and (2) the accounting change firms have a decreased emphasis on earnings-based compensation subsequent to the accounting change.

To evaluate whether the structural change in the compensation–earnings relation offsets the effect of the accounting change on salary and bonus awards, we examine the distribution of average percentage prediction errors in compensation subsequent to the depreciation change for both the test and control firms. These results are presented in table 11 and are similar to the inventory findings. There is a 7.9 (9.5) percent mean (median) increase in bonus and salary compensation for the control firms. The t-statistic that evaluates the significance of the mean increase is significant at the five percent level, implying that there is an economy- or industry-related increase in compensation in the period following the depreciation method changes, the 1970s. The test firm CEOs had a 6.9 (4.8) percent average (median) increase in salary and bonus compensation during these years which is also significant. However, the t-statistic evaluating the difference in the mean estimates for the control and test samples is not significant. We therefore cannot reject the null hypothesis that the compensation committee adjusts the compensation model parameters to offset the effect of the accounting change.

Table 12

Summary statistics for compensation effects of depreciation method change as a percentage of actual compensation for the year of the depreciation change and the subsequent ten years.[a]

	Year relative to accounting change[b]		
	0	1 to 10	0 to 10
Mean	2.36%	2.73%	2.69%
Mean standard deviation[c]	—	2.51	2.49
First quartile	0.00	0.05	0.05
Median	0.78	1.45	1.43
Median standard deviation[c]	—	1.19	1.21
Third quartile	4.65	5.50	5.29

[a] The compensation effect of a depreciation method change as a percentage of actual compensation in year t is $[E(COMP_{1t}) - E(COMP_{2t})/COMP_t] \times 100$, where $E(COMP_{1t})$ and $E(COMP_{2t})$ are expected compensation using reported and adjusted earnings respectively and $COMP_t$ is the actual compensation paid in year t. $COMP_{1t}$ and $COMP_{2t}$ are computed by using eqs. (9) and (10).

[b] The results in years 1 to 10 and 0 to 10 are for the cross-sectional distribution of time-series averages of the compensation effect of the depreciation change as a percentage of actual compensation for 38 firms that change to straight-line depreciation in the period 1967–1974.

[c] No mean or median standard deviations are reported for year 0 since no time-series standard deviations can be calculated for a single year.

Once again, we believe that an equally plausible explanation for the above finding is that the magnitude of the effect of the accounting change on compensation is small relative to the effect of the time-dependent change in compensation, preventing us from discriminating between the null and alternative hypotheses. Table 12 reports the distribution of the percentage effect of the depreciation change on bonus and salary awards assuming that the compensation committee does not adjust the earnings definition or the parameters of the compensation–earnings relation. The mean (median) percentage increase in salary and bonus awards in the year of the depreciation change is 2.4 (0.8) percent. A time-series average of the compensation effect of the change is estimated for each firm for years 0 to 10 and years 1 to 10. The cross-sectional mean (median) of these averages is 2.7 (1.4) percent for years 0 to 10 as well as for years 1 to 10.

4. Discussion of results and conclusion

This paper investigates the effect of accounting policy changes on CEOs' salary and bonus compensation. A number of accounting studies postulate that it is costly for compensation committees to adjust CEOs' bonus and salary awards for changes in accounting procedures. If committees and managers have rational expectations, this 'compensation hypothesis' implies that committees write remuneration contracts anticipating managements' incentives to opportunistically select accounting rules to increase their compensation. No adjustment to managements' compensation schedules will then be observed following a change in accounting rules. In this study, we document the potential impact of accounting changes on CEOs' compensation and perform two tests of the compensation hypothesis. The first test examines whether, subsequent to an accounting change, compensation is based on earnings adjusted for the effect of the change. The second examines whether the compensation model parameters are adjusted to nullify the earnings effect of the accounting change.

Two accounting changes are selected: changes from FIFO to LIFO inventory method and changes from accelerated to straight-line depreciation. These are selected to increase the power of our tests. They both have a large effect on reported earnings. In addition, a change to LIFO typically decreases earnings, whereas a change to straight-line depreciation usually increases earnings.

Our results show that the potential effect of inventory and depreciation accounting changes on CEOs' bonus and salary remuneration is generally small compared to economy-wide changes in compensation over time. The median potential decrease in compensation following a switch from FIFO to LIFO is 6.7% in the year of the switch and 1.5% per year during the next ten years. In contrast, there is an 11.2% median increase in CEOs' compensation per year due to economy- and industry-wide factors that are contemporaneous with, but unrelated to, the accounting changes. The median potential increase in CEOs' compensation following a depreciation accounting change is 0.8% in the first year and 1.5% per year during the next ten years. Once again, there is a 9.5% median increase in CEOs' annual compensation due to industry-wide factors that are contemporaneous with, but unrelated to, the accounting changes.

Our tests of the earnings definition used as a basis for compensation indicate that CEOs' bonus and salary awards are based on reported earnings both before and after the accounting changes. We find no evidence that, subsequent to either the inventory change or the depreciation change, reported earnings are transformed to earnings under the original accounting method for computing compensation awards. The costs of such a transformation do not appear to be significant for the accounting changes considered in this paper: we are able to undo the effects of the changes using publicly available information, even in years subsequent to the method changes. Of course, there may be other costs of adjusting compensation for the effect of the accounting change. For example, it may be costly for the compensation committee to distinguish accounting changes selected by managers to increase their remuneration from those selected to maximize the value of shareholders' wealth. If managers have superior information on future input prices or investment opportunities, it would be costly for the compensation committee to determine whether FIFO or LIFO, or accelerated or straight-line depreciation is appropriate.[16]

The tests of the compensation–earnings relation indicate that there are changes in the parameters of the relation for the test firms subsequent to an accounting change. However, these changes seem to be at least in part due to economy- and industry-wide changes which are unrelated to the accounting changes. This conclusion is based on our finding that there are structural changes in the compensation–earnings relation, and increases in salary and bonus awards comparable to those of the test firms, for a matched sample of control firms. We are unable to reject the hypothesis that CEOs in the test and control firms have the same percentage increases in compensation in years following the accounting changes.

Our tests relating the changes in compensation model parameters of the test firms to the effects of the accounting changes are inconclusive. We cannot reject the hypothesis that the compensation committee nullifies the effect of an accounting change on bonus and salary awards by modifying the parameters of the compensation–earnings relation. We believe that this result is inconclusive because the effect of the accounting change on compensation, as discussed earlier, is too small compared to the time-related effects to allow us to discriminate between the null and alternative hypotheses.

In summary, the potential decline in CEOs' bonus and salary awards following a change to LIFO is 2.3 percent per year. If compensation is not adjusted for this method change, CEOs appear to switch to LIFO despite this loss in their remuneration.[17] Similarly, the potential increase in CEOs' bonus and salary compensation due to the depreciation change is only about 1.5 percent per year. Thus, even if their remuneration is not adjusted for this method change, the benefit to CEOs appears to be small.

---

[16]See Ball (1985) and Demski and Sappington (1985) for a discussion of selection of accounting procedures when managers have inside information on the costs and benefits of alternative accounting and production/investment decisions.

[17]There may be several reasons for this. The potential effect of the LIFO change on compensation may be overstated if firms in our sample have bonus plans with binding upper limits on awards in the year of the inventory method change. As Biddle and Lindahl (1982) and Ricks (1982) document, firms change to LIFO in years of large earnings increases. If there is an upper limit on bonus awards, it is likely to be binding in these years under both FIFO and LIFO. Healy (1985) finds that 46 percent of Fortune 250 industrial firms with usable bonus plans have an upper limit on the pool of funds available for bonus awards. Also, managers own stock in the companies that employ them. Their portfolio wealth will therefore increase following a change in LIFO if equity prices reflect the accompanying tax savings. Finally, executives' human capital is likely to increase following a change to LIFO since the decision benefits shareholders.

References

Abdel-khalik, A.R., 1985, The effect of LIFO-switching and firm ownership on executives' pay, Journal of Accounting Research 23, 427–447.

Ball, Ray, 1985, Accounting, auditing and the nature of the firm, Unpublished paper (Australian Graduate School of Management, and University of Chicago, Chicago, IL).

Biddle, G.C. and F.W. Lindahl, 1982, Stock price reactions to LIFO adoptions: The association between excess returns and LIFO tax savings, Journal of Accounting Research 20, 551–588.

Boyes, W. and D. Schlagenhauf, 1979, Managerial incentives and the specification of functional forms, Southern Economics Journal 45, 1225–1232.

Christie, Andrew, 1986, Aggregation of test statistics: An evaluation of the consistency of evidence on contracting and size hypotheses, Unpublished paper (University of Southern California, Los Angeles, CA).

Demski, Joel S. and David E. Sappington, 1985, Accounting procedures in a principal–agent model, Unpublished paper (Stanford University, Stanford, CA, and University of Pennsylvania, Philadelphia, PA).

Fox, Harland, 1980, Top executive compensation (The Conference Board, New York).

Hagerman, R.L. and M.E. Zmijewski, 1979, Some economic determinants of accounting policy choice, Journal of Accounting and Economics 1, 141–162.

Healy, P.M., 1985, The effect of bonus schemes on accounting decisions, Journal of Accounting and Economics 7, 85–107.

Holthausen, R.W., 1981, Evidence on the effect of bond covenants and management compensation contracts on the choice of accounting techniques: The case of the depreciation switch-back, Journal of Accounting and Economics 3, 73–109.

Holthausen, R.W. and R.W. Leftwich, 1983, The economic consequences of accounting choice: Implications of costly contracting and monitoring, Journal of Accounting and Economics 5, 77–117.

Kaplan, R. and R. Roll, 1972, Investor evaluation of accounting information: Some empirical evidence, Journal of Business 45, 225–257.

Larcker, David F., 1983, The association between performance plan adoption and corporate capital investment, Journal of Accounting and Economics 5, 3–30.

Murphy, K., 1985, Corporate performance and managerial remuneration: An empirical analysis, Journal of Accounting and Economics 7, 11–42.

Ricks, W., 1982, The market's response to the 1974 LIFO adoptions, Journal of Accounting Research 20, 367–387.

Siegel, Sidney, 1956, Nonparametric statistics for the behavioral sciences (McGraw-Hill, New York).

Smith, Clifford and Ross Watts, 1982, Incentive and tax effects of executive compensation plans, Australian Journal of Management 7, 139–157.

Sunder, Shyam, 1973, Relationship between accounting changes and stock prices: Problems of measurement and some empirical evidence, in: Empirical research in accounting: Selected studies 1973, Supplement to Vol. 11 of Journal of Accounting Research, 1–45.

Sunder, Shyam, 1975, Stock price and risk related to accounting changes in inventory valuation, Accounting Review 50, 305–315.

Thiel, H., 1971, Principles of econometrics (Wiley, New York).

Watts, Ross and Jerold Zimmerman, 1986, Positive accounting theory (Prentice Hall, Englewood Cliffs, NJ).

THE ASSOCIATION BETWEEN PERFORMANCE PLAN ADOPTION AND CORPORATE CAPITAL INVESTMENT*

David F. LARCKER

Northwestern University, Evanston, IL 60201, USA

Received September 1981, final version received January 1983

This paper examines the association between one specific change in executive compensation contracts (adoption of performance plans), changes in corporate capital investment, and security market performance. The empirical results indicate that (when compared to similar non-adopting firms) firms adopting performance plans exhibit a significant growth in capital expenditures and a favorable security market reaction to the announcement of the performance plan adoption. These results provide evidence that changes in executive compensation contracts are associated with changes in managerial decisions.

1. Introduction

The agency problems that arise when the owner of a firm contracts with a manager to provide a service have been the focus of considerable theoretical research [e.g., Alchian and Demsetz (1972), Ross (1973), Jensen and Meckling (1976), Demski and Feltham (1978), Harris and Raviv (1979), Fama (1980)]. This research has examined a variety of topics: motivations for contracting between the owner and manager, the optimality of various compensation contracts in selected environmental settings, and the importance of the labor market for managers in agency relationships. Drawing upon this literature, accounting researchers have recently argued that managerial compensation contracts influence managerial decision-making [Watts and Zimmerman (1978), Hagerman and Zmijewski (1979), Dukes et al. (1981), Horwitz and Kolodny (1981)], and thus partially explain the security market reaction associated with accounting changes [Collins and Dent (1979), Dyckman and

*This research was conducted during my tenure as the Hay Group Faculty Research Fellow. I wish to thank Renee Reder for her research assistance, George Goddu of Peat, Marwick, Mitchell & Company for his help with data collection, and Frederic Cook and Lawrence Bickford of Frederic W. Cook & Company for their comments. This paper has greatly benefited from seminar discussion at The University of Rochester, Washington University (St. Louis), University of Pittsburgh, and the Stanford University Summer Workshop. Comments by Nicholas Dopuch, Bruce Johnson, Richard Lambert, Thomas Lys, Robert Magee, William Marshall, Alfred Rappaport, Lawrence Revsine, Ross Watts, Jerold Zimmerman, and an anonymous referee are gratefully acknowledged.

Smith (1979), Lev (1979), Collins et al. (1981), Larcker and Revsine (forthcoming)]. The critical maintained hypothesis in these two streams of research is that compensation contract changes affect a manager's decisions. However, empirical evidence on the association between changes in executive compensation plans and changes in the investment and production decisions of managers is virtually non-existent.

The purpose of this paper is to provide an analysis of the adoption of one specific compensation contract ('performance plans'), changes in corporate capital investment, and security market performance. The empirical results indicate that firms adopting performance plans (relative to similar nonadopting firms) experience a statistically significant growth in capital investment and a favorable security market reaction to the announcement of performance plan adoption. However, it is problematic to directly attribute these results to the 'incentive effects' of performance plans.

The remainder of the paper is divided into five sections. Section 2 describes several common executive compensation contracts and isolates the important contractual characteristics of performance plans. Section 3 discusses the theoretical linkages between performance plan adoption, corporate investment, and security market performance. Section 4 describes the data collection, measurement, and statistical issues. Section 5 presents the empirical results. The research findings are discussed and summarized in section 6.

2. Executive compensation contracts

A wide variety of contractual arrangements are used by major U.S. corporations to determine executive compensation. The contractual provisions of these compensation schemes differ along several important dimensions including the length of time period used to measure performance (e.g., one year or multiple years) and the performance measure (e.g., accounting or share price measures).

Most major corporations sponsor some type of short-term compensation or 'bonus' plan where annual remuneration is based upon yearly performance typically defined in terms of some variant of yearly residual income.[1] A typical bonus plan description is:

> The Corporation's Incentive Compensation Plan provides that the Executive Compensation Committee which administers the Plan may credit to the Incentive Compensation Fund for each fiscal year an

[1]The 1978 and 1979 ExecuComp Surveys [Segal & Associates (1978, 1979)] indicate that approximately 70 percent of the top 1000 firms have a bonus scheme, and the 1979 survey by Towers, Perrin, Forster, and Crosby (TPF&C) indicates that 98 of the top 100 firms have a short-term plan.

amount which does not exceed 12 percent of the Corporation's Net Earnings for such year after deducting an amount equal to 5 percent of the Capital Employed in the Business (as both terms are defined in the Plan) but in no event may the credit to the Fund exceed the aggregate dividends with respect to all classes of stock during such year. [Bendix Corp., 1976 Proxy, p.5].

In addition to using a bonus scheme, most major corporations also sponsor one or more types of long-term compensation contracts.[2,3] Long-term plans differ from bonus schemes in several important respects: the performance is measured over a time period longer than one year (e.g., earnings growth over several years rather than earnings in a single year) and change in share price is commonly used as the performance measure.

There are six basic compensation schemes which are commonly classified as long-term plans: (i) Stock Options (qualified, non-qualified, and incentive stock options), (ii) Stock Appreciation Rights, (iii) Phantom Stock, (iv) Dividend Units, (v) Restricted Stock, and (vi) Performance Plans (performance units or performance shares). *Stock Options* allow an executive to purchase shares of stock at some future date for a fixed option exercise price that is set at the time the option is granted. Qualified plans (recently phased out due to Internal Revenue Service code changes) and incentive stock options differ from non-qualified plans in that the corporation cannot claim a tax deduction for the share price appreciation when options are exercised. In addition, the executive is taxed on the appreciation at the capital gains rate for qualified and incentive stock options, but at the ordinary income rate for nonqualified stock options. *Stock Appreciation Rights* (SARs) are commonly granted in conjunction with stock options, and the executive has the choice of exercising either the stock option or the SAR. Compensation under an SAR is determined by the market appreciation of the underlying stock from the grant date, although an upper limit on SAR appreciation is frequently established. In contrast to stock options, the executive is not required to actually purchase the stock in order to exercise

[2]ExecuComp Surveys indicate that approximately 85 percent of the top 1000 firms sponsor at least one long-term plan, and the 1979 TPF&C survey indicates that 93 of the top 100 firms have at least one long-term incentive plan.

[3]The distinction between short-term and long-term compensation plans is usually based on the time period associated with the performance measure, However, the distinction between short-term and long-term plans is not clear-cut for at least four reasons. First the labor market for managers reduces the possibility that an executive compensated by a bonus plan will have a strictly short-term (one-year) decision-making horizon [Fama (1980)]. Second, earnings are correlated over time, and a manager may be willing to make decisions which have an adverse effect on this year's bonus but a favorable impact on future bonuses. Third, in corporations where a portion of the short-term compensation is deferred, ultimate payment to an executive is sometimes subject to certain long-term constraints (e.g., a prespecified growth in earnings-per-share in years prior to payment). Fourth, the bonus may be paid in stock (sometimes with disposal restrictions), and this will reduce the short-term orientation of bonus plans.

an SAR, and the compensation may be paid in either cash or stock at the discretion of the compensation committee. *Phantom Stock* is equivalent to an SAR except that it is not tied to a non-qualified stock option. A *Dividend Unit* assigns a hypothetical, fixed number of shares of stock to the executive with the amount of compensation paid (either in cash or stock) being equal to the number of shares multiplied by the dividends per share paid to shareholders. *Restricted Stock* plans are stock grants which are earned if the executive remains with the company over some specified time period. However, these grants are not tied to any explicit performance measure.

The remaining category of long-term compensation schemes is *Performance Plans*.[4] Performance plans are of two types: performance units or performance shares. Performance unit plans fix the amount of compensation per unit at the beginning of the award period or assign a unit value which is not related to share price (e.g., book value per share at the end of the award period). In a performance share plan, the compensation per share depends on the market price per share at the end of the performance or award period.

The operation of a performance plan involves several steps:

— Performance goals (usually expressed in terms of earnings-per-share growth) are established by the compensation committee at the beginning of the award period (typically three to six years in duration).
— Each executive participating in the plan is allocated a fixed number of units or shares at the beginning of the award period.
— Each *unit* is assigned a 'fixed' dollar value; the value of each *share* is the share price at the end of the award period.
— The number of units or shares 'earned out' depends upon the degree to which performance goals are met during the award period.
— The amount of compensation paid at the *end* of the award period (in cash and/or stock) is equal to the product of the number of units or shares awarded, percentage of units or shares 'earned out', and value of each unit or share.

The Proxy Statements of Emerson Electric and Toro provide descriptions of typical performance plans (table 1). The board of directors of Emerson Electric adopted a performance share plan in fiscal 1977 where the award period was five years, the performance measure was earnings-per-share (*EPS*) growth, and the number of performance shares 'earned out' was prorated between zero and hundred percent for compounded annual *EPS* growth rates between eleven and twelve percent. In contrast, the performance unit

---

[4]There is one additional type of long-term plan — book units — which operates in a manner similar to performance unit plans (e.g., Roblin). The value of a book unit is equal to the appreciation in book value over the award period, and the remuneration is deferred until the end of the award period. Since this type of plan is essentially identical to a performance plan, book unit plans are considered performance plans in this study.

Table 1

Characteristics of selected performance plans.

Emerson Electric (1977 fiscal year adoption)

Type of plan:	Performance share	
Award period:	5 years	
Performance measure:	Earnings-per-share (EPS)	
		Percentage of shares
Initial targets:	1981 EPS	'earned out'
	$\geq$ $3.60	100
(1976 EPS = $2.05)	< $3.60, but $\leq$ $3.55	70
	< $3.55, but $\leq$ $3.48	50
	< $3.48	0
Form of payment:	20% cash and 80% common stock	

Toro (1976 fiscal year adoption)

Type of plan:	Performance unit	
Award period:	5 years	
Performance measure:	Return-on-invested capital of Toro compared to return-on-invested capital for selected competitors (relative ROI)	
		Percentage of units
Initial targets:	Relative ROI	'earned out'
	$\geq$ 75%	100
	< 75, but $\geq$ 50	Prorated between
	< 50	0
Value of unit:	Book value per common share at the end of the award period	
Form of payment:	Cash or common stock	

plan approved by Toro shareholders in fiscal 1976 assigned each unit a dollar value corresponding to the book value per share of common stock at the end of the five-year award period. More interestingly, the performance measure was the average return-on-invested capital (ROI) for Toro compared to the average ROI for selected competitors over the five-year award period (i.e., a relative ROI performance measure).

Comparing performance plans with the short-term and long-term compensation plans discussed earlier reveals both similarities and differences. First, performance plans have a longer time period for accounting performance evaluation (e.g., three to six years) than the typical short-term plan which provides a bonus based upon yearly accounting performance. Second, performance plans are similar to other long-term plans in that any expected compensation associated with the performance plan is deferred until some future date and is usually forfeited if the executive leaves the corporation during the award period. Third, the performance targets or goals are explicitly stated in terms of growth in accounting-based measures over an award period. This contrasts with, say, stock option plans where performance (and compensation) depends upon increases in market price per share. Finally, performance plans exhibit 'option-like' characteristics similar to stock options, SARs, and phantom stock, in that the payoff is bounded by zero from below and increases as the performance measure exceeds some target.

The number of long-term compensation plans in effect for the top 100 corporations between 1970 and 1979 is presented by type of plan in table 2. As these data suggest, performance plans were virtually non-existent prior to 1972 and have become increasingly popular since the early 1970s. Since the number of corporations adopting performance plans is relatively large and the contractual provisions of these plans are different than prior compensation arrangements, firms adopting and not adopting performance plans provide unique experimental and control groups for determining whether this specific compensation plan change is associated with changes in the decisions of managers and corporate performance.

Table 2

Number of long-term compensation plans in effect for the top 100 corporations (1970–1979).[a]

	1979	1978	1977	1976	1975	1974	1973	1972	1971	1970
Stock options	84	84	86	88	87	87	84	83	89	91
Stock appreciation rights	65	56	45	33	27	20	13	8	—	—
Phantom stock	2	2	3	4	4	4	4	3	3	—
Dividend units	3	5	5	6	5	5	5	6	6	5
Restricted stock	8	7	6	6	—	—	—	—	—	—
Performance units	26	23	17	10	6	3	1	—	—	—
Performance shares	12	8	9	8	5	6	3	1	—	—
No plan	7	7	7	5	5	6	10	11	11	10

[a]*Source:* TPF&C, *Top 100 Compensation Study 1979*, p. 14.

3. Performance plans and managerial decisions

A general theory explaining why compensation contracts are changed or what contractual provisions should be adopted in specific decision settings does not exist, nor will this research attempt to provide such a theory. The purpose of this section is to discuss how the adoption of performance plan compensation contracts can be related to managerial investment decisions and corporate performance. Two research hypotheses are presented for subsequent empirical examination.

In order to analyze the relationships among contractual changes, managerial decisions, and shareholder wealth, some structure must be placed on the decision setting. Three assumptions are made in the following analysis. First, the manager who selects the level of corporate investment is assumed to be risk-averse with respect to the outcomes of these investments. Second, the investment projects being considered by the manager are assumed to be characterized as having negative earnings and cash flows in 'early' years and positive earnings and cash flows in 'later' years. This assumption implies that projects where mandatory 'later-period' negative cash flows are required (e.g., strip mining) are not included in the set of projects being considered by the manager. Finally for ease of analysis, the manager is assumed to be compensated by a fixed salary and a yearly bonus.

The first research question of this study is concerned with whether one should expect the level of corporate investment to change with the addition of the performance plan to the manager's existing remuneration contract. Under a salary plus yearly bonus contract, the manager's remuneration is tied to *yearly* accounting numbers and the manager's decision-making may be heavily influenced by the 'short-term' effects of investment (i.e., the manager's horizon is 'short-term').[5] Now assume that a performance plan is adopted and appropriate changes are made in the salary and bonus contracts.[6] Since all performance plan compensation is deferred until the end of the award period and the compensation forfeited if the manager leaves during the three- to six-year award period, the adoption of a performance plan may lengthen the manager's decision-making horizon to at least three to six years.[7] Given the assumed earnings and cash flows of the projects, the manager will (ignoring effort aversion) increase investment after performance plan adoption. This change in managerial decision-making occurs for two reasons. First, a manager with a longer decision-making horizon considers the positive earnings and cash flows that occur in 'later' periods, and projects that exhibit later payoffs become attractive to the manager. Second, since 'later' period earnings and cash flows are assumed to be positive, any project which was acceptable to the manager before performance plan adoption will also be acceptable after the contractual change lengthens the manager's horizon.

A related attribute of performance plans is that they are based on 'long-term' accounting measures of corporate performance. After performance plan

[5]The reasonableness of this statement depends on the characteristics of the labor market for managers [Fama (1980), Larcker and Magee (1982)]. If the 'ex post settling up' phenomenon discussed by Fama is an effective solution to incentive problems, the manager will exhibit an appropriate decision-making horizon and no change in managerial decision-making will occur. However, little empirical evidence on the extent to which ex post settling up occurs in the labor market for managers is currently available.

[6]In particular, if managers are paid some equilibrium market compensation, the salary and/or bonus contract would be deceased when the performance plan is adopted.

[7]Performance plans are usually designed to allow the executive to participate in *several* separate overlapping plans. For example, a new performance plan (with a separate set of performance goals and a different payoff date) might be established every two years. Thus an executive confronting a series of overlapping plans may have a decision-making horizon which is much longer than the three- to six-year award period associated with any individual plan.

adoption, the manager's compensation arrangement uses two different measures of corporate performance (i.e., 'short-term' and 'long-term' accounting measures). Assuming that neither of the measures is a sufficient statistic for assessing managerial effort, the use of two measures can enable the owner to obtain a more precise determination of managerial effort [Holmstrom (1979)]. Under this new compensation contract, the owner is better able to identify the manager's effort and the overall compensation contract can be designed to encourage the manager to provide a higher level of effort. Moreover, the performance plan will encourage the manager to allocate effort into the search for new investment opportunities and other activities which will increase long-term performance measures, rather than allocating effort into selecting that method of scheduling current production or other activities which only increase the short-term bonus. Thus, the use of long-term accounting measures can induce higher effort levels from the manager which are likely to be required if corporate investment levels increase.

The final characteristic of performance plans is that these contracts exhibit 'option-like' characteristics. Since the expected value of an option increases as the variance of the performance measure (e.g., *EPS* growth) increases, performance plans can reduce the risk-averse manager's natural tendency to reject variance increasing projects [Smith and Watts (1981)]. Thus, the addition of a performance plan may make some high-variance projects (actually projects with a high covariance with the manager's existing projects) more attractive to the manager, and this can lead to an increase in corporate investment. However, the performance plan may also make some previously acceptable low-variance projects less attractive, which results in the opposite prediction regarding corporate investment. Therefore, the influence of the 'option-like' characteristics of the performance plan on corporate investment is ambiguous.

If the option effect of the performance plan leads to an increase in corporate investment, this reinforces the investment changes associated with lengthening the manager's decision-making horizon and encouraging the manager to provide increased effort. Under this circumstance, the discussion above implies that corporate investment should increase with performance plan adoption. The following *research* hypothesis is examined in the subsequent empirical study:

> The adoption of performance plans is associated with an *increase* in corporate investment.

There are two important limitations to the first research hypothesis. First, the hypothesis is limited by the restrictive assumptions used in specifying the decision-setting and the theoretical ambiguity regarding the combined decision-making horizon and option effects on corporate investment. The association between performance plan adoption and corporate investment is, therefore, an empirical issue. Second, the research hypothesis has been developed under the assumption that the compensation contract influences managerial decision-making. Obviously, performance plan adoption and increased investment activity may be joint decisions by the Board of Directors reflecting coincident changes in corporate strategy and executive compensation. In particular, once a new investment is chosen, a compensation arrangement may be adopted which offers high rewards if the program is successful [Salter (1973), Rappaport (1978)]. Therefore, a causal inference from the subsequent empirical results is inappropriate.

The first research hypothesis is only concerned with changes in corporate investment associated with performance plan adoption. A related question is whether the adoption of the performance plan is in the best interests of the shareholders. The impact of the contractual change on shareholder wealth under the assumptions used in developing the first research hypothesis is unclear. That is, the manager may invest in positive or negative net present value projects after performance plan adoption.

A much simpler analysis is to note that the performance plans are generally approved by shareholders (in most cases by explicit vote) and rational shareholders will not approve a managerial compensation contract which will have an adverse effect on their expected wealth. Therefore, shareholder wealth should increase with performance plan adoption. The second *research hypothesis* is:

> The adoption of performance plans is associated with a *favorable* security market reaction.

Note that a favorable security market response to performance plan adoption is not necessarily a signal that the market has a favorable view of the 'incentive' characteristics of performance plans. For example, the market reaction may be a response to corporate strategy changes that are coincident with adoption and for which performance plan adoption is one type of confirmatory information. Alternatively, there may be tax advantages to performance plans relative to qualified stock options because the corporation receives a tax deduction for compensation paid under the performance plan, whereas no tax deduction is typically obtained with qualified stock options [Hite and Long (1982)][8]. Thus, a favorable security market reaction could be the result of the corporation sharing some of the tax savings associated with

---

[8]Additional analysis of the tax consequences of various compensation schemes is provided by Miller and Scholes (1981) and Smith and Watts (1981). Miller and Scholes argue that there are tax advantages to many common executive compensation plans. Thus, it is difficult to argue that compensation plan changes are *purely* incentive or incentive-signaling devices. In contrast, Smith and Watts argue that is is possible to obtain the tax advantage of performance plans more simply via a salary and pension fund scheme. Thus, tax aspects alone cannot explain all of the observed contractual details of performance plans.

the change in compensation plan and have nothing to do with the contractual characteristics of performance plans. However, it seems unlikely that substantial changes in corporate investment and security market performance could be attributed to the slight decrease in corporate taxes resulting from a performance plan tax deduction.

4. Data collection, measurement, and analysis issues

4.1. Sample selection

A list of corporate incentive plans was obtained from a management consulting firm specializing in executive compensation, and a group of companies were identified as potential experimental firms. Each experimental group firm was required to satisfy two criteria. First, the performance plan adoption must have occurred during fiscal years ended in 1971 to early 1978.[9] Second, a firm passing the criterion must have a matching control firm.

A total of twenty-five experimental firms were identified. The experimental firms, fiscal year of performance plan adoption, and selected characteristics of the plans are presented in table 3. Ten different industrial classifications and eight different years of performance plan adoption are represented in the sample of experimental firms.

The *control* firms were required to satisfy the following criteria:

(i)   same industry as the experimental firm (as a minimum the control firms had the same two-digit SIC code in the 1979 COMPUSTAT data base),

(ii)   similar size as the experimental firm (measured by corporate sales in the year prior to performance plan adoption by the experimental firm),[10]

(iii) no formal performance plan over the test period (discussed in section 5),[11]

(iv)   similar fiscal year as the experimental firm.[12]

---

[9]The reason for the 1971 requirement was that Proxy Statements prior to this year (at best) are not available at the Chicago office of the Securities and Exchange Commission (SEC). The 1978 cutoff was necessary in order to obtain investment data after the adoption of the plan.

[10]The size matching was based upon the ratio of sales for the experimental firm to sales for the control firm in the year prior to performance plan adoption. Matches were allowed if this ratio was between 0.25 and 4.00. The majority of the matches had a ratio between 0.51 and 2.00.

[11]Quaker Oats adopted a performance plan in the fiscal year ended June 1980. Thus, the fiscal year ended June 1977 for Quaker Oats was assumed to correspond to the adoption year of Beatrice (February 1978). Midland–Ross modified their short-term plan to include 'contingent awards' in 1979. Although these awards are in some ways similar to performance units, they appear to have prorated vesting features and were first used in 1980 (the year after the test period).

[12]If a firm was a December year-end company, matches were allowed with September through December firms. However, in most cases December experimental companies were matched with December control companies. For non-December firms, a match was allowed with companies whose fiscal year end was close to that of the experimental firm.

The selected control firms are presented in table 3.[13] A profile analysis [Foster (1980)] of the experimental and control firms on selected attributes is presented in table 4. The two groups are not statistically different in the year before performance plan adoption in terms of sales, leverage (long-term debt divided by the market value of the firm), or insider ownership.[14]

4.2. Measurement of corporate investment

Corporate investment includes outlays for capital investment, research and development, advertising, and other similar long-term expenditures. The subsequent empirical analysis considers only capital investment expenditures in the tests of the first research hypothesis because information on research and development and advertising expenditures is typically not available from COMPUSTAT for years prior to performance plan adoption (i.e., the late 1960s and early 1970s).

Capital investment expenditures for the ten years surrounding the plan adoption (seven years before, the year of adoption, and two years after) were collected. The capital investment figures were obtained from COMPUSTAT (data item number 30). The accuracy of a random sample of the data was verified by reference to SEC form 10-K (schedule V).

Corporate capital investment will be analyzed in terms of total dollars of capital investment divided by sales (I/S), and total dollars of capital investment (I). The I/S ratio is used in the empirical tests for three reasons. First, the ratio is an indication of corporate capital investment intensity. Second, dividing investment by sales provides an additional control for firm size.[15] Finally, the empirical results will aggregate time series from *different* calendar years. The advantage of dividing capital investment in specific years

---

[13]The two groups were also selected based upon Tobin's q [Tobin and Brainard (1977), von Furstenberg et al. (1980), Lindenberg and Ross (1981)]. Tobin's q is defined as the ratio of the market value of the firm to the replacement cost of the firm's assets. Tobin's q has been shown to empirically explain capital investment behavior [Malkiel et al. (1979), Ciccolo and Fromm (1979), von Furstenberg et al. (1980)]. The procedures of von Furstenberg et al. (1980) were used to compute Tobin's q. The two groups were not statistically different in terms of average Tobin's q over the period 1960–1976.

[14]The two groups were also compared in terms of their long-term compensation plans. Twenty-four experimental and twenty-four control firms had stock options in place in the year of adoption. Further, five experimental and seven control firms had SARs in place in the year of adoption. Although the time series of performance plan and SAR adoption is similar (table 2), the experimental and control groups do not differ statistically in terms of SAR adoption. Thus, the adoption of SARs is unlikely to explain differences in the capital investment behavior or security market performance of the two groups.

[15]Lev and Sunder (1979) point out that the adequacy of a ratio (such as I/S) in controlling for size requires, among other conditions, that I is proportional to S. Since the proportionality condition is unlikely to be strictly satisfied, the ability of the I/S ratio to control for size may be somewhat limited.

by sales in that same year is that the impact of inflation on the capital investment figure is reduced.[16]

The COMPUSTAT capital investment figure is plagued by a variety of problems [Thies and Revsine (1977)]. The capital investment figure includes (i) additions at cost or the amount spent for the construction and/or acquisition of property, plant, and equipment, (ii) capital expenditures of pooled companies, and (iii) property, plant, and equipment of purchased companies. Perhaps the most serious limitations to the COMPUSTAT capital investment figure are that it does not include acquisitions accounted for as a pooling and it only includes the property, plant, and equipment (not the total cost of the acquisition) of purchased companies. Since acquisitions are conceptually similar to any other type of capital investment and the COMPUSTAT figure does not include all capital investments by the firm,

Table 3

Sample of companies.

Experimental firm	Year[a]	Plan type[b]	Control firm
Industry 20: Foods			
1. Beatrice Foods	1978	Shares/5 yrs/*EPS*	Quaker Oats
2. Nabisco	1976	Units/3 yrs/*EPS*	Campbell Taggart
3. Pillsbury	1975	Shares/4 yrs /*EPS*	International Multifoods
4. Ralston Purina	1975	Units/4 yrs/*Earnings*	Carnation
Industry 22: Textiles			
5. Akzona	1971	Shares/5 yrs/*EPS*	Lowenstein (M.)
Industry 26: Paper			
6. Bemis	1974	Shares/4 yrs/*EPS*	Great Northern Nekoosa
7. Crown Zellerbach	1973	Units/4 yrs/*EPS*	Diamond International
Industry 28: Chemicals			
8. FMC	1973	Shares/4 yrs/*EPS*	DuPont
9. Monsanto	1974	Units/5 yrs/*EPS*	Dow Chemical
10. Nalco	1977	Shares/3 yrs/*EPS*	Schering–Plough
11. Squibb	1975	Units/3 yrs/*EPS*	Pfizer
Industry 29: Petroleum			
12. Atlantic Richfield	1976	Units/5 yrs/*ROE*	Cities Service
13. Sun Co.	1972	Shares/6 yrs/*ROE*	Royal Dutch Petroleum–NY
14. Union Oil of Calif.	1975	Shares/4 yrs/*ROE*	Conoco
Industry 32: Clay, Glass, and Stone			
15. Owens–Illinois	1975	Units/3 yrs/*ROE*	Owens–Corning
16. Vulcan Materials	1973	Shares/3 yrs /*EPS*	Anchor Hocking

[16]The argument that the I/S ratio removes the impact of inflation rests, of course, on the assumption that the price increases for the product (i.e., sales) are the same as the price increases for capital (i.e., investment). This assumption is not likely to be strictly satisfied, and this represents a limitation of the ability of the I/S ratio to control for inflationary influences.

Table 3 (continued)

Experimental firm	Year[a]	Plan type[b]	Control firm
Industry 33: Primary Metals			
17. Cabot	1972	Shares /6 yrs/*EPS*	Handy & Harman
18. Roblin	1977	Units/5 yrs/*BV*	Midland–Ross
Industry 35: Non-electrical Machinery			
19. Dover	1974	Shares/3 yrs / *MULTIPLE*	Harnischfeger
20. Hobart	1977	Units/4 yrs/*EPS*	Scott & Fetzer
21. Toro	1976	Units/5 yrs/*ROI*	Hesston
Industry 36: Electrical Machinery			
22. Emerson Electric	1977	Shares/5 yrs/*EPS*	Whirlpool
Industry 37: Transportation Equipment			
23. Bendix	1974	Units/3 yrs/*EPS*	Fruehauf
24. International Harvester	1975	Units/5 yrs/ *MULTIPLE*	Borg Warner
25. Rockwell International	1977	Shares/3 yrs/*EPS*	General Dynamics

[a]Year refers to the fiscal year end in which the stockholders were notified (via Proxy Statement) that a performance plan was to be adopted. For Ralston Purina, Roblin, and Emerson Electric, the plan was not voted on by the stockholders and the first year in which the executives participated in the plan was used as the year of adoption.

[b]For plan type, *A/B/C*, the following notation is used: *A* = either performance *units* or *shares*, *B* = minimum award period (in years) before payout, and *C* = performance variable (*Earnings* = corporate earnings, *EPS* = earnings-per-share, *ROE* = return on stockholder's equity, *ROI* = return on invested capital, *BV* = book value per share, and *MULTIPLE* = several performance measures are used).

the statistical tests using this figure may be confounded by differences in merger and acquisition (M&A) activity of the experimental and control firms. For example, control firms may exhibit a lower capital investment level than experimental firms because their capital investment is primarily M&A expenditures which are not reported in the COMPUSTAT capital investment figure.

The confounding induced by the COMPUSTAT reporting procedures is most serious when an M&A is accounted for as a pooling. However, a measurement problem also occurs when purchase methods are used because only the property, plant, and equipment of the acquired firm is recorded as capital investment, rather than the total cost of the acquisition. Therefore, the size of the measurement error is affected by both the accounting method selected for the M&A *and* the amount of M&A expenditure.

In an attempt to examine the severity of this measurement problem, the M&A activity of the experimental and control firms (whether accounted for as a purchase or pooling) for the ten-year period surrounding performance plan adoption was collected from *Moody's Industrial Manual.* The announced value of the merger or acquisition was obtained from *Moody's*

Table 4

Profile of experimental and control firms on selected attributes in the fiscal year *prior* to performance plan adoption.

Attribute	Mean difference[a]	Median difference[a]	Wilcoxon Z[b]
Sales (in millions)	$289.593	$217.870	0.901
Long-term debt/ Market value of firm[c]	0.043	0.036	1.305
	Experimental group[d]	Control group[d]	Chi-square[b]
Insider ownership[e]	7 (18)	12 (13)	2.120

[a]The differences are calculated by subtracting the control firm observation from the associated experimental firm observation.

[b]None of the comparisons were statistically significant ($p \leq 0.05$, one-tail).

[c]The long-term debt is measured by book value. The market value of the firm was calculated by adding (i) the average of the high and low common stock price multiplied by the average number of shares of common stock during the fiscal year and (ii) the book value of long-term debt.

[d]The first number is the number of firms where 'insiders' own at least five percent of the firm and the number in parentheses is the number of firms where 'insiders' do not own five percent of the firm.

[e]Equity ownership by officers, directors, families, or related corporations of at least five percent. This data was obtained from *Value Line* and from Proxy Statements for firms not listed by *Value Line*.

Industrial Manual and/or the *Wall Street Journal Index*. The differences in M&A expenditures between the experimental and control groups will be examined for statistical significance in each year in the ten-year test period. If the experimental and control groups exhibit similar M&A expenditures over the test period, the measurement error associated with COMPUSTAT reporting procedures should not be a serious threat to the internal validity of the experimental design.

4.3. Analysis issues

Research hypothesis one posits that performance plan adoption should be associated with shifts in *levels* of corporate investment. Conceptually, a test for changes in capital investment levels can be accomplished by examining changes in levels or growth rates (i.e., a change in level will also be reflected in the growth rates). Since the stochastic process generating capital investment projects in the absence of a performance plan is unknown, it is difficult to determine whether capital investment levels or growth rates are the appropriate measure for statistical analysis. Therefore the tests of research hypothesis one will be performed on both capital investment growth rates and capital investment levels.

In order to control for confounding macroeconomic or industry influences, a two-group matched-pairs experimental design is used in the analysis, with the empirical tests focusing on the *difference* in central tendency for capital investment growth rates or security market performance for each of the matched pairs. The Wilcoxon Matched-Pairs Signed-Ranks Test (hereafter, Wilcoxon) provides a non-parametric test for differences in central tendency of correlated samples and is used in the subsequent analysis [Siegel (1956)]. This non-parametric test was selected because the capital investment data do not meet the strict distributional assumptions required for traditional parametric tests, the Wilcoxon test is less sensitive to the statistical problems posed by modest sample sizes, and the power of this test is close to that of a corresponding parametric test. An estimate of between-group shifts in central tendency for the Wilcoxon test is the *median* of the Walsh average of differences (hereafter, median difference) between the matched pairs [Hollander and Wolfe (1973)]. The mean of the differences (hereafter, mean difference) between matched pairs is reported for comparative purposes. The test statistic for between-groups differences is the Wilcoxon Z-statistic which has approximately a standard normal distribution even in small samples [Siegel (1956)].

5. Results

5.1. Tests of research hypothesis one

5.1.1. Test no. 1

The first test of research hypothesis one was conducted by computing yearly capital investment growth rates for each firm over the nine-year period consisting of the six years before, the year of, and the two years after performance plan adoption. The median difference in yearly growth rates for the matched-pairs of firms was examined for statistical significance in each year. The median difference for I/S growth rates, I growth rates, and associated summary statistics are presented in table 5.[17]

One important result in table 5 is that the experimental and control firms do *not* exhibit statistically significant differences ($p \leq 0.05$, one-tail) in capital investment behavior over periods up to and including the year of performance plan adoption. Thus, the hypothesis that systematic differences existed in the capital investment behavior of the experimental and control firms *prior* to the change in incentive plan is rejected.

In order to test whether performance plan adoption is associated with an *increase* in corporate investment, it is necessary to know something about how the increase will be reflected in the time series of yearly growth rates. One possibility is that the firms have a stable optimal level of current capital

---

[17]Since the yearly statistical tests are related, the traditional problem associated with correlated tests (i.e., an inflated overall Type I error rate) is encountered. However, because it is possible to predict when statistically significant effects should occur, it is unlikely that the observed results are due solely to an inflated Type I error rate.

Table 5

Test no. 1 summary statistics for yearly investment/sales (*I/S*) and investment (*I*) *growth rates.*

Year	Investment/sales (*I/S*)			Investment (*I*)		
	Mean difference[a]	Median difference[a]	Wilcoxon *Z*	Mean difference[a]	Median difference[a]	Wilcoxon *Z*
−6	0.003	−0.055	0.632	0.030	−0.040	0.283
−5	0.112	0.060	0.794	0.121	0.079	0.982
−4	−0.405[b]	−0.129	1.359	−0.462[c]	−0.140	1.251
−3	−0.011	−0.072	0.928	−0.012	−0.060	0.605
−2	0.110	0.079	0.659	0.175	0.080	0.578
−1	−0.001	0.085	1.090	−0.020	0.104	0.928
0	0.030	0.004	0.013	0.015	0.012	0.121
+1	0.251	0.152	2.193[d]	0.251	0.174	1.574
+2	−0.030	0.007	0.040	−0.106	−0.044	0.363

[a]The differences are calculated by subtracting the growth rate of the control firm from the growth rate of the associated experimental firm.

[b]A portion of this difference is due to a large growth rate for Lowenstein. Deleting the Akzona/Lowenstein pair produced a difference in means of −0.184.

[c]A portion of this difference is due to a large growth rate for Lowenstein. Deleting the Akzona/Lowenstein pair produced a difference in means of −0.249.

[d]Statistically significant ($p \leq 0.05$, one-tail).

expenditures from year −7 to year 0 and that adoption of a long-term compensation plan in year 0 results in an increase in this optimal level for subsequent years. Given this scenario, an examination of the time series of yearly capital investment growth rates would reveal the existence of only *one* significant increase, and this increase would occur in year +1 since only in year +1 are the numerator and denominator of the growth rate calculations made under different optimal levels of capital investment.[18] As the data in table 5 indicate, the *I/S* growth rate for the experimental firms is significantly greater than that of the control firms only in year +1. Moreover, the *I* growth rate is close to being statistically significant ($p \leq 0.058$) in year +1. Both of these results are consistent with the scenario just described, and thus hypothesis one is generally *supported* — performance plan adoption is associated with increased corporate capital investment.[19]

[18]The reasonableness of this scenario depends upon the process generating investment opportunities for the firm. The assumption being made is that a sufficient number of acceptable projects exists at the time the executive wishes to increase capital expenditures.

[19]Although the results of Test no. 1 reveal that capital investment for the experimental firms increased in year +1, this increase may be due to some unspecified confounding variable (e.g., changes in corporate investment strategy) and not to the adoption of the performance plan. This is an especially serious problem for this type of study because the firms have self-selected into the experimental control groups, and randomization cannot be relied upon as a control for confounding influences. One method of assessing the seriousness of the self-selection problem is to compare the year +1 *forecasts* of capital investment growth rates for the experimental and

The analysis of capital investment *levels*, as opposed to capital investment growth rates, is presented in table 6. The I/S and I levels are not statistically different in years -7 to year 0 indicating that the experimental and control firms had similar investment levels prior to performance plan adoption. In contrast, the median difference in I/S and I levels is statistically significant ($p \leq 0.10$, one-tail) and positive in year $+1$, a result consistent with the growth rates reported in table 5. Further, the medians in year $+2$ are large relative to years -7 to 0 (table 6). However, the median differences in year $+2$ are not statistically significant and these results are somewhat inconsistent with the analysis of growth rates in table 5. Overall, there is weak evidence that the relative median level of investment has shifted upward for the experimental firms and the analysis of capital investment levels provides results which are generally consistent with the analysis of capital investment growth rates.

Table 6

Test no. 1 summary statistics for yearly investment/sales (I/S) and investment (I) *levels*.

Year	Investment/sales (I/S)			Investment (I)		
	Mean difference[a]	Median difference[a]	Wilcoxon Z	Mean difference[a, b]	Median difference[a, b]	Wilcoxon Z
-7	-0.001	0.000	0.029	-19.829	9.087	1.117
-6	0.006	-0.002	0.094	-26.482	9.444	1.063
-5	0.011	0.002	0.498	-17.571	9.300	0.874
-4	0.001	-0.006	1.063	-22.127	5.320	0.417
-3	-0.007	-0.005	0.632	-28.959	4.364	0.417
-2	0.003	-0.004	0.336	-7.981	9.980	1.063
-1	0.002	-0.003	0.202	8.760	9.088	0.659
0	0.005	0.001	0.094	-15.248	10.814	0.578
$+1$	0.019	0.013	1.413[c]	10.308	27.589	1.440[c]
$+2$	0.014	0.011	0.794	-28.641	22.356	1.117

[a]The differences are calculated by subtracting the level of the control firm from the level of the associated experimental firm.

[b]Investment is expressed in millions of dollars.

[c]Statistically significant ($p \leq 0.10$, one-tail).

control firms (assuming that the forecasts reflect the influence of the confounding variable). If the two groups have, on average, similar forecasts for the capital investment growth rates in year $+1$, it is unlikely that any observed differences in year $+1$ are due to confounding variables.

The first *Value Line* forecasts of year $+1$ capital investment and sales for twenty-three experimental and control firm pairs were used to examine the possibility of confounding influences. The median difference for the forecasted I (I/S) was 0.055 (0.045). The median difference was not statistically significant (Wilcoxon $Z = 0.760$ and 0.578, respectively). Thus, these results provide *no* evidence that the results of Test no. 1 are due to some unspecified confounding variable.

5.1.2. Test no. 2

The second test of the hypothesis was conducted by separating the ten-year time period into three non-overlapping two-year periods and then calculating the two statistics illustrated in table 7. This additional test was conducted to detect possible misspecifications resulting from the use of yearly capital investment growth rates in Test no. 1. If a different analysis of the capital investment time series produces results similar to those of Test no. 1, then the observed results are less likely to be the result of an empirical misspecification.[20]

The internal validity test (table 7) to assess whether the experimental and control firms exhibit similar capital investment growth rates prior to performance plan adoption was conducted first. This test examined the statistical significance of the median difference for the Internal Validity Ratio (growth rates in the period before plan adoption). Consistent with the results of Test no. 1, the two groups of firms were not significantly different in terms of their capital investment behavior (I/S and I growth rates) *prior* to performance plan adoption (table 8).

Table 7

An example illustrating the construction of Test no. 2.

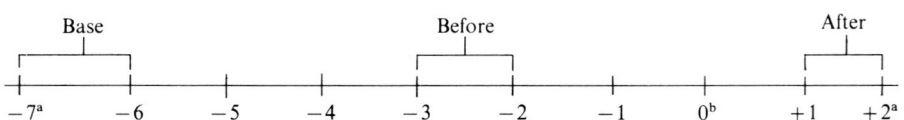

$$I \text{ (after)}^c = \frac{I(+2) + I(+1)}{2} \qquad \text{Internal validity ratio}^c = \left[\frac{I \text{ (before)}}{I \text{ (base)}} - 1 \right]$$

$$I \text{ (before)}^c = \frac{I(-2) + I(-3)}{2} \qquad \text{Research hypothesis ratio}^c = \left[\frac{I \text{ (after)}}{I \text{ (before)}} - 1 \right]$$

$$I \text{ (base)}^c = \frac{I(-6) + I(-7)}{2}$$

[a]Year relative to the year in which the performance plan was adopted (e.g., $+2$ is the second year after adoption).
[b]Year of performance plan adoption.
[c]These statistics are calculated in a similar manner for the I/S measure.

[20]One possible misspecification is that one-year I/S growth rates may behave differently than growth rates calculated over a longer period. Test no. 2 is an attempt to determine whether this type of misspecification is a plausible explanation for the results of Test no. 1.

The test of whether the experimental and control firms exhibit similar capital investment growth rates in the period surrounding performance plan adoption was then conducted (table 7). This test examined the statistical significance of the median difference for the Research Hypothesis Ratio (growth rates in the period before to the period after plan adoption). Consistent with the results of Test no. 1, the experimental firms have a much larger capital investment growth rate in the period surrounding the performance plan adoption than do the control firms (table 8). Since both Test no. 1 and Test no. 2 yield convergent results, research hypothesis one is *supported.*[21]

Table 8

Test no. 2 summary statistics for investment (I) and investment/sales (I/S) growth rates.

Investment/sales (I/S)			Investment (I)		
Mean difference[a]	Median difference[a]	Wilcoxon Z	Mean difference[a]	Median difference[a]	Wilcoxon Z
Internal validity test					
0.133	−0.100	0.982	−0.224[b]	−0.072	0.256
Research hypothesis test					
0.297	0.273	2.220[d]	0.215[c]	0.415	1.735[d]

[a]The differences are calculated by subtracting the control firm observation from the associated experimental firm observation.
[b]A portion of this difference is due to a large investment growth rate for Hesston. Deleting Toro/Hesston pair produced a difference in means of 0.001.
[c]A portion of the difference is due to a large investment growth rate for Harnischfeger. Deleting the Dover/Harnischfeger pair produced a difference in means of 0.563.
[d]Statistically significant ($p \leq 0.05$, one-tail).

[21]Proxy Statements typically describe the performance plan in sufficient detail (see table 3) to determine the length of award period (years). Theory suggests that as the performance evaluation period increases, the levels of capital investment should increase. The Spearman Rank-Order correlation between the award period length and selected relative capital investment growth measures were:

I growth (year +1) = 0.254 ($p > 0.10$, one-tail),

I/S growth (year +1) = 0.191 ($p > 0.10$, one-tail);

I research hypothesis ratio = 0.596 ($p < 0.01$, one-tail),

I/S research hypothesis ratio = 0.578 ($p < 0.01$, one-tail).

Thus, the performance plan attributes appear to explain some of the variance in capital expenditure growth by adopting firms. As the award period increases, capital investment also increases.

Table 9

Summary statistics for yearly levels of merger and acquisition (M&A) activity (in millions of dollars).

Year	Mean difference[a, b]	Median difference[a]	Wilcoxon Z
−7	74.236 (8)	0.000	0.280
−6	7.868 (8)	0.000	0.980
−5	14.942 (12)	0.000	0.628
−4	43.772 (12)	0.000	0.549
−3	−3.470 (10)	0.000	0.153
−2	2.917 (8)	0.000	0.840
−1	−0.125 (10)	0.000	1.274
0	7.176 (9)	0.900	2.310[c]
+1	51.618 (9)	0.000	1.125
+2	8.724 (13)	0.000	0.769

[a]The differences are calculated by subtracting the M&A level of the control firm from the M&A level of the associated experimental firm.

[b]The number in parentheses is the number of experimental/control firm pairs with non-zero M&A activity.

[c]Statistically significant ($p \leq 0.05$, one-tail).

5.2. Merger and acquisition comparisons

As discussed in section 4, the capital investment data used in Tests no. 1 and 2 are plagued by a variety of problems related to the manner in which COMPUSTAT handles merger and acquisition (M&A) activity. In order to assess the severity of this problem, the median difference in M&A level between the experimental and control firms was examined for statistical significance from year −7 to year +2. The summary statistics for these tests are presented in table 9.[22] The only statistically significant result occurred in year 0 (the year of performance plan adoption) where the experimental firms had a slightly *higher* (i.e., the median difference was only $900,000) level of M&A activity than the control firms. Therefore, it does not appear that the two groups of firms had significantly different M&A activity over the test period and the capital investment figure for the control firms is not likely to be understated due to COMPUSTAT reporting procedures for M&A activity. Consequently, the results of Tests no. 1 and no. 2 should not be biased in favor of the research hypothesis.[23]

[22]The M&A tests were also conducted by standardizing M&A by sales and the results were similar to table 9. The computation of M&A growth rates is not possible for individual firms because in most cases the denominator of the ratio would be equal to zero.

[23]The collection of the M&A data revealed that three firms (one experimental and two control completed major reorganizations during the test period. Akzona was formed from American Enka and other companies in 1970, Great Northern Nekoosa was formed from a merger of Great Northern Paper and Nekoosa–Edwards Paper in 1970, and Schering–Plough was formed from the merger of Schering and Plough in 1971. Fortunately, none of these major mergers occurred in the year of performance plan adoption. However, since COMPUSTAT does not restate the capital investment prior to the merger, these major mergers make it very difficult to compare capital investment over time, and this is a limitation to the tine series analysis presented. These three mergers were not included in the analysis in table 9.

5.3. Tests of research hypothesis two

The tests of research hypothesis one indicate that performance plan adoption is associated with increased capital investment. The important question that remains is whether this change has a favorable impact on shareholder wealth. In order to empirically examine the second research hypothesis, a security market reaction test was conducted.

The announcement date selected for analysis was the day on which the SEC *received* the Proxy Statement indicating that the performance plan would be voted on at the annual shareholder meeting. For plans not approved by shareholders, the announcement date was the receipt date of the first Proxy Statement disclosure of the performance plan. Daily stock return data and an equally-weighted daily market index were obtained from the Center for Research on Security Prices (CRSP) tape for an estimation period (day -65 to day -6) and an announcement period (day -5 to day $+5$) centered on the Proxy receipt date.[24]

The single-factor market model was assumed to be an adequate characterization of the rate of return for a stock, or

$$R_{it} = \alpha_i + \beta_i R_{mt} + \varepsilon_{it},$$

where

R_{it} = continuously compounded rate of return for stock i in period t,
R_{mt} = continuously compounded rate of return for the market in period t,
ε_{it} = random error for stock i in period t,
α_i = rate of return on stock i when $R_{mt} = 0$, and
β_i = systematic risk of stock i.

The market model parameters for each stock, α_i and β_i, were estimated via the Scholes and Williams (1977) method using the sixty observations prior to day -5 (i.e., day -65 to day -6). The excess returns ($\hat{e}_{it}$) for each stock were estimated by

$$\hat{e}_{it} = R_{it} - \hat{\alpha}_i - \hat{\beta}_i R_{mt} \quad \text{for} \quad -5 \leqq t \leqq +5.$$

The $\hat{\varepsilon}_{it}$ for each firm was standardized by using the estimated standard deviation of the residuals from the market model and a factor reflecting the increase in variability due to prediction outside the estimation period [see Patell (1976)].[25]

---

[24]The security tests (tables 10 and 11) were conducted with either nineteen or twenty-one matched pairs. Pairs were eliminated because either return data was missing and/or the proxy receipt date was not available.

[25]The precise formula for the standardized excess return is

$$\hat{\hat{\varepsilon}}_{it} = \hat{\varepsilon}_{it}/\hat{\sigma}_i \sqrt{C_{it}} \quad \text{where} \quad C_{it} = 1 + 1/T + \left((R_{mt} - \bar{R}_m)^2 \bigg/ \sum_{t=1}^{T} (R_{mt} - \bar{R}_m)^2 \right),$$

where $\hat{\sigma}_i$ is the standard deviation of the residuals from estimating the market model over days -65 to -6, T is the number of observations in the estimation period, and $\bar{R}_m = (1/T) \sum_{t=1}^{T} R_{mt}$.

Two different control group comparisons were performed — the security market reaction of the control firms at their own proxy receipt date (table 10), and the security market reaction of the control firms at the proxy receipt date of their associated experimental firms (table 11). The results in table 10 control for the possibility that the market reaction of the experimental firms may be due to the information typically contained in a Proxy Statement. This 'proxy effect' may be related to information released on executive remuneration, board of director approval, and shareholder proposals. The results in table 11 control for the possibility that the market reaction of the experimental firms may be due to industry influences. Since the two groups are matched in terms of industry and calendar day of the analysis, the paired comparisons in table 11 control for industry 'events' which are unrelated to the performance plan adoption, but which are reflected in the security market reaction for individual firms.

None of the eleven (day -5 to day $+5$) average standardized excess returns ($\hat{\bar{\varepsilon}}_t$) for the control firms are statistically significant (table 10).[26] Thus, the market does not appear to react to a 'proxy effect' and the security market reaction of the experimental firms is not likely to be confounded with information (other than the announcement of the performance plan) typically contained in the Proxy Statement.[27] In contrast to the control firms, the $\hat{\bar{\varepsilon}}_t$ for the experimental firms is statistically significant and positive on day $+1$[28]. This result is generally reinforced by the matched-pairs t-test and the Wilcoxon Z-test which examine the statistical significance of the mean difference and median difference in market reaction between the experimental

---

[26]The statistical significance of $\hat{\bar{\varepsilon}}_t$ was determined using [see Patell (1976)] the statistic

$$\sum_{i=1}^{n} \hat{\varepsilon}_{it} \bigg/ \left[\sum_{i=1}^{n} (T-2)/(T-4) \right]^{\frac{1}{2}} \sim N(0, 1),$$

where n is the number of firms in the sample.

Day 0 was generally a different calendar day for the firms *within* the experimental and control groups, and thus the $\hat{\varepsilon}_{it}$'s can be viewed as independent. One limitation of this test is that the sample size is not large (i.e., $n = 19$ or 21), and in a strict sense this Z-statistic should be viewed as an approximation. A matched-pairs t-test and the Wilcoxon Z-test were used in assessing statistical significance for differences between the experimental and control groups in tables 10 and 11.

[27]The Proxy Statements of the experimental firms typically contained only one 'unusual' announcement (i.e., performance plan adoption). However, there were other announcements for a small number of firms (e.g., adoption of an employee stock ownership plan, an increase in the number of authorized common shares, and adoption of a restricted stock plan). Although these announcements are limitations to the security market reaction results, there does not appear to be a consistent confounding influence at the time that the performance plan is adopted.

[28]The excess returns for *individual* experimental firms on day $+1$ were examined in order to determine whether the statistically significant test result on this day was due to a small portion of the sample. A binominal test on the signs of the excess returns [Brown and Warner (1981)] was conducted. There were 15 positive and 4 negative signs for the excess returns ($Z = 2.524$, $p < 0.05$, one-tail). Therefore, the security market results were *not* dominated by a small number of firms.

Table 10

Security market reaction of the experimental firms at their proxy receipt date and the control firms *at their proxy receipt date.*

Day	Experimental group ($n=19$) at their proxy receipt date		Control group ($n=19$) at their proxy receipt date		Matched-pairs t-test		Wilcoxon Z-test	
	$\hat{\bar{\varepsilon}}_t$	Z-statistic	$\hat{\bar{\varepsilon}}_t$	Z-statistic	Mean difference[a]	t-statistic	Median difference[a]	Z-statistic
−5	−0.003	−0.012	−0.270	−1.157	0.267	0.900	0.232	0.724
−4	0.076	0.324	−0.107	−0.458	0.183	0.590	0.259	0.765
−3	0.083	0.356	−0.045	−0.192	0.128	0.530	0.167	0.765
−2	0.168	0.718	−0.141	−0.604	0.309	2.200[b]	0.316	2.093[b]
−1	−0.036	−0.153	−0.079	−0.340	0.043	0.130	−0.173	0.483
0	0.277	1.186	−0.064	−0.274	0.341	1.690	0.349	1.248
+1	0.525	2.250[b]	−0.080	−0.342	0.605	2.080[b]	0.513	1.811[b]
+2	−0.158	−0.678	0.050	0.215	−0.208	−0.680	−0.280	0.563
+3	0.186	0.796	0.041	0.178	0.145	0.660	0.237	0.845
+4	−0.209	−0.895	0.224	0.959	−0.433	−1.410	−0.379	1.288
+5	0.042	0.180	0.154	0.661	−0.112	−0.400	−0.111	0.402

[a]The differences are calculated by subtracting the standardized excess return of the control firm from the standardized excess return of the associated experimental firm.

[b]Statistically significant ($p \leqq 0.05$, one-tail).

Table 11

Security market reaction of the experimental firms at their proxy receipt date and the control firms *at the proxy receipt date of the experimental firms*.

Day	Experimental group ($n=21$) at their proxy receipt date		Control group ($n=21$) at the proxy receipt date of the experimental firm		Matched-pairs t-test		Wilcoxon Z-test	
	$\hat{\bar{\varepsilon}}_t$	Z-statistic	$\hat{\bar{\varepsilon}}_t$	Z-statistic	Mean differences[a]	t-statistic	Median differences[a]	Z-statistic
−5	−0.118	−0.530	0.019	0.087	−0.137	−0.500	−0.079	0.434
−4	−0.006	0.028	−0.010	−0.047	0.004	−0.020	−0.051	0.365
−3	0.161	0.724	0.142	0.638	0.019	0.060	−0.038	0.122
−2	0.115	0.518	−0.332	−1.494	0.447	1.760[b]	0.531	2.068[b]
−1	0.018	0.082	−0.216	−0.972	0.234	1.240	0.181	0.921
0	0.218	0.984	−0.342	−1.539	0.560	2.470[b]	0.566	2.138[b]
+1	0.366	1.646[b]	0.173	0.780	0.193	0.770	0.236	0.956
+2	−0.211	−0.948	0.036	0.163	−0.247	−0.790	−0.262	0.539
+3	0.109	0.493	0.124	0.558	−0.015	−0.050	0.001	0.017
+4	−0.233	−1.049	−0.164	−0.739	−0.069	−0.210	0.077	0.365
+5	0.024	0.109	−0.269	−1.212	0.293	1.080	0.300	0.852

[a]The differences are calculated by subtracting the standardized excess return of the control firm from the standardized excess return of the associated experimental firm.
[b]Statistically significant ($p \leqq 0.05$, one-tail).

and control firms, respectively. The parametric and non-parametric matched-pairs tests suggest that the experimental firms experienced a statistically significant and positive market reaction on days -2 and $+1$.[29]

The results which control for 'industry effects' are presented in table 11 and are generally similar to those reported in table 10. The matched-pairs *t*-test and Wilcoxon *Z*-test suggest that experimental firms experienced a statistically significant positive market reaction on days -2 and 0. Since both control group comparisons provide similar results, research hypothesis two is *supported* — the adoption of a performance plan is associated with a favorable security market reaction.[30,31]

6. Discussion and summary

The hypothesis that corporate compensation schemes affect corporate decision-making is an important conceptual linkage in the incentive arguments which are now common in accounting and economic research. However, there has been virtually no empirical examination of this hypothesis. This study has examined one aspect of this incentives question by investigating the association between performance adoption and changes in corporate capital investment. The empirical results indicate that, relative to similar control firms, firms adopting performance plans experienced a statistically significant increase in capital investment following plan adoption,

---

[29]Since Proxy Statements are typically released between the fourth- and first-quarter earnings announcements, the announcement period for each firm was examined to determine if the observed marked reaction could have been due to an earnings release. There were no earnings releases during the announcement period. The *Wall Street Journal Index* was also checked for unusual events in this period for experimental and control firms and none were found.

[30]Similar security market reaction results were also obtained using the unadjusted returns method [Brown and Warner (1980)].

[31]If performance plan adoption is associated with some fundamental change in the expected investment opportunities or strategy of the firm, one might expect to observe differential trading by insiders of the experimental and control firms because insiders should possess superior information about the investment changes.

Data on the *number* of insider buy and sell decisions were collected for nineteen matched pairs of firms from *Value Line* for a 24-month period (month -12 to month $+11$) surrounding the experimental firm's Proxy release month (test period) and a 24-month (month -36 to month -13) comparison period (pre-period). The median difference in net buying activity (buy minus sell decisions) between the experimental and control firms was 2.000 and 2.500 for the pre-period and test period, respectively. The pre-period results were not statistically significant (Wilcoxon $Z = 1.232$). However, the test period results were statistically significant (Wilcoxon $Z = 2.007$).

These results suggest that the expectations of insiders for firms adopting performance plans were, on average, more positive (or less negative) than the expectations of insiders for the control group. Subject to the possibility that the differential insider trading is due to the executives of adopting firms rebalancing their personal investment portfolio as a result of their participation in a new compensation contract, these results are consistent with the conclusion that performance plan adoption is associated with a *favorable* change in corporate investment strategy.

and a positive security market reaction when the adoption of the plan was disclosed to the security market.

There are, of course, many interpretations of the empirical results. One interpretation is that the deferral, 'option-like', and accounting measure characteristics of the performance plan provide managerial incentives to increase capital investment, and thus increase shareholder wealth. Therefore, the empirical results can be explained in terms of the 'incentives' associated with performance plan adoption.

A substantively different explanation is that the performance plans are strictly adopted for tax, as opposed to 'incentive,' purposes [e.g., Miller and Scholes (1981), Hite and Long (1982)]. The favorable security market reaction is consistent with the corporation sharing some of the tax savings associated with performance plan adoption. However, as Smith and Watts (1981) argue, these tax advantages can be obtained with less complex compensation contracts, and the additional complexity of the performance plan is likely to be related to managerial incentives.

It is also difficult to construct a tax argument to explain the substantial change in capital investment behavior observed in conjunction with performance plan adoption. The decrease in corporate taxes that results from performance plans is likely to be small, and provides little (if any) motivation to substantially increase capital investment. Perhaps the appropriate conclusion is that tax effects provide only a partial explanation of the empirical results, and that tax aspects do not impede performance plan adoption. However, it should be noted that the tax aspects of compensation arrangements were not explicitly controlled or examined in this study, and thus tax effects represent an important area for future research.

Another explanation is that the empirical results are due to confounding variables (i.e., the self-selection problem). The experimental and control firms have self-selected into the adopting and non-adopting groups, which suggests that there is something fundamentally different about the two groups. For example, the experimental firms may have changed their corporate investment strategy and simultaneously changed their compensation contracts. The self-selection problem confronts all empirical studies of this type and makes it extremely difficult to conclude that the empirical results are due to incentive and/or tax effects rather than some (unspecified) confounding variable.

References

Alchian, A. and H. Demsetz, 1972, Production information costs, and economic organization, American Economic Review 52, 777–795.

Brown, S.J. and J.B. Warner, 1980, Measuring security price performance, Journal of Financial Economics 8, 205–258.

Ciccolo, J. and G. Fromm, 1979, 'q' and the theory of investment, Journal of Finance 34, 535–547.

Collins, D.W. and W.T. Dent, 1979, The proposed elimination of full cost accounting in the extractive petroleum industry: An experimental assessment of the market consequences, Journal of Accounting and Economics 1, 3–44.

Collins, D.W., D.S. Dhaliwal and M.S. Rozeff, 1981, The economic determinants of market reaction to proposed mandatory accounting changes in the oil and gas industry: A cross-sectional analysis, Journal of Accounting and Economics 3, 37–71.

Demski, J.S. snd G.A. Feltham, 1978, Economic incentives in budgetary control systems, The Accounting Review 53, 336–359.

Dukes, R., T.R. Dyckman and J. Elliott, 1981, Accounting for research and development costs: The impact on research and development expenditures, Journal of Accounting Research, Supplement 18, 1–26.

Dyckman, T.R. and A.J. Smith, 1979, Financial accounting and reporting by oil and gas producing companies: A study of information effects, Journal of Accounting and Economics 1, 45–75.

Fama, E.F., 1980, Agency problems and the theory of the firm, Journal of Political Economy 88, 288–307.

Foster, G., 1980, Accounting policy decisions and capital market research, Journal of Accounting and Economics 2, 29–62.

Hagerman, R.L. and M.E. Zmijewski, 1979, Some economic determinants of accounting policy choice, Journal of Accounting and Economics 1, 141–161.

Harris, M. and A. Raviv, 1979, Optimal incentive contracts with imperfect information, Journal of Economic Theory 20, 231–259.

Hite, G.L. and M.S. Long, 1982, Taxes and executive stock options, Journal of Accounting and Economics 4, 3–14.

Hollander, M. and D.A. Wolfe, 1973, Nonparametric statistical methods (Wiley, New York).

Holmstrom, B., 1979, Moral hazard and observability, The Bell Journal of Economics 10, 74–91.

Horwitz, B. and R. Kolodny, 1981, The economic effects of involuntary unifomity in the financial reporting of R&D expenditures, Journal of Accounting Research, Supplement 18, 38–74.

Jensen, M. and W. Meckling, 1976, Theory of the firm: Managerial behaviour, agency costs and ownership structure, Journal of Financial Economics 3, 305–360.

Larcker, D.F. and R.P. Magee, 1982, Incentive effects and accounting: Accrual issues, Unpublished working paper (J.L. Kellogg Graduate School of Management, Northwestern University, Evanston, IL).

Larcker, D.F. and L. Revsine, forthcoming, The oil and gas accounting controversy: An analysis of economic consequences, The Accounting Review.

Lev, B., 1979, The impact of accounting regulation on the stock market: The case of oil and gas companies, The Accounting Review 54, 485–503.

Lev, B. and S. Sunder, 1979, Methodological issues in the use of financial ratios, Journal of Accounting and Economics 1, 187–210.

Lindenberg, E.B. and S.A. Ross, 1981, Tobin's q ratio and industrial organization, Journal of Business 54, 1–32.

Malkiel, B.G., G. von Furstenberg and H.S. Watson, 1979, Expectations, Tobin's q and industry investment, Journal of Finance 34, 549–561.

Miller, M.H. and M.S. Scholes, 1981, Executive compensation, taxes and incentives, in: K. Cootner and W. Sharpe, eds., Financial economics: Essays in honor of Paul Cootner (Prentice-Hall, Englewood Cliffs, NJ).

Patell, J.M., 1976, Corporate forecasts of earnings per share and stock price behavior: Empirical tests, Journal of Accounting Research 14, 246–276.

Rappaport, A., 1978, Executive incentives vs. corporate growth, Harvard Business Review, 81–88.

Ross, S.A., 1973, The economic theory of agency: The principal's problem, American Economic Review 53, 134–139.

Salter, M.S., 1973, Tailor incentive compensation to strategy, Harvard Business Review, 94–102.

Scholes, M. and J. Williams, 1977, Estimating betas from non-synchronous data, Journal of Financial Economics 5, 309–328.

Segal, Martin E. & Company, Inc., 1978, ExecuComp 1978 review (Segal Associates, New York).

Segal, Martin E. & Company, Inc., 1979, ExecuComp 1979 review (Segal Associates, New York).

Siegel, S., 1956, Nonparametric statistics for the behavioral sciences (McGraw-Hill, New York).

Smith, C.W. and R.L. Watts, 1981, Incentive and tax effects of U.S. executive compensation plans, Unpublished working paper (Center for Research in Government Policy and Business, University of Rochester, Rochester, NY).

Thies, J.B., and L. Revsine, 1977, Capital expenditures data for inflation accounting studies, The Accounting Review 52, 216–221.

Tobin, J. and W.C. Brainard, 1977, Asset markets and the cost of capital, in: B. Belassa and R. Nelson, eds., Economic progress, private values, and public policy: Essays in honor of William Fellner (North-Holland, Amsterdam).

Towers, Perrin, Forester & Crosby, 1979, Top 100 compensation study 1979 (Towers, Perrin, Forester & Crosby, New York).

von Furstenberg, G., B.G. Malkiel and H.S. Watson, 1980, The distribution of investment between industries: A microeconomic application of the 'q' ratio, in: G. von Furstenberg, ed., Capital efficiency and growth (Ballinger, Cambridge, MA) 395–460.

Watts, R.L. and J.L. Zimmerman, 1978, Towards a positive theory of the determination of accounting standards, The Accounting Review 53, 112–134.

INCENTIVE EFFECTS OF STOCK PURCHASE PLANS*

Sanjai BHAGAT, James A. BRICKLEY and Ronald C. LEASE

University of Utah, Salt Lake City, UT 84112, USA

Received August 1984, final version received October 1984

Financial economists are interested in whether alternative compensation plans are adopted primarily for tax, incentive or signaling reasons. As most compensation plans have tax implications, examining for other effects is difficult. In this paper we examine the stock market reaction to employee stock purchase plans which are 'non-tax advantageous' and adopted for incentive/signaling reasons. The results suggest that (1) equity-based compensation schemes have a positive effect on shareholder wealth for reasons other than tax reduction, (2) a motive for adopting these plans is to align managerial and shareholder interests, and (3) equity ownership motivates key executives more than subordinate employees.

1. Introduction

The literature in financial economics increasingly has emphasized the 'agency problem' perhaps originally suggested by Adam Smith (1776) and more recently elaborated upon by Jensen and Meckling (1976), Fama (1980), Fama and Jensen (1983a,b), and others. Much of this literature focused on the incentive conflicts between management and shareholders. Within this context, authors such as Lewellen (1968), Smith and Watts (1982, 1983) and Eaton and Rosen (1983) suggested that equity-based managerial compensation schemes, such as stock and option plans, are important contracts that improve the alignment of management and shareholder interests.

While some authors emphasized the incentive effects of managerial compensation plans, others stressed tax implications.[1] For example, Hite and Long (1982) and Miller and Scholes (1982) demonstrated that most equity-based compensation schemes have tax advantages. The reduction of the total tax bill to firms and their employees makes it difficult to ascertain whether equity-based plans are adopted exclusively for tax reasons or whether incentive effects also

---

* This paper has benefited from helpful comments by Mike Bradley, Ken Eades, Gailen Hite, Prem Jain, Palani-Rajan Kadapakkam, Han Kim, Stan Kon, Bill Kracaw, Ron Masulis, John McConnell, Paul Healy (the referee) and participants of workshops at Purdue University, University of Michigan, University of South Florida, Washington State University, and University of Utah.

[1] Smith and Watts (1982) identify tax and incentive effects.

0304-405X/85/$3.30 © 1985, Elsevier Science Publishers B.V. (North-Holland)

Journal of Financial Economics 14 (1985) 195–215. North-Holland

are important. In addition, equity-based compensation schemes may be adopted to signal to the stock market management's optimism about the firm's future.[2]

Little empirical evidence on the importance of compensation contracts in motivating managerial behavior exists. Larcker (1983) provided evidence that 'performance plans' affect managerial investment decisions. However, Larcker qualified the interpretation of his results because of the lack of controls for possible tax effects.[3] Brickley, Bhagat and Lease (1985) examined the market reaction around the announcement of long-term managerial compensation plans. They found a positive market reaction to these announcements. However, all of the plans they examined had tax implications as well as other possible effects. Similarly, Tehranian and Waegelein (1984) found a positive stock market reaction around short-term bonus plans which also have been shown to have tax implications. To date no empirical study has examined the effects on shareholder wealth of alternative compensation schemes in isolation from tax effects.

This study examines the stock market reaction to stock purchase plans and IRS 423 plans. These plans fall into compensation categories which Miller and Scholes argue do not have tax advantages and are adopted for incentive or signaling reasons.[4] Since the plans are not tax-advantageous, the analysis allows us to study the effects of compensation plans in the absence of tax effects.

Some of the plans examined in this study are directed at top management, while other plans are geared toward lower-level management and other personnel. Since all of the plans are equity-based, we also are able to test the suggestion of Smith and Watts (1983) that share ownership is more likely to motivate top managers than lower-level employees.

The findings in this study support the notion that the market responds positively to stock purchase plans. This evidence is consistent with the hypothesis that equity-based compensation plans are important for reasons

---

[2] If management substitutes equity-based compensation for fixed compensation, they may lose if equity values subsequently decline. Therefore, signaling via the adoption of equity-based compensation schemes meets the Spence (1974) condition for a signaling equilibrium, i.e., the value of the attribute is correlated negatively with the cost of the signal. Note that equity-based compensation schemes often restrict management from immediately selling the stock, e.g., in restricted stock plans. This requirement limits the problem of false signaling and trying to sell the stock before any price decline.

[3] Larcker (1983) also qualified his results because his analysis did not clarify whether shifts in investment policies occurred because of performance plans or simply were coincident with the adoption of these plans. Further, he made several arguments to downplay tax effects and concluded that 'tax effects provide only a partial explanation of the empirical results and do not impede performance plan adoption' (p. 28).

[4] Sometimes IRS 423 plans are referred to as stock purchase plans. In this study when we refer to stock purchase plans we are referring to the stock purchase plans that are not qualified under the tax code [see Miller and Scholes (1982, pp. 192–195)]. IRS 423 plans will be referred to by their specific name. We use the term 'tax-neutral' to refer to either 'tax-neutral' or 'tax-disadvantageous' plans in the sense of Miller and Scholes.

besides tax reduction. Additional analysis provides evidence that the plans have important incentive effects in addition to any possible signaling effects. The less positive market reaction to stock purchase plans that include lower-level management and the zero market reaction that we observe at the announcement of the IRS 423 plans, which makes equity available at a discount to almost all employees, lends support to the Smith–Watts argument.

The following section discusses the plans analyzed in this study. The sample design is outlined in section 3. The fourth section presents empirical evidence on the incentive effects of stock purchase plans. Equity ownership as a motivating device for various levels of employees is analyzed in section 5. Section 6 summarizes the study.

2. Non-tax-motivated compensation plans

The two equity-based compensation plans examined in this study are stock purchase plans and IRS 423 plans. A discussion of these plans and their tax implications follows:

2.1. Stock purchase plans

Stock purchase plans are relatively straightforward. In the most common arrangement, the firm lends the employee funds to purchase the stock at fair market value. Miller and Scholes argue that even when the interest rate charged is below the market rate the plan has no tax consequences:[5]

> When the interest rate charged on the loan to the executive is below the going rate for comparable risks, as is typically the case, a valuable consideration is indeed being given to the executive. But it is a transfer of current (present) value, (not a deferred compensation in our sense), and it has no net tax consequences even for a zero interest rate loan (that is, the value of the interest subsidy doesn't have to be included by the recipient, but it can't be deducted by the firm, so there is no additional tax pie to be shared). With no particular tax-advantage to either party, the presumption that such stock purchase schemes are incentive-related is correspondingly strengthened.   (pp. 194–195)

[5] Long (1983) also demonstrates the tax neutrality of these plans. However, Long argues that under some circumstances the loan variety of a stock purchase plan may have a 'slight tax advantage' over a comparable increase in salary. Since 1972, individuals can deduct only interest expense incurred to hold investments up to the income earned from investments plus $10,000. If this constraint is binding for an executive, it may be tax-advantageous, relative to a salary increase, for the firm to loan money to the executive at below market rates to purchase stock. However, as Long notes, the comparison to straight salary is not valid. The proper comparison would be between stock purchase plans and restricted or phantom stock plans. In any case, Long's argument does not apply to the contribution type of stock purchase plan which we discuss.

Miller and Scholes go on to say:

> In sum, whatever may be the objectives of such stock purchase plans, reaping tax gains is not among them.   (p. 195)

In another variety of the stock purchase plan, the employee pays for only part of the stock, and the firm contributes the remainder. This case also has no tax benefits. The tax consequences are the same as for straight salary. The firm deducts its contribution and the employee includes it as taxable income.

As an example of the board's rationale for the adoption of stock purchase plans, the proxy statement of Univar Corporation of May 30, 1980 says:

> The Board of Directors has long believed that the overall objectives of its compensation program should include a currently competitive salary structure, bonus opportunities based on annual performance, and a long-term incentive program for our key executives. The Executive Stock Purchase Plan is directed toward this latter objective.
>
> The Executive Stock Purchase Plan provides for the purchase of Univar Corporation common stock by key management executives at the current market price on a purchase contract payable over ten years with interest at six percent per annum. Each purchase contract is secured by a pledge of the stock with full recourse against the executive purchaser.

2.2. IRS 423 plans

The employee stock purchase plans provided under Section 423 of the Internal Revenue Code are an option permitting employees to purchase the stock of their employer. The plans *must* be non-discriminatory with respect to full-time employees with the exception that officers, highly paid management personnel, and employees with less than two years of service may be excluded. Any employee who owns greater than or equal to five percent of the outstanding shares of the firm, by statute, is prohibited from participating in the plan. Therefore, if the plan excludes any full-time employee, it is most likely a member of top management.

Miller and Scholes argue that while tax advantages of option plans clearly arise when the employee's marginal tax rate exceeds that of the corporation, salary deferral schemes adopted by taxable corporations for employees in lower tax brackets presumably are adopted for incentive effects (p. 187). IRS 423 plans, adopted for a broad cross-section of employees, seem to qualify as being motivated for incentive reasons.

All of the employees granted the 423 options must have the same rights and privileges. However, the amount of stock that may be purchased may be based on a uniform percentage of compensation, e.g., ten percent, and the plan may limit the total shares that can be purchased by any one employee. Employees may not purchase more than $25,000 of stock under the plan in a given year unless they bought less than the limit in an earlier year and, therefore, have an accrual.

Companies usually offer 423 shares at a discount to the employee. However, the offer price must not be less than the smaller of 85 percent of the market price of the stock when the option is granted or 85 percent of the firm's market value at the time the option is exercised. If the discount is tied to the price at the grant date, the maximum period for exercising the option is five years from the data the option is granted. If the discount is based on the price at exercise, the maximum exercise period is 27 months from the date of the grant.

With the above requirements satisfied under Section 423, the option qualifies for special tax treatment. The employee is not taxed on the option at either the grant date or the exercise date and therefore delays paying taxes until the stock is sold. Employees receive maximum tax advantages if they do not dispose of the stock within two years of the date the option was granted or within one year of the exercise date. If these requirements are met, the difference between the option price and the market price at the time of the grant is taxed as ordinary income when the stock is sold. Any excess is taxed as capital gain. If the employee reaps maximum tax benefits, the employer receives no tax deductions. If, however, the employee does not satisfy the holding period requirements, he or she must include as ordinary income the difference between the market price at exercise and the exercise price. The corporation is entitled to the corresponding deduction.

As an example of the rationale used for adopting these plans, the Electronic Data System's (EDS) August 28, 1978 proxy statement states:

> The Plan is intended to afford the employees of the Company who are responsible for its success, an opportunity to acquire a proprietary interest in the Company, and thus to create in the employees an increased interest in and a greater concern for the welfare of the Company, by offering the employees an opportunity to purchase EDS Common Stock at 85 percent of market value, as described below, through regular payroll deductions up to a maximum of 10% of each participation employee's total compensation.

Firms incur definite costs when they provide stock ownership under 423 such as the discount offered and the lack of tax deductibility (assuming employees satisfy the minimum holding period requirements).[6] Boards, however, argue that the benefits provided by the incentive effects of these plans outweigh the costs and that having the plan available tc all employees is in the stockholders' interest.

---

[6] This argument assumes no adjustment in the employee's salary to reflect the tax benefit.

3. The sample design

A comprehensive list of over 600 New York Stock Exchange firms taking shareholder votes on stock purchase plans and IRS 423 plans from 1970 through 1982 was obtained from the Exchange. The list contained the name of each firm, the shareholder meeting date, and a brief description of the plans voted upon.

The list revealed that often a firm simultaneously took action on other compensation proposals at the same time a stock purchase plan or IRS 423 plan was introduced. Because the intent of our analysis was to isolate the market reaction to non-tax-motivated plans, we eliminated observations that included plans with tax implications.

For the firms satisfying the single compensation plan requirement, we requested the proxy statements containing a detailed description of the plan from the SEC in Washington, D.C.[7] Through this process, we obtained 222 proxy statements containing proposed compensation plans.

After a careful review of the proxy statements, we classified each observation as either 'clean' or 'contaminated'. An event was considered 'clean' if the proxy statement contained no other management-sponsored agenda item except the proposed compensation plan, the election of directors, and the ratification of auditors.[8] An event was considered 'contaminated' if the proxy statement included any other management-sponsored agenda time. Similar to DeAngelo and Rice (1983) and Bhagat and Brickley (1984), 'contaminated' events were eliminated because of the possible confounding effect they might have on the study.[9]

A review of the 'clean' proxies revealed that only a few qualified as tax-neutral stock purchase plans. A majority of the sample were qualified stock purchase plans under Section 423 of the IRS code. A third subset of the 'clean'

---

[7] Initially we requested proxy statements only for firms allocating common stock to their plans equal to at least four percent of the outstanding shares. This criterion was used to hold down the costs involved in collecting old proxy statements. The criterion also had the advantage of screening out smaller plans which were less likely to have a detectable market reaction. Upon a review of these proxies, we found we usually could determine which plans were stock purchase plans and which were IRS 423 plans by using the brief description included on the NYSE list. The stock purchase plans generally were referred to as 'key employee stock purchase plans' while the 423 plans had descriptions such as 'employee stock purchase plans'. As the stock purchase plans were rare, we attempted to obtain additional plans by requesting proxy statements which contained plans below the four percent cut-off but by title appeared to be stock purchase plans.

[8] As a practical matter we could not eliminate proxy statements containing the election of directors and the ratification of auditors. These agenda items are included in almost all proxy statements. Some proxy statements contained shareholder proposals. Since such proposals normally are defeated overwhelmingly, we did not classify such proposals as contaminating.

[9] Both studies use the same definition as we do for 'clean' events.

Table 1

Breakdown of the sample of proxy statements describing the stock purchase plans and IRS 423
plans from 1970 through 1982.

	Number of plans
Clean proxy statements[a]	
IRS 423 plans	69
Stock purchase plans	19
Other plans with tax implications	42
Total	130
Contaminated proxy statements[b]	92
Total proxy statements reviewed	222

[a]'Clean' proxy statements contain no agenda item except for the compensation plan, the election
of directors, ratification of auditors and shareholder proposals.
[b]Contaminated proxy statements include those not meeting the 'clean' criteria.

proxies did not qualify under IRS 423 but has tax implications. This category
consisted mainly of restricted stock purchase plans that typically allow selected
managers to purchase stock at a discount subject to restrictions on ownership
rights. Miller and Scholes showed these plans to be tax advantageous since the
discount is not included as taxable income to the executives or deductible by
the corporation until the restrictions lapse. The tax consequences of these plans
generally occur some years after the initial purchase.

Table 1 shows the total number of proxies reviewed and their classifications.
In total, we reviewed 222 proxy statements of firms proposing compensation
plans. Of these observations, 130 were 'clean' while 92 were 'contaminated'. Of
the 'clean' events, 19 were tax-neutral stock purchase plans, 69 were IRS 423
plans, and 42 were other plans with tax implications. This study focuses on the
tax-neutral stock purchase plans and the IRS 423 plans.

The relatively small number of stock purchase plans from a potential list of
222 proxies supports the findings of Long and the observation by Miller and
Scholes that stock purchase plans are 'relatively rare' (p. 194). Table 2 provides
a detailed description of this sample of 19 plans. As shown in panel A, 11 of
the 19 plans were for top executives only. Panel B lists the three plans that
included top management but also allowed participation by lower-level
managers. One plan (panel C) was directed at managers only and excluded
officers and directors. Finally, four plans included participation by a broad
range of management and non-management employees and are listed in
panel D.

In most of the plans (13), the firm lent the employee the funds to purchase
the common stock. In five cases, the participant paid for part of the purchase while the firm contributed the difference. Finally, in one plan the
purchase had to be funded fully by the employee on a cash basis. Of the 19

Table 2

Description of the characteristics of 19 stock purchase plans over the period 1970 through 1982.

Firm	Proxy mailing date	Plan type[a]	Action
(A) *Plan for key executives only* (11 firms)			
Con Agra	8/24/79	Full purchase	New plan
Con Agra	8/22/80	Loan	Amends existing plan to allow loans to executives
Frigitronics	8/29/80	Loan/discount	New plan
Gamble-Skogmo	5/23/75	Loan	New plan
General Cinema	3/14/75	Loan	New plan
Integon	12/31/74	Loan	New plan
Koracorp Industries	4/21/76	Loan	New plan
Pier 1 Imports	6/20/77	Loan	New plan
Tiger International	4/14/80	Loan	New plan[b]
Tiger International	5/7/82	Loan	New plan[b]
Univar	5/30/80	Loan	New plan
(B) *Plan for key executives and non-top level management personnel* (3 firms)			
Amcord (formerly American Cement)	4/2/76	Loan	Increasing shares under existing plan
Stokely Van Camp	8/29/79	Contribution	New plan
Stokely Van Camp	8/30/82	Contribution	Increasing shares under existing plan
(C) *Plan for managers excluding officers and directors* (1 firm)			
American Cement[c]	4/12/72	Loan	New plan
(D) *Plan for a broad range of employees* (*management and non-management*) *throughout the company, including top management* (4 firms)			
Armstrong Cork	3/14/80	Contribution	New plan
Chesapeake Corp. of Virginia	3/22/74	Contribution	New plan
Dravo	3/27/75	Loan	New plan
Measurex	3/19/80	Contribution	New plan

[a] Plan types include: *Contribution* = participant contributes part of the purchase price and the firm contributes part; the firm's contributions are taxable at ordinary income rates in the year of the award for the participant and the firm deducts the contribution. *Loan* = company loans participant money to buy shares at the fair market value. *Loan/discount* = same as the loan variety except shares are sold at a discount from fair market value; the discount is taxable for the participant at ordinary income rates in the year the purchase is made and deductible by the corporation. *Full purchase* = the firm sells shares to the executive at fair market value on a cash basis.

[b] Tiger International entered into similar loan agreements prior to this plan. However, this plan represents a new agreement.

[c] In 1972 American Cement did not allow officers and directors to participate in the plan. This rule changed by the time of the 1976 amendment.

Table 3

Descriptive statistics for 69 IRS 423 plans over the period 1970 through 1982.[a]

Statistic (1)	Mean value (2)	Standard deviation (3)	Median value (4)
Number of shares authorized (in 000's)	1,285	4,840	300
Percent of shares authorized to total shares outstanding	7.88	4.09	7.20
Percent discount in plan price from market price	12.16	4.44	15.00
Shares authorized per employee[b]	91.7	105.4	59.4
Market value of shares authorized per employee	$1635	$1698	$1037

[a] To be included in this sample, IRS 423 plans had to represent at least four percent of the outstanding common stock.

[b] The total number of employees for each firm was obtained from *Moody's Handbooks*. The number in each case is an approximation of the number of employees eligible for the plan.

plans, 16 were new programs while three were amendments to existing stock purchase arrangements.[10]

Table 3 presents descriptive statistics for the sample of 69 IRS 423 plans. Column 1 identifies the statistic, while column 2 gives the mean value. Columns 3 and 4 present the standard deviation and the median values, respectively. On average, 1,285,000 shares were proposed for these plans (median = 300,000 shares). The plans averaged 7.9 percent of the total shares outstanding.[11] The average discount offered from the market value of the stock was 12.2 percent. On average, firms proposed 92 shares for each employee; the average market value of the shares per employee was $1,635.[12]

---

[10] Why a board decides to propose stock purchase plans after a history of not utilizing this type of compensation scheme provides for interesting speculation. Has the firm been performing poorly and therefore the board proposes the plan to help motivate management? Or are the plans adopted following a major change in the board or top management? Perhaps a new leadership group stimulates the proposal.

We provide an answer to the first possibility in section 4.3. No abnormal performance was found. Regarding the second hypothesis, we searched the *Wall Street Journal Index* for news releases on our sample of firms for three years prior to the adoption date. Of the 19 events itemized in table 2, four plan adoptions or modifications followed significant board or management turnovers in the year of or two years prior to the event. These events were for the Amcord event of April 2, 1976, the Con Agra event of August 24, 1979, the Dravo event of March 27, 1975 and the Stokley Van Camp event of August 29, 1979.

[11] Recall that to be included in the sample of IRS 423 plans, a plan had to constitute at least four percent of the outstanding shares.

[12] The number of employees for each firm was obtained from *Moody's Handbooks*. This number is used as an approximation for the total number of employees eligible under each plan.

4. Empirical evidence on the incentive effects of stock purchase plans

In this section, we discuss the methodology utilized and present the results of our analysis of the market reaction around the announcement of stock purchase plans. We discuss (1) the methodology, (2) the announcement period returns for the stock purchase plans, and (3) our attempt to distinguish between signaling and incentive explanations for the positive market reaction to the stock purchase plans which we find.

4.1. Methodology

To test the null hypothesis that the announcement of stock purchase plans has no impact on shareholder wealth, we utilized the comparison period returns approach (CPR) developed by Masulis (1980) and later modified by Dann (1981). Brown and Warner (1985) compared alternative event study methodology and found the CPR approach at least as powerful as the other approaches given no event clustering in calendar time. See Dann (1981) for a detailed description of the approach.

The statistical significance of the two-day announcement period average stock return was tested using both a t-test and a non-parametric sign test. The announcement period was defined as the official proxy mailing date (contained in every proxy statement) and the following trading day.[13] In the t-test, the null hypothesis is that the two-day announcement period average return is equal to the average of the 75 non-overlapping two-day returns from the comparison period (day -170 to day -21 relative to the announcement date).[14] For the non-parametric (Fisher) sign test, the null hypothesis is that the number of positive two-day announcement period returns equals the average number of positive two-day returns for the non-overlapping two-day intervals in the comparison period.

4.2. Stock returns around the announcement of stock purchase plans

Table 4 presents the time series of average unadjusted returns for 41 trading days centered around the proxy mailing date for the sample of 19 stock purchase plans. Column 1 gives the event day. Column 2 shows the average daily return on each of these days. The cumulative return is reported in column 3, while columns 4 through 6 reflect the percent of the returns that are negative, zero, and positive.

---

[13] This is the same announcement period as used by Bhagat (1983), DeAngelo and Rice (1983) and Bhagat and Brickley (1984) in analyzing proxy statement disclosures.

[14] The standard deviation used in this t-test is calculated from the 75 non-overlapping two-day portfolio returns from the comparison period. This t-test assumes normality and equal variances for the distributions generating announcement period and comparison period two-day portfolio returns. Brown and Warner (1985) note that this t-statistic is 'reasonably well specified' for a portfolio with as few as five securities.

Table 4

Common stock rates of return over the 41-trading-day period around the proxy mailing date for the 19 stock purchase plans over the period 1970 through 1982.

Event day (1)	Mean return (%) (2)	Cumulative return (%) (3)	% negative (4)	% zero (5)	% positive (6)
−20	0.09	0.09	47.4	21.1	31.6
−19	−0.26	−0.17	52.6	5.3	42.1
−18	−0.38	−0.55	42.1	15.8	42.1
−17	−0.72	−1.27	36.8	31.6	31.6
−16	−0.51	−1.78	57.9	15.8	26.3
−15	−0.06	−1.84	31.6	31.6	36.8
−14	−0.45	−2.29	47.4	31.6	21.1
−13	−0.23	−2.52	36.8	31.6	31.6
−12	0.12	−2.40	36.8	15.8	47.4
−11	1.16	−1.24	26.3	31.6	42.1
−10	0.49	−0.75	26.3	36.8	36.8
−9	0.67	−0.09	31.6	21.1	47.4
−8	0.13	0.05	47.4	26.3	26.3
−7	−0.07	−0.03	42.1	15.8	42.1
−6	0.41	0.38	26.3	26.3	47.4
−5	0.34	0.72	21.1	31.6	47.4
−4	0.59	1.31	36.8	21.1	42.1
−3	0.32	1.63	52.6	31.6	15.8
−2	−0.83	0.80	42.1	26.3	31.6
−1	0.53	1.33	42.1	15.8	42.1
0	1.81	3.13	21.1	15.8	63.2
1	1.62	4.75	21.1	31.6	47.4
2	−0.01	4.74	36.8	36.8	26.3
3	−0.04	4.70	52.6	21.1	26.3
4	−0.23	4.47	47.4	10.5	42.1
5	−0.74	3.73	52.6	21.1	26.3
6	−1.04	2.69	57.9	21.1	21.1
7	0.39	3.08	36.8	5.3	57.9
8	0.67	3.75	42.1	5.3	52.6
9	0.64	4.39	26.3	21.1	52.6
10	−0.18	4.21	31.6	26.3	42.1
11	0.43	4.64	26.3	21.1	52.6
12	0.24	4.88	42.1	10.5	47.4
13	−0.42	4.45	57.9	10.5	31.6
14	0.67	5.12	21.1	31.6	47.4
15	−0.05	5.07	27.8	27.8	44.4
16	−0.84	4.23	42.1	36.8	21.1
17	0.75	4.98	42.1	5.3	52.6
18	0.63	5.61	31.6	36.8	31.6
19	0.01	5.62	31.6	21.1	47.4
20	−0.14	5.47	47.4	15.8	36.8

The day 0 (proxy mailing date) average return was 1.81 percent and the day +1 return was 1.62 percent. In contrast, the average return for the 150-day comparison period from day −170 to day −21 was 0.19 percent. With a t-statistic of 3.43, the null hypothesis that the two-day announcement period average return equaled the mean of the non-overlapping two-day returns from the comparison period can be rejected at the one-percent level of significance.[15]

An analysis of the frequency distribution for the announcement period returns for the individual observations in the sample indicated that the results of the t-test are not driven by a few outliers. The number of positive returns was 15 compared to an average of 10.4 positive returns per two-day interval during the comparison period. The binomial probability of 15 or more positive returns using the average proportion of positive returns in the comparison period (55.6%) was 2.6 percent.[16]

The results suggest that compensation schemes that include shares of common stock can, at least in some circumstances, increase shareholder wealth for reasons other than reducing taxes. In the next section we provide evidence to distinguish whether incentive effects are an important component of these plans over and above any pure signaling effects.[17]

4.3. Incentive vs. signaling effects of stock purchase plans

The observed positive market reaction to stock purchase plans is consistent with both an incentive and signaling argument. The market may be reacting to a change in contracting which improves the alignment of management and shareholder interests or responding to a signal by management of an improvement in the firm's outlook. In the latter case, the market may be reacting to the plan purely for signaling reasons even if the plan has no incentive effects.

---

[15] For completeness we conducted the test using returns adjusted by the standard market model. The market model was estimated using the 150 daily returns from day −170 through day −21 relative to the announcement date, and the equally weighted CRSP market index. The t-statistic using market model adjusted returns also was significant at the one-percent level.

We repeated the analysis eliminating five plans. These exclusions included the three plans which were amendments to existing stock purchase arrangements and two plans (Tiger International) where we knew similar agreements existed before the new plan was adopted. The results were consistent with those for the entire sample – an announcement period raw return of 3.63 percent. We also reviewed the *Wall Street Journal Index* around the time of the announcement of each plan. Three of the plans had contemporaneous news releases which may have affected the announcement period returns. After eliminating these 'contaminated' plans, the announcement period raw return was 3.90 percent.

[16] The median announcement period return was 1.82 percent. The median for the announcement period was significantly different from that of the comparison period at the one percent level using the Wilcoxon signed-rank test. This test is distribution-free. See Hollander and Wolfe (1973, pp. 27–33) for a discussion of this test.

[17] Our results do not suggest that all compensation plans involving stock ownership are beneficial to existing shareholders. Shavell (1979) and Smith and Watts (1983) argue that if a manager is compensated overly with shares, the manager may become more risk-averse than desired by shareholders.

Distinguishing between these two explanations is difficult because the major predictions of each hypothesis are equivalent. Each explanation predicts a positive market response to the plans plus a subsequent improvement in cash flows over prior expectations. Since the two explanations are not mutually exclusive, the effects may be reinforcing. In this section we present evidence which collectively provides at least weak support that incentive effects are present in stock purchase plans above and beyond any pure signaling effect.

First, we examined the stated motive in the proxy statements for the adoption of each plan. While a board may misrepresent the intended purpose of the plan, e.g., to say the plans were being adopted for incentive reasons when they actually were adopted to signal the stock market, no obvious reason exists why a board would do so. In 17 of the 19 cases, the board stated that its motive was to improve managerial incentives. A typical reason for adopting a plan was to provide an effective means of attracting, retaining and motivating key employees whose performance is of great importance to the continued success of the company. In two cases, no motive was given.

Second, we examined whether privately-held firms have stock purchase plans. While a privately-held firm may adopt a stock purchase plan to signal creditors, e.g., their bank, concerning the firm's outlook, the plans are not likely to be adopted to signal the general stock market.[18] Finding stock purchase plans among privately-held firms, therefore, would provide additional evidence that other effects besides general market signaling are important.

We utilized Dunn and Bradstreet's 1983 *Billion Dollar Directory* to compile a list of privately-held firms to survey concerning stock purchase plans. Ninety-nine non-insurance, non-publicly-traded firms were identified with sales over $400 million. Each of these companies was sent a questionnaire concerning whether or not they have or ever had a stock purchase plan.[19] Thirty-nine firms responded. Six were co-ops which had no common stock. Of the 33 responses from firms with privately-held stock, seven (21.2%) currently had, or had at one time, stock purchase plans.

Given the relative infrequency of these plans among listed companies, we did not expect to find a large percentage among privately-held firms. However, the *existence* of a substantial portion with stock purchase plans within this

---

[18]At least two reasons explain why adoption of stock purchase plans may not provide a useful signal to creditors. First, creditors may not be concerned about the firm's future outlook in general. They are concerned only about those future states of the world in which the firm is bankrupt, i.e., the company's cash flows are in the left tail of the distribution. The stock-owning managers, on the other hand, are harmed at least equally in bankruptcy but are increasingly better off as the cash flows move to the right in the cash flow distribution. Hence, the interests of creditors and stock-owning managers are likely to be coincidental for only a small portion of the distribution of expected cash flows. Second, if a privately-held firm is interested in signaling creditors regarding the alignment of creditors and managers' interests, it could adopt a 'bond purchase plan'

[19]The questionnaire provided a definition of the stock purchase plans. To encourage responses, we paid the return postage, guaranteed anonymity to respondents, and offered to provide a summary of the results.

sample of privately-held firms provided additional support for the position that these plans are not adopted solely to provide a signal to the stock market.[20]

Finally, we analyzed cumulative abnormal returns prior to the adoption of each plan. Cone (1984) developed a model for financial signaling which predicts that management will tend to signal only after a period of poor performance. In his model, shareholders have the right to fire managers. Managers find it advantageous to bear the costs of signaling only if the firm has been doing poorly and management is in jeopardy of being fired. For the analysis we estimated the standard market model for each firm using month -90 through month -31, relative to the month the proxy statement was mailed, as the estimation period. Then we examined cumulative residuals for our portfolio of 19 firms over the 30-month period, month -30 through month -1. The cumulative abnormal return over this interval for our portfolio of firms was 11.08 percent. The t-statistic of 0.91 did not allow us to reject the null hypothesis of no abnormal performance. The finding tends to further reinforce the incentive hypothesis for plan adoption.

Given our sample and data, distinguishing completely between incentive and signaling arguments for explaining the market reaction to stock purchase plans is impossible. We interpret the evidence as supporting the position that incentive effects are an important motivation for these plans. However, as the two effects are not mutually exclusive, it is possible that both effects are important. The remainder of this paper makes no further attempt to distinguish between the two hypotheses. Rather the data is used to test a hypothesis concerning the effectiveness of equity ownership as an incentive device for different types of employees.

5. Equity ownership as an employee motivating arrangement

Smith and Watts (1983) suggested that since the decisions of top managers are more likely to affect stock price than actions of lower-level employees, stock ownership will motivate key executives more than subordinate personnel. Among lower-level employees a free-rider problem [or a 'cheap-rider' problem as suggested in a different context by Stigler (1974)] may exist. Each employee will hope that the group collectively produces more to increase stock price. However, individuals will have a limited incentive to participate personally because of the small marginal effect they individually contribute to share value. An implication of this reasoning is that equity ownership is more likely to help control agency problems between top managers and shareholders than agency problems between subordinate employees and shareholders, e.g., general effort problems.

---

[20] Those respondents who provided a reason for the use of the plans indicated that they were adopted for incentive reasons.

Table 5

Results of an analysis of variance test of announcement period returns classified by (1) whether the plan was for key executives only, or (2) allowed broader employee participation for the 19 stock purchase plans over the period 1970 through 1982.[a]

	Sample size	Mean unadjusted return (%)	Mean market adjusted return (%)[b]	F-ratio/one-tail p-value (%)	
				Unadjusted returns	Adjusted returns
Group 1 Plan includes key executives only	11	4.86	2.96	3.98/3.1	0.92/17.5
Group 2 Plan allows broader employee participation	8	1.42	1.40		

[a] For this analysis, the announcement period is the proxy mailing date and the following trading day.
[b] Using the standard market model estimated by OLS. The estimation period was day -170 through day -21 relative to the proxy mailing date.

In this section we provide empirical evidence on the effectiveness of equity ownership as a motivating device for various levels of employees. First, we examine cross-sectionally the announcement period stock returns around stock purchase plans based on the categories of participants. Second, we analyze the stock market returns around the introduction of IRS 423 plans. As 423 plans appear geared to reducing the general effort problem throughout an organization, these plans provide an interesting comparison to plans which are directed to management–shareholder agency problems.

5.1. Cross-sectional analysis of announcement period returns around stock purchase plans based on the plan's target groups

Table 5 presents an analysis of variance of the announcement period returns for the sample of stock purchase plans classified by whether the plan is for key executives (group 1) only or allows for broader employee participation (group 2). Both unadjusted and standard market model adjusted returns are reported. Analysis of the data in this table assumes that a plan limited to key executives is directed toward reducing an agency problem between top management and shareholders. In contrast, when lower-level employees are included in the plan, a more general agency problem is assumed to be addressed. These assumptions appear reasonable since the proxies do not single out executives as a special target group in this latter group.

Table 6

Results of an analysis of variance test of announcement period returns classified by (1) plan includes key executives only or key executives and other management personnel, or (2) plan excludes key executives or allows broad participation by management and non-management personnel for the 19 stock purchase plans over the period 1970 through 1982.[a]

	Sample size	Mean unadjusted return (%)	Mean market adjusted return (%)[b]	F-ratio/one-tail p-value (%)	
				Unadjusted returns	Adjusted returns
Group 1 Plan includes key executives only or key executives plus other managers	14	4.35	2.65	3.29/4.4	0.49/24.7
Group 2 Plan excludes key executives or allows broad participation by management and non-management personnel	5	0.79	1.36		

[a] For this analysis, the announcement period is the proxy mailing date and the following trading day.

[b] Using the standard market model estimated by OLS. The estimation period was day -170 through day -21 relative to the proxy mailing date.

The mean announcement period return using unadjusted returns is 4.86 percent for group 1 plans directed toward top management versus 1.42 percent for group 2 plans. The significance level of the difference between these means using the standard F-test is 3.1 percent (one-tail).[21] The significance level (one-tail) for the Wilcoxon rank sum test is 3.2 percent. Using adjusted returns, the average return is 2.96 percent for the top managerial plans and 1.40 percent for the other plans. The means are not significantly different at conventional levels using either the F-test (p-value = 17.5 percent) or the Wilcoxon rank sum test (p-value = 18.1 percent).[22]

Table 6 groups the observations somewhat differently to gain further insights into the differences in the market reaction between plans. Group 1 consists of plans directed exclusively at management – either top management exclusively or all management. Group 2 contains plans that either exclude top management or include non-management employees. The mean for the first group using unadjusted returns is 4.35 percent compared to 0.79 percent for the

[21] A one-tail probability is used since the Smith–Watts hypothesis predicts a larger return for the plans directed at top management.

[22] We are not aware of any study that investigates how the power of cross-sectional tests compares using adjusted and unadjusted returns. Therefore, we are not sure which of the two tests is more reliable.

second group. The significance level of the F-test is 4.4 percent and for the Wilcoxon rank sum test is 6.3 percent, both one-tailed. Using adjusted returns the means are 2.65 percent and 1.36 percent for the two groups, respectively. The means are not significantly different at conventional levels using either test.

Given the small sample sizes for this section of the analysis, and the mixed results using adjusted and unadjusted returns, we interpret the evidence as providing only weak support for the Smith and Watts argument. For more powerful evidence on this hypothesis, IRS 423 plans are examined next.

5.2. Stock returns around IRS 423 plans

IRS 423 plans appear directed toward general incentive problems throughout an organization. The motivation contained in the proxy statement (see section 2.2) for these plans suggests the objective is to increase the stock ownership among a broad cross-section of employees to provide increased incentive to work for the success of the company. These plans most likely exclude top management if any full-time employee group is eliminated.

Table 7 presents the time series of unadjusted returns for 41 trading days centered around the proxy mailing date for the sample of 69 IRS 423 plans. The day 0 (proxy mailing date) average return was 0.13 percent and the day + 1 return was − 0.14 percent. The t-statistic of − 0.27 does not allow rejection of the null hypothesis that the two-day announcement period return equaled the mean (0.13 percent) of the non-overlapping two-day returns from the comparison period (day − 170 to day − 21). The non-parametric sign test also does not allow rejection of the null hypothesis.

In case we mistimed the announcement date for these plans, we also conducted an event study on alternative announcement dates and between possible announcement dates.[23] For 25 of the observations we were able to identify the date where the board first proposed the plan. The average two-day return using the board meeting date and the following trading day as an announcement period was 0.00 percent. Neither the t-test or sign test allowed rejection of the null hypothesis. In addition, we examined returns on the date which the shareholders met and ratified the plan. The average announcement period return for this date and the following trading day was 0.96 percent which also was insignificant using either test. Finally, using the procedure of Dodd and Warner (1983), we analyzed cumulative residuals between the board date and proxy mailing date and between the proxy mailing date and the

---

[23] While information contained in proxy statements appears to be released to the public around the official proxy mailing date, some question exists if the information is always released for all firms on this date. See Brickley, Bhagat and Lease (1985) and Linn and McConnell (1983) for a discussion of announcement dates for proxy statement disclosures.

Table 7

Common stock rates of return over the 41-trading-day period around the proxy mailing date for
the 69 IRS 423 plans over the period 1970 through 1982.

Event day (1)	Mean return (%) (2)	Cumulative return (%) (3)	% negative (4)	% zero (5)	% positive (6)
−20	−0.04	−0.04	36.2	17.4	46.4
−19	0.13	0.09	40.6	11.6	47.8
−18	−0.08	0.01	44.9	15.9	39.1
−17	0.10	0.11	37.7	21.7	40.6
−16	−0.27	−0.16	49.3	10.1	40.6
−15	0.62	0.46	40.6	14.5	44.9
−14	−0.06	0.40	44.9	18.8	36.2
−13	0.54	0.95	42.0	13.0	44.9
−12	0.22	1.17	42.0	21.7	36.2
−11	−0.09	1.08	46.4	17.4	36.2
−10	0.24	1.32	40.6	14.5	44.9
−9	−0.09	1.23	33.3	26.1	40.6
−8	−0.21	1.02	44.9	18.8	36.2
−7	0.16	1.19	46.4	13.0	40.6
−6	0.43	1.62	37.7	17.4	44.9
−5	0.27	1.89	36.2	21.7	42.0
−4	−0.25	1.64	47.8	11.6	40.6
−3	0.13	1.77	40.6	18.8	40.6
−2	0.28	2.05	37.7	21.7	40.6
−1	−0.15	1.90	40.6	23.2	36.2
0	0.13	2.03	44.9	13.0	42.0
1	−0.14	1.90	44.9	20.3	34.8
2	0.65	2.55	30.4	17.4	52.2
3	0.02	2.57	41.2	13.2	45.6
4	0.40	2.96	43.5	21.7	34.8
5	−0.25	2.71	53.6	14.5	31.9
6	−0.32	2.39	44.9	13.0	42.0
7	0.42	2.81	42.0	21.7	36.2
8	−0.03	2.78	44.9	13.0	42.0
9	0.51	3.29	27.5	23.2	49.3
10	−0.10	3.19	46.4	20.3	33.3
11	0.36	3.55	46.4	15.9	37.7
12	−0.24	3.31	46.4	21.7	31.9
13	−0.03	3.28	42.0	15.9	42.0
14	0.37	3.65	30.4	21.7	47.8
15	−0.06	3.59	39.1	21.7	39.1
16	−0.05	3.54	36.2	18.8	44.9
17	−0.15	3.39	40.6	21.7	37.7
18	−0.03	3.36	40.6	15.9	43.5
19	−0.26	3.10	56.5	18.8	24.6
20	0.10	3.20	39.1	18.8	42.0

shareholder meeting date.[24] Consistent with the other results, no abnormal performance was found.[25]

Based on the three possible announcement dates of the IRS 423 plans, and the cumulative abnormal returns between these dates, the market appears indifferent to these plans. However, to explore the impact of these plans further, we examined the market reaction as a function of the size of the plan expressed as a percentage of the total outstanding shares of the firm, i.e., their 'relative size'. Perhaps the smaller plans in our sample could have a market reaction too small to be detected by our methodology.

To see if the announcement period returns were a function of the relative size of the plan, we conducted two tests. In the first test, a simple regression, we used the two-day announcement period return around the proxy mailing date as the dependent variable and relative size as the independent variable. The coefficient (-0.161) for relative size using unadjusted returns was negative and has a t-value of -1.988 that was significant at about the five-percent level (a p-value of 5.09 percent). Using market model adjusted returns, the coefficient of -0.081 had a t-value of -1.104 and a significance level of 27.37 percent.

The second test, a non-parametric test, also tested the relation between the proxy mailing date return and the relative size of the 423 plan. A Spearman rank correlation coefficient for these variables was determined for the 69 firms. The correlation coefficient using unadjusted returns was -0.270 and was significant at the 2.48 percent level. Using adjusted returns the correlation coefficient was -0.181 with a significance level of 13.7 percent.

The results of the analysis of IRS 423 plans supports the notion that, in contrast to stock purchase plans, the market does not react positively and *may* even react negatively to larger IRS 423 plans. This contrast of the market reaction to IRS 423 plans with the market reaction to other managerial incentive plans which provide equity ownership is interesting. Brickley, Bhagat and Lease (1985) analyzed a broad range of managerial stock option plans and stock ownership plans and found a positive and significant market reaction to their introduction.

When viewed in the context of the other evidence in this study and that of Brickley, Bhagat and Lease, the results in this section provide further support for the Smith and Watts argument, i.e., that equity ownership is more likely to motivate top management than lower-level personnel. Why boards of directors

---

[24] See the appendix of Dodd and Warner (1983) for a discussion of the statistical technique which we employed.

[25] The average cumulative residual from the board date through the proxy mailing date was -0.24 percent (Z-statistic $= -0.275$). The average cumulative residual from the proxy mailing date through the shareholder meeting date was 0.70 percent (Z-statistic $= 0.710$).

adopt IRS 423 plans given the apparent non-positive stock market reaction to larger plans is unclear and is a question for further study.[26]

6. Summary and conclusions

This study examines the stock market reaction to equity-based compensation plans which Miller and Scholes suggest are not adopted for tax reasons. These plans are stock purchase plans and IRS 423 plans. The former compensation scheme can be targeted to any employee group within an organization, e.g., top management only, while the latter plans must be non-discriminatory with respect to full-time employees except that top management may be excluded.

The positive market reaction observed at the announcement of stock purchase plans suggests that this form of compensation scheme can increase shareholder wealth for reasons other than tax reduction. Incentive and/or signaling effects seem to be present. Our additional analysis suggests incentive effects are important.

Smith and Watts suggest that equity-based compensation schemes are more likely to motivate top managers than lower-level employees. This hypothesis is tested with the identified plans in this study. The stock purchase plans directed toward key executives have significantly larger announcement period returns than the other plans using unadjusted market returns but insignificantly different returns using adjusted returns. The result weakly supports the Smith–Watts suggestion.

For the IRS 423 plans directed to employees throughout the organization, a zero market reaction occurs at the announcement date. This result, in conjunction with the stock purchase plan evidence and other research, provides additional support for the Smith–Watts contention.

References

Bhagat, S., 1983, The effect of pre-emptive right amendments on shareholder wealth, Journal of Financial Economics 12, 289–310.

Bhagat, S. and J.A. Brickley, 1984, Cumulative voting: The value of minority shareholder voting rights, Journal of Law and Economics 27, 339–365.

Brickley, J.A., S. Bhagat and R.C. Lease, 1985, The impact of long-range management incentive compensation plans on shareholder wealth, Journal of Accounting and Economics 7, 115–129.

Brown, S.J. and J.B. Warner, 1985, Using daily stock returns in event studies, Journal of Financial Economics 14, 3–31.

Cone, K., 1984, Information and outside control: A model of financial signalling, Unpublished manuscript (University of Chicago, Chicago, IL).

Dann, L.Y., 1981, Common stock repurchases: An analysis of returns to bondholders and shareholders, Journal of Financial Economics 9, 113–138.

---

[26] One possibility is that the firm views the larger plans as a major source of raising equity capital. A growing body of empirical literature suggests that on average equity-increasing events lower share price. Perhaps in some cases the board views IRS 423 plans as the least costly method (among costly alternatives) for raising equity. Why the market appears to react negatively to new equity issues is, of course, an interesting question by itself.

DeAngelo, H. and E.M. Rice, 1983, Anti-takeover charter amendments and stockholder wealth, Journal of Financial Economics 11, 329–359.

Dodd, P. and J.B. Warner, 1983, On corporate governance: A study of proxy contests, Journal of Financial Economics 11, 401–438.

Eaton, J. and H.S. Rosen, 1983, Agency, delayed compensation, and the structure of executive remuneration, Journal of Finance 38, 1489–1505.

Fama, E.F., 1980, Agency problems and the theory of the firm, Journal of Political Economy 88, 288–307.

Fama, E.F. and M.C. Jensen, 1983a, Separation of ownership and control, Journal of Law and Economics 26, 301–326.

Fama, E.F. and M.C. Jensen, 1983b, Agency problems and residual claims, Journal of Law and Economics 26, 327–350.

Hite, G.L. and M.S. Long, 1982, Taxes and executive stock options, Journal of Accounting and Economics 4, 3–14.

Hollander, M. and D. Wolfe, 1973, Nonparametric statistical methods (Wiley, New York).

Jensen, M.C. and W.H. Meckling, 1976, Theory of the firm: Managerial behavior, agency costs and ownership structure, Journal of Financial Economics 3, 305–360.

Larcker, D.F., 1983, The association between performance plan adoption and corporate capital investment, Journal of Accounting and Economics 5, 3–30.

Lewellen, W.G., 1968, Executive compensation in large industrial corporations (National Bureau of Economic Research, New York).

Linn, S.C. and J.J. McConnell, 1983, An empirical investigation of anti-takeover amendments on common stock prices, Journal of Financial Economics 11, 361–399.

Long, M.S., 1983, Taxes and executive stock options: The early history, Unpublished manuscript (Federal Home Loan Bank Board, Washington, DC).

Masulis, R.W., 1980, The effects of capital structure change on security prices: A study of exchange offers, Journal of Financial Economics 8, 139–178.

Miller, M.H. and M.S. Scholes, 1982, Executive compensation, taxes and incentives, in: W.F. Sharpe and C.M. Cootner, eds., Financial economics: Essays in honor of Paul Cootner, 179–201.

Shavell, S., 1979, Risk sharing and incentives in the principal and agent relationship, Bell Journal of Economics 10, 55–73.

Smith, A., 1776, The wealth of nations, Cannan ed., 1937 (Modern Library, New York).

Smith, C.W. and R.L. Watts, 1982, Incentive and tax effects of U.S. executive compensation plans, Australian Journal of Management 7, 139–157.

Smith, C.W. and R.L. Watts, 1983, The structure of executive compensation contracts and the control of management, Unpublished manuscript (University of Rochester, Rochester, NY).

Spence, A.M., 1974, Market signaling: Information transfer in hiring and related processes (Harvard University Press, Cambridge, MA).

Stigler, G.J., 1974, Free riders and collective action: An appendix to theories of economic regulation, Bell Journal of Economics and Management Science 5, 359–363.

Tehranian, H. and J.F. Waegelein, 1984, Market reaction to short term executive compensation plan adoption, Unpublished manuscript (Boston College, Boston, MA).

THE IMPACT OF LONG-RANGE MANAGERIAL
COMPENSATION PLANS ON SHAREHOLDER WEALTH*

James A. BRICKLEY, Sanjai BHAGAT and Ronald C. LEASE

University of Utah, Salt Lake City, UT 84112, USA

Received December 1983, final version received August 1984

This study examines the stock price reaction around the announcement of proposed changes in long-term managerial compensation packages. The evidence indicates that on average these plans are met with positive market reactions, i.e., shareholder wealth increases. Further, we are unable to differentiate the market reaction to various types of long-range compensation schemes. This result is consistent with the notion that firms with different characteristics will resolve their managerial compensation requirements differently. Thus no particular compensation package necessarily dominates all others.

1. Introduction

Economists often stress the importance of either incentive or tax features in the design of managerial compensation plans. Authors such as Smith and Watts (1982, 1983) view alternative compensation schemes as important contracts which can improve the alignment of management and securityholder interests and therefore reduce agency costs. Others such as Miller and Scholes (1982) and Hite and Long (1982) think compensation plans generally are designed to provide significant tax benefits. When boards of directors ask shareholders to vote on changes in compensation arrangements for managers, they often stress both the incentive and tax benefits.

While the positive features of compensation contracts are emphasized by many, others oppose certain types of managerial compensation schemes. These groups do not view all compensation arrangements as being in the share-holders' best interest. For example, some shareholder groups, like the ones led by the Gilbert brothers, argue that option plans can harm shareholders by diluting their interests and rewarding managers unjustifiably for improvements in share price. Often an increase in share price might be due more to

*We would like to thank Jeff Coles, Larry Dann, Linda Gorman, Gregg Jarrell, Mike Jensen, Paul Malatesta, Steve Manaster, John McConnell, Ed Rice, Jim Schallheim, Stephen Walsh, Jerry Warner, Jerry Zimmerman, the referee, Richard Ruback, and the participants of workshops at the University of Utah, the University of Washington, and the Conference participants at the University of Rochester for helpful comments.

Journal of Accounting and Economics 7 (1985) 115–129. North-Holland

improvements in the overall economy than managerial effort. Excessive compensation has been the subject of numerous law suits filed against management by shareholders.[1] As another example, former Chairman Patton of the Presidential Commission on Executive, Legislative and Judicial Salaries argued recently that 'CEO salaries now have an Alice-in-Wonderland logic... and that company directors should accept the fact that simply throwing money at top management may be doing more harm than good' [Patton (1983, pp. 24–25)].

Scant empirical evidence exists on whether or not a board is acting in the interest of shareholders when it proposes new compensation schemes. Both Larcker (1983) and Bhagat, Brickley and Lease (1985) provide evidence which supports the hypothesis that alterations in managerial compensation plans can increase shareholder wealth. However, these studies are limited in that their sample sizes are small and each study analyzes only one type of management compensation plan. Larcker examines performance plans, while Bhagat et al. analyze employee stock purchase plans. Both studies utilize samples with less than 30 observations (Bhagat et al. also examine a larger sample of non-managerial compensation plans).

Recent evidence by Bhagat (1983), Bhagat and Brickley (1984), Bradley and Wakeman (1983), Dann and DeAngelo (1983), and DeAngelo and Rice (1983) suggests that management sometimes takes action which decreases shareholder wealth. This evidence leads to the question of whether board actions on compensation plans are wealth-increasing events from the shareholders' perspective.

This paper examines the impact on shareholder wealth of a variety of long-range compensation plans proposed by the board of directors and presented to the shareholders for ratification. Our results are consistent with the hypothesis that these plans increase shareholder wealth. Further, we find no differential market reaction across various types of long-range compensation plans. This finding suggests that various firms face different incentive and/or tax situations and design their compensation packages accordingly. Since we do not differentiate between incentive effects and tax effects, both factors, either separately or jointly, could explain our results. In addition, a proposed change in the management compensation package may provide a favorable 'signal' to the market. Managements' desire to have a bigger equity stake in the firm may be viewed as the disclosure of positive 'inside' information.

The next section describes a variety of long-range compensation plans and discusses managements' rationale for the adoption of these schemes. The sample is described in section 3. Section 4 presents a discussion of announcement dates. The event-time methodology used in the paper and the results are

---

[1]Jones (1980a, b) cites evidence on both the frequency and size of shareholder suits involving 'excessive' managerial compensation.

described in section 5. Cross-sectional analysis of the market reaction to different types of long-range plans is presented in section 6. Finally, section 7 summarizes the findings.

2. Long-range compensation plans

This study focuses on long-range compensation plans.[2] These plans differ from short-term bonus plans in that the compensation is designed to be a function of performance over a longer period of time (normally several years) than in the case of bonus plans which generally reward management for good performance in a given year.

Five major compensation arrangements commonly are classified as long-term plans. These include: stock options, stock appreciation rights (SAR's), restricted stock, phantom stock, and performance plans.[3]

With a stock option plan, the company compensates executives by providing them with options to purchase a given number of shares at a specific price within a given time period. SAR's often are granted with options. These rights allow executives to give up their options and receive the difference between the stock price and the exercise price in cash. SAR's reduce transaction costs in cases where the manager desires cash rather than share ownership.

Restricted stock plans award shares of common stock to executives subject to restrictions on sale. Typically these restrictions are removed if the executive remains with the company for a specified period of time. Until the restrictions are removed, the shares usually are subject to forfeiture if the manager terminates employment. Under a phantom stock plan, the executive is credited as receiving restricted shares by the company but is paid in cash equal to the value of the shares after the restrictions are removed. Similar to SAR's, phantom stock reduces transaction costs if the executive desires cash rather than shares.

Unlike the above plans which compensate managers based on share price performance, performance plans reward managers based on accounting measures. Under these plans, boards establish performance goals (often expressed in terms of earnings-per-share growth) for management at the beginning of an award period – normally three to six years. At the end of the period, executives may receive cash awards, shares of stock, or options which are in varying degrees a function of how well the performance goals have been achieved.

---

[2] This section briefly summarizes the different types of long-range plans. For a more detailed discussion of these plans and the incentive problems which they presumably are designed to reduce, see Smith and Watts (1983). For an analysis of the tax implications of long-range plans, see Miller and Scholes (1982). For a description of short-term compensation plans, see Healy (1983).

[3] Some authors [e.g., Larcker (1983)] classify dividend units as a separate type of plan. These plans base managerial compensation on the amount of dividends paid to shareholders. As these plans seldom are adopted in isolation from other types of long-range plans, they are not included here as a major category.

When boards of directors introduce long-range plans for shareholder voting, they generally stress incentive effects. The following quotes from selected proxy statements containing long-range plan proposals are typical:

> The objective of the program is to further the long-term growth of the company's earnings by offering incentives to those key executives and other employees of the company who contribute substantially to such growth. (Alexander and Alexander Services – 1982 proxy statement)

> In the opinion of the Board of Directors, the program will benefit the company and its shareholders by (a) attracting, motivating and retaining executives of outstanding ability, (b) providing incentives based on pre-established performance objectives, and (c) with respect to the Long-Term Performance Share Plan, increasing the identification of key executives with the company and its shareholders by affording increased ownership of company stock. (Nabisco Brands – 1982 proxy statement)

Occasionally a board stresses the possible tax benefits of a plan. For example:

> The purpose of the amended plan is to make such changes as are required to permit options granted under the plan to qualify as 'incentive stock options' under the Internal Revenue Code... which provides more favorable income tax treatment for persons exercising options. (Federal Signal Corporation – 1982 proxy statement)

Plausible scenarios explain how both an incentive effect and a tax benefit to managers, separately or in combination, could work in the stockholders' best interest. Compensation plans designed to align managerial and shareholder interests more closely (incentive effects) could result in positive stock price reactions at the announcement of the plan.

Alternatively, a compensation package which reduces the tax liability of management could serve shareholder interests in at least two ways. First, lower taxes allow a reduction in gross managerial salaries without reducing net after-tax compensation. The reduction in gross salaries leave a higher residual for the stockholder. Second, even if gross salaries are not reduced, tax-motivated compensation plans for managers benefit shareholders if the increased after-tax benefits attracted higher caliber people or reduced turn-over.

In our sample of plans, it would be difficult if not impossible to differentiate tax from incentive effects. The analysis of Miller and Scholes (1982) indicates that all the plans in our sample have tax implications. The analysis of Smith and Watts (1983) suggests these plans also have incentive effects. Therefore, we explore whether the net effect of any combination of these factors work in the stockholders' best interest. In the remainder of the paper we conduct a standard event-time analysis of the stock market reaction to the introduction of long-range plans.

3. The sample

A comprehensive list of New York Stock Exchange firms voting on 'incentive plans' from 1979 through 1982 was obtained from the Exchange.[4] The list contained the name of each firm, the shareholder meeting date, and a brief description of the plans voted upon.[5] For all the firms on this list, the proxy statements containing a description of the plan were requested from the SEC in Washington, DC. We obtained 344 (94 percent) of the 367 proxies requested.[6]

After a review of the proxy statements, we classified each observation as either 'clean' or 'contaminated'. An event was considered 'clean' if the proxy statement contained no other board-sponsored agenda item except a proposed compensation plan, the election of directors, and the ratification of auditors.[7] An event was considered 'contaminated' if the proxy included any other board-sponsored agenda item. Similar to Bhagat and Brickley (1984) and DeAngelo and Rice (1983), 'contaminated' events were eliminated because of possible confounding effects they might have on the results.

A careful reading of the 'clean' proxies revealed that not all plans were long-range plans. Some were short-term bonus schemes, while others consisted of employee savings plans. Often, companies direct employee savings plans to many employees throughout an organization. Typically the employee contributes money which is matched to some degree by the corporation. Then the funds are invested in one or more alternatives chosen by the employee. Since this study focuses on long-range managerial plans, firms adopting bonus or savings plans were eliminated from the study.[8]

Table 1 summarizes the breakdown of the 344 proxy statements we reviewed. Column 1 classifies the total sample and that portion of the sample which was utilized in the study. Columns 2 and 3 give the number and percent

---

[4]Stephen Walsh, the NYSE proxy specialist, believes this list to be comprehensive. All NYSE firms are required to report executive compensation plans to the Exchange. When reported, these plans are included on the list. Furthermore, Bhagat (1983) cites evidence which indicates the NYSE lists are complete. Mr. Walsh believes that all of the plans we examine were adopted. He has not heard of one case where the plan was not ratified. Executive compensation plans only require a majority vote to pass.

[5]The costs of collecting data for this study were high. We chose 1979 through 1982 as the study period because it was recent and yielded a sufficiently large number of observations.

[6]The SEC librarian was unable to locate the other proxies.

[7]Almost all proxy statements contain agenda items to elect directors and to ratify auditors. Since shareholder proposals normally are defeated overwhelmingly, we did not classify such proposals as contaminating. The definition we used for 'clean' events is the same as used by Bhagat and Brickley (1984) and DeAngelo and Rice (1983).

[8]We have no assurance that the list of short-term bonus or employee savings plans is complete. Plans which are for all employees do not have to be reported to the Exchange. Further, the list concentrates on long-range plans and does not appear complete for bonus plans. Therefore, since it is hard to interpret what type of sample biases may be present for these plans on the list, we chose not to analyse them.

Table 1

Breakdown of the sample of 344 managerial compensation plans analyzed and the 175 plans utilized which were proposed for adoption or modification by boards of directors during the period 1979 through 1982.

Proxy classification (1)	Number of proxies (2)	Percent of proxies (3)
Proxies analyzed		
Contaminated plans	102	30%
Short-term bonus plans	23	6
Employee savings plans	44	13
Useable long-range plans	175	51
Total proxies received	344	100%
Proxies utilized		
Option plans[a]	44	25%
Restricted stock plans[b]	18	10
Performance plans	23	13
Mixed plans[c]	90	51
Useable long-range plans	175	100%

[a] Includes stock appreciation rights plans.

[b] Includes phantom stock plans.

[c] Includes all plans where action was taken on more than one type of long-range compensation scheme. Of the 90 mixed plans, 78 contained an option component. Therefore, 122 plans (44 + 78) were either 'pure' option plans or mixed plans with an option component. The 90 mixed plans also included 56 which contained a restricted stock plan element. Therefore, 74 plans (18 + 56) were either 'pure' restricted stock plans or mixed plans with a restricted stock component. Finally, in the 90 mixed plans there were 67 with a performance plan component. Accordingly, 90 plans (23 + 67) were either 'pure' performance plans or mixed plans which included a performance plan element.

of the proxies in each classification. Of the total 344 proxies received, 102 (30 percent) were contaminated, 23 (six percent) were short-term bonus plans, 44 (13 percent) were savings plans, and 175 (51 percent) were the long-range compensation plans analyzed in the study.

Also summarized in table 1 are the 175 plans utilized in the study. Of these plans, 44 (25 percent) were option plans; 18 (10 percent) were restricted stock plans; 23 (13 percent) were performance plans; and 90 (51 percent) were mixed plans which contained more than one type of long-term compensation scheme.[9] In total, 122 actions were taken on the 'pure' option plans plus mixed plans which contained an option component. Seventy-four votes were taken on restricted stock plans plus mixed plans with a restricted stock element. Finally, 90 actions on performance plans were taken when the mixed plans with a performance component were added to the 'pure' performance plans.

[9] From this point on when we refer to option plans we mean either options and/or SAR's. Also, when we refer to restricted stock plans we include phantom stock plans. These groupings were made because of the similarity of the plans in each case.

Table 2

Distribution of the sample of 175 managerial compensation plans by the year they were voted upon for adoption or modification by the shareholders during the period 1979 through 1982.

Year of shareholder vote	Number of plans	Percent of plans
1979	42	24%
1980	44	25
1981	49	28
1982	40	23
Total	175	100%

Table 2 displays the observations in the sample by year of the shareholder meeting. The observations were distributed evenly over the sample period with between 40 and 49 observations occurring in each year.

Some of the plans consisted of amendments to existing plans while others were new plans. At first we classified a plan as either 'new' or 'amended'. However, due to the complexity and variety of actions taken, as well as to incomplete knowledge of the exact compensation package which existed prior to the plan, such a classification scheme was meaningless.[10] In this study, the market reaction to both new plans and amendments to existing plans were analyzed together.[11]

4. Announcement dates

The financial press rarely reports disclosure of changes in managerial compensation plans. Therefore, considerable uncertainty exists as to the timing of announcement of the plan. Bhagat (1983) and Bhagat and Brickley (1984) found that for some management actions, information is released on the proxy date which is generally the date the proxy statement is mailed. Larcker (1983) found a significant market reaction on the SEC stamp date (as well as two days before and one day after). The stamp date is the date when the SEC mailroom opens the proxy and 'stamps' it as being received. On the other hand, Linn and McConnell (1983) suggested that for some events the information may be released between dates. Because of the uncertainty of the actual announcement

[10] Judging if a plan was new or an amendment to an existing plan was often difficult. For example, a firm might amend an option plan increasing the shares to be optioned and at the same time adopt a performance plan. Alternatively, a firm might adopt a radically different type of option plan than it had previously. However, the firm might have had some type of existing option plan. The number of arbitrary judgments in developing a classification scheme seemed too high to justify the effort.

[11] To the extent amendments to existing plans are anticipated and do not affect shareholder wealth as much as new plans, we are biasing our analysis in favor of the null hypothesis that all these plans do *not* affect shareholder wealth.

Table 3

Distribution of the trading day intervals between possible announcement dates for the sample of 175 managerial compensation plans which were proposed for adoption or modification by boards of directors during the period 1979 through 1982.

Announcement date interval	Median number of trading days	Mean number of trading days	Largest number of trading days	Shortest number of trading days
Board meeting date through the proxy date[a]	33.5	54.9	286	4
Board meeting date through the SEC stamp date[b]	35.0	58.4	290	6
Board meeting date through the shareholder meeting date[a]	60.5	79.8	316	26
Proxy date through the SEC stamp date[c]	3.0	3.2	16	− 4[e]
Proxy date through the shareholder meeting date[d]	27.0	27.1	42	11
SEC stamp date through the shareholder meeting date[c]	23.0	23.2	39	8

[a] Based on the 89 firms where the board date was available.
[b] Based on the 87 firms where both board and SEC stamp dates were known.
[c] Based on the 169 firms where the SEC stamp date was available.
[d] Based on the full sample of 175 firms.
[e] In five cases the SEC stamp date preceded the proxy date.

date in our particular case, we examine all possible event dates as well as a cumulative residual between dates.[12] Event dates analyzed include the board of directors' meeting date (when the plan was first proposed), the date of the proxy statement, the SEC stamp date, and the date on which shareholders voted on the plan.

Board meeting dates are difficult to obtain. Fortunately, in over one-half of our cases (89) the proxy statement contained the board meeting date. We were constrained to use this subsample of firms to analyze the market reaction both on the board date and between the board date and other dates.

---

[12] Discussion with Mr. Walsh of the NYSE suggest that proxy mailing practices differ across firms. While most firms mail proxies out the date the proxy is dated, this is not always the case. In a few instances, the proxies actually have been mailed out before the proxy date, while in other cases the mailing follows the date on the proxy. In addition, some firms mail their proxies first class mail while some proxies are mailed third class. Hence, considerable uncertainty exists about when the information in the proxies becomes publicly available.

The proxy date and the shareholder meeting date were contained in all of the proxy statements. Therefore, we were able to utilize the full sample of 175 plans to analyze market reactions involving these dates.

For 169 of the 175 proxies, the SEC stamp date was readable. Analyses involving the stamp date utilized this subsample of 169.

Table 3 displays information on the number of trading days for various intervals involving the board meeting date, proxy date, SEC stamp date, and the shareholder meeting date. The median number of days in the interval from the board date through the proxy date was 33.5.[13] The median interval for the board date through the SEC stamp date was 35.0 and for the board date through the shareholder meeting date was 60.5.

A median of three days was contained in the interval from the proxy date through the SEC stamp date while 27.0 days was the median interval from the proxy date through the shareholder meeting date. Finally, the median interval from the SEC stamp date through the shareholder meeting date was 23.0 days.

5. Event study results

In this section we report the results of our event-time analysis. First, we report the results for the four possible announcement dates. Then, we report the results for the cumulative analysis between dates.

5.1. Residual returns at the board meeting date, proxy date, SEC stamp date and shareholder meeting date

To test the null hypothesis that the introduction of long-range compensation plans has no impact on shareholder wealth on a given date, we used the standard-event study technique. Dann and DeAngelo (1983) provide a detailed description of the methodology.[14] We measured price effects relative to a benchmark estimated from the following market model:

$$r_{jt} = a_j + B_j R_{mt} + u_{jt},$$

where r_{jt} is the dividend-inclusive rate of return on security j over period t, R_{mt} is the dividend-inclusive rate of return on an equally-weighted market index over period t, $B_j = \mathrm{cov}(r_{jt}, R_{mt})/\mathrm{var}(R_{mt})$, $a_j = \mathrm{E}(r_j) - B_j\mathrm{E}(R_m)$, and u_{jt} is the disturbance term over period t with $\mathrm{E}(u_{jt}) = 0$.[15]

---

[13] When we use the word 'day' we are referring to 'trading days'.

[14] Because of the 'clustering' of our events in calendar time (i.e., the sample period is four years), we reported market adjusted returns. Brown and Warner (1980) suggest market adjustments may be necessary in the presence of such clustering. We also conducted the analysis using the comparison period methodology of Masulis (1980) as modified by Dann (1981). Consistent with the results of Brown and Warner (1983), the results were virtually identical.

[15] In this study we utilized day −170 through day −21, relative to each possible announcement date, for estimating the parameters of the market model for each firm.

Table 4

Abnormal returns for alternative two-day announcement periods for the sample of 175 managerial compensation plans which were proposed for adoption or modification by boards of directors during the period 1979 through 1982.

Alternative announcement dates (1)	Sample size[a] (2)	Two-day announcement period abnormal return (3)	t-statistic (4)
Board date	89	0.3%	0.92
Proxy date	174	−0.1	−0.47
SEC stamp date	169	0.3	1.26
Shareholder meeting date	175	0.2	1.00

	Significance level (5)	Percent negative (6)	Significance level: Sign test (7)
Board date	> 10%	55.8%	> 10%
Proxy date	> 10	54.6	> 10
SEC stamp date	> 10	50.6	> 10
Shareholder meeting date	> 10	45.7	> 10

[a] Sample sizes vary due to lack of board dates and SEC stamp dates and insufficient return data for estimation of the market model parameters.

Table 4 presents the results for the analysis for the four alternative announcement dates. In each case a two-day 'announcement period' is used. This period consists of the announcement date and the following trading day. A two-day period is used in case any information revealed on a given day occurs after the close of trading. Column 1 lists the date being analyzed and column 2 reports the size of the particular subsample. Column 3 reports the average two-day announcement period abnormal return and columns 4 and 5 contain the results of the standard *t*-test. The last two columns report the percentage of negative abnormal returns for each announcement period and the results of the Fisher sign test.[16]

In all cases, both the *t*-test and sign test failed to reject the null hypothesis of no abnormal performance at the ten-percent level of significance. This finding is consistent with either the hypothesis that long-range compensation plans have no impact on shareholder wealth or that the dates which we analyzed were not the correct announcement dates. Next we examine for this second possibility by analyzing returns between dates.

[16] For a description of the Fisher sign test, see Hollander and Wolfe (1973, pp. 39–43).

5.2. Cumulative residuals between announcement dates

Given the empirical literature cited above, we assume that the announcement of the managerial compensation plan would have reached the market by the day following the SEC stamp date. Prior to that date, considerable uncertainty exists as to the timing of the announcement. Therefore, we focus on the cumulative average residuals (*CAR*'s) from the board date through the day after the SEC stamp date. We also analyze the *CAR*'s from two days after the SEC stamp date through the day after the shareholder meeting date for the same sample of firms.

Table 5 reports the results of the *CAR* analysis. The subsample used in this analysis consists of 83 firms for which we knew the board date, the SEC stamp date, and had enough return data to estimate the parameters of the benchmark model. The first column reports the event interval. Column 2 presents the average number of days in the event interval. The third column displays the mean cumulative residual. This number consists of the average *CAR* for the sample firms over the relevant interval. Note that the length of an interval may vary across firms.

To test the significance of the cumulative residuals between dates, we followed the procedure outlined by Dodd and Warner (1983). The

Table 5

Cumulative abnormal returns for the subsample of 83 managerial compensation plans which were proposed for adoption or modification by boards of directors during the period 1979 through 1982 where both the board meeting date and the SEC stamp date were known.[a]

Return interval (1)	Average number of days in the event interval (2)	Mean cumulative residual[b] (3)	Z-statistic (4)	Significance level (5)	Percent positive (6)
Board meeting date through the day after the SEC stamp date	58.4	2.4%	2.18	2.92%	59.0%
Two days after the SEC stamp date through the shareholder meeting date	22.3	1.0	1.09	> 10	54.2

[a] There were 83 firms which had both the board date and the SEC stamp date and which also had enough return data to estimate the market model parameters.

[b] The mean cumulative residual is equal to the average cumulative residual for all firms for the given interval. Note that the length of the interval may vary across firms.

Dodd–Warner procedure tests the hypothesis that the average cumulative risk-adjusted returns (CAR's) for the sample of firms between two specific dates are equal to zero. Again, the length of the interval may vary between firms. The statistic used to test this hypothesis is the Z-statistic shown in the appendix of their paper.[17]

Column 4 in table 5 reports the Z-statistic while column 5 reports the significant level of the test. The percent of the sample which had positive cumulative residual returns is shown in the last column.

The mean cumulative residual for each of the two intervals was positive. Between the board meeting date and the day after the SEC stamp date, the test was significant at the 2.92 percent level, while between two days after the SEC stamp date through the day after the shareholder meeting date the test was insignificant (P-value of 27.57 percent).[18]

The results of this analysis support the notion that the long-range plans in our sample increased shareholder wealth. Further, the results suggest that as one might expect, the information generally is revealed sometime between the board meeting date and the day after the SEC stamp date.[19]

Because of concerns that the significant CAR's from the board date through one day after the SEC stamp date may be due to model misspecification rather than genuine abnormal performance, we also conducted the CAR's test for the 60 days before the board meeting date and the 60 days after the shareholder meeting date. Positive and significant CAR's during these intervals would indicate that what we detected above might not be a favorable market reaction to compensation plans but rather errors in the return benchmark.[20]

[17]See Dodd and Warner (1983, pp. 436–438).

[18]The result of the Z-test for the interval from the board date through one day after the SEC stamp date is not caused by a few outliers. We also calculated a Wilcoxon signed rank test of the hypothesis that the median cumulative abnormal return for this interval equaled zero. Those results were consistent with the results of the Z-test. Note that Brown and Warner (1980) suggest that the Wilcoxon test may be misspecified when using cumulative returns. However, the apparent bias is *against* finding positive abnormal performance.

[19]In our sample, a few of the plans actually were implemented prior to the proxy date contingent on shareholder approval. Therefore, we assume that at least for some firms in our sample the information about the plans may have reached the market before the proxy statement. We also reasoned that in most cases the proxy statement would be received by the market by at least the day after the SEC stamp date (the day after the SEC received the proxy in the mail). Therefore, we were not surprised that no abnormal returns are found between the SEC stamp date plus two and the shareholder meeting date.

[20]If the assumptions of the market model do not hold for our sample [see Fama (1976)], the expected return conditional on the market return may not be linear. Then if the true relation (whatever it is) between the expected return and the market return is constant, use of the standard market model generally will be expected to generate similar 'abnormal' returns between any two arbitrary dates of approximately the same interval. We chose 60-day intervals for this analysis because 60 is approximately equal to the average number of days in the interval from the board date through the day after the SEC stamp date for our sample (58.4 days).

For the 60 days just before the board meeting date, the average cumulative return for the 83 cases was -1.30 percent. The associated Z-statistic was -0.541. Similarly, for the 60 days after the shareholder meeting date, the average cumulative abnormal return was 0.32 percent with an associated Z-statistic of 0.480. Therefore, the cumulative residuals were not statistically different from zero either before or after the evaluation period. These results strengthen the interpretation that the abnormal CAR's found between the board meeting and the day after the SEC stamp date are not an artifact of model misspecification.[21]

6. Cross-sectional analysis: Abnormal returns by type of plan

The previous section provides evidence consistent with the notion that the introduction of long-run compensation plans increases shareholder wealth. In this section we examine whether specific types of long-range plans are associated with different market effects on stock prices.

Table 6 presents an analysis of variance of the CAR's from the board meeting date through the day after the SEC stamp date classified by type of plan.[22] The table displays the mean CAR for plans containing each of the major types of long-range plans and the mean CAR for plans not containing each of these components. The results of standard analysis of variance tests also are reported. The results of the F-tests in all three cases do not allow us to reject the hypothesis that the mean CAR for a plan containing a particular component is the same as for a plan not containing that component.[23]

The results of the analysis of variance suggest that the positive market reaction associated with long-range plans is not generated by a particular type of plan. This finding is consistent with the view of Smith and Watts (1983) that

---

[21]Aside from the possibility that the market model is not specified correctly, the possibility that the parameters of the model are unstable exists. For example, if the announcement of a compensation plan signals a shift in investment or financing policy, the beta may change. Given this possibility, we reconducted our analysis using market model estimates from day $+20$ to day $+170$ relative to the last date for each interval. The significance levels for the analysis using the post-event estimation period were qualitatively identical to those using the pre-event estimation period. (Note: about 15 percent of observations had to be eliminated in the extended analysis because the required returns for the procedure extended into 1983. The 1983 CRSP tapes were not available at the time of the analysis.)

[22]In this paper we reported an analysis of CAR's from the board meeting date through the day after the SEC stamp date using both mixed and unmixed plans. We also conducted a similar analysis for each of the alternative announcement dates and alternative intervals. In addition we reconducted the analysis using the Dodd and Warner (1983) W-statistic as the measure of abnormal returns for each firm (instead of the CAR). We also separately analyzed plans containing only one component (e.g., a plan consisting of only a stock option plan versus a plan containing only a performance plan). All of the additional analyses were consistent with the results reported here.

[23]In addition, the Wilcoxon rank sum test did not allow us to reject the null hypothesis in any case.

Table 6

Analysis of variance: Cumulative abnormal returns from the board meeting date through the day after the SEC stamp date classified by type of plan for a subsample of 83 managerial compensation plans which were proposed for adoption or modification by boards of directors during the period 1979 through 1982.

Description of plan	Mean cumulative abnormal return	Sample size	F-statistic	P-value
(1) Overall plans	2.40%	83		
(2) Plan contains option component	1.46	55	0.68	41.20%
Plan does not contain option component	4.23	28		
(3) Plan contains performance plan component	1.77	43	0.17	68.30
Plan does not contain performance plan component	3.07	40		
(4) Plan contains restricted stock component	4.37	33	1.03	31.38
Plan does not contain restricted stock component	1.09	50		

firms often face a variety of conflicts of interest between managers and the firm's other claimholders and so design compensation contracts which in each case minimize the resulting agency costs. The appropriate compensation package can vary from firm to firm. Alternatively, the tax situation may vary from firm to firm and so the appropriate compensation plan may differ for tax reasons.

7. Summary

Economists often stress the economic benefits of alternative types of managerial compensation schemes. Some groups (e.g., shareholder advocate groups), however, oppose certain types of managerial compensation contracts. These groups argue that some plans benefit managers at the expense of shareholders. The effect of various types of managerial compensation contracts on shareholder wealth is an empirical issue that has received little attention.

In this study we examine the stock market reaction to the introduction of long-range managerial compensation schemes. The results support the notion that these plans represent an improvement in contracting between managers and shareholders which increase shareholder wealth. However, the results do not rule out the possibility that the benefits to shareholders could be derived by a sharing of tax benefits with managers in tax-motivated plans. In addition, managements' desire to have a larger equity stake in the firm could convey positive information to the stock market.

A cross-sectional analysis indicates that no one particular type of long-range plan increases shareholder wealth more than others. This finding supports the notion that different types of plans may be appropriate in different situations.

References

Bhagat, S., 1983, The effect of pre-emptive right amendments on shareholder wealth, Journal of Financial Economics 12, 289–310.

Bhagat, S. and J.A. Brickley, 1984, Cumulative voting: The value of minority shareholder voting rights, Journal of Law and Economics 27, 339–365.

Bhagat, S., J.A. Brickley and R.C. Lease, 1985, Incentive effects of employee stock purchase plans, Journal of Financial Economics, forthcoming.

Bradley, M. and L.M. Wakeman, 1983, The wealth effect of targeted share repurchases, Journal of Financial Economics 11, 301–328.

Brown, S.J. and J.B. Warner, 1980, Measuring security price performance, Journal of Financial Economics 8, 205–258.

Brown, S.J. and J.B. Warner, 1983, Using daily stock returns in event studies, Unpublished manuscript (University of Rochester, Rochester, NY).

Dann, L.Y., 1981, Common stock repurchases: An analysis of returns to bondholders and shareholders, Journal of Financial Economics 9, 113–138.

Dann, L.Y. and H. DeAngelo, 1983, Standstill agreements, privately negotiated stock repurchases, and the market for corporate control, Journal of Financial Economics 11, 275–300.

DeAngelo, H. and E.M. Rice, 1983, Anti-takeover charter amendments and shareholder wealth, Journal of Financial Economics 11, 329–359.

Dodd, P. and J.B. Warner, 1983, On corporate governance: A study of proxy contests, Journal of Financial Economics 11, 401–438.

Fama, E.F., 1976, Foundations of finance (Basic Books, New York).

Healy, P.M., 1983, The impact of bonus schemes on accounting choices, Unpublished dissertation (University of Rochester, Rochester, NY).

Hite, G.L. and M.S. Long, 1982, Taxes and executive stock options, Journal of Accounting and Economics 4, 3–14.

Hollander, M. and D. Wolfe, 1973, Nonparametric statistical methods (Wiley, New York).

Jones, T.M., 1980a, An empirical examination of the resolution of shareholder derivative and class action lawsuits, Boston University Law Review 60, 542–573.

Jones, T.M., 1980b, What's bothering those shareholder-plaintiffs?, California Management Review 22, 5–19.

Larcker, D.F., 1983, The association between performance plan adoption and corporate capital investment, Journal of Accounting and Economics 5, 3–30.

Linn, S.C. and J.J. McConnell, 1983, An empirical investigation of antitakeover amendments on common stock prices, Journal of Financial Economics 11, 361–399.

Masulis, R.W., 1980, The effects of capital structure change on security prices, Journal of Financial Economics 8, 139–178.

Miller, M.H. and M.S. Scholes, 1982, Executive compensation, taxes and incentives, in: W.F. Sharpe and C.M. Cootner, eds., Financial economics: Essays in honor of Paul Cootner (Prentice-Hall, Englewood Cliffs, NJ) 179–201.

Patton, A., 1983, Why so many executives make too much, Business Week, Oct. 17, 24–25.

Smith, C.W. and R.L. Watts, 1982, Incentive and tax effects of U.S. executive compensation plans, Australian Journal of Management 7, 139–157.

Smith, C.W. and R.L. Watts, 1983, The structure of executive compensation contracts and the control of management, Unpublished manuscript (University of Rochester, Rochester, NY).

An Analysis of the Use of Accounting and Market Measures of Performance in Executive Compensation Contracts

RICHARD A. LAMBERT AND DAVID F. LARCKER*

1. Introduction

Prior research has provided useful insights into the structure of compensation plans and their incentive effects.[1] However, one important limitation of these studies is the virtual absence of any cross-sectional analyses of the attributes of compensation contracts.[2] This absence is related, in part, to the problems associated with controlling for "other factors" that affect compensation. That is, compensation contracts are

* University of Pennsylvania. This paper has benefited from workshop discussion at Columbia University, Cornell University, Harvard University, the University of Michigan, and the University of Washington. We would also like to thank an anonymous reviewer and James Anderson for their useful comments. The financial support of Charter Banks and Ernst & Whinney is gratefully acknowledged.

[1] For example, Murphy [1985] and Coughlan and Schmidt [1985] correct some of the econometric problems of earlier research and conclude that executive compensation is, on average, strongly and positively related to the firm's stock market rate of return. Antle and Smith [1986] provide empirical evidence that executive compensation is, on average, more sensitive to the firm's return on equity relative to their industry than to the gross return on equity. Finally, Healy, Kang, and Palepu [1987] and Defeo, Lambert, and Larcker [1987] examine whether compensation contracts seem to be adjusted for accounting changes or the accounting effect of financial reorganizations made by the firm. Lambert and Larcker [1985a; 1985b] provide reviews of this research in the area of executive compensation.

[2] Two recent working papers provide some cross-sectional analysis of executive compensation contracts. Ely [1987] provides evidence that the relative weight placed on alternative measures of performance varies by industry. The theoretical framework employed in Adams [1987] is very similar to ours, although her empirical analysis is substantially different.

Journal of Accounting Research
Vol. 25 Supplement 1987
Printed in U.S.A.

481

thought to be functions of characteristics of the manager, the firm, and the environment.[3] In our attempt to address some of these complexities, we employ an analytical agency theory model to provide a structure for controlling for "other factors" in order to examine the "informational properties" of accounting and market measures of performance.

More specifically, we exploit the results of Holmstrom [1979] and others which suggest that the relative weight placed on a performance measure in a compensation contract is an increasing function of its "signal-to-noise" ratio with respect to the agent's actions. Using this framework, we empirically examine whether the relative use of security market and accounting measures of performance in executive compensation is related to the amount of "noise" inherent in the two signals and the "sensitivity" of these two signals to managerial actions. Our results are consistent with the hypothesis that firms place relatively more weight on market performance (and less weight on accounting performance) in compensation contracts for situations in which (i) the variance of the accounting measure of performance is high relative to the variance of the market measure of performance, (ii) the firm is experiencing high growth rates in assets and sales, and (iii) the value of the manager's personal holdings of his firm's stock is low.

Section 2 provides a theoretical framework for analyzing the use of performance measures in compensation contracts. The sample selection procedures are discussed in section 3. In section 4, we discuss the measurement of the performance variables and managerial compensation and present the results of an analysis of the time-series relation between cash compensation and accounting and market performance. In section 5, we develop a number of hypotheses regarding the informational properties of accounting and market measures of performance. In section 6, we examine whether the cross-sectional variation in the relative weights placed on security market versus accounting performance in compensation contracts is related to the signal-to-noise ratios of these performance variables. The research results are summarized in section 7.

2. Theoretical Framework

Although agency theory does not provide insights into the use of accounting or market numbers as *specific* measures of performance in

---

[3] In contrast, many studies implicitly treat the compensation contract as if it were exogenous. For example, one line of research has examined whether the contracts (either cross-sectional differences in contracts or time-series changes in contracts) are associated with managerial decision making (e.g., Larcker [1983] and Healy [1985]). Unfortunately, it is unclear whether it is appropriate to attribute any association between the adoption of a contract and changes in managerial decisions to (i) the contractual change or (ii) other variables which are the causal determinants of the contractual change. This criticism also applies to studies which have examined the security market reaction to compensation contract changes (e.g., Lambert and Larcker [1985a; 1985b] and Brickley, Bhagat, and Lease [1985]).

compensation contracts, the theory does provide a framework for structuring our empirical analysis. In particular, agency theory can be used to specify the properties of any two generic variables that are relevant for evaluating an agent's performance. Moreover, the theory suggests both a functional form relating the informational properties of the performance variables to parameters of the agent's compensation scheme, and a means of controlling for "other" effects on the form of the compensation scheme so that the analysis can focus on informational properties.

Since most agency models examine incentive problems in a *single-period* setting, we begin our analysis of the use of performance measures in compensation contracts by discussing the implications of these single-period models. We then examine the effect of multiperiod considerations on the relation between compensation and performance.

2.1 SINGLE-PERIOD AGENCY MODELS

The "standard" agency model (see Holmstrom [1979]) analyzes incentive problems that arise when one individual, the principal, delegates decision-making tasks to another individual, the agent.[4] The agent's output, x, is a function of his action, a, and a random state of nature. The agent's action, which is typically interpreted as the amount of effort that he supplies, is assumed to increase the cash flow; however, the effect of the state of nature on the agent's output prevents the principal from using the output to determine unambiguously the amount of effort that was supplied. As a result, the principal must rely on imperfect measures of the agent's actions, such as his output and other information (y) for both evaluation and motivation.

Holmstrom [1979] shows that the agent's compensation as a function of the performance variables x and y, denoted $c(x, y)$, is the solution to the following equation (assuming an interior solution):

$$\frac{1}{U'[c(x, y)]} = \lambda + \mu \frac{f_a(x, y \mid a)}{f(x, y \mid a)} \tag{1}$$

where $U(\cdot)$ is the agent's utility function for money (we assume that the principal is risk neutral), $f(x, y \mid a)$ is the density function of the variables x and y given the agent's effort, $f_a(x, y \mid a)$ is the derivative of the density function with respect to the agent's effort, λ is the Lagrange multiplier on the constraint that specifies the lower bound on the level of expected utility that the contract can provide to the agent, and $\mu > 0$ is the Lagrange multiplier on the constraint that ensures that the agent's choice of effort be incentive compatible.

---

[4] Our analysis concentrates on incentive problems that arise from the unobservability of the agent's action (i.e., moral hazard problems). Other contracting problems, such as those that arise when the agent's skill is unknown (i.e., reputation and screening issues), are beyond the scope of our analysis. Another limitation of the agency models that we employ is that they assume that the agent is responsible only for deciding how much effort to supply; decisions involving a "risk–return" trade-off are ignored.

The performance variables x and y affect the agent's compensation through their effect on the term $f_a(x, y \mid a)/f(x, y \mid a)$. As discussed in Holmstrom [1979] and Milgrom [1981], this term is equivalent to the derivative of the logarithm of the likelihood function $f(x, y \mid a)$ with respect to the agent's effort, a. This provides an informational interpretation to the use of the variables x and y in the contract.[5]

Given the generality of the model, equation (1) provides little guidance regarding the functional form of the relation between the agent's compensation and the performance measures x and y. In order to derive empirical implications from this equation, we place additional structure on the model by making more specific assumptions about the form of the agent's utility function and the form of the probability distributions. In particular, we assume that the agent's utility function is a member of the power class of utility functions, which can be represented as:

$$U(c) = \frac{1}{1 - \kappa} c^{1-\kappa}. \tag{2}$$

This class of utility functions, which exhibits decreasing absolute risk aversion and constant proportional risk aversion, is commonly used in analytical work in agency theory.[6] The parameter κ represents the coefficient of proportional risk aversion for the agent, where higher values of κ correspond to greater degrees of risk aversion. For this class of utility functions, $U'(c) = c^{-\kappa}$ and $1/U'(c) = c^{\kappa}$. Substituting the agent's marginal utility into equation (1) yields:

$$[c(x, y)]^{\kappa} = \lambda + \mu \, \frac{f_a(x, y \mid a)}{f(x, y \mid a)}. \tag{3}$$

We also impose some structure on the form of the probability distributions. As Banker and Datar [1987] show, the term $f_a(x, y \mid a)/f(x, y \mid a)$ is *linear* in x and y for a large class of probability distributions.[7] In particular, we assume that:

$$\frac{f_a(x, y \mid a)}{f(x, y \mid a)} = \delta_0 + \gamma\{\delta_x[x - E(x \mid a)] + \delta_y[y - E(y \mid a)]\}. \tag{4}$$

---

[5] Note that although the principal's utility is a direct function of the firm's stock price (e.g., the variable x), agency theory does not imply that the optimal contract simply ties the agent's compensation exclusively to the firm's stock price. In particular, the random state of nature that affects security prices introduces noise into this performance measure *from the perspective of evaluating the agent's performance.* The existence of this noise implies that there are potential benefits to supplementing security prices with other measures of performance (e.g., accounting numbers) in evaluating the agent's actions.

[6] There are also a variety of empirical studies which lend some support to the use of the power utility function (see Friend and Blume [1975] and Litzenberger and Ronn [1986]).

[7] The class of distributions includes the exponential, normal (where the agent's effort affects the mean of x and y), and the binomial distributions, among others.

For the class of distributions considered in Banker and Datar [1987], the coefficients on the variables x and y can be interpreted as representing the "signal-to-noise ratios" of the performance variables. In particular, we have:

$$\delta_x = \frac{s(x \mid a)}{\text{var}(x \mid a)}, \quad \text{and} \quad \delta_y = \frac{s(y \mid a)}{\text{var}(y \mid a)}$$

where $s(\cdot \mid a)$ is the (conditional) sensitivity of the mean of the signal to the agent's effort, and $\text{var}(\cdot \mid a)$ is the variance of the signal given the agent's effort.[8] Substituting equation (4) into equation (3) implies:

$$[c(x, y)]^\kappa = \lambda + \mu(\delta_0 + \gamma\{\delta_x[x - E(x \mid a)] + \delta_y[y - E(y \mid a)]\}). \quad (5)$$

Combining terms yields a linear expression on the right-hand side of equation (5):

$$[c(x, y)]^\kappa = \beta_0 + \beta_x[x - E(x \mid a)] + \beta_y[y - E(y \mid a)]. \quad (6)$$

The relation specified in equation (6) is complex; it is linear only if $\kappa = 1$, which corresponds to a logarithmic utility function for the agent.[9] Moreover, the parameters λ and μ, which affect the intercept and the slopes on x and y, depend on the attractiveness of the manager's outside employment opportunities, his disutility for effort, the "magnitude" of the agency problem, and the form of the production function. Thus, the slope coefficients (β_x and β_y) on the performance measures of interest are confounded by all of these factors, making interpretations of cross-sectional differences in the slope coefficients problematic.

However, one implication of the model is that for a given firm, if the performance measures are multiplied by their respective "signal-to-noise" ratios, the theory implies that the coefficients on the "rescaled" performance measures will be equal. To see this, equation (5) can be expressed as:

$$[c(x, y)]^\kappa = [\lambda + \mu \cdot \delta_0] + \mu \cdot \gamma\{\delta_x[x - E(x \mid a)]$$
$$+ \delta_y[y - E(y \mid a)]\}. \quad (7)$$

Equation (7) implies that the coefficients on the "rescaled variables" (i.e., $\delta_x[x - E(x \mid a)]$ and $\delta_y[y - E(y \mid a)]$) are equal to $\mu\gamma$. Although the

---

[8] For example, if x and y are distributed as bivariate normal random variables whose means are affected by the agent's effort, we have:

$$s(x \mid a) = \frac{\partial E(x \mid a)}{\partial a} - \frac{\text{cov}(x, y)}{\text{var}(y)}\frac{\partial(E(y \mid a)}{\partial a}.$$

[9] The relation may also be nonlinear because equation (6) applies only for interior solutions for the compensation function. More generally, the optimal sharing rule will include a lower bound. In this case, equation (6) becomes:

$$c^\kappa = \max\{\underline{\beta}, \beta_0 + \beta_x[x - E(x \mid a)] + \beta_y[y - E(y \mid a)]\}.$$

magnitude of the coefficients on the "rescaled variables" will differ cross-sectionally as a function of $\mu\gamma$, the theory predicts that the coefficients on the "rescaled variables" will be equal for a given firm.

Another implication of the model is that the confounding effects of cross-sectional differences in the term $\mu\gamma$ can be reduced by computing the *ratio* of the slope coefficients from equation (6). That is, the ratio of the slope coefficients is:

$$\frac{\beta_x}{\beta_y} = \frac{\mu\gamma\delta_x}{\mu\gamma\delta_y} = \frac{\delta_x}{\delta_y} = \frac{s(x \mid a)}{s(y \mid a)} \frac{\mathrm{var}(y \mid a)}{\mathrm{var}(x \mid a)}. \tag{8}$$

Equation (8) implies that the ratio of the slope coefficients is a function of the ratio of the "signal-to-noise" ratios of the two performance variables. An increase in either the precision (i.e., the inverse of the noise) of a performance variable or its sensitivity to the agent's actions will, ceteris paribus, increase the relative weight the variable receives in the compensation function.

2.2 MULTIPERIOD CONSIDERATIONS

Most multiperiod agency models suggest that compensation contracts have "memory" (e.g., Lambert [1983] and Rogerson [1985]). That is, the agent's compensation in a period will depend not only on the realizations of the performance measures in that period but also on their realizations in *prior* periods.[10] In particular, if we assume that the agent's utility function is additively separable over time (in addition to the assumptions about the agent's utility function and production function discussed in the previous section), Lambert [1983] shows that the optimal contract can be expressed as:

$$[c_t(\cdot)]^\kappa - [c_{t-1}(\cdot)]^\kappa$$

$$= \beta_0 + \beta_{xt}(\cdot)[x_t - E(x_t \mid \cdot)] + \beta_{yt}(\cdot)[y_t - E(y_t \mid \cdot)] \tag{9}$$

where the subscript t refers to time, the expected values for the performance measures x and y are now conditioned upon the actions in that period as well as prior realizations of the performance variables, and the slope coefficients are permitted to depend on the prior realizations of the performance variables.

From a theoretical perspective, little is known about how the realizations of the performance variables in one period affect the slope coefficients in subsequent periods. Moreover, from an empirical perspective, it is difficult to estimate the functional form of a compensation scheme whose slope coefficients vary over time as a function of the prior-period realizations of the performance measures. For these reasons, we suppress any dependence between the slope in one period and the realizations of

---

[10] See Fellingham, Newman, and Suh [1987] for conditions on the form of the agent's utility function for which the optimal contract does *not* involve memory.

the performance measures in prior periods. Therefore, we assume that the slope coefficients, β_x and β_y, are proportional to the time-series average of the signal-to-noise ratios of the performance measures.

Under the above assumptions, the compensation scheme can be expressed as a linear function that relates the *first difference* in compensation raised to the κ power to the "surprise" in the performance measures in the period:

$$c_t^{\kappa} - c_{t-1}^{\kappa} = \beta_0 + \beta_x[x_t - E(x_t \mid \cdot)] + \beta_y[y_t - E(y_t \mid \cdot)]. \qquad (10)$$

In the empirical analysis, we estimate the slope coefficients of equation (10) for each firm using time-series data for compensation, market performance, and accounting performance. The estimated slope coefficients are then used to analyze whether the relative weights assigned to security market and accounting numbers in compensation contracts are related to the signal-to-noise ratios of these performance variables (as predicted in equations (7) and (8)).

3. Sample

Our sample of firms was primarily obtained from the *Forbes* annual compensation survey, which publishes compensation data for firms in at least one of the *Forbes* 500 listings (e.g., assets, sales, market value, or net profits). The survey includes data on cash compensation for the chief executive officer (*CEO*), years as *CEO*, years with the company, and for years 1970 to 1973 the value of shares owned by the *CEO* (and where appropriate, his family). The typical annual survey includes data for 700 to 800 firms.

We include firms in the sample if they satisfy five criteria. First, a complete history for cash compensation from 1970 to 1984 was available from various sources, including the *Forbes* data and proxy statements. Second, each firm was required to have the market value of equity ownership for the *CEO* during each year from 1970 to 1973 in the *Forbes* data. Third, the number of shares owned by the *CEO* (or his family) was reported in either the *Corporate Data Exchange (CDE) Stock Ownership Directory* or proxy statements available to the researchers.[11] Fourth, each firm was required to have selected financial data (discussed below) on the annual *Compustat* or *CRSP* files. Finally, each firm was required to have a constant fiscal year-end from 1970 to 1984.

The final sample of 370 firms consists of 188 industrial (not including natural resource firms) companies; 29 natural resource or petroleum-processing firms, 77 utilities or transportation companies, 25 retail or hotel firms, 48 banks or insurance companies, and 3 firms in unique industrial groups. These firms had a median of one *CEO* change (i.e., two

---

[11] For a small number of banks and finance companies, the *CEO* stock ownership data were obtained for the 1979 fiscal year.

separate *CEO*s) during the 15 years from 1970 to 1984. In addition, the executives had been employed by the firm a median of 27 years and had been the *CEO* of the firm for a median of six years.

4. Estimation of the Slope Coefficients on the Performance Measures

4.1 MEASUREMENT OF THE PERFORMANCE VARIABLES

Because agency theory does not identify the precise procedures for measuring the relevant accounting (corrresponding to the variable *y*) and security market (corresponding to the variable *x*) performance indexes, we make this choice on the basis of observed institutional contractual arrangements and ease in interpreting the empirical results. In order to increase the comparability between the accounting and market measures of performance, we express both variables in terms of rates of return. The security market return (hereafter, *RET*), defined as the sum of the firm's capital gains and dividends divided by the stock price at the beginning of the year, has a natural interpretation as a measure of the firm's performance from the perspective of shareholders. We have chosen Return on Equity (hereafter, *ROE*), which is the firm's earnings before extraordinary items and discontinued operations divided by the average common shareholders' equity, as a "comparable" measure of accounting performance. This measure frequently appears as an explicit performance measure in bonus contracts disclosed in proxy statements.

The discussion in section 2.2 suggested that the relevant measure for each performance variable is its "surprise" component. Since the stochastic process describing the *ROE* performance variable exhibits positive autocorrelation (Foster [1986]), we use the *change in ROE* as our empirical measure of the surprise component.[12] Because the *RET* performance measure is generally considered to be uncorrelated over time, we use its level as our empirical market performance measure.[13]

---

[12] The evidence in Freeman, Ohlson, and Penman [1982] and Foster [1986] indicates that although the *ROE* variable exhibits positive autocorrelation, it is a stationary process. Since the use of the first difference in *ROE* implicitly assumes that *ROE* follows a random walk, we also conducted the analysis with an alternative specification of the *ROE* variable. On the basis of the evidence provided in Foster [1986, table 7.11], we used $ROE_t - .5ROE_{t-1}$ as the "surprise" in the accounting performance variable in period t. The time-series results (e.g., the average explanatory power of the regressions and the average magnitude of the t-statistics), which are not reported, were similar to the results reported in table 1. Although the statistical fit of the cross-sectional analysis (not reported) was generally weaker than the results reported in the text, the overall results were substantively similar.

[13] Ideally, the ex ante expected value of *RET* would be subtracted from the realization of *RET* in order to derive the surprise component of *RET*. In principle, the expected rate of return on the firm's stock price could be estimated by employing an asset pricing model. For example, under the Capital Asset Pricing Model, the expected return on a firm's stock price is a function of the risk-free rate, the firm's beta, and the expected return on the market portfolio. Since estimating the *expected* return on the market portfolio is beyond

4.2 MEASUREMENT OF COMPENSATION

We use *cash compensation* (i.e., salary plus annual bonus) as our measure of executive compensation. Although cash compensation does not value the executive's entire remuneration package, salary plus bonus is almost always a significant portion of total compensation (salary plus bonus, long-term bonuses, perquisites, pensions, grants of stock, and stock options).[14] For example, Benston [1985] and surveys by Booz, Allen, and Hamilton [1983] and Hay Associates [1981] report that salary plus bonus represents between 80% and 90% of total compensation.[15]

Consistent with most studies of compensation, we exclude changes in the value of the manager's holdings of stock and stock options from the measure of compensation.[16] We recognize, however, that the choice between accounting and security market measures of performance in the salary and bonus portion of compensation may depend on the structure of the remainder of the manager's wealth. Therefore (as discussed in more detail below), we examine whether the relative weight placed on market versus accounting performance in the compensation contract is related to the extent to which the manager's other wealth is tied to the firm's stock price.

---

the scope of our analysis, we do not estimate the expected value of *RET* for each period. Instead, our analysis implicitly assumes that the expected value of *RET* is constant over time. Since our empirical analysis uses *real* rates of return, this assumption may not be too unrealistic. If the expected value for *RET* is constant over time, it will simply appear in the intercept of the regression.

[14] See Antle and Smith [1986] and Lambert, Larcker, and Verrecchia [1987] for a discussion of the issues involved in valuing various components of compensation.

[15] This discussion focuses on the level of compensation. For our purposes, the more relevant issue is whether the inclusion of other components of compensation has a significant impact on the *slope coefficients* relating compensation to performance. Jensen and Murphy [1987] provide some evidence on this issue with respect to the slope coefficient on the security market measure of performance. In particular, they find that the slope coefficient that relates salary plus bonus to changes in shareholder wealth is not significantly different from the slope coefficient that relates "total compensation" to changes in shareholder wealth. To our knowledge, there is no evidence regarding whether the slope coefficient on the accounting performance variable would be significantly affected by the inclusion of other components of compensation.

[16] It is unclear whether these gains and losses should be viewed as a component of the manager's compensation (narrowly defined) or as income from personal investments. The value of these components of the manager's wealth are, by definition, directly tied to changes in the firm's stock price. For this reason, our slope coefficients will understate the magnitude of the relation between the manager's *total wealth* and his firm's stock price performance. We attempt to control for any resulting misspecification of our model by including a measure of the magnitude of the manager's stockholdings as an independent variable in the cross-sectional analysis. Consistent with most studies (see Lambert and Larcker [forthcoming] and Jensen and Murphy [1987] for exceptions), we also ignore any future-period effects on cash compensation that arise as a result of current-period performance.

4.3 BOX-COX ESTIMATION

In estimating the relation between compensation and performance, prior research has generally used either compensation or the natural logarithm of compensation as the dependent variable. These specifications are generally made without any guidance from economic theory.[17] In contrast, our analytical agency model, expressed in equation (10), suggests that the relation between compensation and the accounting and market measures of performance can be expressed as:[18]

$$c_t{}^\kappa - c_{t-1}^\kappa = \beta_0 + \beta_{ROE}(ROE_t - ROE_{t-1}) + \beta_{RET}RET_t + e_t \quad (11)$$

where e_t represents a disturbance term.[19] The dependent variable is the change in cash compensation raised to the power κ, where κ is the agent's coefficient or proportional risk aversion.

Since the value of κ is unknown (to the researcher), the parameters of equation (11) cannot be directly estimated using techniques such as multiple regression. However, Box and Cox [1964] have developed a procedure for estimating regression equations in which some or all of the variables are transformed by raising them to a power which is a parameter that must also be estimated. In particular, they show that the parameters κ, β_0, β_{ROE}, and β_{RET} can be estimated via a maximum likelihood approach which utilizes iterative OLS procedures.[20]

4.4 RESULTS OF BOX-COX AND MULTIPLE REGRESSION ANALYSIS

The parameters of equation (11) were estimated separately for each firm, and summary statistics for these parameter estimates are presented in table 1. The mean (median) R-squared of the estimation equations is

---

[17] The choice of the logarithmic transformation is usually defended on unspecified "statistical grounds." In our model, the use of a logarithmic transformation of the dependent variable is not consistent with any member of the power utility functions.

An exception is Masson [1971] who uses compensation (more precisely, the percentage change in compensation) raised to the ⅔ power. Interestingly, Masson states that this procedure is designed to reflect the decreasing marginal utility of compensation in the trade-off between income and leisure (i.e., effort).

[18] Cash compensation and RET are expressed in 1967 dollars using the Consumer Price Index (CPI). The accounting return (ROE) is expressed in nominal terms because of our inability to estimate various asset layers and specific asset price indexes.

[19] The disturbance term arises from other performance measures that may be used by shareholders in compensating the manager but which are not incorporated into our empirical model.

[20] More specifically, for a given value of κ, the maximum likelihood parameters estimates for β_0, β_{ROE}, and β_{RET} can be derived by conducting a multiple regression of the transformed dependent variable on the independent variables. Following Box and Cox [1964], the dependent variable is deflated by the factor $\kappa(\dot{c})^{k-1}$, where $\dot{c}$ is the geometric mean of the compensation variable. Deflating the dependent variable by this factor leaves the magnitudes of the regression coefficients β_{ROA} and β_{RET} relatively unaffected by changes in the parameter κ and makes it easier to calculate the likelihood function.

TABLE 1

Summary Statistics for the Box-Cox Estimation of the Time-Series Relationship Between Compensation (c) and the Change in Return on Equity (ROE) and the Level of Security Market Return (RET) as Expressed in Equation (11):[a]

$$c^\kappa_t - c^\kappa_{t-1} = \beta_0 + \beta_{ROE}(ROE_t - ROE_{t-1}) + \beta_{RET}RET_t + e_t$$

	MEAN	MEDIAN	TRMEAN[c]	STDEV	Q1	Q3
κ[b]	0.784	0.400	0.612	1.800	−0.900	1.800
κ LO	−0.514	−1.000	−0.642	0.876	−1.000	−0.238
κ UP	3.05	2.50	2.86	2.50	1.25	4.10
B O	2.90	2.58	2.85	5.58	−0.16	5.77
T BO	0.494	0.363	0.476	0.874	−0.018	0.953
B ROE	288.2	186.4	256.9	461.9	10.6	499.1
T ROE	1.283	0.939	1.156	1.955	0.069	2.044
B RET	9.54	6.78	8.06	34.08	−7.24	21.89
T RET	0.368	0.337	0.364	1.135	−0.285	1.037
RSQD	0.272	0.205	0.255	0.228	0.083	0.399
DW	2.168	2.164	2.172	0.537	1.782	2.563
AR	−0.040	−0.038	−0.042	0.281	−0.247	0.162

[a] The parameters of equation (11) were estimated separately for each firm using 14 time-series observations. Compensation data is expressed in thousands of dollars. The table presents summary statistics for the 370 estimations.

[b] κ is the power in the BOX-COX transformation (the search for κ was restricted to the interval from −1.0 to 10.0 in increments of .05.), κ LO (κ UP) is the lower (upper) bound for the 95% confidence interval for κ, B O (T BO) is the estimated intercept (t-statistic), B ROE (T ROE) is the estimated slope (t-statistic) on the ROE variable, B RET (T RET) is the estimated slope (t-statistic) on the RET variable, RSQD is the R-squared of the estimation, DW is the Durbin-Watson statistic, and AR is the estimated first-order autocorrelation in the residuals.

[c] TRMEAN trims the smallest 5% and the largest 5% of the observations and averages the remaining observations. Q3 is the third quartile and Q1 is the first quartile.

0.272 (0.205). The mean (median) t-statistic for the ROE slope is 1.283 (0.939), while the mean (median) t-statistic for the RET slope is only 0.368 (0.337). If we aggregate the t-statistics cross-sectionally under the assumption of cross-sectional independence, the corresponding z-statistics for the ROE slope and the RET slope are 22.70 and 6.51, respectively. Since the regressions are conducted over the same time period (i.e., 1970–84), it is unlikely that the slope coefficients are independent across firms; however, only 3 (33) independent observations out of the 370 firms are needed in order for the average t-statistic on the ROE (RET) slope to be significantly different from zero at the 0.05 level (two-tailed). These results suggest that cash compensation is statistically related to both RET and changes in ROE.

The estimates of the parameter κ in table 1 are imprecise; the mean length of the 95% confidence interval is 3.05.[21] Nevertheless, it is instruc-

---

[21] As discussed in Box and Cox [1964, pp. 214–15], the confidence intervals for κ were derived by calculating the range of κ's which yielded values for the logarithm of the likelihood function that were within $.50\chi^2$ ($df = 1$) of the function's maximum value.

tive to compare our estimates of κ with the predictions of the theory and with the values of κ implicitly assumed in prior research. Agency theory implies that the parameter κ represents the agent's coefficient of proportional risk aversion, which should be positive. The mean (median) value of κ was 0.784 (0.400), and only 5.4% of the estimates of κ were negative and statistically significant at the 0.05 level.[22] Many prior studies have analyzed compensation in first differences, which implicitly assumes a value for κ of one. Our results indicate that 74.3% of the confidence intervals for κ included one, which suggests some support for this specification.[23]

Since the confidence interval for κ typically includes the value of one, we also estimated the relation between compensation and *RET* and *ROE* using standard *OLS* multiple regression. The slope coefficients, *t*-statistics, and explanatory power of these mutliple regressions (not reported) are very similar to the results derived from the Box-Cox analysis. This similarity is probably due to the inability of the Box-Cox procedure to distinguish between alternative values of κ.[24]

The results in table 1 suggest that cash compensation is more highly associated with differences in accounting returns than with levels of security market returns.[25] Some additional support for this statement

---

[22] The average *t*-statistics on the performance variables and the *R*-squared of the estimation procedures for the subsample of firms for which the estimate for κ was positive (i.e., the cases that are most consistent with the theory) are virtually identical to the results reported in table 1.

[23] The inability to provide a precise estimate for κ is likely to be due to our small sample size (14 time-series observations per firm) and/or the limited range of compensation numbers. That is, the function c^κ can be well approximated by a linear function of c provided that the range of c is not "too large." To provide some evidence on this issue, we estimated a linear regression between the compensation numbers and the square of compensation for each firm. The mean (median) *R*-squared from these regressions was 0.982 (0.990). Similarly, a linear regression of compensation on the natural logarithm of compensation yielded a mean (median) *R*-squared of 0.970 (0.989). Finally, a regression of the square of compensation on the natural logarithm of compensation yielded a mean (median) *R*-squared of 0.914 (0.959). These results suggest that it would be difficult to determine whether the "best" specification of the dependent variable is the logarithm of compensation ($\kappa = 0$), compensation ($\kappa = 1$), or the square of compensation ($\kappa = 2$), which is consistent with the results in table 1. The finding that a linear specification of the compensation variable works "well" for most firms does not imply, however, that cross-sectional differences in the risk aversion coefficients of managers are unimportant.

[24] As discussed in n. 20, the dependent variable in the Box-Cox estimation was scaled so that the magnitude of the slope coefficients is relatively unaffected by the choice of κ. This will result in the magnitude of the Box-Cox slope coefficient being "close" to the magnitude of the multiple regression slope coefficients (in which κ is exogenously set equal to one).

[25] The magnitude of the coefficient on stock market returns is roughly consistent with the results of other studies. For example, Jensen and Murphy [1987] estimate the slope coefficient from a pooled time-series cross-sectional regression of changes in the real salary plus bonus paid to *CEO*s on the real change in the value of their firm's shareholder wealth to be 0.0000094. To transform this number into a coefficient for a regression in which real stock price *return* is the independent variable, we multiply the coefficient estimated in

can be obtained by examining the results of *univariate* regressions of the change in compensation on the change in *ROE* and the change in compensation on *RET*. In these regressions (not reported), the mean *t*-statistic on *ROE* was 1.18, compared to 0.548 for *RET*. Moreover, the average *R*-squared for the regressions involving *ROE* was 0.186, compared to 0.087 for *RET*. Therefore, the average *incremental* *R*-squared for the *ROE* performance variable was 0.167, whereas the average incremental *R*-squared for *RET* was only 0.068.

5. Hypotheses on the Relative Weights Assigned to the Performance Measures

We discuss two different approaches to testing hypotheses concerning the relative weights assigned to *RET* and *ROE* in compensation contracts. First, we discuss a methodology that tests the agency model prediction that, for a given firm, the slope coefficients on the performance measures scaled by their signal-to-noise ratios should be equal. Second, we discuss a methodology which is designed to address the problems associated with obtaining precise measures of the signal-to-noise ratios of *RET* and *ROE* (the statistical aspects of this approach are presented in section 6 and Appendixes A and B). Finally, we develop specific research hypotheses for empirical examination.

5.1 "EQUALITY OF COEFFICIENTS" APPROACH

Equation (7) implies that if the performance measures *ROE* and *RET* are multiplied by their respective signal-to-noise ratios, then the slope coefficients on the "rescaled" performance measures will be equal. This hypothesis can be tested by conducting a time-series estimation of changes in compensation on the rescaled performance measures, and then testing for equality of the slope coefficients. If it were possible to measure the signal-to-noise ratios for each firm without error, this "equality of coefficients" test procedure would allow for a powerful test of the agency theory relationship developed in section 2.

Although the agency theory model suggests that the "noise" in a performance measure is related to its variance, the theory provides no

---

Jensen and Murphy by the average market value of the firms in our sample, which is $876,000,000 in real $1967, and then divide by 1000.0 to adjust for the fact that we measure compensation in thousands of dollars. The resulting coefficient is 8.23, which is consistent with the mean (median) coefficient of 9.54 (6.78) reported in table 1. Of course, these two sets of results are not strictly comparable because the results in table 1 are based on a *multiple* regression in which both accounting and market measures of performance are used as independent variables, whereas Jensen and Murphy use only a market measure of performance in their regression. In order to achieve a more comparable set of results, we also conducted a simple regression in which the market measure of performance was the only independent variable. The mean slope coefficient from these regressions was 16.67, which is still roughly the same size as the coefficient reported in Jensen and Murphy.

insights into how to measure the sensitivity of the performance measures to the agent's actions. If we make some assumptions about the signal-to-noise ratios of the performance measures, we can use the "equality of coefficients" test procedure to test the *joint* hypothesis that the agency theory model and the assumption about the signal-to-noise ratios are both correct. For example, if the signal-to-noise ratios of *RET* and *ROE* are hypothesized to be equal, the theory predicts that the slope coefficients on the *RET* and *ROE* performance measures will be equal. A crude test of the equality of slope coefficients can be developed by determining whether the *ROE* slope coefficients are statistically different (in central tendency) from the *RET* slope coefficients for our sample of 370 firms. For the Box-Cox estimates, the *ROE* slope coefficient is substantially larger than the *RET* slope coefficient (matched-pairs $t = 11.52$ and Wilcoxon $z = 11.19$).

An alternative hypothesis is that the "noise" of a signal is measured by its time-series variance, and that the sensitivities of the accounting and market measures of performance are equal. After deflating the performance variables by their variances, our results fail to reject the hypothesis that the Box-Cox slope coefficients on the "rescaled" performance variables are (on average) equal (matched-pairs $t = 0.42$ and Wilcoxon $z = -0.45$).

We do not rely on these "equality of coefficients" tests because they are confounded if the signal-to-noise ratios of the two performance measures are measured with error. The resulting estimates for the regression coefficients on the "rescaled variables" would be inconsistent, and the test for equality of coefficients would not produce valid inferences. Specifically, we do not know if the slope coefficients are equal because (*i*) the agency model is actually a good description of contracting, or (*ii*) there is so much measurement error in the estimates of the signal-to-noise variables that this test has no power to reject the research hypothesis, or (*iii*) the coefficient on accounting performance is higher for one group of firms but lower for another group of firms, and the absence of any cross-sectional analysis obscures this fact.

5.2 MOTIVATION FOR CONDUCTING A LATENT VARIABLE CROSS-SECTIONAL ANALYSIS

The problems associated with estimating the signal-to-noise ratios of the performance measures suggest that it is desirable to employ a methodology that explicitly considers measurement error. As developed in equation (8), the agency theory model predicts that the ratio of the regression coefficients on the (unscaled) performance measures provides an estimate of the ratio of the signal-to-noise ratios of the performance measures. Our statistical procedures are designed to assess whether the ratio of these estimated regression coefficients is associated with variables that are hypothesized to have some relationship to the sensitivity and/or noise of the performance variables.

The desirability of this approach is influenced by the degree to which measurement error can be "controlled" in the variables that proxy for the sensitivity and noise of the performance measures. In the remainder of this section, we discuss the variables used to proxy for the relative weights assigned to the *RET* and *ROE* performance measures in the compensation contract, and to proxy for the sensitivity and noise of *RET* and *ROE* with respect to evaluating a manager's performance. In section 6, we use a latent variable analysis to examine whether cross-sectional differences in the relative weights assigned to *RET* versus *ROE* are related to the variables that proxy for the sensitivity and noise of these performance measures. This methodological approach enables us to develop tests of our research hypothesis that "control" measurement error in a manner not available in the "quality of coefficients" test procedure.

5.2.1. Ratio of the Slope Coefficients. Our dependent variable, denoted *PERF MIX*, is the degree to which cash compensation is tied to *RET* relative to *ROE*. As discussed in section 2, we use the ratio of the slope coefficients on the two performance variables to control for other factors that affect the relation between compensation and performance for a particular firm.[26] One important disadvantage of this approach is that the ratio must be calculated from *estimates* of the slope coefficients, and the distribution of the ratio of two random variables can be complicated and possess undesirable properties.

The statistical distribution of the ratio of the slope coefficients is especially sensitive to either measurement error or a near-zero value for the denominator. To reduce these problems, we place the slope coefficient with the more precise (and more positive) estimate in the denominator

---

[26] One problem in interpreting empirical results concerning the ratio of the slope coefficients on the performance variables (β_x/β_y) is that this ratio is sensitive to the *scaling* of the performance variables x and y. For example, if variable x tends to be, on average, ten times as large as variable y in a given firm, then the slope coefficient on x will, ceteris paribus, be approximately $1/10$ as large as the coefficient on y. Clearly, this does not imply that variable y is a more "important" performance measure in contracting than variable x. This problem is exacerbated if the scaling differences between x and y vary cross-sectionally. For example, assume that for another firm, the variable x is only five times as large as variable y. In this situation, the ratio of the slope coefficient on x to y would be approximately $1/5$. More important, it would be inappropriate to conclude that the "informativeness" of variable y relative to variable x is twice as large for the first firm as for the second firm.

A common (statistical) solution to this type of interpretation problem is to deflate the performance measures by their standard deviations. While this will eliminate scaling problems, it also makes it difficult to test hypotheses about the amount of noise in the performance variables. That is, the transformed measures of performance will have, by construction, a variance of one, which tends to eliminate any cross-sectional variation in the relative amounts of noise in the performance measures x and y.

We repeated the analysis using *standardized* performance measures in the time-series regressions. The cross-sectional analysis then related the ratio of the slope coefficients to the *CORR*, *GROWTH*, and *OTHER* constructs. The results, not reported, were similar to the results reported in the text.

of the ratio.[27] As the results in table 1 indicate, the slope coefficient on *ROE* was much more likely to be positive and statistically significant than the coefficient on *RET*. For this reason, the *PERF MIX* construct is defined to be the ratio of the slope coefficient on *RET* to the slope coefficient on *ROE*.

Another problem with the ratio of the slope coefficients arises because the estimated slope coefficients on *RET* and *ROE* can be either positive or negative. As a result, this ratio can be negative if only the numerator is negative or if only the denominator is negative. This complicates the cross-sectional analysis because these outcomes have quite different interpretations for our theoretical analysis. We consider three different means of dealing with this problem, summarized in panel A of table 2. The first approach is to consider only firms with positive slope coefficients on both *ROE* and *RET*. This proxy for the *PERF MIX* variable is denoted *MR-PP* (*BC-PP*) if the slope coefficients were estimated using multiple regression (Box-Cox). A second approach is to allow the numerator of the ratio (i.e., the slope on the *RET* variable) to have any sign but only consider firms with a positive slope coefficient on *ROE*. This proxy is denoted *MR-AP* (*BC-AP*) if the slope coefficients are estimated via multiple regression (Box-Cox). Finally, we compute the ratio after reestimating the slope coefficients on *RET* and *ROE* with the constraint that each slope coefficient and the coefficient of proportional risk aversion be positive.[28] This proxy is denoted *MR-CC* (*BC-CC*) if the slope coefficients are estimated via multiple regression (Box-Cox).

In the subsequent discussion, analysis using *MR-PP* and/or *BC-PP* as the dependent variable is referred to as the "Positive/Positive" case. Similarly, analysis using *MR-AP* and/or *BC-AP* as the dependent variable is referred to as the "Anything/Positive" case. Finally, analysis using the *MR-CC* and/or *BC-CC* variables is referred to as the "Constrained/Constrained" case. The Positive/Positive and Constrained/Constrained cases assume that, a priori, the slope coefficients on both performance measures should be positive. The Anything/Positive case assumes that, a priori, the coefficient on the *RET* variable could be negative, perhaps to "undo" some of the manager's exposure to risk in his other wealth.

5.2.2. Noise in the Performance Measures. The noise in a signal re-

---

[27] The results in table 1 indicate that the precision of the estimates for the slope coefficients varies considerably across firms. This suggests that the ratio of the estimated slope coefficients will possess heteroscedasticity. If the dependent variable in the cross-sectional analysis consisted simply of a single slope coefficient, the heteroscedasticity problem could be solved by deflating the slope coefficients (and the independent variables of the cross-sectional analysis) by the standard error of the slope coefficient estimates. See Saxonhouse [1976] for additional discussion of this point. This approach is not pursued because our dependent variable is the ratio of the slope coefficients, and it is not clear how to compute the standard error of the ratio from the individual standard errors of the slope coefficients.

[28] The slope coefficients were constrained to lie within the interval from .01 to 5000, and the value of κ was constrained to lie in the interval from .01 to 10.

TABLE 2

Description of the Variables Used in the Cross-Sectional Analysis of the Relative Weights
Placed on Performance Measures in Compensation Contracts

A. Proxies for the Relative Weight Placed on *RET* Versus *ROE* (*PERF MIX*)

Variable	Description
MR-PP	The ratio of the slope coefficient on the *RET* variable to the slope coefficient on the *ROE* variable. The slope coefficients were estimated via *M*ultiple *R*egression with the slopes unconstrained. The ratio is used only if both slope coefficient are *P*ositive. The ratio is coded as "missing" if either slope coefficient is negative.
BC-PP	Same as *MR-PP*, except that the slope coefficients are estimated with the *B*ox-*C*ox procedure.
MR-AP	Same as *MR-PP*, except that the slope coefficient on *RET* may take on *A*ny value. That is, the ratio is coded as "missing" if the slope coefficient on the *ROE* variable is negative.
BC-AP	Same as *MR-AP*, except that the slope coefficients are estimated with the *B*ox-*C*ox procedure.
MR-CC	Same as *MR-PP*, except that the slope coefficients are estimated with the coefficients *C*onstrained to be positive.
BC-CC	Same as *MR-CC*, except that the slope coefficients are estimated with the *B*ox-*C*ox procedure.

B. Proxies for the Noise in *ROE* Versus *RET* (*NOISE*)

Variable	Description
RTVAR	*R*atio of the *T*otal *Var*iance (over the period 1970 to 1984) of the change in *ROE* to the total variance of *RET*.
RSVAR	*R*atio of the *S*ystematic Component of the *Var*iance of the change in *ROE* to the systematic component of the variance of *RET*.
ZTRANS	Fisher transformation of the coefficient of correlation for the regression of the real stock price equity return on first differences in the return on assets.

C. Proxies for the Firm's Growth (*GROWTH*)

Variable	Description
A GROW	One plus the Real growth in total assets from 1970 to 1984.
S GROW	One plus the Real growth in sales from 1970 to 1984.

T A B L E 2—*continued*

D. Proxies for the Amount of the Manager's Other Incentives Tied to Stock Price (*OTHER*)

Variable	Description
PER-CENT	Average percentage of the firm owned by the *CEO*. The average is computed using years 1970 to 1973 and 1980.
EQ/COMP	Average ratio of the market value of equity owned by the *CEO* to his cash compensation. The average is computed using years 1970 to 1973 and 1980.
STOCK	Average level for the market value of equity for the *CEO* expressed in thousands of 1967 dollars. The average is computed using years 1970 to 1973 and 1980.

flects the degree to which it is influenced by factors other than the manager's actions. Equation (8) indicates that the appropriate measure of the amount of noise in a signal is the variance of the signal *given the agent's action*. Holding the (conditional) sensitivity of the mean of the signal to the agent's effort constant for both signals, agency theory implies a *positive* relationship between the ratio of the slope on *RET* to the slope on *ROE* and the *inverse* of the ratio of the "noise" in *RET* to the "noise" in *ROE*.

We consider three proxies for the relative amounts of *NOISE* in the two performance measures. The first measure, denoted *RTVAR*, is the ratio of the *time-series* variation in the change in *ROE* to the time-series variation in *RET*.[29] One limitation of this measure is that the time-series

---

[29] It might seem that the ratio of the slope coefficients is related to the inverse of the ratio of the variances of the performance variables by construction. For example, consider the case in which a dependent variable, z, is related to two independent variables, x and y, which are measured without error, in the following fashion:

$$z = \beta_0 + \beta_x x + \beta_y y + e, \quad \text{with} \quad \text{cov}(x, e) = \text{cov}(y, e) = 0.$$

If, for convenience, we assume that x and y are independent, it is well known that the ratio of the slope coefficients on the two independent variables can be written as:

$$\frac{b_x}{b_y} = \frac{\text{cov}(z, x)}{\text{var}(x)} \frac{\text{var}(y)}{\text{cov}(z, y)} = \frac{\text{var}(y)}{\text{var}(x)} \frac{\text{cov}(z, x)}{\text{cov}(z, y)}.$$

This expression makes it seem as if the hypothesized relation between the ratio of the slope coefficients and the ratio of the variances is true by construction. However, if we expand the expressions for $\text{cov}(z, x)$ and $\text{cov}(z, y)$, we have:

$$\frac{b_x}{b_y} = \left[\frac{\text{cov}(\beta_0 + \beta_x x + \beta_y y + e, x)}{\text{var}(x)}\right] \div \left[\frac{\text{cov}(\beta_0 + \beta_x x + \beta_y y + e, y)}{\text{var}(y)}\right]$$

$$= \left[\beta_x + \frac{\beta_y \text{cov}(x, y) + \text{cov}(x, e)}{\text{var}(x)}\right] \div \left[\beta_y + \frac{\beta_x \text{cov}(x, y) + \text{cov}(y, e)}{\text{var}(y)}\right].$$

variation in a signal will not only reflect the amount of "noise" in the signal but also the effect of changes in the agent's action over time. As the results in table 3 indicate, the mean (median) ratio of the variance of *ROE* to the variance of *RET* was 0.051 (0.012).

A second measure for the amount of noise in a signal can be obtained by decomposing the time-series variation in a signal into a market (or industry) component and a firm-specific component. If the market component of the performance measure is thought to be unrelated to the manager's actions, as in the relative performance evaluation literature (see Holmstrom [1982]), then the variance of the *market component* of the performance evaluation measure is a more appropriate measure of the amount of noise in a signal.[30]

The second measure, denoted *RSVAR*, is the ratio of the variance of the systematic component of *ROE* to the variance of the systematic component of *RET*. This ratio was computed by first conducting time-series regressions of the change in *ROE* for the firm on the change in *ROE* for a value-weighted market index and the *RET* for the firm on the value-weighted market *RET*. Descriptive statistics for these "market-model" regressions are presented in table 4 (panels A and B). The market component of the change in *ROE* accounts for (on average) approximately 18% of the total variation in the change in *ROE*, whereas the market accounts for (on average) approximately 37% of the total variation in *RET*. For each firm, the results of these regressions were used to calculate the variance of the systematic component of the change in *ROE* and the variance of the systematic component of *RET*. As the results in table 3 indicate, the mean (median) value of *RSVAR* was 0.064 (0.004).

The final proxy for the *NOISE* construct is derived from discussions in the security price literature which link the magnitude of the correlation between market prices and accounting numbers with the amount of noise in accounting numbers. In fact, Salamon and Smith [1979] have suggested that the correlation between accounting numbers and market prices provides an explicit measure of the amount of "managerial misrep-

---

Since $\text{cov}(x, y) = \text{cov}(x, e) = \text{cov}(y, e) = 0$, it is easy to see that the apparent dependence of the ratio of the slope coefficients on the ratio of the variances disappears. While these covariances will not be exactly equal to zero in a finite sample, they are equally likely to be positive or negative, so there will be no systematic dependence between the size of the ratio of the slope coefficients and the size of the ratio of the variances.

[30] It is not clear that the "market" component of a performance measure constitutes noise when the executive is, in part, responsible for deciding the type of projects (and the industry) in which the firm invests. For example, Dye [1987] shows that a "pure" relative performance evaluation scheme can lead to suboptimal project selections.

Antle and Smith [1986] provide empirical evidence consistent with the hypothesis that *total* executive compensation (including the change in the value of shares of stock and stock options held by the executive) is more sensitive to the firm-specific component of performance than the industry component of performance. However, they do not provide any evidence regarding the use of relative performance evaluation in the salary plus bonus portion of compensation.

TABLE 3

Descriptive Statistics on the Variables Used in the Cross-Sectional Analysis of the Relative
Weights Placed on Performance Measures in Compensation Contracts[a]

	N[b]	MEAN	MEDIAN	TRMEAN	STDEV	$Q1$	$Q3$
MR-PP	166	0.172	0.062	0.104	0.508	0.023	0.170
BC-PP	161	0.384	0.076	0.123	1.782	0.023	0.184
MR-AP	277	0.041	0.012	0.028	0.508	−0.034	0.085
BC-AP	283	−0.032	0.011	0.035	3.851	−0.036	0.089
MR-CC	370	374.8	0.059	146.8	1146.3	0.0002	1.0
BC-CC	370	309.5	0.057	102.8	1034.5	0.0001	0.7320
RTVAR	370	0.051	0.012	0.024	0.180	0.005	0.031
RSVAR	370	0.064	0.004	0.015	0.341	0.001	0.022
ZTRANS	370	0.870	0.838	0.878	1.092	0.246	1.611
A GROW	370	2.184	1.878	1.996	1.852	1.198	2.609
S GROW	370	1.706	1.440	1.567	1.153	1.054	1.994
PER-CENT	370	1.851	0.145	0.832	5.242	0.039	0.450
EQ/COMP	370	82.8	4.4	25.6	292.4	1.4	12.7
STOCK	370	10781	742	3725	36605	197	2390

[a] See table 2 for a definition of the variables.

[b] N is the number of firms with available data. *TRMEAN* trims the smallest 5% and the
largest 5% of the observations and averages the remaining observations. *Q3* is the third
quartile and *Q1* is the first quartile.

resentation" in accounting numbers.[31] However, this correlation measures noise only from the perspective of assessing the *value of the firm.*
As discussed by Gjesdal [1981], an information system that is useful in
valuing the firm need not be useful in assessing a manager's performance.
Therefore, rankings of information systems in terms of their value in
assessing (*i*) a manager's performance and (*ii*) the value of the firm need
not be the same.

The correlation between the *RET* and *ROE* performance measures,
which we denote *ZTRANS*, was obtained by conducting a regression of
the firm's *RET* on its change in *ROE*. The results of these regressions
are summarized in table 4, panel C. For example, the mean (median) *R*-
squared for these regressions was 0.136 (0.084). In order to convert the
correlation coefficient from this regression into a more normally distributed random variable, we defined *ZTRANS* to be the Fisher transformation of the correlation coefficient.

*5.2.3. Sensitivity of the Performance Measures to the Agent's Ac-
tions.* While security market prices are thought to estimate the expected
present value of all future consequences of a manager's actions, accounting numbers are frequently criticized for their inability to reflect future-

---

[31] The accounting literature is replete with articles on earnings manipulation (see Foster
[1986] and Verrecchia [1986]).

TABLE 4

*Summary Statistics for the Results of Regression Analyses of the Systematic Component of
the Change in Return on Assets (ROE), the Systematic Component of Security Market
Return (RET), and the Correlation Between the RET and the Change in ROE for a Sample
of 370 Firms*[a]

A. Time-Series Regression of Change in *ROE* on the Change in Market *ROE*

	MEAN[b]	MEDIAN	TRMEAN	STDEV	Q1	Q3
INT[a]	−0.002	0.000	−0.000	0.013	−0.004	0.003
T INT	0.055	0.058	0.038	0.818	−0.432	0.427
SLOPE	0.937	0.482	0.729	2.410	−0.014	1.541
T SLOPE	1.068	0.945	1.061	1.640	−0.042	2.220
RSQD	0.185	0.118	0.171	0.185	0.023	0.312
DW	2.023	2.010	2.030	0.551	1.636	2.456
AR	0.009	0.016	0.006	0.281	−0.212	0.207

B. Time-Series Regression of *RET* on the Market *RET*

	MEAN	MEDIAN	TRMEAN	STDEV	Q1	Q3
INT	0.024	0.019	0.022	0.049	−0.006	0.050
T INT	0.359	0.393	0.365	0.722	−0.117	0.826
SLOPE	0.999	0.949	0.973	0.459	0.652	1.268
T SLOPE	2.890	2.790	2.840	1.220	2.052	3.525
RSQD	0.373	0.375	0.372	0.174	0.245	0.489
DW	1.845	1.829	1.845	0.443	1.534	2.141
AR	0.097	0.105	0.097	0.226	−0.054	0.255

C. Time-Series Regression of *RET* on Change in *ROE*

	MEAN	MEDIAN	TRMEAN	STDEV	Q1	Q3
INT	0.060	0.052	0.056	0.056	0.024	0.084
T INT	0.734	0.724	0.727	0.577	0.353	1.083
SLOPE	2.351	1.810	2.321	4.332	0.438	4.114
T SLOPE	0.970	0.885	0.958	1.260	0.257	1.750
RSQD	0.136	0.084	0.122	0.146	0.022	0.218
DW	1.892	1.875	1.899	0.418	1.584	2.183
AR	0.076	0.084	0.077	0.214	−0.073	0.233

[a] *INT (T INT)* is the estimated intercept (*t*-statistic) in the regression, *SLOPE (T SLOPE)* is the estimated slope (*t*-statistic), *RSQD* is the coefficient of determination for the regression, *DW* is the Durbin-Watson statistic, and *AR* is the estimated first-order autocorrelation of residuals for the regression.

[b] *TRMEAN* trims the smallest 5% and the largest 5% of the observations and averages the remaining observations. *Q3* is the third quartile and *Q1* is the first quartile.

period consequences of current-period actions (e.g., Rappaport [1986]). While it is possible, in principle, for historical-cost-based accounting rates of return to reflect the present value of the firm's future cash flows by using "economic" depreciation (see the discussion in Beaver [1981]), it is unclear whether conventional accounting practices achieve this result. In particular, constraints imposed by Generally Accepted Accounting Principles may limit the ability of accounting numbers to reflect the cash flows that are expected to arise in the future as a result of the firm's current-period actions.

If accounting-based performance measures are not as sensitive as market-based performance measures to the actions of the manager that have future-period consequences, agency theory predicts that, ceteris paribus, compensation schemes will be less accounting oriented in situations in which firms are in the "early" periods (before the effects of the manager's investments are reflected in accounting numbers), and more sensitive to accounting numbers in "later" periods (when the effects of the manager's investments are reflected in accounting earnings).[32] This hypothesis therefore predicts that the ratio of the RET slope to the ROE slope is *positively* associated with the extent to which the firm is in the "early" versus "later" stages of investment *during the same period* in which the slopes of the compensation function are estimated.

We assume that the extent to which a firm is in the early stages of investment is related to the $GROWTH$ of the firm, as measured by real growth in total assets (denoted $A\ GROW$) and real growth in sales ($S\ GROW$). These growth rates were computed over the period 1970–84, the same period over which the slope coefficients in the compensation function were estimated. We assume that firms in the "early" stages of investment will be experiencing both increases in their asset bases and increasing (as opposed to constant or declining) sales.

5.2.4. Other Components of Managerial Wealth. If the other components of a manager's wealth are highly correlated with the firm's stock price, there may be little incentive benefit to also linking the manager's cash compensation to stock price. Such a link may merely increase the manager's exposure to risk. For this reason, if the manager already has a considerable amount of his wealth tied to the firm's stock price, shareholders may desire to use other informative performance measures in the manager's compensation contract. To test this hypothesis, we examine whether the relative weight placed on RET and ROE is *negatively* associated with the degree to which the manager's other wealth is tied to the firm's stock price.

We consider three proxies for this construct, which is denoted $OTHER$. The first indicator, denoted $STOCK$, is the average dollar value of stock (in 1967 dollars) owned by the CEO or his family. This measure assumes that the manager's "other incentives" are proportional to the size of his equity investment in the firm. For example, the change in the manager's wealth for a given value of RET is proportional to the manager's equity investment. The second indicator, denoted $EQ/COMP$, is the average market value of equity owned by the CEO or his family divided by his cash compensation. This measure assumes that the importance of the manager's equity investment is a function of the size of this investment relative to his cash compensation. The final indicator, denoted PER-

---

[32] See Lambert [1981; 1986] and Ramanan [1986] for agency theory models which support this result.

CENT, is the percentage of the equity held by the *CEO* or his family. This is a commonly discussed measure of the amount of incentive the manager has to increase the firm's stock price.

For our sample of firms, the results in table 3 indicate that the mean (median) percentage of the firm's total stock held by the *CEO* and his family was 1.85% (.145%). Moreover, the mean (median) ratio of equity holdings to annual cash compensation was 82.8 (4.4). These numbers were computed by averaging the values for years 1970 to 1973 and 1980.

6. Cross-Sectional Analysis of Compensation Contracts

The preceding analysis suggests that the relative weight assigned to *RET* versus *ROE* in the cash compensation contract is:
- (*i*) an increasing function of the inverse of the noise ratios of the two performance measures,
- (*ii*) an increasing function of the degree to which the firm is in the "early" stages of investment, and
- (*iii*) a decreasing function of the extent to which the manager's other wealth is tied to stock price.

6.1 CORRELATION ANALYSIS

The results in table 3 indicate that the distributions of many of the variables described above are highly skewed (particularly *MR-CC*, *BC-CC*, *EQ/COMP*, and *STOCK*). In order to obtain more "normal" distributions, we applied a logarithmic transformation to each of the variables.[33] An additional justification for applying a logarithmic transformation is that it converts the multiplicative relation expressed in equation (8) into a more easily estimated additive relation. That is, equation (8) suggests that the ratio of the slope coefficients is related to the ratio of the noise measures *times* the ratio of the sensitivities of the two performance measures. Taking the logarithm of both sides of equation (8) results in an equation in which the logarithm of the ratio of the slope coefficients is related to the logarithm of the ratio of the noise measures *plus* the logarithm of the sensitivities of the performance measures.

The Pearson correlations (after applying the logarithmic transformation) among the proxies for the *PERF MIX*, *NOISE*, *GROWTH*, and

---

[33] Since the variables *MR-AP* and *BC-AP* contain negative values, these variables were not transformed. Moreover, since the variable *ZTRANS* had already been transformed into a normally distributed random variable, no adjustment was made to this variable either.

In addition, each of the distributions for the variables was winsorized (i.e., the "extreme" observations were reset to "less extreme" values—the extreme values were not deleted from the sample). No more than four data points per variable were affected by this procedure. The cutoff points were chosen on the basis of an examination of the univariate histogram for each variable.

OTHER constructs are presented in table 5.[34] These results indicate that the correlations are generally consistent with the hypotheses discussed above. The correlations between the proxies for the *PERF MIX* construct and the *NOISE* construct are generally positive (14 of 18), the correlations between the proxies for the *PERF MIX* and the *GROWTH* construct are also generally positive (9 of 12), and the correlations between the *PERF MIX* proxies and the *OTHER* proxies all have the hypothesized negative sign. Moreover, the results in table 5 also indicate that the proxies for a given theoretical construct are generally highly correlated with each other. The only exception occurs in the *NOISE* construct, where the variables *RTVAR* and *RSVAR* are highly correlated with each other but virtually uncorrelated with *ZTRANS*. This result suggests that the variable *ZTRANS* is not measuring the same underlying variable as *RTVAR* and *RSVAR*. Since the theoretical justification in section 5.2.2 for the variable *ZTRANS* is also considerably different from the justification for the *RTVAR* and *RSVAR* variables, our subsequent empirical tests will analyze the *ZTRANS* variable as a distinct construct, which we refer to as *CORR*.

Although the results in table 5 provide information concerning the relations among the *proxies* for the theoretical constructs, our real concern is with the relations among the underlying *constructs* themselves. For example, we are interested in the correlation between the constructs *PERF MIX* and *NOISE*, as opposed to the correlation between the proxies *MR-PP* and *RTVAR*. There are at least three factors which make it difficult to assess the statistical significance of the relation between the *constructs* on the basis of the correlations among the *proxies*. First, each proxy measures its underlying construct with error. The presence of this measurement error will, ceteris paribus, attenuate the bivariate correlation coefficients. As we discuss below, the existence of multiple proxies for a given construct can, in principle, be used to reduce this problem.

Second, it is difficult to "combine" the correlations among alternative indicators for the same proxy. For example, although the correlations among *all* of the proxies for the *PERF MIX* and the *OTHER* constructs have the predicted signs, the statistical significance of the individual correlations (not presented) varies considerably across proxies. In the case of the *PERF MIX* and the *GROWTH* constructs, this problem is even worse because the signs of the correlations are different for the individual proxies. Inconsistencies in the significance levels and signs of the bivariate correlations make it difficult to draw conclusions concerning the research hypotheses regarding the relations among the underlying constructs.

---

[34] We also computed the Spearman rank-order correlations, which should be less affected by the "nonnormality" of the data, for the untransformed variables. The results (not presented) were very similar to the Pearson correlations applied to the transformed variables presented in table 5.

TABLE 5

Matrix of Pearson Correlation Coefficients for the Variables Used in the Cross-Sectional Analysis of the Relative Weights Placed on Performance Measures in Compensation Contracts[a]

	MR-PP	BC-PP	MR-AP	BC-AP	MR-CC	BC-CC	RTVAR	RSVAR	ZTRANS	A GROW	S GROW	PERCENT	EQ/COMP
BC-PP	0.882												
MR-AP	0.787	0.714											
BC-AP	0.681	0.831	0.837										
MR-CC	0.999	0.645	0.507	0.611									
BC-CC	0.795	0.859	0.549	0.705	0.928								
RTVAR	0.359	0.222	0.062	0.063	−0.023	0.023							
RSVAR	0.157	0.063	0.014	0.004	−0.031	−0.040	0.662						
ZTRANS	0.067	0.139	−0.048	0.111	0.204	0.176	0.029	−0.028					
A GROW	−0.001	0.139	0.038	0.080	0.113	0.117	−0.328	−0.320	0.035				
S GROW	−0.031	0.043	−0.009	0.013	0.017	0.043	−0.337	−0.328	−0.006	0.802			
PER-CENT	−0.292	−0.233	−0.086	−0.075	−0.078	−0.115	0.034	0.028	−0.067	−0.050	0.096		
EQ/COMP	−0.308	−0.265	−0.072	−0.086	−0.090	−0.110	−0.028	−0.013	−0.032	0.019	0.183	0.900	
STOCK	−0.299	−0.266	−0.064	−0.080	−0.113	−0.136	0.011	0.020	−0.043	−0.041	0.140	0.868	0.980

[a] See table 2 for a definition of the variables. The sample size for the correlations is 370, except for comparisons involving MR-PP (n = 166), BC-PP (n = 161), MR-AP (n = 277), and BC-AP (n = 283).

Finally, the individual elements of the correlation matrix are *simple* correlations not *partial* correlations. Although this problem could be solved by conducting a multiple regression of each proxy for *PERF MIX* on all of the proxies for the remaining constructs, this would not solve the other problems discussed above. Moreover, because the proxies for a given construct are typically highly correlated, it may be difficult to obtain precise estimates of the individual coefficients.

6.2 LATENT VARIABLE ANALYSIS

In order to mitigate the measurement and interpretation problems associated with standard multivariate analysis (such as the correlation coefficients in table 5), we estimate each underlying theoretical construct, or *latent variable*, by "combining" each of its proxies.[35] Because such a "combination" should possess less measurement error than the individual proxies, the "measurement error" bias in estimating the relations among the latent variables should be less serious. Moreover, this procedure allows the calculation of a *single* correlation coefficient (or regression coefficient) between any two latent variables, and this avoids difficulties in interpreting several regression coefficients for variables which attempt to measure the same construct.

To implement this procedure, we employ a latent variable structural equation model to estimate the relations among the latent or unobservable variables. Similar to most econometric analyses, we assume that the endogenous latent variable, *PERF MIX*, is related to the exogenous latent variables, *NOISE*, *CORR*, *GROWTH*, and *OTHER*, by the following linear expression:

$$PERF\ MIX = \gamma_0 + \gamma_1 NOISE + \gamma_2 CORR$$
$$+ \gamma_3 GROWTH + \gamma_4 OTHER + \zeta \quad (12)$$

where the γ_i are regression coefficients and ζ is the structural equation residual or disturbance term. The signs and significance levels of the γ_i are used to examine our research hypotheses. The statistical theory underlying this methodological approach and the computational algorithms are described in Joreskog [1969; 1971; 1978], Browne [1984], and Bentler [1983a; 1983b], among others, and are briefly discussed in Appendix A.

6.3 RESULTS OF THE LATENT VARIABLE ANALYSIS

As discussed in Appendix A, our data do not strictly conform to a multivariate normal distribution. This distributional assumption can be

---

[35] Another alternative would be to select a single proxy for each construct and then estimate a multiple regression using the selected proxies. This alternative is not pursued because the selection of the "best" proxy would be arbitrary. Moreover, there is likely to be a loss of information associated with dropping the other proxies for the constructs. Finally, the "best" proxy is likely to be subject to the measurement error problems discussed in the text.

critical to the properties of maximum likelihood parameter estimates of equation (12). In order to assess the sensitivity of our estimates to the absence of multivariate normality, we also provide estimates using elliptical distribution theory (which allows for a common kurtosis for each variable) and unweighted least squares (which makes no distributional assumptions). In addition, several assessments of the degree to which our model characterizes the observed data are presented in Appendix B.

The estimates for the parameters of the structural model are presented in table 6. In general, the maximum likelihood, elliptical distribution, and unweighted least squares procedures provide similar results in terms of coefficient estimates, statistical significance of the estimates, and explanatory power of the structural model. Moreover, the signs of the coefficients are generally the same across the three cases (Positive/Positive, Anything/Positive, and Constrained/Constrained). In general, the slope coefficients on the *NOISE*, *GROWTH*, and *OTHER* variables have the predicted signs (i.e., positive, positive, and negative, respectively), and each variable has a slope coefficient that is statistically significant (at the 0.05 level, two-tailed) in at least one of the cases. The coefficient on the *CORR* variable was positive in every case, which implies that a lower correlation between *ROE* and *RET* is associated with a lower relative weight being placed on *RET* (and a higher relative weight placed on *ROE*), ceteris paribus. It should be noted that the statistical significance of the coefficients varies *across* the three cases. The significance of the *GROWTH* and *OTHER* constructs was the most consistent across the cases, and the significance of the *NOISE* construct was the least consistent.

Finally, the correlation matrix among the constructs (not presented) indicates that two of the exogenous constructs, *NOISE* and *GROWTH*, are significantly *negatively* correlated, while the *GROWTH* and the *OTHER* constructs were significantly *positively* correlated. Although the magnitudes of the correlations vary from case to case, the correlation between *NOISE* and *GROWTH* is approximately -0.35, and the correlation between *GROWTH* and *OTHER* is approximately 0.14. These results suggest that, ceteris paribus, high-growth firms tend to have a lower variance of *ROE* relative to *RET* and high amounts of "other incentives" tied to stock price.[36]

7. Discussion and Summary

This paper examines the usage of accounting return on equity (*ROE*) and security market return (*RET*) as performance measures in the cash compensation (salary plus annual bonus) contracts of chief executive

---

[36] As in multiple regression analysis, a high correlation between independent variables makes it difficult to obtain a precise estimate for the slope coefficients on these variables. As a result, the standard error associated with the estimate of each coefficient becomes large.

TABLE 6

Estimates of the Structural Model in Equation (12):

PERF MIX $= \gamma_1$ NOISE $+ \gamma_2$ CORR $+ \gamma_3$ GROWTH $+ \gamma_4$ OTHER

A. Positive/Positive Case ($n = 148$)—both the RET and ROE slope are positive

	γ_1	γ_2	γ_3	γ_4	R-squared
Maximum Likelihood Coefficient	.346	.083	.135	-.297	21.9%
Maximum Likelihood z-statistic	4.061	1.121	1.750	-3.982	
Elliptical Distribution Coefficient	.345	.083	.134	-.296	22.0%
Elliptical Distribution z-statistic	3.771	1.044	1.625	-3.707	
Unweighted Least Squares Coefficient	.324	.098	.196	-.314	21.9%
Unweighted Least Squares t-statistic	3.593	1.369	2.002	-3.756	

B. Anything/Positive Case ($n = 270$)—RET slope can be positive or negative, but ROE slope is positive

	γ_1	γ_2	γ_3	γ_4	R-squared
Maximum Likelihood Coefficient	.037	.033	.100	-.107	1.9%
Maximum Likelihood z-statistic	.494	.538	1.433	-1.742	
Elliptical Distribution Coefficient	.037	.033	.100	-.107	1.9%
Elliptical Distribution z-statistic	.420	.457	1.214	-1.477	
Unweighted Least Squares Coefficient	.049	.006	.131	-.091	2.1%
Unweighted Least Squares t-statistic	.577	.087	1.833	-1.221	

C. Constrained/Constrained Case ($n = 370$)—both the slope for RET and ROE were constrained to be positive

	γ_1	γ_2	γ_3	γ_4	R-squared
Maximum Likelihood Coefficient	-.015	.200	.043	-.096	5.2%
Maximum Likelihood z-statistic	-.226	3.909	.705	-1.847	
Elliptical Distribution Coefficient	-.016	.200	.040	-.095	5.2%
Elliptical Distribution z-statistic	-.230	3.552	.601	-1.657	
Unweighted Least Squares Coefficient	.022	.190	.096	-.114	5.8%
Unweighted Least Squares t-statistic	.321	3.597	1.427	-2.193	

officers.[37] Our analysis relies on analytical agency models, particularly the results of Holmstrom [1979] and Banker and Datar [1987], for a theoretical framework relating executive compensation to ROE and RET based on the "informational properties" of the two performance measures. We control for the influence of "other factors" on the form of the compensation function (such as differences in the form of the agent's utility function and external opportunities) in order to concentrate on the "informational properties" of ROE and RET.

The theoretical model specifies a linear relation between compensation (raised to a power that is unknown to the researcher) and the performance variables ROE and RET. We estimate the parameters of this relation for each firm using the Box-Cox power transformation estimation procedure. Our results suggest that cash compensation exhibits a strong positive time-series relation with ROE, but only a modest time-series relation with RET. Our estimates of the appropriate power transformation for the compensation number, which can be interpreted as an estimate of the manager's coefficient of proportional risk aversion, are imprecise. This result is consistent with the conclusions of prior researchers who indicate that their results are insensitive to different ad hoc specifications of the compensation variable.

Previous researchers have also suggested that the magnitude of the correlation and/or magnitude of the slope coefficient between compensation and RET provides evidence on the "rationality" of compensation

---

[37] We also conducted the analysis using only the "firm-specific" component of the accounting and security market measures of performance. In order to construct the firm-specific components of performance, we defined the accounting performance index to be the change in the value-weighted ROE for all firms on the *Compustat* tape (excluding the firms in our sample), and the security market performance index to be the (real) value-weighted *CRSP* index of security market returns. For each firm, we estimated a time-series regression of the firm's performance on the performance index over the period 1970–84 (a separate regression was conducted for the accounting and the security market measures of performance). The results of these regressions are summarized in table 4 (panels A and B). We then defined the "firm-specific" components of the firm's performance measure to be the residuals from these regressions.

The firm-specific components of performance were then used in the time-series regressions of compensation on performance. The results of these regressions (not reported) were similar to the results reported in table 1. In particular, the average t-statistic was much higher for the coefficient on the accounting measure of performance than for the market measure of performance. In conducting the cross-sectional analysis, the "independent variables" were constructed in a manner consistent with the time-series analysis. For example, since the time-series analysis regresses compensation on only the firm-specific component of performance, we defined the *NOISE* variable to be the variance of the firm-specific component of the change in *ROE* divided by the variance of the firm-specific component of *RET* in the cross-sectional analysis. The results of the cross-sectional analysis (not reported) were similar to the results reported in the text. For example, the coefficients on the *NOISE*, *CORR*, *GROWTH*, and *OTHER* variables were generally positive, positive, positive, and negative, respectively. The coefficients were most significant for the *NOISE* and *OTHER* variables. Finally, the explanatory power of the cross-sectional analysis was greatest for the Positive/Positive case.

packages (e.g., see Coughlan and Schmidt [1985], Murphy [1986], and Jensen and Murphy [1987]). However, from an agency theory perspective, there is no a priori reason to expect that a high correlation between compensation and *RET* is indicative of a "good" contract or a "bad" contract. Instead, our analysis suggests that the usage of *RET* in the contract will depend on the magnitude of its "signal-to-noise" ratio with respect to evaluating the agent's performance relative to the "signal-to-noise" ratio of other performance measures (such as *ROE*).

Hypotheses regarding cross-sectional differences in the relative amounts of "signal-to-noise" in *ROE* and *RET* were examined using a latent variable analysis. This methodology reduces problems that arise in cross-sectional regression analysis when the dependent and independent variables specified by the theory cannot be directly observed. The results of our cross-sectional analysis suggest that the degree to which compensation is related to *RET* versus *ROE* is positively related to the inverse of the degree of "*NOISE*" in the two performance measures. This result is consistent with the agency theory notion that the influence of factors other than the agent's action (i.e., noncontrollable factors) on a performance measure can decrease the relative weight that it receives in the compensation contract.

In addition, we find that high-"*GROWTH*" firms tend to place relatively more emphasis on *RET* rather than *ROE* as a performance measure. We interpret this result as consistent with the hypothesis that accounting numbers provide a less useful measure of the agent's performance when the consequences of the agent's current-period actions tend to occur in the future and are not reflected in current-period accounting numbers. We also find that firms place less importance on *RET* (relative to *ROE*) in the cash compensation contract when *RET* is of more importance in the *OTHER* components of the agent's wealth. This suggests that the overall structure of the agent's wealth plays a role in the design of each component of the agent's compensation.

Finally, our results suggest that there is a positive association between the relative influence of *RET* versus *ROE* in compensation and the correlation between *RET* and *ROE*. Alternatively stated, this result suggests that a low correlation between *RET* and *ROE* is associated with less relative weight on *RET* and more relative weight on *ROE* in the compensation function. This is consistent with the hypothesis that a lack of correlation between *RET* and *ROE* does not imply that accounting earnings contain "measurement error" from the perspective of evaluating the agent's performance. As discussed in Gjesdal [1981], an information system that does not provide very informative signals regarding the value of the firm can provide signals that are valuable in evaluating the agent's performance.

One important limitation to our analysis arises from the "undesirable" distributional properties of the *ratio* of the estimated slope coefficients of compensation on *RET* versus *ROE*. As discussed in section 2, calculating the ratio of the two slope coefficients, in principle, allows us to control for "other factors" that affect the relation between compensation and performance. However, it is not clear how to handle negative slope coefficients, or how to assess the moments of the distribution of the ratio.

A related limitation is that our cross-sectional results are affected by the operational definition of the ratio of the slope coefficients. The results were strongest for the subsample of firms for which the slopes on both *RET* and *ROE* were positive (i.e., the Positive/Positive case). However, including firms with a negative slope coefficient on *RET* (i.e., the Anything/Positive case) substantially reduced the statistical significance of the results.

Finally, our results are limited by the restrictive structural model relating the constructs of interest. Specifically, we assume a simple recursive structure in which *PERF MIX* is an endogenous variable and *NOISE, CORR, GROWTH,* and *OTHER* are exogenous variables. If some of these constructs are endogenous, it would be desirable to develop a more complicated nonrecursive model in order to avoid the bias in the coefficients that results from ignoring the simultaneous equations aspects of the system.

APPENDIX A

Overview of Latent Variable Analysis

In a latent variable analysis, each observed variable, or proxy, is assumed to be composed of the "true score" for its underlying construct and "measurement error." In particular, it is assumed that the observed variables have a common factor analysis structure. For the Positive/Positive case, this structure can be represented as:

$$
\begin{bmatrix}
MR\text{-}PP \\
BC\text{-}PP \\
RTVAR \\
RSVAR \\
ZTRANS \\
A\,GROW \\
S\,GROW \\
PERCENT \\
EQ/COMP \\
STOCK
\end{bmatrix}
=
\begin{bmatrix}
\lambda_1 & 0 & 0 & 0 & 0 \\
\lambda_2 & 0 & 0 & 0 & 0 \\
0 & \lambda_3 & 0 & 0 & 0 \\
0 & \lambda_4 & 0 & 0 & 0 \\
0 & 0 & 1 & 0 & 0 \\
0 & 0 & 0 & \lambda_6 & 0 \\
0 & 0 & 0 & \lambda_7 & 0 \\
0 & 0 & 0 & 0 & \lambda_8 \\
0 & 0 & 0 & 0 & \lambda_9 \\
0 & 0 & 0 & 0 & \lambda_{10}
\end{bmatrix}
\begin{bmatrix}
PERF\,MIX \\
NOISE \\
CORR \\
GROWTH \\
OTHER
\end{bmatrix}
+
\begin{bmatrix}
\delta_1 \\
\delta_2 \\
\delta_3 \\
\delta_4 \\
0 \\
\delta_6 \\
\delta_7 \\
\delta_8 \\
\delta_9 \\
\delta_{10}
\end{bmatrix}
\quad (A1)
$$

where the λ_i are regression parameters, and the δ_i are "measurement errors" or disturbance terms. The disturbance terms in equation (A1) are assumed to be uncorrelated with the underlying constructs and uncorrelated with each other. Since the *CORR* construct has only a single variable (i.e., *ZTRANS*), the relation between *CORR* and *ZTRANS* is expressed as an identity.[38]

Statistical procedures for estimating the relations among the latent variables, such as those implied by the structure imposed by equation (A1), have been developed by Joreskog [1969; 1971; 1978], Browne [1984], and Bentler [1983a; 1983b], among others. These procedures exploit the fact that the covariance matrix among the *observed* variables can be expressed as a function of the parameters λ_i and var(δ_i) from equation (A1) and the parameters of the variance–covariance matrix among the *latent* variables.[39] Specifically, let $\sum (\theta)$ denote the variance–covariance matrix implied by a given set of basic parameters θ (i.e., the parameters λ_i, var(δ_i), and the parameters of the variance–covariance matrix of the latent variables). Intuitively, the estimation procedure can be thought of as choosing the parameters θ whose corresponding variance–covariance matrix, $\sum (\theta)$, most closely reproduces the empirical variance–covariance matrix for the observed variables, S. Given the estimates for the variance–covariance matrix for the latent variables, the partial correlation coefficients (and their associated standard errors) between the latent variables, which correspond to the parameters γ_i in equation (12), can then be obtained in a straightforward manner.

More formally, the basic parameters θ are chosen to minimize the fit function:

$$(\mathbf{s} - \boldsymbol{\sigma}(\theta))' \mathbf{W} (\mathbf{s} - \boldsymbol{\sigma}(\theta)), \qquad (A2)$$

where $\mathbf{s}$ is a (55×1) vector of the variances and covariances of the observed variables, and σ is the corresponding (55×1) vector of variances and covariances implied by the basic parameters θ.[40] The vector ($\mathbf{s} - \boldsymbol{\sigma}(\boldsymbol{\theta})$) therefore represents the *residual* variances and covariances of the observed variables (i.e., the portion of the variances and covariances that cannot be explained by the underlying parameters θ).

The matrix $\mathbf{W}$ determines the weight that each *residual* variance or covariance receives in selecting the basic parameters θ to minimize the fit function. The choice of the matrix $\mathbf{W}$ depends on the assumptions made about the distributions of the observed variables. For example, if the observed variables are independent and follow a multivariate normal distribution, the weight matrix can be specified so that the estimation procedure provides full information *maximum likelihood* (*FIML*) esti-

---

[38] We also constrain the variances of the latent variables to be equal to one in order to identify the system (see Long [1976] for a discussion of this issue).

[39] For example, the covariance between the variables *MR-PP* and *RTVAR* is $\lambda_1\lambda_3 \cdot$ cov(*PERF MIX, NOISE*), and the covariance between the variables *BC-PP* and *RSVAR* is $\lambda_2\lambda_4 \cdot$ cov(*PERF MIX, NOISE*). As discussed in n. 38, since the variances of the latent variables are constrained to equal one, the covariances among the latent variables are equal to the correlations between the latent variables.

[40] In particular, s is the lower triangular elements (including the diagonal elements) of the estimated variance–covariance matrix of the observed variables.

mates and standard errors for the coefficients relating the latent variables to other latent variables and for the coefficients relating the latent variables to their observed proxies.[41] Under these conditions, the *FIML* estimates are consistent, asymptotically normally distributed, and asymptotically efficient.

To provide some evidence on how well our data satisfy the assumption of multivariate normality, table 7 presents the skewness and kurtosis of each variable used in the cross-sectional analysis. The results indicate that, even after the data have undergone a logarithmic transformation, the assumption of multivariate normality can be rejected (for an overall test of the assumption of multivariate normality, we use the Mardia [1970] test, which is distributed as a standard normal variable in large samples). Multivariate normality is least seriously violated for the Positive/Positive case, followed by the Constrained/Constrained case and the Anything/Positive case. For the proxies for the exogenous constructs, the *EQ/COMP* and *STOCK* variables are positively skewed, and the *S GROW* variable has a more positive kurtosis than would be expected in a normal distribution. For the proxies for the endogenous constructs, the Positive/Positive proxies are closest to satisfying the normality assumption, the Anything/Positive proxies are leptokurtic, and the Constrained/Constrained proxies are positively skewed.

Bentler [1985, pp. 53–54] reports that "there is little empirical or theoretical guidance available as to when a statistically significant variation from normality becomes large enough to affect structural modeling conclusions." The maximum likelihood *parameter* estimates are generally robust to violations of normality. However, the standard errors must be interpreted with caution when the variables are not normally distributed. In order to provide some evidence on the appropriateness of the maximum likelihood procedures for our problem, we also conduct the estimation using procedures that allow for distributions that are more general than multivariate normal.

For situations in which the primary violation of normality results from the kurtosis of the variables, Browne [1984] has developed estimation procedures (i.e., the specification of the form of the **W** marix) based on *elliptical distribution theory*. In particular, the elliptical distribution estimation procedures are based on the assumption that the variables have a *common* coefficient of kurtosis. Under these conditions, the resulting elliptical estimators are consistent and asymptotically efficient. The estimation procedure also provides standard errors for the parameter estimates which allow significance tests to be performed. For our data

---

[41] In particular, if the weight matrix is iteratively updated during estimation, minimizing equation (A2) is equivalent to minimizing the function $\log[\det(\Sigma)] + \text{trace}[\mathbf{S} \ \Sigma^{-1}] - \log[\det(S)] - p$, where log is the natural logarithm, det is the determinant of a matrix, trace is the trace of a matrix, and p is the number of observed variables ($p = 10$ for our model). See Browne [1984, p. 65] for a discussion of this point. This function corresponds to the standard likelihood function for latent variable estimation.

TABLE 7

Descriptive Statistics for the Variables Used in the Cross-Sectional Analysis of the Performance Measures Used in Compensation Contracts

A. Positive/Positive Case ($n = 148$ firms)—both the *RET* and *ROE* slopes are positive

Variable:[a]	MR-PP	BC-PP	RTVAR	RSVAR	ZTRANS	A GROW	S GROW	PERCENT	EQ/COMP	STOCK
SKEWNESS	−.4009	−.1263	.4288	−.3222	−.0063	.0990	.0115	.5183	.9607	.6918
KURTOSIS	−.1808	−.1386	−.0223	−.0357	.0917	.1832	1.2314	−.0166	.4909	.2400

Standard Error for Univariate Tests of Skewness: .201[b]
Standard Error for Univariate Tests of Kurtosis: .401[c]
z-statistic for Mardia Test for Multivariate Normality: 7.27

B. Anything/Positive Case ($n = 270$ firms)—*RET* slope can be positive or negative, but *ROE* slope is positive

Variable:	MR-AP	BC-AP	RTVAR	RSVAR	ZTRANS	A GROW	S GROW	PERCENT	EQ/COMP	STOCK
SKEWNESS	−.2267	.6440	.6162	−.2691	−.2268	.1945	.0561	.4016	.7843	.5225
KURTOSIS	6.8142	6.7658	.1873	−.1834	.1654	.2926	.8706	−.1191	.2615	.0973

Standard Error for Univariate Tests of Skewness: .149
Standard Error for Univariate Tests of Kurtosis: .298
z-statistic for Mardia Test for Multivariate Normality: 24.64

C. Constrained/Constrained ($n = 370$ firms)—both the slopes for *RET* and *ROE* were constrained to be positive

Variable:	MR-CC	BC-CC	RTVAR	RSVAR	ZTRANS	A GROW	S GROW	PERCENT	EQ/COMP	STOCK
SKEWNESS	.9621	1.0719	.8384	−.1590	−.0656	.0144	.0242	.5128	.8477	.5748
KURTOSIS	−.1641	.0425	.8560	−.1925	.3006	.1846	.6602	−.1307	.3334	.0385

Standard Error for Univariate Tests of Skewness: .127
Standard Error for Univariate Tests of Kurtosis: .254
z-statistic for Mardia Test for Multivariate Normality: 16.15

[a] See table 2 for a definition of the variables.
[b] In a large sample, the coefficient of skewness is distributed normally with a standard error that is approximately equal to $\sqrt{6/(N+1)}$.
[c] In a large sample, the coefficient of kurtosis is distributed normally with a standard error that is approximately equal to $\sqrt{24/(N+1)}$.

(see the results in table 7), the assumption of equal coefficients of kurtosis is more likely to be met for the Positive/Positive and the Constrained/Constrained cases than for the Anything/Positive case.

In order to provide estimates under even more general assumptions regarding the distributions of the variables, we also estimate the coefficients using *unweighted least squares*.[42] While the coefficients provided by this method are consistent, they are not asymptotically efficient. One further disadvantage of the unweighted least squares estimation procedure is that the standard errors of the coefficients cannot be directly calculated. Joreskog [1981] suggests that the standard errors can be calculated using jackknifing methods. Therefore, our empirical results present jackknifed standard errors for the coefficients estimated using the unweighted least squares method. It should be noted, however, that jackknifing methods can be sensitive to skewness in the data (see Mosteller and Tukey [1977]).

APPENDIX B
Assessment of the Latent Variable Model

Before the parameter estimates can be interpreted, it is important first to examine how well the estimated model implied by the theory characterizes the data. In particular, it is critical to demonstrate that each proxy measure has a positive and statistically significant relationship with its construct. This examination is done by determining whether each λ is positive and has a "large" z-statistic.[43] The results in table 8

---

[42] In this case, the estimation procedure is equivalent to minimizing $(\mathbf{s} - \boldsymbol{\sigma}(\theta))'\mathbf{W}(\mathbf{s} - \boldsymbol{\sigma}(\theta))$, where $\mathbf{W}$ is an identity matrix. This is equivalent to minimizing the sum of the squared covariance residuals.

An alternative estimation procedure is to use the Arbitrary Distribution Function (ADF) estimators developed by Browne [1984]. These estimators impose no distributional restrictions except that the first four moments and the eighth moment of the distributions exist. This procedure is computationally intensive relative to the ones that we employ and sensitive to the starting values provided to the algorithm. The ADF estimators provided results similar to those reported in tables 6 and 8 for the Positive/Positive case. However, we experienced convergence problems in attempting to estimate the parameters of the other two cases. This result may be due to the fact that the relations between the variables appear to be much stronger in the Positive/Positive case than in the other two cases. Moreover, the simulation results in Browne [1984] seem to suggest that the ADF estimates can be biased in small samples. Despite these problems, the distribution-free nature of the ADF estimators may make them attractive in research studies in which multivariate normality is a tenuous assumption.

[43] For ease of comparison, the parameters reported in tables 6 and 8 are *standardized* (i.e., computed as if the latent variables have unit variances and the observed variables also have unit variances). Since the scales for the variables are irrelevant for our purposes, this does not affect the substantive inferences made regarding the research hypotheses. However, the z-statistics reported in the tables are based on the unstandardized solution (because the input into the estimation algorithm is the covariance matrix not the correlation matrix). The covariance matrix is used as the input because the mathematical statistics that form the basis of the estimation are developed from knowledge of the distribution of the covariance matrix (e.g., if the data are multivariate normal, the covariance matrix is Wishart distributed). The distribution of the correlation matrix is less obvious.

TABLE 8

Estimation of the Parameters of the Latent Variable Model Expressed in Equation (A1)

CONSTRUCT:	PERF MIX		NOISE		CORR	GROWTH		OTHER			GOODNESS-OF-FIT INDEXES[c]			
PROXY: PARAMETER:	MR-PP λ_1	BC-PP λ_2	RTVAR λ_3	RSVAR λ_4	ZTRANS λ_5	A GROW λ_6	S GROW λ_7	PERCENT λ_8	EQ/COMP λ_9	STOCK λ_{10}	BENT-BON	CHISQ	prob.	% sig.
A. Positive/Positive Case (n = 148 firms)—both the RET and ROE slopes are positive														
ML[b] Coefficient:	0.991	0.889	0.979	0.716	1.000[a]	0.797	1.000	0.883	1.000	0.980	.960	50.948	.002	1.8%
ML z-statistic:	13.728	11.963	9.318	7.517	—	11.701	—	13.716	—	16.484				
EL[b] Coefficient:	0.992	0.889	0.980	0.714	1.000	0.797	1.000	0.883	1.000	0.980	.939	42.091	.024	1.8%
EL z-statistic:	12.546	10.978	8.612	6.944	—	10.736	—	12.519	—	14.918				
ULS[b] Coefficient:	0.975	0.900	0.930	0.734	1.000	0.825	0.912	0.871	1.000	0.975	.985	N/A	N/A	0.0%
ULS t-statistic:	17.412	15.497	6.940	5.243	—	3.986	3.948	34.701	—	87.865				
B. Anything/Positive Case (n = 270 firms)—RET slope can be positive or negative, but ROE slope is positive														
ML Coefficient:	0.837	1.000	0.828	0.827	1.000	0.815	0.982	0.888	1.000	0.979	.965	75.188	<.001	3.6%
ML z-statistic:	17.046	—	10.967	10.967	—	12.316	14.357	18.696	—	22.237				
EL Coefficient:	0.837	1.000	0.828	0.827	1.000	0.814	0.982	0.888	1.000	0.979	.948	48.172	.005	3.6%
EL z-statistic:	14.017	—	9.183	9.181	—	10.276	11.922	15.278	—	17.900				
ULS Coefficient:	0.830	1.000	0.822	0.826	1.000	0.813	.978	0.875	1.000	0.969	.991	N/A	N/A	0.0%
ULS t-statistic:	21.015	—	12.422	9.741	—	12.357	12.256	47.831	—	155.815				

C. Constrained/Constrained ($n = 370$ firms)—both the slopes for RET and ROE were constrained to be positive

ML	Coefficient:	0.989	0.938	0.823	0.804	1.000	0.820	0.979	0.900	1.000	0.980	.956	146.496	<.001	5.4%
ML	z-statistic:	17.163	16.435	12.810	12.611	—	15.017	17.593	22.403	—	26.105			
EL	Coefficient:	0.991	0.936	0.823	0.804	1.000	0.818	0.981	0.900	1.000	0.980	.932	106.668	<.001	5.4%
EL	z-statistic:	15.350	14.664	11.496	11.324	—	13.421	15.711	19.767	—	22.820			
ULS	Coefficient:	0.928	0.999	0.818	0.803	1.000	0.843	0.947	0.891	1.000	0.977	.987	N/A	N/A	5.4%
ULS	t-statistic:	48.353	230.396	15.212	12.360	—	12.730	12.829	65.044	—	227.200			

[a] Parameter was constrained.

[b] ML refers to maximum likelihood estimates and standard errors, EL refers to elliptical distribution estimates and standard errors, and ULS refers to unweighted least squares jackknifed estimates and standard errors.

[c] BENT-BON is the Bentler-Bonnet index described in Appendix B, CHISQ is likelihood ratio test statistic, prob. is the probability of observing a chi-squared value at least as large as CHISQ under the null hypothesis that the theoretical model describes the observed data, and % sig. refers to the percentage of standardized residuals that are statistically significant at the 0.05 level (two-tailed).

indicate that for each case and for each estimation method, each λ is close to one and is highly significant.[44] It is also desirable to observe that the structural equation has a nontrivial coefficient of determination.[45] The explanatory power of the structural model varied considerably across the three cases (table 8). The Positive/Positive case had the highest R-squared (21.9%), followed by the Constrained/Constrained (5.2%) and the Anything/Positive (1.9%) cases.[46]

Several common indexes are used to assess the "goodness of fit" for the estimated theoretical specification. One index is the maximum likelihood chi-square statistic, which is computed by multiplying the sample size by the minimum of the maximum likelihood fit function (see n. 41). If the theoretical model is able to reproduce the observed variance–covariance matrix, the chi-squared value will be small (with an associated large probability level). The probability value associated with the chi-squared is typically compared to a standard "cutoff" of 0.01 or 0.05. For each of our three cases, we can reject (at the 0.01 level) the hypothesis that our model explains the covariance structure of the observed variables. However, as discussed by Joreskog and Sorbom [1984], among others, the chi-square is very sensitive to sample size and departures from multivariate normality. In particular, large sample sizes and lack of multivariate normality tend to increase the chi-square above what can be expected from specification error in the theoretical model.

An alternative goodness-of-fit statistic has been developed by Bentler and Bonett [1980]. This index compares the value (denoted Q) of the fit

---

[44] Several of the loadings were constrained to be equal to one in table 8. This was done because the unconstrained estimation exhibited an "improper solution" (i.e., a standardized loading, λ, greater than one and an associated negative measurement error variance). Following the procedures recommended in Van Driel [1978] and Gerbing and Anderson [forthcoming], the cause of the improper solution appeared to be sampling variation, as opposed to model misspecification. Therefore, the loading for the improper solution was constrained at one, and the respecified model was estimated. For the constrained λ's, we do not report z-statistics.

It is important to note, however, that this type of respecification can produce biased estimates for the loadings and correlations between latent variables. Specifically, the simulation results in Gerbing and Anderson [forthcoming] suggest that the λ's for the factor containing the improper solution are "too large" and the correlations between latent variables are "too small." In addition, the standard errors for the parameter estimates are "too large." This type of bias is a limitation to our empirical analysis.

[45] See Fornell and Larcker [1981], Bagozzi, Fornell, and Larcker [1981], and Joreskog and Sorbom [1984] for a discussion of various indexes of explanatory power in a latent variable context.

[46] In psychometric terms, the large, positive λ's suggest that the proxies exhibit *convergent validity* (i.e., different measures of the same construct are highly correlated). In addition, the results also suggest that the proxies exhibit *discriminant validity* (i.e., different measures of different constructs are less highly correlated than different measures of the same construct). Discriminant validity can be demonstrated if none of the confidence intervals for the bivariate correlations between constructs includes one. Although not reported in table 8, none of our confidence intervals includes the value of one.

function in equation (A2) for the theoretical model to the value (denoted Q_0) of the fit function for a "null model" (i.e., a model where each proxy variable is its own latent variable and each of these latent variables is constrained to be independent). The Bentler and Bonett index is computed as $[1 - Q/Q_0]$. This index can be thought of as providing some indication of how much better the theoretical model fits the data relative to the severely constrained null model. Bentler [1985] suggests that the Bentler and Bonett index should exceed 0.90 in reasonable models. For each of our cases, the Bentler-Bonett index exceeds this suggested "cutoff".

Finally, we also examine the standardized residual covariance (or correlation) matrix, $(\mathbf{s} - \sigma(\theta))$, for large and statistically significant values. Many large residuals are indicative of an inability of the theoretical model to reproduce the observed variance–covariance matrix. Therefore, we report the percentage of standardized residual covariances that are statistically significant at the 0.05 level (two-tailed). For the Positive/Positive case, less than 2% of the standardized residual covariances were significant. For the Anything/Positive case, less than 4% were significant, and for the Constrained/Constrained case, less than 6% were significant. Overall, we conclude that our model has a "reasonable" ability to reproduce the observed variance–covariance matrix.

REFERENCES

ADAMS, H. "Factors Affecting the Use of Performance Variables in Executive Compensation Contracts." Working paper, Northwestern University, 1987.

ANTLE, R., AND A. SMITH. "Measuring Executive Compensation: Methods and an Application." *Journal of Accounting Research* (Spring 1985): 296–325.

———. "An Empirical Investigation into the Relative Performance Evaluation of Corporate Executives." *Journal of Accounting Research* (Spring 1986): 1–39.

BAGOZZI, R. P., C. FORNELL, AND D. F. LARCKER. "Canonical Correlation Analysis as a Special Case of a Structural Relations Model." *Multivariate Behavioral Research* (October 1981): 437–54.

BANKER, R., AND S. DATAR. "Sensitivity, Precision, and Linear Aggregation of Accounting Signals." Working paper, Carnegie Mellon University, 1987.

BAUMOL, W. J. *Business Behavior, Value, and Growth.* New York: Harcourt, Brace & World, 1967.

BEAVER, W. *Financial Reporting: An Accounting Revolution.* Englewood Cliffs, N.J.: Prentice-Hall, 1981.

BENSTON, G. "The Self-Serving Hypothesis: Some Evidence." *Journal of Accounting and Economics* (April 1985): 67–84.

BENTLER, P. M. "Some Contributions to Efficient Statistics for Structural Models: Specification and Estimation of Moment Structures." *Psychometrika* (December 1983a): 493–517.

———. "Simultaneous Equation Systems as Moment Structure Models." *Journal of Econometrics* (May/June 1983b): 13–42.

———. *Theory and Implementation of EQS: A Structural Equations Program.* Los Angeles: BMDP Statistical Software, 1985.

———, AND D. G. BONETT. "Significance Tests and Goodness of Fit in the Analysis of Covariance Structures." *Psychological Bulletin* 88 (1980): 588–606.

BOOZ, ALLEN AND HAMILTON. *Executive Pay in the Eighties: Major Exposures Ahead.* New York: Booz, Allen and Hamilton, 1983.

Box, G., AND D. Cox. "An Analysis of Transformations." *Journal of the Royal Statistical Society*, series B, no. 2 (1964): 211–52.

Brickley, J. A., S. Bhagat, AND R. C. Lease. "The Impact of Long-Range Managerial Compensation Plans on Shareholder Wealth." *Journal of Accounting and Economics* (April 1985): 115–29.

Browne, M. W. "Asymptotically Distribution-Free Methods for the Analysis of Covariance Structures." *British Journal of Mathematical and Statistical Psychology* (May 1984): 62–83.

Coughlan, A. T., AND R. M. Schmidt. "Executive Compensation, Management Turnover, and Firm Performance: An Empirical Investigation." *Journal of Accounting and Economics* (April 1985): 43–66.

Defeo, V., R. Lambert, AND D. Larcker. "The Executive Compensation Effects of Equity-for-Debt Swaps." Working paper, University of Pennsylvania, 1987.

Dye, R. "Relative Performance Evaluation and Project Selection." Working paper, Northwestern University, 1987.

Ely, K. "Cross-Sectional Variations in the Relationship Between Accounting Variables and the Chief Executive's Compensation." Working paper, University of Chicago, 1987.

Fellingham, J., P. Newman, AND Y. Suh. "Contracts Without Memory in Multiperiod Agency Models." *Journal of Economic Theory* (1987).

Fornell, C. *A Second Generation of Multivariate Analysis.* Vols. 1 and 2. New York: Praeger, 1982.

———, AND D. F. Larcker. "Evaluating Structural Equation Models with Unobservable Variables and Measurement Error." *Journal of Marketing Research* (February 1981): 39–50.

Foster, G. *Financial Statement Analysis.* Englewood Cliffs, N.J.: Prentice-Hall, 1986.

Freeman, R., J. Ohlson, AND S. Penman. "Book Rate-of-Return and Prediction-of-Earnings Changes: An Empirical Investigation." *Journal of Accounting Research* (Autumn 1982): 639–53.

Friend, I., AND M. Blume. "The Demand for Risky Assets." *American Economic Review* (December 1975): 901–22.

Gerbing, D. W., AND J. C. Anderson. "Improper Solutions in the Analysis of Covariance Structures: Their Interpretability and a Comparison of Alternative Respecifications." *Psychometrika* (forthcoming).

Gjesdal, F. "Accounting for Stewardship." *Journal of Accounting Research* (Spring 1981): 208–31.

Hay Associates. "Fifth Annual Hay Report on Executive Compensation." *Wharton Magazine* (Fall 1981): 50–56.

Healy, P. "The Effect of Bonus Schemes on Accounting Decisions." *Journal of Accounting and Economics* (April 1985): 85–107.

———, S. Kang, AND K. Palepu. "The Effect of Accounting Procedure Changes on Executives' Remuneration." *Journal of Accounting and Economics* (March 1987): 7–34.

Holmstrom, B. "Moral Hazard and Observability." *Bell Journal of Economics* (Spring 1979): 74–91.

———. "Moral Hazard in Teams." *Bell Journal of Economics* (Autumn 1982): 324–40.

Jensen, M., AND K. Murphy. "Are Executive Compensation Contracts Structured Properly?" Working paper, University of Rochester, 1987.

Joreskog, K. G. "A General Approach to Confirmatory Maximum Likelihood Factor Analysis." *Psychometrika* (June 1969): 183–202.

———. "Statistical Analysis of Sets of Congeneric Tests." *Psychometrika* (June 1971): 109–33.

———. "Structural Analysis of Covariance and Correlation Matrices." *Psychometrika* (December 1978): 443–77.

———. "Covariance Structures." *Scandinavian Journal of Statistics* 8 (1981): 65–83.

———, AND D. A. Sorbom. *LISREL: Analysis of Structural Relationships by the Method of Maximum Likelihood (Version VI).* Chicago: National Educational Resources, 1984.

LAMBERT, R. "Managerial Incentives in Multiperiod Agency Relationships." Ph.D. dissertation, Stanford University, 1981.

———. "Long Term Contracts and Moral Hazard." *Bell Journal of Economics* (Autumn 1983): 441–52.

———. "Executive Effort and Selection of Risky Projects." *Rand Journal of Economics* (Spring 1986): 77–88.

———, AND D. LARCKER. "Executive Compensation, Corporate Decision-Making, and Shareholder Wealth: A Review of the Evidence." *Midland Corporate Finance Journal* (Winter 1985a): 6–22.

———, AND D. LARCKER. "Golden Parachutes, Executive Decision-Making and Shareholder Wealth." *Journal of Accounting and Economics* (April 1985b): 179–203.

———, AND D. LARCKER. "The Executive Compensation Effects of Large Corporate Acquisitions." *Journal of Accounting and Public Policy* (forthcoming).

———, D. LARCKER, AND R. VERRECCHIA. "Portfolio Issues in the Valuation of Executive Compensation." Working paper, University of Pennsylvania, 1987.

LARCKER, D. "The Association Between Performance Plans and Corporate Capital Investment." *Journal of Accounting and Economics* (April 1983): 3–30.

LEWELLEN, W. G. *Executive Compensation in Large Industrial Organizations.* New York: National Bureau of Economic Research, 1968.

LITZENBERGER, R., AND E. RONN. "A Utility-Based Model of Common Stock Prices Movements." *Journal of Finance* (March 1986): 67–92.

LONG, J. S. "Estimation and Hypothesis Testing in Linear Models Containing Measurement Error: A Review of Joreskog's Model for the Analysis of Covariance Structures." *Sociological Methods and Research* (November 1976): 157–206.

MARDIA, K. "Measures of Multivariate Skewness and Kurtosis with Applications." *Biometrika* 57, no. 2 (1970): 519–30.

MASSON, R. T. "Executive Motivations, Earnings, and Consequent Equity-Performance." *Journal of Political Economy* (November 1971): 1278–92.

MILGROM, P. "Good News and Bad News: Representation Theorems and Applications." *Bell Journal of Economics* (Autumn 1981): 380–91.

MOSTELLER, F., AND J. TUKEY. *Data Analysis and Regression.* Reading, Mass.: Addison-Wesley, 1977.

MUELLER, D. C. "A Theory of Conglomerate Mergers." *Quarterly Journal of Economics* (November 1969): 643–59.

MURPHY, K. "Corporate Performance and Managerial Remuneration: An Empirical Analysis." *Journal of Accounting and Economics* (April 1985): 11–42.

———. "Top Executives Are Worth Every Nickel They Get." *Harvard Business Review* (March/April 1986): 125–32.

RAMANAN, R. "Managerial Incentives, Accounting for Interest Costs and Investment Related Decisions." Ph.D. dissertation, Northwestern University, 1986.

RAPPAPORT, A. *Creating Shareholder Value.* New York: Free Press, 1986.

ROGERSON, W. "Repeated Moral Hazard." *Econometrica* (June 1985): 69–76.

ROLL, R., AND S. ROSS. "An Empirical Investigation of the Arbitrage Pricing Model." *Journal of Finance* (December 1980): 1073–1103.

SALAMON, G., AND E. SMITH. "Corporate Control and Managerial Misrepresentation of Firm Performance." *Bell Journal of Economics* (Spring 1979): 319–28.

SAXONHOUSE, G. "Estimated Parameters as Dependent Variables." *American Economic Review* (March 1976): 178–83.

VAN DRIEL, O. P. "On Various Causes of Improper Solutions in Maximum Likelihood Factor Analysis." *Psychomerika* (June 1978): 225–43.

VERRECCHIA, R. "Managerial Discretion in the Choice Among Financial Reporting Alternatives." *Journal of Accounting and Economics* (October 1986): 175–95.

The Executive Compensation Effects of Equity-for-Debt Swaps

Victor J. Defeo, Richard A. Lambert, and David F. Larcker

ABSTRACT: This paper provides an analysis of the association between the accounting gain produced by an equity-for-debt swap and executive compensation. Our results suggest that the executives of firms completing a swap transaction experience an increase in cash compensation (salary plus bonus). The increase is largest both in absolute magnitude and in statistical significance for firms whose compensation plans are more "accounting-oriented" (i.e., firms whose executives would be expected to experience the greatest increase in compensation under the hypothesis that firm's compensation plan is not adjusted for the accounting gain produced by the swap). We also find that, on average, the value of the executives' personal equity holdings decreases in the period surrounding the announcement of the swap. The magnitude of this decrease is, on average, comparable in size to the increase in their compensation. However, there is some weak evidence that executives of firms whose compensation plans are more "accounting-oriented" experience a statistically significant increase in their total wealth (i.e., the sum of excess compensation and the value of personal equity holdings) as a result of the swap transaction.

ACCOUNTING research has directed increasing attention to the relations among accounting numbers, compensation plans, and managerial incentives (e.g., see Antle and Smith [1985, 1986], Dukes et al. [1980], Healy [1985], Holthausen [1981], Horwitz and Kolodny [1980], Lambert and Larcker [1985, 1987a, and 1987b], Larcker [1983, 1987], Larcker and Revsine [1983], and Watts and Zimmerman [1978]). In particular, researchers are beginning to examine whether compensation contracts with senior-level executives, which are often written explicitly on the basis of accounting numbers, are adjusted for the effects of managerial "manipulation" of earnings.[1] Evidence on this issue can provide insight into the factors that influence the selection of accounting numbers and the motivation of executives to engage in earnings manipulation.

[1] Abdel-khalik [1985], Healy et al. [1987], and Simon [1983] analyze the compensation effects associated with a change from LIFO to FIFO, and Healy et al. [1987] examine the compensation effects associated with changes from accelerated to straight-line depreciation.

The financial support of Atlantic Richfield, Charter Banks, Ernst & Whinney, and Peat Marwick Main & Co. is gratefully acknowledged. This paper has benefited from discussion comments at Drexel University, the University of Kansas, the University of Maryland, and the American Accounting Association 1986 annual meeting. The comments of two anonymous reviewers, Paul Healy, and Maureen McNichols were especially helpful.

Victor J. Defeo is an Assistant Professor, Richard A. Lambert is an Associate Professor, and David F. Larcker is a Professor, all at The Wharton School, University of Pennsylvania.

Manuscript received September 1987.
Revision received August 1988.
Accepted November 1988.

THE ACCOUNTING REVIEW
Vol. LXIV, No. 2
April 1989

In this paper, we analyze the relation between the earnings effects associated with an equity-for-debt swap (hereafter swap) and changes in executive compensation and wealth. In a swap transaction, an investment banking firm purchases previously issued corporate bonds that are selling at a discount, and exchanges them with the corporation for new equity shares. As with other types of corporate recapitalizations, relatively little is known about why firms engage in swaps. At the anecdotal level, Peavy and Scott [1985, p. 44] state that many financial analysts argue that "swaps are just an accounting ploy designed to boost earnings without increasing the firm's economic value." In particular, a swap transaction enables the corporation to report an accounting gain equal to the difference between the book value and the market value of the debt (adjusted for any transaction costs). The "earnings manipulation" aspect of swaps is also discussed in Sloan and Spragins [1981] and Anders [1982].

According to Finnerty [1985], the first swap occurred shortly after the enactment of the Bankruptcy Act of 1980, which allowed firms to avoid taxation on the accounting gain produced by extinguishing the debt. The accounting gain produced by a swap transaction was made taxable in the Tax Reform Act of 1984, and very few swaps occurred after this date. The timing of swaps relative to tax law changes suggests that swaps are at least partially motivated by tax considerations. However, even if the accounting gain is tax-free, it is not clear that repurchasing debt in order to report an accounting gain has any real economic benefits to the firm.

In fact, even though these recapitalizations produce a positive effect on accounting earnings, their announcement is associated with a security market reaction that is, on average, *negative* and sta-

tistically significant.[2] To the extent that a negative security price reaction constitutes evidence concerning the desirability of an action from the perspective of shareholders (which we discuss in more detail in Section IV), there is greater potential for a conflict of interest between managers and shareholders with swaps than for other accounting transactions (e.g., changes in inventory method or depreciation method). This suggests that swap transactions are potentially informative events for examining shareholder-manager conflicts.

Swap transactions are also interesting events because of the amount of information that is typically disclosed regarding these transactions. Specifically, the firms in our sample disclose that they have completed a swap transaction and report the magnitude of the swap's effect on accounting earnings in their annual report in the year in which the swap takes place. The disclosure of this information, which is similar to the information disclosed regarding voluntary changes in accounting methods, should make it easy, in principle, for shareholders to control any conflicts of interest with the managers that might arise regarding the desirability of swap transactions. For example, it would be relatively simple to

---

[2] There are many empirical studies that have examined the security market reaction to recapitalizations. At least five recent studies have analyzed large samples of swaps: (a) Finnerty [1985] estimates the cumulative excess return from day 0 to day +1 to be -1.19 percent, (b) Peavy and Scott [1985] estimate the cumulative excess return from day -5 to day +5 to be -1.84 percent, (c) Rogers and Owers [1985] estimate the cumulative excess return from day -1 to day 0 to be -1.29 percent for firms involved in a "refunding strategy" and -0.60 percent for the remaining firms, (d) Lys and Sivaramakrishnan [1987] estimate the cumulative excess return from day 0 to day +1 to be -1.11 percent, and (e) Hand [1987] estimates the cumulative excess return from day 0 to day +1 to be -1.30 percent. Moreover, each of these cumulative excess returns is statistically significant at conventional levels.

remove the accounting gain produced by the swap transaction and base executive bonuses on the adjusted accounting earnings. In fact, Demski et al. [1984] suggest that managerial decisions that are observable by the shareholders (or the board of directors), such as accounting changes, swap transactions, or mergers, can be explicitly included in the terms of managerial compensation contracts. In this way, shareholders have the ability to preclude actions from being selected which, based on the information they possess, they believe to be contrary to their own interests.

In this paper, we assess the impact of the increase in accounting earnings produced by the swap on the compensation and wealth of top-level executives. Our empirical results indicate that the executives of firms completing a swap transaction experience an *increase* in cash compensation (salary plus bonus). The increase is largest both in absolute magnitude and in statistical significance for firms whose compensation plans are more "accounting-oriented" (i.e., firms whose executives would be expected to experience the greatest increase in compensation under the hypothesis that the firm's compensation plan is not adjusted for the accounting gain produced by the swap). We also find that the value of the executives' personal equity holdings decreases in the period surrounding the announcement of the swap. The magnitude of the decrease in the value of their personal equity holdings is, on average, comparable in size to the increase in their compensation. However, there is some weak evidence that executives of firms whose compensation plans are more "accounting-oriented" experience a statistically significant increase in their "total" wealth (defined as the sum of excess compensation and the value of personal equity holdings) as a result of the swap transaction.

The remainder of the paper is divided into five sections. Section I describes the sample selection criteria and discusses some general characteristics of the sample. In Section II, we use data from the period prior to the swap to empirically estimate the relation between accounting earnings and executive compensation for each firm in our sample. In Section III, we analyze the excess compensation for executives in the year of the swap transaction. Section IV presents the results of the security market reaction to the swap announcement, the impact of the swap on the stock-related components of executive wealth, and the "total" effect of the swap on the executives' wealth. The study is summarized in Section V.

I. SAMPLE

A sample of swaps was developed from data provided by three investment banking firms and data on registrations of equity-for-debt transactions contained in the *Investment Dealer's Digest*. These sources produced an initial sample of 273 individual swap transactions. The following selection criteria were used to develop the final sample:

- compensation data (salary plus annual bonus) for the chief executive officer (CEO) must be available for the period from 1970 to the year of the swap,
- the effect of the swap transaction on annual earnings (hereafter, the swap gain) must be disclosed in the annual report, and
- data on earnings before extraordinary and discontinued operations and data on extraordinary and discontinued operations must be available on either the industrial or research COMPUSTAT file from 1970 to the year of the swap.

The application of these selection criteria produced a sample of 179 swap transactions from 1981 to 1984.[3] If a firm completed multiple swaps in a given year, we aggregated these swaps into a single observation and computed the total effect on earnings from swap transactions within the year. This approach is used because we have only *annual* compensation data for assessing the association between the accounting gain provided by the swap and executive compensation. This aggregation procedure reduced the sample size to 159 *firm-years* with swap transactions. There were 22, 76, 35, and 26 firms that engaged in swap transactions in the fiscal years ending in 1981, 1982, 1983, and 1984, respectively. There were 92 firms who completed swaps in only one of these years, 26 firms with swaps in two years, and five firms with swaps in three years. The sample includes firms engaged in durable manufacturing, nondurable manufacturing, banking, and regulated utilities. The firms in the sample are some of the largest public corporations in the United States. For example, the mean (median) market value of the common shares outstanding at the end of the fiscal year prior to the swap date was $1,902MM ($1,039MM).

Data on the accounting treatment and size of the swap gain are presented in Table 1. SFAS No. 4 generally requires that material gains that arise from the early extinguishment of debt be reported as extraordinary items. Panel A of Table 1 indicates that 107 of the 159 firms included the swap gain in *ordinary* income. Although this would suggest that the majority of the firms viewed the effect of the swap on net income to be immaterial, in many cases the earnings effect of the swap was nontrivial. For example, the mean (median) accounting gain produced by the swap is $11.5MM ($7.2MM), with a range from $0.0MM to $89.0MM.

Moreover, panel B of Table 1 indicates that these gains had the effect of increasing net income by a mean of 8.0 percent and a median of 4.8 percent in the year of the swap.

The results in Table 1 suggest that firms are more likely to treat the swap gain as an extraordinary item as the gain becomes large relative to the earnings of the firm. Using a parametric two-sample t-test ($t=2.51$) and a nonparametric two-sample Mann-Whitney test ($z=5.15$), we can reject the hypothesis that the size of effect of the swap gain on net income is independent of whether the gain is included in ordinary income or treated as an extraordinary item. However, note that the swap transaction frequently has a nontrivial effect on reported earnings even for the firms that included the swap gain in ordinary income. For this set of firms, the median effect on net income was 3.9 percent, and one-fourth of these firms increased their net income by at least 6.8 percent via the swap transaction.

It is also of interest to examine the earnings performance of the sample in the year of the swap transaction. We compared the earnings in the year of the swap, excluding the swap gain, to the earnings number that would be expected assuming that the earnings process follows a random walk with a drift term (see Foster [1986] for a review of earn-

---

[3] Hand [1987] reports that the total population of swaps over the period from 1981 to 1984 consists of 291 transactions. Therefore, our initial sample of 273 swaps is essentially equivalent to the population of these corporate recapitalizations. A total of 59 firms (with 65 swap transactions) were lost due to insufficient compensation data. For the most part, these were smaller firms whose compensation data from the early 1970s could not be obtained from proxy statements available to us. In addition, 15 firms (with 23 swap transactions) were eliminated because the annual report did not mention the effect of the swap transaction on accounting earnings. Finally, six firms were eliminated because of missing data on the COMPUSTAT file.

TABLE 1

DESCRIPTIVE STATISTICS FOR THE ACCOUNTING ASPECTS OF EQUITY-FOR-DEBT SWAPS
(1981–1984)

Panel A. Treatment of Swap Gain:

	Number of Firms
Gain Treated as Ordinary Income	107
Gain Treated as Extraordinary Income	52

Panel B. Size of Swap Gain Relative to Net Income:[a]

	Total Sample	Firms that Treated Swap Gain as	
		Ordinary Income	Extraordinary Income
n[b]	142	99	43
Mean	0.080	0.054	0.139
Median	0.048	0.039	0.090
TMean	0.065	0.047	0.108
StDev	0.133	0.049	0.221
Max	1.484	0.274	1.484
Min	0.000	0.002	0.000
Q3	0.096	0.068	0.145
Q1	0.029	0.023	0.059

[a] The net income figure in the denominator of this ratio is net income without the swap gain. Firms with negative earnings in the year of the swap ($n = 17$) are excluded.

[b] Notation: n = sample size, Mean = sample average, Median = sample median, TMean = trimmed mean (upper and lower five percent of observations removed), StDev = sample standard deviation, Max = largest observation, Min = smallest observation, Q3 = value corresponding to the upper quartile, and Q1 = value corresponding to lower quartile.

ings expectation models). For 95 (60 percent) of the firms, earnings before extraordinary items in the year of the swap (excluding the swap gain) was below the expectation, and for 96 (60 percent) of the firms, net income was below the expectation. Moreover, 17 (11 percent) of the firms had a net loss in the year of the swap.

To conduct significance tests, we standardized the earnings forecast error in the year of the swap for each firm using the standard deviation of its forecast errors from 1970 to the year prior to the swap. The mean (median) standardized forecast error for income before extraordinary items and discontinued operations was −0.44 (−0.41), with similar results for net income. If the standard-

ized forecast errors for earnings are assumed to be independent, the unexpected decrease in earnings is statistically significant using both a parametric t-test and nonparametric Wilcoxon rank-sum test at the 0.01 level (two-tail). Due to time period and industry clustering, it is likely that the 159 observations exhibit some degree of positive cross-sectional correlation, which suggests that these significance levels are likely to be overstated. These results indicate that swaps tend to occur during years in which firms are experiencing adverse annual earnings performance relative to time-series expectation models.[4] This finding is

[4] Given the research method discussed in Sections II and III, the relevant benchmark for earnings performance

consistent with the results in Lys and Sivaramakrishnan [1987], who examine annual earnings, and in Hand [1987], who examines quarterly earnings performance.

II. Estimation of Executive Compensation Contracts

Model of Executive Compensation and Accounting Earnings

The most direct means of assessing whether executive compensation contracts are adjusted for the effect of swap transactions on accounting earnings would be to obtain access to the precise form of the executives' compensation contracts. Unfortunately, there are a number of factors which prevent us from adopting this approach. Although approximately 95 percent of the firms in the sample report that their executive compensation contracts contain annual bonus plans that are based on accounting earnings, only 67 of the 159 firms (i.e., 42 percent) disclose the precise functional form of their bonus funding formulas in their proxy statements.[5] Moreover, almost all firms provide their compensation committees with the discretion to adjust the reported bonus formulas. Therefore, even if the bonus formulas do not explicitly state that they are adjusted for the effects of swap transactions or other accounting changes, the compensation committee may do so implicitly (see Antle and Smith [1985, pp. 313–314] for additional discussion of this issue).

Finally, the bonus formulas and the compensation data that are disclosed in proxy statements are for different groups of executives. This prevents the researcher from using the compensation data disclosed in proxy statements to determine whether the disclosed bonus formulas are implicitly adjusted. Proxy statements disclose only individual compensation data for the top five officers and for all officers and directors as a group. However, the bonus plans described in proxy statements are used to calculate a bonus *pool* that is shared among a much larger group of executives. Neither the aggregate compensation paid to this group nor the precise formula for allocating the bonus pool to individual executives or subgroups of executives is typically disclosed.

Because of the problems associated with using the bonus formulas described in proxy statements, an empirical model was developed of the relation between cash compensation (salary plus annual bonus) and earnings for each firm. In prior studies, some researchers have estimated the form of the relation between compensation and performance using

---

is the time-series expectation model discussed in the text. However, it is also of interest to compare the earnings performance of the firms in our sample to the earnings performance of firms that did not engage in swap transactions. This information would be relevant, for example, for research studies that attempt to predict why some firms engage in swap transactions while other firms do not. To provide some evidence on this issue, the standardized forecast errors for the swap firms were compared to the standardized forecast errors for the *industry* portfolio composed of all firms on either the annual or research COMPUSTAT file in the same two-digit SIC code as the swap firm (again using an expectation model for earnings in the form of a random walk with a drift). The Wilcoxon matched-pairs signed-rank test was then applied to the swap firm's standardized forecast error and the corresponding forecast error for the industry portfolio for the year of the swap. The results provide weak evidence that the swap firms had more negative standardized forecast errors than their industry comparison group for earnings before extraordinary items and discontinued operations ($z = -1.622$, $p < 0.10$, one-tail) and for earnings after extraordinary items and discontinued operations ($z = -0.787$, $p > 0.10$, one-tail). Because both groups of firms appear to have been experiencing adverse earnings performance, it is unlikely that firms engage in swap transactions solely as a result of their adverse earnings performance.

[5] This percentage is slightly higher than that found in Healy [1985], who found that approximately 38 percent of the *Fortune 250* disclose the precise functional form of their bonus funding formulas in their proxy statements.

cross-sectional data (e.g., Abdel-khalik [1985, 1988], Adams [1987], and Ely [1987]), while other researchers have used time-series data (e.g., Antle and Smith [1986], Healy et al. [1987], and Lambert and Larcker [1987b]). Since the evidence in the latter group of papers suggests that the slope coefficients of compensation plans vary considerably across firms, and because the firms from the sample belong to a diverse set of industries, we have chosen to adopt the time-series approach to empirically estimating the relation between compensation and earnings.

We assume that cash compensation for firm i can be characterized by

$$(C_{it}-r_iC_{i,t-1})=a_i+b_i(E_{it}-r_iE_{i,t-1})$$
$$+u_{it} \qquad (1)$$

where

C_{it} = the cash compensation for firm i in year t,

E_{it} = the earnings for firm i in year t,

u_{it} = the random error (residual) for firm i in year t,

a_i and b_i = the regression parameters, and

r_i = the first-order autocorrelation coefficient.

The relation in equation (1) is a regression with an adjustment for first-order autocorrelation.[6] If the autocorrelation coefficient is equal to zero, the regression is equivalent to a regression of cash compensation on earnings in levels. If the autocorrelation coefficient is equal to one, the regression is equivalent to a regression of first differences in compensation on first differences in earnings. Note that equation (1) permits the parameters a_i, b_i, and r_i to be firm-specific.

As in Healy et al. [1987], Abdel-khalik [1985], and Simon [1983], we use cash

compensation (i.e., salary plus annual bonus) as our measure of compensation in equation (1). Compensation data for the CEO (or top corporate executive) from 1970 to the year of the swap was obtained from proxy statements and the annual compensation surveys in *Business Week* and *Forbes*. In order to avoid the confounding effects of changes in the price level on the analysis of time-series data, the cash compensation and earnings numbers were converted to 1967 dollars by applying the relevant Consumer Price Index (CPI).

While cash compensation is not a complete measure of executive compensation, it is almost always a significant portion of total compensation.[7] Moreover, since bonus plans are frequently explicitly written in terms of accounting numbers, whereas other forms of compensation are not, we would expect cash compensation to be more sensitive to accounting

[6] The relation between compensation and earnings expressed in equation (1) is similar to that estimated in Healy et al. [1987] with the following exceptions. First, our analysis uses the Cochrane-Orcutt procedure to adjust for serial correlation in the residuals, whereas the results reported in Healy et al. do not use this adjustment. However, Healy et al. note [p. 18] that they repeated their analysis using the Cochrane-Orcutt adjustment procedure and obtained similar results. We also found that our results were insensitive to whether the Cochrane-Orcutt method was applied. Second, our dependent and independent variables are compensation and earnings, respectively, while Healy et al. use the logarithm of compensation and the logarithm of earnings. Lambert and Larcker [1987b] provide evidence that suggests that the results of compensation studies are generally insensitive to whether logarithmic transformations are applied to the data.

[7] Cash compensation typically represent 70 to 80 percent of a CEO's yearly compensation (see Hay Associates [1981], Booz Allen & Hamilton [1985], and Murphy [1985]). Moreover, Jensen and Murphy [1987] provide some evidence that the slope coefficient relating cash compensation to performance (as measured by the change in the market value of the firm's stock) is not significantly different than the coefficient relating total compensation to performance. To our knowledge, there is no evidence regarding whether the slope coefficient on accounting performance would be significantly affected by the inclusion of other components of compensation.

numbers than would other forms of compensation.[8] This suggests that it may be easier to detect whether the accounting gain produced by the swap transaction is allowed to "flow through" the bonus contract than through the complete compensation contract.[9] In particular, if we find that firms go to the trouble of removing the effect of the swap gain on accounting earnings in determining their executive bonuses, we believe that it would be unlikely that they would make the executives "whole" by increasing another component of their compensation.

However, if we find that firms do not adjust their cash compensation contracts for the accounting gain produced by the swap, we cannot be sure that there are no offsetting effects in the other components of compensation. For example, an examination of the proxy statements of the firms in our sample in the year of the swap indicated that 88.1 percent of the firms had stock option plans, 64.8 percent had stock appreciation rights, 18.9 percent had restricted stock plans, 54.1 percent had performance plans, and 5.7 percent had other performance-based plans. Unfortunately, the information disclosed about these plans is generally insufficient to allow us to determine the amount of compensation paid from these plans as a function of performance in any particular year.[10] The absence of a complete analysis of the total wealth of the executives is a limitation to the analysis of the motivations of executives to engage in swaps. In particular, the finding that firms permit the accounting gain to flow through the cash compensation contract is consistent with, but does not imply, the proposition that executives personally profit from the swap.

Since some firms include the swap gain as ordinary income and other firms report it as an extraordinary item, the effect of the swap gain on compensation depends, in part, on whether the firm's compensation plan is based on earnings before extraordinary items or after extraordinary items. While it is frequently difficult to determine whether a particular firm excludes extraordinary items in calculating its executive bonuses, summary data provided by consulting firms indicate that approximately 50 percent of firms with formal short-term bonus plans measure performance on the basis of earnings before extraordinary items, 40 percent base their bonuses on earnings after extraordinary items, and the choice of the earnings measure varies by organization level for the remaining ten percent of firms. Because both types of plans appear to be commonly used, we will estimate the relation between compensation and accounting earnings for all firms using income before extraordinary items and discontinued operations as the accounting measure of performance, and then repeat the analysis using net income (i.e., income after extraordinary items and discontinued operations).

Results of Estimating Equation (1)

Equation (1) is estimated in two steps.

[8] In a related context, Murphy [1985] finds that the salary plus bonus component of executive compensation has a stronger statistical relationship with performance (as measured by stock price return and sales) than does total compensation.

[9] This argument would suggest that the sensitivity of our tests could be improved by further restricting our definition of compensation to the annual bonus (and excluding salary). Unfortunately, few firms separately disclose salaries and annual bonuses, especially over long periods of time. Since most firms disclose only the sum of salary and bonus, but not the individual components, we use salary plus bonus in our empirical analysis.

[10] Moreover, it is difficult to assign a value to "long-term" compensation whose ultimate payoff is contingent upon the realization of future performance measures. For example, Lambert et al. [1988] suggest that the value of an executive stock option to an executive will depend on his degree of risk aversion and his degree of diversification, and will generally be smaller than the Black-Scholes value.

First, the first-order autocorrelation coefficient is estimated from the residuals obtained from a regression of compensation on earnings in levels.[11] Second, the autocorrelation coefficient is used to transform the data as indicated in equation (1), and ordinary least squares procedures are used to estimate $\hat{a}_i$, $\hat{b}_i$, and the standard deviation of the regression residuals ($\hat{s}_i$). In each step, compensation and earnings data from 1970 to year $t-1$ are used in estimating equation (1), where year t denotes the swap year.[12]

Descriptive statistics associated with the estimation of equation (1) using earnings before extraordinary items and discontinued operations indicate that, on average, cash compensation has a statistically significant positive relation with earnings (Table 2, panel A). Moreover, the relation exhibits a substantial degree of explanatory power (e.g., the median adjusted R^2 is 0.350). Similar results are obtained using net income as the accounting measure of performance (Table 2, panel B). However, the explanatory power for the regressions is slightly smaller when extraordinary items and discontinued operations are included in the earnings number. These results provide some empirical confirmation that accounting performance measures, which are typically observed in funding formulas disclosed in proxy statements, have some relation with executive compensation. Interestingly, executive compensation has a much higher association with accounting earnings (R^2s of approximately 30 to 35 percent) than with security price returns (i.e., R^2s of approximately three to nine percent reported in Murphy [1986]).

Results in Table 2 also suggest that the intercepts and slope coefficients exhibit considerable differences across firms. While it is common for empirical studies in the executive compensation literature

to estimate separate intercepts for each firm, many studies constrain the slope coefficient to be the same across firms (e.g., Abdel-khalik [1985; 1988], who regresses compensation on accounting earnings, and Murphy [1985] and Coughlan and Schmidt [1985], who regress compensation on firm size and stock price return). For our sample of firms, the hypothesis that the slope coefficients are the same for all firms can be rejected at the 0.01 level of significance both for the case in which accounting performance is measured using earnings before extraordinary items and discontinued operations and when accounting performance is measured using net income.

III. ANALYSIS OF EXCESS COMPENSATION

Computation of Excess Compensation

Given the empirical model in equation (1), the unexpected portion of the manager's compensation for firm i in year t (or excess compensation) can be expressed as:

$$\Delta C_{i,t} = [(C_{i,t} - \hat{r}_i C_{i,t-1})] - [\hat{a}_i + \hat{b}_i (E^*_{i,t} - \hat{r}_i E_{i,t-1})] \quad (2)$$

---

[11] The median first-order autocorrelation coefficient for the residuals of the regression estimated in levels using earnings before extraordinary items and discontinued operations was 0.177, with a range from -0.495 to 0.751. Twenty-five percent of the sample had an autocorrelation coefficient greater than 0.408. Similar values for the first-order autocorrelation coefficient were obtained when accounting performance was measured using earnings after extraordinary items and discontinued operations. Based on these results, we estimate the association between compensation and earnings using the autocorrelation adjustment. However, estimating equations (1) and (2) in levels, and conducting the associated tests on unexpected compensation with these estimates did not have a substantive effect on the empirical results.

[12] For firms that completed swap transactions in more than one year, the estimation period for the later swap transactions will include earnings numbers that have been affected by the earlier swap transactions. To avoid any problems that this might cause in estimating the parameters of the compensation function, we removed the effect of the earlier swap transactions from the earnings numbers from those periods.

TABLE 2

DESCRIPTIVE STATISTICS FROM THE FIRM-SPECIFIC REGRESSIONS OF CASH COMPENSATION ON EARNINGS[a]

Regression Model for Executive Compensation of Firm i:

$$(C_{it} - r_i C_{i,t-1}) = a_i + b_i (E_{it} - r_i E_{i,t-1}) + u_{it}$$

Panel A. *With Earnings Measured Using Income Before Extraordinary Items:*[b]

	$\hat{a}$	t-statistic$_a$	$\hat{b}$	t-statistic$_b$	R^2	Adjusted R^2
Mean	109.9	5.89	1.59	2.67	0.422	0.359
Median	97.5	5.04	1.13	2.48	0.415	0.350
TMean	102.3	5.38	1.45	2.55	0.418	0.355
StDev	93.5	5.22	2.27	3.08	0.263	0.291
Max	561.4	35.89	12.46	18.91	0.978	0.975
Min	−65.9	−2.26	−10.79	−9.43	0.000	−0.124
Q3	143.9	7.90	2.35	3.97	0.645	0.606
Q1	56.4	2.70	0.38	1.17	0.198	0.108

Panel B. *With Earnings Measured Using Net Income:*[b]

	$\hat{a}$	t-statistic$_a$	$\hat{b}$	t-statistic$_b$	R^2	Adjusted R^2
Mean	111.9	6.36	1.41	2.55	0.384	0.318
Median	101.3	5.41	0.91	2.30	0.383	0.319
TMean	108.3	5.89	1.20	2.36	0.376	0.309
StDev	74.2	5.19	1.80	3.08	0.267	0.296
Max	401.6	35.22	12.46	18.61	0.977	0.975
Min	−65.6	−2.26	−1.09	−9.52	0.000	−0.124
Q3	147.1	8.05	1.96	3.56	0.589	0.548
Q1	61.4	3.24	0.41	1.05	0.141	0.055

[a] In the regression estimation, compensation is expressed in thousands of (1967) dollars and earnings are expressed in millions of (1967) dollars. A separate regression was estimated for each of the 159 firms. The regressions were estimated using data from 1970 to the year prior to the swap.

[b] For notation, see Table 1.

where $E_{i,t}^*$ is the earnings number that *would have been reported in the absence of the swap*. For the regressions that measure accounting performance using income before extraordinary items and discontinued operations, we calculate $E_{i,t}^*$ by subtracting the swap gain from the reported earnings number for those firms that included the swap gain in ordinary income (i.e., $E_{i,t}^* = E_{i,t} - swap\ gain_i$). For the firms that reported the swap gain as an extraordinary item, the swap gain has already been excluded from $E_{i,t}$, so no adjustment to the reported earnings number is necessary. For the regressions in which accounting per-formance is measured using net income, we calculate $E_{i,t}^*$ by removing the swap gain from the reported income number for all firms (i.e., $E_{i,t}^* = E_{i,t} - swap\ gain_i$).

Equation (2) calculates the difference between the actual compensation received in the year of the swap and the level of compensation that would be expected given the compensation function estimated in equation (1) and the level of earnings that would have been reported in the absence of the swap transaction. This provides a direct means of assessing whether the accounting gain that arises due to the swap transaction is permitted to flow through the compensation function. [13,14] One critical assumption of this approach is that other managerial actions that have an effect on earnings would have remained the same had the swap not occurred. If these other actions are correlated with the swap decision, the computation of actual earnings minus the reported swap gain is, of course, not equal to the earnings number that would have been reported in the absence of the swap. [15]

One limitation to using equation (2) to calculate the excess compensation in the year of the swap is that it assumes that the contract is linear even if earnings in the year of the swap are extremely low. For example, if b_i is positive and $E_{i,t}^*$ is sufficiently negative, equation (1) would predict that compensation is negative. Since most CEOs have employment contracts that provide a positive lower bound to their compensation in a given year, a simple linear extrapolation of the compensation function estimated in equation (1) is likely to systematically underestimate the expected level of compensation and, thus, overestimate the level of excess compensation. In an attempt to address this problem, we modified equation (2) so that predicted compensation was at least equal to the estimated intercept from equation (1). This modification is used throughout the subsequent analysis. [16,17]

Benchmarks for Comparison

In order to test the null hypothesis that the swap gain is not allowed to flow through the compensation contract, we compare the measure of excess compensation, $\Delta C_{i,t}$, to four different (although related) benchmarks. In particular, two within-sample (compensation comparisons involving only the swap firms) and two between-sample (compensation comparisons involving the swap firms and

[13] In contrast, studies by Simon [1983], Abdel-khalik [1985], and some of the tests conducted in Healy et al. [1987] focus on whether the parameters of the compensation contract are adjusted when the transaction of interest occurs. While the results of these tests can be used to test whether the form of the compensation contract has changed, it is often difficult to use the results of these tests to infer whether the change leads to an increase in compensation. For example, if the intercept of the contract increases, but the slope decreases (or vice versa), the executive's compensation could either increase or decrease relative to what it would have been in the absence of the change.

[14] Our analysis examines only the swap's effect on the *level* of compensation. However, the analysis is incapable of determining whether the swap has an effect on other parameters of the distribution of the CEO's compensation (e.g., the riskiness of compensation). In particular, a swap transaction typically has the effect of decreasing the firm's debt-to-equity ratio, which may result in a decrease in the variance of the firm's accounting earnings. If the riskiness of the executive's compensation also decreases, the swap may result in an increase in his utility even if he does not experience an increase in the level of compensation.

[15] As an example of this type of omitted variables problem, suppose a manager is contemplating a new capital investment program. In the early years of the program, the earnings of the firm may be adversely affected by the program, especially if the returns do not occur until subsequent time periods. The negative impact on short-term accounting earnings may have such a large effect on managerial compensation that the manager turns down the investment program. However, the manager may be willing to undertake the investment program if he or she is able to use the accounting gain produced by a swap transaction to, at least partially, offset the investment program's negative impact on short-term earnings. Under this scenario, the manager's decision to begin the investment program is related to the decision to complete the swap transaction. Therefore, the accounting gain due to the swap that is reported in the financial statements does *not* equal the total effect of the change on earnings. Moreover, it is precisely because the compensation scheme is not adjusted for "earnings manipulation" that the manager implements the capital investment program. The "gain" that the manager appears to receive from manipulating earnings merely compensates him for the short-term loss that he would have suffered from the investment program's effect on earnings. Ramanan [1985] provides related empirical evidence on the relation between capital investment and the decision to change from expensing interest to interest capitalization.

[16] We also calculated the results without this modification. Not surprisingly, the compensation comparison W_0 was significantly higher than the results reported here, but the overall interpretation of the results are very similar to the results reported in the text. The mean (median) ratio of the intercept to the average level of cash compensation for our sample of 159 firms is .561 (.536). This ratio is similar to the "typical" ratio of fixed salary to cash compensation reported in consulting firm surveys

a matching set of control firms) research designs are developed to attempt to control for various confounding influences on $\Delta C_{i,t}$. The four compensation comparisons are as follows (the superscript e refers to experimental firms and the superscript c refers to control firms):

$$W_0 = \Delta C^e_{i,t} - 0, \tag{3a}$$

$$W_{-1} = \Delta C^e_{i,t} - \Delta C^e_{i,t-1}, \tag{3b}$$

$$B_0 = \Delta C^e_{i,t} - \Delta C^c_{i,t}, \text{ and} \tag{3c}$$

$$B_{-1} = [\Delta C^e_{i,t} - \Delta C^c_{i,t}] - [\Delta C^e_{i,t-1} - \Delta C^c_{i,t-1}]. \tag{3d}$$

The first compensation comparison (denoted W_0) assumes that the regression model estimated using data from 1970 to $t-1$ is an appropriate characterization of the compensation model used by the firm in period t. Under these conditions, the expected value of $\Delta C^e_{i,t}$ is, by construction, equal to zero under the null hypothesis that the swap gain does not flow through the compensation function. This general approach is similar to standard event study procedures, and is well established in the accounting literature examining security market reactions.

The disadvantage of model W_0 is that it does not control for any other factors that systematically affect $\Delta C^e_{i,t}$. One example of a confounding factor is that the reporting requirements concerning the types of remuneration that are included in cash compensation are not constant over time. In particular, many companies included the payouts from long-term performance plans in the cash compensation figures over the period 1979 to 1982. It ' is typically very difficult to isolate the size of the performance plan payouts or even to determine whether the cash compensation figures contain performance plan payouts.

This reporting problem is likely to result in an overestimation of the excess compensation for firms whose swap occurred in 1981 or 1982, and an underestimation of the excess compensation for firms whose swap occurred in 1983 to 1984. To see this, suppose the "extra payouts" from performance plans are only included in the measure of cash compensation in years 1979 to 1982. Since the compensation model is estimated using the data from 1970 through the year prior to the swap, some of the data in the estimation period will contain the extra payments and some will not. Therefore, the estimated compensation model will *partially* incorporate the extra payments from performance plans. If a swap occurs in 1981 or 1982, the compensation in the event year will include the extra payment. Therefore, the excess compensation is likely to be positive in the year of the swap even without the swap gain. On the other hand, firms whose swap occurred in 1983 or 1984 have the extra payments in the estimation period, but not in the year of the swap. Therefore, these firms will tend to have a negative excess compensation, even without the swap gain.

The three remaining compensation

(e.g., Sibson & Co. [1986]) and provides some indirect support for the use of the estimated intercept as a lower bound for expected compensation.

[17] To further ensure that the results are not driven by the measure of expected compensation being biased in situations in which earnings is unusually low, we split the sample on the basis of the firm's standardized earnings forecast error in the year of the swap. The group with the most negative unexpected earnings had a median standardized forecast error of -1.39, so any bias in the compensation benchmark that might arise in years with low earnings would be greatest for these firms. In contrast, the median standardized forecast error for the subgroup with the highest standardized forecast error was 0.67. Since the median forecast error is positive for this subgroup, these firms should not be subject to the bias discussed above. We conducted the four compensation comparisons for these two groups of firms, and could not reject the hypothesis that the excess compensation is the same for both groups.

comparisons attempt to provide a greater degree of control for confounding events such as those described above. The second comparison (denoted W_{-1}) attempts to control for systematic misspecifications of equation (1) that are stable over time for a given firm. In this comparison, the excess compensation in the year of the swap is compared to the excess compensation in the year prior to the swap. If the confounding factor has an equal effect on both $\Delta C^e_{i,t}$ and $\Delta C^e_{i,t-1}$, the effect of this factor will be eliminated with model W_{-1}. For example, if long-term performance plan payouts are included in the compensation measure in both the year of the swap and the year prior to the swap, this confounding effect on compensation is less likely to be a problem with comparison W_{-1} than with comparison W_0.

The two remaining compensation comparisons utilize a control group of firms to provide the benchmark for $\Delta C^e_{i,t}$. These between-sample tests assume that a comparison sample can be constructed that will remove (or reduce) any industry-specific and time period effects on compensation that are unrelated to the swap transaction. Our control group is composed of firms in the *Forbes 500* that (1) did not engage in a swap, (2) have cash compensation data from 1970 to the year of the associated experimental firm's swap, and (3) have earnings data (both before and after extraordinary items and discontinued operations) on the annual or research COMPUSTAT files for the same period. A total of 398 firms in our compensation data base satisfied these three criteria.

From this group of potential control firms, each swap firm was matched with the control firm in the same two-digit SIC code whose market value of equity in the year prior to the swap was closest to that of the swap firm. Control firms were found for 154 of the 159 swap firms. The five firms without a control group were in SIC codes 21 and 41, which have relatively small numbers of firms. The swap firms were slightly larger than their corresponding control firms. Specifically, the mean difference in the market value of equity of the swap and control firms was \$393.26MM (matched-pairs $t=2.27$, $p<.05$, two-tail) and the median difference was \$37.38MM (Wilcoxon $Z=1.99$, $p<.05$, two-tail). However, the difference in firm size (especially the median difference) is small relative to the average size of the swap firms.

In the third compensation comparison (denoted B_0), the benchmark for the excess compensation of experimental firm i in the year of the swap is the excess compensation of its control firm in that year. This comparison assumes that both $\Delta C^e_{i,t}$ and $\Delta C^c_{i,t}$ are similarly affected by any systematic industry-specific or time period effects on compensation, so that their difference will reduce these effects. The disadvantage of this comparison (similar to the problem with model W_0) is that it does not consider the possibility that the regression models in equation (1) may be systematically misspecified over time for both swap and control firms.

The fourth compensation comparison (denoted as B_{-1}) is an attempt to provide a control for any systematic misspecification of the regression model in equations (1) and (2) within a firm over time *and* any industry-specific and time period effects on executive compensation. Similar to the between-sample analysis in B_0, our basic measure of interest is $[\Delta C^e_{i,t} - \Delta C^c_{i,t}]$. However, rather than comparing this difference to zero, we compare it to the corresponding difference computed in the year prior to the swap (i.e., $[\Delta C^e_{i,t-1} - \Delta C^c_{i,t-1}]$). This should control any misspecifications that are stable over time for the swap and control firms related to the regression analysis in equations (1) and (2).

To summarize, the excess compensation in the year of the swap is compared to four different benchmarks in order to assess whether the observed compensation is larger than would be expected if the accounting gain produced by the swap is not permitted to flow through the compensation function. Although somewhat conjectural, we believe that the above four comparisons are roughly ranked in terms of threats to internal validity. For example, comparison W_0 is perhaps the weakest research design and comparison B_{-1} the strongest. However, we are cognizant of the fact that each research design has unique advantages and disadvantages and, thus, we do not attempt to simply rely on one comparison. Our approach to interpreting the multiple comparisons is to assess whether the results tend to converge to an overall conclusion regarding whether executives implementing swaps earn additional compensation.

Statistical Tests

The primary statistical tests used in our analysis are the parametric one-sample or matched-pairs t-test (in which the measure of central tendency is the mean of the observations) and the nonparametric Mann-Whitney or Wilcoxon matched-pairs signed-rank test (in which the measure of central tendency is the median of the Walsh averages of the observations).[18] The null hypothesis is that the swap gain does not flow through the compensation contract, or that the central tendencies of the compensation comparisons W_0, W_{-1}, B_0, B_{-1} are equal to zero.

Swap Gain and Executive Compensation Results

Descriptive statistics and statistical tests for shifts in the central tendency of the four compensation comparisons are presented in Table 3. Panel A of Table 3 indicates that when the compensation function is estimated using earnings before extraordinary items and discontinued operations, the median excess compensation relative to the four compensation models ranges from $5,050 to $9,800 (in 1967 dollars). For comparison purposes, the median compensation from 1970 to year $t-1$ for the swap firms is $188,600. Therefore, the magnitude of the excess compensation represents an increase in compensation of approximately four percent. While this may appear to be a small number, it is important to note that the size of this increase is comparable to the magnitude of the swap's effect on earnings reported in Table 1.

The results in Table 3 also indicate that the excess compensation relative to the four benchmarks is generally statistically insignificant at conventional levels. The one exception is comparison W_0.

[18] We also conducted statistical tests using *standardized* measures of excess compensation. The standardization was achieved by dividing the excess compensation for firm i by the standard deviation of the residuals from the time period used to estimate the parameters of equation (1) and a confidence interval adjustment due to forecasting outside the estimation period [Patell, 1976]. The confidence interval adjustment is similar to that applied in security market event study analysis. This procedure for standardizing the prediction errors has the effect of placing a smaller weight on firms with unusual earnings in the year of the swap. As a result, this procedure will help to mitigate problems that arise if our compensation benchmark is systematically biased in situations in which earnings are unusually low. Although the statistical tests using standardized measures of excess compensation are likely to be better specified than the tests using unstandardized measures, we report only the unstandardized results for two reasons. First, the standardization procedure had little effect on the results of the tests for excess compensation. Second, the unstandardized measures of excess compensation are expressed in terms of dollars, whereas the standardized measures of compensation are dimensionless. Therefore, the unstandardized measures of compensation are more easily compared to the change in the value of the executive's stockholdings (which is also expressed in terms of dollars).

TABLE 3

DESCRIPTIVE STATISTICS FOR THE DIFFERENCE BETWEEN EXCESS COMPENSATION IN THE YEAR OF THE SWAP AND THE FOUR BENCHMARKS FOR EXCESS COMPENSATION[a]

Panel A. With Earnings Measured Using Income Before Extraordinary Items:

Compensation Comparison	n	Mean	Median	TMean	StDev	Min	Max	Q1	Q3	t-stat[b]	Wilcoxon Z[b]
W_0	159	8.32	9.80	10.45	64.64	−310.15	239.34	−18.62	44.71	1.62	2.58
W_{-1}	159	0.85	5.05	1.14	57.98	−193.76	266.23	−25.39	29.91	0.18	0.73
B_0	154	1.99	7.33	5.63	78.67	−354.29	193.27	−35.63	45.59	0.31	1.00
B_{-1}	154	6.05	6.79	5.89	85.79	−261.01	284.53	−43.14	49.93	0.87	1.04

Panel B. With Earnings Measured Using Net Income:

Compensation Comparison	n	Mean	Median	TMean	StDev	Min	Max	Q1	Q3	t-stat	Wilcoxon Z
W_0	159	12.10	8.43	11.37	54.54	−128.91	239.34	−16.73	43.46	2.80	2.72
W_{-1}	159	1.38	1.65	0.87	63.29	−200.26	266.23	−27.61	33.50	0.27	0.36
B_0	154	2.68	1.40	2.37	71.82	−217.24	207.83	−39.62	42.08	0.46	0.37
B_{-1}	154	3.93	7.42	1.38	84.45	−258.96	284.14	−47.41	38.18	0.58	0.34

[a] The four compensation comparisons utilize benchmarks for excess compensation that are defined in Section III. Compensation is expressed in thousands of (1967) dollars.

[b] Notation: t-stat is the t-statistic for a test that the mean of the excess compensation is equal to zero, and Wilcoxon Z is the Z-statistic for a test that the median of the excess compensation is equal to zero.

However, as discussed above, this compensation model is likely to have low internal validity because it does not control for systematic misspecification of the regression model in equation (1) over time for a specific firm and does not control for systematic industry-specific or time period effects on executive compensation.

The lack of statistical significance is consistent with the hypothesis that the swap gain has no effect on compensation or the hypothesis that the effect is, on average, too small to be detected by our tests. To provide some evidence on this issue, we repeated the analysis after partitioning the firms on the basis of the anticipated size of the effect on compensation. Our procedures for partitioning the firms are similar in spirit to, but more sophisticated than, the procedures used in earlier studies on the managerial incentives related to accounting transactions. Specifically, prior researchers have generally partitioned the firms on the basis of whether their proxy statement contains a description of an explicit accounting-based bonus plan. Since 151 (95 percent) of the firms in our sample report that they have a formal accounting-based bonus plan, this is not a very useful partitioning variable for our study.

The first procedure for partitioning the firms assumes that the effect of the swap gain on executive compensation depends on the estimated slope of the firm's compensation plan, the magnitude of the swap gain, and whether the swap gain is included in ordinary income or reported as an extraordinary item. For the case in which we estimate the form of the compensation plans using income *before* extraordinary items and discontinued operations as the accounting measure of performance, the swap gain should have no effect on compensation for firms that report the gain as an *extraordinary* income. On the other hand, if the swap gain is included in ordinary income, equation (1) predicts that, if the compensation plan is not adjusted for the accounting gain produced by the swap, the effect on executive compensation should be $b_i \times swap\ gain_i$.[19]

The second procedure for partitioning the firms is identical to the first, except that we use the terms of the compensation plan described in the firm's proxy statement to predict the magnitude that the firm's *bonus pool* would increase due to the swap gain. Although we argued in Section II that the information disclosed in proxy statements regarding the terms of the compensation plans is generally insufficient to allow us to develop a measure of the expected compensation of the CEO, some firms provided enough information to allow us to predict the magnitude of the increase in the bonus pool under the hypothesis that the bonus pool is not adjusted for the effect of the swap gain on earnings. We further assume that if the effect of the swap gain is predicted to be greater for the bonus pool of firm A than for firm B, the effect will also be greater on the compensation of the CEO of firm A than for firm B. The 67 firms that disclosed enough information in their proxy statements to calculate the potential size of the swap gain effect on their bonus pools were ranked on this basis, and the remaining firms were eliminated from this comparison.[20]

[19] If the form of the compensation function was estimated using net income as the measure of accounting performance, the firm's decision to report the swap gain as ordinary income or as an extraordinary item is irrelevant to our determination of compensation. In this case, the effect of the swap gain on compensation equals $b_i \times swap\ gain_i$ for $firm_i$. The mean (median) value of $b_i \times swap\ gain_i$ was $3,312 ($1,678), which is slightly smaller than the compensation effects calculated in Table 3.

[20] For the 67 firms that disclosed sufficient information, the mean (median) increase in the size of the bonus pool was $338,100 ($15,000) in 1967 dollars under the hypothesis that the bonus formula is not adjusted for the swap gain.

TABLE 4

COMPARISON OF EXCESS COMPENSATION FOR SUBGROUPS OF FIRMS AFTER
PARTITIONING FIRMS ON THE BASIS OF THE EXPECTED MAGNITUDE OF
THE SWAP'S EFFECT ON EXECUTIVE COMPENSATION[a]

Panel A. Compensation Contract is Assumed to be Written in Terms of Income Before *Extraordinary Items:*

Variable Used to Construct Subgroups	Low Subgroup		High Subgroup		Difference Between Subgroups	
	Mean	Median[b]	Mean	Median[b]	t-stat[c]	MW z-stat[c]
Estimated Slope × Swap Gain						
Model W_0 (n=159)	−7.4	−0.9	23.8	26.0	3.11	2.88
Model W_{-1} (n=159)	2.8	6.5	−1.1	1.1	−0.42	−1.04
Model B_0 (n=154)	−16.7	−13.2	20.7	15.8	3.03	2.62
Model B_{-1} (n=154)	6.6	16.5	5.5	5.7	−0.08	−0.56
Δ Bonus Pool from Swap Gain						
Model W_0 (n=67)	0.1	3.7	22.2	26.4	1.47	1.77
Model W_{-1} (n=67)	−10.6	−1.5	20.0	11.3	1.96	1.83
Model B_0 (n=64)	−7.0	−6.1	15.7	19.2	1.12	1.52
Model B_{-1} (n=64)	−3.2	−2.8	28.0	18.9	1.22	1.35
Estimated Slope of Contract						
Model W_0 (n=159)	−5.0	−1.3	21.8	19.6	2.67	2.47
Model W_{-1} (n=159)	3.4	4.8	−1.7	6.5	−0.56	−0.19
Model B_0 (n=154)	−15.1	0.9	18.2	11.6	2.64	2.20
Model B_{-1} (n=154)	6.7	16.4	5.4	6.1	−0.10	−0.18
Slope From Funding Formula						
Model W_0 (n=67)	−2.1	8.6	30.4	30.7	2.07	2.07
Model W_{-1} (n=67)	−9.6	−5.1	25.4	20.9	2.13	2.67
Model B_0 (n=64)	−9.6	0.9	24.3	32.7	1.79	1.77
Model B_{-1} (n=64)	−5.0	−6.3	36.9	21.9	1.73	1.80
OVERALL MEAN OF COMPARISON STATISTICS					1.49	1.44

The final two variables used to partition the firms are based on the compensation scheme slope coefficient magnitude. Under the hypothesis that the compensation scheme is not adjusted for the swap gain, the swap's effect on executive compensation is, *ceteris paribus*, an increasing function of the magnitude of the compensation contract slope coefficient. The third partitioning variable uses the estimated slope from equation (1), and the fourth partitioning variable uses the slope of the bonus funding formula described in the firm's proxy statement (if sufficient information about the bonus formula is disclosed). Therefore,

the first and third partitioning variables are based on empirical estimates of the form of the compensation plan, and the second and fourth partitioning variables are based on the bonus formulas described in proxy statements.

These four variables are used to separately partition the sample into a "HIGH" and a "LOW" subgroup on the basis of the magnitude of the swap gain's expected effect on compensation under the hypothesis that the compensation scheme is not adjusted for the accounting gain produced by the swap transaction. For each of the four partitioning variables, the four models of

TABLE 4—*Continued*

Panel B. Compensation Contract is Assumed to be Written in Terms of Net Income (Income After Extraordinary Items):

	Low Subgroup		High Subgroup		Difference Between Subgroups	
Variable Used to Construct Subgroups	Mean	Median[b]	Mean	Median[b]	t-stat[c]	MW z-stat[c]
Estimated Slope × Swap Gain						
Model W_0 $(n=159)$	1.6	−0.5	22.5	22.3	2.44	2.61
Model W_{-1} $(n=159)$	7.6	1.6	−4.7	1.6	−1.23	−0.36
Model B_0 $(n=154)$	−12.1	−11.7	17.1	13.5	2.55	2.51
Model B_{-1} $(n=154)$	4.1	10.4	3.7	3.6	−0.03	0.38
Δ Bonus Pool from Swap Gain						
Model W_0 $(n=67)$	0.5	3.3	20.4	26.9	1.30	1.55
Model W_{-1} $(n=67)$	−11.1	−1.4	−4.7	10.7	1.84	1.78
Model B_0 $(n=64)$	1.4	−0.2	17.1	12.0	0.33	0.55
Model B_{-1} $(n=64)$	−1.0	2.5	23.0	20.0	0.98	1.45
Estimated Slope of Contract						
Model W_0 $(n=159)$	5.4	−1.1	18.9	16.9	1.58	1.67
Model W_{-1} $(n=159)$	7.5	6.5	−4.8	−2.8	−1.23	−1.06
Model B_0 $(n=154)$	−7.5	−11.0	12.4	9.1	1.71	1.66
Model B_{-1} $(n=154)$	5.8	10.6	2.2	2.0	−0.27	−0.42
Slope From Funding Formula						
Model W_0 $(n=67)$	−3.6	−3.3	30.9	26.9	2.19	2.22
Model W_{-1} $(n=67)$	−9.7	−3.4	23.1	13.6	1.94	2.26
Model B_0 $(n=64)$	−5.4	−3.8	20.1	29.0	1.35	1.58
Model B_{-1} $(n=64)$	−5.4	5.2	34.9	15.9	1.69	1.56
OVERALL MEAN OF COMPARISON STATISTICS					1.07	1.25

[a] Compensation measures are expressed in thousands of (1967) dollars.

[b] Median of the Walsh Averages.

[c] t-stat is the t-statistic for a test of the equality of the means of the LOW and HIGH subgroups. MW z-stat is the Mann-Whitney z-statistic for a test of the equality of the medians for the LOW and HIGH subgroups. A positive value for these statistics indicates that the central tendency for the HIGH subgroup exceeded the central tendency for the LOW subgroup.

excess compensation given in equation (3) are used, resulting in a total of 16 comparisons. For each comparison, a parametric t-test and a nonparametric Mann-Whitney z-test are used to test the hypothesis that the excess compensation is equal for the two subgroups.

The results in Table 4 indicate that, relative to the compensation benchmarks, the excess compensation for the HIGH subgroup exceeds the excess compensation for the LOW subgroup in 12 of 16 of the comparisons. Taken individ-

ually, ten of the 16 Mann-Whitney z-statistics are significant at the 0.10 level (two-tail). The overall mean of the 16 Mann-Whitney z-statistics is 1.44. While it is difficult to calculate a precise measure of significance for this overall mean without knowing the correlation between the 16 comparisons, the overall mean is significant at the five percent level as long as the 16 correlated observations constitute the equivalent of at least two independent observations. The results using the parametric t-test, and the results in which accounting performance is measured using net income are similar.

The results are not completely consistent across the four partitioning variables and the four models for excess compensation. The results are most consistent when the firms are partitioned on the basis of the compensation contract parameters observed in proxy statements. Results of these comparisons yield a positive difference between the subgroups in every case. On the other hand, the results are not as consistent when the firms are partitioned on the basis of the estimated parameters of the compensation contracts. The results tend to be either positive and strongly significant (models W_0 and B_0) or negative and insignificant (models W_{-1} and B_{-1}).

Our overall interpretation of the results in Tables 3 and 4 is that the executives of firms completing a swap transaction experience an increase in compensation. The increase is largest (both in absolute magnitude and in statistical significance) for firms whose compensation plans and swap transactions would be expected to produce the greatest increase in compensation under the hypothesis that the accounting gain is allowed to flow through the compensation function. We interpret these results as being consistent with the hypothesis that firms do not adjust their salary plus bonus contracts for the accounting gain produced by the swap.

IV. ANALYSIS OF EXECUTIVE WEALTH

While the analysis in the previous section focused on the swap transactions' effect on the executives' salary plus bonus compensation, it is also of interest to examine the swaps' effect on other components of the executives' wealth. As established in prior research (see the references in fn. 2), the announcement of a swap transaction is associated with a

stock price reaction that is, on average, negative. Therefore, it is tempting to conduct an event study to assess the change in the value of the executives' equity holdings, and then add this to the compensation comparisons calculated in Section III in order to compute the "total" effect of the swap transaction on the wealth of the executives. A problem with this approach is that it implicitly assumes that the security price reaction constitutes a measure of the desirability of the swap transaction from the perspective of shareholders. In particular, an adverse effect on shareholder wealth is assumed to be a sign that shareholders view a swap as a negative net present value transaction.

Prior research has generally been unable to determine any negative cash flow implications of swap transactions that would explain the magnitude of the security price response. In particular, the magnitude of the reaction is too large to be explained by the fee paid to the investment banking firm that participates in the swap transaction, the loss of the tax shield on the interest payments of the debt that is extinguished, or the "excess" compensation paid to managers as a result of the swap gain. Lys and Sivaramakrishnan [1987] suggest that the negative reaction may be due to the signalling aspects of the swap, rather than to the swap *per se*. That is, they suggest that managers take leverage-decreasing actions (such as swaps) when they acquire information that causes them to make downward revisions in their assessment of the firm's future earnings performance (see Ross [1977], Harris and Raviv [1985], and Miller and Rock [1985] for additional discussion). Lys and Sivaramakrishnan [1987] find that analysts revise their forecasts for annual earnings downward in the period surrounding the swap announcement, and the results in

Section II demonstrated that the earnings number that is reported at the end of the year is, on average, lower than time-series expectation models would predict. These results are consistent with the hypothesis that the market decreases the price of the firm's stock because it perceives the announcement of a swap as information that the firm's earnings prospects will be worse than expected.[21]

Although we cannot determine which of the above explanations for the security market reaction has descriptive validity, it is important to note that they have different implications regarding the method of computing the total impact of the swap on executive wealth. If the negative stock price reaction arises solely because the swap conveys information about the firm that would have been ultimately released (e.g., at the time of the next earnings announcement), then the swap, *per se*, has no adverse effect on either shareholder wealth or the value of the CEO's stock holdings (other than timing considerations). Under this scenario, it is not appropriate to add the decrease in the value of the CEO's stock holdings associated with the announcement of the swap to his excess compensation. Given the results in Tables 3 and 4, we would conclude that the executives do personally profit from swap transactions (especially the executives of firms with highly "accounting-oriented" compensation schemes).

In fact, the negative security market reaction could occur even if the swap, by itself, is a positive net present value transaction given the unfavorable private information possessed by the manager. The market reaction to the swap would then be composed of (1) the favorable effect of the swap itself and (2) the unfavorable effect of the information that the swap conveys about the firm's future earnings prospects. Assum-

ing that the information about the firm's future earnings prospects would have ultimately been disclosed, the appropriate measure of the "total" effect of the swap on the executives' wealth would be the unexpected compensation calculated in Section III and the favorable effect of the swap *per se* discussed above (which we cannot measure). In this case, the excess compensation calculated in Section III provides a lower bound on the "total" effect of the swap transaction on executive wealth.

However, if the market reaction is the result of the swap transaction having a negative net present value, it is appropriate to add the change in the value of the CEO's stock holdings to the excess compensation computed in the previous section. In the following subsections, we discuss the method used to compute the change in the value of the CEO's stock holdings at the announcement of the swap, and the "total" effect of the swap on the executive's wealth.

Method

The changes in shareholder wealth associated with the swaps were analyzed by estimating the security market reaction in an event period centered on the day that the swaps were announced in *The Wall Street Journal*.[22] Daily returns and

---

[21] To provide some insight into whether managers possess unfavorable private information at the time of the swap transaction, we examined the insider trading behavior of managers in the period surrounding the swap transaction. Specifically, we examined the dollars of insider buying minus the dollars of insider selling (for both open market and private transactions) in the six months prior to the swap relative to the same calendar period in the year prior to the swap. We could not reject the null hypothesis that the amount of insider trading was the same in these two time periods. These results suggest that either managers did not possess unfavorable private information at the time of the swap transaction, or they did not choose to use this information in making trading decisions.

[22] Alternatively, we could have used the date on which the preliminary registration statement concerning the

the daily value-weighted market index were obtained from the Center for Research on Security Price (CRSP) tape for an estimation period from day -120 to day -21 and an event period from day -20 to day $+20$. The single factor market model was assumed to be an adequate characterization of the return generating process, and this model was estimated via ordinary least squares in the estimation period. The daily excess returns, standardized excess returns, and squared standardized excess returns were estimated in the event period using the regression parameters, standard deviation of the market model residuals in the estimation period, and the confidence interval adjustment due to forecasting outside the estimation period (see Patell [1976] for a discussion of these statistics). The statistical significance of the average standardized excess returns and squared standardized excess returns was determined by using Normal theory tests and jackknifing methods.

Results of Security Market Reaction to Swap Announcement

The average excess returns and associated statistical tests for the swap announcement were very similar to the results reported in prior research (see fn. 2). The security market reaction to the swap occurred in a short time interval prior to and including day zero.[23] The swap was, on average, associated with a *decrease* in shareholder wealth of approximately -1.01 percent over the time period from day -1 to day 0 ($p < 0.05$, two-tail). The cumulative excess return from day -1 to day 0 corresponds to a mean decrease in shareholder wealth of \$14.5MM, and a median decrease of \$9.0MM.

The change in the value of the executive's equity holdings associated with the swap ($Stk\ Chg_i$) is computed by

$$Stk\ Chg_i = Shares_i \times Price_i \times CER_i,$$

where

$Shares_i$ = number of shares owned by the CEO of firm i in the year prior to the date of the swap,

$Price_i$ = price per share at the end of the fiscal year prior to the date of the swap, and

CER_i = cumulative excess return from day -1 to day 0 for firm i.

Expressed in 1967 dollars, the mean value of the CEO's equity ownership (i.e., $Shares_i \times Price_i$) for our sample was \$1,268,645, and the median value was \$271,800. When multiplied by the security market reaction to the announcement of the swap, the mean change in the value of the executives' stock holdings was $-\$17,825$, and the median change was $-\$1,625$. In addition, approximately 69 percent of the CEOs experienced a decrease in the value of their stock holdings over the period from day -1 to day 0.

---

equity used in the swap was filed with the Securities and Exchange Commission. This filing date was available in the *Investment Dealer's Digest* for 85 of our firms. For this subsample, similar to the results in Hand [1987], the registration date precedes the *WSJ* date by a median distance of one trading day. Since the *WSJ* date is easily obtained and this date is very close to the date of the preliminary registration statement, the *WSJ* announcement for the swap is used as the event date.

[23] The sample size for the event study is only 157 because we could not find a *WSJ* announcement date or security price data was not available on the CRSP tape. There are several firms with multiple swap dates within a given fiscal year (e.g., 6/82 and 9/82). These two dates are treated as *separate* observations for the security market reaction computations. Since we use compensation changes in a given fiscal year as the unit of analysis, we sum the market response for the multiple swaps during a fiscal year in order to measure the total effect on executive wealth. After combining multiple swaps that occurred in the same fiscal year for a given firm, the total number of swap-years was equal to 139.

TABLE 5

ANALYSIS OF THE TOTAL EFFECT OF THE SWAP ON THE CEO's WEALTH[a]

Panel A. With Earnings Measured Using Income Before Extraordinary Items:

	n	Mean	Median	TMean	StDev	Min	Max	Q1	Q3	t-stat[c]	Wilcoxon Z[c]
Total W_0[b]	139	-11.7	6.4	5.1	279.8	-2989.7	1130.6	-23.4	36.7	-0.49	1.16
Total W_{-1}	139	-17.4	0.8	-2.0	278.5	-3016.5	1079.1	-36.4	33.9	-0.74	-0.21
Total B_0	134	-19.7	4.6	-2.9	279.7	-2888.1	1140.3	-39.5	37.7	-0.82	-0.31
Total B_{-1}	134	-13.1	-1.2	0.2	281.0	-2897.1	1083.2	-45.5	47.2	-0.54	-0.07

Panel B. With Earnings Measured Using Net Income:

	n	Mean	Median	TMean	StDev	Min	Max	Q1	Q3	t-stat	Wilcoxon Z
Total W_0[b]	139	-7.2	2.3	5.9	276.8	-2982.6	1131.8	-22.1	36.5	-0.31	1.24
Total W_{-1}	139	-16.7	1.0	-2.2	279.8	-3012.9	1079.7	-42.8	34.4	-0.70	-0.22
Total B_0	134	-17.7	-0.2	-3.4	290.7	-3052.1	1141.5	-44.7	32.5	-0.70	-0.65
Total B_{-1}	134	-15.5	2.5	-3.0	289.5	-2998.6	1083.9	-56.6	42.8	-0.62	-0.43

[a] The Total effect on CEO wealth is expressed in thousands of (1967) dollars.

[b] The four measures of the total effect on CEO wealth are defined in equations (4a) to (4d).

[c] Notation: t-stat is the t-statistic for a test that the mean of the total effect on wealth is equal to zero and Wilcoxon Z is the z-statistic for a test that the median of the total effect on wealth is equal to zero.

*Executive Wealth Effects
of the Swap Transaction*

Assuming that the security price reaction to the announcement of a swap provides a measure of the swap's desirability from the perspective of shareholders, we compute the "total" effect of the swap on the CEO's wealth by adding the excess compensation calculated in Section III to the change in the value of the CEO's equity holdings associated with the swap's announcement. As discussed in Section II, our executive compensation measure is salary plus annual bonus; therefore, our measure of the "total" wealth of the executives includes only (1) salary plus bonus and (2) the value of the shares owned in their firms.

Given the four benchmarks for excess compensation, the total effect of the swap can be expressed as:

$$\text{Total } W_0 = Stk\ Chg_i + \Delta C_{i,t}^e \qquad (4a)$$

$$\text{Total } W_{-1} = Stk\ Chg_i \\ + \Delta C_{i,t}^e - \Delta C_{i,t-1}^e \qquad (4b)$$

$$\text{Total } B_0 = Stk\ Chg_i \\ + \Delta C_{i,t}^e - \Delta C_{i,t}^c \qquad (4c)$$

$$\text{Total } B_{-1} = Stk\ Chg_i \\ + [\Delta C_{i,t}^e - \Delta C_{i,t}^c] \\ - [\Delta C_{i,t-1}^e - \Delta C_{i,t-1}^c]. \qquad (4d)$$

The null hypothesis is that the total effect on executive wealth is equal to zero.

Analysis of the total effect of the swap on executive wealth is presented in Table 5. The large differences between the mean, median, and trimmed mean indicate that several "outliers" are present in the data. For this reason, we will concentrate on the nonparametric results, which should be less influenced by the presence of these outliers. The results in Table 5 suggest that the total effect on executive wealth is relatively small and statistically insignificant.

The analysis of the swap's total effect

Defeo, Lambert, and Larcker

was then repeated using the same procedure for partitioning the firms as in Table 4. Recall that the partitioning variables attempt to predict the anticipated size of the swap's effect on compensation under the hypothesis that the compensation scheme is not adjusted for the effect of the swap transaction on accounting income. The results of the comparisons of the total wealth effects for the subgroups are presented in Table 6. Overall, the results for the total wealth comparisons are similar to the excess compensation comparisons that are contained in Table 4, although not as statistically significant. The nonparametric results in Table 6 indicate that the total wealth effect for the HIGH subgroup exceeded the total wealth effect for the LOW subgroup in 14 of the 16 comparisons. Taken individually, six of the 16 Mann-Whitney z-statistics are significant at the 0.10 level (two-tail). The overall mean of the 16 Mann-Whitney z-statistics is 1.49. This overall mean is significant at the five percent level as long as the 16 correlated observations constitute the equivalent of at least two independent observations. The results for the case in which earnings was measured using net income are similar.

Similar to the results in Table 4, the total wealth comparisons were most consistent when the firms were partitioned on the basis of the compensation contracts parameters observed in proxy statements, and less consistent when the firms were partitioned on the basis of the estimated parameters of the compensation contracts. Although the tests that compare the total effect for the two subgroups are less conclusive than the tests for the compensation effect, our overall interpretation of these tests is that the executives of the firms in the "HIGH" subgroups experience a marginally greater increase in wealth than the executives of the firms in the "LOW" subgroups.

TABLE 6

COMPARISON OF TOTAL EFFECT OF THE SWAP ON THE CEO'S WEALTH FOR SUBGROUPS
OF FIRMS AFTER PARTITIONING FIRMS ON THE BASIS OF THE EXPECTED
MAGNITUDE OF THE SWAP'S EFFECT ON EXECUTIVE COMPENSATION

Panel A. Compensation Contract is Assumed to be Written in Terms of Income Before Extraordinary Items:

Variable Used to Construct Subgroups	Low Subgroup		High Subgroup		Difference Between Subgroups	
	Mean	Median	Mean	Median	t-stat[a]	MW z-stat[a]
Estimated Slope × Swap Gain						
Total W_0 ($n=139$)	1.0	−4.6	−25.0	19.7	−0.53	2.67
Total W_{-1} ($n=139$)	14.0	3.2	−51.0	−7.7	−1.35	−0.93
Total B_0 ($n=134$)	−9.0	−15.0	−32.0	10.1	−0.45	2.20
Total B_{-1} ($n=134$)	18.0	3.1	−47.0	−7.4	−1.29	−0.75
Δ Bonus Pool from Swap Gain						
Total W_0 ($n=62$)	−3.0	−1.6	11.2	21.0	0.95	1.32
Total W_{-1} ($n=62$)	−12.0	−4.5	7.6	7.4	1.26	1.23
Total B_0 ($n=59$)	−10.8	−14.0	5.3	18.4	0.81	1.23
Total B_{-1} ($n=59$)	−0.3	−10.5	14.0	1.4	0.54	0.56
Estimated Slope of Contract						
Total W_0 ($n=139$)	−42.0	−7.8	23.2	19.7	1.47	3.79
Total W_{-1} ($n=139$)	−33.0	−0.9	0.1	4.5	0.74	0.94
Total B_0 ($n=134$)	−57.0	−21.4	19.7	14.0	1.64	3.69
Total B_{-1} ($n=134$)	−35.0	−7.7	10.0	4.1	0.95	1.17
Slope From Funding Formula						
Total W_0 ($n=62$)	−5.3	5.4	18.0	19.3	1.59	1.50
Total W_{-1} ($n=62$)	−12.4	−13.7	12.9	19.7	1.62	2.22
Total B_0 ($n=59$)	−12.2	−1.4	11.1	29.1	1.32	1.32
Total B_{-1} ($n=59$)	−8.0	−15.1	28.0	9.5	1.52	1.71
OVERALL MEAN OF COMPARISON STATISTICS					0.67	1.49

V. SUMMARY

In this paper, we examine the relation between the increase in accounting earnings generated via an equity-for-debt swap and the change in executive compensation and wealth. Our results indicate that, on average, the accounting gain produced by a swap is associated with an increase in cash compensation (i.e., salary plus bonus) that is both small in magnitude and statistically insignificant. These results are similar to the executive compensation effects of accounting changes reported in Healy et al. [1987]. In that paper, the authors conclude that executives appear to earn slightly higher levels of compensation after an accounting change, but that the increase is not statistically significant when compared to a matched-pairs control group. The lack of statistical significance in our paper is consistent with the hypothesis that the swap gain has no effect on compensation or the hypothesis that the swap gain is, on average, too small to be detected by our tests.

To provide more detailed evidence on the relation between the swap gain and compensation, we partitioned the sample of firms into a HIGH and a LOW subgroup according to the magnitude of the

TABLE 6—Continued

Panel B. Compensation Contract is Assumed to be Written in Terms of Net Income (Income After Extraordinary Items):

Variable Used to Construct Subgroups	Low Subgroup		High Subgroup		Difference Between Subgroups	
	Mean	Median	Mean	Median	t-stat[a]	MW z-stat[a]
Estimated Slope × Swap Gain						
Total W_0 (n=139)	13.0	−5.0	−26.0	16.3	−0.84	1.98
Total W_{-1} (n=139)	22.0	1.3	−54.0	−7.3	−1.64	−1.14
Total B_0 (n=134)	0.0	−12.4	−34.0	5.6	−0.69	1.81
Total B_{-1} (n=134)	18.0	9.7	−47.0	−7.7	−1.33	0.64
Δ Bonus Pool from Swap Gain						
Total W_0 (n=62)	−3.1	1.2	9.6	19.0	0.83	1.02
Total W_{-1} (n=62)	−11.8	−1.0	6.8	10.7	1.14	1.36
Total B_0 (n=59)	−1.3	−7.6	−1.9	9.0	−0.03	0.39
Total B_{-1} (n=59)	0.8	7.2	10.0	10.3	0.36	0.77
Estimated Slope of Contract						
Total W_0 (n=139)	−29.0	−5.0	17.3	16.9	1.04	2.35
Total W_{-1} (n=139)	−27.0	0.8	−5.0	1.1	0.49	−0.13
Total B_0 (n=134)	−46.0	−13.5	11.2	8.7	1.15	2.51
Total B_{-1} (n=134)	−33.0	3.1	2.5	2.5	0.72	0.30
Slope From Funding Formula						
Total W_0 (n=62)	−6.9	−5.4	18.4	19.0	1.71	1.64
Total W_{-1} (n=62)	−12.0	−11.1	11.6	15.0	1.46	1.86
Total B_0 (n=59)	−7.3	−9.2	7.4	9.0	0.80	1.01
Total B_{-1} (n=59)	−7.1	−0.1	24.3	7.4	1.32	1.15
OVERALL MEAN OF COMPARISON STATISTICS					0.41	1.10

[a] t-stat is the t-statistic for a test of the equality of the means of the LOW and HIGH subgroups. MW z-stat is the Mann-Whitney z-statistic for a test of the equality of the medians for the LOW and HIGH subgroups. A positive value for these statistics indicates that the central tendency for the HIGH subgroup exceeded the central tendency for the LOW subgroup.

predicted effect of the swap gain on executive compensation under the hypothesis that the accounting gain produced by the swap is allowed to "flow through" the compensation function. This approach provides a more sophisticated means of assessing whether a firm's compensation scheme is highly accounting-oriented than the typical procedure used in the accounting literature, which is to partition firms on the basis of whether their proxy statement contains a description of an explicit accounting-based bonus plan. Our results indicate that the excess compensation for the HIGH subgroup exceeded the excess compensation for the LOW subgroup. We interpret these results as being consistent with the hypothesis that firms do *not*, on average, adjust their annual bonus plans for the effect of the swap gain on accounting earnings.

One interpretation of the finding that firms do not use their annual bonus plans to penalize managers for engaging in swap transactions is that shareholders do not perceive these transactions *per se* to adversely affect their wealth. Under this scenario, the negative stock price reaction associated with the announcement of swaps might be interpreted as arising because swaps convey bad news about the firms' future earnings prospects, and not because swaps themselves are negative net present value projects.

Alternatively, if the adverse market reaction to the announcement of the swap is the result of the swap being a negative net present value transaction from the perspective of shareholders, our evidence suggests that there is an unresolved conflict of interest between managers and shareholders with respect to swap transactions. That is, we find that managers experience an increase in their cash compensation despite the adverse effect on shareholder wealth. While the magnitude of the compensation increase is not especially large, the percentage increase in compensation is comparable in magnitude to the percentage increase in earnings produced by the swap.

The absence of a complete examination of all of the components of executive wealth is, of course, a limitation to this interpretation of our results. In particular, we cannot be certain that executives are not penalized via other components of their compensation. For example, we find that the top executives experience a decrease in the value of their equity holdings in their firms that is, on average, comparable in size to the increase in their compensation. However, there is some weak evidence that the total effect of the swap transaction on executive wealth is positive for firms whose compensation plans are more "accounting-oriented" (i.e., the increase in compensation exceeds the decrease in the value of personal equity holdings).

REFERENCES

Abdel-khalik, A., "The Effect of LIFO-Switching and Firm Ownership on Executives' Pay," *Journal of Accounting Research* (Autumn 1985), pp. 427–447.

——, "Incentives for Accruing Costs and Efficiency in Regulated Monopolies Subject to ROE Constraint," Supplement to *Journal of Accounting Research* (Forthcoming 1988).

Adams, H., "Factors Affecting the Use of Performance Measures in Executive Compensation Contracts," Working paper (Northwestern University, 1987).

Anders, G., "Corporations Find Help for Balance Sheets: Swap Costly Debt for Low-Yielding Stock," *The Wall Street Journal* (June 30, 1982), p. 25.

Antle, R., and A. Smith, "Measuring Executive Compensation: Methods and an Application," *Journal of Accounting Research* (Spring 1985), pp. 296–325.

——, and ——, "An Empirical Investigation of the Relative Performance Evaluation of Corporate Executives," *Journal of Accounting Research* (Spring 1986), pp. 1–39.

Booz Allen & Hamilton, "Creating Shareholder Value: A New Mission for Executive Compensation," *Midland Corporate Finance Journal* (Winter 1985), pp. 56–66.

Coughlan, A., and R. Schmidt, "Executive Compensation, Managerial Turnover, and Firm Performance: An Empirical Investigation," *Journal of Accounting and Economics* (April 1985), pp. 43–66.

Demski, J., J. Patell, and M. Wolfson, "Decentralized Choice of Monitoring Systems," THE ACCOUNTING REVIEW (January 1984), pp. 16–34.

Dukes, R., T. Dyckman, and J. Elliott, "Accounting for Research and Development Costs: The Impact on Research and Development Expenditures," Supplement to *Journal of Accounting Research* (1980), pp. 1–26.

Ely, K., "Cross-Sectional Variations in the Relation Between Accounting Variables and the Chief Executive's Compensation," Working paper (University of Chicago, 1987).

Finnerty, J., "Stock-for-Debt Swaps and Shareholder Returns," *Financial Management* (Autumn 1985), pp. 5–17.

Foster, G., *Financial Statement Analysis,* Second Edition (Prentice-Hall, 1986).

Hand, J., "Debt-Equity Swaps," Unpublished working paper (University of Chicago, Graduate School of Business, 1987).

Harris, M., and A. Raviv, "Capital Structure and Corporate Control," Working paper (Northwestern University, J. L. Kellogg Graduate School of Management, 1985).

Hay Associates, "Fifth Annual Hay Report on Executive Compensation," *Wharton Magazine* (Fall 1981), pp. 50–56.

Healy, P., "The Effect of Bonus Schemes on Accounting Decisions," *Journal of Accounting and Economics* (April 1985), pp. 85–107.

———, S. Kang, and K. Palepu, "The Effect of Accounting Procedure Changes on CEO's Cash Salary and Bonus Compensation," *Journal of Accounting and Economics* (April 1987), pp. 7–34.

Holthausen, R., "Evidence on the Effect of Bond Covenants and Management Compensation Contracts on the Choice of Accounting Techniques: The Case of the Depreciation Switch-Back," *Journal of Accounting and Economics* (March 1981), pp. 73–109.

Horwitz, B., and R. Kolodny, "The Economic Effects of Involuntary Uniformity in the Financial Reporting of R&D Expenditures," Supplement to *Journal of Accounting Research* (1980), pp. 38–74.

Jensen, M., and K. Murphy, "Are Executive Compensation Contracts Structured Properly?" Unpublished working paper (University of Rochester, 1987).

Lambert, R., and D. Larcker, "Executive Compensation, Corporate Decision-Making, and Shareholder Wealth: A Review of the Evidence," *Midland Corporate Finance Journal* (Winter 1985), pp. 6–22.

———, and ———, "Executive Compensation Effects of Large Corporate Acquisitions," *Journal of Accounting and Public Policy* (Winter 1987a), pp. 231–243.

———, and ———, "An Analysis of the Use of Accounting and Market Measures of Performance in Executive Compensation Contracts," Supplement to *Journal of Accounting Research* (1987b), pp. 85–125.

———, ———, and R. Verrecchia, "Portfolio Issues in the Valuation of Executive Compensation," Working paper (University of Pennsylvania, Wharton School, 1988).

Larcker, D., "The Association Between Performance Plan Adoption and Corporate Capital Investment," *Journal of Accounting and Economics* (April 1983), pp. 3–30.

———, "Short-Term Executive Compensation Contracts and Executive Expenditure Decisions: The Case of Commercial Banks," *Journal of Financial and Quantitative Analysis* (March 1987), pp. 33–50.

———, and L. Revsine, "The Oil and Gas Accounting Controversy: An Analysis of Economic Consequences," THE ACCOUNTING REVIEW (October 1983), pp. 706–732.

Lys, T., and S. Sivaramakrishnan, "Earnings Expectations and Capital Restructuring: The Case of Equity-for-Debt Swaps," Unpublished working paper (Northwestern University, J. L. Kellogg Graduate School of Management, 1987).

Miller, M., and K. Rock, "Dividend Policy Under Asymmetric Information," *Journal of Finance* (September 1985), pp. 1031–1051.

Murphy, K., "Corporate Performance and Managerial Remuneration: An Empirical Analysis," *Journal of Accounting and Economics* (April 1985), pp. 11–42.

———, "Incentives, Learning, and Compensation: A Theoretical and Empirical Investigation of Managerial Labor Contracts," *Rand Journal of Economics* (Spring 1986), pp. 59–76.

Patell, J., "Corporate Forecasts of Earnings per Share and Stock Price Behavior: Empirical Tests," *Journal of Accounting Research* (Autumn 1976), pp. 246–276.

Peavy, J., and J. Scott, "A Closer Look at Stock-for-Debt Swaps," *Financial Analysts Journal* (May-June 1985), pp. 44–50.

Ramanan, R., "Managerial Incentives, Accounting for Interest Costs, and Investment Related Decisions of the Firm," Unpublished Ph.D. dissertation (Northwestern University, 1985).

Rogers, R., and J. Owers, "Equity for Debt Exchanges and Stockholder Wealth," *Financial Management* (Autumn 1985), pp. 18–26.

Ross, S., "The Determination of Financial Structure: The Incentive-Signalling Approach," *The Bell Journal of Economics* (Spring 1977), pp. 23–40.

Sloan, A., and E. Spragins, "It's a Super Deal," *Forbes* (December 7, 1981), pp. 39–40.

Sibson & Company, Inc., *Facts & Issues 1986* (Sibson & Company, 1986).

Simon, D., "Compensation Effects and Accounting Changes: An Empirical Examination," Unpublished Ph.D. dissertation (Northwestern University, 1983).

Watts, R., and J. Zimmerman, "Towards a Positive Theory of the Determination of Accounting Standards," THE ACCOUNTING REVIEW (January 1978), pp. 112–134.

THE EFFECT OF OWNER VERSUS MANAGEMENT CONTROL ON THE CHOICE OF ACCOUNTING METHODS*

Dan S. DHALIWAL

University of Arizona, Tucson, AZ 85721, USA

Gerald L. SALAMON

University of Iowa, Iowa City, IA 52242, USA

E. Dan SMITH

University of Florida, Gainesville, FL 32611, USA

Received January 1982, final version received March 1982

This paper examines the relationship between the ownership control status of firms and the accounting methods they adopt. The arguments of Watts and Zimmerman's positive theory are integrated with those of managerial economists to generate the prediction that management controlled firms are more likely than owner controlled firms to adopt accounting methods which increase reported earnings. This prediction is inconsistent with Fama's hypothesis that the market for managerial talent will prevent management controlled firms from acting differently than owner controlled firms. This paper compares the depreciation methods used by a sample of management and owner controlled firms for financial reporting purposes. The comparison considers and controls for the factors of firm size, leverage, and the depreciation method used for tax reporting purposes. The comparison reveals that there is a significant difference in the depreciation methods adopted by management controlled and owner controlled firms for financial reporting purposes.

1. Introduction

In the early and middle sixties the existence of a 'corporate personality' [Sorter et al. (1964, 1966)] was given as an explanation of the particular accounting methods chosen by firms. This theory suggested that there was a non-economic dimension to 'corporate personality' [Sorter et al. (1966, p. 200)] and thus, a non-economic dimension to the process which characterizes the selection of accounting methods by firms. Recently, this 'corporate

*We wish to thank an anonymous referee for his valuable comments on a previous draft of this paper. Helpful comments were also received from Russ Barefield, Mark Rusbarsky, Ross Watts, Jerold Zimmerman, and participants in accounting workshops at the University of Washington and University of Oregon.

0165–4101/82/0000–0000/$02.75 © 1982 North-Holland

Journal of Accounting and Economics 4 (1982) 41–53. North-Holland Publishing Company

personality' explanation has been partially supplanted by an alternative one which is based upon positive economic theory [Watts and Zimmerman (1978)]. Basically, this positive economic theory suggests that the accounting methods adopted by a firm are systematically related to certain characteristics of the firm and/or its industry. The work of Watts and Zimmerman (1978), Hagerman and Zmijewski (1979), Dhaliwal (1980, 1982), Bowen, Lacey and Noreen (1981) and Zmijewski and Hagerman (1981) all suggest that there is an association between firm and/or industry characteristics and the relative income effect of the accounting methods chosen by the firm from the set of available methods.

It is clear from the empirical work conducted so far that firms do not choose accounting methods in a random manner. However, it is also clear from the empirical work conducted so far that there is still quite a bit to learn about the choice of accounting methods by firms. Theory development and the associated empirical work is still at the stage where the set of firm and/or industry characteristics which are relevant to the choice of accounting methods are not yet well delineated. The purpose of this paper is to examine the relationship between the ownership control status of the firm and the accounting methods it adopts. In particular, we examine whether the depreciation method selected for financial reporting purposes is independent of ownership control status. Our results suggest that, in general, accounting methods chosen by a firm will not be independent of the firm's ownership control status. The prior work on this topic is reviewed in the next section of this paper.

2. Ownership control status and choice of accounting methods: Theory and prior evidence

The field of managerial economics provides theory and evidence that the set of accounting methods adopted by the firm is related to its ownership control status.[1] Williamson (1964, 1967), and Monsen and Downs (1965) argue that the managers of large corporations with diffuse ownership (hereafter called management-controlled or MC firms) have considerable discretion in guiding the affairs of their firms and that this discretionary power is used to divert some resources from corporate shareholders. Hindley (1970, p. 195) argues that the current market value of the shares of MC firms will be smaller than their potential value if the managers of MC firms divert a significant amount of firm resources to themselves. This difference between the potential value and current market value of the firm's shares provides an incentive for an outside group to gain control of the corporation. Hindley

[1]The arguments regarding the behavior of management-controlled firms are taken from Salamon and Smith (1979, pp. 319–320).

(1970, pp. 199–200) and Williamson (1967, p. 13) hypothesize that the managers of MC firms exercise control over the information released regarding firm performance in an attempt to present the results of firm operations in a most favorable way. The attempt to control information is intended to keep current shareholders satisfied and unwilling to support any takeover attempts by outside groups.[2] This line of argument suggests that the managers of MC firms are likely to choose accounting methods which result in higher or early reported earnings and higher reported equity.

An alternative argument for expecting managers to prefer those accounting methods which result in higher reported earnings has been summarized by Gagnon (1967, pp. 191–192) as follows:

'The basic argument is that the managers of the firms maximize their own monetary and nonmonetary income by maximizing reported income. In principle, a top executive will be paid the maximum amount of money which he could obtain by taking some other job. In a competitive market, that amount will be equal to his marginal product. Now, it is conceivable that accounting profits are the main data available to the shareholders to measure the productivity of the executive team. As a matter of fact the National Industrial Conference Board has accumulated evidence that, in a large number of companies listed on the New York Stock Exchange, part of the executive compensation is formally based on company profits. That type of contract should constitute an incentive to maximize reported earnings.'

. . .

'Finally, there is some nonmonetary gain for a group of executives in reporting higher rather than lower profits. In a summary of the literature on managerial motivation, Williamson (1964, pp. 30–32) reports that theorists largely agree on the fact that managers seem to pay great attention to their "security" and "reputation for excellence". It may be assumed that security and reputation are in some way dependent on reported profits. Consequently, executives maximizing their own utility would pay some attention to the reporting methods their firm uses.'

The hypothesis that closely-held firms (hereafter, referred to as owner-controlled or OC firms) are likely to choose accounting methods with different income effects than the accounting methods chosen by MC firms is also implied by the positive theory of accounting method choice developed

[2]Note that these arguments are consistent with an efficient stock market. In particular, these arguments do not assume that management can influence stock returns by choosing one set of accounting methods over others. The arguments only assume that the accounting methods chosen by management can convince *some* of the firm's shareholders that management is doing a creditable job and thus make these shareholders unwilling to support a takeover.

by Watts and Zimmerman (1978). Zmijewski and Hagerman (1981, p. 131) describe the Watts and Zimmerman positive theory as being based on the two propositions that (1) managers attempt to maximize their utility, and (2) that their utility is positively related to their compensation. The notion that management utility is tied to the amount and timing of compensation leads to the hypothesis that MC firms will be more inclined than OC firms to choose accounting methods which result in higher or earlier reported income. In OC firms, the owners can motivate and monitor the behavior of managers directly so the need for incentive compensation schemes based upon reported income is not great. On the other hand, the outside owners of MC firms must devise mechanisms to motivate the firm managers to act in a manner which does not ignore the interests of the outside owners. One common mechanism used for this purpose is the adoption of incentive compensation schemes (of either the cash bonus or stock option type) which depend upon reported income. Consequently, it is likely that MC firms are more likely than OC firms to have incentive compensation schemes based upon reported income.[3] This means that the managers in MC firms are more likely to benefit than are the managers in OC firms from the selection of accounting methods which result in high and/or early reported income.

The managers of OC firms do not have the same incentives to increase reported earnings as do the managers of MC firms. Smith (1976, p. 708) argues that the owner-managers of OC firms will be concerned with the acceleration of expense deductions for tax purposes and perhaps, for reporting purposes, in order to influence labor's bargaining position. This reasoning suggests that the owner-managers in OC firms are more likely than the managers of MC firms to adopt reporting alternatives which lower or delay reported income.

In summary, several arguments lead to the hypothesis that, ceteris paribus, MC firms are more likely than OC firms to choose those accounting methods which result in higher (or early) reported earnings and higher reported equity. There does exist, however, a contrary view [Fama (1980)]. As described by Holthausen (1981, pp. 75–76), this view suggests that the managers of MC firms bear the full cost of failing to maximize firm value and thus, would be reluctant to elect accounting methods that did not maximize this value. If Fama's arguments are correct then we would expect to see no difference in the accounting methods adopted by MC and OC firms. Thus, the results of this paper will help determine whether the positive theory of Watts and Zimmerman (1978) (and of the managerial economists

---

[3]There is some evidence consistent with this observation. In particular, Collins, Rozeff and Dhaliwal (1981, p. 59, table 4) reported that income-based compensation plans and firm size are significantly positively correlated. Later in this paper, it is reported that MC firms are significantly larger than OC firms. These results are consistent with the expectation that MC firms are more likely than OC firms to have incentive compensation plans.

such as Williamson) or the theory of Fama (1980) that the market for managerial talent is efficient has the most predictive ability in the context of the problem of accounting method choice. It should be noted, however, that there already exists some evidence that the accounting policy decisions of firms are not independent of their ownership control status. Smith (1974, 1976) provides evidence that the managers of MC firms make accounting method changes in a pattern which is significantly different from that of OC firms. Additionally, Salamon and Smith (1979) provide evidence that the timing of the accounting method changes of MC firms is different from that of OC firms. Finally, Salamon and Smith (1979) find that the relationship between accounting information signals and shares prices is influenced by the ownership control status of firms.

The work reviewed in this section of the paper suggests that there may be a systematic difference in the accounting methods adopted by MC and OC firms. However, there is no published work which has conducted an examination and comparison of the accounting methods of MC and OC firms. The major purposes of this paper is to conduct a direct test of the null hypothesis that there is no difference in the accounting methods of MC and OC firms against the alternative hypothesis that MC firms have more of a tendency than OC firms to choose income or equity increasing accounting methods. In order to conduct such a test, other factors which influence the accounting methods chosen by the firm must be considered and controlled. In the next section of this paper a brief review of the prior work on the relationship between other firm and/or industry characteristics and the accounting methods chosen by the firm is conducted in order to pinpoint those factors which must be controlled during the test of our main hypothesis.

3. Determinants of accounting policy choice

Watts and Zimmerman (1978) argue that management's preferences with regard to accounting methods depend upon the relative income effects of the methods and the size of the firm. In particular, they hypothesize that larger firms will tend to adopt accounting methods which will reduce (or delay) the reporting of income. Watts and Zimmerman (1978), Hagerman and Zmijewski (1979), Bowen, Lacey and Noreen (1981) and Zmijewski and Hagerman (1981) have all found some empirical support for the hypothesized relationship between firm size and the income effect of the accounting methods of the firm. Therefore, in determining whether there is or is not an association between ownership control status and accounting methods, we must control for the effect of firm size.

Dhaliwal (1980) argues that financial leverage and accounting methods will be associated because of the existence of restrictive covenants in the firm's credit agreements. In particular, firms with large amounts of debt relative to equity will tend to choose accounting methods which result in higher or earlier reported earnings. Evidence consistent with this hypothesis was found in studies dealing with the firm's choice between the full cost and the successful efforts methods of accounting for exploration and development costs [Deakin (1979), Dhaliwal (1980)] and in studies dealing with the firm's choice between capitalization and expensing of interest incurred during construction [Dhaliwal (1982), Bowen et al. (1981)]. In addition, Leftwich (1981) and Holthausen (1981) found that leverage was a significant factor in explaining the degree of stock price reaction to changes in accounting methods. Thus, the firm's debt to equity ratios must be controlled for when we examine the effect of ownership control status on the accounting methods used by the firms.

Hagerman and Zmijewski (1979) argue that firms with high systematic risk or which are highly capital intensive or which are in highly concentrated industries would prefer accounting alternatives which result in lower (or later) reported earnings. Their argument is based upon the belief that high accounting profits by firms with these characteristics are likely to lead politicians to subject these firms to negative wealth transfers through regulation. However, Dhaliwal (1980) points out that application of accounting methods which result in lower or delayed reported earnings are also likely to result in lower reported equity and total capital. Thus, the effect of such accounting methods on the firm's rate of return is unclear. Because reported rate of return is one of the variables likely to be used in regulatory decisions, it is not clear that the management of firms with high systematic risk or which are highly capital intensive or which are in highly concentrated industries would adopt accounting methods which reduce (or delay) reported income. This ambiguity is, perhaps, the reason why Hagerman and Zmijewski (1979) did not find that the variables they studied had a consistent relationship with the income effect of the accounting methods they examined.

The work reviewed above suggests that two firm specific characteristics — size and leverage — have a consistent influence on the accounting methods adopted by the firm in a variety of contexts. The results with respect to other firm and/or industry characteristics are weak and mixed. Consequently, our test of the null hypothesis that there is no difference in the accounting methods chosen by MC and OC firms will be conducted in a manner which considers the effect of potential size and leverage differences between the MC and OC firms in our sample. In the next section of this paper, we describe the empirical investigation which was conducted to test the hypothesized relationship between the type of firm control and the accounting methods adopted by the firm.

4. Formulation of research hypothesis, sample selection and tests of hypothesis

4.1. Research hypothesis

The general hypothesis addressed in this paper is whether there exist systematic differences between the accounting methods adopted by firms of different ownership control status. To construct a powerful test of that hypothesis, it is desirable to use accounting methods which have a significant effect on reported income and a time period in which firms explicitly evaluated the alternative methods.

Prior to the passage of the Internal Revenue Code of 1954, almost all firms used straight-line depreciation for both tax and financial reporting purposes. However, the Internal Revenue Code of 1954 allowed firms to use accelerated depreciation methods (such as double-declining balance and sum-of-the-year's-digits) for tax reporting purposes. Immediately after the passage of the 1954 Code, Accounting Research Bulletin (ARB) 44 authorized firms to use these methods for financial reporting purposes. Furthermore, firms could use an accelerated depreciation method for tax purposes and the straight-line method for financial statement purposes.

It is also important to note that the use of straight-line depreciation instead of accelerated depreciation method can lead to materially higher reported earnings and equity. Archibald (1967) conducted a study of 55 firms that changed from accelerated depreciation to straight-line depreciation method for financial reporting purposes while retaining accelerated depreciation for tax reporting purposes. He summarized the impact of this change on reported net income in the year of change as follows (p. 165):

> 'The median improvement (in income) is 10.8 percent and the range runs from 0 (where the footnote indicated there was no material effect) to 72.70 percent. Accountants traditionally use this percentage as a basis for assessing the materiality of the change. It is interesting to note there are 10 firms for which the profit improvement was less than the rule-of-thumb 5 percent but also more than half the firms improved profits by more than 10 percent.'

The above points suggest that a reasonable test of our general hypothesis could be based on an examination of the depreciation methods used by a group of MC and OC firms following ARB 44 in 1954. The particular hypothesis to be examined in this paper, then, is

> 'MC firms are more likely than OC firms to use straight-line depreciation method for financial reporting purposes.'

4.2. Sampling procedure and firm characteristics

The firms used in this study were selected from those listed in the U.S.

Senate Staff Report, *Factors Affecting the Stock Market* (1955). The list was essentially all the firms on the New York Stock Exchange in December 1954. 150 non-regulated firms were randomly selected from this list and included in the sample if they could be classified as either management- or owner-controlled on the basis of the criteria specified below.

Firms were classified as owner-controlled if one party owned 10 percent or more of the voting stock and exercised active control, or if one party owned 20 percent or more of the voting stock. Representation on the board of directors or in the management of the firm was taken to be evidence of active control. A firm was classified as management-controlled if no single block of stock greater than 5 percent was controlled by any party. The firms were required to meet these control criteria for each of the years 1954–1962. Form 10-K and definitive proxy statements for each firm were examined to verify that the ownership position reported in 1954 was maintained through 1962.

This first step in the sampling procedure yielded 57 firms which were classified as MC firms and 53 firms which were classified as OC firms. The next step was to examine 10-K and proxy statements to determine the depreciation method used by each firm for financial reporting and tax purposes during 1959 and 1962. In this manner the depreciation method used by all firms except three OC firms was determined. Table 1 provides a breakdown of the resulting sample firms by depreciation method and by ownership control status.

Table 1

Depreciation methods and ownership control status in 1962 and 1959.

Depreciation method[a]	Ownership control status	
	Management-controlled	Owner-controlled
A/A	24 (23)[b]	29 (28)
A/S	18 (17)	12 (10)
S/S	15 (17)	9 (12)

[a]A/A is accelerated depreciation method for both tax and financial reporting purposes, A/S is accelerated depreciation method for tax and straight-line for financial reporting purposes, S/S is straight-line method for both tax and financial purposes.
[b]Figures in parentheses denote the number of firms classified in 1959.

The arguments made earlier relating the accounting methods adopted by firms to their ownership control status suggest that, in general, MC firms have incentives to adopt income increasing accounting methods. It was also argued that OC firms do not have the same incentives to adopt income increasing methods and will, perhaps, be disposed toward adopting income decreasing methods. The arguments were made in reference to the methods adopted for financial reporting purposes and assumed there were no direct cash flow differences for the firms associated with adopting one method versus another. In this case, this means that the earlier arguments lead to predictions regarding the depreciation methods adopted by MC and OC firms for financial reporting purposes given that each group uses the same depreciation method for tax reporting. All the firms which used straight-line depreciation for tax reporting — whether MC or OC firms — also used straight-line depreciation for financial reporting. Thus, this group is not a very fertile one for the purpose of testing our theory. Consequently, the remainder of this study focuses on those 42 (40) MC and 41 (38) OC firms which used accelerated depreciation for tax reporting in 1962 (1959). This group is appropriate for our purposes because all of the firms used the same depreciation method for tax reporting but did not all use the same depreciation method for financial reporting.

The work reviewed in the previous section of this paper suggests that an examination of the size and leverage characteristics of our remaining MC and OC firms should be conducted before or coincident with any statistical evaluation of the differences in the depreciation methods chosen by them. The reason is that we want to ensure that any observed differences in the accounting methods adopted by these MC and OC firms is attributable to differences in their ownership control status rather than to differences in their size or leverage characteristics. Consequently, we obtained information on total assets and the debt-to-equity ratios for 1962 and 1959 for the firms remaining in the sample.

We have conducted an analysis of the differences between the firms in our sample for the years 1959 and 1962. The results for both years are quite similar and only those for 1962 are reported here. The choice of 1959 and 1962 was dictated by the availability of data regarding firms' depreciation methods.

We conducted tests of the null hypotheses that there was no difference in the size and debt-to-equity ratios of these MC and OC firms by the Mann–Whitney U test. The results of these tests are given in table 2. The evidence in table 2 suggests that the leverage characteristics of MC and OC firms are not significantly different but that MC firms are somewhat larger than OC firms. It should be recalled that prior research has shown that large firms are more likely to choose income reducing accounting methods than small firms. Thus, this evidence which suggests that MC firms are larger than OC firms would have a tendency to counteract the prediction of our main (alternative) hypothesis that MC firms are more likely to adopt income increasing accounting methods than OC firms when the hypothesis is tested by using a univariate statistical technique.

In order to determine the impact of the contaminating effect of the size

Table 2

Size and leverage characteristics (1962) Mann–Whitney U-test.[a]

	Mean rank	U-statistic	Z-score
(a) *Total assets*			
Management-controlled firms	45.3		
Owner-controlled firms	37.7	688	1.41[b]
(b) *Debt-to-equity ratio*			
Management-controlled firms	41.7		
Owner-controlled firms	41.3	831	0.08

[a]The variables are ranked from lowest to highest in all cases and firms using S/S are omitted.
[b]Significant at an alpha level of 0.08 (one-tailed test).

variable we have conducted both a univariate and multivariate analysis of the differences in the depreciation methods used by MC and OC firms. A univariate test is conducted of the difference in the proportion of MC and OC firms which used straight-line depreciation for financial reporting (given that they used accelerated depreciation for tax purposes). The Z-score associated with this test is 1.29 which is significant at an alpha level of 10%. This is modest support for the prediction that MC firms are more likely than OC firms to adopt income increasing accounting methods.

It should be noted that this understates the significance of the difference between MC and OC firms given the direction of the size difference between these firms. In the next section of this paper, a multivariate probit analysis is conducted in order to see just how much the size variable has contaminated the univariate results.

5. Probit analysis of the relationship between depreciation method and the type of firm control

Probit analysis is appropriate in those situations where the dependent variable takes the values 0 or 1. In essence, probit analysis predicts the probability that the dependent variable will take the value 1 given the values of the independent variables. Procedurely, it is postulated that the dependent variable W takes the values 0 or 1, depending upon the values of the independent variables, $x_1, \ldots, x_k$. Then, an index Z is constructed as a linear combination of the independent variables, i.e., for ith observation,

$$Z_i = \beta_0 + \beta_1 X_{1i} + \cdots + \beta_k X_{ki}.$$

It is assumed that there is a threshold value of Z_i above which the dependent variable takes the value 1 and below which it takes the value 0. The threshold values are assumed to be normally distributed over the population and the parameters of the model are typically estimated using maximum likelihood methods.

In this study, probit analysis was conducted using the depreciation method adopted by a firm as the dependent variable which was assigned a value of 0 if the firm used A/A and 1 if it used A/S. The size, debt-to-equity ratio and the type of firm control were used as independent variables. The firm control variable was assigned the value 0 if the firm was owner-controlled and 1 if it was management-controlled. Summary statistics for and the correlation matrix of these variables are presented in tables 3 and 4, respectively. The correlation coefficients reported in table 4 are consistently small so that multi-collinearity is not a problem in this application.

Table 3

Summary statistics of variables in the probit model (1962).

Variable	Sample mean	Sample variance
Depreciation method	0.3614	0.2320
Size	0.277×10^9	0.115×10^{18}
Debt/equity	0.2899	0.1668
Firm control (OC=0; MC=1)	0.5060	0.2499

Table 4

Correlation matrix of variables in the probit model (1962).

Method	Size	Debt/equity	Firm control
Size	1.0000		
Debt/equity	0.0256	1.0000	
Firm control	0.1989	−0.0979	1.0000

The results of the probit analysis are presented in table 5. These results indicate that the model is significant at an α level of less than 0.01 based on a chi-square statistic of 13.2589 with 3 degrees of freedom. The coefficient of the debt-equity variable has the expected positive sign which is significant at the $\alpha = 0.01$ and the coefficient of the size variable has the expected negative sign and is significant at an α level of 0.15.

The probit analysis results indicate that the coefficient of the variable Firm Control has a positive sign and is statistically significant at the $\alpha = 0.03$. These results are consistent with our hypothesis that management controlled firms are more likely than owner controlled firms to select straight-line depreciation

Table 5

Probit analysis results (1962) (dependent variable: $A/A = 0$ and $A/S = 1$).

Variable	Coefficient	t-statistic	χ^2 (d.f.)
Constant	−1.1467	−3.432	13.2589[a] (3)
Size[b]	−0.6464	−1.054	
Debt/equity	2.2291	2.939[a]	
Firm control (MC = 1) (OC = 0)	0.5886	1.860[c]	

[a]Significant at an alpha level of 0.01.
[b]For estimation purposes, the size variable was scaled by 10^{-9} in the probit analysis.
[c]Significant at an alpha level of 0.03.

method for financial reporting. It should be noted that the control status variable is statistically significant at a lower level in the multivariate analysis [0.03 than it was in the univariate analysis (0.10)]. This suggests that the probit analysis was at least partially successful in controlling for the size differences between the MC and OC firms in the sample so that the effect of the ownership control variable could be more cleanly determined.[4]

6. Summary and conclusions

In this paper, the arguments of the Watts and Zimmerman positive theory are integrated with those of managerial economists to generate the hypothesis that the accounting methods adopted by a firm are influenced by whether a firm is management or owner controlled. Specifically, this line of argument lead to the prediction that management controlled firms are more likely than owner controlled firms to adopt accounting methods which result in increased or early reported earnings. This prediction contrasts with one developed by Fama (1980). Fama theorizes that the market for managerial talent is such that there will be no difference in behavior between the managers of MC and OC firms. Our results indicate that there exists a difference in the depreciation methods adopted by MC and OC firms in the direction hypothesized by the theory and, thus, the results are inconsistent with the prediction of Fama's theory.

---

[4]The results of the probit analysis for 1959 were similar to those for 1962 but were weaker overall ($\chi^2_{(3)} = 9.08$). All variables in the probit analysis had their expected signs with the debt/equity ratio significant at an $\alpha < 0.01$ and the ownership control variable significant at an $\alpha < 0.08$. The size variable was significant at an $\alpha < 0.15$.

References

Archibald, R.T., 1967, The return to straight-line depreciation: An analysis of a change in accounting method, Journal of Accounting Research, Empirical Studies in Accounting: Selected Studies, 164–180.

Bowen, R., J. Lacey and E. Noreen, 1981, Determinants of the decision by firms to capitalize interest costs, Journal of Accounting and Economics, Aug., 151–179.

Collins, D., M. Rozeff and D. Dhaliwal, 1981, The economic determinants of the market reaction to proposed mandatory accounting changes in the oil and gas industry: A cross-sectional analysis, Journal of Accounting and Economics, March, 37–71.

Deakin, E.B., 1979, An analysis of differences between non-major oil firms using successful efforts and full cost methods, The Accounting Review, Oct., 722–734.

Dhaliwal, D., 1980, The effect of the firm's capital structure on the choice of accounting methods, The Accounting Review, Jan., 78–84.

Dhaliwal, D., 1982, Economic considerations in the management decision to lobby for alternative accounting methods: Evidence from the accounting for interest costs issue, Journal of Business Finance and Accounting, Summer, forthcoming.

Fama, F., 1980, Agency problems and the theory of the firm, Journal of Political Economy, April, 288–307.

Gagnon, J., 1967, Purchases versus pooling of interests: The search for a predictor, Journal of Accounting Research, Empirical Studies in Accounting: Selected Studies, 187–204.

Hagerman, R. and M. Zmijewski, 1979, Some economic determinants of accounting policy choice, Journal of Accounting and Economics, April, 141–161

Hindley, B., 1970, Separation of ownership and control in the modern corporation, The Journal of Law and Economics, April, 185–222.

Holthausen, R., 1981, Evidence on the effect of bond covenants and management compensation contracts on the choice of accounting techniques: The case of depreciation switch-back, Journal of Accounting and Economics, March, 73–109.

Kallay, A., 1978, Towards a theory of corporate dividend policy, Unpublished manuscript (University of Rochester, Rochester, NY).

Leftwich, R., 1981, Evidence of the impact of mandatory changes in accounting principles on corporate loan agreements, Journal of Accounting and Economics, March, 3–36.

Monsen, R.J. and A. Downs, 1965, A theory of large managerial firms, The Journal of Political Economy, June, 231–236.

Salamon, G.L. and E.D. Smith, 1979, Corporate control and managerial misrepresentation of firm performance, The Bell Journal of Economics, Spring, 319–328.

Smith, E.D., 1974, The effect of the separation of ownership from control on accounting policy decision, Unpublished Ph.D. dissertation (The Ohio State University, Columbus, OH).

Smith, E.D., 1976, The effect of the separation of ownership from control on accounting policy decisions, Accounting Review, Oct., 707–723.

Sorter, G.H., S.W. Becker, T.R. Archibald and W.H. Beaver, 1964, Corporate personality as reflected in accounting decisions: Some preliminary findings, The Journal of Accounting Research, Autumn, 183–196.

Sorter, G.H., S.W. Becker, T.R. Archibald and W.H. Beaver, 1966, Accounting and financial measures as indicators of corporate personality — Some empirical findings, in: Jaedicke, Ijiri, Nielsen, eds., Research in accounting measurement (American Accounting Association, Sarasota, FL) 200–210.

U.S. Senate, 1955, Factors affecting the stock market (Staff report) (U.S. Government Printing Office, Washington, DC).

Watts, R. and J. Zimmerman, 1978, Towards a positive theory of the determination of accounting standards, The Accounting Review, Jan., 112–134.

Williamson, O.E., 1964, The economics of discretionary behavior: Managerial objectives in a theory of a firm (Prentice-Hall, Englewood Cliffs, NJ).

Williamson, O.E., 1967, A dynamic stochastic theory of managerial behavior, in: A. Phillips and O. Williamson, eds., Prices: Issues in theory, practice, and public policy (University of Pennsylvania Press, Philadelphia, PA) 11–31.

Zmijewski, M. and R. Hagerman, 1981, An income strategy approach to the positive theory of accounting standard setting/choice, Journal of Accounting and Economics, Aug., 129–149.

WHY DO FIRMS TERMINATE THEIR OVERFUNDED PENSION PLANS?

Jacob K. THOMAS*

Columbia University, New York, NY 10027, USA

Received May 1988, final version received March 1989

Financial and pension variables are analyzed to test predictions of a number of explanations for the recent surge in reversions of excess assets from terminations of overfunded pension plans. Terminations are apparently motivated by cash needs, rather than tax, accounting, or wealth transfer considerations. These cash needs arise from large unexpected declines in funds from operations or financial restructuring subsequent to hostile takeover attempts. However, terminations appear to be a costly source of funds, since firms seek funds from numerous other sources (dividend cuts, 'slow' withdrawals of pension assets, and investment cuts) before resorting to terminations.

1. Introduction

Asset reversions from terminations of *overfunded* defined benefit plans currently provide significant resources for corporations. Unlike defined contribution plans, assets need not equal – and often exceed – accrued or legal liabilities for plans with defined future benefits. Based on a Pension Benefit Guaranty Corporation (PBGC) list of reversions exceeding a million dollars, more than 12.5 billion dollars were paid to sponsors from 1,137 plan terminations initiated between May 1980 and March 1986. More important, annual flows from plan reversions doubled in each of those years and exceeded 6 billion dollars during 1985 – for these large reversions alone. This amount is almost 20 percent of all common stock offerings during 1985 (estimated by the Census Bureau to equal 36 billion dollars). While pension contracts specifically allow reversions of excess assets and no request for asset reversion has yet been refused by regulatory agencies, plan terminations have been a contentious legal and political issue. Considerable opposition exists to the thesis

*I am grateful to Vic Bernard (the referee), Ray Ball (the editor), Hank Bessembinder, Jim Brickley, Harry DeAngelo, Linda DeAngelo, Kathy McGahran, Averil Preston-Thomas, Mike Weisbach, Jerry Zimmerman, and many workshop participants for their helpful comments. I thank the Managerial Economics Research Center (University of Rochester) for financial support, and the National Bureau of Economics Research and Ben Friedman for providing the Form 5500 data.

Journal of Accounting and Economics 11 (1989) 361–398. North-Holland

that sponsors are entitled to any excess assets, evidenced by testimony at the congressional hearings on asset reversions.[1]

This paper seeks to understand why firms terminate overfunded plans. Terminations could be motivated by the cash flow, financial statement, or tax effects of excess pension assets reverting to the sponsoring firm. Alternatively, reversions could represent wealth transfers to stockholders from workers, lenders, and the PBGC. While several alternative explanations are investigated, three explanations are discussed in detail. First, excess pension assets, representing a source of financial slack, are withdrawn by firms facing an unexpected decline in 'available funds', defined as funds from operations less anticipated investments and 'sticky' dividend payouts. Informational asymmetries between managers and investors [Myers and Majluf (1984)] explain why firms build financial slack, and how different reserves of financial slack are liquidated to offset unexpected shortfalls in available funds. Second, reversions expropriate wealth from workers [Ippolito (1986)], since firms renege on an implicit promise to pay pension benefits that vest later in a worker's career. Finally, for firms anticipating financial distress, asset reversions allow wealth transfers to stockholders from lenders and the PBGC. Terminations could also be driven by the tax and accounting effects of assets reverting to the sponsoring firm. However, analysis of these two explanations suggests that neither factor is likely to be the primary motivation for terminations.

Section 2 offers a brief overview of relevant institutional details. Plan terminations, characterized as immediate withdrawals of excess assets, are compared with 'slow' withdrawals effected by changes in actuarial assumptions. Although both alternatives achieve similar results, terminations appear to be more costly while the slower alternative takes longer to execute. In section 3, each explanation is evaluated in terms of its ability to answer three important questions. First, why do only a subset of overfunded firms terminate their plans (cross-sectional predictions)? Second, why is the year of termination the optimal year to do so (time-series predictions)? Finally, in terms of alternative withdrawal routes, what factors determine the choice between plan terminations and slow withdrawals of excess assets?

Most explanations and related predictions are based on various imperfections, representing (1) an inability to write first-best contracts and (2) institutional features of the pension funding process. While being unable to observe magnitudes of the costs of such imperfections results in less precise predictions, analyzing each explanation's ability to answer the three questions above provides a clearer description of the conditions required to explain plan terminations. The qualitative predictions derived for each explanation are

---

[1]'A proliferation of these self-interested employer activities is spreading unchecked like some insidious disease, striking down the retirement security of the worker, infecting one employer after the other, while the agencies merely stand by and ponder.' Representative Edward R. Roybal, Chairman, House Committee on Aging.

compared with observed characteristics of terminating firms to discriminate among competing explanations.

Section 4 conducts cross-sectional comparisons of terminating firms with two other reference samples of overfunded firms: a set of firms initiating slow withdrawals and a benchmark sample of firms making no withdrawals. Analysis of summary financial measures indicates that terminating firms fall into two distinct groups. The first group, representing firms not associated with corporate control changes, appear to face 'tight' financial conditions, characterized by profits and cash flows that are lower than the benchmark sample of no withdrawal firms. (The slow withdrawal reference sample exhibits characteristics between these two samples.) In contrast, firms terminating their pension plans after a control change appear very similar to the benchmark sample (based on pre-control change data).

Given these apparent differences between the two terminating groups, each group is analyzed separately in sections 5 and 6, respectively. Examination of the time series of cash inflows and outflows for the first group (without control changes) reveals large and persistent declines in funds from operations for a number of years prior to termination. Moreover, a systematic pattern of responses to these unexpected shortfalls in available funds is observed. Initially, working capital accounts are liquidated (current liabilities increase and current assets decrease) and long-term investments are scaled back. Subsequently, dividends are cut and slow withdrawals of excess pension assets are initiated. Finally, terminations are undertaken and the funds obtained are used to retire debt. These results suggest that excess pension assets represent financial slack, and slow withdrawals and terminations represent liquidation of this slack. The evidence is less supportive of the two wealth transfer explanations.

The second group of terminating firms (with control changes) is associated with a stable pattern of inflows and outflows of funds leading up to the control change. As in the cross-sectional results, the control-change group appears more similar to the benchmark sample (without pension asset withdrawals) than the first group of terminating firms. This apparent puzzle is partly resolved by examining terminating firms immediately after the control change. For a subset of these firms, associated with 'friendly' control changes (not resisted by incumbent management), terminations appear to be motivated by plan consolidation considerations. In contrast, for terminations following hostile takeover attempts and going-private control changes, financial resource constraints similar to the first terminating group appear to play an important role. Evidence from other studies [Kaplan (1988) and Marais et al. (1987)] indicates that such control changes are typically followed by drastic financial restructuring (such as large increases in debt levels). To alleviate the ensuing tightness in available resources, new owners/managers seek funds from a number of sources, including asset sales and plan terminations.

While most terminations (except for those following friendly control changes) appear to be a response to tight financial conditions, no tightness is observed before the control change for the sample associated with hostile control changes. If such control changes eliminate inefficiencies, these firms should not have been overfunded. Why is overfunding optimal only for some firms? To answer this question, I examine differences between the hostile control change sample and the benchmark sample along a number of dimensions and document some evidence consistent with the 'free cash flow' theory [Jensen (1986)].

In addition to providing new evidence on theories of corporate finance, this study adds to prior pension research examining the same issue [Hamdallah and Ruland (1986), Mittlestaedt (1988), and Stone (1987)]. Typically, logit or probit regressions are used to compare terminating and benchmark nonterminating firms along explanatory variables that proxy for various alternative explanations. However, collinearity among these explanatory variables as well as similarities in the descriptive characteristics of terminating firms predicted by alternative explanations make it difficult to reject particular hypotheses. Both Stone and Mittelstaedt conclude that terminations appear to be primarily driven by the cash flow effects of termination.

In this paper, the traditional explanations (as well as some new ones) are analyzed in greater detail to generate numerous testable predictions. The inclusion of time-series comparisons, a reference slow withdrawal group of overfunded firms, and additional pension variables enables several new tests of these predictions. Finally, including terminations following control changes allows a more general analysis of why terminations occur. These research design improvements increase the statistical power of the empirical procedures and allow identification of the cash flow effects of reversions as being the primary motivation for pension plan terminations.

2. Background

Excess pension assets can be withdrawn in either of two ways.[2] The first route, labelled here as slow withdrawals, requires 'correcting' actuarial choice variables to reduce present values of plan liabilities and generate an over-funded status. This overfunding is then amortized through reduced future contributions (allowable amortization periods lie between ten and thirty years). The second and faster route requires plan termination and is typically

---

[2] Details of institutional features can be obtained from McGill (1984), and evidence supporting empirical generalizations discussed in this section is referenced in Ippolito (1986). Plans become overfunded either because of unexpected increases in plan assets and unexpected decreases in legal liabilities, or because sponsors intentionally select conservative actuarial variables that require funding towards larger *actuarial* liabilities than those resulting from less conservative (more realistic) actuarial variables. Intentional overfunding could be driven by tax [Tepper (1981)] and other reasons [Francis and Reiter (1987)].

completed within a year or two. After informing employees and obtaining approval from the PBGC, the sponsor collects all assets in excess of legal liabilities (both vested and nonvested). Employees are usually enrolled in a replacement plan, which could be either a defined contribution plan or a defined benefit plan.[3] While plan terminations provide faster access to surplus assets, relative to slow withdrawals, the sponsor bears certain associated costs. First, all unvested benefits vest upon termination. Second, terminations cause certain explicit transaction costs, related to purchasing annuities and implementing a replacement plan. Finally, potential employee discontent could dissipate significant resources.

Asset reversions initiated by 'ongoing' entities, a recent phenomenon, have caused bitter property rights disputes, with employee groups claiming ownership to all pension assets.[4] Numerous attempts have been made through legal and legislative channels to block such reversions. Interestingly, slow withdrawals have never been contested. The evolution of this property rights debate towards the current position that sponsors are indeed entitled to excess assets has impacted the way plan terminations are structured.[5] Initially, when the ultimate legal resolution of this dispute was in considerable doubt, some 'sweetening' of benefits was offered to overcome employee resistance. Also, replacement plans were typically defined contribution plans, since terminations were linked to alleged deficiencies of defined benefit plans. Subsequently, replacement defined contribution plans were used less frequently and smaller, if any, benefit increases were offered. The frequency and dollar magnitude of reversions increased steadily until 1985 (see section 4 for evidence of these patterns). This trend reverses sharply after 1985, probably due to a 10 percent excise tax on reversions levied by the Tax Reform Act of 1986.

3. The alternative hypotheses

Three competing explanations for plan terminations are examined here. A general description of the prototypical terminating firm is developed for each

[3] Often when replacement defined benefit plans are desired, firms elect to use a spinoff/termination combination. All benefits for retired employees and assets in excess of legal liabilities for active employees are spunoff to another plan which is immediately terminated to achieve the desired reversion.

[4] While asset reversions caused by 'terminal' events (such as plant closings and firm liquidations) have always existed, reports of reversions by ongoing entities appeared in the financial press only during the 1980's. Also, the PBGC's list of asset reversions only documents terminations since May 1980.

[5] In May 1984, the ERISA agencies issued Joint Implementation Guidelines that allowed reversions of surplus assets as long as certain conditions were met, which include (1) all benefits vest and are guaranteed by purchased contracts, (2) funding methods for successor plans should provide for faster amortization of unfunded liabilities, and (3) spinoff/terminations and termination/reestablishments are allowed only once every fifteen years.

Table 1

Predictions of competing explanations.

Nature of predictions	Competing hypotheses		
	Liquidation of financial slack	Wealth transfers from bondholders and PBGC	Breach of implicit contracts
Cross-sectional (relative to benchmark overfunded firms)	• Low cash flows relative to investment opportunities • Low stock of internal slack	• Low equity values, in financial distress	• High proportion of workers of intermediate tenure (with highest pension bonds)
Time series	• Decline in operating cash flows and/or increases in investments • Depletion of lower cost sources of financial slack	• Substantial decline in profitability and equity value • Alter portfolio of firm assets to increase risk • Increase payouts to equityholders • No equity issues/debt repurchases	• Reversion preceded by control change
Relation between terminations and slow withdrawals	• Terminations represent an extreme case, and are used if slow withdrawals are insufficient	• No systematic relation	• Slow withdrawals are not breaches of implicit contracts
Type of replacement plan	• Defined benefit	• Defined benefit	• Defined contribution

hypothesis and summarized in table 1. Section 3.4 summarizes three other plausible explanations that were also considered, and briefly discusses why they are unlikely to explain terminations.

3.1. Liquidation of financial slack

Myers (1984) and Myers and Majluf (1984) argue that, in the presence of sticky dividend policies and informational asymmetries between managers and investors, firms follow a pecking order when seeking new financing. They prefer internal sources to external sources, and prefer less risky external funds (riskless debt followed by risky debt) to more risky external funds (equity).[6] As a result managers build financial slack, in the form of liquid assets and unused borrowing capacity, which is drawn down first (before external financing is sought) when internally generated funds from operation fall below levels required to finance profitable investments and dividends. While the original financial slack hypothesis does not specifically consider pension funding, the same arguments can be extended to cover pension assets. Specifically, excess pension assets represent financial slack, and withdrawals of excess assets are viewed as liquidation of financial slack.[7]

Changes in available funds, representing the excess of inflows from operations over outflows required for profitable investments and stable dividends, are not easily determined. Moreover, since the cash flow identity requires that inflows (funds from operations and net external financing) equal outflows (net investments and dividends), neither the accumulation and liquidation of financial slack nor exogenous shocks and related firm responses are easily identified. Here a simple random-walk model is used to predict components of the cash flow identity; i.e., deviations from expectation are measured by observed changes in these separate components. Further, the investment opportunity set and internally generated funds from operations are assumed to be exogenously determined.

Both slow withdrawals and terminations can be used to liquidate financial slack stored as excess pension assets. Given the lower cost of slow withdrawals, plan terminations are expected only if funds from slow withdrawals and other preferred nonpension sources are insufficient to cover the unexpected decline in available funds. Note that the position in the pecking order of these two pension sources of financial slack, relative to nonpension sources,

---

[6] Here risk is defined in terms of value changes when managers' inside information is revealed. As firms climb up the pecking order, costs increase along two dimensions: positive net present value projects that are not accepted and costs of financial distress.

[7] Why should firms use excess pensions assets to store financial slack? Bodie et al. (1984) argue that the corporate tax advantages of holding financial slack inside the funding (explained further in section 3.4), relative to outside the fund, provide an answer to this question.

cannot be predicted without estimates of relevant costs, and thus remains an empirical issue to be explored in later sections.

Despite the inability to make specific predictions regarding pension and nonpension sources of financial slack, a number of general predictions are possible. Unexpected declines in available funds are necessary but not sufficient to cause plan terminations. Terminations are not expected for 'small' declines that can be covered by slow withdrawals or by depleting the stock of preferred sources of nonpension financial slack. Also, firms with gradual and persistent declines in available funds that occur over a number of years are likely to seek slow withdrawals before the cumulative effect of these declines can no longer be offset by slow withdrawals and the declining stock of nonpension financial slack. Therefore, slow withdrawals are generally expected to precede terminations. While this prediction would not apply to firms that terminated their plans in response to sudden declines in available funds that are larger than can be offset by slow withdrawals, it would still hold *on average* for the sample of terminating firms.

The financial slack explanation generally expects replacement plans to also be defined benefit plans. The choice between defined benefit and defined contribution plans and, more generally, the choice between current and deferred compensation is probably influenced by many factors other than those discussed here [Thomas (1988)]. As long as the recent decline in available funds leading up to the termination does not change the desirability of deferred compensation in the form of defined benefit pensions, this prediction is true. If, however, firms select defined benefit plans only to store (and subsequently liquidate) financial slack, then replacement plans are not expected to be defined benefit plans if such firms do not expect to overfund and liquidate in the future.

Predictions of the financial slack hypothesis (see table 1)

- Both slow withdrawals and plan terminations follow unexpected declines in funds from operations and/or increases in profitable investment opportunities. However, plan terminations (slow withdrawals) are expected after relatively larger (smaller) cumulative declines in funds available to finance profitable investments and maintain stable dividends.
- Cross-sectionally, slow withdrawal firms should exhibit intermediate characteristics between those of terminating firms and the no withdrawal benchmark sample.
- Over time, the sample of terminating firms should, on average, exhibit a gradual decline in available funds and initiate slow withdrawals over the years preceding the termination.
- Terminated plans are expected to be replaced by defined benefit plans.

3.2. Wealth transfers from lenders and the PBGC

For firms associated with an increased likelihood of financial distress, wealth transfers from lenders to stockholders provide a second motivation for plan terminations. Terminations represent a potential reduction in debtholder security, if they occur before bankruptcy. Subsequent to reorganization/ liquidation, excess pension assets are available to stockholders only after senior claims have been satisfied. However, if terminations precede bankruptcy and funds from reversions are paid out as dividends or stock repurchases (or are used for projects riskier than those anticipated by lenders), stockholders gain at the expense of lenders.

Similarly, terminations could represent attempts to transfer wealth to stockholders from the PBGC. Overfunded firms experiencing a sudden decline in equity values can strip excess pension assets via terminations, pay out these funds to stockholders, and then *underfund* their plans to maximize the value of the pension 'put' [Treynor (1976)]. The PBGC insures pension liabilities, and holds a lien on pension assets plus 30 percent of the sponsor's equity. Despite minimum funding requirements, designed to reduce the PBGC's exposure, firms facing financial distress can seek to transfer pension obligations to the PBGC by underfunding their plans.[8] Decreases in funding levels and increases in the risk of firm assets and assets in the pension fund increase the value of the pension put created by the PBGC's guarantee. However, the value of this pension put is constrained by the PBGC's ability to enforce its claims (all terminations require the PBGC's approval, for example). Moreover, very few firms obtain permission to underfund, and even less have actually exercised the pension put [Thomas (1988)]. Given the limited relevance of these arguments to the vast majority of firms, only wealth transfers from lenders are considered hereafter.

Obtaining testable predictions for the wealth transfer hypothesis is complicated by several factors. First, since the wealth transfer hypothesis is silent on motives for overfunding, it provides only a partial explanation for pension funding behavior. If firms overfund for other unspecified reasons, such as taxes [see Francis and Reiter (1988) for other factors], then withdrawals could also be motivated by these unknown factors. This inability to explicitly incorporate other relevant factors limits the precision of predictions that can be made. Second, as explained below, many predictions of the financial slack hypothesis are also consistent with the wealth transfer hypothesis. Finally,

---

[8] Normally, the minimum funding requirements of the Employee Retirement Income Security Act of 1974 ensure sufficient pension assets to cover legal liabilities, and the claim on 30 percent of equity provides a cushion to offset unexpected events. However, as equity values decline this cushion is reduced, and firms can obtain minimum funding waivers by claiming that minimum funding jeopardizes future contributions.

given that terminations almost certainly create conditions that allow potential reduction in debtholder wealth, determining whether or not terminations were primarily caused by wealth transfer considerations is difficult without estimates of the magnitudes of benefits from terminations under alternative hypotheses.

Predictions for the wealth transfer hypothesis are obtained by analyzing the link between overfunding/withdrawals and wealth transfers. Overfunding transfers wealth to lenders only if 'external' funds (dividends not paid or new equity issues) are used to finance overfunding. Given the seniority of their claims on firm and excess pension assets, debtholders in aggregate remain unaffected by asset transfers between the firm and the pension fund. Moreover, even if external funds are used for overfunding, the magnitudes of gains to lenders are a function of default risk of the outstanding debt; the more secure the debt the lower the wealth transferred to lenders. Conversely, withdrawals of excess pension assets represent wealth transfers from lenders only when these funds are paid out to stockholders, and the magnitudes of potential wealth transfers increase with the risk of financial distress.[9] Since financial distress is highly correlated with declines in profitability and funds from operations, the predictions of this hypothesis are similar to the case when liquidation of financial slack is caused by declines in operating flows. However, unlike the financial slack explanation, this hypothesis does not predict terminations following unexpected increases in investment opportunities.

Certain other predictions unique to the wealth transfer explanation can also be derived. First, new issues of equity around termination dates are inconsistent with wealth transfers from lenders. Second, terminations are not expected to be associated with retirement of outstanding debt. Third, to complete the wealth transfer process firms are expected to pay out reversions as dividends or stock repurchases and/or firms are expected to invest funds from terminations in assets riskier than those held in the pension fund.

The relation between slow withdrawals and terminations is not as well-defined as in the financial slack explanation. Given the incentives of lenders to anticipate and prevent such wealth transfers, slow withdrawals over a number of years could be inappropriate devices to increase stockholder wealth. Since lending agreements contain restrictions on financing and investment decisions designed to protect lenders, declining accounting measures in these future years could cause technical default, thereby enabling lenders to restructure their claims before the slow withdrawal process is substantially complete. Thus, a comparison of the higher costs of terminations with the increased probability of being unable to pay out all excess pension assets to stockholders

---

[9]This explanation does not require that the hypothesized wealth transfers be unexpected. Reduction of lender security via plan terminations and payouts to stockholders under certain states of the world could be anticipated and suitably priced by lenders.

under the slow withdrawal alternative is expected to determine the withdrawal route selected under the wealth transfer explanation.

Since slow withdrawals could be caused by other factors, they are not generically similar to terminations and slow withdrawal firms are not necessarily expected to exhibit intermediate characteristics between terminating firms and the benchmark no withdrawal sample. Moreover, since slow withdrawals are not always preferred to terminations, the wealth transfer explanation does not make specific predictions about slow withdrawals preceding terminations.[10]

Similar to the financial slack explanation, the wealth transfer explanation does not generally expect firms to change the mix between current and deferred compensation or use replacement defined contribution plans after the termination.

Predictions of the wealth transfer hypothesis (see table 1)

- Terminations are expected to follow substantial declines in profitability resulting in increased probabilities of financial distress.
- Terminations are not expected to be associated with equity issues and debt repurchases.
- Terminations are expected to be associated with increased payouts to stockholders and/or increases in the risk of assets held by the sponsoring firm.
- Terminated plans are expected to be replaced by defined benefit plans.

3.3. Breach of implicit contracts

Economists have noted [see Lazear (1979), for example] that most pension contracts are structured such that pension benefit accruals are skewed toward older workers, since total compensation profiles (current wages plus present values of deferred vested pensions) are likely to be steeper than marginal product profiles. In accounting terminology, workers provide output based on promised 'projected' benefits while firms are only legally liable for 'accumulated' benefits. In effect, workers post a pension 'bond' by being underpaid early in their careers, relative to their marginal product, and receiving compensating overpayments later in their careers. While the actual amounts of hypothesized overpayments and underpayments vary with plan features (such as benefit formulas and employee demographics) and assumptions used, two generalizations are possible: cumulative underpayments are highest for work-

---

[10]Slow withdrawals are expected to precede terminations under the following conditions: (1) if slow withdrawals are caused by factors other than wealth transfer considerations, and these factors are correlated with declining cash flows and profits from operations, or (2) if slow withdrawals are used (along with increased dividend payouts) to transfer wealth to stockholders until violation of a lending covenant appears imminent, at which point terminations are used to complete the wealth transfer process.

ers of intermediate tenure, and these underpayments are potentially large, relative to employee compensation.[11]

Workers would not post such bonds if firms did not generally honor implicit contracts. If plan terminations represent an expropriation of a pension bond, why were implicit contracts breached in these cases?[12] One possible factor is the sharp increase in unfriendly corporate control changes during the 1980's fueled perhaps by innovations in takeover technology, such as junk bonds. These control changes could create incentives to disregard implicit contracts entered into by previous management/owners [see Shleifer and Summers (1987)]. While these and other reasons to renege on implicit contracts are not considered further here, an important aspect of the hypothesized breach of contract is explained below. Excess assets do not belong to employees, and the magnitude of expropriation is unrelated to the amount of excess assets. Funding levels are irrelevant for this explanation; even termination of under-funded plans expropriate pension bonds. Since legal liabilities are insured by the PBGC, all compensating overpayments that vest later in a worker's tenure are collected by workers provided the plan survives. Therefore, expropriations occur only because terminations deny workers the opportunity to continue with the plan and receive the compensating overpayments that refund the posted pension bonds.[13]

Since replacement defined benefit plans also allow collection of future overpayments, only replacement defined contribution plans result in workers losing their pension bonds. Note that not offering a replacement plan or using a replacement defined benefit plan that offers less than full credit for past service is also consistent with breach of implicit contracts. However, some form of retirement plan is almost always offered for ongoing operations (no

---

[11] To illustrate the magnitude of potential underpayments, take a plan that pays an annual benefit at age 65 equal to $1\frac{1}{2}$ percent of final year's wages times number of years of service. Assume that nominal interest rates are expected to be 9 percent, that cash compensation and marginal product are expected to grow at a nominal rate of 6 percent, and that the 'average' employee joins at age 30, retires at age 65, and expects to live to age 75 [based on an example developed by Bulow (1982)]. If firms equate total compensation (cash wages plus accrued pensions) and marginal product over each worker's tenure, then the *annual* difference between total compensation and marginal product is approximately negative 5 percent in the first few years of service, approaches 0 around year 20, and increases to a maximum of approximately 20 percent before retirement. The *cumulative* underpayment reaches a maximum of approximately one year's marginal product around year 24.

[12] More generally, breaches of implicit contracts could involve nonpension forms of compensation, and the ability to expropriate wealth from workers using other devices, such as unilateral wage reductions, is not precluded. Here plan terminations are viewed as a convenient vehicle to breach implicit contracts, as argued by Ippolito (1986).

[13] Since pension bonds are lost upon liquidation and are jeopardized subsequent to reorganization in bankruptcy, employees of firms facing financial distress could voluntarily forsake their pension bonds to assist in firm survival. However, this case is not characteristic of the breaches of implicit contracts envisaged by Ippolito (1986) and Shleifer and Summers (1987) as it does not represent opportunistic managerial behavior.

terminations without a replacement plan were uncovered for the sample analyzed later), and most replacement defined benefit plans have provided for past service credits [see FASB (1985)]. Therefore using a dichotomous separation between replacement defined benefit and defined contribution plans to proxy for the absence and presence, respectively, of a desire to expropriate pension bonds is expected to be a reasonable working assumption.

Predictions of the breach of implicit contracts hypothesis (see table 1)

- Terminated plans should have the highest proportions of beneficiaries of intermediate tenure (across all overfunded plans and over time).
- Terminations are expected more frequently after control changes.
- Slow withdrawals do not serve as substitutes for plan terminations, since continuation of the plan allows workers to collect future overpayments. Thus, no time-series or cross-sectional links between terminations and slow withdrawals are predicted by this explanation.
- Replacement plans are expected to be defined contribution plans.

3.4. Other explanations

One explanation, frequently offered in the financial press, alleges that terminations represent wealth transfers from workers since *all* pension assets belong to workers (see footnote 1). This view runs counter to a legal interpretation of the pension contract. It is also at odds with the regulatory authorities routinely granting permission for terminations (see footnote 5). Moreover, Landsman (1986) documents evidence suggesting that excess pension assets are capitalized in stock prices, and therefore do not belong to workers.[14] Two other explanations, relating to tax and financial statement effects, are discussed below in greater detail.

3.4.1. Decline in tax status

The tax benefits of overfunding and withdrawing from pension plans arise from tax code provisions that allow a tax deduction for excess contributions,

---

[14]Another common explanation encountered in the financial press argues that if overfunding was fortuitously caused by unexpected increases (decreases) in pension assets (liabilities), and firms expect this situation to reverse, then terminations enable firms to settle legal liabilities and collect excess assets. Note that this explanation assumes mean reversion in asset prices or interest rates (used to compute present values of liabilities). In any case, the evidence does not support this view. Most terminated plans were already overfunded prior to 1980. Also, comparing the time series of stock market indices and the inverse of long-term bond yields, proxying for plan assets and plan liabilities respectively, with the frequency of terminations each year offers no discernable patterns. A dollar investment in the 'equity' and 'bond' portfolios at the beginning of 1980 is followed through the end of 1985. While the excess of the equity portfolio over the bond portfolio exhibits large increases and decreases over the period, the 'flow' of terminations grows exponentially.

and exempt from corporate taxes all income earned within the fund [see Tepper (1981) and Black (1980)]. By incorporating institutional constraints to overfunding/withdrawal and intertemporal tax rate changes to the Tepper–Black analysis, Thomas (1988) argues that desired levels of overfunding are determined by current marginal tax rates as well as expected 'unshielded' taxable income – representing expectations of future taxable income before discretionary pension contributions, but after endogenously determined non-pension tax deductions. A decline in tax status causes desired funding levels to drop, thereby causing firms to withdraw excess pension assets. Notwithstanding potential errors in measurement of tax status, and the difficulty in controlling for an associated decline in profitability and cash flows, Thomas's results document a significant link between tax status declines and declines in pension funding.

While tax status declines provide incentives to withdraw prior overfunding, this argument does not distinguish between slow and quick withdrawals. As long as the lower tax status persists long enough to complete a slow withdrawal, the tax benefits under both withdrawal routes are similar. Therefore, under this view, plan terminations are preferred only if tax status is expected to increase again before a slow withdrawal can be substantially completed; i.e., only 'temporary' tax status declines result in terminations. For example, firms with expected future taxable income that is positive but insufficient to cover current carryforwards of net operating losses (NOL) and investment tax credits (ITC) prior to their expiration, if slow withdrawals are used, would seek to accelerate income by initiating plan terminations.

Cross-sectional analyses of tax attributes confirm that both slow withdrawal and terminating groups are associated with unusually high proportions of low tax status firms (currently not paying taxes or carrying forward NOLs and ITCs), relative to the benchmark group. Similarly, time-series analyses indicate that tax status declined for both groups. While this evidence suggests that tax status declines are associated with withdrawals of excess assets, it does not explain why terminations were used in some cases. As argued earlier, the tax benefits explanation predicts terminations only for temporary tax status declines. While problems with measuring tax status hamper tests of this hypothesis, preliminary evidence indicates that the declines in tax status observed for the terminating group are unlikely to be temporary, in the sense of tax attribute carryforwards expiring before slow withdrawals can be completed. The Economic Recovery Tax Act (ERTA) of 1981 had *increased* the number of years for which NOLs and ITCs could be carried forward from seven to fifteen years. (The sample studied consists of terminations between 1980 and 1985). Examination of tax footnotes to annual reports indicates that for the 27 firms (of 88 firms in the termination sample without control changes) disclosing any NOL or ITC carryforwards, the median (mean) for the earliest year of expiration of ITC or NOL carryforwards is 11 (10). Of these 27 firms, only 13 firms had carryforwards that were expected to expire within ten years of the termination year. Another tax motivation for terminations, over slow with-drawals, would be an impending increase in the statutory tax rates. Again, the evidence is at odds with this view, since a tax rate *decrease* was forecast towards the end of the period studied (and legislated by the Tax Reform Act of 1986). Overall, this analysis indicates that tax factors could only have motivated terminations for a few firms, if any at all. However, slow with-drawals could potentially be caused by tax factors.

3.4.2. Financial statement effects

Asset reversions, after taxes, cause an increase in cash and a corresponding increase in income and owners' equity. Managers have incentives to initiate such income-increasing and leverage-reducing transactions for two general reasons [see Watts and Zimmerman (1986)]. First, managerial compensation is increased to the extent that compensation depends on contracts such as bonus and performance plans that are based on reported accounting income [see Healy (1985) for details and exceptions to this general rule]. Second, income increases and leverage decreases can reduce the probability, and the associated costs, of facing technical default on lending contracts containing covenants defined in the terms of accounting ratios [see Smith and Warner (1979)].

There are, however, a number of institutional factors that reduce the likelihood of terminations being driven by the financial statement effects. First, accounting guidelines were formalized in 1982, before the bulk of all terminations were made, to require that the gain be either amortized over at least ten years, for replacement defined benefit plans, or classified as extraordi-nary income otherwise.[15] The first treatment spreads the income over a number of years, similar to a slow withdrawal, and creates an offsetting liability (corresponding to the unamortized reversion) which *increases* lever-age.[16] The second treatment causes the reversion to have no effect on firms whose accounting-based contracts specifically exclude extraordinary income [see Healy (1985, table 1)]. Second, since delays in obtaining approval from the PBGC and the Internal Revenue Service (IRS) are both long (often exceeding a year) and unpredictable, plan terminations are a risky alternative for firms seeking to 'time' improvements in their accounting ratios. Therefore, financial statement considerations, while relevant, are unlikely to be the primary moti-vation for plan terminations.

---

[15]See SEC Staff Accounting Bulletin No. 52 (dated May 16, 1983) and FASB Action Alert No. 82-46 (dated November 24, 1982). These rules were superseded by SFAS No. 88 [FASB (1985)], which called for immediate recognition of gain for terminations after 1985. However, this rule change does not apply to my sample, as the terminations analyzed here occurred before the standard was applied.

[16]Examination of annual reports indicates that after 1982, when the relevant accounting rules were changed, for an increasing proportion of terminations (corresponding to the increased use of replacement defined benefit plans reported in table 6) the reversion was amortized over ten years.

4. Sample selection and descriptive statistics

The research design involves examining financial and pension variables for terminating firms to determine the extent to which the data is consistent with the predictions of each explanation summarized in table 1. Prior studies [Bodie et al. (1984), Francis and Reiter (1987), and Thomas (1988)] indicate that desired funding levels are determined by financial measures (such as profitability, leverage, cash flows, and tax status) as well as pension variables (such as plan demographics). Thus, withdrawals of excess assets, representing a decline in desired funding levels, are expected to be associated with changes in these explanatory variables. Therefore variables suggested by prior studies (namely profitability, leverage, cash flows, and tax status) as well as those identified in section 3 are considered in the empirical tests. Cross-sectional tests compare relevant variables across terminating, slow withdrawal, and benchmark no withdrawal firms, while time-series tests examine changes in these variables over the period leading up to the termination. In effect, the tests provide evidence on whether the same set of explanatory variables

Table 2

Descriptive characteristics of the PBGC termination sample.

Panel A: Distribution of terminations over time

Year	Frequency	Percent	Reversion (in millions of $)	Percent
1980	9	1.5	18.3	0.3
1981	35	5.7	158.5	2.8
1982	81	13.3	405.6	7.1
1983	161	26.3	1,603.2	28.3
1984	319	52.2	3,461.5	61.0
1985	6	1.0	25.1	0.4
Total	611		5,672.2	

Panel B: Ownership status around termination date [a]

Ownership after termination date	Ownership before termination date			
	Parent	Sub./div.	Missing	Total
Parent	**187**	15	32	234
Sub./div.	40	**68**[b]	18	126
Missing	46	24	**181**	251
Total	273	107	231	611

[a]Sponsors are classified as parents or subsidiaries/divisions based on examination of the S&P Register and the Million Dollar Director. All sponsors not located are coded as missing. (For a subsample, examined in detail, the Wall Street Journal Index is also used to identify ownership changes.) The before (after) termination status is based on the directory published one (two) year(s) before (after) the year of termination.

[b]Six of these subsidiaries/divisions changed parents during the period examined. For all other entries on the main diagonal (in boldface) ownership status remains unchanged.

explain all withdrawals (i.e., are terminations caused by more extreme values of these variables, relative to slow withdrawals). Alternatively, does one set of explanatory variables explain withdrawals, and another set explain the incremental decision to use the termination route?

A PBGC list of large reversions, exceeding a million dollars, is examined first to report descriptive characteristics. To facilitate detailed examination of financial information, only those terminations with sponsors on Compustat are selected to form the termination sample. Since Compustat does not provide pension funding information, comparison overfunded firms without terminations (slow withdrawal or no withdrawal groups) are selected from the FASB36 tape (Version IV, Columbia University).

The PBGC sample of 611 plans, representing 514 completed terminations and 97 proposed terminations, is based on a PBGC list of asset reversions dated June 13, 1985. This list was edited to eliminate duplicates and to include six sponsors omitted from an earlier list (dated August 29, 1984). Table 2, panel A, reports the growth of terminations over the sample period, which extends primarily from 1980 to 1984.

To assess the importance of the potential link between control changes and terminations hypothesized by the implicit contracts explanation, a preliminary measure of ownership status before and after the termination date is examined.[17] The S&P Register and the Million Dollar Directory are used to classify ownership status one year before and two years after the termination date, for all 611 sponsors in the initial sample.[18] The results of this analysis, reported in panel B of table 2, indicate that many terminations (all 135 terminations not on the main diagonal, plus 6 of 68 terminations in the middle cell) are associated with ownership changes.[19] Note that this preliminary measure of changes in ownership underestimates the true proportion of control changes,

---

[17] The first announcement of intended termination, which is the relevant date here, does not appear to be publicly available, except for the few cases in which the announcement was carried in the financial press. Conversations with officials of the PBGC's disclosure section indicate that the termination date provided in their list of terminations, which is the date used here, generally represents the date as of which benefit accruals are proposed to be frozen. They indicated that the date on their list can both precede and succeed the announcement date, and appears to be selected for bookkeeping convenience. Examination of annual reports for a subsample (described later) indicates that the dates on the PBGC list coincide with financial year-ends in a majority of cases.

[18] Since both directories are based on information compiled as of the fall of that year, the previous year's edition is used to code ownership status before termination. Since many changes are noted with a lag (often as late as two years), the edition two years after the termination year is used to code the post-termination ownership status.

[19] Given that the S&P directory includes over 45,000 companies (criteria for inclusion not specified) and the Million Dollar Directory includes over 160,000 companies (net worth exceeding $500,000), it is surprising that as many as 181 firms (30 percent of the sample) are coded as missing both before and after the termination date. While most missing sponsors are probably associated with small private firms not covered in the directories, errors in the PBGC list are responsible for some cases. Note that for the subsample of terminations analyzed in detail, ownership status was also checked using the Wall Street Journal Index (WSJI) and annual reports.

since it cannot detect changes that occurred within the category coded as missing both before and after the termination date. It also excludes changes such as proxy contests in which the legal entity sponsoring the plan remained unchanged. Given the potential importance of control changes for this sample, terminations preceded by control changes are analyzed separately.

A subset of these 611 plans, where the sponsor (or the sponsor's parent, if sponsor is a subsidiary) is on the 1984 edition of Compustat (Annual Industrial and Research tapes), is selected for detailed analysis. This subset includes 147 Compustat firms, representing 181 plans. These firms are screened to delete the following:

- 12 firms with 'immaterial' reversions, defined as less than one percent of equity market value,
- 3 firms where the termination related to a plant closing,
- 9 firms where annual reports could not be obtained from the University of Rochester Library, and
- 4 firms where annual reports indicate no reversion occurred (excess assets returned to new plan).

Annual reports and the Wall Street Journal Index (WSJI) are examined for all firms not deleted to identify a 'change' (T-C) sample, consisting of 31 firms (36 plans) with control changes occurring up to two years prior to the termination date, and a 'no change' (T-NC) sample, consisting of the remaining 88 firms (113 plans). Control changes include 15 explicit ownership changes (mergers and acquisitions) and 16 other changes in corporate control (going-private transactions and proxy contests).

To provide a comparison, two other samples are identified from the 887 overfunded firms on the FASB36 tape not associated with plan terminations.[20] Overfunding is determined by comparing plan assets with accrued liabilities standardized for cross-sectional variation in discount rates [see Thomas (1988, app. B-2) for procedure employed]. First, a slow withdrawal (SW) sample of 199 overfunded firms with at least one year between 1980 and 1984 that satisfies all of the following three conditions is identified:

(1) percent change in pension expense, scaled by assets, $[(P/A)_t - (P/A)_{t-1}]/(P/A)_{t-1}$, is less than -25%,
(2) percent change in pension expense, scaled by employees, $[(P/E)_t - (P/E)_{t-1}]/(P/E)_{t-1}$, is less than -25%,
(3) change in pension expense, as a percent of assets, $(P_t - P_{t-1})/A_t$, is less than -0.15%,

---

[20]Of the 1119 firms on the FASB36 tape with at least one year of complete data available to estimate funding levels, 115 firms were underfunded on average. Of the remaining 1004 overfunded firms, another 117 firms were deleted because they initiated a termination or because a terminating sponsor was a subsidiary/division either before or after the termination.

where P, E, and A represent the annual pension expense, total employees and total assets, respectively. While the three filters are *ad hoc*, they represent an effort to ensure that the decline in pension expense was large relative to the preceding year (the first two percent change filters) as well as important in dollar terms (the third filter).[21] The remaining 688 overfunded firms form the no withdrawal (NW) sample. This sample is used as a benchmark for comparison with the two terminating samples and the slow withdrawal sample.

As the FASB36 tape comprises the largest firms on Compustat (total assets exceed a billion dollars or gross fixed assets plus inventory exceed 125 million dollars), both the benchmark no withdrawal sample and the slow withdrawal samples are on average significantly larger than the two terminating samples. However, since none of the competing hypotheses posit that firm size is a relevant variable, and to enable larger sample sizes, sponsors not on the FASB36 tape are also included in the two terminating samples, with and without control changes.[22]

Table 3, panel A, indicates that the distribution over time of the year of termination (coded as year 0) for the two Compustat samples of terminating firms is similar to that reported in table 2 for the full sample of terminations. For the slow withdrawal sample, the first year that satisfies all three conditions for a decline in pension expense is coded as the slow withdrawal year (year 0). Year 0 for this sample exhibits a distribution similar to the two terminating samples. The 688 firms in the no withdrawal benchmark group are randomly assigned a year 0 to maintain proportions of firms in each calendar year similar to the proportions reported by the slow withdrawal sample. Maintaining a representative distribution across calendar years for the slow withdrawal and benchmark samples and observing similar distributions for the two termination samples reduces the likelihood of time-period effects causing any observed differences among the four samples. Specifically, economy-wide effects (such as the 1981–1982 recession) appear to be distributed uniformly across all samples.

Panel B in table 3 reports industry membership [see Sharpe (1982) for industry definitions] for the four samples of overfunded firms and compares them to industry membership for the two Compustat populations (Active and Research firms). Some intersample differences exist: utilities are absent from both terminating samples, and firms from the capital and consumer industries

---

[21] See Thomas (1988, app. B-1) for details on pension flow measures used. Mittelstaedt (1988) uses a 40 percent change in pension expense (not scaled by assets or employees) to select his slow withdrawal sample.

[22] Requiring that terminating firms also be on the FASB36 tape reduces the change and no change samples to 53 and 20 firms, respectively. The significant differences between the no change terminating sample and the no withdrawal benchmark sample reported in table 4 (discussed later) also exist for the reduced sample of terminating firms on the FASB36 tape. Interestingly, the reduced termination sample remains significantly smaller than the benchmark and slow withdrawal samples.

Table 3

Descriptive characteristics of terminating and comparison groups.

Panel A: Distribution of year 0[a]

| | Terminating samples | | | | | | | |
| | No control changes (T-NC) | | With control changes (T-C) | | Slow withdrawal sample (SW) | | Benchmark no withdrawal sample (NW) | |
Year	#	%	#	%	#	%	#	%
1980	2	2%	1	3%	13	7%	52	8%
1981	8	9%	1	3%	21	10%	53	8%
1982	11	13%	8	26%	32	16%	122	18%
1983	21	24%	6	19%	59	30%	208	30%
1984	43	49%	15	48%	74	37%	253	37%
1985	3	3%	0	0%	0	0%	0	0%
Total	88		31		199		688	

Panel B: Industry membership

Firms with overfunded plans

| | Terminating | | Slow withdrawal sample (NW) | No withdrawal benchmark (SW) | Compustat firms | |
Industry[b]	No control changes (T-NC)	With control changes (T-C)			Active	Research
Basic	9 (10%)	2 (7%)	25 (13%)	46 (7%)	212 (7%)	177 (9%)
Capital	26 (30%)	3 (10%)	38 (19%)	53 (8%)	717 (22%)	460 (22%)
Construction	4 (5%)	3 (10%)	17 (9%)	19 (3%)	142 (4%)	102 (5%)
Consumer	33 (38%)	15 (48%)	67 (34%)	200 (36%)	1179 (46%)	946 (29%)
Energy	6 (7%)	4 (13%)	11 (5%)	29 (4%)	192 (6%)	100 (5%)
Finance	6 (7%)	2 (7%)	11 (5%)	158 (23%)	406 (13%)	152 (7%)
Transportation	4 (5%)	2 (7%)	12 (6%)	34 (5%)	132 (4%)	101 (5%)
Utilities	0 (0%)	0 (0%)	18 (9%)	149 (22%)	255 (8%)	24 (1%)
Total	88	31	199	688	3235	2062

[a] Year 0 is the year of termination for the two terminating samples (T-NC and T-C), the first year of slow withdrawal for the SW sample and a randomly assigned year (designed to maintain a distribution similar to the SW sample) for the benchmark (NW) sample.

[b] Industries are as defined in Sharpe (1982).

are underrepresented and the finance industry is overrepresented in the no withdrawal benchmark sample. Despite these apparent differences, most industries are represented proportionally in all four samples. Therefore, terminations are unlikely to be caused by institutional factors unique to certain industries.[23]

Table 4 reports the median values of relevant financial and pension variables for all four samples as of the year before termination (year − 1). (Definitions for and sources of all variables used in the paper are provided in appendix 1.) The *p*-values for nonparametric rank sum comparisons of the two terminating samples (and the slow withdrawal sample) with the benchmark no withdrawal group are also reported in parentheses. Data as of the end of year 0 is not used since it includes the cash and accounting effects of terminations for a majority of the sample (the reversion occurred after year 0 for the rest of the sample). Unfortunately, these effects were not disclosed for all terminating firms and therefore could not be adjusted for in the year 0 financial data.[24]

The termination group *with* control changes is not significantly different from the benchmark group along any of the financial measures examined. In contrast, the termination group *without* control changes is significantly less profitable, more highly levered, and has lower amounts of funds from operations than the no withdrawal benchmark group. Tax status is lower for this group, evidenced by a significantly lower proportion of taxpayers and a significantly higher proportion of firms with NOL carryforwards (based on chi-squared tests), relative to the benchmark group. This difference should not be interpreted as unequivocal support for the tax benefits hypothesis, however, because of the high expected correlation between profitability and tax status. The observed differences in profitability and tax status are also generally consistent with the financial slack and wealth transfer hypotheses.

The slow withdrawal group exhibits profitability, cash flow and leverage measures that are in between those exhibited by the no change termination group and the benchmark no withdrawal group. The slow withdrawal group also exhibits an intermediate level of taxpayers (which is significantly less than the benchmark group). However, the proportion of firms with NOL carryforwards is not significantly different from the benchmark group.

A measure of the proportions of employees of intermediate tenure indicates that all four samples are similar; i.e., no statistically significant differences

---

[23] To confirm that interperiod and interindustry differences are not responsible for the significant differences reported later in table 4, all variables (except the two tax measures) were recomputed by subtracting industry medians of the corresponding variables for that year. The results remain essentially unchanged.

[24] In many cases it appeared that the financial statement effects of termination were not separately disclosed because they were not material. However, disclosures were not made for some cases with substantial reversions. Interestingly, considerable heterogeneity was observed in the tax rates used to disclose after-tax cash flow effects.

Table 4

Median attributes of samples with overfunded pension plans.[a]

	Terminating firms		Nonterminating firms	
Financial and pension variables[b]	No control changes (T-NC) (88 firms)	With control changes (T-C) (31 firms)	Slow withdrawal (SW) (199 firms)	No withdrawal benchmark (NW) (688 firms)
Book Debt / Book Equity	0.63 (0.01)	0.43 (0.41)	0.34 (0.00)	0.46
Book Debt / Mkt. Equity	0.67 (0.02)	0.38 (0.08)	0.28 (0.00)	0.44
Op. Income / Total Assets	0.06 (0.00)	0.10 (0.31)	0.11 (0.84)	0.11
Net Income / Mkt. Equity	0.05 (0.00)	0.10 (0.02)	0.15 (0.00)	0.17
W.C. Flows / Mkt. Equity	0.14 (0.00)	0.20 (0.46)	0.17 (0.26)	0.18
Cash Flows / Mkt. Equity	0.16 (0.01)	0.22 (0.30)	0.19 (0.43)	0.18
# Vested / Total Benef.	0.30 (0.43)	0.29 (0.52)	0.34 (0.19)	0.30
% Taxpayers[c]	51% (0.00)	70% (0.11)	74% (0.02)	82%
% NOL Cfwd.[c]	35% (0.00)	11% (0.82)	9% (0.89)	9%

[a] Values reported in parentheses below the medians are p-values from two-tailed rank sum tests of the null hypothesis that the median for that sample equals the median for the benchmark (NW) sample. For the last two variables (% taxpayers and % NOL cfwd.) the p-values are based on chi-squared tests of equal proportions.

[b] Additional details regarding variable definitions are provided in the appendix. All variables are based on beginning-of-year values for the year of termination for the (T-C) terminating sample, the first year of slow withdrawal for the SW sample, and a randomly assigned year (designed to maintain a distribution similar to the SW sample) for the benchmark (NW) sample. For the T-NC terminating sample, the most recent year prior to termination with available data is used.

[c] Taxpayers and NOL cfwd. refer to firms with positive current federal tax payments (data item #63), and positive NOL carryforwards (data item #52) reported on Compustat, respectively.

relative to the benchmark group are observed. For purposes of determining relative pension bond magnitudes, employee tenure is classified as follows: (1) *early*, representing unvested and partially vested employees, (2) *intermediate*, representing fully vested active employees, and (3) *late*, representing retired and separated beneficiaries.[25] Median values of the proportion of fully vested employees (intermediate tenure) to total beneficiaries range from a low of 28 percent for the control change group to a high of 34 percent for the slow withdrawal group.[26]

Given that the two terminating samples appear to differ in many respects, the subsequent detailed analysis is conducted separately for the two samples. Section 5 examines terminations without control changes and the sample with control changes is analyzed in section 6.

5. Terminations not associated with control changes

5.1. Liquidation of financial stock

To examine if plan terminations are a response to unexpected declines in cash available to fund future investments and dividend payouts, both time-series and cross-sectional analyses are conducted to compare the termination sample without control changes and the two reference samples of overfunded firms.[27] The time-series analysis examines measures of components of the cash flow identity (operating cash flows plus net external financial equal net investments plus dividends) to determine patterns in the pre-termination period. Specifically, if terminating firms faced a reduction in available funds, did cash flows from operations decline or did investment levels increase? Also, how do dividends and external financing change in response? The cross-sectional test is a multivariate analog of the univariate tests in table 4 and determines if slow withdrawals and terminations represent ordered withdrawal alternatives. Observing that terminations are similar to (but an extreme form

---

[25] These measures are fairly representative of the early, intermediate, and late tenure groups. For the example described in footnote 11, the pension bond remains below approximately half the current annual cash wage prior to full vesting (early tenure). Throughout the fully vested (intermediate) stage, the pension bond exceeds half the current wage, except for the last two years before retirement, and the pension bond drops to zero after retirement (late tenure). Thus, the proxy is in error only during the last two years of active service, at which time the employee should correctly belong to the late tenure group.

[26] This measure is computed separately for each plan, based on 1977 data obtained from a database described in Friedman (1982). Average values, weighted by plan assets, are then computed for each firm. For the two termination samples, the ratio only considers terminated plans and plans that were not terminated are excluded.

[27] Consistent with the results reported in table 4, both cash flows from operation and net investments exhibit a stable time-series pattern for the termination sample with control changes. Also, no significant differences are observed, relative to the benchmark sample, along any of the variables examined in this subsection.

of) slow withdrawals supports the financial slack hypothesis. On the other hand, evidence indicating that terminations and withdrawals of pension assets are explained by different sets of variables is inconsistent with this hypothesis.

The time-series analysis, reported in panel A of table 5, is based on median values of cash flow variables for the three samples for year 0 and five prior years (years -1, -2, etc.). The associated p-values for nonparametric rank sum tests that compare the terminating and slow withdrawal samples with the benchmark sample are also reported. All variables, except where noted, are scaled by the same variable – book value of total assets – to allow comparisons across firms, across cash flow components, and over time. Cash from operations is separated into two parts: working capital from operations (W.C. flows) and cash from changes in noncash current accounts (Δ current accounts).[28] This separation identifies cash flows generated by liquidating investments in working capital (such as decreases in inventories and accounts receivable, and increases in current liabilities) – a fairly liquid reserve of financial slack.

Consistent with the predictions of the financial slack hypothesis, terminations are preceded by large declines in funds from operations. The median working capital from operations declines from a high of 10 percent (of total assets) to a low of 5 percent by year -1 (also see fig. 1). This decline begins in year -3 and reduces further in years -2 and -1. Note that the year 0 data is contaminated, since it includes the effects of excess pension assets reverting to the sponsor for some cases.

Analysis of investment behavior (Net Investment) indicates that terminating firms did not liquidate financial slack to finance increased investment opportunities. In fact, median Net Investments declined from 8 percent of total assets (before year -3) to 5 percent (by year 0). While such a decline is consistent with the view that investment opportunities decreased, it is also consistent with the view that some investments were deferred or cancelled and/or some existing investments were disposed of in response to the large decline in funds from operations. Analysis of dividends, the remaining component of cash outflows, indicates that firms waited until year -1 before reducing dividends (from 1.3 percent to 0.7 percent of total assets). Note that decreases in investments and dividends do not completely offset the observed declines in working capital flows.

This shortfall in funds available to finance investments and dividend payments appears to be made up almost entirely by depleting investments in working capital (increasing current liabilities and decreasing investments in

---

[28]Although cash flows and working capital flows are labelled as being 'from operations', Compustat includes the effects of discontinued operations and extraordinary items (similar to net income) in computing these flows. Also, current liabilities include the current portion of long-term debt. These current liabilities were not reclassified as long-term debt because Compustat did not identify the amounts separately in many cases.

Table 5

Comparison of terminating firms (without control changes) versus slow withdrawal and benchmark groups.

		Panel A: Time-series analysis of median cash flow components [a]		
Financial measures [b]	Rel. year [c]	No change in control (T-NC sample)	Slow withdrawal (SW sample)	No withdrawal benchmark (NW sample)
W.C. Flows ___ Total Assets	−5	0.096/(0.00)	0.122/(0.32)	0.123
	−4	0.100/(0.00)	0.118/(0.30)	0.123
	−3	0.092/(0.00)	0.118/(0.29)	0.124
	−2	0.079/(0.00)	0.112/(0.10)	0.123
	−1	0.052/(0.00)	0.107/(0.00)	0.122
	0	0.065/(0.00)	0.103/(0.00)	0.121
Δ Current Accounts ___ Total Assets	−5	−0.024/(0.31)	−0.019/(0.60)	−0.016
	−4	−0.006/(0.31)	−0.012/(0.82)	−0.012
	−3	−0.009/(0.20)	−0.012/(0.83)	−0.013
	−2	0.009/(0.04)	−0.003/(0.77)	−0.004
	−1	0.006/(0.15)	0.004/(0.05)	0.000
	0	0.012/(0.04)	−0.002/(0.90)	−0.003
Net Investment ___ Total Assets	−5	0.079/(0.15)	0.078/(0.01)	0.090
	−4	0.079/(0.04)	0.077/(0.02)	0.086
	−3	0.071/(0.00)	0.088/(0.05)	0.094
	−2	0.067/(0.00)	0.081/(0.03)	0.091
	−1	0.054/(0.00)	0.069/(0.00)	0.085
	0	0.050/(0.00)	0.070/(0.00)	0.084
Dividends ___ Total Assets	−5	0.013/(0.00)	0.020/(0.00)	0.018
	−4	0.013/(0.00)	0.021/(0.00)	0.018
	−3	0.013/(0.01)	0.021/(0.01)	0.018
	−2	0.013/(0.00)	0.021/(0.01)	0.019
	−1	0.010/(0.00)	0.012/(0.07)	0.019
	0	0.007/(0.00)	0.021/(0.18)	0.019
Net Ext. Fin. ___ Total Assets	−5	0.005/(0.94)	0.003/(0.21)	0.006
	−4	0.002/(0.13)	0.002/(0.09)	0.008
	−3	0.006/(0.41)	0.009/(0.54)	0.007
	−2	0.003/(0.13)	0.001/(0.01	0.007
	−1	0.006/(0.87)	−0.002/(0.01)	0.001
	0	−0.011/(0.01)	0.000/(0.45)	0.000
$\dfrac{(P/A)_t - (P/A)_{t-1}}{(P/A)_{t-1}}$	−5	−0.009/(0.26)	0.023/(0.76)	0.019
	−4	−0.001/0.57)	0.020/(0.78)	0.011
	−3	−0.008/(0.07)	−0.011/(0.32)	−0.002
	−2	−0.029/(0.10)	0.003/(0.83)	−0.006
	−1	−0.141/(0.00)	−0.051/(0.12)	−0.014
	0	−0.216/(0.00)	−0.464/(0.00)	−0.038
Excess Returns [d]	−5	−0.061/(0.30)	−0.077/(0.63)	−0.083
	−4	−0.101/(0.07)	−0.075/(0.00)	−0.066
	−3	−0.159/(0.00)	−0.035/(0.98)	−0.050
	−2	−0.174/(0.00)	−0.084/(0.00)	0.019
	−1	−0.096/(0.00)	−0.031/(0.67)	−0.010
	0	0.059/(0.00)	−0.024/(0.00)	0.019

Table 5 (continued)

Panel B: Ordered probit analysis of pension asset withdrawals[e]

$$Y = \alpha + \beta_1 \Delta\left(\frac{\text{Book Debt}}{\text{Book Equity}}\right) + \beta_2 \Delta\left(\frac{\text{Op. Income}}{\text{Total Assets}}\right) + \beta_3 \Delta\left(\frac{\text{W.C. Flows}}{\text{Total Assets}}\right)$$

Coefficient	0.12	−2.81	−15.22
t-statistic	0.48	−1.01	−4.06
p-value	(0.63)	(0.31)	(0.00)

$$\chi_3^2 = 27.27 \qquad p\text{-value} = 0.00 \qquad N = 685$$

The degree of withdrawal is coded as follows: 0 for the no withdrawal benchmark (NW) sample, 1 for the slow withdrawal (SW) sample, and 2 for no control change (T-NC) termination sample.

[a] Median values of components of the cash flow identity (operating flows plus net external financing equal net investments plus dividends) are reported for each sample. The values reported in parentheses are *p*-values from two-tailed rank sum tests of the null hypothesis that the median for that sample equals the median for the benchmark (NW) sample.

[b] Additional details regarding variable definitions are provided in the appendix.

[c] Rel. year is the year relative to year 0, which is the year of termination for the terminating sample (T-NC), the first year of slow withdrawal for the SW control sample, and a randomly assigned year (designed to maintain a distribution similar to the SW sample) for the benchmark (NW) sample.

[d] Excess returns measure the difference between firm stock returns and the equally weighted CRSP index.

[e] All statistics and *p*-values reported are based on the McKelvey and Zavoina (1975) method. Δ represents the median value of annual changes in these variables over the five-year period leading up to the year of termination (rel. year = −5 to rel. year = −1). The appendix provides additional details on variables used.

current assets). Median changes in noncash current accounts indicate that up to year −3 terminating firms made net investments in working capital (negative values of Δ current accounts). After year −3, however, firms generated cash by reducing their investments in working capital. Net external financing (Net Ext. Fin.) remains relatively constant at around 0.5 percent of total assets, except in year 0 when it drops to −1%. Analysis of issues and repurchases of debt and equity (results not reported) indicates that the observed year 0 decline in net external financing is caused entirely by debt repurchases.

While the benchmark sample reports relatively stable median values for the cash flow variables, the slow withdrawal sample reports changes in cash flow components that are similar to but smaller in magnitude than the changes observed for the terminating sample. Similar results are documented in Mittelstaedt (1988). Also, analysis of percent changes in pension flows (P/A) indicates that the terminating sample initiated slow withdrawals in year −1, prior to the termination (see table 5). Similarly, the slow withdrawal sample registers a small year −1 decrease in pension flows. (Note that the large year 0 declines in pension flows are a direct consequence of the sample

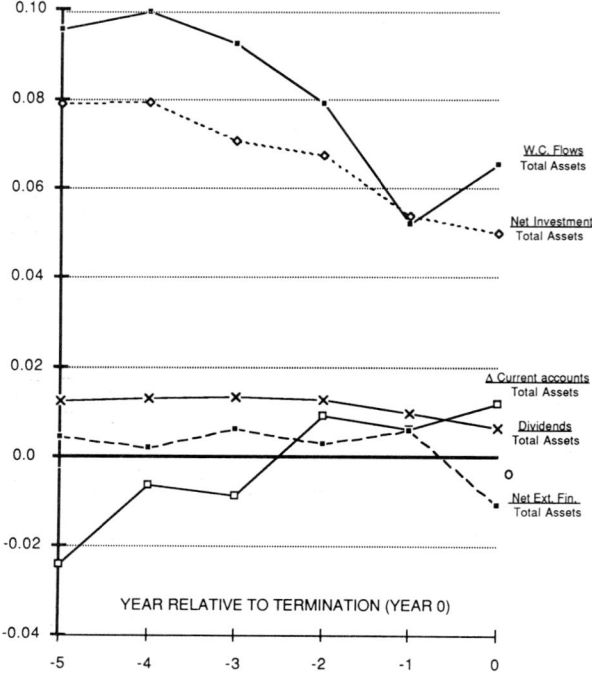

Fig. 1. Time-series analysis of median cash flow components; termination sample without control changes. The components of the cash flow identity are related as follows: Operating cash flows (W.C. Flows + Δ Current Accounts) + Issues − repurchases of debt and equity (Net Ext. Fin.) = Purchases less sales of long-term assets (Net Inv.) + Dividends.

selection process, since a 25 percent decline in pension flows is one of three minimum requirements.)

Assuming that the financial slack hypothesis is valid, the results in fig. 1 and table 5 allow some inferences regarding the position in the pecking order of funds from both pension and nonpension sources. Firms view excess pension assets as financial slack and prefer slow withdrawals to terminations. Also, some forms of nonpension slack appear to be preferred over pension slack since firms liquidate their investments in working capital and scale down their long-term investments before resorting to slow withdrawals of pension assets. Equity appears to be a very costly source of funds, since new issues of equity are almost never used. The evidence regarding debt issues is less clear. Although new issues of debt (net of retirements) are not observed either, the unusually high leverage values reported in table 4 for this terminating sample suggest that fairly high levels of debt are preferred to plan terminations. Alternatively, declines in equity value causes leverage to increase. However, the year 0 debt retirements suggest that plan terminations are preferred once risky debt exceeds a certain level.[29]

From a corporate finance perspective, these results also provide a description of the relative magnitude of the levels, as well as potential changes in levels, of various cash flow components. While funds from operations (working capital) and net investments are the largest components (around 10 percent of total assets), dividends (between 1 and 2 percent of total assets), and net external financing (less than 1 percent of total assets) are relatively small. Interestingly, although the level of net investments in current accounts is small (normally around 2 percent of total assets), the magnitude of the change in this component (to a disinvestment of about 1 percent of total assets) is almost as large as the changes in the two larger components.

The results of a multivariate cross-sectional test using an ordered probit analysis [see McKelvey and Zavoina (1975)], reported in panel B of table 5, generally confirm the univariate results reported in panel A.[30] The dependent variable, representing extent of withdrawal of excess pension assets, codes no withdrawal, slow withdrawal, and terminating firms as 0, 1, and 2, respectively. Median changes in explanatory variables measuring profitability, leverage, and funds from operations, between year -5 and year -1, are used to explain the pension withdrawal choice. Changes in funds from operations (W.C. flows) is highly significant and appears to be the most important factor motivating withdrawals of excess assets. Moreover, the ordered probit model suggests that larger (smaller) declines in funds from operations are associated with terminations (slow withdrawals). Using alternative measures for cash flows, profitability, and leverage does not change this basic result.

5.2. Wealth transfers from debtholders

The wealth transfer hypothesis predicts that firms approaching financial distress seek to transfer wealth from debtholders (or the PBGC) by stripping excess pension assets and paying it out to shareholders. The low profitability values exhibited by the no control change terminating sample in table 4 as well as the declines in profitability in table 5 are consistent with predictions that

---

[29] The year -1 decline in dividends are also consistent with terminating firms facing restrictive lending covenants, with the year 0 debt repurchases representing an effort to 'buy out' some of these restrictions.

[30] A conventional regression analysis on ordinal level dependent variables causes correlation between the error and regressor which results in a based coefficient. McKelvey and Zavoina offer a maximum likelihood technique that corrects for the bias, assuming that the observed dependent variable lumps into categories an underlying continuous dependent variable that is described by a linear regression model. Mittelstaedt (1988) uses a choice-based trichotomous logit model that separately compares the terminating and slow withdrawal firms with the benchmark group. Constraining the three samples to represent ordered propensities to make withdrawals, as in this paper, is inappropriate for the hypotheses tested there.

are common to both the financial slack and wealth transfer hypotheses. The large declines in market values (excess returns in table 5, panel A) also support the prediction that terminating firms appear closer to financial distress. Note that the systematic relation between slow withdrawals and terminations observed in tables 4 and 5 do not reject this wealth transfer view.

However, predictions unique to the wealth transfer view are not supported by the evidence. The year 0 repurchases of debt are inconsistent with firms seeking to transfer wealth from debtholders. Similarly, the decline in dividend payments after year -2 is inconsistent with a strategy of increased payouts to stockholders. While dividends might have fallen further without these withdrawals of excess assets, the time-series evidence is inconsistent with terminating firms seeking to maximize payouts to shareholders. First, dividends do not increase in year $+1$ despite an increase in cash flows (since year $+1$ data was not available for all firms, this year is excluded from table 5). Second, the dividend cut in year -1 could have been avoided (or reduced) by terminating the plan earlier than year 0.

Unfortunately, additional evidence on predictions unique to the wealth transfer explanation is not easily obtained. An event study approach that analyzes the effects of termination on stockholder and bondholder wealth is unlikely to resolve this issue because of two major problems. First, the announcement date is not clearly identifiable (see footnote 17). Second, given a wider 'event' window, confounding due to related events is a major problem. Terminations appear to be a response to exogenous events that have large wealth effects. The many downward revisions of bond ratings observed in WSJI for this sample could be due to the general decline in financial health for the termination sample, rather than the hypothesized wealth transfers caused by terminations. Similarly, the incidence of takeover attempts, albeit unsuccessful (see section 6), appears to have raised stock prices for many sample firms. Therefore, the effects of termination announcements on stockholder and debtholder wealth are not easily identified.

5.3. Breach of implicit contracts

The evidence on the proportions of vested employees (of intermediate tenure with the highest pension bonds), reported in table 4, is inconsistent with the view that magnitudes of pension bonds motivate breaches of implicit contracts via plan terminations. Also, comparing terminated plans with plans not terminated for both termination samples (results not reported) reveal similar proportions of vested beneficiaries. Apparently, employee groups with the highest pension bonds are not targeted for terminations. However, the substantial proportion of terminations associated with control changes (table 2) is consistent with the view that new owners/managers renege on implicit contracts entered into by previous owners/management.

Table 6

Analysis of replacement plans following asset reversions.[a]

Panel A: 63 firms from Compustat sample

Year	Frequency			Reversion (in millions of $)		
	DB	DC	Total	DB	DC	Total
1980–1982	0	11	11	0	431	431
	0%	100%		0%	100%	
1983	8	11	19	661	278	939
	42%	58%		70%	30%	
1984	14	17	31	685	155	840
	45%	55%		82%	18%	
1985	2	0	2	23	0	23
	100%	0%	—	100%	0%	—
Total	24	39	63	1369	864	2233
	38%	62%		61%	39%	

Panel B: 73 proposed terminations from PBGC list (dated June 13, 1985)

Ownership change[b]	Frequency			Reversion (in millions of $)		
	DB	DC	Total	DB	DC	Total
No	23	25	48	104	104	208
	48%	52%		50%	50%	
Yes	15	10	25	397	42	439
	60%	40%	—	90%	10%	—
Total	38	35	73	501	146	647
	52%	48%		77%	23%	

[a] Replacement plans are coded as DB (DC) for defined benefit (defined contribution) plans.
[b] Ownership changes are based on examination of the S&P Register and the Million Dollar Directory to identify changes that occurred between the year prior to the termination and two years following the termination.

Regardless of the link between control changes and motivation to expropriate pension bonds, plan terminations breach implicit pension contracts only if employees are not allowed the opportunity to receive future 'overpayments', proxied here by the presence of replacement defined contribution plans. Table 6, panel A, reports replacement plan data obtained from annual reports for 63 of the 88 terminating firms not associated with control changes. (Either post-termination annual reports could not be obtained or replacement plan information was not disclosed for the remaining 25 firms in this sample as well as the 31 control change terminating firms.) While all replacement plans for terminations before 1983 are defined contribution plans, the use of replacement defined benefit plans appear to increase thereafter. Also, since terminations with replacement defined benefit plans are associated with larger reversion amounts, they represent almost all of the assets reverting to sponsors in

1984 and 1985 (82 and 100 percent, respectively). The higher proportions of replacement defined contribution plans earlier in the sample period appear to be caused by an initial uncertainty as to how the courts and employees would react to replacement defined benefit plans (see footnote 5). The patterns for replacement plans observed subsequently do not support the breach of implicit contracts view.

To provide additional evidence on replacement plans, panel B of table 6 examines 73 proposed terminations with replacement plan data provided in the PBGC list (eight firms appear in both panels A and B).[31] Using the ownership change categories described in table 2, the relative proportions of defined benefit and defined contribution plans are reported separately for terminations with and without ownership changes. Again, the data appear to contradict the breach of implicit contracts view since replacement defined benefit plans are employed in 52 percent of the terminations, and represent 77 percent of the assets reverting to sponsors.[32] Moreover, replacement defined benefit plans are used more often after terminations following ownership changes, relative to terminations not associated with ownership changes.

6. Terminations following control changes

Two puzzling results relating to terminations following control changes have been presented so far. They are: (1) the presence of substantial differences between the two termination samples (with and without control changes) and (2) the absence of observable differences between the control change sample and the no withdrawal benchmark sample. Analysis of WSJI news items for the control change sample reveal that a third of the control changes (11 firms) represent 'friendly' acquisitions (not resisted by incumbent management) by other firms. Examination of annual reports for acquiring firms suggests that the terminations were due to the acquired firm's plan(s) being consolidated with the much larger plan of the acquiring entity. Note that the acquiring firms and not the sponsors of the terminated plans are being examined here. The annual report footnotes suggest that a reduction in administration costs and a desire for uniformity across the workforce, rather than any of the effects discussed in the paper, motivated these terminations. Two other pieces of evidence support this view. First, benefit levels increased after the termination in some cases. Second, a detailed time-series and cross-sectional examination similar to that conducted in tables 4 and 5 (results not reported) for a sample

---

[31] The PBGC list does not provide replacement plan data for plans that were already terminated. Note that replacement plan data is obtained from annual reports in panel A and the PBGC list in panel B. While panel A offers a time-series perspective on the type of replacement plan used, panel B includes data on terminations associated with control changes.

[32] A more recent PBGC list (as of June 30, 1987) indicates that replacement defined benefit plans represent 72 percent of the terminations and 95 percent of assets reverting to sponsors.

of 29 friendly acquiring firms indicated no significant differences relative to the benchmark no withdrawal group. This sample consisted of 11 firms making the friendly acquisitions noted above and 18 firms that acquired smaller sponsors that were not on Compustat and were therefore excluded from the terminating samples analyzed so far.

The remaining two-thirds of the control change terminating sample are associated with at least one hostile takeover attempt, and the control change typically involves a going-private transaction. Mittelstaedt (1988) finds that his measure of 'susceptibility to takeover' is higher for terminating firms, relative to slow withdrawal and benchmark firms. Based on evidence documented in other studies of similar control changes [see Kaplan (1988) and Schipper and Smith (1988), for example], these firms undergo massive financial restructuring that results in highly leveraged positions (and low marginal tax rates) similar to those associated with the no control change terminations described in section 5. To alleviate the resulting constraints on available resources, such firms often seek cash from internal sources such as asset sales. Plan terminations represent a similar source of funds.

This description of terminating firms after the hostile control change provides a potential explanation for the first puzzle regarding the differences observed between the termination sample without control changes and the pre-control data for the other termination sample. Additional analysis of these firms after the control change was not conducted because of the difficulty in obtaining financial information. However, the absence of any observed differences between the benchmark sample and the termination sample with control changes (the second puzzle) remains to be explained. A time-series analysis of pre-control change data (results not reported) does not reveal any unusual changes immediately prior to the control change, and confirms that the hostile control change sample is not significantly different from the benchmark sample along the variables analyzed in table 5. Why were these particular firms targets of hostile control changes? Moreover, unlike the first termination sample where the financial stress arises exogenously from declining operating profits, here the tightness is self-induced from financial restructuring. In the absence of exogenous changes, why does the desirability of overfunded plans change after the control change?

While seeking to retrieve funds from acquired firms is consistent with undercapitalized investors attempting to 'finance' such takeovers (assuming capital constraints), Jensen (1986) offers a more specific alternative explanation. He argues that some incumbent managers seek to maximize total resources under their control, rather than shareholder wealth, and cause firms to grow beyond the optimal size. Managers are reluctant to release 'free' cash flows, in excess of those required to fund all positive net present value (NPV) projects, via payments to equity claimants. Instead they dissipate such funds by investing in negative NPV projects, by creating unused debt capacity, and by increasing organizational inefficiencies. Ceteris paribus, Jensen expects such firms to be associated with stable cash flows, high profitability (due to economic rents/quasirents), and low growth opportunities.[33] Successful efforts to discipline such managers through internal and external control mechanisms are followed by asset divestitures and increased debt loads, with the proceeds being paid out to shareholders via increased dividends and share repurchases.

To understand better the link between Jensen's view and terminations for this sample, a 'hostile' control change sample of 30 firms was obtained by deleting 11 friendly control changes from the termination sample with control changes and including 10 firms from the no control change termination sample with at least one mention in the WSJI of a hostile takeover attempt; i.e., targets of both successful and unsuccessful hostile takeover attempts are assumed to be similar *ex ante*.

Univariate comparisons of the sample with hostile takeover attempts and the benchmark sample, reported in table 7, offer preliminary evidence supporting the view that firms with excess free cash flows are targets of hostile takeover attempts. Despite similarities between the two samples along dimensions analyzed in tables 4 and 5, three measures of valuation that compare market values of equity to book values (based on historical costs and replacement values) and cash flow measures indicate that both assets and cash flows for this termination sample are capitalized at lower market values than the benchmark sample. This difference suggests that the termination sample is associated with lower growth opportunities and/or inefficient management. The stability of median cash flow measures over time, similar to that reported in table 5 for the benchmark sample, as well as the higher profitability of this sample relative to the termination sample without control changes is also consistent with Jensen's description. However, the profitability measures in table 7 do not indicate the presence of economic rents, since the termination sample is less profitable than the benchmark sample, especially when replacement-cost-based measures of equity are used. Also, the termination sample appears to be associated with a lower level of investments, contrary to Jensen's prediction. Finally, the termination sample is not associated with a significantly lower level of dividend payouts or higher unused debt capacity (lower leverage).

A multivariate comparison of the two groups using a logit regression model indicates that the two groups of firms are significantly different based on these

---

[33]Jensen suggests that activities generating economic rents or quasirents tend to generate free cash flows. Unlike rapidly growing organizations with numerous profitable investment projects, he identifies industries with few growth opportunities and stable operating cash flows as likely candidates that fit this description. Examples he provides are the oil, tobacco, forest products, broadcasting, and food products industries.

Table 7

Comparison of terminating firms associated with hostile takeover attempts and the no withdrawal benchmark sample.

Financial variables[a]	Terminations with hostile takeover attempts		No withdrawal benchmark sample	Logit regression results[b]	
	Medians	(*p*-value)[c]	Median	Coefficients	(*p*-value)
Book Equity / Mkt. Equity	1.256	(0.21)	1.069	0.897	(0.19)
Repl. Value / Mkt. Equity	2.398	(0.00)	1.633	−0.446	(0.10)
Cash Flows / Mkt. Equity	0.283	(0.01)	0.196	2.780	(0.13)
Net Income / Repl. Value	0.061	(0.00)	0.140	−18.746	(0.01)
Op. Income / Book Assets	0.101	(0.13)	0.109	−0.524	(0.95)
Book Debt / Book Equity	0.458	(0.57)	0.446	−0.673	(0.29)
Int. Exp. / PP & E	0.033	(0.59)	0.034	−0.000	(1.00)
Net Investment / Book Assets	0.066	(0.05)	0.088	−0.758	(0.87)
Dividends / Mkt. Equity	0.052	(0.11)	0.049	3.387	(0.79)

Overall model: $N = 404$

$\chi_9^2 = 27.65$ p-value = 0.00

[a] Median values are computed for each firm over the period extending from year -5 to 0. Additional details regarding variable definitions are provided in the appendix.

[b] A logit regression is estimated for the two groups of firms with the dependent variable coded as 1 (0) for the termination sample with hostile takeover attempts (benchmark no withdrawal sample).

[c] Values reported in parentheses are p-values from two-tailed rank sum tests of the null hypothesis that the median for the termination sample equals the median for the benchmark sample.

explanatory variables. However, the coefficient estimates and associate *p*-values reported in the last two columns of table 7 suggest that only one profitability measure (net income scaled by replacement cost of assets) is significant. One explanation for this drop in the number of significant explanatory factors is the high degree of multicollinearity present in the data.[34] Overall, the univariate and multivariate comparisons reported in table 7 suggest that overfunded firms that subsequently became targets for hostile takeover attempts are significantly different, along a number of financial variables, from overfunded firms that did not subsequently withdraw excess pension assets (the benchmark sample). Since the variables used here are likely to measure relevant conceptual variables (such as growth opportunities) with considerable error, these results should be considered preliminary and interpreted with caution.

In summary, the observed differences between the two terminating samples (with and without control changes) are partially explained by splitting the control change sample into two subsamples representing hostile and friendly control changes. Terminations for the friendly control change subsample are probably motivated by relatively innocuous plan consolidation considerations. Differences between the subsample with hostile control changes and the termination sample without control changes could disappear if post-control-change data is examined. Descriptions of restructuring following hostile takeovers suggest that such firms face tight financial conditions similar to those observed for the termination sample without control changes. Thus the same factors could potentially motivate all plan terminations (excluding the friendly control change subsample). While the specific link between terminations and attempted corporate control changes is not addressed here, examination of financial measures prior to hostile control changes provides some support for Jensen's predictions regarding the type of firms likely to be associated with such control changes.

7. Conclusion

To understand why some overfunded plans are terminated, this paper empirically examines a number of plausible explanations. The results indicate that terminating firms fall into three general groups: (a) terminations not associated with control changes, (b) terminations followed by hostile attempts to change control, and (c) terminations following friendly control changes. Unlike the first two groups, terminations for the third group appear to be

---

[34] Most pair-wise correlations coefficients are highly significant. However, the condition indexes [based on Belsley, Kuh, and Welsch (1980)] are below 25, suggesting the absence of severe multicollinearity.

motivated by plan consolidation considerations and are, therefore, not examined in detail. Results of analyses for the other two groups provide no support for the view that terminations represent a breach of implicit contracts. Also, analysis of accounting rules suggest that financial statement based incentives are unlikely to be the prime factor motivating plan terminations. For the sample of terminations not associated with corporate control changes, large and persistent declines in cash flows from operations are observed prior to the year of termination. Similarly, the sample of terminations associated with hostile takeover attempts also appear to be characterized by tight financial conditions engendered by the financial restructuring that typically follows such takeover attempts.

These characteristics are generally consistent with the predictions of three other explanations considered: the tax benefit hypothesis, the wealth transfer from debtholders and PBGC hypothesis, and the financial slack hypothesis. However, analysis of the tax benefits argument suggests that it can only explain terminations in special cases associated with temporary tax status declines. While difficulties in identifying empirically such tax status declines limit tests of the tax hypothesis, preliminary evidence indicates that only a small proportion of terminating firms fall into this category.

Similarly, although the results do not overwhelming reject the wealth transfer explanation, they appear to contradict certain predictions unique to the wealth transfer explanation. First, there is evidence of the proceeds from terminations being used to repurchase debt. Second, the absence of increased payouts to stockholders both before and after terminations is inconsistent with terminating firms seeking to reduce debtholder wealth. Finally, this explanation is not supported by the financial restructuring associated with terminations following hostile control changes. Marais et al. (1987) and Kaplan (1988) conclude that wealth transfers from debtholders are unlikely to motivate such control changes. Existing debt is often renegotiated to allow additional new debt, and announcements of these control changes are not associated with large value decreases for outstanding debt.

The financial slack explanation appears to provide a simple rationale for terminations undertaken by firms with and without control changes. Excess pension assets represent financial slack and slow withdrawals and terminations represent liquidation of such slack. Smaller declines in available funds are satisfied by slow withdrawals and/or liquidations of preferred sources of nonpension slack. Continued declines in available funds that exhaust the stock of preferred sources of financial slack are associated with terminations. For terminations without control changes, the decline in available funds is gradual and terminations are preceded by slow withdrawals. For terminations with control changes, however, the decline in available funds is sudden (created by new management) and terminations are not preceded by slow withdrawals.

Appendix

Table 8

Variable	Description	Data item	Source[a]
Book Debt	= Book value of long-term debt	#9	Compustat
Book Equity	= Book value of common equity	#60	Compustat
Net Income	= After-tax income (before extraordinary items and discontinued operations)	#18	Compustat
Op. Income	= Income before interest and taxes	#16 + #18 + #15	Compustat
Total Assets	= Book value of total assets	#6	Compustat
Δ Current Accounts	= Cash from changes in noncash current accounts	Δ(#5) $-\Delta$(#4 − #1)	Compustat
Mkt. Equity	= Market value of common equity	#24 × #25	Compustat
NOL Cfwd.	= 0 for firms with no NOL carry forwards = 1 for firms with positive NOL carryforwards	#52	Compustat
Taxpayer	= 0 for firms with zero or negative tax payments = 1 for firms with positive tax payments	#63	Compustat
W.C. Flows	= Working capital provided from operations	#110	Compustat
Cash Flows	= Cash flows provided from operations	110 + Δ current accounts	Compustat
Net Investment	= Net investments in long-term assets	#128 + #129 −(#107 + #109)	Compustat
Dividends	= Cash dividends to common equity	#21	Compustat
Net Ext. Fin.	= Issues less purchases of debt and equity	#108 + #111 −(#114 − #115)	Compustat
P/A	= Pension expense, scaled by total assets	#43/#6	Compustat
Excess Return	= Difference between actual stock return and market return (equally weighted index), annual value = sum of 12 monthly returns	—	CRSP
Int. Exp.	= Total interest expense	#15	Compustat
PP&E	= Book value of Property, Plant & Equipment (Gross)	#7	Compustat
Repl. Value	= Book value of equity (replacement cost basis)	—	FASB33 tape
Vested	= Total vested benefits	—	FASB36 tape
Accrued	= Total accrued benefits	—	FASB36 tape
# Vested[b]	= Number of vested beneficiaries	—	Friedman tape
Total Benef.[b]	= Number of total beneficiaries	—	Friedman tape

[a] The Compustat data is from the active and research files for the Expanded Annual Industrial plus OTC sample. The CRSP data is from the monthly return files. The two FASB tapes are obtained from Columbia University, and the Friedman tape is from the National Bureau of Economic Research [see Friedman (1982)].

[b] Computed by plan. For the slow withdrawal and benchmark samples an average, weighted by plan assets, is computed for each firm.

References

Belsley, D.A., E. Kuh, and R.E. Welsch, 1980, Regression diagnostics (Wiley, New York, NY).

Black, F., 1980, The tax consequences of long-run pension policy, Financial Analysts Journal, July-Aug., 21–28.

Bodie, Z., J.O. Light, R. Morck, and R.A. Taggart, Jr., 1984, Funding and asset allocation in corporate pension plans: An empirical investigation, National Bureau of Economic Research working paper no. 1315 (NBER, Cambridge, MA).

Bulow, J.I., 1982, What are corporate pension liabilities?, Quarterly Journal of Economics 95, 435–452.

Financial Accounting Standards Board (FASB), 1985, Statement of financial accounting standard no. 88: Employers' accounting for settlements and curtailments of defined benefit plans and for termination benefits, Dec. (FASB, Stamford, CT).

Francis, J.R. and S.A. Reiter, 1987, Determinants of corporate pension funding strategy, Journal of Accounting and Economics 9, 35–60.

Friedman, B.F., 1982, Pension funding, pension asset allocation, and corporate finance: Evidence from individual company data, National Bureau of Economic Research working paper no. 957 (NBER, Cambridge, MA).

Hamdallah, A.E. and W. Ruland, 1986, The decision to terminate overfunded pension plans, Journal of Accounting and Public Policy 5, 77–91.

Healy, P., 1985, The effect of bonus schemes on accounting decisions, Journal of Accounting and Economics 7, 85–108.

Ippolito, R.A., 1986, Pensions, economics and public policy (Pension Research Council and Dow Jones–Irwin, Homewood, IL).

Jensen, M.C., 1986, Agency costs of free cash flow, corporate finance and takeovers, American Economic Review, Papers and Proceedings 76, 323–329.

Kaplan, S.N., 1988, Sources of value in management buyouts, Ph.D. dissertation, May (Harvard University, Cambridge, MA).

Landsman, W., 1986, An empirical investigation of pension fund property rights, Accounting Review 61, 662–691.

Lazear, E.P., 1979, Why is there mandatory retirement?, Journal of Political Economy 87, 1261–1284.

McGill, D.M., 1984, Fundamentals of private pensions (Richard D. Irwin, Homewood, IL).

McKelvey, R. and W. Zavoina, 1975, A statistical model for the analysis of ordinal level dependent variables, Journal of Mathematical Sociology 4, 103–120.

Marais, L., K. Schipper, and A. Smith, 1987, Management buyouts and securityholder wealth effects, Working paper, Sept. (University of Chicago, Chicago, IL).

Mittelstaedt, H.F., 1988, An empirical analysis of the factors underlying the decisions to make extreme reductions in pension plan funding, Journal of Accounting and Economics, this issue.

Myers, S.C., 1984, The capital structure puzzle, Journal of Finance 39, 575–592.

Myers, S.C. and N.S. Majluf, 1984, Corporate financing and investment decisions when firms have information that investors do not have, Journal of Financial Economics 15, 187–221.

Schipper, K. and A. Smith, 1988, Corporate income tax effects of management buyouts, Working paper, June (University of Chicago, Chicago, IL).

Sharpe, W.F., 1982, Factors in New York Stock Exchange security returns, 1933–1979, Journal of Portfolio Management 8, 5–19.

Schleifer, A. and L.H. Summers, 1987, Breach of trust in hostile takeovers, National Bureau of Economic Research working paper no. 2342 (NBER, Cambridge, MA).

Smith, C. and J. Warner, 1979, Financial contracting: An analysis of bond covenants, Journal of Financial Economics 7, 117–162.

Stone, M., 1987, A financing explanation for overfunded pension plan terminations, Journal of Accounting Research 25, 317–326.

Tepper, I., 1981, Taxation and corporate pension policy, Journal of Finance 36, 1–13.

Thomas, J.K., 1988, Corporate taxes and defined benefit pension plans, Journal of Accounting and Economics 10, 199–237.

Treynor, J.L., 1977, The principles of corporate pension finance, Journal of Finance 32, 627–638.

Watts, R.L. and J.L. Zimmerman, 1986, Positive accounting theory (Prentice-Hall, Englewood Cliffs, NJ).

Labor Union Contract Negotiations and Accounting Choices

Susan E. Liberty and Jerold L. Zimmerman

ABSTRACT: This paper examines the hypothesis that managers reduce reported earnings during labor union contract negotiations relative to earnings released before and after contracts are negotiated. Analyzing earnings around labor negotiations provides evidence regarding when managers manipulate accounting earnings and, hence, information regarding the costs and benefits of managing earnings. We find no evidence of lower than expected earnings during negotiations. Time series of quarterly and annual unexpected earnings, using several measures of expected earnings, are examined around labor talks for a sample of 105 unionized companies over the period 1968-1981. Both random and matched samples of firms not engaged in labor negotiations also are chosen. The time series of earnings during labor talks for the unionized sample is indistinguishable from that of the random and matched samples. An analysis of these firms' quarterly earnings time-series properties and their abnormal stock returns suggests that in this sample period unionized firms had less incentive to reduce earnings because they already were performing poorly.

PRIOR research finds that managers' accounting choices are systematically affected by firm contracts based explicitly on accounting numbers and situations which implicitly use accounting numbers.[1] Management compensation plans and corporate bond covenants often are based explicitly on accounting numbers. The evidence suggests that these contracts and their specific terms influence managers' accounting choices. Government regulatory agencies (e.g., public utility rate regulators) that explicitly use accounting numbers to restrict managers' actions also affect managers' choices of accounting procedures. In addition, the firm's political sensitivity, frequently measured by firm size, appears to affect managers' accounting decisions even though accounting numbers are used only implicitly in the political process (see Christie [1986] for relevant studies).

This paper analyzes another set of corporate contracts hypothesized to affect managers' accounting choices—labor contracts.[2] Unlike most executive compensation contracts and debt agreements, few labor contracts are explicitly based

[1] Holthausen and Leftwich [1983] and Watts and Zimmerman [1986, Chapter 11] review the literature.

[2] See Watts and Zimmerman [1978, p. 117]; Watts and Zimmerman [1986, Ch. 10]; Holthausen and Leftwich [1983, p. 87]; and Larcker and Balkcom [1984, p. 9].

Helpful comments from Harry DeAngelo, Linda DeAngelo, Jacob Thomas, Jerold Warner, Ross Watts, the participants of workshops at UCLA, Stanford University, University of Florida, University of Toronto, University of Michigan, and University of Rochester and the two referees are gratefully acknowledged.

Susan E. Liberty is a doctoral student and Jerold L. Zimmerman is Alumni Distinguished Professor of Accounting, both at the University of Rochester.

Manuscript received May 1985.
Revisions received November 1985 and April 1986.
Accepted May 1986.

on accounting numbers,[3] although a leading labor economics textbook suggests that earnings are used in labor contract negotiations: "If profits are high and the business outlook is good, [the union leader] can afford to make large demands. If business is declining and profits are failing, he may have to be content with holding the present wage level" [Reynolds, 1978, p. 390]. The financial press provides additional examples:

> Mr. Fraser (United Auto Workers) and Thomas Miner, Chrysler's vice president of labor relations, both noted that because of the company's weak financial condition and the auto industry's continued poor outlook, workers couldn't expect big gains in this pact [*Wall Street Journal*, 9/17/82].

> The union (United Auto Workers) says it deserves some wage-and-benefit gains. It points to the company's (Caterpillar) earnings of $3 billion for the past six years . . . [*Wall Street Journal*, 10/6/82].

The hypothesized effect of reported accounting numbers on labor negotiations is similar to the hypothesized effect of earnings on the political process. In both cases, managers' reports of lower earnings are assumed to affect the process implicitly. Voters, politicians, and union members presumably do not adjust completely the reported numbers for managers' expected manipulations because such adjustments are costly. The existence of information costs is assumed to create incentives for managers to report lower earnings, thereby influencing both the political process and labor talks. The two situations differ if labor unions have greater incentives to undo managers' manipulations or have lower information costs than participants in the political process.

This paper develops and tests the hypothesis that managers reduce earnings released during contract talks relative to earnings released before and after the negotiations. Analyzing earnings around labor negotiations provides evidence regarding when managers manipulate accounting earnings and, hence, information regarding the costs and benefits of managing earnings. The evidence in this study is inconsistent with the view that managers depress earnings during contract talks.

The next section discusses how accounting earnings might affect labor talks, followed by a section explaining the data sources and sampling procedures. A fourth section describes our research method, which is to examine various time series of quarterly and annual unexpected earnings around contract negotiations. A section on results indicates no evidence that managers of unionized firms report lower than expected earnings during labor negotiations. Several measures of expected earnings are employed. Both random and matched samples of firms not engaged in labor negotiations also are chosen. The time series of earnings during labor talks is indistinguishable from that of the random and matched samples. However, the quarterly earnings time-series properties of firms with labor contracts differ from those of the random sample. In particular, over the sample period of 1974–1981, the firms with labor contracts exhibit, on average, a downward drift in seasonally differenced quarterly earnings as compared to the random sample. The drift also occurs in the sample of firms matched by firm size and

---

[3] In rare cases, union members' wages are explicitly tied to reported earnings. Eastern Airlines, for example, has a union contract directing the firm to pay back workers 3.5 percent in withheld wages plus a bonus of as much as 3.5 percent if Eastern earns at least two percent on revenue [*Wall Street Journal*, 9/17/82].

industry. An analysis of these firms' abnormal stock returns indicates that this negative earnings drift is consistent with their generally poor real operating performance which was anticipated by the stock market. This finding suggests that in this sample period, unionized firms had less incentive to reduce earnings because they already were performing poorly. A final section interprets and summarizes the findings.

DEVELOPMENT OF THE HYPOTHESIS

The accounting literature and popular press present the hypothesis that managers manipulate earnings surrounding labor contract talks. This section explores a possible argument for this hypothesis. The argument assumes unions want information regarding the firm's economic rents, and accounting earnings provide information about economic rents. It is then asserted that the benefits to managers of depressing earnings during contract talks exceed the costs.

Economic rents either arise from monopoly profits or are the returns from previous firm-specific investments (i.e., quasi-rents). Economic rents affect union bargaining if either of two models of labor unions is adopted: the *monopoly model* that assumes the union maximizes the wage bill [Cartter, 1959, pp. 80–84; Rees, 1973, pp. 126–133; and Baldwin, 1983] or the *bargaining model* that assumes the union uses its power to strike to appropriate some of the firm's (quasi- or monopoly) rents [Ashenfelter and Johnson, 1969 and Tracy, 1985]. Under the monopoly model, the firm's rents are likely correlated with the firm's derived demand for labor. As a rational monopolist, the union provides labor up to the point at which the marginal revenue of supplying labor is equated with its marginal cost. Under the bargaining

model, the union's resolve to strike depends on the firm's economic rents. As profits increase, the union expects larger wage concessions. To increase the probability of realizing these concessions, the union uses its power to strike as a bargaining device. Under both the monopoly and bargaining models of unions, economic rents affect the union's demand.

Accounting earnings act as surrogates for economic rents as long as less costly alternative sources do not provide similar or better information on rents. If unions can observe outputs, inputs, and prices, then alternative sources of information on economic rents exist. In addition, if unions can collect and organize these sources to provide, at less cost, similar or more accurate information than accounting earnings, unions will not rely on reported profits as surrogates for economic rents. Therefore, the hypothesis that managers manipulate reported earnings surrounding contract talks requires the assumption that alternative information sources do not eliminate totally the unions' reliance on accounting earnings.

The anticipated benefits to managers of manipulating earnings are the lower wage bills. That is, wages will be higher if earnings are not reduced during contract talks. Managers' costs of manipulating earnings are (1) the increased default costs due to greater likelihood of technical default on bond covenants, and/or (2) reduced managerial pay from executive compensation packages based on reported earnings. Both of these costs are bounded by the non-zero costs of renegotiating debt and/or compensation contracts. Presumably, these renegotiation costs are low since debtholders and shareholders benefit from lower wage bills, *ceteris paribus*.

The benefits of manipulating earnings

can be diminished for several reasons. First, labor officials can adjust the reported earnings, to some extent undoing accounting manipulations. If the information used in making these adjustments is costless, union leaders can adjust earnings completely. Hence, the hypothesis that managers depress reported earnings during labor talks requires the assumption that these information costs are positive. Second, union leaders may learn over time of managers' manipulations. Contract talks usually occur every three years. In this repeated game, it is assumed that either managers do not reduce earnings during every negotiation or that turnover in union leadership precludes unions from completely adjusting earnings. The validity of these various assumptions is an empirical issue.

Given that managers have incentives to manipulate earnings, the manipulation can take several forms. By deferring revenue recognition or accelerating cost recognition, reported earnings during labor negotiations are reduced and earnings following the talks are raised relative to what they would have been absent management's manipulations. Such accounting effects can be induced by altering accounting accruals [Healy, 1985]. For example, obsolete inventories can be written off or allowances for uncollectible receivables can be increased unexpectedly in the current period. Future period earnings will be higher than previously anticipated to the extent inventory write-offs and uncollectible allowances are lower. Such accounting accrual decisions do not involve changes in accounting procedures (e.g., changing depreciation methods) and are within the scope of management's normal discretion. Moreover, the accrual manipulations are implemented more easily during the first three fiscal quarters since

these earnings are not audited. It is unlikely that managers will change accounting procedures during contract talks since these manipulations are easily observed and the repeated game nature of labor contracts necessitates switching back to the previous procedure after the talks. Hence, this paper examines the time-series pattern of earnings surrounding labor contract talks. In particular, earnings released during contract talks are hypothesized to be lower than earnings released before and after negotiations.

DATA SOURCES

The information regarding union employers, unions, and contract negotiation dates was drawn from two sources. The *Wage Calendar*, published yearly by the U.S. Department of Labor, lists bargaining agreements that cover at least 5,000 employees and that are scheduled to expire in the calendar year. The *Wage Calendar* only follows selected industries, however, so the *Wall Street Journal Index* (*WSJI*) was searched for additional contract signings during the period 1965-1981. Since our tests are conducted on both annual earnings and quarterly earnings, annual and quarterly contract samples were constructed. To be included in the samples, labor contracts identified in the *Wage Calendar* or *WSJI* must meet the following criteria:

1. The negotiating employer is a company with annual earnings data on Compustat for the negotiation year and the following year, or quarterly earnings data, including earnings release dates, on Compustat for the period 1974-1981;
2. The contract is negotiated during the years 1965 through 1981 for the

annual analysis or the years 1974 through 1981 for the quarterly analysis;[4]

3. For annual analysis purposes, the company is listed in *Moody's Industrial Manual* and reports on a calendar-year basis. A calendar-year basis is chosen to simplify assumptions regarding timing of earnings releases (see section on tests of annual data [pp. 709–710]).

4. If the company negotiates with several unions, all labor contracts expire on the same date (If contracts expire at different times, management's incentive to shift income across periods is reduced.);

5. Twenty percent or more of the firm's employees are covered by the contract. Alternative cut-offs of zero and 50 percent also were used without altering the results. The *Wage Calendar* lists the number of employees covered by the contract and Compustat's annual database lists the total number employed.

Table 1 summarizes the data collection results. In the annual sample, each labor contract is negotiated every three or four years, except for ten contracts (representing nine different firms) which cover only 18 months to two years. In the quarterly sample, four contracts of four firms cover less than three years. For the annual and quarterly samples, 576 and 303 company-year contract observations, respectively, are available from the *Wage Calendar* and 658 and 401 are available from the *Wall Street Journal* (*WSJ*). The final annual sample size of 242 contracts represents 105 firms, while in the quarterly sample, 134 contracts represent 85 firms. For both the annual and quarterly contract samples, about 40 to 50 percent of the observations are lost

because the necessary financial information regarding the company is not available on Compustat.

RESEARCH METHOD

This section describes tests of the hypothesis that managers depress earnings during contract talks. Quarterly and annual accounting earnings reported during contract talks were compared to earnings reported at other times. In conducting these tests, certain issues were addressed, such as timing issues involving earnings release dates, the construction and use of control samples of firms, and the selection of earnings expectation models. These issues are discussed in the following subsections.

Timing Issues

Testing whether earnings are reduced during union negotiations requires specifying the particular quarter's or year's earnings number subject to management manipulation. Examining the *WSJI* for 1974–1978 revealed the opening date of negotiations was reported for 19 contracts listed in the *Wage Calendar*. In these instances, the mean duration of the talks was 2.53 months, indicating that, on average, only one quarterly earnings report is released during contract talks. Four of the 19 contract talks exceeded three months. Quarterly or annual earnings numbers released just prior to contract approval are defined as the "negotiation period earnings" and denoted as

---

[4] The year 1965 was selected for the annual earnings tests because this was the first year labor contracts were reported in the *Wage Calendar*. The year 1974 was selected for the quarterly tests because the 1983 Compustat files do not have quarterly earnings data available prior to 1973. Note that mandatory wage and price controls (Nixon's Phase II) were in effect from 11/14/71 to 1/11/73 [Ruback, 1982]. Those controls precede the quarterly test period, but they fall in the middle of the annual earnings test period. Excluding observations during wage and price controls does not alter the results of the annual tests.

TABLE 1

SUMMARY STATISTICS OF THE QUARTERLY AND ANNUAL CONTRACT SAMPLE SELECTION PROCEDURE.
ORIGINAL SAMPLE SIZE BY SOURCE, NUMBER OF CONTRACTS DELETED FOR
VARIOUS REASONS, AND FINAL SAMPLE SIZE.

	Samples			
	Annual		Quarterly	
Number of contracts listed in *Wage Calendar*				
1968–1981	576			
1974–1981			303	
Number of contracts reported in *Wall Street Journal*				
1965–1981		658		
1974–1981				401
Less:				
a) Contracts where company not listed in *Moody's Industrial Manual*	5	—	—	—
b) Contracts listed in *Wage Calendar*	—	89	—	42
c) Contracts where company not on calendar year	43	61	—	—
d) Contracts where information not available on Compustat	240	242	113	222
e) Contracts where employer negotiated with several unions in overlapping time periods	72	82	33	60
f) Contracts covering less than 20% of all employees	56	102	70	30
Total by Source	160	82	87	47
Final Sample (all sources):				
Total number of contracts	242		134	
Number of companies	105		85	
Final sample as a percentage of total possible sample	19.6%		19.0%	

$t=0$ earnings. For example, suppose a contract is signed on August 1, 1976. If earnings for the second quarter ended June 30, 1976 are released in July, the second quarter would be considered as "negotiation period earnings" and denoted $t=0$. If the second quarter's earnings are released in August, the first quarter's income is denoted $t=0$.

Determining the "negotiation period earnings" requires a comparison of the earnings release date to the date the contract was approved. The contract approval date is not available for all the contracts selected from the *Wage Calendar*. Restricting the sample to only those cases where both earnings release dates and contract approval dates are available reduces the sample size by roughly two-thirds. Accordingly, the following procedures determine the negotiation period earnings for the quarterly tests. (The procedure for defining the negotiation period earnings for the annual tests is described later.)

1. For those observations selected from the *Wage Calendar*, the contract approval date is assumed to be the date reported in that publication as the beginning of the new contract period. If the *WSJI* indicates a different date, that date is used as the contract approval date.
2. The negotiation period ($t=0$) is defined as the latest quarter of the fiscal year for which the earnings release date reported on Compustat precedes the contract approval date.

The tests reported in this paper examine the one quarterly earnings number released prior to contract approval or the beginning of the new contract. Subsequent tests reveal that combining quarters $t=0$ and $t=-1$ or defining quarter $t=-1$ as the negotiation quarter does not alter the results.

Control Samples

Two control samples are selected: a random sample and a matched sample. A random sample of 85 firms was chosen to provide information regarding how the contract sample differs from an average Compustat firm. Specifically, every 28th firm of the alphabetically ordered Compustat Quarterly Industrial file was selected to obtain a total of 85 firms. If a randomly selected firm also appeared in the contract sample, it was disregarded and the next alphabetical firm was selected. Each random sample firm was assigned the contract dates of a contract sample firm, where both samples were alphabetically organized.

A sample of matched firms also was selected to control for possible industry

and size effects on the unionized firms' performance. All the tests were replicated substituting this matched control sample for the randomly selected control sample. The matched control sample was constructed by selecting firms in the same four-digit SIC industry with 1978 sales within 25 percent of the contract firm's 1978 sales. When a match did not exist at the four-digit SIC level, three-digit and then two-digit industries were examined for possible matches. Firms that engaged in union contract negotiations but failed to meet the criteria for inclusion in the contract sample were not included in the matched sample. The process reduced the original sample size by 32 percent, from 134 contracts to 91 contracts, because 23 firms could not be matched at the two-, three-, or four-digit SIC level. Contract firms without suitable matches are predominantly in the auto, can, farm equipment, and electrical equipment manufacturing industries.

The matched sample is composed of 61 contracts matched at the four-digit SIC level, seven contracts matched at the three-digit level, and 23 contracts matched at the two-digit level. The matched and random samples produce very similar results, except where noted.

Table 2 summarizes the differences between the contract and random samples. The first two columns indicate that the mean 1978 sales, total assets, number of employees, market value, and the ratio of long-term debt to market value of the contract firms exceed the respective means of the random sample firms at the .05 level (two-tail t-test).[5] These

---

[5] Since some of the firms have multiple labor contracts, data for the year 1978 are used to compare the contract and random sample firms. This procedure prevents firms with multiple contracts from dominating the results by entering the comparison more than once. The year 1978 is chosen because it is the middle year of the quarterly contract sample period.

TABLE 2

COMPARISON OF CONTRACT SAMPLE AND RANDOM SAMPLE FIRMS IN 1978
(LEVELS IN MILLIONS OF DOLLARS)

	1978 Levels		Ratio of 1981 to 1974 Levels	
	Contract Sample	Random Sample	Contract Sample	Random Sample
Number of firms*	85	85	85	85
Mean Sales	$3,537	$ 675	1.987	3.115
Standard Deviation	8,550	1,353	.761	3.417
Median	980	191	1.785	2.328
t-statistic		3.05***	−2.88***	
Mean Total Assets	$2,464	$ 580	1.909	2.636
Standard Deviation	4,602	1,066	.628	2.465
Median	942	187	1.880	2.000
t-statistic		3.68***	−2.56***	
Mean Number of Employees	48,984	10,003	1.037	1.992
Standard Deviation	114,776	18,664	.483	3.202
Median	18,195	2,762	.982	1.206
t-statistic		3.07***	−2.62***	
Mean Firm Market Value**	$1,420	$ 480	2.255	4.529
Standard Deviation	2,570	1,091	1.141	6.679
Median	561	121	1.991	2.467
t-statistic		3.10***	−3.02***	
Mean (Long-Term Debt/ Market Value)	.389	.309	1.081	1.091
Standard Deviation	.208	.228	1.148	1.652
Median	.394	.287	.856	.812
t-statistic		2.39***	−.04	
Mean (Net Income/Total Assets)	−.041	.059	.836	.545
Standard Deviation	.880	.089	3.350	10.060
Median	.047	.067	.984	.905
t-statistic		1.04	.25	
Mean Market Model Beta	.851	1.010		
Standard Deviation	.321	.413		
Median	.799	.932		
t-statistic		−22.16***		

* Firms remaining after excluding contracts where less than 20 percent of employees are covered.
** Book Value of Long-Term Debt + Book Value of Preferred Stock + Market Value of Common Stock at Year-End.
*** Difference in means of contract and random sample firms is significant at .05 level (two-tail t-test).

findings reveal that our sample of contract firms is biased toward larger firms. The contract firms also have statistically significantly smaller common stock betas. While not statistically significant, the contract firms have lower returns on assets than the random sample firms in 1978. Additional evidence on the relative profitability of the two samples is provided in the section on test results.

The last two columns of Table 2 report growth ratios for the two samples over the period 1974–1981. The contract sample experienced nominal growth in sales, assets, number of employees, and market value. The random sample experienced statistically significantly greater growth in these variables over the same period.

Recomputing the Table 2 summary statistics using the matched sample and the reduced contract sample (not reported) produces no statistically significant differences in any of the first two columns' variables, except that the unionized firms continue to have a lower mean market model beta (t-statistic of -8.46). Thus, the matching procedure controls for firm size, number of employees, market value, and leverage. However, some mean growth ratios still differ significantly betwen the contract and matched samples. The ratios of 1981 to 1974 levels for sales and market values are lower for the contract than the matched samples (t-statistics of -1.72 and -2.17, respectively). The matched sample performed better than the unionized firms over the period 1974 to 1981.

Earnings Expectation Models

To assess whether annual or quarterly earnings are manipulated by management, we compare actual to expected earnings for all negotiation and surrounding periods. Annual earnings are assumed to follow a random walk. Unexpected annual earnings are then the difference between the current year's and the previous year's earnings.[6] Unexpected quarterly earnings are estimated using two expectations models. The first model [see Foster, 1977 and Benston and Watts, 1978] accounts for the seasonality

of quarterly earnings and any trend contained in the most recent quarterly income figures. Unexpected earnings for firm i at quarter t, FE_{it}, are calculated as:

$$FE_{it} = Q_{it} - (Q_{it-4} + \hat{a}_i + \hat{b}_i(Q_{it-1} - Q_{it-5})) \quad (1)$$

where Q_{it} is firm i's earnings per share in the year t and $\hat{a}_i$ and $\hat{b}_i$ are the estimated coefficients.

Forty quarters of earnings data, the maximum available on Compustat, are employed in the analysis.[7] Reported tests use nominal earnings per share figures adjusted for changes in the number of shares. (Deflating earnings in quarter t by the Consumer Price Index at the start of quarter t does not alter the findings.) All quarters except negotiation quarters are included in the estimation.[8] As an alternative estimation procedure, only quarters preceding the negotiation quarter are used, provided that at least ten quarterly observations are present. This alternative procedure, whereby the earnings expectation model is re-estimated for each contract negotiation, produces results (not reported) very similar to those reported.

The second quarterly expectations

[6] Analysts' forecasts were not used as expected earnings because analysts might factor into their forecasts managers' income-reducing tendencies surrounding labor contract negotiations, thereby reducing the power of the tests.

[7] Compustat figures are the final earnings numbers, not the "as reported," preliminary numbers in the WSJ. To check the possibility that managers release lower preliminary numbers during contract negotiations and report higher final numbers, we compared the Compustat figures to earnings as announced in the WSJI. Tests based on a subsample of the firms over the fiscal years 1974–1978 failed to reject the null hypothesis that earnings revisions and negotiation quarters are independent.

[8] The negotiation quarter is excluded only when calculating the dependent variable $Q_{it} - Q_{it-4}$, where the negotiation quarter is Q_{it}. This results in about one of every 12 observations being deleted (since labor contracts generally are negotiated every three years).

model employed assumes expected earnings this quarter are equal to actual earnings four quarters ago. Hence, unexpected earnings are:

$$FE'_{it} = Q_{it} - Q_{it-4} \qquad (2)$$

Neither unexpected earnings model controls for real production (cash flow) effects produced by union wage negotiations. For example, if wages rise following negotiations, earnings in quarters +1, +2, . . . are lower than in quarter 0. The lack of Compustat data on total wage bills precludes adequate control for these wage adjustments. Accordingly, the tests assume these effects are small and do not mask managers' accounting manipulations.

Besides testing whether unexpected annual earnings in negotiation periods differ from unexpected earnings in non-negotiation periods, unexpected annual accounting accruals also are examined.[9] Using accounting accruals is a more powerful test if accruals are subject to managerial manipulation surrounding contract talks and cash flows are not manipulated. Annual accruals are assumed to follow a random walk. The hypothesis is that management manipulates accounting accruals (the difference between reported earnings and cash flows) during contract negotiations. Three approximations of accounting accruals are used: (1) the sum of the changes in accounts receivable and inventories less the sum of depreciation, the change in accounts payable, the change in income taxes payable, and deferred taxes (see Healy [1985]); (2) the change in accounts receivable; and (3) the change in inventory balances. For each of the three accrual measures, the total accruals for the negotiation period and the preceding period are compared. Increases or decreases in a measure from one period to the next are noted.

TEST RESULTS

The test results do not support the hypothesis that managers depress earnings released during labor contract talks. The quarterly results are presented first, followed by the annual results.

Tests of Quarterly Data

As described above, equation (1) is used as one method for estimating unexpected quarterly earnings in the negotiation quarter. Individual time-series models are estimated for each firm in the contract, matched, and random samples using up to 35 quarterly observations. The fewest number of observations in any estimation is 20. We first present various time series of quarterly earnings surrounding the negotiation quarter. Then the results of estimating expected quarterly earnings time-series models and their interpretations are presented.

The Time-Series Behavior of Quarterly Earnings Surrounding Labor Negotiations. The analysis examines the time-series behavior of earnings surrounding the negotiation quarter (quarter 0). To measure unexpected earnings activity around the negotiation quarter, two standardized variables are calculated for each firm in "event time." The results are presented in Table 3, where $t=0$ denotes the quarterly earnings release preceding the end of the contract negotiation. The variables are calculated beginning seven quarters prior to and ending four quarters following the negotiation period. A three-year time span is employed, as most contracts examined were renegotiated every three years. In only four cases was a contract negotiated to cover an 18-month to two-year time period. For these observations, only

---

[9] Quarterly accruals are not examined due to the lack of balance sheet data on the quarterly Compustat database.

those quarters between contracts are included in the calculations.

Two standardized variables are reported. Computed for each contract, they then are weighted equally in averaging the results across observations in event time.[10]

$$(Q_t - E(Q_t))/SD_{FE} \qquad (3)$$

$$(Q_t - Q_{t-4})/SD_{lag} \qquad (4)$$

where

Q_t = earnings per share in quarter t, adjusted for changes in the common stock base;

$Q_t - E(Q_t)$ = unexpected earnings per share in quarter t using equation (1);

SD_{FE} = standard deviation of the forecast error, $Q_t - E(Q_t)$;

SD_{lag} = standard deviation of the seasonally differenced quarterly earnings per share $Q - Q_{t-4}$.

The first ratio is unexpected earnings from equation (1) deflated by the standard deviation of the forecast errors. The second ratio, based on equation (2), is the change in earnings from the fourth preceding quarter deflated by the standard deviation of that change in earnings. Time series of the standardized variables' cross-sectional means (equations 3 and 4) are computed and reported for both the contract and random samples. Also, the time series of cross-sectional mean *differences* between the contract and random samples are computed. Differences are computed for each matched pair (i.e., the contract sample firm's standardized variable less the corresponding random sample firm's standardized variable). All tests were replicated (not reported) using the reduced contract and matched samples.

As noted earlier, event time for the random and matched sample firms corresponds to the negotiation quarter of the corresponding contract firm. The first alphabetically arranged random firm is assigned the contract dates of the first alphabetically arranged contract firm, and so forth. A matched sample firm is assigned the contract dates of its corresponding contract firm.

Table 3 indicates that quarters 0 and -1 are not depressed relative to other quarters. Hypothesis tests are conducted on both the contract sample's time series of standardized variables (the first two columns of Table 3) and the differenced (contract less random sample) time series (last two columns of Table 3). Two empirical tests are conducted: (1) mean standardized unexpected earnings in quarters -1 and 0 are compared to mean standardized unexpected earnings in quarters -7 to -2, and (2) the mean standardized unexpected earnings in quarter zero is compared to the mean in quarter $+1$. Parametric two-tail t-tests and nonparametric Wilcoxon ranks tests are used to assess statistical significance.

The first test (i.e., the mean standardized unexpected earnings in quarters -1 and 0 compared to mean standardized unexpected earnings in quarters -7 to -2) does not result in any statistically

---

[10] Alternative measures (not reported) also were calculated without changing any inferences. For example, quarterly earnings or seasonally differenced quarterly earnings were divided by either the firm's share price at the beginning of quarter t or the share price at the end of quarter t. These two variables control for the market's expectations of changes in cash flows. If managers depress reported earnings and not cash flows during contract talks, earnings will fall but share price will not change. These ratios bias the tests in favor of finding the hypothesized time-series pattern if wages unexpectedly rise following contract talks. In this case, unexpected cash flows and stock prices fall, causing the earnings-to-price ratio to rise during the talks. In spite of this bias, the calculated mean earnings-to-price ratios are inconsistent with managers depressing earnings during labor negotiations.

TABLE 3

AVERAGE STANDARDIZED QUARTERLY EARNINGS IN EVENT TIME.
QUARTER ZERO IS THE EARNINGS RELEASED PRIOR TO THE END OF CONTRACT NEGOTIATION

Quarter	Contract Sample		Random Sample		Differenced Ratios (Contract—Random)	
	$(Q_t - E(Q_t))$ $/SD_{FE}$	$(Q_t - Q_{t-4})$ $/SD_{lag}$	$(Q_t - E(Q_t))$ $/SD_{FE}$	$(Q_t - Q_{t-4})$ $/SD_{lag}$	$(Q_t - E(Q_t))$ $/SD_{FE}$	$(Q_t - Q_{t-4})$ $/SD_{lag}$
-7	-.032	.056	-.028	.054	-.004	.002
-6	.310	.353	.006	.089	.304	.264
-5	.139	.242	.013	.111	.126	.131
-4	.003	.159	.051	.231	-.048	-.072
-3	.106	.180	-.062	.145	.168	.035
-2	-.074	.083	-.004	.217	-.070	-.134
-1	-.100	.001	.007	.159	-.107	-.158
0	.082	.138	-.062	.108	.144	.030
1	-.182**	-.069*	.060	.205	-.242**	-.274**
2	-.036	-.030	.035	.141	-.071	-.171
3	-.063	.006	-.108	.109	.045	-.103
4	-.031	-.008	-.053	.112	.022	-.120

* Significantly different from quarter zero at .10 level using two-tail t-test.
** Significantly different from quarter zero at .05 level using two-tail t-test and Wilcoxon two-tail ranks tests.

Q_t = earnings per share in quarter t,
$E(Q_t)$ = expected quarterly earnings from the autoregressive time-series model,
SD_{FE} = standard deviation of the forecast errors from the autoregressive time-series model, and
SD_{lag} = standard deviation of $Q_t - Q_{t-4}$.

significant differences using either the t-test or Wilcoxon test. Under the second test, both standardized variables' means in quarter zero are statistically larger than the corresponding means in quarter $+1$ at the .10 level (two-tail t-test) in the contract sample (first two columns of Table 3) and when contract and random samples are differenced (last two columns). However, the decline in the standardized variables from quarter 0 to quarter $+1$ is opposite the hypothesized change (i.e., managers are predicted to increase earnings following contract talks). Wages rising and accounting earnings falling following contract signing would induce the observed time-series pattern. All the preceding tests were repeated using the matched control sample in place of the random sample and no test statistic achieved statistical

significance. These findings are inconsistent with the hypothesis that managers depress earnings before wage settlements.[11]

[11] The reported standardized earnings' means in Table 3 are higher in quarter zero than the two quarters preceding contract talks and in the quarter following contract signing. Real production effects that mask any accounting manipulations might explain this time-series pattern. For example, during labor talks, production might be raised in anticipation of labor strikes. Higher production levels cause unit costs to fall and total profits to rise under absorption costing. If production is cut after contract signing, unit costs rise and total profits fall.

To test for real changes in production levels surrounding labor talks, quarterly inventory data were collected. Forty-eight of the 121 sample contracts for industrial firms reported quarterly inventory levels in *Moody's Industrial Manual*. Two ratios were calculated: inventory in quarter t divided by quarter $t-1$ sales and the change in inventory from quarter $t-1$ to t divided by quarter $t-1$ sales. The ratios were calculated for t ranging from quarter -7 to $+4$. There is no evidence indicating that inventory levels rise during or preceding contract talks. These findings are consistent with those

TABLE 4

SUMMARY STATISTICS FROM ESTIMATING THE AUTOREGRESSIVE MODEL OVER
1974–1981 FOR 85 CONTRACT FIRMS AND 85 RANDOM SAMPLE FIRMS.
NEGOTIATION QUARTERS ARE EXCLUDED FROM THE ESTIMATION.

$$Q_{it} - Q_{it-4} = a_i + b_i(Q_{it-1} - Q_{it-5}) + \epsilon_{it}$$

Contract Sample (N=85)

	Intercept	Slope	R^{2a}	Residual Autocorrelation Coefficients				
				Lag 1	Lag 2	Lag 3	Lag 4	Lag 5
Mean	−.011	.357	.183	.039*	.006	−.026	−.271*	−.021
Median	.009	.375	.120	.006	−.005	−.019	−.295	−.023
Std. Dev.	.146	.278	.196	.118	.140	.154	.188	.155
% Negative	43.5%	10.5%	—	44.7%	52.9%	57.6%	90.6%	56.5%

Random Sample (N=85)

	Intercept	Slope	R^2	Residual Autocorrelation Coefficients				
				Lag 1	Lag 2	Lag 3	Lag 4	Lag 5
Mean	.031	.317	.154	.011	.026	−.020	−.195*	.000
Median	.017	.312	.087	.002	.009	−.013	−.174	−.004
Std. Dev.	.100	.282	.170	.102	.157	.155	.188	.163
% Negative	25.8%	10.6%	—	47.0%	44.7%	52.9%	85.9%	51.8%

Results of two-tail t-tests of differences of means for contract and random samples:

	t-statistic	Significance
Intercept	−2.226	.027
Slope	.921	.358

* Significantly different from zero at 1% level (two-tail t-test).
^a Unadjusted R^2.

Results of Estimating the Quarterly Time-Series Model. Summary statistics of the autoregressive model estimations for the contract and random samples are presented in Table 4. Included are the average estimated coefficients, unadjusted R^2 figures, and residual autocorrelation coefficients.

A relatively large proportion (43.5 percent) of contract sample firms has a negative estimated intercept. In comparison, 25.8 percent of the random sample firms have negative intercepts. The esti-

mated mean intercepts of the two samples differ significantly, as indicated by the two-tail t-tests of the differences of means. The mean slope coefficient in the contract sample, while not statistically significantly larger than in the random sample, indicates that seasonally differenced

---

reported by Tracy [1985]. He finds that changes in inventory to sales are unrelated to strike activity around contract talks.

The preceding tests do not control for the higher wage bills after contract signing.

earnings are more highly serially correlated in the contract sample than in
the random sample. This higher correlation likely is due to the contract
sample being composed of larger firms,
whose year to year fluctuations are typically less pronounced than the fluctuations in the random sample's smaller
firms. On average, the contract sample
firms have slightly higher unadjusted
R^2's than the random sample firms.
Both samples have relatively large fourth-
order residual autocorrelation. This
residual autocorrelation is not captured
by the simple autoregressive model. A
second regressor, $(Q_{t-4}-Q_{t-8})$, was
added to the regression to include the
dependence (results not reported). This
reduced the contract sample's mean
fourth-order autocorrelation to $-.079$,
while that of the random sample was
lowered to $-.049$. These autocorrelations still differ significantly from zero
but are substantially smaller than those
calculated without the additional regressor. Other parameters in Table 4 were
not materially altered by the addition of
the second regressor, except the mean
and median unadjusted R^2 rose to
approximately .40 for both samples. All
the tests were replicated using the multiple regression with $(Q_{t-4}-Q_{t-8})$, and
none of the study's inferences are
changed.

Summary statistics in Table 4 were
recomputed using the 62 contract firms
and their matched counterparts (not
reported). The mean intercepts of the
matched and reduced contract samples
are no longer statistically different. The
contract sample mean and median intercepts ($-.007$ and .012) are slightly higher
than those reported in Table 4 and the
matched sample mean and median intercepts ($-.001$ and .015) are slightly lower
than the random sample's mean and
median.

The smaller intercepts of the contract
firms relative to those of the random
sample indicate that these firms had
smaller drift in seasonally differenced
quarterly earnings than the randomly
selected firms over the time period of
1974–81.[12] The contract sample's smaller
drift is consistent with the contract firms
exhibiting poor operating performance
relative to that of the random sample.[13]
This possibility is examined next.

If the contract firms incurred real cash
flow declines over the period 1973–1982,
and if these declines were not fully anticipated by the market, then stock returns
of the contract firms should exhibit
negative abnormal performance and the
random sample should not. Monthly
equity rates of returns are obtained from
the CRSP file for the period 6/69–12/81.
For each sample firm i, abnormal performance in month t is calculated using the
simple market model estimated over the
60 months preceding month t. Then the
one-period forward prediction error,
PE_{it}, is calculated using the estimated
market model coefficients:

$$PE_{it}=R_{it}-(\hat{\alpha}_{it}+\hat{\beta}_{it}R_{mt})$$

$R_{it}=$continuously compounded
(log transform) rate of return
of firm i in month t;

$R_{mt}=$continuously compounded
(log transform) equally-
weighted market index in
month t;

---

[12] The sign of the drift of seasonally differenced earnings depends on the sign of the intercept if the process is
stationary. See Pindyck and Rubinfeld [1981, p. 520].

[13] Poor operating performance and the smaller intercepts in the quarterly earnings time-series models might
be due to managers in the unionized firms using different accounting procedures than managers in randomly selected firms. No differences were found between
the accounting method choices of the two samples.
Examined choices included depreciation, inventory,
investment tax credits, and amortization of past service
costs.

TABLE 5

CUMULATIVE ABNORMAL RETURNS (CAR) FROM MARKET MODEL REGRESSIONS 7/74–12/81
EQUALLY WEIGHTED MARKET INDEX
CONTRACT, RANDOM, AND MATCHED SAMPLES
(Z-STATISTICS IN PARENTHESES)

Time Period	No. of Months	Contract Less Random Sample (85 firms)			Contract Less Matched Sample (62 firms)		
		Contract	Random	Difference	Contract	Matched	Difference
A. 7/74–12/81	90	−.233 *	.009	−.242	−.119	−.099	−.020
		(−1.530)	(.060)	(−1.220)	(−.890)	(−.730)	(−.130)
B. 7/74–12/76	30	.000	−.007	.007	.066	.036	.030
		(.000)	(−.070)	(.060)	(.760)	(.400)	(.260)
C. 1/77–6/79	30	−.226 **	−.006	−.220 **	−.185 **	−.131 **	−.054
		(−2.760)	(−.120)	(−1.990)	(−3.050)	(−2.050)	(−.870)
D. 7/79–12/81	30	−.008	.022	−.030	−.008	−.004	.004
		(−.080)	(.290)	(−.250)	(−.080)	(−.050)	(.040)

* Statistically significant at the .10 level (one-tail *t*-test)
** Statistically significant at the .05 level (one-tail *t*-test)

$\hat{\alpha}_{it}, \hat{\beta}_{it}$ = coefficients from estimating the market model over t-61 to t-1.

The estimated coefficients ($\hat{\alpha}_{it}$ and $\hat{\beta}_{it}$) are updated for each month t by reestimating the market model using the most recent 60 observations. The average monthly portfolio abnormal rate of return, PE_{pt}, where p is the contract or random sample, is generated by equally weighting the monthly prediction errors of the sample p firms. The monthly prediction errors are then summed to derive cumulative abnormal returns (CAR) for each sample over the period 7/74 to 12/81.

Table 5 reports cumulative abnormal returns for the contract, random, and matched samples over the entire period of 7/74 to 12/81 (Row A) and the three equal subperiods comprising the entire period (Rows B, C, and D). The first three columns of Table 5 compare the entire contract sample to the random sample. The last three columns of Table 5 compare the reduced contract sample

to the matched control sample. Matching by industry and size decreases the contract sample from 85 firms to 62 firms. Over the entire period (row A), the contract sample experiences a statistically insignificant relative decline of 24.2 percent compared to the random sample and a two percent relative decline compared to the matched sample.[14] Only for the subperiod 1/77 to 6/79 are cumulative abnormal returns of the contract sample relative to those of the random sample statistically different from zero. During this same subperiod, the reduced contract and matched samples have sta-

[14] Under the assumption that the monthly average prediction errors are independent and identically distributed, a Z-statistic is calculated to assess significance. The Z-statistic is computed as:

$$Z = \frac{\frac{1}{n} \sum_{i=1}^{n} PE_{pi}}{(\sigma^2(PE_{pi})/n)^{1/2}}$$

where n is the number of months in the cumulation and $\sigma^2(PE_{pi})$ is the variance of the calculated portfolio prediction errors across time.

tistically significant negative CAR's of 18.5 percent and 13.1 percent, respectively. However, the paired difference (contract less matched) is not different from zero.

The findings in Table 5 are consistent with the contract firms experiencing unanticipated cash flow declines over at least a portion of the sample period. These reduced cash flows were not restricted to unionized firms but extended to similarly sized firms in the same industry.

The contract firms reported a negative mean earnings to total assets ratio in 1978 (Table 2) while the random firms reported a positive mean accounting rate of return. The matched sample firms also had a positive mean accounting rate of return in 1978 (not presented). These results are consistent with a study by Clark [1984] who finds that the presence of unions reduces accounting rates of return after controlling for firm, industry, and market differences.

Sensitivity Analysis. Additional tests were conducted to ascertain the sensitivity of the results to various assumptions. These are described briefly below.

(a) The preceding tests assume that the last quarterly earnings announced before the new contract begins is the one likely to be depressed. However, in some contract talks, quarters -1, -2, or -3 might be reduced. To test this possibility, for each contract and the two standardized measures, the quarter with the smallest earnings measure over quarters -7 through $+4$ is identified. Then, for each quarter i, the frequency across contracts of the smallest measure is constructed. A Kolmogorov-Smirnov test using the random sample's distribution of frequencies as the expected distribution fails to reject the null hypothesis of no difference between the random and contract samples.[15]

(b) The net benefits of earnings manipulations might be less in times of financial distress than at other times. Managers' incentives to reduce earnings decline if the likelihood of bond covenant default is higher. Likewise, unions might have better alternative sources of information regarding firm performance during financial downturns (e.g., layoffs and plant closings) than during other times. To test this possibility, the contract sample is split based on the sign of the time-series model intercept. Tests conducted in Table 3 on the standardized variables are repeated first for firms with negative time-series model intercepts and then for firms with positive intercepts. Under the hypothesis being tested, the positive intercept subsample should exhibit earnings manipulations more frequently in quarter zero than firms with negative intercepts. The evidence (not reported) does not support this hypothesis.

Labor strikes also reduce the power of the tests if strikes increase earnings fluctuations or if strikes affect managers' incentives to manipulate earnings. The evidence (not reported) does not support this conjecture. The *WSJI* was examined for evidence of strike activity surrounding contract talks. The contract sample is split according to whether a strike did or did not occur in the three months preceding the new contract's approval. The 85 contract talks (63 percent of the sample) not involving strikes have statistically insignificantly greater earnings in quarter 0 than quarter $+1$ under both standardized measures.

Finally, since layoffs are easily ob-

---

[15] A chi-squared test which assumes that the expected frequency of the lowest earnings measure is equal across quarters also is calculated for the two standardized measures. The null hypothesis of no difference between the actual and expected frequencies is not rejected.

served by unions, earnings manipulations are likely to have less impact on negotiations when firm employment is declining. The contract sample is split on the negative or non-negative firm-wide employment change in the year of contract talks from the preceding year. Neither subsample (i.e., decreased and not decreased employment) evidences depressed earnings during labor talks.

(c) Each preceding test uses average results across all observations. It is possible that managers systematically reduce only the large positive unexpected earnings, the effect of which is diluted in the means. One possibility is that managers are more likely to decrease earnings when forecast errors (i.e., unexpected earnings) are positive. To test this hypothesis, the largest 20 percent of standardized forecast errors in negotiation quarters is compared to the largest 20 percent of forecast errors in non-negotiation quarters.

The means of the largest 20 percent of standardized unexpected earnings in negotiation quarters are not statistically significantly smaller than the means of the top 20 percent of forecast errors in all other quarters. These findings reject the hypothesis of earnings manipulations when large positive unexpected earnings are realized in negotiation quarters.

(d) We further hypothesize that the motivation to manipulate earnings is greater if the employer is the first company in the industry to negotiate a new (three-year) contract with a specific union. Using the companies reported in the *Wage Calendar*, the test statistics in Table 3 are recomputed for contracts in which the company was the first in its industry (as defined by two-digit SIC code) to have contract talks. It is concluded that the timing of contract negotiation within the industry does not alter the previous findings.

(e) Finally, if the negotiation quarter (i.e., quarter zero) was the fourth quarter, it is deleted and the analysis is performed using the remaining data. This test eliminates two potentially confounding effects: (1) the presence of an annual audit, which reduces management's discretion over fourth-quarter results, and (2) the effect of management compensation plans. Managers are less likely to reduce reported earnings in the fourth quarter, because the bonus pool, and hence, management compensation, is reduced.[16] If negotiation period earnings occur prior to the fourth fiscal quarter and they are depressed, the compensation pool is unaffected to the extent earnings following $t=0$ are raised. Deleting all fourth-quarter negotiation quarters does not alter the previous findings.

Tests of Annual Data

Like the quarterly findings, tests of annual earnings reject the hypothesis that managers depress earnings during labor talks. In particular, the following analyses were conducted:

Alternative Earnings Measures. The annual sample of contract firms is examined using a random walk model for expected earnings, as described earlier. We use three alternative measures of earnings: (1) adjusted earnings per share, (2) net income after extraordinary items, and (3) income available to common stockholders. In addition, three alternative definitions for changes in annual accounting accruals are used: total accruals, the change in receivables, and the change in inventories. Use of these measures is unable to reject the null hypoth-

---

[16] This statement assumes that annual earnings are between the lower and upper bounds that constrain the size of the bonus pool. See Healy [1985].

esis of no depressed earnings during union contract talks.

Alternative Timing Conventions. As noted earlier, all firms in the annual sample report on a calendar-year basis. In all annual analyses, when contracts are negotiated within seven months of a calendar year's close, the "negotiation period" chosen as year zero is the most recently completed fiscal year (e.g., all contract negotiations completed from January 1976 through July 1976 defined 1975 earnings as the negotiation period earnings). To test the sensitivity to this July timing convention, May, June, and August conventions also are used. Also, the sample of firms is restricted further in one test to only those contracts signed between May and July. These contract talks are the most likely to have been exposed to last year's earnings and, hence, the test should have the most power. Again, there is no evidence that managers depress earnings during contract talks.

Alternative Test Statistics. Test statistics are calculated defining year 0 as the negotiation period and years -1 and $+1$ as the non-negotiation periods. Two-by-two contingency tables of the frequencies of positive/negative unexpected earnings (or accruals) in the negotiation and non-negotiation periods are constructed. Then, chi-squared statistics are computed. Negotiation periods will show larger frequencies of negative unexpected earnings than non-negotiation periods if managers depress earnings during contract talks. Chi-squared statistics fail to reject the hypothesis that managers reduce earnings during labor talks. Also, the mean standardized unexpected earnings (or accruals) in the negotiation year and the subsequent year are calculated and found to be insignificantly different. In no case is the proportion of negative unexpected earnings in the negotiation period significantly greater than in the following year. In most cases, the proportion of negative forecast earnings is greater in the year after the negotiation period. The proportion of the annual sample with declines in accruals also is calculated for the two periods, with no change in the results.

INTERPRETATIONS AND SUMMARY

The tests reported in this paper are inconsistent with the hypothesis that managers reduce earnings reported during labor contract negotiations. Three (non-mutually exclusive) interpretations of the findings exist. First, as the firms were experiencing poor real operating performance, managers did not adjust earnings during the sample period. Second, no manipulations occurred, as unions can undo them. Third, the tests lack sufficient power to detect management's earnings adjustments. These explanations are discussed below.

(1) During the sample period (roughly 1969–1981), the unionized firms performed poorly and, hence, managers in these firms had little incentive to depress reported earnings during contract talks. Three pieces of evidence suggest that the unionized firms had financial difficulties during the test period. First, negative accounting rates of return and smaller growth rates for the contract sample compared to the random sample are reported in Table 2. Second, average negative drift in seasonally differenced earnings among contract firms is reported in Table 4. And third, Table 5 shows that the unionized firms had negative abnormal stock returns during the sample period. A matched sample of similarly sized firms from related industries also performed poorly over the sample period, providing some evidence that the contract sample's poor performance should not be attributed entirely

to unionization. However, the contract sample had statistically significantly smaller growth in sales and market value during 1974 to 1981 than its matched counterparts, indicating some real costs of unionization.

Under this interpretation of the findings, the costs to managers of further depressing accounting earnings during contract talks likely exceed the benefits. This suggests that managers of these unionized firms possibly depressed earnings during contract talks when their firms were profitable, but such earnings manipulations were abandoned when the firms were less profitable.

(2) The unions can undo managers' accounting manipulations. Managers engage in (costly) earnings manipulations if the unions are unable to adjust completely the reported numbers. However, union officials have incentives to undo managers' accounting manipulations if such manipulations affect labor negotiations. Reynolds [1978, p. 390] claims that, with so much at stake, union officials are financially sophisticated and able to accurately assess the firm's and industry's financial position independently of management's disclosures. If the unions are able to undo managers' manipulations, there is no reason for managers to engage in this costly exercise.

The tests performed in this paper rely on publicly available data (i.e., past earnings). Labor officials can undo managers' adjustments to the same extent that our tests can detect such manipulations unless, because of large sample sizes, our tests are more powerful than the unions' ability to adjust the numbers. The implicit assumption in this and other papers is that the tests are sufficiently powerful to detect manipulations given that they occur, while non-managers (voters, politicians, unions, or boards of directors) are unable to completely adjust for such manipulations.

(3) Managers manipulate reported earnings to affect labor negotiations but the tests lack sufficient power to detect such manipulations. Several reasons can explain the low power of the tests. First, the normal variability in quarterly or annual earnings is large relative to the amount of earnings manipulation during labor talks. While our tests are based on at most 242 observations, this might not be large enough to reduce standard errors.

Second, the tests lack power because it is difficult to specify which quarterly or annual figure is subject to manipulation. Although different timing assumptions are used, it is unlikely that any given assumption applies to all observations. In contrast, Healy [1985] can identify which annual earnings number is subject to manipulation since the compensation contract specifies how the bonus pool is related to reported earnings.

Finally, the tests lack power because they do not control for the effect of union contract talks on the firm's cash flows. For example, higher wages following the contract reduce earnings, thereby masking any managerial accounting manipulations and reducing the power of the tests.

Contracts that explicitly use accounting numbers have been found to affect managers' accounting choices. Presumably, implicit uses of accounting numbers also can affect accounting decisions. It was expected that labor contract talks, while not explicitly based on accounting numbers, would implicitly use those numbers in the negotiation process, thereby creating incentives for managers to manipulate earnings. Labor contract talks are like the political process in their implicit use of accounting numbers, but are unlike the political process in that only earnings released during contract talks are subject to manipulation. In our sample of firms, there is no evidence that the benefits of adjusting earnings (i.e., the anticipated wage savings) exceed the cost (i.e., reduced management compensation and/or technical default costs on debt covenants). Alternatively, the benefits might exceed the costs, but the earnings adjustments, being too small relative to the normal variance of earnings, are difficult to detect.

Three related papers also examine managers' incentives to manipulate earnings. Healy [1985] analyzes the role of accounting numbers in executive compensation contracts. DeAngelo [1986a and 1986b] analyzes the time-series behavior of accounting numbers surrounding (a) proxy contests and (b) negotiated management buyouts in "going private" transactions. Healy hypothesizes that managers can increase their bonuses by manipulating accounting accruals. In DeAngelo [1986a], managers are hypothesized to raise reported earnings before the resolution of proxy contests to increase their likelihood of winning the election. DeAngelo [1986b] hypothesizes that managers can decrease the price they pay outside shareholders when they take the firm private by low-ering reported income prior to the "going private" transaction. Like the present study, these three papers assume that costly information prevents non-managers (e.g., unions, boards of directors, stockholders, and their financial advisors) from fully adjusting the reported numbers for any managerial opportunism.

Healy [1985] and DeAngelo [1986a] find evidence of managerial manipulation of earnings surrounding bonus determination and proxy contests, whereas DeAngelo [1986b] and the present study are unable to document any managerial opportunism. Assuming that the tests have sufficient power to detect manipulation and that such manipulation benefits managers because the outside parties are unable to make offsetting adjustments, the four studies' conflicting results suggest that (a) managers' perceived benefits of earnings manipulation differ across contracts and situations and/or (b) non-managers have either different information costs or different incentives to acquire information. These four studies and subsequent ones will help delineate the nature and magnitude of managers' perceived benefits of earnings adjustments and non-managers' information costs and their incentives for information acquisition.

REFERENCES

Ashenfelter, O., and G. Johnson, "Bargaining Theory, Trade Unions, and Industrial Strike Activity," *American Economic Review* (March 1969), pp. 35–49.

Baldwin, C., "Productivity and Labor Unions: An Application of the Theory of Self-Enforcing Contracts," *Journal of Business* (April 1983), pp. 155–185.

Benston, G., and R. Watts, "The Market's Forecast of Earnings," Unpublished paper (University of Rochester, 1978).

Cartter, A. M., *Theory of Wages and Employment* (Richard D. Irwin, Inc., 1959).

Christie, A., "Aggregation of Test Statistics: An Evaluation of the Consistency of Evidence on Contracting and Size Hypotheses," Unpublished paper (University of Southern California, 1986).

Clark, K. B., "Unionization and Firm Performance: The Impact on Profits, Growth, and Productivity," *American Economic Review* (December 1984), pp. 893–919.

DeAngelo, L. E., "Managerial Competition, Information Costs, and Corporate Governance: The Use of Accounting Performance Measures in Proxy Contests," Working paper (University of Rochester, 1986a).

———, "Accounting Numbers as Market Valuation Substitutes: A Study of Management Buyouts of Public Stockholders," THE ACCOUNTING REVIEW (July 1986b), pp. 400–420.

Farber, H. S., "Bargaining Theory, Wage Outcomes and the Occurrence of Strikes: An Econometric Analysis," *American Economic Review* (June 1978), pp. 267–271.

Foster, G., "Quarterly Accounting Data: Time Series Properties and Predictive Ability Results," THE ACCOUNTING REVIEW (January 1977), pp. 1–21.

Healy, P. M., "The Impact of Bonus Schemes on Accounting Choices," *Journal of Accounting & Economics* (April 1985), pp. 85–107.

Holthausen, R. W., and R. W. Leftwich, "The Economic Consequences of Accounting Choice: Implications of Costly Contracting and Monitoring," *Journal of Accounting & Economics* (August 1983), pp. 77–117.

Larcker, D., and J. Balkcom, "Executive Compensation Contracts and Investment Behavior: An Analysis of Mergers," Working paper (Northwestern University, 1984).

Pindyck, R. S., and D. L. Rubinfeld, *Econometric Models and Economic Forecasts*, 2nd Ed. (McGraw-Hill Book Company, 1981).

Rees, A., *The Economics of Work and Pay* (Harper and Row Publishers, 1973).

Reynolds, L. G., *Labor Economics and Labor Relations*, 7th Edition (Prentice-Hall, Inc., 1978).

Ruback, R. S., "The Effect of Discretionary Price Control Decisions on Equity Values," *Journal of Financial Economics* (March 1982), pp. 83–105.

Tracy, J. S., "Contract Negotiations and Strikes," Unpublished working paper (Yale University, 1985).

Watts, R. L., and J. L. Zimmerman, *Positive Accounting Theory* (Prentice-Hall, Inc., 1986).

——— and ———, "Towards a Positive Theory of the Determination of Accounting Standards," THE ACCOUNTING REVIEW (January 1978), pp. 112–134.

IV

APPLICATION TO SPECIFIC ACCOUNTING CHOICES

1 Zmijewski, Mark E. and Robert L. Hagerman, "An Income Strategy Approach to the Positive Theory of Accounting Standard Setting/Choice," *Journal of Accounting and Economics*, 3 (1981), pp. 129–149.

2 Lee, Chi-wen Jevons and David A. Hsieh, "Choice of Inventory Accounting Methods: Comparative Analyses of Alternative Hypotheses," *Journal of Accounting Research*, 23 (1985), pp. 468–485.

3 Daley, Lane A. and Robert L. Vigeland, "The Effects of Debt Covenants and Political Costs on the Choice of Accounting Methods: The Case of Accounting for R&D Costs," *Journal of Accounting and Economics*, 5 (1983), pp. 195–211.

4 Lys, Thomas, "Mandated Accounting Changes and Debt Covenants: The Case of Oil and Gas Accounting," *Journal of Accounting and Economics*, 6 (1984), pp. 39–65.

5 Mian, Shehzad L. and Clifford W. Smith, Jr., "Incentives for Unconsolidated Financial Reporting," *Journal of Accounting and Economics*, 12 (1990a), pp. 141–171.

6 Mian, Shehzad L. and Clifford W. Smith, Jr., "Incentives Associated with Changes in Consolidated Reporting Requirements," *Journal of Accounting and Economics*, 13 (1990b), pp. 249–266.

7 Leftwich, Richard W., Ross L. Watts and Jerold L. Zimmerman, "Voluntary Corporate Disclosure: The Case of Interim Reporting," *Journal of Accounting Research*, 19 (1981, Supplement), pp. 50–77.

8 Imhoff, Eugene A., Jr., and Jacob K. Thomas, "Economic Consequences of Accounting Standards: The Lease Disclosure Rule Change," *Journal of Accounting and Economics*, 10 (1988), pp. 277–310.

9 Zimmer, Ian, "Accounting for Interest by Real Estate Developers," *Journal of Accounting and Economics*, 8 (1986), pp. 37–51.

10 Wong, Jilnaught, "Economic Incentives for the Voluntary Disclosure of Current Cost Financial Statements," *Journal of Accounting and Economics*, 10 (1988), pp. 151–167.

The articles reproduced in this section attempt to apply costly-contracting ideas to a range of accounting policy choices. They offer a variety of conclusions and research design issues. **Zmijewski and Hagerman (1981)** observe that firms make *portfolios* of accounting policy choices. If various accounting choices are substitutes, in that more than one alternative exists to achieve the same objective, then the power of a research design that explains accounting choice is reduced by focusing on just one. For example, if the research hypothesis is that managers reduce reported income in a particular situation, and if that can be achieved through the selection of either a depreciation method or an inventory valuation method, then studying depreciation policy alone reduces the likelihood of observing the hypothesized effect. However, there is little hard evidence on the extent to which the firm's independent accountants (auditors) allow managers the wide discretion assumed in this reasoning. **Zmijewski and Hagerman** adopt a portfolio research design and observe a significant relation between accounting policy choice and variables that proxy for properties of debt and compensation contracts, as well as political costs.

Lee and Hsieh (1985) study a single accounting policy choice, LIFO versus FIFO for inventory valuation purposes. They confront several important research design issues, including:

1. testing alternative hypotheses;
2. the unobservability of contracting costs and political costs; and
3. the possibility that proxy variables such as size and leverage are correlated with omitted variables such as firms' production-investment opportunity sets. Their results do not support the contracting-cost or political-cost hypotheses in this context.

This conclusion perhaps is not surprising, since the LIFO conformity rule suggests that tax motives dominate inventory method choices in the U.S.

Daley and Vigeland (1982) and **Lys (1984)** investigate accounting for R&D and oil and gas expenditures, respectively. **Daley and Vigeland** report a significant relation between the decision to capitalize R&D expenditures, prior to FAS 2 in 1974, and leverage, closeness to dividend restrictions in debt covenants, public versus private debt financing, and size. They do not address the endogeneity of the independent variables (that is, that the efficient accounting capitalization method could be determined by similar variables as the efficient financing method).[1] **Lys** observes that the commonly-used proxy for debt default risk (reported leverage) can be improved by introducing a second instrument—the standard deviation of asset returns. A given closeness to a debt covenant will imply higher expected costs for firms with less predictable asset values. Adopting this modification, **Lys** documents a significant relation between debt financing and equity returns around the times FAS 19 and ASR 253 were announced, in 1977–78.

Mian and Smith (1990a, 1990b) investigate FAS 94, which was released in 1987. FAS 94

---

[1]An extended discussion of this issue is in Ball (1980).

changed GAAP by eliminating the option to not consolidate minority-owned subsidiaries whose affairs are materially different than those of their parent. **Mian and Smith (1990a)** test and reject the hypothesis, used by the FASB to justify eliminating the nonconsolidation option, that financial statement users demand uniformity in accounting methods across firms. They report a variety of evidence that the option to not consolidate previously had been exercised by firms on rational contracting grounds. This evidence is consistent with that reported earlier by Francis (1986) and Whittred (1987).

    Mian and Smith (1990b) report further evidence, on lobbying the FASB for and against FAS 94, on how the affected firms responded, and on the effect on those firms' share prices. The lobbying evidence includes two notable results. First, the users on whose behalf the FASB claimed to be acting, on average lobbied against the change, which is difficult to reconcile with the FASB's justification for its decision. Second, nine firms that voluntarily did not consolidate financial subsidiaries actually lobbied the FASB for compulsory consolidation, apparently on purely strategic grounds. None of the nine had debt covenants that restricted leverage and hence, ignoring the accounting costs of consolidation (which competitors would also incur), the nine would be relatively indifferent to the new rule. However, the lobbying firms' competitors tended to have debt covenants and to have a larger effect of consolidation on their reported leverage ratios. This suggests they were lobbying strategically, in order to impose costs on their competitors. **Watts and Zimmerman (1978)** introduced the then-controversial notion that lobbying the FASB is an economic act, based on self interest. **Mian and Smith (1990b)** takes the notion one step further, by observing that self interest sometimes implies strategic lobbying.

    Imhoff and Thomas (1988) study responses to FAS 13 in 1976, which required all capital leases to be recorded as debt-financed assets, at their present values. FAS 13 thus increased reported leverage for those firms affected. The documented responses include renegotiating lease contracts so as not to trigger capital leasing, a reduction in use of leasing and a reduction in use of nonlease debt. We again see that an accounting change, with no direct cash flow implications, is associated with real effects because contracts are written in terms of the reported accounting numbers.

    Zimmer (1986) and **Wong (1988)** apply the theory to Australian and New Zealand data, respectively. **Zimmer** investigates the decision by property developers to capitalize on expense interest costs. **Wong** investigates the decision to voluntarily adopt inflation-adjusted (current cost) accounting. These papers illustrate the role of contracting costs and political costs in accounting policy choice, as initially hypothesized by **Watts and Zimmerman (1978)** and **Watts (1977)**.

AN INCOME STRATEGY APPROACH TO THE POSITIVE THEORY OF ACCOUNTING STANDARD SETTING/CHOICE

Mark E. ZMIJEWSKI and Robert L. HAGERMAN*

State University of New York at Buffalo, NY 14214, USA

Received May 1979, final version received April 1981

This paper is designed to provide additional evidence on the positive theory of accounting policy choice by combining individual accounting principles into firm income strategies. These strategies were the dependent variable in a probit analysis where the independent variables were size, management compensation, industry concentration ratio, systematic risk, capital intensity and the total debt to total asset ratio. The results indicate that four of these factors (size, management compensation, concentration ratio, and the total debt to total asset ratio) have a significant association with the choice of a firm's income strategy. This test provides strong evidence consistent with the positive theory of accounting standard setting/choice. We also present evidence that smaller firms and/or firms in less concentrated industries do not appear to make accounting policy choice decisions that are consistent with this theory.

1. Introduction

A recent series of articles has re-examined and augmented the phenomenon first addressed by Gordon (1964), when he proposed a theory which attempted to manifest the economic incentives which motivate managers' choices of accounting principles.[1] These papers have extended Gordon's query by attempting to determine the economic incentives which motivate managers' concern with the set of accounting principles utilized to generate the firms' financial statements. This concern is exhibited through two economic phenomena. The first is the firms' lobbying activities for or against a proposed accounting standard. These actions are designed to influence the set of generally accepted accounting principles (GAAP) from which a firm may choose. The second is the choice of, and/or changes in, the set of accounting principles utilized by a firm. Both phenomena involve real economic costs to the firm. The question is, assuming economic rationality, what are the benefits justifying these costs? In response to this question a

---

*We would like to thank J. Boness, L. Brown, D. Dhaliwal, L. Kelly, R. Watts and J. Zimmerman and the members of the Accounting and Finance Workshop at the State University of New York at Buffalo for their helpful comments and suggestions.

[1]See Watts (1974, 1977), Watts and Zimmerman (1978), Hagerman and Zmijewski (1979) and Dhaliwal (1980).

0165–4101/81/0000–0000/$02.50 © North-Holland

Journal of Accounting and Economics 3 (1981) 129–149. North-Holland Publishing Company

positive theory of the determination and choice of accounting principles is being developed.

The purpose of this paper is to further develop and test this positive theory of accounting by using an income strategy approach. This approach treats the firm's set of accounting choices as a single comprehensive decision.[2] We also test whether or not this theory is generally applicable to all firms.

A positive theory of accounting that explains why firms lobby for and choose particular accounting principles could be very useful. Such a theory could identify the economic motives that influence managers to make certain choices and thus indicate how these incentives could be altered. This theory could also be used by accounting regulatory bodies and other accounting policy-makers to predict how corporations and possibly other related parties, i.e., auditors, would react to proposed changes in accounting rules and hence, predict the economic effect of these changes. Such forecasts could aid policy-makers in anticipating which corporations are most likely to lobby for or against a given proposal.

The paper is organized as follows. In section 2 we discuss the positive theory of accounting and the previous empirical tests. Next we discuss the multi-dimensional nature of the accounting policy decisions made by managers and develop our income strategy approach. Section 4 contains the results of our empirical tests. Finally, in section 5 we present a summary and our conclusions.

2. Prior work

2.1. A positive theory of accounting policy choice

Gordon (1964) was the first to seriously analyze the economic motives management might have in choosing accounting principles. He concluded that managers will choose accounting principles that smooth the net income series. Gordon's analysis is suspect because it implicitly assumes that investors cannot, or will not, fully adjust for alternative accounting principles. The empirical work conducted by Ball (1972), Sunder (1975), and others, indicate that, at the aggregate market level, adjustments are made in accordance with the efficient market hypothesis.[3] Thus, managers are probably not motivated to choose accounting principles which necessarily smooth income or growth for this reason.

---

[2]This type of approach could also be applied to the following areas of research: positive theory of accounting, income smoothing, and changes in accounting principles.

[3]In addition, the income smoothing research such as: Copeland (1968), Cushing (1969), White (1970), Ball and Watts (1972), Barefield and Comiskey (1972), and Smith (1976), has been less than conclusive on this issue.

Watts and Zimmerman (1978), hereafter W–Z, formally developed a theory hypothesizing the economic incentives managers have in selecting accounting principles and developed an empirically testable model. W–Z tested this model on manager's lobbying positions that were submitted to the FASB concerning the general price level accounting (GPLA) exposure draft. Hagerman and Zmijewski (1979), hereafter H–Z, extended this theory and tested it on the managers' choice of individual accounting policies.

The theory developed by W–Z is based on the proposition that managers attempt to maximize their utility which is directly related to their compensation and hence wealth. Management compensation is increased by either increasing the value of management stock option plans and/or by increasing the cash paid through incentive cash bonuses. Therefore, W–Z argued that the following factors would increase management wealth: (i) decreased or delayed tax payments, (ii) favorable government regulations, (iii) decreased political costs, e.g., threats of nationalization, expropriation, anti-trust suits, etc., (iv) decreased information production costs, and (v) increases in the income measure used as the base for the incentive bonus plans. Increased firm cash flows from the first four factors would, ceteris paribus, lead to higher stock prices, while the last factor would result in a direct increase in management compensation.

Based on this logic, managers will lobby for and choose those accounting policies which decrease or defer tax payments, help secure favorable regulations (or decisions by regulators), decrease political costs, decrease information production costs, and/or increase managers' cash bonuses. Except for the reduction of information production costs which directly decrease cash outflows, accounting policies affect these factors by the impact they have on reported net income. An accounting policy which reduces income can reduce or delay a firm's tax payments (assuming it must be used for both accounting and tax purposes, i.e., LIFO). If a firm is regulated, accounting policies which reduce net income would allow management to argue that profits are too low and that a price increase is justified. Lower earnings also reduce political costs because the firm is less visible and hence less likely to be attacked by political activists than are firms with higher earnings. Finally, if a company bases its incentive plan on reported earnings, managers have an incentive to favor those methods which increase reported income.

Watts (1977), using the results of Jensen and Meckling (1976), was the first to suggest that debt covenants might also influence the choice of accounting policies. Collins, Rozeff and Dhaliwal (1980), Dhaliwal (1980), Holthausen (1980), and Leftwich (1980) made the argument that the higher is the debt/equity ratio of the firm, the more binding are the debt covenants on the firm. The firm can attempt to loosen some of these covenants, e.g., the dividend covenant, by choosing accounting policies that increase reported income. Hence, they hypothesized that high debt/equity ratios are associated with income increasing accounting alternatives and, with the exception of Holthausen (1980), they found that debt/equity ratio was significant in the various issues they tested.

2.2. Empirical tests

W–Z tested their positive theory of accounting by examining the lobbying position c. the firms which made submissions to the FASB about the proposed GPLA standard. They examined the empirical relationship of a firm's adjusted lobbying position (adjusted for the effect GPLA would have on its income) to size and market share, used as proxy variables for political costs, the existence of a management profit-sharing plan, two proxy variables for possible tax effects, and whether or not the firm was regulated.[4] The variable with the most discriminating power was firm size, with the larger firms lobbying for lower earnings. The other variables had little explanatory power.

Hagerman and Zmijewski (1979) also tested this theory. They used probit analysis to determine if the choice of four individual accounting policies (i.e., depreciation and inventory methods, the treatment of the investment tax credit, and the amortization of past service costs) by 300 firms could be explained by the theory. The H–Z model consisted of firm size and management incentive plan variables as did the W–Z model. H–Z substituted an eight firm concentration ratio variable for the W–Z market share variable. The concentration ratio is assumed to be a proxy variable for the ability of a firm to earn monopoly rents, which can result in large political costs. Corporations which earn monopoly rents and report them are more likely to face anti-trust action and entry by other firms. Thus it was hypothesized that corporations which earn monopoly rents will choose accounting principles which reduce reported income to forestall entry as well as anti-trust suits. Two additional variables were tested by H–Z: systematic risk and capital intensity. Riskier firms will tend to earn higher returns to compensate them for the additional systematic risk they bear. Therefore, to the extent that accounting income reflects economic income, riskier firms will show higher accounting profits. Likewise, capital intensive firms will appear to earn higher profits than labor intensive firms because the total cost of capital is not a recognized expense in computing net income. Since riskier firms and more capital intensive firms will appear to earn abnormal profits, they will have an incentive to choose those accounting principles that will reduce reported income.

H–Z treated Last-In-First-Out (LIFO), accelerated depreciation, the deferral of the investment tax credit, and the amortization of past service

---

[4]The GPLA effect on income was estimated via the adjusting procedure developed by Davidson and Weil (1975a, b), and Davidson, Stickeny and Weil (1976).

costs over a period of less than 30 years as income deflating alternatives. The income inflating choices were First-In-First-Out (FIFO), straight-line depreciation, the flow-through method for the investment tax credit, and amortization periods of 30 years or more for pension past service costs. The model was statistically significant for only two of the four policies: inventory and depreciation methods. What was even more disturbing was the fact that the same variables were not consistently significant across each of the four policies tested. This evidence indicates that, while the independent variables may have explanatory power in general, they are not individually consistent determinants of accounting policy choice. This could be interpreted to infer that either different decision processes are used for each accounting policy choice (which seems unlikely) or that the accounting policies which were tested are not individual decisions.

3. The income strategy approach

3.1. Income strategies

Although many studies have assumed that the choice of accounting policies are independent,[5] it is unlikely that managers act in this manner. If management uses the H–Z or the W–Z model in their accounting policy lobbying and choice decisions, these decisions will not be independent because the values of the model's independent variables are identical for each decision. Based on the economic factors which influence these decisions, managers will attempt to achieve the optimal reported net income over time and will choose a set of accounting policies accordingly. Essentially, management will adopt a multi-dimensional income strategy for the firm, with each policy being one dimension of that decision.

Both W–Z and H–Z models made the assumption of independence. W–Z did not discuss the effect of the other policy decisions made by the firm. A firm would not incur lobbying costs if it could counteract the effect of a decision made by the FASB by changing its set of accounting principles if the cost of this change would be less than the cost of lobbying. H–Z assumed that managers would choose an accounting principle based on its individual effect on reported income and the economic variables of the model. Since the set of independent variables is the same for each firm at any point in time, the model should predict either all income increasing or all income decreasing accounting policy choices for each of the firms. Therefore, for a particular firm, the model would infer a conservative (all income decreasing policies) or liberal (all income increasing policies) firm income strategy.

---

[5]See for example: Abdel-khalik and McKeown (1978), Ball (1972), Cushing and Deakin (1974), Eggleton, Penman and Twomby (1976), and Kaplan and Roll (1972) (changes in accounting principle); Watts and Zimmerman (1978) (lobbying decisions); and Hagerman and Zmijewski (1979) (accounting policy choice decisions).

However, only 12.33% of the H–Z sample fell into these extreme categories (see table 1). This result is consistent with our argument that firms follow an overall income strategy.

An optimal strategy need not be extreme because of the trade-offs the managers face. Some variables such as size induce managers to use deflating policies while other variables such as management compensation plans encourage managers to choose income inflating alternatives. The result of these trade-offs mean that any combination of the available set of alternative GAAP may be optimal for a given firm.

If firms follow an overall firm income strategy, then the firm's strategies should be used as the dependent variable in a statistical analysis conducted to test the choice of accounting principles. This will provide a stronger test of the hypothesis. Given the four policy choices analyzed by H–Z (depreciation, inventory, investment tax credit, and pension past service costs) and two choices for each policy (income increasing or income decreasing) there are 2^4, or 16 combinations that firms could follow. It is necessary to consider how these 16 combinations can be partitioned into an ordinal ranking of distinct income strategies across all firms.[6] The first set of strategies we test is based on the assumption that the choices of inventory and depreciation methods, the amortization of pension costs, and the treatment of the investment tax credit, all have an equal effect on reported income. This assumption yields five alternative strategies, each with a different magnitude of effect on reported income. The five strategies are: income decreasing policies for all four methods, one income increasing policy and three income decreasing policies, two income increasing policies and two income decreasing policies, three increasing policies and one decreasing policy, and finally, all income increasing policies. The combinations of policies that make up these five strategies are shown in table 1.

The assumption that all the alternative accounting principles have an equal effect on reported income is arbitrary. However, as it is not possible to measure the exact effects of the various accounting principles, we make two additional sets of assumptions regarding the impact of alternative principles. We then test the resulting sets of strategies to see if the results are sensitive to the assumptions of the individual accounting policies on the alternative aggregation procedures. The first additional set of assumptions is that the pension cost and investment tax credit alternatives have exactly one-half of the effect of the inventory and depreciation alternatives. This assumption results in a set of seven distinct strategies. The combination of accounting principles choices that make up these seven strategies are also presented in

---

[6]We have reviewed the literature for articles and empirical evidence which would provide us with a methodology which would divide the 16 combinations of accounting policies into an ordinal ranking of firm income strategies. Unfortunately, we were unable to find any such references. Although the assumptions which we have made may appear somewhat *ad hoc*, we feel that they are rational and are adequate surrogates for the true ordinal rankings.

Table 1

Alternative combinations of accounting policies and income strategies for Watts–Zimmerman (W–Z) and Hagerman–Zmijewski (H–Z) samples.

Combination	Possible policy alternatives				W–Z sample		H–Z sample		Classification of strategies		
	Depreciation	Inventory	Pension costs	Investment tax credit	#	%	#	%	5	7	9
Most decreasing 1	0	0	0	0	4	11.77	10	3.33	1	1	1
2	0	0	1	0	2	5.88	0	0.00	2	2	2
3	0	0	0	1	0	0.00	9	3.00	2	2	2
4	0	0	1	1	0	0.00	1	0.33	3	3	3
5	1	0	0	0	0	0.00	29	9.67	2	3	4
6	0	1	0	0	0	0.00	11	3.67	2	3	4
7	1	0	1	0	4	11.77	8	2.67	3	4	5
8	0	1	1	0	2	5.88	1	0.33	3	4	5
9	1	0	0	1	4	11.77	68	22.67	3	4	5
10	0	1	0	1	0	0.00	12	4.00	3	4	5
11	1	0	1	1	6	17.64	24	8.00	4	5	6
12	0	1	1	1	0	0.00	1	0.33	4	5	6
13	1	1	0	0	1	2.94	17	5.67	3	5	7
14	1	1	1	0	1	2.94	7	2.33	4	6	8
15	1	1	0	1	2	5.88	75	25.00	4	6	8
Most increasing 16	1	1	1	1	8	23.53	27	9.00	5	7	9
					34	100%	300	100%			

where

Policy	0 Income decreasing policy	1 Income increasing policy
Depreciation	Accelerated method	Straight line method
Inventory	LIFO	FIFO
Amortization of past costs	Less than 30 years	30 years or more
Investment tax credit	Deferral method	Flow-through method

table 1. The second alternative set of assumptions is that the pension costs and tax credits have an equal but less than one-half of the effect that inventory and depreciation alternatives have on reported income. This assumption yields a set of nine strategies. The combinations that make up these strategies are again shown in table 1.

We propose to test the model previously developed by H–Z augmented with the debt/equity ratio on the income strategy adopted by the firm, rather than on the individual lobbying or policy choice decisions. We assert that accounting policy decisions must be analyzed as part of an overall firm strategy and not as independent decisions. If, in fact, the firm does make its accounting policy decisions via some type of income strategy decision process, the model should be able to classify the firms according to the strategies chosen.

3.2. Methodological considerations

These strategies, given our previous assumptions, can be ranked in the order of the assumed magnitude of the effect on net income. The first strategy is the most income decreasing possibility while the last strategy is the most income increasing strategy. This treatment of the firms' income strategies has resulted in certain data limitations which will be a determinant in the choice of an appropriate statistical methodology.

The first limitation is that the actual effect on reported income of a particular strategy cannot be observed. Because of this, we are only able to hypothesize the ranking of the strategies. The second limitation is that, at best, the hypothesized rankings are ordinal. Hence, the choice to assign the same size interval to each strategy cannot be used to infer that each strategy will have the same magnitude of effect on reported income.

Given these data limitations, regression analysis is an inappropriate statistical technique for the following two reasons. First, there is a violation of the assumptions which must be made about the properties of the error terms in regression analysis. The error terms in the regression model where the dependent variable is categorical: (i) will *not* have an expected value of zero, (ii) will *not* be normally distributed but in fact have a discrete distribution, and (iii) will be heteroskedastic. The severity of these violations will decrease as the number of categories is expanded. This can be intuitively seen by expanding the number of categories to the limit, i.e., when the number of categories approaches infinity, the dependent variable becomes continuous and the violations no longer exist. Hence, one may justifiably utilize regression analysis if the dependent variable has a sufficient number of categories to reduce the severity of this problem. The second problem is that regression analysis implicitly assumes that the dependent variable has a cardinal scale.

An alternative statistical technique is the *n*-chotomous probit analysis developed by McKelvey and Zaviona (1975). The assumption of this methodology is that, although unobservable, the dependent variable has a continuous underlying normal distribution. Hence, if the true values could be observed, the previously discussed regression model would satisfy the necessary assumptions. Given this assumption, the objective of n-chotomous probit analysis is to simultaneously estimate the regression coefficients of the true underlying regression model as well as the parameters of the cardinal scale of category intervals. The resulting estimated parameters will provide an estimation of the probability that an observed vector of independent variables is within any particular category bounded by that category's estimated cardinal intervals.

The estimation of these parameters is calculated by use of the maximum likelihood estimation procedure via the Newton–Ralphson iterative method of solution for nonlinear systems.[7] The advantage of using parameters estimated by this method is the appealing statistical properties of the estimators. These estimates are asymptotically efficient and have a known asymptotic sampling distribution. Therefore, we are able to perform hypothesis tests on the significance of both the overall model and the individual independent variables. Another appealing feature of this technique is that it is possible to make certain inferences about the estimated size of the intervals chosen. We are able to test the hypothesis that the size of the estimated cardinal interval is significantly different from zero. This test will provide some indirect evidence on the appropriateness of our choice of income strategies.

To test the overall model the likelihood ratio will be used. This is done by taking minus two times the log likelihood ratio which is distributed as a chi-square with $k-1$ (k being the number of independent variables) degrees of freedom, cf., McKelvey and Zavonia (1975). The asymptotic t-test will be used to test the significance of both the estimated coefficients of the independent variables and the size of the estimated cardinal intervals.[8]

The independent variables are measured in the following ways. Size is measured by the log of net sales. Capital intensity is calculated by the ratio of gross fixed assets to sales. Concentration ratio, which is defined as the percentage of total industry sales made up by the top eight firms,[9] is our proxy for the firm's ability to earn monopoly rents. The debt/equity ratio is defined as total debt to total assets. The systematic risk of the corporation is

[7]For an excellent discussion of both categorical dependent variables and the Newton–Ralphson method of nonlinear estimation, see Maddala (1977, pp. 162–166, 171–174).

[8]One may question our choice of n-chotomous probit analysis over multiple discriminant analysis (MDA). The decision is quite clear, MDA does not provide a direct statistical test of either the coefficients of the individual independent variables or the size of the estimated intervals. Furthermore, the MDA model assumes that all of the independent variables are normally distributed. Given our binary management profit-sharing variable, this assumption would be violated.

[9]Concentration ratios have obvious shortcomings as measures of monopoly rents but they are widely used because no better proxy is readily available.

measured by beta estimated from the market model. A zero-one dummy variable represents the existence or non-existence of a management profit sharing plan based on reported net income.

4. Empirical tests

4.1. Data

The data used in our analyses consist of the 34 unregulated firms of W–Z and the 300 unregulated firms of H–Z.[10] For each of the firms, the previously discussed economic variables and the choice of the four accounting principles were collected from either the firms' 1975 SEC 10K or annual reports. It should be noted that the 300 H–Z firms represent a random sample of firms, while the 34 W–Z firms represent the population of unregulated firms which made submissions to the FASB in regard to the GPLA discussion memorandum (a non-random sample). Therefore, it is interesting to compare the two samples and the characteristics of the data.

Since firms with extreme strategies (all increasing or decreasing policy choices) have less ability to counteract the effect of a mandated accounting policy change/standard, one may anticipate that firms which made submissions to the FASB tend to have extreme policies. This hypothesis can be tested by examining the distributions of the firm strategies of the two samples. The distribution of the 16 possible combinations of the four accounting policies for the two samples is shown in table 1. The distributions for the five, seven, and nine strategy cases can also be easily derived from this table. The main difference between the distributions of the two samples is the percentage of W–Z observations in the two extreme strategies. The W–Z sample has a much larger percentage of firms in these two strategies than does the H–Z sample. This supports our hypothesis that firms with extreme strategies will tend to make submissions to the FASB.

To test the statistical significance of this difference, the binomial test was used. The proportion of firms in each combination (strategy) of the H–Z sample was used as an unbiased estimator of the probability of the population's combination (strategy). Using the Clopper–Pearson methodology, a 95% confidence interval was calculated for the estimator.[11] The upper bound of the 95% confidence interval was then used as the estimated population probability of the two extreme combinations for the binomial test. This was done to intentionally bias the estimator in favor of the null hypothesis to provide for a stronger test. The upper bound of the 95% confidence interval for the extreme income deflating and income inflating combinations are 0.053 and 0.123, respectively. Basing the binomial

---

[10]Twenty-one of the 34 W–Z firms were also in the H–Z sample.
[11]See Hollander and Wolfe (1973, pp. 15–24).

tests on these probabilities resulted in rejecting the null hypothesis for both of the extreme combinations. The income deflating combination was rejected at the 0.0475 level of significance and the income inflating combination was rejected at the 0.0239 level. Thus the data indicate that the W–Z sample has significantly more firms with extreme strategies than can be expected (assuming that the H–Z sample is representative of the population).

In their discussion of firm size, W–Z asserted that smaller firms would either not make a submission or make an unfavorable submission to the FASB regarding the GPLA discussion memorandum. Therefore, one would hypothesize that the mean size of the W–Z sample would be much larger than that of the H–Z sample. We performed the Mann–Whitney U test to test this hypothesis. The mean size of the W–Z sample is more than twice that of the H–Z sample. The null hypothesis was rejected at the 0.001 level of significance. The fact that the firms in the W–Z sample are so large may explain why W–Z did not find the management compensation or regulatory proxy variables useful in classifying the firms' lobbying choices. The potential political costs borne by large firms may be so large that they dominate the benefits from increasing reported income. In addition, the political pressures for large firms may be so great as to induce the firms to act as if they were regulated. Thus, the regulatory and compensation variables could be insignificant for the firms examined by W–Z.

The Mann–Whitney U test was also performed on the other economic variables discussed (the five, seven and nine strategy cases, concentration ratio, capital intensity, total debt to total assets, and risk) but we were not able to reject the null hypothesis with any reasonable degree of significance.

4.2. Empirical test of the income strategy approach

If our proposed income strategies are representative of managements' income strategies, and if these income strategies are generated by the decision process represented by the model, then one would expect that this model would be able to classify firms according to their choice of a particular strategy.

Specifically, the model is

$$Strategy_i = \alpha_0 + \alpha_1 MGTC + \alpha_2 Conc + \alpha_3 Beta$$
$$+ \alpha_4 Size + \alpha_5 CI + \alpha_6 TD + e,$$

where

$Strategy_i$ = Income strategy (i = 5, 7, or 9),
$MGTC$ = Management compensation plan (0 = no, 1 = yes),
$Conc$ = Eight-firm concentration ratio,

Beta	= Systematic risk,
Size	= Log of net sales (proxy for political costs),
CI	= Capital intensity (gross fixed assets/sales),
TD	= Total debt/total assets,
e	= Error term

This hypothesis was tested by using the 300 firm H–Z sample and estimating the coefficients of the model with firm income strategy as the dependent variable. The coefficients, estimated via *n*-chotomous probit analysis, and the other results of the tests are presented in table 2. What is immediately clear from the data is that the results for five, seven, and nine strategies are virtually identical. This evidence indicates that our results are not sensitive to the admittedly arbitrary choice of income strategies.

Some inferences can be made about the appropriateness of our strategies by examining the significance of the magnitude of the bounded cardinal intervals estimated by the *n*-chotomous probit analysis. The ranges of the estimated cardinal intervals and their *t*-statistics are presented in table 3. Note that there are two less bounded intervals than the number of strategies in each case. This is because the two outer strategies are only bounded on one side and must therefore, have statistically significant magnitudes. The *t*-statistics indicate that all bounded estimated cardinal intervals are statistically significant for both the five and seven strategy cases. The nine strategy case has three intervals which are not statistically significant. This may suggest that some of the strategies of this case are not unique. The data indicate that in the five and seven strategy cases the strategies are, in fact, different from one another, although we cannot state if they are in fact the 'true' strategies. Given these results, however, we feel that the strategy assumptions previously discussed are acceptable and that the model is not biased by the choice of a particular set of assumptions regarding the effect of the accounting policies on net income.

The model is statistically significant at the 0.001 level for all three cases tested.[12] For the five strategy case, 40% of the sample observations were properly classified. The percent correctly classified for both the seven and nine strategy case was 33%. One way to determine how good these predictions are is to compare them to a naive policy which assumes an equal probability of each strategy. The prediction rates of the model are much better than under this naive classification and the differences are very significant. An alternative comparison is to assume that the naive forecaster will always choose the most common strategy in the sample. The model's predictions are better than those from this approach and are significant at

---

[12]This level of significance is much greater than the level of significance reported by Hagerman and Zmijewski (1979) when they tested the policy decisions individually. The largest of the chi-squares reported in the H–Z analysis was 16.944, while the smallest of these tests is 26.35. Both studies used the same sample of firms.

Table 2

Probit analysis of accounting strategies.

Independent variables and statistics	Dependent variable		
	5 strategy case	7 strategy case	9 strategy case
Constant	3.10356[b]	3.03981	3.03283
	(7.515)	(7.598)	(7.592)
Management compensation ($+$)[a]	0.31259	0.26812	0.26055
	(2.409)	(2.112)	(2.055)
Concentration ratio ($-$)	-0.63437	-0.61523	-0.61678
	(-2.214)	(-2.193)	(-2.200)
Systematic risk-beta ($-$)	-0.13656	-0.09032	-0.08168
	(-0.765)	(-0.518)	(-0.469)
Size-log of net sales ($-$)	-0.32095	-0.32406	-0.32351
	(-2.638)	(-2.720)	(-2.717)
Capital intensity ($-$)	-0.12651	-0.12218	-0.12091
	(-0.959)	(-0.945)	(-0.935)
Total debt to total assets ($+$)	0.35747	0.40935	0.40930
	(1.718)	(2.005)	(2.005)
Estimated R^2	0.09030	0.09066	0.08983
Probit analysis χ^2 (d.f. $=6$)	26.3675	26.5813	26.3490
% correctly classified	40.00%	33.00%	33.00%
Sample size	300	300	300

[a]Expected sign of coefficient.
[b]Coefficient
(asymptotic t-statistic).

the 25% level. The estimated R^2 for the five, seven and nine strategy cases are 0.0903, 0.0907, and 0.0898, respectively.

The 'true' ranking of the combinations of accounting policies, and hence the 'true' strategies may differ from the proposed strategies for two reasons. The first is that the *ad hoc* assumptions which were made about the magnitude of the effect of the accounting policies on net income across all firms may have been incorrect. The result of this type of error would be that many of the estimated cardinal intervals would not be statistically significant. As previously discussed, we do not feel we have a serious problem of this nature. The second reason that any of the strategies tested may differ from the 'true' strategies is because of individual firm effects of the accounting policies. For a specific firm the inventory effect could be larger than, less than, or equal to the depreciation effect. The same holds for the other policies. To examine the effect of this error, the number of firms which were classified within one strategy was calculated. The percentage of correctly classified firms for the five, seven, and nine strategy cases was 88.33%, 68.67%, and 56.67%, respectively.

Table 3

Significance of bounded estimated cardinal intervals from probit analysis.

Bounded interval	Five strategy case	Seven strategy case	Nine strategy case
First	0.00000–1.02335[a] (7.396)	0.00000–0.31626 (3.103)	0.00000–0.31611 (3.103)
Second	1.02335–2.06368 (6.112)	0.31626–1.02697 (4.354)	0.31611–0.34278 (0.173)
Third	2.06368–3.32887 (5.376)	1.02697–1.90344 (5.219)	0.34278–1.02498 (4.180)
Fourth	N.A.[b]	1.90344–2.28248 (2.114)	1.02498–1.90135 (5.225)
Fifth	N.A.	2.28248–3.32511 (4.167)	1.90135–2.12352 (1.261)
Sixth	N.A.	N.A.	2.12352–2.28009 (0.855)
Seventh	N.A.	N.A.	2.28009–3.32281 (4.186)

[a]Range of estimated cardinal interval
(t-statistic).
[b]N.A. — Not applicable.

A hold-out sample was also used to test this model. The model was estimated using 150 observations and then was used to predict the accounting strategies of the remaining 150 hold-out sample firms. This was repeated by using the first hold-out sample to estimate the model and then predicting the strategies for the other 150 firms. The percentage of correct predictions was 39%, 30% and 28.6%, for the five, seven, and nine strategies, respectively. This is significantly different at the 5% level from the naive classification model of equal probability for each strategy for all three strategies. Thus, our model also appears to have significant predictive ability.

What is of most interest in the formulation of a positive theory of accounting is the statistical significance of the overall model and of the individual independent variables which were hypothesized to be important factors in the firm's choice of accounting policies. Therefore, our main concern is with the significance of the individual independent variables.[13] The log of net sales is negatively related to the choice of accounting strategies at the 1% level of significance in all three cases.[14] This supports

[13]To use the asymptotic t-test, the residuals of the probit analysis are assumed to be normally distributed. We tested the residuals of the five, seven, and nine strategy cases using the Kolmogorov–Smirnov goodness of fit test. The null hypothesis, that the sample is normally distributed could not be rejected at any reasonable level of significance [see Hollander and Wolfe (1973, pp. 219–228)].

[14]Net sales was also tested in place of the log of net sales variable. This substitution resulted in a lower asymptotic t-value for this variable and a slightly lower chi-square value for the overall significance of the model.

the argument that larger firms have incentives to reduce accounting profits. This is identical to the result of both the W–Z and H–Z analyses. Thus, there is considerable evidence that large firms face political costs which they attempt to minimize by reducing net income.

Concentration ratio, which is our proxy for the ability of a firm to earn monopoly rents, is significant at the 5% level in all three cases. The sign of the maximum likelihood estimate (MLE) indicates that firms in more concentrated industries tend to adopt accounting strategies that reduce net income. This is consistent with our reasoning that such firms will attempt to reduce reported profits in order to avoid entry and anti-trust action. This result is of particular interest to students of industrial organization since it indicates a bias against finding a positive relationship between profitability and concentration. This is inconsistent with the results of Hagerman and Senbet (1976) which indicate that concentration ratios and the choice of accounting principles are independent, although they did not control for size or any of the other independent variables.

The existence of a management profit-sharing plan is significant at the 5% level in all three cases. The sign of the MLE indicates that managers are more likely to choose accounting strategies that increase net income if such plans are available to them. This result is not consistent with the results of W–Z. Thus it appears that the existence of management incentive plans does influence the choice of accounting principles when a random sample of firms is examined.

Total debt to total assets is significant at the 10% level in the five strategy case and is significant at the 5% level in the seven and nine strategy cases. The sign of the coefficient of this factor is positive which suggests that firms which use relatively more debt financing choose accounting policies which tend to increase net income. This is consistent with the hypothesis that firms with more debt are more constrained by their debt covenants, and hence, attempt to loosen these constraints by choosing accounting policies which increase net income.[15]

The two remaining variables, beta and capital intensity, are not significant although they are of the expected sign. It may well be that the effect of risk and capital intensity on profits, as reflected in net income may be too small to induce managers to use accounting principles to reduce the reported income.

These results support our hypothesis that firms act as though they choose accounting policies relative to an income strategy decision process. The

---

[15]Equivalent results were obtained when total debt to equity was used for leverage instead of total debt to total assets. Substituting either long-term debt to equity or long-term debt to total assets for the leverage factor was not significant.

combination of accounting policy decisions made by a firm appear to be associated with a firm income strategy.[16]

4.3. General applicability of the model

The positive theory of accounting developed by W–Z predicts that firms will attempt to report lower income via the choice of accounting principles if they are regulated or subject to political pressure. W–Z state: 'In small (i.e., low political cost) unregulated firms we would expect that managers do have incentives to select accounting standards which report higher earnings, if the expected gain in incentive compensation is greater than the foregone tax consequences'.[17] This is interpreted to mean that the management compensation variable would be more important for firms facing low political costs than those facing high political costs. Likewise, other variables should be more important for the high political cost firms than for low political cost firms. To test this hypothesis, we partitioned our sample into low political cost firms and high political cost firms to see if the same model fits both sub-samples.

The firms in the H–Z sample were partitioned into high and low political cost subsamples by ranking the firms on a political cost variable, dividing the sample at the median and classifying firms above (below) the median as having high (low) political costs. Since both size and concentration ratios are proxy variables for political costs the division was done twice, once by using size to partition the sample and then by partitioning the sample based on concentration ratios. Thus, four probit analyses were conducted.

The subsample means and variances for the income strategies and the independent variables are reported for each subsample in table 4. The data show that the large size firms and the firms in highly concentrated industries follow, on average, more income deflating strategies than smaller firms or firms in less concentrated industries. These differences are statistically significant at the 5% level. This is expected since the high political cost groups have more incentives to reduce reported net income. These data also show that large firms tend to be in more highly concentrated industries than smaller firms. This statistically significant difference suggests an association between size and concentration ratios.

The results of the four probit analyses are presented in table 5. It is quite apparent that the model is significant for both of the high political cost subsamples and not significant for either of the low political cost subsamples at the 5% level. Thus, the evidence indicates that the model is not generally applicable to all firms.

---

[16]Regression analysis was also used and the results were equivalent to those reported in the text.

[17]Watts and Zimmerman (1978, p. 118).

Table 4

Descriptive statistics of economic variables partitioned on political cost proxy variables; seven strategy case.

Criterion variables		Economic variables						
		Income strategy	Concentration ratio	Management profit sharing	Risk (beta)	Capital intensity	Size log of net sales	Total debt to total assets
Size	Large	4.440[a] (2.166)	0.7108 (0.0329)	0.7000 (0.2100)	1.030 (0.0871)	0.6024 (0.1343)	3.259 (0.1519)	0.4518 (0.0259)
	Small	4.880 (2.066)	0.5958 (0.0653)	0.5133 (0.2598)	0.8951 (0.1519)	0.5762 (0.3196)	2.400 (0.0759)	0.4747 (0.1535)
Concentration ratio	High	4.387 (1.917)	0.8422 (0.0124)	0.6200 (0.2356)	0.9687 (0.1210)	0.6225 (0.2967)	2.981 (0.3368)	0.4563 (0.0649)
	Low	4.933 (2.262)	0.4645 (0.0211)	0.5933 (0.2413)	0.9564 (0.1257)	0.5561 (0.1553)	2.678 (0.2137)	0.4702 (0.1146)

[a] Mean (variance).

Table 5

Probit analysis of high and low political cost subsamples; seven strategy case.

Independent variables and statistics	Criterion variables			
	Size (net sales)		Concentration ratio	
	Large	Small	High	Low
Constant	4.46783[b]	1.94250	3.61505	2.4801
	(5.142)	(2.302)	(4.056)	(4.124)
Management compensation $(+)$[a]	0.43603	0.17400	0.63754	−0.00657
	(2.289)	(0.979)	(3.354)	(−0.037)
Concentration ratio $(-)$	−0.43965	−0.71274	−0.83081	−0.06863
	(−0.897)	(−2.058)	(−1.025)	(−0.105)
Systematic risk-beta $(-)$	−0.45036	0.15334	−0.14823	−0.04759
	(−1.532)	(0.692)	(−0.585)	(−0.192)
Size-log of net sales $(-)$	−0.60938	0.13515	−0.48054	−0.14675
	(−2.652)	(0.429)	(−3.015)	(−0.732)
Capital intensity $(-)$	−0.40863	−0.00183	0.11850	−0.51667
	(−1.675)	(−0.012)	(0.713)	(−2.337)
Total debt to total assets $(+)$	−0.08460	0.46989	0.43733	0.35128
	(−0.154)	(2.095)	(1.275)	(1.346)
Estimated R^2	0.12369	0.08039	0.13219	0.06695
Probit analysis χ^2 (d.f. = 6)	18.4801	11.4547	19.4534	9.7193
% correctly predicted	33.33%	30.67%	38.67%	34.67%
Sample size	150	150	150	150

[a]Expected sign of coefficient.
[b]Coefficient
  (asymptotic t-statistic).

For the high political cost subsample partitioned on size, all independent variables except concentration ratio and debt to total assets are significant at the 15% level or less. Concentration ratio may not be significant because the additional political costs due to earning potential monopoly profits may be small if the company is already very visible to political activists because of its size. This evidence indicates that, for large firms, the concentration ratio proxy for political costs provides no information beyond that provided by the size variable. This could explain the results of W–Z. They did not find a significant amount of discriminatory power for the market share variable but the evidence above indicates that the size of the unregulated firms of the W–Z study was very large.

For the low political cost subsample partioned on size, only the concentration ratio and the debt to asset ratio were significant and the overall model is not significant. This suggests that smaller firms only consider potential competition, anti-trust action and debt covenants when they decide on the set of accounting principles to follow. This evidence also indicates that concentration ratio provides information beyond that provided by firm size when size is below the threshold point for political costs. This result is expected since concentration ratio may be a proxy variable for industry political costs and hence, all firms within a concentrated industry may be scrutinized by regulators, political activists, etc.

For the high political costs subsample partitioned on concentration ratio, two variables (management profit sharing and size) are significant at the 15% level or less and the overall model is significant. These results are very similar to the high political cost subsample partitioned on size. This may be due to the similar partitioning of the size variable for both of the high political cost subsamples. The reason size is significant may be due to the fact that it is the larger firms in concentrated industries that face the major political costs. This suggests political costs are a function of size, given the concentration of the industry.

For the low political cost subsample partitioned on concentration ratio, only capital intensity is significant. Again, the overall model for this subsample is not significant. What is unexpected in the two low political cost subsamples is lack of significance of the management profit-sharing variable. These results are inconsistent with the contention of W–Z who argue that this variable should be more important for firms that face lower political costs. One possible explanation is that smaller firms tend to be owner controlled, making profit-sharing plans less important to these managers.[18]

These results confirm W–Z's argument that there is a threshold effect. That is, smaller firms and firms in less concentrated industries do not choose accounting principles as if they considered political costs. The model, however, works very well for large firms and firms in highly concentrated industries. Thus, the model is not generally applicable to all firms and further research is required to determine what influences the choice of accounting principles by managers of smaller firms.

5. Summary and conclusions

This paper is an attempt to answer two questions. First, are accounting policy decisions made jointly? By developing a variety of alternative accounting strategies we tested them against the proposed positive theory. The results indicated that size, the existence of a profit-sharing plan, degree of concentration and debt to total assets ratio all influence the accounting strategy of a firm. These results are much stronger than when individual policy choices are tested, i.e., Hagerman and Zmijewski (1979). Thus it appears that firms choose an overall income strategy.

[18]This analysis was also conducted on the five and nine strategy cases. The results are equivalent to those reported for the seven strategy case.

We also conducted tests to ascertain if the model was generally applicable to all firms (i.e., small firms or firms in less concentrated industries) and found that it was only significant for large firms and those in highly concentrated industries.

Thus, the evidence in this study suggests that individual accounting policy choice decisions are part of an overall firm strategy. Although further refinements must still be made (e.g., testing for the actual dollar effects on net income and considering all accounting policy decisions), this evidence is important to researchers examining income smoothing, changes in accounting principles, and the effects of accounting standard setting. Individual accounting policies should be examined as part of an overall firm strategy. A second point to be considered is that the model, in its present form, is not universally applicable. It appears as though only the larger firms and those in more concentrated industries fit the model. Additional factors must be added to the model so that it can be applied to all firms. Finally, it is apparent that neither size nor concentration ratio individually represent perfect proxy variables for political costs. Thus, further research into the measurement and quantification of political costs is needed.

References

Abdel-khalik, A.R. and J.C. McKeown, 1978, Understanding accounting changes in an efficient market: Evidence of differential reaction, The Accounting Review 53, 851–868.

Alchian, Armen A. and Reuben A. Kessel, 1959, Redistribution of wealth through inflation, Science 130, 535–539.

Ball, R., 1972, Changes in accounting techniques and stock prices, empirical research in accounting: Selected studies 1972, Supplement to the Journal of Accounting Research 10, 1–38.

Ball, R. and R. Watts, 1972, Some time series properties of accounting income, Journal of Finance 28, 633–682.

Barefield, R.M. and E.E. Comiskey, 1972, The income smoothing hypothesis: An alternative test, The Accounting Review 47, 291–298.

Collins, Daniel W., Michael S. Rozeff and Dan Dhaliwal, 1980, The economic determinants of market reaction to propose mandatory accounting changes in the oil and gas industry: A cross-sectional analysis, Journal of Accounting and Economics 3, 37–71.

Copeland, R., 1968, Income smoothing, Journal of Accounting Research 5, 101–116.

Cushing, B.E., 1969, An empirical study of changes in accounting policy, Journal of Accounting Research 6, 196–203.

Cushing, B.E. and E.B. Deakin, 1974, Firms making accounting changes: A comment, The Accounting Review 49, 104–112.

Davidson, Sidney and Roman L. Weil, 1975a, Inflation accounting: What will general price level adjusted income statements show?, Financial Analysts Journal 31, 27–31, 70–81.

Davidson, Sidney and Roman L. Weil, 1975b, Inflation accounting: Public utilities, Financial Analysts Journal 31, 30–34, 62.

Davidson, Sidney, Clyde P. Stickney and Roman L. Weil, 1976, Inflation accounting (McGraw-Hill, New York).

Dhaliwal, D.S., 1980, The effect of the firm's capital structure on the choice of accounting methods, The Accounting Review 55, 78 85.

Eggleton, J.R., S.H. Penman and J.R. Twombly, 1976, Accounting changes and stock prices: An examination of selected uncontrolled variables, Journal of Accounting Research 14, 89–137.

Gordon, Myron J., 1964, Postulates, principles and research in accounting, The Accounting Review 39, 251–263.

Hagerman, R. and L. Senbet, 1976, A test of accounting bias and market structure, Journal of Business 49, 509–514.

Hagerman, R. and M. Zmijewski, 1979, Some economic determinants of accounting policy choice, Journal of Accounting and Economics 1, 142–161.

Hollander, M. and D.A. Wolfe, 1973, Nonparametric statistical methods (Wiley, New York).

Holthausen, Robert W., 1980, Theory and evidence on the effect of bond covenants and management compensation contracts on the choice of accounting techniques: The case of the depreciation switch-back, Unpublished Ph.D. dissertation (University of Rochester, Rochester, NY).

Kaplan, R.S. and R. Roll, 1972, Investor evaluation of accounting information: Some empirical evidence, Journal of Business 45, 225–257.

Leftwich, Richard, 1980, Private determination of accounting methods in corporate bond indentures, Unpublished Ph.D. dissertation (University of Rochester, Rochester, NY).

Maddala, G., 1977, Econometrics (McGraw-Hill, New York).

McKelvey, R. and W. Zavoina, 1975, A statistical model for the analysis of ordinal level dependent variables, Journal of Mathematical Sociology 4, 146–163.

Smith, D.E., 1976, The effect of the separation of ownership from control on accounting policy decisions, The Accounting Review 51, 707–723.

Sunder, S., 1975, Empirical analysis of stock price and risk as they relate to accounting changes in inventory valuation, The Accounting Review 50, 305–315.

Watts, Ross, 1974, Accounting objectives, Working paper series no. 7408 (Graduate School of Management, University of Rochester, Rochester, NY).

Watts, Ross, 1977, Corporate financial statements: Product of market and political processes, Australian Journal of Management, 53075.

Watts, Ross and Jerold Zimmerman, 1978, Toward a positive theory of the determination of accounting standards, The Accounting Review, 53.

Watts, Ross and Jerold Zimmerman, 1979, The demand and supply of accounting theories: The market for excuses, The Accounting Review 54, 273–305.

White, G., 1970, Discretionary accounting decisions and income normalization, Journal of Accounting Research 8, 260–275.

Choice of Inventory Accounting Methods: Comparative Analyses of Alternative Hypotheses

CHI-WEN JEVONS LEE* AND DAVID A. HSIEH†

1. Introduction

In the past decade, hundreds of firms switched to the *LIFO* accounting method for their inventories in response to high rates of inflation. Nevertheless, many others continue to use the *FIFO* method. Biddle [1980] estimated that each of the 105 *FIFO* firms in his study paid an average of nearly $26 million in additional federal income tax. What makes these *FIFO* firms so reluctant to switch accounting methods?

A review of the literature provides three possible explanations for inventory accounting choices: political costs, agency costs, and divergent production and investment characteristics. Because the required economic variables to test these three alternative explanations are not observable, the empirical tests are based on examination of proxy variables. Many of the proxy variables of the first and third explanations are the same, so it is difficult to discriminate one from the other using univariate statistical methods. For example, there is consistent evidence of an association between size and inventory accounting choices. But size can serve as a proxy for either political costs, or divergent production and investment opportunities, or both. Similarly, there is also strong evidence that the type of industry is associated with inventory choice, which could also be consistent with both explanations.

The major purpose of this paper is to test the three explanations cited above in a simultaneous manner using multivariate probit methods.

* Associate Professor, University of Pennsylvania; † Associate Professor, University of Chicago. The helpful comments of Chris Petruzzi, Gary Biddle, and an anonymous referee are gratefully acknowledged. [Accepted for publication November 1984.]

Probit is a useful statistical technique for discriminating between alternative hypotheses with overlapping proxy variables. For purposes of exposition, we term the third explanation a Ricardian hypothesis. The hypothesis is "Ricardian" in three senses. First, it assumes that all firms are endowed with different production-investment opportunity sets. Second, it assumes that there is perfect intrafirm congruence among the interests of manager, stockholders, and creditors and that there is no economic externality between the firm and the rest of the world. In short, the firm is assumed to be a classical Ricardian firm. Third, the hypothesis postulates that the differences in production-investment opportunity sets provide firms with different comparative advantages in adopting *LIFO* or *FIFO*, and that managers choose inventory accounting methods primarily to minimize tax costs according to the Ricardian principle of comparative advantage. Several new proxy variables consistent with the Ricardian hypothesis are used in our multivariate hypothesis tests. The proxy variables consistent with the political cost and agency cost hypotheses are drawn from the literature.

We find that size and industry are very significant variables in univariate statistical tests. However, their statistical significance disappears in the multivariate probit tests. This finding casts doubt on the political cost hypothesis since it relies on size as a significant determinant of inventory accounting choices. We also do not find a significant effect of the debt/equity ratio on inventory method choices, which is inconsistent with the agency cost hypothesis. Our results seem more consistent with our Ricardian hypothesis. Nevertheless, since the three hypotheses are not mutually exclusive, our findings do not conclusively refute the political cost and agency cost hypotheses. They do underlie the need for future research to develop more precise proxy variables for these two hypotheses if we desire more conclusive results.

In section 2, we synthesize three hypotheses of inventory accounting choice within the framework proposed by Holthausen and Leftwich [1983], which assumes rational accounting choices are made in response to various monitoring and contracting costs. In section 2 we also summarize the proxy variables used in previous tests of inventory accounting choices. The details of the Ricardian hypothesis and its appropriate proxy variables are discussed in section 3. Section 4 describes the attributes of our data and the results of our univariate tests. The results of our multivariate probit tests are discussed in section 5. Conclusions appear in section 6.

Hypotheses and Proxy Variables in the Literature

2.1 MANAGER'S INVENTORY ACCOUNTING CHOICE AND MONITORING-CONTRACTING COSTS

Consider an economy with three major transaction costs: corporation income taxes, monitoring costs, and contracting costs. The corporation income tax laws are contracts made between the firm and the government. The inventory accounting method is a measurement rule used in those contracts. Changing inventory accounting methods can redistribute wealth between firms and the government.

Contracting costs encompass the costs of evaluating, negotiating, and renegotiating the terms of contracts. Monitoring costs are costs of collecting and interpreting information about performance under and enforcement of contracts between parties to the contracts.

The economy is composed of four classes of economic agents: managers, stockholders, bondholders, and the "government." All economic agents are assumed to be rational and to maximize their own objective functions with respect to given constraints. Depending on the relative magnitude of various transaction costs, we test our three hypotheses against a benchmark of a random-choice hypothesis regarding inventory accounting choices.

A random-choice hypothesis would be consistent with a world in which all monitoring–contracting costs are negligible. In such a world, users of accounting numbers can costlessly unravel those numbers and all contracts can be instantaneously renegotiated. Hence, the choice of inventory accounting method would have no effect on the wealth of any economic agent. Formally, the random-choice hypothesis can be stated as follows.

Random-Choice Hypothesis. When all monitoring–contracting costs are negligible, there are no systematic differences in attributes between *LIFO* and *FIFO* firms.

Since we know that previous evidence indicates systematic differences between *LIFO* and *FIFO* firms, the random-choice hypothesis is known to be empirically invalid. We use it merely to set the stage for the other three hypotheses.

Consider now a world where tax laws are the only nominal contracts with high monitoring–contracting costs. Any difference in the interests of managers, stockholders, and bondholders can be completely negotiated away (they have perfect goal congruence). There is no economic externality between the firm and the rest of the world. The government's function is simply to impose taxes and to provide goods and services. A firm operating in this world is a classical Ricardian firm in that the manager's objective is simply to maximize the firm's value—hence, to minimize tax costs—with respect to the given constraints imposed by tax laws and production-investment opportunity sets. The manager's choice of inventory accounting method will be based on the firm's comparative advantage in tax costs minimization arising from the firm's endowed production-investment opportunity set. This leads to what we have termed the Ricardian hypothesis.[1] Formally, it can be stated as follows.

---

[1] This hypothesis is loosely stated in the literature as a "tax hypothesis." However, the

Ricardian Hypothesis. If (1) the corporation income tax laws are nominal contracts but the monitoring–contracting costs for all other transactions are negligible and (2) firms are endowed with different production-investment opportunity sets, then the managers' inventory accounting choice can be predicted by the comparative advantage in tax costs minimization associated with the production-investment opportunity set of each.

Next, change the above conditions such that transactions between the government and the firm are subject to high monitoring–contracting costs. Other transactions remain relatively free of such costs. It is reasonable to assume that the high monitoring–contracting costs between governments and firms will lead the former to base their economic policy and regulation on accounting numbers. If so, different accounting numbers from different accounting methods will trigger political action that changes the economic environment in which the firm operates. The additional costs arising from policy-induced changes in the economic environment reflect the political costs of choosing a particular accounting method (say, *FIFO*) over its alternative (say, *LIFO*).

This political cost scenario implies that in the real world political costs are larger than *LIFO–FIFO* tax differentials. Hence, managers' inventory accounting choices will be based on political cost considerations instead of tax considerations. This suggests that two firms which have identical production-investment opportunity sets but face different political environments would choose different inventory accounting methods. More formally, this can be stated as follows.

Political Cost Hypothesis. If the relevant political costs are larger than the *LIFO–FIFO* tax differentials, the choices of inventory accounting methods will be based on political considerations instead of tax considerations.

Finally, consider a world wherein intrafirm transactions among managers, stockholders, and bondholders involve high monitoring–contracting costs, but tax and political costs are negligible. In this case, all managers maximize their own objective functions with respect to the constraints of given nominal contracts. Since contract negotiation and monitoring are costly, stockholders and bondholders would tolerate the potential goal incongruence of managers' actions.

In a real setting the agency cost scenario would imply that relevant intrafirm monitoring–contracting costs are larger than *LIFO–FIFO* tax differentials. As a result, managers' inventory accounting choices will be based on intrafirm contractual environments such as compensation schemes and bonds covenants. Accordingly, two firms with identical

---

essence of the Ricardian hypothesis in contrast to the political cost and the agency cost hypotheses is that the manager operates a classical Ricardian firm, so his objective is strictly to maximize the value of his firm (in this case, to minimize tax costs). The term of "Ricardian hypothesis" seems better to reflect the underlying economic assumptions.

production-investment opportunity sets but with different sets of intra-firm contracts would use different inventory accounting methods. Formally, this can be stated as follows.

Agency Cost Hypothesis. If the relevant agency costs are larger than the *LIFO–FIFO* tax differential, the managers' choices of inventory accounting methods can be predicted by the constraints of intrafirm contracts they face.

The Ricardian, political cost, and agency cost hypotheses need not be independent or mutually exclusive. For example, if the political cost hypothesis leads to the objective of minimizing accounting incomes, then the Ricardian hypothesis and the political cost hypothesis will be empirically indistinguishable. Similarly, if both political costs and agency costs are high, managers' inventory accounting choices could be jointly determined by political and intrafirm contractual considerations.

2.2 PROXY VARIABLES IN THE LITERATURE

As a preliminary step to our study, we review previous literature on the *FIFO/LIFO* choices in order to identify proxy variables which might be linked to the three hypotheses. These are summarized in table 1, along with our interpretations of the linkage and main results of these prior studies.

Table 1 shows that 16 proxy variables have been used in studies of inventory accounting choices. Eleven of these 16 variables were not statistically significant in explaining managers' choices. The five that were statistically significant are (1) absolute firm size, (2) potential tax savings of *LIFO* over *FIFO*, (3) industry, (4) auditor, and (5) a ratio of total debts/total assets.

Since Big Eight accounting firms tend to develop a comparative expertise in certain industries, the identity of the auditor in the Eggleton, Penman, and Twombly [1976] study may be simply another proxy for industry. As a result, we omitted this variable in our paper. The other four variables are relevant to our hypotheses and were included in our empirical work. Their linkages are discussed in the next section, along with other variables used in the empirical tests.

3. Proxy Variables and the Ricardian Hypothesis

According to Gonedes [1979], differences in inventory accounting methods can affect the net present value of firms. If managers behave in conformity with the Ricardian hypothesis, all firms with identical production-investment opportunity sets will choose the same inventory accounting methods. For firms with heterogeneous production-investment opportunity sets, value-maximizing managers will adopt inventory accounting methods according to the Ricardian principle of comparative advantage.

TABLE 1
Proxy Variables in the Literature on Choice of Inventory Accounting Methods

Proxy Variables	Authors	Theories	Significance at 5% Level
1. Absolute firm size	Hagerman and Zmijewski [1979][a]	Political cost	No
	Morse and Richardson [1983]	Political cost or Ricardian	Yes
	Abdel-khalik [1985]	Political cost	Yes
2. Growth of accounting income	Morse and Richardson	Political cost	No
3. Dividend/unrestricted R.E.	Morse and Richardson	Agency cost	No
4. Income/interest expense	Morse and Richardson	Agency cost	No
5. $\frac{\text{Net tangible assets}}{\text{Long-term debts}}$ ...	Morse and Richardson	Agency cost	No
6. *As if* cost of goods (potential tax savings of *LIFO* over *FIFO*)	Biddle [1980]	Ricardian	Yes
	Morse and Richardson	Ricardian	Yes
7. Concentration ratio...	Hagerman and Zmijewski	Political cost	No
8. Capital intensity	Hagerman and Zmijewski	Political cost	No
	Abdel-khalik	Political cost	Yes
9. Risk (beta)	Hagerman and Zmijewski	Political cost	No
10. Effective tax rate.....	Hagerman and Zmijewski	Agency cost and political cost	No
11. Change of corporate personnel	Eggleton-Penman-Twombly [1976]	N/A[b]	No
12. Industry	Eggleton-Penman-Twombly	N/A	Yes
13. Auditor	Eggleton-Penman-Twombly	N/A	Yes
14. Management profit-sharing dummy	Hagerman and Zmijewski	Agency cost	No
15. *CEO* compensation ...	Abdel-khalik	Agency cost	No
16. Total debt/total assets	Zmijewski-Hagerman [1981]	Agency cost	Yes[c]

[a] The number in brackets indicates the publication year.
[b] Eggleton-Penman-Twombly did not elaborate any theory of management motivation.
[c] It is significant only in the sample of small firms.

3.1 IRS TAX REGULATION AND THE RICARDIAN PRINCIPLE OF COMPARATIVE ADVANTAGE

The use of *LIFO* is under strict IRS regulation. The four main rules relevant to its implementation are: (1) Only the cost method of valuation can be used in conjunction with the *LIFO* method. There cannot be any write-downs to market value. (2) *LIFO* may not be used if the taxpayer uses any other inventory method for credit purposes or for financial reports. (3) In general, once a taxpaper elects the *LIFO* method, a subsequent change is not available without approval from the IRS commissioner. Automatic approval is available if the taxpayer agrees to a ten-year spread of any positive adjustments. (4) The IRS has established a list of four situations that may warrant the termination of the *LIFO* election: (*a*) violation of the reporting conformity requirements; (*b*) failure to restate inventories for the preceding year to cost; (*c*) failure to elect properly; and (*d*) failure to maintain adequate records with respect to *LIFO*.

According to rule (1), the *LIFO* method precludes the use of the lower of cost or market rule for *LIFO* inventories. This suggests that firms with large inventory price fluctuations may have a comparative advantage in adopting the *FIFO* method, whereas firms with steady price movements should have a comparative advantage in adopting *LIFO*. Rules (2) and (3) imply that the *LIFO* method requires high bookkeeping costs and is under closer scrutiny by the IRS. Therefore, larger and technologically more advanced firms will have a comparative advantage in adopting the *LIFO* method.

The achievement of maximum tax benefit from the *LIFO* method requires stable year-end inventory levels. Firms with large year-end inventory fluctuations should have comparative advantages in adopting the *FIFO* method. Moreover, according to rule (3), firms are free to switch from *FIFO* to *LIFO* but not vice versa. Hence, *FIFO* firms hold a valuable timing option which allows them to switch to the *LIFO* method at a future optimal time. This timing option is freely disposable, so its value is nonnegative.[2] The opportunity cost of holding this timing option is the current tax savings a firm could otherwise derive from the *LIFO* method. Consequently, a firm will "kill" this timing option and switch to the *LIFO* method when the inflation rate is high and the increase of year-end inventory is large, which make the opportunity costs of the timing option higher than its value. Those firms with high inflation rates should have a comparative advantage in using the *LIFO* method, whereas other firms should have a comparative advantage in keeping the *FIFO* method.

3.2 THE PRODUCTION-INVESTMENT OPPORTUNITY SET AND PROXY VARIABLES

The foregoing discussion implies that comparative advantages in adopting a particular inventory accounting method depend primarily on three factors: (1) the stochastic process of inventory prices, (2) the stochastic process of inventory quantities, and (3) bookkeeping and tax-reporting costs. In this study, we hypothesize that the exogenously given production-investment opportunity set will have a dominant influence on these three factors. We used eight proxy variables to reflect the characteristics of the production-investment opportunity set that are relevant to the choice of inventory accounting method. They are: price variability, inventory variability, accounting income variability, absolute

---

[2] Lee [1984] provides two formulas to evaluate the timing option. Based on Lee's [1984] model, Lee and Petruzzi [1985] developed a stochastic model for optimal timing of inventory accounting switches.

firm size, relative firm size, capital intensity, inventory intensity, and industry classification.

Accounting income variability serves as a proxy for a firm's operational volatility. Operational volatility depends on the nature of the output market, production technology, and the general economic environment. When a firm operates smoothly, it should be less costly to control inventory, so such a firm will have a comparative advantage in adopting the *LIFO* method.

The *LIFO*-related bookkeeping and tax-reporting costs seem to be mostly fixed in nature. Consequently, larger firms will have a comparative cost advantage in adopting the *LIFO* method. The absolute size of the firm may also be a proxy for operational volatility and inventory controllability in that due to economies of scale, larger firms seem to be better able to attain smooth operations and inventory control. Since the nature of the output market and production technology and factoral intensity differ from industry to industry, economies of scale may also be reflected in relative firm size within each industry.[3]

Another important aspect of the production-investment opportunity set is the relative factoral intensity. Capital-intensive firms will have higher proportions of fixed to variable costs which increase the importance of financial and production planning. Since the *LIFO* method itself requires more control and planning than the *FIFO* method, a capital-intensive firm should have a comparative advantage in adopting the *LIFO* method.

The ability to control inventory is also reflected in such ratios as the inventory turnover. We assume that a high inventory turnover indicates an efficient inventory management.

Finally, since production-investment opportunity sets will vary from industry to industry, we used industry classification as a proxy variable for production-investment opportunity sets. However, this is a very robust proxy variable that could also be consistent with other competing theories.

3.3 MEASUREMENT OF VARIABLES

We could not obtain data on bookkeeping and tax-reporting costs. The data collected for the other eight variables are discussed in this subsection.

3.3.1. Inventory variability. Inventory variability was measured by the coefficient of variation (variance/mean ratio) for year-end inventories.

3.3.2. Accounting income variability. We used the variance/mean ratios of before-tax accounting income to measure the accounting income variability.

---

[3] To the extent that many firms are diversified across several industries, the measurement of relative size within an industry would be very noisy. The measurement errors can reduce the power of our test or even lead to biased results. According to Judge et al. [1980], the bias is toward a zero relative-size effect.

3.3.3. Price variability. The data for inventory prices were collected from the DRI (Data Resources Institute) tape. Although we tried to match the descriptions of price indices in the DRI tape and the SIC code used in the *Compustat* tape as closely as possible, measurement errors may not have been totally resolved. To avoid the measurement error problem, we chose a simple but robust measurement—the relative frequency of positive inflation.[4] For each SIC four-digit industry, we calculated the relative frequency of positive price changes for the period 1960–80. A large relative frequency of positive inflation implies that the mean inflation rate is high, the variance of inflation rate is small, or both.[5] Consequently, a higher frequency of positive inflation should lead to a comparative advantage in adopting the *LIFO* method.

3.3.4. Absolute firm size. Absolute firm size was measured by both assets and net sales.

3.3.5. Relative firm size. Relative firm size was measured both as the ratio of a firm's assets to the total industry assets and a firm's sales to total industry sales, based on the SIC four-digit industry codes.

3.3.6. Capital intensity. Two measures were used here: the ratio of gross fixed assets to net sales (gross capital intensity) and net fixed assets to net sales (net capital intensity).

3.3.7. Efficiency of inventory management. Efficiency of inventory management was measured by the inventory/net sales ratio and the inventory/total assets ratio.

3.3.8. Industry dummies. To keep the number of industry dummy variables small and manageable, we assigned a dummy variable to each of the two-digit SIC industries. This yielded 20 industry dummy variables as a result.

4. Data and Univariate Analysis

The financial data were collected from the *Compustat* file. All firms in the sample had to have adopted either the *LIFO* method or the *FIFO* method for at least seven uninterrupted years.[6] The data collection period of each firm varied from 7 years to 20 years. The sample consists of 127 firms which had adopted *LIFO* and 672 firms which had adopted *FIFO* (a total of 799 firms). Table 2 lists the distribution of data in terms of

---

[4] We also measured the price variability in terms of the coefficient of variations of inflation rates. Our estimation of the effect of price variability on choice of accounting method is not statistically significant using this measure.

[5] Since the mean inflation rate is positive, when the variance of the inflation rate approaches zero, the relative frequency of positive inflation will approach one.

[6] Beginning in 1972, if more than one inventory accounting method is used to value inventory, then all applicable codes of methods will be noted in the *Compustat* file. We eliminated all the firms with more than one code of inventory accounting method. Hence our data are less pure before 1972 than after. However, the inventory accounting method that is identified for each sampled firm is at least the primary method used.

TABLE 2

Distribution of Sample Data

SIC Code	Description	Number of LIFO Firms	Number of FIFO Firms	Subtotal
2000	Food and Beverages	7	24	31
2200	Textile Products	7	13	20
2300	Textile-Apparel Mfrs.	3	59	62
2400	Forest Products	2	16	18
2500	Home Furnishings	1	14	15
2600	Paper Products.	5	6	11
2700	Publishing.	0	12	12
2800	Chemicals	5	53	58
2900	Petroleum Products.	5	13	18
3000	Rubber and Plastic	3	17	20
3300	Steel Products	30	15	45
3400	Metal Products.	12	50	62
3500	Machinery.	15	124	139
3600	Appliances	8	123	131
3700	Motor Vehicles and Aircraft. . . .	5	32	37
3800	Instruments	4	39	43
3900	Leisure Goods.	2	21	23
5100	Drug Stores.	1	14	15
5300	Department Stores	6	6	12
5400	Grocery Stores	6	21	27
	Total	127	672	799

SIC two-digit codes and inventory accounting methods. The *FIFO* method is the method adopted by the majority of firms of each industry except in the steel industry.

The means of test variables, the predicted differences, the *t*-statistics, and the appropriate underlying theory are provided in table 3 for the *LIFO* firms and the *FIFO* firms. The first 11 variables will be examined extensively throughout the remainder of this paper. The variables V_{12} to V_{15} are briefly discussed in this section. The univariate tests of the hypotheses of mean differences were based on simple *t* tests.[7] The

$$[7]\ t_i = \frac{\sum_{l=1}^{127} \frac{V_{il}}{127} - \sum_{f=1}^{672} \frac{V_{if}}{672}}{\sqrt{\frac{(127-1)S_{il}^2 + (672-1)S_{if}^2}{127+672-2}}};$$

where

i = attribute index;

l = index of *LIFO* firms, $l = 1, \ldots, 127$;

f = index of *FIFO* firms, $f = 1, \ldots, 672$;

V_{il}, V_{if} = value of variable V_i of firm l and f respectively;

S_{il}^2, S_{if}^2 = sample variance of variable V_1 of all *LIFO* firms and *FIFO* firms, respectively.

TABLE 3

Univariate Analysis of Inventory Accounting Choice

	Variables	(1) LIFO Firms	(2) FIFO Firms	(3) Behavioral Theory	(4) Hypothesis	(5) t-statistic[c]
V_1	Net sales	445M[a]	152M[a]	P.C., R.	$t_1 > 0$	6.35
V_2	Total assets	349M	110M	P.C., R.	$t_2 > 0$	5.04
V_3	Variability of inventories .	0.294[b]	0.537[b]	R.	$t_3 < 0$	−10.8
V_4	Variability of before-tax income	0.397	0.931	R.	$t_4 < 0$	−1.59
V_5	Long-term debt/equity ratio	0.63	0.55	A.C.	$t_5 < 0$	1.14
V_6	Inventories/net sales	0.182	0.218	R.	$t_6 < 0$	−3.42
V_7	Inventories/total assets . . .	0.278	0.	R.	$t_7 < 0$	−3.87
V_8	Relative size in net sales . .	1.32	0.87	P.C., R.	$t_8 > 0$	3.44
V_9	Relative size in total assets	1.28	0.87	P.C., R.	$t_9 > 0$	3.05
V_{10}	Gross capital intensity	0.55	0.34	P.C., R.	$t_{10} > 0$	7.38
V_{11}	Relative frequency of price increases	0.74	0.62	R.	$t_{11} > 0$	4.76
V_{12}	Debt/equity ratio	1.43	.34	A.C.	$t_{12} < 0$	0.64
V_{13}	Net capital intensity	0.29	0.20	P.C., R.	$t_{13} > 0$	4.28
V_{14}	Variability of inflation rates	0.07	0.06	R.	$t_{14} < 0$	1.55
V_{15}	Effective tax rate	0.42	0.45	N.A.	—	−1.40

[a] M represents million dollars.

[b] P.C. stands for political cost theory; R. for Ricardian hypothesis; A.C. for agency cost theory; and N.A. for no particular theory applied.

[c] With degrees of freedom of 797, the t-statistics are normally distributed.

predicted signs of t_i are given in column (4) and the calculated t-statistics in column (5).

The test results for the two agency variables are not consistent with the agency cost hypothesis. However, the proxy variables (debt/equity ratios) might be too weak to capture the effect of agency costs on inventory accounting choices. Although the test results are more consistent with the Ricardian and the political cost hypotheses, we cannot differentiate between the two hypotheses because both are tested with an overlapping set of proxy variables.

Table 4 shows the correlations among the ten proxy variables, V_1–V_{10}, and the correlations between inventory accounting choices and each of the ten proxy variables.[8] Several interesting features appear in table 4. First, the size variables (V_1 and V_2) are significantly correlated with inventory accounting choices, but they are also significantly correlated with many other proxy variables (e.g., V_6, V_7, V_8, V_9, and V_{10}), which are also significantly correlated with inventory accounting choice. Hence the correlation between size variables and inventory accounting choices

---

[8] The relative frequency of price increases (V_{11}) is not a firm-specific proxy variable. Table 4 only observes the correlations among the firm-specific proxy variables.

TABLE 4
Pearson Correlation Coefficients

	V_1	V_2	V_3	V_4	V_5	V_6	V_7	V_8	V_9	V_{10}
$V_2{}^a$	.855*b									
V_3	−.103*	−.067								
V_4	−.021	−.016	.024							
V_5	−.036	−.033	−.079	−.002						
V_6	−.152*	−.056	.090	−.025	.045					
V_7	−.171*	−.237*	−.088	.027	−.075	.453*				
V_8	.555*	.400*	−.063	−.026	−.062	−.057	−.081			
V_9	.543*	.428*	−.053	−.034	−.033	−.003	−.105*	.979*		
V_{10}	.306*	.452*	−.085	−.058	.140*	.214*	−.468*	.095*	.152*	
*LIFO/FIFO*c	.218*	.174*	−.358*	−.072	.040	−.118*	−.136*	.121*	.108*	.249*

a A description of the variables is given in table 3.
b Asterisk sign indicates significance at 1% level.
c *LIFO/FIFO* is a dummy variable where 0 is a *FIFO* firm and 1 is a *LIFO* firm.

could be spurious. As a result, the size effect cannot provide unequivocal support for any specific hypothesis.

Second, the variability of inventory (V_3) is significantly correlated with inventory accounting choices, but it is not correlated with other proxy variables except Net Sales (V_1). Even there, the correlation is relatively small (−0.103). This indicates that the univariate test of V_3 is reasonably independent of other proxy variables. Finally, except for the correlation between V_1 and V_2 (both are size variables), the correlations among proxy variables are all smaller than 0.6. Hence, the issue of multicollinearity in a multivariate test does not seem to be overwhelming here.[9]

Before leaving this section, we briefly discuss V_{12} to V_{15}. The three pairs of proxy variables, namely, (V_{12}, V_5), (V_{13}, V_{10}), and (V_{14} and V_{11}), measure the same underlying economic determinants. Since the t-statistics of V_5, V_{10}, and V_{11} are respectively more significant than V_{12}, V_{13}, and V_{14}, they are included in our multivariate probit tests but the latter are omitted.

Hagerman and Zmijewski [1979] presumed that the *LIFO* method has a tax benefit over the *FIFO* method, in which case the larger the effective tax rate, the more desirable the *LIFO* method would be. However, the *LIFO* method does not necessarily result in tax savings for all firms. A good counterexample is that in an industry with a declining price level, the *FIFO* method should have a tax benefit over the *LIFO* method. Hence the effective tax rate (V_5) cannot represent the relative attractiveness of the *LIFO* method. We do not find significant differences in effective tax rate between *LIFO* firms and *FIFO* firms. Hence, V_{15} is also omitted from the multivariate probit tests.

---

[9] According to Judge et al. [1980, p. 459], a rule of thumb for a serious multicollinearity problem is when the correlations among the explanatory variables are higher than 0.8. An alternative version of this rule is to compare the simple correlation coefficients to R^2 and conclude that multicollinearity is deemed harmful if these correlation coefficients are greater than R^2.

5. Multivariate Analyses

It has been well documented that size and industry are associated with choices of inventory accounting methods (for example, Eggleton, Penman, and Twombly [1976] and Morse and Richardson [1983]). The general interpretation is that size and industry proxy for more fundamental economic variables which determine accounting choices. In this section, we examine some potential underlying economic variables, using multivariate probit analysis.

We begin the multivariate analysis by measuring industry effects. Twenty dummy variables were used to represent the 20 SIC two-digit industries defined in table 2. Probit modes were then estimated and the results appear as Analysis 1 in table 5. Each entry in table 5 is the t-statistic of the marginal effect of a given proxy variable on the inventory accounting choice.[10] If the t-statistic is larger than two, then the given proxy variable has significant marginal explanatory power.[11] The marginal explanatory power of all industry dummies is measured by the likelihood ratio test statistic:

$$LR = -2(-349.900) - (-293.030) = 113.740.$$

With degrees of freedom of (10.798), LR is significant at the 0.01% level.

From Analysis 1, we see that the industry effect does significantly "explain" managers' choices of inventory accounting methods. Knowing the SIC two-digit code of each firm allows us to predict correctly the firms' inventory accounting methods 85.98% of the time. This prediction power is much better than Hagerman and Zmijewski's [1979] model which had only a 58.00% correction rate.

The industry effect may actually reflect differential industrial price movements. When the prices of inventories go up, firms will benefit from adopting the *LIFO* method. To examine whether industrial price movements actually explain this industry effect, we included industry dummies and V_{11} (relative frequency of price increases in each industry during 1960–79) in our estimations of the probit models. The results are reported as Analysis 2 in table 5. If the industry dummies are nothing but proxies for inventory price movements, then including V_{11} in the estimation of the probit models should greatly reduce the significance of the t-statistics of the dummy variables. The evidence from Analysis 2 suggests that the industry dummies are not proxies for inventory price movements. In fact,

---

[10] As far as the examination of industry effect is concerned, we could apply the χ^2 independency test and obtain essentially the same result. By using a multivariate probit method, however, we are able to show that the industry effect is simply a proxy for some other more fundamental economic variables.

[11] The t-statistics in Analysis 1 are similar to those of univariate tests. Because the industry dummies D are mutually independent by construction, the regression in Analysis 1 is in fact a canonical regression. Hence, the t-statistic of each industry is independent of other variables.

the industry dummies and V_{11} jointly and complementarily determine the inventory accounting choice. When V_{11} is included in the estimation, the values of the t-statistic of many industry dummies actually increase.

A second possible explanation of the industry effect is that firms in different industries have different production-investment opportunity sets. Except for the long-term debt/equity ratio (V_5), the ten variables, V_1–V_{10}, listed in table 5 are intended to be proxy variables for production-investment opportunity sets. Variables V_3 (variability of inventory), V_4 (variability of income), V_6 (inventory/sales), and V_7 (inventory/assets) are derived from the Ricardian hypothesis. The other five variables, V_1 (net sales), V_2 (total assets), V_8 (relative size in sales), V_9 (relative size in assets), and V_{10} (capital intensity), could be interpreted as proxies for both the Ricardian and the political cost hypotheses.

V_1, V_2, V_8, and V_9 are basically size variables measured in different ways. If the Ricardian hypothesis is descriptively valid, then these size variables can be replaced by the proxy variables representing production-investment opportunity set. Including size and the proxies for production-investment characteristics should lead to reductions in the significance of the size coefficients, if size is merely proxying for the same phenomenon. Similarly, if the industry effect noted above is also proxying for the same characteristics, including industry dummy variables together with these other proxy variables in a multivariate probit analysis should reduce the significance of industry effects. Of course, multicollinearity would reduce the statistical significance of all the explanatory variables. But a good proxy variable should only wipe out the statistical significance of a bad proxy variable.

Analyses 3 and 4 are similar except that the size variable in Analysis 3 is measured by net sales and that in Analysis 4 is measured by total assets. The statistical significances for most variables, especially those related to the Ricardian hypothesis, are somewhat higher in Analysis 3 than Analysis 4, suggesting that V_6 is a better measurement of inventory turnover than V_7. Both analyses show that the size effect is no longer significant when included in multivariate analyses employing proxy variables for production-investment opportunity sets.

Since neither the size effect nor the debt/equity ratio effect is significant in Analyses 3 and 4, we conclude that our evidence does not support either the political cost hypothesis or the agency cost hypothesis. However, our results by no means conclusively reject these two hypotheses. More careful development of proxy variables for these two hypotheses is needed before any conclusive statements can be made.

Analyses 5 and 6 differ only in the measurement of the size variable— net sales in Analysis 5 and total assets in Analysis 6. These two analyses include the industry dummies along with variables V_1–V_{11}. Note that the significance of industry effects observed in Analyses 1 and 2 disappears. This result also implies that the significant industry effects probably

TABLE 5

Multivariate Analysis of Inventory Accounting Choice

Determinant Variables	Behavioral	Theoretical Sign	Analysis 1	Analysis 2	Analysis 3	Analysis 4	Analysis 5	Analysis 6
V_1 Sales	P.C., R.	+	—	—	+0.376	—	+0.500	—
V_2 Assets	P.C., R.	+	—	—	—	+0.159	—	+0.352
V_3 Inv. Var.	R.	−	—	—	−7.668	−7.377	−6.153	−5.727
V_4 Inc. Var.	R.	−	—	—	−2.136	−1.924	−1.944	−1.854
V_5 Long-Term D/E	A.C.	−	—	—	−0.318	−0.505	−0.721	−1.045
V_6 Inv/Sales	R.	−	—	—	−3.247	—	−3.613	—
V_7 Inv/Assets	R.	−	—	—	—	−1.761	—	−2.234
V_8 Rel. Sales	P.C., R.	+	—	—	+0.998	—	+1.429	—
V_9 Rel. Assets	P.C., R.	+	—	—	—	+0.927	—	+1.573
V_{10} Cap. Int.	P.C., R.	+	—	—	+3.883	+2.711	+1.360	+0.494
V_{11} Price Movement	R.	+	—	+2.714	—	—	+2.548	+2.561
D_1 (2000)			−3.012	−4.050	—	—	+0.037	+0.573
D_2 (2200)			−1.341	−2.786	—	—	+0.913	+0.903
D_3 (2300)			−6.071	−6.081	—	—	−1.160	−0.944
D_4 (2400)			−3.121	−4.114	—	—	−0.167	+0.096
D_5 (2500)			−3.012	−4.044	—	—	−1.418	−1.228
D_6 (2600)			−0.301	−2.010	—	—	+0.036	+0.289
D_7 (2700)			−67.589	−12.478	—	—	−7.216	−7.253
D_8 (2800)			−5.821	−6.039	—	—	−0.629	−0.493
D_9 (2900)			−1.872	−3.173	—	—	−0.769	−0.374
D_{10} (3000)			−3.027	−3.993	—	—	−0.016	+0.211
D_{11} (3300)			+2.228	+1.303	—	—	+1.698	+1.670
D_{12} (3400)			−4.731	−4.481	—	—	−0.427	−0.285
D_{13} (3500)			−8.765	−5.439	—	—	+0.105	−0.069
D_{14} (3600)			−8.954	−9.570	—	—	−0.274	−0.278
D_{15} (3700)			−4.262	−4.731	—	—	−0.610	−0.409

D_{16} (3800)	−4.894	−5.022	—	—	−0.708	−0.700
D_{17} (3900)	−3.662	−4.521	—	—	−0.743	−0.621
D_{18} (5100)	−3.012	−3.928	—	—	−1.655	−0.547
D_{19} (5300)	0.000	−1.785	—	—	+0.773	−0.964
D_{20} (5400)	−2.845	−3.932	—	—	−0.798	+0.348
Estimated R^2	0.471	0.481	0.538	.526	.590	.580
% Correctly Predicted	85.98	85.98	85.98	85.98	87.98	87.86
Value of Log-Likelihood Function	−293.030	−287.525	−255.741	−262.474	−227.304	−232.716

D_i, $i = 1, \ldots, 20$, are dummy variables for the SIC two-digit industries indicated in parentheses. A description of SIC codes is given in table 2.
V_{1i} is the relative frequency of price increases in each industry during 1960–1979.
The value of the log-likelihood function when all coefficients are restricted to be zero is −349.900.
The entry is the t-statistic of the estimated coefficient of each proxy variable. Because the degree of freedom is very large, each t-statistic is deemed normally distributed.
P.C. stands for political cost hypothesis; A.C. for agency cost hypothesis; and R. for Ricardian hypothesis.

reflect cross-industry differences in production-investment opportunity sets.

Across the six multivariate analyses in table 5, four variables are consistently significant throughout—(1) inventory variability (V_3), (2) inventory turnover (V_6), (3) relative frequency of inventory price increases (V_{11}), and (4) dummy for publishing industry (D_7). The first three are derived from the Ricardian hypothesis. That is, the inventory variability and inventory turnover are related to the efficiency of inventory control, and the relative frequency of inventory price increases is an important factor in the firm's production-investment opportunity set. It would be difficult to imagine a scenario that could attribute their effects to either the political cost hypothesis or the agency cost hypothesis.

The dummy variables for the publishing industry may merely reflect the phenomenon of the short economic lives of books. Writing down year-end inventories of unsold first editions is a common practice in the publishing industry. Hence the whole publishing industry uses the *FIFO* method that affords them the write-down opportunity. The variable V_{11} measures the average price movement in each industry, and this may not capture the write-down feature precisely.

Two econometric issues need to be addressed. First, as pointed out by Biddle [1980], the efficiency of inventory control is not exogenous to inventory accounting choice. The endowed differences in inventory variability and inventory turnover can affect inventory accounting choices. But the inventory accounting choice can also affect inventory variability and inventory turnover. Hence, our results may be subject to simultaneous equations bias. To circumvent this problem, we estimated the equations using an instrumental-variable approach. Similar results were obtained (available upon request). Second, as pointed out by McFadden [1982], both logit and probit methods are nonlinear approximations of underlying choice models, and there is no theoretical basis on which to choose between these two methods. Our results, however, were the same using both methods.

6. Conclusion

In this study, we examined systematic differences in characteristics between *LIFO* and *FIFO* firms, using both univariate and multivariate analyses. Three hypotheses of managers' inventory accounting choices were explored—agency cost, political cost, and Ricardian. Our univariate results did not support the agency cost hypothesis, and were equally consistent with the other two hypotheses. However, our multivariate analyses, which allow us to assess each hypothesis separately, were more consistent with the Ricardian hypothesis. We conclude that the size and industry effects noted in prior studies of inventory accounting choices more likely reflect differences in production-investment characteristics of firms than differences in political costs.

REFERENCES

ABDEL-KHALIK, A. R. "The Effect of LIFO-Switching and Firm Ownership on Executives' Pay." *Journal of Accounting Research* (Autumn 1985): 427–47.

BIDDLE, G. "Accounting Methods and Management Decisions: The Case of Inventory Costing and Inventory Policy." *Journal of Accounting Research* (Supplement 1980): 235–80.

EGGLETON, I. R. C., S. H. PENMAN, AND J. R. TWOMBLY. "Accounting Changes and Stock Prices: An Examination of Selected Uncontrolled Variables." *Journal of Accounting Research* (Spring 1976): 66–88.

GONEDES, N. J. "Accounting Techniques and Firms' Equilibrium Values: Tax Methods and the LIFO/FIFO Choice." Report 7911, Center for Mathematical Studies in Business and Economics, University of Chicago, 1979.

HAGERMAN, R., AND M. ZMIJEWSKI. "Some Economic Determinants of Accounting Policy Choice." *Journal of Accounting and Economics* (August 1979): 141–61.

HOLTHAUSEN, R. W., AND R. W. LEFTWICH. "The Economic Consequences of Accounting Choice: Implications of Costly Contracting and Monitoring." *Journal of Accounting and Economics* (August 1983): 77–118.

JUDGE, G. G., ET AL. *The Theory and Practice of Econometrics.* New York: Wiley, 1980.

LEE, C. J. "Tax Effect Hypothesis and Inventory Accounting Methods." Working paper, University of Pennsylvania, 1984.

———, AND C. PETRUZZI. "A Stochastic Model of Inventory Accounting Choice." Working paper, University of Pennsylvania, 1985.

MCFADDEN, D. "Econometric Models of Probabilistic Choice." In *Structural Analysis of Discrete Data: With Econometric Applications*, edited by C. Manski and D. McFadden. Cambridge, Mass.: M.I.T. Press, 1982.

MORSE, D., AND G. RICHARDSON. "The LIFO/FIFO Decision." *Journal of Accounting Research* (Spring 1983): 106–27.

ZMIJEWSKI, M. E., AND R. L. HAGERMAN. "An Income Strategy Approach to the Positive Theory of Accounting Standard Setting/Choice." *Journal of Accounting and Economics* (August 1981): 129–49.

THE EFFECTS OF DEBT COVENANTS AND POLITICAL COSTS ON THE CHOICE OF ACCOUNTING METHODS

The Case of Accounting for R&D Costs

Lane A. DALEY and Robert L. VIGELAND*

University of Minnesota, Minneapolis, MN 55455, USA

Received October 1982, final version received September 1983

Until 1974, firms could capitalize or expense all or part of their research and development (R&D) costs. Managerial choice between these two alternatives is hypothesized to be affected by the existence of debt covenants which employ accounting numbers relating to leverage, interest coverage, and ability to pay dividends. In addition, the use of public versus private debt is hypothesized to affect the accounting choice due to differential renegotiation costs. Lastly, a political cost hypothesis is tested. This study uses a multivariate statistical technique, the generalized jackknife. The results suggest that firms which capitalized R&D costs were more highly levered, used more public debt, were closer to dividend restrictions, and were smaller than firms which expensed R&D costs.

1. Introduction

In 1974, the Financial Accounting Standards Board (FASB) adopted Statement No. 2 which required firms to expense, rather than capitalize, research and development (R&D) costs. Prior to that time, firm managers could choose which of the two accounting treatments they wished to apply.

Recent research by Hagerman and Zmijewski (HZ) (1979), Zmijewski and Hagerman (ZH) (1981), Bowen, Noreen and Lacey (BNL) (1981), and Dhaliwal (1980), among others, has begun to investigate the motivation for management's choice among alternative accounting principles. Using agency theory and other economic factors, models have been developed to distinguish between firms choosing different accounting alternatives (e.g., capitalization vs. expensing) for apparently similar events and transactions. This study seeks to extend this analysis to the choice of an accounting method for R&D expenditures prior to FASB No. 2.

The study focuses on two opposing incentives which affect management's choice between capitalization or expensing R&D costs. First, we examine the

*The comments of participants at the 1982 UBC–Washington–Oregon conference and the University of Minnesota workshop as well as Pete Frost, Jerry Zimmerman, and especially Bob Bowen, have been most helpful and are gratefully acknowledged. Any errors remaining are the responsibility of the authors.

potential for contracting costs in the form of bond covenant limitations on leverage, dividend payments, and interest coverage to motivate this choice. Along with these variables we also investigate the effect of using public debt on this choice. Second, a political cost hypothesis, similar to that originally proposed by Watts and Zimmerman (1978), is also employed.

Generally, the results support the hypothesis that firms with higher leverage and tighter dividend restrictions (both typical types of debt covenant restrictions) are more likely to capitalize some R&D costs. In addition, larger firms are more likely to expense as suggested by the political cost hypothesis.

The remainder of the paper is organized as follows. Section 2 develops the hypotheses to be tested. Section 3 discusses issues of experimental design and sample selection. In section 4 some descriptive statistics on the variables used in this study are given. Section 5 develops the multivariate analysis used in this study to test the hypotheses, while section 6 discusses the results. Section 7 discusses various sensitivity tests and the paper closes with a summary in section 8.

2. Hypotheses

The hypotheses employed here to explain the choice of an accounting method for R&D costs are similar to those used elsewhere [e.g. BNL (1981)] to explain other choices of accounting methods. A brief summary of recent work in this area can be found in Holthausen and Leftwich (1983). This section consists of two parts. The first develops hypotheses related to financial variables present in debt covenants while the second does the same for political costs.

2.1. Financial variables

The use of restrictive covenants in debt agreements to reduce management's ability to create wealth transfers between debt and equity holders has been recognized for some time [see Jensen and Meckling (1976), and Smith and Warner (1979)]. These restrictions generally focus on financial variables and set maximum limits for both leverage and dividend distributions. Leverage limitations are typically of two types: (1) limits on long term debt/total assets, and (2) limits on the interest coverage ratio. Dividends are restricted to a maximum available pool (unrestricted retained earnings) from which dividends may be paid. Since generally accepted accounting principles are used to measure these financial variables, capitalization of R&D costs will (ceterius paribus) tend to relax these debt constraints (relative to expensing R&D costs) by increasing earnings, retained earnings, and total assets. This motivates the first three hypotheses of this study, stated in their alternative form:

H_A^1.   Firms which capitalized R&D were more heavily levered.[1]

H_A^2.   Firms which capitalized R&D had lower interest coverage ratios.

H_A^3.   Firms which capitalized R&D had higher ratios of dividends to unrestricted retained earnings.

Leftwich (1981) hypothesizes that when a firm finds it necessary to alter its debt constraints, public debt agreements are more costly to renegotiate than private debt agreements. This suggests that firms which use public debt more extensively are more likely to use accounting principles to avoid covenant restrictions since for the same probability of violation the expected costs are higher for a firm with more public debt.[2] This leads to the fourth hypothesis,

H_A^4.   Firms which capitalized R&D cost had more public debt in their capital structure.

2.2. Political costs

Managers, particularly those of larger firms, may undermine their credibility by adopting reporting rules which are perceived as unorthodox by financial statement users. As discussed in BNL (1981), such a loss in credibility may create additional transactions costs. Thus, managers will only choose unorthodox reporting standards if the expected benefits exceed the increased costs. While this cost may not be large on average, for larger firms far from covenant constraints it may be sufficient to cause avoidance of an accounting policy such as capitalization of R&D costs which was not widely followed.[3]

Since capitalization is likely to make reported income higher (on average) it may be that the expected costs of government scrutiny are also increased by this choice [see Watts and Zimmerman (1978) for a further discussion of this issue]. Presumably if firms report higher incomes, regulators will be more likely to place tighter constraints on such firms' operations. There may be less risk of this for small firms if regulators tend to focus on large

---

[1]The level of a firm's leverage is only a proxy for the firm's proximity to a constraint on leverage if the maximum leverage specified in debt covenants is constant across firms. Cross-sectional differences in maximum leverage will introduce measurement error.

[2]The existence of public debt will also likely alter the nature of the constraints within the bond covenants. Smith and Warner (1979) report that private debt agreements are more likely to specify the use of particular accounting treatments in determining critical accounting ratios (e.g. leverage, etc.) than are public debt agreements. Public indentures are more likely to rely on GAAP as a way of reducing monitoring costs. If constraints are measured using GAAP, management may use alternatives within GAAP to reduce the probability of violating a debt constraint.

[3]See Gellein and Newman (1973) for a survey of reporting practices for R&D costs prior to the adoption of FASB Statement No. 2.

recognizable firms to obtain the greatest political benefits. Each of these factors leads to the last alternative hypothesis of this study.

·H_A^5.   Firms which capitalized R&D tended to be smaller firms.

3. Experimental design and sample selection

To test the hypotheses developed in section 2 we employ a treatment and control group design (capitalizers and expensers, respectively). The capitalizers were identified by reference to the *Disclosure Journal Index of Corporate Events* covering the period from May, 1974 to April, 1976.[4] These firms all changed their accounting method to expensing R&D costs as incurred in response to or in anticipation of FASB No. 2. Firms complying with FASB No. 2 in reports filed with the SEC after April, 1976, or those switching before May, 1974, are not included in the sample of capitalizers. Whether this results in our sample being unrepresentative is not clear, since those switching early are likely to be least affected by the switch, but those waiting the longest are likely to be most affected.

Once this population of 433 capitalizers was identified, the expensers were randomly selected from a set of firms identified as having R&D expense reported for 1972 on the *Compustat Annual Industrial File*, but not listed as being a capitalizer.[5] This set totalled 843 firms, of which 215 (approximately 25%) were randomly drawn for inclusion in the control group.[6] Since a Compustat limitation was imposed to identify the control group, a similar constraint was placed on the capitalizers so as not to create a size bias which would affect the hypothesis test. This, of course, introduces a survivorship bias into the study. A sample of 152 capitalizers in the Compustat file were identified. Inability to obtain a required data item resulted in the firm being dropped from the sample. The final sample consisted of 313 firms (178 R&D expensing firms and 135 R&D capitalizing firms). Table 1 gives a breakdown of the sample by two-digit SIC codes.

All of the data items used in this study are the 1972 amounts. The year 1972 was chosen because it was the year immediately preceding the start of the FASB's deliberations on the R&D accounting issue and, thus, the last

---

[4]Publication of the *Disclosure Journal* was terminated as of April, 1976.

[5]Firms in regulated industries such as banks, insurance, railroads and air transportation, were excluded due to possible limitations on accounting principle choice imposed by industry regulators. These industries were also omitted from the capitalizing sample. The industries excluded were SIC codes 4000–4999 inclusive, except for SIC code 4950 — Pollution control services.

[6]A sample size of 215 firms was selected arbitrarily with the intention of achieving a representative sample while keeping data collection costs manageable. Since the size of the population of all capitalizers and expensers is unknown, the relative frequency of each group in the sample may be unrepresentative.

Table 1

Industry membership of sample firms.

SIC	Industry	Expensers	Capitalizers
10	Metal mining	2	1
13	Oil and gas exploration	1	5
15	Building construction	0	1
17	Construction — special trade	0	1
20	Food and kindred products	13	1
21	Tobacco	1	0
22	Textile products	6	0
23	Apparel	3	4
24	Lumber and wood products	2	2
25	Home furnishings	1	0
26	Paper and allied products	4	2
27	Printing and publishing	2	2
28	Chemicals and allied products	25	7
29	Petroleum refining	5	1
30	Rubber and miscellaneous plastics	6	2
32	Stone, clay, glass, and concrete products	6	4
33	Primary metal industries	5	2
34	Fabricated metal products	8	7
35	Machinery, except electrical	25	21
36	Electrical and electronic machinery, equipment, and supplies	20	21
37	Transportation equipment	16	13
38	Instruments	8	9
39	Miscellaneous manufacturing	7	9
49	Electric, gas, and sanitary services	0	1
50	Wholesale trade — durable goods	1	3
51	Wholesale trade — non-durable goods	2	2
54	Retail trade — food	1	0
56	Retail trade — apparel	1	0
59	Retail trade — other	1	0
65	Real estate	0	1
70	Hotels	1	1
73	Business services	3	8
75	Automotive services	0	1
78	Motion pictures	0	1
99	Conglomerates	2	2
	Total	178	135

year in which firms' choices of R&D accounting methods were likely to be unaffected by actual or anticipated policy changes. All data items except public debt and unrestricted retained earnings were obtained from the Compustat file. Values for public debt and unrestricted retained earnings were obtained from *Moody's Industrial Manual* and *Moody's OTC Manual.*

Using 1972 data collected from Compustat and *Moody's*, the following variables were computed for each firm:

$NPLEV$ = (Total LTD − Public LTD − Capitalized lease obligations)/
(Total assets − Intangible assets),

$PLEV$ = Public LTD/(Total assets − Intangible assets),

DIV/URE = Cash dividends/Unrestricted retained earnings,

$INTCOV$ = Income before extraordinary items/Interest expense,

$SIZE$ = Sales,

where

$NPLEV$ = Non-public leverage,

$PLEV$ = Public leverage,

DIV/URE = Ratio of dividends to unrestricted retained earnings,

$INTCOV$ = Interest coverage ratio, and

LTD = Long-term debt.

The form of the leverage variables ($NPLEV$ and $PLEV$), especially the treatment of capitalized lease obligations and intangible assets, was suggested by Smith and Warner (1979, pp. 136–137).

A problem existed in defining the DIV/URE and $INTCOV$ variables for some firms when the denominators were zero. In such cases, the DIV/URE ratio was assigned a value of 5.0 and the $INTCOV$ ratio was assigned a value of 2,000. Both of these values were selected so that the value of the ratio would exceed that of any firm in the sample with a non-zero value in the denominator.[7] Sensitivity analysis was performed to assess the degree to which this coding affected the results and is discussed in section 7.

4. Descriptive statistics/univariate tests

Descriptive statistics for the variables of interest are presented in table 2.[8] As can be seen, in every case the mean differences are in the hypothesized direction. Using the non-parametric Mann–Whitney U-test, all the differences (with the exception of that for the DIV/URE measure) are highly significant.

Table 3 contains the correlation matrix for the variables. Below the correlation matrix are the multiple correlations obtained by regressing each independent variable on all other independent variables [a procedure

[7]The number of firms so coded is as follows.

	DIV/URE		INTCOV	
	Capitalizer	Expenser	Capitalizer	Expenser
	32	18	4	9

[8]No attempt has been made to control for the effect of R&D capitalization. The variables *PLEV, NPLEV,* and *DIV/URE* would all be expected to have higher values under the current expensing alternative while *INTCOV* would be expected to have a lower value. Our inability to adjust for this accounting difference makes the differences between the two groups appear generally less significant than otherwise.

Table 2

Univariate tests of the relationship between debt covenant constraints and political cost variables, and the method of accounting for R&D costs.

| Variable[a] | Hypothesis | (1) R&D capitalizers | | (2) R&D expensers | | Significance | |
		Mean Std. dev. (N = 135)	Maximum Minimum	Mean Std. dev. (N = 178)	Maximum Minimum	t-test	U-test[b]
NPLEV	(1) > (2)	0.171	0.776	0.130	0.540	0.004	0.005
		0.143	0.0	0.117	0.0		
INTCOV	(1) < (2)	62.695	2000.0	127.607	2000.0	0.076	0.001
		340.588	−282.0	459.347	−12.2		
DIV/URE	(1) > (2)	1.330	5.0	0.661	5.0	0.001	0.200
		2.081	0.0	1.447	0.0		
PLEV	(1) > (2)	0.062	0.475	0.042	0.393	0.028	0.001
		0.102	0.0	0.071	0.0		
SIZE	(1) < (2)	250.0	4071.5	487.3	9759.1	0.013	0.001
		633.2	0.956	1039.2	2.621		

[a]For a description of the variables, see section 3.
[b]Mann–Whitney U-test used.

Table 3

Correlation among explanatory variables.

| Variable | Pairwise correlation coefficients | | | | |
	NPLEV	INTCOV	DIV/URE	PLEV	SIZE
NPLEV	1.000	—	—	—	—
INTCOV	−0.267[a]	1.000	—	—	—
DIV/URE	0.318[a]	−0.123[a]	1.000	—	—
PLEV	−0.105	−0.140[b]	0.196[a]	1.000	—
SIZE	−0.067	−0.079	−0.088	0.124[b]	1.000
Multiple R[c]	0.442	0.326	0.404	0.332	0.187

[a]Significant at the 0.01 level.
[b]Significant at the 0.05 level.
[c]Obtained by regressing the variable on all other variables; for a description of these, see section 3.

suggested by Johnston (1972)] to gain insight into the degree of multicollinearity among the variables.

The largest bivariate correlation is 0.318 (R^2 of 0.101) between the *DIV/URE* and *NPLEV* variables. The multivariate correlations range from 0.187 (R^2 of 0.035) to 0.442 (R^2 of 0.195). In general the results do not appear to be indicative of high multicollinearity, but some caution is warranted in interpreting the univariate tests above. To avoid misinterpretation of the results, a multivariate analysis technique was also applied.

5. Multivariate analysis

To simultaneously test the significance of the variables developed from the hypotheses in section 2, several models are available. Two models frequently used in cases where only the *ex post* group membership can be observed as a dependent variable are probit and logit analysis. A third alternative, employed here, is the use of a jackknife procedure combined with ordinary least squares (OLS) estimation.

Simple OLS (with binary dependent variables) creates unbiased estimates of coefficients, but leads to statistical problems because the error terms are heteroscedastic and non-normal. For this reason the standard errors of coefficients are inefficient and standard significance tests are potentially misleading.

Probit and logit are two alternative econometric models which overcome this limitation by imposing an assumption concerning the distributional characteristics of the dependent variable. These models assume that the dependent variable is an estimate of the probability an observation belongs in one of the two groups. The assumption imposed is the shape of the probability density function for the distribution. Probit employs a normal density function and logit a logistic density function using information concerning the marginal probability of an observation being in one group (derived from sample data). The methods develop asymptotically efficient estimates of coefficients and standard errors using maximum likelihood estimators, which allow for asymptotic t-test to assess statistical significance.

The generalized jackknife procedure was developed by Quenouille (1956) and applied to the regression problem presented here by Mosteller and Tukey (1977). This estimation procedure (described more fully in the appendix) utilizes the unbiased nature of the OLS estimators, and develops multiple estimates of the regression coefficients (pseudo coefficients) via repetitive estimation of the model, while systematically leaving out a new observation at each repetition. No specific assumption concerning the density function of the dependent variable is necessary for estimation.

Once the set of estimated pseudo-coefficients is developed, the means and variances of these coefficients are used to develop t-statistics which are asymptotically distributed as a standard normal [Arveson (1969)]. The only critical assumption is that the pseudo-coefficient estimates are sufficiently independent that the central limit theory can be invoked to ensure that the sampling distribution of the mean is asymptotically normal. Tukey (1958) proposes such a treatment.

There have been several studies comparing the jackknife to other estimators. These are summarized in Miller (1974). In the accounting literature the only application of which we are aware is for ratio estimation by Frost and Tamura (1982). The very weak assumptions necessary to rely on the jackknife may make it more robust than probit or logit should the underlying assumptions of these latter models be violated. Further discussion on this issue is contained in section 7.2.

The jackknife procedure estimates the following model:

$$Y_i = \gamma_0 + \gamma_1 NPLEV_i + \gamma_2 PLEV_i + \gamma_3 INTCOV_i$$

$$+ \gamma_4 SALES_i + \gamma_5 DIV/URE_i + e_i, \tag{1}$$

where $Y_i = 1$ if the firm i capitalized any R&D cost, $Y_i = 0$ if not, and all other variables are as defined in section 3.

A second and separate issue in this type of study relates to the external validity (generalizability) of the findings with respect to the power of the model to correctly classify firms into the capitalizer or expenser groups. In some studies the classification success ('hit rate') is estimated using the same sample from which the model parameters are developed [e.g. BNL (1981) and HZ (1979)]. This procedure overstates the discriminatory power of the model since the estimation process (in general) maximizes the rate of successful classification by minimizing the variance of the error terms. Other research has employed a holdout sample for cross-validation [e.g. Altman (1968), Beaver (1966), and Kaplan and Urwitz (1979)]. This gives unbiased estimates of hit rates, but the exclusion of firms from the estimation sample reduces the efficiency of the coefficient estimates and thus makes hypothesis testing more difficult.

Mosteller and Tukey (1977) discuss an alternative method of cross-validation which provides information on the predictive ability of the discriminant function and increases the number of observations used to estimate (1).[9] This procedure systematically omits one observation from each pass through the estimation procedure as described above. After (1) is estimated over the remaining 312 observations, the resulting model parameters are used to classify the omitted observation. This results in predictions for each of the 313 observations using information from the other 312.

To this point nothing has been said about the classification rule used once a firm's discriminant score ($\hat{Y}$) has been generated via the cross-validation procedure. Theoretically this rule can only be determined after the costs of

---

[9]Note that this cross-validation procedure can be employed with any discrimination process (e.g. probit, logit, jackknife, etc.).

type I and type II errors have been specified. Since we see no clear way to assess this relative loss function in this context, we employ the following traditional rule:

$\hat{Y} \geq 0.5$: classify as a capitalizer;
$\hat{Y} < 0.5$: classify as an expenser.

This rule may not optimize the hit rate but is comparable to previous studies where no specified alternative hypothesis was present.

6. Results

Results of the jackknife estimation procedure are presented in table 4. The signs of the coefficients are all consistent with the theoretical predictions. The success rate from the cross-validation procedure was 65.2%, which is significantly different from random assignment at the 0.01 level using either binomial or chi-squared tests.

Table 4

Jackknife estimates of multivariate model of the relationship between debt covenant constraints, political costs, and methods of accounting for R&D costs.

| | Variables[a] | | | | | |
	—	NPLEV	INTCOV$\times 10^{-2}$	DIV/URE	SIZE$\times 10^{-2}$	PLEV
Coefficient	γ_0	γ_1	γ_2	γ_3	γ_4	γ_5
Expected sign	(?)	(+)	(−)	(+)	(−)	(+)
Estimated value	0.330	0.448	−0.003	0.031	−0.007	0.669
t-value	6.39	1.92	−0.44	1.84	−2.18	2.07
Probability under H_0	(0.001)	(0.025)	(0.330)	(0.034)	(0.015)	(0.020)

Correctly classified = 65.2%   Value of chi-squared statistic = 8.80
                                Probability under $H_0 < 0.005$

Dependent variable = 1   if capitalizer
                    = 0   if expenser

[a]For a description of the variables, see section 3.

The coefficients on the bond covenant variables have predicted signs, although not all are significant. Both the private and public debt variables are positive and significant at the 0.05 level. As predicted the public debt variable coefficient is larger, but the difference between public and private debt is insignificant (at the 0.10 level). The dividends to unrestricted retained earnings variable is also positive and significant (at the 0.05 level) as predicted. Only the interest coverage ratio is insignificant, but even this coefficient is of predicted sign.

The size variable is also highly significant (0.02 level) in the direction predicted by the political cost hypothesis. Overall, we interpret these results to be consistent with the alternative hypotheses suggested above.

7. Sensitivity analyses

This section describes the four major steps which were undertaken to examine the sensitivity of the results to (1) the use of a random control group design, (2) the use of jackknife in lieu of probit analysis, (3) the special coding rules employed, and (4) omitted variables. Also described here is an examination of the 'threshold effect' in firm size documented by Zimmerman (1983) and ZH (1981).

7.1. Random control group vs. Matched pairs

When using a random control group, the possibility exists that the results are driven by omitted variables.[10] Of particular concern in this study is the industry membership of sample firms. DeAngelo and Masulis (1980) suggest that industries differ with respect to their optimal leverage ratios due to differences in non-cash tax deductions such as depreciation and the investment tax credit. Bowen, Daley, and Huber (1982) provide empirical support for this theory. If optimal leverage differs by industry, bondholders should take this into account and set different leverage limits in bond covenants for firms in different industries. Thus, the assumption that the leverage constraint is a cross-sectional constant is questionable. Matching firms on industry classification should add power to the leverage test by controlling somewhat for this lack of cross-sectional consistency.[11] However, this matching may limit the variation of other explanatory variables, thus reducing their power to discriminate between R&D capitalizers and expensers.

To determine whether differences in industry classification affected the results in the random control group tests, another test was conducted with a control group matched on industry classification (four-digit SIC code).[12] Firms for which no suitable match could be found were dropped, resulting in a sample of 111 matched pairs of firms. The results of the jackknife estimation procedure were as expected. All coefficients were of the predicted

---

[10]Of course these factors could be incorporated specifically as variables in a random control group design, but such factors as industry membership may not have sufficient observations to allow discrimination (i.e., each industry has only one firm represented).

[11]Ideally the measure desired is the distance between the maximum allowable leverage and actual leverage. This was not obtainable from available data. Thus, matching may partially compensate for the noise in the surrogate variable.

[12]The control group was also matched on firm sizes (sales) to control for other confounding variables.

sign but only the leverage variables (*PLEV* and *NPLEV*) were significant. Both of these variables were more highly significant in the matched pairs test than in the random control group test, but all other variables were less significant. The matching process, then, did create more powerful tests on the leverage variables, but at the cost of less powerful tests on the other variables.

7.2. Jackknife vs. Probit

The weaker assumptions necessary to rely on the jackknife procedure do not necessarily imply that jackknife dominates probit and logit in all cases. The jackknife procedure requires an OLS regression for each firm in the sample and is therefore much more costly than probit or logit as sample size increases. Moreover, as sample sizes increase, violations of the distributional assumptions of probit and logit may well be of less concern.

To assess this trade-off, probit analysis was used to estimate model (1) with virtually identical results. Thus, in a sample as large as that used in this study, the added cost of using jackknife is probably not justified. Research on smaller sample properties of the techniques is necessary to determine at what point the benefits of jacknife become apparent.

7.3. Special coding rules

Since several ad hoc coding rules were utilized (described in section 4) sensitivity analysis was undertaken to determine whether these results are robust to alternative measurement rules. Each of the following procedures was undertaken:

(1) All observations for which any special coding was necessary were dropped from the sample. This loss of sample size caused a decrease in the power of the test and lowered the significance levels of the coefficients. Only *NPLEV* and *SALES* were still significant at the 0.10 level. However, the signs and magnitudes of the coefficients were basically unchanged.

(2) Several firms had interest coverage ratios with very large absolute values. To determine whether these outliers were driving the results for *INTCOV*, the ratio for these firms was recoded to ± 50.0 as appropriate. The results are similar to those in table 4 except that the leverage variables are slightly less significant and *INTCOV* is significant at the 0.10 level.

In general, it can be concluded that the overall results are quite robust to the coding rules and the basic conclusions are not being driven by outliers, with the possible exception of the *INTCOV* variable.

7.4. Omitted variables

It is conceivable that some firms selected capitalization for financial reporting purposes because it was employed for tax purposes and wished to avoid the costs of maintaining separate financial records. Tax law allowed deferral of some R&D costs, and firms without sufficient taxable income to absorb current deductions for R&D costs might indeed have preferred deferral, since the amortization period for the capitalized R&D cost could exceed the operating loss carryforward period.[13]

As a precaution, the analysis was rerun after deleting those sample firms with net operating loss carryforwards disclosed in 1972. These are the only firms for which the above arguments seem plausible. The results of this analysis were virtually unchanged, although the reduction of sample size and resulting loss of power reduced the significance of the coefficients. Thus, it seems safe to regard the bookkeeping cost issue as trivial.

The magnitude of R&D expenditures might affect the accounting method selected. It is significant to note that in 1972 R&D expense was not a required disclosure. Only firms which felt that this amount was material chose to disclose this item. Thus, the hypothesis that expensing firms are simply those with an immaterial amount of R&D expenditures seems questionable. This is borne out by the fact that there is essentially no difference in R&D intensity (the ratio of R&D expense to sales) for capitalizing versus expensing firms in our samples.[14,15]

7.5. Issues related to firm size

Previous studies [ZH (1981) and Zimmerman (1983)] have shown that the effect of firm size on the choice of accounting methods is non-linear. In

---

[13]Ideally we would like to identify the accounting methods used for both book and tax. If the bookkeeping cost arguments are insignificant, then there should be no greater propensity for firms in the treatment group to choose a particular tax procedure compared to the control group. Unfortunately, it was not mandatory at this time to reconcile the tax expense and current tax payments in the tax footnote. This prevents a direct examination of this issue. We did identify firms which had an operating loss carryforward on the Compustat tape in 1972. These firms may have a greater probability of deferring for tax purposes in order to spread out the timing of the tax deductions.

[14]36 capitalizers did not disclose R&D expense in 1972. Thus the comparison of R&D expense to sales does not include these firms. Of course, these firms are not subject to the criticism that they expense due to immateriality since some R&D was capitalized prior to or in 1972. The results described above were replicated including an R&D/sales variable and dropping the firms not reporting R&D expense. The R&D variable was insignificant and other results were fundamentally unchanged.

[15]The ratio of R&D expense to sales had mean values of 1.94 percent for the capitalizers and 1.79 percent for expensers. This difference is insignificant at the 0.20 level. This test suffers from omitting capitalizers whose R&D intensity may be small (see footnote 13), and from an inability to obtain R&D expenditures for the numerator for some firms. The net effect of these two limitations is unknown, since they tend to have opposing biases.

particular, these studies have shown that variables related to political costs are much less important in explaining the choice of accounting principles for smaller firms than for larger firms. ZH (1981) partitioned their sample into large-firm and small-firm sub-samples and found that the size variable was only significant in the large-firm sub-sample. The same technique was applied here with opposite results. The sample of 313 firms was partitioned into a large-firm sub-sample (156 firms) and a small-firm sub-sample (157 firms). Jackknife estimates were obtained for each of the sub-samples. For the larger firms, only the coefficients on the two leverage variables were significant at the 0.05 level. For the small firms, both leverage variables and size were significant at the 0.05 level and *INTCOV* was significant at the 0.10 level. These results are inconsistent with ZH (1981) and suggest that the role of size variables in the choice of accounting methods is not yet well understood.

Zimmerman (1983) has shown that the size variable does not explain the choice of accounting principles, as hypothesized, for firms in the trade industries (SIC codes 5000–5999). As shown in table 1, the present sample includes very few firms from the trade industries and test on this issue were not possible. However, it is noteworthy that the multivariate model used here performed badly on these firms. None of the five R&D capitalizing firms in our sample was correctly classified, while five of the six R&D expensing firms were correctly classified. This poor performance does not appear to be attributable to an anomalous size effect, however, as the R&D capitalizers were smaller than the R&D expensers, as hypothesized.[16] Moreover, deleting these firms from the sample and re-estimating model (1) actually results in a slight decrease in the predictive ability of the model.

8. Conclusions

Prior to 1974, firms could capitalize or expense their R&D costs. This study investigates whether this choice was related to significant differences in variables which attempt to capture the firms' proximity to constraints imposed by debt covenants, the cost of violating these covenants, and political costs. Specifically, it is observed that R&D capitalizing firms were more highly levered, employed more public debt, had a higher ratio of dividends to unrestricted retained earning, and were smaller in size than R&D expensing firms. The study is unable to reject the null hypothesis with regard to interest coverage, probably due to the effect of outliers in the sample.

The extensions of previous research are fourfold. First, a variable related to the amount of public debt employed in a firm's capital structure is used to explain the choice of accounting principles. The results are consistent with

---

[16]This difference is significant at the 0.05 level in a Mann–Whitney *U*-test.

the hypothesis that the higher renegotiation costs associated with public debt provide an additional incentive for firms to choose accounting techniques to avoid constraints imposed by debt covenants. However, these results are only marginally significant.

Second, a multivariate technique is employed which is relatively new to accounting research and may have significant advantages over probit and discriminant analysis in small samples since it requires less restrictive assumptions than probit, but allows for asymptotical significance tests. Third, a cross-validation procedure is introduced which provides greater external validity for assessing the predictive power of the proposed model. Finally, both a matched pairs design and a random control group design are used in an effort to gain insight into the effects of this choice on our results. The conclusion concerning matching appears to be mixed, gaining power on some dimensions (leverage) but sacrificing power on others (dividend restrictions and political costs).

The results confirm previous findings by BNL (1981), Dhaliwal (1980) and ZH (1981) with respect to the relationship between accounting principle choice and leverage. The findings are also generally consistent with BNL (1981) for the effects of dividend restrictions. This is in contrast to Elliott et al. (1983) who found no difference between R&D capitalizers and expensers on this dimension, probably due to their matched-pairs design.

Appendix

To briefly describe the jackknife estimation process in detail, the specific model used in this study, eq. (1), is introduced,

$$Y_i = \gamma_1 + \gamma_1 NPLEV_i + \gamma_2 PLEV_i + \gamma_3 INTCOV_i + \gamma_4 SALES_i$$

$$+ \gamma_5 DIV/URE_i + e_i,$$

where $Y_i = 1$ if firm i capitalized any R&D cost, $Y_i = 0$ if not, and all other variables are as defined in section 3.

To generate the jackknife estimates of the γ_j, (γ_j^J) a matrix of 'pseudo' values must be generated for the coefficients in (1). These 'pseudo' values are determined using the following procedure.

(1) Estimate eq. (1) using all the observations.
(2) Re-estimate (1) by systematically dropping a different observation each pass (313 regressions are generated for the random control group design).
(3) Calculate the 'pseudo' value of each coefficient for each dropped observation as

$$\gamma_{jk}^P = n\gamma_{j\,\text{all}} - (n-1)\gamma_{jk}, \qquad k = 1,\ldots,313, \quad j = 0,1,\ldots,5,$$

where

$\gamma_{j\,\text{all}}$ = estimated value of the jth coefficient (γ) over all firms,

γ_{jk} = estimated value of the jth coefficient (γ) over $n-1$ firms where firm k is omitted,

n = total number of firms,

γ_{jk}^{P} = 'pseudo' value for the jth coefficient associated with the kth observation

Application of this procedure produces a (6×313) matrix of 'pseudo' values. The variance–covariance matrix for the coefficients can then be generated from this matrix and the standard error derived from (A.2) below. Taking the mean value (A.1) of the γ_{jk}^{P} gives an unbiased estimate of γ_j,

$$\gamma_j = \frac{1}{n}\sum_{k=1}^{n} \gamma_{jk}^{P}, \tag{A.1}$$

$$S_{\gamma_j}^2 = \left(\sum_{k=1}^{n} (\gamma_{jk}^{P} - \gamma_j)^2\right) \Big/ (n-1). \tag{A.2}$$

References

Altman, E., 1968, Financial ratios, discriminant analysis, and the prediction of corporate bankruptcy, Journal of Finance 23, 589–609.

Arveston, J., 1969, Jackknifing U-statistics, Annals of Mathematical Statistics 40, 2067–2100.

Beaver, W., 1966, Financial ratios as predictors of failure, Empirical Research in Accounting: Selected Studies, supplement to Journal of Accounting Research 4, 71–111.

Bowen, R., L. Daley and C. Huber, 1982, Evidence on the existence and determinants of inter-industry differences in leverage, Financial Management, Winter, 10–20.

Bowen, R., E. Noreen and J. Lacey, 1981, Determinants of the corporate decision to capitalize interest, Journal of Accounting and Economics 3, 151–179.

DeAngelo, H. and R. Masulis, 1980, Optimal capital structure under corporate and personal taxation, Journal of Financial Economics 8, 3–29.

Dhaliwal, D., 1980, The effect of the firm's capital structure on the choice of accounting methods, The Accounting Review 50, 78–84.

Elliott, J., G. Richardson, T. Dyckman and R. Dukes, 1983, The impact of SFAS No. 2 on firm expenditures on research and development: Replications and extensions, Journal of Accounting Research, forthcoming.

Frost, P. and H. Tamura, 1982, Jackknifed ratio estimation in statistical auditing, Journal of Accounting Research 20, 103–120.

Gellein, O. and M. Newman, 1973, Accounting for research and development expenditures (AICPA, New York).

Hagerman, R. and M. Zmijewski, 1979, Some economic determinants of accounting policy choice, Journal of Accounting and Economics 1, 142–161.

Holthausen, R., 1981, Evidence on the effect of bond covenants and management compensation contracts on the choice of accounting techniques: The case of the depreciation switch-back, Journal of Accounting and Economics 3, 73–109.

Holthausen, R. and R. Leftwich, 1983, The economic consequences of accounting choice: Implications of costly contracting and monitoring, Journal of Accounting and Economics 5, 75–117.

Jensen, M. and W. Meckling, 1976, Theory of the firm: Managerial behavior, agency costs and ownership structure, Journal of Financial Economics 3, 305–360.

Johnston, J., 1972, Econometric methods (McGraw Hill, New York).

Kaplan, R. and G. Urwitz, 1979, Statistical models of bond ratings: A methodological inquiry, Journal of Business 52, 231–262.

Leftwich, R., 1981, Evidence of the impact of mandatory changes in accounting principles on corporate loan aggreements, Journal of Accounting and Economics 3, 3–36.

Miller, R., 1974, The jackknife — A review, Biometrika 61, 1–15.

Mosteller, F. and J. Tukey, 1977, Data analysis and regression (Addison-Wesley, Reading, MA).

Quenouille, M., 1956, Notes on bias in estimation, Biometrika 61, 353–360.

Smith, C. and J. Warner, 1979, On financial contracting: An analysis of bond covenants, Journal of Financial Economics 7, 117–161.

Tukey, J., 1958, Bias in confidence in not-quite large samples, Annals of Mathematical Statistics 29, 614.

Watts, R. and J. Zimmerman, 1978, Toward a positive theory of the determination of accounting standards, The Accounting Review 53, 112–134.

Zimmerman, J., 1983, Taxes and firm size, forthcoming Journal of Accounting and Economics 5, 119–149.

Zmijewski, M. and R. Hagerman, 1981, An income strategy approach to the positive theory of accounting standard setting/choice, Journal of Accounting and Economics 3, 129–149.

MANDATED ACCOUNTING CHANGES AND DEBT COVENANTS
The Case of Oil and Gas Accounting*

Thomas LYS

Northwestern University, Evanston, IL 60201, USA

Received February 1983, final version received February 1984

The relationships among mandated accounting changes, bond covenants and security prices has been the focus of several studies. These studies have provided mixed evidence on the existence of a bond covenant effect on security prices. This paper suggests that inconclusive prior results are a consequence of inappropriately measuring the default risk of debt. Using an option pricing framework, it is shown that the debt to equity *alone* is not an adequate measure of default risk. In particular, both the debt to equity ratio *and* the total risk of the firm are necessary to adequately model the bond covenant effects of an accounting change. These theoretical propositions are supported by the empirical analysis of the security market reaction to changes in oil and gas accounting.

1. Introduction

The consequences of accounting changes on shareholder wealth have been the subject of several studies [e.g., Holthausen (1981), Leftwich (1981) and Collins et al. (1981)]. These papers argue that binding debt covenants are one reason for the observed security price reactions following accounting changes. However, tests of the existence of debt covenant effects have achieved only modest levels of statistical significance and conflicting results. The purpose of this paper is to provide a more rigorous examination of the existence of debt covenant effects from mandated accounting changes, with specific focus upon the security market reaction associated with the announcement of Financial Accounting Standard 19 (FAS 19). It is shown in subsequent sections, that inconclusive prior results may be caused by an inadequate proxy for the default risk of the debt. The results indicate that the more precise measures of

*This paper has been adapted from my Ph.D. dissertation at the University of Rochester. I thank my dissertation committee: Ross Watts (Chairman), G. William Schwert, Clifford Smith and Jerold Zimmerman for their helpful criticism and persistent guidance. I also wish to thank Andrew Christie, Daniel Collins, Peter Dodd, Nicholas Dopuch, Kenneth French, Paul Healy, Robert Holthausen, Bruce Johnson, Richard Lambert, David Larcker, Richard Leftwich, Robert Magee, Abbie Smith, and the referee, William Beaver, for valuable comments on previous drafts. Financial support from the Center for Research in Government Policy and Business, The University of Rochester, the Swiss Foundation for the Sciences, and the Accounting Research Center, Northwestern University, is gratefully acknowledged.

Journal of Accounting and Economics 6 (1984) 39–65. North-Holland

the default risk of debt used in this paper detect a bond covenant effect and explain a significant portion of the cross-sectional variation in security price returns at the exposure draft release date.

The remainder of this paper is organized into five sections. Section 2 discusses the relationship between mandated accounting changes, debt covenants, and changes in equity value of the affected firms. Sample selection is described in section 3. Section 4 presents time series results. The cross-sectional research method and results are presented in section 5. Finally, the results are summarized in section 6.

2. Research hypotheses

Debt covenants limit shareholders' ability to redistribute the value of the firm to themselves after issuance of the debt. By voluntarily constraining their future actions, shareholders increase the expected net present value of the debt, and therefore, the issue price of the debt. Debt covenants typically include (i) dividend restrictions, (ii) leverage restrictions and (iii) investment restrictions [see Smith and Warner (1979) and Kalay (1978) for a discussion of these constraints]. These contracts often are expressed in terms of *accounting* numbers. Therefore, mandated accounting changes that have a large impact on accounting numbers used in debt covenants can result in a wealth redistribution between debtholder and shareholder.

A recent example of such an accounting change is the elimination of full cost accounting (FAS 19). This accounting standard was expected to significantly alter the accounting numbers of small non-integrated oil and gas producers. Companies forced to change from full cost to successful efforts were expected to experience reduced retained earnings, reduced unrestricted retained earnings, and increased debt to equity ratios.[1,2] Since these numbers are used in debt covenants, this accounting change increases the likelihood of violations of covenants for affected companies and therefore can reduce shareholder wealth.

For example, a large number of the oil and gas firms affected by FAS 19 have debt that was issued when interest rates were lower than interest rates prevailing at the time of the proposed accounting change. Covenant violations give debtholders specific rights such as to terminate the lending agreement and demand immediate repayment of the loan. Repayment of the debt following a

---

[1]For example, a study of 36 full cost companies by Touche Ross & Co. showed that the implementation of FAS 19 would: (1) reduce reported earnings by an average of 20%, (2) reduce asset carrying values of oil and gas properties by an average of 30%, and (3) reduce shareholders' equity by an average of 16%. Letter dated March 29, 1977 from Touche Ross & Co. to the Ad Hoc Committee on Full Cost Accounting.

[2]For an analysis of properties of accounting numbers under alternative accounting methods, see Sunder (1976), Deakin (1979), and Lilien and Pastena (1982).

covenant violation will result in a wealth transfer from shareholders to debtholders since the par value of the debt exceeds its market value.

Faced with an increased probability of (costly) debt covenant violations, management will be forced to (i) adjust financing and investment policies or to (ii) attempt to renegotiate the covenants with the lender(s). Notice that these actions were available *prior* to the announcement of the accounting change, but were not chosen by management. Assuming that managers are attempting to maximize the wealth of shareholders, the managerial response to the accounting change is not likely to result in an increase of security prices (compared to the pre FAS 19 levels.) Hence, the first research hypothesis is:

H_1: Security prices of full cost companies are *reduced* following announcements that *increase* the probability of implementation of FAS 19.

Research hypothesis one specifies the *mean* security price response to a mandated accounting change. However, additional evidence on the existence of debt covenant effects can be obtained by analyzing cross-sectional differences in security price responses to the announcement of FAS 19. Five additional research hypotheses are developed by analyzing the impact of FAS 19 on the firm's investment and financing policies and the cost of renegotiating debt covenants and/or refinancing the debt.

2.1. Changes of investment and financing policies

If managers maximize shareholder wealth, the investment and financing policies selected before the announcement of FAS 19 are optimal given the firm's debt covenants. However, as discussed above, FAS 19 was expected to make covenants more binding. Therefore, affected companies will be forced to reduce current and/or future dividends, issue additional equity and/or sell less debt relative to the levels that would have been chosen in absence of FAS 19. As a result, current and/or future investments will be higher and debt/equity ratios will be lower relative to the levels that management would have selected in the absence of the accounting change. Since the increase in investment is entirely financed by shareholders through reduced dividend payments, the ex-dividend value of the firm will increase, the default risk of the outstanding debt will be reduced, and a wealth redistribution from shareholder to debtholder will occur.

Since changes in investment and financing policies occur because of changes in the accounting data used in covenants, the magnitude of the security price effect will be positively related to the FAS 19 induced change in the accounting numbers used in covenants. Therefore, the second research hypothesis is:

H_2: The magnitude of the security price response is positively related to the impact of FAS 19 on the firm's accounting numbers.

The effect of an increase in firm value on the equity of a levered firm that is entirely financed by shareholders can be explicitly analyzed in an option pricing framework. The equity of a levered firm can be viewed as a call option on the firm's assets with an exercise price equal to the face value of the debt [see Smith (1976)]. For example, using the Black and Scholes (1973) option pricing model, the change in equity value following an unexpected change in firm value can be represented as[3]

$$\partial S/\partial V = N(d_1),\qquad(1)$$

where

$$d_1 = \left\{\ln(V/X) + (r + 1/2\sigma^2)T\right\}/\sigma\sqrt{T},$$

and

S = market value of the equity,
V = market value of the firm,
X = face value of the debt,
σ = instantaneous standard deviation of V,
T = time to maturity of the debt,
r = instantaneous riskless rate of return,
$N(\cdot)$ = cumulative standard normal distribution function.

The cross-sectional implication of the accounting change can be derived from eq. (1) by analyzing differences in $N(d_1)$ depending upon firm specific parameters.[4] These are (i) the leverage ratio X/V, (ii) total firm risk σ and (iii) the time to maturity T.

The differential impact of the accounting change based on the firm's leverage ratio is derived from (1) as

$$\frac{\partial}{\partial(X/V)}\frac{\partial S}{\partial V} = -n(d_1)\frac{V}{X}\frac{1}{\sigma\sqrt{T}} < 0,\qquad(2)$$

where $n(\cdot)$ is the standard normal probability density function. Eq. (2) is consistent with the claim of prior research that security prices of firms with higher leverage will be more adversely affected by mandatory accounting

---

[3]Notice that the Black and Scholes option pricing model cannot be strictly applied, since it assumes, among other things, no dividend payments, no bankruptcy cost and no interest payments on the debt. Therefore, eq. (1) should be viewed as a simplified approximation, whose validity remains an empirical question.

[4]Notice that the 'net' effect of the accounting change on shareholder wealth is $N(d_1) - 1.0$, since the increase in V is entirely financed by reducing dividends. Since $0.0 \leq N(d_1) \leq 1.0$, the net effect is negative, as derived in the first research hypothesis.

changes. Consistent with existing literature, the third research hypothesis is:

H_3: The security price response following announcement of FAS 19 will be negatively related to the firm's leverage ratio.

The differential impact of the accounting change is also a function of total firm risk (σ) and the debt's time to maturity (T). The partial derivatives of (1) are

$$\frac{\partial}{\partial \sigma} \frac{\partial S}{\partial V} = -\mathrm{n}(d_1) \frac{d_1 - \sigma\sqrt{T}}{\sigma},$$ (3)

and

$$\frac{\partial}{\partial T} \frac{\partial S}{\partial V} = -\mathrm{n}(d_1) \frac{d_1 - \sigma\sqrt{T}}{\sqrt{T}}.$$ (4)

The value of d_1 is an inverse function of the probability of default and can assume values between $-\infty$ and $+\infty$. Therefore, both expressions cannot be signed unambiguously. However, substituting estimated values for V, X, T, σ, and r (see section 5 and the appendix for the procedures used in estimating these variables), the value of $d_1 - \sigma\sqrt{T}$ is positive for each of the sample firms. Given positive estimates of $d_1 - \sigma\sqrt{T}$, (3) and (4) imply:

H_4: The security price response following announcement of FAS 19 will be negatively related to total firm risk (σ).

H_5: The security price response following announcement of FAS 19 will be negatively related to the time to maturity of the debt (T).

Prior research analyzing the linkage between mandated accounting changes and bond covenants hypothesizes that the wealth redistribution is proportional to the pre-accounting change distance to the benchmark specified in the covenants. This distance, in turn, is assumed to be positively related to the default risk of the outstanding debt. Therefore, firms with riskier debt are assumed to be more adversely affected by the accounting change. Since default risk is unobservable, prior research uses the debt to equity ratio as a proxy for the debt's risk [e.g. Collins et al. (1981)]. However, leverage only proxies for the debt's risk if total firm risk is held constant. For example, public utilities have high leverage ratios, but relatively low risk debt.

The omission of σ from the analysis is likely to cause serious problems because this variable is likely to be negatively correlated with leverage. For example, due to bankruptcy cost, firms with high uncertainty regarding the terminal value of the firm (high σ) will tend to issue less debt, thus having low debt to equity ratios. Indeed, the correlation between debt to equity ratio and total firm variance is estimated to be -0.632 in the current sample (see table 4). Therefore, a structural equation using only the leverage variable is plagued by the econometric problems of correlated omitted variables, resulting in biased coefficient estimates for the included variables and can, therefore, result in inappropriate inferences with respect to the existence of a bond covenant effect [see Maddala (1977, p. 155)]. Empirical evidence on this issue is provided in section 5.

2.2. Renegotiation cost

Finally, an alternative course of action available to shareholders is to renegotiate the covenants in order to reduce the security price impact of the accounting change. Renegotiations, however, will impose negotiation cost, as well as necessary interest rate concessions [see Benston (1978)], in order to achieve lender approval to the covenant change. The associated transaction costs represent an upper bound on the impact of FAS 19 on security prices. Therefore, the sixth research hypothesis is:

H_6: The security price impact is an increasing function of the lower of (i) renegotiation cost and (ii) the cost associated with retiring the debt.

The procedures used to generate the sample for the empirical analysis is presented in the next section. Research hypothesis 1 is tested in section 4. The empirical implications of research hypotheses 2, 3, 4, 5, and 6 are investigated in section 5.

3. Sample selection

The sample firms consist of all firms identified in Dyckman and Smith (1979) and Lev (1979). Additionally, firms that lobbied with the Financial Accounting Standard Board (FASB) against the exposure draft and firms that were members of the Ad Hoc Committee on Full Cost Accounting were also included in the original test sample.

After excluding corporations not listed on the New York or American Stock Exchanges, a total of 114 oil and gas companies using full cost accounting in 1977 remain in the sample. In addition, firms are excluded from the sample if they: (i) are not incorporated within North America, (ii) have more than four missing consecutive daily returns in the period starting December 20, 1974 to January 19, 1979 on the CRSP file, (iii) are not involved in production of oil and/or natural gas, and (iv) are not listed in the 1978 *Moody's Industrial* or *Public Utilities Manual*.

These additional requirements reduced the original sample by 25 firms to a total of 89 companies (portfolio *ALL*). This sample is composed of 64 firms listed in Moody's *Industrial Manual* (1978) (portfolio *IND*), and 25 companies classified by Moody's (1978) as *Public Utilities* (portfolio *UTL*). Of the 64 industrial companies, 48 are incorporated in the United States (portfolio *INDUS*) and 16 in Canada (portfolio *INDCA*).[5] In addition, a control group of 40 oil and gas producing firms using the *successful efforts* method of accounting previously identified by Lev (1979) and by Collins and Dent (1979), is also analyzed. Two additional portfolios are constructed: (i) an equally weighted portfolio of the 40 successful efforts companies (portfolio *SE*) and (ii) an equally weighted zero investment portfolio with a *long* position in portfolio *SE* and a *short* position in portfolio *ALL* (portfolio *SE-ALL*).

4. Time series analysis

This section investigates whether the observed security market reaction is consistent with the first research hypothesis. Event days on which a security price reaction is observed are then used in section 5 to test research hypotheses 2 through 5.

Three events are analyzed – Exposure Draft, FAS 19 and ASR 253. The Exposure Draft outlines the FASB's proposal to eliminate full cost accounting. The proposed accounting change was accepted in FAS 19 and reversed by the SEC in ASR 253.[6] For each of the analyzed events the date of publication of the relevant *Wall Street Journal* (WSJ) article is used as announcement date. Three hundred trading days starting March 10, 1976 to May 16, 1977 are used to estimate the parameters of the market model [see Fama (1976)]. That is, the continuously compounded daily returns of each portfolio ($R_{j,t}$) are regressed on the continuously compounded returns of the value-weighted market index of the same day ($R_{m,t}$), or

$$R_{j,t} = \alpha_j + \beta_j R_{m,t} + e_{j,t}. \tag{5}$$

The estimated parameters of the market model are then used to compute prediction errors around each of the investigated events for each of the seven portfolios, or

$$\hat{e}_{j,t} = R_{j,t} - \hat{\alpha}_j - \hat{\beta}_j R_{m,t}. \tag{6}$$

For each event day in the test period and each portfolio the *t*-statistic is computed as

$$t_{j,t} = \hat{e}_{j,t} / \hat{s}_{j,t}, \tag{7}$$

---

[5] Oil and gas firms incorporated in Canada are retained in the sample even though Canada was not expected to follow U.S. practices on oil and gas accounting. The reason is that most of these Canadian firms have debt placements with U.S. lenders and it is likely that the associated covenants are expressed in U.S. GAAP.

[6] See Lev (1979), Foster (1980), and Lys (1982) for a discussion of the numerous announcements of oil and gas accounting changes.

Table 1

Daily prediction errors surrounding announcement of the Exposure Draft (*t*-values in parentheses).[a]

Calendar date	Event	Portfolios and number of companies						
		ALL 89	*IND* 64	*INDUS* 48	*INDCA* 16	*UTL* 25	*SE* 40	*SE-ALL* 129
07/11/77		0.23 (0.54)	0.23 (0.41)	0.28 (0.47)	0.08 (0.10)	0.25 (0.57)	0.41 (0.99)	0.17 (0.40)
07/12/77		0.06 (0.15)	0.97 (0.18)	0.25 (0.04)	0.31 (0.38)	0.02 (−0.03)	0.41 (1.00)	0.34 (0.81)
07/13/77		0.87 (1.99)	1.45 (2.62)	1.31 (2.20)	1.88 (2.30)	−0.61 (−1.36)	0.99 (2.42)	0.12 (0.28)
07/15/77	ED Dated	−0.27 (−0.60)	−0.37 (−0.67)	−0.61 (−1.03)	0.34 (0.41)	−0.00 (−0.00)	−0.77 (−1.88)	−0.50 (−1.19)
07/18/77		−0.66 (−1.49)	−0.91 (−1.63)	−1.18 (−1.97)	−0.11 (−0.14)	−0.03 (−0.06)	−0.27 (−0.66)	0.39 (0.91)
07/19/77	ED issued	−1.41 (−3.22)	−1.71 (−3.07)	−1.75 (−2.92)	−1.59 (−1.95)	−0.68 (−1.53)	−0.16 (−0.38)	1.25 (2.45)
07/20/77	WSJ article	−1.05 (−2.40)	−1.63 (−2.94)	−1.63 (−2.74)	−1.61 (−1.98)	0.38 (0.86)	−0.66 (−1.62)	0.39 (0.92)
07/21/77		0.26 (0.60)	0.35 (0.62)	0.30 (0.50)	0.48 (0.59)	0.05 (0.11)	−0.01 (−0.02)	−0.27 (−0.64)
07/22/77		−0.04 (−0.09)	−0.06 (−0.11)	0.01 (0.01)	−0.26 (−0.32)	0.02 (0.04)	−0.31 (−0.76)	−0.27 (−0.64)
07/25/77		−0.13 (−0.30)	−0.15 (−0.27)	−0.10 (−0.16)	−0.30 (−0.37)	−0.08 (−0.17)	−0.22 (−0.54)	−0.09 (−0.21)
07/26/77		−0.74 (−1.68)	−0.98 (−1.76)	−0.77 (−1.28)	−1.59 (−1.95)	−0.12 (−0.28)	−0.44 (−1.08)	0.29 (0.69)
07/27/77		−1.37 (−3.08)	−1.77 (−3.16)	−1.95 (−3.23)	−1.23 (−1.49)	−0.35 (−0.77)	−0.88 (−2.13)	0.48 (1.11)
07/28/77		0.12 (0.27)	0.43 (0.77)	0.75 (1.25)	−0.51 (−0.63)	−0.67 (−1.50)	0.32 (0.78)	0.20 (0.48)
07/29/77		0.00 (0.01)	−0.21 (−0.37)	−0.16 (−0.28)	−0.32 (−0.40)	0.53 (1.20)	−0.15 (−0.38)	−0.16 (−0.37)

[a] Portfolio description:

ALL = Sample of companies using the full cost method of accounting.
IND = Subsample of portfolio *ALL* listed in Moody's *Industrial Manual*.
INDUS = Subsample of portfolio *ALL* listed in Moody's *Industrial Manual* and incorporated in the U.S.A.
INDCA = Subsample of portfolio *ALL* listed in Moody's *Industrial Manual* and incorporated in Canada.
UTL = Subsample of portfolio *ALL* listed in Moody's *Public Utilities Manual*.
SE = Sample of companies using the successful efforts method of accounting.
SE-ALL = Equally weighted zero investment portfolio with a long position in portfolio *SE* and a short position in portfolio *ALL*.

where

$$\hat{s}_{j,t}^2 = MSE\left[1 + 1/300 + \left(R_{m,t} - \overline{R}_m\right)^2 \Big/ \sum_{i=1}^{300}\left(R_{m,t} - \overline{R}_m\right)^2\right],$$

and

MSE = estimated mean square error of the market model regression,
$\overline{R}_m$ = average return on the market in the estimation period.

Prediction errors for portfolios *ALL*, *IND*, *INDUS*, *INDCA*, *UTL*, *SE* and *SE-ALL* for the 14 trading days surrounding announcement of the

Table 2

Daily prediction errors surrounding announcement of FAS 19 (*t*-values in parentheses).[a]

Calendar date	Event	Portfolios and number of companies						
		ALL 89	*IND* 64	*INDUS* 48	*INDCA* 16	*UTL* 25	*SE* 40	*SE-ALL* 129
11/25/77		0.42 (0.96)	0.58 (1.05)	0.36 (0.60)	1.24 (1.52)	0.01 (0.01)	0.33 (0.81)	−0.09 (−0.21)
11/28/77		−0.04 (−0.09)	−0.12 (−0.22)	−0.16 (−0.26)	−0.03 (−0.03)	0.18 (0.41)	0.51 (1.26)	0.55 (1.30)
11/29/77		−0.08 (−0.18)	−0.15 (−0.26)	−0.50 (−0.82)	0.88 (1.06)	0.09 (0.21)	−0.00 (−0.01)	0.08 (0.19)
11/30/77		0.25 (0.56)	0.47 (0.85)	0.13 (0.22)	1.47 (1.80)	−0.33 (−0.75)	−0.46 (−1.15)	−0.72 (−1.70)
12/01/77		0.71 (1.61)	0.97 (1.74)	0.58 (0.97)	2.09 (2.56)	0.05 (0.11)	0.72 (1.75)	0.01 (0.03)
12/02/77		1.09 (2.49)	1.30 (2.34)	0.94 (1.58)	2.34 (2.87)	0.57 (1.29)	0.42 (1.03)	−0.67 (−1.60)
12/05/77		−0.10 (−0.24)	−0.10 (−0.19)	−0.20 (−0.33)	0.17 (0.21)	−0.10 (−0.23)	−0.30 (−0.73)	−0.19 (−0.45)
12/06/77	FAS 19 announced	−0.40 (−0.89)	−0.79 (−1.40)	−0.56 (−0.93)	−1.45 (−1.75)	0.59 (1.32)	0.00 (0.00)	0.39 (0.92)
12/07/77		−0.09 (−0.20)	0.22 (0.39)	0.06 (0.10)	0.69 (0.85)	−0.87 (−1.95)	−0.14 (−0.35)	−0.05 (−0.13)
12/08/77		0.33 (0.76)	0.52 (0.94)	0.02 (0.03)	1.98 (2.42)	−0.14 (−0.32)	−0.06 (−0.15)	−0.39 (0.94)
12/09/77		0.34 (0.77)	0.66 (1.19)	0.43 (0.72)	1.33 (1.62)	−0.48 (−1.07)	0.59 (1.44)	0.25 (0.59)
12/12/77		0.04 (0.09)	−0.05 (−0.09)	0.07 (0.11)	−0.38 (−0.47)	0.26 (0.57)	0.24 (0.58)	0.20 (0.47)
12/13/77		−0.30 (−0.69)	−0.45 (−0.81)	−0.34 (−0.57)	−0.77 (−0.94)	0.06 (0.14)	−0.19 (−0.46)	0.12 (0.28)
12/14/77		−0.07 (−0.15)	0.13 (0.23)	0.26 (0.44)	−0.29 (−0.35)	−0.57 (−1.27)	−0.24 (−0.58)	−0.17 (−0.40)

[a]See footnote to table 1.

Exposure Draft (July 20, 1977), FAS 19 (December 6, 1977) and ASR 253 (August 30, 1978) are reported in tables 1 to 3. The results for each release date are:

(i) *Exposure Draft* (table 1): The Exposure Draft is *dated*, July 15, 1977, but was not made public until July 19, and was first mentioned in the WSJ on July 20. No significant abnormal returns are observed on July 15 or July 18. However, a statistically significant security price reaction is observed on July

Table 3

Daily prediction errors surrounding announcement of ASR 253 (*t*-values in parentheses).[a]

Calendar date	Event	Portfolios and number of companies						
		ALL 89	IND 64	INDUS 48	INDCA 16	UTL 25	SE 40	SE-ALL 129
08/21/78		0.30 (0.63)	0.21 (0.39)	0.26 (0.44)	0.08 (0.10)	0.44 (0.99)	0.27 (0.65)	−0.01 (−0.02)
08/22/78		−0.14 (−0.31)	0.02 (0.04)	0.19 (0.32)	−0.57 (−0.70)	−0.54 (−1.21)	−0.09 (−0.21)	(0.05) (0.12)
08/23/78		−0.58 (−1.32)	−0.62 (−1.11)	−0.89 (−1.48)	0.28 (0.34)	−0.50 (−1.11)	0.20 (0.48)	0.78 (1.84)
08/24/78		0.07 (0.16)	−0.09 (−0.16)	−0.41 (−0.69)	1.00 (1.22)	0.47 (1.05)	0.35 (0.86)	0.28 (0.67)
08/25/78		−0.54 (−1.30)	−0.86 (−1.55)	−0.78 (−1.30)	−1.16 (−1.42)	0.26 (0.59)	−0.54 (−1.33)	−0.01 (−0.01)
08/28/78		−0.30 (−0.68)	−0.65 (−1.17)	−0.58 (−0.97)	−0.86 (−1.05)	0.58 (1.29)	−0.50 (−1.22)	−0.20 (−0.47)
08/29/78	Public announcement	−0.10 (−0.23)	0.01 (0.01)	0.19 (0.31)	−0.59 (−0.72)	−0.36 (−0.81)	−0.25 (−0.60)	−0.15 (−0.34)
08/30/78	WSJ article	0.45 (1.03)	0.75 (1.35)	0.51 (0.85)	1.55 (1.90)	−0.29 (−0.65)	−0.03 (−0.09)	−0.48 (−1.15)
08/31/78		0.54 (1.24)	0.57 (1.03)	0.26 (0.43)	1.64 (2.01)	0.48 (1.09)	0.03 (0.09)	−0.51 (−1.21)
09/01/78		1.04 (2.37)	1.56 (2.81)	0.48 (0.80)	5.17 (6.34)	−0.27 (−0.62)	0.31 (0.75)	−0.74 (−1.75)
09/05/78		−0.63 (−1.43)	−0.66 (−1.18)	−0.64 (−1.08)	−0.73 (−0.90)	−0.56 (−1.26)	−0.58 (−1.42)	0.05 (0.12)
09/06/78		−0.48 (−1.10)	−0.56 (−1.02)	0.00 (0.01)	−2.59 (−3.16)	−0.28 (−0.62)	0.34 (0.82)	0.82 (1.94)
09/07/78		−0.29 (−0.65)	−0.42 (−0.76)	−0.35 (−0.59)	−0.68 (−0.83)	0.06 (0.12)	0.13 (0.32)	0.42 (0.99)
09/08/78		0.62 (1.40)	1.06 (1.90)	0.30 (0.50)	3.58 (4.36)	−0.50 (−1.11)	0.54 (1.32)	−0.07 (−0.17)

[a]See footnote to table 1.

19 (the exposure draft issue date) and July 20 (the WSJ report date). On these two days, portfolio *ALL* fell by 1.41% and 1.05%, respectively (*t*-values of −3.22 and −2.40); the value of industrial companies decreased by 1.71% and 1.63% (*t*-values of −3.07 and −2.94); the value of companies incorporated in the U.S. fell by 1.75% and by 1.63% (*t*-values of −2.92 and −2.74); and the value of companies incorporated in Canada fell by 1.59% and 1.61% (*t*-values of −1.95 and −1.98). Public utilities experienced an abnormal price change of −0.68% on July 19 and 0.38% on July 20 (*t*-values of −1.53 and 0.86).

Oil and gas firms employing the *successful efforts* method of accounting experienced a small (and insignificant) security price reaction on July 18, 19 and 20, 1977. However, a comparison between full cost and successful efforts firms reveals that the two groups' performances are significantly different only on *July 19, 1977* (i.e., portfolio *SE-ALL* realized an abnormal performance of 1.25%; *t* = 2.45).[7,8]

(ii) *FAS 19* (table 2): A negative but statistically *insignificant* security price reaction is observed on December 5 and 6, 1977. The results on December 6 appear to be due to the Canadian sample, which experienced a marginally significant negative abnormal price performance of −1.45% (*t* = −1.75). The performance of portfolios *SE* and *SE-ALL* confirms the observation that no significant security price changes occurred at the announcement date of FAS 19. Portfolio *SE* remained unchanged at that date while portfolio *SE-ALL* increased by 0.39% (*t* = 0.92).[9]

(iii) *ASR 253* (table 3): A small positive performance for full cost companies is found on August 30, 1978, the day the WSJ reports the SEC's decision to overrule FAS 19. However, only Canadian firms appear to have benefited from this decision with a price increase of 1.55% (*t* = 1.90), and it is likely that confounding events are responsible for this result.[10] No abnormal performance to *SE* firms is observed on this date. In addition, a comparison of portfolios *SE* and *ALL* reveals that full cost companies did not significantly outperform

---

[7] The results reported above are consistent with Lev's (1979) findings. He reports an abnormal performance of 0.57%, −2.32% and −1.66% for full cost companies and −0.42%, 0.09% and −0.69% for successful efforts companies for the three trading days July 18–20, 1977.

[8] Successful efforts companies are an imperfect control group, since they are also affected by the accounting change. To test whether an impact is observed, Lys (1982) uses a sample of oil and gas companies incorporated in Canada and not traded on U.S. exchanges to the sample of Canadian firms traded on U.S. exchanges. Since Canada was not expected to follow U.S. GAAP on oil and gas accounting [see Collins and Dent (1979)], this control portfolio is not expected to be affected by the events. Only monthly data are available. However, the control sample outperformed U.S. traded Canadian firms in July, the month the Exposure Draft is announced.

[9] The positive performance on December 1 and 2, 1977 reflects oil and gas discoveries in Alberta, Canada. See the WSJ, December 1, 1977.

their *SE* counterparts (portfolio *SE-ALL* realized an abnormal performance of −0.48% with $t = -1.15$).[11]

Overall, the event-tests performed find empirical support for the first research hypothesis only on July 19, 1977, the announcement date of the exposure draft. These results are generally consistent with Haworth et al. (1978), Collins and Dent (1979), Lev (1979) and Smith (1981a). The following section uses a cross-sectional analysis to provide additional evidence on whether bond covenant effects can explain the security market reaction at the exposure draft release date.

5. Cross-sectional analysis

5.1. Cross-sectional sample

The firm sample is further reduced for the cross-sectional test. First, only the *industrial* sample (portfolio *IND*), is used in the cross-sectional tests since this is the only portfolio that showed any impact in the time series tests. Second, twenty-nine companies failed to disclose information about the financial statement impact of FAS 19 in their 1977 10-K forms and are deleted from the test sample.[12] Finally, one company incorporated in Canada, is deleted from the sample because it has no debt in its capital structure.[13] These additional requirements reduced the cross-sectional sample from 64 to 34 oil and gas producing firms employing the full cost method of accounting.

5.2. Measures for the independent variables

5.2.1. Default risk

Section two hypothesizes that the equity of firms with riskier debt will be more adversely affected by FAS 19 (research hypotheses 3, 4 and 5). The analysis identifies three measures of default risk – firm variance (S), leverage

---

[10] The WSJ reports: 'Dome Petroleum Ltd. shares soared Friday, fueled by rumors of a major oil discovery in the Beaufort Sea Area of the Canadian arctic.' Exclusion of Dome from the Canadian sample did not affect the results. It is likely, however, that other Canadian petroleum companies also benefit from this oil discovery. Also, on Monday, September 5, 1978, the WSJ reports of rumors of a major oil discovery in the Beaufort Sea Area of the Canadian arctic.

[11] This result is also found in Smith (1981b). She reports an abnormal performance of −0.46% on August 30, 1978.

[12] These 29 firms fall into two groups. The first is composed of U.S. incorporated companies using a fiscal year ending prior to issuance of the Exposure Draft. The second group consists of Canadian firms that did not disclose the expected consequences of the proposed elimination of full cost accounting.

[13] Since the hypothesis maintains that the accounting change resulted in a redistribution of wealth from shareholder to debtholder, it is unable to analyze equity changes of unlevered firms. The equity of this company (Prairie Oil) fell by 2.18% ($t = -0.73$) on July 19, 1977.

(*TD/E*) and time to maturity (*TM*). The following proxies are used for these variables:

(*S*) The daily standard deviation of the returns on the *firm* is estimated from the standard deviation of daily security prices adjusted for the firm's capital structure. Estimation of this variable is derived in the appendix. The standard deviation of the daily firm returns is predicted to be *negatively* related to the security market reaction.

(*TD/E*) Debt to equity ratio is computed by dividing the book value of the debt by the market value of the equity. Preferred stock is treated as equity and its market value is used when available.[14] *TD/E* is hypothesized to be negatively related to the security market reaction.

(*TM*) For each firm the average time to maturity of the debt is computed by weighing the time to maturity of each debt issue by its book value relative to total long-term debt. The analysis predicts a *negative* relation between time to maturity and the security market reaction.[15]

5.2.2. Accounting impact

Research hypothesis 2 predicts a *positive* relationship between the size of FAS 19's impact on the firm's accounting data and the change in security prices of the affected firms. Three variables are used to proxy for this effect:

(*CRD*) The first variable is the relative reduction in unrestricted retained earnings. The data to compute this variable is collected from the 10-K statements for the fiscal year ending 1977. For firms with available data ($n = 14$), the change in the contractual restrictions on dividends (*CRD*) is computed as the relative reduction in unrestricted retained earnings,

$$CRD_j = -\Delta RE_j / FD_j, \tag{8}$$

where for firm j

ΔRE_j = expected reduction in the book value of retained earnings,
FD_j = unrestricted retained earnings prior to the issuance of the Exposure Draft.

CRD_j is set equal to zero for firms that did not report unrestricted retained earnings in their 10-K forms or their annual reports ($n = 20$).[16] Research

---

[14] Reestimation of the cross-sectional model with preference treated as junior debt had no impact on the results.

[15] In addition, *TM* also proxies for the time that a binding covenant will affect managerial decisions if no renegotiation takes place.

[16] There appears to be no difference in the dividend policies of these two groups. Of the 14 companies in the first group, 12 or 86% paid cash dividends in 1977. Of the 20 companies with missing data, 14 or 70% paid cash dividends in 1977.

hypothesis 2 predicts that the change in unrestricted retained earnings is positively related to changes in dividend policy and to the security market reaction.

(*SRD*) In addition to the change in unrestricted earnings, the relative impact on (total) retained earnings is investigated to test whether *statutory restrictions* on dividends are binding. These dividend restrictions are imposed by state incorporation statutes. In general, lawful dividends can only be paid out of retained earnings.[17] For each firm, the extent to which these restrictions are binding is computed by comparing the expected reduction in retained earnings to the *cash dividends* paid by the company in 1977. It is assumed that firms do not alter their dividend policy as long as retained earnings are non-negative. In order to quantify the severity of statutory restrictions on dividends the following algorithm is used:

(i) *SRD* is set equal to zero for firms that did not pay cash dividends during 1977 *or* for firms whose retained earnings, after adjustment for the accounting change, exceed the dividends paid in 1977.

(ii) *SRD* is set equal to -1.0 for firms that paid cash dividends in 1977 *and* whose retained earnings, after adjustment for the accounting change, are negative.

(iii) Finally, for firms that paid cash dividends in 1977 but whose retained earnings after adjustment for the accounting change are positive but smaller than the 1977 cash dividends, *SRD* is set

$$SRD_j = (RE_j - \Delta RE_j)/DIV_j - 1.0, \tag{9}$$

where for firm j

ΔRE_j = reduction of the book value of retained earnings,
RE_j = book value of retained earnings,
DIV_j = cash dividends paid in 1977.

The larger (more negative) the relative reduction in retained earnings the higher the likelihood that statutory restrictions will become binding and the more negative the security price impact. Therefore, a positive association between *SRD* and the security market reaction is expected.

(*OR/TR*) The percentage of revenues derived from oil and gas operations is computed by dividing oil and gas revenue by total revenue. This variable proxies for the likely impact of the accounting ruling on the firm's accounting

---

[17]See for example Deer (1978). A complicating factor in determining whether a given dividend is lawful is caused by conflicting state laws. Corporations incorporated in one state can also be subjected to the laws of the states where major business is conducted and/or where creditors and shareholders reside.

data.[18] That is, change in oil and gas accounting should be most pronounced for firms heavily involved in oil and gas production. Since covenants become more binding with larger adverse changes in accounting numbers, a negative relationship between OR/TR and the security market is expected.

5.2.3. Renegotiation cost

Research hypothesis 5 predicts that the security price impact will be a function of the cost to renegotiate, call or repurchase the debt. The variables used to proxy for these costs are:

(RC/E)   The cost of refinancing the debt. These costs arise if companies are forced to renegotiate the covenants of the loan agreement *and* debtholders make their consent conditional on an adjustment in the coupon rate towards the current market rate of interest. Obviously, the renegotiation costs are largest (more negative) for firms which have debt selling below book value (i.e., for firms which have issued debt in the past when interest rates were lower than current rates). Therefore, refinancing costs are computed as (i) the difference between the present value of the actual coupon payments and (ii) the present value of interest payments of equal maturity and risk in 1977 (plus any call premiums).[19] The relative refinancing costs are obtained by deflating total refinancing cost by the value of the equity.[20] The refinancing costs (RC/E) are expected to be positively related to the security market reaction.

(PD/TD)   The relative amount of publicly traded debt is computed by taking the ratio of public to total long term debt. Leftwich (1981) and Holthausen (1981) hypothesize that renegotiation costs differ between public and private debt issues. The security market reaction is expected to be negatively related to (PD/TD).

5.3. Summary statistics for the independent variables

Descriptive statistics for the independent variables are reported in table 4. On average, elimination of full costing would result in a reduction in unre-

---

[18]Since the variables *SRD* and *CRD* were formally *unavailable* to market participants at the announcement date of the exposure draft, it is possible that market participants used *OR/TR* to assess the likely impact of the exposure draft on the companies' debt covenants.

[19]All public and some privately placed debt have call provisions with call prices ranging from 101% to 110.375% of the book value of the debt. The ratio between the proceeds received from the sale of the debt to the issue price ranged from 97.75% to 99%.

[20]Since the current yield on the debt is not observable, the following algorithm is used: (i) For companies which issued debt in 1977, that rate is used. (ii) Companies with rated debt are assigned the yield to maturity of equally risky debt in 1977. (iii) The coupon rate on the *most recent* debt issue is compared to the yield on rated corporate debt in that year. The yield on corporate debt corresponding to this rating in 1977 is then assigned as the refinancing rate. (iv) For companies when methods (i) through (iv) could not be applied the refinancing rate is set equal to the yield of Moody's B-rated debt for 1977.

Table 4

Summary statistics for the independent variables.

Variable	Description	Mean	Standard error	Simple correlation coefficients							
				S	TD/E	TM	CRD	SRD	OR/TR	RC/E	
S	Daily standard deviation on the return on the firm.	0.0086	0.0035	1.000							
TD/E	Book value of the debt to market value of equity.	1.2398	0.9020	−0.632	1.000						
TM	Average time to maturity on the debt (in years).	7.9868	5.1222	−0.369	−0.077	1.000					
CRD	Reduction of unrestricted retained earnings.	−1.6744	5.5827	−0.082	0.140	−0.119	1.000				
SRD	Reduction on dividends due to statutory restrictions.	−0.1129	0.3148	−0.253	0.234	0.002	0.337	1.000			
OR/TR	Oil and gas revenue to total revenue.	0.6402	0.3225	0.203	−0.103	0.195	−0.177	−0.302	1.000		
RC/E	Total estimated refinancing cost to total equity.	−0.0252	0.0349	0.485	−0.225	−0.667	−0.031	−0.219	−0.003	1.000	
PD/TD	Book value of public debt to total debt.	0.0867	0.1611	−0.161	−0.057	0.587	−0.333	0.063	0.015	−0.386	

stricted retained earnings by 167% with numerous firms having a deficit in this account. However, this estimate is likely to overestimate the actual reduction in the funds for dividends account because the computations are based on the companies' assessment of the likely impact of FAS 19 in response to a request by the SEC. Since most of the sample firms *opposed* the accounting change, these firms have an incentive to overstate the expected impact in order to influence the SEC to reverse FAS 19.

If the accounting change was implemented in 1977, the sample firms would have to cut dividends by at least 11.29% due to statutory dividend restrictions. As discussed above, the incentive to overstate the likely impact of the accounting ruling is likely to bias this measure downwards. The refinancing cost for the sample firms is, on average, 2.5% of the market value of the equity. This figure is comparable to the magnitude of security price reduction following announcement of the exposure draft reported by Lev (1979). Finally, the debt of the full cost firms is typically privately held and the sample firms derive on average 64% of their revenues from oil and gas operations.

The simple correlation coefficients between the independent variables are also reported in table 4. It was argued in section 2 that total firm risk and debt to equity are likely to be negatively correlated. As implied by the assumption of costly bankruptcy, *low risk firms* (i.e., firms with a relatively low standard deviation) tend to issue *more debt* than *high risk firms* [a correlation of -0.632 is found between firm risk (S) and the relative amount of debt in the companies capital structure].

5.4. Cross-sectional regression model

Section 2 uses an option pricing framework to derive the independent variables that determine the wealth consequence of FAS 19 on shareholder wealth. However, the structural form of the cross-sectional equation cannot be derived, and a linear relationship is assumed. Using the variables defined above, the cross-sectional model is estimated as

$$e_{j,t} = a_0 + a_{1,t}S_j + a_{2,t}(TD/E)_j + a_{3,t}TM_j + a_{4,t}CRD_j + a_{5,t}SRD_j$$
$$+ a_{6,t}(OR/TR)_j + a_{7,t}(RC/E)_j + a_{8,t}(PD/TD)_j + u_{j,t},$$

where $e_{j,t}$ is the abnormal return to equity holders of firm j at event date t, $u_{j,t}$ is a random error term, and the $a_{i,t}$'s $(i = 1, \ldots, 8)$ are the regression coefficients.

5.5. Cross-sectional test results

Although section 4 concludes that a significant security price reaction is observed only on the date of the exposure draft, the cross-sectional model is estimated for all three events (Exposure Draft, FAS 19, and ASR 253) in interest of completeness. If the results are not spurious we should find significant results only at the exposure draft event date.

The estimated coefficients for July 19, 1977 are reported in table 5. The first row of table 5 reports the full model results and subsequent rows report the results for reduced models, excluding independent variables that are not statistically significant.[21]

The F-statistic for the full model is 3.41, implying that the null hypothesis (i.e., no statistical relationship) is rejected at the 5% level of confidence. Overall, the model explains 52% of the cross-sectional variation of the dependent variable on July 19, 1977. Thus, the independent variables explain a non-trivial portion of the variation in security prices at the exposure draft announcement date.

The t-statistics of the individual regression coefficients reveal that only S and TD/E significantly differ from zero at the 5% level. Two coefficients, PD/TD and RC/E, have the wrong sign, but are not significantly different from zero. The insignificance of the refinancing costs (RC/E) is likely to be caused by measurement error. The insignificant coefficient for the relative amount of publicly traded debt does not suggest private lenders impose lower costs to renegotiate covenants. This latter result is consistent with Leftwich (1981) and with Collins et al. (1981).

The second row of table 5 reports the coefficients of a reduced model. CRD and SRD are excluded as measures of accounting impact and RC/E is omitted as a measure of transaction cost. This model explains 48% of the cross-sectional variations (the F-statistic is 5.17, exceeding the 95% fractile of the F-distribution). The reduction of explanatory power due to the exclusion of these three variables is not statistically significant (the F value is 2.19).

Row 3 of table 5 reports the estimated coefficients by additionally excluding PD/TD and row 4 also excludes TM, since both are found not to be statistically significant. The R^2 of these two models are 46.1% and 44.9%, respectively, with F-statistics of 6.20 and 8.16 (both exceeding the 95% fractile of the F-distribution).

As noted earlier, prior research only uses the debt to equity ratio as a risk measure. Therefore, it is of interest to investigate the sensitivity of the approach to the omission of the firm's risk. Regression (10) is reestimated without S, the proxy of firm risk, and the results are reported in row 5 of table 5. There are two important results. First the regression loses almost all of its explanatory power. This suggests that S is an important variable. Second, the coefficient of debt to equity has the predicted sign, but is not statistically

---

[21]Six sample firms had earnings announcements in the WSJ in the ten trading day period surrounding issuance of the Exposure Draft. To ensure that these announcements do not bias the test results, the cross-sectional model was reestimated excluding these six firms. The test results remained virtually unchanged.

Table 5

Cross-sectional model; event date: 07/19/77; event: Exposure Draft; mean value of dependent variable: −2.6% (t-statistics in parentheses).

| | | Independent variables [predicted signs in brackets] | | | | | | | | | |
| | | Risk | | | Accounting impact | | | Transaction cost | | | |
Row	Intercept	S [−]	TD/E [−]	TM [−]	SRD [+]	CRD [+]	OR/TR [−]	RC/E [+]	PD/TD [−]	R^2	F
1	0.056 (2.63)[a]	−5.138 (−3.45)[a]	−0.014 (−2.70)[a]	−0.001 (−1.17)	0.007 (0.60)	0.001 (1.07)	−0.016 (−1.45)	−0.006 (−0.05)	0.033 (1.29)	52.2	3.41[a]
2	0.055 (2.64)[a]	−5.132 (−3.52)[a]	−0.013 (−2.60)[a]	−0.001 (−1.23)			−0.021 (−1.95)[b]		0.025 (1.02)	48.0	5.17[a]
3	0.056 (2.69)	−4.920 (−3.41)[a]	−0.013 (−2.52)[a]	−0.001 (−0.79)			−0.023 (−2.15)[a]			46.1	6.20[a]
4	0.040 (2.71)	−4.241 (−3.68)[a]	−0.011 (−2.44)[a]				−0.026 (−2.60)[a]			44.9	8.16[a]
5	−0.001 (−0.75)		−0.002 (−0.38)	0.000 (0.33)	0.010 (0.70)	0.001 (0.69)	−0.029 (−2.29)[a]	−0.037 (−0.23)	0.020 (0.63)	29.4	1.55

[a]Significant at the 2.5% level one-tail test for t-statistics, or exceeds the 95% fractile of F-distribution.
[b]Significant at the 5% level one-tail test for t-statistics.

significant. The results imply that the inability of prior studies [e.g., Leftwich (1981), Collins et al. (1981)] to find evidence of a debt covenant effect may be due to model misspecification.

The cross-sectional model is also estimated on the other event dates described in the time series test (table 6).[22] The results are consistent with the prediction errors of the time series tests. For example, on July 20, 1977, full cost companies did not experience a statistically significant security price performance relative to the control group (see table 1). This suggests that the security market return on this day is not related to the proposed accounting change. The lack of statistical significance for the cross-sectional tests on this date reinforces this result. Similarly, no statistically significant variation is explained on the other dates examined in table 6.

5.6. Validation of cross-sectional tests

One important question concerns the relevant critical values for the *t*-statistics and the *F*-statistics for interpreting the results in tables 5 and 6. That is, if there is a systematic misspecification of the market model, the estimated coefficients of the cross-sectional regression could differ from zero under the null hypothesis of no security market reaction to the accounting change and, therefore, result in an inappropriate rejection of the null hypothesis.[23] Specifically, it can be shown (using option pricing analysis) that the coefficient on leverage is biased in favor of a rejection of the null hypothesis (i.e., of no relationship between leverage and the security price change). Finally, it can be shown that the coefficient on the standard deviation of the firm's returns is biased in favor of acceptance of the null hypothesis [see Lys (1982)].[24] Therefore, it is important to determine the size of the estimated coefficients on non-event dates.

Evidence on the relevant critical values in the present sample is obtained by performing four different cross-sectional validation tests using 'non-event' security returns. The market model coefficients for each of the 34 sample firms are estimated using a two hundred day trading period starting March 1, 1976. The market model parameters are then used to compute abnormal returns for each of the sample firms for a 531 trading day period from December 14, 1976 to January 19, 1979. The cross-sectional model is reestimated on each of these 'non-event dates', and the resulting *t* and *F* values are sampled.

---

[22] The independent variable are estimated using 1977 accounting data and the variables have not been updated for ASR 253 which occurred in 1978. This will induce an error in variables problem which biases the results in favor of the null hypothesis.

[23] For example, Banz (1981) and Reinganum (1981) find that abnormal returns are correlated with firm size.

[24] Jain (1982) estimates the magnitude of these biases and finds that the effect is sufficiently large as to produce inappropriate inferences. His results suggest that a different interpretation of the reported *t* and *F* values is required.

Table 6

Cross-sectional model; summary of 'other event dates' [predicted coefficients in brackets] (t-statistics in parentheses).

Event	Date	Mean value of dependant variable	Intercept	Risk			Accounting impact			Transaction cost		R^2	F
				S	TD/E	TM	SRD	CRD	OR/TR	RC/E	PD/TD		
Exposure Draft	07/20/77	[−] −2.1%	−0.019 (−0.73)	[−] −0.255 (−0.14)	[−] −0.004 (−0.56)	[−] 0.000 (0.02)	[+] −0.031 (−2.15)[a]	[+] 0.000 (0.15)	[−] −0.006 (−0.46)	[+] −0.209 (−1.24)	[−] 0.003 (0.09)	24.3	1.00
FAS 19	12/05/77	[−] 0.2%	0.006 (0.21)	[−] 0.848 (0.42)	[−] −0.008 (−1.05)	[−] −0.001 (−0.85)	[+] −0.009 (−0.58)	[+] 0.000 (0.53)	[−] 0.005 (0.33)	[+] −0.204 (−1.09)	[−] 0.007 (0.10)	17.6	0.62
FAS 19	12/06/77	[−] −1.1%	−0.014 (−0.53)	[−] −0.028 (−0.02)	[−] −0.003 (−0.38)	[−] 0.001 (0.47)	[+] −0.008 (−0.53)	[+] 0.000 (0.21)	[−] −0.009 (−0.63)	[+] −0.147 (−0.85)	[−] 0.026 (0.77)	22.1	0.88
ASR 253	08/29/78	[+] 0.2%	0.009 (0.36)	[+] −0.523 (−0.30)	[+] −0.006 (−1.01)	[+] −0.000 (−0.33)	[+] 0.007 (0.48)	[+] 0.000 (0.41)	[+] 0.029 (2.05)[b]	[−] 0.081 (0.50)	[−] 0.018 (0.57)	13.8	0.50
ASR 253	08/30/78	[+] 0.7%	−0.007 (−0.25)	[+] 0.636 (0.33)	[+] −0.002 (−0.23)	[+] 0.002 (1.29)	[−] −0.006 (−0.39)	[−] 0.001 (1.38)	[+] 0.001 (0.09)	[−] 0.387 (2.18)[a]	[+] 0.007 (0.21)	24.0	0.99

[a]Significant at the 2.5% level one-tail test.
[b]Significant at the 5% level one-tail test.

The results of this procedure are presented in table 7. The first test consisted of estimating the cross-sectional model [eq. (10)] on each of the 531 trading days. The sample statistics of the individual *t-coefficients* and the sample statistics for the *F-values* are reported in column 1 of table 7. The second test estimated the cross-sectional coefficients only on those 'non-event dates' on which the equally weighed 34 firm portfolio had a significant abnormal performance. Forty-six such 'event days' are found in the 531 day period considered. Eq. (10) is estimated on these 46 days and the results are reported in column 2 of table 7. In both tests, the average *t-statistic* of the regression coefficient is small relative to the standard deviation of these estimates. This suggests that the *t*-tests in tables 5 and 6 are not confounded by market model misspecifications. The average *F*-statistic is close to 1.0, again suggesting no model misspecification.

Tests 1 and 2 investigate whether the values significantly differ from zero in 'non-event' days. However, they do not take into account whether the particu-

Table 7

Test for specification errors; cross-sectional model estimated in non-event period; average *t*-statistic of coefficients (sample standard deviations in parentheses).

	Unsigned model		Signed model	
	All days	Only significant days	All days	Only significant days
	Number of observations			
	531	46	531	46
Intercept	0.0087	−0.2440	−0.1976	−0.6856
	(1.1326)	(1.2726)	(1.1153)	(1.1042)
S	−0.0792	−0.0075	0.4365	1.2556
	(1.2125)	(1.7620)	(1.1340)	(1.2363)
TD/E	−0.1331	−0.2941	0.4274	1.4440
	(1.2402)	(1.8562)	(1.1718)	(1.2029)
TM	−0.1680	−0.2072	0.1077	0.4342
	(0.9734)	(0.8815)	(0.9819)	(0.7947)
PD/TD	0.0590	0.3423	−0.0898	−0.1694
	(0.8119)	(0.8072)	(0.8091)	(0.8603)
SRD	0.0384	−0.3676	−0.0212	0.2149
	(0.9854)	(1.0041)	(0.9859)	(1.0475)
CRD	0.0174	0.0988	−0.0172	−0.2565
	(0.9154)	(0.8673)	(0.9154)	(0.8344)
RC/E	−0.1236	−0.1883	0.0983	0.3465
	(0.9953)	(1.0444)	(0.9981)	(1.0031)
OR/TR	0.0040	(−0.0329)	(0.0085)	−0.0204
	(1.0038)	(1.0497)	(1.0038)	(1.0500)
F-statistic	1.0603	1.3826	1.0603	1.3826
	(0.6526)	(0.7649)	(0.6526)	(0.7649)

lar day had 'good' or 'bad' news, i.e., whether firm values *increased* or *decreased*. Tests 3 and 4 explicitly take the sign of the portfolio performance in the 531 and 46 'non-event dates' into account. Days on which the portfolio fell in value are labeled *negative* events, while days in which the portfolio value rose are labeled *positive* events. The cross-sectional model is reestimated by multiplying the dependent variables by minus one for negative event dates. These results are reported in columns 3 and 4 of table 7, and again suggest no misspecifications.[25]

6. Summary

This paper investigates whether debt covenants are related to changes in firm value occurring with mandated accounting changes. The results suggest that the proposed elimination of full cost accounting had an adverse impact on security prices of oil and gas companies. More importantly, default risk and the accounting impact are negatively related to the security price performance. This result suggests that debt covenants are important and that these contracts can have an impact on the wealth of shareholders when accounting changes occur.

The paper provides two additional insights that should be useful in future research on bond covenants effects. First, prior tests of bond covenant effects of accounting changes [e.g., Leftwich (1981), Holthausen (1981) and Collins et al. (1981)] use the debt to equity ratio as a measure of the debt's default risk, but find little explanatory power for this variable. As shown in the above analysis, this result may be due to the absence of an adjustment for the total risk of the firm. That is a statistically significant negative correlation exists between total firm risk and leverage, which implies that omission of one of these factors can result in a traditional omitted variable problem. Therefore, omitting one of these variables in the cross-sectional regression can produce an insignificant coefficient for the other factor. The empirical results suggest that this type of omitted variable problem exists for the oil and gas firm sample and that both variables (total firm risk and leverage) are necessary to isolate bond covenant effects. Second, the paper analyzes whether systematic misspecifications of the cross-sectional model are responsible for the test results. For this sample, the results suggest that the cross-sectional model is not misspecified, a result inconsistent with Jain (1982).

Two important reservations are, however, in order. First, the theory is not powerful enough to specify the structural equation for the cross-sectional cost function linking debt covenants and shareholder wealth. Since a rigorous link

---

[25]The results (see table 7) do not indicate a misspecification of the cross-sectional model. Moreover, Jain's (1982) results cannot be replicated in the present sample. Overall, the four tests performed indicate that the benchmark used in computing the *t*-statistics in tables 5 and 6 (i.e., 0) is, in fact, appropriate for the current sample.

between the theory and the empirical method has not been established, the analysis is limited by the traditional problems arising from misspecifying the structural equation (e.g., omitted variables and measurement errors). Second, data is available for only 34 oil and gas firms in the cross-sectional tests, and generalization can only be made from this modest sample. Subject to these limitations, the paper offers a more powerful approach to testing the debt covenant effect of mandated accounting changes.

Appendix

Derivation of the standard deviation of the return on the firm[26]

The standard deviation of the firm's return (σ), the leverage ratio and the average maturity of the debt are used as measures of the debt's default risk. However, market estimates of σ cannot be easily obtained, since market values for non-traded claims (mainly privately placed debt) are not available. Therefore, estimates of the standard deviation of the firm's returns are derived using contingent claim models. A similar approach is followed by Christie (1981), who studies the implications of three contingent claim models on the variances of the equity of levered firms. The models are:

(i)   the *consol bond model* studied by Black and Cox (1976),
(ii) the *discount bond model* with no safety covenant based on the Black and Scholes (1973) option pricing model, and
(iii) a simplified estimator based on the Black and Scholes (1973) option pricing model.

The cross-sectional regression is estimated using all three estimators of $\hat{\sigma}$. The results appear to be insensitive to the specific estimator used. However, estimators (i) and (ii) occasionally produce *negative* estimates of σ (the relative frequencies for the sample are 6% for the consol bond model and 14% for the discount bond model). Therefore, only the results using the simplified Black and Scholes option pricing model are described below and reported in section 5.

The standard deviation of the return of the firm can be written as a weighted average of the standard deviations of debt and equity, or

$$\sigma_V = (D/(D+E))\sigma_D + (E/(D+E))\sigma_S, \qquad (A.1)$$

where

σ_S = instantaneous standard deviation of the return on the equity,
σ_V = instantaneous standard deviation of the return on the firm,

---

[26]I am indebted to Andrew Christie, Graduate School of Management, University of Rochester, for helpful comments on this section.

σ_D = instantaneous standard deviation of the return on the debt,
D = market value of the debt,
E = market value of the equity.

Assume that σ_D is relatively *small* when compared to σ_V and σ_S, and can be 'neglected'. Then (A.1) becomes

$$\sigma_S = \sigma_V(1 + D/E). \tag{A.2}$$

The standard deviation on the returns on the firm, σ_V, can be estimated as the slope coefficient in a time series interpretation of eq. (A.2). However, the *market* value of the debt is unavailable. To estimate σ_V from (A.2), the debt's book value is substituted for the market value and a time series regression using 400 daily returns starting March 1, 1976 to September 29, 1977 is estimated. Estimates of the daily standard deviation of the equity are obtained by taking the absolute value of the difference between the daily security return and the average security return for the 400 day period,

$$\left|\left(R_{j,t} - \overline{R}_j\right)\right| = s_j\left(1 + D_j/E_{j,t}\right), \tag{A.3}$$

where

$R_{j,t}$ = return on the equity of firm j on day t,
$\overline{R}_j$ = average daily return on security j in the 400 trading day period.

The estimated value of s_j from the regression (A.3), which does not include an intercept, is used in section 5 as an estimator of the daily standard deviation of the returns of the firm.

References

Alchian, A.A. and H. Demsetz, 1972, Production, information costs and economic organization, The American Economic Review 62, 777–795.
Benston, G.J., 1978, Statement before the Securities and Exchange Commission: An evaluation of studies on the effect of the FASB's exposure draft and Statement 19 on the share prices of oil and gas producing companies.
Banz, R.W., 1981, The relationship between market value and returns of common stocks, Journal of Financial Economics 9, 3–18.
Black, F. and Jhon Cox, 1976, Valuing corporate securities: Some effects of bond indenture provisions, Journal of Finance 31, 351–367.
Black, F. and M. Scholes, 1973, The pricing of options and corporate liabilities, Journal of Political Economy, May–June, 637–654.
Collins, D.W. and W.T. Dent, 1979, The proposed elimination of full cost accounting in the extractive petroleum industry: An empirical assessment of the market consequences, Journal of Accounting and Economics 1, 3–44.
Collins, D.W., M.S. Rozeff and D.S. Dhaliwal, 1981, A cross-sectional analysis of the economic determinants of market reaction to the proposed mandatory accounting change in the oil and gas industry, Journal of Accounting and Economics 3, 37–72.

Collins, D.W., M.S. Rozeff and W.K. Salatka, 1982, The SEC's challenge of FAS No. 19: A test of market reversal, The Accounting Review, Jan., 1–17.

Cox, J. and S.A. Ross, 1976, The valuation of options for alternative stochastic processes, Journal of Financial Economics 3, 145–166.

Christie, A.A., 1981, The stochastic behavior of common stock variances: Value and leverage effects, Unpublished working paper (Graduate School of Management, University of Rochester, Rochester, NY).

Deakin, E.B., 1979, Analysis of differences between non-major oil firms, The Accounting Review, Oct., 722–734.

Deer, R.E., 1978, The lawyer's basic corporate practice manual, Joint Committee on Continuing Professional Education of the American Law Institute and the American Bar Association, 2nd ed. (Philadelphia, PA).

Dyckman, T.R. and A.J. Smith, 1979, Financial accounting and reporting by oil and gas producing companies: A study of information effects, Journal of Accounting and Economics 1, 45–74.

Fama, E.F., 1976, Foundation of finance (Basic Books, New York).

Fogelson, J.H., 1978, The impact of changes in accounting principles on restrictive covenants in credit agreements and indentures, The Business Lawyer 33, 769–787.

Foster, G., 1980, Accounting policy decisions and capital market research, Journal of Accounting and Economics 2, 29–62.

Haworth, H., J. Matthews and C. Tuck, 1978, Full cost versus successful efforts: A study of a proposed accounting change's competitive impact, SEC Directorate of Economic and Policy Research, Feb.

Holthausen, R.W., 1981, Theory and evidence on the effect of bond covenants and management compensation contracts on the choice of accounting techniques: The case of depreciation switch-back, Journal of Accounting and Economics 3, 73–109.

Jain, P.C., 1982, Cross-sectional association between abnormal return and firm specific variables, Journal of Accounting and Economics 4, 205–228.

Jensen, M. and W.H. Meckling, 1976, Theory of the firm: Managerial behavior, agency costs and ownership structure, Journal of Financial Economics 3, 305–360.

Kalay, A., 1978, Corporate dividend policy: A collection of related essays, Unpublished Ph.D. thesis (University of Rochester, Rochester, NY).

Larcker, D.F. and L. Revsine, 1983, The oil and gas accounting controversy: An analysis of economic consequences, The Accounting Review, forthcoming.

Leftwich, R., 1981, Evidence of the impact of mandatory changes in accounting principles on corporate loan agreements, Journal of Accounting and Economics 3, 3–30.

Leftwich, R., 1983, Accounting information and private markets: Evidence from private lending agreements, The Accounting Review, Jan., 23–42.

Lev, B., 1979, The impact of accounting regulation on the stock market: The case of oil and gas companies, The Accounting Review, July, 485–503.

Lilien, S. and V. Pastena, 1982, Determinants of intra-method choice in the oil and gas industry, Journal of Accounting and Economics 4, 145–170.

Lys, T., 1982, Selection of accounting procedures and implications of changes in generally accepted accounting principles: A case study using oil and gas accounting, Unpublished Ph.D. thesis (University of Rochester, Rochester, NY).

Maddala, G.S., 1977, Econometrics (McGraw-Hill, New York).

Myers, S.C., 1977, Determinants of corporate borrowing, Journal of Financial Economics 2, 147–175.

Reinganum, M.R., 1981, Misspecification of capital asset pricing: Empirical anomalies based on earning yields and market values, Journal of Financial Economics 9, 19–46.

Scholes, M. and J. Williams, 1977, Estimating betas from nonsynchronous data, Journal of Financial Economics 5, 309–329.

Smith, A.J., 1981a, An empirical investigation of the information effects of a change in the financial reporting standards for oil and gas producers: The proposed elimination and subsequent retention of full cost accounting, Unpublished dissertation (Cornell University, Ithaca, NY).

Smith, A.J., 1981b, The SEC reversal of FASB statement No. 19: An investigation of information effects, Journal of Accounting Research 19, Suppl.

Smith, C.W., 1976, Option pricing: A review, Journal of Financial Economics 1, 3–52.

Smith, C.W. and J.B. Warner, 1979, On financial contracting: An analysis of bond covenants, Journal of Financial Economics 7, 117–161.

Sunder, S., 1976, Properties of accounting numbers under full-costing and successful-efforts costing in the petroleum industry, The Accounting Review, Jan., 1–18.

Wakeman, L.M., 1980, Bond rating agencies and the capital markets, Unpublished working paper (Graduate School of Management, University of Rochester, Rochester, NY).

Watts, R.L., 1977, Corporate financial statements: A product of the market and political processes, Australian Journal of Management 2, 53–75.

Watts, R.L. and J.L. Zimmerman, 1978, Towards a positive theory of the determination of accounting standards, The Accounting Review, Jan., 112–134.

INCENTIVES FOR UNCONSOLIDATED
FINANCIAL REPORTING

Shehzad L. MIAN

Emory University, Atlanta, GA 30322, USA

Clifford W. SMITH, Jr.

University of Rochester, Rochester, NY 14627, USA

Received July 1988, final version received June 1989

We provide a positive analysis of a firm's decision to report the operations of a financial subsidiary on a consolidated versus an unconsolidated basis. Our evidence indicates that the firm is more likely to choose consolidated reporting the greater the operating, financial, and informational interdependencies between parent and subsidiary. Moreover, our evidence offers no support for the FASB hypothesis that firms use unconsolidated financial subsidiaries to understate the fixed claims on their balance sheets.

1. Introduction

In statement 94, the Financial Accounting Standards Board requires consolidation of all majority-owned subsidiaries. In presenting FAS 94 the board argues:

> Present practice has been criticized not only because apparently similar enterprises use different consolidation policies but also because excluding some subsidiaries from consolidation results in the omission of significant amounts of assets, liabilities, revenues, and expenses from the consolidated statements of many enterprises. Omissions of large amounts of liabilities, especially those of finance and similar subsidiaries, have led to the criticism that not consolidating those subsidiaries is an important factor in what is often called 'off-balance-sheet financing'.

This statement suggests the FASB is concerned that the option to use unconsolidated financial reporting produces too much variation in reported accounting numbers across firms.

*We thank M. Barclay, G. Benston, J. Brickley, A. Christie, S.P. Kothari, P. Meyers, W. Scott, R. Watts, J. Zimmerman and especially R. Ball (the editor), R. Holthausen (conference discussant), and G. Whittred (the referee). The research was partially supported by the John M. Olin Foundation, the Lynde and Harry Bradley Foundation, and the Bradley Policy Research Center at the Simon School.

Journal of Accounting and Economics 12 (1990) 141–171. North-Holland

In contrast, much effort by academic accountants recently has focused on the development of a positive theory of accounting policy choice. This theory assumes that accounting choices are the product of purposeful maximizing decisions by informed individuals interacting in competitive markets. It assumes that the variation in the use of accounting methods is in response to variation in firm circumstances. Although numerous papers have examined aspects of consolidated versus unconsolidated reporting, little work has focused on the development of a positive theory of the firm's consolidation decision.[1] Without a positive theory of this accounting policy choice, rational evaluation of whether the observed variation in reporting practice is 'too great' is problematic. Such a theory is necessary to understand the relevant costs and benefits of reducing the accounting choice set.

In this paper, we provide a positive theory of the firm's consolidation decision, developing hypotheses to explain the cross-sectional variation in pre-FAS 94 reporting practice for firms with financial subsidiaries. We hypothesize that the more interdependent the parent–subsidiary activities, the more likely the subsidiary's operations will be reported on a consolidated basis. We focus on three dimensions in which these interdependencies can occur: operating interdependencies, information interdependencies, and financial interdependencies. We recognize that other hypotheses might also usefully explain aspects of firms' consolidation decisions, however the limited prior analysis of this policy choice has produced no other alternatives. We therefore focus on our interdependence and the FASB's off-balance-sheet financing hypotheses.

Overview. In section 2, we analyze incentives for choosing whether to report a subsidiary's performance on a consolidated or an unconsolidated basis given that both are feasible. In section 3, we describe our data set. Our tests in section 4 indicate the evidence generally is consistent with our interdependence hypothesis. We also examine the FASB's hypothesis that firms employ unconsolidated reporting specifically to reduce the fixed claims that appear on the firm's balance sheet. Our evidence is inconsistent with this off-balance-sheet financing hypothesis. In section 5, we offer our conclusions.

2. Hypotheses

We view the consolidation choice as an organizational decision that lies on a continuum: at one extreme, a specific activity can be retained within the firm and performed by a department or division; at the other extreme, the activity can be subcontracted to an independent firm. Between these extremes, the activity can be carried on within a subsidiary. Closer to the external subcontracting end of the spectrum would be an externally-controlled partially-owned

---

[1] The exceptions are the papers by Francis (1986) and Whittred (1986, 1987) that focus on the relation between consolidation policy and debt guarantees.

affiliated corporation, while closer to the internal department/division end would be a wholly-owned subsidiary. Pre-FAS 94 accounting practice requires reporting the activities of an externally-controlled affiliated corporation on an unconsolidated basis, but reporting the activities of departments/divisions on a consolidated basis. Majority-owned operating subsidiaries generally are consolidated as well. Thus prior to FAS 94, the major discretion in reporting practice is limited to majority-owned financial subsidiaries.

Klein, Crawford, and Alchian (1978) argue that the more firm-specific the activity, the more likely it is performed internally within a department or division and the less likely it is subcontracted to an independent firm. Extending their analysis, we hypothesize that the more interdependent the parent and subsidiary activities, the more likely is the subsidiary's performance to be reported on a consolidated basis. Hence, consolidated reporting is closer to the end of the organizational spectrum where the activity is performed internally, while reporting on an unconsolidated basis is closer to the subcontracting end of the spectrum. Thus we suggest that this accounting decision reflects the firm's choice of organizational structure and is determined by the interdependence between the parent and subsidiary activities.

Note that our interdependence hypothesis ultimately relies on the proposition that if one set of accounting numbers is more appropriate for internal control purposes, that set also will tend to be reported externally. Of course, a firm could use consolidated numbers for internal control purposes but report unconsolidated numbers; however, we believe such a policy imposes costs: (1) Watts and Zimmerman (1986) argue that there are potential political costs associated with employing different numbers for external reporting and internal control. They suggest that were the internal numbers made public, those seeking wealth transfers would use the set which furthers their ends. (2) Watts (1977) notes the demand for external audits of the firm's financial reports by the corporation's security holders, but the internal use of accounting numbers in judging managerial performance and setting compensation also provides a derived demand for their external verification. By employing the same figures for both internal control and external financial reporting, a single external audit satisfies both demands. (3) Conditioning contracts on numbers employed for a wide variety of purposes controls the incentive to manipulate the numbers for any single purpose.[2]

2.1. Operating interdependence

There is significant variation in the interdependence of the real production activities between parents and their subsidiaries across firms. For example, finance subsidiaries appear to fall into two major categories: (1) subsidiaries

---

[2]See also the discussion of 'fairness' in Ball (1989).

that extend credit to the firm's operating units (these are frequently named capital companies) and (2) subsidiaries that extend credit to the firm's customers (these are frequently named acceptance or credit companies). For subsidiaries in the first category, we expect that parent–subsidiary activities are more interdependent and hence more likely to be consolidated; for subsidiaries in the second category, we expect activities are more independent and thus more likely to be unconsolidated. However, in special cases we expect subsidiaries engaged in customer financing to be consolidated. For example, in our analysis of accounts-receivable financing policies [Mian and Smith (1989a)], we note that if credit extension terms are employed to engage in effective price discrimination, the firm must coordinate output and credit prices. We suggest that such coordination is facilitated by retaining the credit extension function within the firm. The more market power the firm has in the product market, the more likely it employs credit terms as a price discrimination tool, and the more likely it reports the subsidiary's activities on a consolidated basis.

Similarly, leasing subsidiaries fall into two major categories, manufacturer-lessors and third-party lessors. We expect subsidiaries acting as manufacturer-lessors to be more frequently consolidated (especially if the firm has market power[3]), while those acting as third-party lessors are more likely to be unconsolidated. We expect to observe differences in consolidation policy between real estate subsidiaries which acquire properties for use by the firm versus subsidiaries which act as general real estate developers. Since in the first case the subsidiary is the landlord for the parent while in the second there is no necessary relation between subsidiary and parent, our analysis predicts the former will be consolidated while the latter will be unconsolidated. Finally, insurance subsidiaries write insurance policies to companies within the group as well as to external policy holders. Our analysis implies that the greater the fraction of business within the group, the more likely is the subsidiary to be consolidated.

2.2. Information interdependence

The original justification for unconsolidated financial subsidiaries is a section of ARB 51 which states:

> Separate statements or combined statements would be preferable for a subsidiary or group of subsidiaries if the presentation of financial information concerning the particular activities of such subsidiaries would be more informative to shareholders and creditors of the parent company than would the inclusion of such subsidiaries in the consolidation. For

---

[3]Smith and Wakeman (1985) argue that if leasing is used for price discrimination, then the required coordination of leasing terms and sales prices is facilitated by retaining the leasing activities within the firm.

example, separate statements may be required for a subsidiary which is a bank or an insurance company and may be preferable for a finance company where the parent and the other subsidiaries are engaged in manufacturing operations.

Based on this paragraph, finance, insurance, leasing, and real estate subsidiaries are frequently included in the parent's balance sheet only through its equity interest in the subsidiary.

Employing the criteria in ARB 51 suggests that the greater the difference in accounting practice between the firm's core business and that of its subsidiary, the more likely is the firm to choose unconsolidated reporting. Thus, the information-heterogeneity hypothesis implies: (1) Firms in the financial services industry should report financial subsidiary performance on a consolidated basis more frequently than firms in manufacturing industries. (2) Manufacturing firms should report insurance subsidiaries performance on an unconsolidated basis more frequently than finance, leasing, or real estate subsidiaries because regulation of insurance has produced more specialized accounting conventions for insurance than for the other types of financial subsidiaries. (3) Foreign subsidiaries should be consolidated less frequently than domestic subsidiaries.

We believe that this information-heterogeneity hypothesis is deficient in that it focuses on only the benefits of disclosure, rather than on both costs and benefits. While some information disclosure is mandated by law, other disclosure is at the discretion of corporate management. For that set of information over which corporate officers exercise discretion, to maximize firm value they must disclose any information for which the incremental benefits exceed the costs. These costs have two components, the out-of-pocket costs of the accounting procedures and the costs associated with proprietary information. By proprietary information, we mean information where there is reduction in the present value of the firm's expected cash flows due to the publication of the information. For example, the information might be of value to the firm's competitors. Thus managers have incentives not to disclose proprietary information.[4]

Unconsolidated financial statements are generally more informative than consolidated financial statements in the sense that the information in a set of unconsolidated statements generally allows a user to perform a homemade consolidation, particularly if the magnitude of within-group contracting is either reported or small. The converse is not true – there is insufficient information for a user to take a consolidated statement and produce home-

---

[4]Note that the favorable financing effects of the provision of such information still could be obtained by privately contracting with a creditor (such as a bank) or a private equity supplier and supplying the information in confidence as part of the contract.

made unconsolidated statements. Therefore the information-interdependence hypothesis implies that the higher the potential information costs associated with the subsidiary's activities, the more likely those activities are to be reported on a consolidated basis.[5] Hence, if subsidiaries engaging in more firm-specific activities face greater costs of disclosure (perhaps because data on internal funding allocations would reveal information on which parts of the business management plans to expand), then the activities of these subsidiaries should be reported on a consolidated basis. Also if disclosures of foreign financial subsidiaries are more costly than that of domestic financial subsidiaries (perhaps because it would reveal valuable information about the company's growth rates in specific foreign markets), we expect foreign financial subsidiaries to be consolidated more frequently than domestic.

2.3. Financial interdependence

Direct guarantees. If a wholly-owned subsidiary issues debt that is not guaranteed by the parent, then unrestricted nonarmslength transactions between parent and subsidiary present potential problems. For example, the transfer of assets to a related corporation not subject to the initial debt agreement at nonmarket prices can reduce the coverage afforded subsidiary-company creditors. Whittred (1987) argues that cross-guarantees among related companies avoid the costs of prohibiting asset transfers within the group while controlling incentives to use such transactions to transfer wealth from borrowing company creditors. Both Francis (1986) and Whittred (1987) suggest that consolidation facilitates monitoring compliance with contracts where guarantees are offered. However, there are potentially important differences between Francis' and Whittred's analyses. Francis is concerned only with parent-provided guarantees of the subsidiary's debt. He hypothesizes that if such guarantees are provided, consolidated reporting will be employed, while if such guarantees are not provided, parent-only reporting will be employed. Whittred recognizes that guarantees can be more complex. He hypothesizes that with either parent-provided guarantees of the subsidiary's debt or subsidiary-provided guarantees of the parent's debt, consolidated reporting will be employed.

Our analysis suggests the debt guarantees produce a specific form of interdependence between parent and subsidiary activities – a financial interdependence. We thus expect firms with such guarantees to be more likely to report the activities of a financial subsidiary on a consolidated basis.

Indirect guarantees. While Francis and Whittred examine only direct guarantees, there are also several methods of providing indirect guarantees to

[5] Note that the FASB's segment reporting requirements limit the extent to which consolidation can be employed to aggregate information.

subsidiary company creditors. For example, some firms negotiate joint lines of credit between the parent and subsidiary, thus obligating both to repay the credit. In some firms the parent sells receivables to their finance subsidiary with recourse, thus providing a guarantee of the assets instead of the liabilities. Finally, Ronen and Sondhi (1989) note that some firms negotiate an operating agreement between the parent and its captive finance subsidiary that impose various constraints on their joint activities: (1) The operating agreement can include an income-maintenance agreement where the parent guarantees that the subsidiary's net income will be at least a prespecified multiple of its fixed charges (the parent is required to make direct payments to the subsidiary if earnings are below the required level). (2) The agreement can include provisions requiring maintenance of other balance-sheet items such as debt ratios or cash flows. (3) The agreement can restrict dividends paid by the subsidiary, funds transfers, loans, and advances. (4) The agreements can specify holdback reserves where the subsidiary is allowed to withhold a prespecified portion of the purchase price that is refunded when the receivables are collected. Such provisions in the parent–subsidiary operating agreement are alternate mechanisms for the parent to provide effective guarantees of the subsidiary's debt.

One potentially important difference between the direct debt guarantees and the indirect guarantees provided through arrangements such as joint lines of credit, sales of receivables with recourse, and operating agreements between parent and subsidiary is their treatment in debt agreements. Standard bond covenants typically require that long-term debt with direct guarantees be included in the calculation of funded debt of the parent, while such inclusion is not required with indirect guarantees. If a parent has outstanding bonds with covenants specifying financing limitations in terms of the ratio of funded debt to net tangible assets and if the parent offers direct guarantees of an unconsolidated subsidiary's debt, then the subsidiary's long-term debt would be included in the calculation of this ratio, but the subsidiary's assets would not be.[6] Hence the form of the guarantee should be related to the reporting policy for the subsidiary: We expect direct guarantees to be associated with consolidated reporting and indirect guarantees to be associated with unconsolidated reporting.

In addition, monitoring and enforcing the restrictions in operating agreements requires the disclosure of subsidiary activities. The more interdependent the parent–subsidiary activities, the more costly is such disclosure. Therefore, if the activities undertaken through financial subsidiaries are more interdependent, we expect them to employ direct guarantees. Conversely, if the activities undertaken through financial subsidiaries are more independent, we expect them to employ indirect guarantees.

---

[6] We would like to thank Greg Whittred for this observation.

We also expect to observe an association between the form of the guarantee and the type of subsidiary. For bank, savings and loan, insurance, leasing, and real estate subsidiaries, the asset substitution problems can be controlled by other mechanisms, thus parent-provided guarantees are less valuable. For example, bank, savings and loan, and insurance subsidiaries are regulated. This regulation limits opportunities for asset substitution. In addition, banks, savings and loans, and some insurance subsidiaries receive subsidized government-provided guarantees through the Federal Deposit Insurance Corporation, Federal Saving and Loan Insurance Corporation, or state insurance guarantee funds [see also Kane (1986)]. Parent-provided guarantees would reduce the value of these subsidies. Leasing and real estate subsidiaries are more likely to collateralize their debt, thus controlling the asset substitution problem. Thus we expect to observe guarantees primarily provided to finance subsidiaries.

3. Data

We form an initial sample of the 1985 Fortune 500 industrials (listed in the 4/28/86 issue) plus the ten largest firms in each of Fortune's eight service industries (listed in the 6/9/86 issue).[7] From these 580 firms, we exclude 72 firms that are not on CRSP or Compustat. Of the remaining 508 firms, 24 have insufficient information in their annual reports or *Moody's*[8] to determine their consolidation policy with respect to their subsidiaries (for example, out of these 24 firms, 7 have no 1985 annual report because they are acquired or go private). Thus our final sample includes 484 firms.

Of the 484 firms, 246 have at least one majority-owned finance (including bank, savings and loan, financial, credit, capital, and acceptance), insurance, leasing, or real estate subsidiary. Table 1 reports the number of firms with consolidated and unconsolidated financial subsidiaries by SIC code. In this table we report categorical observations. If a firm has three unconsolidated insurance subsidiaries, they are counted only once; however, if a particular subsidiary engages in both financing and leasing, we count it in both categories. Thus the number of subsidiaries reported could be either greater or less than the actual number of financial subsidiaries established by a given company. Approximately half the firms in the sample have financial subsidiaries (246 firms) and half do not (238 firms). Of the firms with financial subsidiaries, half are consolidated (148 firms) and half are unconsolidated (148 firms).

Table 2 reports the distribution of consolidated policies for financial subsidiaries for our sample of 484 firms. Since we report categorical observations,

---

[7]The eight service industry classifications used by Fortune are: commercial banking, life insurance, transportation, retailing, utilities, savings institutions, diversified financials, and diversified service.

[8]Throughout the paper, we employ the 1986 *Moody's* Industrials, Public Utility, Bank and Finance, and Transportation Manuals which report 1985 data.

Table 1

Consolidation policy for finance, insurance, real estate, and leasing subsidiaries[a] for 484 firms by SIC code using 1985 data (U is unconsolidated and C is consolidated).

Industry	SIC code	Finance[b]		Insurance		Real estate		Leasing		Total[c]			Firms without subsidiaries	All firms
		C	U	C	U	C	U	C	U	C	U	Total[d]		
Mining	10–14	2	4	2	2	3	1	2	0	5	5	7	9	16
Construction	15–17	0	0	0	0	0	0	0	0	0	0	0	3	3
Food & tobacco	20–21	8	7	6	4	3	1	4	2	15	11	19	19	38
Textiles & apparel	22–23	0	0	0	0	0	0	0	0	0	0	1	14	15
Lumber & furniture	24–25	2	0	0	0	0	0	1	0	2	0	2	5	7
Paper & printing	26–27	6	3	4	6	2	5	2	0	12	9	19	23	42
Chemicals	28	10	8	5	9	4	1	2	2	15	15	24	29	53
Petroleum, rubber & plastics	29–30	7	9	6	5	1	3	1	4	10	11	18	12	30
Leather, stone, clay, concrete & glass	31–32	0	3	1	1	1	2	1	0	3	3	5	11	16
Primary & fabricated metals	33–34	4	7	2	6	3	4	1	4	6	13	16	27	43
Machinery & electrical machinery	35–36	12	34	8	14	4	4	3	9	19	34	45	39	84
Transportation equipment	37	7	17	1	11	1	9	4	12	9	23	26	2	28
Measurement instruments & miscellaneous	38–39	2	6	3	2	1	1	1	1	6	7	10	11	21
Transportation, communication, gas, electric & sanitary service	40–49	3	4	1	2	5	2	2	0	7	4	11	10	21
Wholesale trade	50–51	2	1	0	2	0	1	1	1	2	3	4	3	7
Retail trade	53–59	3	2	1	2	1	2	1	0	3	3	5	5	10
Financial services	60–67	22	5	16	4	12	2	12	2	31	6	32	12	44
Services	72–89	0	1	0	0	1	0	2	0	2	1	2	4	6
Totals	10–89	90	111	56	70	43	38	40	37	148	148	246	238	484

[a] We report categorical observations; for example, if a firm has three unconsolidated insurance subsidiaries, they are counted only once, but if a subsidiary engages in both financing and leasing, it is counted both places.

[b] Includes subsidiaries with finance, financial, credit, acceptance, bank, savings and loan, or capital in its name.

[c] Total will not be the sum of finance, insurance, real estate, and leasing if a firm has multiple subsidiaries.

[d] Total will not be the sum of the consolidated and unconsolidated figures if a firm has both consolidated and unconsolidated subsidiaries.

Table 2

Distribution of consolidation policy across finance, insurance, leasing, and real estate subsidiaries[a] for 484 firms using 1985 data.

Number of consolidated subsidiaries	Number of unconsolidated subsidiaries					
	0	1	2	3	4	Total
0	238	45	37	10	6	336
1	51	24	7	6	1	89
2	30	6	1	2	2	41
3	13	1	0	0	0	14
4	4	0	0	0	0	4
Total	336	76	45	18	9	484

[a]We report categorical observations; for example, if a firm has three unconsolidated domestic insurance subsidiaries, they are counted only once, but if a subsidiary engages in both financing and leasing, it is counted both places. Thus, the number of subsidiaries reported could be either greater or less than the number established by a given firm. Since we report firm-class observations, the maximum number for any firm would be eight – in that case the firm would have at least one consolidated and one unconsolidated finance, insurance, leasing, and real estate subsidiary.

the maximum number for any firm would be eight – in which case the firm would have both consolidated and unconsolidated finance, insurance, leasing, and real estate subsidiaries. In our sample, 238 firms have no financial subsidiaries, 98 firms have only unconsolidated financial subsidiaries, 98 firms have only consolidated financial subsidiaries, and 50 firms have both consolidated and unconsolidated financial subsidiaries.

The data in tables 1 and 2 indicate that prior to FAS 94 among our sample of firms (1) reporting the financial performance of financial subsidiaries on an unconsolidated basis is a widely employed accounting option, and (2) there is significant cross-sectional variation in the use of unconsolidated financial subsidiaries.

4. Evidence

4.1. Interdependence hypothesis

Operating interdependence. To test our operating-interdependence hypothesis, we examine the names of the 209 finance subsidiaries[9] as potentially observable proxies for interdependence. Each of these subsidiaries has either finance, financial, bank, savings and loan, credit, acceptance, or capital in its

[9]The number of observations reported here does not match the number of observations reported in table 1 for two reasons: (1) In table 1, we report categorical observations, while here the individual subsidiary is the unit of observation. (2) Here we require knowledge of the name of the subsidiary, while we do not in table 1.

name. We expect the capital subsidiaries are more likely to be engaged in intra-firm financing, while bank/S&L/credit/acceptance subsidiaries are more likely to be engaged in external financing. Finance/financial subsidiaries can be either. Of the 63 acceptance/credit subsidiaries, 47 (74.6%) are unconsolidated. Conversely, 11 of 12 capital subsidiaries (91.6%) are consolidated. Only 4 of the 20 bank/S&L subsidiaries (20%) are unconsolidated; however, if we eliminate those subsidiaries of firms in the financial services industry, all 4 remaining subsidiaries (100%) are unconsolidated. Finally, of the 114 finance/financial subsidiaries, 68 (59.6%) are consolidated. For 29 of these 114 subsidiaries, there is a description of the subsidiary's primary activities in *Moody's* or the firm's annual reports. Of those described as primarily engaged in receivables or sales financing, 22 of 24 (91.7%) are unconsolidated; of those described as financing acquisitions/general corporate purposes/capital outlays and investments, all 5 (100%) are consolidated. This evidence is generally consistent with our operating-interdependence hypothesis.

A second test of the operating-interdependence hypothesis focuses on the 25 pairs of subsidiaries of those 22 firms in table 2 with both consolidated and unconsolidated financial subsidiaries in the same class. (The other 28 firms with mixed consolidation policy have variation in consolidation policy across types of subsidiaries – for example, an unconsolidated finance subsidiary and a consolidated real estate subsidiary.) We review these 22 firms' annual reports, SEC filings, FASB lobby letters, and finally call each company in an attempt to find the specific activities undertaken by the subsidiaries and basis for their consolidation decision. Our findings are summarized in table 3.

Although our interpretation of this evidence obviously is subjective, we believe that the consolidation decision for nineteen observations (76%) is consistent with the interdependence hypothesis: For Borg–Warner, Chrysler, Coca Cola, Cummins Engine, Eaton, General Electric, General Motors, Harris, Honeywell, Occidental Petroleum, J.C. Penney, Phillip Morris, Phillips Petroleum, Sara Lee, and Union Carbide, the unconsolidated finance subsidiary engages in sales financing, while the consolidated finance subsidiary engages in intra-firm financing. For Illinois Tool and Chrysler, the unconsolidated leasing subsidiary engages in more third-party leasing, while the consolidated leasing subsidiary engages in more manufacturer leasing; for General Motors, the unconsolidated subsidiary leases GM automobiles to GM customers, while the consolidated leasing subsidiary leases GM signs to GM dealers. Finally, Penney's unconsolidated real estate subsidiary participates in joint ventures to develop shopping centers, while the consolidated real estate subsidiary owns buildings in which the parent operates stores. In four cases (16%), Aetna, Dexter, Hewlett-Packard, and NCR, we can document no substantive difference in the operating activities of the subsidiaries (however, in each case one of the subsidiaries is foreign). In one case (4%), we can obtain an activity description for only one of the pair: For Ingersoll Rand, the

Table 3

Consolidation policy information for 25 pairs of subsidiaries of 22 firms with different consolidation policies across subsidiaries of the same type (finance, insurance, leasing, real estate).

Parent firm	SIC code	Subsidiary type	Incorporation of unconsolidated subsidiary	Incorporation of consolidated subsidiary
A.M. International	50	Leasing	Domestic	Foreign

Subsidiaries activities are undisclosed.

Aetna Life and Casualty	63	Insurance	Foreign	Domestic

Consolidation of foreign subsidiaries results in distortion of reported information. This distortion is caused by two major factors: (1) Foreign exchange fluctuations will distort year-to-year trends, indicating changes in U.S. $ value and not the level of activity conducted by foreign operation. (2) Foreign subsidiaries operate in different environment. Therefore products and services offered in foreign countries are often diverse and unlike those offered in the U.S. Because of this, little or no GAAP guidance is available. To translate such foreign products and services to a U.S. basis on a detailed level will most likely create incomprehensible results.

Borg–Warner Company	28	Finance	Domestic	Domestic, Foreign

Unconsolidated subsidiary engages in sales financing and commercial financing; it has a joint line of credit with the parent; sales of accounts receivable by the parent are with recourse. Consolidated subsidiaries engage in intra-firm financing and sales financing, and the subsidiary's debt is guaranteed by the parent.

Chrysler Corporation	37	Finance	Domestic	Domestic

Unconsolidated subsidiary engages in sales financing; consolidated subsidiary engages in intra-firm financing and capital raising for general corporate purposes. Unconsolidated financial services subsidiary operates in a business and economic environment which differs drastically from that of its parent. Consolidation would result in financial statements for which there is no substance or basis in reality.

		Leasing	Domestic	Foreign

Unconsolidated subsidiary engages in leasing of both parent-related and non-parent-related assets. Consolidated subsidiary's activities also include leasing of both parent-related and non-parent-related assets, but their primary focus is on auto leasing.

Coca Cola Company	20	Finance	Domestic	Foreign

The unconsolidated subsidiary engages in sales financing and credit related activities, it has a joint line of credit with the parent. Subsidiary's debt is guaranteed by parent. Consolidated subsidiary actively engages in intra-firm financing of parent's subsidiaries; subsidiary's debt guaranteed by parent.

Cummings Engine	35	Finance	Domestic	Foreign

Unconsolidated subsidiary engages in sales financing and credit related activities; it has a joint line of credit with the parent. Consolidated subsidiary makes investments in connection with the parent's foreign operations.

Table 3   (continued)

Parent firm	SIC code	Subsidiary type	Incorporation of unconsolidated subsidiary	Incorporation of consolidated subsidiary
Dexter Corporation	28	Leasing	Domestic	Foreign

Unconsolidated subsidiary engages in leasing of non-parent-related assets. Consolidated subsidiary engages in leasing of non-parent-related assets.

Eaton Corporation	37	Finance	Domestic	Foreign

Unconsolidated subsidiary primarily engages in non-parent-related sales financing activities. Consolidated subsidiary engages in business more closely related with parent's activities, like intra-firm financing; parent guarantees this subsidiary's debt.

General Electric Corporation	36	Finance	Domestic	Domestic

Unconsolidated subsidiary engages in general financial services; it has a joint line of credit with the parent. Consolidated subsidiary engages in intra-firm financing (capital raising for acquisitions/general corporate purposes); parent guarantees this subsidiary's debt. If activities of finance subsidiary are primarily to support operations of parent, it should be consolidated. If the converse is true, then consolidation only creates confusion.

General Motors Corporation	37	Finance	Domestic	Foreign

Unconsolidated subsidiary engages in sales financing activities. Consolidated subsidiary borrows in the Eurodollars market and lends the proceeds back to other GM operating units. The domestic finance subsidiary is unconsolidated to avoid problems arising from consolidation of nonclassified balance-sheet-dominated finance company with income-statement-oriented manufacturing operations of the parent.

		Leasing	Domestic	Domestic

Unconsolidated subsidiary engages in leasing of GM produced automobiles. Consolidated subsidiary engages in leasing of GM signs to GM dealers.

Harris Corporation	36	Finance	Domestic	Foreign

Unconsolidated subsidiary engages in parent-related sales financing. Consolidated subsidiary engages in intra-firm financing and capital raising for general corporate purposes.

Hewlett Packard	38	Finance	Domestic	Foreign

Unconsolidated subsidiary engages in parent-related sales-financing. Consolidated subsidiary engages in parent-related sales-financing.

Honeywell, Incorporated	34	Finance	Domestic	Foreign

Unconsolidated subsidiary engages in parent-related sales financing. Consolidated subsidiary has multiple intra-company financing activities; subsidiary's debt guaranteed by the parent.

Ingersoll Rand	35	Finance	Domestic	Foreign

Unconsolidated subsidiary engages in sales financing. Consolidated subsidiary's activities are undisclosed.

Table 3 (continued)

721

Parent firm	SIC code	Subsidiary type	Incorporation of unconsolidated subsidiary	Incorporation of consolidated subsidiary
Illinois Tool Works	34	Leasing	Domestic	Domestic

Unconsolidated subsidiary engages in non-parent-related leasing activities. Consolidated subsidiary engages in leasing activities related to parent's activities.

NCR Corporation	35	Finance	Domestic	Foreign

Unconsolidated subsidiary engages in sales financing. Consolidated subsidiary's engages in sales-financing; parent guarantees the subsidiary's debt.

Occidental Petroleum	13	Finance	Domestic	Foreign

Unconsolidated subsidiary engages in sales financing. Consolidated subsidiary engages in intra-firm financing (capital raising for acquisition/general corporate purposes); parent guarantees debt of this subsidiary.

J. C. Penney Corporation	53	Finance	Domestic	Domestic

Unconsolidated subsidiary is a bank which operates in industry different from parent's principal business and has minimal contribution to consolidated operations. Consolidated subsidiary has the sole purpose of financing parent's operations and consolidation best portrays the financial structure of parent's operations.

		Real Estate	Domestic	Domestic

Unconsolidated subsidiary's real estate activities are not closely related to parent firm's activities (developing and operating real estate, primarily shopping centers, through participation in joint ventures). Consolidated real estate subsidiary has operations more closely related to parent's line of business (subsidiary owns buildings in which parent operates stores).

Phillip Morris	21	Finance	Domestic	Foreign

Unconsolidated subsidiary engages in sales financing of parent's products; it has an income maintenance agreement with the parent. Consolidated subsidiary engages in intra-firm financial planning.

Phillips Petroleum	29	Finance	Domestic	Foreign

Unconsolidated subsidiary finances sales of parent's products. Consolidated subsidiary engages in intra-firm financing (capital raising for acquisition/general corporate purposes) and financial planning.

Sara Lee Corporation	20	Finance	Domestic	Foreign

Unconsolidated subsidiary engages in sales financing; it has a joint line of credit and an income maintenance agreement with the parent. Consolidated subsidiary provides intra-firm financing (capital raising for acquisitions/general corporate purposes); this subsidiary's debt is guaranteed by the parent.

Union Carbide	28	Finance	Domestic	Foreign

Unconsolidated subsidiary engages in sales financing; it has an income maintenance agreement with the parent. Consolidated subsidiary provides intra-firm financing (capital raising for acquisitions/general corporate purposes); subsidiary's debt is guaranteed by the parent.

unconsolidated finance subsidiary engages in sales financing and the consolidated subsidiary's activities are undisclosed. In this case the activity description is not obviously inconsistent with our hypothesis. In the case of AM International (4%), we have insufficient information to classify the subsidiaries' activities. Thus, 19 of the 25 observations are qualitatively consistent with our hypothesis, none are obviously inconsistent, and six are indeterminate.

A final potential test of the operating-interdependence hypothesis is a joint test. We hypothesize that the more interdependent the parent–subsidiary activities, the more likely the subsidiary is wholly-owned. This implies that majority-owned (but not wholly-owned) financial subsidiaries are more likely to be unconsolidated. Unfortunately, when we examine the ownership data reported in *Moody's* for the 555 majority-owned financial subsidiaries of the 246 firms reported in table 1, we find only seven subsidiaries that are not wholly-owned. Even though five of the seven firms (71%) are unconsolidated, with such a low observation frequency, we hesitate to argue that this result is statistically significant.[10]

Information interdependence. In our examination of corporate consolidation policy choices we find two cases of firms voluntarily changing their consolidation policy for a financial subsidiary. In both cases, the changes are justified as being more informative. Control Data Corporation changed from a consolidated to an unconsolidated basis in accounting for Commercial Credit Corporation in 1985. Their annual report states: 'The equity method is intended to provide stockholders with a more appropriate view of the computer business results than was provided under the consolidated basis. The change is due to the disparity of the businesses and changes in strategies related to commercial credit resulting in greater separateness of the business.'[11] In 1985 J.C. Penney consolidated their previously unconsolidated finance subsidiary. In the annual report they say that the change is made 'to more appropriately reflect the financial structure of the company'. Although we want to be careful in interpreting these statements literally – the list of feasible justifications for accounting policy changes by firms is limited – these statements suggest that information implications potentially are important.

We argue above that the information-heterogeneity hypothesis implies differences in consolidation policy for financial subsidiaries between parent firms

---

[10] The seven financial subsidiaries that are not wholly-owned are three unconsolidated banks, two unconsolidated insurance subsidiaries, and two consolidated leasing subsidiaries. If we rely on the symmetry in table 2 to argue that the probability of reporting the activities of a financial subsidiary on an unconsolidated basis is 0.5, then the probability of observing five unconsolidated financial subsidiaries out of seven subsidiaries is 0.16.

[11] In 1986, Control Data sold 81.6% of the stock of Commercial Credit to the public and in 1987 their remaining shares, so that it was no longer a wholly-owned subsidiary. If the change in ownership also reflects changes in operating activities, then this observation also is consistent with the operating-interdependence hypothesis.

Table 4

Consolidation decision and subsidiary location for our sample of 246 firms with 555 financial subsidiaries[a] using 1985 data.

	Foreign	Domestic	Total
Consolidated	93	180	273
Unconsolidated	28	254	282
Total	121	434	555

$\chi^2 = 47.40$ p-value < 0.001

[a]We report categorical observations; for example if a firm has three consolidated foreign insurance subsidiaries, they are counted only once, but if a subsidiary engages in both financing and leasing, it is counted both places. Thus, the number of subsidiaries reported could be either greater or less than the number established by a given firm. Note that the number of observations reported in this table differs from those in table 1 because here the subsidiary is the unit of observations while there the firm is.

in the manufacturing and financial services industries, between insurance and other financial subsidiaries, and between foreign and domestic subsidiaries. The data in table 1 indicate that for the entire sample, the use of consolidated and unconsolidated subsidiaries is equal (148 for each). A 2×2 contingency table indicates that there is a marginally significant difference between the financial services industry, where consolidated subsidiaries predominate, and the metals, machinery, and transportation equipment industries, where unconsolidated subsidiaries predominate ($\chi^2 = 3.65$).[12]

The data in table 1 indicate insurance subsidiaries are most likely to be unconsolidated by nonfinancial firms (62%), while real estate subsidiaries are most likely to be consolidated (46%); however, this observed variation across subsidiary types is not statistically significant ($\chi^2 = 0.53$).[13]

A third dimension of potential information heterogeneity involves foreign versus domestic subsidiaries. Table 3 indicates that although Aetna offers precisely this rationale for reporting its foreign subsidiary on an unconsolidated basis, for every other firm with matched pairs of subsidiaries in this sample, the foreign subsidiary is consolidated. In table 4 we segregate the 555 subsidiaries of the 246 firms from table 1 by consolidation policy and location of the subsidiary. There is a significant association between consolidation

[12]This is well as all other χ^2 statistics reported in this paper have one degree of freedom. For a χ^2 with one degree of freedom, the 95% critical value is 3.84.

[13]Note that this observed variation also could be related to regulation. Statutory accounting principles specified in the insurance law of some states do not permit mutual life insurance companies to consolidate any subsidiaries. Although this regulation does not directly affect any of the firms in our sample (they are all common stock firms), such explicit regulation of accounting practice for one set of firms may indirectly affect this choice either by establishing expectations about the appropriate method of accounting for specific activities, or by altering the costs of being different.

Table 5

Consolidation decision and direct debt guarantees for our sample of 246 firms with 555 financial subsidiaries[a] using 1985 data.

	Subsidiaries with debt guarantees	Subsidiaries without debt guarantees	Total
Consolidated	42	231	273
Unconsolidated	11	271	282
Total	53	502	555
	$\chi^2 = 21.18$	p-value < 0.001	

[a] We report categorical observations; for example if a firm has three consolidated foreign finance subsidiaries, they are counted only once, but if a subsidiary engages in both financing and leasing, it is counted twice. Thus, the number of subsidiaries reported could be either greater or less than the number established by a given firm.

policy and whether the subsidiary is foreign or domestic ($\chi^2 = 47.40$). But the association is not the one implied by the information-heterogeneity hypothesis – foreign financial subsidiaries are significantly more frequently consolidated than unconsolidated (93 versus 28).[14] However, this data is consistent with the informational-interdependence hypothesis if the use of unconsolidated financial reporting would reveal valuable information in specific foreign markets to their competition.

Financial interdependence. To analyze the financial-interdependence hypothesis, we examine the annual reports and *Moody's* for the 246 firms with financial subsidiaries from table 1 to see if the frequency of parent-provided direct guarantees is greater for firms with consolidated financial subsidiaries than it is for those with unconsolidated financial subsidiaries. For the total sample of 555 financial subsidiaries in table 5 the association between the consolidation decision and the use of direct guarantees is significant ($\chi^2 = 21.18$).

The consistency between our evidence and Whittred's is noteworthy given the differences in the data: (1) Whittred focuses on operating subsidiaries, while we examine financial subsidiaries. There could be important differences between operating and finance subsidiaries; for example, one might establish a captive finance subsidiary specifically to segregate the accounts receivable from the firm's operating assets because they have different characteristics as collateral [see Mian and Smith (1989a)]. Cross-guarantees might undercut this distinction. (2) Whittred examines Australian data while we examine Ameri-

---

[14] From the consolidation requirements of major countries, as detailed in OECD (1987) in the appendix, these requirements do not appear systematically more restrictive than those of the U.S. prior to FAS 94. Thus it is not obvious that foreign consolidation requirements explain this observed association between consolidation and subsidiary location.

can data. One might expect differences in legal systems to lead to a difference in frequency (or forms) of guarantees provided to subsidiaries. (3) Whittred's data comes from 1930–1960, while ours is from 1985. Evolution in the contracting technology over this period is expected to affect observed practices.

In table 6, we segregate the 555 subsidiaries of the 246 firms from table 5 by consolidation policy, subsidiary location, and the use of direct and indirect guarantees. For our sample of firms, data from the firms' annual reports and *Moody's* indicates that there is significant overlap in the types of guarantees offered. For example, there are eight firms reported in table 6 with both direct and indirect guarantees. There are 29 firms with joint lines of credit, 10 firms where the parent sells receivables to the subsidiary with recourse, and 32 firms with an operating agreement between parent and subsidiary. The operating agreements include: an income maintenance agreement in 21 cases, provisions requiring maintenance of balance sheet or cash flow items in 13 cases, restrictions on subsidiary dividends, funds transfers, loans and advances in 4 cases, and holdback reserves in 6 cases. Each of the 62 subsidiaries that receive indirect guarantees is unconsolidated.

Table 6 indicates that the debt of only 11 unconsolidated subsidiaries receives direct guarantees.[15] We examine these apparent exceptions in more detail. The 11 unconsolidated subsidiaries involve only 9 parent firms. In 7 of the cases, the parent firm's debt does not include a restriction related to the ratio of funded debt to net tangible assets. In the other 2 cases we calculate the ratio of funded debt of the subsidiary to the net tangible assets of the parent to see how much this constraint would be affected. In both cases this ratio is less than 1%. We believe this provides additional indirect evidence that the rules under which debt guarantees are administered in the firm's bond contracts are an important component of the consolidation decision.

We hypothesize above that the nature of the subsidiaries' activities and the existence and form of the guarantee should be interrelated. Table 6 indicates that direct debt guarantees are provided primarily to consolidated finance subsidiaries, while indirect guarantees are provided primarily to unconsolidated finance and leasing subsidiaries. Debt of insurance, real estate, or consolidated leasing subsidiaries is rarely guaranteed. Although the data in table 6 suggest that unconsolidated leasing subsidiaries receive guarantees, we believe that this is primarily an artifact of our data classification system. Eight of the ten subsidiaries receiving indirect guarantees and the two subsidiaries receiving both direct and indirect guarantees are finance subsidiaries that also engage in leasing. When these double-counted subsidiaries are eliminated, only three unconsolidated leasing subsidiaries receive guarantees. Thus, the data in

---

[15] These 11 are the 3 unconsolidated subsidiaries with direct guarantees plus the 8 unconsolidated subsidiaries with both.

Table 6

Consolidation decision, subsidiary location, type of subsidiary, and form of debt guarantee for the 246 firms with 555 financial subsidiaries[a] using 1985 data (C is consolidated, U is unconsolidated, and T is total).

Form of debt guarantee	Finance		Insurance		Leasing		Real estate		Total		
	C	U	C	U	C	U	C	U	C	U	T
Domestic											
Direct	15	1	0	1	0	1	0	0	15	3	18
Indirect[b]	0	42	0	0	0	10	0	2	0	54	54
Both	0	6	0	0	0	2	0	0	0	8	8
Neither	55	65	31	63	36	24	43	37	165	189	354
Total	70	114	31	64	36	37	43	39	180	254	434
Foreign											
Direct	27	0	0	0	0	0	0	0	27	0	27
Indirect[b]	0	0	0	0	0	0	0	0	0	0	0
Both	0	0	0	0	0	0	0	0	0	0	0
Neither	30	13	28	13	8	2	0	0	66	28	94
Total	57	13	28	13	8	2	0	0	93	28	121
Total											
Direct	42	1	0	1	0	1	0	0	42	3	45
Indirect[b]	0	42	0	0	0	10	0	2	0	54	54
Both	0	6	0	0	0	2	0	0	0	8	8
Neither	85	78	59	76	44	26	43	37	231	217	448
Total	127	127	59	77	44	39	43	39	273	282	555

[a] We report categorical observations; for example, if a firm has four unconsolidated domestic finance subsidiaries, they are counted only once, but if a subsidiary engages in both financing and leasing, it is counted both places. Thus, the number of subsidiaries reported could be either greater or less than the number established by a given firm. Note that the number of observations here differs from those reported in table 1 because here the subsidiary is the unit of observations while there the firm is.

[b] Includes joint lines of credit between parent and subsidiary, operating agreements between parent and subsidiary, and sales of receivables to subsidiary with recourse.

table 5 suggest that debt guarantees are provided primarily to finance subsidiaries.

We next focus on the 209 cases where we have the specific name of the finance subsidiary. In table 7 we segregate these subsidiaries by name, consolidation policy, subsidiary location, and the use of direct and indirect guarantees. We find: (1) consolidated finance/financial/capital subsidiaries receive 90% of the direct guarantees, (2) unconsolidated finance/financial/credit/acceptance subsidiaries receive 100% of the indirect guarantees, and (3) S&L/banks receive no guarantees.

The form of the guarantee and subsidiary location are related. Of the 42 firms where consolidated subsidiaries receive direct guarantees, 27 of the subsidiaries are foreign, while none of the unconsolidated subsidiaries that receive guarantees are foreign. In contrast, all of the indirect guarantees are provided to domestic subsidiaries; foreign subsidiaries receive no indirect guarantees.[16] While there is a significant association between the use of direct guarantees and subsidiary location ($\chi^2 = 29.19$),[17] table 6 indicates that this cannot account for the entire relation between subsidiary location and consolidation policy. For the subset of 448 subsidiaries with no guarantees, there is still a significant association between consolidation policy and location ($\chi^2 = 16.57$).[18] While we believe that consolidating foreign financial subsidiaries avoids the publication of costly information and that the form of debt guarantee has important implications for the consolidation decision, we do not understand fully why the form of the guarantee should be related to subsidiary location.[19]

Thus our evidence in tables 6 and 7 on the use of guarantees suggests the problem is richer than recognized by previous authors: (1) The activities of the subsidiary and the use of guarantees are related. Bank, S&L, and insurance subsidiaries receive virtually no guarantees. This is consistent with the hypothesis that regulation controls the asset substitution problem and that parent-provided guarantees would reduce the value of subsidized government-provided guarantees. Leasing and real estate subsidiaries receive virtually no guarantees. This is consistent with the hypothesis that the debt of these subsidiaries is more likely to be explicitly collateralized. Capital subsidiaries

---

[16] If *Moody's* provides different levels of contractual detail for domestic versus foreign subsidiaries, this result could simply reflect a reporting bias in *Moody's*.

[17] From the last column in table 6, the first row of the contingency table is $18 + 8 = 26$ and $27 + 0 = 27$, the second is $54 + 354 = 408$ and $0 + 94 = 94$.

[18] From the Neither rows under the Total columns in table 6, the first row of the contingency table is 165 and 189, the second is 66 and 28. Repeating the test for the 502 subsidiaries with no direct guarantees produces equivalent results ($\chi^2 = 27.26$).

[19] Investment bankers argue that names or reputations are particularly important in Eurobond markets. This raises the possibility that explicit guarantees are offered for debt of foreign subsidiaries to lower information costs.

receive direct guarantees, while acceptance/credit subsidiaries receive indirect guarantees. (2) The form of the guarantee and the consolidation decision are related. Among finance/financial subsidiaries, direct guarantees imply consolidation, but indirect guarantees do not. (3) The form of the guarantee and subsidiary location are related. Foreign subsidiaries are more likely to receive direct guarantees, but are less likely to receive indirect guarantees.

Whittred (1987) and Francis (1986) also argue that if debt covenants are defined at the separate-entity level, then unconsolidated reporting is appropriate, but if covenants are defined at the consolidated-entity level, consolidated reporting is appropriate. To examine this hypothesis, we again examine the 196 firms from table 2 with consistent consolidation policies. From *Moody's*, we find that of the 98 firms with unconsolidated subsidiaries, 73 have public debt outstanding; of the 98 with consolidated subsidiaries, 76 have public debt outstanding. *Moody's* reports three types of covenants which employ balance sheet data: the dividend covenant, restrictions on creation of additional debt, and a covenant restricting security sales and leasebacks. Table 8 demonstrates that from the evidence in *Moody's* the covenants for firms with unconsolidated captives appear to employ only unconsolidated balance sheet data, while the firms with consolidated captives employ only consolidated balance sheet data.[20] Thus, our cross-sectional data apparently is consistent with this hypothesis without exception. However, this evidence is also consistent with the hypothesis that customized accounting numbers are more likely to be included in private than in public debt agreements [Smith and Warner (1979) and Leftwich (1981, 1983)]. Thus, a stronger test of this hypothesis would examine private lending agreements where the costs of employing tailored non-GAAP definitions are lower.

Summary of evidence on the interdependence hypothesis. We estimate a regression employing our sample of 555 financial subsidiaries where the dependent variable is the consolidation policy for the subsidiary and the independent variables are also dummy variables: (1) subsidiary provides customer financing,[21] (2) subsidiary is foreign, (3) parent is a nonfinancial corporation, (4) subsidiary is an insurance firm, (5) parent provides a direct guarantee of the subsidiary's debt, (6) parent provides an indirect guarantee of the subsidiary's debt. The regression is significant ($\bar{r}^2 = 0.30$, $F = 41.23$) and five of the six coefficients are of the expected sign and significant at the 1%

---

[20] However, *Moody's* does not provide the requisite detail on definitions to be certain in this determination. As indicated in *Commentaries* (1971), the definition of restricted subsidiaries can differ across firms; it appears that the most frequent consolidated subsidiary excluded under the indenture's definition of a restricted subsidiary is a foreign subsidiary. (*Commentaries* suggests that this is because of potential currency controls or expropriation risks.)

[21] Either there is a reference in the firm's annual report or *Moody's* that indicates that this is the primary activity of the subsidiary or the name of the subsidiary includes credit/acceptance.

Table 7

Consolidation decision, subsidiary location, subsidiary name, and form of debt guarantee for the 209 finance subsidiaries[a] using 1985 data (C is consolidated, U is unconsolidated, and T is total).

Form of debt guarantee	Capital		Finance/Financial		S&L/Bank		Credit/Acceptance		Total		
	C	U	C	U	C	U	C	U	C	U	T
Domestic											
Direct	6	0	12	0	0	0	0	0	18	0	18
Indirect[b]	0	0	0	19	0	0	0	20	0	39	39
Both	0	0	0	1	0	0	0	3	0	4	4
Neither	1	1	25	23	14	2	14	24	54	50	104
Total	7	1	37	43	14	2	14	47	72	93	165
Foreign											
Direct	4	0	12	0	0	0	0	0	16	0	16
Indirect[b]	0	0	0	0	0	0	0	0	0	0	0
Both	0	0	0	0	0	0	0	0	0	0	0
Neither	0	0	19	3	2	2	2	0	23	5	28
Total	4	0	31	3	2	2	2	0	39	5	44
Total											
Direct	10	0	24	0	0	0	0	0	34	0	34
Indirect[b]	0	0	0	19	0	0	0	20	0	39	39
Both	0	0	0	1	0	0	0	3	0	4	4
Neither	1	1	44	26	16	4	16	24	77	55	132
Total	11	1	68	46	16	4	16	47	111	98	209

[a] Here, the number observations differs from that in table 6 for two reasons: (1) individual finance subsidiaries are the unit observation rather than categorized observations; (2) we require knowledge of the specific name of the subsidiary.

[b] Includes joint lines of credit between parent and subsidiary, operating agreements between parent and subsidiary, and sales of receivables to subsidiary with recourse.

Table 8

Use of balance-sheet data in specifying covenant restrictions by 196 firms with consistent consolidation policy (246 firms with financial subsidiaries minus 50 mixed consolidation policy firms) using 1985 data.

Type of bond covenant	73 firms with public debt outstanding of 98 firms with only unconsolidated subsidiaries			76 firms with public debt outstanding of 98 firms with only consolidated subsidiaries		
	Number using bond covenant[a]	Number using balance-sheet data[b]	Number using no balance-sheet data	Number using bond covenant[a]	Number using balance-sheet data[b]	Number using no balance-sheet data
Dividend covenant	30	5	25	29	4	25
Debt creation restriction	22	19	3	19	15	4
Security, sales and lease back provision	60	48	12	55	39	16
Total[c]	67	56	11	64	43	21

[a] Bond provisions were obtained from *Moody's*.
[b] Assets, liabilities, stockholder equity or debt ratios.
[c] Total will not be the sum of the column frequencies because bond issues contain multiple covenants.

level.[22] Thus, the implications from our separate examination of operational, informational, and financial interdependence are confirmed in this multivariate context.

4.2. Off-balance-sheet financing hypothesis

The FASB argues that an important aspect of the use of unconsolidated financial subsidiaries is that the procedure keeps the subsidiary's debt off the parent's balance sheet. Although this off-balance-sheet financing hypothesis is the primary rationale offered for FAS 94, it has been subjected to little empirical testing. Much of the published research on consolidation focuses on documenting differences between reported numbers employing consolidated versus unconsolidated methods; for example, see Benis (1979), Beranek and Clayton (1985), Beranek and Dillon (1982a, b), Burnett, King, and Lembke (1979), Copeland and McKinnon (1979), Heian and Thies (1989), and Mohr (1988).

---

[22] The customer-financing variable is significant at the 10% level. A multiple logistic regression provides similar results, except the indirect guarantee variable is not significant.

The off-balance-sheet financing hypothesis has two components: (1) unconsolidated financial reporting causes users to form biased estimates of the fixed claims in the parent firm's capital structure, and (2) firm's use of unconsolidated financial reporting is motivated by an incentive to exploit this bias. Comiskey, McEwen, and Mulford (1987) demonstrate that the betas of parent firms with unconsolidated finance subsidiaries are more highly correlated with the leverage derived from a proforma consolidation than with the parent's reported leverage. Mian and Smith (1989b) find that user firms overwhelmingly lobby against FAS 94. Both studies raise questions about the asserted bias in expectations produced by the use of unconsolidated reporting. However, neither study examines firms' motives for employing unconsolidated financial subsidiaries.

Under the off-balance-sheet financing hypothesis, variation in observed reporting policy across firms reflects variation in firms' incentives to attempt to structure their accounting balance sheet to understate the fixed claims on their economic balance sheet. If the off-balance-sheet hypothesis is an important explanation for the use of unconsolidated financial reporting, then the use of unconsolidated financial subsidiaries should be associated with the use of other forms of off-balance-sheet financing such as operating leases and unfunded pension benefits. Firms with strong incentives to engage in off-balance-sheet financing are more likely to employ all three off-balance-sheet financing techniques, while firm's with weak incentives should employ few or none.[23]

Value Line reports firms' use of operating leases and their unfunded pension liabilities. In table 9 we report the joint frequency of the use of consolidated versus unconsolidated financial subsidiaries, operating leases, and unfunded pension liabilities for the subset of 462 firms with *Value Line* data from our sample of 484 firms.

We estimate a regression with a dummy variable set equal to one if the firm has an unconsolidated financial subsidiary. The independent variables are the use of operating leases and unfunded pension liabilities. This regression indicates no significant association whether we measure the use of operating leases and unfunded pension liabilities deflated by assets ($\bar{r}^2 = -0.001$, $F = 0.702$) or simply as a dummy variable ($\bar{r}^2 = 0.001$, $F = 1.18$).

Although we believe that this result of no significant association is evidence against the FASB's off-balance-sheet financing hypothesis, more powerful tests are feasible. A more powerful test would simultaneously estimate a system of equations that control for the economic incentives to employ unconsolidated financial subsidiaries, operating leases, and unfunded pension liabilities. Such

---

[23] Note that our test of the off-balance-sheet financing hypothesis is consistent with the Holthausen and Leftwich (1983) suggestion to examine the consistency across the set of accounting policies chosen by firms.

Table 9

Association between consolidation policy for financial subsidiaries, the average use of operating leases ($\overline{OL}$) and unfunded pension liabilities ($\overline{UPL}$) in $ millions for a sample of 462 firms[a] using 1985 data.

| | Firms with unfunded pension liabilities | | | | | Firms without unfunded pension liabilities | | | |
| | Firms with operating leases | | | Firms without operating leases | | Firms with operating leases | | Firms without operating leases | |
Consolidation policy	$\overline{UPL}$	$\overline{OL}$	N	$\overline{UPL}$	N	$\overline{OL}$	N	N	
Unconsolidated subsidiaries only	236	50	6	85	3	65	64	25	
Both consolidated and unconsolidated	150	43	4	—	0	83	34	11	
Consolidated subsidiaries only	42	13	5	11	3	64	59	31	
No financial subsidiaries	42	40	11	91	5	27	139	62	
Total	103	38	26	67	11	49	296	129	

[a] Our average operating lease ($\overline{OL}$) and average unfunded pension liability ($\overline{UPL}$) data from *Value Line* is in $ millions. N is the number of observations in each category. Data on 22 firms from our sample of 484 firms is unavailable, thus our sample is 462 firms.

a test is required to control for the potential interrelation among corporate policies [see Smith and Watts (1989)].

5. Conclusions

We analyze firm's incentives to report the operations of a financial subsidiary on an unconsolidated versus a consolidated basis. We extend the Klein, Crawford, and Alchian (1978) analysis and argue that the more interdependent the parent–subsidiary activities, the more likely the subsidiary's operations will be reported on a consolidated basis. These interdependencies can occur in three dimensions: operating interdependencies, information interdependencies, financial interdependencies. We thus treat the firm's consolidation decision as simply a special case of the firm's organizational structure decision.

We find that when given the choice, firms in our sample choose to report on an unconsolidated basis with approximately the same frequency as on a consolidated basis. Our hypotheses explain a significant amount of the observed variation in pre-FAS 94 reporting practice for firms with financial subsidiaries. The evidence indicates that a firm is more likely to choose to report the performance of a financial subsidiary on a consolidated basis: (1) the greater the operating, financial, or informational interdependencies among the parent–subsidiary activities; (2) in the case of foreign subsidiaries rather than domestic; (3) when the parent provides a direct guarantee of the subsidiary's debt rather than an indirect guarantee; and (4) when the parent is in the financial services industry.

We document a richer structure of parent-provided guarantees of financial subsidiaries debt than has been suggested by previous authors: (1) Bank, S&L, leasing, insurance, and real estate subsidiaries receive virtually no parent-provided guarantees. (2) Consolidated finance, financial, and capital subsidiaries tend to receive direct debt guarantees. (3) Unconsolidated finance, financial, credit, and acceptance subsidiaries tend to receive indirect guarantees. (4) Foreign consolidated finance subsidiaries are more likely to receive direct guarantees, but foreign unconsolidated financial subsidiaries receive no indirect guarantees.

We also examine the FASB's hypothesis that firms employ unconsolidated reporting to understate the fixed claims on their balance sheets. Our evidence offers no support for this hypothesis. We believe that this evidence in conjunction with that offered by Comiskey, McEwen, and Mulford (1987) and Mian and Smith (1989b) raises serious questions about the validity of the FASB's expressed rationale for its adoption of FAS 94. We thus conclude that the FASB in reducing the accounting choice set through the adoption of FAS 94 has eliminated a valuable accounting alternative; that of reporting the activities of a majority-owned financial subsidiary on an unconsolidated basis.

Our analysis has several limitations: (1) Potentially the most severe is that we do not have a theory that explains why firms manage some activities within the firm, segregate some activities into divisions, establish a wholly-owned subsidiary corporation to perform some activities, and contract with external companies through market transactions for other activities. While some work exists along these lines, the profession lacks a coherent theory of this organizational choice and any conclusions we reach about the incentives to report a subsidiary's activities on a consolidated versus an unconsolidated basis must be somewhat tentative. (2) Data on the size of consolidated financial subsidiaries would allow more powerful tests. (3) Much of our data on the structure of the firms' contracts comes from *Moody's* rather than from the original set of corporate contracts. For example, data not detailed in *Moody's*, such as those on private lending agreements, would allow more powerful tests of hypotheses about the use of tailored accounting numbers in section 4. (4) Data on compensation of subsidiary and divisional executives would permit more powerful tests of the interdependence hypotheses. Smith and Watts (1982) argue that the accounting system provides the ability to decompose total firm performance; thus accounting-based compensation plans (such as bonus plans) are particularly valuable in providing incentive compensation to divisional executives who control only a portion of the firm's cash flows. They note that observed bonus plans differ with respect to the weight given aggregate firm performance versus the performance of individual operating units. They argue that the more independent the profits of individual operating units, the smaller the weight on total firm performance. This implies that firms which report a subsidiary's performance on a consolidated basis will place greater weight on aggregate firm performance in the subsidiary CEO's bonus payments.

There are three aspects of our analysis that we believe are novel yet have potentially broader applicability: (1) In testing the interdependence hypothesis, we focus on the details of the firms' contracts rather than employing less specific proxies like firm size and debt–equity ratios. We believe that our analysis provides a richer understanding of these accounting policy choices specifically because it focuses more directly on the firms' contractional provisions. (2) We offer a joint test of the FASB hypothesis that firms employ unconsolidated financial subsidiaries to mislead investors by understating the fixed claims on the firms' balance sheet. We argue that under this off-balance-sheet financing hypothesis, firms also should employ other off-balance-sheet financing methods like operating leases and unfunded pension liabilities. We believe that our evidence of no significant association between operating leases or unfunded pension liabilities and the use of unconsolidated reporting is evidence against the FASB hypothesis. (3) We derive more powerful tests and a richer understanding of the theory by focusing on apparently inconsistent observations. For example, the eleven unconsolidated subsidiaries that receive direct guarantees are owned by firms that either have no restrictions on funded debt in their bond contracts or have low ratios of subsidiary funded debt to parent net tangible assets (less than 1%).

Appendix

Table 10

Summary of accounting rules for excluding an entity from consolidation for a sample of 14 foreign countries.

Country	Activities differ from the rest of the group	Located abroad	Long-term restrictions on funds transfer	Effective control not exercised	Holdings temporary	Subsidiary immaterial in size	Undue expense and/or delay	Other reasons
Australia	Yes[a]	In the case of hostilities or threat of approbation	Yes[a]	Yes, especially in the case of liquidation or scheme of arrangement	Yes[a]	No	Yes[a]	If consolidated accounts would be misleading or harmful to the subsidiary
Belgium	No	If high inflation	Yes	If effective control is impossible	Yes	Yes	Yes	If sale of participation is intended
Canada	If financial statements are dissimilar and consolidated accounts could not be meaningful	No	Yes	No	Yes	Yes	No	Bank or insurance company if financial statements do not conform with GAAP
Denmark	No	No	Yes	No	Yes	Yes	No	In respect of the true and fair value
Finland	So that consolidation would distort the picture	No, if the financial standards to be applied by foreign subsidiaries are different from the Finnish	Yes	No[b]	Yes	—	—	—
Germany	Yes, required	Yes	—	If no unified management, exclusion is required		Yes	No	—
Italy	If risks or restrictions impair control	Yes	Yes	Yes	Yes	Yes	Yes	—

Country	Activities differ from the rest of the group	Located abroad	Long-term restrictions on funds transfer	Effective control not exercised	Holdings temporary	Subsidiary immaterial in size	Undue expense and/or delay	Other reasons
Japan	No	No	No, in principle	Yes	Yes	As an option to the parent	No	Subsidiary is not deemed to be a going concern, or result would be misleading
Netherlands	Yes, if unified management is not feasible	—	Yes	Yes	Yes	Yes	Yes	In all cases the excluded entity is considered not to be a group entity
New Zealand[c]	So that they cannot be treated as a single undertaking[d]	—	—	—	—	The amount of investment is immaterial	Yes	Result would be misleading or harmful[d] to one of the companies
Norway	—	—	Yes	—	—	—	E.g., newly acquired foreign subsidiary	Result would be misleading
Spain	No	In war or political instability or with severe inflation	No	No	Yes	Yes	Yes	Major solvency problems: liquidation
Sweden	No	No	No	No	No	No	No	No
United Kingdom	So that they cannot be treated as a single entity	No	Yes	In cases of no control of voting power and membership of the board	If intended to be temporary	Yes	Yes	Results would be misleading or harmful to the parent or any subsidiary

[a] No legislative exclusions but represents common practice.
[b] In the case of majority of voting rights.
[c] In opinion of parent entity's directors.
[d] Approval of the Governor-General In Counsel is required.

References

American Bar Foundation, 1971, Commentaries on model debenture indenture provisions 1965, Model debenture indenture provisions all registered issues 1967, and Certain negotiable provisions which may be included in a particular incorporating indenture (ABF, Chicago, IL).

Ball, Ray, 1989, The firm as a specialized contracting intermediary: Application to accounting and auditing, Journal of Accounting and Economics, forthcoming.

Benis, Martin, 1979, The non-consolidated finance company subsidiary, The Accounting Review 54, 808–814.

Beranek, William and Ronnie Clayton, 1985, Risk differences and financial reporting, Journal of Financial Research 8, 323–334.

Beranek, William and Gadis J. Dillon, 1982a, Consolidated financial statements: Sufficient for loan decisions, Journal of Commercial Bank Lending, 71–76.

Beranek, William and Gadis J. Dillon, 1982b, Consolidated financial statements and risk, Journal of Financial Education, 32–39.

Burnett, Tom, Thomas E. King, and Valdeau C. Lembke, 1979, Equity method reporting for major finance company subsidiaries, The Accounting Review 54, 815–823.

Comiskey, Eugene E., Ruth Ann McEwen, and Charles W. Mulford, 1987, A test of proforma consolidation of finance subsidiaries, Financial Management 16, 45–50.

Copeland, Ronald M. and Sharon McKinnon, 1987, Financial distortion and consolidation of captive finance subsidiaries in the general merchandising industry, Journal of Business Finance and Accounting 14, 77–97.

Francis, Jere R., 1986, Debt reporting by parent companies: Parent-only versus consolidated statements, Journal of Business Finance and Accounting 13, 393–403.

Heian, James B. and James B. Thies, 1989, Consolidation of finance subsidiaries: $230 billion in off-balance-sheet financing comes home to roost, Accounting Horizons, 1–9.

Holthausen, Robert W. and Richard W. Leftwich, 1983, The economic consequences of accounting choice: Implications of costly contracting and monitoring, Journal of Accounting and Economics 5, 77–117.

Kane, Edward J., 1986, Appearance and reality in deposit insurance: The case for reform, Journal of Banking and Finance, 175–188.

Klein, Benjamin, Robert Crawford, and Armen A. Alchian, 1978, Vertical integration, appropriable rents and the competitive contracting process, Journal of Law and Economics 21, 297–326.

Leftwich, Richard W., 1981, Evidence on the impact of mandatory changes in accounting principles on corporate loan agreements, Journal of Accounting and Economics 3, 3–36.

Leftwich, Richard W., 1983, Accounting information in private markets: Evidence from private lending agreements, The Accounting Review 58, 23–42.

Mian, Shehzad L. and Clifford W. Smith, 1989a, Accounts receivable management policy: Theory and evidence, Unpublished manuscript (University of Rochester, Rochester, NY).

Mian, Shehzad L. and Clifford W. Smith, 1989b, Incentives associated with changes in consolidated reporting requirements, Unpublished manuscript (University of Rochester, Rochester, NY).

Mohr, Rosanne M., 1988, Unconsolidated finance subsidiaries: Characteristics and debt/equity effects, Accounting Horizons 2, 27–34.

Organization for Economic Cooperation and Development, 1987, Consolidation policies in OECD countries, Report by the Working Group on Accounting Standards (OECD, Paris).

Ronen, Joshua and Ashwinpaul C. Sondhi, 1989, Debt capacity and financial contracting: Finance subsidiaries, Journal of Accounting Auditing and Finance 4, 237–265.

Smith, Clifford W. and Lee Wakeman, 1985, Determinants of corporate leasing policy, Journal of Finance 40, 895–908.

Smith, Clifford W. and Jerold B. Warner, 1979, On financial contracting: An analysis of bond covenants, Journal of Financial Economics 7, 117–161.

Smith, Clifford W. and Ross Watts, 1982, Incentive and tax effects of executive compensation plans, Australian Journal of Management 7, 139–157.

Smith, Clifford W. and Ross Watts, 1989, The investment opportunity set and corporate policy choices, Unpublished manuscript (University of Rochester, Rochester, NY).

Watts, Ross L., 1977, Corporate financial statements, a product of the market and political processes, Australian Journal of Management 2, 53–75.

Whittred, Greg, 1986, The evolution of consolidated financial reporting in Australia, Abacus 22, 103–120.

Whittred, Greg, 1987, The derived demand for consolidated financial reporting, Journal of Accounting and Economics 9, 259–285.

INCENTIVES ASSOCIATED WITH CHANGES IN CONSOLIDATED REPORTING REQUIREMENTS*

Shehzad L. MIAN

Emory University, Atlanta, GA 30322, USA

Clifford W. SMITH, Jr.

University of Rochester, Rochester, NY 14627, USA

Received February 1990, final version received August 1990

We examine the effects of mandated changes regarding consolidation. Analysis of FAS 94 submissions indicates: firms with unconsolidated subsidiaries lobby against FAS 94; strategic lobbying; accounting-data users lobby against FAS 94; and accounting firms support the proposal more than industrials. FAS 94 adoption produced negative returns in affected firms. In response to FAS 94, firms with unconsolidated financial subsidiaries were more likely to sell, close, or reorganize the subsidiary, retire debt, or securitize corporate assets. Finally, Canadian firms switch to unconsolidated reporting after a 1978 amendment to Canadian GAAP eliminating limitations on its use. Collectively this evidence suggests FAS 94 eliminated a valuable reporting alternative.

1. Introduction

Given no externalities, firms have private incentives to establish accounting policies that maximize both firm value and social welfare. However, as Watts and Zimmerman (1986) recognize, feasible accounting practices are determined not just by private market forces; they are determined through a quasi-political process. In this paper, we seek to further our understanding of this process by focusing on changes in accounting standards governing consolidated reporting.

There are two general categories of incentives that can be examined regarding consolidation policy: (1) incentives for choosing whether to report a subsidiary's performance on a consolidated or an unconsolidated basis given that both are feasible, and (2) incentives associated with changing from one basis to another given a mandated change in the set of feasible accounting provisions.

*We thank R. Ball, M. Barclay, G. Benston, J. Brickley, A. Christie, R. Holthausen, S.P. Kothari, P. Meyers, W. Scott, C. Smithson, R. Watts, G. Whittred, and especially R. Vigeland (referee) and J. Zimmerman (editor). The research was partially supported by the John M. Olin Foundation, the Lynde and Harry Bradley Foundation, the University Research Committee, Emory University, and the Managerial Economics Research Center at the Simon School.

Journal of Accounting and Economics 13 (1990) 249–266. North-Holland

We address the first set of issues in Mian and Smith (1990a). In that paper, we provide a positive theory of firms' incentives to employ unconsolidated financial reporting. We examine the set of firm and subsidiary characteristics that lead the firm to choose consolidated or unconsolidated reporting. Our evidence suggests that for some firms, the option to report a subsidiary's performance on an unconsolidated basis is valuable.

In this paper, we address the second set of issues. Here, we assume that the firm has chosen its reporting policy optimally. Given their consolidation decision we analyze the reaction to Financial Accounting Standard 94. Adopted on 30 October 1987, FAS 94 requires that a firm's majority-owned subsidiaries be included on a consolidated basis for accounting periods ending after 15 December 1988. We examine whether firms with unconsolidated financial subsidiaries: (1) are more likely to lobby against the exposure draft for the proposed accounting change, (2) are more likely to observe a negative abnormal return associated with the announcement of the adoption of FAS 94, and (3) are more likely to engage in transactions that would reduce the cost of FAS 94 compliance.

In section 2, we examine the submissions to the Financial Accounting Standards Board lobbying on FAS 94. We analyze the submissions of various groups: manufacturing firms, accounting-statements users, and auditors. In section 3, we examine the wealth effects of the adoption of FAS 94, since by restricting accounting techniques, wealth transfers among various market participants can be generated. In section 4, we analyze organizational restructurings, debt restructuring, or asset securitization as potential adjustments to reduce the costs of complying with FAS 94. In section 5, we examine a complementary change in accounting standards, the response of Canadian firms to the 1978 amendment to Canadian GAAP which relaxes constraints on reporting a financial subsidiary's performance on an unconsolidated basis. We offer our conclusions in section 6.

2. Lobbying on FAS 94

Language in Accounting Research Bulletin 51 allowed managers to report the performance of financial subsidiaries on an unconsolidated basis.

> Separate statements or combined statements would be preferable for a subsidiary or group of subsidiaries if the presentation of financial information concerning the particular activities of such subsidiaries would be more informative to shareholders and creditors of the parent company than would the inclusion of such subsidiaries in the consolidation. For example, separate statements may be required for a subsidiary which is a bank or an insurance company and may be preferable for a finance company where the parent and other subsidiaries are engaged in manufacturing operations.

In December 1986, the FASB issued an exposure draft of their proposal to eliminate the option to exclude subsidiaries from consolidation on the grounds that their operations are nonhomogeneous.

The FASB received 232 letters on the exposure draft. We obtained copies of these submissions and examined each to determine its lobbying position. The appendix contains a summary of the frequency with which various arguments appear in the submissions classified by occupational category (as established by the FASB). Some *agree* without reservation; for example, 3M states: 'We support the issuance of the ED [exposure draft] as a final standard. Nonhomogeneity should not preclude consolidation of majority owned entities.' Others *agree* with reservations; for example. Exxon states: 'However, even though we agree with the board's basic conclusion in this exposure draft, we take exceptions to certain provisions.' Some are forthright in stating that they *disagree*; for example, General Mills states: 'We disagree with the proposed statement's concept of consolidating financial service entities with nonfinancial parent companies.' Finally some firms only *comment*; for example, DuPont states: 'We express no view with respect to the basic thrust of the ED that all majority-owned subsidiaries should be consolidated unless control is temporary or does not rest with the majority owner, but we offer the following comments on other provisions of the ED for your consideration.'

Across the letters that express reservations or disagreement there are six basic arguments that appear repeatedly: (1) *Time Extension* – for example, Navistar states: 'Finally we strongly urge that the effective date be set back to December 15, 1988.' (2) *Use of Cost Method* – for example, IBM states: 'We object at this time to the Board mandating the cost method of accounting for all majority-owned subsidiaries where control does not rest with the majority owner.' (3) *Continued Unconsolidated Disclosures* – for example, Exxon states: 'We feel that the requirement for the continued disclosures about formerly unconsolidated subsidiaries is not evenhanded and sets a very undesirable precedent of different disclosure based solely on past accounting practices.' (4) *Increased Costs* – for example, Marine Midland Bank states: 'In general, we believe that the proposal requiring consolidation of all majority-owned and/or controlled subsidiaries will place an increased reporting burden on issuers of financial statements while potentially reducing the value of those statements to users such as ourselves.' (5) *Exceptions* – for example, Gulf States Utilities states: 'For this reason, the company, although agreeing with the theoretical basis for this Exposure Draft, believes that an exception to such consolidated accounting and reporting should be provided for rate-regulated enterprises.' (6) *Reporting Entity Project* – for example, Hewlett Packard states: 'We do not see the need for the proposed accounting standard or the benefit of separating this issue from the project on the reporting entity. It appears this proposal was formulated in an effort to cure an urgent reporting deficiency which we do not believe exists. We urge the board to withdraw this proposal and evaluate the nonhomogeneity issue in connection with the broader project on the reporting entity.'

Because these letters tend to be worded diplomatically we believe some discretion is required to map these statements into a summary lobby position. For example, we do not believe that an agree-with-reservations letter, which first states that it agrees with the exposure draft but then argues that their previously unconsolidated subsidiary be exempted from the requirement to consolidate, is appropriately classified as supporting the proposal. Thus, in table 1, we regroup lobbying positions from the appendix into three categories: FOR, AGAINST, and COMMENT. Under FOR we include both firms that *agree* without reservation and those that *agree* with minor reservations (firms that raise only issues of time extension, continued unconsolidated disclosures, or use of cost method). Under AGAINST we include firms that *disagree* as well as those that say they either *agree* or *comment* with major reservations (firms that raise issues of exceptions, the reporting entity project, or increased costs). Finally, under COMMENT we include firms that *comment* without major reservations. (Note that this basic coding scheme was applied prior to conducting any of our tests; subsequently, we tried other classifications and our results are robust to reasonable modifications of this classification scheme.)

In panel A of table 1, respondents are classified by occupational category (as established by the FASB) and lobbying position. Among the respondents there are: 131 industrial firms, 28 banking firms, 17 public accounting firms, 9 securities firms, 27 representational organizations, and 20 others (including academic, government, and law). Entities that in their submissions identify themselves as users of this data are subdivided in panel B; there are 18 banking firms, 8 securities firms, and 3 representational organizations.

FAS 94 and accounting statement users. The FASB argues that firms' financial subsidiaries are typically more highly levered than those engaged in manufacturing. By not consolidating, firms show lower leverage than they would if the subsidiaries were consolidated. They argue that this off-balance-sheet financing is potentially misleading to users. This implies that potential users (e.g., the banking and securities industries and risk-rating firms) should be more likely to lobby for FAS 94. Mian and Smith (1990a) suggest an alternate hypothesis: that potential users of accounting statements prefer to have more disaggregated information. This hypothesis implies potential users would lobby against FAS 94.

We examine the lobbying position of the user firms in panel B of table 1. We identify submissions by 18 firms in the banking industry and 8 firms in the securities industry, as well as three letters from representational groups which state explicitly that they are users of the accounting statements. Of these 29 submissions three lobby FOR the exposure draft, 23 lobby AGAINST, and three COMMENT without expressing an opinion. Thus, at

Table 1

Frequency of lobbying position on 232 lobby letters to the FASB on the consolidation exposure draft classified by occupational category. FOR includes all lobby letters that agree without major reservations ('Increased Costs', 'Exceptions', and 'Reporting Entity Projects' – see appendix); AGAINST includes all lobby letters that disagree plus those that agree or comment with major reservations; COMMENT includes all lobby letters that comment without major reservations. Figures in parentheses are percentage of respondents within each category that adopt the specified lobbying position.

| | Lobbying position | | | |
	FOR	AGAINST	COMMENT	Total
Panel A: Occupational category				
Industrials	35 (26.7)	88 (67.2)	8 (6.1)	131
Banking	3 (10.7)	24 (85.7)	1 (3.6)	28
Public accounting	5 (29.4)	10 (58.8)	2 (11.8)	17
Securities	0 (0.0)	9 (100.0)	0 (0.0)	9
Representational organizations	16 (59.3)	7 (25.9)	4 (14.8)	27
Other	8 (40.0)	9 (45.0)	3 (15.0)	20
Total	67 (28.9)	147 (63.4)	18 (7.8)	232
Panel B: Financial statement users				
Banking	2 (11.1)	15 (83.3)	1 (5.6)	18
Securities	0 (0.0)	8 (100.0)	0 (0.0)	8
Representational organizations	1 (33.3)	0 (0.0)	2 (66.7)	3
Total	3 (10.3)	23 (79.4)	3 (10.3)	29

least among this sample of users who lobby, there appears to be little support for the hypothesis that the use of unconsolidated reporting is misleading or confusing.[1]

Lobbying and consolidation policy. When alternate accounting techniques represent close substitutes, small differences in expected net benefits can

[1]This result also is consistent with the evidence in Comiskey, McEwen, and Mulford (1987) that suggests firms' betas are more closely associated with financial leverage based on a pro forma consolidation than financial leverage based on unconsolidated data.

drive firms to choose one procedure over another. If a firm has instituted a particular accounting technique, and if it has negotiated outstanding long-term contracts assuming the use of that accounting procedure, then a mandated change in feasible accounting standards force that firm either to renegotiate existing contracts or bear the costs of operating under a set of inefficient contractual constraints. Note that these recontracting and opportunity costs are not bounded by the magnitude of the cost difference on which the original accounting procedure was chosen; thus the ex post recontracting costs can be substantial even though the ex ante cost difference motivating the original choice is trivial. Moreover, the distribution of these recontracting costs provides particular firms incentives to lobby for or against an accounting-method change.

Mandated consolidation of insurance, leasing, real estate, and finance subsidiaries generally increases leverage, decreases the reported return on assets, and decreases the reported interest coverage of the parent firm's debt [see Copeland and McKinnon (1987), Mohr (1988), and Heian and Thies (1989)]. Thus required consolidation of financial subsidiaries increases the probability of covenant violation for a parent firm with debt contracts employing restrictive covenants based on unconsolidated subsidiary reporting [see Smith and Warner (1979)]. Since contracts are costly to renegotiate, the stockholders of such parent firms face potential losses from the adoption of FAS 94. Therefore, we expect firms with unconsolidated financial subsidiaries to be more likely to lobby against the standard than other firms. We also expect some firms currently without unconsolidated financial subsidiaries to lobby against the proposal because it would restrict their accounting opportunity set, and the firm values the option to establish an unconsolidated financial subsidiary in the future. However, firms' incentives to lobby can be more subtle. For example, firms without unconsolidated financial subsidiaries have incentives to lobby for adoption of the FASB exposure draft if adoption eliminates a valuable accounting option employed by their competitors. Because its elimination would impose more costs on their competition than on themselves, the firm's competitive position is enhanced by lobbying for adoption of the exposure draft. Moreover, this argument also implies that a firm with an unconsolidated subsidiary could have an incentive to lobby for passage of FAS 94, even though it imposes costs on itself, so long as the benefit from imposing costs on its competitors outweighs the self-imposed costs.

We examine the consolidation policies of the 131 industrial corporations that lobby with the FASB on the consolidation exposure draft. Of the 131, we eliminate eight firms that only submit comments and nine firms where we cannot determine the firm's consolidation policy. Table 2 presents the contingency table of consolidation policy and lobbying position on the exposure draft for the 114 remaining industrial firms. Table 2 provides strong evidence

Table 2

Contingency table of consolidation policy versus lobbying position on the exposure draft for 114 manufacturing firms which express either a favorable or unfavorable opinion in lobbying with the FASB and have a discernable consolidation policy with respect to their subsidiaries.

| Lobbying position | Does the firm have an unconsolidated financial subsidiary? | | Total |
	No	Yes	
FOR	22	9	31
AGAINST	11	72	83
Total	33	81	114

$$\chi^2 = 36.55 \qquad p\text{-value} < 0.001$$

that firms with unconsolidated subsidiaries are more likely to lobby against the exposure draft and firms without unconsolidated subsidiaries are more likely to lobby for it ($\chi^2 = 36.55$).[2]

To analyze whether the nine firms with unconsolidated subsidiaries that lobby for FAS 94 do so to impose costs on their competitors, we examine these firms and their horizontal rivals. The nine firms all fall into five 3-digit SIC codes. Using the data reported in *Moody's* and corporate annual reports, we find that of the Fortune 500, 16 firms with unconsolidated financial subsidiaries are in the same 3-digit industries. None of the nine firms that lobby for FAS 94 has covenants restricting funded debt to net tangible assets, while four (25%) of their rivals do. [Note that although *Moody's* only covers public debt issues, these are the issues of greatest concern because of their higher renegotiation costs – see Smith and Warner (1979) and Leftwich (1981).] We estimate the average change in the debt/equity ratio implied by FAS 94 for the two groups. It increases by 8% for the firms that lobby FOR FAS 94, but by 27% for their rivals. We interpret this difference as suggesting that FAS 94 adoption imposes higher costs on the firm's competitors than on itself.

As an alternate control group we also examine the rivals to the eleven firms without unconsolidated subsidiaries that lobbied against FAS 94. We expect strategic issues should be less important for this group than for the nine firms with unconsolidated financial subsidiaries who lobby FOR FAS 94. We find that of the Fortune 500, 23 firms with unconsolidated subsidiaries are in the same 3-digit industries. Of those, five firms have covenants restricting funded debt to net tangible asset. We estimate that the average change in the debt/equity ratio for these firms is 13%. Thus, we believe that

[2]This as well as all other χ^2 statistics reported in this paper have one degree of freedom. For a χ^2 with one degree of freedom the 95% critical value is 3.84.

this data on average debt/equity ratio changes also is consistent with the nine firms engaging in strategic lobbying, attempting to employ the FASB's accounting-standard-setting process to improve their competitive position by imposing costs on their competitors.

Auditor lobbying on FAS 94. Accounting firms have various incentives to lobby which are not mutually exclusive: (1) Accounting firms have incentives to lobby for standards that increase their value [Watts and Zimmerman (1986)]. FAS 94 is expected to increase auditing revenues for two reasons – to provide a consolidated statement, the auditor must examine both the previously unconsolidated statements as well as the process of consolidation, also FAS 94 requires firms to furnish separate summarized financial statements or previously unconsolidated subsidiaries so that information is not lost through aggregation. (2) Accounting firms have incentives to lobby for rules that reduce their potential legal liability [see Kothari, Lys, Smith, and Watts (1988)]. Thus, if less client discretion with respect to accounting choice reduces auditors' legal liability, then accounting firms have incentives to support the standard. (3) Accounting firms have an incentive to support the FASB. They might reason that if the FASB fails, whatever succeeds it (some governmental body such as the SEC) is likely to be worse for the auditing industry [see Watts and Zimmerman (1986)]. (4) Accounting firms have incentives to lobby as their client firms do [see Haring (1979) and Watts and Zimmerman (1986)]. (5) Accounting firms are expected to be more concerned about the position of their large clients than of their smaller clients, if audit fees are a positive function of firm size [see Watts and Zimmerman (1986)].

Thus in the case of FAS 94 the first three motives imply that accounting firms should be more likely to lobby FOR the exposure draft than industrial firms. Table 3 provides strong evidence that submissions by public accounting firms and public accounting representational organizations lobby FOR the exposure draft more frequently than industrial firms and their representational organizations ($\chi^2 = 6.21$).

Table 3

Contingency table of 155 public accounting firms/representational organizations and industrial firms/representational organizations versus lobbying position with the FASB on the consolidation exposure draft.

Lobbying position	Industrial firms/ representational organizations	Accounting firms/ representational organizations	Total
FOR	37	14	51
AGAINST	92	12	104
Total	129	26	155
	$\chi^2 = 6.21$	p-value = 0.01	

Table 4

Contingency table of lobbying position of public accounting firms versus lobbying position of 117 client firms which express either a favorable or unfavorable opinion in lobbying with the FASB on the consolidation exposure draft.

Lobbying position of client firms	Lobbying position of public accounting firms		
	FOR	AGAINST	Total
FOR	9	22	31
AGAINST	15	71	86
Total	24	93	117
	$\chi^2 = 1.88$	p-value = 0.17	

In addition, table 4 tests the importance of the fourth incentive by examining accounting firms' lobbying positions against that of their client firms for the 117 of the 131 industrial firms where their auditor could be identified and where the auditor lobbied on FAS 94. We find no significant association between the auditor and client-firm lobbying position ($\chi^2 = 1.88$).

To test the importance of the fifth incentive, we obtain data on assets from COMPUSTAT and *Moody's* on 116 of the 117 firms (one firm is private and declines to disclose data on firm size). We divide the sample, and examine the correspondence between auditor and client lobbying for the 58 firms above the median firm size. Within this subsample of larger firms, there again is no statistically significant association between auditor and client lobbying on FAS 94 ($\chi^2 = 0.04$). We also estimate a logistic regression where the independent variable is the ratio of sales by the auditors client firms' who lobby for FAS 94 to sales of all clients who lobby. Again, there is no significant association between auditor and client lobbying on FAS 94.

While differential interests of auditor and client firms might obscure the relation between their lobbying position in terms of FOR versus AGAINST, clients' lobbying positions might affect auditors' opinions with respect to individual arguments about the effect of FAS 94. To test this hypothesis, we examine the association between auditor and client lobby position on the six arguments summarized in the appendix. The χ^2 statistics are all less than 1.89, and thus are insignificant. Thus, client-firm positions appear to be less important in determining auditor lobbying positions on FAS 94 than in the case of other FASB rulings summarized in Watts and Zimmerman (1986, ch. 13).

3. Wealth effects of FAS 94

To estimate the value effects associated with the adoption of FAS 94, we examine the abnormal returns to the firms with unconsolidated financial subsidiaries around the time of the potentially relevant announcements. Adopted on 30 October 1987 and reported in the *Wall Street Journal* on 2 November 1987, it requires a company's majority-owned subsidiaries be included on a consolidated basis for accounting periods ending after December 15, 1988 (extended from December 15, 1987 in the exposure draft). The decision is preceded by six *Wall Street Journal* articles discussing the issue. Moreover there are two other potentially important announcements in the FASB *Action Alert* but not the *WSJ*. In table 5 we report the stock-price reactions in these announcements for various subsets of firms. We look at the firms on CRSP that have unconsolidated finance, insurance, leasing, or real estate subsidiaries, the firms that lobby FOR and AGAINST the FASB exposure draft, and firms that are mentioned specifically in the *Wall Street Journal* articles.

The combined market-adjusted abnormal-return evidence suggests that the identifiable stock-price reaction is limited to the November 1987 announcement. The -1.38% abnormal return for the 169 firms with unconsolidated financial subsidiaries provides weak evidence ($t = -1.69$) that the passage of FAS 94 eliminates a valuable accounting option. We believe that the most significant result is the -3.26% abnormal return for the 75 firms which lobby AGAINST the proposal ($t = -2.94$); however, the 29 firms that lobby FOR the proposal have a -0.88% abnormal return. This result is consistent with the proposition that those firms with the most to lose from the adoption of FAS 94 incur the costs to lobby against its passage.

To see whether the difference among the abnormal returns is significant, we estimate a regression where the October 30/November 2, 1987 two-day abnormal return (AR) is the dependent variable and where the independent variables are dummies for whether the firm submits a letter to the FASB lobbying FOR the exposure draft, for whether the firm submits a letter to the FASB lobbying AGAINST the exposure draft, for whether the firm is mentioned in the November 2 *Wall Street Journal* article on the adoption of FAS 94 (*WSJ*), and a measure of the relative size of their unconsolidated subsidiaries (SIZE – the ratio of subsidiaries' assets to parents' assets). SIZE is included because the costs of FAS 94 adoption are likely to be greater the larger the firm's unconsolidated financial subsidiary. We estimate the following cross-sectional regression across the 106 firms with the required data (*t*-statistics are in parentheses):

$$AR_j = \underset{(-1.00)}{-0.74} + \underset{(0.57)}{1.46\ FOR_j} - \underset{(-2.21)}{2.26\ AGAINST_j} - \underset{(-0.30)}{0.58\ WSJ_j}$$

$$+ \underset{(0.17)}{0.42\ SIZE_j} + e_j.$$

The estimated coefficient on the AGAINST dummy is statistically significant

Table 5

Summary of two-day market-adjusted announcement returns for firms with unconsolidated subsidiaries around the major *Wall Street Journal* and FASB *Action Alert* reports on the progress of FAS 94, requiring consolidation (sample size in parentheses).

Event	Firms with unconsolidated subsidiaries	Firms that lobby for FAS 94	Firms that lobby against FAS 94	Firms mentioned in *WSJ*
3 Feb 1982	FASB *Action Alert* reports that consolidation project was put on the Board's agenda – Board meeting 27 Jan 1982.			
	-0.37 (187)	-0.32 (26)	-0.45 (71)	—
30 Apr 1984	*WSJ* discussion of FASB project to require consolidation.			
	0.08 (194)	-0.30 (29)	-0.02 (77)	—
1 Oct 1986	FASB *Action Alert* reports that on 24 Sep 1986 it was tentatively agreed to proceed to an exposure draft.			
	0.24 (184)	0.74 (29)	0.67 (77)	—
17 Dec 1986	*WSJ* reports that FASB has proposed consolidation rule. Notes that comments are requested by 14 Apr 1987. If adopted it does not become effective until 15 Dec 1987.			
	0.15 (181)	0.20 (29)	-0.03 (77)	-1.43 (2)
29 Jan 1987	*WSJ* notes proposed FASB rule requiring consolidation faces big battle.			
	0.26 (177)	-0.47 (29)	0.02 (77)	-1.41 (1)
6 Feb 1987	*WSJ* discussion of consolidation as issue to face new FASB Chairman Beresford. Notes Board plans to issue final rule in late 1987.			
	0.32 (177)	-1.17^{b} (29)	-0.70 (77)	—
12 Oct 1987	*WSJ* announces Tenneco will create a holding company.			
	-0.33 (169)	0.40 (29)	-0.32 (75)	-1.17 (1)
2 Nov 1987	*WSJ* reports that FASB issued rule 94 on 30 Oct 1987. It is effective 15 Dec 1988, a year later than originally proposed.			
	-1.38^{a} (169)	-0.88 (29)	-3.26^{b} (75)	-3.71^{b} (9)

[a]Statistically significant at the 10% confidence level.
[b]Statistically significant at the 5% confidence level.

($t = -2.21$); the adjusted R^2 for the regression is 0.02 and the F statistic is 1.65. Note that if the abnormal return in table 5 were significant simply due to chance variation, then there should be no predictable cross-sectional pattern in the abnormal returns; thus, the significance of the cross-sectional regression coefficient increases our confidence in the table 5 results. However, multicollinearity is present in this regression (this is not surprising given the small number of lobby letters classified as COMMENT). A simple regression of abnormal returns on the FOR dummy variable is positive and statistically significant. Additional analysis also suggests that, the AGAINST result is driven largely by the *increased-costs* firms from the appendix; a simple regression of abnormal returns on an *increased-costs* dummy variable is statistically significantly negative. Because of this multicollinearity, precise estimates of the effects of the individual variables is difficult to estimate.

We expect the *WSJ* coefficient to be negative; these firms are singled out because they are adversely affected by the adoption of FAS 94. For example, the estimated impact of FAS 94 on leverage and accounting returns is substantial for this set of firms. Using 1986 data, the average change in the firms' debt/equity ratios is +163% and the average change in the return on assets is −39%. Of the nine firms, eight have accounting-based compensation plans. Of the nine firms, seven have debt covenants restricting future financing based on the book value of the firm's debt. We thus are surprised that this coefficient is not significant.

4. Adjustments to FAS 94

To better understand the abnormal stock-price reactions to the announcement of FAS 94 reported in table 5, we examine ways in which corporations adjust to this restriction of the accounting opportunity set. We examine *Moody's*, corporate Annual Reports, and the *Wall Street Journal* for corporate announcements of the sale of financial subsidiaries, the closing of financial subsidiaries, and corporate reorganizations involving financial subsidiaries. We also note cases of voluntary debt retirement as a potential method of eliminating debt covenants that FAS 94 would make binding. Finally, we note the sale of securitized assets[3] such as accounts receivable or auto loans as a method of reducing the liabilities reported on the firm's consolidated balance sheet.

In some cases, we are very confident that these transactions are a direct response to the adoption of FAS 94. For example, in response to the FASB's October 30, 1987 announcement of the adoption of FAS 94, Tenneco, Inc. announced a special meeting of stockholders to approve a significant corpo-

---

[3]See Hess and Smith (1988). We thank Charles W. Smithson for providing the data on securitized transactions.

rate reorganization on November 2, 1987. The announcement states:

> As a result of this accounting change, indebtedness of the Company's finance subsidiaries will for the first time be included in consolidated debt for purposes of computing the Company's borrowing capacity under a number of its outstanding debt instruments. This result, which was unforseen and unintended at the time these debt instruments were originally created, will unacceptably restrict the ability of the Company and its subsidiaries to issue long-term debt and thus significantly impair the Company's future financing flexibility.

However, the motive for other announcements is unclear. For example the Deere and Company 1989 Annual Report States:

> In November 1988, the United States retail finance subsidiaries announced a change in organizational structure.... These changes were made to increase the operating and financial autonomy of the retail finance subsidiaries, with the objectives of realizing operating efficiencies and of establishing procedures to enable the retail finance subsidiaries to expand their acquisitions to finance receivables from sources other than Deere & Company.

Because we cannot be sure of the motives for these announcements, we separately report the frequency of these transactions by the 85 firms with unconsolidated financial subsidiaries and 35 firms without unconsolidated subsidiaries of the 120 firms with discernable consolidation policies that lobby on FAS 94. *Accounting Trends and Techniques* (1989) reports that of the 600 firms surveyed, the implementation of FAS 94 occurs both in 1987 and 1988 (the number of companies consolidating all significant subsidiaries in 434 in 1986, 456 in 1987, and 546 in 1988). Thus we note these transactions in both 1987 and 1988.

Table 6 summarizes our data on these transactions for the 120 firms that lobby FOR FAS 94 [see also Comiskey and Mulford (1989)]. As panel A of table 7 indicates, these transactions in 1987 and 1988 are significantly more likely among firms with unconsolidated financial subsidiaries than among firms without them ($\chi^2 = 4.34$). We interpret this as evidence of costs imposed on firms with unconsolidated financial subsidiaries by the implementation of FAS 94. Panel B indicates similar results for the 114 firms that lobbied FOR or AGAINST FAS 94 ($\chi^2 = 4.26$). Given the evidence in table 2 of a significant relation between lobbying position and consolidation policy, the results in panel A and B are not independent. However, they focus on complementary questions.

We believe that the table 6 evidence understates the costs of adjustment to FAS 94 because some firms began the adjustment process prior to FAS 94 adoption. For example, the automobile manufacturers negotiated profit-sharing plans for hourly employees with the UAW. The Ford Motor Company plan bases payments on 'income (loss) before income taxes of Ford and its consolidated subsidiaries'.[4] By requiring consolidation of Ford Motor Credit and First Nationwide, FAS 94 would have increased the profit base under this plan by almost 20% and increased benefits under the plan by almost 33%. However, the plans were amended; specifically a supplemental agreement between General Motors and the UAW dated October 8, 1987 states:

> In the event the proposed FASB rule regarding consolidation of majority-owned subsidiaries becomes final, appropriate adjustments will be made to 'Profits' and 'Sales and Revenues' for the purpose of the Profit Sharing Plan. These adjustments will be made to achieve the same results as would be achieved under the present practice of reporting the after-tax results of unconsolidated subsidiaries (majority-owned 'nonhomogeneous' operations) on a single line basis in the consolidated results of the parent Corporation and of excluding the revenues of these subsidiaries.

We have no way of knowing what concessions were required to produce this Supplemental Agreement. However, because it is dated before the final announcement of FAS 94, it underscores the fact that we do not have clean event dates. Thus, we expect some transactions motivated by FAS 94 as well as some stock-price adjustment to FAS 94 precede the announcement of its adoption on October 30, 1987. This reduces the power of our tests that employ abnormal returns in section 3. It also suggests that we understate the transactions motivated by FAS 94.

5. Consolidation in Canada

While FAS 94 restricts the accounting opportunity set with respect to consolidation policy, a 1978 amendment to Canadian GAAP expands it. Briefly, there have been two major changes in Canadian GAAP affecting the choice of reporting a financial subsidiary's performance on a consolidated or unconsolidated basis. In January 1973, Section 3050.10 of the Canadian

---

[4]Agreement Concerning Profit Sharing Plan and Ford Motor Company Profit Sharing Plan for Hourly Employees in the United States, paragraph 19.

Table 6

Summary of the 1987–1988 transactions that are potential adjustments to the adoption of FAS 94 by 120 firms that lobby with the FASB and have a discernable consolidation policy with respect to their subsidiaries.

Type of announcement	1987		1988	
	Firm has an unconsolidated financial subsidiary	Firm has no unconsolidated financial subsidiary	Firm has an unconsolidated financial subsidiary	Firm has no unconsolidated financial subsidiary
Sale of a financial subsidiary	4	4	7	1
Cease operation of a financial subsidiary	0	0	3	0
Reorganization affecting a financial subsidiary	5	0	3	0
Voluntary debt retirement	10	2	3	2
Sale of securitized assets	3	0	3	1
Total number of announcements	22	6	19	4
Total number of firms with announcements	21	4	18	3
Total number of firms examined	85	35	85	35

Institute of Charted Accountants Handbook was revised:

> The fact that the nature of the business carried on by a subsidiary differs from that of the parent is not a valid reason for, and should not be used to justify, exclusion of a subsidiary from consolidation.

In August 1978, this provision was deleted.

We believe that it is informative to focus on the 1978 amendment. While both the 1973 CICA amendment and FAS 94 impose more restrictions on the use of unconsolidated reporting, the 1978 CICA amendment expands the accounting opportunity set. By examining the change in the use of unconsolidated financial subsidiaries associated with the change in reporting requirements, we can obtain an independent estimate of the value of the option to report a subsidiary's performance on an unconsolidated basis.

We employ the data on the consolidation choice for finance subsidiaries summarized in *Financial Reporting in Canada* from 1975 to 1987. (Earlier issues do not report separately the consolidation choice for finance subsidiaries.) The data indicate that the frequency of use of finance subsidiaries is much lower in Canada than in the United States. Over the period from

Table 7

Contingency table of 1987–1988 transactions that are potential adjustments to FAS 94 adoption versus consolidation policy and lobbying position.

Panel A: Transactions versus consolidation policy for 120 firms that lobby with the FASB and have a discernable consolidation policy with respect to their subsidiaries

Announcement of a transaction	Does the firm have an unconsolidated financial subsidiary?		
	Yes	No	Total
Yes	31	6	37
No	54	29	83
Total	85	35	120

$\chi^2 = 4.34$ p-value = 0.04

Panel B: Transactions versus lobbying position for 114 firms which express either a favorable or unfavorable opinion in lobbying with the FASB and have a discernable consolidation policy with respect to their subsidiaries

Announcement of a transaction	Lobbying position		
	AGAINST	FOR	Total
Yes	30	5	35
No	53	26	79
Total	83	31	114

$\chi^2 = 4.25$ p-value = 0.04

1973 to 1986 fewer than 5% of the firms in the Canadian sample report the existence of finance subsidiaries, compared to 26% of the firms in our sample reported in Mian and Smith (1990b).

For the Canadian firms with finance subsidiaries over the years prior to 1978, the average fraction of finance subsidiaries reported on an unconsolidated basis is 19%; after 1978, that fraction is 44%. This difference is significant at the 1% level. When the feasible set of accounting techniques is expanded, firms should switch only if the net benefits are positive. Hence we believe that this Canadian experience provides independent evidence that the option to report the performance of a financial subsidiary on an unconsolidated basis is valuable.

6. Conclusions

From our examination of lobbying with the FASB over the proposal to require consolidation, we conclude that firms with unconsolidated subsidiaries tend to lobby against the exposure draft; firms with only consolidated subsidiaries tend to lobby for it; public accounting firms typically support the exposure draft more frequently than their client firms; and, contrary to FASB arguments, users generally lobby against the exposure draft. In contrast to other studies of lobbying on FASB exposure drafts, we find no significant association between client and auditor lobbying on FAS 94. We offer weak evidence of a negative stock-price reaction to the announcement of FAS 94, especially among those firms that lobby against the exposure draft. However, the power of this test is low because of the difficulty in event-date identification. Our examination of firms' response to the imposition of FAS 94 indicates that the frequency of certain transactions firms could use to reduce the cost of FAS 94 compliance is higher among firms with unconsolidated subsidiaries. Specifically, our evidence suggests that these firms: (1) retire outstanding long-term debt contracts that are conditional on reported accounting numbers, (2) change the corporate activities to mitigate the implications of the accounting change (for example, by either the sale, closing, or reorganization of their financial subsidiaries or the securitization and sale of assets). Finally, our Canadian evidence indicates that when the accounting opportunity set is expanded by imposing fewer restrictions on the use of unconsolidated reporting, then firms switch from consolidated to unconsolidated reporting. We believe that this evidence is especially important since in this case the fixed costs of contract renegotiation argue against switching.

In summary, although there are limitations associated with each of the individual pieces of evidence we offer in this paper, when taken collectively they suggest that the FASB in reducing the accounting opportunity set has eliminated a valuable alternative, that of reporting the activities of a wholly-owned financial subsidiary on an unconsolidated basis. This has occurred despite widespread use of the technique and strong lobbying against the proposal by both reporting firms and users.

There are two aspects of our analysis that we believe are novel yet have potentially broader applicability: (1) We examine the impact of FAS 94 on the horizontal rivals of the nine firms with captive financial subsidiaries that lobby for passage of the proposal. Others have not previously documented that firms lobby for a proposal that would impose costs on themselves in order to impose greater costs on their competitors. (2) We provide an integrated analysis of lobbying with respect to the proposed change, wealth effects of the announced change, and firm responses to this change in accounting standards. Specifically, we argue that the firms that expect to bear the largest costs if the exposure draft is adopted have the greatest incentive to lobby against the proposal. We thus document that firms that lobby against the adoption of FAS 94 realize more negative wealth effects are more likely to sell, reorganize or close a financial subsidiary, retire debt, or securitize assets than other firms.

Appendix

Table 8

Frequency of 232 lobby letters to the FASB on the consolidation exposure draft classified by occupational category. Note that the letters typically contain multiple arguments.

	Industrials	Banking	Public accounting	Securities	Representational organizations	Others	Total
Agree	46	5	8	0	18	8	85
Disagree	77	22	7	9	5	9	129
Comment	8	1	2	0	4	3	18
Total number of letters	131	28	17	9	27	20	232
Time extension	44	3	9	0	10	1	67
Use of cost method	29	2	5	0	5	0	41
Continued unconsolidated disclosures	54	4	9	0	11	1	79
Increased costs	70	22	4	8	4	7	115
Exceptions	14	2	4	2	3	0	25
Reporting entity project	30	9	7	5	3	2	56

References

Amershi, Amin H., Joel S. Demski, and Mark A. Wolfson, 1982, Strategic behavior and regulation research in accounting, Journal of Accounting and Public Policy 1, 19–32.

Comiskey, Eugene E. and Charles W. Mulford, 1989, Financial statements and the adoption of SFAS 94, Working paper (Georgia Institute of Technology, Atlanta, GA).

Comiskey, Eugene E., Ruth Ann McEwen, and Charles W. Mulford, 1987, A test of proforma consolidation of finance subsidiaries, Financial Management 16, 45–50.

Copeland, Ronald M. and Sharon McKinnon, 1987, Financial distortion and consolidation of captive finance subsidiaries in the general merchandising industry, Journal of Business Finance and Accounting 14, 77–97.

Haring, J.R., 1979, Accounting rules and the accounting establishment, Journal of Business 52, 507–519.

Heian, James B. and James B. Thies, 1989, Consolidation of finance subsidiaries $230 billion in off-balance-sheet financing comes home to roost, Accounting Horizon 3, 1–9.

Hess, Alan C. and Clifford W. Smith, 1988, Elements of mortgage securitization, Journal of Real Estate Finance and Economics 1, 331–346.

Kothari, S.P., Tom Lys, Clifford W. Smith, and Ross Watts, 1988, Auditor liability and information disclosure, Journal of Accounting, Auditing and Finance 3, 307–339.

Leftwich, Richard, 1981, Evidence of the impact of mandatory changes in accounting principles on corporate loan agreements, Journal of Accounting and Economics 3, 3–36.

Mian, Shehzad L. and Clifford W. Smith, 1990a, Incentives for unconsolidated financial reporting, Journal of Accounting and Economics 12, 141–171.

Mian, Shehzad L. and Clifford W. Smith, 1990b, Accounts receivable management policy: Theory and evidence, Working paper (University of Rochester, Rochester, NY).

Mohr, Rosanne M., 1988, Unconsolidated finance subsidiaries: Characteristics and debt/equity effects, Accounting Horizons 2, 27–34.

Smith, Clifford W. and Jerold B. Warner, 1979, On financial contracting: An analysis of bond covenants, Journal of Financial Economics 7, 117–161.

Watts, Ross L. and Jerold L. Zimmerman, 1986, Positive accounting theory (Prentice-Hall, Englewood Cliffs, NJ).

Voluntary Corporate Disclosure: The Case of Interim Reporting

RICHARD W. LEFTWICH,* ROSS L. WATTS,† AND
JEROLD L. ZIMMERMAN††

1. Introduction

In the absence of mandatory interim reporting requirements, some firms voluntarily published interim reports. Attempts to mandate interim reporting encountered strong opposition from other firms. In this paper, we investigate the economic incentives of managers of corporations to provide interim reports voluntarily. In particular, we analyze why corporations choose a particular reporting frequency for external purposes. Our approach is in direct contrast to the predominantly normative thrust of much of the accounting literature dealing with interim reporting. Prescriptions concerning the desirable frequency of corporate reporting are common in that literature[1] and much attention is devoted to two related issues: (1) how frequently "should" corporations be required to report to their stockholders (i.e., semiannually, quarterly, or even monthly)? and (2) how "should" interim reports relate to annual reports? Little attention is given to the incentives of managers to choose a particular reporting frequency for external purposes.

_____
* University of Chicago; † University of Rochester; †† University of Rochester. We received helpful comments on earlier versions of this paper from Nick Dopuch, Robert Holthausen, Robert McCormick, Abbie Smith, Jerry Warner, and participants in the Accounting Workshop at the University of Queensland, Australia. We are grateful for those comments, but accept all responsibility for any remaining errors in the paper. This research was partially supported by the Managerial Economics Research Center, Graduate School of Management, University of Rochester and the Institute of Professional Accounting, Graduate School of Business, University of Chicago.

[1] For a summary of such prescriptions see Bollom and Weygandt [1972].

Watts [1977] explains voluntary corporate financial reporting as the residual of individual maximizing in both the market and the political processes. He develops several hypotheses concerning the voluntary presentation of audited financial statements. However, publication of audited annual financial statements in the United States has been mandatory for more than 40 years as a result of requirements of the Securities and Exchange Commission (SEC).[2] As a result, it would be very costly to collect the data necessary for an investigation of annual financial reporting. Instead, we investigate the voluntary provision of interim financial reports prior to when those reports were required by the SEC. In this paper, we explore whether the monitoring process associated with issuing capital to parties outside the firm can explain why managers exceed minimum reporting requirements. The data analysis in the paper is primarily descriptive, but it does yield some conclusions. There are associations between the firms' use of monitoring devices (including interim reporting) and their asset and capital structures. However, there are some puzzling features of the data. The firms that we expect to be most likely to report quarterly, report semiannually.

OUTLINE OF THE PAPER

In Section 2 of the paper, "Attempts to Mandate Interim Reports," we examine the history of interim reporting requirements and opposition to them. Section 3, "Incentives for Voluntary Disclosure," considers the cost–benefit trade-offs influencing managers' decisions to report more frequently than is required. In Section 4, we describe the characteristics of a sample of firms drawn from a time period relatively free of mandated interim reporting. We analyze the capital structures, asset composition, and monitoring devices employed by those firms. We identify some features of firms which report more frequently than is mandated. Section 5 contains our conclusions.

2. Attempts to Mandate Interim Reports

For many years, stock exchanges and the SEC were unsuccessful in their attempts to elicit interim accounting reports from corporations. The endeavors of the NYSE date from the 1920s, before the SEC was established. Both the SEC and the NYSE encountered strong opposition from corporations before eventually achieving their objectives. At least one stock exchange, the American (ASE), opposed interim reporting requirements as recently as 1955. However, despite the opposition from some corporations, other corporations voluntarily provided interim reports, even in the 1920s.

---

[2] To some extent, corporate disclosure laws are simply codification of existing practice (Hunt [1935]). However, as a result of the political process, those laws often serve other functions, such as increasing the resources under the control of politicians and bureaucrats. See Jensen [1976] for a discussion of the incentives of politicians and regulators to increase their own welfare by creating and solving "crises."

In this section of the paper, we trace the history of attempts by the exchanges (primarily the NYSE) and the SEC to mandate interim reporting.

A. STOCK EXCHANGES

In order to satisfy listing requirements, corporate managers must make certain reports to the exchange, for example, notification of proposed dividends. These reporting requirements are part of a "package" of restrictions on listed firms' behavior. In this paper, we are concerned with only part of the package offered by exchanges—accounting reports which enable investors to monitor managers' behavior.

Stock exchanges are intermediaries offering financial services to both corporations and investors. Exchanges establish a market for corporate capital by providing investors with facilities for trading risk and return packages. The survival of an exchange depends on how well it responds to the demand for financial services by corporations and investors.[3]

Different exchanges offer different products, just as different manufacturers of automobiles offer different products. We do not address the question of why any one exchange offers the specific products that it does. Nor do we explain how and why the products offered by one particular exchange differ from those offered by other exchanges. Exchanges must attract and retain customers. Consequently, listing requirements cannot be imposed capriciously.

Different exchanges impose, explicitly or implicitly, different monitoring standards on corporations, and even within an exchange, those standards vary across corporations. Reporting standards are costly, so they can be "imposed" only to the extent that they are demanded (at that price) by investors (who select an exchange for trading) and corporations (who select an exchange for listing).[4] Consider the following example explicitly recognizing constraints on an exchange's power to require interim reports: "This exchange favors the filing of Interim Reports but has not insisted in some cases because *some listings would be lost to the over-the-counter markets where there is no such requirement....* We have talked to our companies at one time or another regarding this subject and we find that some of the smaller corporations object to the filing because their competitors are not listed on the stock exchange and do not make similar information available. Other companies

---

[3] We realize that restrictions on entry and regulation of stock exchanges weaken these arguments about survival. However, the existence of substitute financial intermediation services such as mutual funds and private placement markets reinforces the survival arguments.

[4] We do not imply that each customer gets the exact package he wants. When there are economies of scale in production (or negotiation and contracting) firms offer several standard packages rather than a spectrum of products. For example, automobiles could be (and are) made to order to reflect specific individual tastes, but, given the technology of production, such tailor-made products are so expensive that few customers choose them.

have objected because of the seasonal nature of their business claiming that an Interim Report would be misleading."[5]

Of all the stock exchanges in the U.S., the NYSE has shown the greatest interest in encouraging quarterly reporting, but its attempts to mandate quarterly reports were not immediate successes. Although some corporations listed on the NYSE voluntarily produced quarterly reports in the early 1900s (Taylor [1963, pp. 80–84]), it should be remembered that, in 1900, some listed firms did not even distribute annual accounts to stockholders. The NYSE attempted to require all listed firms to distribute annual accounts, but it admitted its inability to force compliance: "The demand of the investing public for publicity in corporate affairs was not a sufficient force at that time to make effective the request of the Stock Exchange and it was some time before such an agreement was obtained from substantially all listed companies."[6]

Agreements to publish quarterly earnings numbers were obtained by the NYSE from some corporations,[7] but, by 1926, the NYSE admitted its dissatisfaction with the progress: "The Exchange continued to exert its influence to bring about the publication of interim-earnings statements, and, although its efforts in this direction met with ready response in many quarters, it became evident, in 1926, that progress was not being made as rapidly as was consistent with the growing public demand for more frequent publicity. All companies not already under agreement to publish quarterly reports were therefore approached with the request that earnest consideration be given to the matter of publishing their future statements of earnings quarterly."[8]

Some summary statistics from the *NYSE Bulletin* provide evidence of the rate of progress. Of the 957 "active domestic" corporations listed on the NYSE in 1926, 25 percent had agreed to publish quarterly earnings and 8 percent had agreed to publish semiannual earnings. In 1927, the corresponding figures were 37 and 15 percent and the NYSE attributed the increase to its 1926 requests. In 1931, the NYSE again approached corporations not publishing quarterly earnings and claimed that the approach was successful, although no details of the degree of success were cited. After the 1931 approach, 63 percent of active domestic corporations were publishing quarterly earnings and 17 percent were

---

[5] Letter from the President of the Cincinnati Stock Exchange to Robert Taylor, November 1962. Cited in Taylor [1963, p. 16], emphasis added.

[6] *New York Stock Exchange Bulletin*, 10, no. 8 (August 1939). Reprinted in *Journal of Accountancy* (October 1939): 286–88. The quoted material is on page 286 of the reprint. Subsequent references are to *NYSE Bulletin*, with page numbers from the reprint.

[7] Apparently, listing agreements are seldom renegotiated until corporations apply to list a new issue of stock or bonds. Thus, even if listing conditions for new issues are revised, there can be a considerable time lag before those conditions apply to all issues which are listed. Taylor [1963, p. 11] describes this negotiation process.

[8] *NYSE Bulletin* [1939, p. 286]. An interesting question, beyond the scope of the present study, is why the NYSE became interested in requiring its listed firms to publish interim reports in the 1920s and not, say, in the late 1800s?

publishing semiannual earnings. How much of the increase from 1927 to 1931 was due to NYSE action is a moot point. The 1927 figures refer to those companies "under agreement" to publish at those intervals, but the 1931 figures refer to those companies actually publishing. The NYSE admitted that "these figures included companies which were regularly but informally following the practice of publishing more frequent earnings, although not under agreement to do so."[9]

By 1939, the NYSE listing agreement required quarterly earnings reports, with exceptions made "only upon presentation of convincing reasons that such reports would be impractical or misleading." Nevertheless, approximately 100 active domestic corporations did not publish any interim reports. The NYSE itself admitted that "many of these companies are engaged in similar lines of business as, and are otherwise comparable to, other listed companies which now publish quarterly reports"[10]—not particularly convincing testimony to support the view that the NYSE was able to impose its requirements on listed corporations.

Only two other exchanges in the U.S. require quarterly reports—the Philadelphia-Baltimore-Washington and the American.[11] The American was not an ardent advocate until relatively recently. When the SEC proposed mandatory quarterly reporting in 1955, the American expressed its opposition to the proposal. It was not until 1962 that the ASE listing agreement was modified to require firms seeking new listings to publish quarterly earnings.

B. SECURITIES AND EXCHANGE COMMISSION

The SEC had the authority to require quarterly reports when it was established in 1934, but its attempts to require them met considerable opposition. The first quarterly reporting requirements were imposed by the SEC in 1945, but only as a part of a program to provide investors with information about firms' transition from wartime contracts to peacetime production. In particular, quarterly sales and unfilled orders pursuant to war contracts were to be disclosed. In 1946, the SEC proposed mandatory quarterly income reports for corporations under its jurisdictions. After adverse comments were received, the proposal was withdrawn and replaced by a requirement to file quarterly sales or gross revenues on form 8–K. In 1952, the SEC again proposed that the quarterly reporting requirements be extended to encompass the entire income statement. This proposal encountered strong opposition from corporations and stock exchanges.[12] At that time the SEC's authority did not extend to the over-the-counter market and the exchanges expressed concern at the potential loss of business: "A listed corporation may delist its securities in the event that any rule or regulation published by the Commission substan-

---

[9]*NYSE Bulletin* [1939, p. 287].
[10]*NYSE Bulletin* [1939, p. 288].
[11] Taylor [1963, p. 15].
[12] Taylor [1963, pp. 28–31].

tially alters or adds to the obligation of the corporation. In extending this open invitation to delisting, ... the Commission should study whether this move is in the best interests of investors and whether the risk of complete loss of information to investors is not greater than the relatively minor gains proposed."[13]

After reviewing the comments on its proposal, the SEC reversed its position. The 1952 proposal for quarterly income statements was dropped and, in addition, the requirement for quarterly sales reporting on form 8-K was abandoned. Some corporations responded by ceasing to publish that quarterly data. The Financial Analysts Federation (FAF) expressed concern at the loss of information valuable to investors (and, incidentally, to analysts) and mounted a campaign to obtain agreement from corporations to publish quarterly data voluntarily. The FAF was disillusioned by the negative response to its friendly overtures and resorted instead to intensive lobbying with the SEC because it was "necessary to have a certain amount of regulations and laws in order to get the things that are the greatest good for the greatest number."[14]

In 1955, the SEC proposed a semiannual filing of form 9-K covering both sales and earnings. The report was to be filed only once per year, 45 days after the end of the first half of the fiscal year. Most corporations reporting to federal regulatory bodies were exempt from the requirement. Due to a change in SEC policy, the 201 comment letters were made public. Only 2 of the 70 favorable responses were from corporations—the remainder came from security analysts or their professional associations. Corporations accounted for 57 of the 63 unfavorable responses, and they objected essentially on two grounds: (i) the distortion caused by seasonal factors, and (ii) the difficulty of interim income measurement. However, the SEC enforced its proposal the same year.

The SEC extended its interim reporting requirements to quarterly reports in 1970. A 1964 amendment to the Securities and Exchange Commission Act of 1934 gave the SEC power to impose reporting requirements on corporations traded in the over-the-counter market. This amendment overcame the objections of the exchanges concerning voluntary delisting of securities to avoid SEC reporting requirements. Following the Wheat Report, the SEC rescinded the semi-annual form 9-K in 1970 and introduced a detailed quarterly income report on form 10-Q.[15]

None of the SEC or stock exchange regulations concerning interim reports requires that such reports be sent to stockholders. The stock exchanges require publication (e.g., through press releases) and the SEC requires filing in public record. There are no auditing requirements.

---

[13] Letter to the SEC from the President of the American Stock Exchange in February 1955. Cited by Taylor [1963, p. 19].

[14] From the report of the chairman of the Corporate Information Committee of the FAF to the directors of the FAF. Cited by Taylor [1963, p. 35].

[15] For the purposes of this paper, later modifications of the requirements are not relevant.

The history we have sketched in this section reveals that opposition to interim reporting requirements was not universal. Some corporations voluntarily provided those reports long before the SEC required them. In the next section, we explore the economic incentives for some managers to produce interim reports voluntarily and for other managers to oppose mandatory interim reporting.

3. Incentives for Voluntary Disclosure

Traditional theories of the firm in accounting and finance view the stockholders as "owners" of the firm. Recent advances in the theory of the firm suggest a richer model of the firm—the firm represents a "nexus of contracts," implicit and explicit, between suppliers of various factors of production.[16] The nexus of contracts view has particular appeal for accounting because many of those contracts are defined and monitored in terms of accounting numbers. We focus on one particular subset of the contracts—those associated with the supply of capital, in particular, debt and equity capital. To investigate the monitoring arrangements associated with those contracts, we resort to the framework of analysis developed in Jensen and Meckling [1976], now commonly known as "agency theory." We first discuss the benefits of monitoring whenever managers do not hold all of the firm's capital. We then outline various methods of monitoring this agency relationship. We conclude the section by discussing the costs of various forms of monitoring and the derived demand for accounting reports as a monitoring device.

A. BENEFITS OF MONITORING

If a firm issues any form of capital to outsiders (nonmanagers), an agency relationship exists between the holders of outside capital (the principals) and the managers (the agents).[17] An agency relationship gives rise to "agency costs" because the agent is expected to act in his own interest, which need not be consistent with the interests of the principals.[18] Of course, the holders of outside capital are aware of the potential agency problems and anticipate the behavior of the agents when they

---

[16] Jensen and Meckling [1976]. Also, see Alchian and Demsetz [1972] and Fama [1980].

[17] Jensen and Meckling [1976, p. 308] define an agency relationship as "a contract under which one or more persons (the principal(s)) engage another person (the agent) to perform some services on their behalf which involves delegating some decision making authority to the agent."

[18] The nature of the outside capital determines what form the agency costs assume. If the outside capital has residual claims (e.g., equity), the agent (manager) has incentives to divert the firm's resources to his own use. If the outside capital has a fixed claim against the firm's cash flows (e.g., debt), the holders of the residual claims (both internal and external) can benefit if the firm's investment policy is changed in favor of more risky assets or if the firm pays out its assets in dividends and leaves the fixed claim holders with the "shell" of the corporation. See Jensen and Meckling [1976, pp. 312–43] for a detailed analysis of the agency costs of debt and equity financing.

price their claims. Agents have incentives to devote resources to reduce the divergence between their actual behavior and that desired by the principal. The principal can constrain and monitor the agents' behavior and the agents can offer to impose certain restrictions on their own behavior through bonding arrangements, rather than have holders of outside capital price the claims to reflect all the anticipated divergence.

Expenditures on monitoring can reduce agency costs. Consequently, the higher the level of agency costs, the greater the incentives for managers to employ monitoring. We expect that expenditure on monitoring is an increasing function of the proportion of the firm's assets that is financed by outside capital, because the incidence of agency costs is higher for firms of the same size with a greater proportion of outside capital. Moreover, the benefits of monitoring (and thus the expenditure on monitoring) depend on the asset structure of the firm (e.g., assets in place vs. growth opportunities)[19] and the composition of the financial claims (e.g., inside vs. outside capital)[20] because agency costs depend on both those factors.

Managers incur expenditures on one or more of the following monitoring devices:[21] (i) publication of accounting reports, (ii) appointment of outside directors, (iii) listing requirements of stock exchanges.

(i) *Publication of accounting reports.* Before there were any requirements by statute or administrative law, owners of corporations "going public" contracted in the articles of incorporation or bylaws to provide audited annual financial statements (Watts [1977] and Watts and Zimmerman [1979; 1980]).[22] These statements enable outside common and preference shareholders and fixed-claim holders to determine if contract provisions have been violated. Moreover, it is in the interests of the manager to provide these reports voluntarily: "Suppose, for example, that the bondholders (or outside equity holders) would find it worthwhile to produce detailed financial statements such as those contained in the usual published accounting reports as a means of monitoring the manager. If the manager himself can produce such information at lower costs than they (perhaps because he is already collecting much of the data for his own internal decision making purposes), it would pay him to agree in

---

[19] See Myers [1977].

[20] See Jensen and Meckling [1976].

[21] This is not an exhaustive list of monitoring devices. For example, information gathering by security analysts and the market for managers can monitor and discipline corporate managers. Similarly, stock option plans can provide incentives for managers to take the interests of stockholders into account. We do not discuss these monitoring devices in this paper because we have no data to enable us to determine how they impact the sample of firms we describe below. Like other omitted variables, these variables could affect our sample of firms cross-sectionally and confound or reinforce any results we obtain in our tests.

[22] Further, the auditors were liable for breaches of covenants in the corporations' articles or bylaws (Watts [1977, p. 59]). The ability of an auditor to reduce agency costs is reflected in the auditor's reputation, i.e., in the auditor's "brand name."

advance to incur the cost of providing such reports and to have their accuracy testified to by an independent outside auditor."[23]

Trustees for fixed-claim holders and insurance companies holding fixed claims monitor lending agreements. Typically, in the indenture agreements for public and private debt, we observe covenants requiring corporate managers to file annual and interim accounts with the trustee or insurance company.[24] The annual financial statements must be audited, but there is no such requirement for the interim reports. Thus, even private lenders, such as insurance companies, do not obtain audited interim reports. Lending agreements usually require the officers of the corporation to certify compliance with the covenants,[25] and private lending agreements often require the auditors to certify that they have not obtained any knowledge of a breach of the covenants during their annual audit.[26] The officers' and auditors' certificates combined with the annual audit enable the interim reports to serve as a monitoring device even though they are not audited. We investigate the public provision of interim financial reports as a monitoring device because those reports were provided voluntarily in a period for which we can obtain data, while annual reports were mandatory.

(*ii*) *Appointment of outside directors.* When outside capital is raised, outside directors are often appointed to the corporation's board of directors. Juran and Louden [1966, pp. 19–21] suggest that outside directors of publicly-held corporations perform two functions:[27] (1) they increase the effectiveness of the chief executive officer (CEO) by providing expertise and experience; and (2) they serve as trustees for the nonmanager owners, especially as the corporation grows and the shares are more widely held.

As an alternative function to (2), we suggest that outside directors monitor the manager's behavior for external suppliers of fixed capital, for example, debt holders. The lender can monitor the manager's actions at lower cost if it has a representative on the borrower's board of directors. The most common occupations of outside directors are banker and

---

[23] Jensen and Meckling [1976, p. 338].

[24] For example, see the Indenture Agreement between Household Finance Corporation and Mellon Bank NA (as trustee) dated January 15, 1977 (section 9.04) and between the Southland Corporation and Mercantile National Bank at Dallas (as trustee) dated February 15, 1977 (section 5.03) and the Note Agreement between Brunswick Corporation and the Prudential Insurance Company of America dated May 11, 1976 (section 5A).

[25] See sections 4.05, 4.11, and 5A of the Household Finance, Southland Corporation, and Brunswick Corporation agreements referred to in n. 24. Making managers of the corporation liable for defaults in the lending agreement avoids some agency problems. The manager is made legally liable for all damages from the breach, but receives only a fraction of the benefits.

[26] See section 5A of the Brunswick Agreement. It is not clear why public placements restrict themselves to the officer's certificate and do not require the auditor to certify compliance.

[27] Fama [1980] argues that directors serve a much broader constituency. In Fama's view, directors monitor the contracts with suppliers of factors of production and thus can represent creditors, employees, etc.

insurance company director.[28] In the sample of listed firms below, we note that commercial banks often have a representative on the board of companies to which they make loans.[29]

(iii) *Listing requirements of stock exchanges.* The stock exchanges' monitoring of corporate management behavior takes two forms. First, in order to meet listing requirements, corporate bylaws have to contain certain covenants, which, in turn, reduce agency costs. Second, as we discuss in Section 2, stock exchanges require listed firms to publish accounting reports on a regular basis. The reporting requirements of the NYSE are more stringent than those of other exchanges. It appears that the NYSE offers investors more intensive monitoring and thus attracts listings from corporations that value the monitoring, that is, given that the NYSE offers an intensive monitoring package, we expect some natural selection among firms choosing that exchange for listing.

B. COSTS OF MONITORING

Managers of firms can choose any level and combination of the monitoring devices (i), (ii), and (iii) above, that is, managers can determine the frequency of external reporting, the exchange listing, and the number of outside directors. Managers select a monitoring package, and the composition of the chosen package depends on the costs and benefits of the various monitoring devices. In part A above, we discuss the benefits of employing different forms of monitoring. Below, we discuss the costs of monitoring.

(i) *Publication of accounting reports.* The most commonly cited costs of interim reporting are: (a) the advantage such information could give to competitors, (b) the out-of-pocket costs associated with taking inventory, calculating accruals, etc., for interim income determination, and (c) the allegedly misleading nature of the information in a seasonal business.[30]

Without necessarily endorsing the validity of these arguments, we could test them by trying to construct proxies for such variables as the cost to the firm of providing competitors with additional information, the out-of-pocket costs of interim reporting, and the costs due to the seasonal variability of the firm's earnings. For example, it could be argued that interim reporting by diversified firms would provide less information to competitors than would be provided by interim reports of firms in single

---

[28] See the 1961 National Industrial Conference Board survey of 431 manufacturing firms reported in Koontz [1967]. Juran and Louden [1966, p. 203] state that "commercial bankers are the most usual category of outsider on the board."

[29] We also offer some tangential evidence that outside banker-directors serve a monitoring function. The NYSE requires that listed firms have an audit committee composed solely of directors "independent of management control" and explicitly states that commercial bankers with whom the corporation has dealings qualify as directors "independent of management control." See "Rules of Board—Listing Policies and Procedures," *New York Stock Exchange Guide,* Poor's 2495 G and H (New York: Commerce Clearing House).

[30] For a sample of these arguments, see *NYSE Bulletin* [1939, p. 287] and Taylor [1963, pp. 131–78].

industries. If taking inventory accounted for most of the out-of-pocket costs of interim reporting, we could use the value of inventory as a proxy for out-of-pocket costs.

We suspect that the marginal out-of-pocket costs of external reporting are low for many listed firms because they have some form of internal interim reporting. However, the marginal cost of reporting that information externally could be high because of the potential legal liability resulting from public disclosure. Taylor [1963, pp. 8–9] cites a similar argument by Gilman [1939, p. 77]: "It is, of course, true that most business organizations do prepare monthly or at least quarterly reports, but these are generally regarded as operating reports for the guidance of operating men and are seldom considered sufficiently reliable in certain respects for general publication."

(*ii*) *Appointment of outside directors.* We expect that the costs of employing outside directors on the board comprise the higher decision-making costs due to the increased size of the board (or the opportunity cost of a displaced insiders' expertise if the board size remains constant) and the cost of potential leakage of information to competitors.

(*iii*) *Listing requirements of stock exchanges.* Firms must conform to the restrictions in the stock exchange listing requirements. Thus, listing requirements impose costs on a firm to the extent that the benefits of particular restrictions are less than the costs of those restrictions. The costs of listing are the net costs of the actual set of requirements less the net costs of the set of restrictions the firm would choose if those restrictions could be "tailor-made."

C. DERIVED DEMAND FOR INTERIM REPORTING

We recognize that, in equilibrium, the optimal level and form of monitoring depends on the costs and benefits of the various forms of monitoring. However, as we discuss in Appendix A, there are theoretical and econometric problems in estimating the equilibrium relation. We attempt to abstract from those problems by assuming that there is no cross-sectional or time-series variation in the costs of monitoring. Consequently, any cross-sectional or time-series variation in the costs (and endogeneity problems) can confound the analysis we conduct in the next section. We return to these problems when we interpret the results.

In this paper, we are concerned primarily with examining how the use of one monitoring method (the frequency of external reporting) varies across firms and through time. We investigate whether any of that cross-sectional and time-series variation is a function of variables that are suggested by agency theory, that is, differences in firms' capital structures, asset structures, and choices of other monitoring devices. We analyze the cross-sectional variation by estimating the following derived demand function for interim reporting:

$$R = h(A, V, L, P, OD, R', X) \qquad (1)$$

where:[31] R = reporting frequency, A = ratio of assets in place, V = size of the firm, L = leverage ratio for debt, P = leverage ratio for preferred stock, OD = use of outside directors, R' = reporting frequency ten years beforehand, X = exchange listing.

Similarly we analyze the time-series variation by estimating the function:

$$\Delta R = k(\Delta A, \Delta V, \Delta L, \Delta P, \Delta OD, \Delta X) \qquad (2)$$

where Δ indicates the change in the above variables over time.

We include the assets-in-place variable (A) to control for the asset structure of the firm. Myers [1977] suggests that, for a given level of fixed claims, agency costs are lower, the higher the ratio of the value of the corporation's assets in place (assets already owned) to the value of its growth opportunities because it is more costly to shift the risk of existing assets than future assets. Thus, we expect that the frequency of reporting is greater if more of the total value of the firm is represented by future growth opportunities.

The size variable is included in equations (1) and (2) to control for the agency costs of outside capital. We have no data on the amount of outside capital issued by firms, but we suggest that the larger the firm, the higher the proportion of the capital held by outsiders.[32] However, we cannot predict the effect of size on the reporting frequency because of omitted supply-side variables. For example, there are more sources of information (other than accounting reports) for larger firms. Further, firm size also will proxy for industry, political costs, exchange listing, etc., thereby diluting its effectiveness as a proxy for agency costs of outside capital.[33]

According to Jensen and Meckling [1976], the agency cost of outside capital depends on the form of the claims held by outsiders. Thus, we include leverage variables (L and P) to control for cross-sectional and time-series variation in the types of outside capital issued by firms. We do not include a variable in the equation for the proportion of equity because the leverage variables will capture that effect.

We include variables in (1) and (2) to represent the exchange listing (X) and the presence of outside directors (OD) because we expect managers to choose a package of monitoring arrangements, that is, the use of one form of monitoring (interim reporting) depends on the use of other forms of monitoring. However, in addition to the problems we discuss above and in Appendix A, a priori we cannot determine whether, in equilibrium, monitoring activities of outside directors and exchanges substitute for or complement an increased reporting frequency. For example, if they are complements, the presence of an outside director on

---

[31] In the next section, we give precise definitions of these variables and their proxies.

[32] This is consistent with Jensen and Meckling [1976, pp. 346–51].

[33] Other proxies for outside capital were also tried: number of outside shareholders and proportion of common stock owned by outsiders.

a corporation's board is a signal that managers have selected an "intensive" monitoring package and there is a higher probability that the corporation publishes interim reports. On the other hand, if they are substitutes, the presence of an outside director on a firm's board indicates that the firm is being closely monitored already and there is a lower probability that the firm publishes interim reports.

The variable representing the historical reporting frequency of the firm (R') is included in the cross-sectional analysis to capture any "inertia" effect. We are interested in whether monitoring has any marginal explanatory power with regard to a firm's reporting frequency when compared with alternative explanations. A naive view is that firms choose a particular reporting frequency virtually at random, for example, based on what directors consider is the "norm" for a particular industry, and adhere to this frequency once it has been adopted.

In the next section of the paper, we discuss the data and the methodology used to estimate equations (1) and (2) and present the results.

4. Data, Methodology, and Results

After describing the data and presenting some descriptive statistics, this section presents estimates of both cross-sectional and time-series functions.

A. DATA

For the cross-sectional analysis we chose a random sample of industrial corporations with common stocks listed on either the NYSE or the ASE in 1948. 1948 was selected because initially we used a data source to determine frequency of reporting that spanned the years 1935–48. We wanted a time period as far removed from the depression and World War II as possible, to avoid any major recapitalizations or governmental influences due to the depression or the War, but yet before the SEC mandated quarterly income reports. Every fifth corporation listed alphabetically in the *Commercial and Financial Chronicle* quotations for the NYSE on December 31, 1948 was included in the sample.[34] An approximately equal number of ASE firms was obtained by adjusting the selection frequency. This selection procedure yielded 83 NYSE firms and 82 ASE firms.

In the time-series investigation we examine the change in reporting frequency of the 1948 sample of firms over the period 1937–48.[35] We used Moody's *News Reports*, a twice-weekly publication, to classify firms as quarterly, semiannual, or annual earnings reporters in 1948. As a check

---

[34] The first company was selected by choosing a random number between one and five. Thereafter, every fifth company was chosen. If that company was a railroad or utility, the next company in alphabetical order was substituted.

[35] 1937 was "chosen" by our research assistant, who, when told to gather 1938 data, used the 1938 *Moody Manual*. The existence of this footnote is evidence of agency costs of research assistants.

on this classification procedure we examined NYSE listing applications for details of the required reporting frequency in the debt contracts of our sample firms. Unfortunately, too few firms actually include debt covenants for us to make a systematic codification of the data. However, in the few cases where we did find the details in the listing applications, the covenants require a greater frequency of reports than we observed in the *News Reports*.

There are at least two possible explanations for the discrepancy between Moody's and the debt covenants: (*i*) Moody's publish only a subset of interim reports, and (*ii*) the firms report to debt holders or trustees for debt holders more frequently than to shareholders. To the extent that the first reason is correct, we are less likely to find any relationship between the reporting frequency in Moody's and the variables we describe in Section 3. If the second reason is correct, it suggests (given that the marginal out-of-pocket costs of reporting to shareholders in addition to debt holders are small) that other costs of publicizing the data are behind the decision not to publish the interim reports. These other costs could include: legal costs (due to increased frequency of lawsuits), costs of providing information to competitors, costs of providing information to labor unions, and political costs.

Table 1 reports the frequency of interim reporting across the two exchanges according to Moody's *News Reports*. NYSE firms report significantly more frequently than ASE firms, indicating that the NYSE firms were subject to more intense monitoring than ASE firms. Only 7 of the 83 NYSE firms produce no interim reports, whereas 47 of the ASE firms produce no interim reports.

Financial data for each firm in our sample was obtained from the 1938 and 1949 editions of Moody's *Industrial Manual*. The empirical proxies used to estimate the cross-sectional model (equation (3)) are:

(*i*) *Assets in place* (A) is proxied by the ratio of property (land, buildings, and equipment) net of depreciation to firm value, V. $A4$ and $A3$ denote assets in place in 1948 and 1937, respectively.

(*ii*) *Value of the firm* (V) is the sum of the market value of the common[36] and the book values of current liabilities, long-term debt, and preferred stock. $V4$ and $V3$ denote the value of the firm in 1948 and 1937, respectively.

(*iii*) *Debt* (L) is measured by the ratio of the sum of the book values of bank loans, public, and private debt to firm value, V. $L4$ and $L3$ denote the proportion of long-term debt in 1948 and 1937, respectively.

(*iv*) *Preferred stock* (P) is measured by the ratio of book values of preferred equity to firm value, V. $P4$ and $P3$ denote the proportion of preferred stock in 1948 and 1937, respectively.

---

[36] Market value of the common is computed as the product of the number of shares outstanding on the balance sheet date and the average of the high and low prices as reported in Moody's.

TABLE 1

Number of Firms and Frequency of Interim Reporting by Stock Exchange for 1948

	Stock Exchange		Total Number of Firms
	ASE	NYSE	
Annual reports only	47	7	54
Semiannual reports	13	19	32
Quarterly reports	22	57	79
Total	82	83	165

$\chi^2 = 46.26$ with 2 degrees of freedom, significant at .01.

(v) *Outside directors (OD).* The outside director variable is proxied by a dummy variable which is set to one if any nonmanager director is a manager or director of a bank or insurance company.[37] We identified each sample firm's directors from the 1948 edition of Moody's *Industrial Manual,* and the occupation of nonmanager directors was determined from Poor's *Register of Directors and Executives* (1948) and *Who's Who in Finance and Industry* (volume 6).

(vi) *Reporting frequency (R).* The extent of interim reporting is a dichotomous variable, taking the value of zero or one depending on the frequency of reporting as disclosed by Moody's *News Reports.* $R4$ and $R3$ denote the frequency of reporting in 1948 and 1937, respectively.

(vii) *Exchange (X).* The exchange listing is represented by a dummy variable which takes the value of one for NYSE firms and zero for ASE firms. $X4$ and $X3$ denote the firm's exchange listing in 1948 and 1937, respectively.

B. DESCRIPTIVE STATISTICS

Table 2 presents means and standard deviations of the firm's assets and capital structure by exchange. The average firm listed in the NYSE is over five times larger than its ASE counterpart as measured by total assets, has almost five times as much debt, has a higher proportion of fixed assets and funded debt, and is more likely to have a banker or insurance director on the board. Although NYSE firms are more highly levered than ASE firms, the average firm on both exchanges has relatively little debt in its capital structure.

Table 3 contains the simple correlations among the measures of capital structure for each exchange. The top correlation is for the NYSE firms

---

[37] As an alternative proxy for the *OD* variable, we calculate the ratio of the number of outside directors from banks and insurance companies to the total number of directors. The results of our tests are insensitive to the form of the proxy. Due to the high cost of collecting this information, we collected it for 1948 only. (Note: Professor Burton, in his comments, suggests using proportion of outside directors on the board. This variable also was used and the above definition produced slightly superior results.)

TABLE 2

Summary Statistics Means and Standard Deviations of Variables Classified by Stock Exchange for 164 Sample Firms in 1948

Variable	Label	Exchange			
		NYSE		ASE	
		Mean	Standard Deviation	Mean	Standard Deviation
Total assets (000s)		160,231**	362,238	29,826**	114,005
Debt (000s)		14,730**	38,298	3,094**	14,560
Market value	V4	146,182**	267,685	35,800**	175,779
Fixed assets/market value	A4	.394*	.288	.321*	.232
Debt/market value	L4	.077	.102	.053	.102
Preferred stock/market value	P4	.068	.098	.056	.109
Outside directors dummy	OD	.639	.483	.531	.502
No. firms in sample		83		81†	

* Means are different at the 10-percent level of significance using pooled variances.
** Means are different at the 5-percent level of significance using pooled variances.
† One firm was deleted due to missing data.

TABLE 3

Simple Correlations Between Variables for 164 Sample Firms in 1948/Top Correlation Is for the 83 NYSE Firms and Bottom Correlation Is for the 81 ASE Firms

	Fixed Assets to Market Value (A4)	Debt to Market Value (L4)	Outside Director (OD)	Market Value of Firm (V4)	Preferred Stock to Market Value (P4)
A4	1.00				
	1.00				
L4	.064	1.00			
	.388*	1.00			
OD	.118	−.034	1.00		
	.197	.045	1.00		
V4	.218	.128	.111	1.00	
	.050	.070	−.075	1.00	
P4	−.141	.082	−.130	.034	1.00
	.045	.111	.095	−.059	1.00

* Greater than two standard errors from zero.

and the bottom correlation is for the ASE firms. The only correlation coefficient that is at least two standard errors from zero is the correlation between the ratio of debt to market value and the ratio of fixed assets to market value for ASE firms, which is .388. The critical value for 81 firms is .22. This is consistent with Myers' [1977] prediction.

C. PROBIT ESTIMATES OF INTERIM REPORTING IN 1948

In this subsection we estimate equation (1) in the following form using 1948 data:

$$R4_i = \beta_0 + \beta_1 A4_i + \beta_2 V4_i + \beta_3 L4_i + \beta_4 P4_i$$
$$+ \beta_5 OD_i + \beta_6 R3_i + \beta_7 X4_i + \epsilon_i \tag{3}$$

where: $R4$ = frequency of interim reporting in 1948,
       $A4$ = assets in place in 1948,
       $V4$ = the value of the firm in 1948,
       $L4$ = debt in 1948,
       $P4$ = preferred stock in 1948,
      OD = outside directors (as of 1948),
       $R3$ = frequency of interim reporting in 1937,
       $X4$ = stock exchange listing in 1948.

Table 4 reports the results of estimating equation (3) using the probit probability model.[38]

Four different definitions of 1948 interim reporting are used in table 4. In the first definition, numbered 1, $R4_i$ is zero if the firm is an annual reporter and one otherwise. In the second definition, $R4_i$ is zero for annual reporters and one for quarterly reporters, that is, the 32 semiannual reporters are excluded from the estimation. In the next definition, numbered 3, $R4_i$ is again zero for annual reporters, but one for semiannual reporters, that is, the 79 quarterly reporters are excluded from the estimation. In the final definition, numbered 4, the 54 annual reporters are excluded—$R4_i$ is zero for semiannual reporters and one for quarterly reporters. Thus, in the definitions, $R4_i$ is zero for "less intensive" reporters and one for "more intensive" reporters.

There are three estimations for each definition of $R4_i$ using different samples. The first sample, the pooled sample, includes all firms with a dummy variable, $X4$, for the exchange. (The dummy is one for NYSE firms and zero for ASE firms.) The other two estimations are for the NYSE and ASE subsamples. Four features of the results are noted.

(*i*) The result in table 1 that NYSE firms are more likely to report quarterly is also apparent in the significance of the exchange variable, $X4$, in table 4 (definitions 1–3) after controlling for the other variables. However, when the annual reporters are excluded in definition 4, NYSE firms are no more likely to report semiannually than ASE firms.

(*ii*) The only variable on the NYSE that is statistically significant is the 1937 reporting frequency, $R3$. On the NYSE, $R3$ is significant and has the same sign across all four definitions. In contrast, $R3$ is significant in only one of the definitions (definition 2) for ASE firms. This suggests that firms on the NYSE in 1948 had more stable reporting frequencies over this period. This is not necessarily attributable to NYSE reporting policies.

---

[38] Probit is a nonlinear maximum likelihood estimation procedure that assumes that the dependent variable, the probability that the firm chooses to issue an interim report, is a continuous random variable that is normally distributed. See Finney [1964]. Inclusion of the dummy variables OD, $R3$, and X does not seriously affect the estimation. Deleting these dummy variables has little effect on the remaining coefficients or their t-statistics. Ordinary least squares (OLS) regressions also were estimated. OLS produced slightly higher t-statistics, with remarkably similar signs and magnitudes of the transformed coefficients.

TABLE 4

Probit Models of the Reporting Frequency in 1948 by Stock Exchange and Pooled Firms

(Asymptotic t-statistics in parentheses)

Dependent Variable	Sample	$\bar{R}^2$	X^2	N	C	A4	V4	LA	P4	OD	R3†	X4
0 = Annual report, 1 = Semiannual or quarterly	Pooled	.33	69.8*	164	-.91 (-3.2)*	-.44 (-.9)	-.25 (-.4)	2.50 (1.9)*	1.11 (.9)	.50 (2.0)*	.93 (3.7)*	1.41 (4.9)*
	NYSE	.20	19.3*	83	.17 (2.5)*	-1.15 (-1.1)	-.28 (-.3)	3.24 (.8)	-2.63 (-.7)	.88 (1.3)	2.42 (2.8)*	
	ASE	.06	10.9*	81	-.65 (-1.9)*	-.77 (-1.1)	-.55 (-.4)	2.50 (1.6)	1.28 (.9)	.58 (1.9)*	.49 (1.6)	
0 = Annual report, 1 = Quarterly	Pooled	.40	67.9*	132	-1.22 (-3.7)*	-.14 (-.3)	-.36 (-.4)	1.86 (1.2)	-.25 (-.2)	.56 (2.0)*	1.24 (3.8)*	1.41 (4.4)*
	NYSE	.23	19.1*	64	-.11 (-.1)	-1.34 (-1.2)	-.20 (-.1)	3.98 (.9)	-1.66 (-.4)	.87 (1.1)	2.86 (2.5)*	
	ASE	.02	8.2	68	-1.05 (-2.5)*	.27 (.4)	-7.80 (-.7)	.66 (.3)	-.77 (-.4)	.65 (1.9)*	.70 (1.7)*	
0 = Annual report, 1 = Semiannual	Pooled	.35	39.8*	85	-1.48 (-3.9)*	-1.22 (-1.7)*	.01 (.01)	4.15 (2.6)*	2.81 (1.9)*	.49 (1.4)	.90 (2.2)*	1.53 (3.8)*
	NYSE	.23	14.0*	26	-.42 (-.4)	-1.04 (-.8)	.45 (.3)	-.82 (-.2)	-5.18 (-.8)	1.03 (1.2)	3.45 (2.2)*	
	ASE	.22	21.0*	59	-.99 (-2.2)*	-3.78 (-2.7)*	.35 (.2)	6.79 (3.1)*	5.27 (2.4)*	.49 (1.1)	.08 (.1)	
0 = Semiannual, 1 = Quarterly	Pooled	.10	19.0*	111	.38 (1.1)	1.41 (2.1)*	-.92 (-1.6)	-2.62 (-1.9)*	-.52 (-.4)	-.18 (-.6)	.51 (3.0)*	.10 (.3)
	NYSE	.09	12.8*	76	.39 (1.0)	.64 (.9)	-.74 (-1.3)	-.90 (-.5)	1.88 (.9)	-.17 (-.4)	.62 (2.9)*	
	ASE	.44	30.2*	35	.15 (.2)	16.0 (1.8)*	-54.3 (-1.7)*	-23.7 (-1.9)*	-9.36 (-1.5)	-.75 (-.6)	.21 (.5)	

* Significant at 10-percent level two-tail test for t-statistics or exceeds 95-percent fractile of X^2 distribution. $\bar{R}^2$ is the adjusted R^2 from estimating the corresponding ordinary least squares regression.

† If a firm's reporting frequency in 1937 was not reported in Moody's *News Reports*, it was assumed to be an annual.

(*iii*) For the ASE firms, the variable—outside directors (*OD*)—is statistically significant in definitions 1 and 2. This result is due primarily to the greater frequency of outside directors on boards of ASE quarterly reporters. (We confirm this below.)

(*iv*) There is an anomaly with semiannual reporters on the ASE. In definition 3, the higher the assets in place the less likely the firm will report more frequently, whereas in definition 4 the higher the assets in place the more likely the firm will report more frequently. There are similar sign reversals for debt, *L*4, and preferred stock, *P*4.

In summary, the capital structure variables (*V*4, *L*4, and *P*4) and the asset structure variable (*A*4) are significant only in definitions 3 and 4 for the ASE firms. And the signs of these coefficients are inconsistent across these two cases if semiannual reporting is considered less intensive monitoring than quarterly reporting. As noted, one of the alternative monitoring inputs—the exchange variable, *X*4—is generally significant, and the other monitoring variable, *OD*, is significant for ASE firms except when semiannual reporters are considered separately.[39]

We investigated the ASE semiannual reporting anomaly further. We could not find any evidence of an industry effect among the semiannual reporters. Those firms include mining, tobacco, department store, steel, and paper companies. For virtually every semiannual reporting firm in our sample, there is another firm in the same industry that does not report semiannually. Table 5 reports summary statistics by exchange for each type of reporting firm. For both NYSE and ASE firms, mean market and total asset values are larger for semiannual reporters than for either annual or quarterly reporters. However, these differences are not significant at the 0.1 level. Two of the three largest firms on both the NYSE and ASE are semiannual reporters, although an examination of the size distribution reveals that semiannual reporters are uniformly distributed across the various size categories.[40] Thus, semiannual reporters are among the largest and smallest of firms and come from most industries sampled.

While the differences are not significant, the frequency of outside directors is highest among ASE firms for quarterly reporters. This result

---

[39] A number of diagnostic and specification tests were performed on the estimated models reported in table 4: (*i*) Scaling assets in place, debt, and preferred stock by total assets instead of market value of the firm produced generally slightly higher *t*-statistics, but no sign reversals on the estimated coefficients. (*ii*) Deleting *R*3, the firm's interim reporting frequency in 1937, does not alter the significance levels of the remaining coefficients (excluding the constant). (*iii*) Age of the firm was included as a proxy for when the firm was listed. Newly listed firms are more likely to have signed a listing application requiring interim reporting than older firms that were listed before the NYSE became interested in interim reporting. The coefficient on age was statistically insignificant, and deleting it did not affect the remaining coefficients. (*iv*) Firm size as measured by total assets was substituted for market value. The results were essentially the same.

[40] The distribution of total assets is very skewed. The total assets of the two largest NYSE firms are 4 and 6.5 standard deviations from the mean. The largest semiannual reporter on the ASE is 5 standard deviations from the mean of total assets of ASE firms. If firms are ranked by total assets and the number of semiannual reporters in each tricile is

is consistent with the significant coefficients of *OD* previously reported in table 4. Table 5 also reveals that semiannual ASE reporters have lower assets in place than either annual or quarterly reporters and higher debt and preferred leverage ratios (the leverage ratio differences are statistically significant but the assets-in-place differences are not). These differences are consistent with the anomaly reported in table 4. This evidence, like the ASE probit estimates (definitions 3 and 4) in table 4, suggests that reporting frequency and capital and asset structures are associated, albeit not all in the direction expected. The semiannual firms have the lowest assets in place and highest leverage ratios and, therefore, we expect the highest agency costs, but they are not the most monitored in terms of reporting frequency.

Further analysis of the semiannual reporters was conducted. They do not have a different dividend payment frequency from quarterly or annual reporters; nor do they have abnormally good or bad earnings records prior to 1948; nor do they have abnormal stock price rates of return around 1948.[41] Moreover, there is no association between frequency of reporting and state of incorporation. However, there is an association between reporting frequency and auditor for the ASE firms. Semiannual ASE reporters are less likely to engage a Big Six auditor (Haskins & Sells, Price Waterhouse, Arthur Andersen, Ernst & Ernst, Peat Marwick, and Lybrand Ross & Montgomery) than ASE quarterly or annual reporters.[42] Only 15 percent of the ASE semiannual reporters have a Big Six auditor, whereas 43 and 59 percent of the ASE annual and quarterly reporters, respectively, had a Big Six auditor. These differences are significant at the 0.1 level. If a dummy variable representing auditor (one is Big Six and zero otherwise) is added to the regression[43] in table 4, coefficients on these dummy variables have *t*-statistics of -2.77 and 3.53 in definitions 3 and 4 for ASE firms.

calculated, the following distribution results:

Number of Semiannual Reporters in Each Size Category

	Ranks of Firms by Total Assets			Total
	1–27	28–54	55–83	
ASE	4	4	5	13
NYSE	7	5	7	19
Total	11	9	12	32

[41] This evidence is inconsistent with the hypothesis that managers choose reporting frequency to *signal* future expected performance.

[42] We chose to classify auditors by the number of clients in our sample. The largest six auditors had between 10 and 27 clients in our sample. The remaining 46 auditors in the sample had fewer than five clients each.

[43] Regression *t*-statistics are reported because the probit algorithm failed to converge on these estimations.

TABLE 5

Summary Statistics Means and Standard Deviations of Variables Classified by Type of Reporting and Stock Exchange for Sample Firms in 1948

Variable	Label	ASE			NYSE		
		Annual Reporters	Semiannual Reporters	Quarterly Reporters	Annual Reporters	Semiannual Reporters	Quarterly Reporters
Number of firms		46	13	22	7	19	57
Market value (000s)	$V4$						
Mean		46,570	40,643	10,420	145,839	216,357	122,830
Std. dev.		228,224	94,117	9,430	188,576	420,400	205,130
Total assets (000s)							
Mean		30,021	59,589	11,821	127,829	278,464	124,799
Std. dev.		125,200	160,903	10,673	145,242	641,888	226,475
Debt (000s)							
Mean		1,869	11,769	586	19,627	21,392	11,908
Std. dev.		6,645	34,024	1,701	47,869	53,485	30,928
Outside director	OD						
Mean		.435	.615	.682	.571	.684	.632
Std. dev.		.501	.506	.477	.535	.478	.487
Fixed assets/market value	$A4$						
Mean		.331	.235	.351	.419	.371	.399
Std. dev.		.253	.204	.196	.384	.282	.284
Debt/market value	$L4$						
Mean		.041*	.118	.039**	.043	.086	.079
Std. dev.		.097	.125	.086	.090	.109	.101
Preferred/market value	$P4$						
Mean		.044*	.135	.034**	.060	.047	.076
Std. dev.		.080	.183	.089	.090	.073	.107

* Means of annual and semiannual reporters are significantly different at the .1 level.
** Means of quarterly and semiannual reporters are significantly different at the .1 level.

Our results suggest that firms reporting semiannually have lower monitoring costs for reasons we are unable to explain. Because of the lower monitoring costs, the ASE semiannual reporters are able to obtain more capital (debt and preferred stock) with lower proportions of assets in place. NYSE semiannual reporters also have lower assets in place and more debt than quarterly or semiannual reporters. Two possible omitted variables could account for lower monitoring costs for these firms—the firms could have lower risk[44] or employ other monitoring devices such as sinking funds, collateral for their debt, or internal control systems.

D. PROBIT ESTIMATES OF CHANGES IN REPORTING FREQUENCY: 1937–48

Besides the 1948 cross-sectional estimates of interim reporting (table 4), we also examine those firms that changed interim reporting frequency and the correlates of that change. Table 6 displays the transition matrix for 161 firms whose reporting frequency in 1937 could be determined. Sixty-one switched reporting frequency, with 36 increasing their reporting frequency and 25 decreasing their reporting frequency. Of the 36 firms that increased their reporting frequency, 26 did not change exchanges, but the other 10 went to an exchange that had tighter reporting requirements.[45]

The 61 firms that changed reporting frequency were analyzed further. Equation (2) was estimated using probit. The dependent variable is one if the firm increased its reporting frequency (e.g., an annual reporter becomes quarterly or semiannual or a semiannual reporter becomes quarterly) and zero if it decreased its reporting frequency. The independent variables are defined above. The variable outside directors (OD) is not included due to the high cost of collecting this data for 1937.

---

[44] We estimated the market model for 7 of the 19 NYSE semiannual reporters over various subperiods from 1926–48. The average beta of these 7 firms was .76 and six of the seven had betas less than one. These seven were all the NYSE semiannual reporters on the HP 3000 CRSP files. The firms included American Chain and Cable, McGraw-Hill, J.C. Penney, Phelps-Dodge, Phillip Morris, Safeway, and Standard Oil of Indiana. Further stock price tests of ASE firms were not conducted due to the lack of machine readable data for this time period.

[45] From table 6, the following table can be constructed:

Change in Exchange	Change in Reporting Frequency		
	Increase	Decrease	Total
No change	26	22	48
Weaker to stronger*	10	2	12
Stronger to weaker**	0	1	1
Total	36	25	61

  * Other or ASE to NYSE.
 ** NYSE to ASE.

TABLE 6

Transition Matrix of Reporting Frequencies in 1937 and 1948 by Stock Exchange

1937	Reporting Frequency	1948						
		American Stock Exchange (ASE)			New York Stock Exchange (NYSE)			Total
		Annual	Semiannual	Quarterly	Annual	Semiannual	Quarterly	
ASE	Annual	29	7	5	1	1	3	46
	Semiannual	6		6			2	14
	Quarterly	7	3	6			1	17
NYSE	Annual				5	3	2	10
	Semiannual		1			10	3	14
	Quarterly	1		1	1	5	43	51
Other Exchanges	Annual			3			1	4
	Semiannual	2	2					4
	Quarterly						1	1
	Total	45	13	21	7	19	56	161*

* Three firms were deleted because their reporting frequency in 1937 could not be determined.

The results of the estimation of equation (2) are:

$$\text{Prob}(\Delta R) = N[-.1 + 1.1 \, \Delta A - .4 \, \Delta L + .8 \, \Delta X - .6 \, \Delta P - .6 \, \Delta V].$$
$$\quad\;\; (.4) \;\; (1.8) \quad (-.2) \quad (1.4) \quad (-.6) \quad (-.0)$$

Asymptotic t-statistics are in parentheses. $X^2 = 6.6$ (significant at the 0.75 level). N denotes the cumulative normal density function.

Only one of the capital and asset structure variables, the change in assets in place, is significant at the 0.1 level. However, the sign of that coefficient is anomalous. There is slight confirmation that changing exchanges affects reporting frequency. This result is consistent with the transition matrix in table 6.

We suspect that substantial measurement errors in the independent variables are adversely affecting these results. Take the case of a firm that changes its reporting frequency in 1938 and maintains the same reporting frequency until 1948. For this firm, most of the change in capital structure would have occurred by 1937 or 1938 and measuring the change in the right-hand side variables over 1937–48 adds noise to the independent variables.

5. Conclusions

In this paper we examine the empirical relation beween reporting frequency and variables suggested by agency theory, in particular capital structure, asset structure, and other monitoring devices. Overall, the results are not strong. Three empirical regularities emerge:

(i) *Stock exchange effect.* Firms on the NYSE in 1948 report with a higher frequency than ASE firms. Further, firms which changed exchange listing from any exchange to the NYSE or from exchanges other than the NYSE to the ASE in the period 1937 to 1948 are more likely to increase their frequency of reporting in that period. Since managers have the freedom to choose the exchange on which to list their shares, this result cannot be construed as being due to coercion on the part of the exchange.

(ii) *Inertia.* The reporting frequency of firms listed on the NYSE in 1948 is significantly associated with the firm's reporting frequency in 1937.

(iii) *Anomalies.* The debt and preferred leverage ratios of semiannual reporters on the ASE in 1948 are significantly higher than the corresponding ratios for the other reporting frequencies. The asset structure ratio of semiannual reporters on the ASE in 1948 is lower than the asset structure ratios for other ASE reporters. Although that difference is not significant, the coefficient on asset structure is significant in the cross-sectional probit estimates in 1948, which involve the semiannual reporters as a separate group. In the time-series estimates the coefficient on the change in asset structure is also significant. However, the direction of these associations between asset structure variables and reporting frequency is counterintuitive.

The absence of stronger results and the presence of the anomalies are probably due to several methodological problems. These problems include:

(*i*) *Specification of theory*. As indicated above and in Appendix A, we do not have a finance theory of capital structure. Without such a theory we are unable to specify a relationship between frequency of reporting and the exogenous variables. The variables used in this paper are endogenous. We tried to overcome this problem by assuming there was no cross-sectional or time-series variation in the supply-side (i.e., the production function was stationary and the same for all firms). The results suggest this assumption was inappropriate.

(*ii*) *Measurement errors in the dependent variables*. There is evidence that some firms report to debt holders more frequently than indicated in Moody's *News Reports*. Either Moody's does not report all interim reports they receive or firms choose different reporting frequencies for shareholders and debt holders. If there is a bias in Moody's reporting, then the associations reported can be spurious or obfuscating the actual associations. If firms choose different reporting frequencies, then the specification of the derived demand for interim reporting should exclude debt variables.

(*iii*) *Measurement errors in the independent variables*. As described above, the independent variables are measured with error in the time-series estimation since the changes in the capital structure and asset structure variables span an eleven-year period.

We cannot overcome the lack of a theory of capital structure. But there are some methodological refinements we would incorporate in a replication:

(*i*) Instead of examining the cross-sectional variation in interim reporting, concentrate on the changes in the variables around the time of the change in reporting frequency. This would reduce the measurement error in the independent variables.

(*ii*) Investigate the stock price performance of the firms changing reporting frequency around the time of the change. If managers voluntarily change reporting frequency to increase shareholders' wealth (and the stock price tests are powerful enough to detect the benefits), positive abnormal performance should be observed, subject to the problem of confounding events. (For example, firms may change their reporting frequency when they change industries or undertake new investment projects.)

(*iii*) Examine the firms' interim reporting frequency over time and identify those firms which have multiple changes. If the frequent changes are due to Moody's publication decisions, elimination of those firms would reduce the measurement error in the dependent variable. If multiple changes in reporting frequency are due to these firms being close to the margin, eliminating these firms will increase the power of the tests.

(*iv*) Examine the attributes of the financial reports (other than reporting frequency) of ASE semiannual and quarterly reporters. If semiannual reporters supply more detailed reports than quarterly reporters, our assumption that the semiannual reports necessarily represent a lower level of monitoring is false.

APPENDIX A

The purpose of this appendix is to illustrate some of the econometric problems in the empirical results and not to construct a formal model of the derived demand for interim reporting.

Suppose the firm faces the following demand for monitoring:

$$Q = hT^{\gamma}L^{\gamma_1}P^{\gamma_2}V^{\gamma_3}A^{\gamma_4} \qquad (A1)$$

where:

$T =$ the market price for each additional unit of monitoring, Q,
$P =$ preferred stock,
$L =$ debt,
$V =$ market value of firm,
$A =$ assets in place,
$h, \gamma, \gamma_1, \gamma_2, \gamma_3, \gamma_4 =$ firm-specific parameters,

and the following production function for monitoring:[46]

$$Q = \alpha R^{\beta_1}OD^{\beta_2}X^{\beta_3} \qquad (A2)$$

where:

$R =$ reporting frequency
$OD =$ outside directors
$X =$ exchange listing.

Solving equation (A2) for R yields:

$$\ln R = -\frac{\ln \alpha}{\beta_1} + \frac{\ln Q}{\beta_1} - \frac{\beta_2 \ln OD}{\beta_1} - \frac{\beta_3 \ln X}{\beta_1}. \qquad (A3)$$

Substituting (A1) into (A3) yields:

$$\ln R = \frac{\ln(h/\alpha)}{\beta_1} + \frac{\gamma}{\beta_1} \ln T + \frac{\gamma_1}{\beta_1} \ln L + \frac{\gamma_2}{\beta_1} \ln P \qquad (A4)$$
$$+ \frac{\gamma_3}{\beta_1} \ln V + \frac{\gamma_4}{\beta_1} \ln A - \frac{\beta_2}{\beta_1} \ln OD - \frac{\beta_3}{\beta_1} \ln X.$$

The firm chooses the profit-maximizing set of inputs—R^*, OD^*, and X^*, given $T, L, P, V,$ and A. Equation (A4) is the input demand function (i.e., the derived demand) for interim reporting. Estimates of equation

---

[46] The demand and production functions are not assumed to be Cobb-Douglas because the exponents are not constrained to sum to one.

(A4) can be obtained if all the variables are continuous and observable. All the variables in (A4) are observable, except T, the market price of monitoring. Coefficient estimates in equation (A4) are biased because the omitted variable (price) is likely not independent of the other included variables. Moreover, the coefficient estimates are not efficient (Maddala [1977, p. 156]).

Besides suffering from an omitted variables problem, estimating equation (A4), which contains right-hand side variables that are endogenous (L, P, V, OD, and X) again is likely to produce biased and inconsistent estimates (Maddala [1977, pp. 220–51]). The only way to solve the endogeneity problem is to specify completely the system of equations. That is, each endogenous variable would have to be stated in terms of exogenous variables (i.e., reduced form equations) and then the whole system estimated using, for example, indirect least squares. However, there are two problems with this solution, the first theoretical, the other empirical. At present, there is little finance theory that explains firms' capital structure and three of the endogenous variables (L, P, and V) are capital structure variables. A necessary condition for specifying the reduced form monitoring equations is a finance theory to guide us in specifying the capital structure equations. The second problem is an econometric problem whereby a system of equations must be solved where some of the endogenous variables are dichotomous (e.g., R and X) and others are continuous. For a solution of the econometric problem see Warren and Strauss [1979].

REFERENCES

ALCHIAN, A. A., AND H. DEMSETZ. "Production, Information Costs, and Economic Organization." *American Economic Review* (December 1972): 777–95.

BOLLOM, W. J., AND J. J. WEYGANDT. "An Examination of Some Interim Reporting Theories for a Seasonal Business." *The Accounting Review* (January 1972): 75–84.

FAMA, E. F. "Agency Problems and the Theory of the Firm." *Journal of Political Economy* (April 1980): 288–307.

FINNEY, D. J. *Probit Analysis.* 2d ed. Cambridge: Cambridge University Press, 1964.

GILMAN, S. *Accounting Concepts of Profit.* New York: Ronald Press Co., 1939.

HUNT, B. C. "Auditor Independence." *Journal of Accountancy* (June 1935): 453–59.

JENSEN, M. C. "Towards a Theory of the Press." Working paper, Graduate School of Management, University of Rochester, June 1976.

———, AND W. H. MECKLING. "Theory of the Firm: Managerial Behavior, Agency Costs and Ownership Structure." *Journal of Financial Economics* (October 1976): 305–60.

JURAN, J. M., AND J. K. LOUDEN. *The Corporate Director.* New York: American Management Association, 1966.

KOONTZ, H. *The Board of Directors and Effective Management.* New York: McGraw-Hill, 1967.

MADDALA, G. S. *Econometrics.* New York: McGraw-Hill, 1977.

MYERS, S. C. "Determinants of Corporate Borrowing." *Journal of Financial Economics* (November 1977): 147–75.

TAYLOR, R. G. "An Examination of the Evolution, Content, Utility and Problems of Published Interim Reports." Ph.D. dissertation, University of Chicago, 1963.

WARREN, R. S., AND R. P. STRAUSS. "A Mixed Logit Model of the Relationship Between

Unionization and Right-to-Work Legislation." *Journal of Political Economy* (June 1979): 648–55.

WATTS, R. L. "Corporate Financial Statements: A Product of the Market and Political Processes." *Australian Journal of Management* (April 1977): 53–75.

————, AND J. L. ZIMMERMAN. "The Demand for and Supply of Accounting Theories: The Market for Excuses." *The Accounting Review* (April 1979): 273–305.

————. "The Markets for Independence and Independent Auditors." Working paper, Graduate School of Management, University of Rochester, 1980.

ECONOMIC CONSEQUENCES OF ACCOUNTING STANDARDS
The Lease Disclosure Rule Change*

Eugene A. IMHOFF, Jr.

University of Michigan, Ann Arbor, MI 48109, USA

Jacob K. THOMAS

Columbia University, New York, NY 10027, USA

Received May 1986, final version received April 1988

We examine capital structure changes to investigate the impact of SFAS No. 13 on lessees. While this accounting standard essentially rearranged capital lease disclosures (from footnotes to the balance sheet), mandated capitalization substantially altered key accounting ratios. Our results document a systematic substitution from capital leases to operating leases and nonlease sources of financing. In addition, lessees appear to reduce book leverage by increasing equity and reducing conventional debt. The magnitudes of these responses are cross-sectionally related to preadoption levels of footnoted capital leases.

1. Introduction

This paper documents a significant change in the capital structure of lessee firms in response to Statement of Financial Accounting Standard (SFAS) No. 13, 'Accounting for Leases' [FASB (1976)]. Before the accounting rule change, most leases that were effectively purchases of assets (hereafter 'capital leases') were reported in footnotes to the financial statements.[1] SFAS No. 13 changed the form of capital lease disclosures by requiring all capital leases to be reported as assets and debt – effectively moving capital leases from the footnotes to the balance sheet. Lease capitalization was expected to increase

---

*The authors acknowledge Krishna Palepu's (the referee) helpful suggestions along with comments from Ray Ball, Vic Bernard, Linda DeAngelo, Harry DeAngelo, Robert Lipe, Greg Niehaus, Patricia O'Brien, Jay Ritter, Jay Shanken, Dennis Sheehan, Cliff Smith, Ross Watts, Jerry Zimmerman, and workshop participants at Michigan State University, University of Colorado at Boulder, and University of Notre-Dame.

[1]Prior to SFAS No. 13, firms had the option of reporting capital leases either in the footnotes or in the body of the financial statements. Most lessees, especially firms with relatively large amounts of capital leases, elected footnote disclosure for their capital leases. Technically, these off-balance sheet capital leases are termed 'financing' leases, under ASR No. 147 [SEC (1973)]. Here we ignore this distinction and refer to all leases that are essentially purchases of assets as capital leases.

Journal of Accounting and Economics 10 (1988) 277–310. North-Holland

book leverage ratios and reduce accounting rates of return. Based on contracting-costs arguments [summarized in Holthausen and Leftwich (1983) and Watts and Zimmerman (1986)], we hypothesize that financial statement changes caused by the standard increased the cost of using capital leases, thereby causing lessees to reduce the proportion of assets financed through capital leases.

The most pervasive effect we observe is substitution from capital leases to operating leases (all leases not classified as capital leases).[2] Firms employing relatively larger amounts of capital leases reported substantial declines in capital leases and corresponding increases in operating leases around adoption of the standard. We also find substitution towards nonlease financing, indicated by a decline in total leasing (operating and capital combined). Finally, the standard is associated with leverage-reducing changes within nonlease sources of financing, evidenced by increases in equity and decreases in conventional long-term debt. The magnitude of these capital structure changes, which offset the expected financial statement impact of the standard, are cross-sectionally related to preadoption levels of footnoted capital leases.

We examine the lease accounting rule change because it had a major impact on lessees' financial statements. Balance sheet debt is expected to double for our sample of lessees with relatively higher preadoption levels of footnoted capital leases.[3] The existence of prepronouncement 'as-if capitalized' footnote disclosures enables us to predict the standard's impact on lessees' financial statements, thereby allowing cross-sectional analyses. Footnote disclosures also identify cash flows for capital and operating leases both before and after the change, thereby allowing estimation of firm responses to the standard along a number of dimensions.

The regression methodology employed here uses control periods from before and after the new standard to identify unexpected capital structure changes associated with the rule change. This procedure controls for two statistical problems that potentially bias inferences based on analyses of financial statement variables: heteroskedasticity and regression to the mean. To provide additional control for confounding effects, we analyze a well-defined subsample of lessees. We also offer a nonparametric analysis that is used to complement the regression results. Unlike earlier studies that analyze only one

---

[2]All long-term leases that are not effectively purchases of assets are classified as operating leases. (Short-term leases and rental contracts are excluded from the analysis.) While the distinction between capital and operating leases is assumed to be dichotomous, the degree to which ownership rights and risks can be transferred to lessees is clearly a continuous variable. Here we use the accounting definitions of capital and operating leases to represent two groups of leases that transfer relatively more and relatively less ownership rights to the lessee, respectively.

[3]Other factors supporting the perceived importance of this standard include the number of comment letters received by the Financial Accounting Standards Board (FASB) concerning SFAS No. 13, during its development, and the fact that the FASB has issued thirteen subsequent pronouncements related to leases.

response variable (discussed in section 4.1) we analyze potential responses along many dimensions. Our results demonstrate the importance of considering alternative responses that firms affected by a new standard might use to offset the financial statement effects of the rule change.

Section 2 of this paper develops the research hypothesis. Section 3 reports results of empirical tests, and section 4 discusses the methodology employed and provides a summary of the results and their implications.

2. Research hypothesis

Fig. 1 describes the lease disclosure environment before and after SFAS No. 13. The notation introduced in fig. 1 and used throughout the paper identifies the net present values (PV) of capital lease obligations reported in footnotes ($PVCAP_f$) and balance sheets ($PVCAP_b$), as well as minimum scheduled cash flows (FL) for both capital leases ($FLCAP$) and operating leases ($FLOP$). While some leases were capitalized ('booked') as assets and debt prior to the standard, most capital leases were reported in footnotes in accordance with existing accounting rules [AICPA (1964, 1973), SEC (1973)]. After the standard, the present values of preadoption capital lease obligations reported in footnotes are required to be capitalized retroactively as debt and the corresponding unamortized asset values included as assets. Because of differences in the timing of expenses for capital and operating leases, owners' equity is expected to decline after capitalization and net income is expected to decrease for most lessees (with increasing nominal amounts of capital leases) [El-Gazzar et al. (1986)].[4]

The financial statement impact of lease capitalization and the consequences expected by managers of affected firms are well documented elsewhere [Abdel-khalik (1981)]. Increases in debt and assets combine with decreases in equity and income to cause expected increases in accounting measures of leverage and decreases in accounting rates of return. Managers specifically mentioned debt covenant violations as a problem caused by increased accounting leverage ratios [FASB (1976)]. Also accounting rates of return are frequently used either explicitly as a measure of managerial performance in compensation contracts [Healy (1985)] or implicitly by compensation committees in setting overall compensation [Antle and Smith (1986)]. Managers of lessee firms with debt contracts, managerial compensation agreements, or other contracts affected by SFAS No. 13 had economic incentives to offset the

---

[4] Unlike the uniform balance sheet effect of the standard, lease capitalization can either increase or decrease income. Relative to operating leases, expenses are higher (lower) for capital leases early (late) in the lease life. However, examination of preadoption footnote data that disclosed 'as-if-capitalized' information, for a subsample of lessees described in the appendix, uncovered no income-increasing firms and indicated a high cross-sectional correlation between increases in leverage and percent decreases in income.

Lease disclosures available before and after SFAS No. 13[1]

PANEL A: **Present values of all future lease payments (STOCKS)[2]**

TYPE OF LEASE (source of information)	PRE SFAS NO. 13	POST SFAS NO. 13
CAPITAL[3] (balance sheet and footnotes)	1) Booked as asset/liability $\boxed{PVCAP_b}$ .... 2) Off-Balance Sheet $\boxed{PVCAP_f}$	Booked as asset/liability $\boxed{PVCAP_b}$
OPERATING	Present values are not reported for operating leases	

PANEL B: **Next five year's lease payments (FLOWS)[2]**

TYPE OF LEASE (source of information)	PRE SFAS NO. 13	POST SFAS NO. 13
CAPITAL[3] (footnotes)	1) Booked as asset/liability $FLCAP_b$ (not reported) .... 2) Off-Balance Sheet $\boxed{FLCAP_f}$	Booked as asset/liability $\boxed{FLCAP_b}$
OPERATING (footnotes)	$\boxed{FLOP}$ (reported combined)	$\boxed{FLOP}$

[1] Summary notation used to present lease disclosures is as follows. The first two letters, *PV* and *FL*, represent present values (in panel A) and cash flows (in panel B), respectively. The remaining letters (*CAP* or *OP*) represent capital and operating leases, respectively. The subscripts *b* and *f* indicate that present values for capital leases are reported in the balance sheet and footnotes, respectively.

[2] Only boxed items were disclosed in Annual Reports. In Panel B, $FLCAP_b$ was not reported and $FLCAP_f$ and FLOP were reported as a combined amount in the pre SFAS No. 13 period. To obtain separate values for flows in this period, an average ratio FLCAP/PVCAP is computed for each firm in the post SFAS No. 13 period. This ratio is multiplied by $PVCAP_b$ and $PVCAP_f$, for each firm, to impute $FLCAP_b$ and $FLCAP_f$ for the pre SFAS No. 13 period. FLOP is estimated by subtracting the imputed value of $FLCAP_f$ from the total for FLOP and $FLCAP_f$ reported in the pre SFAS No. 13 period.

[3] Most capital leases in the pre SFAS No.13 period were not booked as assets and liabilities on the balance sheet. Instead they were labelled "financing" leases and footnote disclosures reported the financial statement effects that would have occurred if these leases had been booked as assets and liabilities. After SFAS No. 13, all capital leases are booked on the balance sheet.

Fig. 1

financial statement effects of lease capitalization. While stockholders and managers are the parties adversely affected by the standard and managers are expected to determine appropriate responses, for expositional purposes we refer to the firm (or the lessee) as the party being affected by and determining responses to the standard.

Each firm's response to the standard depends on factors such as the cost of violating debt contract restrictions, the way accounting-based restrictions are stated and measured, and the upper and lower limits in compensation arrangements. Potential responses include 1) renegotiating parameters of contracts affected by lease capitalization, 2) violating debt covenants and entering into technical default, and 3) mitigating the financial statement impact of lease capitalization by undertaking offsetting capital structure changes. This last response includes a host of capital structure changes representing substitution from capital leases and conventional debt into equity and other forms of off-balance sheet financing (including operating leases). In general, the specific response (or mix of responses) selected by each lessee is determined by the relative costs and benefits of alternative responses, and magnitudes of firm responses are determined by factors such as the magnitude of the standard's impact on relevant accounting ratios and the amount of preadoption 'slack' relative to limits specified in affected contracts.

Our research strategy is to examine actual lessee responses to the standard to provide evidence on the relative costs and benefits of alternative responses. Additional confirmation that the responses observed are a consequence of the standard is provided by examining the cross-sectional relation between the magnitudes of firm responses and the expected impact of the standard. In the absence of data on relevant parameters of affected contracts, preadoption levels of footnoted capital leases ($PVCAP_f$ reported immediately prior to the standard) are assumed to proxy for the expected impact of the standard.[5] In effect, we assume that cross-sectional variation along omitted contractual variables (such as limits specified in debt contracts and preadoption 'slack' relative to these limits) is random, or at least sufficiently unrelated to the proxy used to allow statistically significant relations to be observed. To enable comparisons across lessees, $PVCAP_f$ is deflated by long-term capitalization (LTC), which equals the book value of long-term conventional debt and equity plus the present values of all capital lease obligations ($PVCAP_f +$ $PVCAP_b$). The same ratio was employed by the SEC (1973) to measure the

---

[5]Examination of footnote data indicates that, while the expected liability increase due to lease capitalization ($PVCAP_f$) is correlated with expected asset increases, equity decreases, and income reductions across lessees, the dollar value of this liability effect differs slightly from the asset and equity effects and varies substantially from the income effect (see footnote 4). We assume that the liability-based proxy used here is cross-sectionally related to expected changes in accounting measures of leverage and rates of return, despite the fact that these accounting measures are based on financial statement items that include both liability and nonliability accounts.

extent to which firms employ footnoted capital leases. Despite potential measurement error, we believe this proxy for the expected impact of the standard is the best available, and it is used as the explanatory variable for all empirical tests.

In summary, the research hypothesis is motivated by the effects of lease capitalization on key accounting ratios used explicitly and implicitly in lending and compensation contracts. Cross-sectionally, the hypothesis predicts that lessees with larger amounts of preadoption footnoted capital leases, scaled by long-term capitalization, are relatively more active in their efforts to offset financial statement changes caused by the standard. In contrast, the null hypothesis (of no economic consequences) predicts that lessees mechanically apply the new lease disclosure rules by booking all capital leases previously reported in the footnotes.

3. Empirical tests and results

To test the null hypothesis, we identify unexpected capital structure changes based on available financial disclosures. We first examine the cross-sectional relation between unexpected changes in capital leases around SFAS No. 13 and preadoption levels of footnoted capital leases for all Compustat firms reporting leases. We then examine the same relation for a subsample of 158 firms, to address certain limitations of the Compustat sample results. Since reducing capital leases represents only one of many possible responses to the standard, we also examine four other measurable responses for this subsample: changes in operating leases, changes in overall leasing, changes in conventional (nonlease) debt, and changes in equity.[6]

3.1. Changes in capital leases – Compustat sample

If lessees affected by SFAS No. 13 seek to reduce capital leases, the research hypothesis predicts an unexpected decline in reported capital leases, subsequent to the adoption of SFAS No. 13, that is positively related to preadoption levels of footnoted capital leases. This simple statement of the hypothesis requires adjustment to incorporate several institutional details.

The standard allowed for a lengthy transition period that varied across firms. Annual reports for years ending on or before December 1976 disclosed leases under the old rules. Annual reports for years ending on or after December 1978 were expected to have completed retroactive adoption of the

---

[6]Only a subset of the many responses observed are analyzed in depth, since analysis of all potential responses for all lessees is prohibitively expensive (see section 4.2).

standard for all capital leases.[7] Thus, the time between the last report in the preadoption period and the first report in the postadoption period is two years for calendar-year-end firms and three years for all other firms. Moreover some lessees adopted the standard early (typically firms with relatively low amounts of capital leases), while a few others delayed capitalization beyond the 1978 deadline to settle contractual violations caused by adoption of the standard [Pfeiffer (1980)].

To avoid reading individual annual reports to identify firm-specific transition periods, we assume a uniform two-year transition period for all lessees on Compustat. The first year in the postadoption period (called 1978) consists of firm-years with year-ends between December 1978 and November 1979. Similarly, we treat firm-years with year-ends between December 1976 and November 1977 as the last year in the preadoption period and label this year as 1976. All subsequent tests conducted on a subsample of 158 lessees (described in the appendix) use firm-specific transition periods and years are classified as defined by Compustat. While the two-year transition period assumed here causes potential measurement errors, the actual transition period for 128 of 158 firms in the subsample (81 percent) was included within this two-year period. Using an approximate transition period causes underestimation of lessee responses, thereby biasing tests on the Compustat sample in favor of the null hypothesis.[8]

In addition to the complexity regarding transition periods, SFAS No. 13 altered the definition of capital leases to include some leases previously classified as operating leases and also redefined the discount rate used to compute present values of lease obligations.[9] These changes result in a small but indeterminable upward bias in postadoption present values for capital leases, relative to expectations based on preadoption levels of capital leases.

---

[7]Initially the FASB allowed a five-year grace period, to 1981, before retroactive capitalization was required. This concession was in response to lessee complaints that capitalization would cause them to violate extant contractual agreements. The SEC intervened with ASR 225 [SEC (1977)] and reduced this period to two years. However, the SEC allowed firms to delay capitalization if more time was needed to settle contractual violations caused by adoption of the new standard, provided reasons for the delay were disclosed.

[8]Since lessees were aware of the proposed standard prior to 1976, firm responses could precede the two-year transition period considered here. However, a three-year transition period starting in 1975 is not used since lease data is available only after 1973. The data required for a three-year preadoption control period (introduced later) would not be available.

[9]Under ASR 147 [SEC(1973)], leases had to be both noncancellable and their term exceed 75 percent of the economic life of the asset to qualify as 'capital' leases (more correctly, financing leases). Under SFAS No. 13, however, even cancellable leases can be classified as capital leases. Also, leases meeting any one of four conditions, including the 75 percent of economic life criterion, are classified as capital leases. Under ASR 147, the relevant discount rate was the interest rate implicit in the lease payments. Under SFAS No. 13, the relevant discount rate is the lower of the implicit rate and the 'incremental' borrowing rate of the lessee (defined as the rate the lessee would have to pay to borrow funds at lease inception to purchase the leased asset). This potential reduction in discount rates implies higher present values.

Again, not accounting for this change in definitions biases statistical tests against observing a *decreasing* in capital leases as predicted by the research hypothesis.

To incorporate the two-year transition period and underestimation of expected postadoption values of *PVCAP*, the null and research (alternate) hypotheses are stated in terms of the following cross-sectional model:

$$(PVCAP/A)_{1978} - E[(PVCAP/A)_{1978}]$$

$$= \gamma + \delta(PVCAP_f/LTC)_{1976} + \zeta, \tag{1}$$

$$H_0: \quad \gamma > 0, \quad \delta = 0, \qquad H_a: \quad \gamma > 0, \quad \delta < 0,$$

where

$PVCAP$ = present value of future lease commitments for all capital leases,
A = book value of nonlease assets,
$PVCAP_f$ = present value of future lease commitments for capital leases reported in footnotes,
LTC = long-term capitalization equals $PVCAP_f$ plus book value of debt and equity, and
$E[\cdot]$ = expected value, based on preadoption levels of capital leases.

Since specifications of the independent and dependent variables and their exact functional relation is hampered by lack of theory, we make certain choices to allow empirical tests. In addition to assumptions made in section 2 regarding the explanatory variable, we assume that unexpected changes in capital leases, representing the dependent variable, are linearly related to the explanatory variable. Present values for capital leases (*PVCAP*) are scaled by the book value of nonlease assets (*A*) to control for changes in firm size and inflation during the lengthy transition period.[10] Extensive sensitivity analyses summarized later reveal that our results are not driven by these choices. Given that expected postadoption values of capital leases, based on preadoption levels, are potentially downward biased (due to the definitional changes per SFAS No. 13), the intercept (γ) is expected to be positive under both hypotheses. Note that both the null and alternative hypotheses predict zero values for the intercept if expectations are correctly specified. Any bias due to the definitional change is assumed to be entirely captured by the intercept.[11]

---

[10]Assets financed through capital leases are specifically excluded from the measure used to deflate *PVCAP* to avoid any bias caused by a decline in capital leases in the postadoption period as predicted by the alternate hypothesis. *LTC*, the deflator used for the explanatory variable, is not used as a deflator for *PVCAP* for the same reason.

[11]If, however, the underestimation of postadoption values is positively related to preadoption levels of footnoted capital leases, then estimates for δ will be biased towards zero.

For notational simplicity, we drop firm subscripts (subscript i for the ith firm) used to signify that individual firms are being analyzed in a cross-section regression.

To identify firm responses in the absence of a theory predicting levels of capital leases, we could assume that observed changes in capital leases equal unexpected changes during the transition period (a random walk expectation model).[12] However, if high-lease firms normally reduce leasing and low-lease firms normally increase leasing, a cross-sectional mean-reverting relation would exist between levels and changes in levels of capital leases.[13] Since preadoption levels of capital leases, $(PVCAP/A)_{1976}$, are highly correlated empirically with the independent variable specified in eq. (1), $(PVCAP_t/LTC)_{1976}$, the null hypothesis would be incorrectly rejected in this case. To provide an expectation model that controls for reversion towards a cross-sectional mean, the following relation is estimated over three two-year periods extending from 1974 to 1980:

$$(PVCAP/A)_t - (PVCAP/A)_{t-2} = \alpha + \beta(PVCAP/A)_{t-2} + \eta_t. \quad (2)$$

This cross-sectional relation (firm subscripts dropped for convenience) pools observations for each firm from the transition period and two adjacent control periods defined as follows:

P_1 = a preadoption control period, $t = 1976$,
P_2 = the transition period, $t = 1978$, and
P_3 = a postadoption control period, $t = 1980$.

The presence of reversion towards a cross-sectional mean is indicated by estimated values of the intercept (α) and slope (β) that are greater than and less than zero, respectively. If the slope is not different from zero, the expectation model reduces to a random walk model (with the intercept representing the drift term). In either case, the residuals obtained from this regression measure unexpected changes in capital leases.

Combining eqs. (1) and (2) provides a convenient single-stage regression that simultaneously estimates the expectation model and also tests the null

---

[12] Smith and Wakeman (1985) summarize the literature on the determinants of leasing. Current theory has not developed sufficiently to suggest a model, that predicts the (optimal) quantity of leasing that firms employ. Also, since useful preadoption disclosures for capital leases originated in 1973, after ASR 147, there is insufficient data to fit firm-specific time-series models. However, the random walk model provides excellent predictions of $PVCAP/A$ for individual years during the preadoption period (R^2 values in excess of 0.95).

[13] This form of mean reversion is different from regression towards firm-specific time-series means. See Freedman, Pisani, and Purvis (1978) for additional details.

hypothesis as follows:

$$Y_t = (PVCAP/A)_t - (PVCAP/A)_{t-2}$$

$$= \alpha + \beta(PVCAP/A)_{t-2}$$

$$+ D\{\gamma + \delta(PVCAP_f/LTC)_{1976}\} + \varepsilon_t, \tag{3}$$

$$H_0: \quad \delta = 0, \quad H_a: \quad \delta < 0,$$

where

Y	= two-year change in $PVCAP/A$, from year $t-2$ to t,
$PVCAP$	= present value of all future lease payments on all capital leases,
A	= book value of all nonlease assets,
$PVCAP_f$	= present value of all future lease payments for capital leases reported in footnotes,
LTC	= long-term capitalization $= PVCAP_f$ plus book value of long-term debt and equity, and
D	= 1 if $t = 1978$ (transition period, P_2) and
	= 0 if $t = 1976$ (preadoption period, P_1) or $t = 1980$ (postadoption period, P_3).

Note that the first right-hand-side variable uses observations from all three periods to estimate the expectation model in eq. (2). Transition period residuals, representing unexpected changes in capital leases, are then used to measure the cross-sectional relation of interest, expressed in eq. (1). This is done by activating the second right-hand-side variable in eq. (3), through the dummy variable, only for observations from the transition period.[14] Since both the null and alternate hypotheses predict positive values for γ, it is deleted from the hypothesis specification.

A sample obtained from the 1980 edition of the Annual Industrial Compustat tape is used to estimate eq. (3). Firms are included in the three periods if 1) positive values are reported in year t for either capital or operating leases and 2) the data necessary for estimating eq. (3) are available on the tape. Results obtained using the White (1980) correction for heteroskedasticity are

---

[14] The high correlation during 1976 between the two right-hand-side variables in eq. (3) might suggest that the expectation model in eq. (2) should be estimated over the control periods only (excluding the transition period) to avoid biasing the expectation model and reducing the likelihood of detecting the hypothesized [eq. (1)] effect. Note, however, that this dilution of the hypothesized effect is only a problem when eqs. (1) and (2) are estimated separately, since the combined single-stage regression in eq. (3) estimates only the incremental effects of each explanatory variable on the dependent variable. A benefit of estimating the expectation model over all three periods, rather than the control periods alone, is that the number of observations used to estimate the expectation model increases by approximately 50 percent.

Table 1

Analysis of changes in capital leases around adoption of SFAS No. 13 – Compustat sample.[a]

Panel A: Regression analysis of changes in capital leases

$$Y_t = (PVCAP/A)_t - (PVCAP/A)_{t-2}$$
$$= \alpha + \beta (PVCAP/A)_{t-2} + D\{\gamma + \delta(PVCAP_f/LTC)_{1976}\} + \varepsilon_t$$

	α	β	γ	δ
Estimate	0.0017	−0.11	0.021	−0.55
t-statistic[b]	0.49	−1.94	4.47	−7.07
p-value[c]	0.062	0.05	0.00	0.00

$$n = 1987 \qquad R^2 = 0.32$$

Y	= two-year change in $PVCAP/A$
$PVCAP$	= present value of all future lease payments on all capital leases
A	= book value of all nonlease assets
$PVCAP_f$	= present value of all future lease payments on capital leases reported in footnotes
LTC	= long-term capitalization = book value of long-term debt and equity plus $PVCAP_f$
D	= 1 if $t = 1978$ (transition period, P_2) and
	= 0 if $t = 1976$ (preadoption period, P_1) or if $t = 1980$ (postadoption period, P_3)

Panel B: Description of observations by change type

Type of change	$(PVCAP/A)_t$ [d]	$(PVCAP/A)_{t-2}$ [e]	P_1 1974–1976	P_2 1976–1978	P_3 1978–1980	N	Percent
1	= 0	= 0	165	83	63	311	(16%)
2	= 0	> 0	22	18	17	57	(3%)
3	> 0	= 0	36	78	8	122	(6%)
4	> 0	> 0	520	474	503	1497	(75%)
Totals			743	653	591	1987	(100%)

(Two-year change periods; Totals)

[a] While SFAS No. 13 was enacted in 1976, most firms adopted the standard in 1978. Therefore changes in capital leases during this two-year transition period (P_2) are compared with changes over similar two-year periods during preadoption (P_1) and postadoption (P_3) periods to determine an effect of SFAS No. 13.

[b] *t*-statistics have been computed based on White (1980) to correct for heteroskedastic error terms.

[c] *p*-value for δ is based on a one-tailed test. All other *p*-values refer to two-tailed tests.

[d] End-of-period value.

[e] Beginning-of-period value.

reported in table 1, panel A.[15] The highly significant negative *t*-statistic on δ indicates rejection of the null hypothesis and is consistent with the alternate

[15] Error terms are heteroskedastic – both cross-sectionally and over time. The dispersion in error terms increases with both right-hand-side variables and is higher in P_2 than it is in the two control periods. While the parameter estimates are unbiased in this case, the standard errors are biased [Kmenta (1971, p. 256)]. The regression procedure PROC REG when used with the ACOV option estimates a heteroskedasticity-consistent variance–covariance matrix for parameter estimates suggested by White (1980) [see SAS (1986)]. It also recomputes the *F*-tests provided with the TEST statement and reports a χ^2-test (based on asymptotic estimates) and *p*-values using the consistent variance–covariance matrix. All *t*-statistics reported equal $\sqrt{\chi^2}$-statistics .

hypothesis.[16] Assuming as a first-order approximation that the two scaling variables, *LTC* and *A*, equal each other, the magnitude of δ can be interpreted as a 55 percent marginal decline in reported capital leases; i.e., at the margin, only 45 percent of footnoted capital leases were booked after the standard.[17] The positive value of $\gamma = 0.02$ can be interpreted as follows: firms with no footnoted capital leases in 1976 exhibit an increase in capital leases equal to two percent of their nonlease assets. Presumably this increase is due to the more stringent definitions after SFAS No. 13.

These results indicate considerable cross-sectional variation in firm responses. While firms with relatively low amounts of footnoted leases report unexpected increases in capital leases, firms with larger amounts of footnoted capital leases report unexpected declines in capital leases. Also this decline, as a percent of preadoption levels of capital leases, is larger for firms with larger amounts of footnoted capital leases. Estimates obtained for α and β indicate that the data display some regression to the mean, since β is significantly negative at the five percent level.

We observe clustering of prediction errors caused by lessees reporting no capital leases in either year t or $t - 2$. This violates the ordinary least squares (OLS) regression model's assumption of normally distributed error terms.[18] Table 1, panel B reports the numbers of firms in each of four possible categories (labelled types 1 through 4) depending on whether the amounts of capital leases in years t and $t - 2$ are equal to or greater than zero. Observations of types 1, 2, and 3 form the clusters that violate the normality assumption of the OLS model. Ex ante we could not predict which firms that reported no capital leases in year $t - 2$ were going to report a positive amount in year t. To be consistent we would either have to exclude all firms that reported no capital leases in year $t - 2$ or else include all such firms. We opted for the latter strategy, to allow a more representative sample. Eq. (3) was reestimated on subsets of the Compustat sample obtained by deleting observa-

---

[16]Correcting for heteroskedasticity has opposite effects on γ and δ. It increases (reduces) the standard error estimates and decreases (increases) the *t*-statistics for $\delta(\gamma)$. The *t*-statistic on δ is approximately -17 without the White adjustment.

[17]More correctly, as footnoted capital leases increase by x percent of *LTC* (say from 15 percent to 25 percent of *LTC*), unexpected declines in capital leases increase by $0.55x$ percent of *A* (from 6.15 percent of *A* to 11.65 percent of *A* – using estimated values of γ and δ from table 1). These changes are not strictly comparable given the different deflators used. Reestimating eq. (3) with *A* as the deflator for the explanatory variable (instead of *LTC*) provides the following estimates: $\gamma = 0.014$ and $\delta = -0.47$. Thus 53 percent of incremental capital leases were booked after SFAS No. 13.

[18]Cross-sectional dependence in error terms, because of industry concentration, is another potential violation of the standard assumptions of the OLS regression model (positive dependence biases downward the standard errors for parameter estimates). However, given the absence of sufficient time-series data, we are unable to estimate (and correct for) any bias due to this effect.

tions of types 1, 2, and 3 (both individually and collectively) and the results remained essentially unchanged.[19]

We conducted several additional tests to determine if the table 1 results are sensitive to alternate specifications of the regression model and choice of proxy variables. Examination of scatter plots for alternate specifications of the dependent and independent variables over each period indicates that the eq. (3) model is well-specified both in terms of the variables selected as well as the linear relation assumed. Similarly, numerous attempts to reestimate eq. (3) using alternate variables revealed a consistent rejection of the null hypothesis.[20] Finally, alternative methods to adjust for heteroskedasticity provided similar results to those reported here using White's procedure.[21]

3.2. Limitations of Compustat sample results

Smith and Wakeman (1985) suggest that levels of leasing are endogenously determined and correlated with other variables such as tax status, asset structure, contracting costs, and investment opportunities. Therefore changes in these variables, rather than SFAS No. 13, could have altered the costs and benefits of using capital leases, relative to other financing sources.[22] If so, the previous tests are biased due to the omitted correlated variables problem [Kmenta (1971, ch. 10)]. For example, we observe lessees with relatively large amounts of capital leases are concentrated in a few industries, such as airlines and retailers. Our results are consistent with the alternative explanation that an exogenous change that mainly affected these industries caused them to

[19] The type 1 observations, consisting of firms that report no capital leases in both years, form the largest of the three groups. Removing type 1 observations that are concentrated at the origin increases the absolute value of estimates for γ and δ as well as the t-statistics on δ.

[20] We used *proportional* changes in capital leases, both with and without scaling by total nonlease assets, instead of the change measure used in eq. (3). The heteroskedasticity increased significantly, since firms with very low amounts of capital leases report large proportional changes. Using proportional changes reduces sample size since all observations of types 1 and 3 (see table 1, panel B) are deleted because the denominator ($PVCAP_{t-2}$) is equal to zero. However, the effect of SFAS No. 13 is still significant, since δ remains significantly less than zero (t-statistic ≈ -4) when eq. (3) was reestimated using these alternative measures of firm response. We also replaced the scaling variable, nonleased assets (A), with other reasonable candidates such as total assets including capital leases and long-term capitalization. While the absolute value of the t-statistic on δ declined, because of the bias mentioned in footnote 10, in no case did it drop below 5.

[21] Weighted least-squares regressions [Kmenta (1971, ch. 8)] using linear functions of the independent variable eliminated most of the heteroskedasticity present. Although the estimated values of γ and δ differ from those reported in table 1, due to the weighting employed, the t-value on δ always remains highly significant at approximately -6.

[22] Endogeneity of the standard could explain why the new standard and the exogenous change that reduced the benefits of leasing occurred at the same time. Ball (1980) argues that the enactment of a rule change could signal that resistance to the change had declined and the standard was 'allowed' to pass. A decline in the attractiveness of capital leases due to a change in tax laws (for example) could be the reason why firms became less concerned about the effects of SFAS No. 13.

reduce capital leasing. In this case, eq. (3) is misspecified since the relevant explanatory variable, effect of the exogenous change (or its proxy, industry membership), is omitted and a spurious relation is observed with the amount of preadoption footnoted capital leases.

While extant theory has identified variables that influence leasing behavior, a model that specifies how these variables determine levels of leasing is yet to be determined. One research design recommended in such cases is to use matching to control for these relevant explanatory variables [Runkel and McGrath (1972)]. Three variables that are correlated with the proportion of assets financed through capital leases, and are expected to proxy for the determinants of capital leasing, are: industry membership, total leverage (including capital leases), and firm size.[23] We selected a subsample of 79 pairs of firms with each pair consisting of a high-lease firm and a low-lease firm from the same industry with similar size and leverage. High and low levels of leasing are based on preadoption levels of footnoted capital leases. An eq. (3) regression estimated on this subsample is less likely to be confounded by omitted correlated variables, since by construction the sample correlation between the included independent variable and the three omitted variables is reduced, relative to the Compustat sample.[24]

Matching procedures possess certain limitations in quasi-experiments where the researcher does not determine levels of control variables. If all variables relevant to the choice of capital leases have been identified, why do firms in the same industry with similar size and leverage choose different amounts of capital leases? Perhaps the optimal level of capital leases is not a uniquely determined amount; i.e., there is sufficient randomness in the choice of lease financing in the population to allow selection of a reasonable sample of high- and low-lease firms matched on the three control variables. Alternatively, our model is incomplete and matching only for industry, size, and leverage still leaves open the possibility of other omitted correlated variables. Despite these

---

[23]See the appendix for additional details on these control variables. The Compustat sample showed highly significant correlations (at less than one percent) between capital leases and these three variables. Certain industries, especially airlines and retailers, and highly levered firms employed more capital leases. Firm size had a more complex effect, since it was positively related to capital leases for certain industries and negatively related for others.

[24]An alternative strategy is to reestimate the table 1 regression with the three control variables as additional explanatory variables. The coefficient for δ remained significantly negative when 1976 values of leverage and size and industry membership are included as regressors. Industry membership is represented by dummies for each of eight broad industry groupings with lessee firms [see Sharpe (1982) for industry definitions]. Also separate regressions were estimated for each industry group with leverage and size as additional regressors. Only in three industry groups (construction, energy, and utilities) was the estimate for δ not significantly below zero, at the five percent level. Lessees in these three industries comprised only nine percent of the Compustat sample and consisted almost entirely of low-lease firms. Since the coefficients for size and leverage varied in sign and significance across industries, we conclude that complex interactions exist among the three control variables, and simply including them in an eq. (3) regression is likely to cause misspecification.

potential limitations, attempts to control for omitted correlated variables are not without benefits. If the null hypothesis is rejected again for the subsample, then the likelihood that SFAS No. 13 induced the results reported in table 1 is increased; if there is an omitted correlated variable, it is not one of these three. Alternatively, if the null hypothesis cannot be rejected, further investigation might identify the omitted variable(s) underlying the table 1 results.

3.3. Changes in capital leases – Subsample results

The appendix details the procedure employed to select the 79 matched pairs of high- and low-lease firms. For the subsample, the correlation between the three control variables and footnoted capital leases is reduced, relative to the Compustat sample.[25] Also, using firm-specific adoption dates to delineate the transition period, instead of the uniform two-year period used for the Compustat sample, provides additional control against contemporaneous effects. The number of firms with one-, two-, and three-year transition periods are 27, 120, and 11, respectively, and actual transition periods started as early as 1975 and extended as late as 1980. As in the Compustat sample, the preadoption and postadoption periods represent the two years immediately before and after the transition period. Individual years in the preadoption period are coded from -3 to -1 with year -1 being the last preadoption year. Similarly, years in the postadoption period are coded from $+1$ to $+3$ with year $+1$ being the first postadoption year.

Eq. (3) is adjusted to accommodate firm-specific transition periods as follows:

$$Y_t = (PVCAP/A)_t - (PVCAP/A)_{t-2}$$

$$= \alpha + \beta (PVCAP/A)_{t-2} \tag{3'}$$

$$+ D\{\gamma + \delta (PVCAP_f/LTC)_{-1}\} + \varepsilon_t,$$

$$H_0: \quad \delta = 0, \qquad H_a: \quad \delta < 0.$$

Here changes in capital leases are measured from year -3 to -1 in P_1 (two

---

[25] Unlike size and industry membership, leverage is still significantly related (p-value below 0.05) to footnoted capital leases for the 158-firm subsample. However, residual correlation between footnoted capital leases and the three control variables is unlikely to explain the subsample results (described later in section 3.3), since including all three control variables as additional explanatory variables does not affect the basic result (δ remains significantly less than zero).

years), from year -1 to $+1$ in P_2 (one, two, or three years), and from year $+1$ to $+3$ in P_3 (two years).[26] The expected impact of the standard (second right-hand-side variable) is now the value of $PVCAP_t/LTC$ in the last firm-specific preadoption year, year -1, and is activated by the dummy variable only if the observation relates to the transition period.

The results of estimating eq. (3') for the subsample, reported in panel A of table 2, are similar to the table 1 results observed for the Compustat sample. While the estimate for δ changes from -0.55 (in table 1) to -0.46, unexpected declines in capital leases during the transition period are still significantly related to preadoption levels of footnoted capital leases. Panel B of table 2 provides additional confirmation, by examining median changes in capital leases for high- and low-lease firms and median differences between changes for high- and low-lease firms in each matched pair over the transition and control periods. The overall comparison in the bottom row of panel B, based on a nonparametric signed rank test, significantly rejects the null hypothesis that matched pairs difference in the transition period equal those in the two control periods. This test is conceptually similar to the regression in eq. (3'), since matched pairs differences measure cross-sectional variation and interperiod comparisons measure unexpected changes. Given that the alternate hypothesis expects matched pairs differences to be more negative during the transition period, reported p-values are based on one-tailed tests.

The median changes in capital leases reported in each cell of panel B provide a description of the magnitudes of these changes in each period. We report p-values for Wilcoxon signed rank tests of the null hypothesis that each median change equals zero to compare the relative magnitudes of changes across cells. The high-lease group reported median changes in capital leases, expressed as a percent of total nonlease assets, of -0.9 percent, -6.8 percent, and -1.8 percent during P_1, P_2, and P_3, respectively. For low-lease firms, the corresponding median declines are -0.4 percent, -0.9 percent, and -0.4 percent, respectively. The matched pairs differences confirm these separate comparisons. Note that reporting changes as a percent of nonlease assets does not portray a representative picture of the substantial declines that occurred. For example, the 6.8 percent decline in capital leases (relative to nonlease assets) for the high-lease sample during P_2 represents a 45-percent decline relative to preadoption levels of capital leases.

---

[26] Relative to low-lease firms, high-lease firms are a smaller proportion (37 percent) of the 27 firms with one-year transition periods and a larger proportion (64 percent) of the 11 firms with three-year transition periods. Therefore allowing for firm-specific transition periods could create an unintended bias in favor of the alternate hypothesis. However, no bias appears to exist, since the results reported in table 2 remain unchanged (actually, the null hypothesis is rejected even more strongly) when firm-specific preadoption and postadoption periods, of duration equal to each firm's transition period, are employed.

Table 2

Analysis of changes in capital leases around adoption of SFAS No. 13 for a subsample of 158 firms.[a]

Panel A: Regression analysis of changes in capital leases

$$Y_t = (PVCAP/A)_t - (PVCAP/A)_{t-2}$$
$$= \alpha + \beta(PVCAP/A)_{t-2} + D\{\gamma + \delta(PVCAP_f/LTC)_{-1}\} + \varepsilon_t$$

	α	β	γ	δ
Estimate	0.010	-0.16	0.012	-0.46
t-statistic[b]	2.77	-4.26	1.61	-6.31
p-value[c]	0.01	0.00	0.11	0.00

$$n = 409 \qquad R^2 = 0.57$$

Y	= two-year change in $PVCAP/A$
$PVCAP$	= present value of all future lease payments on all capital leases
A	= book value of all nonlease assets
$PVCAP_f$	= present value of all future lease payments on capital leases reported in footnotes
LTC	= long-term capitalization = book value of long-term debt and equity plus $PVCAP_f$
D	= 1 if $t = 1$ (transition period, P_2) and
	= 0 if $t = -1$ (preadoption period, P_1) or if $t = 3$ (postadoption period, P_3)

Panel B: Median changes in capital leases

$$Y_t \text{ (as \% of } A) = (PVCAP/A)_t \times 100 - (PVCAP/A)_{t-2} \times 100$$

		P_1 Years -3 to -1[a]	P_2 Years -1 to 1[a]	P_3 Years 1 to 3[a]
High-lease group	Median (p-value)[c]	-0.9% (0.07)	-6.8% (0.00)	-1.8% (0.00)
Low-lease group	Median (p-value)[c]	-0.4% (0.00)	-0.9% (0.00)	-0.4% (0.00)
Difference high–low	Median (p-value)[c]	0.2% (0.65)	-5.9% (0.00)	-1.1% (0.03)
Overall comparison	(p-value)[d]		(0.00)	

[a]SFAS No. 13 was enacted in 1976, and most firms adopted the standard in 1978. Here firm-specific adoption periods are used and the years coded as follows: The year of (before) adoption is coded 1 (-1) and the two years following year 1 (preceding year -1) are coded 2 (-2) and 3 (-3), respectively. Therefore changes in capital leases for all firms are measured over two-year preadoption (P_1) and postadoption (P_3) periods. For the transition period (P_2), most firms (120 out of 158) have two years between years -1 and 1. For 27 (11) firms the transition period extended over one (three) years.

[b]t-statistics have been computed based on White (1980) to correct for heteroskedastic error terms.

[c]In panel A, the p-value for δ is based on a one-tailed test; all other p-values refer to two-tailed tests. In panel B, p-values refer to two-tailed Wilcoxon signed rank tests of the null hypothesis that median changes in present values of capital leases = 0.

[d]p-value refers to a one-tailed rank sum test of the null hypothesis that matched pairs differences (high–low) in P_2 equal differences in P_1 and P_3, versus the alternative that differences in P_2 are more negative than differences in P_1 and P_3.

The nonparametric comparisons in panel B complement the regression analysis in panel A.[27] Our results are unlikely to be artifacts of the methodology selected, since we observe similar results using different methodologies. Similarities between the results reported in tables 1 and 2 suggest that the Compustat sample results are not due to an omitted variable and that our subsample seems to be representative of the Compustat sample. Since data required for additional tests had to be hand-collected from footnotes in annual reports, only the subsample is used for additional tests discussed below.

3.4. Changes in operating leases – Subsample results

The observed decline in reported capital leases after the standard suggests that offsetting increases in other sources of financing occurred at the same time. Since operating leases remained outside the purview of SFAS No. 13, firms could escape lease capitalization by restructuring capital leases to qualify as operating leases. An unexpected increase in operating leases in combination with the observed unexpected decrease in capital leases represents a substitution from capital to operating leases. Fig. 1 indicates that only flows (minimum commitments for the next five years), not present values, are disclosed for operating leases, and in the preadoption period operating lease flows are reported in combination with flows for footnoted capital leases.[28] To obtain separate flows during the preadoption period, we assume that for each firm the relation between flows and present values for capital leases remains stationary over time. An average value of this relation, K_i, is computed for each firm i using data from each year in the postadoption period ($t = 1, 2, 3$) as follows:

$$K_i = \sum_{t=1}^{3} (FLCAP_b)_{it} \bigg/ \sum_{t=1}^{3} (PVCAP_b)_{it},$$

where the variables are as defined in fig. 1. The present values of capital leases in the balance sheet and footnotes in each preadoption year ($t = -1, -2, -3$) for each firm i are then multiplied by K_i to obtain estimates of corresponding

---

[27]Unlike nonparametric comparisons of medians, the regression analysis is sensitive to deviations from the linear relationship hypothesized and to violations of the assumptions of the OLS model. (Note that ignoring cross-sectional dependencies affects reported significance levels for both the regression analysis as well as the median comparisons.) Also, the matched pairs differences provide more control for omitted variables, since each pair is individually matched along all three control variables. On the other hand, the regression model uses variation along the independent variable more efficiently, since the nonparametric comparisons use only a high/low dichotomy. Finally, the regression model includes an expectation model that controls for mean reversion.

[28]Rental commitments for the next year were also disclosed. These one-year-ahead flows are highly correlated, by firm, with the five-year-ahead flows analyzed in the paper. The results in sections 3.4 and 3.5 remain essentially unchanged when one-year-ahead flows are analyzed.

values of flows:

$$(FLCAP_b)_{it} = (PVCAP_b)_{it} \times K_i$$

and

$$(FLCAP_f)_{it} = (PVCAP_f)_{it} \times K_i.$$

Flows for operating leases ($FLOP$) during each year in the preadoption period are determined by subtracting the imputed value of $FLCAP_f$ from the flows reported for operating and footnoted capital leases combined.

A regression model similar to eq. (3′) is estimated on operating lease flows to determine if they increased unexpectedly ($\delta > 0$) during the transition period. $PVCAP/A$ in eq. (3′) is replaced by $FLOP/A$, while the second variable on the right-hand side, $(PVCAP_f/LTC)_{-1}$, remains unchanged. The results reported in table 3, panel A indicate significant unexpected increases in operating leases, suggesting substantial substitution from capital to operating leases. As in tables 1 and 2, the magnitude of δ can be interpreted as a marginal increase in operating leases of approximately 37 percent.[29] The overall comparison reported in the bottom row of panel B, based on rank sum tests, also significantly rejects the null hypothesis (p-value = 0.0). High-lease firms report a median increase in operating leases of 4.6 percent (as a percent of nonlease assets) during the transition period, which is significantly greater than zero. This increase is also significantly larger than the 1.1 percent increase registered by matched low-lease firms during the same period. Changes in operating leases are not significantly different from zero (at the five percent level) outside the transition period for either group. These results indicate that much of the unexpected decline in capital leases is offset by increases in operating leases, suggesting that many capital leases were restructured during the transition period to qualify as operating leases.

3.5. Changes in overall leasing flows – Subsample results

Can substitution into operating leases account entirely for the observed capital lease declines or did some substitution into nonlease financing also occur? Since the measures used for analyzing declines in capital leases (present values in table 2) and increases in operating leases (cash flows in table 3) are not comparable, we examine total leasing flows (FLTOT) to determine if the

---

[29] Unlike tables 1 and 2, the estimate for γ is now negative. Since definitional changes regarding discount rates only affect present values not flows, this sign reversal for the intercept suggests that the broader definition of capital leases after SFAS No. 13 resulted in some operating leases being reclassified as capital leases. Not accounting for this definitional change causes underestimation (overestimation) of postadoption levels of capital (operating) leases resulting in the positive (negative) intercept observed in tables 1 and 2 (table 3).

Table 3

Analysis of changes in cash flows for operating leases around adoption of SFAS No. 13 for a subsample of 158 firms.[a]

Panel A: Regression analysis of changes in operating lease flows

$$Y_t = (FLOP/A)_t - (FLOP/A)_{t-2} = \alpha + \beta(FLOP/A)_{t-2} + D\{\gamma + \delta(PVCAP_f/LTC)_{-1}\} + \varepsilon_t$$

	α	β	γ	δ
Estimate	0.017	-0.26	-0.015	0.37
t-statistic[b]	4.14	-4.58	-1.64	5.94
p-value[c]	0.00	0.00	0.10	0.00

$$n = 369 \qquad R^2 = 0.34$$

Y	= two-year change in $FLOP/A$
$FLOP$	= cash flow commitments for operating leases over next five years
A	= book value of all nonlease assets
$PVCAP_f$	= present value of all future lease payments on capital leases reported in footnotes
LTC	= long-term capitalization = book value of long-term debt and equity plus $PVCAP_f$
D	= 1 if $t = 1$ (transition period, P_2) and
	= 0 if $t = -1$ (preadoption period, P_1) or if $t = 3$ (postadoption period, P_3)

Panel B: Median changes in operating lease cash flows

$$Y_t \text{ (as \% of } A) = (FLOP/A)_t \times 100 - (FLOP/A)_{t-2} \times 100$$

		P_1 Years -3 to -1[a]	P_2 Years -1 to 1[a]	P_3 Years 1 to 3[a]
High-lease group	Median (p-value)[c]	0.2% (0.20)	4.6% (0.00)	-0.0% (0.77)
Low-lease group	Median (p-value)[c]	0.2% (0.56)	1.1% (0.00)	0.0% (0.73)
Difference high–low	Median (p-value)[c]	0.3% (0.56)	3.1% (0.00)	0.1% (1.00)
Overall comparison	(p-value)[d]		(0.00)	

[a]SFAS No. 13 was enacted in 1976, and most firms adopted the standard in 1978. Here firm-specific adoption periods are used and the years coded as follows: The year of (before) adoption is coded 1 (-1) and the two years following year 1 (preceding year -1) are coded 2 and 3 (-2 and -3), respectively. Therefore changes in operating lease cash flows for all firms are measured over two-year preadoption (P_1) and postadoption (P_3) periods. For the transition period (P_2), most firms (120 out of 158) have two years between years -1 and 1. For 27 (11) firms the transition period extended over one (three) years.

[b]t-statistics have been computed based on White (1980) to correct for heteroskedastic error terms.

[c]In panel A, the p-value for δ is based on a one-tailed test; all other p-values refer to two-tailed tests. In panel B, p-values refer to two-tailed Wilcoxon signed rank tests of the null hypothesis that the median changes in operating lease cash flows = 0.

[d]p-value refers to a one-tailed rank sum test of the null hypothesis that matched pairs differences (high–low) in P_2 equal differences in P_1 and P_3, versus the alternative that differences in P_2 are more positive than differences in P_1 and P_3.

two changes completely offset each other. If no unexpected changes in total leasing flows are observed, then increases in operating leases completely offset capital lease declines. If, however, total leasing flows decline unexpectedly, then a portion of the observed decrease in capital leases represents substitution into nonlease sources of financing.[30]

The results of estimating eq. (3′), adjusted to replace present values of capital leases by total leasing flows, are reported in panel A of table 4. Total leasing flows are obtained by combining flows for capital and operating leases ($FLTOT = FLCAP + FLOP$). While the estimate for δ is negative, it is not significantly different from zero. Since γ is also insignificantly different from zero, no significant decline in total leasing flows occurred during the transition period. In contrast, the panel B results indicate significant rejection of the null hypothesis (p-value on overall comparison is 0.01). During the transition period high-lease firms report a median decline in total lease flows of 1.6 percent (as a percent of total nonlease assets), which is significantly less than zero. The smaller decline of 0.1 percent reported by low-lease firms (not significantly different from zero) results in differences between matched pairs that are also significantly different from zero.

Inconsistencies between the two panels are explained by examining changes during the postadoption period reported in panel B. High-lease firms continue to reduce total leasing flows after adopting the standard, since the median decline of 1.3 percent in P_3 is also significantly less than zero. This continued large decline during P_3 is captured by the expectation model in panel A (significantly negative value of β) leaving only a small and statistically insignificant unexpected decline during P_2 to be explained by the level of footnoted capital leases. Estimating the expectation model over P_1 alone results in a significantly negative (at the five percent level) estimate for δ.[31] The absence of declines in operating leases during P_3 (table 3, panel B) suggests that the continued decline in total leases during P_3 is caused entirely by capital lease declines during this period.[32] Perhaps, some capital leases

---

[30]A simple measure indicates that most, but not all, of the decline in capital leases during P_2 is offset by a corresponding increase in operating leases. The ratio of adoption period changes in operating lease flows ($FLOP$) to changes in capital lease flows ($FLCAP$) has a median value of -0.69. This value is significantly lower than zero, which is the expected value if there was no relation between the two changes. However, it is also significantly different from -1, which is the expected value if the two changes completely offset each other.

[31]The coefficients obtained for α and β based on an eq. (2) regression estimated over P_1 alone were used to identify unexpected changes in total leasing during P_2. Regressing these unexpected changes against preadoption levels of footnoted capital leases [eq. (1)] resulted in an estimate for $\delta = -0.097$ (p-value = 0.05). Note that any mean reversion effects are considered in the expectation model estimated over P_1.

[32]Analysis of median changes in leasing flows for capital leases ($FLCAP$, not $PVCAP$ as in table 2) indicates a -1.2% decline, as a percent of nonlease assets, for high-lease firms during P_3. Therefore, most of the P_3 decline in total leasing flows of -1.3% (table 4, panel B) for this group of firms is explained by capital lease declines.

Table 4

Analysis of changes in cash flows for all leases around adoption of SFAS No. 13 for a subsample of 158 firms.[a]

Panel A: Regression analysis of changes in total leasing cash flows

$$Y_t = (FLTOT/A)_t - (FLTOT/A)_{t-2}$$
$$= \alpha + \beta(FLTOT/A)_{t-2} + D\{\gamma + \delta(PVCAP_t/LTC)_{-1}\} + \varepsilon_t$$

	α	β	γ	δ
Estimate	0.017	-0.13	-0.0031	-0.023
t-statistic[b]	2.45	-2.44	-0.40	-0.39
p-value[c]	0.01	0.01	0.69	0.35

$$n = 388 \qquad R^2 = 0.07$$

Y = two-year change in $FLTOT/A$
$FLTOT$ = cash flow commitments for total leases (operating and capital) over next five years
A = book value of all nonlease assets
$PVCAP_t$ = present value of all future lease payments on capital leases reported in footnotes
LTC = long-term capitalization = book value of long-term debt and equity plus $PVCAP_t$
D = 1 if $t = 1$ (transition period, P_2) and
   = 0 if $t = -1$ (preadoption period, P_1) or if $t = 3$ (postadoption period, P_3)

Panel B: Median changes in total leasing cash flows

$$Y_t \text{ (as \% of } A) = (FLTOT/A)_t \times 100 - (FLTOT/A)_{t-2} \times 100$$

		P_1 Years -3 to -1[a]	P_2 Years -1 to 1[a]	P_3 Years 1 to 3[a]
High-lease group	Median (p-value)[c]	-0.2% (0.58)	-1.6% (0.00)	-1.3% (0.03)
Low-lease group	Median (p-value)[c]	-0.6% (0.05)	-0.1% (0.83)	-0.3% (0.47)
Difference high–low	Median (p-value)[c]	0.7% (0.21)	-1.5% (0.00)	-1.1% (0.19)
Overall comparison	(p-value)[d]		(0.01)	

[a]SFAS No. 13 was enacted in 1976, and most firms adopted the standard in 1978. Here firm-specific adoption periods are used and the years coded as follows: The year of (before) adoption is coded 1 (-1) and the two years following year 1 (preceding year -1) are coded 2 (-2) and 3 (-3), respectively. Therefore changes in total lease cash flows for all firms are measured over two-year preadoption (P_1) and postadoption (P_3) periods. For the transition period (P_2), most firms (120 out of 158) have two years between years -1 and 1. For 27 (11) firms the transition period extended over one (three) years.

[b]t-statistics have been computed based on White (1980) to correct for heteroskedastic error terms.

[c]In panel A, the p-value for δ is based on a one-tailed test; all other p-values refer to two-tailed tests. In panel B, p-values refer to two-tailed Wilcoxon signed rank tests of the null hypothesis that the median changes in total lease cash flows = 0.

[d]p-value refers to a one-tailed rank sum test of the null hypothesis that matched pairs differences (high–low) in P_2 equal differences in P_1 and P_3, versus the alternative that differences in P_2 are more negative than differences in P_1 and P_3.

maturing soon after the transition period were not terminated or renegotiated as operating leases during the transition period, they were allowed to expire at maturity.

To summarize, total leases declined during the transition period, relative to the pattern in the preadoption period, and this decline is larger for high-lease firms. Therefore, transition period declines in capital leases (table 2) are only partly offset by increases in operating leases (table 3) and the overall importance of leasing (capital and operating combined) as a source of financing declined after SFAS No. 13. However, since high-lease firms continued to decrease total leasing even after adopting the standard, transition period declines were not unusual compared to the postadoption control period. Apparently the process of substitution into nonlease financing was gradual, and not completed within the transition period.

3.6. Changes in equity and conventional debt – Subsample results

Despite the firm responses documented in tables 2, 3, and 4, some high-lease firms did not report a decline in capital leases or in overall leasing. Such firms were either unaffected by the standard or were able to find alternative ways to mitigate any potential adverse consequences of capitalization (see section 4 for examples of other responses we observe). Abdel-khalik (1981) suggests that decreases in conventional debt and increases in equity may have been employed to reverse the leverage-increasing effect of lease capitalization. He documents unexpected increases in equity issues during a three-year transition period (1975 to 1978) for a sample of high-lease firms, relative to equity issues during a three-year preadoption period (1972 to 1975). This finding motivates our last test which examines the null hypothesis that the mix of nonlease financing for lessees remained unaffected by the standard. The alternate hypothesis predicts that lessees undertook equity-increasing and debt-reducing changes to offset the leverage-increasing effects of the standard on their balance sheets.

Changes in equity and debt are reexamined using our methodology, which includes a postadoption control period, and also tests for a cross-sectional relation between the magnitudes of unexpected debt and equity changes and levels of footnoted capital leases. Consistent with Abdel-khalik's methodology, we use annual changes in debt and equity reported in the Statement of Changes in Financial Position (SCFP) and define net changes in equity and debt as issues less repurchases scaled by year-end book values of nonlease assets. Since lease capitalization is expected to affect contracts that are denominated in book values, these variables attempt to capture managerial efforts to alter the book values of equity and debt. With the exception of *early* retirement of debt trading above or below face value, all amounts obtained from the SCFP represent book values.[33]

The transition and control periods employed are defined as follows:

T_1 = preadoption period, employs changes reported in SCFP for 1973, 1974, and 1975,

T_2 = transition period, employs changes reported in SCFP for 1976, 1977, and 1978, and

T_3 = postadoption period, employs changes reported in SCFP for 1979, 1980, and 1981.

Note that the three-year periods selected here are different from the two-year periods used in section 3.1 and the firm-specific transition periods used in sections 3.2 to 3.5. This specification maintains consistency with Abdel-khalik (1981) and reflects the fact that the transition period used here is more representative of the total period available for firms to respond to the new standard.[34]

Attempts to estimate the regression in eq. (3′) to changes in equity and debt for the subsample uncovered no significant unexpected changes during the transition period. Further examination of the data reveals that, while there are some lessees with increases in equity and decreases in debt during the transition period, these changes are on average not large enough (as a percent of nonlease assets) to generate estimates of δ that are significantly different from zero. As an alternative analysis, changes in debt and equity are investigated to determine if the *frequency* of extreme changes varied systematically over the three periods.

To identify extreme changes in debt and equity we first computed annual debt and equity changes for all Compustat firms from 1973 to 1980. Distributions of both changes, reported in table 5, seem fairly stationary, suggesting that Abdel-khalik's results are probably not due to economy-wide effects. Next we coded all debt and equity changes for our 158-firm subsample to emphasize extreme changes, using the mean (over 1973 to 1980) 5th, 10th, 90th, and 95th percentile points indicated in the bottom rows of panels A and B in table 5.

---

[33] Note that the equity change measure specifically excludes changes in the book value of equity due to retained earnings (net income less dividends). We concur with Abdel-khalik that including changes in retained earnings would reduce our ability to detect managerial efforts to change the book value of equity. In effect, this assumes that changes in realized net income, not including shifting of income between adjacent periods, is largely outside managerial control and that managers prefer not to change dividends as a vehicle to adjust the book value of owner's equity.

[34] As mentioned in footnote 8, lease capitalization was expected by lessees prior to enactment of the standard in 1976 and therefore some changes could have preceded the transition period considered here. Note that the availability of a slightly longer time series of SCFP data on debt and equity changes, relative to the lease data required for previous tests, allowed the three-year periods used in this subsection.

Table 5

Issues and repurchases of equity and debt between 1973 and 1980 for all Compustat firms.

Year	N	Percentiles of distribution						
		1%	5%	10%	50%	90%	95%	99%

Panel A: Changes in paid-in-equity = (Equity issues − Equity repurchases)/Total nonleased assets[a]

Year	N	1%	5%	10%	50%	90%	95%	99%
1973	1911	−0.06	−0.023	−0.0120	0.000	0.0120	0.040	0.21
1974	1947	−0.06	−0.014	−0.0058	0.000	0.0060	0.020	0.11
1975	1971	−0.06	−0.011	−0.0040	0.000	0.0072	0.020	0.11
1976	2015	−0.07	−0.013	−0.0039	0.000	0.0110	0.030	0.14
1977	2023	−0.09	−0.019	−0.0059	0.000	0.0086	0.020	0.13
1978	2024	−0.10	−0.022	−0.0062	0.000	0.0150	0.046	0.17
1979	2013	−0.10	−0.024	−0.0086	0.000	0.0186	0.060	0.22
1980	1768	−0.11	−0.019	−0.0071	0.000	0.0360	0.100	0.25
Mean		*−0.08*	*−0.0174*	*−0.0059*	*0.000*	*0.0146*	*0.042*	*0.16*

Panel B: Changes in debt = (Debt issues − Debt retirements)/Total nonleased assets[a]

Year	N	1%	5%	10%	50%	90%	95%	99%
1973	1905	−0.18	−0.054	−0.330	0.000	0.110	0.16	0.25
1974	1940	−0.19	−0.060	−0.036	0.000	0.110	0.15	0.27
1975	1964	−0.25	−0.094	−0.058	−0.001	0.084	0.12	0.25
1976	2002	−0.22	−0.088	−0.054	−0.001	0.079	0.13	0.25
1977	1999	−0.20	−0.074	−0.037	0.000	0.099	0.16	0.30
1978	2002	−0.20	−0.061	−0.034	0.000	0.110	0.16	0.30
1979	2001	−0.27	−0.067	−0.037	0.000	0.110	0.16	0.29
1980	1767	−0.19	−0.080	−0.043	0.000	0.110	0.16	0.29
Mean		*−0.22*	*−0.075*	*−0.043*	*0.000*	*0.100*	*0.15*	*0.28*

[a] The variables are obtained from Compustat as follows: *Equity issues* (Compustat data item #108), *Equity repurchases* (#115), *Debt issues* (# 111), *Debt retirements* (#114), *Total nonleased assets* (#6 less #84).

Annual changes in debt and equity below the 5th and above the 95th percentile points are considered to be 'very large', and changes between the 5th and 10th and between the 90th and 95th percentile points are considered 'large' changes. Debt and equity changes for all firm-years are coded a value between −2 and +2 as follows:

Code	Change	Description
+2 (−2)	'very large'	if change for that year is greater (less) than the mean 95th (5th) percentile point for all Compustat changes (see table 5)
+1 (−1)	'large'	if change for that year is greater (less) than the mean 90th (10th) percentile point for all Compustat changes (see table 5)
0	'normal'	for all annual changes between the 10th and 90th percentiles

All observed changes are adjusted for offsetting changes in adjacent years. This adjustment is often necessary for debt changes, since debt approaching maturity is typically refinanced. For example, if a firm reported a very large decrease in debt (coded as -2) in one year only to be followed by a very large increase in debt (coded as $+2$) of approximately the same magnitude in the next year, then both years' debt changes are coded as '0'. The scores are then summed over each three-year period to get an overall coded value for that period. The few cases that had summed values for a period that were greater (less) than $+2$ (-2) had the change codes set to $+2$ (-2).

Table 6 reports frequencies of the five coded values over all three periods. While most firms fall into the normal category (coded '0'), some report extreme changes. For example, the high-lease group in T_1 (upper panel, first column) consists of 4, 4, 65, 1, and 5 firms with equity changes coded -2, -1, 0, $+1$, and $+2$, respectively. The bottom row in each panel presents p-values for Wilcoxon signed rank tests of the null hypothesis that the median change in each period equals zero. The high p-value ($=1$) reported here indicates that extreme decreases of equity (four -2's and four -1's) approximately equal extreme increases (one $+1$ and five $+2$'s) during T_1 for high-lease firms.

Examination of debt and equity changes for the high-lease group during T_2 indicates more extreme equity increases (21) than decreases (11) and more extreme debt decreases (24) than increases (15). Note that both changes reduce balance sheet leverage and similar changes are not observed for T_1 and T_3. Unlike the leverage-reducing pattern observed for high-lease firms, both equity and debt changes for low-lease firms (reported in the middle panel) exhibit consistent patterns over all three periods. Equity changes reveal more extreme decreases than increases in T_1, more increases than decreases in T_3, and an intermediate response during T_2. Debt changes reveal consistently more extreme increases than decreases for all three periods. Also, nonparametric rank sum tests (not reported) indicate that changes during T_2 for high-lease firms are significantly different from changes in T_1 and T_3 (p-values equal 0.05 and 0.045 for equity and debt changes, respectively). For low-lease firms, however, changes in T_2 are not significantly different from those in T_1 and T_3.

While the frequencies for extreme debt and equity changes for high- and low-lease firms are consistent with the alternate hypothesis, the overall comparisons reported in the bottom row of the bottom panel are unable to reject (at the five percent level of significance) the null hypothesis that matched pairs differences in T_2 equal differences in the two control periods. Further investigation using rank sum tests (not reported) reveals that matched pairs differences (bottom panel) in T_2 are significantly different from differences in T_3 (p-values equal 0.035 and 0.03 for equity and debt changes, respectively). However, since similar tests indicate that the matched pairs differences in T_1 are not significantly different from those in T_2, for both equity and debt changes, the overall tests are unable to reject the null hypothesis at the five percent significance level.

Table 6

Changes in equity and debt around adoption of SFAS No. 13 for a subsample of 158 firms.

Coded change value		Equity changes[a]			Debt changes[a]		
		T_1 1972–1975	T_2 1975–1978	T_3 1978–1981	T_1 1972–1975	T_2 1975–1978	T_3 1978–1981
Panel A: High-lease group							
Very large decrease	−2	4	7	11	10	11	7
Large decrease	−1	4	4	3	3	13	5
Normal	0	65	47	49	51	40	48
Large increase	1	1	10	5	8	11	12
Very large increase	2	5	11	10	7	4	5
(*p*-value)[b]		(1.00)	(0.18)	(0.92)	(0.73)	(0.07)	(0.87)
Panel B: Low-lease group							
Very large decrease	−2	10	8	6	2	2	2
Large decrease	−1	4	5	5	1	4	6
Normal	0	59	45	41	50	47	51
Large increase	1	4	13	8	9	10	8
Very large increase	2	2	8	17	17	16	11
(*p*-value)[b]		(0.03)	(0.51)	(0.02)	(0.00)	(0.00)	(0.01)
Panel C: Differences between matched pairs of firms (high-low)							
Max. negative difference	−4	1	0	0	3	3	2
	−3	2	1	1	3	6	2
	−2	2	12	18	13	12	9
	−1	3	9	9	9	15	11
No difference	0	52	31	33	41	29	32
	1	8	15	8	6	10	16
	2	10	8	5	1	3	4
	3	0	1	1	3	1	0
Max. positive difference	4	1	2	1	0	0	0
(*p*-value)[b]		(0.14)	(0.87)	(0.03)	(0.00)	(0.00)	(0.11)
Overall comparison (*p*-value)[c]			(0.25)			(0.08)	

[a]Extreme equity changes reported are coded values between −2 and +2 based on annual changes in paid-in-capital (stock issuances less repurchases, deflated by nonleased assets) over each of the three periods. Similarly, extreme debt changes are coded values based on issuances less retirements of conventional (nonlease) debt, deflated by nonleased assets. Extreme increases (decreases) for both debt and equity are coded as +1 and +2 (−1 and −2) if the changes are in the top (bottom) 90th and 95th percentiles, respectively, of changes reported by all Compustat firms.

[b]*p*-values, in parentheses, refer to two-tailed Wilcoxon sign rank tests of the null hypotheses that the median change is 0.

[c]*p*-values refer to one-tailed rank sum tests of the null hypothesis that matched pair differences (high–low) in T_2 equal matched pair differences in T_1 and T_3, versus the alternative hypothesis that matched pairs differences for equity (debt) changes are more positive (negative) in T_2.

In summary, the results support Abdel-khalik's view that high-lease firms used leverage-reducing changes with nonlease sources of financing to reverse the balance sheet impact of the standard. Several tests comparing transition period changes separately with each control period and separate analyses of the two groups indicate that high-lease firms exhibit an unusual number of extreme debt decreases and equity increases during the transition period. However, the overall results reported here are only marginally significant for debt changes (p-value = 0.08) and not significant for equity changes (p-value = 0.25).[35]

4. Summary

4.1. Methodology employed

Often an 'event study' methodology, based on security prices, is used to measure economic effects of new standards.[36] This approach is indirect because firm responses are hypothesized but not investigated. Instead, security price movements around the release date of new information relating to the standard are examined to observe economic consequences [Leftwich (1981)]. Some researchers have explored alternative methods, focusing on the direct link between accounting changes and firm responses. Typically, financial statement variables have been investigated to infer responses attributable to new accounting standards.[37] For example, the impact of SFAS No. 2, 'Accounting for Research and Development Costs' [FASB (1974)], on reported R&D expenditures has been investigated in several studies [Dukes et al. (1980), Horwitz and Kolodny (1980), Elliott et al. (1984), Selto and Clouse (1985)].

Application of the direct approach to the lease standard requires consideration of several methodological problems noted by Ball (1980) and Wolfson (1980). Unlike earlier studies using the direct approach, we consider firm responses along many dimensions. The effect of other (unknown) contemporaneous changes is minimized by using control periods from before and after the transition period and by analyzing cross-sectional variation in firm responses. We also validate our results by using multiple analyses (regressions and

[35]See the appendix for evidence of significant debt changes (and insignificant equity changes), based on overall comparisons for a subset of high- and low-lease firms. Also, note that the debt changes reported in table 6 are unlikely to be due to mean reversion. Since high-lease firms have less conventional debt than low-lease firms (see table 8), the presence of mean reversion would cause more debt increases for the high-lease group, in contrast with the debt decreases observed here.

[36]For example, FASB pronouncements on oil and gas accounting, foreign currency translation, and changing prices have each been examined using the event study approach.

[37]Other response variables that have been examined include auditor changes [DeAngelo (1982)] and lobbying behavior [Watts and Zimmerman (1978)].

nonparametric matched pairs comparisons) on different samples (Compustat sample and subsample). After examining the data and obtaining an intuitive understanding of what changes occurred, we develop innovative ways to transform and analyze these data. While this study considers variables and relations that are specific to the lease standard examined, we believe many aspects of the methodology employed here are valuable for research studying the impact of other accounting standards.

4.2. Results

Overall our results support the hypothesis that the financial statement effects of lease capitalization required by SFAS No. 13 had a significant impact on lessees. Capital leases as a source of financing declined sharply after the standard. The substantial amount of substitution into operating leases we observe suggests that renegotiation of lease contracts is a low-cost alternative, relative to other responses that potentially mitigate the financial statement effects of the standard. To a lesser extent, other capital structure changes were also selected in some instances, evidenced by an increased use of nonlease financing and leverage-reducing changes in the mix of nonlease financing (decreasing in debt and increases in equity). Overall, most lessees apparently elected not to renegotiate contracts affected by lease capitalization nor to enter into technical default, and employed various capital structure changes instead.

While the magnitudes of firm responses are on average related to the expected impact of the standard, individual firm responses show considerable variation. In addition to the firm responses analyzed here, we observed numerous other actions undertaken by firms to mitigate the effects of the standard, such as 1) successfully renegotiating contracts affected by complying with the standard [American Seating Company's Annual Report for 1978], 2) delaying capitalization to obtain additional time to renegotiate affected contracts [Pfeiffer (1980)], and 3) lobbying by trade groups to obtain special dispensation when applying the standard to leases that are unique to their industries [Barrons (11/12/1977, p. 5)]. What factors determine the choice among alternative responses? Hopefully future research on cross-sectional variation in the mix of firm responses will provide further evidence on the relative costs of alternative responses.

Appendix: Selection of subsample

The subsample provides additional control to help interpret the results for the Compustat sample by attempting to reduce the bias caused by omitted correlated variables. Three omitted variables that could potentially explain firm responses and also be correlated with the included independent variable,

Table 7

Sample selection procedure.

High-lease sample[a]	
Firms in 1980 edition of Compustat (Annual Industrial) tape	2,457
Firms with footnoted capital leases ($PVCAP_f$) reported from 1973 to 1976	388
Firms with $PVCAP_f/LTC > 10\%$	269

Matching procedures[a]	
Initial set of high lease firms	269
Less firms excluded because no matches available due to:	
no low-lease control firms in 4-digit SIC industry group[b]	(122)
no matches on *SIZE*	(49)
no matches on leverage (*LEVR*)	(31)
Initial set of matched pairs	67
Plus high-lease firms moved to low-lease group	12
Final set of matched pairs	79

[a] Variables are obtained from Compustat as follows: $PVCAP_f$ (footnoted capital leases) = #88, LTC (long-term capitalization) = #88 + #9 + #10 + #60, $SIZE$ (total assets) = #6 + #88, $LEVR$ (leverage) = (#9 + #88)/(#9 + #88 + #10 + #60).

[b] Low-lease firms were firms that disclosed any form of leasing during the period 1973 to 1976 and had footnoted capital leases amounting to less than 10 percent of total long-term capitalization, except for the 12 relatively low-lease firms in the four industries with significant amounts of leasing (SIC #4511, 5311, 5411, 5812) that had footnoted capital leases below 20 percent of LTC.

$PVCAP_f/LTC$, are:

(1) industry (4-digit SIC code),
(2) total assets (including capital lease), *SIZE*, and
(3) total leverage (including capital lease), *LEVR*.

These variables are defined in table 7. Matching requires identification of pairs of high- and low-lease firms in the same industry that are reasonably matched along *SIZE* and *LEVR*. The 338 firms on Compustat reporting $PVCAP_f$ from 1973 to 1976 are examined to form a 'high-lease' sample. We identified a total of 269 firms with present values of footnoted capital leases ($PVCAP_f$) in excess of 10 percent of total long-term capitalization (LTC) for 1976.[38] Firms in this sample are expected to be most affected by lease capitalization since they report the highest amounts of footnoted capital leases. Matches for these 269 high-lease firms are sought by identifying all low-lease firms ($PVCAP_f < 10\%$ of LTC) in the same 4-digit SIC code that reported a positive amount of

[38] The total 'long-term capitalization' measure was used in ASR No. 147 [SEC(1973)]. Firms with footnoted capital (financing) leases in excess of five percent of this capitalization measure were required to disclose them in their footnotes. Interestingly, many firms below the five percent criterion also disclosed this information.

leasing activity, and then selecting one firm with reasonably similar size (represented by total assets plus $PVCAP_f$) and leverage (long-term debt plus $PVCAP$ divided by long-term capitalization) as of 1976. The size and leverage parameters used to obtain reasonable matches are:

$$SIZE:^{39} \quad 0.40 < \frac{\text{Size of high-lease firm}}{\text{Size of low-lease firm}} < 2.50,$$

and

$$LEVR:^{40} \quad |\text{Leverage of high-lease firm} - \text{Leverage of low-lease firm}| \leq 0.25.$$

Note that these parameters are based on visual evaluation of sample firms and have no theoretical basis. They are the smallest ranges we could have selected to leave a reasonably large number of pairs of firms matched on industry, size, and leverage. Similarly, the 10 percent hurdle for high-lease firms is based on a tradeoff between larger sample sizes and potential misclassification of firms. The search for low-lease firms, matched on these three dimensions, was repeated for all 269 firms and resulted in a sample of 67 matched pairs. In observing the firms that were dropped from the sample, we noted that four industries with significant amounts of leasing activity had been almost completely deleted (airlines, retail department stores, retail grocery stores, and fast food chains). These industries comprised the bulk of all lease firms examined in the FASB's research report on leases [Abdel-khalik (1981)] and are considered important to this study.

To include these industries in the study, we permit low-lease firms in these four industries to have a value of the explanatory variable, $PVCAP_f/LTC$, be as high as 20 percent, with their high lease counterparts reporting values in excess of 20 percent. This adjustment is in keeping with the relatively high–relatively low approach to matching and yet maintains a reasonably low probability of misclassifying firms.[41] This adjustment allowed the addition of 12 matched pairs, bringing the sample size to 158 companies (or 79 matched pairs).[42] Note that a 20 percent filter for high-lease industries and a 10 percent

---

[39] This is a proportional parameter allowing the high-lease firm to be 40 percent as large as the low-lease firm (e.g., \$40/\$100) or the low-lease firm to be 40 percent as large as the high-lease firm (e.g., \$100/\$40).

[40] The absolute difference in leverage is less than or equal to 0.25.

[41] For example, if the filter that determines high- and low-lease groups varied by industry, all industries could have been represented, yet a large number of firms would have been misclassified. 'Low'-lease firms with large amounts of leasing and 'high'-lease firms with low levels of leasing would exist, thereby biasing downwards the probability of observing an effect in the matched pairs comparisons.

[42] For the 12 pairs, the mean and median difference in financing leases (as a percent of long-term capitalization) is 20 percent, with differences between pairs ranging from 5 to 28 percent.

Table 8

Summary data on attributes on high-lease and low-lease samples.

Variable[a]	High-lease group		Low-lease group		Difference high–low	
	Mean	Median	Mean	Median	Mean	Median
$PVCAP/LTC$	0.2241	0.1823	0.0633	0.0563	0.1608[b]	0.1350[b]
$PVCAP_f/LTC$	0.2101	0.1607	0.0434	0.0	0.1667[b]	0.1358[b]
$LOG(SIZE)$	5.1808	4.9471	5.2389	4.9698	0.0580	0.0427
$SALES$	1212.16	208.21	1019.21	191.11	192.95	17.52
$LEVR$	0.4535	0.4641	0.4147	0.4046	0.0388[b]	0.0402[b]
$DEBT\ RATIO$	0.3099	0.3202	0.3895	0.3932	−0.0795[b]	−0.0576[b]
$INTCOV$	5.6414	3.9887	5.6645	4.2658	0.2111	−0.3342
$RONA$	0.0768	0.0754	0.0972	0.0923	−0.0205[b]	−0.0169[b]

[a] The variables are computed as defined below. All values refer to book values as reported by Compustat, except for *Preferred equity* where liquidation values are used. The Compustat data item numbers are in parentheses. $PVCAP_f$ = Footnoted capital leases (#88), $PVCAP$ = Total capital leases (#88 + #84), LTC = Long-term capitalization = $PVCAP_f$ (#88) + *Long-term debt* (#9) + *Common equity* (#60) + *Preferred equity* (#10), $SIZE$ = *Total assets* (#6) + $PVCAP_f$ (#88) (in 1976), $SALES$ = *Net sales* (#12) (in 1976), $LEVR$ = (*Long-term debt* (#9) + $PVCAP_f$ (#88))/LTC (in 1976), $DEBT\ RATIO$ = *Long-term debt* (#9)/(*Long-term debt* (#9) + *Common equity* (#60) + *Preferred equity* (#10)) (in 1976), $INTCOV$ = Median value of *interest coverage* (between 1971 and 1980) defined as (*Interest expense* (#15) + *Pre-tax income* (#18 + #16))/*Interest expense* (#15), $RONA$ = Median value of *Return on assets* (between 1971 and 1980) defined as *Pre-tax income/SIZE*.

[b] Significant at 5% level, based on two-tailed tests.

filter for all other industries has no effect on the regression results in panels A of tables 2, 3, and 4. Also, it biases against finding a significant difference for the matched pairs comparisons reported in panels B of these tables.[43] We do not believe that the matching requirements, which tend to delete many high-lease firms, bias our results in favor of the alternative hypotheses, since the subsample results in table 2 are similar to the Compustat sample results in table 1. The results in footnote 43 indicate that the matching requirements are likely to bias the subsample results against rejecting the null hypothesis.

Table 7 summarizes the effect of each selection criterion on the original set of 388 high-lease firms, and table 8 provides summary statistics that compare the two groups. Consistent with the sample construction procedures, the high-lease group has significantly more footnoted capital leases ($PVCAP_f$) than the low-lease group. Also, high-lease firms have significantly more capital leases ($PVCAP$). Matched pairs are of similar size, based on natural loga-

[43] To gauge the amount of bias, all overall comparisons in panels B of tables 2, 3, and 4 and table 6 were repeated without these 12 additional pairs. As expected, the differences between high- and low-lease groups are even more significant for the reduced subsample of 67 pairs than they are for the 79 pairs. Note that the debt changes in table 6 become significant at the three percent level. (However, the equity changes remain insignificant at the five percent level.)

rithms of *SIZE*. Also, *SALES*, another measure of firm size is well-matched across the pairs of high- and low-lease firms. However, the total leverage (*LEVR*) match is not completely successful as high-lease firms report significantly higher values of *LEVR* (debt plus capital leases). Given that the high-lease group was constructed to have more footnoted capital leases and similar values of *LEVR*, the low-lease group should have higher amounts of conventional debt (*DEBT RATIO*). Table 8 confirms this expectation. [The interest coverage ratio (*INTCOV*), however, is not significantly different.] The low-lease group is significantly more profitable (*RONA*). Two other measures, not reported in table 8, are the number of years, between 1971 and 1980, that firms reported a tax loss carryforward and the number of years that the firm paid no dividends. While the high-lease group has a slightly lower number of firms that always paid some dividends (58 versus 63 out of the 79 pairs of firms) and also fewer firms that did not report a tax loss carryforward (43 versus 49 out of 79 firms), the differences are not statistically significant using chi-squared tests of independence. To summarize, our subsample of pairs of high- and low-lease firms are similar along all relevant dimensions, except for leverage differences.

References

Abdel-khalik, A., 1981, The economic effects on lessees of FASB statement no. 13: Accounting for lessees (FASB, Stamford, CT).

American Institute of Certified Public Accountants (AICPA), 1964, Accounting Principles Board (APB) opinion no. 5: Reporting of leases in financial statements of lessees (AICPA, New York, NY).

American Institute of Certified Public Accountants (AICPA), 1973, Accounting Principles Board (APB) opinion no. 31: Disclosure of lease commitments by lessees (AICPA, New York, NY).

Antle, R. and A. Smith, 1986, An empirical investigation of the relative performance evaluation of corporate executives, Journal of Accounting Research 24, 1–39.

Ball, R., 1980, Discussion of Accounting for research and development costs: The impact on research and development expenditures, Supplement to the Journal of Accounting Research 18, 27–37.

DeAngelo, L., 1982, Mandated successful efforts and auditor choice, Journal of Accounting and Economics 4, 171–203.

Dukes, R., T. Dyckman, and J. Elliott, 1980, Accounting for research and development costs: The impact on research and development expenditures, Supplement to the Journal of Accounting Research 18, 1–26.

Elliott, J., G. Richardson, T. Dyckman, and R. Dukes, 1984, The impact of SFAS no. 2 on firm expenditures on research and development: Replications and extension, Journal of Accounting Research 22, 85–102.

El-Gazzar, S., S. Lillien, and V. Pastena, 1986, Accounting for leases by lessees, Journal of Accounting and Economics 8, 217–238.

Financial Accounting Standards Board (FASB), 1974, Statement of financial accounting standard no. 2: Accounting for research and development costs (FASB, Stamford, CT).

Financial Accounting Standards Board (FASB), 1976, Statement of financial accounting standard no. 13: Accounting for leases (FASB, Stamford, CT).

Freedman, D., R. Pisani, and R. Purves, 1976, Statistics (Norton, New York, NY).

Healy, P., 1985, The effect of bonus schemes on accounting decisions, Journal of Accounting and Economics 7, 85–108.

Holthausen, R. and R. Leftwich, 1983, The economic consequences of accounting choice: Implications of costly contracting and monitoring, Journal of Accounting and Economics 5, 77–118.

Horwitz, B. and R. Kolodny, 1980, The economic effect of involuntary uniformity in financial reporting and R&D expenditures, Supplement to the Journal of Accounting Research 18, 38–74.

Kmenta, J., 1971, Elements of econometrics (Macmillan, New York, NY).

Leftwich, R., 1981, Evidence on the impact of mandatory changes in accounting principles on corporate loan agreements, Journal of Accounting and Economics 3, 3–36.

Pfeiffer, G., 1980, The economic consequences of lease accounting changes, Working paper (Cornell University, Ithaca, NY).

Runkel, P.J. and J.E. McGrath, 1972, Research on human behavior: A systematic guide to method (Holt, Rinehart, and Winston, New York, NY).

SAS, 1986, SAS user's guide: Statistics (SAS Institute, Cary, NC).

Securities and Exchange Commission (SEC), 1973, Accounting series release (ASR) no. 147: Notice of adoption of amendments to regulation six requiring improved disclosure of rules (SEC, Washington, DC).

Securities and Exchange Commission (SEC), 1977, Accounting series release (ASR) no. 225: Lease accounting and disclosure rules (SEC, Washington, DC).

Selto, F. and M. Clouse, 1985, An investigation of manager's adaptations to SFAS no. 2: Accounting for research and development costs, Journal of Accounting Research 23, 700–717.

Sharpe, W., 1982, Factors in New York Stock Exchange security returns, 1931–1979, Journal of Portfolio Management 8, 5–19.

Smith, C. and L. Wakeman, 1985, Determinants of corporate leasing policy, Journal of Finance 40, 895–908.

Watts, R. and J. Zimmerman, 1986, Positive accounting theory (Prentice-Hall, Englewood Cliffs, NJ).

Watts, R. and J. Zimmerman, 1978, Towards a positive theory of the determination of accounting standards, The Accounting Review 53, 112–134.

Wolfson, M., 1980, Discussion of The economic effects of involuntary uniformity in the financial reporting of R&D expenditures, Supplement to the Journal of Accounting Research 18, 76–83.

ACCOUNTING FOR INTEREST BY
REAL ESTATE DEVELOPERS

Ian ZIMMER*

University of Queensland, St. Lucia, Brisbane, Australia 4067

Received January 1984, final version received April 1985

This paper investigates accounting for interest by Australian real estate developers. It argues that management's choice of accounting technique is the result of *ex ante* contracting to prevent management opportunistic behavior, rather than a manifestation of opportunistic behavior *per se*. The argument provides a richer description of accounting choice and explains why, in Australia, leverage and the accounting method choice are correlated in the absence of bond covenants. The argument also explains why, inconsistent with political cost arguments, larger firms are more likely to capitalize than expense interest.

1. Introduction

Although accounting for interest costs has been prescribed in the U.S. (FASB 34), this matter has not, until very recently, come under regulatory scrutiny in Australia. However, a discussion memorandum has been issued by the Australian Accounting Research Foundation on the topic of accounting for real estate development [Phin (1983)], signalling impending regulatory activity. Accounting for interest costs is one issue marked for attention by the memorandum. In this paper, current practice in accounting for interest by Australian real estate developers is described, and the determinants of management's decision to capitalize or expense interest are considered. This leads to hypotheses about the attributes of firms that capitalize interest. Tests of these hypotheses are reported.

It is argued that managers of real estate development firms are more likely to increase reported income by capitalizing (rather than expensing) interest where the firm writes contracts under which interest directly increases the revenues of the firm. It is proposed that this is a manifestation of contracting procedures aimed at maximization of firm value by preventing opportunistic behavior by managers, in contrast to previous studies that have predicted that opportunistic

*This paper has benefited from the comments of Peter Dodd, Richard Morris, Ross Watts, Greg Whittred, Jerold Zimmerman, the reviewer (Eric Noreen of the University of Washington) and participants in workshops at Monash, New South Wales and Queensland Universities.

behavior by managers (such as loosening bond covenants and minimizing political costs) determines the accounting method choice. This distinction is important. Apart from providing a richer description of the accounting choice setting, the arguments explain why leverage and rule selection are correlated even in the absence of bond covenants and why, inconsistent with political cost arguments [Watts and Zimmerman (1978)] larger firms have previously been found to be more likely to capitalize interest [Bowen, Noreen and Lacey (1981)].

The next section of the paper provides necessary institutional background by describing the nature of contracts written by real estate developers with customers, lenders and coventurers. This leads to two lines of argument about the determinants of accounting for interest. The first implies that interest capitalization is the result of maximization of firm value via contracting processes and hypothesizes relations between rule selection and (a) the existence of certain types of contracts with customers and/or coventurers and (b) the use of project-specific financing by the firm. The second line adapts conventional arguments that the choice is a result of opportunistic accounting decisions taken by managers after certain contracts are put in place. The sample selection and research design are outlined in section 3, and empirical results consistent with the hypotheses are presented in section 4. Discussion and conclusions are presented in section 5.

2. Hypothesis development

2.1. Ex ante contracting processes

Developers often write contracts in which the project's price is dependent on the project's cost. For example, contracts sometimes include 'rise and fall' clauses whereby, if the cost of raw materials or other factors change, the price changes. Such 'cost plus' contracts are a device for shifting risk to a buyer with lower costs of bearing risk. The definition of 'allowable' or 'recoverable' costs in such contracts is a matter of concern to the customer and developer, since it is a mechanism by which wealth can be transferred between them.

If the developer seeks to have interest included in the definition of cost, then the customer will be cautious with respect to the determination of both the 'amount of funds employed' and the rate of interest applicable to those funds, particularly where the developer intends to finance the project from either retained earnings or a general pool of debt capital. There are at least two solutions to this problem. First, the contracting parties can negotiate both the definition of funds employed and the rate. However, the possibility of opportunistic behavior by management through arbitrary allocations means that this arrangement will be costly to negotiate and monitor. Alternatively, the parties could agree that the project is to be financed using funds 'tied' to the project.

In this context 'project-specific finance' has several attractive features. In general it minimizes the monitoring costs arising from the conflict of interest between the firm and both its customers and lenders. From the point of view of the customer, the use of project-specific finance eliminates the need to monitor arbitrary allocations or assignment of interest charges to the project. Turning to the lender, since project-specific loans are secured[1] over the assets of the project, they also reduce the problem of asset substitution (i.e., replacement of low-variance projects with high-variance projects after the firm has raised debt valued at prices commensurate with low-variance activities) and claim dilution (i.e., the subsequent issue of debt of the same or higher priority). This has the effect of minimizing the interest cost that is eventually borne by the purchaser. Project-specific financing is a special case of secured debt financing as discussed by Smith and Warner (1979).

These relations are schematized in fig 1. Risk shifting via cost plus contracts induces agreements in which interest is included as a defined cost. These contracts, if they extend across fiscal years, provide the basis for interest capitalization for financial reporting for at least two reasons:

(a) The first is a manifestation of financial executive incentive schemes which are, to an increasing extent, dependent on accounting earnings [Smith and Watts (1982)]. Tying compensation to accounting earnings creates incentives for managers to capitalize interest. Shareholders, through a representative such as a compensation committee, are likely to restrict management discretion with respect to the transfer of expenses between periods via interest capitalization. However, the shareholders are likely to allow capitalization where the incurrence of interest directly results in increased revenues, such as in the circumstances of a cost plus pricing contract. In that case capitalization is in both the firms' and managers' interest. Accordingly, allowing capitalization in only these circumstances is likely to be a rule that reduces opportunistic actions and increases firm value. While it is less likely that shareholders will permit capitalization on *all* project-specific debt, such permission is *more* likely than allowing management absolute discretion. The reason is it limits the amount of interest that can be capitalized because (in accordance with Australian securities legislation) these projects must be valued at the lower of cost or realizable value.

(b) Apart from the effects of financial executive incentive schemes, a further reason for the same rule being followed in invoicing and external reporting is

---

[1] In circumstances of default the lender usually has recourse to the other assets of the firm. However, the lender does not have direct access to such assets, indeed they may be secured by other lenders. Even if they are not secured to others, it is usually much more costly to obtain repayment from liquidation of assets not secured. For example, under some charge documents (e.g. a legal mortgage) the lender 'owns' the asset. Therefore, there are fewer restrictions on the lender's power to possess and sell such an asset than is the case with those that are unsecured.

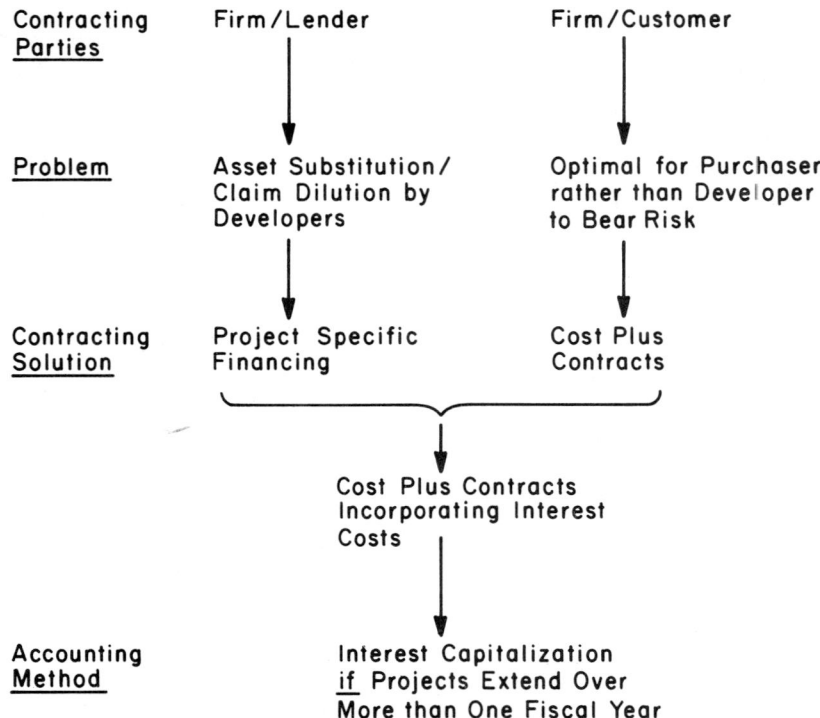

Fig. 1. The relation between opportunistic action reducing and risk shifting contracts and interest capitalization.

that such consistency reduces costs of negotiation time with auditors and (more particularly) cost investigators where the customer is a governmental agency or the contract allows inspection of cost records by an outside party.

The analysis schematized in fig. 1 implies several hypotheses. For example, it predicts an association between interest capitalization and cost plus contracts that include interest as a cost and extend across fiscal periods. This is perhaps the most powerful test of the model. Other hypotheses relate likelihood of interest capitalization to *both* the existence of project-specific financing and cost plus contracts. Initial investigations indicated difficulty in ascertaining the nature of contracts written between the firm and its customers. In contrast, the type of financing used by developers is ascertainable. Therefore the primary hypothesis selected for testing in this study was:

H.1.   Firms that finance projects by a project-specific loan are more likely to capitalize interest than firms that do not finance projects by a project-specific loan.

Joint venture agreements. Developers use other types of contracts that lead to almost identical expectations. For example, they frequently become involved in joint venture partnerships.[2] A typical joint arrangement used by Australian real estate developers involves one party (the 'financing coventurer') providing equity finance and the other party developing the project. On completion, the development is sold and the coventurers share profits in proportions agreed before the development commenced. The 'financing coventurer' as well as providing funds on an equity basis, may also contribute debt funds on which interest is charged. The same problems of asset substitution and claim dilution mentioned previously occur under these arrangements. The financing coventurer is concerned that contributed funds are used only in the project subject to the joint venture agreement, and the other coventurer is concerned that the amount of interest charged to the project is not excessive. One way to reduce these uncertainties is to legally tie these debt funds to the job. The interest payment is made before the amount of profit to be shared is calculated. Therefore it is efficient bookkeeping to account for this as part of the cost of the job in the records of the joint development.

Often further debt funds for the project are obtained from another party, such as a banker. However, whether debt funds come from either the financing coventurer or an external party, profit sharing is partly affected by the interest charged to the project. Again, at least one of the coventurers is concerned that the amount of interest charged to the project is not excessive, and at least one of the coventurers is concerned that the funds are used only in the project. Similar to the previous example, these concerns lead to a project-specific loan being raised and the interest thereon being accounted for as part of the cost of the job in records pertaining to the joint development. Therefore, in the context of a joint venture agreement, the optimal contracting method again implies capitalization of interest only on project-specific loans to *prevent* opportunistic behavior.

2.2. Ex post opportunistic actions

The *ex ante* argument is that interest capitalization is *allowed* if cost plus or joint venture contracts and consequent project-specific financing exist. It does not imply that capitalization necessarily follows from the existence of such contracts. Indeed, the probability of capitalization is increased where *ex post* opportunistic actions by management are cost-effective.[3] For example, it has

[2] Note that the term 'joint venture', as used in the Australian real estate development industry, denotes a partnership of two or more corporations for the purpose of a project of limited duration. Although the power of American corporations to form partnerships is prohibited in several U.S. jurisdictions, such constraints do not exist in Australia.

[3] For a review of evidence of *ex post* opportunistic actions affecting accounting policy choices, see Holthausen and Leftwich (1983).

been frequently argued that firms that are closer to debt covenants are more likely to use income increasing accounting techniques to minimize debt agreement renegotiation costs. This suggests that firms with higher leverage are more likely to capitalize rather than expense interest:

H.2.   Firms with higher leverage are more likely to capitalize interest than firms with lower leverage.

Similarly, the existence of management compensation schemes based on accounting earnings increases the probability of capitalization. However, due to difficulties in observing the nature of management compensation schemes in place, this proposition is not tested here.

3. Method

3.1. Other factors

To determine the research procedure it is necessary to consider factors not included in the proposed model that could plausibly affect the choice. For example, Watts and Zimmerman (1978) have argued that firm size proxies for political costs, leading to hypothesized negative relations between firm size and the adoption of income increasing techniques. However, size could proxy for many factors [Ball and Foster (1982)]. Indeed, it is unlikely that size would proxy for political costs of Australian property developers, as such firms do not appear to have been 'threatened' by government, unions or other organizations as a result of reporting higher profits over the period of this study. There is no evidence that they are as 'politically sensitive' as, say, the U.S. oil industry.

However, the *ex ante* analysis presented here implies that the size of real estate developers is *positively* associated with adoption of interest capitalization, i.e., larger firms are more likely to capitalize interest. This is expected because larger firms in the industry tend to be involved in longer projects. For example, it is the larger firms that are likely to successfully tender for large government and other contracts because they have a greater range of expertise at their disposal. Further, many of the smaller firms' activities are limited to residential house construction projects of 6–8 weeks duration. Therefore, the larger firms are more likely to be involved in projects that extend across fiscal periods. The greater the length of projects completed by the firm, the greater the incentive for management to defer interest charges by capitalization. Perhaps for similar reasons, Bowen, Noreen and Lacy (1981) found that when firms in the (politically sensitive) oil industry were excluded from their sample, larger firms were more likely to capitalize interest (thereby increasing income) than smaller firms.

The 'pool' of retained earnings available for distribution as dividends could also affect the choice. Bowen et al. (1981) found unrestricted retained earnings, a measure of closeness to dividend-related covenants, to be significant in explaining the choice of accounting for interest in the United States. However, this is not relevant in the context of this paper, as a recent survey of Australian public and private debt agreements [Whittred and Zimmer (1984)] shows that dividend-constraining covenants are not included in debt agreements. Indeed, the only financial ratios included in Australian continuing covenants relate to (variously defined) debt/assets ratios, which are included in all public debt contracts examined in the survey.

The 'pool' of retained earnings may also affect the choice through the effect of legal restrictions on dividends, i.e., dividends can only be paid out of profits, not capital. Therefore, if a dividend policy is being hampered by a lack of retained earnings, it is functional for management to use income increasing techniques. However, given the scope allowed management to increase reserves available for distribution under current Australian dividend law, this ratio is at best only a very weak proxy for the extent to which management is so restricted, and is not considered further.

The tax deductibility of interest may also be an important factor. In Australia, interest is deductible for tax purposes the *earlier* of when it is either paid or accrued [Richards (1984)]. Accordingly, if the terms of a debt issue imply that interest is not payable until maturity, then the firm has an incentive to expense, rather than capitalize interest. This type of debt, referred to as 'deferred' debentures or notes is relatively unusual in Australia. None of the firms analyzed included such debt. Under more normal circumstances, where interest is payable periodically during the period of issue, tax planning should have no effect on the accounting policy choice.

3.2. Sample selection and research method

The 1982 annual reports of all (61) companies listed in either the 1981 (latest available) copy of Jobson's Yearbook of Australian Companies or the most recent stock exchange journal as being active in real estate development were requested from the 'company secretaries' (i.e., chief administrative officers) of each firm. Where no reply was received within a reasonable time copies of the reports were obtained from the stock exchange library. In three cases the report was not available as the firm had ceased to exist. In another five cases the firms were no longer involved in real estate development. Two firms were deleted because they had a deficiency in assets (i.e., negative shareholder's equity) and two were primarily finance companies. This left a sample of 49 firms for analysis.

Identification of a firm's method of accounting for interest is not always straightforward as neither the method used, nor disclosure of the method actually used, is explicitly required by Australian regulations. The Companies' Act requires disclosure of interest paid and the format suggested by an appendix to the professional standard on the format of a profit and loss statement (AAS1) recommends disclosure of the amount of interest charged to profit and loss. Accordingly, companies who capitalize interest often provide a reconciliation of the differences between interest paid and interest expense. However, many firms do not follow the professional recommendation and the amount capitalized is often not disclosed.[4] For the purpose of this study a firm is initially identified as an interest capitalizer if:

(a) an amount of interest capitalized is disclosed in the accounts, or
(b) the company states that it capitalizes interest as part of real estate development costs in the 'statement of accounting policies' section of the annual report.

Every company was telephoned and their accounting policy confirmed. Firms included in the sample and their categorization are reported in table 1.

To test the first hypothesis, firms' financing procedures must be observed. As these are not publicly disclosed it is necessary to gather this data by a telephone survey. Admittedly, data gathered in this way can lack credibility. However, a telephone survey was used in this case because (a) the question asked required a simple, factual answer, (b) there was no reason to expect the interviewees to be dishonest, and (c) the answers, in aggregate, were verified by an analysis of annual report debt structures. Accordingly, the company secretaries (chief administrative officers) of each firm in the sample were telephoned. They were asked:

> 'Do you normally finance projects by a project-specific facility secured against the project'?

Replies indicated that they either 'never' financed developments in this way, or they did in most if not all cases. This answer was coded as a YES or NO.

If the answers are correctly coded, then *ceteris paribus* there should be observable differences in the liabilities section of the balance sheets between those companies that are recorded as using different financing procedures. In particular, those firms that use project-specific finance, which by definition involves loan security that takes the form of a 'fixed charge' (or encumbrance

---

[4] For example, companies frequently show 'interest, rates and taxes and other holding charges capitalized' as one aggregate amount.

Table 1

Australian property developers and method of accounting for interest in 1982.

Firms capitalizing interest	Firms not capitalizing interest
1. Acron Pacific Ltd	1. A.H. Hodge and Son Ltd
2. Ariadne Australia Ltd	2. Barina Corporation Ltd
3. Austmark International Ltd	3. Central Management & Finance Ltd
4. Bond Corp. Holdings Ltd	4. Entrad Ltd
5. CDL Developments Ltd	5. Hooker Corporation Ltd
6. Charles Davis Ltd	6. Impala Securities Ltd
7. Jack Chia (Australia) Ltd	7. Ipec Holdings Ltd
8. Consolidated Press Hold. Ltd	8. Jonray Holdings Ltd
9. Costain Australia Ltd	9. Kimberley Securities Ltd
10. CSR Ltd	10. Kingsway Group Ltd
11. Dainford Holdings Ltd	11. McDonald Industries Ltd
12. General Corp. of Aust. Ltd	12. Martin Properties Ltd
13. Hawkstone Investments Ltd	13. Myer Realty Ltd
14. Henry & Walker Ltd	14. Newmetal Mines Ltd
15. Interwest Ltd	15. Orlit Holdings Ltd
16. Jennings Industries Ltd	16. Paynter Dixon Hold. Ltd
17. Katanning Holdings Ltd	17. Peter Kurts Properties Ltd
18. Kemtron Ltd	18. West Coast Projects Aust. Ltd
19. Kern Corp. Ltd	
20. Latec Investments Ltd	
21. Leighton Holdings Ltd	
22. Lend Lease Corp. Ltd	
23. Mallina Holdings Ltd	
24. Oceanic Equity Ltd	
25. Parrys Esplanade Ltd	
26. Pennant Holdings Ltd	
27. Southern Farmers Group Ltd	
28. Stirling Properties Ltd	
29. The Adelaide Steamship Co. Ltd	
30. Valinda Properties Ltd	
31. Westfield Holdings Ltd	

on a specific asset), should reflect a higher proportion of debt secured by such a charge than those firms that do not use project-specific finance. As disclosure of the nature of security pertaining to debt agreements is a statutory requirement in Australia, the data to calculate this ratio could be obtained directly from the annual report of each firm. A Mann–Whitney test[5] indicated that these proportions are significantly different at $p = 0.01$ (one-tailed), supporting the accuracy of the company secretaries' statements and my coding of their statements. Proportions are detailed in table 3.

---

[5] When conducting tests of differences between means, I rely on *t*-tests where it is known that the population distribution is approximately normal (e.g. debt/assets and total assets logged) and Mann–Whitney tests for other variables.

Table 2

The relation between method of accounting for interest and type of
debt finance raised for Australian real estate developers in 1982.

		Are project-specific financing facilities used?	
		YES	NO
Is interest	YES	25	6
capitalized?	NO	5	13

4. Results

4.1. Interest capitalization and financing procedure

Initially, a test of the first hypothesis was made by relating the answer to the question about financing procedures to method of accounting by analysis of the contingency table shown at table 2.

This resulted in a chi-square of 13.40 significant at $p = 0.0003$ in the hypothesized direction, implying that those that use project-specific facilities are much more likely to capitalize interest than those that do not. In reply to the question, secretaries of two companies indicated that although they 'generally' do not use project-specific funds, *if* they did use such a facility they would capitalize interest.

Subsequent to the question on methods of financing, the company secretaries were asked to describe their accounting policy in detail. These descriptions revealed that of the 25 capitalizers that normally use project-specific facilities, 23 do not capitalize interest when they do not use project-specific finance. When they capitalize interest, the amount capitalized is the amount actually paid. The other two companies are CDL Developments Ltd (in receivership at time of writing) which imputed a rate 'based on the current market rate of project-specific debt funds' during the period of study, and Jack Chia (Australia) Ltd which, when not using a project-specific facility, impute interest on a weighted average cost of debt basis. Six firms capitalize interest but do not use project-specific debt contracts. Three of these use the current market rate for debt funds applicable to such projects. Two use a weighted average cost of debt capital. One company uses a 'notional' (apparently subjectively determined) rate of 10%

The diversity in these practices has at least two implications. First, the dependent variable could be respecified so that the policy, instead of being viewed as a choice between capitalization/expense, could be considered a choice between capitalization on project-specific loans only or any of a number of other policies. The significance of chi-square on this data set is robust to such a respecification. Second, it suggests that there are factors, other than those explicitly discussed in the model proposed here, that also partially determine policy choice. Discussions with the firms that do not fit the schema outlined in this paper did not indicate any systematic differences in the contracts written by these firms from the others. However, future research on larger samples, perhaps with actual inspection of contracts by researchers, may reveal the distinguishing features of these firms.

4.2. Significance of leverage and size

Leverage and size were also tested for significance. Descriptive data pertaining to these factors are provided in table 3.

In view of the arguments proposed in the *ex post* analysis in this paper and elsewhere, and results reported previously [Holthausen and Leftwich (1983)] it is predicted that firms with higher leverage are more likely to capitalize. A *t*-test indicated that the debt/assets ratio is significant ($t = 3.20$, $p = 0.001$, one-tailed).[6] Of course, the debt/assets ratio is not independent of the method of accounting for interest. Everything else equal, a firm that capitalizes interest must have a *lower* debt/assets ratio than one that expenses interest. Due to incomplete disclosures, it is not possible to adjust the numbers; however, it should be noted that if the effect of the interest accounting policy was undone, the difference in leverage between the two groups would be *more* significant. Accordingly, it is concluded that a significant positive relation between leverage and likelihood of capitalization exists.

Note that such a correlation is equivocal evidence of opportunistic behaviour by management. Indeed, it may be considered further evidence in support of the *ex ante* analysis prescribed earlier because there is an (almost tautological) relationship between the likelihood of firms raising project-specific loans and the extent of debt in their capital structure. To illustrate, consider an extreme case of an all equity firm, that has not previously been a party to one of the contracts described earlier but accepts a positive NPV project that does involve such a contract. In such a case acceptance of the project causes leverage to increase from zero to a positive value. In more general circumstances, involvement of firms in these contracts implies some type of debt being raised; therefore firms that sign these types of contracts are likely to have greater debt than firms that do not.

The significant correlation reports only a directional association. It is not possible to infer that both of these non-mutually exclusive explanations are operative based on this significant difference alone. Nevertheless, the practice of limiting interest capitalized to that attributable to project-specific loans by most firms is supportive of the customer/coventurer contracting arrangements explanation, as Australian lenders do not specify the method of accounting for

---

[6] Mann-Whitney test significant at $p = 0.002$ (one-tailed).

Table 3

Descriptive statistics for Australian real estate developers in 1982 according to whether they do or do not capitalize interest.

	Interest capitalizers ($n = 31$)	Interest expensers ($n = 18$)	Total sample ($n = 49$)
Debt / assets ratio			
Mean	0.613	0.437	0.548
Median	0.621	0.411	0.586
Standard deviation	0.170	0.208	0.202
Total assets (000s)			
Mean	188248	71628	145408
Median	52602	8049	24805
Standard deviation	479613	158310	394805
Total assets (*logged*)			
Mean	4.698	4.107	4.481
Median	4.721	3.906	4.395
Standard deviation	0.708	0.786	0.784
Market value of equity plus book value of debt (000s)			
Mean	163218	58548	124768
Median	50360	8299	23992
Standard deviation	397555	124482	326908
Market value of equity plus book value of debt (*logged*)			
Mean	4.6678	4.0483	4.4402
Median	4.7020	3.9190	4.3800
Standard deviation	0.697	0.768	0.776
Proportion of debt secured by a fixed charge			
Mean	0.517	0.426	0.484
Median	0.560	0.342	0.500
Standard deviation	0.342	0.348	0.343

interest for the purpose of calculating financial ratio constraints in debt agreements [Whittred and Zimmer (1984)]. However, further analysis indicates that (although subsets of the sample contains few degrees of freedom) leverage remains significant at liberal levels when the analysis is limited to (a) those companies that normally raise project-specific finance ($t = 1.23$, $p = 0.12$, one-tailed),[7] or (b) those that do not ($t = 1.76$, $p = 0.05$, one-tailed).[8] Accord-

[7] Mann–Whitney test significant at $p = 0.101$ (one-tailed).

[8] Mann–Whitney test significant at $p = 0.198$ (one-tailed).

Table 4

Correlations between the independent variables used to explain accounting choice ($n = 49$), with two-tailed test probabilities of the correlations being different from zero shown in parentheses.

	$\dfrac{\text{Debt}}{\text{Assets}}$	Size
Financing procedure (0 = project-specific loans not raised) (1 = project-specific loans raised)	0.3523 ($p = 0.01$)	−0.2068 ($p = 0.14$)
$\dfrac{\text{Debt}}{\text{Assets}}$		0.0257 ($p = 0.86$)

ingly, it is tentatively concluded that both the *ex ante* and *ex post* factors are affecting the choice.

It is also expected that larger firms are more likely to capitalize than smaller firms. A *t*-test of the difference in size, measured by the log of the sum of the market value of equity and the book value of debt of each firm, indicates a statistically significant difference in size in the hypothesized direction ($t = 2.80$, $p = 0.003$, one-tailed).[9] This is inconsistent with the 'political costs' argument conventionally proposed in policy choice research; but it is consistent with the arguments in this paper and the U.S. findings of Bowen et al. The difference in size is significant when the analysis is limited to (a) those companies that normally raise project-specific finance ($t = 1.96$, $p = 0.03$, one-tailed)[10] or (b) those that do not ($t = 2.69$, $p = 0.007$, one-tailed).[11]

4.3. Multivariate analysis

The interpretation of univariate tests in the presence of multicollinearity is problematic. The extent to which the variables tested are independent is reflected in the correlation matrix shown in table 4.

In view of the argued relationship between the raising of project-specific finance and leverage proposed earlier, the significant relation between these factors is expected. The extent to which each factor is significant when controlling for others was investigated by running a multivariate probit regression. The dependent variable was coded either 0 (= interest expensed) or 1 (= interest capitalized). Further, the financing procedure variable was coded either 0 (= project-specific finance *not* raised) or 1 (= project-specific finance

[9] Mann–Whitney test significant at $p = 0.008$ (one-tailed).

[10] Mann–Whitney test significant at $p = 0.030$ (one-tailed).

[11] Mann–Whitney test significant at $p = 0.220$ (one-tailed).

Table 5

Coefficients of probit regression of interest accounting policy choice against financing procedure, leverage and size ($n = 49$) with asymptotic t-statistics in parentheses.

	Financing procedure	$\dfrac{\text{Debt}}{\text{Assets}}$	Size	Model R^2
Predicted coefficient sign	+	+	+	
Estimated coefficient	1.80	1.27	0.39	0.49
Asymptotic t-statistics	(3.33)	(0.95)	(2.54)	

raised). The resultant coefficients are shown in table 5. The values in the parentheses are the maximum likelihood estimate divided by the standard error of the estimate. Asymptotically, this ratio is a t-statistic. The R^2 for the model is 0.49. The significance tests indicate that both financing procedure and size remain significant when other variables are controlled for, however debt/assets does not.

5. Discussion and conclusion

Results indicate that an important explanation of the accounting policy choice pertains to the way that contracts between the firm and (a) customers, (b) lenders and (c) coventurers are written so as to prevent opportunistic behavior by management. Factors implied by such an explanation, such as the existence of project-specific loans, leverage and size of the firm, are significantly correlated with the choice; although leverage is not significant when other factors are controlled.

The argument proposed and tested here is different from previous explanations of economic determinants of policy choice in at least two ways. First, it stresses the effect of procedures for the *prevention* of opportunistic behavior; whereas previous studies have described accounting choices as manifestations of attempts to (for example) minimize political costs and loosen debt covenants. This enables explanations of rule selection to be proposed even where the firm is not politically sensitive and there are either no relevant debt constraints or where the debt contract prescribes the method of accounting for interest for the purpose of such covenants. A second difference is that it is specifically concerned with accounting for interest; whereas previous studies have described general determinants of income effects. For example, the closeness to debt covenants arguments could be tested on many valuation or allocation choices available to management.

References

Ball, R.J. and G. Foster, 1982, Corporate financial reporting: A methodological review of empirical research, in: Studies on current research methodologies in accounting: A critical evaluation, Supplement to Journal of Accounting Research, 161–234.

Bowen, R.M., C.W. Noreen and J.M. Lacey, 1981, Determinants of the corporate decision to capitalize interest, Journal of Accounting and Economics 3, 151–179.

Holthausen, R.W. and R.W. Leftwich, 1983, The economic consequences of accounting choice: Implications of costly contracting and monitoring, Journal of Accounting and Economics 5, 77–117.

Phin, P.A., 1982, Accounting for real estate development (Australian Accounting Research Foundation, Melbourne).

Richards, R., 1984, When is interest deductible?, The Australian Accountant, March, 97–99.

Smith, C. and J. Warner, 1979, On financial contracting: An analysis of bond covenants, Journal of Financial Economics 7, 117–161.

Smith, C.W. and R.L. Watts, 1982, Incentive and tax effects of executive compensation plans, Australian Journal of Management, Dec., 14–155.

Watts, R.L. and J.L. Zimmerman, 1978, Towards a positive theory of the determination of accounting standards, The Accounting Review, Jan., 112–134.

Whittred, G.P. and I.R. Zimmer, 1984, Accounting information in the market for debt: Australian evidence, Working paper (Department of Commerce, University of Queensland, St. Lucia, Australia).

ECONOMIC INCENTIVES FOR THE VOLUNTARY DISCLOSURE OF CURRENT COST FINANCIAL STATEMENTS

Jilnaught WONG*

University of Auckland, Auckland, New Zealand

Received October 1985, final version received September 1987

This study examines why some New Zealand listed companies voluntarily present current cost financial statements. The results suggest that tax and political cost considerations are influential in the voluntary disclosure of current cost information.

1. Introduction

This study examines whether New Zealand listed companies' voluntary disclosure of current cost financial statements is a product of the political process. It makes two contributions to understanding motives for accounting choices. First, it extends the domain of accounting choices beyond those under the historic cost model, on which most studies have focused,[1] by empirically testing the economic factors influencing management's decision to present current cost financial statements.[2] Second, the study provides a test of the economic consequences of accounting decisions in a different institutional environment. Most of the studies to date are based on United States corporations.[3] Although these studies focus on different accounting issues using different samples, thereby contributing towards the external validity of the

---

*I wish to thank Ray Ball, Allan Barton, Michael Bradbury, Andrew Christie, David Emanuel, Dale Morse, Alastair Scott, Ian Stewart, David Tweedie, Ross Watts, Greg Whittred, Jerold Zimmerman, and Paul Healy (the referee) for their valuable comments. I also wish to thank Russell Fulton and Jim Manegold for their assistance with computer programming. The financial support of the New Zealand Society of Accountants' Peter Barr Research Fellowship, the University of Auckland's Research Fund, and Coopers and Lybrand, Auckland, are gratefully acknowledged.

[1] Holthausen and Leftwich (1983), Kelly (1983), and Watts and Zimmerman (1986) provide summaries of the work in this area.

[2] Watts and Zimmerman (1978) and McKee et al. (1984) examine firms' lobbying behavior with respect to a proposed requirement that firms use general price-level accounting, whereas this study examines a voluntary accounting choice.

[3] Trotman (1980), Bazley, Brown and Izan (1985), Zimmer (1986), and Whittred (1987), which are Australian studies, are some exceptions.

Journal of Accounting and Economics 10 (1988) 151–167. North-Holland

results, it is not known whether these results generalize to other institutional domains.

The remainder of the paper is organized as follows. Section 2 presents an outline of the current cost accounting adjustments. This provides the background for the research hypotheses in section 3. The sample selection and research design are outlined in section 4, and the results are presented in section 5, followed by the conclusions in section 6.

2. Current cost accounting

In November 1975, the New Zealand Government set up a Committee of Inquiry into Inflation Accounting (known as the Richardson Committee) to 'assess the merits of alternative standards and methods [of accounting] that might be adopted in New Zealand... in the light of rapidly changing price levels.' The Richardson Committee released its report in December 1976. The Richardson Committee recommended:

(1) Assets should be valued at current replacement cost.
(2) Three adjustments (the cost of sales, depreciation, and circulating monetary asset adjustments) should be charged to the income statement in arriving at the current cost operating profit of the enterprise.
(3) A leverage adjustment, being the leveraged portion of the holding gains on the non-monetary assets, should be credited to the current cost operating profit in arriving at the profit attributable to the shareholders.

In general, the net effect of the current cost accounting adjustments was to reduce net income (see section 4).

In December 1978, the New Zealand Society of Accountants issued 'CCA Guidelines', GU-1, that recommended the voluntary disclosure of current cost financial statements which were to be prepared in accordance with the Richardson Committee's proposals. This voluntary disclosure terminated in April 1982 when the New Zealand Society of Accountants mandated the supplementary disclosure of current cost information [New Zealand Society of Accountants (1982)]; however, the majority of New Zealand companies (which are virtually the same companies making up the control group in this study) did not comply with this mandate, and in February 1986 the standard was withdrawn.

3. Research hypotheses

Accounting researchers have developed and tested hypotheses relating political incentives facing managers to their choice of accounting procedures [see, for example, Watts and Zimmerman (1978), Zmijewski and Hagerman (1981), Daley and Vigeland (1983), and Ayres (1986)]. This section presents the hypotheses to be tested without repeating much of the underlying theoretical reasoning.

3.1. Taxes

Some companies in New Zealand unequivocally state that their decision to publish current cost financial statements is to influence Government's decision to eliminate taxes on 'fictitious' gains. For example, the 1981 annual report of Ivon Watkins–Dow Limited contains the following statement:

> 'It is hoped that CCA [current cost accounting] will eventually be THE method of accounting and that its recognition and acceptance by Government bodies will lead to taxation relief by recognition of a lower level of assessable income in times of rising prices.' (Emphasis in original.)

A priori, one would expect that companies with heavy tax burdens are those most likely to use current cost accounting as a means of influencing tax policy. The first hypothesis tested in this paper is:

(H.1) Ceteris paribus, companies that voluntarily disclose current cost financial statements have higher effective tax rates than those not disclosing such statements.

Previous studies indicate a firm's leverage (proxy for debt contracting costs) is important in explaining accounting policy choices [Holthausen and Leftwich (1983), Kelly (1983), and Watts and Zimmerman (1986)]. In this study, the leverage ratio is also examined, but not for a debt covenant effect. Within the context of current cost accounting, leverage would not proxy for debt contracting costs because current cost financial statements are supplementary, while accounting-based debt covenants rely on the primary financial statements. The hypothesis tested here is that only firms with low leverage ratios use current cost accounting to influence tax reform. For highly leveraged firms, much of the current cost (debit) adjustments' impact and, hence, potential tax benefits are eliminated by the leverage adjustment.[4] This implies that:

(H.2) Ceteris paribus, companies that voluntarily disclose current cost financial statements have lower leverage ratios than those not disclosing such statements.

---

[4]An interview survey by McRae and Dobbins (1974) found that companies in the United Kingdom were ambivalent to the preparation of inflation accounts because the tax benefits of the inflation adjustments would be significantly offset by the tax on the gain from debt.

3.2. Regulation

Companies that enjoy 'monopolistic' shares of the market are potentially vulnerable to political costs [Hagerman and Zmijewski (1979)]. In New Zealand, the Commerce Commission, set up under the Commerce Act 1975, is responsible for investigating trade practices that are alleged to be contrary to the public interest. In this study, a firm's market concentration ratio is used as a proxy for the likelihood that the Commission will scrutinize the firm's affairs. This suggests:

(H.3) Ceteris paribus, companies that voluntarily disclose current cost financial statements have larger market concentration ratios than those not disclosing such statements.

The Commerce Act also makes provisions for the use of accounting information for price regulation. S 98 of this Act states:

> 'The profitability of the manufacturer or distributor of the goods or the supplier of the services, in relation to shareholders' funds, or, as the case may be, to the equity capital invested by the proprietor or partners, or to the assets employed in, or to the annual sales of, the whole of that person's business...'

can be used to regulate prices. That no mention is made of historical cost accounting in this regulation suggests that current cost accounting could help justify price increases. In periods of increasing prices, current cost accounting reduces profits[5] and increases assets (or capital), thereby reducing the return on assets (or capital) relative to historical cost accounting. This suggests:

(H.4) Ceteris paribus, companies that voluntarily disclose current cost financial statements have higher historical return on assets than those not disclosing such statements.

Hagerman and Zmijewski (1979) suggest that a firm's profitability is positively associated with its capital intensity since capital-intensive firms do not include the opportunity cost of capital in calculating income. Consequently, capital-intensive firms are more likely to view current cost accounting as a means for dampening reported income, thereby reducing accusations of profiteering. This implies:

(H.5) Ceteris paribus, firms that voluntarily disclose current cost financial statements are more capital-intensive than firms not disclosing such statements.

---

[5] This assumes that the sum of the debit adjustments (cost of sales, depreciation, and circulating monetary asset adjustments) are larger than the credit (leverage) adjustment; this would generally be the case. See table 1 in section 4.

3.3. Firm size

Watts and Zimmerman (1978) argue that because large firms are politically visible, they prefer accounting practices that minimize reported income, thereby reducing their political exposure. Since current cost accounting reduces income, large firms are more likely to present current cost financial statements. This paper uses reported net income as the size proxy[6]. This sixth hypothesis tested is:

(H.6) Ceteris paribus, companies that voluntarily disclose current cost financial statements have larger reported net income than those not disclosing such statements.

4. Method

4.1. Sample selection and research method

The tests conducted in this study compare the effective tax rate, leverage, market concentration ratio, historical return on assets, capital intensity, and net income between two groups of firms: a treatment group that voluntarily discloses current cost financial statements and a control group that does not disclose such statements. Both univariate and multivariate tests are conducted to assess the statistical difference in these variables.

The treatment sample is obtained by examining New Zealand listed companies' annual reports following publication of the Report of the Committee of Inquiry into Inflation Accounting in 1976. The treatment sample consists of 15 companies; four companies first disclose current cost financial statements in 1977, while one commenced disclosure in 1979, eight in 1980, and two in 1981. Recall that 1981 is the last year for voluntary disclosure because disclosure became mandatory from April 1982.

The effect of current cost accounting for the treatment group for 1980 and 1981[7] is presented in table 1, which shows the means and medians of the current cost adjustments. The sum of these adjustments, on average, reduce historic cost pre-tax income by 49 percent and 43 percent in 1980 and 1981, respectively. In each year, the largest debit adjustment is for depreciation, reflecting the low turnover of fixed assets relative to other types of assets.

The decline in the monetary working capital adjustment in 1981 is due to a change in the definition of the adjustment. In 1980, 13 of the treatment firms report a circulating monetary asset adjustment (following the Richardson

---

[6] Watts and Zimmerman (1986, p. 239) suggest that while net income and other size measures (e.g., sales) are highly correlated, the former better differentiates 'firms that are receiving from those providing wealth transfers'. The results reported in section 5 do not differ materially when sales or log(sales) is used instead of net income.

[7] The two companies that commence disclosure in 1981 present comparisons for 1980.

Table 1

Income impact of current cost accounting ($n = 15$) (percentage of mean historic cost pre-tax income in parentheses) ($ in thousands).

Mean historic cost pre-tax income	1980 $6,327			1981 $7,848		
Current cost adjustments[a]	Mean	Median	Minimum Maximum	Mean	Median	Minimum Maximum
COSA (debit)	1,644 (26%)	1,292 (20%)	129 5,912	1,809 (23%)	1,376 (18%)	188 7,491
MWCA (debit)	2,011 (32%)	1,094 (17%)	−361 10,090	1,757 (22%)	888 (11%)	−515 11,717
DA (debit)	2,095 (33%)	1,913 (30%)	102 5,355	2,482 (32%)	2,471 (31%)	122 6,456
LA (credit)	2,684 (42%)	1,623 (26%)	280 10,733	2,672 (34%)	1,935 (25%)	254 10,551
Total (debit)	3,096 (49%)	2,577 (41%)	446 9,697	3,377 (43%)	2,285 (29%)	495 10,241

[a] COSA = cost of sales adjustment, being the difference between current and historic cost of sales,

MWCA = monetary working capital adjustment, being the loss in purchasing power from holding monetary working capital,

DA = depreciation adjustment, being the difference between current and historic cost depreciation,

LA = leverage adjustment, being the leveraged portion of the realized and unrealized holding gains.

Committee's recommendations), while in 1981 only eight firms report this adjustment and the other seven use a monetary working capital adjustment in accordance with the New Zealand Society of Accountants' exposure draft [New Zealand Society of Accountants (1981)].[8]

The explanatory variables representing proxies for the potential economic incentives are taken from the 1980 financial statements on the New Zealand Companies Database.[9] Of the 216 companies on this database, 15 are dropped because of missing data. The remaining 201 companies are then split into the treatment group of 15 companies and the other 186 firms form the control group.

[8] It is interesting to note that if current cost accounting was adopted for tax purposes, and the existing tax rate retained, the treatment companies would have received, on average, tax relief of 58 percent and 63 percent of the income tax expense in 1980 and 1981, respectively.

[9] This database was set up, and is maintained, by the Department of Accounting and Finance, University of Otago, Dunedin, New Zealand. It contains financial statement data for New Zealand listed companies since 1976.

The following explanatory variables are computed for each company:

TR = income tax expense (net of deferred tax)/net income before taxes,

LR = long-term liabilities/total assets less current liabilities,[10]

MCR = $NI_i / \sum_{j=1}^{n} NI_j$, where NI_i is the NI (defined below) for company i in industry of size n,

ROA = net income before interest and taxes/total assets,

CI = gross fixed assets/total assets,[11]

NI = net income after taxes before extraordinary items.

Eleven firms in the control group have pre-tax losses. Ten of these firms have zero income tax expense, yielding zero effective tax rates, while one firm has a positive income tax expense and its effective tax rate is set to one (i.e., 100 percent).

Industry classifications of the sample firms are reported in table 2. Because of the small expected frequencies in 60 percent of the cells, it is inappropriate to use the chi-square distribution to assess the significance of the association between industry membership and the decision to disclose current cost information. Instead, a randomization test [Noreen (1986)], which is described in section 5.3, is conducted. This test indicates an association ($p = 0.042$) between industry membership and the current cost disclosure decision.

The cells with the largest discrepancy between the observed and expected frequencies are disclosing firms in the drugs and chemicals (code 14) and transport and tourism (code 29) industries. Other than cross-sectional industry differences that are considered in the test variables, there is no obvious explanation for these clusterings. However, Ball and Foster (1982) point out that firm size, which is considered in H.6, is likely to vary across industries with a possibility that firm size could proxy for omitted variables which are industry-related. Further, cross-sectional dependence results in overstated t-statistics and hence the likelihood of a type I error. While the next section attempts to mitigate the concern over omitted variables, caution should nevertheless be exercised in interpreting the results.

4.2. Other factors

Raising capital could motivate firms to disclose current cost information. Of the treatment companies in this study, only one made a rights issue in the year following the initial reporting of current cost information. Such a result

---

[10] This computation is set out in New Zealand Society of Accountants (1978,1981).

[11] The number of employees per dollar of fixed assets would be a better proxy for capital intensity. Unfortunately, information on employee numbers is not disclosed by New Zealand companies.

Table 2

Industry membership of firms disclosing and not disclosing current cost financial statements.

Industry code[a]	Industry name	Treatment Disclosing	Control Non-disclosing
1	Meat freezing and preserving	1	5
2	Beverages and other food	1	10
10	Woolen mills	0	4
11	Clothing manufacturers	0	5
12	Forestry and wood	0	7
13	Printing and packaging	0	13
14	Drugs and chemicals	3	5
15	Non-metallic minerals	2	7
16	Metals and machinery	1	17
17	Electrical appliances	0	10
18	Other manufacturing	3	14
21	Construction	0	6
22	Gas	1	2
23	Wholesale	1	24
24	Retail	0	22
26	Pastoral	0	11
27	Investment	0	8
29	Transport and tourism	2	6
30	Miscellaneous services	0	10
		15	186

[a] Reserve Bank of New Zealand industry codes.

suggests that the reduction of agency costs associated with the raising of equity finance is unlikely to be related to the voluntary disclosure of current cost financial statements. Hence, it is not considered further.

Another factor that could influence firms to disclose current cost information is the average age of their assets. Ceteris paribus, the older the assets of the firm, the greater the problems with historical cost. Thus, it can be hypothesized that the likelihood of disclosing current cost data increases with the average age of assets, because the historical cost statements become an increasingly inefficient basis for contracting. Indeed, this very problem is recognized in New Zealand where revaluation of fixed assets is permitted for debt contracting purposes. Further, nearly all New Zealand companies' financial statements include asset revaluations, a practice permitted by New Zealand accounting standards. Hence, where a revaluation system is already in use for contracting, it is less likely that current cost statements would be demanded for this purpose.

Nevertheless, the average age of a firm's assets, proxied by the ratio of accumulated depreciation to cost, is tested. The results (not presented in section 5) indicate that this factor is not significantly different between firms disclosing and those not disclosing current cost information.[12] This result suggests that asset age is unlikely to be an important omitted variable.

Other omitted variables are management compensation plans and book-keeping costs associated with the preparation of current cost financial statements. With respect to the former, contracted compensation arrangements that link bonuses to reported income are not common in New Zealand. However, it could be argued that a manager's compensation is implicitly tied to earnings [Bowen, Noreen and Lacey (1981) and Larcker and Revsine (1983)], and the omission of this variable could affect the results.

Because New Zealand firms frequently revalue fixed assets, it is unlikely that additional information production costs for preparing current cost financial statements would be material. Further, it is unlikely that these additional costs would vary significantly across firms, and this factor is not considered further.

5. Results

5.1. Descriptive statistics and univariate results

The descriptive statistics in table 3 indicate skewness in some of the explanatory variables: the effective tax rate variable (TR) is skewed to the left, while the market concentration ratio (MCR) and net income (NI) variables are skewed to the right, thereby causing problems in applying the t-test. The exponential transformation is therefore applied to TR, while the natural logarithmic transformation is applied to MCR and NI. Table 3 indicates that skewness is reduced substantially as a result of the transformations.

Table 3 indicates that, in every case, the difference in the means of the treatment and control subsamples are in the hypothesized directions. Using the t-test, the differences in the effective tax rate [$\exp(TR)$; H.1], leverage ratio [LR; H.2], and return on assets [ROA; H.4] are significant at the five percent level, while the differences in the market concentration ratio [$\ln(MCR)$; H.3], capital intensity [CI; H.5], and firm size [$\ln(NI)$; H.6] are significant at the one percent level.

The overall significance of these results is overstated because some of the variables are correlated. Table 4 contains the correlation matrix for these variables. Many of the correlations are significant at the one percent level. The Belsley, Kuh and Welsch (1980) diagnostics indicate a strong dependency between the market concentration ratio [$\ln(MCR)$] and firm size [$\ln(NI)$].

---

[12]A t-test indicates that the difference in the means is not significant at the ten percent level. In the logit analysis, the asset age variable is not significant ($p = 0.419$). When the logit model is re-estimated after dropping the two variables with which it is significantly correlated (H.2's leverage ratio and H.5's capital intensity), the asset age variable is still not significant at the ten percent level.

Table 3

Summary statistics and univariate tests of the relation between explanatory variables and the voluntary disclosure of current cost financial statements.

Hypothesis	Variable[a]	Descriptive statistics						Test variable[a]	Univariate tests						One-tailed probability
		(1) Treatment			(2) Control				(1) Treatment			(2) Control			
		Mean	Median	Std.dev.	Mean	Median	Std.dev.		Mean	Median	Std.dev.	Mean	Median	Std.dev.	
		($n=15$)			($n=186$)				($n=15$)			($n=186$)			t-test
1. (1) > (2)	TR	0.376	0.409	0.118	0.293	0.371	0.199	exp(TR)	1.465	1.505	0.153	1.367	1.448	0.273	0.019
2. (1) < (2)	LR	0.178	0.202	0.062	0.219	0.199	0.165	LR	0.178	0.202	0.062	0.219	0.199	0.165	0.026
3. (1) < (2)	MCR	0.195	0.162	0.172	0.092	0.032	0.152	ln(MCR)	2.923	3.010	0.731	2.152	1.987	1.054	0.001
4. (1) > (2)	ROA	0.153	0.146	0.081	0.110	0.110	0.097	ROA	0.153	0.146	0.081	0.110	0.110	0.097	0.036
5. (1) > (2)	CI	0.700	0.766	0.269	0.502	0.454	0.281	CI	0.700	0.766	0.269	0.502	0.454	0.281	0.007
6. (1) > (2)	NI($m)	3.850	3.299	3.362	2.509	0.770	5.345	ln(NI)	15.449	15.483	0.529	14.958	14.834	1.277	0.003

[a]TR = income tax expense (net of deferred tax)/net income before tax,
LR = long-term liabilities/total assets less current liabilities,
$MCR = NI_i / \sum_{j=1}^{n} NI_j$, where NI_i is the reported net income of company i in industry of size n,
ROA = net income before interest and tax/total assets,
CI = gross fixed assets/total assets,
NI = net income after tax before extraordinary items,
$\exp$ = exponential,
$\ln$ = natural log.

Table 4

Correlations among the independent variables used to explain the voluntary disclosure of current cost financial statements with two-tailed probabilities in parentheses ($n = 201$).

Variable[a]	exp(TR)	LR	ln(MCR)	ROA	CI	ln(NI)
exp(TR)	1.000					
LR	−0.192 (0.006)	1.000				
ln(MCR)	0.174 (0.013)	−0.063 (0.371)	1.000			
ROA	0.324 (0.000)	−0.274 (0.000)	0.320 (0.000)	1.000		
CI	−0.035 (0.624)	0.158 (0.025)	0.203 (0.004)	0.116 (0.101)	1.000	
ln(NI)	0.063 (0.371)	−0.163 (0.021)	0.845 (0.000)	0.330 (0.000)	0.102 (0.148)	1.000

[a]exp(TR) = exponential [income tax expense (net of deferred tax)/net income before tax],
LR = long-term liabilities/total assets less current liabilities,
ln(MCR)= natural log($NI_i / \sum_{j=1}^{n} NI_j$), where NI_i is the reported income of company i in industry of size n,
ROA = net income before interest and tax/total assets,
CI = gross fixed assets/total assets,
ln(NI)   = natural log (net income after tax before extraordinary items).

This should be borne in mind when interpreting the results of the logit regression.

5.2. Logit analysis

Setting the dependent variable to one if the firm presents current cost financial statements, and zero otherwise, the logit model can be written as:

$$\text{logit}(p) = a + b_1 \exp(TR) + b_2 LR + b_3 \ln(MCR)$$

$$+ b_4 ROA + b_5 CI + b_6 \ln(NI),$$

where p is the probability that the dependent variable equals one, and the independent variables are as previously defined. With the exception of b_2, which is predicted to be negative, all the coefficients are predicted to be positive.

Before presenting the results, it is worth noting that the maximum likelihood estimates of the logit model parameters are based on a large-sample convergence assumption, which may not be met in this study because of the small number of firms presenting current cost information. Consequently, caution should be exercised in interpreting the results. To assess the sensitivity of these results to possible violation of this assumption, a randomization test [Noreen (1986)] is conducted.

The estimated coefficients, their t-statistics, and significance levels for the logit model are presented in table 5. The model likelihood ratio chi-square statistic is 19.56 (6 d.f.), implying the null hypothesis of no statistical relation is rejected at the one percent level of confidence. The likelihood ratio index is 0.18.

The tax-related hypothesis, which is stated in H.1 and H.2, predicts that firms with high tax rates and low leverage ratios are more likely to voluntarily disclose current cost information. Table 5 shows that tax rate [exp(TR); H.1] is positive as predicted and moderately significant ($p = 0.154$), while the leverage ratio [LR; H.2] has the predicted negative sign and is moderately significant ($p = 0.126$). These results provide some support for the argument that firms presenting current cost financial statements are those likely to benefit most from tax relief if the tax system was modified to incorporate current cost adjustments.

The results in table 5 also provide support for the political cost hypothesis which is stated in H.3 to H.6. The market concentration ratio [ln(MCR); H.3] is positive as predicted and significant ($p = 0.075$), supporting the hypothesis that firms with high concentration ratios are more susceptible to criticisms of profiteering and, hence, have an incentive to reduce reported earnings through current cost accounting. There is only weak support for the direct relation between the return on assets [ROA; H.4] and the voluntary disclosure of current cost information ($p = 0.180$). Capital intensity [CI; H.5] is positive and significant ($p = 0.013$), providing support for Hagerman and Zmijewski's (1981) argument that capital-intensive firms are more likely to use earnings decreasing procedures. Finally, while firm size [ln(NI); H.6] has the predicted positive sign, it is not significant ($p = 0.344$); the collinear relation between the market concentration ratio [ln(MCR)] and firm size [ln(NI)], as previously noted, appears to seriously degrade the firm size coefficient.[13] Overall, these results provide some support for the political cost hypothesis.

Using the coefficients of the logit model in table 5 to calculate each observation's probability of disclosing current cost information, the mean and median estimated probabilities (0.189 and 0.179) are higher for the 15 disclosing firms than the mean and median probabilities (0.065 and 0.035) for the 186 non-disclosing firms. A t(chi-square)-test indicates that the difference in the means (medians) is significant beyond the one percent level. This provides further evidence that the variables in the logit model explain the decision by managers to disclose current cost financial statements.

---

[13] The logit model is also reestimated after dropping variables that are collinear. However, this procedure leads to a specification bias and hence biased estimators. With this caveat in mind, the results of those regressions, which are not presented, indicate that all the variables have their predicted signs and are significant at the five percent level or better.

Table 5

Logit analysis of the relation between explanatory variables and the voluntary disclosure of current cost financial statements ($n = 201$).[a]

Explanatory variables[b]	Predicted sign	Coefficient	t-statistic	One-tailed probability
exp(TR)	+	1.466	1.021	0.154
LR	−	−3.515	−1.147	0.126
ln(MCR)	+	0.766	1.437	0.075
ROA	+	3.059	0.913	0.180
CI	+	2.609	2.224	0.013
ln(NI)	+	0.249	0.402	0.344
Likelihood ratio index[c]		0.18		
Likelihood ratio statistic[d]		19.56 (6 d.f., $p = 0.003$)		
% correctly classified		93.50		

[a] Dependent variable = 1 if disclosed current cost financial statements ($n = 15$), = 0 if did not disclose current cost financial statements ($n = 186$).

[b] exp(TR) = exponential [income tax expense (net of deferred tax)/net income before tax],

  LR = long-term liabilities/total assets less current liabilities,

  ln(MCR) = natural log ($NI_i / \sum_{j=1}^{n} NI_j$), where NI_i is the reported income of company i in industry of size n,

  ROA = net income before interest and tax/total assets,

  CI = gross fixed assets/total assets,

  ln(NI) = natural log (net income after tax before extraordinary items).

[c] The log likelihood ratio index is defined as $1 - \log$ likelihood at convergence/log likelihood at zero. It is similar to a R^2 measure in a multiple-regression model and provides an indication of the logit model's explanatory power.

[d] The likelihood ratio statistic is used to test the hypothesis that all the parameters in the model are simultaneously equal to zero. Under this null hypothesis, the statistic has an asymptotic distribution which is a chi-square with degrees of freedom equalling the number of explanatory variables in the model.

Based on a 0.33 probability cutoff that minimizes the number of misclassifications, table 5 indicates that the logit model correctly classifies 93.5 percent of the observations. This percentage is overstated because the same firms are used to develop the model and to test its predictive power. With this caveat in mind, the logit model performs slightly better than a naive model that classifies all firms as non-reporters (186/201 = 92.5 percent), but the difference in predictive accuracy is not statistically significant. Nevertheless, the results indicate that management's disclosure decision varies with the tax and political cost variables. These variables provide a richer explanation of the phenomenon than the naive model's, which is not intuitively appealing.

5.3. Randomization test

Because the distribution of the maximum likelihood estimates of the logit model parameters is restricted to its large-sample (asymptotic) properties, estimators generated from small samples may not be reliably analyzed using asymptotic methods. To test the sensitivity of the logit results to possible violation of the large-sample assumption, a randomization test is also conducted.

Noreen (1986) states that the randomization procedure is valid regardless of sample size and/or the distribution of variables. In this section, the randomization method is used to assess the significance of each explanatory variable's coefficient and the likelihood ratio statistic, by comparing them to their respective probability distributions under the assumption that the null hypothesis is true.

The following procedures are conducted. First, the dependent variable is shuffled relative to the matrix of explanatory variables; this ensures the dependent variable is stochastically independent of the explanatory variables and thus the null hypothesis is true. Second, a logit analysis is performed using the shuffled dependent variable and the explanatory variables; this produces pseudo coefficients for each explanatory variable and a pseudo likelihood ratio statistic.

The above procedures are carried out 500 times, yielding 500 pseudo coefficients for each explanatory variable, and 500 pseudo likelihood ratio statistics (i.e., an empirical distribution of each test statistic under the null hypothesis is constructed).[14] The significance of each test statistic for the original (unshuffled) data is assessed relative to its empirically generated distribution. The null hypothesis is rejected if the actual value of the test statistic (based on the unshuffled data) is unusually large relative to the test statistic for the shuffled data. Noreen (1986, p. 24) presents the test statistic's significance level as

$$p = (nge + 1)/(NS + 1),$$

where *nge* is the number of times the pseudo test statistic is as large (small) as the actual test statistic when a direct (inverse) association is hypothesized, and *NS* is the number of shuffles.

Table 6 contains the results of the randomization test. The table presents the actual test statistics, the mean and standard deviation of the pseudo test statistics that result from shuffling the dependent variable and running the logit regression 500 times, and the significance level of the actual test statistics. These results support those in table 5; all the four variables that show some significance in table 5 [i.e., exp(*TR*), LR, ln(*MCR*), and *CI*] are even more significant in the randomization test. The effective tax rate [exp(*TR*)] and leverage ratio [*LR*], which are significant at the 15 percent level in table 5, are now significant at the ten percent level. The market concentration ratio [ln(*MCR*)] and capital intensity [*CI*], which are significant at the ten and five

---

[14] Noreen (1986, p. 5) suggests computing the test statistic 100 to 1,000 times.

Table 6

Randomization test of the relation between explanatory variables and the voluntary disclosure of current cost financial statements (number of shuffles of the dependent variable = 500).

Variable[a]	Predicted sign	Actual test statistic (table 5)	Mean (std.dev.) of pseudo test statistic	No. of times pseudo test statistic is greater (less) than actual test statistic	One-tailed probability[b]
exp(TR)	+	1.466	0.041 (1.179)	45	0.092
LR	−	− 3.515	− 0.450 (2.235)	(39)	0.080
ln(MCR)	+	0.766	− 0.133 (0.612)	23	0.048
ROA	+	3.059	0.403 (3.071)	95	0.192
CI	+	2.609	0.079 (1.076)	2	0.006
ln(NI)	+	0.249	0.259 (0.612)	230	0.461
Likelihood ratio statistic		19.560	6.170 (3.714)	2	0.006

[a]exp(TR) = exponential [income tax expense (net of deferred tax)/net income before tax],
LR = long-term liabilities/total assets less current liabilities;
ln(MCR) = natural $\log(NI_i/\sum_{j=1}^{n}NI_j)$, where NI_i is the reported income of company i in industry of size n,
ROA = net income before interest and tax/total assets,
CI = gross fixed assets/total assets;
ln(NI) = natural log (net income after tax before extraordinary items).
[b]The one-tailed probability is $(nge + 1)/(NS + 1)$, where nge is the number of times the pseudo test statistic is greater (less) than the actual test statistic when a direct (inverse) relation is hypothesized, and NS is the number of shuffles.

percent levels in table 5, are now significant at the five and one percent levels, respectively. Consistent with table 5 the likelihood ratio statistic is significant beyond the one percent level. Overall, the results of the randomization test support those from the logit analysis.

6. Conclusions

This study investigates whether tax and political cost variables influence New Zealand listed companies' decisions to voluntarily disclose current cost financial statements. It is found that voluntary presenters of current cost financial statements have: (1) higher effective tax rates, (2) lower leverage ratios, (3) larger market concentration ratios, and (4) are more capital-intensive. These results are consistent with the view that companies subject to wealth transfers by way of taxes and government regulation attempt to affect the probability of such transfers via an accounting choice: the voluntary disclosure of supplementary current cost financial statements.

A limitation of the study is its statistical conclusion validity. The number of observations, particularly the size of the treatment group, is small by U.S. standards. While the randomization test mitigates this concern, tests of the tax and political cost hypotheses in other accounting choices with larger samples should provide further evidence of the political effect on financial reporting.

Another limitation is the potential misspecification of the theoretical constructs. Take the tax hypothesis, for example, where not only are the firm's tax rate and leverage ratio important, but so is the magnitude of the potential tax relief (i.e., the tax effect of the current cost adjustments). An additional powerful test would be to compare the potential tax relief (as proxied by the magnitude of the current cost adjustments) across the two samples. Unfortunately, this is not possible because the current cost adjustments could not be determined for the non-disclosing companies, even when such disclosure became 'mandatory' in 1982; as noted in section 2, these companies did not comply with the standard [New Zealand Society of Accountants (1982)]. Subject to these limitations, it is, nevertheless, encouraging to find economic determinants of accounting policy choices prevalent in a different institutional environment, New Zealand.

References

Ayre, F.L., 1986, Characteristics of firms electing early adoption of SFAS 52, Journal of Accounting and Economics 8, 143–158.

Ball, R. and G. Foster, 1982, Corporate financial reporting: A methodological review of empirical research, Supplement to the Journal of Accounting Research, 161–234.

Bazley, M., P. Brown and H.Y. Izan, 1985, An analysis of lease disclosures by Australian companies, Abacus, 44–62.

Belsley, D.A., E. Kuh and R.E. Welsch, 1980, Regression diagnostics: Identifying influential data and sources of collinearity (Wiley, New York).

Bowen, R.E., E. Noreen and J. Lacey, 1981, Determinants of the corporate decision to capitalize interest, Journal of Accounting and Economics 3, 151–179.

Daley, L.A. and R.L. Vigeland, 1983, The effects of debt covenants and political costs on the choice of accounting methods: The case of accounting for R&D costs, Journal of Accounting and Economics 5, 195–211.

Hagerman, R.L. and M.E. Zmijewski, 1979, Some economic determinants of accounting policy choice, Journal of Accounting and Economics 1, 141–161.

Holthausen, R.W. and R.W. Leftwich, 1983, The economic consequences of accounting choice: Implications of costly contracting and monitoring, Journal of Accounting and Economics 5, 77–117.

Kelly, L., 1983, The development of a positive theory of corporate management's role in external financial reporting, Journal of Accounting Literature 2, 111–150.

Larcker, D.F. and L. Revsine, 1983, The oil and gas accounting controversy: An analysis of economic consequences, The Accounting Review 58, 706–732.

McKee, J.A., T.B. Bell and J.R. Boatsman, 1984, Management preferences over accounting standards: A replication and additional tests, The Accounting Review 59, 647–659.

McRae, T.W. and R. Dobbins, 1974, Behavioural aspects of the inflation accounting controversy, Accounting and Business Research, Spring, 135–140.

New Zealand Society of Accountants, 1978, CCA Guidelines: GU-1 (New Zealand Society of Accountants, Wellington).

New Zealand Society of Accountants, 1981, ED 25: Current cost accounting (New Zealand Society of Accountants, Wellington).

New Zealand Society of Accountants, 1982, CCA-1: Information reflecting the effects of changing prices (New Zealand Society of Accountants, Wellington).

Noreen, E., 1986, An introduction to testing hypotheses using computer-intensive methods, Unpublished manuscript (University of Washington, Seattle, WA).

Richardson Committee, 1976, The report of the committee of inquiry into inflation accounting (Government Printer, Wellington).

Trotman, K.T., 1980, The effect of the firm's capital structure on the choice of accounting methods for long-term construction contracts, Australian Journal of Management 5, 141–144.

Watts, R.L. and J.L. Zimmerman, 1978, Towards a positive theory of determination of accounting standards, The Accounting Review 53, 112–134.

Watts, R.L. and J.L. Zimmerman, 1986, Positive accounting theory (Prentice Hall, Englewood Cliffs, NJ).

Whittred, G.P., 1987, The derived demand for consolidated financial reporting, Journal of Accounting and Economics 9, 259–285.

Zimmer, I., 1986, Accounting for interest by real estate developers, Journal of Accounting and Economics 8, 37–51.

Zmijewski, M. and R. Hagerman, 1981, An income strategy approach to the positive theory of accounting standard setting/choice, Journal of Accounting and Economics 3, 129–149.

Alchian, Armen A., "Uncertainty, Evolution, and Economic Theory," *Journal of Political Economy*, 58 (1950), pp. 211–221.

Alchian, Armen A., and Harold Demsetz, "Production, Information Costs, and Economic Organization," *American Economic Review*, 62 (December 1972), pp. 777–795.

Ball, Ray, "Discussion of Accounting for Research and Development Costs: The Impact on Research and Development Expenditures," *Journal of Accounting Research*, 18 (1980, Supplement), pp. 27–37.

Ball, Ray, and George Foster, "Corporate Financial Reporting: A Methodological Review of Empirical Research," *Journal of Accounting Research* (1982, Supplement), pp. 161–234.

Benston, George, "Required Financial Disclosure and the Stock Market: An Evaluation of the Securities and Exchange Act of 1934," *American Economic Review*, 63 (March 1973), pp. 132–155.

Brickley, James A., and Frederick H. Dark, "The Choice of Organizational Form," *Journal of Financial Economics*, 18 (1987), pp. 401–420.

Coase, Ronald H., "The Nature of the Firm," *Economica*, n.s., 4 (November 1937), pp. 386–405.

Crystal, Graef S., *In Search of Excess*, W. W. Norton & Co.: New York (1991).

Fama, Eugene F., and Michael C. Jensen, "Separation of Ownership and Control." *Journal of Law and Economics* 26 (June 1983), pp. 301–325.

Francis, Jere R., "Debt Reporting by Parent Companies: Parent-Only versus Consolidated Statements." *Journal of Business Finance and Accounting*, 13 (1986), pp. 393–403.

Hayek, Friedrich, "The Use of Knowledge in Society," *American Economic Review*, 35 (1945), pp. 519–530.

Holmstrom, Bengt R., "Moral Hazard and Observability," *Bell Journal of Economics* (Spring 1979), pp. 74–91.

Jensen, Michael C., and William H. Meckling, "Theory of the Firm: Managerial Behavior, Agency Costs and Ownership Structure," *Journal of Financial Economics*, 3 (October 1976), pp. 305–360.

Jensen, Michael C., and Kevin J. Murphy, "CEO Incentives—It's Not How Much You Pay, But How," *Harvard Business Review 90*, (1990), pp. 138–153.

Rosenberg, Nathan, and L. E. Birdzell, Jr., *How the West Grew Rich: The Economic Transformation of the Industrial World*. New York: Basic Books (1986).

Watts, Ross L., "Corporate Financial Statements: A Product of the Market and Political Processes," *Australian Journal of Management* (April 1977), pp. 52–75.

Watts, Ross L., and Jerold L. Zimmerman, *Positive Accounting Theory*, Englewood Cliffs, N.J.: Prentice-Hall (1986).

Watts, Ross L., and Jerold L. Zimmerman, "Towards a Positive Theory of the Determination of Accounting Standards," *Accounting Review* (JanuPary 1978), pp. 112–134.

Whittred, Greg, "The Derived Demand for Consolidated Financial Reporting in Australia," *Journal of Accounting and Economics*, 9 (1987), pp. 259–285.